MINI WORKSHOP MANUAL 1959-1976

SALOON · COUNTRYMAN · TRAVELLER
CLUBMAN · ESTATE · 1275 GT · VAN
PICK-UP · MOKE · COOPER · COOPER 'S'
INCLUDING
AUSTRALIAN SUPPLEMENT

Workshop Manual

Publication No. AKD 4935 (9th Edition) with Australian Supplement Publication No. TP832C (1976)

Australian Supplement

The first section of this manual applies to all Mini models manufactured in England and Spain up to 1976. A supplement will be found at the back of the manual which covers the differences between the British and Australian assembled vehicles during this period and covers the following models:

850 • 998 DELUXE • 998 MINI MATIC • 1100 and K • 850 VAN
998 VAN • 1100 VAN • 997 COOPER • 998 COOPER
COOPER 'S' • CLUBMAN • CLUBMAN GT • 850 MOKE
998 MOKE • 1100 MOKE • 1275 MOKE
Plus all other body versions e.g. TRAVELLER etc. •

Owners of Australian produced vehicles should first consult the required section in the main body of the manual and then check the appropriate section and appendix in the supplement. Information in the supplement does not supersede that given in the main body of the book but should be used in conjunction with it.

Brooklands Books Ltd., P.O. Box 904,
Amersham, Bucks, HP6 9JA, UK
brooklandsbooks.com

Part No. AKD 4935 (9th Edition) with Australian Supplement TP832C (1976)

ISBN: 9781855201613 4W4//3018 Ref: M13AWH

CONTENTS

INTRODUCTION

DESCRIPTION

This Manual is intended to assist the skilled mechanic in carrying out repairs and replacements in a minimum time.

References to left- or right-hand side in this Manual are made when viewing the car from the rear.

MANUAL ARRANGEMENT

The first part of the Manual includes the General Data, Engine Tuning Data, and Maintenance which incorporates the Recommended Lubricants Chart.

A Service Tools section is featured at the end of the Manual.

The remainder of the Manual is divided into sections, and each section carries a reference letter that identifies the section with an assembly or a major component. Each section is prefixed with a contents page and is sub-divided numerically. The pages and illustrations are numbered consecutively within each section and the section title and letter are shown at the top of each page.

Sections having the suffix **'a'** contain supplementary information dealing with the Mini fitted with Automatic transmission.

Sections having the suffix **'b'** contain supplementary information applicable to the Mini range, i.e. 850, 1000, Clubman, 1275 GT, and the Cooper 'S' Mk. III. These vehicles have **NEGATIVE** earth electrical systems.

To reduce repetition, operations covered in this manual do not include reference to testing the vehicle after repair. It is essential that work is inspected and tested after completion and if necessary a road test of the vehicle is carried out particularly where safety related items are concerned.

REPAIRS AND REPLACEMENTS

When replacement parts are required it is essential that only genuine British Leyland parts and Unipart replacements are used.

Attention is particularly drawn to the following points concerning repairs and the fitting of replacement parts and accessories:

Safety features embodied in the car may be impaired if other than genuine parts are fitted.

In certain territories, legislation prohibits the fitting of parts not to the vehicle manufacturer's specification.

Torque wrench setting figures given in the Manual must be strictly adhered to.

Locking devices, where specified, must be fitted. If the efficiency of a locking device is impaired during removal it must be renewed.

Owners purchasing accessories while travelling abroad should ensure that the accessory and its fitted location on the car conform to mandatory requirements existing in their country of origin.

The terms of the Owners Service Statement may be invalidated by the fitting of other than genuine British Leyland parts and Uniparts.

All British Leyland parts and Unipart replacements have the full backing of the Owners Service Statement.

British Leyland Distributors and Dealers are obliged to supply only genuine service parts.

INTRODUCTION

SPECIFICATION

British Leyland UK Limited is constantly seeking ways to improve the specification of its vehicles and alterations take place continually. While every effort is made to produce up-to-date literature this Manual should not be regarded as an infallible guide to current specifications. Further the specification details set out in this Manual apply to a range of vehicles and not to any particular one.

Distributors and Dealers are not agents of British Leyland UK Limited and have absolutely no authority to bind British Leyland UK Limited by any express or implied undertaking or representation.

During the period of running-in from new, certain adjustments may vary from the specification figures given in this Manual. These adjustments will be reset by the Distributor or Dealer at the After Sales Service, and thereafter should be maintained at the figures specified in the Manual.

Self-locking nuts

Deformed thread stiffnuts must not be re-used where the lacquer coating (SMT65) is affected in any way, and they must not be degreased in any circumstances. New nuts must always be used if their clamping torque has been lowered.

IMPORTANT. Insert-type stiffnuts must be used on the front suspension tie rods and front end to frame fixings. Deformed thread stiffnuts must not be used in these positions even if originally fitted. New stiffnuts must always be used on drive shafts.

Cars produced by AUTHI, Pamplona, Spain

The vehicle specification differs in some respects from those models produced in the U.K. The basic information contained in this Manual applies to cars from both sources of production.

EMISSION CONTROL SYSTEMS

Servicing and adjusting engine emission control equipment must be carried out in accordance with the instructions given in Section T.

The service operations and adjustments showing this symbol must be followed by an exhaust emission check.

DATA CONTENTS

* To European emission control requirements (ECE 15).

GENERAL DATA

MINI MK. I & II (848 c.c.) & MK. II (998 c.c.)

	(848 c.c.)	(998 c.c.)
ENGINE		
Type	8MB.	99H.
Number of cylinders	4.	4.
Bore	2.478 in. (62.94 mm.).	2.543 in. (64.588 mm.).
Stroke	2.687 in. (68.26 mm.).	3.00 in. (76.2 mm.).
Capacity	51.7 cu. in. (848 c.c.)	60.96 cu. in. (998 c.c.).
Firing order	1, 3, 4, 2.	1, 3, 4, 2.
Valve operation	Overhead by push-rod.	Overhead by push-rod.
B.M.E.P.	128 lb./sq. in. (9 kg./cm.^{2}) at 2,900 r.p.m.	130 lb./sq. in. (9.14 kg./cm.^{2}) at 2,700 r.p.m.
Torque	44 lb. ft. (6.08 kg. m.) at 2,900 r.p.m.	52 lb. ft. (7.28 kg. m.) at 2,700 r.p.m.
Oversize bores: 1st	+ .010 in. (.254 mm.).	+ .010 in. (.254 mm.).
2nd	+ .020 in. (.508 mm.).	+ .020 in. (.508 mm.).

CRANKSHAFT

Main journal diameter	1.7505 to 1.751 in. (44.46 to 44.47 mm.).	
Minimum regrind diameter	1.7105 in. (43.45 mm.).	
Crankpin journal diameter	1.6254 to 1.6259 in. (41.28 to 41.29 mm.).	
Crankpin minimum regrind diameter	1.5854 in. (40.27 mm.).	
Main bearings		
Number and type	3 shell type.	
Material	Steel-backed white metal.	Steel-backed copper-lead; thin wall.
Running clearance	.0005 to .002 in. (.013 to .051 mm.).	.001 to .0027 in. (.025 to .069 mm.).
Length	1.187 in. (30.16 mm.).	
End-clearance	.002 to .003 in. (.051 to .076 mm.).	
End-thrust	Taken on centre main bearing.	

CONNECTING RODS

Length between centres	5.75 in. (14.605 cm.).
Big-end bearings	
Bearing side-clearance	.008 to .012 in. (.203 to .305 mm.).
Bearing diametrical clearance	.001 to .0025 in. (0.25 to .063 mm.).
Bearing length	.875 in. (22.22 mm.).

PISTONS

	(848 c.c.)	(998 c.c.)
Type	Split skirt.	Solid skirt.
Clearances: Bottom of skirt	.0006 to .0012 in. (.015 to .030 mm.).	.0005 to .0011 in. (.013 to .028 mm.).
Top of skirt	.0026 to .0032 in. (.066 to .081 mm.).	
Oversizes	+ .010 in., + .020 in., + .030 in. + .040 in. (.254 mm., .508 mm., .762 mm., 1.016 mm.).	+ .010 in., + .020 in. (.254 mm., .508 mm.).

PISTON RINGS

	(848 c.c.)	(998 c.c.)
Compression: Plain	Top ring.	Top ring, chrome-faced.
Tapered	Second and third rings.	Second and third rings.
Width	.069 to .070 in. (1.75 to 1.78 mm.).	.0620 to .0625 in. (1.574 to 1.588 mm.).
Thickness	.095 to .101 in. (2.41 to 2.56 mm.).	.106 to .112 in. (2.692 to 2.835 mm.).
Fitted gap	.007 to .012 in. (.178 to .305 mm.).	
Clearance in groove	.0015 to .0035 in. (.038 to .089 mm.).	

MINI MK. I & II (848 c.c.) & MK. II (998 c.c.)—continued

	(848 c.c.)	(998 c.c.)
Oil control type	Slotted scraper.	
Width	.124 to .125 in. (3.15 to 3.175 mm.).	
Thickness	.095 to .101 in. (2.41 to 2.56 mm.).	
Fitted gap	.007 to .012 in. (.178 to .305 mm.).	
Clearance in groove	.0015 to .0035 in. (.038 to .089 mm.).	

GUDGEON PIN

	(848 c.c.)	(998 c.c.)
Type	Clamped in little-end.	Fully floating, with circlip location.
Fit in piston	Hand push-fit.	Hand push-fit.
Diameter (outer)	.624 in. (15.86 mm.).	

VALVES AND VALVE GEAR

Valves

	(848 c.c.)	(998 c.c.)
Seat angle: Inlet	45°.	
Seat angle: Exhaust	45°.	
Head diameter: Inlet	1.093 to 1.098 in. (27.76 to 27.89 mm.).	
Head diameter: Exhaust	1.000 to 1.005 in. (25.40 to 25.53 mm.).	
Stem diameter: Inlet	.2793 to .2798 in. (7.096 to 7.109 mm.).	
Stem diameter: Exhaust	.2788 to .2793 in. (7.081 to 7.096 mm.).	
Valve lift	285 in. (7.24 mm.).	.28 in. (7.14 mm.).
Valve stem to guide clearance: Inlet	.0015 to .0025 in. (.038 to .064 mm.).	
Valve stem to guide clearance: Exhaust	.002 to .003 in. (.051 to .076 mm.).	
Valve rocker clearance; Running	.012 in. (.305 mm.) (cold).	
Valve rocker clearance; Timing	.019 in. (.48 mm.).	
Timing markings	Dimples on timing wheels, marks on flywheel.	
Chain pitch and number of pitches	⅜ in. (9.525 mm.). 52.	
Inlet valve: Opens	5° B.T.D.C.	
Inlet valve: Closes	45° A.B.D.C.	
Exhaust valve: Opens	40° B.B.D.C.	
Exhaust valve: Closes	10° A.T.D.C.	
Valve rocker bush bore (reamed)	.5630 to .5635 in. (14.30 to 14.312 mm.).	

VALVE GUIDES

Length: Inlet and exhaust	1.687 in. (42.86 mm.).
Diameter: Outside: Inlet and exhaust	.469 in. (11.91 mm.).
Diameter: Inside: Inlet and exhaust	.2813 to .2818 in. (7.145 to 7.257 mm.).

VALVE SPRINGS

Free length: Inlet and exhaust	1.625 in. (41.27 mm.).
Number of working coils	4½.
Pressure: Inlet and exhaust: Valve open	70 lb. (31.8 kg.).
Pressure: Inlet and exhaust: Valve closed	37.5 lb. (17.027 kg.).

TAPPETS

Diameter	.812 in. (20.64 mm.).
Length	1.5 in. (38.10 mm.).

MINI MK. I & II (848 c.c.) & MK. II (998 c.c.)—continued

	(848 c.c.)	(998 c.c.)
CAMSHAFT		
Journal diameters: Front		1.6655 to 1.666 in. (42.304 to 42.316 mm.).
Centre		1.62275 to 1.62325 in. (41.218 to 41.231 mm.).
Rear		1.3725 to 1.3735 in. (34.862 to 34.887 mm.).
End-float		.003 to .007 in. (.076 to .178 mm.).
Bearings: Type: Front		White-metal-lined, steel-backed.
Centre and rear		Plain (running in block).
Inside diameter (reamed in position)		1.667 to 1.6675 in. (42.342 to 42.355 mm.).
Clearance: Front		.001 to .002 in. (.025 to .051 mm.).
Centre and rear		.00125 to .00275 in. (.0317 to .0698 mm.).
Bearings: number and type		3. Steel-backed white metal.
Inside diameter (reamed in position): Front		1.667 to 1.6675 in. (42.342 to 42.355 mm.).
Centre		1.6245 to 1.6255 in. (41.261 to 41.287 mm.).
Rear		1.3748 to 1.3755 in. (34.914 to 34.937 mm.).
Running clearance		.001 to .002 in. (.025 to .051 mm.).
ENGINE LUBRICATION SYSTEM		
Oil pump		
Type		Concentric or Hobourn-Eaton.
Relief pressure valve opens		60 lb./sq. in. (4.2 kg./cm.^{2}).
Relief valve spring: Free length		2 $\frac{55}{64}$ in. (72.63 mm.).
Fitted length		2 $\frac{5}{32}$ in. (54.77 mm.).
Oil filter		
Type		Full-flow.
Capacity		1 pint (1.2 U.S. pints, .57 litre).
Oil pressure		
Normal running		60 lb./sq. in. (4.22 kg./cm.^{2}).
Idling (minimum)		15 lb./sq. in. (1.05 kg./cm.^{2}).
COOLING SYSTEM		
Type		Pressurized radiator, thermo-siphon, pump- and fan-assisted.
Pressure cap		13 lb./sq. in. (.91 kg./cm.^{2}).
Thermostat setting		82°C. (180°F.).
Cold climates		88°C. (188°F.).
Hot climates		74°C. (165°F.).
FUEL SYSTEM		
Carburetter refer to **'TUNING DATA'**.		
Fuel pump		
Make and type: Early saloons	S.U. electric. PD.	
Later vehicles	S.U. electric. SP.	S.U. electric. SP and AUF 201 type.

MINI MK. I & II (848 c.c.) & MK. II (998 c.c.)—continued

	(848 c.c.)	(998 c.c.)
Delivery rate: PD type		45 pints/hr. (25.5 litres/hr.).
SP and AUF 201 type		56 pints/hr. (32 litres/hr.).
Delivery pressure; PD type		2 to 3 lb./sq. in. (.14 to .21 kg./cm.^{2}).
SP and AUF 201 type		2½ to 3 lb./sq. in. (.17 to .21 kg./cm.^{2}).

CLUTCH

	(848 c.c.)	(998 c.c.)
BMC single dry plate		
Diameter		7⅛ in. (180.9 mm.).
Facing material		Wound yarn.
Pressure springs		6.
Colour		Red spot.
Diaphragm-spring clutch		
Make		Borg and Beck.
Diameter		7⅛ in. (180.9 mm.).
Facing material		Wound yarn.
Diaphragm-spring colour code	Brown	Light green.

TRANSMISSION

Gearbox

Number of forward speeds	4.
Synchromesh	Second, third, and fourth gears.
Ratios: Top	1.0 : 1.
Third	1.412 : 1.
Second	2.172 : 1.
First	3.627 : 1.
Reverse	3.627 : 1.
Overall ratios: Top	3.765 : 1.
Third	5.317 : 1.
Second	8.176 : 1.
First	13.657 : 1.
Reverse	13.657 : 1.

Final drive

	(848 c.c.)	(998 c.c.)
Type	Helical gears and differential.	
Ratio: Saloon	3.765 : 1 (17/64).	3.44 : 1 (18/62).
Van and Pick-up		3.76 : 1 (17/64).

Gearbox	**(From Engine No. 8AM-WE-H101)**	**(From Engine Nos. 99H-159-H101 and 99H-251-H101)**
Number of forward speed	4.	4.
Synchromesh	All forward gears.	All forward gears.
Ratios: Top	1.00 : 1.	1.00 : 1.
Third	1.43 : 1.	1.43 : 1.
Second	2.21 : 1.	2.21 : 1.
First	3.52 : 1.	3.52 : 1.
Reverse	3.54 : 1.	3.54 : 1.
Overall ratios: Top	3.76 : 1.	3.44 : 1.
Third	5.40 : 1.	4.93 : 1.
Second	8.32 : 1.	7.63 : 1.
First	13.25 : 1.	12.13 : 1.
Reverse	13.30 : 1.	12.19 : 1.
Road speed at 1,000 r.p.m. in top gear	15.2 m.p.h. (24.3 km.p.h.).	16.2 m.p.h. (25.75 km.p.h.).

MINI MK. I & II (848 c.c.) & MK. II (998 c.c.)–continued

DRIVE SHAFTS

Type	Solid shaft, reverse spline.
Make and type of joint	Hardy Spicer, hemispherical joint.

STEERING

Type	Rack and pinion.	
Steering-wheel turns–lock to lock	2⅓	
Steering-wheel diameter	15¾ in. (40 cm.).	
Camber angle	1° positive to 3° positive.	
Castor angle	3°	with vehicle in an unladen condition.
King pin (swivel hub) inclination	9° 30′	
Toe-out	$\frac{1}{16}$ in. (1.6 mm.)	
Lock angle: outer wheel at 20°, inner wheel	23°	

FRONT SUSPENSION

Early models, 1959-1964	Rubber cone spring.
Later models	Hydrolastic displacers.
Fluid capacity	4 pints (5 U.S. pints, 2.27 litres).
Fluid pressure: Early models (unladen)	263 lb./sq. in. (18.49 kg./cm.²).
Later models (unladen)	282 lb./sq. in. (19.74 kg./cm.²).
(Car Nos. given in Section H.10)	

REAR SUSPENSION

Type	Rubber cone spring.
Toe-in	⅛ in. (3.18 mm.).
Camber	1° positive.
Radius arm bushes (reamed bore)	.8125 to .8130 in. (20.63 to 20.65 mm.).

HYDRAULIC DAMPERS (Rubber suspension only)

Type: Front and rear	Tubular telescopic.

BRAKES (Up to Chassis Nos. 296256 and 638878)

Lockheed hydraulic	Single-leading shoe.
Drum size	7 in. (17.8 cm.) diameter.
Lining dimensions: Front or rear	6.75 in. x 1.25 in. (17.14 cm. x 3.17 cm.).
Lining area: Front or rear	33.75 sq. in. (217.7 cm.²).
Lining material	Don 202.
Master cylinder bore diameter	¾ in. (19.05 mm.).

Wheel cylinders

Cylinder bore diameter: Front	$\frac{13}{16}$ in. (20.64 mm.).
Rear	⅝ in. (15.87 mm.).

MINI MK. I & II (848 c.c.) & MK. II (998 c.c.)—continued

BRAKES (From Chassis Nos. 296257 and 638879)

Lockheed hydraulic	Two-leading shoe.
Lining dimensions	6.75 x 1.5 in. (17.4 x 3.18 cm.).
Lining area per wheel: Front	20.5 sq. in. (132.3 cm.^{2}).
Rear	17.1 sq. in. (110.3 cm.^{2}).
Swept area per wheel: Front	33 sq. in. (213 cm.^{2}).
Rear	27.5 sq. in. (177.4 cm.^{2}).
Master cylinder bore diameter	0.7 in. (17.78 mm.).
Lining material	Don 202.
Wheel cylinders	
Cylinder bore diameter: Front	$\frac{15}{16}$ in. (23.81 mm.).
Rear	¾ in. (19.05 mm.).

WHEELS

Type: ventilated disc	3.50B x 10.

TYRES

Size:	
Standard	5.20–10 tubeless.
Radial ply	145–10 tubeless.
Pressures:	
Standard—normal conditions	Front 24 lb./sq. in. (1.7 kg./cm.^{2}). Rear 22 lb./sq. in. (1.55 kg./cm.^{2}).
fully loaded	Front and rear 24 lb./sq. in. (1.7 kg./cm.^{2}).
Radial ply, all conditions	Front 28 lb./sq. in. (1.97 kg./cm.^{2}). Rear 26 lb./sq. in. (1.83 kg./cm.^{2}).

ELECTRICAL EQUIPMENT

System	12-volt, positive earth.
Charging system	Compensated voltage control.
Battery	Lucas BLT7A, BLTZ7A, BT7A, BTZ7A.
Capacity: BLT7A, BLTZ7A	34 amp.-hr. at 20-hr. rate.
BT7A, BTZ7A	43 amp.-hr. at 20-hr. rate.
Starter motor	Lucas M35G.
Dynamo	Lucas C40.
Maximum output	22 amps. at 2,250 r.p.m.
Cut-in speed	1,450 r.p.m. at 13.5 volts.
Control box	Lucas RB106/2.
Cut-out: Cut-in voltage	12.7 to 13.3.
Drop-off voltage	8.5 to 11.0.
Reverse current	5.0 amps. (max.).
Regulator (at 3,000 r.p.m. dynamo speed):	
Open-circuit setting at 20°C. (68°F.)	16.0 to 16.6 volts.
For ambient temperatures other than 20° C. (68°F.) the following allowances should be made to the above setting: For every 10°C. (18°F.) above 20°C. (68°F.) subtract .1 volt. For every 10°C. (18°F.) below 20°C. (68°F.) add .1 volt.	
Alternator	Lucas 11AC (12 volts).
Maximum output	43 amperes.
Rotor windings: Resistance	3.8 ± .2 ohms at 20°C. (68°F.).
Current	3.2 amps. at 12 volts.

MINI MK. I & II (848 c.c.) & MK. II (998 c.c.)—continued

Minimum brush length	$\frac{5}{32}$ in. (3.97 mm.).
Brush spring pressure:	
$\frac{25}{32}$ in. (19.84 mm.) compressed length	4 to 5 oz. (113 to 142 gm.).
$\frac{13}{32}$ in. (10.32 mm.) compressed length	7½ to 8½ oz. (212 to 241 gm.).
Control unit	
Type	Lucas 4TR.
Voltage setting at 3,000 alternator r.p.m.	13.9 to 14.3 volts.
Circuit resistance (max.)	.1 ohm.
Field isolating relay	Lucas 6RA.
Warning light control	Lucas 3AW.

GENERAL DIMENSIONS

Wheelbase: Saloon	6 ft. 8 $\frac{5}{32}$ in. (2.036 m.).
Van, Pick-up, Traveller, and Countryman	7 ft. 0 $\frac{5}{32}$ in. (2.138 m.).
Moke	6 ft. 8 $\frac{5}{32}$ in. (2.036 m.).
Overall length: Saloon	10 ft. 0¼ in. (3.05 m.).
Van, Traveller, and Countryman	10 ft. 9 $\frac{7}{8}$ in. (3.259 m.).
Pick-up	10 ft. 10½ in. (3.315 m.).
Moke	10 ft. 0 in. (3.04 m.).
Overall width	4 ft. 7½ in. (1.41 m.).
Moke	4 ft 3½ in. (1.36 m.).
Overall height: Saloon	4 ft. 5 in. (1.35 m.).
Van	4 ft. 6½ in. (1.38 m.).
Traveller, Countryman, and Pick-up	4 ft. 5½ in. (1.36 m.).
Moke	4 ft. 8 in. (1.42 m.).
Ground clearance	6 $\frac{5}{32}$ in. (15.63 cm.).
Moke	6½ in. (16.2 cm.).
Track: Front	47 $\frac{7}{16}$ in. (1.205 m.).
Rear	45 $\frac{7}{8}$ in. (1.164 m.).
Turning circle: Saloon	31 ft. 7 in. (9.63 m.) } Mk. I models.
Van, Pick-up, Traveller, and Countryman	32 ft. 9 in. (9.893 m.) } Mk. I models.
Moke	31 ft. (9.4 m.) } Mk. I models.
Turning circle: Saloon	28 ft 6 in. (8.55 m.) } Mk. II models
Van, Pick-up, Traveller, and Countryman	29 ft. (8.84 m.) } Mk. II models
Kerbside weight: Saloon (Rubber suspension models)	1,294 lb. (587 kg.).
Saloon (Hydrolastic suspension models)	1,398 lb. (634.5 kg.).
Van	1,334 lb. (605 kg.) approx.
Traveller and Countryman	1,456 lb. (660 kg.) approx.
Pick-up	1,328 lb. (604 kg.) approx.
Moke	1,240 lb. (562 kg.).
Maximum permissible towing weight (suitable for 1 in 8 gradient in bottom gear):	
Saloon and Moke	8 cwt. (406.4 kg.).
Van, Pick-up, Traveller, and Countryman	6 cwt. (304.7 kg.).

WEIGHT OF COMPONENTS

Engine and transmission assembly	333 lb. (151 kg.).

MINI MK. I & II (848 c.c.) & MK. II (998 c.c.)—continued

CAPACITIES

Transmission casing (including filter)	8½ pints (10.2 U.S. pints, 4.83 litres).
Cooling system	5¼ pints (6.3 U.S. pints, 3 litres).
With heater	6¼ pints (7.5 U.S. pints, 3.55 litres).
Fuel tank: Saloon	5½ gallons (6.6 U.S. gallons, 25 litres).
Van and Pick-up	6 gallons (7.2 U.S. gallons, 27.3 litres).
Traveller and Countryman: Early models	6½ gallons (7.8 U.S. gallons, 29.6 litres).
Later models with underfloor tank	6 gallons (7.2 U.S. gallons, 27.3 litres).

TORQUE WRENCH SETTINGS

	lb. ft.	kg. m.
Engine		
Camshaft nut	60 to 70	8.3 to 9.7
Connecting rod big-end bolts	35 to 38	4.8 to 5.3
Crankshaft pulley nut	70 to 80	9.7 to 11.1
Cylinder head stud nuts	40	5.5
Cylinder side cover	3 to 4	0.42 to 0.55
Clutch spring housing to pressure plate set screws	16	2.2
Driving strap to flywheel set screw	16	2.2
Flywheel centre bolt	110 to 115	15.2 to 15.9
Flywheel housing bolts and stud nuts	18	2.5
Gudgeon pin clamp screws	22 to 25	3.0 to 3.5
Heater control to cylinder head	6 to 8	0.83 to 1.11
Main bearing set screws	60 to 65	8.3 to 9.0
Manifold to cylinder head	12 to 16	1.7 to 2.2
Oil filter bowl centre bolt	12 to 16	1.7 to 2.2
Oil pump	6 to 9	0.83 to 1.25
Oil pipe banjo	35 to 40	4.8 to 5.5
Oil pressure release valve—dome nut	40 to 45	5.5 to 6.2
Rocker cover	3 to 4	0.41 to 0.55
Rocker shaft bracket nuts	22 to 25	3.0 to 3.5
Spark plugs (cast iron cylinder head)	18	2.5
Timing cover and front plate:		
¼ in. dia. UNF bolts	4 to 6	0.55 to 0.83
$\frac{5}{16}$ in. dia. UNF bolts	10 to 14	1.4 to 1.9
Water pump	14 to 18	1.9 to 2.5
Water outlet elbow	6 to 9	0.83 to 1.25
Thermal transmitter	16	2.2
Gearbox and transmission		
Third motion shaft bearing retainer screws	13	1.8
First motion shaft nut	150	20.7
Third motion shaft nut	150	20.7
Transmission case to crankcase	6	.8
Transmission drain plug	25	3.5
Transmission case studs—$\frac{3}{8}$ in. dia. UNC.	8	1.1
Transmission case studs—$\frac{5}{16}$ in. dia. UNC.	6	.8
Transmission case stud nuts—$\frac{3}{8}$ in. UNF.	25	3.4
Transmission case stud nuts—$\frac{5}{16}$ in. UNF.	18	2.5
Bottom cover set screws—¼ in. dia. UNC. (change-speed tower)	6	.8
Final drive		
Driven gear to differential cage	60	8.3
Driving flange to differential nut	70	9.6 (and align to next split pin hole)
End cover bolts (differential housing)	18	2.5

MINI MK. I & II (848 c.c.) & MK. II (998 c.c.)—continued

TORQUE WRENCH SETTINGS

Suspension and steering	**lb. ft.**	**kg. m.**
Drive shaft coupling 'U' bolt nuts	8 to 12	1.11 to 1.66
Drive shaft nut (front hub)	60	8.3 (align to next slot)
Front suspension tie-rod to front sub-frame	20 to 24	2.8 to 3.3
Front suspension tie-rod to lower wishbone	17 to 20	2.4 to 2.8
Front suspension—upper support arm pivot shaft nut	45 to 60	6.2 to 8.3
Front suspension lower wishbone pivot shaft nut	30 to 35	4.1 to 4.8
Road wheel nuts	40 to 45	5.5 to 6.2
Steering-column/rack pinion clamp bolt	8 to 10	1.11 to 1.38
Steering lever to swivel hub	30 to 35	4.1 to 4.8
Steering tie-rod ball joint to steering arm	20 to 24	2.8 to 3.3
Steering-wheel nut	32 to 37	4.5 to 5.1
Swivel hub ball pin retainer	70 to 80	9.6 to 11.1
Swivel hub ball pins to wishbone arms	35 to 40	4.8 to 5.5
Steering tie-rod ball joint to rack locknut	35 to 40	4.8 to 5.5
Steering rack assembly 'U' bolts to floor	10 to 12	1.4 to 1.7
Steering-column clip bracket to column clip and parcel shelf	13 to 18	1.8 to 2.5
Rear suspension rear hub nut	60	8.3 (align to next slot)
Rear radius arm pivot shaft nut	45 to 60	6.2 to 8.3
Backplate to rear radius arm bolts	18 to 22	2.5 to 3.0

Alternator (11AC)	**lb. in.**	**kg. m.**
Brush box fixing screws	10	.115
Diode heat sink fixings	25	.288
Through-bolts	45 to 50	.518 to .576

Distributor		
Distributor clamp bolt: Fixed nut type	50	.576
Fixed bolt type	30	.345

GENERAL DATA

MINI COOPER 997 c.c. & 998 c.c.

The following information is applicable to the Mini-Cooper and should be used in conjunction with the preceding specification for the Mini Mk. I and II (848 c.c.) and Mk. II (998 c.c.).

	(997 c.c.)	(998 c.c.)
ENGINE		
Type	9F.	9FA.
Number of cylinders	4.	4.
Bore	2.458 in. (62.43 mm.).	2.543 in. (64.588 mm.).
Stroke	3.20 in. (81.28 mm.).	3.00 in. (76.2 mm.).
Capacity	60.87 cu. in. (997 c.c.).	60.96 cu. in. (998 c.c.).
B.M.E.P.: High compression	134 lb./sq. in. (9.42 kg./cm.^{2}) at 3,500 r.p.m.	142 lb. sq. in. (10 kg./cm.^{2}) at 3,000 r.p.m.
Low compression	129 lb./sq. in. (9.07 kg./cm.^{2}) at 3,500 r.p.m.	135 lb./sq. in. (9.5 kg./cm.^{2}) at 3,000 r.p.m.
Torque: High compression	54 lb. ft. (7.46 kg. m.) at 3,600 r.p.m.	57 lb. ft. (7.881 kg. m.) at 3,000 r.p.m.
Low compression	53 lb. ft. (7.32 kg. m.) at 3,500 r.p.m.	56 lb. ft. (7.74 kg. m.) at 2,900 r.p.m.

CRANKSHAFT

Main bearings

Material	Steel-backed copper-lead or aluminium-tin; thin wall.
Running clearance	.001 to .0027 in. (.025 to .069 mm.).
Length	1.0625 in. (26.99 mm.).

CONNECTING RODS

Big-end bearings

Material	Steel-backed copper-lead or aluminium-tin; thin wall.
Bearing length	.875 in. (22.22 mm.).

PISTONS

Type	Solid skirt.	Solid skirt.
Clearance:		
Bottom of skirt (pressure face)	.0016 to .0022 in. (.041 to .056 mm.).	.0005 to .0011 in. (.013 to .028 mm.).
Oversizes: 1st	+.010 in. (.254 mm.).	
2nd	+.020 in. (.508 mm.).	

PISTON RINGS

Compression: Top	Plain, chrome-faced.
Second and third	Tapered.
Width	.0620 to .0625 in. (1.574 to 1.588 mm.).
Thickness (all rings)	.106 to .112 in. (2.692 to 2.835 mm.).

GUDGEON PIN

Type	Fully floating, with circlip location.
Fit in piston	.0001 in. (.0025 mm.) tight to .00035 in. (.0089 mm.) slack.
Fit in small end	.0002 in. (.005 mm.) slack, to size.
Diameter	.6244 in. (15.86 mm.) to .6247 in. (15.867 mm.).

MINI-COOPER (997 c.c. & 998 c.c.)—continued

VALVES AND VALVE GEAR

	(997 c.c.)	(998 c.c.)
Valves		
Throat diameter: Inlet	.098 in. (23.06 mm.).	1.172 in. (29.77 mm.).
Exhaust	.312 in. (7.92 mm.).	.908 in. (23.06 mm.).
Head diameter: Inlet	1.156 in. (29.4 mm.).	1.219 in. (30.86 mm.).
Exhaust	1.00 in. (25.40 mm.).	1.00 in. (25.4 mm.).
Valve lift	.312 in. (7.92 mm.).	.312 in. (7.92 mm.).
Inlet valve: Opens	16°B.T.D.C. *	5°B.T.D.C. *
Closes	56°A.B.D.C. *	45°A.B.D.C. *
Exhaust valve: Opens	51°B.B.D.C. *	51°B.B.D.C. *
Closes	21°A.T.D.C. *	21°A.T.D.C. *

* With .019 in. (.48 mm.) valve rocker clearance (for checking purposes only).

VALVE SPRINGS

	(997 c.c.)	(998 c.c.)
Free length: Inner		1.672 in. (42.47 mm.).
Outer	1.75 in. (44.45 mm.).	1.75 in. (44.45 mm.).
Pressure: Inner: Valve closed		18 lb. (8.17 kg.).
Valve open		30 lb. (13.6 kg.).
Outer: Valve closed	55 lb. (24.9 kg.).	55½ lb. (25.13 kg).
Valve open	90 lb. (40.8 kg.).	88 lb. (39.9 kg.).

CAMSHAFT

Journal diameters: Front	1.6655 to 1.6666 in. (42.304 to 42.316 mm.).
Centre	1.62275 to 1.62325 in. (41.218 to 41.231 mm.).
Rear	1.3725 to 1.3735 in. (34.862 to 34.887 mm.).
End-float	.003 to .007 in. (.076 to .178 mm.).
Bearings: Number and type	3. Steel-backed white metal.
Inside diameter (reamed in position): Front	1.667 to 1.6675 in. (42.342 to 42.355 mm.).
Centre	1.6245 to 1.6255 in. (41.261 to 41.287 mm.).
Rear	1.3748 to 1.3755 in. (34.914 to 34.937 mm.).

ENGINE LUBRICATION SYSTEM

Oil pump	
Type	Concentric or Hobourn-Eaton.
Relief pressure valve operates	70 lb./sq. in. (4.92 kg./cm.^{2}).
Relief valve spring: Free length	2 $\frac{39}{64}$ in. (66.28 mm.).
Fitted length	2 $\frac{5}{32}$ in. (54.77 mm.).
Oil pressure	
Normal running	70 lb./sq. in. (4.92 kg./cm.^{2}).
Idling (minimum)	15 lb./sq. in. (1.05 kg./cm.^{2}).

FUEL SYSTEM

Carburetter refer to 'TUNING DATA'.

Fuel pump	
Make and type	S.U. electric. Type SP.
Delivery rate	56 pts./hr. (67.2 U.S. pts./hr., 32 litres/hr.).
Delivery pressure	2½ to 3 lb./sq. in. (.18 to .21 kg./cm.^{2}).

MINI-COOPER (997 c.c. & 998 c.c.)—continued

AIR CLEANERS

Type	Oil-wetted gauze.
Later models	Paper elements

IGNITION SYSTEM

Coil, **Distributor**, **Sparking plugs** — Refer to 'TUNING DATA'.

CLUTCH

Pressure springs—colour	Black enamel with white spot.
Diaphragm spring colour code	Light green.

GEARBOX

Ratios: Top	1.0 : 1.	
Third	1.357 : 1.	
Second	1.916 : 1.	
First	3.2 : 1.	
Reverse	3.2 : 1.	
	STANDARD	AVAILABLE ALTERNATIVE
Overall ratios: Top	3.765 : 1.	3.444 : 1.
Third	5.11 : 1.	4.674 : 1.
Second	7.213 : 1.	6.598 : 1.
First	12.05 : 1.	11.03 : 1.
Reverse	12.05 : 1.	11.03 : 1.

DIFFERENTIAL

Ratio	3.765 : 1 standard. 3.444 : 1 optional (available as a Service item only).

BRAKES

Brake fluid	Lockheed (Series 329).

Front

Type	Disc.
Disc diameter	7 in. (177.8 mm.).
Pad area (total)	13.8 sq. in. (89 cm.^{2}).
Swept area (total)	101 sq. in. (651.5 cm.^{2}).
Pad material	M78 (Red/green/red/green/red).
Minimum pad thickness	$\frac{1}{16}$ in. (1.6 mm.).

Rear

Drum size	7 in. (17.8 cm.) diameter.
Lining dimensions	6.75 x 1.5 in. (17.4 x 3.18 cm.).
Lining area total	40.5 sq. in. (261.29 cm.^{2}).
Lining material	Don 202.

MINI-COOPER (997 c.c. & 998 c.c.)—continued

GENERAL DIMENSIONS

Kerbside weight: Rubber suspension models	1,400 lb. (635 kg.).
Hydrolastic suspension models	1,433 lb. (650 kg.).
Maximum permissible towing weight (suitable for 1 in 8 gradient in bottom gear):	8 cwt. (406.4 kg.).

TORQUE WRENCH SETTINGS

	lb. ft.	**kg. m.**
Calliper retaining bolts	35 to 40	4.8 to 5.5
Steering lever ball joint	25 to 30	3.4 to 4.1.

GENERAL DATA

MINI-COOPER 'S' MK. I (970 c.c., 1071 c.c. & 1275 c.c.) and COOPER 'S' MK. II & III (1275 c.c.)

The following information is applicable to the Mini-Cooper 'S' and should be used in conjunction with the preceding specifications. See Workshop Manual Supplement AKD 4957 for engine tuning data on cars fitted with exhaust emission control equipment (Exhaust Port Air Injection).

ENGINE

Number of cylinders	4.
Bore (all models)	2.780 in. (70.6 mm.).
Stroke: 970 c.c.	2.4375 in. (61.91 mm.).
1071 c.c.	2.687 in. (68.26 mm.).
1275 c.c.	3.2 in. (81.33 mm.).
Cubic capacity: 970 c.c.	59.1 cu. in. (970 c.c.).
1071 c.c.	63.35 cu. in. (1071 c.c.).
1275 c.c.	77.9 cu. in. (1275 c.c.).
Capacity of combustion chamber (valves and sparking plug fitted)	1.306 cu. in. (21.4 c.c.).
B.M.F.P.: 970 c.c.	142 lb./sq. in. (9.98 kg./cm.^{2}) at 4,500 r.p.m.
1071 c.c.	143 lb./sq. in. (10.05 kg./cm.^{2}) at 4,500 r.p.m.
1275 c.c.	153 lb./sq. in. (10.76 kg./cm.^{2}) at 3,000 r.p.m.
Torque: 970 c.c.	57 lb. ft. (7.88 kg. m.) at 5,000 r.p.m.
1071 c.c.	62 lb. ft. (8.58 kg. m.) at 4,500 r.p.m.
1275 c.c.	79 lb. ft. (10.92 kg. m.) at 3,000 r.p.m.

CRANKSHAFT

Main journal diameter	2.0005 to 2.0010 in. (50.81 to 50.82 mm.).
Minimum regrind diameter	1.9805 to 1.9810 in. (50.30 to 50.31 mm.).
Main bearings	
Material	Steel-backed copper-lead; thin wall.
Length	1.000 in. (25.4 mm.).
Running clearance	.001 to .0027 in. (.025 to .068 mm.).

CONNECTING RODS

Little-end bore diameter	.8110 to .8115 in. (20.60 to 20.61 mm.).

PISTONS

Type	Solid skirt.
Clearance: Bottom of skirt (pressure face)	.0019 to .0025 in. (.048 to .063 mm.).
Top of skirt	.0025 to .00283 in. (.063 to .072 mm.).

PISTON RINGS

Compression: Plain	Top ring.
Tapered	Second and third ring.
Width	.0459 to .0469 in. (1.16 to 1.19 mm.).
Thickness	.116 to .122 in. (2.94 to 3.09 mm.).
Fitting gap	.008 to .013 in. (.20 to .33 mm.).
Clearance in groove	.0015 to .0035 in. (.04 to .09 mm.).
Oil control type	
Width	.1553 to .1563 in. (3.94 to 3.96 mm.).
Thickness	.116 to .122 in. (2.94 to 3.09 mm.).
Fitted gap	.008 to .013 in. (.20 to .33 mm.).
Clearance in groove	.0015 to .0035 in. (.04 to .09 mm.).

MINI-COOPER 'S' MK. I (970 c.c., 1071 c.c., & 1275 c.c.) & COOPER 'S' MK. II & III (1275 c.c.)—continued

GUDGEON PIN

Type	Pressed in connecting rod.
Fit in piston	Hand push-fit.
Diameter (outer)	.8123 to .8125 in. (20.63 to 20.64 mm.).
Fit in connecting rod	.0008 to .0015 in. (.020 to .038 mm.) interference.

VALVES AND VALVE GEAR

Valves

Head diameter: Inlet	1.401 to 1.406 in. (35.58 to 35.71 mm.).
Exhaust	1.214 to 1.219 in. (30.83 to 30.96 mm.).
Valve lift	.318 in. (8.08 mm.), nominal.
Stem diameter: Exhaust	.2788 to .2793 in. (7.08 to 7.09 mm.).
Inlet	.2793 to .2798 in. (7.09 to 7.11 mm.).
Valve rocker clearance: Standard	.012 in. (.30 mm.) cold.
Competition	.015 in. (.38 mm.) cold.
Timing	.021 in. (.53 mm.).
Inlet valve: Opens	5° B.T.D.C.
Closes	45° A.B.D.C.
Exhaust valve: Opens	51° B.B.D.C.
Closes	21° A.T.D.C.

(Inlet and exhaust valve timing: with .021 in. (.53 mm.) valve rocker clearance (for checking purposes only).)

VALVE SPRINGS

Free length: Inner	1.705 in. (43.31 mm.).
Outer	1.740 in. (44.19 mm.).
Number of working coils: Inner	6¼.
Outer	4½.
Pressure: Inner: Valve closed	26.6 lb. (12.065 kg.).
Valve open	46 lb. (20.865 kg.).
Outer: Valve closed	49.6 lb. (22.498 kg.).
Valve open	94 lb. (42.638 kg.).

CAMSHAFT

Journal diameter: Rear	1.37275 to 1.3735 in. (34.87 to 34.88 mm.).
Inside diameter (reamed in position): Rear	1.3745 to 1.3750 in. (34.91 to 34.92 mm.).
Running clearance: Rear	.001 to .00225 in. (.025 to .057 mm.).
Bearing length: Rear	$\frac{49}{64}$±.010 in. (19.45±.25 mm.).

ENGINE LUBRICATION SYSTEM

Oil pressure (normal running)	60 lb./sq. in. (4.22 kg./cm.^{2}) at 70° C. (158° F.) oil temperature.

COOLING SYSTEM

Thermostat setting	82° C. (180° F.).
Cold climates	88° C. (188° F.).
Hot climates	74° C. (165° F.).

FUEL SYSTEM

Carburetter refer to 'TUNING DATA'.

MINI-COOPER 'S' MK. I (970 c.c., 1071 c.c., & 1275 c.c.) & COOPER 'S' MK. II & III (1275 c.c.)—continued

CLUTCH

Make and type: Early type	BMC single dry plate.
Later type	Diaphragm spring.
Diameter	7.125 in. (180.9 mm.).
Facing material: Standard	Wound yarn, riveted.
Pressure springs (early type): Inner	6.
Outer	6.
Colour: Inner	Green spot.
Outer	White spot.

GEARBOX (3-speed Synchromesh)

Ratios:	Standard	Optional (close ratio)
Top	1.0 : 1	1.0 : 1
Third	1.357 : 1	1.242 : 1
Second	1.916 : 1	1.78 : 1
First	3.200 : 1	2.57 : 1
Reverse	3.200 : 1	2.57 : 1

Overall gear ratios (as applicable):

Standard gearbox

Final drive ratio	1st and reverse	2nd	3rd	4th
3.765 (17/64)	12.05 : 1	7.21 : 1	5.11 : 1	3.765 : 1
3.444 (18/62)	11.02 : 1	6.60 : 1	4.67 : 1	3.444 : 1
3.939 (16/63)	12.06 : 1	7.54 : 1	5.34 : 1	3.939 : 1
4.133 (15/62)	13.27 : 1	7.92 : 1	5.61 : 1	4.133 : 1
4.267 (15/64)	13.65 : 1	8.18 : 1	5.79 : 1	4.267 : 1

Optional gearbox (close ratio)

Final drive ratio	1st and reverse	2nd	3rd	4th
3.444 (18/62)	8.84 : 1	6.13 : 1	4.28 : 1	3.444 : 1
3.647 (17/62)	9.37 : 1	6.49 : 1	4.53 : 1	3.647 : 1
3.765 (17/64)	9.66 : 1	6.70 : 1	4.68 : 1	3.765 : 1
3.939 (16/63)	10.12 : 1	7.02 : 1	4.89 : 1	3.939 : 1
4.133 (15/62)	10.61 : 1	7.35 : 1	5.13 : 1	4.133 : 1
4.267 (15/64)	10.90 : 1	7.61 : 1	5.30 : 1	4.267 : 1
4.35 (15/65)	11.18 : 1	7.74 : 1	5.40 : 1	4.35 : 1

Road speed in top at 1,000 r.p.m.

Ratio	
3.444	16.07 m.p.h. (25.71 km.p.h.).
3.647	15 m.p.h. (24.14 km.p.h.).
3.765	14.7 m.p.h. (23.52 km.p.h.).
3.939	14.06 m.p.h. (22.5 km.p.h.).
4.133	13.4 m.p.h. (21.44 km.p.h.).
4.267	12.96 m.p.h. (20.74 km.p.h.).
4.35	12.57 m.p.h. (20.23 km.p.h.).

DIFFERENTIAL

Ratio—standard: 970 c.c.	3.765 : 1.
1071 c.c.	3.765 : 1.
1275 c.c. (Mk. I and II)	3.444 : 1.
Alternative ratios	3.939 : 1, 4.267 : 1, and 4.35 : 1.

MINI-COOPER 'S' MK. I (970 c.c., 1071 c.c., & 1275 c.c.) & COOPER 'S' MK. II & III (1275 c.c.)—continued

GEARBOX (4-speed Synchromesh) — **Standard (close ratio)**

Ratios	
Top	1.0 : 1
Third	1.35 : 1
Second	2.07 : 1
First	3.30 : 1
Reverse	3.35 : 1

Overall gear ratios (4-speed synchromesh)

Final drive ratio	Reverse	1st	2nd	3rd	4th
3.65 : 1 (17/62)	12.21	12.04	7.56	4.93	3.65

Road speed in top at 1,000 r.p.m.

Ratio

3.65 : 1 .. .. 15 m.p.h. (24.14 km.p.h.).

DIFFERENTIAL

Ratio—standard: 1275 c.c. .. .. 3.65 : 1.

Alternative ratios .. .. 3.939 : 1, 4.267 : 1, and 4.35 : 1.

BRAKES

Type .. .. Lockheed hydraulic with vacuum servo.

Servo Unit

Type: (Mk. I and II models) .. .. Lockheed 5½ in. (140 mm.).

(Mk. III models) .. .. Lockheed type 6.

Front

Type .. .. Disc.

Disc diameter .. .. 7½ in. (190.5 mm.).

Pad material (Up to Commission No. 000573A) .. .. Ferodo DA6.

(From Commission No. 000574A) .. .. Mintex M78 (Red/green/red/green/red).

Pad area (total) .. .. 17.3 sq. in. (111.4 cm.²).

Swept area (total) .. .. 122 sq. in. (787 cm.²).

Minimum pad thickness .. .. 1/16 in. (1.6 mm.).

FRONT HUBS

Bearings .. .. Timkin taper roller.

WHEELS

Type: Ventilated disc .. .. 3.50B x 10 or 4.5J x 10.

TYRES

Size: Standard .. .. 145–10 SP, tubed, or 5.20–10 C41 tubed.

Optional .. .. 500L–10, tubed.

Tyre pressures (145–10SP and 5.20–10 C41 only):

Front .. .. 28 lb./sq. in. (1.97 kg./cm.²).

Rear .. .. 26 lb./sq. in. (1.83 kg./cm.²).

MINI-COOPER 'S' MK. I (970 c.c., 1071 c.c., & 1275 c.c.) & COOPER 'S' MK. II & III (1275 c.c.)—continued

CAPACITIES

Fuel tank: (early models)	$5\frac{1}{2}$ galls. (25 litres).
Twin tanks (later Mk. II and Mk. III models)	11 galls. (50 litres).

GENERAL DIMENSIONS

Track: Front: 3·5 in. rim	$47\frac{17}{32}$ in. (1·207 m.).
4·5 in. rim	$48\frac{17}{32}$ in. (1·233 m.).
Rear: 3·5 in. rim	$46\frac{5}{16}$ in. (1·176 m.).
4·5 in. rim	$47\frac{5}{16}$ in. (1·202 mm.).
Kerbside weight: Rubber suspension models	1,411 lb. (640 kg.) approx.
Hydrolastic suspension models	1,540 lb. (698 kg.) approx.

TORQUE WRENCH SETTINGS

	lb. ft.	*kg. m.*
Cylinder head nuts (10 off)	42	5·8
Cylinder head bolt (front, 1 off)	25	3·5
Connecting rod big-end nuts (assemble dry only)	40	5·5
Main bearing set screws (early type)	67	9·3
Main bearing nuts (later type)	57	7·9
Drive shaft nut	150	20·7

GENERAL DATA

MINI AUTOMATIC (848 c.c. & 998 c.c.)

The following information is applicable to the Mini Automatic and should be used in conjunction with the preceding specification for the Mini Mk. I and II (848 c.c.) and Mk. II (998 c.c.).

ENGINE

	(848 c.c.)	(998 c.c.)
Type	8AH.	9AG.
B.H.P.	39 at 5,250 r.p.m.	41 at 4,850 r.p.m.
B.M.E.P.		130 lb./in.^{2} (9.14 kg./cm.^{2}) at 2,750 r.p.m.
Torque	44 lb. ft. (6.08 kg. m.) at 2,500 r.p.m.	52 lb. ft. (7.19 kg. m.) at 2,750 r.p.m.

LUBRICATION SYSTEM

Oil pump

Type .. .. Hobourn-Eaton.

Oil filter

Type .. .. Full-flow.

Capacity .. .. 1 pint (1.2 U.S. pints, .57 litre).

Oil pressure

Normal running speed and temperature .. .. 60 lb./sq. in. (4.22 kg./cm.^{2}).

Idling (minimum) at normal running temperature .. .. 15 lb./sq. in. (1.05 kg./cm.^{2}).

COOLING SYSTEM

Pressure cap (up to 1974) .. .. 13 lb./sq. in. (0.91 kg./cm.^{2}).

(To ECE 15 regulations–1974 on) .. .. 15 lb./sq. in. (1.05 kg./cm.^{2}).

FUEL SYSTEM

Carburetter refer to 'TUNING DATA'.

IGNITION SYSTEM

Coil
Distributor
Sparking plugs } Refer to 'TUNING DATA'.

DIFFERENTIAL

Ratio .. .. 3.27 : 1.

AUTOMATIC TRANSMISSION

Ratios:	Top	1.0 : 1.
	Third	1.46 : 1.
	Second	1.845 : 1.
	First	2.69 : 1.
	Reverse	2.69 : 1.
Overall ratios:	Top	3.76 : 1.
	Third	5.49 : 1.
	Second	6.94 : 1.
	First	10.11 : 1.
	Reverse	10.11 : 1.
Speedometer		7/17.

MINI AUTOMATIC—continued

TORQUE CONVERTER

Type	3-element.
Ratio	2 : 1 maximum.
Converter output gear ratio	1.15 : 1.
End-float	.0035 to .0065 in. (.089 to .164 mm.).

DRIVE SHAFTS

Make and type of joint	Hardy Spicer, flange joint.

CAPACITIES

Transmission casing (including filter)	13 pints (7.38 litres, 16 U.S. pints).
Refill capacity (approx.)	9 pints (5 litres, 11 U.S. pints).

WEIGHT OF COMPONENTS

Engine and transmission assembly	357 lb. (162 kg.).
Automatic transmission	112 lb. (50.8 kg.).

GENERAL DIMENSIONS

Kerbside weight: Mini Mk. I Saloon	1,390 lb. (630.8 kg.).
Mini Mk. II Saloon	1,442 lb. (654 kg.).
Mini 850/1000 Saloon	1,442 lb. (654 kg.).
Mini Clubman Saloon	1,450 lb. (658 kg.).

TORQUE WRENCH SETTINGS

	lb. ft.	kg. m.
Converter centre bolt	110 to 115	15.2 to 15.9
Converter (six central bolts)	22 to 24	3.0 to 3.3
Converter drain plugs	18 to 20	2.5 to 2.8
Converter housing bolts	18	2.5
Differential driving flange securing bolts	40 to 45	5.5 to 6.2
Gear train bearing caps	12	1.6
Gear train carrier strap	12	1.6
Governor to auxiliary pump housing bolts	10 to 15	1.4 to 2
Kickdown control assembly to transmission casing (on nyloc housing)	5	.7
Oil filter bowl	12 to 16	1.6 to 2.2
Input shaft nut	70	9.6
Servo unit securing bolts	17	2.4
Top and reverse clutch hub nut	150	20.7
Transmission to engine securing nut	12	1.6
Valve block securing bolts	10	1.4
Valve block bolts (securing three sections)	7	0.97
$\frac{5}{16}$ in. UNF. bolts	18 to 20	2.5 to 2.8
$\frac{3}{8}$ in. UNF. bolts	30	4.1

GENERAL DATA

MINI 850/1000 SALOON, VAN, & PICK-UP

The following information refers specifically to new or modified components fitted to the above Mini range coincident with the introduction of NEGATIVE earth electrical systems and must be used in conjunction with the preceding specifications for the Mini Mk. I (848-c.c. engine) and the Mini Mk. II (998-c.c. engine).

ENGINE

Type (848c.c.)	85H.
(998c.c.)	99H.

COOLING SYSTEM

Pressure cap (up to 1974)	13 lb./sq. in. (0.91 kg./cm.^{2}).
(To ECE 15 regulations–1974 on)	15 lb./sq. in. (1.05 kg./cm.^{2}).

ENGINE LUBRICATION SYSTEM

Oil filter

Type	Full flow, renewable element or cartridge.
Capacity	1 pint (1.2 U.S. pints, 0.57 litre).

IGNITION SYSTEM

Coil
Distributor
Sparking plugs
} Refer to '**TUNING DATA**'.

FUEL SYSTEM

Carburetter refer to '**TUNING DATA**'.

Fuel pump

Make/type	S.U. mechanical; AUF 700 (AUF 705 model).
Suction (min.)	6 in. (152 mm.) Hg.
Pressure (min.)	3 lb./sq. in. (.21 kg./cm.^{2}).

TRANSMISSION (Fitted to 998 c.c.)*

Gearbox

Number of forward speeds	4.
Synchromesh	All forward gears.
Ratios: Top	1.00 : 1.
Third	1.43 : 1.
Second	2.21 : 1.
First	3.52 : 1.
Reverse	3.54 : 1.
Overall ratios: Top	3.44 : 1.
Third	4.93 : 1.
Second	7.63 : 1.
First	12.13 : 1.
Reverse	12.19 : 1.
Road speed at 1,000 r.p.m. in top gear	16.2 m.p.h. (25.75 km.p.h.).
Speedometer gear ratio	4/14.

Final drive

Type	Helical gears and differential.
Ratio	3.44 : 1 (18/62).

* Up to 1974 (ECE 15 regulations)–Van and Pick-up as 848 c.c.

MINI 850/1000 SALOON, VAN, & PICK-UP—continued

TRANSMISSION (Fitted to 848 c.c.)

Gearbox

Number of forward speeds	4.
Synchromesh	All forward gears.
Ratios: Top	1.00 : 1.
Third	1.43 : 1.
Second	2.21 : 1.
First	3.52 : 1.
Reverse	3.54 : 1.
Overall ratios: Top	3.76 : 1.
Third	5.40 : 1.
Second	8.32 : 1.
First	13.25 : 1.
Reverse	13.30 : 1.
Road speed at 1,000 r.p.m. in top gear	15.2 m.p.h. (24.3 km.p.h.).
Speedometer gear ratio	4/16.

Final drive

Type	Helical gears and differential.
Ratio	3.76 : 1 (17/64).

DRIVE SHAFT

Make	Hardy Spicer.
Type of shaft	Solid shaft, reverse spline.
Joint at wheel end	Constant velocity.
Coupling/joint at differential end: Later models	Pre-lubricated offset-sphere joint.
Early models	Pre-lubricated sliding joint with rubber coupling and 'U' bolts.

SUSPENSION

Type	Rubber cone spring. (Hydrolastic special market fitment.)

Hydraulic dampers

Type: Front and rear	Tubular telescopic.

BRAKES

Master cylinder	
Bore diameter	0.7 in. (17.78 mm.).
Wheel cylinders	
Bore diameter: Front	$\frac{15}{16}$ in. (23.81 mm.).
Rear	¾ in. (19.05 mm).
Tandem master cylinder	
Bore diameter	0.7 in. (17.78 mm.).
Brake fluid	UNIPART 550 BRAKE FLUID, alternatively use a high-boiling-point brake fluid conforming to specification S.A.E. J1703c, with a minimum boiling point of 260°C. (500°F.).

ELECTRICAL EQUIPMENT

System	12-volt, negative earth	
Charging system	Compensated voltage control.	
Battery:		
Lucas 'Pacemaker' type	A7	A9
Capacity at 20 hr. rate	30 amps.	40 amps.
Lucas type	CL7	CLZ7
Capacity at 20 hr. rate	34 amps.	34 amps.
Exide battery	Type 6 VTP 9–BR.	
Capacity at 20 hr. rate	35 amps.	

MINI 850/1000 SALOON, VAN, & PICK-UP—continued

Dynamo	Lucas C40.
Maximum output	22 amps. at 2,250 r.p.m.
Cut-in speed	1,450 r.p.m. at 13.5 volts.
Control box	Lucas RB106/2.
Cut-out: Cut-in voltage	12.7 to 13.3.
Drop-off voltage	8.5 to 11.0.
Reverse current	5.0 amps. (max.).
Regulator (at 3,000 r.p.m. dynamo speed):	
Open-circuit setting at 20°C. (68°F.)	16.0 to 16.6 volts.
For ambient temperatures other than 20°C. (68°F.) the following allowances should be made to the above setting.	
For every 10°C. (18°F.) above 20°C. (68°F.) subtract .1 volt.	
For every 10°C. (18°F.) below 20°C. (68°F.) add .1 volt.	
Starter motor	Lucas M35G or M35J.
M35G Type: Brush spring tension	15 to 25 oz. (425 to 709 gm.).
M35J Type: Brush spring tension	28 oz. (794 gm.).
Light running current	65 amperes at 8,000-10,000 r.p.m.
Lock torque	7 lb. ft. (.97 kg. m.) with 350-375 amps.
Alternator	Lucas 16ACR.
Nominal output	34 amps. at 6,000 r.p.m. (engine–2,800 r.p.m.).
Nominal system voltage	14.2 volts at 20% nominal output.
Maximum continuous speed	12,500 r.p.m.
Resistance of rotor winding at 20°C. (68°F.)	4.33 ohms ±5%.
Brush spring tension	7 to 10 oz. (198 to 283 gm.).
Windscreen wiper	Lucas 14W.
Light running speeds (rack disconnected)	46 to 52 r.p.m. (normal speed), 60 to 70 r.p.m. (fast speed).
Light running current	1.5 amps. (normal speed), 2 amps. (fast speed).
Brush spring pressure	5 to 7 oz. (140 to 200 gm.).
Minimum brush length	$\frac{3}{16}$ in. (4.8 mm.).
Armature end-float	.002 to .008 in. (.05 to .2 mm.).
Maximum pull to move rack in tube	6 lb. (2.7 kg.).
Windscreen wiper arm spring pressure	7 to 9 oz. (200 to 255 gm.).

GENERAL DIMENSIONS AND WEIGHTS

Track: Models up to 1974: Front	47$\frac{7}{16}$in. (1.205 m.).
Rear	45$\frac{7}{8}$ in. (1.164 m.).
Models to ECE 15 regulations–1974 on:	
Front	47$\frac{13}{16}$in. (1.214 m.).
Rear	46$\frac{15}{32}$in. (1.180 m.).
Kerbside weight:	
850 Saloon (Synchromesh)	1,363 lb. (619 kg.) approx.
1000 Saloon (Synchromesh)	1,410 lb. (640 kg.) approx.
(Automatic)	1,442 lb. (654 kg.) approx.
Van	1,334 lb. (605 kg.) approx.
Pick-up	1,328 lb. (603 kg.) approx.

TORQUE TIGHTENING FIGURES

	lb. ft.	kg. m.
Brakes (split brake system)		
Tandem master cylinder reservoir flange screws	5	0.7
Cylinder body outlet plugs	20 to 33	2.8 to 4.5
Pressure failure switch	12 to 15	1.6 to 2.1
Pressure failure switch body end plug	20 to 33	2.8 to 4.5
Inertia valve plug	40 to 50	5.5 to 6.8
Alternator (Type 16ACR)		
Shaft nut	25 to 30	3.5 to 4.2

Refer to pages **General Data 8 and 9** for all other Torque figures.

GENERAL DATA

MINI CLUBMAN

The following information is applicable to the Mini Clubman Saloon and Estate fitted with the 99H engine. Use in conjunction with the preceding specification for the Mini Mk. II.

ENGINE

Type	99H.
Number of cylinders	4.
Bore	2.543 in. (64.588 mm.).
Stroke	3.00 in. (76.2 mm.).
Capacity	60.96 cu. in. (998 c.c.).
Compression ratio: High compression	8.3 : 1.
Low compression	7.6 : 1
B.M.E.P. High compression	130 lb/sq. in. (9.14 kg./cm.^{2}) at 2,700 r.p.m.
Low compression	———
Torque: High compression	52 lb. ft. (7.28 kg. m.) at 2,700 r.p.m.
Low compression	———

COOLING SYSTEM

Pressure cap (up to 1974)	13 lb./sq. in. (0.91 kg./cm.^{2}).
(To ECE 15 regulations – 1974 on)	15 lb./sq. in. (1.05 kg./cm.^{2}).

ENGINE LUBRICATION SYSTEM

Oil filter

Type	Full flow, renewable element or cartridge.
Capacity	1 pint (1.2 U.S. pints, 0.57 litre).

IGNITION SYSTEM

Coil, **Distributor**, **Sparking plugs** — Refer to **'TUNING DATA'**.

FUEL SYSTEM

Carburetter refer to **'TUNING DATA'**.

Air cleaner

Type	Paper element with warm/cold air intake and silencer tube.

Fuel pump

Make/type	S.U. mechanical; AUF 700 (AUF 705 model).
Suction (min.)	6 in. (152 mm.) Hg.
Pressure (min.)	3 lb./sq. in. (.21 kg./cm.^{2}).

TRANSMISSION

Gearbox

Number of forward speeds	4.
Synchromesh	All forward gears.
Ratios: Top	1.00 : 1.
Third	1.43 : 1.
Second	2.21 : 1.
First	3.52 : 1.
Reverse	3.54 : 1.
Overall ratios: Top	3.44 : 1.
Third	4.93 : 1.
Second	7.63 : 1.
First	12.13 : 1.
Reverse	12.19 : 1.
Road speed at 1,000 r.p.m. in top gear	16.2 m.p.h. (25.75 km.p.h.).
Speedometer gear ratio	4/14.

Final drive

Type	Helical gears and differential.
Ratio	3.44 : 1 (18/62).

MINI CLUBMAN—continued

● **DRIVE SHAFTS**

Make	Hardy Spicer.
Type of shaft	Solid shaft, reverse spline.
Joint at wheel end	Constant velocity.
Coupling/joint at differential end: Later models	Pre-lubricated offset-sphere joint.
Early models	Pre-lubricated sliding joint with rubber coupling and 'U' bolts. ●

STEERING

Type	Rack and pinion.
Steering-wheel turns—lock to lock	2.7.
Steering-wheel diameter	15.0 in. (380 mm.).
Front wheel alignment—toe-out	$\frac{1}{16}$ in. (1.6 mm.) or 0° 15′ included angle } vehicle unladen.
● Lock angle: outer wheel at 20°, inner wheel	21.50°±1.50°. ●

SUSPENSION

Saloon—up to Commission Nos. S 20 S 48644A (Manual gearbox)
S 20 S 48267A (Automatic transmission)

Type	Hydrolastic suspension.
Fluid capacity	4 pints (5 U.S. pints, 2.27 litres), approx.
*Fluid pressure (unladen)	292 lb./sq. in. (20.6 kg./cm.^{2}), approx.
Trim height: Front and rear	13½ ± $\frac{3}{8}$ in. (343 ± 9.5 mm.).

* Adjust to trim height.

Saloon—from Commission Nos. S 20 S 48645A (Manual gearbox)
S 20 S 48268A (Automatic transmission)

Type	Rubber cone springs.

Estate

Type	Rubber cone springs.

HYDRAULIC DAMPERS (Estate car and later saloons)

Type: Front and rear	Tubular telescopic.

ELECTRICAL EQUIPMENT

System	12-volt, negative earth.	
Charging system	Compensated voltage control.	
Battery		
Lucas 'Pacemaker' type	A7	A9
Capacity at 20 hr. rate	30 amps.	40 amps.
Lucas type	CL7	CLZ7
Capacity at 20 hr. rate	34 amps.	34 amps.
Exide battery	Type 6 VTP 9–BR.	
Capacity at 20 hr. rate	35 amps.	
Dynamo	Lucas C40.	
Maximum output	22 amps. at 2,250 r.p.m.	
Cut-in speed	1,450 r.p.m. at 13.5 volts.	
Control box	Lucas RB106/2.	
Cut-out: Cut-in voltage	12.7 to 13.3.	
Drop-off voltage	8.5 to 11.0.	
Reverse current	5.0 amps. (max.).	
Regulator (at 3,000 r.p.m. dynamo speed):		
Open-circuit setting at 20°C. (68°F.)	16.0 to 16.6 volts.	

For ambient temperatures other than 20°C. (68°F.) the following allowances should be made to the above setting: For every 10° C. (18° F.) above 20° C. (68° F.) subtract .1 volt. For every 10°C. (18°F.) below 20°C. (68°F.) add .1 volt.

Starter motor	Lucas M35G or M35J.
M35G Type: Brush spring tension	15 to 25 oz. (425 to 709 gm.).
M35J Type: Brush spring tension	28 oz. (794 gm.).
Light running current	65 amperes at 8,000–10,000 r.p.m.
Lock torque	7 lb. ft. (.97 kg. m.) with 350–375 amps.
Alternator	Lucas 16ACR.
Nominal output	34 amps. at 6,000 r.p.m.
Nominal system voltage	14.2 volts at 20% nominal output.
Maximum continuous speed	12,500 r.p.m.
Resistance of rotor winding at 20° C. (68° F.)	4.33 ohms ± 5%.
Brush spring tension	7 to 10 oz. (198 to 283 gm.).
Windscreen wiper	Lucas 14W.
Light running speeds (rack disconnected)	46 to 52 r.p.m. (normal speed), 60 to 70 r.p.m. (fast speed).
Light running current	1.5 amps. (normal speed), 2 amps. (fast speed).
Brush spring pressure	5 to 7 oz. (140 to 200 gm.).
Minimum brush length	$\frac{3}{16}$ in. (4.8 mm.).
Armature end-float	.002 to .008 in. (.05 to .2 mm.).
Maximum pull to move rack in tube	6 lb. (2.7 kg.).
Windscreen wiper arm spring pressure	7 to 9 oz. (200 to 255 gm.).

GENERAL DIMENSIONS

Wheelbase: Saloon	6 ft. 8 $\frac{5}{32}$ in. (2.036 m.).
Estate	7 ft. 0 $\frac{5}{32}$ in. (2.138 m.).
Overall length: Saloon	10 ft. 4 $\frac{5}{8}$ in. (3.16 m.).
Estate	11 ft. 2 in. (3.4 m.).
Overall width	4 ft. 7½ in. (1.41 m.).
Overall height: Saloon	4 ft. 5 in. (1.35 m.).
Estate	4 ft. 5½ in. (1.36 m.).
Ground clearance	6 $\frac{5}{32}$ in. (15.63 mm.).
Turning circle: Saloon	28 ft. 6 in. (8.55 m.)
Estate	29 ft. (8.84 m.).
Track: Models up to 1974: Front	47 $\frac{7}{16}$ in. (1.205 m.).
Rear	45 $\frac{7}{8}$ in. (1.164 m.).
Models to ECE 15 regulations–1974 on:	
Front	47 $\frac{13}{16}$ in. (1.214 m.).
Rear	46 $\frac{13}{32}$ in. (1.180 m.).

WEIGHTS

Kerbside weight: Saloon	1406 lb. (638 kg.) approx.
Estate	1514 lb. (686 kg.) approx.
Maximum towing weight: Saloon	8 cwt. (406.4 kg.) } (suitable for 1 in 8 gradient in bottom gear).
Estate	6 cwt. (304.7 kg.) } (suitable for 1 in 8 gradient in bottom gear).

CAPACITIES

Transmission casing (including filter)	8½ pints (10.2 U.S. pints, 4.83 litres).
Cooling system	5¼ pints (6.3 U.S. pints, 3 litres).
With heater	6¼ pints (7.5 U.S. pints, 3.55 litres).
Fuel tank: Saloon	5½ gallons (6.6 U.S. gallons, 25 litres).
Estate	6 gallons (7.2 U.S. gallons, 27.3 litres).

TORQUE TIGHTENING FIGURES

Alternator (type 16ACR)

Shaft nut	25 to 30 lb. ft. (3.5 to 4.2 kg. m.).

Refer to pages **General Data 8 and 9** for all other Torque figures.

GENERAL DATA

MINI 1275 GT

ENGINE

Type	12H.
Number of cylinders	4.
Bore	2.78 in. (70.61 mm.).
Stroke	3.2 in. (81.28 mm.).
Capacity	77.8 cu. in. (1274.86 c.c.).
Firing order	1, 3, 4, 2.
Valve operation	Overhead by push-rod.
Compression ratio: H.C.	8.8 : 1.
L.C.	8 : 1.
B.M.E.P.: H.C.	134 lb./sq. in. (9.4 kg./cm.^{2}) at 3,500 r.p.m.
Torque: H.C.	69 lb. ft. at 3,500 r.p.m.
Oversize bore: 1st	.010 in. (.25 mm.).
Max.	.020 in. (.51 mm.).

Crankshaft

Main journal diameter	2.0005 to 2.0010 in. (50.81 to 50.82 mm.).
Crankpin journal diameter	1.7504 to 1.7509 in. (44.45 to 44.47 mm.).
Crankshaft end thrust	Taken in thrust washers at centre main bearing.
Crankshaft end-float	.002 to .003 in. (.05 to .07 mm.).

Main bearings

Number and type	Three thin-wall; split shells copper-lead-indium.
Material	VP3, lead-indium at NFM/3B.
Length	.975 to .985 in. (24.76 to 25.02 mm.).
Diametrical clearance	.001 to .0027 in. (.025 to .07 mm.).
Undersizes	.020 in. (.51 mm.) and .040 in. (1.02 mm.).

Connecting rods

Type	Horizontally split lug end, plain small end.
Length between centres	5.748 to 5.792 in. (21.36 to 21.59 mm.).

Big-end bearings

Type and material	Thin-wall; steel-backed, copper-lead-indium plated.
Length	.840 to .850 in. (21.33 to 21.59 mm.).
Diametrical clearance	.001 to .0025 in. (.02 to .06 mm.).
End-float of crankpin	.006 to .010 in. (.15 to .25 mm.).

Pistons

Type	Aluminium, solid skirt, dished crown.
Clearance in cylinder: Top of skirt	.0029 to .0037 in. (.07 to .09 mm.).
Bottom of skirt	.0015 to .0021 in. (.04 to .05 mm.).
Number of rings	4 (3 compression, 1 oil control).
Width of ring grooves: Top, second, third	.0484 to .0494 in. (1.23 to 1.25 mm.).
Oil control	.1578 to .1588 in. (4.01 to 4.03 mm.).
Gudgeon pin base	.8125 to .8129 in. (20.64 to 20.65 mm.).

Piston rings

Compression: Type: Top	Internally chamfered chrome.
Second and third	Tapered cast iron.
Width Top / Second and Third	.0615 to .0625 in. (1.57 to 1.60 mm.).
Fitted gap: Top	.011 to .016 in. (.28 to .40 mm.).
Second and third	.008 to .013 in. (.20 to .33 mm.).
Ring to groove clearance: Top / Second and third	.0015 to .0035 in. (.04 to .09 mm.).
Oil control:	
Type	Duaflex 61.
Fitted gap: Rails / Side spring	.012 to .028 in. (.30 to .70 mm.).

Gudgeon pin

Type	Pressed in connecting rod.
Fit in piston	Hand push fit.
Diameter (outer)	.8123 to .8125 in. (20.63 to 20.64 mm.).
Fit to connecting rod	.0008 to .0015 in. (.02 to .04 mm.) interference.

Camshaft

Journal diameters: Front	1.6655 to 1.6660 in. (42.304 to 42.316 mm.).
Centre	1.62275 to 1.62325 in. (41.218 to 41.231 mm.).
Rear	1.37275 to 1.37350 in. (34.866 to 34.889 mm.).
Bearing liner inside diameter:	
Un-reamed after fitting: Front	1.652 in. (41.98 mm.).
Centre	1.61 in. (40.89 mm.).
Rear	1.36 in. (34.52 mm.).
Reamed after fitting: Front	1.6670 to 1.6675 in. (42.34 to 42.35 mm.).
Centre	1.62425 to 1.62475 in. (41.25 to 41.37 mm.).
Rear	1.3745 to 1.3750 in. (34.91 to 34.92 mm.).
Bearings: Type	White-metal-lined, steel-backed.
Diametrical clearance	.001 to .002 in. (.02 to .05 mm.).
End-thrust	Taken on locating plate.
End-float	.003 to .007 in. (.07 to .18 mm.).
Cam lift	.318 in. (8.07 mm.).
Drive	Duplex chain and gear from crankshaft.
Timing chain	$\frac{3}{8}$ in. (9.52 mm.) pitch x 52 pitches.

Tappets

Type	Bucket.
Outside diameter	.81125 to .81175 in. (20.60 to 20.62 mm.).
Length	1.495 to 1.505 in. (37.97 to 38.23 mm.).

Rocker gear

Rocker shaft: Diameter	.5615 to .5625 in. (14.26 to 14.29 mm.).
Rocker arm: Bore	.686 to .687 in. (17.45 mm.).
Bush inside diameter	.5630 to .5635 in. (14.3 to 14.31 mm.).

MINI 1275 GT—continued

Valves

Seat angle: Inlet and exhaust	45°.
Head diameter: Inlet	1.307 to 1.312 in. (33.2 to 33.21 mm.).
Exhaust	1.1515 to 1.1565 in. (29.24 to 29.37 mm.).
Stem diameter: Inlet	.2793 to .2798 in. (7.09 to 7.11 mm.).
Exhaust	.2788 to .2793 in. (7.08 to 7.09 mm.).
Stem to guide clearance: Inlet and exhaust	.0015 to .0025 in. (.04 to .08 mm.).
Valve lift: Inlet and exhaust	.318 in. (8.07 mm.).

Valve guides

Length: Inlet	1.6875 in. (42.87 mm.).
Exhaust	1.8437 in. (46.83 mm.).
Fitted height above seat: Exhaust / Inlet	.540 in. (13.72 mm.).

Valve springs

Free length	1.95 in. (49.13 mm.).
Fitted length	1.383 in. (34.715 mm.).
Load at fitted length	79.5 lb. (36.03 kg.).
Load at top of lift	124 lb. (56.3 kg.).
No. of working coils	4½.

Valve timing

Timing marks	Dimples on timing gears.
Rocker clearance: Running	.012 in. (.305 mm.) cold.
Timing	.021 in. (.533 mm.).
Inlet valve: Opens	5° B.T.D.C.
Closes	45° B.B.D.C.
Exhaust valve: Opens	51° B.B.D.C.
Closes	21° A.T.D.C.

ENGINE LUBRICATION SYSTEM

Oil pump

Type	Internal gear, splined drive from camshaft.
Oil pressure relief valve	50 lb./sq. in. (3.5 kg. cm.^{2}).
Relief valve spring: Free length	2.86 in. (72.64 mm.).
Fitted length	2.156 in. (54.77 mm.).
Load at fitted length	13 to 14 lb. (5.90 to 6.35 kg.).

Oil filter

Type	Full flow, renewable element or cartridge.
Capacity	1 pint (1.2 U.S. pints, .57 litre).

System pressure

Running	70 lb./sq. in. (4.92 kg. cm.^{2}) approx.
Idling	15 lb./sq. in. (1.05 kg. cm.^{2}) approx.

MINI 1275 GT—continued

IGNITION SYSTEM

Coil
Distributor
Sparking plugs
} Refer to 'TUNING DATA'.

COOLING SYSTEM

Thermostat settings

Standard	82° C. (180° F.).
Hot countries	74° or 77° C. (165° or 170° F.).
Cold countries	88° C. (190° F.).
Pressure cap: (engines up to 1974)	13 lb./sq. in. (.91 kg./cm.^{2}).
(engines to ECE 15 Regulations)	15 lb./sq. in. (1.05 kg./cm.^{2}).

FUEL SYSTEM

Carburetter refer to 'TUNING DATA'.

Air cleaner

Type: (engines up to 1974)	Paper element with warm/cold air intake and silencer tube.
(engines to ECE 15 Regulations)	Paper element with air temperature control.

Fuel pump

Make/type	S.U. mechanical; AUF 700 (AUF 705 model).
Suction (min.)	6 in. (152 mm.) Hg.
Pressure (min.)	3 lb./sq. in. (.21 kg./cm.^{2}).

CLUTCH

Make and type	Borg & Beck diaphragm type.
Clutch plate diameter	$7\frac{1}{8}$ in. (180.9 mm.).
Facing material	Wound yarn.
Diaphragm-spring colour code	Green/Blue.
Clutch fluid	Unipart 410 or 550 Brake Fluid.

TRANSMISSION

Gearbox

Number of forward speeds	4.	
Synchromesh	All forward gears.	
	From Engine No. 12H 389S, H6901	**Early cars**
Ratios: Top	1.00 : 1	1.00 : 1.
Third	1.35 : 1	1.35 : 1.
Second	2.07 : 1	2.07 : 1.
First	3.30 : 1	3.30 : 1.
Reverse	3.35 : 1	3.35 : 1.
Overall ratios: Top	3.44 : 1	3.65 : 1.
Third	4.66 : 1	4.93 : 1.
Second	7.21 : 1	7.64 : 1.
First	11.47 : 1	12.14 : 1.
Reverse	11.53 : 1	12.21 : 1.
Road speed at 1,000 r.p.m. in top gear	16.2 m.p.h. (25.75 km.p.h.)	15 m.p.h. (24.14 km.p.h.)
Speedometer gear ratio	4/14	4/16.

MINI 1275 GT—continued

Final drive

Type	Helical gears and differential.
Ratio	3.44 : 1 (18/62) 3.65 : 1 (17/62).

DRIVE SHAFTS

Make	Hardy Spicer.
Type of shaft	Solid shaft, reverse spline.
Joint at wheel end	Constant velocity.
Coupling/joint at differential end (later models)	Pre-lubricated offset-sphere joint.
(early models)	Pre-lubricated sliding joint with rubber coupling and 'U' bolts.

STEERING

Type	Rack and pinion.
Steering-wheel turns—lock to lock	2.7.
Steering-wheel diameter	15.0 in. (380 mm.).
Front wheel alignment—toe-out	$\frac{1}{16}$ in. (1.6 mm.) or 0° 15′ included angle } car unladen.

SUSPENSION—up to Commission No. S 20 D 8155A

Type	Hydrolastic suspension.
Fluid capacity	4 pints (5 U.S. pints, 2.27 litres) approx.
*Fluid pressure (unladen)	292 lb./sq. in. (20.6 kg./cm.^{2}), approx.
Trim height—front and rear	13½ ± $\frac{3}{8}$ in. (343 ± 9.5 mm.).

* Adjust to trim height.

Later cars—from Commission No. S 20 D 8156A

Type	Rubber cone springs.

HYDRAULIC DAMPERS (Later cars only)

Type: Front and rear	Tubular telescopic.

BRAKES

Type	Lockheed hydraulic.
Servo unit (Models up to 1974)	Lockheed (Type 6).
Master cylinder bore diameter	.7 in. (17.9 mm.).

Split brake system

(Tandem master cylinder)	Refer to Mini 850/1000 Data.
Brake fluid	Unipart 550 BRAKE FLUID, alternatively use a high-boiling-point brake fluid conforming to specification S.A.E. J1703c, with a minimum boiling point of 260° C. (500° F.).

MINI 1275 GT—continued

Front

Type ..	Disc.
Disc diameter (Models up to 1974) ..	7.5 in. (190.5 mm.).
(Models to ECE 15 Regulations) ..	8.4 in. (213.4 mm.).
Pad material (Models up to 1974) ..	Mintex M78 (Red/green/red/green/red).
(Models to ECE 15 Regulations) ..	Mintex M121 (LDB 751).
Pad area—total (Models up to 1974) ..	17.3 sq. in. (111.6 cm.^{2}).
(Models to ECE 15 Regulations) ..	16.6 sq. in. (107 cm.^{2}).
Swept area—total (Models up to 1974) ..	122 sq. in. (787 cm.^{2}).
(Models to ECE 15 Regulations) ..	134.46 sq. in. (864.5 cm.^{2}).
Minimum pad thickness ..	$\frac{1}{16}$ in. (1.6 mm.).

Rear

Drum size ..	7 in. (17.8 cm.) diameter.
Lining dimensions ..	6.75 x 1.5 in. (17.4 x 3.18 cm.).
Lining area total ..	40.5 sq. in. (261.29 cm.^{2}).
Lining material ..	Don 202.
Wheel cylinder diameter (Models up to 1974) ..	.75 in. (19.05 mm.).
(Models to ECE 15 Regulations) ..	.50 in. (12.7 mm.).

WHEELS

Type ..	Pressed steel disc.
Size (Models up to 1974) ..	4.5J x 10.
(Models to ECE 15 Regulations) ..	4.5J x 12.

TYRES

Size ..	145–10 Radial ply (tubed).
Pressures all conditions: Front ..	28 lb./sq. in. (1.97 kg./cm.^{2}).
Rear ..	26 lb./sq. in. (1.83 kg./cm.^{2}).
Size (Models to ECE 15 Regulations) ..	145/70SR–12.
Pressures all conditions: Front and Rear ..	28 lb./sq. in. (1.97 kg./cm.^{2}).

DENOVO WHEELS AND TYRES

Wheels

Type ..	Divided inner and outer pressed steel rim with replaceable lubricant canisters.
Size ..	80 mm.x 310 mm.

Tyres

Size ..	155/65 SF–310.
Pressures (cold) all conditions: Front ..	26 lb./sq. in. (1.8 kg./cm.^{2}).
Rear ..	24 lb./sq. in. (1.7 kg./cm.^{2}).

ELECTRICAL EQUIPMENT

System ..	12-volt, negative earth.
Charging system ..	Compensated voltage control.

Battery:

Lucas 'Pacemaker' type ..	A9	A11/9.
Capacity at 20 hr. rate ..	40 amps.	50 amps.
Lucas type ..	C9	CZ9.
Capacity at 20 hr. rate ..	43 amps.	43 amps.

Dynamo	Lucas C40.
Maximum output	22 amps. at 2,250 r.p.m.
Cut-in speed	1,450 r.p.m. at 13.5 volts.
Control box	Lucas RB106/2.
Cut-out: Cut-in voltage	12.7 to 13.3.
Drop-off voltage	8.5 to 11.0.
Reverse current	5.0 amps. (max.).
Regulator (at 3,000 r.p.m. dynamo speed):	
Open-circuit setting at 20° C. (68° F.)	16.0 to 16.6 volts.
For ambient temperatures other than 20° C. (68° F.) the following allowances should be made to the above setting: For every 10° C. (18° F.) above 20° C. (68° F.) subtract .1 volt. For every 10° C. (18° F.) below 20° C. (68° F.) add .1 volt.	
Starter motor	Lucas M35G or M35J.
M35G Type	
Brush spring tension	15 to 25 oz. (425 to 709 gm.).
M35J Type	
Brush spring tension	28 oz. (794 gm.).
Light running current	65 amperes at 8,000–10,000 r.p.m.
Lock torque	7 lb. ft. (.97 kg. m.) with 350–375 amps.
Alternator	Lucas 16ACR.
Nominal output	34 amps. at 6,000 r.p.m. (engine–2,800 r.p.m.).
Nominal system voltage	14.2 volts at 20% nominal output.
Maximum continuous speed	12,500 r.p.m.
Resistance of rotor winding at 20° C. (68° F.)	4.33 ohms ± 5%.
Brush spring tension	7 to 10 oz. (198 to 283 gm.).
Windscreen wiper	Lucas 14W.
Light running speeds (rack disconnected)	46 to 52 r.p.m. (normal speed), 60 to 70 r.p.m. (fast speed).
Light running current	1.5 amps. (normal speed), 2 amps. (fast speed).
Brush spring pressure	5 to 7 oz. (140 to 200 gm.).
Minimum brush length	3/16 in. (4.8 mm.).
Armature end-float	.002 to .008 in. (.05 to .2 mm.).
Maximum pull to move rack in tube	6 lb. (2.7 kg.).
Windscreen wiper arm spring pressure	7 to 9 oz. (200 to 255 gm.).

GENERAL DIMENSIONS

Wheelbase	6 ft. 8 5/32 in. (2.036 m.).
Overall length	10 ft. 4 21/32 in. (3.16 m.).
Overall width	4 ft. 7½ in. (1.41 m.).
Overall height (Models up to 1974)	4 ft. 5 in. (1.35 m.).
(Models 1974 on with standard 12 in. wheels)	4 ft. 5½ in. (1.358 m.).
(Models with DENOVO wheels/tyres)	4 ft. 5 21/64 in. (1.354 m.).
Ground clearance (Models up to 1974)	6 in. (152.4 mm.).
(Models with standard 12 in. wheels)	6½ in. (165 mm).
(Models with DENOVO wheels/tyres)	6 21/64 in. (161 mm.).
Turning circle	28 ft. 6 in. (8.55 m.).

MINI 1275 GT—*continued*

Track (Models up to 1974):	Front	48½ in. (1232 mm.).
	Rear	47⅝ in. (1210 mm.).
(Models with 12 in. wheels):	Front	48¾ in. (1238 mm.).
	Rear	$47\frac{7}{16}$ in. (1205 mm.).
(Models with DENOVO wheels/tyres):	Front	$48\frac{37}{64}$ in. (1234 mm.).
	Rear	47¼ in. (1200 mm.).

WEIGHTS

Kerbside weight (Models with standard wheels)	1,555 lb. (707 kg.) approx.
(Models with DENOVO wheels)	1,481 lb. (671 kg.) approx.
Maximum permissible towing weight (suitable for 1 in 8 gradient in bottom gear):	8 cwt. (406.4 kg.).

WEIGHT OF COMPONENTS

Engine and transmission assembly	339 lb. (154 kg.).

Capacities

Transmission casing (including filter)	8½ pints (10.2 U.S. pints, 4.83 litres).
Cooling system	5¼ pints (6.3 U.S. pints, 3 litres).
With heater	6¼ pints (7.5 U.S. pints, 3.55 litres).
Fuel tank (Models up to 1974)	5½ gallons (6.6 U.S. gallons, 25 litres).
(Models to ECE 15 Regulations)	7½ gallons (9 U.S. gallons, 43 litres).

TORQUE TIGHTENING FIGURES

	lb. ft	**kg. m.**
Engine		
Cylinder head nuts	50	7
Connecting rod bolt nuts (including multi-sided type nuts—oiled)	31 to 35	4.3 to 4.8
Alternator (type 16ACR)		
Shaft nut	25 to 30	3.5 to 4.2
Brakes		
Calliper retaining bolts	35 to 40	4.8 to 5.5
Suspension and steering		
Drive shaft nut	150	20.7
Steering lever ball joint	25 to 30	3.5 to 4.2

Refer to pages **General Data 8 and 9** for all other Torque figures

GENERAL DATA

MINI CLUBMAN 1100

The following information is applicable to the Mini Clubman 1100 Saloon and Estate fitted with the 10H engine. Use in conjunction with the specification for the Mini Clubman.

ENGINE

Type	10H
Number of cylinders	4
Bore	2.543 in (64.58 mm)
Stroke	3.296 in (83.72 mm)
Capacity	1098 cm^3 (67 in^3)
Firing order	1, 3, 4 2
Valve operation	Overhead by push-rod
Compression ratio	8.5 : 1
Oversize bores	0.020 in (0.51 mm)
Torque (gross)	60 lbf ft (8.3 kgf m) at 2,450 rev/min

Crankshaft

Main journal diameter	1.7505 to 1.7512 in (44.46 to 44.48 mm)
Minimum regrind diameter	1.7105 in (43.45 mm)
Crankpin journal diameter	1.6252 to 1.6259 in (41.28 to 41.29 mm)
Minimum regrind diameter	1.5852 in (40.27 mm)
Crankshaft end-thrust	Taken on thrust washers at centre main bearing
Crankshaft end-float	0.001 to 0.005 in (0.03 to 0.13 mm)

Main bearings

Number and type	3 thin wall type
Width	1$\frac{1}{16}$ in (27 mm)
Diametrical clearance	0.001 to 0.0027 in (0.03 to 0.07 mm)
Undersizes	0.010 in 0.020 in 0.030 in 0.040 in (0.25 mm 0.51 mm 0.76 mm 1.02 mm)

Connecting rods

Type	Diagonally split big-end, bushed small end
Length between centres	5.75 in (146.1 mm)

Big-end bearings

Type	Thin wall
Diametrical clearance	0.001 to 0.0025 in (0.03 to 0.06 mm)
Undersizes	0.010 in 0.020 in 0.030 in 0.040 in (0.25 mm 0.51 mm 0.76 mm 1.02 mm)

Gudgeon pin

Type	Fully floating
Fit in piston	Hand push-fit

MINI CLUBMAN 1100—continued

Pistons

Type	Solid skirt
Clearances:	
Bottom of skirt	0.0005 to 0.0015 in (0.01 to 0.04 mm)
Top of skirt	0.0021 to 0.0033 in (0.05 to 0.08 mm)
Oversizes	0.020 in (0.51 mm)

Piston rings

Compression:	
Type: Top	Chrome-faced
Second and third	Tapered, cast iron alloy
Width	0.0615 to 0.0625 in (1.57 to 1.60 mm)
Fitted gap	0.007 to 0.012 in (0.18 to 0.30 mm)
Ring to groove clearance	0.002 to 0.004 in (0.05 to 0.10 mm)
Oil control:	
Type	Duaflex
Fitted gap: Rails	0.012 to 0.028 in (0.30 to 0.71 mm)
Side spring	0.10 to 0.15 in (2.5 to 3.8 mm)

Camshaft

Journal diameters: Front	1.6655 to 1.6660 in (42.30 to 42.32 mm)
Centre	1.62275 to 1.62325 in (41.22 to 41.23 mm)
Rear	1.3725 to 1.3735 in (34.87 to 34.89 mm)
Bearing liner inside diameter (reamed after fitting):	
Front	1.6670 to 1.6675 in (42.34 to 42.35 mm)
Centre	1.62425 to 1.62475 in (41.26 to 41.27 mm)
Rear	1.3745 to 1.3750 in (34.91 to 34.93 mm)
Diametrical clearance	0.001 to 0.002 in (0.02 to 0.05 mm)
End-thrust	Taken on locating plate
End-float	0.003 to 0.007 in (0.08 to 0.18 mm)

Rocker gear

Rocker shaft diameter	0.5615 to 0.5625 in (14.26 to 14.29 mm)
Rocker bush inside diameter (reamed in position)	0.5630 to 0.5635 in (14.30 to 14.31 mm)

Tappets

Type	Barrel
Outside diameter	0.812 in (20.64 mm)
Length	1.5 in (38.10 mm)

Valves

Seat angle: Inlet	45°
Exhaust	45°
Head diameter: Inlet	1.151 to 1.156 in (29.23 to 29.36 mm)
Exhaust	1.0 to 1.005 in (25.4 to 25.53 mm)
Stem diameter: Inlet	0.2793 to 0.2798 in (7.09 to 7.11 mm)
Exhaust	0.2788 to 0.2793 in (7.08 to 7.09 mm)
Stem to guide clearance: Inlet and exhaust	0.0015 to 0.0025 in (0.04 to 0.06 mm)
Valve lift: Inlet and exhaust	0.285 in (7.24 mm)

MINI CLUBMAN 1100—continued

Valve guides

Length: Inlet and exhaust	1.531 in (38.89 mm)
Outside diameter: Inlet and exhaust	0.4695 to 0.4700 in (11.93 to 11.94 mm)
Inside diameter: Inlet and exhaust	0.2813 to 0.2818 in (7.15 to 7.16 mm)
Fitted height above spring seat: Inlet and exhaust	0.5938 in (15.08 mm)
Interference fit in head: Inlet and exhaust	0.0005 to 0.0015 in (0.01 to 0.04 mm)

Valve springs

Free length	1.750 in (44.45 mm)
Fitted length	1.258 in (31.95 mm)
Load at fitted length	55.5 lbf (25.2 kgf)
Load at top of lift	88 lbf (39.9 kgf)
Number of working coils	4½

Valve timing

Timing marks	Dimples on timing wheels, marks on flywheel
Rocker clearance: Running	0.012 in (0.31 mm) cold
Timing	0.029 in (0.74 mm)
Inlet valve: Opens	5° B.T.D.C.
Closes	45° A.B.D.C.
Exhaust valve: Opens	51° B B.D.C.
Closes	21° A.T.D.C.

ENGINE LUBRICATION SYSTEM

System	Wet sump, pressure fed
System pressure: Running	60 lbf/in² (4.21 kgf/cm²)
Idling	15 lbf/in² (1.05 kgf/cm²)
Oil pump	Rotor type
Oil filter	Full flow, with renewable cartridge
Oil pressure relief valve	60 lbf/in² (4.21 kgf/cm²)
Relief valve spring: Free length	2.86 in (72.62 mm)
Fitted length	2.156 in (54.77 mm)

IGNITION SYSTEM

Coil
Distributor
Sparking plugs
} Refer to 'TUNING DATA'.

FUEL SYSTEM

Carburetter refer to 'TUNING DATA'.

Air cleaner

Type	Paper element with air temperature control

Fuel pump

Make/type	S.U. mechanical; AUF 700 (AUF 722 model)
Suction (min.)	6 in (152 mm) Hg
Pressure (min.)	3 lbf/in² (.21 kgf/cm²)

MINI CLUBMAN 1100—continued

COOLING SYSTEM

Pressure cap	15 lbf/in² (1.05 kgf/cm²)

GENERAL DIMENSIONS

Track:	Front	47 13/16 in (1.214 m)
	Rear	46 13/32 in (1.180 m)

CAPACITIES

Fuel tank:	Saloon	7½ gallons (9 U.S. gallons, 34 litres)
	Estate	6 gallons (7.2 U S. gallons, 27.3 litres)

TORQUE WRENCH SETTINGS

	lbf ft	kgf m
Engine		
Cylinder head stud nuts	50	6.91
Connecting rod big-end bolts	37	5.11
Main bearing bolts	63	8.70
Flywheel centre-bolt	113	15.61
Rocker bracket nuts	24	3.32
Cylinder side cover bolt	4	0.55
Timing cover—¼ in U.N.F. bolt	6	0.83
5/16 in U.N.F. bolt	12	1.66
Water pump bolts	16	2.21
Water outlet elbow nuts	8	1.10
Oil filter centre bolt	14	1.94
Oil filter head nuts	14	1.94
Oil pump bolts	8	1.10
Manifold to cylinder head nuts	14	1.94
Rocker cover nuts	4	0.55
Crankshaft pulley nut	75	10.37
Sump drain plug	25	3.46
Flywheel housing bolts and stud nuts	18	2.5

ENGINE TUNING DATA

Model:			Year:
MINI Mk. I	**–Saloon and variants**	(848 c.c.)	**1959–67**
	–Moke		**1965–69**
MINI Mk. II	**–Saloon and variants**		**1967–69**
MINI 850	**–Saloon and variants**		**1969–72**

ENGINE

Type: Mk. I and II models	8AM.	
850 models	85H.	
Capacity	848 c.c. (51.7 cu. in.).	
Compression ratio	8.3 : 1.	
Firing order	1, 3, 4, 2.	
Compression pressure	150 lb./sq. in. (10.5 kg./cm.^{2}).	
Idling speed	500 r.p.m.	
Fast idle speed	900 r.p.m.	
Valve rocker clearance	.012 in. (.305 mm.) (cold).	
Timing marks	Dimples on timing wheels, marks on flywheel.	
	PREMIUM FUEL	REGULAR (COMMERCIAL)
Ignition timing:	DISTRIBUTOR	FUEL DISTRIBUTOR
Static	T.D.C.	7°B.T.D.C.
*† Stroboscopic at 600 r.p.m.	3°B.T.D.C.	10°B.T.D.C.

DISTRIBUTOR

Make/type: Early type	Lucas DM2 or 25D4.	
Later type	Lucas 45D4.	
Contact breaker gap	.014 to .016 in. (.35 to .40 mm.).	
Rotation of rotor	Anti-clockwise.	
Dwell angle: DM2 and 25D4	60°±3°.	
45D4	51°±5°.	
Condenser capacity	.18 to .24 mF.	
Serial No.: DM2 and 25D4	40768, 41026	40767, 41007.
45D4	41411	41410.
	PREMIUM FUEL	REGULAR (COMMERCIAL)
Centrifugal advance	DISTRIBUTOR	FUEL DISTRIBUTOR
Decelerating check*†	30° to 34° at 3,400 r.p.m.	22° to 26° at 5,000 r.p.m.
	24° to 28° at 2,500 r.p.m.	15° to 19° at 3,900 r.p.m.
	16° to 20° at 1,300 r.p.m.	1° to 5° at 1,700 r.p.m.
	9° to 15° at 900 r.p.m.	
	1° to 7° at 700 r.p.m.	
No advance below	500 r.p.m.	850 r.p.m.
Vacuum advance		
Starts	7 in. (17.7 cm.) Hg.	5 in. (12.7 cm.) Hg.
Finishes†	10° at 13 in. (33 cm.) Hg.	16° at 11 in. (27.9 cm.) Hg.

SPARK PLUGS

Make	Champion.
Type	N9Y or N5.
Gap	.025 in. (.625 mm.).

IGNITION COIL

Make/type	Lucas LA12.
Primary resistance at 20°C. (68°F.)	3.2 to 3.4 ohms (cold).
Consumption–ignition on	3.9 amps.

CARBURETTER

Make/type	S.U. Type HS2.
Piston spring	Red.
Jet size	.090 in. (2.29 mm.).
Needle: Standard	EB.
Rich	M.
Weak	GG.

* Crankshaft degrees and r.p.m. † Vacuum pipe disconnected.

ENGINE TUNING DATA

Model: **MINI Mk. II–Saloon and variants** } (998 c.c.) Year: **1967–69**
MINI 1000–Saloon **1969–72**

ENGINE		
Type	99H.	
Capacity	998 c.c. (60.96 cu. in.).	
Compression ratio	8.3 : 1.	
Firing order	1, 3, 4, 2.	
Compression pressure	150 lb./sq. in. (10.5 kg./cm.²).	
Idling speed	500 r.p.m.	
Fast idle speed	900 r.p.m.	
Ignition timing:		Van/Pick-up
Static	5°B.T.D.C.	7°B.T.D.C.
*† Stroboscopic at 600 r.p.m.	8°B.T.D.C.	10°B.T.D.C.
Timing marks	Dimples on timing wheels, marks on flywheel.	
Valve rocker clearance (cold)	.012 in. (.305 mm.)	
DISTRIBUTOR		
Make/type	Lucas 25D4 or 45D4.	
Rotation of rotor	Anti-clockwise.	
Dwell angle: 25D4	60°±3°.	
45D4	51°±5°.	
Contact breaker gap	.014 to .016 in. (.35 to .40 mm.).	
Condenser capacity	.18 to .24 mF.	
		Van/Pick-up
Serial No.: 25D4	40931, 41030	41007.
45D4	41412	41410.
Centrifugal advance		
Decelerating check*†	22° to 26° at 5,000 r.p.m.	22° to 26° at 5,000 r.p.m.
	16° to 20° at 3,400 r.p.m.	15° to 19° at 3,900 r.p.m.
	9° to 13° at 1,600 r.p.m.	1° to 5° at 1,700 r.p.m.
	6° to 10° at 1,300 r.p.m.	
	0° to 4° at 900 r.p.m.	
No advance below	600 r.p.m.	850 r.p.m.
Vacuum advance		
Starts	5 in. (12.7 cm.) Hg.	5 in. (12.7 cm.) Hg.
Finishes†	14° at 11 in. (27.9 cm.) Hg.	16° at 11 in. (27.9 cm.) Hg.
SPARK PLUGS		
Make	Champion.	
Type	N5 or N9Y.	
Gap	.025 in. (.625 mm.).	
IGNITION COIL		
Make/type	Lucas LA12.	
Primary resistance at 20°C. (68°F.)	3.2 to 3.4 ohms (cold).	
Consumption–ignition on	3.9 amps.	
CARBURETTER		
Make/type	S.U. Type HS2.	
Piston spring	Red.	
Jet size	.090 in. (2.29 mm.).	
Needle: Standard	GX.	
Rich	M.	
Weak	GG.	

* Crankshaft degrees and r.p.m. † Vacuum pipe disconnected.

ENGINE TUNING DATA

Model: **MINI Mk. I and II AUTOMATIC** **(848 c.c.)** Year: **1965–69**

ENGINE	
Type	8AH.
Capacity	848 c.c. (51.7 cu. in.).
Compression ratio	8.9 : 1.
Firing order	1, 3, 4, 2.
Compression pressure	160 lb./sq. in. (11.25 kg./cm.²).
Idling speed	650 r.p.m.
Fast idle speed	1,050 r.p.m.
Ignition timing:	
Static	3° B.T.D.C.
*† Stroboscopic at 600 r.p.m.	6° B.T.D.C.
Timing marks	Dimples on timing wheels, marks on converter.
Valve rocker clearance (cold)	.012 in. (.305 mm.)
DISTRIBUTOR	
Make/type	Lucas 25D4 or 45D4.
Rotation of rotor	Anti-clockwise.
Dwell angle: 25D4	60° ± 3°.
45D4	51° ± 5°.
Contact breaker gap	.014 to .016 in. (.35 to .40 mm.).
Condenser capacity	.18 to .24 mF.
Serial No.: 25D4	41134, 41242, 41251.
45D4	41417.
Centrifugal advance	
Decelerating check*†	26° to 30° at 5,500 r.p.m. 24° to 28° at 4,800 r.p.m. 15° to 19° at 1,800 r.p.m. 12° to 16° at 1,600 r.p.m. 0° to 4° at 800 r.p.m.
No advance below	600 r.p.m.
Vacuum advance	
Starts	3 in. (7.62 cm.) Hg.
Finishes†	18° at 15 in. (38.1 cm.) Hg.
SPARK PLUGS	
Make	Champion.
Type	N5 or N9Y.
Gap	.025 in. (.625 mm.)
IGNITION COIL	
Make/type	Lucas LA12.
Primary resistance at 20° C. (68° F.)	3.2 to 3.4 ohms (cold).
Consumption–ignition on	3.9 amps.
CARBURETTER	
Make/type	S.U. Type HS4.
Piston spring	Red.
Jet size	.090 in. (2.29 mm.).
Needle: Standard	AN.
Rich	H6.
Weak	EB.

* Crankshaft degrees and r.p.m. † Vacuum pipe disconnected.

ENGINE TUNING DATA

Model: **MINI Mk. II AUTOMATIC** (998 c.c.) Year: **1967–69**
MINI 1000 and CLUBMAN AUTOMATIC **1969–74**

ENGINE	
Type	9AG, 99H.
Capacity	998 c.c. (60.96 cu. in.).
Compression ratio	8.9 : 1.
Firing order	1, 3, 4, 2.
Compression pressure	160 lb./sq. in. (11.25 kg./cm.²).
Idling speed	650 r.p.m.
Fast idle speed	1,050 r.p.m.
Ignition timing:	
Static	4°B.T.D.C.
*† Stroboscopic at 600 r.p.m.	6°B.T.D.C.
Timing marks	Dimples on timing wheels, marks on converter.
Valve rocker clearance (cold)	.012 in. (.305 mm.)
DISTRIBUTOR	
Make/type	Lucas 25D4 or 45D4.
Rotation of rotor	Anti-clockwise.
Dwell angle: 25D4	60°±3°.
45D4	51°±5°.
Contact breaker gap	.014 to .016 in. (.35 to .40 mm.).
Condenser capacity	.18 to .24 mF.
Serial No.: 25D4	41134, 41242.
45D4	41417.
Centrifugal advance	
Decelerating check*†	26° to 30° at 5,500 r.p.m. 24° to 28° at 4,800 r.p.m. 15° to 19° at 1,800 r.p.m. 12° to 16° at 1,600 r.p.m. 0° to 4° at 800 r.p.m.
No advance below	600 r.p.m.
Vacuum advance	
Starts	3 in. (7.62 cm.) Hg.
Finishes†	18° at 15 in. (38.1 cm.) Hg.
SPARK PLUGS	
Make	Champion.
Type	N5 or N9Y.
Gap	.025 in. (.625 mm.).
IGNITION COIL	
Make/type	Lucas LA12.
Primary resistance at 20°C. (68°F.)	3.2 to 3.4 ohms (cold).
Consumption–ignition on	3.9 amps.
CARBURETTER	
Make/type	S.U. Type HS4.
Piston spring	Red.
Jet size	.090 in. (2.29 mm.).
Needle: Standard	AC.
Rich	M1.
Weak	HA.

* Crankshaft degrees and r.p.m. † Vacuum pipe disconnected.

ENGINE TUNING DATA

Model: **MINI COOPER** (997 c.c.) Year: **1961–64**

ENGINE

Type ..	9F.
Capacity ..	997 c.c. (60.87 cu. in.).
Compression ratio: High compression ..	9 : 1.
Low compression ..	8.3 : 1.
Firing order ..	1,3,4,2.
Compression pressure ..	———
Idling speed (approx.) ..	500 r.p.m.
Fast idle speed ..	900 r.p.m.
Ignition timing:	
Static: High compression ..	7° B.T.D.C.
Low compression ..	5° B.T.D.C.
Stroboscopic at 600 r.p.m.:	
*High compression ..	9° B.T.D.C.
Low compression ..	7° B.T.D.C.
Timing marks ..	Dimples on timing wheels, marks on flywheel.
Valve rocker clearance ..	.012 in. (.305 mm.) (cold).

* Crankshaft degrees and r.p.m.

DISTRIBUTOR

Make/type ..	Lucas 25D4.	
Rotation of rotor ..	Anti-clockwise.	
Dwell angle ..	60° ± 3°.	
Contact breaker gap ..	.014 to .016 in. (.35 to .40 mm.).	
Condenser capacity ..	.18 to .24 mF.	
Serial No. ..	40774.	40873.
Centrifugal advance	HIGH COMPRESSION	LOW COMPRESSION
Decelerating check*† ..	16° to 22° at 1,600 r.p.m.	26° to 30° at 2,600 r.p.m.
	2° to 8° at 1,000 r.p.m.	21° to 25° at 2,000 r.p.m.
	0° to 3° at 800 r.p.m.	15° to 19° at 1,200 r.p.m.
		8° to 12° at 900 r.p.m.
		0° to 5° at 600 r.p.m.
No advance below ..	600 r.p.m.	300 r.p.m.
Vacuum advance		
Starts ..	3 in. (7.62 cm.) Hg.	4 in. (10.1 cm.) Hg.
Finishes† ..	14° at 8 in. (20.3 cm.) Hg.	14° at 7 in. (17.7 cm.) Hg.

* Vacuum pipe disconnected. † Crankshaft degrees and r.p.m.

SPARKING PLUGS

Make ..	Champion.
Type ..	N5.
Gap ..	.025 in. (.625 mm.).

IGNITION COIL

Make/type ..	Lucas HA12.
Primary resistance at 20° C. (68° F.) ..	3.0 to 3.4 ohms. (cold).
Consumption–ignition on ..	3.9 amps.

CARBURETTERS

Make/type ..	Twin S.U. Type HS2.
Piston spring ..	Red.
Jet size ..	.090 in. (2.29 mm.).
Needle: Standard ..	GZ.

ENGINE TUNING DATA

Model: **MINI COOPER (998 c.c.)** Year: **1964–69**

ENGINE

Type	9FA.	
Capacity	998 c.c. (60.96 cu. in.).	
Compression ratio: High compression	9 : 1.	
Low compression	7.8 : 1.	
Firing order	1,3,4,2.	
Compression pressure: High compression	165 lb./sq. in. (11.6 kg./cm.^{2}).	
Low compression	150 lb./sq. in. (10.5 kg./cm.^{2}).	
Idling speed	500 r.p.m.	
Fast idle speed	900 r.p.m.	
Ignition timing	HIGH COMPRESSION	LOW COMPRESSION
Static	5° B.T.D.C.	5° B.T.D.C. (91 to 96 octane fuel).
*Stroboscopic at 600 r.p.m.	7° B.T.D.C.	7° B.T.D.C.
Timing marks	Dimples on timing wheels, marks on flywheel.	
Valve rocker clearance (cold)	.012 in. (.305 mm.).	

* Crankshaft degrees and r.p.m.

DISTRIBUTOR

Make/type	Lucas 24D4.	
Rotation of rotor	Anti-clockwise.	
Dwell angle	60° ± 3°.	
Contact breaker gap	.014 to .016 in. (.35 to .40 mm.)	
Condenser capacity	.18 to .24 mF.	
Serial No.	40955, 41032.	40958, 41031.
Centrifugal advance	HIGH COMPRESSION	LOW COMPRESSION
Decelerating check*†	30° to 34° at 6,000 r.p.m.	28° to 32° at 5,500 r.p.m.
	28° to 32° at 5,400 r.p.m.	26° to 30° at 4,400 r.p.m.
	24° to 28° at 4,200 r.p.m.	22° to 26° at 2,200 r.p.m.
	18° to 22° at 2,300 r.p.m.	16° to 20° at 1,800 r.p.m.
	12° to 16° at 1,800 r.p.m.	3° to 9° at 1,000 r.p.m.
	1° to 5° at 800 r.p.m.	0° to 3° at 600 r.p.m.
No advance below	300 r.p.m.	400 r.p.m.
Vacuum advance		
Starts	3 in. (7.62 cm.) Hg.	3 in. (7.62 cm.) Hg.
Finishes†	14° at 8 in. (20.32 cm.) Hg.	16° at 7 in. (17.7 cm.) Hg.

* Vacuum pipe disconnected. † Crankshaft degrees and r.p.m.

SPARKING PLUGS

Make	Champion.
Type	N5.
Gap	.025 in. (.625 mm.).

IGNITION COIL

Make/type	Lucas HA 12.
Primary resistance at 20° C. (68° F.)	3.0 to 3.4 ohms. (cold).
Consumption–ignition on	3.9 amps.

CARBURETTERS

Make/type	Twin S.U. Type HS2.
Piston spring	Blue.
Jet size	.090 in. (2.29 mm.).
Needle: Standard	GY.
Rich	M.
Weak	GG.

ENGINE TUNING DATA

Model: **MINI COOPER 'S' (970 c.c. and 1071 c.c.)** Year: **1963–65**

ENGINE

Type	9FC, 10F.
Capacity: 970 c.c.	59.1 cu. in.
1071 c.c.	63.35 cu. in.
Compression ratio: 970 c.c.	10 : 1.
1071 c.c.	9.0 : 1.
Firing order	1,3,4,2.
Compression pressure	190 to 200 lb./sq. in. (13.36 to 14.07 kg./cm.^{2}).
Idling speed	600 r.p.m. approx.
Fast idle speed	1,000 r.p.m.
Ignition timing:	
Static: 970 c.c.	12° B.T.D.C.
1071 c.c.	3° B.T.D.C.
Stroboscopic at 600 r.p.m.*: 970 c.c.	14° B.T.D.C. at 600 r.p.m.
1071 c.c.	5° B.T.D.C. at 600 r.p.m.
Timing marks	Dimples on timing wheels, marks on flywheel.
Valve rocker clearance: Standard	.012 in. (.30 mm.) cold.
Competition	.015 in. (.38 mm.) cold.

* Crankshaft degrees and r.p.m.

DISTRIBUTOR

Make/type	Lucas 23D4.
Rotation of rotor	Anti-clockwise.
Dwell angle	60° ± 3°.
Contact breaker gap	.014 to .016 in. (.35 to .40 mm.).
Condenser capacity	.18 to .24 mF.
Serial No.	40819.

Centrifugal advance

Decelerating check*	28° to 32° at 7,000 r.p.m.
	22° to 26° at 5,200 r.p.m.
	10° to 14° at 1,600 r.p.m.
	6° to 12° at 1,000 r.p.m.
	0° to 3° at 600 r.p.m.
No advance below	450 r.p.m.

* Crankshaft degrees and r.p.m.

SPARKING PLUGS

Make	Champion.
Type	N9Y.
Gap	.025 in. (.625 mm.).

IGNITION COIL

Make/type	Lucas HA 12.
Primary resistance at 20° C. (68° F.)	3.0 to 3.4 ohms. (cold).
Consumption–ignition on	3.9 amps.

CARBURETTERS

Make/type	Twin S.U. Type HS2.
Piston spring	Red.
Jet size	.090 in. (2.29 mm.).
Needle: 970 c.c.	AN (Standard).
1071 c.c.	H6 (Standard).

ENGINE TUNING DATA

Model: **MINI COOPER 'S' (Mk. I, II, & III)** Year: **1964/70 onwards**

ENGINE

Type: Mk. I and II models	12FA.
Mk. III models	12H.
Capacity	1275 c.c. (77.9 cu. in.).
Compression ratio	9.75 : 1.
Firing order	1,3,4,2.
Compression pressure	190 to 200 lb./sq. in. (13.36 to 14.07 kg./cm.^{2}) at 500 r.p.m.
Idling speed	600 r.p.m. approx.
Fast idle speed	1,000 r.p.m. approx.
Ignition timing:	
Static	2° B.T.D.C.
Stroboscopic at 600 r.p.m.	4° B.T.D.C.
Timing marks	Dimples on timing wheels, marks on flywheel.
Valve rocker clearance: Standard	.012 in. (.30 mm.) cold.
Competition	.015 in. (.38 mm.) cold.

* Crankshaft degrees and r.p.m.

DISTRIBUTOR

Make/type	Lucas 23D4.
Rotation of rotor	Anti-clockwise.
Dwell angle	60° ± 3°.
Contact breaker gap	.014 to .016 in. (.35 to .40 mm.).
Condenser capacity	.18 to .24 mF.
Serial No.	40819, 41033.

Centrifugal advance

Decelerating check*	28° to 32° at 7,000 r.p.m.
	22° to 26° at 5,200 r.p.m.
	10° to 14° at 1,600 r.p.m.
	6° to 12° at 1,000 r.p.m.
	0° to 3° at 600 r.p.m.
No advance below	450 r.p.m.

* Crankshaft degrees and r.p.m.

SPARKING PLUGS

Make	Champion.
Type	N9Y.
Gap	.025 in. (.625 mm.).

IGNITION COIL

Make/type	Lucas HA12.
Primary resistance at 20° C. (68° F.)	3.0 to 3.4 ohms. (cold).
Consumption–ignition on	3.9 amps.

CARBURETTERS

Make/type	Twin S.U. Type HS2.
Piston spring	Red.
Jet size	.090 in. (2.29 mm.).
Needle: Standard	M.
Rich	AH2.
Weak	EB.

ENGINE TUNING DATA

Model: **MINI CLUBMAN** Year: **1969–72**

ENGINE

Type	99H.
Capacity	998 c.c. (60.96 cu. in.).
Compression ratio	8.3 : 1.
Firing order	1, 3, 4, 2.
Compression pressure	150 lb./sq. in. (10.5 kg./cm.²).
Idling speed	500 r.p.m.
Fast idling speed	900 r.p.m.
Ignition timing :	
Static	5°B.T.D.C.
*†Stroboscopic at 600 r.p.m.	8°B.T.D.C.
Timing marks	Dimples on timing wheels, marks on flywheel.
Valve rocker clearance (cold)	.012 in. (.305 mm.).

DISTRIBUTOR

Make/type	Lucas 25D4 or 45D4.
Rotation of rotor	Anti-clockwise.
Dwell angle: 25D4	60°± 3°.
45D4	51°± 5°.
Contact breaker gap	.014 to .016 in. (.35 to .40 mm.).
Condenser capacity	.18 to .24 mF.
Serial No.: 25D4	41030.
45D4	41412.

Centrifugal advance

Decelerating check*†	22° to 26° at 5,000 r.p.m.
	16° to 20° at 3,400 r.p.m.
	9° to 13° at 1,600 r.p.m.
	6° to 10° at 1,300 r.p.m.
	0° to 4° at 900 r.p.m.
No advance below	600 r.p.m.

Vacuum advance

Starts	5 in. (12.7 cm.) Hg.
Finishes*	14° at 11 in. (27.9 cm.) Hg.

SPARK PLUGS

Make	Champion.
Type	N9Y or N5.
Gap	.025 in. (.625 mm.).

IGNITION COIL

Make/type	Lucas LA12.
Primary resistance at 20°C. (68°F.)	3.2 to 3.4 ohms (cold).
Consumption–ignition on	3.9 amps.

CARBURETTER

Make/type	S.U. Type HS2.
Piston spring	Red.
Jet size	.090 in. (2.29 mm.).
Needle: Standard	GX.
Rich	M.
Weak	GG.

* Crankshaft degrees and r.p.m. † Vacuum pipe disconnected.

ENGINE TUNING DATA

Model: **MINI 1275 GT** Year: **1969–72**

ENGINE	
Type	12H.
Capacity	1274.86 c.c. (77.8 cu. in.).
Compression ratio: HC	8.8 : 1.
LC	8 : 1.
Firing order	1, 3, 4, 2.
Compression pressure	175 lb./sq. in. (12.3 kg./cm.^{2}).
Idling speed	650 r.p.m.
Fast idle speed	1,050 r.p.m.
Ignition timing:	
Static	8°B.T.D.C.
*†Stroboscopic at 600 r.p.m.	10°B.T.D.C.
Timing marks	Dimples on timing wheels, marks on flywheel.
Valve rocker clearance (cold)	.012 in.(.305 mm.).
DISTRIBUTOR	
Make/type	Lucas 25D4 or 45D4.
Rotation of rotor	Anti-clockwise.
Dwell angle: 25D4	60°± 3°.
45D4	51°± 5°.
Contact breaker gap	.014 to .016 in. (.35 to .40 mm.).
Condenser capacity	.18 to .24 mF.
Serial No.: 25D4	41257.
45D4	41419.
Centrifugal advance	
Decelerating check*†	18° to 22° at 4,000 r.p.m. 11° to 15° at 2,800 r.p.m. 6° to 10° at 2,000 r.p.m. 4° to 8° at 1,600 r.p.m. 0° to 3° at 800 r.p.m.
No. advance below	300 r.p.m.
Vacuum advance	
Starts	3 in. (7.62 cm.) Hg.
Finishes*	18° to 22° at 10 in. (25.4 cm.) Hg.
SPARK PLUGS	
Make	Champion.
Type	N9Y.
Gap	.025 in. (.625 mm.).
IGNITION COIL	
Make/type	Lucas LA12.
Primary resistance at 20°C. (68°F.)	3.2 to 3.4 ohms (cold).
Consumption–ignition on	3.9 amps.
CARBURETTER	
Make/type	S.U. type HS4.
Piston spring	Red.
Jet size	.090 in. (2.29 mm.).
Needle: Standard	AC.
Rich	BQ.
Weak	HA.

* Crankshaft degrees and r.p.m. † Vacuum pipe disconnected.

ENGINE TUNING DATA

Model: **Mini 1000 (CANADA)** Year: **1970 on**

ENGINE

Type	99H.
Capacity	998 c.c. (60.96 cu.in.).
Compression ratio	8.9 : 1.
Firing order	1, 3, 4, 2.
Compression pressure	120 lb/sq. in. (8.44 kg./cm².).
Idling speed	800 r.p.m. (to 1973), 850 r.p.m. (1973 on)
Fast idle speed	1,200 to 1,300 r.p.m.
Ignition timing:	
Static	1° B.T.D.C. (to 1972), 2° B.T.D.C. (1972), 6° B.T.D.C. (1973 on).
*† Stroboscopic: at 1,000 r.p.m.	9° B.T.D.C.
at 1.500 r.p.m.	8° B.T.D.C. (1973 on).
Timing marks	Dimples on timing wheels, marks on flywheel
Valve rocker clearance (cold)	.012 in. (.30 mm.).

DISTRIBUTOR

Make/type	Lucas 25D4.
Rotation of rotor	Anti-clockwise.
Dwell angle	60° + 3°
Contact breaker gap	.014 to .016 in. (.35 to .40 mm).
Condenser capacity	.18 to .24 mF.
Serial No.	41134 (to 1972), 41395 (1972 only), 41532 (1973 on).

Centrifugal advance	**Up to 1972**	**1973 on**
Decelerating check*†	24° ± 2° at 3,000 r.p.m.	32° ± 2° at 5,200 r.p.m.
	16° at 1,400 to 1,600 r.p.m.	18° at 2,800 to 3,400 r.p.m.
	4° at 600 to 800 r.p.m.	8° at 1,500 to 2,100 r.p.m.

Vacuum advance	**Up to 1972**	**1972 only**	**1973 on**
Starts	3 in. Hg.	5 in. Hg.	10 in. Hg.
Finishes	15 in.Hg.	8 in. Hg.	15 in. Hg.
Total crankshaft degrees	18° ± 2°.	6° ± 2°.	10° ± 2°.

* Crankshaft degrees and r.p.m. † Vacuum pipe disconnected.

SPARK PLUGS

Make/type	Champion N 9Y.
Gap	.025 in. (.65 mm.).

IGNITION COIL

Make/type	A.C. Delco or Lucas 11C 12.
Primary resistance at 20° C (68° F)	1.43 to 1.58 ohms.
Consumption–ignition on	4.5 to 5 amps.
Ballast resistance	1.3 to 1.4 ohms.

CARBURETTER

Make/type	S.U. HS4.
Type specification	AUD 398 (up to 1972), AUD 548 (1972 only), AUD 618 (1973 on).
Choke diameter	1½ in. (38 mm.).
Jet size	.090 in. (3 mm).
Needle	AAG (to 1973), ABJ (1973 on).
Piston spring	Red.
Initial jet adjustment	11 flats from bridge.
Throttle to damper	.080 in. (2.0 mm.).

EXHAUST EMISSION

Exhaust gas analyser reading at engine idle speed	4.5% CO (maximum).

ENGINE TUNING DATA

Model: **MINI CLUBMAN (SWEDEN)** Year: **1972 on**

ENGINE

Type	99H.
Capacity	998 c.c. (60.96 cu. in.).
Compression ratio	8.3 : 1.
Firing order	1, 3, 4, 2.
Compression pressure	150 lb/sq. in. (10.5 kg./cm^2.).
Idling speed	800 r.p.m.
Fast idle speed	1,100 to 1,200 r.p.m.
Ignition timing:	
Static	1° B.T.D.C.
*† Stroboscopic at 1,000 r.p.m.	9° B.T.D.C.
Timing marks	Dimples on timing wheels, marks on flywheel.
Valve rocker clearance (cold)	.012 in. (.30 mm.) (cold).

* Crankshaft degrees and r.p.m. † Vacuum pipe disconnected.

DISTRIBUTOR

Make/type	Lucas 25D4.
Rotation of rotor	Anti-clockwise.
Dwell angle	60° ± 3°.
Contact breaker gap	.014 to .016 in. (.35 to .40 mm.).
Condenser capacity	.18 to .24 mF.
Serial No.	41212.

Centrifugal advance

Decelerating check*†	24° to 28° at 5,000 r.p.m. 20° to 24° at 3,400 r.p.m. 12° to 16° at 1,600 r.p.m. 7° to 11° at 1,300 r.p.m. 1° to 4° at 900 r.p.m.
No advance below	600 r.p.m.

Vacuum advance

Starts	3 in. (7.62 cm.) Hg.
Finishes*	18° at 15 in. (38.1 cm.) Hg.

† Vacuum pipe disconnected. * Crankshaft degrees and r.p.m.

SPARK PLUGS

Make/type	Champion N9Y.
Gap	.025 in. (.65 mm.).

IGNITION COIL

Make/type	Lucas LA12.
Primary resistance at 20°C. (68°F.)	3.2 to 3.4 ohms (cold).
Consumption–ignition on	3.9 amps.

CARBURETTER

Make/type	S.U. type HS4.
Specification	AUD 450.
Piston spring	Red.
Jet size	.090 in. (2.3 mm.).
Needle	AAG.

EXHAUST EMISSION

Exhaust gas analyser reading at engine idle speed	3.5 to 4.5% CO.

ENGINE TUNING DATA

Model: **MINI 850 Saloon and variants** **(848 c.c.)** Year: **1972–74** ●

ENGINE

Type	85H.	
Capacity	848 c.c. (51.7 cu. in.).	
Compression ratio	8.3 : 1.	
Firing order	1, 3, 4, 2.	
Compression pressure	150 lb./sq. in. (10.5 kg./cm.²).	
Idling speed	800 r.p.m.	
Fast idle speed	1,100 to 1,200 r.p.m.	
Valve rocker clearance	.012 in. (.30 mm.) (cold).	
Timing marks	Dimples on timing wheels, marks on flywheel.	
Ignition timing:		
Static	T.D.C.	‡ 9°B.T.D.C.
*† Stroboscopic at 1,000 r.p.m.	19°B.T.D.C.	‡ 14° B.T.D.C.

DISTRIBUTOR

Make/type	Lucas 25D4 or 45D4.	
Contact breaker gap	.014 to .016 in. (.35 to .40 mm.).	
Rotation of rotor	Anti-clockwise.	
Dwell angle: 25D4	60°±3°	
45D4	51°±5°.	
Condenser capacity	.18 to .24 mF.	
Serial No.: 25D4	41026.	41569. ‡
45D4	41411.	41570. ‡

Centrifugal advance

Decelerating check*†	30° to 34° at 3,400 r.p.m.	18° to 22° at 4,000 r.p.m.
	24° to 28° at 2,500 r.p.m.	11° to 15° at 2,800 r.p.m.
	16° to 20° at 1,300 r.p.m.	4° to 8° at 1,600 r.p.m.
	9° to 15° at 900 r.p.m.	0° to 3° at 800 r.p.m.
	1° to 7° at 700 r.p.m.	
No advance below	500 r.p.m.	300 r.p.m.

Vacuum advance

Starts	7 in. (17.8 cm.) Hg.	5 in. (12.7 cm.) Hg.
Finishes*	10° at 13 in. (33 cm.) Hg.	20° at 13 in. (33 cm.) Hg.

SPARK PLUGS

Make/type	Champion N9Y.
Gap	.025 in. (.65 mm.).

IGNITION COIL

Make/type	Lucas LA12.
Primary resistance at 20°C. (68°F.)	3.2 to 3.4 ohms (cold).
Consumption–ignition on	3.9 amps.

CARBURETTER

Make/type	S.U. Type HS2.
Specification	AUD 449.
Piston spring	Red.
Jet size	.090 in. (3 mm.).
Needle	AAV.

EXHAUST EMISSION

Exhaust gas analyser reading at engine idle speed	3.5 to 4.5% CO.

* Crankshaft degrees and r.p.m. † Vacuum pipe disconnected. ‡ 1974 on: Fitted to a limited number of manual transmission engines.

ENGINE TUNING DATA

Model: **MINI CLUBMAN** (998 c.c.)
MINI 1000–Saloon and variants

Year: 1972–74

ENGINE		
Type	99H.	
Capacity	998 c.c. (60.96 cu. in.).	
Compression ratio	8.3 : 1.	
Firing order	1, 3, 4, 2.	
Compression pressure	150 lb./sq. in. (10.5 kg./cm.²).	
Idling speed	800 r.p.m.	
Fast idle speed	1,100–1,200 r.p.m.	
Ignition timing:		
Static	5°B.T.D.C.	‡ 10°B.T.D.C.
†* Stroboscopic at 1,000 r.p.m.	11°B.T.D.C.	‡ 13°B.T.D.C.
Timing marks	Dimples on timing wheels, marks on flywheel.	
Valve rocker clearance (cold)	.012 in. (.30 mm.)	
DISTRIBUTOR		
Make/type	Lucas 25D4 or 45D4.	
Rotation of rotor	Anti-clockwise.	
Dwell angle: 25D4	60°±3°.	
45D4	51°±5°.	
Contact breaker gap	.014 to .016 in. (.35 to .40 mm.).	
Condenser capacity	.18 to .24 mF.	
Serial No.: 25D4	41254.	41246.‡
45D4	41212.	41418.‡
Centrifugal advance		
Decelerating check*†	22° to 26° at 5,000 r.p.m.	18° to 23° at 5,600 r.p.m.
	16° to 20° at 3,400 r.p.m.	14° to 18° at 4,000 r.p.m.
	9° to 13° at 1,600 r.p.m.	9° to 13° at 2,400 r.p.m.
	6° to 10° at 1,300 r.p.m.	6° to 10° at 1,500 r.p.m.
	0° to 4° at 900 r.p.m.	0° to 1° at 900 r.p.m.
No advance below	600 r.p.m.	800 r.p.m.
Vacuum advance		
Starts	5 in. (12.7 cm.) Hg.	6 in. (15.2 cm.) Hg.
Finishes*	14° at 11 in. (27.9 cm.) Hg.	16° at 14 in. (35.6 cm.) Hg.
SPARK PLUGS		
Make/type	Champion N9Y.	
Gap	.025 in. (.65 mm.).	
IGNITION COIL		
Make/type	Lucas LA12.	
Primary resistance at 20°C. (68°F.)	3.2 to 3.4 ohms (cold).	
Consumption–ignition on	3.9 amps.	
CARBURETTER		
Make/type	S.U. Type HS2.	
Specification	AUD 509.	
Piston spring	Red.	
Jet size	.090 in. (3 mm.).	
Needle	AAV.	
EXHAUST EMISSION		
Exhaust gas analyser reading at engine idle speed	3.5 to 4.5% CO.	

* Crankshaft degrees and r.p.m. † Vacuum pipe disconnected. ‡ 1974 on: Fitted to a limited number of manual transmission engines.

ENGINE TUNING DATA

To European emission control requirements (ECE 15)

Model: **MINI 1275 GT** — Year: **1972–74**, **1974 on**

ENGINE

Type	12H.
Capacity	1274.86 c.c. (77.8 cu. in.).
Compression ratio	8.8 : 1.
Firing order	1, 3, 4, 2.
Compression pressure	175 lb./sq. in. (12.3 kg./cm.²).
Idling speed	750 r.p.m.
Fast idle speed	1,100 to 1,200 r.p.m.
Ignition timing:	
Static	8°B.T.D.C.
*† Stroboscopic at 1,000 r.p.m.	13°B.T.D.C.
Timing marks	Dimples on timing wheels, marks on flywheel.
Valve rocker clearance (cold)	.012 in. (.30 mm.)

DISTRIBUTOR

Make/type	Lucas 25D4 or 45D4.
Rotation of rotor	Anti-clockwise.
Dwell angle: 25D4	60°± 3°.
45D4	51°±5°.
Contact breaker gap	.014 to .016 in. (.35 to .40 mm.).
Condenser capacity	.18 to .24 mF.
Serial No.: 25D4	41257, 41214.
45D4	41419.

Centrifugal advance

Decelerating check*†	18° to 22° at 4,000 r.p.m.
	11° to 15° at 2,800 r.p.m.
	6½° to 10° at 2,100 r.p.m.
	4° to 8° at 1,600 r.p.m.
	0° to 3° at 800 r.p.m.
No advance below	300 r.p.m.

Vacuum advance

Starts	3 in. (7.6 cm.) Hg.
Finishes*	20° at 10 in. (25.4 cm.) Hg.

SPARK PLUGS

Make/type	Champion N9Y.
Gap	.025 in. (.65 mm.).

IGNITION COIL

Make/type	Lucas LA 12.
Primary resistance at 20°C. (68°F.)	3.2 to 3.4 ohms (cold).
Consumption—ignition on	3.9 amps.

CARBURETTER

Make/type	S.U. Type HS4.
Specification	AUD 567.
Piston spring	Red.
Jet size	.090 in. (3 mm.).
Needle	ABB.

EXHAUST EMISSION

Exhaust gas analyser reading at engine idle speed	3 to 4.5% CO.

* Crankshaft degrees and r.p.m. † Vacuum pipe disconnected.

ENGINE TUNING DATA

To European emission control requirements (ECE 15)

Model: **MINI 850–Saloon and variants** **(848 c.c.)** Year: **1974 on**

ENGINE

Type	85H.
Capacity	848 c.c. (51.7 cu. in.).
Compression ratio	8.3 : 1.
Firing order	1, 3, 4, 2.
Compression pressure	150 lb./sq. in. (10.5 kg./cm.^{2}).
Idling speed	800 r.p.m.
Fast idle speed	1,100 to 1,200 r.p.m.
Valve rocker clearance	.012 in. (.30 mm.) (cold).
Timing marks	Dimples on timing wheels, marks on flywheel.
Ignition timing:	
Static	6°B.T.D.C.
*† Stroboscopic at 1,000 r.p.m.	11°B.T.D.C.

DISTRIBUTOR

Make/type	Lucas 45D4.
Contact breaker gap	.014 to .016 in. (.35 to .40 mm.).
Rotation of rotor	Anti-clockwise.
Dwell angle	51°± 5°.
Condenser capacity	.18 to .24 mF.
Serial number	41570.

Centrifugal advance

Decelerating check*†	18° to 22° at 4,000 r.p.m. 11° to 15° at 2,800 r.p.m. 4° to 8° at 1,600 r.p.m. 0° to 3° at 800 r.p.m.
No advance below	300 r.p.m.

Vacuum advance

Starts	5 in. (12.7 cm.) Hg.
Finishes*	20° at 13 in. (33 cm.) Hg.

SPARK PLUGS

Make/type	Champion N9Y.
Gap	.025 in. (.65 mm.).

IGNITION COIL

Make/type	Lucas LA12.
Primary resistance at 20°C. (68°F.)	3.2 to 3.4 ohms (cold).
Consumption–ignition on	3.9 amps.

CARBURETTER

Make/type	S.U. Type HS4.
Specification	AUD 611.
Piston spring	Red.
Jet size	.090 in. (3 mm.).
Needle	ABS.

EXHAUST EMISSION

Exhaust gas analyser reading at engine idle speed	3.5 to 4.5% CO.

* Crankshaft degrees and r.p.m. † Vacuum pipe disconnected.

ENGINE TUNING DATA

To European emission control requirements (ECE 15)

Model: **MINI CLUBMAN (Manual and Automatic)**
MINI 1000–Saloon and variants (Manual) **(998 c.c.)**
–Saloon (Automatic)

Year: **1974 on**

ENGINE

Type	99H.
Capacity	998 c.c. (60.96 cu. in.).
Compression ratio	8.3 : 1.
Firing order	1, 3, 4, 2.
Compression pressure	150 lb./sq. in. (10.5 kg./cm.^{2}).
Idling speed	750 r.p.m.
Fast idle speed	1,100–1,200 r.p.m.
Ignition timing:	
Static	4°B.T.D.C.
*† Stroboscopic at 1,000 r.p.m.	7°B.T.D.C.
Timing marks	Dimples on timing wheels, marks on flywheel.
Valve rocker clearance (cold)	.012 in. (.30 mm.)

DISTRIBUTOR

Make/type	Lucas 45D4.
Rotation of rotor	Anti-clockwise.
Dwell angle	51°±5°.
Contact breaker gap	.014 to .016 in. (.35 to .40 mm.).
Condenser capacity	.18 to .24 mF.
Serial No.	41418.
Centrifugal advance	
Decelerating check*†	14° to 18° at 4,000 r.p.m.
	9° to 13° at 2,400 r.p.m.
	6° to 10° at 1,500 r.p.m.
	0° to 1° at 900 r.p.m.
No advance below	800 r.p.m.
Vacuum advance	
Starts	6 in. (15.2 cm.) Hg.
Finishes*	16° at 14 in. (35.6 cm.) Hg.

SPARK PLUGS

Make/type	Champion N9Y.
Gap	.025 in. (.65 mm.).

IGNITION COIL

Make/type	Lucas LA12.
Primary resistance at 20°C. (68°F.)	3.2 to 3.4 ohms (cold).
Consumption–ignition on	3.9 amps.

CARBURETTER

Make/type	S.U. Type HS4.
Specification	AUD 679.
Piston spring	Red.
Jet size	.090 in. (3 mm.).
Needle	ABX.

EXHAUST EMISSION

Exhaust gas analyser reading at engine idle speed	3.5 to 4.5% CO.

* Crankshaft degrees and r.p.m. † Vacuum pipe disconnected.

ENGINE TUNING DATA

To European emission control requirements (ECE 15)

Model: **MINI CLUBMAN** (1098 c.c.) Year: **1974 on**

ENGINE

Type	10H.
Capacity	1098 c.c. (67 cu. in.).
Compression ratio	8.5 : 1.
Firing order	1, 3, 4, 2.
Cranking pressure	165 lb./sq. in. (11.6 kg./cm.^{2}).
Idling speed	750 r.p.m.
Fast idle speed	1,100 to 1,200 r.p.m.
Ignition timing:	
Static	9°B.T.D.C.
*† Stroboscopic at 1,000 r.p.m.	12°B.T.D.C.
Timing marks	Dimples on timing wheels, marks on flywheel.
Valve rocker clearance (cold)	.012 in. (.30 mm.).

DISTRIBUTOR

Make/type	Lucas 25D4 or 45D4.
Rotation of rotor	Anti-clockwise.
Dwell angle: 25D4	60°± 3°.
45D4	51°± 5°.
Contact breaker gap	.014 to .016 in. (.35 to .40 mm.).
Condenser capacity	.18 to .24 mF.
Serial No.: 25D4	41246.
45D4	41418.
Centrifugal advance	
Decelerating check*†	20 to 24° at 6,000 r.p.m. 14 to 18° at 4,000 r.p.m. 9 to 13° at 2,400 r.p.m. 6 to 10° at 1,500 r.p.m. 0 to 1° at 900 r.p.m.
No advance below	800 r.p.m.
Vacuum advance	
Starts	6 in. (15.2 cm.) Hg.
Finishes*	16° at 14 in. (35.6 cm.) Hg.

SPARK PLUGS

Make/type	Champion N9Y.
Gap	.025 in. (.65 mm.).

IGNITION COIL

Make/type	Lucas LA12.
Primary resistance at 20°C. (68°F.)	3.2 to 3.4 ohms (cold).
Consumption–ignition on	3.9 amps.

CARBURETTER

Make/type	S.U. Type HS4.
Specification	AUD 508.
Piston spring	Red.
Jet size	.090 in. (3 mm.).
Needle	ABP.

EXHAUST EMISSION

Exhaust gas analyser reading at engine idle speed	3 to 4.5% CO.

* Crankshaft degrees and r.p.m. † Vacuum pipe disconnected.

MAINTENANCE

CONTENTS

SERVICE OPERATIONS–SUMMARY

After sales service = 1,000 miles (1500 km)
A Every 6,000 miles (10000 km) or 6 months
B Every 12,000 miles (20000 km) or 12 months
Items included in the 3,000 miles (5000 km) or 3 months interval Optional Inspection Check are indicated in **column C**

After Sales	A	B	C	ACTION ● / OPERATION X — BRITISH LEYLAND **Leycare Service**
●	●	●	●	Fit seat cover
	X	X	X	Check condition and security of seats and seat belts
●	●	●	●	Drive on lift; stop engine
X	X	X	X	Check operation of lamps
X	X	X	X	Check operation of horn(s)
X	X	X	X	Check operation of warning indicators
X	X	X	X	Check/adjust operation of windscreen washers
X	X	X	X	Check operation of windscreen wipers
X	X	X	X	Check operation of hand brake; release fully after checking
X	X	X	X	Check rear view mirrors for cracks and crazing
X				Check operation of window controls
X	X	X		Check steering-column clamp bolt
●	●	●	●	Open bonnet, fit wing covers. Raise lift to convenient working height with wheels free to rotate
●	●	●	●	Remove hub cap
	●	●		Mark stud to wheel relationship
	●	●		Remove road wheel
	X	X	X	Check tyre complies with manufacturer's specification
	X	X	X	Check tyre for tread depth
X	X	X	X	Check tyre visually for external cuts in fabric
X	X	X	X	Check tyre visually for external exposure of ply or cord
X	X	X	X	Check tyre visually for external lumps or bulges
X	X	X	X	Check/adjust tyre pressures
		X		Front: Remove brake drum, wash out dust, inspect linings for wear and drum for condition, refit drum
X	X	X	X	Front: Adjust brakes
	X	X		Front: Inspect brake pads for wear and discs for condition
X	X	X	X	Check for oil leaks from steering and fluid leaks from suspension system
X	X	X	X	Check condition and security of steering unit joints and gaiters
		X		Rear: Remove brake-drum, wash out dust, inspect linings for wear and drum for condition, refit drum
X	X	X	X	Rear: Adjust brakes
X	X	X		Lubricate all grease points (excluding hubs)
	●	●		Refit road wheel in original position
X	X	X	X	Check tightness of road wheel nuts
●	●	●	●	Refit hub cap
●	●	●	●	Raise lift to full height
X	X	X		Drain engine/transmission oil
X	X	X	X	Check visually brake pipes and unions for chafing, leaks and corrosion
X	X	X	X	Check visually fuel and clutch pipes for chafing, leaks and corrosion
X	X	X	X	Check exhaust system for leakage and security
	X	X		Lubricate hand brake mechanical linkage and cables
X				Check security of accessible engine mountings
X				Check security of suspension fixings
	X	X		Renew engine oil filter element (Manual gearbox)
●	●	●		Refit engine drain plug
●	●	●	●	Lower lift
●	●	●		Fit exhaust extractor pipe
●	●	●	●	Remove ignition shield (Clubman and 1275 GT)
	X	X		Renew engine oil filter element (Automatic transmission)
X				Check/adjust torque of cylinder head nuts
X				Check/adjust torque of rocker shaft nuts
X				Check security of manifold nuts
X		X		Check/adjust valve clearance

(Operations from "Remove hub cap" to "Refit hub cap":) Starting at the right-hand front complete these operations at each wheel

After Sales	A	B	C	ACTION ● OPERATION X
X	X	X		Fill engine with oil
			X	Check/top up engine oil
		X		Lubricate water pump (early models only)
	X	X		Lubricate dynamo bearing (early models only)
X	X	X		Top up carburetter piston damper(s)
X	X	X		Lubricate accelerator control linkage and pedal pivot
		X		Renew air cleaner element(s)
X				Check security of accessible engine mountings
X	X	X	X	Check driving belt; adjust or renew
	X			Clean/adjust spark plugs
		X		Renew spark plugs
X	X	X	X	Check/top up clutch fluid reservoir
X	X	X	X	Check/top up brake fluid reservoir
X	X	X	X	Check/top up windscreen washer reservoir
X	X	X	X	Check/top up cooling system
		X		Clean brake servo filter
		X		Clean and test crankcase breather valve (when fitted)
		X		Renew engine breather filter/oil filler cap (when fitted)
		X		Clean engine breather filter (when fitted)
	X	X		Check/adjust clutch return stop clearance
X	X	X		Check cooling and heating systems for leaks
	●	●		Run engine and check sealing of oil filter; stop engine
X	X	X		Recheck/top up engine oil
●	●	●		Connect electronic instruments
X	X	X		Check visually distributor points; renew if necessary
X	X	X		Check volt drop between coil CB and earth
X	X	X		Lubricate distributor
●	●	●		Run engine
X	X	X		Disconnect vacuum pipe, check dwell angle, adjust points as necessary } Refer to Engine Tuning Data
X	X	X		Check stroboscopic ignition timing
X	X	X		Check distributor automatic advance
X	X	X		Check advance increase as vacuum pipe is re-connected
X	X	X		Check throttle operation, set to fast idle until engine reaches normal running temperature
X	X	X		Lubricate all locks and hinges (not steering lock)
	X	X	X	Check and if necessary renew windscreen wiper blades
X	X	X		Check/adjust engine idle speed and carburetter mixture settings
●	●	●		Stop engine and disconnect instruments
●	●	●	●	Refit ignition shield (Clubman and 1275 GT)
●	●	●	●	Remove wing covers
	●	●		Fill in details and fix appropriate Unipart underbonnet stickers
●	●	●	●	Close bonnet
●	●	●		Remove exhaust extractor pipe
●	●	●	●	Remove spare wheel
	X	X	X	Check spare tyre complies with manufacturer's specification
	X	X	X	Check depth of tread
X	X	X	X	Check visually for external cuts in tyre fabric
X	X	X	X	Check visually for external exposure of ply or cord
X	X	X	X	Check visually for external lumps or bulges
X	X	X	X	Check/adjust tyre pressure
●	●	●	●	Refit spare wheel. Drive car off lift
X	X	X	X	Check/top up battery electrolyte
	X	X		Clean and grease battery connections
X	X	X	X	Check/adjust headlamp alignment
X	X	X		Check/adjust front wheel alignment
X	X	X		Carry out road or roller test and check function of all instrumentation
X	X	X	X	Report any additional work required
X	X	X	X	Ensure cleanliness of controls, door handles, steering-wheel, etc.
●	●	●	●	Remove seat cover

LUBRICATION DIAGRAM

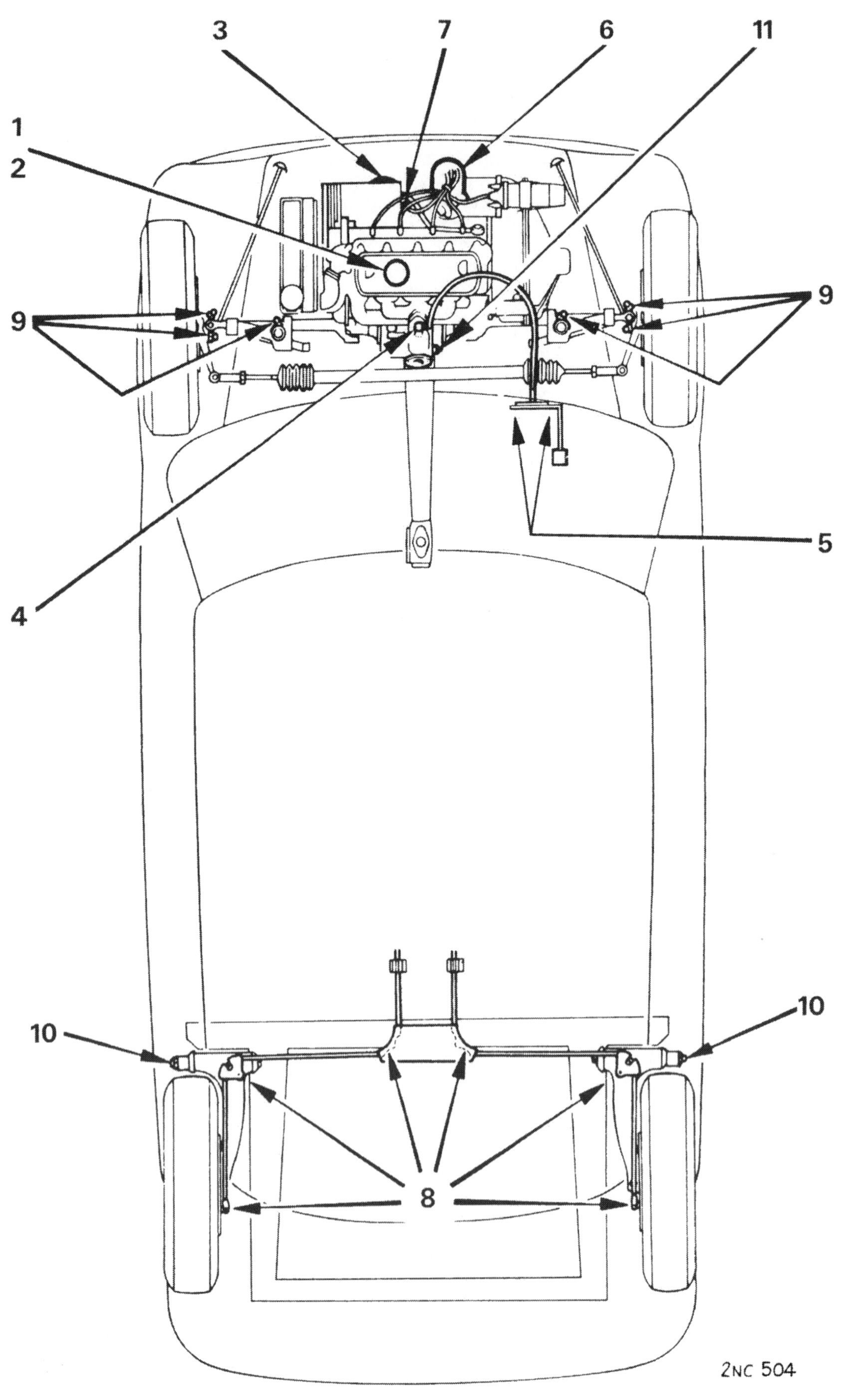

KEY TO LUBRICATION DIAGRAM

Every 3,000 miles (5000 km.) or 3 months Optional Lubrication

(1) ENGINE/TRANSMISSION. Inspect the oil level with the dipstick, and top-up if necessary.

Every 6,000 miles (10000 km.) or 6 months

(2) ENGINE/TRANSMISSION. Drain off the old oil and refill with new oil.

(3) OIL FILTER. Fit a new cartridge or filter element.

(4) CARBURETTER. Remove the cap from the top of the suction chamber and top up to the correct level with oil.

(5) ACCELERATOR. Lubricate accelerator control linkage and pedal fulcrum.

(6) DISTRIBUTOR. Lubricate the cam, contact breaker pivot, weights and centre spindle.
Do not oil the cam wiping pad.

(7) DYNAMO. Add a few drops of recommended engine oil through the oil hole in the commutator end bearing.
An alternator does not require periodic lubrication.

(8) HAND BRAKE. Lubricate the sector pivots and cable linkages.

(9) STEERING JOINTS.
(10) REAR SUSPENSION RADIUS ARMS.
} Lubricate as detailed in '**MAINTENANCE**'.

LOCKS AND HINGES. Lubricate the bonnet release, safety catch, and all locks and hinges.
Do not oil the steering lock.

NOTES:
The lubricating nipple shown on indicator 11 is fitted to earlier vehicles and only requires attention at major overhaul periods when grease should be used. Later cars are fitted with the single rod change mechanism and a lubricating nipple is not fitted.

Recommended oils and greases are given overleaf.

SERVICE LUBRICANTS

Component	Engine/Transmission Unit Distributor, Carburetter Dashpot, Oil Can			Grease Points	Upper Cylinder Lubrication
Climatic conditions	**All temperatures above −10°C (15°F)**	**Temperatures 10°C to −20°C (50°F to −5°F)**	**All temperatures below −10°C (15°F)**	**All conditions**	**All conditions**
Minimum performance level	British Leyland Service Fill Lubricating Oil Specification for Passenger Car and Light Commercial Petrol Engines B.L.S. OL.02			Multipurpose Lithium Grease N.L.G.1 Consistency No. 2	Upper Cylinder Lubricant
MOBIL	Mobiloil Special 20W/50 or Super 10W/50	Mobiloil Super 10W/50	Mobiloil 5W/20	Mobilgrease M.P.	Mobil Upperlube
SHELL	Shell Super 20W/50	Shell Super 10W/50	Shell Super 5W/30	Shell Retinax A	Shell Upper Cylinder Lubricant
BP	BP Super Visco-Static 20/50 or 10W/40	BP Super Visco-Static 10W/30 or 10W/40	BP Super Visco-Static 5W/20	BP Energrease L 2	BP Upper Cylinder Lubricant
CASTROL	Castrol GTX	Castrolite	Castrol GTZ	Castrol LM Grease	Castrollo
DUCKHAMS	Duckhams Q. 20–50	Duckhams Q. 5500	Duckhams Q. 5–30	Duckhams L.B. 10 Grease	Duckhams Adcoid Liquid
ESSO	Esso Uniflo 10W/50	Esso Uniflo 10W/50	Esso Extra Motor Oil 5W/20	Esso Multipurpose Grease H	Esso Upper Cylinder Lubricant
TEXACO	Havoline 20W/50 or 10W/40	Havoline 10W/40	Havoline 5W/30	Marfak All purpose	Special Upper Cylinder Lubricant
PETROFINA	Fina Supergrade 20W/50 or 10W/50 or 10W/40	Fina Supergrade 10W/50 or 10W/40	Fina Supergrade 5W/20	Fina HTL 2	Fina Cyltonic

LUBRICATION

The lubrication systems of your new car are filled with a high quality oil. You should always use a high quality oil of the correct viscosity range in the engine/transmission during subsequent maintenance operations or when topping up. The use of oils not to the correct specification can lead to high oil and fuel consumption and ultimately to damage to the engine or gearbox components.

Oils to the correct specification contain additives which disperse the corrosive acids formed by combustion and also prevent the formation of sludge which can block oilways. Additional oil additives should not be used. Servicing intervals must be adhered to.

Engine/transmission unit Use a well-known brand of oil to B.L.S. OL.02 or MIL–L–2104B or A.P.1, SE quality with a viscosity band spanning the temperature range of your locality.

S.A.E. VISCOSITY

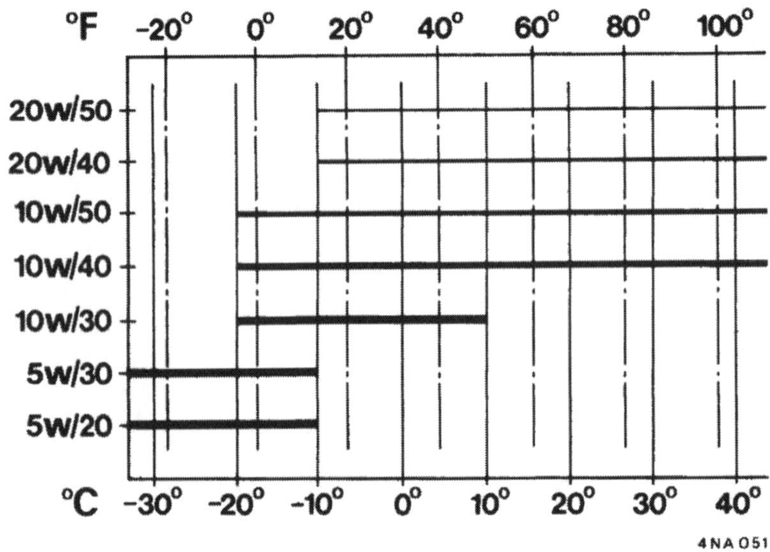

Steering rack Use E.P. 90 (MIL–L–2105) above – 15°C (10°F).
Use E.P. 80 (MIL–L–2105) below – 15°C (10°F).

Grease points Use Multipurpose Lithium Grease N.L.G.1. consistency No. 2.

RECOMMENDED FLUIDS, ANTI-FREEZE, CAPACITIES

ANTI-FREEZE SOLUTIONS

Use Bluecol Anti-freeze or an anti-freeze conforming to B.S. 3151 or B.S. 3152. The correct quantities of anti-freeze for different degrees of frost protection are given below:

ANTI-FREEZE	AMOUNT OF ANTI-FREEZE			COMMENCES TO FREEZE		FROZEN SOLID	
%	PTS.	U.S. PTS.	LITRES	°C.	°F.	°C.	°F.
25	1½	1.8	.85	−13	9	−26	−15
33⅓	2	2.5	1.2	−19	−2	−36	−33
50	3¼	3.75	1.8	−36	−33	−48	−53

BRAKE AND CLUTCH FLUID

Vehicles with all drum system: Use UNIPART 410 or 550 Brake Fluid; alternatively use a brake fluid conforming to specification S.A.E. J1703c.

Vehicles with disc/drum system: Use UNIPART 550 Brake Fluid or alternatively use a fluid to specification S.A.E. J1703c with a minimum boiling-point of 260°C. (500°F.) DO NOT use any other type of brake fluid.

CAPACITIES

	PINTS	U.S. PINTS	LITRES
Engine with manual gearbox (including filter) ..	8½	10.2	4.82
Engine with automatic transmission (including filter):			
Total capacity	13	16	7.38
Refill capacity	9	11	5
Cooling system: Without heater	5¼	6.3	3
With heater	6¼	7.5	3.55

ENGINE AND TRANSMISSION (Synchromesh)

Checking oil level

NOTE: Ensure that the vehicle is standing on a level surface.

1. Maintain the level at the 'MAX' mark on the dipstick; the difference in quantity between the 'MIN' and 'MAX' marks is approximately 1 pint (0.6 litre).

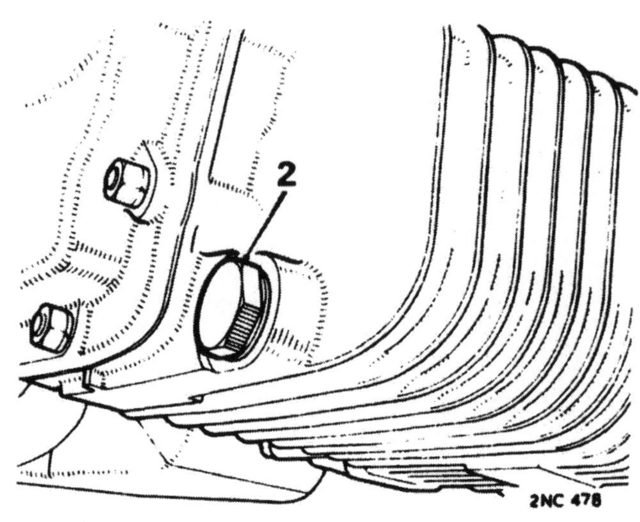

Draining and refilling

2. Drain the oil while the engine is warm; clean the magnetic drain plug, and fit a new sealing washer if necessary. Tighten the plug to the torque figure given in **'GENERAL DATA'**.
3. Refill with a recommended oil, see **'RECOMMENDED LUBRICANTS'**, up to the 'MAX' mark on the dipstick. Run the engine for a short while, then allow it to stand for a few minutes before re-checking the level; top up if necessary.

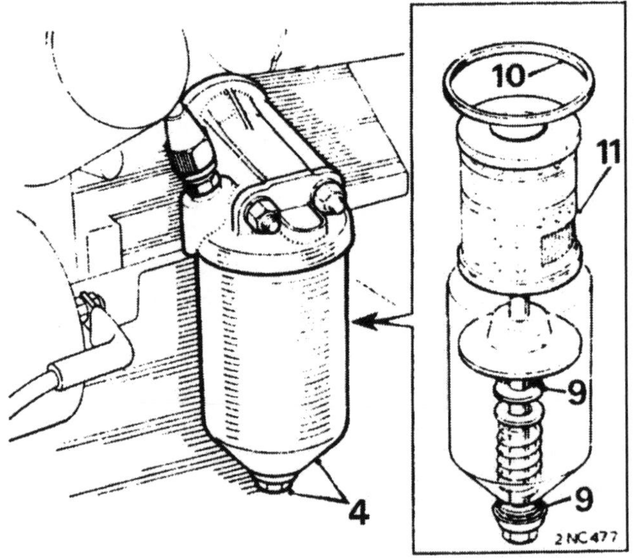

Filter element renewal

4. Unscrew the filter bowl securing bolt and remove the filter assembly.
5. Discard the used element.
6. Remove the circlip from the centre bolt.
7. Withdraw the centre bolt and remove the pressure plate, rubber and steel washers, and the spring.
8. Thoroughly wash the casing and components in a cleaning fluid.
9. Examine the sealing washers, and replace if necessary.
10. Extract the sealing ring from the filter head recess and fit a replacement.
11. Reassemble the filter bowl components and fit a new element.
12. Refit the filter assembly; rotate the bowl while tightening to ensure that it is correctly located on the sealing ring. Tighten the retaining bolt to the torque figure given in **'GENERAL DATA'**.
13. Check for oil leakage immediately the engine is started.

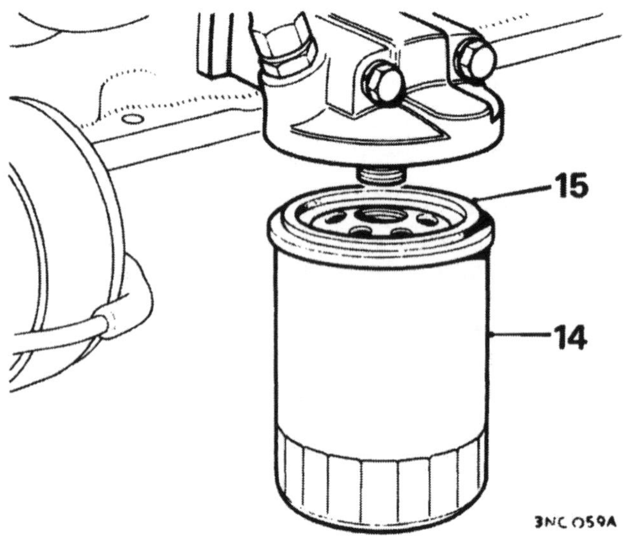

Disposable cartridge filter

14. Unscrew the filter cartridge from the filter head and discard the used cartridge and seal.
15. Lubricate the seal on the new cartridge with engine oil and screw the cartridge onto the filter head. **TIGHTEN BY HAND FORCE ONLY: DO NOT OVERTIGHTEN.**

ENGINE AND TRANSMISSION (Automatic)

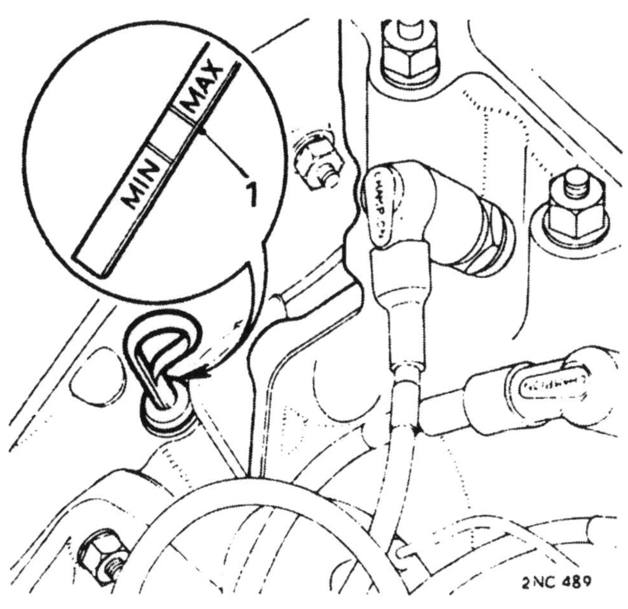

Checking oil level

NOTE:Ensure that the vehicle is standing on a level surface.

1. Start the engine and run it for 1-2 minutes. Stop the engine and wait for 1 minute, then check the oil level with the dipstick. Maintain the oil level up to the 'MAX' mark on the dipstick; the difference in quantity between the 'MIN' and the 'MAX' marks is approximately 1 pint (0.6 litre).

Draining and refilling

2. Draining the oil is as detailed for the 'Synchromesh' transmission except that the full quantity will not drain out at each oil change.
3. Refill the engine with the correct quantity of oil, see **'GENERAL DATA'**. Use one of the oils listed in the **'RECOMMENDED LUBRICANTS'** chart.
4. Run the engine for 1-2 minutes, check the oil level, and top up if necessary.

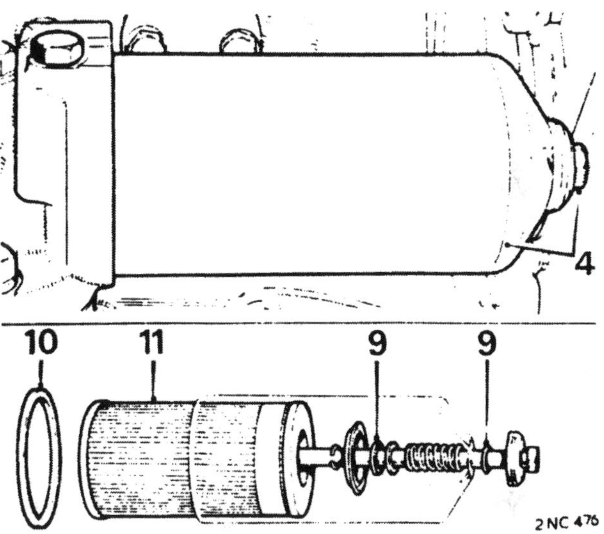

Filter element renewal

5. **All models except 'Clubman'**. Remove the front grille (16 screws) and place a container beneath the filter bowl. On 'Clubman' models sufficient clearance exists for filter bowl removal.
6. Filter element renewal is as detailed for the 'Synchromesh' transmission except that the filter bowl is removed and refitted through the grille aperture (where applicable).

DYNAMO

1 Add a few drops of oil through the central hole in the rear bearing housing. Avoid over-lubricating.

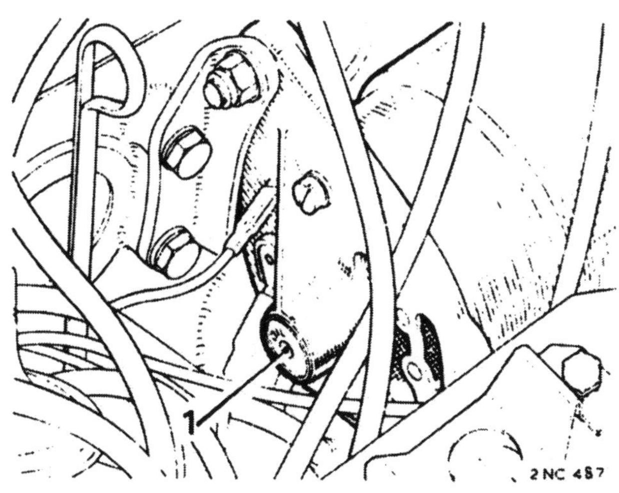

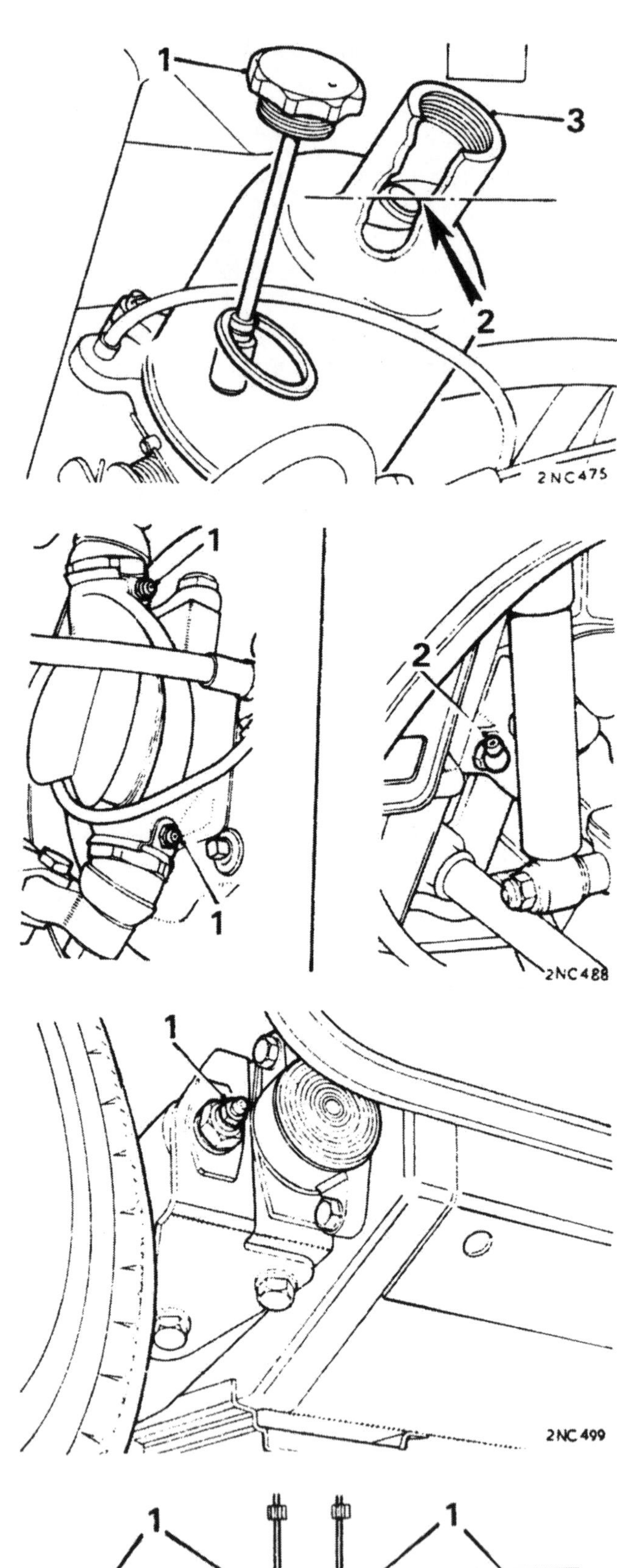

CARBURETTER

1. Unscrew the damper cap and withdraw the damper.
2. Check the oil level, and top up if necessary until the level is ½ in. (13 mm.) above the top of the hollow piston rod.
   NOTE: Under no circumstances should a heavy-bodied lubricant be used.
3. Push the damper assembly back into position and screw the cap firmly by hand into the suction chamber.

FRONT SUSPENSION

Swivel hub ball joints

1. Use one of the recommended greases shown in the **'RECOMMENDED LUBRICANTS'** chart and charge the two nipples on each swivel hub with grease. If the joints are already filled with grease, no further grease can usually be forced in.

Upper support arm inner pivot

2. Apply grease to the lubricating nipple on each unit on both sides of the vehicle.

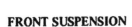

REAR SUSPENSION

Radius arms

1. Using the same recommended grease as used for **'FRONT SUSPENSION'** lubrication, charge the nipple on each unit with grease until excess grease appears from the inner bush on the opposite end of the radius arm.

HAND BRAKE CABLE

1. Smear grease around the cable guide channels.
2. Lubricate the swivel sector pivots with oil.
3. Smear grease around the operating lever clevis pin and the cable adjacent to the spring anchor brackets.

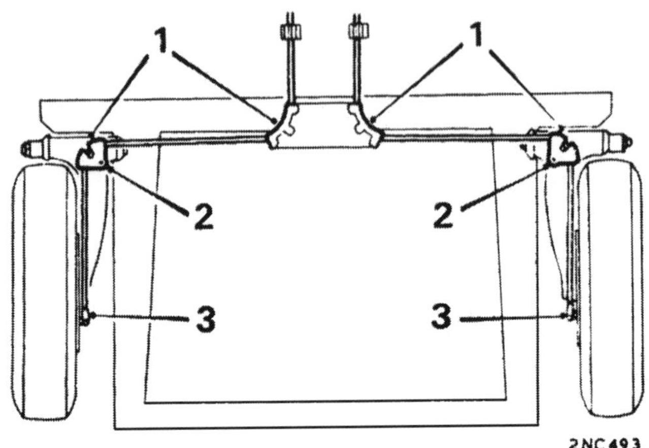

ROUTINE MAINTENANCE–
MECHANICAL

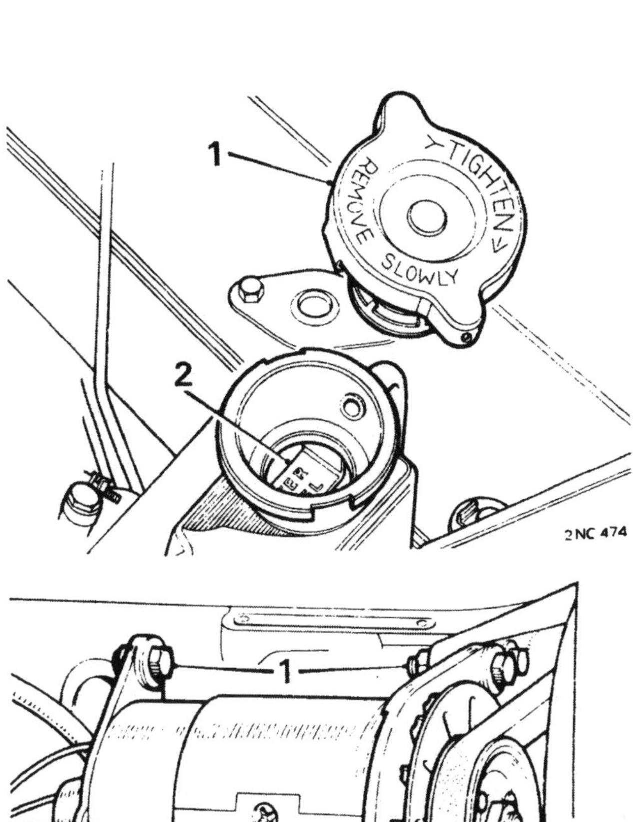

COOLING SYSTEM

The cooling system is under pressure while the engine is hot. Allow the system to cool before removing the filler cap.

NOTE: If it is essential to remove the filler cap while the engine is HOT, take great care to protect the hands and arms from scalding by the escaping steam, and turn the cap to the safety stop to release pressure.

1. Remove the radiator filler cap.
2. Top up with sufficient coolant to bring the level up to the 'level indicator' inside the header tank. When the system contains anti-freeze ensure that the specific gravity of the coolant is maintained.

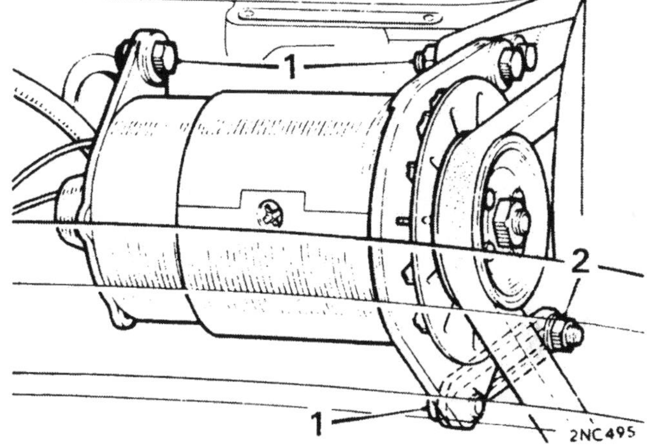

FAN BELT ADJUSTMENT

When correctly tensioned it should be possible, under moderate hand pressure, to deflect the longest run of the belt by ½ in. (13 mm.).

Adjusting

1. Slacken the dynamo or alternator securing bolts.
2. Slacken the adjusting link nut.
3. Move the dynamo or alternator to the required position; apply any leverage necessary to the drive-end bracket and not to any other part of the alternator. The lever used should preferably be of wood or soft metal. DO NOT OVERTENSION as this will impose an excess loading on the drive bearings and stretch the belt.
4. Tighten the adjusting link bolt, the dynamo or alternator securing bolts and re-check the tension.

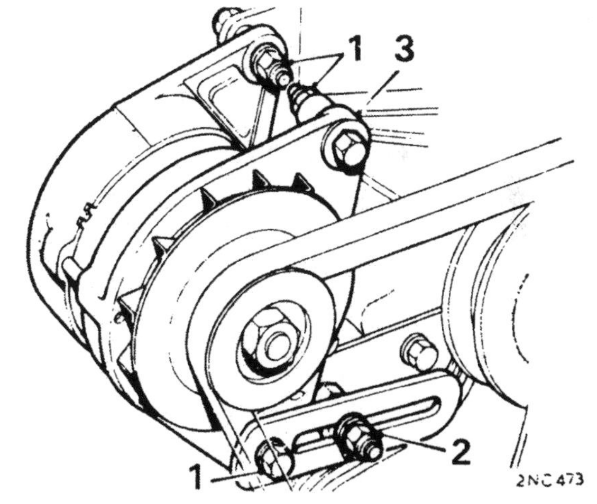

CLUTCH

Release lever clearances

A clearance of 0.020 in. (0.5 mm.) must be maintained between the clutch release lever and its return stop. Use a feeler gauge to check the clearance.

Checking

1. Pull the release lever outwards until all movement is taken up and check the clearance 'A'.

Adjusting

2. Slacken the locknut.
3. Turn the stop until the correct clearance is obtained, and retighten the locknut.

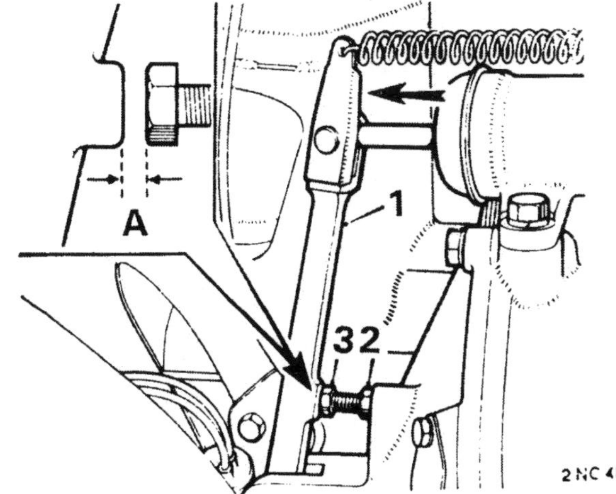

Master cylinder reservoir

Refer to **'BRAKE AND CLUTCH RESERVOIRS'**.

BRAKE AND CLUTCH RESERVOIRS

Fluid levels

Brake. One of three types of master cylinder may be fitted, according to the regulations of the country for which the vehicle was produced.

Checking

1. The fluid level in the brake 'B' and clutch 'C' master cylinder reservoirs must be maintained at the bottom of the filler necks.
2. BRAKE RESERVOIR WITH TRANSLUCENT EXTENSION: The fluid must be maintained up to the 'FLUID LEVEL' mark on the translucent extension.
3. SPLIT BRAKING SYSTEM RESERVOIR: The fluid must be maintained up to the 'FLUID LEVEL' mark on the side of the reservoir (arrowed).

Topping up

4. Remove the plastic filler cap and top up with UNIPART 410 or 550* BRAKE FLUID. Alternatively, use a high-boiling-point brake fluid conforming to specification S.A.E. J1703c with a minimum boiling point of 260°C. (500°F). DO NOT use any other type of fluid.

   Frequent topping-up is indicative of a leak in the system which must be detected and rectified immediately.

   NOTE: Brake fluid can have a detrimental effect on paintwork. Ensure that fluid is not allowed to contact paint-finished surfaces.
5. Check that the breather holes in the filler caps are clear and screw on the caps.

*Use UNIPART 550 BRAKE FLUID for disc brake models.

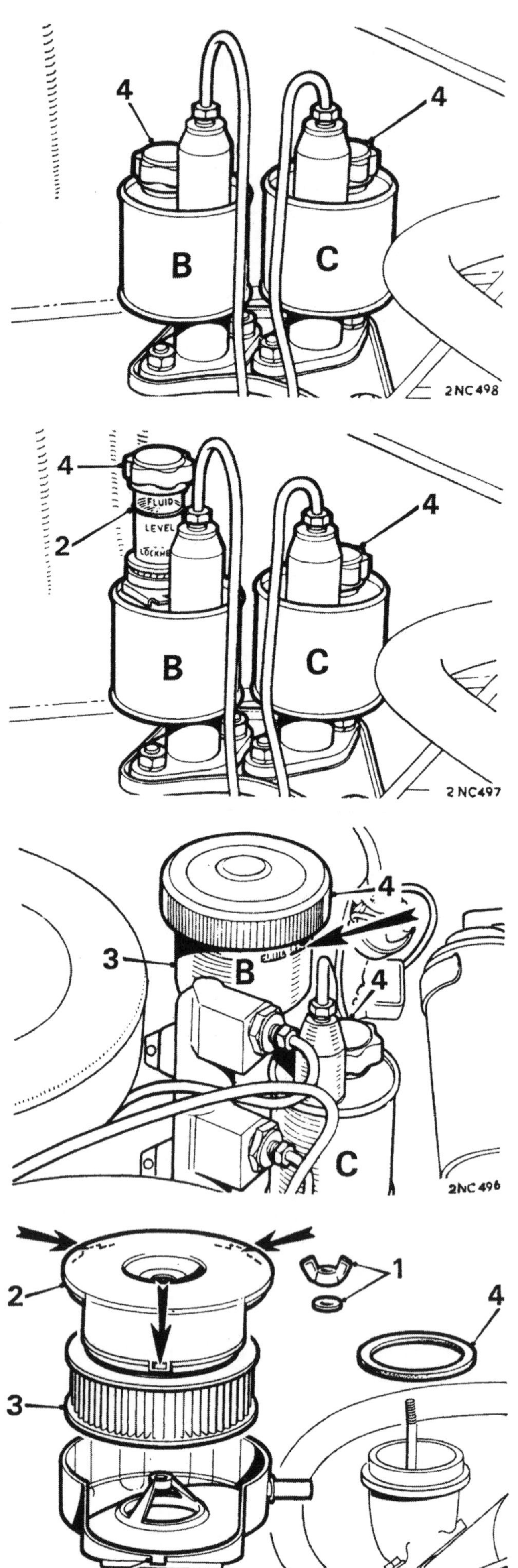

AIR CLEANER

Renew the air cleaner element at the intervals given in the 'MAINTENANCE SUMMARY'. In dusty operating conditions the element may require renewal more frequently than recommended.

Element replacement

1. Unscrew the wing nut(s) and disconnect the breather hose (when fitted).
2. METAL CASE TYPE: Lift off the top cover.

   PLASTIC CASE TYPE: Use a screwdriver in the slots (arrowed) to lever up the top cover, then release it from its locating lug (arrowed) adjacent the air intake pipe.
3. Remove and discard the old element(s) and thoroughly clean the container.

4. Ensure that the rubber seal is correctly positioned; on the plastic-type cleaner it should be in the groove on the underside of the top cover, and on the metal-type around the central boss of the container.

5. Fit new element(s) and refit the cover as detailed below:
   SMALL PLASTIC TYPE: Engage the locating lug (5) into the top cover (arrowed) and snap-fit the cover onto the container. Refit and tighten the wing nut.
   LARGE PLASTIC TYPE: Align the 'arrow' marked on the cover with the locating lug (5) and snap-fit the cover onto the container. Refit and tighten the two wing nuts.

6. Reconnect the breather hose (when fitted).

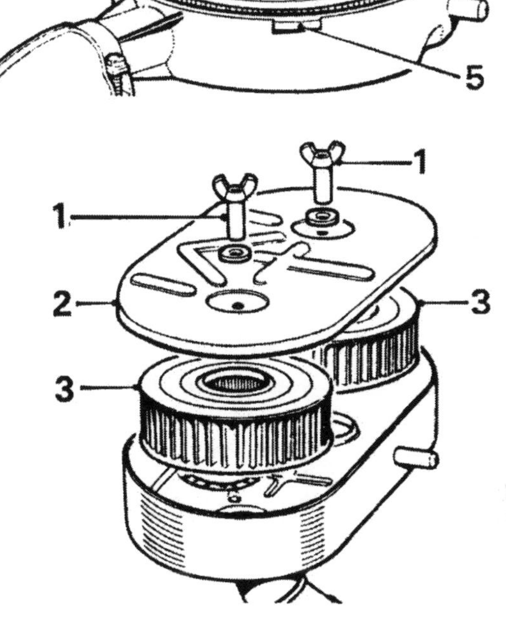

VALVE ROCKER CLEARANCES

Checking

1. Disconnect the breather hose (when fitted).

2. Unscrew the rocker cover securing screws and lift off the cover.

3. Turn the engine; on automatic models rotate the starter ring gear using a screwdriver inserted through the aperture on the converter housing (adjacent to the oil dipstick).

4. Insert a 0.012 in. (0.305 mm.) feeler gauge between the valve rocker arms and the valve stems and check the clearances in the following order:

   Check No. 1 valve with No. 8 fully open.
   " " 3 " " " 6 " "
   " " 5 " " " 4 " "
   " " 2 " " " 7 " "
   " " 8 " " " 1 " "
   " " 6 " " " 3 " "
   " " 4 " " " 5 " "
   " " 7 " " " 2 " "

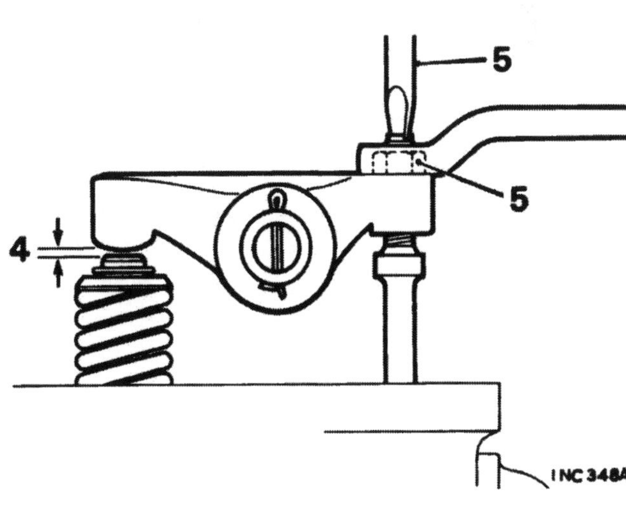

Adjusting

5. Slacken the adjusting screw locknut and turn the screw, clockwise to reduce the clearance or anti-clockwise to increase it. Retighten the locknut when the feeler gauge is a sliding fit, holding the adjusting screw against rotation with a screwdriver.

6. Check that its cork gasket is serviceable, refit the rocker cover and connect up the breather hose (when fitted).

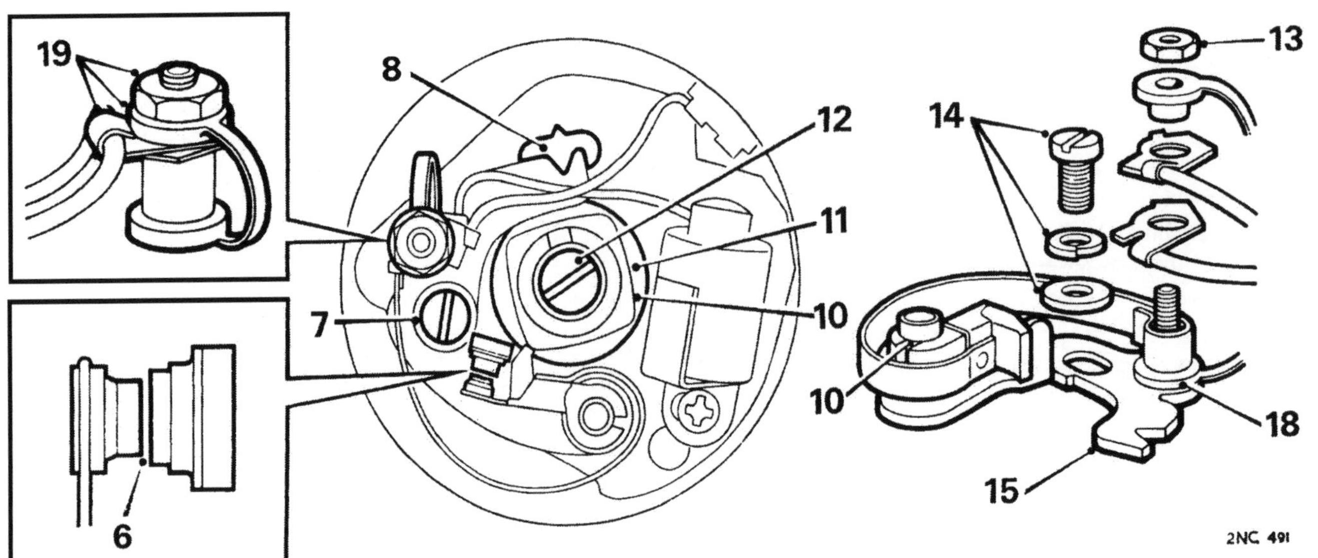

IGNITION

Distributor

Contact breaker–cleaning

1. Remove the ignition shield (Clubman and 1275 GT).
2. Remove the distributor cap and rotor arm.
3. Turn the engine until the contact points are fully open.
4. Inspect the contact points and if burned or blackened, clean them with fine emery-cloth or a fine carborundum file. The points are easier cleaned if the contact set is removed, see operations 13 to 20.
5. After cleaning, wipe the contact points with a fuel-moistened cloth and check the gap setting.

Contact breaker–gap setting

6. With the contact points fully open, check the gap setting with a feeler gauge, it should be 0.014 to 0.016 in. (0.35 to 0.40 mm.).

Contact breaker–adjusting

7. Slacken the contact plate securing screw.
8. Insert a screwdriver into the notched hole of the plate and turn it clockwise to decrease and anti-clockwise to increase the gap.
9. Tighten the securing screw and re-check the gap setting.

Contact breaker–lubrication

10. Lightly smear the pivot post and spindle cam with grease.
11. Lubricate the centrifugal weights with a few drops of oil through the hole in the base plate.
12. Remove the rotor arm and add a few drops of engine oil around the screw in the cam spindle. Do not remove the screw as clearance is provided for oil to pass.

IMPORTANT. Avoid over-lubrication, wipe away all surplus lubricant and ensure that the contact points are clean and dry.

Contact breaker–renewing

13. Remove the nut and lift off the top insulating bush and both electrical leads from the pivot stud.
14. Remove the contact plate securing screw, spring and plain washer.
15. Remove the contact set.
16. Before fitting a new contact set, wipe the points clean.
17. Lubricate the contact set and spindle cam as detailed in operations 10 to 12.
18. Position the contact set on the distributor base plate and refit the securing screw and washers.
19. Locate the electrical terminals onto the top insulating bush and fit the bush so that the terminals make contact with the moving contact spring. Refit and tighten the pivot nut.
20. Adjust the gap setting as detailed in operations 6 to 9.

NOTE: Whenever a new contact set has been fitted, re-check the gap after the first 500 miles (800 km.). During this period the heel of the moving contact will have bedded in on the spindle cam and consequently reduced the gap setting.

Sparking plugs

Servicing

1. Remove the sparking plugs and clean them, preferably with an air-blast service unit.
2. Clean the exterior insulators.
3. Check and re-set the points gap to 0.025 in. (0.65 mm.). Use a plug gauge setting tool and move the side electrode to obtain the correct setting.
4. Replacement. When fitting new plugs ensure that only the recommended type is used, see **'GENERAL DATA'**. Check the gap setting before installation. Tighten to a torque figure of 18 lb. ft. (2.5 kg. m.).

CARBURETTER TUNING (SINGLE)

The efficient operation of the engine and any exhaust emission control equipment which may be fitted depends not only on correct carburetter adjustment but also on correct ignition timing, rocker clearance, distributor contact breaker and plug gaps. It is essential that these items are checked before adjusting the carburetter.

Carburetter tuning must be confined to setting the idle and fast idle speeds and the mixture at idle speed. A reliable tachometer should be used if possible.

IMPORTANT. Where vehicles must conform to exhaust emission control regulations, adjustments should only be carried out if the use of a reliable tachometer and an exhaust gas analyser (CO meter) are available.

1. Top up the carburetter piston damper if necessary.
2. Check that the throttle functions correctly.
3. Ensure that the mixture control (choke) will return fully, that the cable (3) has $\frac{1}{16}$ in. (2 mm.) free play before it starts to pull on the lever.
4. Check that a small clearance exists between the fast idle screw and the cam.
5. Check that the piston falls freely onto the bridge of the carburetter. Raise the piston lifting pin (5); when released, the piston should fall freely, indicated by a distinct metallic click.
6. On vehicles fitted with Automatic Transmission select 'N' on the gear quadrant and apply the hand brake.
7. Start the engine and run it at a fast idle speed until it attains normal running temperature, and continue for a further five minutes.
8. Increase the engine speed to 2,500 r.p.m. for 30 seconds.

NOTE: Tuning can now be commenced. If delay prevents the adjustments being completed within three minutes, increase the engine speed to 2,500 r.p.m. for 30 seconds and then continue tuning. Repeat this clearing procedure at three-minute intervals until tuning is completed.

9. Check the idle speed with a tachometer (see **'TUNING DATA'**), and adjust by turning the throttle adjusting screw.

   If a smooth idle at the correct speed is not obtainable, adjust the idle speed mixture setting as follows:
10. Turn the jet adjusting nut up to weaken, or down to enrich, one flat at a time, to obtain the fastest speed. Turn the nut up slowly until the speed just commences to fall, then turn the nut down to the weakest position for maximum speed.
11. Re-check the idle speed and adjust as necessary.
12. Pull the mixture control knob until the linkage is about to move the carburetter jet.
13. Turn the fast idle screw (4) to give the correct fast idling speed (see **TUNING DATA'**).

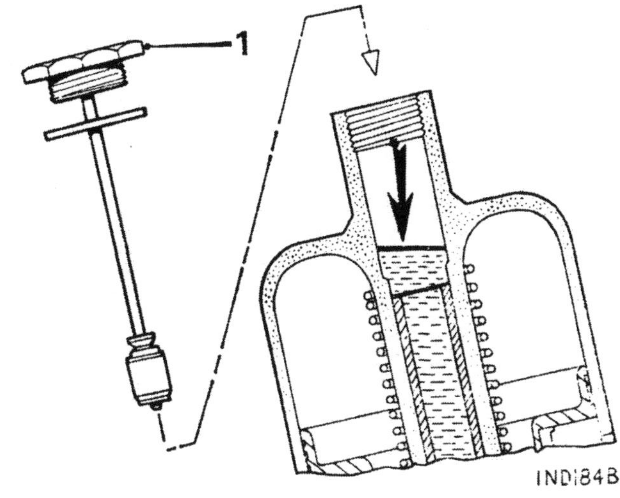

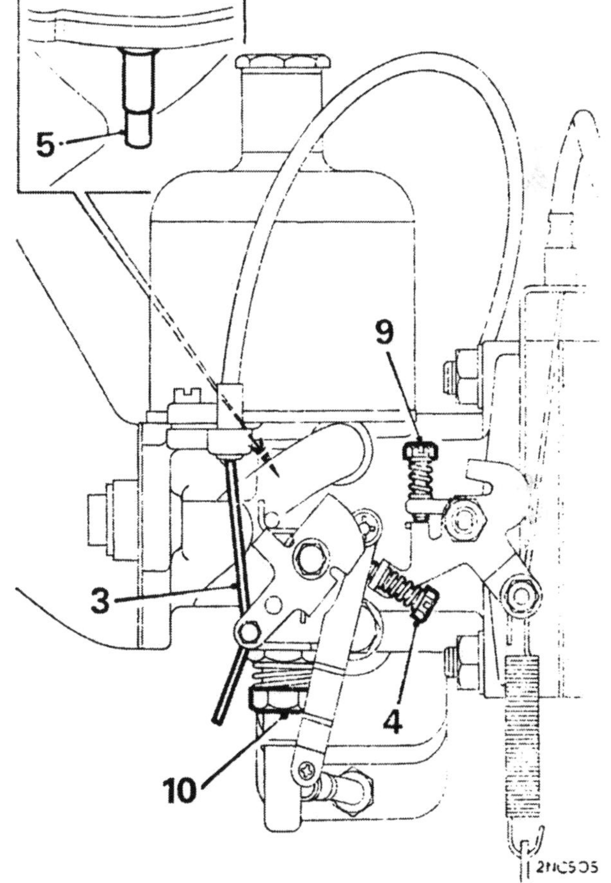

CARBURETTER TUNING (TWIN)

The efficient operation of the engine and any exhaust emission control equipment which may be fitted depends not only on correct carburetter settings but also on correct ignition timing, tappet clearance, distributor contact breaker and plug gaps. It is essential that these items are checked before adjusting the carburetters.

Carburetter tuning must be confined to setting the idle and fast idle speeds and mixture at idle speed. A reliable tachometer and a carburetter intake balancing meter should be used if possible.

IMPORTANT. Where a vehicle must conform to exhaust emission control regulations, adjustments should only be carried out if a reliable tachometer, balancing meter and an exhaust gas analyser (CO meter) are available.

1. Top up the carburetter piston dampers if necessary.
2. Check that the throttle functions correctly.
3. Remove the air cleaner assembly.
4. Remove the air intake manifold.
5. Ensure that the mixture control (choke) will return fully, that the cable (5) has $\frac{1}{16}$ in. (2 mm.) free play before it starts to pull on the lever.
6. Check that a small clearance exists between the fast idle screws and their cams.
7. Raise each carburetter piston lifting pin (7), release the pin and check that the piston falls freely onto the bridge of the carburetter, indicated by a distinct metallic click.
8. Start the engine and run it at a fast idle speed until it attains normal running temperature and continue for a further five minutes.
9. Increase the engine speed to 2,500 r.p.m. for thirty seconds.

NOTE: Tuning can now be commenced. If delay prevents the adjustment being completed within three minutes, increase the engine speed to 2,500 r.p.m. for 30 seconds and then continue tuning. Repeat this clearing procedure at three-minute intervals until tuning is completed.

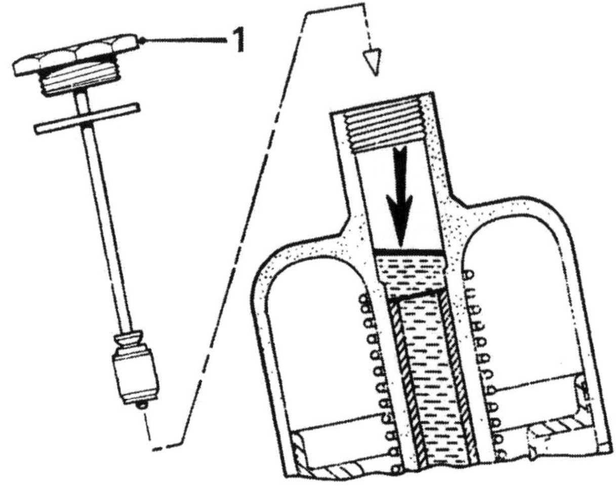

Slow running adjustment and synchronization

10. Check the idle speed with a tachometer, see **'TUNING DATA'**, and check the carburetters for balanced air intake using a balance meter.
11. If the balance is not correct, adjust by turning the throttle adjusting screw on one of the carburetters. Then adjust the idle speed by turning the throttle adjusting screw on each carburetter by the same amount until the correct idle speed is obtained.
12. Check the throttle shaft pin clearance and adjust if necessary—see items 21 to 23.

    If a smooth idle at the correct speed and balance is not obtainable, stop the engine, and adjust the idle speed mixture setting as follows.

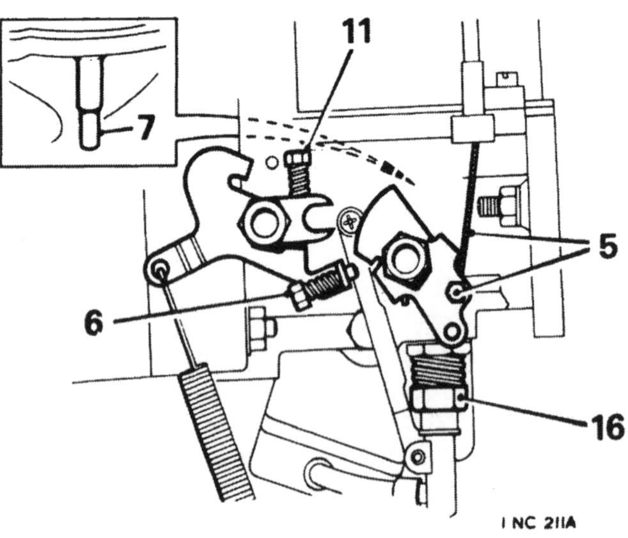

Mixture setting

13. Slacken the clamp bolt on one of the throttle spindle interconnections.
14. Disconnect the clamp bolt on one of the jet control interconnections.
15. Remove each suction chamber and piston and screw the jets up until they are flush with the bridge of the carburetter or as fully up as possible.
16. Turn down the jet adjusting nut on each carburetter two complete turns.
17. Refit the piston and suction chambers and top up the piston damper oil levels.

NOTE: Operations 15 to 17 need not be carried out if it is known that the jets are in the same relative position.

18. Restart the engine and run at idle speed.

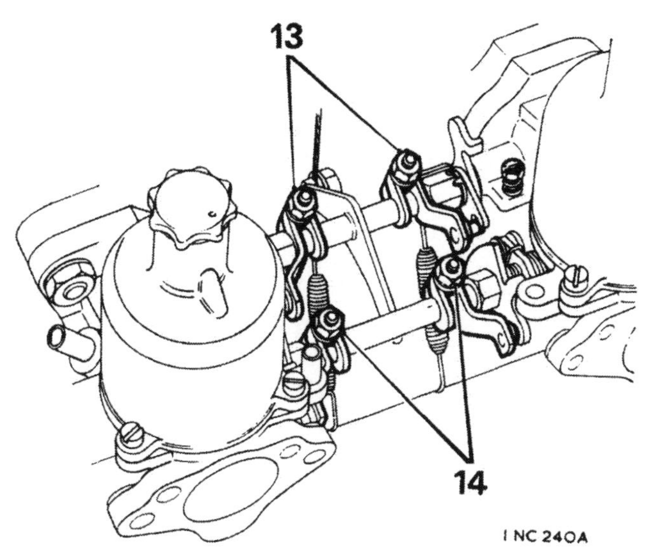

Adjusting

19. Turn the jet adjusting nut, 16, on both carburetters in the same direction, one flat at a time, up to weaken or down to enrich, until the fastest speed is recorded on the tachometer. Now turn the nuts up slowly until the speed just commences to fall; finally, turn each nut down equally very slowly by the minimum amount until maximum speed is regained.
20. Re-check the idle speed and carburetter intake balance; adjust as necessary with the throttle adjusting screws, 11.

    EMISSION CONTROLLED CARS: Use the exhaust gas analyser and check that the percentage CO reading is within the prescribed limits. If the reading falls outside the limits, reset both jet adjusting nuts equally by the minimum amount necessary to bring the reading just within the limits.

Throttle linkage adjustment

21. Slacken the throttle shaft lever clamping screws.
22. Place a 0.012 in. (0.31 mm.) feeler gauge between the tail of the throttle shaft operating lever and the choke control interconnecting rod.
23. Move each throttle shaft lever downwards until the lever (or pin) rests on the lower arm of the throttle spindle operating fork. Maintain this position, and with the feeler gauge still in position, tighten both throttle shaft lever clamping screws, 21, and withdraw the feeler gauge. The levers (or pins) should now have a clearance 'A' in the forks.

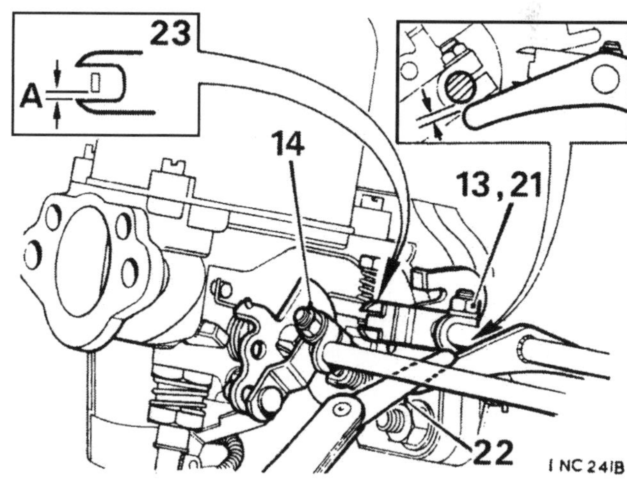

Fast idle adjustment

24. Pull out the mixture control knob (choke) until the linkage is about to move the carburetter jets. Lock the knob in this position.
25. Turn each fast idle screw, 6, until it just contacts its cam.
26. Re-start the engine and turn each fast idle screw equally to give the correct fast idle speed, see **'TUNING DATA'**. Stop the engine.
27. Refit the air intake manifold.
28. Refit the air cleaner assembly.

BRAKES

Adjustment

1. Jack up the vehicle and place supports under the sub-frames. Deal with one adjuster at a time.

FRONT

2. Turn the adjuster in the same direction as the forward rotation of the road wheel until the wheel is locked. Back off the adjuster the minimum amount necessary to allow the wheel to revolve freely.
3. Spin the wheel, apply the foot brake hard to centralize the brake-shoes, and re-check the adjustment.
4. Repeat this procedure with each adjuster and repeat the same operation on the other front wheel.

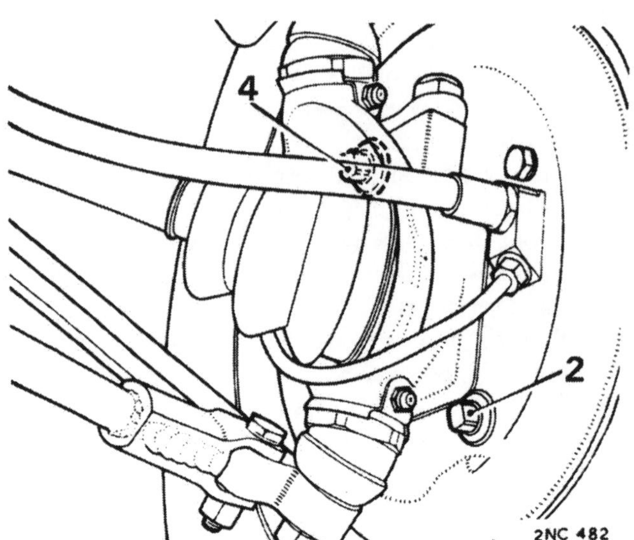

REAR

5. Turn the single squared adjuster in a clockwise direction (when viewed from under the centre of the vehicle) until the wheel is locked. Back off the adjuster the minimum amount necessary to allow the wheel to revolve freely.
6. Repeat the above operation on the other rear wheel.

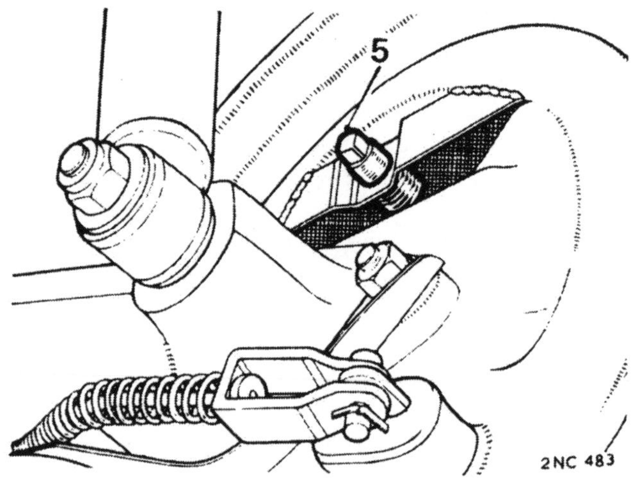

Hand brake

7. Adjust the brake-shoes as detailed in 1 to 6.
8. Apply the hand brake to the third notch on the ratchet.
9. Turn each cable adjusting nut at the lever trunnion until both wheels can only just be turned by heavy hand pressure.
10. Ensure that the wheels rotate freely when the hand brake is released.

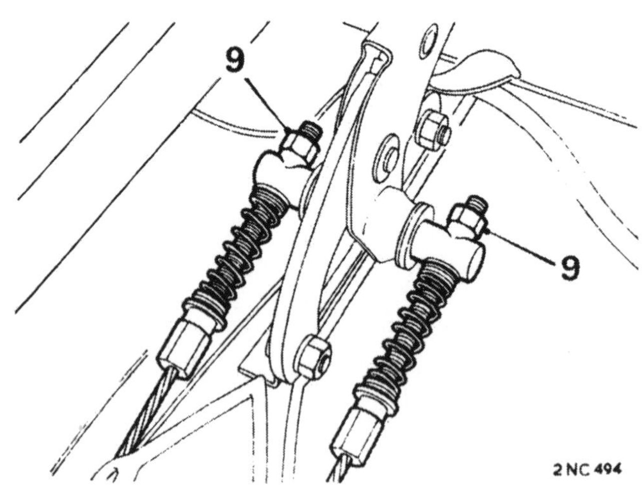

BRAKE LININGS

Checking

1. Jack up the vehicle and place supports under the sub-frames.
2. Back off the brake adjusters and release the hand brake when dealing with the rear brakes.
3. Remove the brake-drum securing screws and pull off the drums.
4. Examine the linings for wear or contamination and clean dust from the linings, backplate and brake-drum.

   IMPORTANT. Ensure that sufficient lining material remains to allow the vehicle to be used until the next service interval for this check, without the lining thickness wearing below the safe limit.

5. Fit replacement brake-shoe assemblies as complete axle sets if replacements are required, and refer to Section M.
6. Refit the brake-drums, adjust the shoes, and refit the road wheels.

DISC BRAKE PADS

Inspecting

1. Jack up the front of the car, place supports under the sub-frame and remove the road wheels.
2. Check the thickness of the pads, and renew them if the pad linings are approaching the minimum thickness of $\frac{1}{16}$ in. (1.6 mm.). Always ensure that sufficient pad material remains for the car to be used until the next service interval.

Replacing

3. Remove the pad-retaining split pins.
4. Withdraw the pads and anti-squeak shims.
5. Press the pistons into the calliper, using Service tool 18G 672.
6. Refit the new pads, with the anti-squeak shims correctly located, and fit new split pins. DO NOT renew the pads on one side of the car only.
7. Apply the brakes hard several times to adjust the pad to disc clearance. No other adjustment is necessary.
8. Check and correct the fluid level in the brake master cylinder reservoir.

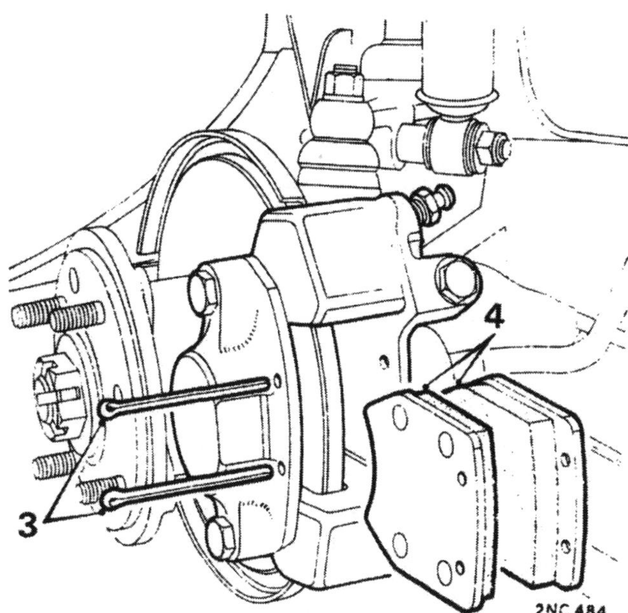

BRAKE SERVO FILTER

The filter should be cleaned at the intervals recommended in the **'MAINTENANCE SUMMARY'**.

Removing

1. Lever the dome off the valve cover with a screwdriver (a rrowed).
2. Remove the filter and clean it with compressed air at low pressure. DO NOT use cleaning fluid or lubricant of any description on the filter.

Refitting

3. Ensure that the air valve spring is securely located onto the valve.
4. Refit the filter and snap-fit the dome onto the valve cover.

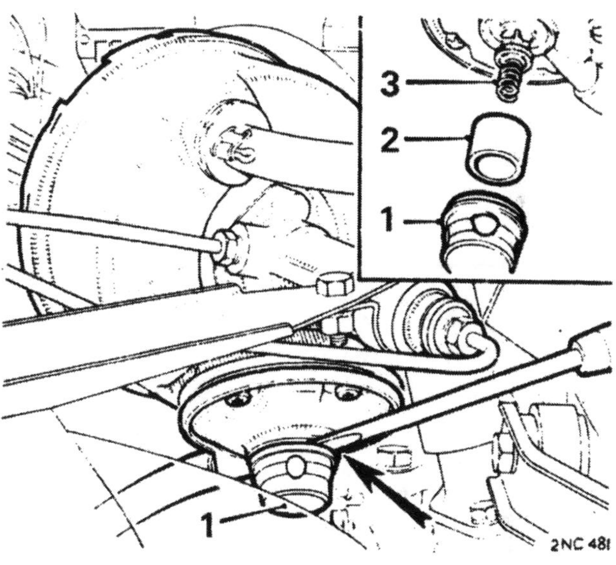

BRAKES (PREVENTIVE MAINTENANCE)

In addition to the recommended periodical inspection of brake components it is advisable as the car ages and as a precaution against the effects of wear and deterioration to make a more searching inspection and renew parts as necessary.

It is recommended that:

1. Disc brake pads, drum brake linings, hoses, and pipes should be examined at intervals no greater than those laid down in the **'MAINTENANCE SUMMARY'**.
2. Brake fluid should be changed completely every 18 months or 18,000 miles (30000 km.) whichever is the sooner.
3. All fluid seals in the hydraulic system and all flexible hoses should be examined and renewed if necessary every three years or 36,000 miles (60000 km.) whichever is the sooner. At the same time the working surfaces of the pistons and of the bores of the master cylinder, wheel cylinders, and other slave cylinders should be examined and new parts fitted where necessary.

Care must be taken always to observe the following points:

a. At all times use the recommended brake fluid.
b. Never leave fluid in unsealed containers; it absorbs moisture quickly and can be dangerous if used in your braking system in this condition.
c. Fluid drained from the system or used for bleeding is best discarded.
d. The necessity for absolute cleanliness throughout cannot be over-emphasized.

WHEELS AND TYRES

Checking

1. Check that the tyres on the same axle are of the same size and make and that cross-ply and radials have not been incorrectly mixed, see 'NOTES'.
2. Examine all tyres for cuts in the fabric, exposure of ply or cord, structure, lumps or bulges.
3. Check the depth of the tyre tread; those which are approaching the minimum tread depth of 1 mm. or will have worn to this limit before the next service interval should be replaced.
4. Check and adjust the tyre pressures, including the spare, when the tyres are cold, see 'GENERAL DATA'.
5. Check the wheel nuts for tightness–torque tightening figure is 42 lb. ft. (5.8 kg. m.).

NOTES: Radial-ply tyres should only be fitted in sets of four, although in certain circumstances it is permissible to fit a pair on the rear wheels; tyres of different construction MUST NOT be used on the same axle. Radial-ply tyres must never be fitted to the front wheels with conventional cross-ply tyres at the rear.

STEERING

Wheel alignments

1. Check the front wheel alignment with the car unladen and with the tyres at their correct pressures, see 'GENERAL DATA'.
2. Carry out the alignment check as detailed in Section J.4.

Checking for wear

3. Check all moving parts for wear and security.
4. Examine the steering rack and drive shaft gaiters for condition and oil leakage.
5. Check tightness of the column to rack pinion clamp bolt; the torque tightness is 8 to 9 lb. ft. (1 to 1.2 kg. m.).

ROUTINE MAINTENANCE– ELECTRICAL

General checks

1. Check the functioning of all lamps, horns, direction indicators and windscreen wipers.
2. Examine the windscreen wiper blades, and replace if showing signs of deterioration.

Headlamp beam alignment

The headlamp beams should be set with the normal load on the car. They should be set parallel to each other in the straight-ahead position and ½±¼ below horizontal or in accordance with local regulations of the country for which the car was produced.

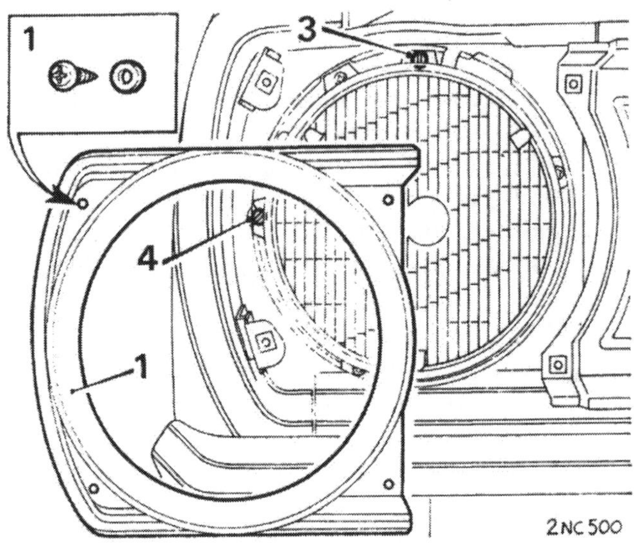

Adjusting

1. Clubman and 1275 GT models: To obtain access to the beam adjusting screws, remove the front grille extensions (four screws each).
2. All other models: Remove the rim retaining screw, pull the rim forwards and upwards to release it from the lamp retaining lugs.
3. Use beam setting equipment to check the alignment; turn the top screw for vertical adjustment.
4. Turn the screw on the side of the lamp unit for horizontal adjustment.
5. Refit the headlamp rims or the grille extensions as applicable to the model.

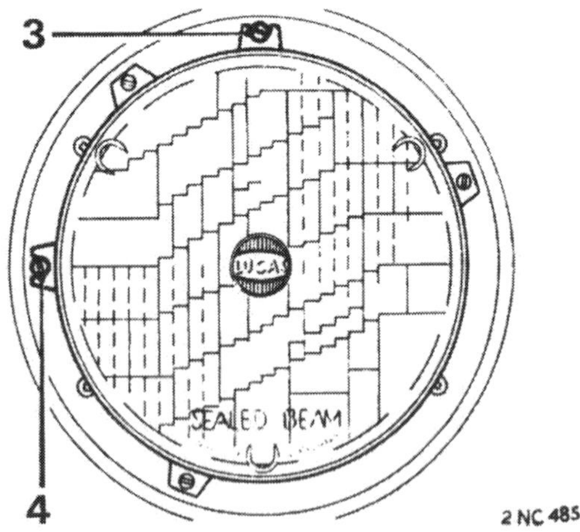

Battery

GENERAL MAINTENANCE

1. Wipe away all dirt and moisture from the top of the battery. Check that the terminals are secure, and smear with petroleum jelly.

NOTE: One of two types of battery may be fitted, therefore refer to the applicable procedure for topping-up.

TOPPING-UP

2. **Lucas Pacemaker (type A7, A9, A11/9).** The electrolyte levels (1) are visible through the translucent battery case or may be checked by fully raising the vent cover (2) and tilting it to one side. The electrolyte level in each cell must be maintained so that the separator plates (3) are just covered. To avoid flooding, the battery must not be topped up within half an hour of it having been charged from any source other than the generating system fitted to the car.

   To top up the levels, raise the vent cover and pour distilled water into the trough (4) until all the rectangular filling slots (5) are full and the bottom of the trough is just covered. Press the cover firmly into position: the correct quantity of distilled water will automatically be distributed to each cell. In extremely cold conditions, run the engine immediately after topping-up to mix the electrolyte.

IMPORTANT. The vent cover must be kept closed at all times, except when topping-up. The electrolyte will flood if the cover is raised while trickle charging the battery. A single-cell heavy discharge tester cannot be used on this type of battery. On no occasion should the vent cover be detached from the battery.

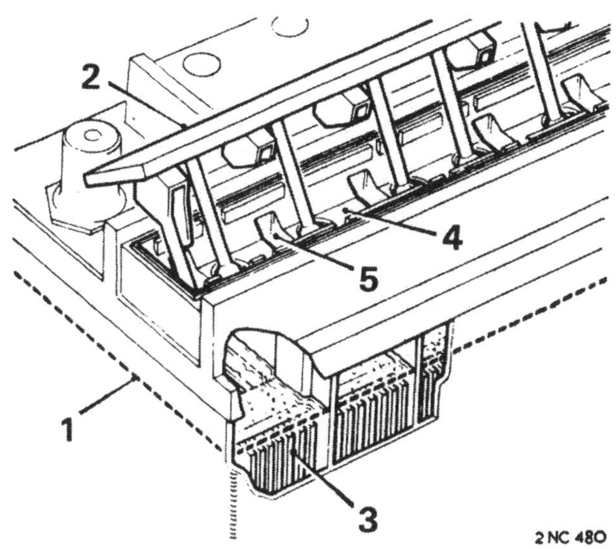

TOPPING UP

3. **Lucas (Type CL7, CL9).** Remove the manifold (1) and check the electrolyte level (2) in each cell.

   Top up if necessary with distilled water until the separator guard is just covered; do not overfill.

NOTE: Do not use tap-water and do not use a naked light when examining the condition of the cells. More frequent topping-up may be necessary in hot climates or if long daily runs are made.

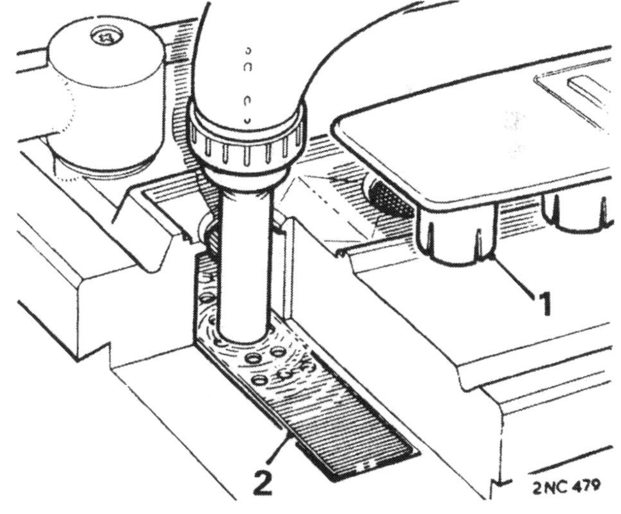

CHECKING SPECIFIC GRAVITY

4. Take hydrometer readings from each cell. If the electrolyte level is low, top up with distilled water and recharge the battery for at least 40 minutes.

   HYDROMETER READINGS:

   Climates below 27° C. (80° F.):

	Specific gravity	Degrees Baumé
Cell fully charged	1.270–1.290	30.5–32.5
Cell about half-charged ..	1.190–1.210	23.0–25.0
Cell completely discharged ..	1.110–1.130	14.5–16.5

   Climates frequently above 27° C. (80° F.):

	Specific gravity	Degrees Baumé
Cell fully charged	1.210–1.230	25.0–27.0
Cell about half-charged ..	1.130–1.150	16.5–19.0
Cell completely discharged ..	1.050–1.070	7.0–9.5

   The figures given are corrected to an electrolyte temperature of 16 °C. (60 °F.) and readings obtained must also be corrected to suit the temperature of the electrolyte.

   For every 3 ° C. (5 ° F.) above 16°C. (60°F.) add 0.002 S.G. (0.2° B.).

   For every 3°C. (5°F.) above 16°C. (60°F.) subtract 0.002 S.G. (0.2° B.).

5. All cells should give approximately the same readings. A cell that differs unduly from the rest, in its level or specific gravity, may be damaged.

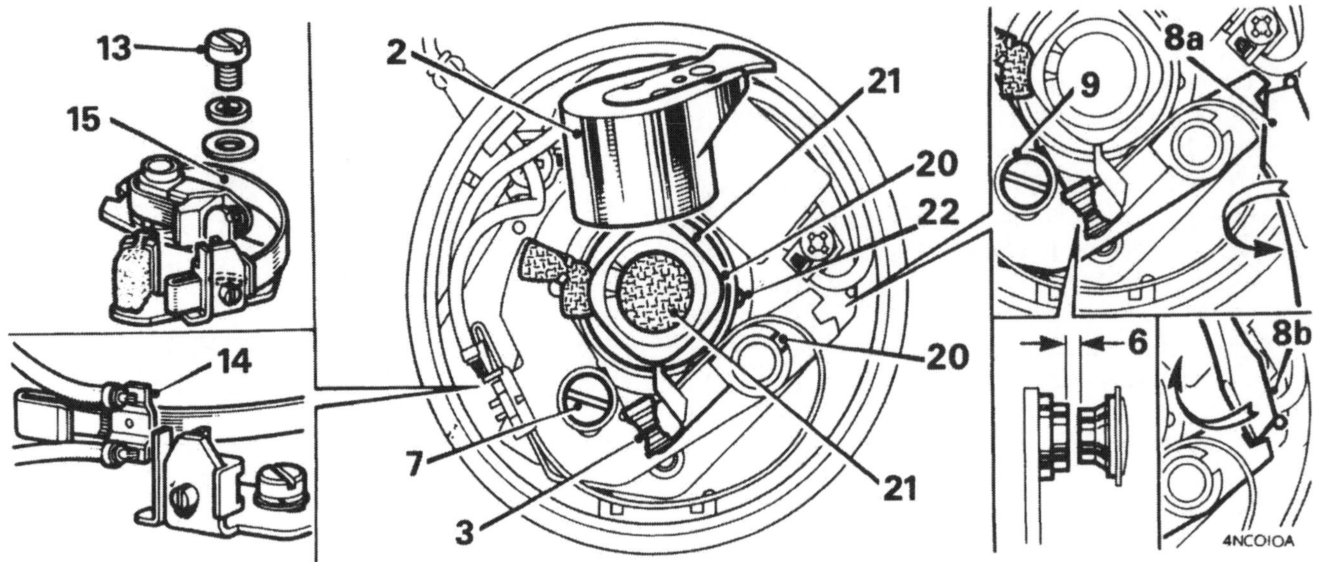

●IGNITION

Distributor–type 45D4

Contact breaker–cleaning

1. Remove the ignition shield (Clubman and 1275 GT).
2. Remove the distributor cap and rotor arm.
3. Turn the engine until the contact points are fully open.
4. Inspect the contact points and if burned or blackened, clean them with fine emery-cloth or a fine carborundum file. The points are easier cleaned if the contact set is removed, see operations 13 to 19.
5. After cleaning, wipe the contact points with a fuel moistened cloth and check the gap setting.

Contact breaker–gap setting

6. With the contact points fully open, check the gap setting with a feeler gauge, it should be 0.014 to 0.016 in. (0.35 to 0.040 mm).

Contact breaker–adjusting

7. Slacken the contact plate securing screw.
8. Insert a screwdriver into the notched hole of the plate and lever against the pip provided on the base plate.
   a. Turn anti-clockwise to decrease the gap.
   b. Turn clockwise to increase the gap.
9. Tighten the securing screw and re-check the gap setting.
10. Turn the crankshaft until the heel of the contact is on the highest point of an alternative cam lobe.
11. Re-check the contact gap.
12. Repeat 10 and 11 for each remaining cam lobe.

Contact breaker–renewing

13. Remove the contact plate securing screw, spring and plain washer.
14. Press the contact breaker spring from the insulated post and release the terminal plate.
15. Remove the contact set.
16. Wipe the points of the new contact set clean, using a fuel-moistened cloth.
17. Connect the terminal plate to the contact breaker spring.
18. Position the contact set on the base plate and fit the retaining screw and washers.
19. Position the spring on the insulated post between the two locating shoulders.

Lubrication

20. Very lightly smear the cam and pivot post with grease.
21. Add a few drops of oil to the felt pad in the top of the cam spindle and through the gap between the contact plate and the cam spindle to lubricate the centrifugal weights. **Do not oil the cam wiping pad.**
22. Every 24,000 miles (40000 km): Add a drop of oil to the two holes in the base plate to lubricate the centre bearing.
23. Wipe away all surplus lubricant and ensure the contact points are clean and dry.
24. Refit the rotor arm, wipe the inside and outside of the distributor cover clean, refit the distributor cover.

General

After fitting a new contact breaker set the contact breaker should be checked, adjusted, and lubricated according to the instructions given.

Whenever a new contact set has been fitted, re-check the gap after the first 500 miles (800 km). During this period the heel of the contact will have bedded to the spindle cam and reduced the initial contact gap setting.

BODY AND GENERAL INSPECTION

Lubrication

1. Inject a small quantity of engine oil through the key slots and around the push-buttons.
2. Lubricate the door hinges with engine oil.
3. Apply grease to the moving surfaces of the bonnet release mechanism and oil to the release lever and safety-catch pivot points.

General checks

4. Check the condition and security of seats and seat belts; report if attention is required.
5. Check the rear view mirror for looseness, cracks or crazing.
6. Check that the body and door drain holes are clear; use a piece of stiff wire to probe the apertures and remove any obstruction.

GENERAL INSPECTION

Visual checks

1. Check the fuel and clutch pipes and unions for chafing, leaks and corrosion.
2. Check the exhaust system for security, leakage, or severe corrosion likely to cause leakage before the next check is called for.

SECTION A

THE ENGINE

† These operations must be followed by an exhaust emission check 

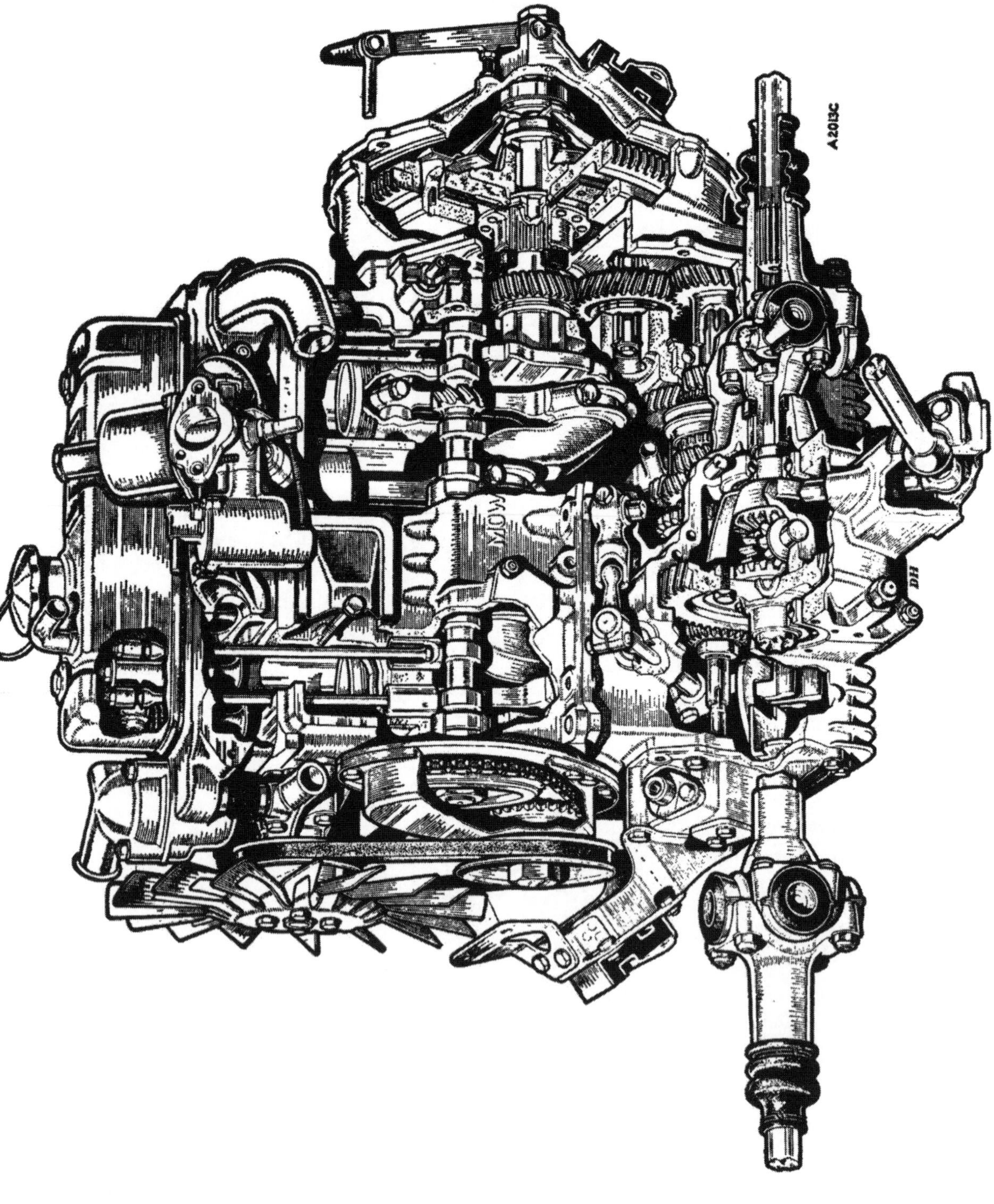

THE POWER UNIT AND SYNCHROMESH TRANSMISSION ASSEMBLY

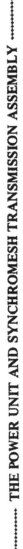

Section A.1

AIR CLEANER

Removing

1. Disconnect the breather hose from the rocker cover, unscrew the wing nut and lift off the cleaner.

COOPER

Removing

1. Disconnect the breather pipe from the rocker cover.
2. Remove the four securing screws to remove the gauze-type cleaner, unscrew the two wing nuts to remove the paper-element-type cleaner.

Section A.2

CARBURETTER

Removing

1. Remove the cleaner.
2. Disconnect the mixture and throttle cables.
3. Disconnect the suction advance pipe.
4. Disconnect the fuel delivery hose.
5. Unscrew the two nuts and lift off the carburetter cable abutment plate and two gaskets.

When refitting, make sure the gaskets are in good condition.

COOPER

Removing

1. Remove the bonnet and disconnect the battery.
2. Disconnect the choke and throttle cables and the main flexible feed pipe.
3. Disconnect the interconnecting pipe support clip.
4. Unhook the three return springs.
5. Disconnect the vacuum advance pipe.
6. Remove the nuts and withdraw both carburetters together.

Refitting

Reverse the removing instructions and adjust the linkage as in Section D.6 (35).

Section A.3

EXHAUST PIPE

Removing

Slacken the exhaust pipe to manifold clamp and disconnect the fixing points on the gear change extension and the rear sub-frame.

Refitting

1. Disconnect the engine tie-rod from the cylinder block.
2. Assemble the exhaust pipe to the engine leaving the fixing bolts and the manifold clamp loose.
3. Push the engine forward to line up the tie-rod bolt holes and wedge it in position with a wooden block. If necessary, slacken the two engine to sub-frame bolts and then retighten them.
4. Reconnect the tie-rod.
5. Insert slip packings, as required, between the transmission case and the pipe bracket, and then tighten the bolt, the sub-frame fixings, and the manifold clamp.
6. Remove the wooden block.

COOPER

Removing

1. Remove the screw securing the exhaust pipe to manifold clamp from the front end of the gear change extension.
2. Unscrew the nuts and bolts at the intermediate and rear mountings and withdraw the pipe.

Refitting

Reverse the removing instructions.

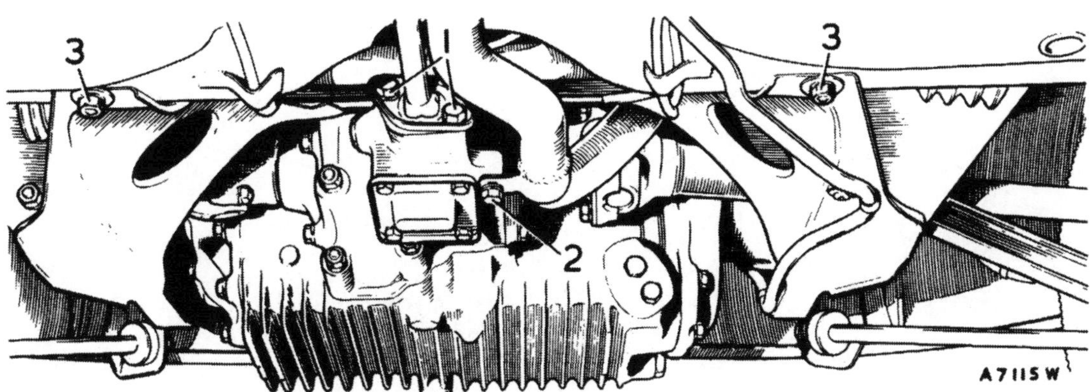

Fig. A.1
The front sub-frame and transmission casing viewed from beneath the car, showing (1) the gear change lever retaining screws, (2) the exhaust system fixing point, (3) the front sub-frame rear mounting point (four set screws)

Section A.4

EXHAUST MANIFOLD

Removing

1. Carry out instructions in Sections A.1 and A.2.
2. Slacken the pipe clamp, unscrew the six nuts and withdraw the manifold.

COOPER

3. Jack up the vehicle and remove the bonnet.
4. Remove the exhaust pipe assembly, Section A.3, and carburetters, Section A.2.
5. Remove the inlet manifold.
6. Unscrew the 'U' bolts and withdraw them from the right-hand universal joint.
7. Remove the right-hand wheel and disconnect the steering tie-rod.
8. Disconnect the top and bottom swivels, partly withdraw the hub and drive shaft.
9. Support the hub to avoid damage to the brake hose.
10. Turn the differential flange until it is upright, withdraw the exhaust manifold from the studs, manoeuvre it to the right to clear the sub-frame and transmission casing and lift upwards.

Refitting

Reverse the removing instructions.

Section A.5

ROCKER SHAFT 

Removing and dismantling

1. Remove the air cleaners (Section A.1).
2. Drain the cooling system (Section C.1).
3. Remove the rocker cover.
4. Slacken the rocker shaft bracket and cylinder head nuts gradually in the order shown in Fig. A.4. When the load is released remove the rocker shaft bracket nuts and the shaft and brackets.

Fig. A.2
The pressed-steel type of valve rocker

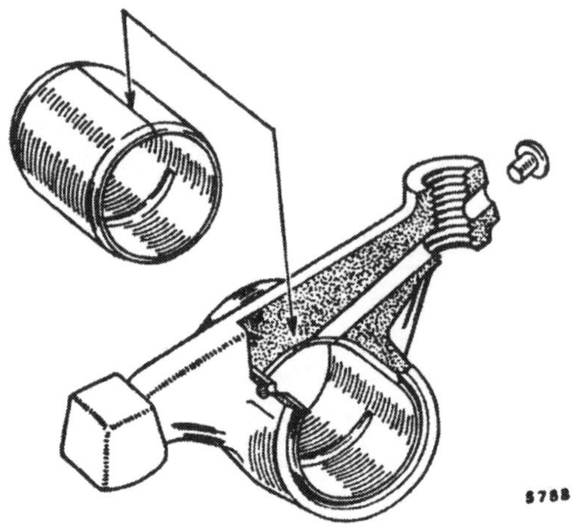

Fig. A.3
The forged-type valve rocker

5. Remove the shaft locating screw from the front bracket.
6. Withdraw the split pin and washers from the front end of the shaft.
7. Slide the rockers, brackets and springs from the shaft, noting their relative positions for correct refitting.
8. Unscrew the plug from the front end of the shaft and clean out the oilways.

Rockers and bushes

Check the rockers for wear. Two types of rocker are in use—pressed steel or forged; if the forged type is fitted the rockers can be rebushed, but worn pressed-steel rockers must be renewed.

To fit new bushes

9. Remove the old and press in new bushes with Service tool 18G 226 and 18G 226 A.
10. Locate the joint of the bush at the top as shown in Fig. A.3.
11. Remove the adjuster screw.
12. Drill out the plug in the end of the rocker with a No. 43 drill (2.26 mm.) and continue the oilway through the bush.
13. Replug the end hole with a rivet welded in position.
14. Continue the hole in the top of the rocker barrel with a No. 47 drill (1.98 mm.).
15. Burnish-ream the bush to the dimension given in 'GENERAL DATA'.

Reassembling

16. Reverse the dismantling procedure.
17. Fit the plugged end of the shaft and the tapped bracket at the front of the engine.
18. Tighten the cylinder head and rocker shaft nuts to the recommended torque and in the order shown in Fig. A.4.

Adjustment

19. Remove the sparking plugs, engage top gear and push the car forward to rotate the crankshaft. This operation can be also effected by jacking up one side of the front suspension until the road wheel can be rotated, and thus turn the crankshaft to the required position.
20. Rotate the crankshaft until the valve being checked has its tappet resting opposite the peak on the camshaft, i.e. valve completely closed. This cannot be observed accurately, therefore if checking is carried out according to the adjustment chart, this will avoid turning the crankshaft more than is necessary. The valve rocker clearance is given in **'GENERAL DATA'**.
21. Hold the adjusting screw against rotation while slackening the locknut, insert the feeler gauge and turn the adjustment screw until the gauge is a sliding fit, tighten the locknut and recheck the clearance.
22. Refit the rocker cover with a new joint washer if necessary, and lower the car (if jacked up).

Adjust	No.	1	rocker	with	No.	8	valve	fully	open
,,	,,	3	,,	,,	,,	6	,,	,,	,,
,,	,,	5	,,	,,	,,	4	,,	,,	,,
,,	,,	2	,,	,,	,,	7	,,	,,	,,
,,	,,	8	,,	,,	,,	1	,,	,,	,,
,,	,,	6	,,	,,	,,	3	,,	,,	,,
,,	,,	4	,,	,,	,,	5	,,	,,	,,
,,	,,	7	,,	,,	,,	2	,,	,,	,,

Section A.6

CYLINDER HEAD

Removing

1. Remove the bonnet.
2. Drain the cooling system (Section C.1).
3. Disconnect the battery and electrical connections from the cylinder head.
4. Remove the carburetter air cleaner (Section A.1).
5. Remove the carburetter (with cables attached) from the manifold and position it clear of the cylinder head.
6. Disconnect the exhaust pipe from the manifold flange. **Cooper 'S'**. Remove the exhaust manifold as detailed in Section A.4.
7. Release the automatic advance suction pipe and remove the rocker cover.
8. **Cooper 'S'**. Remove the bolt (A) and nut (B) before releasing the remaining cylinder head nuts.
9. Progressively slacken and remove the cylinder head nuts in the reverse sequence shown in **Fig. A.4.**
10. Remove the rocker shaft, push-rods, and the radiator tie-plate from the thermostat housing.
11. Disconnect the top water hose and slacken the clip securing the water pump to cylinder head by-pass hose.
12. Disconnect the heater hose and cable from the water valve on the rear of the cylinder head.
13. Lift the cylinder head squarely off the studs; if the head does not release easily from the block, tap each side of the head with a soft-faced mallet. Lift the gasket from the studs.

Refitting

14. Reverse the removing procedure, noting the following points:
    a. Thoroughly clean the faces of the cylinder head and the top of the block; fit a new gasket without jointing compound or grease, it is marked 'TOP' and 'FRONT'.
    b. Progressively tighten the cylinder head and rocker shaft nuts, and finally tighten to the torque figures given in **'GENERAL DATA'** and in the sequence shown on Fig. A.4.
    Cooper 'S'. The additional bolt and nut (Fig. A.4) must be tightened last.
15. Adjust the valve rocker clearances as detailed in **'Adjustment'** (Section A.5). Start the engine, and when at normal running temperature re-check the clearances.

Section A.7

DECARBONIZING

1. Remove the cylinder head and gasket (Section A.6) and the valves (Section A.8).
2. Scrape the carbon from the piston crowns, cylinder head, valves, and cylinder block, leaving a ring of carbon around the periphery of each piston and the top of each bore. Blow all deposits of carbon from the head and block.
3. Refit the cylinder head (Section A.6).

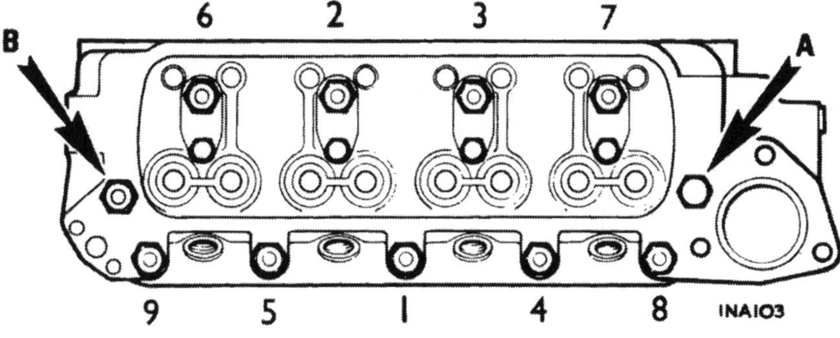

Fig. A.4

The releasing and tightening sequence of the cylinder head retaining nuts. Arrows 'A' and 'B' indicate the additional bolt and nut on the Cooper 'S' head

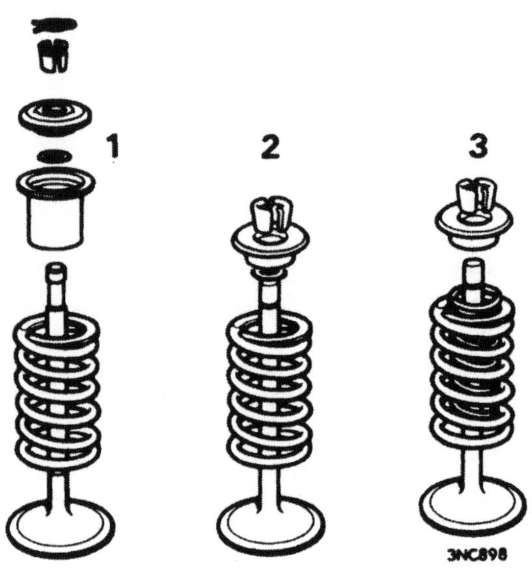

Fig. A.5
The component parts of the valve assembly

1. Early 'Mini' type. 2. Later 'Mini' type.
3. Cooper and Cooper 'S' type.

Section A.8

VALVES 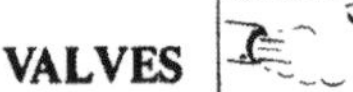

Removing

1. Remove the cylinder head and gasket (Section A.6).
2. Withdraw the cotter clip (when fitted).
3. Compress the spring and extract the two halves of the cotter.
4. Slowly release the spring, remove the spring compressor and withdraw the retaining cap, shroud valve spring, and rubber seal.
5. Remove the valve. If the heads of the valves are not numbered, store them in such a way that they can be replaced in their original positions.

The Cooper 'S' has no cotter clips or shroud, and the rubber seal is fitted over the valve guide. Double valve springs are fitted.

Grinding

Clean the valves and seatings and examine them for pitting and unevenness. If the valves are in a very poor condition, fit new, otherwise reface them on a valve grinder.

Reface the valve seats if necessary, using special cutters, see Service tools Section 'S'. Confine valve seat and valve refacing to the minimum and finally grind the valves onto their respective seats with fine grinding paste. Thoroughly clean the valves and seats with petrol (fuel) or paraffin (kerosene) before reassembling.

Valve seat inserts

When it becomes necessary to fit inserts, machine the cylinder head to the dimensions given in Fig. A.7. The inserts should have an interference fit of .0025 to .0045 in. (.063 to .11 mm.) and must be pressed, not driven, into the cylinder head.

Valve guides

Remove by drifting the guide(s) downwards into the combustion chambers. Drift in the new guide(s) to the depth illustrated, see Fig. A.6.

Fit the inlet guides with the largest chamfer at the top, and the exhaust with the counterbore at the bottom.

Refitting

Reverse instructions 1 to 5 above.

Section A.9

TAPPETS 

(Engines with tappet side-covers)

Removing

1. Remove the air cleaner(s) and carburetter(s) (Sections A.1 and A.2).
2. Remove the rocker cover and shaft assembly (Section A.5).
3. Remove the manifold (Section A.4) and the push-rods.
4. Remove the tappet covers and tappets.
5. Fit new tappets by selective assembly so that they just fall into their guides under their own weight, when lubricated.

Refitting

Reverse the removing operations, taking care to refit the tappets in their original positions.

Section A.10

DISTRIBUTOR DRIVE SHAFT 

Removing

1. Remove the distributor (Section B.1).
2. Take out the screw securing the distributor housing to the cylinder block and carefully withdraw the housing to avoid damage to the 'O' ring seal (later models only). The upper end of the shaft is drilled and tapped with a $\frac{5}{16}$-in. UNF. thread; screw in a suitable bolt and withdraw the shaft.

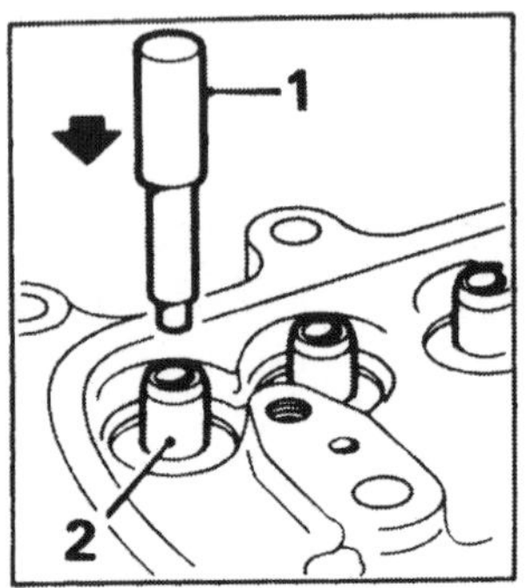

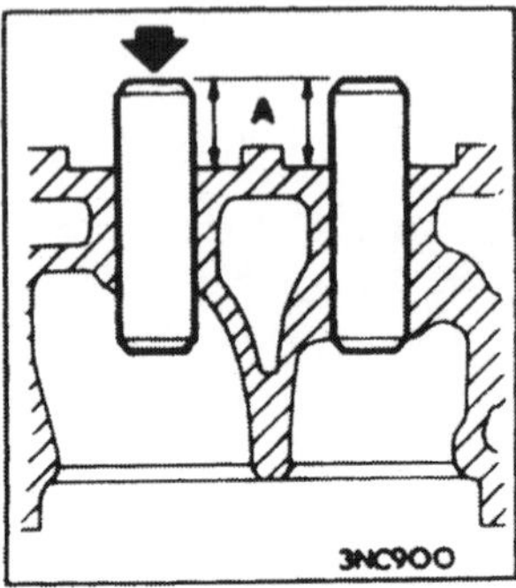

Fig. A.6
Using a drift (1) to fit the valve guide (2) to the correct depth. 'A' = $\frac{19}{32}$ in (15.08 mm)

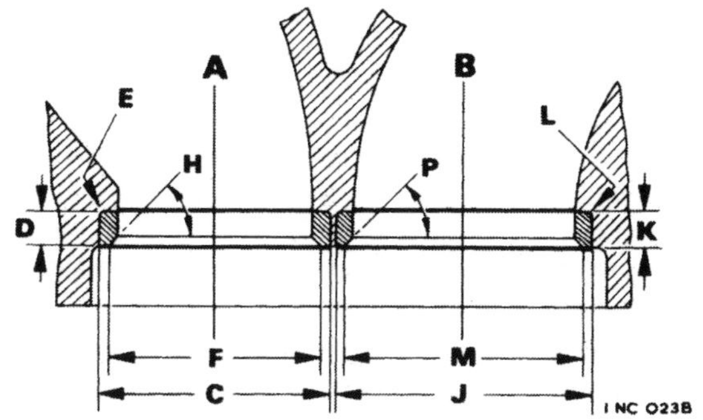

Fig. A.7
Valve seat insert machining dimensions. Machine the throats of the inserts to blend with those of the cylinder head

EXHAUST 'A'					
	C	D	E	F	H
MINI	1.124 to 1.125 in. (28.55 to 28.58 mm.)	0.186 to 0.188 in. (4.72 to 4.77 mm.)	Maximum radius 0.015 in. (0.38 mm.)	1.0235 to 1.0435 in. (25.99 to 26.50 mm.)	45°
997-c.c. COOPER	1.124 to 1.125 in. (28.55 to 28.58 mm.)	0.186 to 0.188 in. (4.72 to 4.77 mm.)	0.015 in. (0.38 mm.)	1.0235 to 1.0435 in. (25.99 to 26.50 mm.)	45°
998-c.c. COOPER	1.124 to 1.125 in. (28.55 to 28.58 mm.)	0.186 to 0.188 in. (4.72 to 4.77 mm.)	0.015 in. (0.38 mm.)	1.0235 to 1.0435 in. (25.99 to 26.50 mm.)	45°
970-c.c. COOPER 'S'	1.2465 to 1.2475 in. (31.6 to 31.7 mm.)	0.186 to 0.188 in. (4.72 to 4.77 mm.)	0.015 in. (0.38 mm.)	1.2065 to 1.2265 in. (30.65 to 31.16 mm.)	45°
1071-c.c. COOPER 'S'	1.2465 to 1.2475 in. (31.66 to 31.7 mm.)	0.186 to 0.188 in. (4.72 to 4.77 mm.)	0.015 in. (0.38 mm.)	1.2065 to 1.2265 in. (30.65 to 31.16 mm.)	45°
1275-c.c. COOPER 'S'	1.2465 to 1.2475 in. (31.66 to 31.7 mm.)	0.186 to 0.188 in. (4.72 to 4.77 mm.)	0.015 in. (0.38 mm.)	1.2065 to 1.2265 in. (30.65 to 31.16 mm.)	45°

INLET 'B'					
	J	K	L	M	P
MINI	1.187 to 1.188 in. (30.16 to 30.17 mm.)	0.186 to 0.188 in. (4.72 to 4.77 mm.)	Maximum radius 0.015 in. (0.38 mm.)	1.0855 to 1.1055 in. (27.58 to 28.07 mm.)	45°
997-c.c. COOPER	1.3075 to 1.3085 in. (33.21 to 33.23 mm.)	0.186 to 0.188 in. (4.72 to 4.77 mm.)	0.015 in. (0.38 mm.)	1.116 to 1.136 in. (28.34 to 29.2 mm.)	45°
998-c.c. COOPER	1.3745 to 1.3755 in. (34.90 to 34.95 mm.)	0.186 to 0.188 in. (4.72 to 4.77 mm.)	0.015 in. (0.38 mm.)	1.206 to 1.226 in. (30.60 to 31.15 mm.)	45°
970-c.c. COOPER 'S'					
1071-c.c. COOPER 'S'					
1275-c.c. COOPER 'S'	1.4365 to 1.4375 in. (36.5 to 36.52 mm.)	0.186 to 0.188 in. (4.72 to 4.77 mm.)	0.015 in. (0.38 mm.)	1.3935 to 1.4135 in. (35.41 to 35.91 mm.)	45°

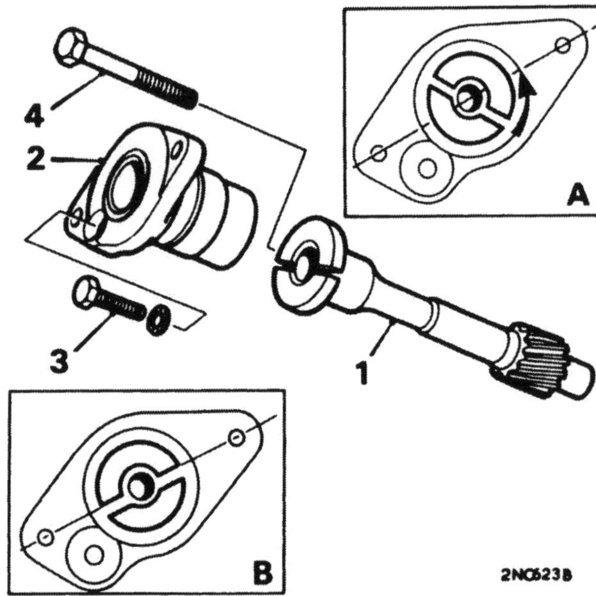

Fig. A.8
The distributor drive shaft. Inset 'A', shows the position of the slot to engage the shaft. Inset 'B', shows the correct fitted position

1. Drive shaft.
2. Housing.
3. Screw—housing.
4. Bolt—$\frac{5}{16}$ in UNF (used to remove and refit shaft).

Refitting

3. Turn the crankshaft until No. 1 piston is at T.D.C. on the compression stroke (No. 4 cylinder exhaust and inlet valves rocking and the 1/4 mark on the flywheel against the pointer).
4. Hold the spindle so that the drive slot is in the position shown (Fig. A.8) with the large offset uppermost, and enter the gear. As the gear engages the camshaft the spindle will turn anti-clockwise.
5. Refit the distributor (Sections B.1 and B.2).

Section A.11

FLYWHEEL AND CLUTCH

Removing

1. Disconnect the coil (or solenoid) leads and remove the coil (or solenoid).
2. Remove the starter (Section N.3).
3. Unhook the clutch lever spring, withdraw the lever pivot pin, pull the push-rod from the slave cylinder and remove the lever from the clutch housing.
4. Take off the slave cylinder.
5. Disconnect the exhaust pipe/manifold clamp.
6. Detach the radiator support bracket from the thermostat housing.
7. Unscrew the two nuts and set screws securing the right-hand engine mounting to the sub-frame side-member.
8. Take out the clutch cover screws.
9. Raise the engine just enough to allow the removal of the clutch cover. Do not let the fan blades damage the radiator.
10. Remove the three nuts and the clutch thrust plate from the pressure spring housing. When a diaphragm clutch is fitted, release the spring retainer to detach the thrust plate.
11. Bring Nos. 1 and 4 pistons to T.D.C. to prevent the primary gear 'C' washer from falling and being wedged behind the flywheel. With the crankshaft in any other position this could happen and result in damage as the flywheel is withdrawn.
12. Tap up the locking washer and slacken the flywheel retaining screw three or four threads. Use Service tools 18G 304 and 18G 304 M to free the flywheel from the taper on the crankshaft. Remove the tool as soon as the flywheel is free.
13. Unscrew the flywheel retaining screw and take off the key plate.
14. Withdraw the flywheel and clutch together.
15. Dismantle the clutch as described in Section E.1.

NOTES:

A. As the flywheel is pulled from the shaft, oil from the annulus behind the flywheel oil seal may spill down the face of the flywheel onto the clutch driven plate. Look out for this when dismantling to avoid assuming that the oil has passed the seal during normal running.

B. In early engines a rubber plug was fitted into the rear end of the crankshaft as an added precaution against oil leaking past the normal brass taper plug. An improved brass plug is now fitted and the rubber is discontinued.

C. Later engines have non-lubricated bushes in the crankshaft primary gear and the flywheel oil seal is not fitted.

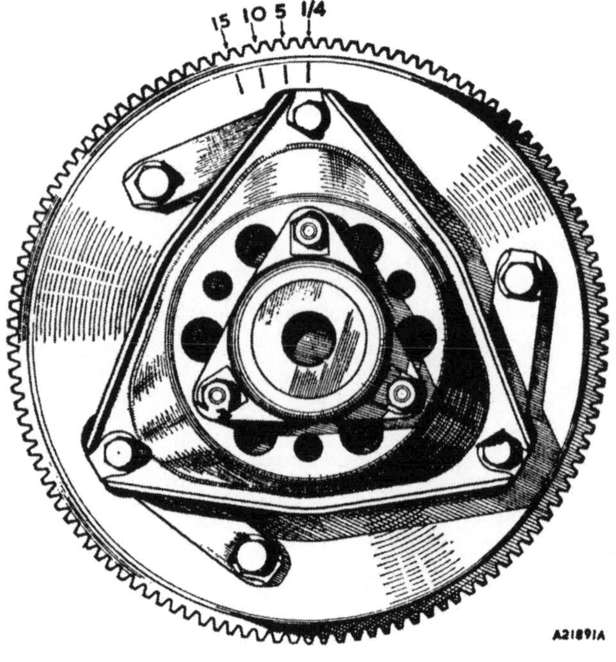

Fig. A.9
The flywheel and clutch assembly
(Coil spring type clutch)

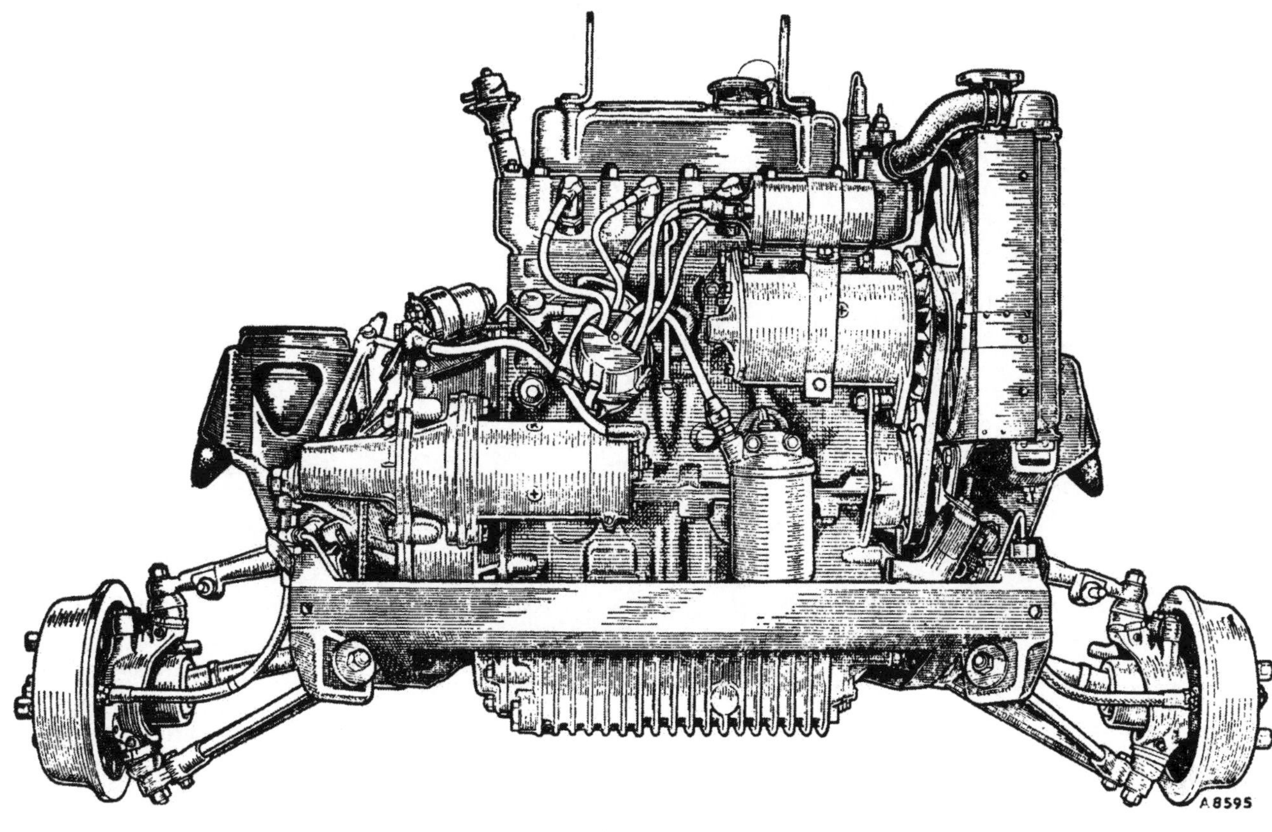

Fig.A.10
The engine and front suspension assembly

Starter ring

If a new starter ring is needed, split the old one with a cold chisel. Clean the bore of the new ring and the mating surface of the flywheel, heat the ring to a temperature of 300 to 400°C. (575 to 752°F.), indicated by a light blue colour, and fit it to the flywheel with the lead of the teeth towards the flywheel register. Allow it to cool naturally.

Refitting

16. Assemble the clutch.
17. Lubricate the flywheel oil seal (if fitted).
18. Ensure that the 'C' washer is correctly positioned and then turn the crankshaft to bring Nos. 1 and 4 pistons to T.D.C.
19. The crankshaft primary gear splines should be lightly wiped with Duckham's M–B grease.
20. Clean and dry the crankshaft and flywheel tapers; they must be assembled dry.
21. Fit the flywheel and clutch assembly to the shaft, replace the washer and retaining screws.
22. Tighten the screw to the recommended torque (see **'GENERAL DATA'**) and tap over the locking washer.
23. Refit the clutch thrust plate.
24. Lower the engine and carry out the removal operations 1 to 8 in reverse order.

Section A.12

ENGINE AND SUB-FRAME ASSEMBLY

Removing

1. Remove the bonnet, drain the cooling system and remove the front grille.
2. Disconnect the battery.
3. Disconnect the electrical connections from the engine.
4. Disconnect the speedometer cable from the instrument.
5. Disconnect the heater hoses.
6. Disconnect the brake pipes at the three-way union.
7. Use Service tool 18G 1063 and disconnect the steering-rack ball joints.
8. Disconnect the tie-rod from the cylinder block and swing the rod away from the engine.
9. COOPER 'S'. Detach the servo vacuum pipe from the inlet manifold.
10. Remove the front hydraulic dampers (fitted to non-Hydrolastic suspension vehicles only).
11. Remove the exhaust pipe (Section A.3).
12. Remove the air cleaner and carburetter (Sections A.1 and A.2).
13. COOPER AND MK. II MODELS. Remove the remote control gear-change extension (Section A.32).
14. Remove the hexagon plug with the anti-rattle spring and plunger from the gear change extension.

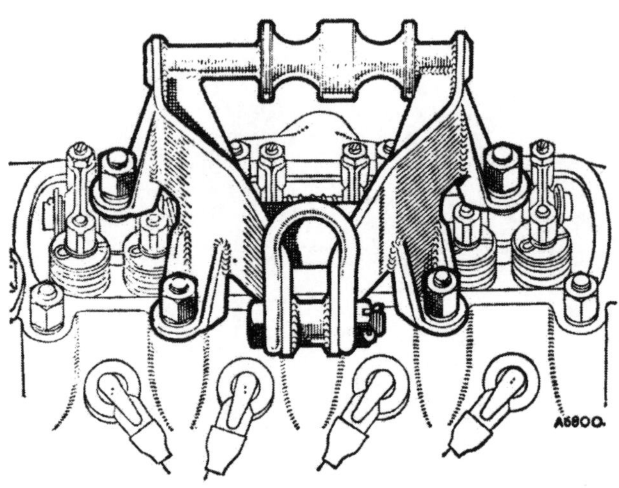

Fig. A.11
Use the individual front lifting eye of the attachment to give an angled lift when removing and refitting the power unit

15. Remove the gear lever retaining plate; pull the lever out of the casing into the car.
16. Remove the slave cylinder securing bolts and attach the unit to the bulkhead (do not disconnect the hose).
17. Depressurize and evacuate the models fitted with Hydrolastic suspension (Section H.7) and disconnect both hoses.
18. Support the body with slings under the front wings, and the engine below the transmission casing.
19. Knock back the locking tabs and withdraw the four body to sub-frame bolts (nuts if studs are fitted), two on each side of the bulkhead cross-member. Take out the four set screws securing the rear of the sub-frame to the front floor and the two screws securing the front of the frame to the bottom of the grille panel.
20. Lift the body clear of the engine and withdraw the sub-frame and engine assembly.

Removing engine from sub-frame

21. Remove the rocker cover nuts and fit the engine lifting bracket (Fig. A.11).
22. Drain the oil. Disconnect the drive shafts at the differential (Section G).
23. Support the sub-frame under both side-members and take the weight of the engine on the lifting equipment. Take out the two screws securing each engine mounting to the sub-frame.
24. Lift the engine out of the frame.

Refitting

25. Reverse the removal instructions.
    NOTE.—On vehicles NOT fitted with the remote control gear-change pull the gear lever up into the interior of the car before the body is lowered onto the frame. Bleed the brakes and clutch.

Section A.13

ENGINE AND TRANSMISSION

Removing

1. The engine and transmission assembly can be taken out through the bonnet aperture as follows:
2. Refer to Section A.12 and carry out instruction Nos. 1 to 5, 8 and 12 to 16.
3. Remove the windscreen washer bottle and bracket (if necessary).
4. Disconnect the drive shafts at the differential.
5. Disconnect the exhaust pipe from the manifold and secure the pipe against the bulkhead.
6. Remove the rocker cover nuts and fit the engine lifting bracket (Fig. A.11).
7. Take the weight of the engine on the lifting equipment and unscrew the two set screws securing each engine mounting to the sub-frame and lift out the engine.

Refitting

8. Reverse the removal instructions.
    NOTES.—On vehicles NOT fitted with the remote control gear-change pull the gear lever up into the interior of the car before the engine is lowered into position. Keep the sliding joints pushed well onto the drive shaft splines while the flexible couplings are moved into position.

COOPER

Removing

1. Carry out the instructions 1 to 9 and 16 in Section A.12.
2. Remove the fresh-air motor (when fitted).
3. Disconnect the oil gauge pipe.
4. Take off the distributor cap.
5. Remove the carburetters and air cleaners (Sections A.1 and A.2).
6. Remove the exhaust pipe assembly (Section A.3).
7. Remove the three bolts securing the rear extension mounting to the floor (Fig. A.12).

8. Unscrew the gear lever knob and take out the screws with the rubber cover and plate.
9. Remove the gear-change extension. Disconnect the hydraulic and vacuum pipe and remove the brake servo (Cooper 'S').

Refitting

Reverse the removing instructions.

Section A.14

ENGINE MOUNTINGS

Removing

LEFT-HAND

1. Remove the radiator (Section C.3).
2. Support the engine with the attachment shown in Fig. A.11; use the central 'straight lift' position and take the weight off the mounting.
3. Remove the nuts securing the mounting bracket to the transmission casing and the two set screws securing the mounting to the sub-frame side-members; withdraw the bracket and mounting assembly.

RIGHT-HAND

4. Remove the clutch cover and engine mounting together as detailed in Section A.11.

Refitting

Reverse the removing instructions.

Fig. A.12
The securing points for the remote control gear-change extension

Section A.15

TIMING COVER

Removing

If the fan cowling is not the later split-type the engine will have to be removed as in Section A.13; otherwise proceed as follows

1. Remove the radiator (Section C.3).
2. Slacken the dynamo or alternator bolts and remove the fan belt.
3. Withdraw the crankshaft pulley.
4. Remove the cover securing screws and lift off the cover.

Refitting

5. Reverse the removing instructions when refitting the cover. The oil seal in the cover must be renewed if it shows signs of deterioration, using Service tool 18G 134 together with adaptor 18G 134 BD.
6. The oil thrower behind the crankshaft pulley must be fitted with the face marked 'F' away from the engine. Fill the annular groove of the seal with grease and use Service tool 18G 1044 to centralize the cover to the crankshaft.

   NOTE.—The early type front cover and oil thrower must only be used together. The oil thrower must be fitted with its concave side facing away from the engine.
7. Use Service tool 18G 138 to centralize the seal to the crankshaft or use the crankshaft pulley.
8. Fill the groove of the seal with grease, lubricate the pulley hub and rotate the hub through the cover oil seal.
9. To ensure correct centralization the cover and hub should now be fitted together, aligning the keyway in the pulley with the key in the crankshaft.
10. Insert the cover retaining screws and tighten them evenly.
11. Refit and tighten the crankshaft pulley bolt to the torque figure given in 'GENERAL DATA' and tap over the locking washer.

Section A.16

TIMING GEARS AND CHAIN

Removing

1. Remove the timing cover (Section A.15).
2. Withdraw the oil thrower.
3. Unlock the camshaft chain wheel nut, unscrew and remove the nut and lock washer.

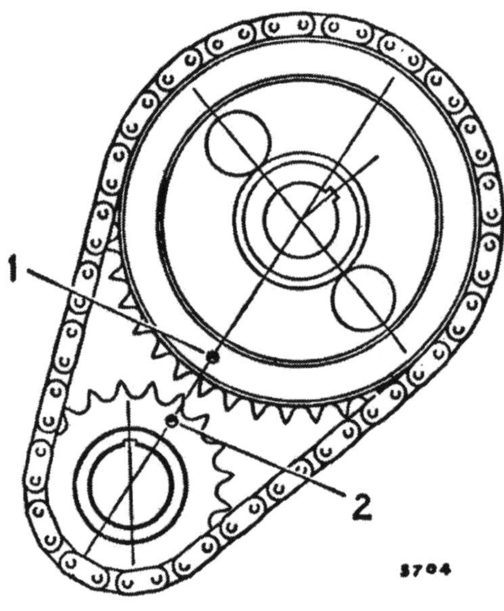

Fig. A.13
The timing gears assembled into the timing chain with the two marks on the gears opposite each other

4. Pull both chain wheels, with the chain at the same time. Note the thickness of the packing shims behind the crankshaft wheel.
5. Extract the wheels from the chain.

Refitting

6. Place the crankshaft gear packing shims in position and turn the shaft to bring the key to the top.
7. Bring the camshaft keyway to the position shown in Fig. A.13 (approx. 1 o'clock).
8. Assemble the two wheels in the chain with the marks opposite each other as in Fig. A.13. Push the wheels onto the shafts, turning the camshaft slightly as required to line up the key. Push the wheels as far as they will go and secure the camshaft gear with the lock washer and nut.
9. Check the alignment of the wheels by placing a straight-edge across the teeth of the camshaft and crankshaft gears and measuring the gap between the straight-edge and the crankshaft gear. Adjust with shims behind the crankshaft gear as required.
10. Refer to Section A.15 **'Refitting'** items 5 to 11.

Section A.17

VALVE TIMING

Checking

1. Adjust the rocker clearance of No. 1 inlet valve to .019 in. (.48 mm.), .021 in. (.53 mm.) Cooper 'S', and turn the crankshaft until the valve is about to open.
2. Take off the flywheel inspection hole cover. The pointer should now be opposite the 5° mark on the flywheel.
3. After checking, reset the rocker clearance of No. 1 inlet valve to .011 in. (.28 mm.)—engine hot.

Section A.18

FLYWHEEL HOUSING AND PRIMARY GEAR

Removing

1. Remove the engine (Section A.13).
2. Remove the flywheel and clutch assembly (Section A.11).
3. Remove the screws and nuts securing the housing; note their positions for correct replacement.
4. When withdrawing the housing and to avoid damage to the oil seal use Service tool 18G 570, or 18G 1043 if a red silicon rubber oil seal is fitted (Fig. A.15).
5. Extract the circlip and remove the primary gear.

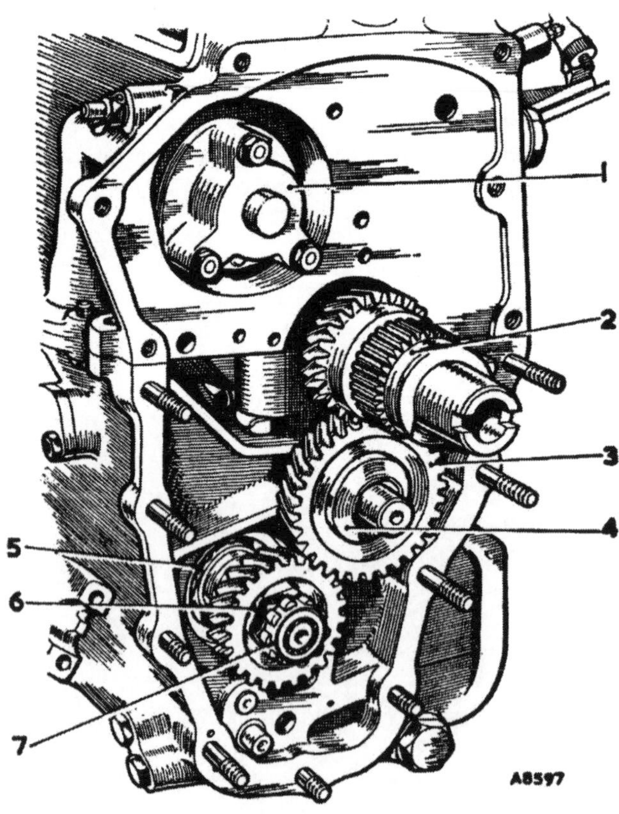

Fig. A.14
The engine and transmission assembly with the flywheel housing removed, showing the gear train to the first motion shaft

1. Oil pump.
2. Crankshaft primary gear.
3. Idler gear.
4. Idler gear thrust washer.
5. First motion shaft bearing.
6. First motion shaft driving gear.
7. Roller bearing.

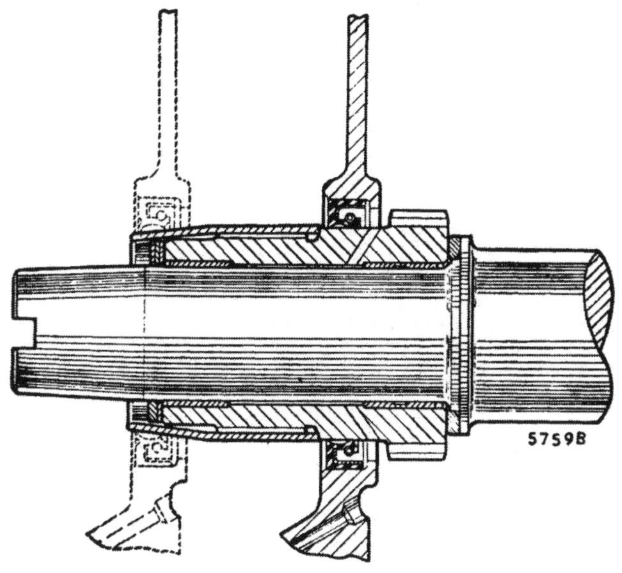

Fig. A.15
The Service tool 18G 1043 positioned over the clutch splines of the crankshaft primary gear to prevent damage to the lip of the oil seal

Refitting

6. Check the primary gear running clearance (Fig. A.16). Fit the inner thrust washer with its chamfered bore against the crankshaft flange.
7. Renew the crankshaft primary gear oil seal if it shows signs of damage or oil leakage, using Service tool 18G 134 and adaptor 18G 134 BC.
   This seal can also be renewed without removing the housing or draining the engine/transmission unit (see Section A.30).
8. Refit the housing, using 18G 1043 to protect the red silicon rubber oil seal. Service tool 18G 570 must only be used for assembly with the old-type oil seal. Lubricate the oil seal before assembly. Fit a new joint washer.
9. Tighten the nuts and set screws to the recommended torque see **'GENERAL DATA'**. It is important to return the set screws to the positions from which they were removed.

Later engines were fitted with non-lubricated bushes in the primary gear. No oil feed is provided from the crankshaft and no oil seal is fitted in the flywheel.

10. Remove the primary gear as described in Section A.18.
11. When refitting, check the running clearance (Fig. A.17).
12. Adjust by fitting the appropriate thrust washer with the chamfered inner edge of the washer to face the crankshaft (see Fig. A.17).

Primary gear bushes

If new bushes are fitted, line-ream them to the dimensions given in Fig. A.18.

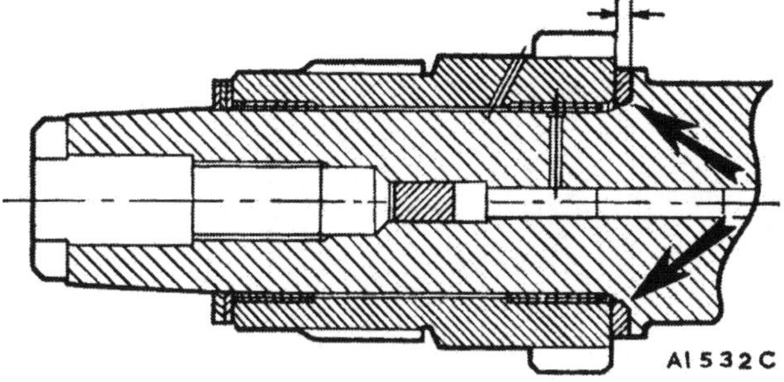

Fig. A.16
The crankshaft primary gear with lubricated bushes must be assembled with the correct running clearance of between .003 and .006 in. (.076 and .152 mm.). Measure the gap indicated and use the following table to determine the correct thickness of the thrust washer required to obtain this clearance

WHEN GAP IS	USE WASHER THICKNESS
.1295 to .1315 in. (3.27 to 3.34 mm.)	.125 to .127 in. (3.17 to 3.22 mm.)
.1315 to .1335 in. (3.34 to 3.39 mm.)	.127 to .129 in. (3.22 to 3.27 mm.)
.1335 to .1345 in. (3.39 to 3.42 mm.)	.129 to .131 in. (3.27 to 3.32 mm.)

First motion shaft outer race

Removing

1 Extract the spring ring from above the outer race.
2. Expand the housing by immersion in very hot water. **Do not use other methods of heating the housing.**

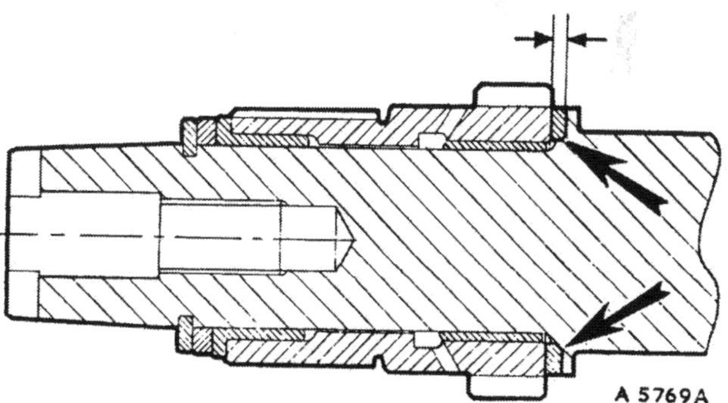

Fig. A.17
The correct running clearance is .0035 to .0065 in. (.0885 to .1645 mm.). Measure the gap indicated and fit the appropriate thrust washer as given below to obtain this clearance

WHEN GAP IS	USE WASHER THICKNESS
.1175 to .119 in. (2.875 to 3.025 mm.)	.112 to .114 in. (2.848 to 2.898 mm.)
.119 to .121 in. (3.025 to 3.076 mm.)	.114 to .116 in. (2.898 to 2.949 mm.)
.121 to .123 in. (3.076 to 3.127 mm.)	.116 to .118 in. (2.949 to 3.000 mm.)
.123 to .125 in. (3.127 to 3.18 mm.)	.118 to .120 in. (3.000 to 3.051 mm.)

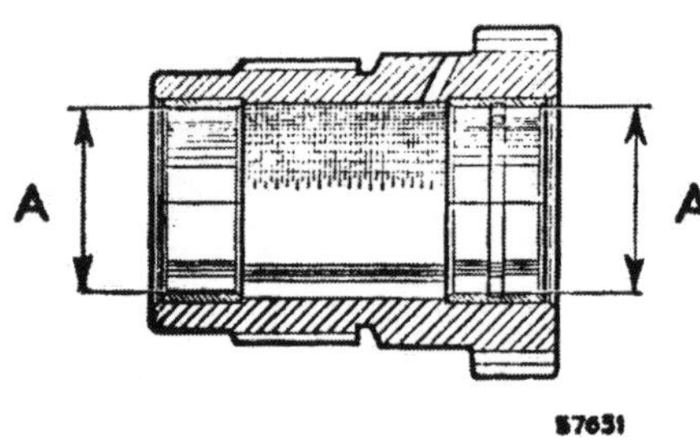

Fig. A.18
A section through the crankshaft primary gear. The bushes (A) must be line-reamed to 1.3775 to 1.3780 in. (34.98 to 35.00 mm.) after fitting (lubricated bushes only)

3. Withdraw the race with Service tool 18G 617 A. This operation may also be carried out using Service tool 18G 617 B with the sleeve from the original Service tool 18G 617.

Refitting

4. Reverse the removal instructions, driving the race into position with Service tool 18G 617 A.

Section A.19

TRANSMISSION HOUSING

Removing

1. Remove the engine from the car (Section A.13).
2. Remove the flywheel and clutch (Section A.11), and the flywheel housing (Section A.18).
3. Remove the starter motor.
4. Lift the engine to separate it from the transmission.

Dismantling

See Section F.1.

Refitting

Reverse the removing instructions.

NOTE.–It is important to insert the short transmission housing to crankcase screw before the crankcase is lowered onto the transmission housing and to screw it in as far as possible before the two housings are finally brought together.

Section A.20

OIL PRESSURE

The differential pressure switch fitted to the oil filter head on later models gives an indication when an oil change is required. If the warning light in the instrument panel appears and continues to glow when the engine is running at or above idling speed, both the engine oil and the filter element must be changed as soon as possible within a maximum of the next 300 miles (500 km.).

If the oil pressure falls appreciably, check:

1. The quantity of oil in the sump.
2. The condition of the pump.
3. The union on the suction side of the pump.
4. The pick-up filter for sludge.
5. The condition of the bearings.

Section A.21

OIL PRESSURE RELIEF VALVE

To examine, unscrew the hexagonal domed nut and remove the folded copper washer, the valve and the spring. Check the length of the spring against the dimensions given in **'GENERAL DATA'**.

If the valve cup is worn reseat it using metal polish with Service tool 18G 69.

Section A.22

OIL PUMP

Removing

1. Remove the engine as detailed in Section A.13.
2. Remove the flywheel and clutch assembly and the flywheel housing as detailed in Sections A.11 and A.18.
3. Bend back the lock washers, remove the bolts securing the pump to the crankcase, and withdraw the pump.

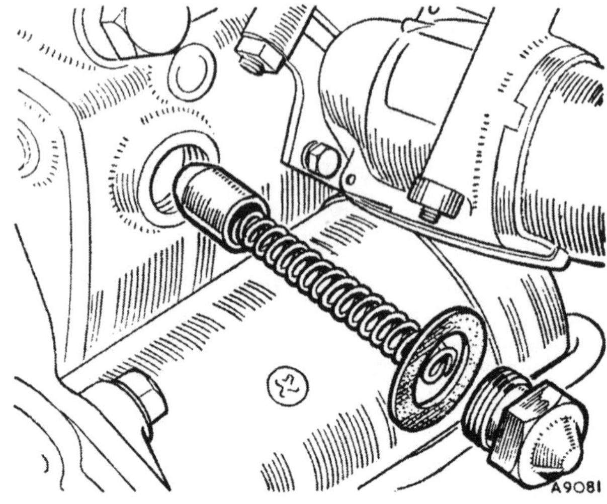

Fig. A.19
The oil pressure relief valve

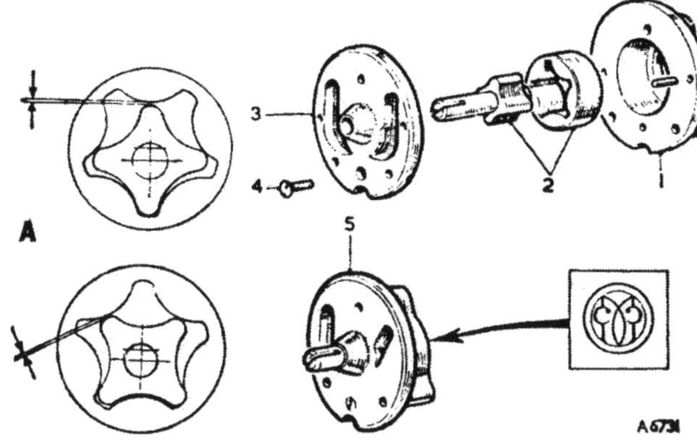

Fig. A.20
Two types of oil pump which may be fitted to this engine.
'A' indicates the lobe positions for checking clearances

HOBOURN-EATON
1. Body
2. Shaft and rotor.
3. Cover.
4. Screw–cover to body.

CONCENTRIC PUMPS LTD.
5. Pump (serviced as an assembly only).

Dismantling and reassembling (Hobourn-Eaton)

4. The pump cover is located on the pump body by two dowels and a machine screw. When the screw is removed the pump can be separated for examination and replacement where necessary.
5. Install the rotors in the pump body.
6. Place a straight-edge across the joint face of the pump body, and measure the clearance between the top face of the rotors and the underside of the straight-edge. The clearance should not exceed .005 in. (.127 mm.). In cases where the clearance is excessive this may be remedied by removing the two cover locating dowels and lapping the joint face of the pump body.
7. Install the rotors in the pump body and measure the clearance between the rotor lobes when they are in the position shown in Fig. A.20. If the clearance is in excess of .006 in. (.152 mm.) the rotors must be renewed.
8. Reassembly is a reversal of the dismantling procedure.
9. After reassembling, check the pump for freedom of action.

Refitting

The refitting of the pump to the cylinder block is a reversal of the removal procedure; ensure that the intake and delivery ports are not obstructed when fitting a new paper joint washer.

Section A.23

CAMSHAFT 

Removing

1. Remove the engine (Section A.13), the rocker shaft assembly (Section A.5), the push-rods and tappets (Section A.9), and the distributor (Section A.10).
2. Unscrew the camshaft locating plate and withdraw the camshaft.
3. If the camshaft bearings are worn, remove the flywheel housing and transmission case (Sections A.18 and A.19).

FRONT LINER

Extract worn liners and fit new with Service tool 18G 124 A and adaptor 18G 124 K. Line ream the new liners with Service tools 18G 123 A, 18G 123 AH, 18G 123 AJ.

COOPER
FRONT AND REAR LINERS

Extract worn liners and fit new using Service tools 18G 124 A with adaptor 18G 124 K for the front liner, and adaptor 18G 124 M for the rear liner. Line ream the new liners with Service tools 18G 123 A, 18G 123 BA, 18G 123 AP, 18G 123 AT, 18G 123 AN, and 18G 123 AQ.

CENTRE LINER

Use Service tool 18G 124 A with adaptors 18G 124 K and 18G 124 B to extract the worn liner and fit a new one. Line ream the new liner, using Service tools 18G 123 A, 18G 123 BB, 18G 123 B, and 18G 123 BC.

Refitting

Reverse the dismantling and removing instructions.

Section A.24

PISTONS AND CONNECTING RODS

Pistons and bores are stamped with a number in a diamond and the number on the piston must be the same as that on the bore to which it is fitted.

Oversize pistons are marked on the crown with the oversize; this is the boring dimension and running clearance has been allowed for. Pistons are available in the sizes shown in **'GENERAL DATA'**.

Removing

1. Remove the engine (Section A.13), the flywheel and clutch (Section A.11), the flywheel housing (Section A.18), the transmission (Section A.19), and the cylinder head (Section A.6).
2. Unlock and unscrew the big-end bolts; remove the bearing caps and push the connecting rod assemblies upwards through the bores.

Dismantling

3. Lift the rings out of their grooves and slide them off the piston. Always remove and refit rings over the top of the piston.
4. Hold the gudgeon pin in a vice between two plugs and unscrew the clamp bolt. Push out the gudgeon pin.

Reassembling

5. With the piston and gudgeon pin cold, the pin must be thumb push-fit for three-quarters of its travel and finally be tapped in with a hide mallet. Tighten the clamp bolt to the recommended torque (see **'GENERAL DATA'**).
6. Use new locking plates and tighten the connecting rod bolts to the recommended torque (see **'GENERAL DATA'**).

NOTE.–The second and third rings are tapered and the upper sides are marked 'T'.

Fig. A.21
The piston markings

COOPER
(998-c.c. engine)

The gudgeon pins are fully floating with a bush in the small end of the connecting rod. The pins are retained in the piston by a circlip at either end. Should damage or wear occur, the gudgeon pin must not be renewed independently of the piston, and the small-end bush must not be renewed on its own, but only as a new connecting rod assembly.

Cooper 'S'

The gudgeon pin is a press fit in the small end of the connecting rod, and the bearing surfaces for the pin are in the piston bosses. The interference fit of the pin in the small end is the only method used to retain the gudgeon pin in its correct relative position. It is essential that the specified interference fit is maintained (see **'GENERAL DATA'**).

Service tool 18G 1002 must be used to remove and replace the gudgeon pin and great care is necessary to avoid damage to the piston. Mark the piston and pin before dismantling to ensure that the pin is replaced in the same side of the piston from which it was removed.

Refitting

Reverse the removal instructions, items 1 and 2.

Cylinder liners

Dry liners may be fitted and machining dimensions are given below.

A press capable of 3 tons (3000 kg.) is required to fit new liners, and of 8 tons (8000 kg.) to press out old. The dimensions of the pilots needed are given in Fig. A.22.

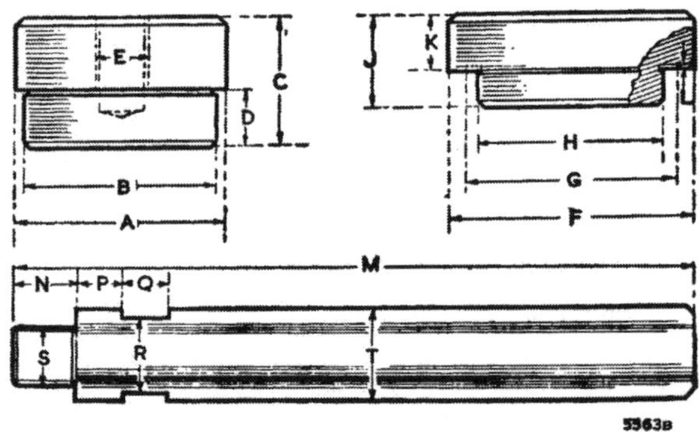

Fig. A.22
Cylinder liner pilots should be made to the above dimensions from case-hardening steel and case-hardened. The pilot extension should be made from 55-ton hardening and tempering steel, hardened in oil, and then tempered at 550°C. (1,020°F.)

DIMENSIONS: PRESSING-OUT PILOT

Illustration application	Engine (c.c.)	Inches (in.)		Metric (mm.)	
A.	848	2.578	+.005 –.000	65.48	+.127 –.000
	997	2.593		65.88	
	998	2.625		66.68	
	1070, 1275	2.778		70.56	
B.	848	2.465	+.000 –.005	62.61	+.000 –.127
	997	2.452		62.28	
	998	2.537		64.44	
	1070, 1275	2.859		72.63	
C.	All engines	1.75		44.45	
D.	All engines	75		19.05	
E.	All engines	¾ B.S.W. Thread			

DIMENSIONS: PRESSING-OUT PILOT

Illustration application	Engine (c.c.)	Inches (in.)		Metric (mm.)	
F.	848, 997	3.00		76.20	
	998	3.062		77.79	
	1070, 1275	3.312		84.14	
G.	848, 997	2.625		66.68	
	998	2.687		69.26	
	1070, 1275	2.906		73.82	
H.	848	2.455	+.000 –.005	62.35	+.000 –.127
	997	2.430		61.72	
	998	2.515		63.88	
	1070, 1275	2.753		69.85	
J.	All engines	1.25		31.75	
K.	All engines	.75		19.05	
L.	All engines	.015		.38	

DIMENSIONS: PILOT EXTENSION

Illustration application	Engine (c.c.)	Inches (in.)	Metric (mm.)
M.	All engines	10.5	317.5
N.	All engines	.875	22.22
O.	All engines	.625	15.87
Q.	All engines	.625	15.87
R.	All engines	1.00	25.4
S.	All engines	¾ B.S.W. thread	
T.	All engines	1.25	31.75

Engine type	Liner Part No.	Machine bores of cylinder block to this dimension before fitting liner	Outside diameter of liner	Interference fit of liner in cylinder block bore	Machine liner bore to this dimension after fitting
848 c.c.	2A 784	2.6035 to 2.604 in. (66.128 to 66.14 mm.)	2.606 to 2.60675 in. (66.19 to 66.21 mm.)	.002 to .00325 in. (.05 to .08 mm.)	2.477 to 2.4785 in. (62.915 to 62.954 mm.)
997 c.c. (9F)	12A 391				2.4570 to 2.4585 in. (62.408 to 62.445 mm.)
998 c.c. (9FA) 998 c.c. (99H)	12G 164	2.64075 to 2.64125 in. (67.076 to 67.099 mm.)	2.64325 to 2.644 in. (67.139 to 67.158 mm.)		2.542 to 2.5435 in. (64.571 to 64.608 mm.)
1070 c.c. (9FD/SA) 1275 c.c. (12FA, 12H)	AEG 239 AEG 428	2.8750 to 2.8755 in. (73.0 to 73.0012 mm.)	2.8775 to 2.87825 in. (73.179 to 73.306 mm.)		2.779 to 2.7805 in. (70.58 to 70.622 mm.)

Section A.25

CRANKSHAFT AND MAIN BEARINGS

Removing

1. Carry out the operations described in Section A.24, items 1 and 2, and remove the timing cover (Section A.16).
2. Check the crankshaft end-float.
3. Prise out the circlip and slide the primary gear from the shaft.
4. Note that the main bearing caps and crankcase are numbered; withdraw the caps and bearing shells. Do not interchange caps and shells. The bottom halves of the two thrust washers will be removed with the centre bearing cap.
5. Lift out the crankshaft with the remaining halves of the thrust washer and the top half-shells of the main bearings.
6. Inspect the crankpins and journals, and the bearing shells; regrind the shaft and renew the bearings as necessary. Permissible regrind dimensions and undersize bearing sizes are given in 'GENERAL DATA'. Ensure that all oilway countersinks are machined to their original dimensions.
7. Inspect the thrust washers, and fit new if necessary.
8. Thoroughly clean the crankshaft and bearings.

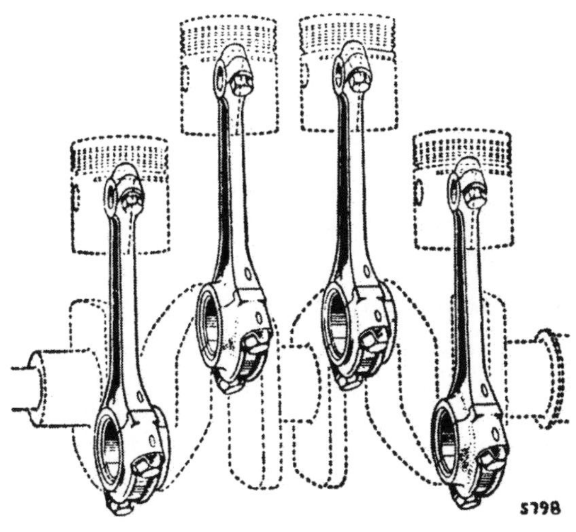

Fig. A.23
The correct assembly of connecting rods to the pistons and crankshaft

Refitting

Reverse the removal instructions.

Section A.26

CRANKSHAFT AND PRIMARY GEAR

See Section A.18.

Section A.27

CRANKCASE CLOSED-CIRCUIT BREATHING (When fitted)

Fresh air enters the engine through two holes and a filter in the filler cap on the rocker cover. The air then passes to the crankcase down the push-rod drillings. The crankcase fumes leave the engine through a breather outlet pipe on the front engine side cover. Oil droplets and mist are trapped in an oil separator before the fumes pass through a breather control valve and to the intake manifold, thus providing closed-circuit crankcase breathing.

Testing

With the engine at normal running temperature, run it at idling speed. Remove the oil filler cap. If the valve is functioning correctly the engine speed will increase by approximately 200 r.p.m. as the cap is removed, the change in speed being audibly noticeable. If no change in speed occurs, service the valve as follows.

Servicing

The crankcase breather unit should be serviced at the periods recommended in the Driver's Handbook or the Passport to Service.

OIL FILLER CAP

1. Remove the combined oil filler cap and breather filter and fit a replacement at the recommended servicing period.

BREATHER CONTROL VALVE

2. Remove the retaining clip 1, and dismantle the valve.
3. Clean all metal parts with solvent (trichlorethylene, fuel, etc.). If deposits are difficult to remove, immerse in boiling water before applying the solvent. Do not use an abrasive.
4. Clean the diaphragm (3) with detergent or methylated spirit.
5. Replace components showing signs of wear or damage.
6. Reassemble the valve, ensuring the metering needle (4) is in the cruciform guides (6) and the diaphragm is seated correctly.
   NOTE.–The 1st type valve assembly (without the cruciform guides) is serviced as an assembly.

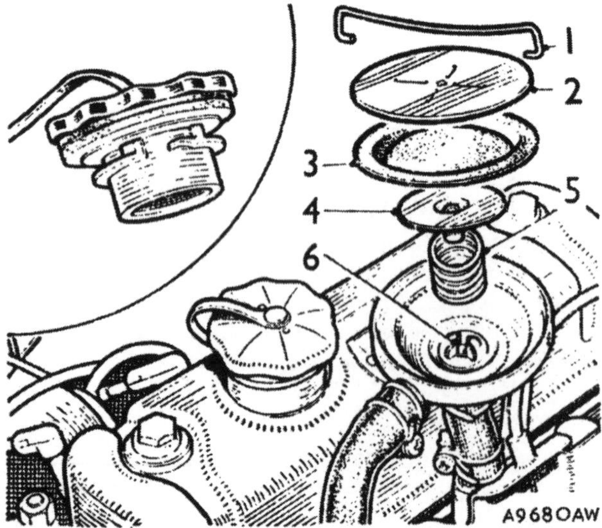

Fig. A.24
The crankcase closed-circuit breathing installation. (Inset) the oil filler cap filter

1.	Retaining clip.	4.	Metering needle.
2.	Cover.	5.	Spring.
3.	Diaphragm.	6.	Cruciform guides.

Section A.28

FLYWHEEL AND CLUTCH
(Diaphragm Spring Clutch)

Removing

1. Remove the engine as in Section A.13.
2. Remove the clutch cover.
3. Mark the pins and the cover to ensure refitting in their original positions.

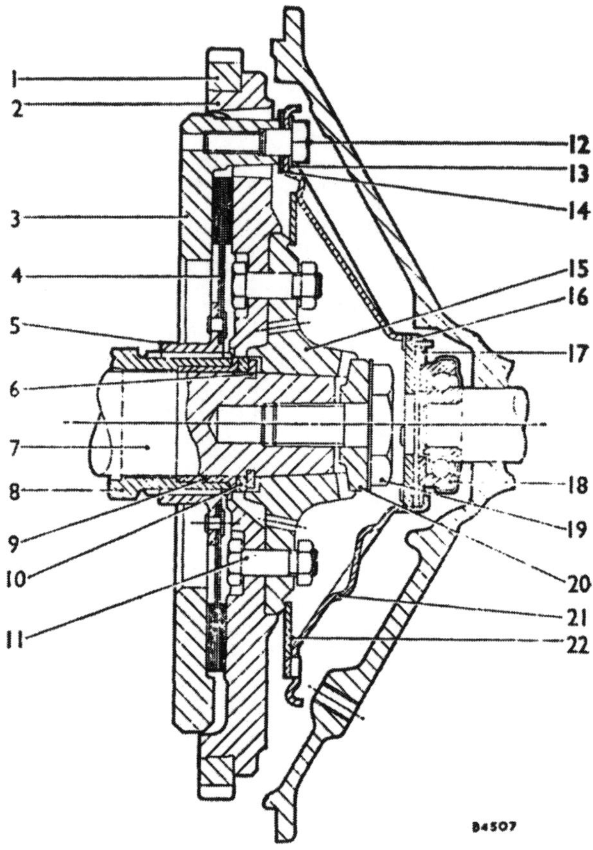

Fig. A.25
A section through the flywheel and diaphragm clutch assembly

1.	Starter ring.	12.	Driving pin.
2.	Flywheel.	13.	Lock washer.
3.	Pressure plate.	14.	Driving strap
4.	Driven plate.	15.	Flywheel hub.
5.	Driven plate hub.	16.	Thrust plate.
6.	Circlip.	17.	Plate retaining spring.
7.	Crankshaft.	18.	Thrust bearing.
8.	Crankshaft primary gear.	19.	Flywheel screw.
9.	Primary gear bearing.	20.	Keyed washer.
10.	Thrust washer.	21.	Cover.
11.	Flywheel hub bolt.	22.	Diaphragm spring.

4. Slacken the three clutch driving pins evenly to release the spring pressure. Replace the pins as they are removed one at a time with three $\frac{5}{16}$ in. UNF. x 2 in. studs to prevent the pressure plate moving out of alignment.
5. Remove the cover and spring assembly.
6. Bring Nos. 1 and 4 pistons to T.D.C. to prevent the primary gear 'C' washer falling and being wedged behind the flywheel. With the crankshaft in any other position this could happen and result in damage as the flywheel is withdrawn.
7. Knock up the locking washer and remove the flywheel retaining screw using Service tool 18G 587. Remove the keyed washer and insert the plug from Service tool adaptor set 18G 304 N in the screw hole.

8. Use Service tools 18G 304 with adaptor set 18G 304N (cadmium-plated) to remove the flywheel.
   NOTE.—The black screws from set 18G 304 M must not be used on the diaphragm clutch.
9. Screw the three adaptor screws into the flywheel and fit the plate of tool 18G 304 over the screws with the retaining nuts screwed on evenly to keep the plate parallel with the flywheel.
10. Screw the centre bolt of adaptor set 18G 304 N through the plate of tool 18G 304. Hold the flywheel from turning and tighten the centre bolt against the adaptor set plug until the flywheel is released from the crankshaft taper.
11. Withdraw the flywheel assembly and remove the Service tool.

Inspecting

12. Inspect the cover for elongation of the driving pin holes.
13. Inspect the driving pins for ridging and wear; fit three new pins if any are worn.
14. Inspect the driving straps; fit three new ones if any are worn.

Refitting

15. If the driving straps have been removed from the flywheel ensure that the spacing washers are fitted between the straps and the flywheel face.
16. Refer to instruction 6.
17. Locate the cover and spring assembly with the clutch balance mark 'A' adjacent to the 1/4 timing mark on the flywheel (see Fig. E.2). Fit the driving pins in their original positions, tightening each a turn at a time by diametrical selection to the torque figure given in 'GENERAL DATA'.
    Ensure that the dowel portion of the driving pins has entered the holes in each pair of driving straps. Incorrect assembly can cause 'clutch judder'.
18. Tighten the flywheel retaining screw to the torque figure given in the 'GENERAL DATA', tap up the locking washer and refit the clutch cover.
19. Refit the engine (see Section A.13).

Section A.29

OIL COOLER
(Cooper 'S')

Removing

1. Remove the front grille, taking care not to lose the spacers used for each securing screw.
2. Hold each union on the cooler from turning and disconnect both hoses from the cooler unit.
3. Complete removal of both hoses is effected in this manner—holding each union in turn on the oil filler head and the crankcase whilst releasing the hoses.

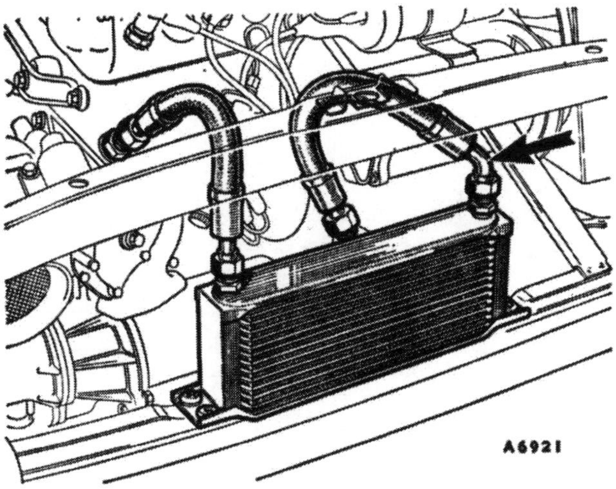

A6921

Fig. A.26
The 13 tube oil cooler fitted to the Cooper 'S'. The arrow indicates the angled hose connection

4. Remove the cooler unit securing screws and remove the unit through the grille aperture.

Refitting

5. Refit the cooler unit and tighten the securing screws.
6. Connect each hose to its respective position on the oil cooler. If replacement hoses are fitted connect the hose with the angled connection to the oil cooler with its other end connected to the filter head. Ensure that the hoses are not under stress from twist—hold each union with a spanner whilst tightening the hose connections.
7. Start and run the engine and check for oil leakage.
8. Top up the engine oil to the 'MAX' level on the dipstick.
9. Refit the front grille, see item 1.

Section A.30

PRIMARY GEAR OIL SEAL REPLACEMENT

Removing

1. a. Remove the engine/transmission assembly (Section A.13).
   b. Remove the engine/rod change-type transmission assembly (Section A.33).
2. Remove the flywheel and clutch, Section A.11 (coil spring type) or Section A.28 (diaphragm spring type).
3. Remove the 'C' shaped thrust washer and backing ring securing the primary gear to the crankshaft.
4. Screw the centre bolt of tool 18G 1068B securely into the crankshaft, Fig. A.27.

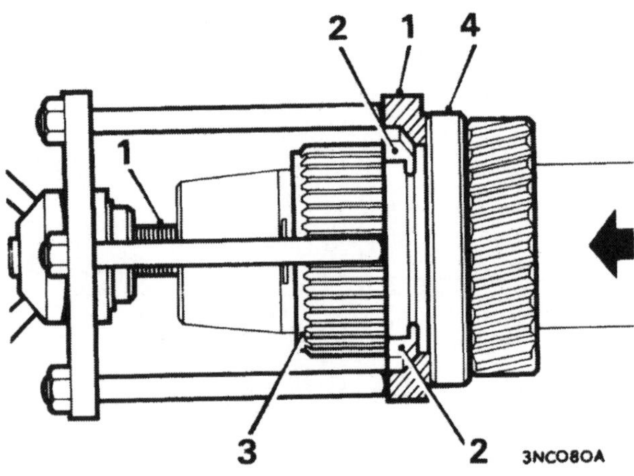

Fig. A.27
Showing tool in position to withdraw the primary gear and oil seal.

1. Service tool 18G 1068B.
2. Tool collets.
3. Primary gear.
4. Oil seal.

5. Pull the primary gear outwards as far as possible.
6. Pull the body of tool 18G 1068B over the centre bolt until the groove in the primary gear is visible inside the tool body, Fig. A.27.
7. Fit the two half collets of the tool into the groove in the gear, Fig. A.27.
8. Turn the winged nut anti-clockwise to withdraw the primary gear and oil seal clear of the housing, Fig. A.27.

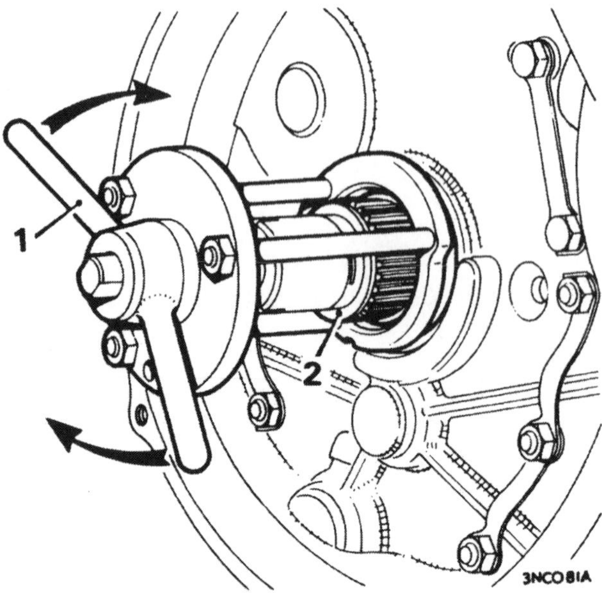

Fig. A.28
Refitting the primary gear and oil seal

1. Service tool 18G 1068B.
2. Primary gear.

Refitting

9. Fit tool 18G 1043 over the primary gear.
10. Liberally lubricate the new oil seal with engine oil and fit it over the protector sleeve onto the primary gear.
11. Smear the primary gear front thrust washer with grease and refit it (with its chamfered inner edge against the shoulder on the crankshaft).
12. Locate the primary gear onto the crankshaft until the gear teeth are starting to engage with those of the idler gear, and with the oil seal contacting the housing bore whilst still seated on the sealing surface of the gear.
13. Pass the body of tool 18G 1068B over the crankshaft and screw the winged nut in a clockwise direction down the centre bolt to press the seal into the housing, Fig. A.28. The seal is correctly fitted when the base of the tool contacts the lip of the housing bore.
14. Refit the backing ring and 'C' shaped thrust washer (with the back of the 'C' washer adjacent to the timing marks on the flywheel).
15. Refit the clutch/flywheel assembly, Section A.11 or A.28.
16. a. Refit the engine/transmission assembly (Section A.13).
    b. Refit the engine/rod change-type transmission assembly (Section A.33).●

Section A.31

FLYWHEEL RETAINING SCREW THREAD

The flywheel retaining screw thread in the end of the crankshaft is not Standard Whitworth but is Whitworth form:

Diameter $\frac{5}{8}$ in. 16 T.P.I. $1\frac{1}{16}$ in. full thread

If it is found necessary to clean up the thread, the operation must be confined to cleaning up. This thread is highly stressed and must always be up to full size.

Section A.32

PRIMARY DRIVE GEAR TRAIN
(Rod change transmission)

Removing

1. Remove the clutch/flywheel assembly, Section A.28.
2. Remove the flywheel housing, Section A.18.
3. Remove the primary gear rear thrust washer and backing ring, Fig. A.29.
4. Pull off the primary gear, Fig. A.29.
5. Remove the primary gear front thrust washer.
6. Remove the circlip retaining the first motion shaft roller bearing, using tool 18G 1004, Fig. A.29.

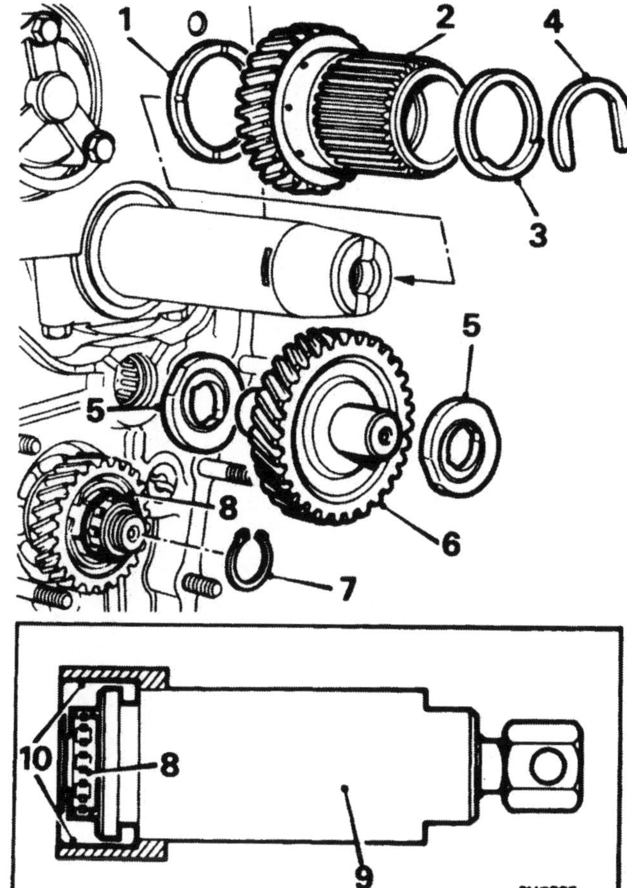

Fig. A.29
Removing the primary and idler gear assemblies. Inset shows Service tools fitted to remove the first motion shaft spigot roller bearing.

1. Rear thrust washer.
2. Primary gear.
3. Backing ring.
4. Front thrust washer.
5. Idler gear thrust washers.
6. Idler gear.
7. Circlip–first motion shaft bearing.
8. Roller bearing–first motion shaft.
9. Service tool 18G 705.
10. Service tool 18G 705C.

7. Use tool 18G 705 and 18G 705C to pull off the first motion shaft roller bearing, Fig. A.29.
8. Remove the idler gear and thrust washers.
9. Make up and use a tool to lock the gear train while the first motion shaft gear retaining nut is slackened. Make the tool using an old idler gear and a piece of steel bar to the dimensions given in Fig. A.30.
10. Drill a ¾ in (19.05 mm) dia. hole in the bar as shown in Fig. A.30 and arc-weld the bar to the old idler gear. Wrap several thicknesses of tape around the bar where it will contact the crankshaft.
11. Position the tool into the idler gear bearing with the handle against the crankshaft, Fig. A.31.
12. Knock back the lock washer tab securing the first motion shaft gear retaining nut.
13. Remove the retaining nut and lift off the first motion shaft gear.

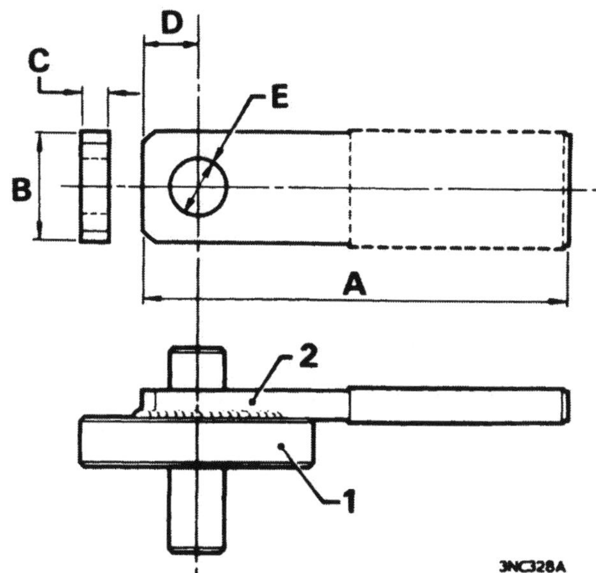

Fig. A.30
Showing make up of tool to hold the gear train.

1. Idler gear. 2. Steel bar.

A. = 5¼ in (133 mm)
B. = 1½ in (38 mm)
C. = ⅜ in (9.5 mm)
D. = ¾ in (19.05 mm)
E. = ¾ in (19.05 mm)

Inspecting

14. Examine all gears for undue wear or damage, and replace as a complete set if necessary. Check the thrust washers and replace as required with those selected after checking the idler gear and primary gear end-float.

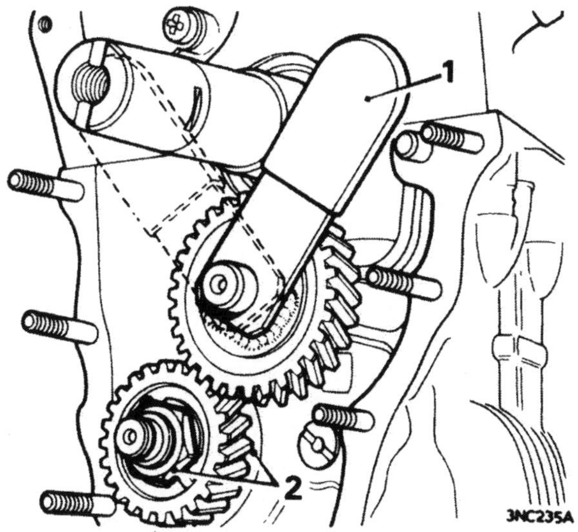

Fig. A.31
Using tool to hold the gear train to enable the first and third motion shaft nuts to be removed and refitted.

1. Made-up tool. 2. First motion gear and retaining nut.

Refitting

15. Fit the first motion shaft gear with a new lock washer.
16. Position the gear train holding tool on the opposite side of the crankshaft, Fig. A.31.
17. Refit and tighten the first motion shaft gear retaining nut to 150 lbf ft (20.7 kg m).
18. Remove the gear train holding tool.
19. Primary gear end-float: Refit the primary gear with its front thrust washer, with the chamfered side of the washer (arrowed) towards the crankshaft.
20. Refit the rear backing ring and thrust washer.
21. Check the primary gear end-float with feeler gauges, see Fig. A.32; the amount of end-float should be from 0.0035 to 0.0065 in (0.089 to 0.165 mm). Adjust if necessary by fitting the correct thickness thrust washer from the range given below.

Primary gear thrust washer chart

0.112 to 0.114 in (2.84 to 2.89 mm)
0.114 to 0.116 in (2.89 to 2.94 mm)
0.116 to 0.118 in (2.94 to 2.99 mm)
0.118 to 0.120 in (2.99 to 3.04 mm)

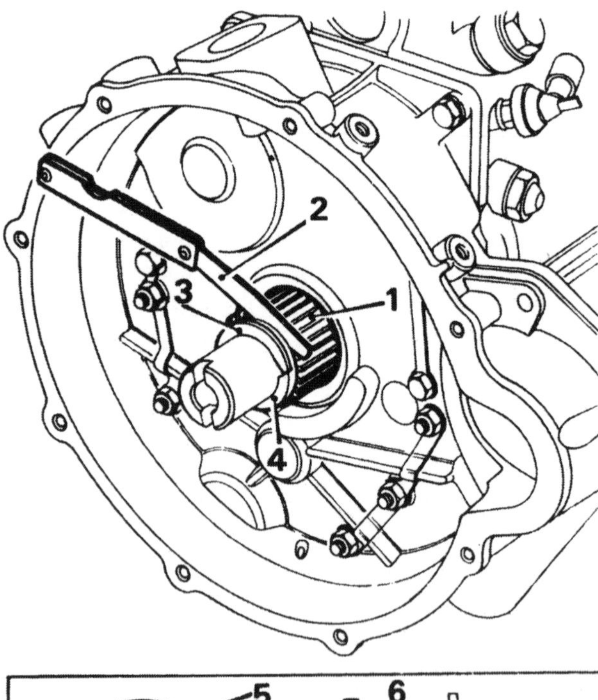

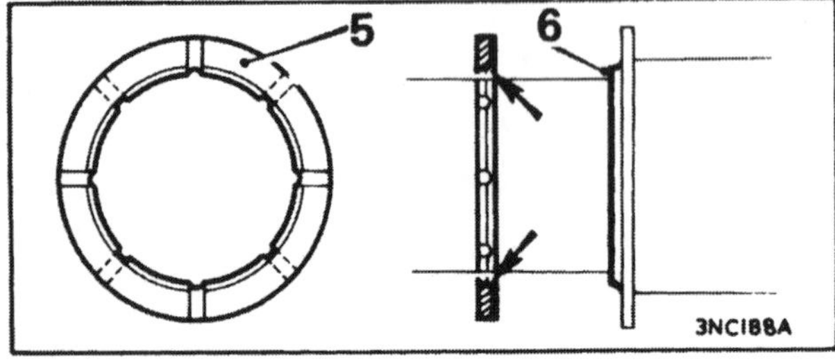

Fig. A.32
Checking the primary gear end float with feeler gauges. Fit thrust washer with chamfered side 'arrowed' towards the crankshaft.

1. Primary gear.
2. Feeler gauges.
3. 'C' shaped thrust washer.
4. Rear backing ring.
5. Front thrust washer.
6. Crankshaft.

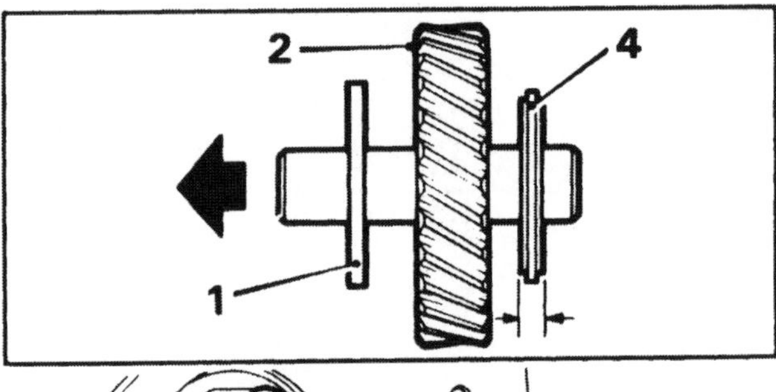

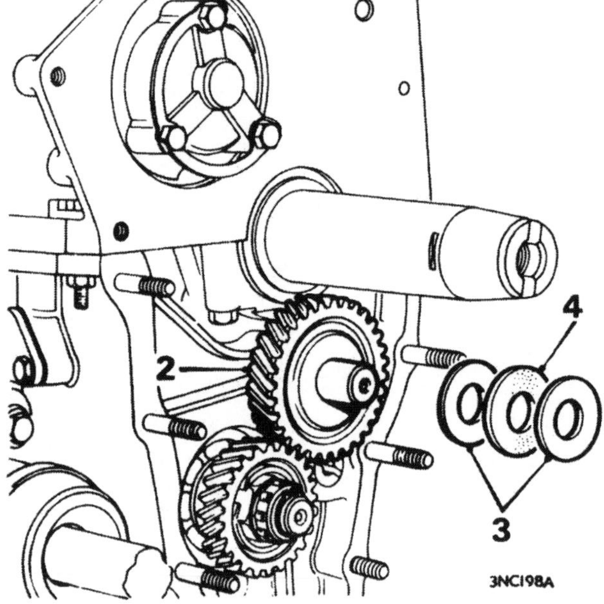

Fig. A.33
Using Service tool 18G 1089 to determine the thickness of thrust washers required. Inset shows the assembly of tool and thrust washer onto the idler gear.

1. Thrust washer.
2. Idler gear.
3. Service tool 18G 1089 (two washers).
4. Dental wax washer.

22. Remove the primary gear assembly after adjustment.
23. Idler gear end-float: Assemble the idler gear to the transmission (longer spindle into the transmission) with a nominal washer from the range available, onto the transmission side of the idler gear, Fig. A.33.
24. Assemble the thin washers of tool 18G 1089 interposed with a dental wax washer onto the flywheel side of the idler gear.
25. Fit a new flywheel housing joint washer.
26. Refit the flywheel housing and tighten the securing bolts and nuts to 18 lbf ft (2.5 kgf m).
27. Remove the housing and discard the joint washer.
28. Remove the tool 18G 1089 (washers with dental wax interposed) and measure the thickness of the assembly with a micrometer. From the measurement figure taken, subtract 0.004 to 0.007 in (0.102 to 0.178 mm). Select and fit a thrust washer of the required thickness from the chart given below.

Idler gear thrust washer chart

0.132 to 0.133 in (3.35 to 3.37 mm)
0.134 to 0.135 in (3.40 to 3.42 mm)
0.136 to 0.137 in (3.45 to 3.47 mm)
0.138 to 0.139 in (3.50 to 3.53 mm)

29. Fit a new flywheel housing joint washer; do not re-use the one used when carrying out the idler gear adjustment.
30. Refit the primary gear with its selected front thrust washer, backing ring, and rear thrust washer, Fig. A.32.
31. Fit tool 18G 1043 over the primary gear and screw the two guides into the two bottom holes in the crankcase.
32. Refit the flywheel housing, Section A.18.
33. Refit the clutch/flywheel assembly, Section A.28.

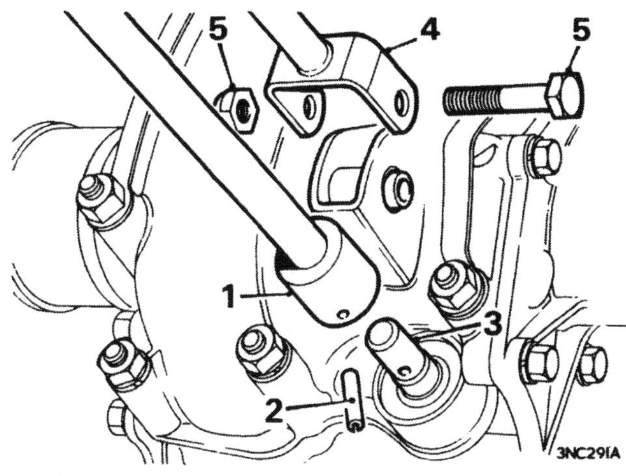

Fig. A.34
Disconnect the rod gear change remote control from the transmission.

1. Extension rod.
2. Roll pin–extension rod.
3. Selector shaft.
4. Steady rod.
5. Nut and bolt –steady rod fork.

Section A.33

ENGINE AND GEARBOX ASSEMBLY (Rod-change gearbox)

Removing

1. Disconnect the battery.
2. Remove the bonnet.
3. Remove the air cleaner.
4. Disconnect the petrol feed hose, vacuum advance pipe and the breather hose from the carburetter.
5. Remove the carburetter and place it to one side clear of the power unit.
6. Disconnect both hoses from the fuel pump.
7. Disconnect the two-piece type speedometer cable at its centre joint.
8. Remove the cylinder block drain plug and drain the coolant.
9. Disconnect the heater hose from the radiator bottom hose connection.
10. Remove the heater water control valve from the cylinder head and place to one side.
11. Disconnect the exhaust down pipe from the exhaust manifold flange.
12. Disconnect and remove the horn.
13. From beneath the right hand front wing, release the pipe from the air intake.
14. Remove the air intake from the wing valance.
15. Disconnect the starter cable connection from the starter solenoid.
16. Disconnect the engine earth cable from the clutch cover.
17. Remove the distributor cap and rotor arm.
18. Disconnect the alternator plug connector and the electrical connections from the ignition coil and oil pressure switch.
19. Disconnect the clutch operating lever return spring, remove the slave cylinder securing bolts and place the unit clear of the power unit.
20. Release the engine tie-rod from the rear of the cylinder block, slacken the bolt securing the opposite end and swing the rod clear of the power unit.
21. Remove the rocker cover and fit the engine lifting attachment, see Fig. A.11.
22. Follow the procedure 1, 2 and 4 to 9 in Section G.5 to withdraw the drive shafts out of the inboard joints.
23. Drift out the roll-pin securing the remote control extension rod to the selector shaft, see Fig. A.34.
24. Remove the securing nut and bolt from the remote control steady fork on the final drive housing and detach the fork, see Fig. A.34.
25. Disconnect the exhaust steady bracket from the final drive end-cover.
26. Remove the four bolts and nuts securing the engine mountings to the sub-frame.
27. Attach lifting equipment to the front lifting eye of the attachment to give an angled lift, and lift the power unit out of the vehicle.

Refitting

28. Reverse the removing procedure noting the following:
    a. Remove the engine lifting attachment; refit and tighten the cylinder head nuts to the torque figure given in **'GENERAL DATA'**.
    b. Refill the cooling system.

SECTION Aa

THE ENGINE

The information given in this Section refers specifically to engines fitted with automatic transmission and must be used in conjunction with Section A

These operations must be followed by an exhaust emission check 

Section Aa.1

LUBRICATION

Checking oil level

NOTE: Ensure that the vehicle is standing on a level surface.

1. Start the engine and run it for 1-2 minutes. Stop the engine and wait for 1 minute, then check the oil level with the dipstick.
2. Maintain the oil level up to the 'MAX' mark on the dipstick; the difference in quantity between the 'MIN' and 'MAX' marks is approximately 1 pint (0.6 litre).

Draining and refilling

The oil should be renewed at the periods given in the **MAINTENANCE SUMMARY'**. Drain the oil while the engine is warm, and clean the magnetic drain plug using lint-free cloth.

3. Remove the drain plug and allow the oil to drain, clean the drain plug and fit a new sealing washer if necessary. Tighten the plug to the torque figure given in **GENERAL DATA'**.
4. Refill with a recommended oil, see **'RECOMMENDED LUBRICANTS'**, up to the 'MAX' mark on the dipstick.
5. Repeat the procedures in 1 and 2.

Section Aa.2

OIL FILTER

Filter element renewal

REMOVING

1. **All models except 'Clubman'.** Remove the front grille (16 screws).
   On 'Clubman' models sufficient clearance exists for filter bowl removal.
2. Place a suitable container beneath the oil filter.
3. Unscrew the central retaining bolt and remove the bowl and element assembly.

CLEANING

4. Thoroughly clean the filter bowl with petrol (fuel) and dry off.
5. Wipe the filter head clean and fit a new sealing ring in the filter head recess.

REFITTING

6. Reassemble the filter bew! with a new element and the internal components fitted in the order shown in Fig. Aa.1. Ensure that the internal sealing washer is in good condition and a snug fit on the retaining bolt.

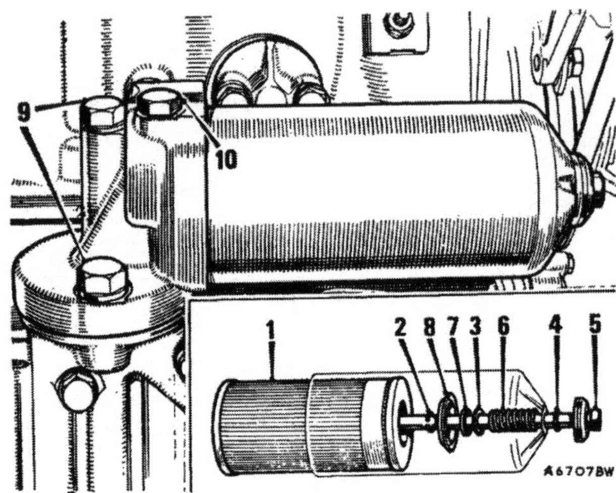

Fig. Aa.1
The engine/automatic transmission oil filter. (Inset) the filter components

1. Filter element.
2. Circlip.
3. Steel washer.
4. Sealing ring.
5. Centre bolt.
6. Spring
7. Sealing washer.
8. Sealing plate.
9. Filter head retaining bolts
10. Oil pressure check plug.

7. Refit the filter bowl assembly and tighten the central retaining bolt to the torque figure given in **'GENERAL DATA'**.
8. Check for oil leakage immediately the engine is started.
9. Top up the engine oil level following the instructions in Section Aa.1.
10. Refit the front grille (where applicable).

Filter head and bowl assembly

REMOVING

11. Release the distributor cap.

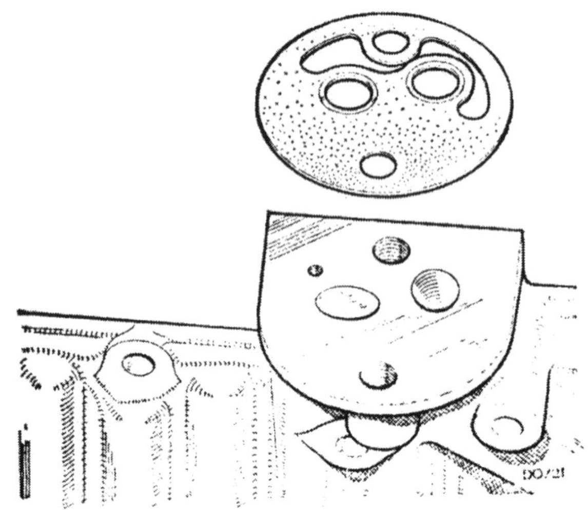

Fig. Aa.2
The correct location of the later-type filter head/front cover joint washer

12. Unscrew the filter head retaining bolts and remove the assembly.

    NOTE.–The oil filter head to front cover joint washer (with copper inserts) fitted to later units is **not** interchangeable with those fitted to the earlier units. The two 'O' ring oil seals are not used on the later units (see Fig. Aa.2 for correct location of the later-type joint washer).

REFITTING

13. Reverse the removal instructions, fitting a new joint washer and seals (if fitted). Tighten the securing bolts to the torque figure in **'GENERAL DATA'**.
14. Carry out items 8 and 9.

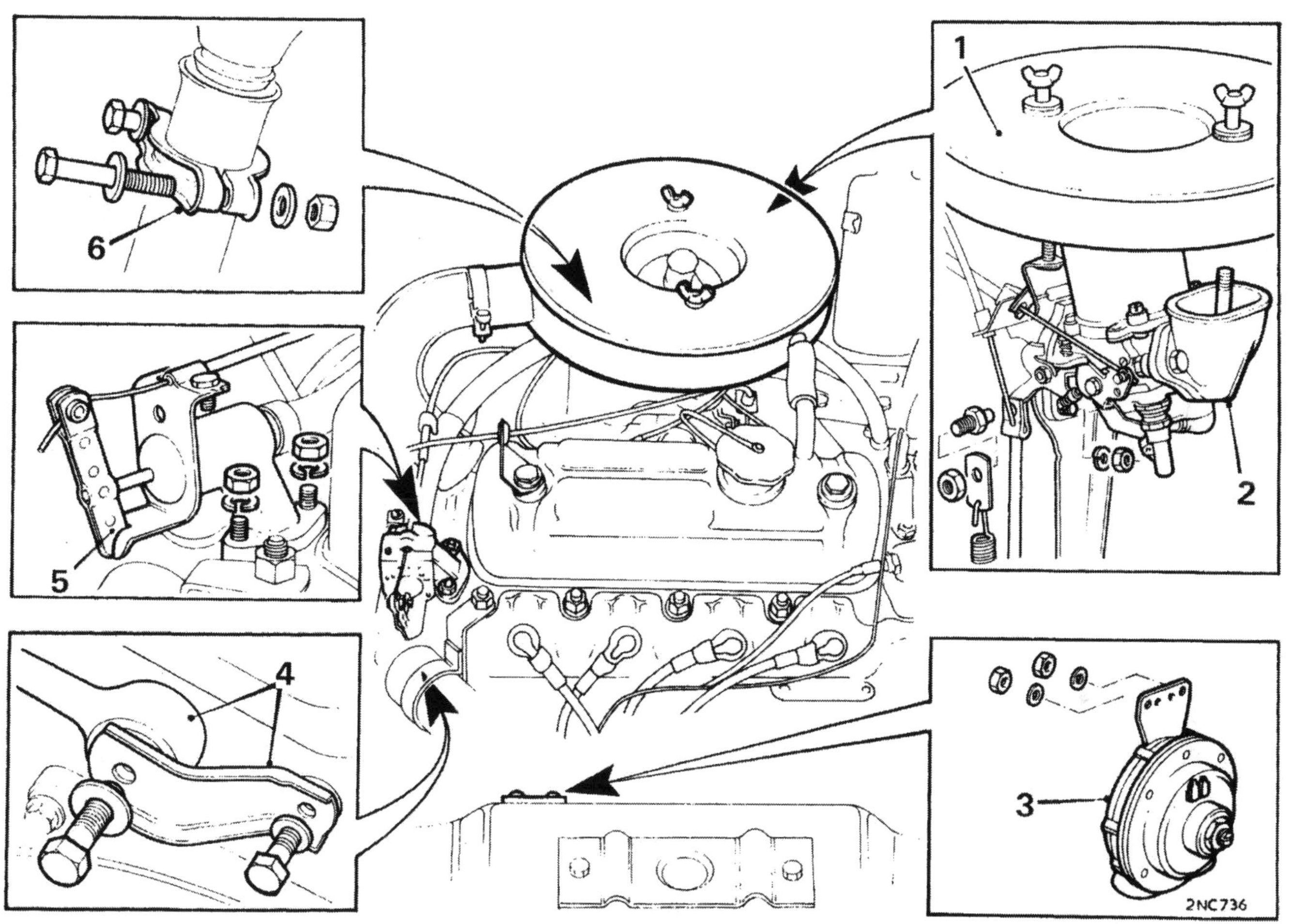

Fig. Aa.3
The main components to be disconnected or removed from inside the engine compartment before removing the engine and transmission unit

1. Air cleaner.
2. Carburetter.
3. Horn.
4. Engine tie-rod.
5. Heater water valve.
6. Exhaust pipe clamp.

Section Aa.3

ENGINE AND TRANSMISSION

Removing

1. Disconnect the battery earth cable.
2. Mark the fitted position of the bonnet to its hinges and remove the bonnet
3. Raise the front of the car until the wheels are free to rotate and remove the drive shaft flange securing nuts.
4. Remove the bellcrank lever guard or, on early units, pull back the rubber boot; disconnect the selector cable yoke from the bellcrank lever.
5. Remove the exhaust bracket from the final drive cover. The larger nut is secured by a locking tab (see Fig. Aa.4).
6. Drain the cylinder block and release the heater control water valve from the rear of the cylinder head and retain it clear of the engine.

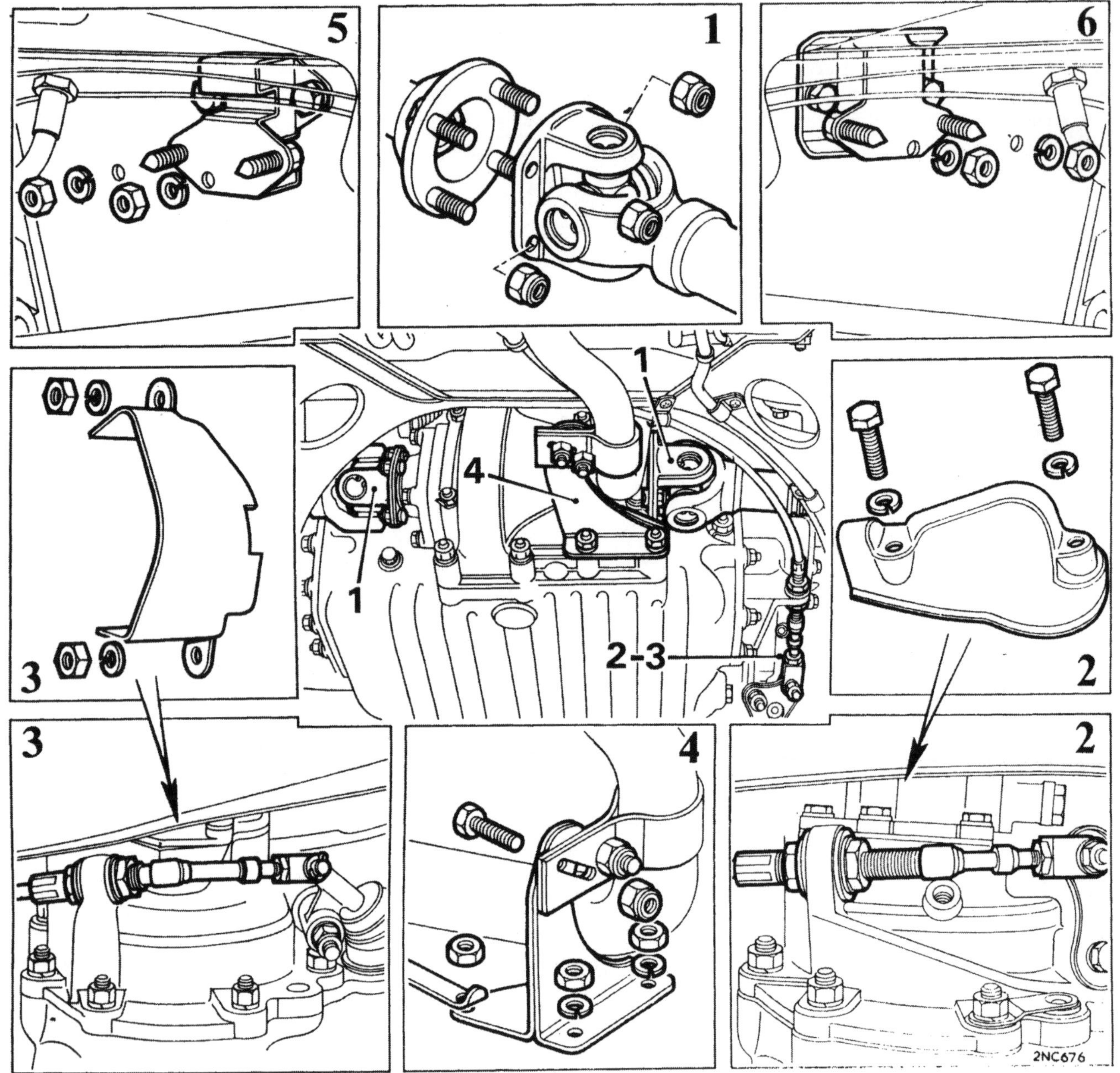

Fig. Aa.4
The main components to be disconnected or removed from below the car before removing the engine and transmission unit

1. Drive shaft universal joints.
2. Gearchange cable and cover (latest type).
3. Gearchange cable and cover (early type)
4. Exhaust pipe bracket.
5. L.H. front engine mounting.
6. R.H. front engine mounting.

7. Disconnect the heater hose from radiator bottom hose adaptor.
8. Release the heater air intake tube (when fitted) from the front grille and wing valance and retain it clear of the engine.
9. Disconnect all electrical connections from the engine.
10. Remove the distributor cap.
11. Remove the air cleaner as in Section Da.1.
12. Release the carburetter from the engine and attach it to the bulkhead clear of the engine.
13. Unscrew and release the speedometer cable from its pinion on the transmission casing, or from the rear of the speedometer on models where the the instrument is centrally situated.
14. Disconnect the oil pressure hose (when fitted).
15. Disconnect and remove the horn (when attached to the bonnet locking platform).

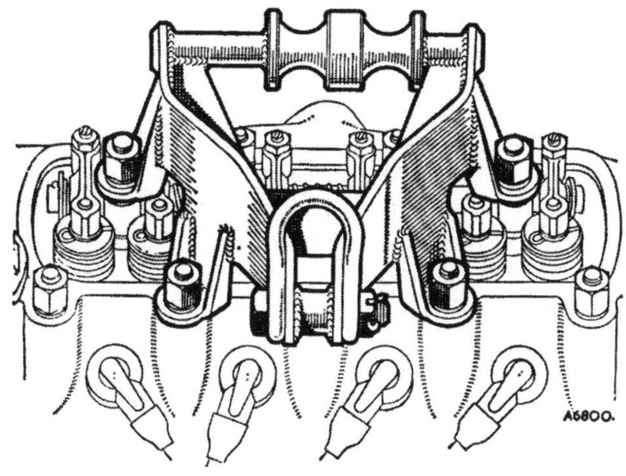

Fig. Aa.5
Use the individual front lifting eye of the attachment to give an angled lift when removing and refitting the power unit

16. Disconnect the exhaust pipe from the manifold and secure the pipe against the bulkhead.
17. Detach the engine tie-rod from its locations on the cylinder block and bulkhead bracket.
    Early models: Release the tie-rod from the rear of the cylinder head and swing it away from the engine.
18. Remove the rocker cover nuts and fit the engine lifting bracket (Fig. Aa.5).
19. Remove the set screws securing each engine mounting to the sub-frame.
20. Lift the engine sufficiently to release the drive shafts from the driving flanges, and remove the engine/transmission unit from the car.

Refitting

21. Reverse the removal instructions with particular attention to the following points.
22. Lower the engine/transmission unit to a position where the drive shafts can engage the driving flange studs and screw the securing nuts on approximately four threads. Lower the unit completely into the car.
23. Adjust the selector lever cable and transverse rod as detailed in Section Fa.2.
24. Tighten all hose connections and refill the cooling system.
25. Top up the engine with oil as described in Section Aa.1.

Section Aa.4

TRANSMISSION UNIT

Removing

1. Remove the engine and transmission (see Section Aa.3).
2. Remove the radiator mounting bracket from the transmission case.
3. Remove the starter motor, with the distance piece (if fitted) and the converter cover.
4. Drain the transmission.
5. Knock back the lock washer on the converter centre bolt. Hold the converter from turning with a suitable screwdriver inserted through the hole in the converter housing. Using Service tool 18G 587, remove the centre bolt (Fig. Aa.6).

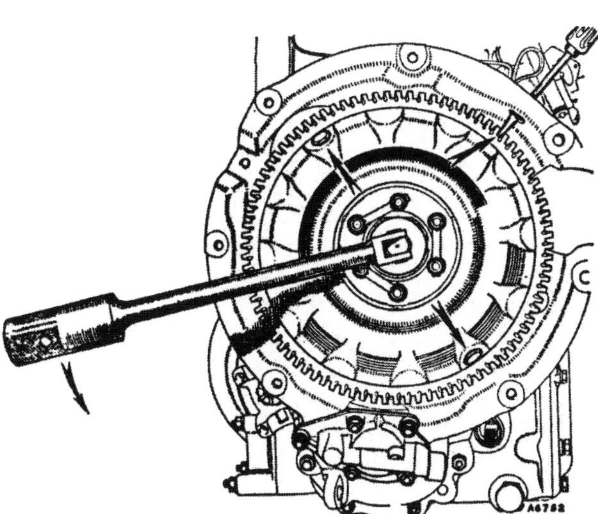

Fig. Aa.6
Removing the converter centre bolt, using Service tool 18G 587. A suitable screwdriver inserted through the converter housing to stop the converter turning, and the converter drain plugs, are indicated by arrows

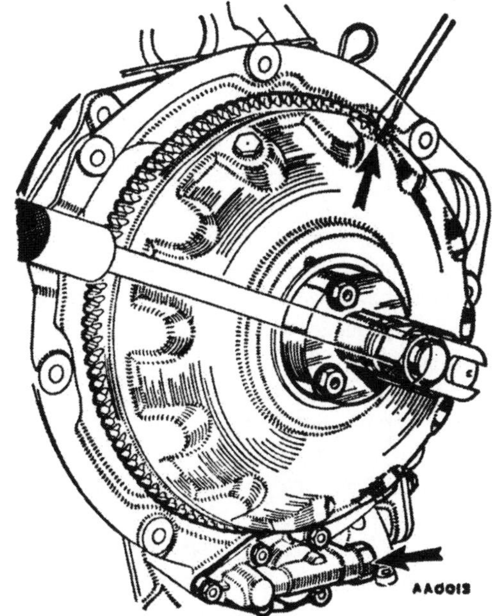

Fig. Aa.7
Removing the converter using Service tool 18G 1086. A screwdriver to stop the converter turning, and the low pressure valve, are indicated by the arrows

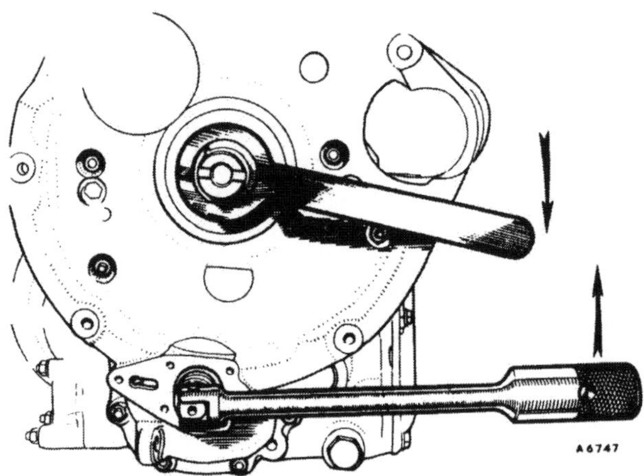

Fig. Aa.8
Using Service tool 18G 1088 to hold the converter output gear when removing the input gear nut

6. Knock back the locking tabs and remove three equally spaced set screws from the converter centre. Ensure that the slot in the end of the crankshaft is horizontal. Using Service tool 18G 1086 with the adaptor correctly positioned, remove the converter (Fig. Aa.7). Remove the Service tool and refit the three screws.
7. Remove the low pressure valve from the converter housing. Note that later valves are fitted with a screwed plug, which replaces a welch plug and must not be removed.
8. Fit Service tool 18G 1088 onto the converter output gear and remove the input gear self-locking nut (Fig.Aa.8).
9. Disconnect the transverse rod from the bell-crank assembly, remove the nut securing the bell-crank to its pivot and withdraw the bell-crank. Knock back the locking washer securing the bell-crank pivot, unscrew and remove the pivot.
10. Fit the nylon protector sleeve Service tool 18G 1098 over the converter output gear.
11. Remove the nuts and set screws securing the converter housing to the transmission and lift away the housing. Remove the converter oil outlet pipe from the housing.
12. Lever the main oil feed pipe from the transmission and oil pump.
13. Remove the idler gear, thrust washers, and the converter output gear assembly.
14. Remove the oil filter assembly and disconnect the engine oil feed pipe together with (on early units) its rubber seal and spring washer (see Fig. Aa.9).
15. Remove the nuts and set screws securing the engine to the transmission and with suitable lifting equipment lift the engine away from the transmission.

Inspecting

Ensure that the oil rings fitted to the main oil pipe, oil filter, transmission to engine oil feed pipe, and the main oil strainer pipe are in perfect condition. All joint faces must be free from burrs and new joint washers should be used.

Check that the converter housing bush has not come loose in its housing.

Inspect the idler gear bearings and renew if necessary, using Service tool 18G 581 to remove the bearings from the casings. Inspect the input gear bearing and renew if necessary by removing the circlip and pressing the bearing from the housing.

Check the main oil seals and renew if necessary. If it is necessary to renew the converter housing oil seal this operation is detailed in Section Aa.15. To renew the converter output gear oil seal, remove the rear case assembly and carefully remove the seal. Lubricate the new seal and press into the casing, using Service tools 18G 134 and 18G 134 CN (Fig. Aa.11).

NOTE.–Before refitting the transmission unit, check the casing to determine whether it is the later type with a cast-in oil reservoir (to improve idler gear bearing lubrication). Should it be an earlier type casing, it is advisable to modify the unit as detailed in Section Fa.17.

Refitting

16. Immerse the front main bearing cap moulded rubber oil seal in oil and fit with the lip facing the rear of the engine.

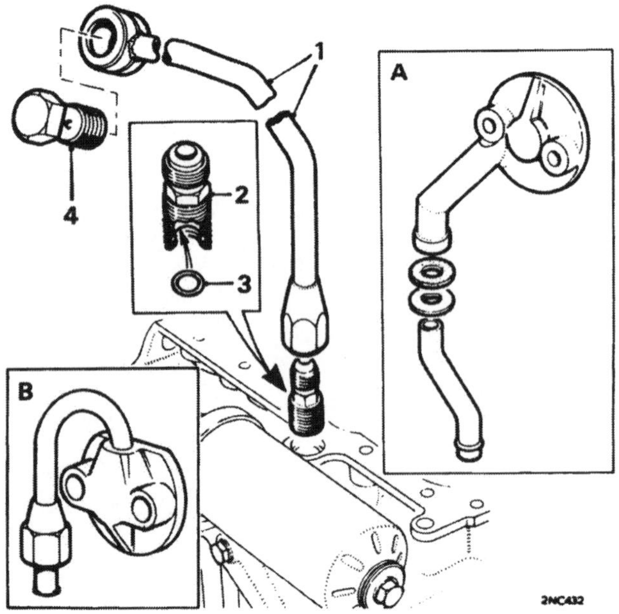

Fig. Aa.9
Inset 'A'–Pipe assembly fitted to early units
Inset 'B'–Pipe assembly to be used to enable the later transmission unit, with the screwed union (2), to be fitted to an early type engine not fitted with items 1 and 4

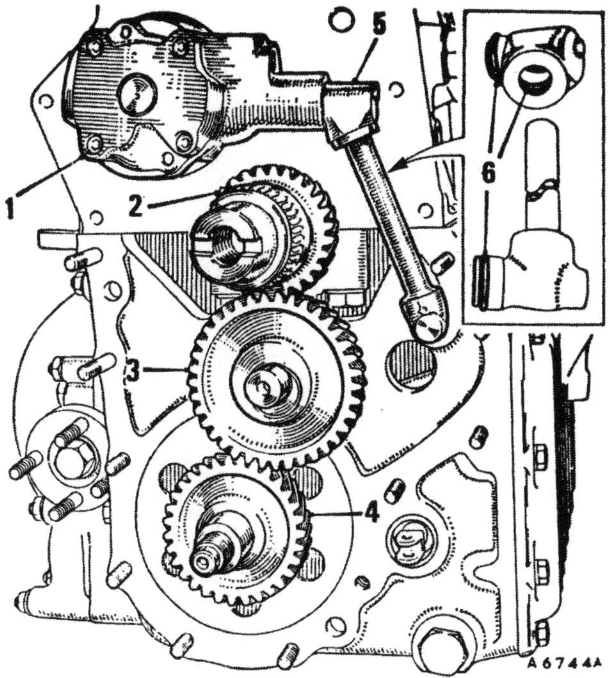

Fig. Aa.10
The converter housing removed showing:

1. Main oil pump.
2. Converter output gear.
3. Idler gear.
4. Input gear.
5. Oil feed pipe.
6. Sealing rings.

17. Fit the rubber sealing ring on to the main oil strainer pipe and fit new gaskets to the transmission case.
18. Lower the engine on to the transmission. Ensure that the moulded rubber seal is correctly located. Tighten the set screws and nuts as the transmission is being lowered in position.
19. Refit the transmission to engine oil feed pipe (both types of pipe assemblies are shown in Fig. Aa.9).
20. Refit the oil filter assembly (see '**NOTE**' in Section Aa.2 regarding joint washer location).
21. Refit the main oil pump to transmission oil pipe.
22. Trim off any excess transmission joint from the rear of the unit. Clean the surfaces and fit a new converter housing gasket.
23. Refit the converter output gear. When refitting, make certain that the correct running clearance of .0035 to .0065 in. (.089 to .165 mm.) is maintained between the inner thrust washer and the converter output gear. If the clearance is outside these limits, select and fit the appropriate washer from the size range, with the chamfered inner edge of the washer to face the crankshaft.

Converter output gear thrust washers

.112 to .114 in. (2.848 to 2.898 mm.)
.114 to .116 in. (2.898 to 2.949 mm.)
.116 to .118 in. (2.949 to 3.0 mm.)
.118 to .120 in. (3.0 to 3.051 mm.)

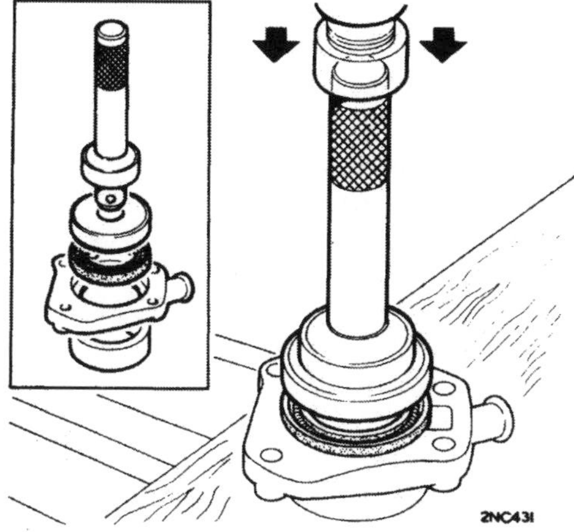

Fig. Aa.11
Replacing the converter output gear oil seal. Pressing the seal in, using Service tools 18G 134 and adaptor 18G 134 CN, with (inset) showing exploded view

NOTE.—Two types of input gears have been used, those fitted to earlier units have two thrust washers (Fig. Aa.14). The later gear (of increased hub thickness) has a number of thin shims fitted to the outer hub face of the gear for adjustment (see Fig. Aa.19).

Idler and input gear adjustment (Early Models)

24. Assemble the idler gear to the transmission with a nominal washer (from the range fitted), on the transmission side of the idler gear. Assemble Service tool 18G 1089 with a dental wax washer interposed on to the converter housing side of the idler gear. To cut the holes in the wax strip, place the larger washers of 18G 1089 one on either side of the wax, opposite each other, and press together.

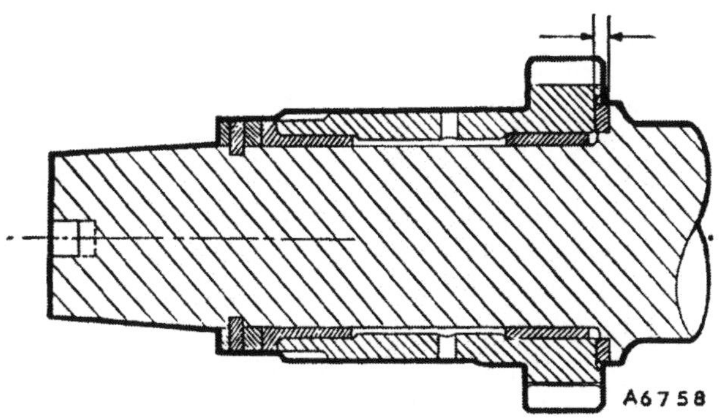

Fig. Aa.12
The converter output gear. Measure the gap indicated and fit the appropriate thrust washer

25. Fit input Service tool 18G 1098 interposed with a dental wax washer (Fig. Aa.13).

 NOTE.–If the input gear will not fully mesh with the idler gear, this indicates that the third speed reaction gear thrust washer has become displaced. Therefore it is necessary to remove, dismantle, and reassemble the gear train as detailed in Section Fa.12 (all items except (1)).

26. Screw the two pilot bars of Service tool 18G 1043 into the two bottom tapped holes in the crankcase. Fit the nylon protector sleeve Service tool 18G 1098 over the converter output gear and refit the converter housing; tighten into position to the correct torque figure given in **'GENERAL DATA'**. The input shaft nut must not be fitted.

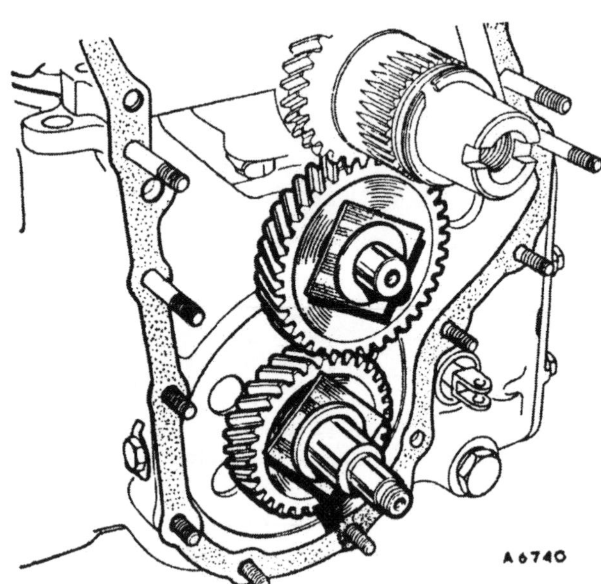

Fig. Aa.13
The idler and input gears fitted with the Service tool 18G 1089 (two sets of special washers, each set interposed with wax washer)

27. Remove the converter housing.
28. Measure the thickness of the idler gear thrust washer plus the thickness of the Service tool 18G 1089 and its dental wax washer. From this figure subtract .004 to .007 in. (.102 to .178 mm.) to give the total thickness of the thrust washers to be fitted to provide the correct idler gear end-float.

Idler gear thrust washer
.130 to .131 in. (3.30 to 3.32 mm.)
.132 to .133 in. (3.35 to 3.37 mm.)
.134 to .135 in. (3.40 to 3.42 mm.)
.136 to .137 in. (3.45 to 3.47 mm.)
.138 to .139 in. (3.50 to 3.53 mm.)

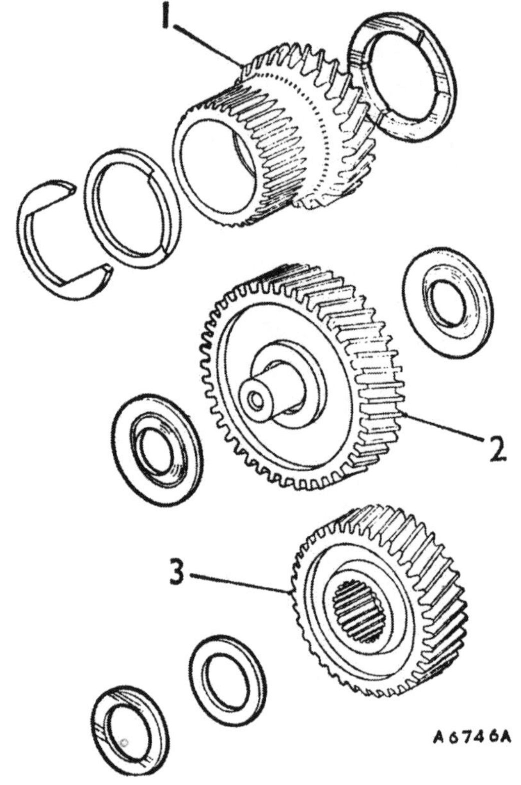

Fig. Aa.14
The converter output 1, idler 2, and input gear 3 with their respective thrust washers

29. Measure the thickness of the input gear Service tool 18G 1089 plus its dental wax washer. Add .001 to .003 in. (.025 to .076 mm.) to the figure to give the total thickness of the thrust washers to be fitted to provide the required 'nip' on the input gear bearing.

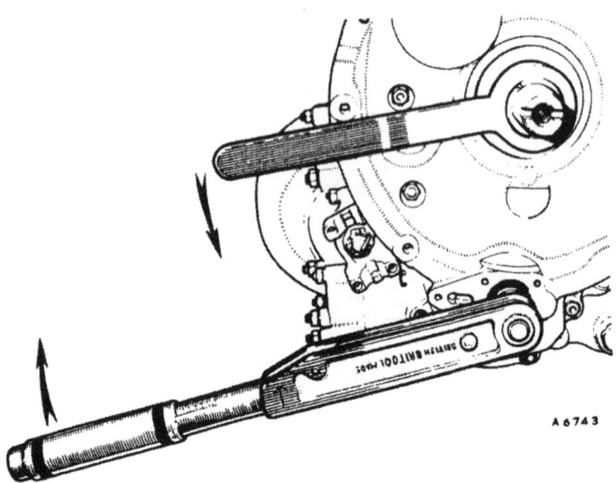

Fig. Aa.15
Using Service tools 18G 1088 to hold the converter output gear and 18G 592 to tighten the input gear nut to the correct torque figure

Fig. Aa.16
Using Service tools 18G 191 and 18G 191 A, with the dial test indicator set at zero

Input gear thrust washers
.128 to .130 in. (3.25 to 3.30 mm.)
.132 to .134 in. (3.35 to 3.40 mm.)
.140 to .142 in. (3.55 to 3.61 mm.)
.148 to .150 in. (3.76 to 3.81 mm.)
.152 to .154 in. (3.86 to 3.91 mm.)

30. a. Fit one washer on each side of the idler gear as calculated in item 28.
    b. Fit two washers to make up the calculated thickness onto the input gear shaft. Both washers must be fitted to the outside of the input gear (see Fig. Aa.14), with the chamfered inside edge of one washer towards the gear.

Idler and input gear adjustment (Later Models)

31. Carry out item 24.
32. Place the input gear on a surface plate or onto Service tool 18G 191 A and use a dial test indicator gauge, Service tool 18G 191, to take a mean reading. Set the dial gauge to zero as shown in Fig. Aa.16.
33. Fit Service tool adaptor 18G 1089 A over the input shaft. Use Service tool 18G 1089/1 to cut a dental wax washer, and fit the wax washer with Service tool 18G 1089/1 over the input shaft (see Fig. Aa.17).
34. Carry out items 26 and 27.
35. Fit a new converter housing joint washer and ensure that NO shims are sticking to the input gear bearing. Lubricate the oil seal lip, refit the housing and tighten to the torque figure given in '**GENERAL DATA**'. The input shaft nut must not be fitted.
36. Remove the converter housing and withdraw the adaptor assembly 18G 1089 A, wax washer, and 18G 1089/1. Substitute this complete assembly for the input gear on the surface plate (see Fig. Aa.18).
37. Use the dial test indicator gauge. Service tool 18G 191, and measure the thickness of this assembly (see Fig. Aa.18). The mean reading obtained indicates the total thickness of shims required to eliminate end-float. To this figure add shims to the value of .001 to .003 in. (.025 to .076 mm.) to give the required input bearing preload.

Input gear adjustment shims
.003 in. (.076 mm.)
.012 in. (.305 mm.)

38. Measure the thickness of the idler gear thrust washer plus the thickness of the Service tool 18G 1089 and its dental wax washer. From this figure subtract .004 to .007 in. (.102 to .178 mm.) to give the total thickness of the thrust washers to be fitted to provide the correct idler gear end-float.

Idler gear thrust washers
.132 to .133 in. (3.35 to 3.37 mm.)
.134 to .135 in. (3.40 to 3.42 mm.)
.136 to .137 in. (3.45 to 3.47 mm.)
.138 to .139 in. (3.50 to 3.53 mm.)

39. a. Fit the required thickness of shims as calculated in item 37 onto the outside of the input gear (see Fig. Aa.19).
    b. Fit one washer on each side of the idler gear (see Fig. Aa.19) as calculated in item 38.

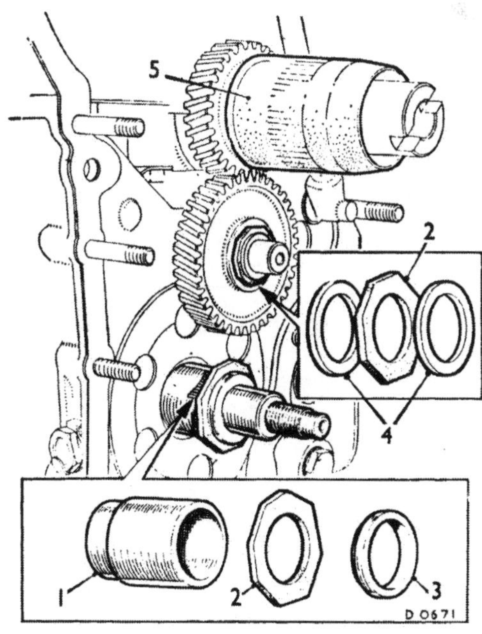

Fig. Aa.17

1. Service tool 18G 1089 A.
2. Wax washer.
3. Service tool 18G 1089/1.
4. Service tool 18G 1089 with wax washer interposed.
5. Service tool 18G 1098.

Refitting

40. Refit and align the converter outlet pipe.
41. Discard the converter housing joint washer used during the idler and input gear adjustment operations. Refit the converter housing with a new joint washer, remove the pilot bars of Service tool 18G 1043 and tighten the securing nuts and set screws to the torque figure given in **'GENERAL DATA'**.
42. Refit the input gear shaft nut and tighten to the correct torque figure (see **'GENERAL DATA'**), using Service tools 18G 1088 and 18G 592.
43. Remove each pair of bolts in turn from the converter and fit new locking plates. Tighten the bolts to the torque figure given in **'GENERAL DATA'**, and tap up the locking tabs.
    NOTE.–Do not remove all six screws from the converter centre at one time.
44. Lubricate the converter oil seal and refit the converter. Refit the washer (offset pegs) and the centre bolt with its lock washer. Tighten the bolt to the correct torque figure (see **'GENERAL DATA'**) with Service tools 18G 587 and 18G 592 and lock up the lock washer.
45. Refit the low pressure valve and gasket.
46. Refit the gear selector bell-crank lever and its pivot, and reconnect it with the transverse rod. See that either the rubber boot (early models) or guard (later models) is refitted.
47. Refit the converter cover, the starter motor, and the rear engine mounting.
48. For refitting the engine and transmission to the car (see Section Aa.3).

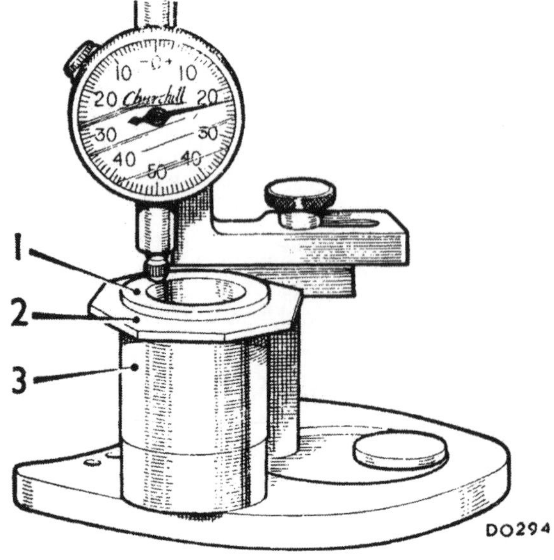

Fig. Aa.18
Measuring the adaptor assembly

1. Service tool 18G 1089/1. 2. Wax washer. 3. Service tool 18G 1089 A.

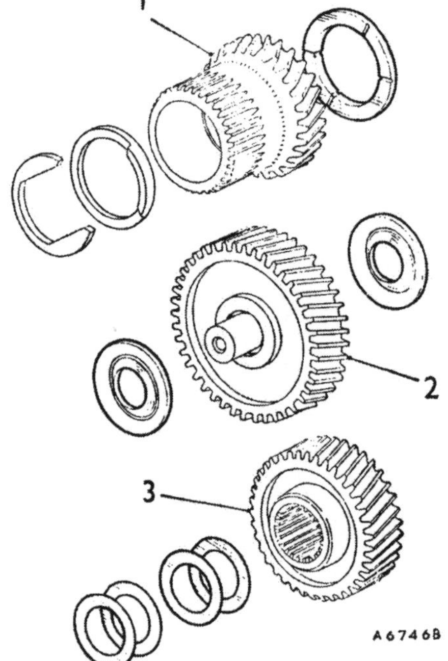

Fig. Aa.19
The converter output 1, idler 2, and input gear 3 with their respective thrust washers and shims

Section Aa.5

EXHAUST SYSTEM

Removing

1. Slacken the exhaust pipe to manifold clamp.
2. Release the pipe from the bracket on the final drive casing (Fig. Aa.3) and from the two locations on the rear sub-frame.

Refitting

3. Refit the exhaust system to the car with the intermediate and rear support clips loose to allow articulation at the manifold spherical flange.
4. Align the pipe flange with the manifold, refit and tighten the manifold clamp.
5. Ensure correct alignment of the system and tighten the remaining fixing points.

Section Aa.6

DISTRIBUTOR DRIVING SPINDLE 

Removing

1. Remove the distributor and driving spindle as detailed in Section A.10.

Refitting

2. Refitting is described in Section A.10 with the following exceptions.

3. To rotate the crankshaft, insert a screwdriver through the aperture (adjacent the oil dipstick) on the converter housing or end cover, and turn the converter starter ring gear to the position described in Section A.10.
4. Check that the correct timing mark on the converter is in line with the pointer on the converter housing (see Figs. Ba.1 and Ba.2).

Section Aa.7

VALVE TIMING 

1. Follow the instructions given in Section A.17 with the following exceptions.
2. Rotate the crankshaft as described in Section Aa.6 until the 5° B.T.D.C. timing mark on the converter is opposite the pointer on the converter cover.

Section Aa.8

OIL PUMP

Removing

1. Remove the engine and transmission as detailed in Section Aa.3.
2. Remove the converter and converter housing as detailed in Section Aa.4, items 3 to 12.
3. Remove the pump securing screws and withdraw the pump.

Dismantling and reassembling

4. Follow the instructions given in Section A.22 for the Hobourn-Eaton pump.

Refitting

5. Reverse the removal instructions fitting new joint washers as required.

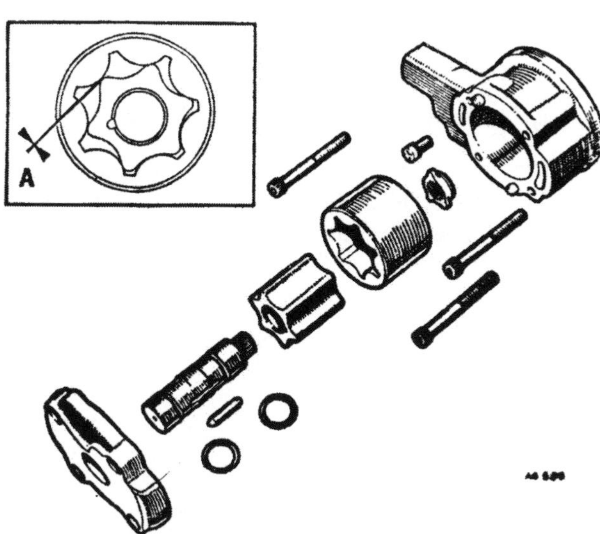

Fig. Aa.20
The oil pump components. 'A' indicates the lobe positions for checking clearances

Section Aa.9

CAMSHAFT 

NOTE.—Extreme care is necessary when removing the camshaft. The oil pump drive coupling may stick by oil adhesion to the camshaft and possibly fall into the transmission unit. Ensure therefore when refitting the camshaft that this drive coupling is fully located on the splined oil pump spindle.

Removing

1. Follow the instructions given in Section A.23 with the following exceptions.
2. Remove the engine and transmission as detailed in Section Aa.3.
3. Should the front camshaft bearing clearance be excessive, a new bearing liner must be fitted and as this will entail line-reamering after fitting, both the converter, converter housing, and the transmission unit must be removed as in Section Aa.4.
4. For removing, fitting, and reaming a new liner follow the instructions in Section A.23.

Refitting

5. Refitting is a reversal of the removal procedure given in Section A.23.

Section Aa.10

PISTONS AND CONNECTING RODS

Removing

1. Follow the instructions given in Section A.24 with the following exceptions.
2. Remove the engine and transmission unit as detailed in Section Aa.3.
3. Remove the converter, converter housing, and the transmission unit from the engine as detailed in Section Aa.4.

Refitting

4. Refitting is a reversal of the removing procedure (see Sections A.24 and Aa.3-4).

Section Aa.11

CRANKSHAFT AND MAIN BEARINGS

Removing

1. Follow the instructions given in Section A.25 with the following exceptions.
2. Remove the engine and transmission unit as detailed in Section Aa.3.
3. Remove the converter, converter housing, and the transmission unit from the engine as detailed in Section Aa.4.

Refitting

4. Follow the refitting instructions for installation of the crankshaft and bearings given in Section A.25.
5. Carry out the inspection and refitting of the transmission unit as detailed in Section Aa.4.

Section Aa.12

ENGINE MOUNTINGS

Removing

LEFT-HAND MOUNTING

1. Follow the instructions in Section A.14.

RIGHT-HAND MOUNTING

2. Disconnect the battery earth cable.
3. Disconnect the electrical connections from the starter solenoid and remove it from the wing valance.
4. Disconnect the engine tie-rod from the rear of the cylinder block and the exhaust down pipe from the manifold flange.
5. Remove the two nuts and set screws securing the mounting to the sub-frame.
6. Lift the rear of the engine sufficiently to remove the securing nuts and bolts from the converter cover and the starter motor. Turn the cover slightly anti-clockwise and remove the cover complete with the engine mounting.
7. Unscrew the set screws to release the mounting from the cover.

Refitting

8. Refitting is a reversal of the removal procedure.

Section Aa.13

CONVERTER OUTPUT GEAR

Removing

1. Remove the engine and transmission as detailed in Section Aa.3.
2. Carry out the removing instructions as detailed in Section Aa.4, items 3 to 11 and 13.

Adjusting

3. Carry out the instruction given in Section Aa.4, item 23.

Refitting

4. Refitting is a reversal of the removal procedure.

Section Aa.14

CYLINDER LINERS

Follow the instructions in Section A.24 with the following exceptions.

1. Remove the engine and transmission from the car as detailed in Section Aa.3.
2. Remove the transmission unit from the engine as detailed in Section Aa.4.

Section Aa.15

CONVERTER HOUSING OIL SEAL REPLACEMENT

Removing

1. Remove the engine from the car as detailed in Section Aa.3.
2. Remove the starter motor and converter cover.
3. Remove the converter (Section Aa.4, items 5 and 6).
4. Remove the old seal, using Service tool 18G 1087. Hook the tool into the oil seal groove and tap outwards on the tool, working round the seal until it is removed.

Refitting

The new seal must be fitted to the correct depth in order that the oil drain hole behind the seal remains open.

5. Take a depth measurement from any convenient point on the periphery of the housing bore of the front face of the housing to the undercut face (see Fig. Aa.21).

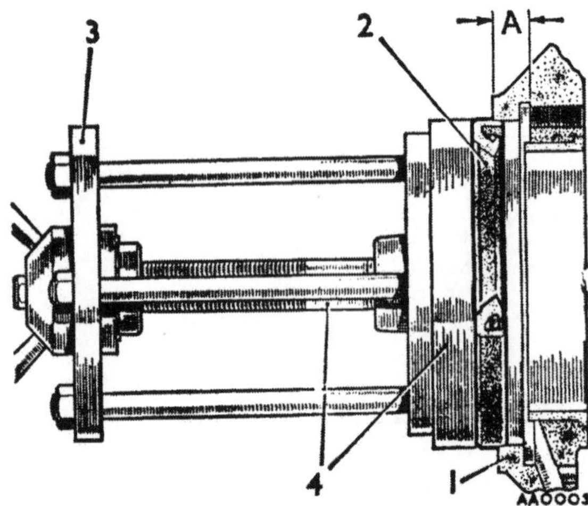

Fig. Aa.21

A section through of fitting the converter housing oil seal. A = the depth measurement to be taken

1. Converter housing.
2. Oil seal.
3. Service tool 18G 1068 B.
4. Service tool adaptor set 18G 1068 A.

This measurement will be approximately ⅜ in. (9.5mm.), but should it be more or less than this measurement this must be taken into account and either added to or subtracted from ⅜ in. (9.5 mm.).

EXAMPLE: If the measurement is ⅜ in. (9.5 mm.) fit the new seal to be flush with the front face of the converter housing. If measurement is less than ⅜ in. (9.5 mm.) fit the seal proud of the face by the difference of measurement obtained.

NOTE.–The converter housing face is not machined, therefore, the initial measurement position and that used when fitting a new seal must always be taken from the same position on the housing.

6. Screw in the short threaded end of Service tool 18G 1068 A securely into the crankshaft.
7. Liberally lubricate the new oil seal.
8. Assemble the new seal together with Service tool 18G 1068 B into position (see Fig. Aa.22).
9. Screw in the wing nut of the tool until the seal is pressed in to the depth of the measurement (see item 5).
10. The remainder is a reversal of the removing procedure.
11. Check and top up oil level (Section Aa.1).

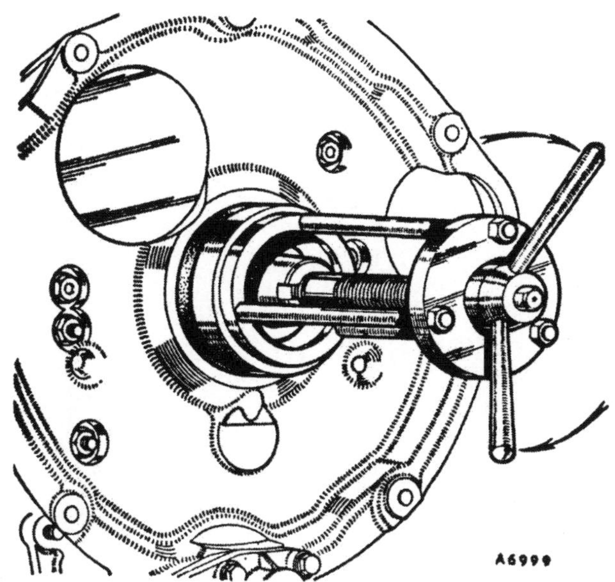

Fig. Aa.22
Fitting the converter output gear oil seal, using Service tool 18G 1068 B with adaptor 18G 1068 A

SECTION B

THE IGNITION SYSTEM

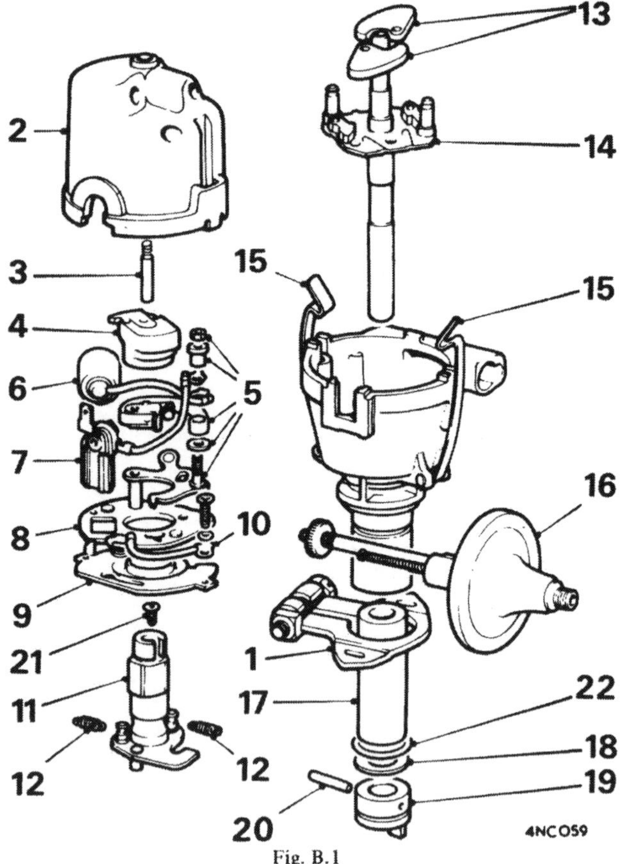

Fig. B.1

The components of the 25D4 distributor

1. Clamping plate
2. Moulded cap
3. Brush and spring
4. Rotor arm
5. Contacts (set)
6. Capacitor
7. Terminal and lead (low tension)
8. Moving contact breaker plate
9. Contact breaker base plate
10. Earth lead
11. Cam assembly
12. Automatic advance springs
13. Weight assembly
14. Shaft and action plate
15. Cap-retaining clips
16. Vacuum unit
17. Bush
18. Thrust washer
19. Driving dog
20. Taper pin
21. Cam screw
22. 'O' ring oil seal

Section B.1

DISTRIBUTOR (Type 25D4)
– Remove and refit

Removing

1. Remove the cover or grommet from the timing hole in the clutch/converter cover and rotate the crankshaft until the flywheel/converter is at the correct static setting, see **'ENGINE TUNING DATA'**; the appropriate timing mark should be adjacent to the pointer in the timing hole.
2. Unclip the distributor cap and place it to one side.
3. Detach the low tension cable from the terminal blade on the distributor body.
4. Disconnect the vacuum pipe from the vacuum timing control unit.
5. Take out the two screws securing the clamp plate and pull out the distributor. Do not loosen the clamp plate pinch bolt.

Refitting

6. Reverse the removing procedure, noting the following:
   a. Position the offset tongues of the driving dog with the larger offset uppermost.
   b. Later type distributors have an 'O' ring oil seal on the mounting shank.
   c. Recheck and adjust if necessary the stroboscopic timing to the figure quoted in **'ENGINE TUNING DATA'**.

Section B.2

DISTRIBUTOR (Type 25D4)
– Overhaul

Dismantling

1. Remove the distributor from the engine, Section B.1.
2. Remove the high tension cables from the distributor cap.
3. Withdraw the brush and spring from inside the cap.
4. Withdraw the rotor arm from the top of the cam.
5. Remove the nut from the terminal pillar on the fixed contact plate and detach the upper insulating bush and the two leads from the terminal pillar.
6. Remove the moving contact from the contact breaker moving plate.
7. Remove the lower insulating bush from the terminal pillar.
8. Remove the screw to release the fixed contact plate from the contact breaker moving plate.
9. Remove the screw to release the condenser from the contact breaker moving plate.
10. Detach the vacuum unit link from the contact breaker moving plate.

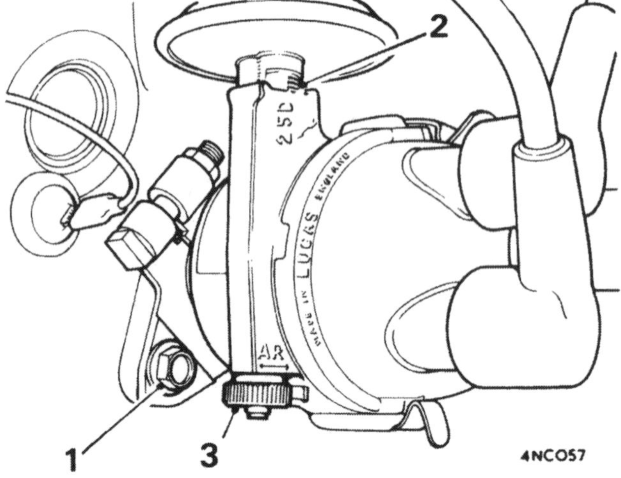

Fig. B.2
The 25D4 type distributor

1. Clamp screw
2. Vernier scale
3. Knurled adjuster nut

11. Remove the rubber seals and the two screws to release the contact breaker base plate and the earthing lead from the distributor body.
12. Turn the contact breaker base plate clockwise in relation to the contact breaker moving plate and detach the moving plate from the base plate.
13. Remove the circlip from the end of the micrometer adjusting screw and unscrew the micrometer adjusting nut to release the vacuum timing control unit and coil spring from the distributor body.
14. Remove the micrometer adjusting nut ratchet spring from the distributor body.
15. Detach the two springs from the pillars on the cam and the action plate.
16. Remove the screw and withdraw the cam, and the centrifugal timing control weights from the distributor shaft and action plate.
17. Drive the pin out of the distributor driving dog to release the dog and the thrust washer from the distributor shaft.
18. Withdraw the shaft and action plate from the distributor body.
19. Withdraw the distance collar and steel washer(s) from the distributor shaft.
20. Remove the 'O' ring from the distributor body.

NOTE.–The Cooper 'S' distributor is not fitted with a suction advance device; therefore items 13 and 14 are not applicable.

Inspection

21. Check all components for wear and damage.
22. Inspect the distributor cap for cracks and signs of tracking.

Reassembling

23. Reverse the procedure in 2 to 20, noting:
    a. Lubricate the distributor shaft and bearing with one of the recommended engine lubricants. Add a few drops of this lubricant to the auto-advance mechanism.
    b. Lubricate the bearing surfaces of the contact breaker base plate and the moving plate with Ragosine molybdenized non-creep oil.
    c. Fit the cam so that the rotor arm driving slot on the top of the cam is uppermost and the large offset of the distributor shaft driving dog is to the left, when viewed from the base of the distributor.
    d. Lightly smear the cam and the outside of the contact breaker hollow pivot post with Retinax 'A' or equivalent grease.
    e. Adjust the contact breaker gap to the dimension given in **'ENGINE TUNING DATA'**.
    f. Rotate the micrometer adjustment nut until it is in the mid position of its adjustment.
24. Check the distributor performance, see **'ENGINE TUNING DATA'**.
25. Refit the distributor, Section B.1.

Section B.3

DISTRIBUTOR (Type 45D4)
– Remove and refit

NOTE.–This distributor is fitted to engines from 1974 on, see **'ENGINE TUNING DATA'** for the particular model application and tuning figures.

Removing

1. Follow the removing procedure given in Section B.1, with the following exception:
    a. Disconnect the low tension cable from the 'Lucar' connector.

Refitting

2. Follow the refitting procedure in Section B.1.

Section B.4

DISTRIBUTOR (Type 45D4)
– Overhaul

Dismantling

1. Remove the rotor arm and extract the felt pad from the cam.
2. Remove the two screws retaining the vacuum unit, tilt the unit to disengage the operating arm and remove the vacuum unit.
3. Push the low tension lead and grommet into the inside of the body.
4. Remove the base plate securing screw.
5. Lever the slotted segment of the base plate from its retaining groove and lift out the base plate assembly.
6. Drift out the parallel pin retaining the drive dog.
7. Remove the drive dog and thrust washer.
8. Remove the shaft complete with automatic advance mechanism, steel washer and nylon spacer.
   NOTE.–Do not dismantle the advance mechanism beyond removing the control springs, see item 12.
9. Push the moving contact spring inwards and detach the low tension connector from the spring loop.
10. Remove the screw to release the earth lead and capacitor.
11. Remove the securing screw and lift off the contact set.

Inspecting

12. If any of the moving parts or the cam are worn or damaged, renew the complete shaft assembly.
13. Check the fit of the shaft in its bearing, if the bearing allows excessive side play, renew the complete distributor.

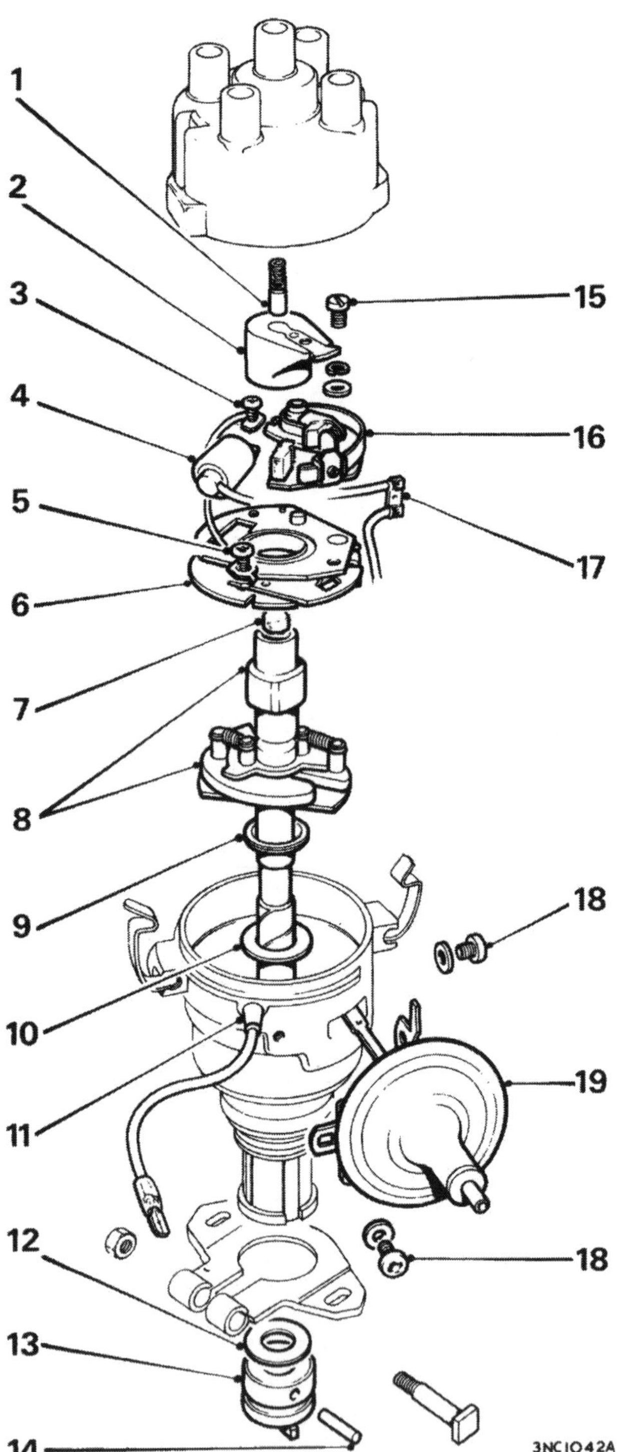

Fig. B.3
The components of the 45D4 distributor

1. Pick-up brush and spring
2. Rotor arm
3. Retaining screw – capacitor
4. Capacitor
5. Retaining screw – base plate
6. Base plate
7. Felt pad – cam
8. Cam spindle and automatic advance weight assembly
9. Spacer
10. Steel washer
11. Low tension lead
12. Thrust washer–drive dog
13. Drive dog
14. Retaining pin–drive dog
15. Retaining screw–contact set
16. Contact set
17. Low tension lead connector
18. Retaining screws–vacuum unit
19. Vacuum unit

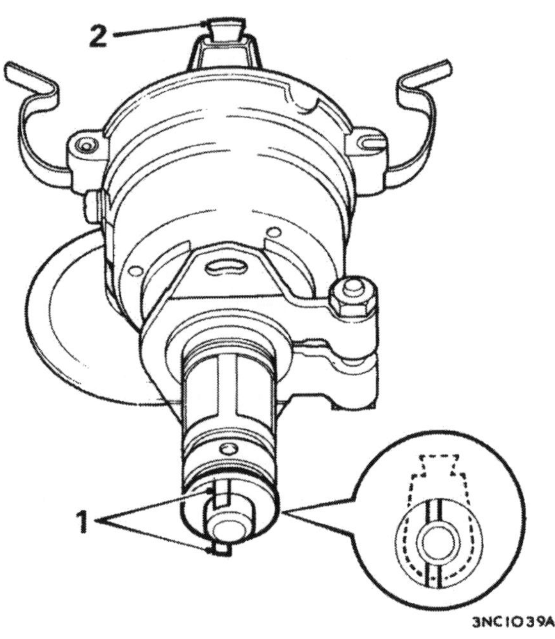

Fig. B.4
Fitting the drive dog to a new distributor, note the driving tongues (1) are parallel with the rotor arm electrode (2)

14. Check the base plate assembly; if the spring between the plates is damaged or if the plates do not move freely, renew the assembly.
15. Check the distributor cap for signs of tracking or cracks and check that the pick-up brush moves freely in its holder.
16. Check the rotor arm for damage, electrode security, and burning or tracking.

Reassembling

17. Reverse the procedure in 1 to 11, noting the following:
    a. Lubricate the contact pivot post with Retinax 'A' or equivalent grease.
    b. Ensure that the nylon spacer and steel washer are fitted on the shaft and lubricate the shaft with Rocol MP (Molypad).
    c. Fit the thrust washer with its raised pips towards the drive dog.
    d. Fit the drive dog so that the driving tongues are parallel with the rotor arm electrode and to the left of its centre line when the rotor arm points upwards as shown in Fig. 4.
    NOTE.–If a new shaft is fitted, it must be drilled with a $\frac{3}{16}$ in. (4.76 mm.) drill through the hole in the drive dog. During drilling, push the shaft from the cam end, pressing the drive dog and washer against the body shank.
    e. Secure the pin in the drive dog by ring punching the holes. If the shaft is new, tap the end of the drive dog with a hammer to flatten the washer pips and ensure the correct end-float.

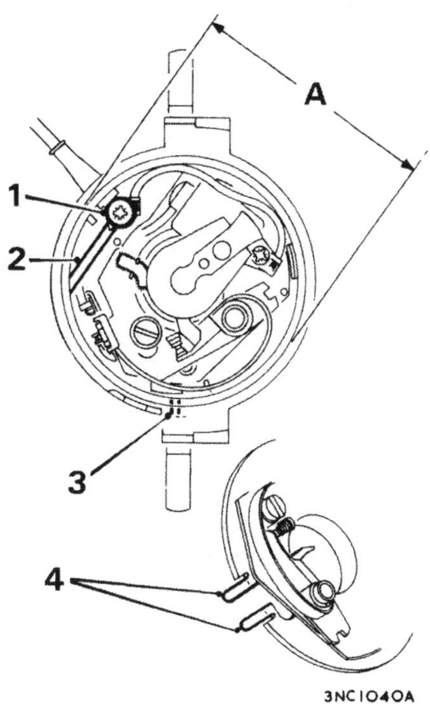

Fig. B.5

1. Base plate securing screw
2. Slot in base plate
3. Screw hole
4. Prongs

'A' = Diameter checking position

f. Position the base plate assembly so that the two downward pointing prongs will straddle the screw hole below the cap clip, see Fig. B.5. Press the base plate into the body until it engages the undercut.
g. Take an accurate measurement across the distributor cap register on the body at right angles to the slot in the base plate, Fig. B.5. Position the earth lead and fit and tighten the base plate securing screw. Re-measure across the cap register; if the measurement has not increased by at least 0.006 in. (9.15 mm.), renew the base plate assembly.
h. Check that the base plate prongs still straddle the screw hole and refit the vacuum unit, engaging the operating arm with the moving plate pin.
j. Set the contact points gap to 0.014 to 0.016 in. (0.36 to 0.40 mm.).

Section B.5

TIMING

NOTE.—The method of checking the 'static' timing given below will give a reasonable degree of accuracy, but to obtain optimum performance from the engine, the 'stroboscopic' timing should be checked using electronic tuning equipment.

Before commencing to check the ignition timing, ensure that the distributor contact points are set to the correct gap; clean and adjust if necessary, see **'MAINTENANCE'**.

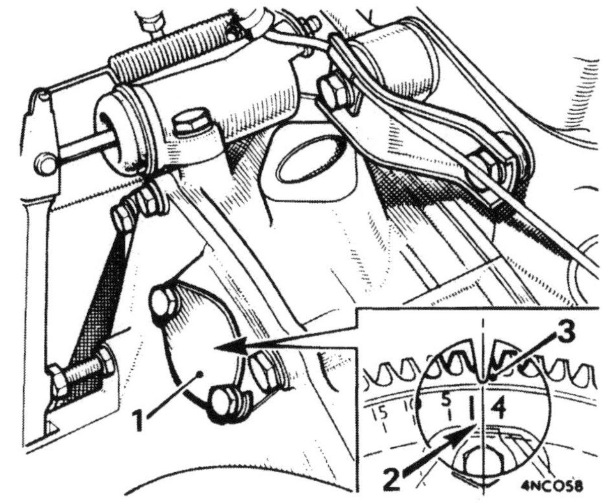

Fig. B.6
Remove the inspection plate (1) and use a mirror to see the timing marks (2) and pointer (3)

Checking – Static

1. Remove the cover or grommet from the timing inspection aperture in the clutch/converter cover. Use a mirror to see the timing marks on the flywheel/converter, see Fig. B.6 or Figs. **Ba.1/Ba.2** (Automatic). Rotate the crankshaft in the direction of engine rotation until the correct static timing mark (see **'ENGINE TUNING DATA'**) is opposite the timing mark pointer in the inspection aperture.
2. With the pointer opposite the correct timing mark and No. 1 piston on compression, the distributor rotor electrode should be pointing to No. 1 segment in the cap and the contact points just about to break.

Adjusting

3. **Distributor with adjuster nut:** Turn the knurled adjuster (Fig. B.2) towards **'A'** or **'R'** to correct the adjustment as follows:
   a. If the points are open, turn the adjuster towards **'R'** until they just close.
   b. If the points are closed, turn the adjuster towards **'A'** until they are just about to open.

Each graduation on the vernier scale is equal to approximately 5° of flywheel/converter movement and 55 clicks on the knurled adjuster.

4. **Cooper 'S' and engines with 45D4 type distributor:** Slacken the distributor clamp bolt and turn the distributor clockwise to advance and anti-clockwise to retard the ignition firing point. Tighten the clamp bolt and recheck the setting.

Checking points opening – electrical

5. Connect a 12-volt bulb between the low-tension terminal on the side of the distributor and a good earth point on the engine; switch on the ignition.

6. a. **Distributor with adjuster nut**: If the bulb lights, turn the knurled nut towards **'R'** until the light goes out and then back towards **'A'** until it just lights.
   If the bulb does not light, turn the nut towards **'A'** until it just lights.
   b. **45D4 distributor and Cooper 'S' type**: Slacken the distributor clamp bolt. If the bulb lights, turn the distributor body anti-clockwise (to retard) until the light goes out and then turn clockwise (to advance) until it just lights.
   If the bulb does not light, turn the distributor body clockwise (to advance) until the bulb just lights. Tighten the clamp bolt.
7. Refit the distributor cap.

Stroboscopic check

8. Disconnect the vacuum advance pipe from the distributor.
9. Paint the timing marks on the flywheel/converter with white paint.
10 Start and run the engine at the speed recommended in **'ENGINE TUNING DATA'** for the particular model application.
11. Adjust as necessary, see operations 3 or 4 as applicable to model and distributor type. Run the engine to above 2,000 r.p.m. and check that the automatic advance is working.
12. Connect up the vacuum advance pipe and refit the inspection plate/grommet.

SECTION Ba

THE IGNITION SYSTEM

The information in this Section refers specifically to engines fitted with automatic transmission and must be used in conjunction with Section B

† This operation must be followed by an exhaust emission check 

Fig. Ba.1
The timing mark location on early units. The T.D.C. position is indicated by the 1/4 marking on the converter, 5° and 10° B.T.D.C. marks are also provided. Shown inset, the hole (arrowed) for inserting a suitable tool to turn the converter

Fig. Ba.2
The timing mark location on later units. The converter is marked in degrees from 20° B.T.D.C. to 10° A.T.D.C., the 'O' mark indicates the T.D.C. position. Turn the converter with a suitable tool inserted through the hole (arrowed) in the cover

Section Ba.1

TIMING THE IGNITION 

1. Follow the instructions given in Section B.2 with the following exceptions.
2. To rotate the crankshaft, insert a screwdriver through the aperture (adjacent to the oil dipstick) on the converter housing or end cover, and turn the starter ring gear in the direction of engine rotation to the position described in Section B.2, item 5.
3. The timing marks can be seen on the converter (Figs. Ba.1 and Ba.2) after removal of the rubber grommet on the converter end cover.

SECTION C

THE COOLING SYSTEM

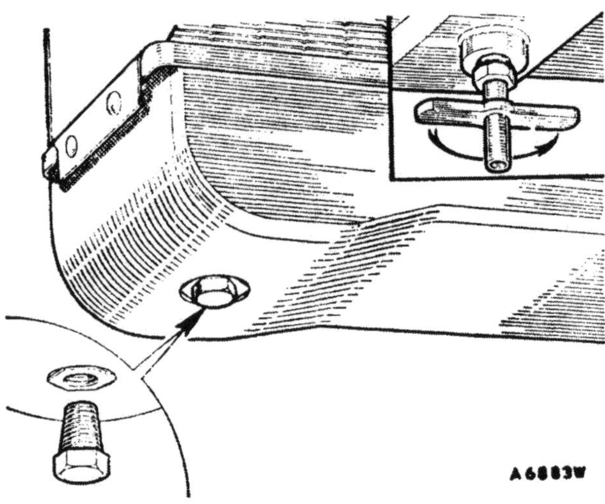

Fig. C.1
The radiator drain plug or tap

Section C.1

RADIATOR

The cooling system is under considerable pressure when hot.

Take off the cap slowly, turning it anti-clockwise until you feel the tongues engage the lobes on the end of the filler cam. Allow the pressure to fall before turning further and removing the cap.

Draining

1. Drain the system, using the taps (or plugs if fitted) at the base of the radiator and at the rear of the cylinder block.

Flushing

2. Flush the system periodically by running water through until it comes out clear. If the radiator is excessively furred up, remove it and flush through in the reverse direction (in through the bottom hose connection) using the reverse flush adaptor 18G 187 with a 1 in. (25 mm.) hose.

Filling

3. Close the drain tap(s) or refit the drain plug(s). Fill to the level indicator in the radiator top tank. Use only the recommended anti-freeze when necessary.

Removing

4. Remove the bonnet and drain the system.
5. Remove the cowling upper support bracket and the two bolts securing the lower support bracket to the engine mounting.

One-piece cowling

6. Disconnect the top hose and completely remove the lower.
7. Take out the four screws securing the radiator to the cowling and lift off the radiator and cowling.

TWO-PIECE COWLING

8. Disconnect the top and bottom hoses.
9. Take out the six screws securing the radiator to the cowling and remove the top half of the cowling.
10. Bend the lower hose to the outside of the cowling and lift out the radiator.

COOPER

Removing

11. Drain the system and remove the bonnet and grille.
12. Disconnect the top hose.
13. Detach the upper mounting bracket.
14. Remove the top half of the cowling.
15. Take out the two screws in the bottom half of the cowling securing the lower mounting bracket.
16. Disconnect the heater hose from the bottom radiator hose and the radiator hose.
17. Remove the fan and lift out the radiator.

Refitting

Reverse the removal instructions.

Section C.2

FAN BELT

Removing

1. Slacken the dynamo pivot and adjusting link bolts.
2. Lift the dynamo and run the belt off the crankshaft pulley.
3. Manoeuvre the belt between the fan blades and the right-hand top of the cowling.

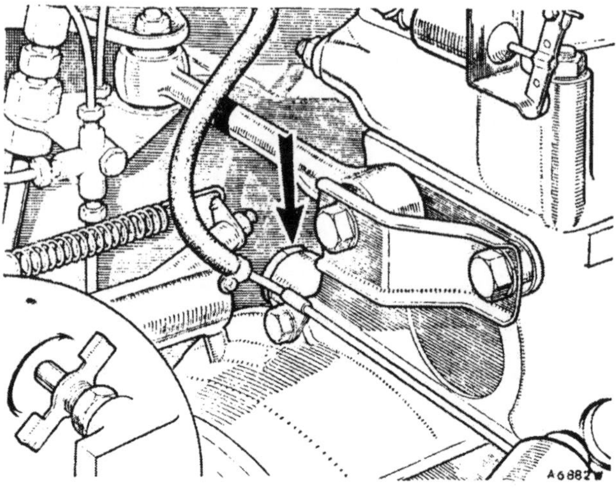

Fig. C.2
The cylinder block drain plug or tap

Fig. C.3
The filler cap of the sealed cooling system removed, showing the water level indicator

4. If the fan is 16-bladed, feed the belt between individual blade tips and the cut-out in the cowling flange.

Refitting

Reverse the removing instructions.

Adjusting

Adjust the tension by moving the dynamo so that the belt can be moved 1 in. (25 mm.) at the centre of its longest run.

Section C.3

WATER PUMP

Removing

1. Drain the system and remove the radiator.
2. Disconnect the hose from the water pump inlet connection and slacken the top clip of the by-pass hose.
3. Unscrew four set screws and lift off the pump.

Dismantling

4. Withdraw the bearing locating wire through the hole in the top of the pump body.
5. Tap the spindle backwards to extract the spindle and bearing assembly.
6. Pull the vane from the spindle and remove the seal.

Reassembling

Reverse the dismantling instructions.

Refitting

Reverse the removing instructions.

Section C.4

FROST PRECAUTIONS

Damage due to freezing can be prevented by draining the system when the car is not in use, or by the addition of anti-freeze. When a heater is fitted anti-freeze must be used as there is no provision for satisfactorily draining the heater matrix.

Use only the anti-freeze of the ethylene glycol type: Bluecol is recommended. Also, any anti-freeze to B.S.3151 or B.S.3152 is approved.

Quantity of anti-freeze required

Anti-freeze	Commences to freeze		Frozen solid		Amount of anti-freeze		
%	°C.	°F.	°C.	°F.	Pts.	US pts	Litres
25	−13	9	−26	−15	1½	1.8	.85
33⅓	−19	−2	−36	−33	2	2.5	1.18
50	−36	−33	−48	−53	3¼	3.75	1.8

Section C.5

THERMOSTAT

Removing

1. Drain the cooling system (Section C.1).
2. Disconnect the top hose and remove the cowling upper support bracket.
3. Remove the securing nuts and spring washers from the thermostat cover and the cover from its studs.
4. Remove the paper joint washer and lift out the thermostat.

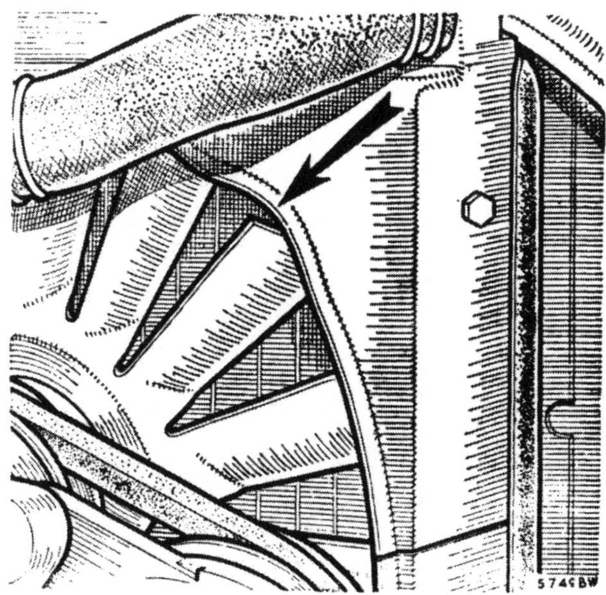

Fig. C.4
Turn the fan blades to the position indicated where the fan belt can be extracted through the recess provided in the radiator cowling

Testing

5. Test the thermostat opening temperature by immersing it in water and raising the temperature of the water to the thermostat opening temperature as given under **'GENERAL DATA'**. If the thermostat valve fails to open or sticks in the fully open position, fit a new one; do not attempt to repair it.

Refitting

6. Installation of the thermostat assembly is the reverse of the removal procedure. Fit a new joint washer if the existing one is damaged.
7. A wax-element-type thermostat together with a modified thermostat water outlet cover is fitted to later vehicles.
8. When refitting this type of thermostat it is essential that the threaded stem faces upwards.

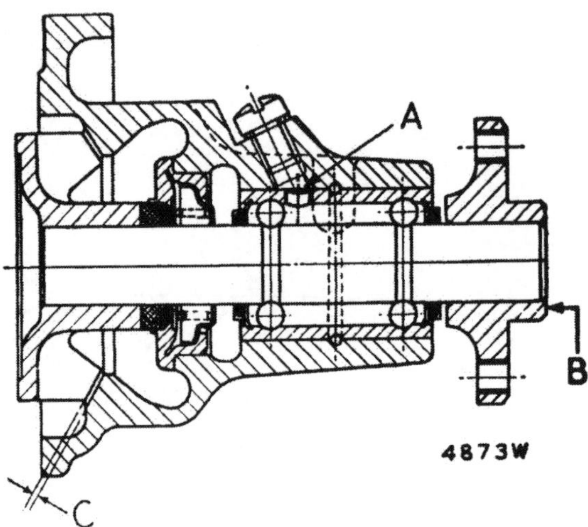

Fig. C.5
A section through the water pump showing the location of the components. When assembled, the hole (A) in the bearing must coincide with the lubricating hole in the water pump and the face of the hub (B) must be flush with the end of the spindle. The clearance at (C) must be .020 to .030 in. (.508 to .762 mm.)

SECTION D

THE FUEL SYSTEM

† These operations must be followed by an exhaust emission check 

Fig. D.1
The fuel tank located on the left-hand side of the luggage compartment

Section D.1

FUEL TANK

Removing

1. Unscrew the tank drain plug (when fitted) approximately three turns, otherwise, disconnect the flexible hose from the pump and drain the tank.
2. Take off the filler cap, disconnect the lead from the gauge unit and unscrew the bolt from the securing strap. Release the vent pipe clip and remove the tank from the luggage compartment, at the same time drawing the fuel and vent pipes through the floor. Note the locating plate fitted below the tank.

VAN, PICK-UP, AND LATER TRAVELLER

3. Remove the six flange screws and spacers and lower the tank.

TRAVELLER (EARLY MODELS)

4. Remove the trim liner from the body above the tank, and the metal finishers from the rear seat squab support.
5. Lift out the luggage platform, disconnect the battery and ease the trim panel away from the tank.
6. Drain the tank and disconnect the drain and fuel delivery pipes. Take off the filler cap.
7. Disconnect the fuel gauge lead and pull the breather pipe from the tank.
8. Unscrew the support bracket screws and lift the tank from the vehicle.

Refitting

SALOON

9. Reverse the removal instructions. Note that the vent pipe passes through the same hole as the wiring harness. The seal between the drain pipe housing and the body must be watertight. Refit the locating strip before the strap is tightened.

VAN, PICK-UP, AND TRAVELLER

Reverse the removal instructions.

Section D.2

TANK GAUGE UNIT

Removing

1. Disconnect the battery earth cable and the electrical connection from the fuel gauge tank unit.
2. Ensure that the fuel level in the tank is below that of the fuel gauge unit aperture.
3. Remove the six securing screws to remove the unit. On later models remove the tank unit locking ring with Service tool 18G 1001 and carefully remove the unit from the tank.

Refitting

4. When refitting the gauge unit, use a new joint washer coated with a suitable sealing compound.
5. On later models fit a new rubber sealing ring and tighten the unit locking ring with the Service tool.

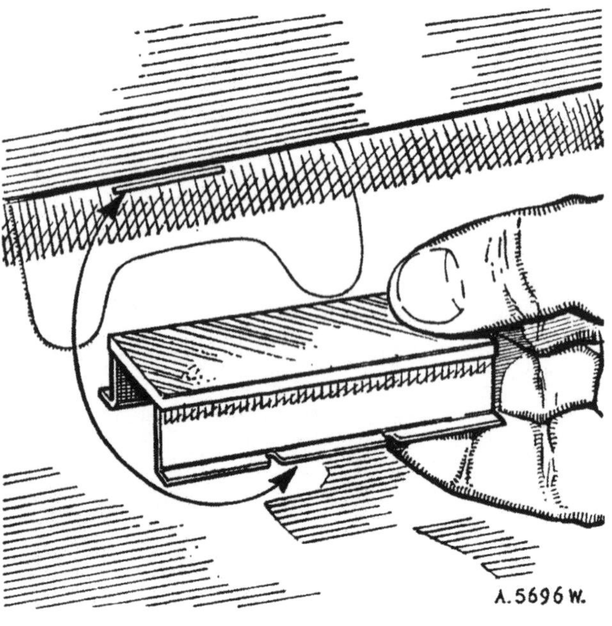

Fig. D.2
The tongue of the fuel tank locating plate must be secured in the slot in the luggage compartment floor

Section D.3

FUEL PUMP–TYPE PD

Apart from cleaning the filter and contact points, no servicing is possible; if the pump fails a new one must be fitted.

Removing

1. Disconnect the leads, slacken the clamp screws, and pull off the fuel pipes. Unscrew the bracket screws and remove the pump and bracket.

CLEANING THE FILTER

2. Remove the pump and take off the bottom cover plate. Extract the filter and clean it with a brush and petrol (fuel). Fit a new cover gasket.

POINTS

3. Lift off the top cover and clean the points by drawing a piece of clean paper between them.
4. Check that the points make good contact and that the gap between the end of the upper blade and its stop face is not less than .015 in. (.4 mm.).

Refitting

5. Reverse the removing instructions.

Fig. D.3
The PD-type fuel pump

Section D.4

FUEL PUMP–TYPE SP AND AUF 201

The pump is mounted on the lower left-hand flange of the rear sub-frame.

Removing

1. Disconnect the battery, the pump leads, and both hoses.
2. Unscrew the nut securing the pump clamp to the bracket and lift off the pump and clamp.

Refitting

3. Reverse the removing instructions.

Dismantling

4. Screw the inlet nozzle from the pump body and withdraw the filter and fibre washer.
5. Unscrew the six screws securing the coil housing to the body, separate the housing, diaphragm, and body.
6. Withdraw the retainer screw, retainer, and valves.
7. Unscrew the armature from the inner rocker trunnion and remove the brass rollers, feed spring and impact washer from the armature.
8. Remove the terminal nut, Lucar connector and washer from the terminal screw and take off the bakelite cap.
9. Unscrew the spring blade securing screw and disconnect the coil lead. Remove the terminal screw retaining nut; cut the lead washer.
10. Unscrew the two pedestal retaining screws and disconnect the braided copper earth lead.
11. Remove the remaining coil lead from the terminal screw and the screw from the pedestal.
12. Push the rocker pivot pin from the pedestal and remove the rocker assembly. Do not remove the toggle spring.

Inspecting

13. Clean and examine all parts.
14. Check the feed spring; test figures are given in **'GENERAL DATA'**.
15. Check the condition of the valves and springs.
16. If the points are pitted or burnt, fit a new rocker assembly.

Assembling

17. Refit the valves and retainer.
18. Screw the nozzle, with a new washer, into the body.
19. Refit the rocker assembly.
20. Refit the terminal screw, spring washer, short coil lead, new lead washer and nut.
21. Connect the braided copper earth lead to the nearest pedestal screw with the tag next to the head of the screw; screw the pedestal to the coil housing.
22. Refit the remaining coil lead and the spring blade. The blade must bear against the small rib on the top face of the pedestal, and the tag of the solenoid lead must be on top of the blade.
23. Adjust the spring blade so that the points are making good contact and the points on the blade wipe over the centre line of the other points when the rocker arm is moved up and down. Tighten the spring blade screw.

THE AUF 201 and SP FUEL PUMP COMPONENTS

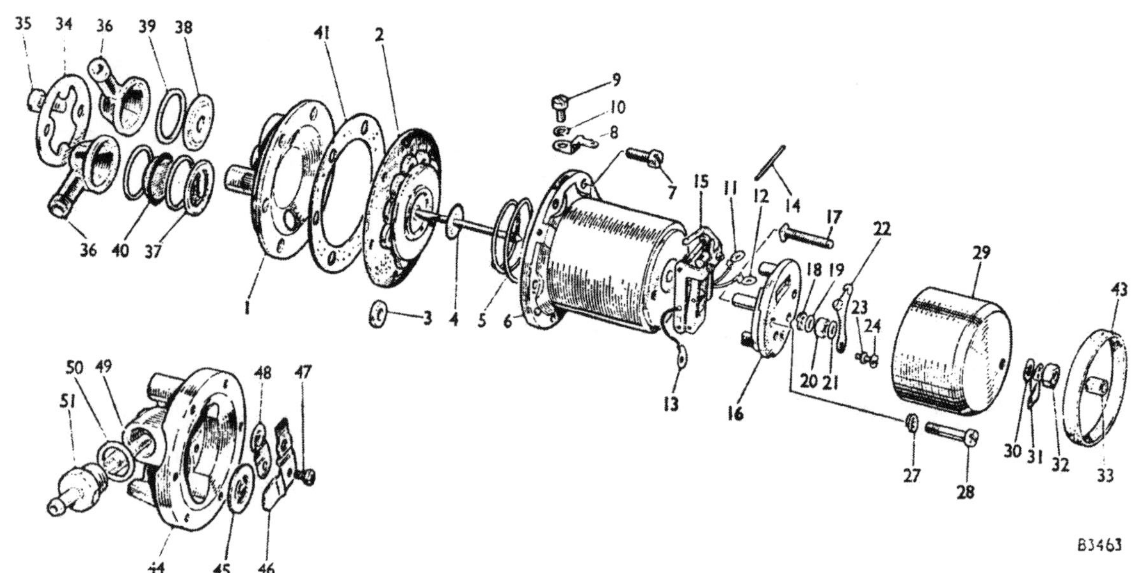

No.	Description	No.	Description	No.	Description	
1.	Pump body (AUF 201 only).	17.	Terminal stud.	35.	Set screw.	
2.	Diaphragm and spindle assembly.	18.	Spring washer.	36.	Inlet and outlet nozzles.	
3.	Armature centralizing roller.	19.	Lead washer.	37.	Inlet valve.	AUF 201 only. (35–40)
4.	Impact washer.	20.	Terminal nut.	38.	Outlet valve.	
5.	Armature spring.	21.	End-cover seal washer.	39.	Sealing washer.	
6.	Coil housing.	22.	Contact blade.	40.	Filter.	
7.	Set screw.	23.	Washer.	41.	Gasket.	
8.	Earth connector.	24.	Contact blade screw.	43.	Sealing band.	
9.	Set screw.	27.	Spring washer.	44.	Pump body.	
10.	Spring washer.	28.	Screw.	45.	Outlet valve.	
11.	Terminal tag.	29.	End-cover.	46.	Valve retainer.	
12.	Terminal tag.	30.	Shakeproof washer.	47.	Screw.	SP type only. (43–51)
13.	Earth tag.	31.	Connector.	48.	Inlet valve.	
14.	Rocker pivot arm.	32.	Nut.	49.	Filter.	
15.	Rocker mechanism.	33.	Insulating sleeve.	50.	Washer.	
16.	Pedestal.	34.	Clamp plate (AUF 201 only).	51.	Inlet nozzle.	

24. The free end of the spring blade must be deflected away from the rib on the pedestal so that a gap exists between the under-side of the blade and the rib.
25. Refit the impact washer and the spring to the armature spindle, pass the spindle through the centre of the coil housing and screw it into the trunnion on the inner rocker.
26. Screw the spindle into the trunnion until a steady pressure on the armature just fails to cause the outer rocker to snap over. Then unscrew the spindle seven holes (for body and coil housing screws).
27. Position the rollers, fit the body to the coil housing and tighten the securing screws.
28. Refit the bakelite cap, spring washers, Lucar connector, nut and terminal screws.
29. Refit the rubber sleeve, and the dust excluders to the inlet and outlet connections.

AUF 201 type pump

This type of pump is fitted to later vehicles. The instructions given for the SP pump apply, with the exception of items, 4, 6, and 18; for item 4 substitute instructions 30 and 31.

30. Unscrew the two screws securing the spring clamp plate which holds the inlet and outlet nozzles. Remove the nozzles, filter and valve assemblies, being careful to note their correct positions for replacement.

Rocker finger settings (AUF 201)

31. After reassembly the spring blade of the contacts should rest against the ridge of the pedestal mounting when the outer rocker is pressed onto the coil housing and a gap of .030 in. (.76 mm.) should exist between the points. When the outer rocker is released the spring blade should be deflected away from the ridge. If necessary, set the blade and/or rocker fingers to achieve this position.

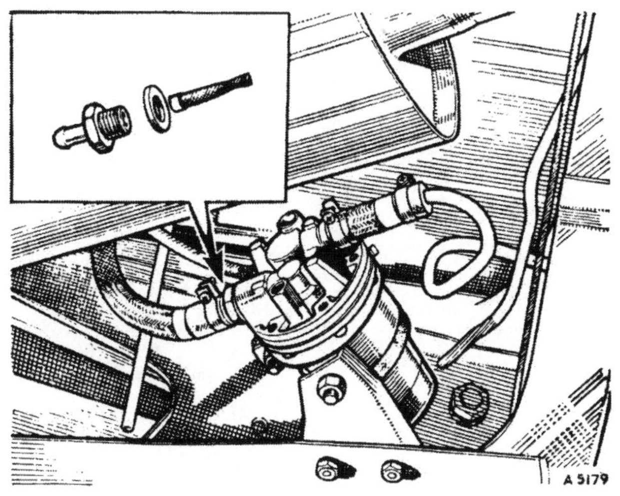

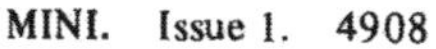

Fig. D.4
The SP-type fuel pump

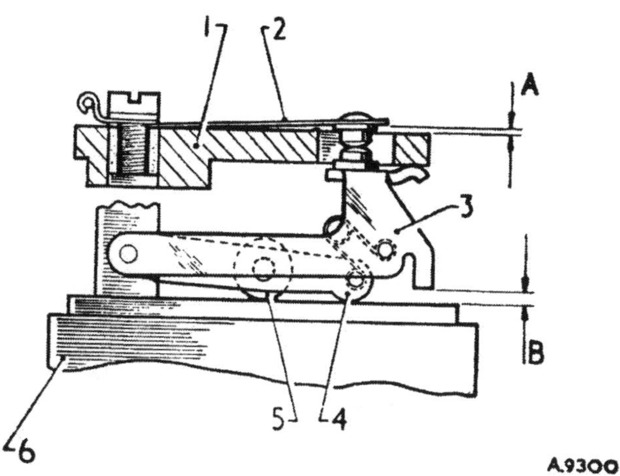

Fig. D.5
The rocker finger settings

A. .035 in.±.005 in. (.89 mm.±.12 mm.).
B. .070 in.±.005 in. (1.78 mm.±.12 mm.).

1. Pedestal.
2. Contact blade.
3. Outer rocker.
4. Inner rocker.
5. Trunnion.
6. Coil housing.

Section D.5

FUEL PUMP TESTING

1. Fit the SP adaptor set to a test rig, and a cut-away cap to the pump. Connect the pump to a 12-volt battery with a voltmeter and resistance in circuit.

Priming

2. The pump should prime from dry in 10 to 15 seconds and the paraffin (kerosene) should rise in the glass container until it runs from the overflow drain pipe. If the level does not rise above the small hole in the drain pipe, the pump is faulty. Initial air bubbles should cease after a minute or two; if they do not, there is an air leak on the suction side.

Valves

3. Run the pump for about 10 minutes and turn off the fuel tap. If the pump beats within 12 seconds, the inlet valve is not seating correctly.

Minimum delivery

4. Partly open the fuel tap and gradually depress the spring blade to reduce the stroke. The pump should continue working with increasing frequency until it stops owing to the lack of a gap between the points.

Reduced voltage

5. The pump should work satisfactorily at a minimum of 9.5 volts.

THE CARBURETTER COMPONENTS

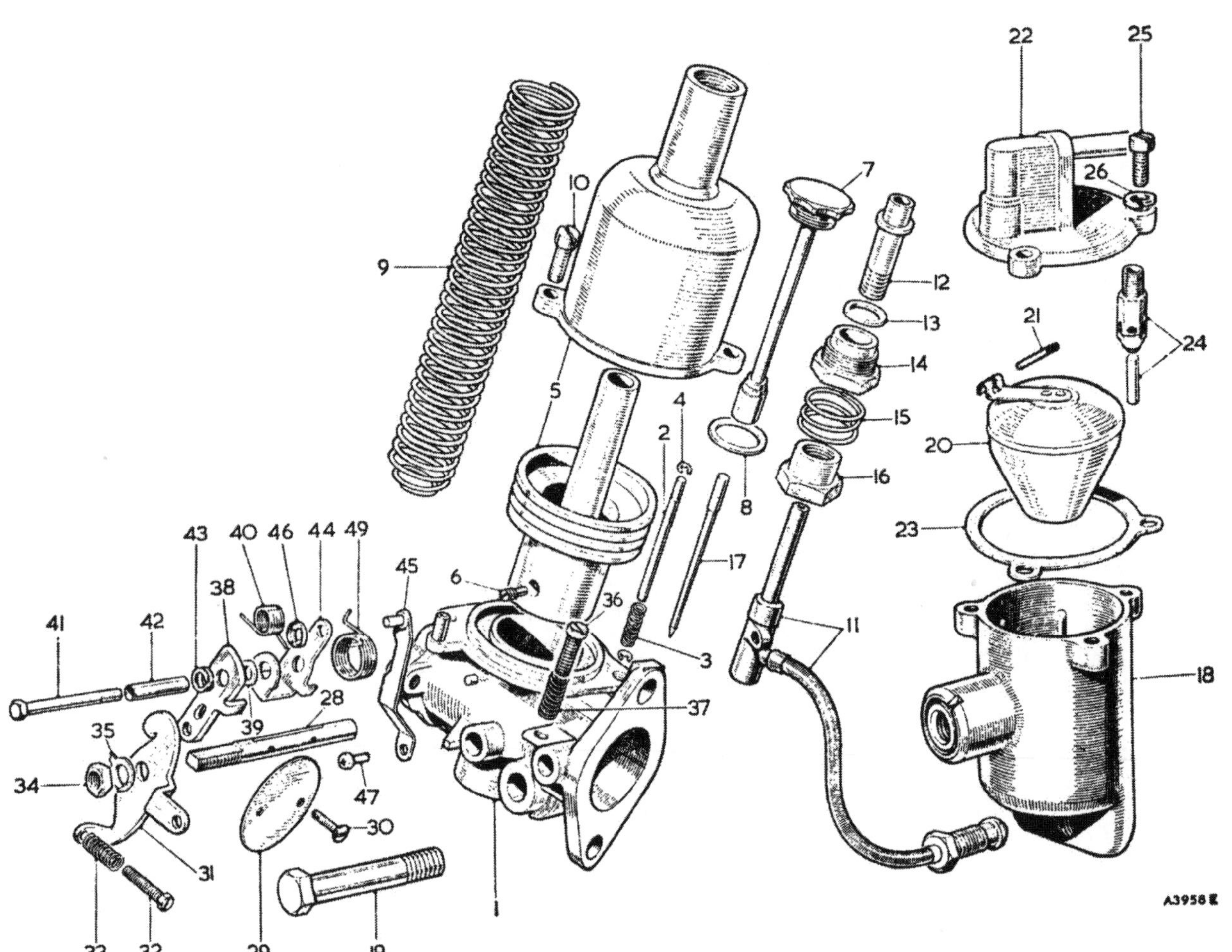

No.	Description	No.	Description	No.	Description
1.	Body.	17.	Jet needle.	34.	Throttle spindle nut.
2.	Piston lifting pin.	18.	Float-chamber body.	35.	Tab washer for nut.
3.	Spring for pin.	19.	Float-chamber securing bolt.	36.	Idling stop screw.
4.	Circlip for pin.	20.	Float and lever assembly.	37.	Spring for stop screw.
5.	Suction chamber and piston assembly.	21.	Lever hinge pin.	38.	Cam lever.
6.	Needle locking screw.	22.	Float-chamber lid assembly.	39.	Washer.
7.	Piston damper assembly.	23.	Washer for lid.	40.	Cam lever spring.
8.	Washer for damper cap (fibre).	24.	Needle and seat assembly.	41.	Cam lever pivot bolt.
9.	Piston spring.	25.	Screw–float-chamber lid to body.	42.	Pivot bolt tube.
10.	Screw–suction chamber to body.	26.	Spring washer.	43.	Spring washer.
11.	Jet assembly.	28.	Throttle spindle.	44.	Pick-up lever assembly.
12.	Jet bearing.	29.	Throttle disc.	45.	Jet link.
13.	Washer for jet bearing (brass).	30.	Screw–throttle disc.	46.	Jet link retaining clip.
14.	Lock screw for jet bearing.	31.	Throttle lever.	47.	Jet link securing screw.
15.	Lock spring	32.	Cam stop screw.	49.	Spring for pick-up lever.
16.	Jet adjusting screw.	33.	Spring for stop screw.		

Section D.6

CARBURETTERS 

IMPORTANT.–The instructions given in this section for adjusting, dismantling and reassembling the carburetters applies only to **cars not fitted with exhaust emission control equipment.** Carburetters fitted to **cars with exhaust emission control equipment** must be tuned and serviced in accordance with the instructions given in **Workshop Manual Supplement AKD 4957 A.**

Dismantling

1. Unscrew the plug and withdraw the piston damper.
2. Take out the two suction chamber securing screws, lift off the suction chamber and withdraw the piston and jet needle.
3. Disconnect the rod from the bottom of the jet, and the nylon feed tube from the base of the float-chamber; pull out the jet and tube.
4. Unscrew and remove the jet adjusting nut and the spring.
5. Unscrew the jet bearing locking nut.
6. Remove the float-chamber securing bolt and the float-chamber.
7. Take out three screws and lift off the top of the float-chamber; withdraw the float.
8. Screw out the needle valve assembly.

Inspecting

9. Note the condition of the needle valve and seating; fit a new needle and seating if necessary.
10. If the jet needle is bent or otherwise damaged, withdraw the locking screw in the piston and fit a new needle. Push the needle in until the shoulder is flush with the lower face of the piston.
11. Clean and dry the piston assembly; lubricate the piston rod only with thin oil.

Reassembling

Reverse the dismantling instructions and centre the jet.

Jet centring

12. Screw the jet adjusting nut up as far as possible, lift the piston with the lifting pin and allow it to drop; it should drop freely onto the bridge with a soft metallic click. Repeat with the adjusting nut screwed fully down. If the piston does not fall freely in either of the tests, proceed as follows.
13. Carry out instructions 3 and 4 above.
14. Refit the adjusting nut without the spring and screw it up as far as possible.
15. Slacken the jet bearing lock nut until the bearing can be turned with the fingers.
16. Remove the piston damper and press the piston down onto the bridge. Tighten the lock nut.

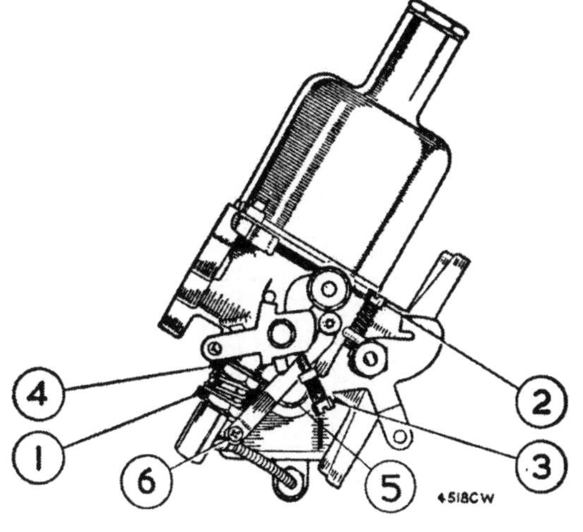

Fig. D.6
The carburetter adjusting screws

1. Jet adjusting nut.
2. Throttle adjusting screw.
3. Fast-idle adjustment screw.
4. Jet locking nut.
5. Float-chamber bolt.
6. Jet link securing screw.

17. Lift the piston and note whether it falls freely; fully lower the adjusting nut and check again. If the second check produces a sharper click than the first, repeat the centring.
18. Refit the parts that have been removed, pour thin oil into the hollow rod of the piston damper to within .5 in. (12.7 mm.) of the top of the rod.

Adjustments

SLOW RUNNING

19. Turn the throttle adjusting screw as necessary.

MIXTURE.

20. Run the engine until it is at its normal temperature.
21. Disconnect the choke cable.
22. Unscrew the throttle adjusting screw until the throttle is fully closed and then screw it up about one turn.
23. Hold the jet up against the adjusting nut and then turn the nut until the engine runs smoothly without missing or hunting.
24. Raise the piston about $\frac{1}{32}$ in. (1 mm.). If there is a momentary increase in speed the adjustment is correct; if the engine stops the mixture is too weak; and if it continues to increase even when the piston is raised ¼ in. (7 mm.) the mixture is too rich.
25. Adjust the idling speed as required.
26. Set the fast idling screw so that there is a clearance of about $\frac{1}{64}$ in. (.4 mm.) between the cam and the end of the screw when the engine is warm and idling with closed throttle. Alteration may be needed after the mixture has been adjusted. Re-connect the choke cable.

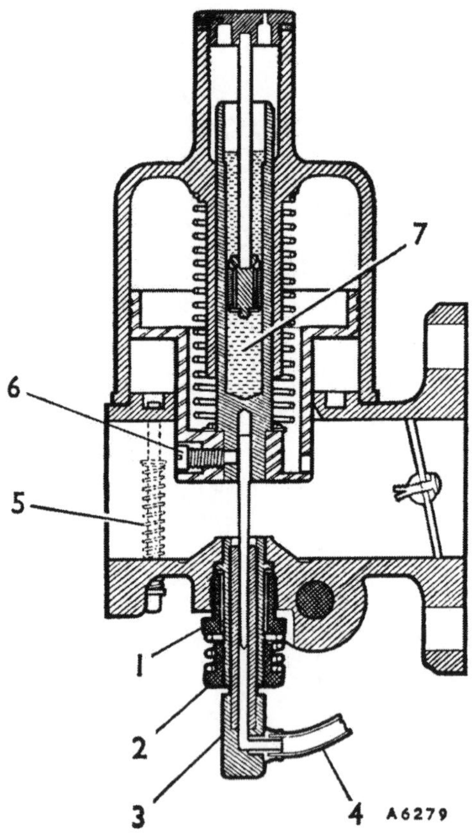

Fig. D.7
A section through the carburetter showing:

1. Jet locking nut.
2. Jet adjusting nut.
3. Jet head.
4. Nylon fuel pipe.
5. Piston lifting pin.
6. Needle securing screw.
7. Piston damper oil well.

27. Fuel starvation or flooding may be caused by an incorrect float level. To check the level, insert a $\frac{5}{16}$ in. (8 mm.) bar between the lip of the float-chamber and the hinged lever. Adjust by bending the lever where the curved portion meets the shank. On carburetters fitted with a nylon float use a test bar of $\frac{1}{8}$ in. (3.18 mm.) diameter.

Flooding

This may be caused by an incorrect float level or by a faulty needle valve.

28. Remove, clean, and inspect the needle valve and seating; fit a new assembly if necessary.
29. Check the float level.

COOPER
SLOW-RUNNING

30. As instruction 19 but turn both screws an equal amount. Listen to the hiss at the carburetter intake and adjust the screws until the intensity of the hiss at each is the same.

MIXTURE

31. Carry out instructions 20 to 23 on each carburetter moving both nuts the same number of turns.
32. Raise the piston on the left-hand carburetter about $\frac{1}{32}$ in. (.8 mm.). If the engine speed increases the mixture is too rich; if the engine speed immediately decreases the mixture is too weak; if the engine speed momentarily increases very slightly the mixture is correct.
33. Repeat 32 on the right-hand carburetter.
34. Re-adjust the slow-running speed as necessary.

LINKAGE ADJUSTMENT, FIG. D.8

35. Disconnect the choke cable. With the throttle shaft levers free on the shaft, put a .012 in. (.30 mm.) feeler between the shaft stop and the choke inter-connecting spindle. Move each throttle lever downwards until the pin rests lightly on the lower arm of the fork in the carburetter throttle lever. Tighten the clamp of the throttle shaft lever. When both carburetters are adjusted the pins on the throttle levers should then have the correct clearance in the forks. Re-connect the choke cable and ensure that the jet heads return against the jet adjusting nuts when the choke knob is pushed fully in. Adjust the fast idling screws.

Section D.7

AIR CLEANER 

Renew the filter element at the recommended periods.

Removing

1. Unscrew the wing nut at the top of the cleaner, remove the cover and extract the element.

Refitting

2. Reverse the removal procedure.

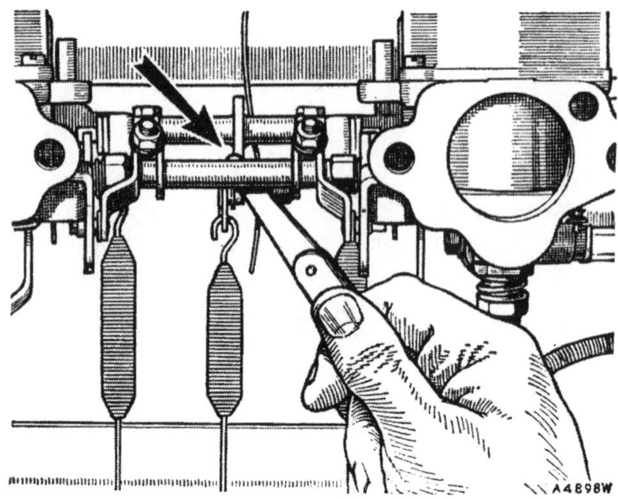

Fig. D.8
The feeler between the throttle shaft stop and the choke interconnecting spindle

COOPER
Gauze filters
Removing
3. Detach the breather hose and remove the four retaining screws to remove the air cleaners.

CLEANING
4. Wash the gauzes thoroughly in fuel, dry and re-oil with engine oil.

REFITTING
5. Reverse the removal procedure, fitting new joint washers if necessary.

COOPER
Dry element filter
Renew the filter elements at the recommended periods.

REMOVING
6. Remove the two wing nuts and washers and remove the cover, lift out the paper elements and wipe the inside of the container to remove all dust deposit. The container may also be removed if required by careful manoeuvring over the carburetters, after releasing the throttle lever return spring and the breather hose (if fitted).

REFITTING
7. Reverse the removal procedure, ensuring that the air manifold rubber seals are correctly positioned if the container has been removed.

Section D.8

FUEL PUMP
(Moke)

The fuel pump is located in the pannier of the left-hand side-member (Fig. D.9).

Removing
1. Disconnect the battery.
2. Remove the pannier side cover (two quick-release fasteners).
3. Disconnect the lead from the pump terminal.
4. Slacken the clips and pull the hose from the delivery pipe, and the suction hose from the pump.
5. Remove two nuts to release the mounting bracket.

Dismantling and assembling
6. Follow the instructions in Section D.4.

Refitting
7. Reverse the removing instructions, tighten all clips, and secure the earth lead with one of the mounting bracket nuts.

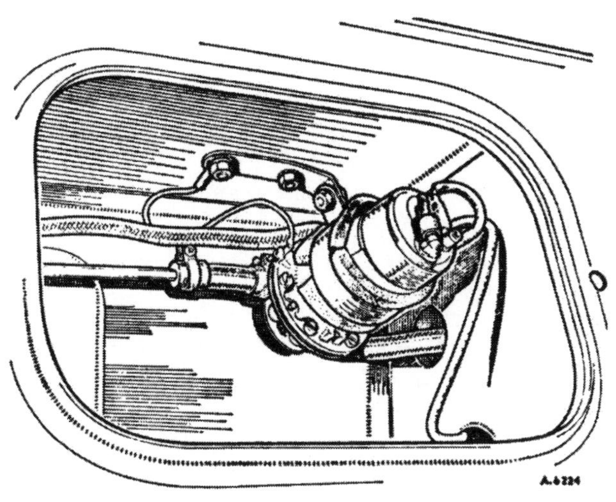

Fig. D.9
The fuel pump location in the left-hand side-member

Section D.9

FUEL TANK
(Moke)

The fuel tank is located in the left-hand side-member. Remove the tank for access to the gauge unit.

Removing
1. Remove the forward pannier side cover and disconnect the lead from the fuel gauge unit terminal.
2. Drain the fuel tank (see Fig. D.10).
3. Disconnect the suction hose from the fuel pump.
4. Remove the bottom cover-plate from the side-member.
5. Extract the tank-retaining screw from the top face of the side-member.
6. Remove the support bracket and lower the tank.

Refitting
7. Reverse the removal instructions.

Section D.10

TWIN FUEL TANKS
(Cooper 'S')

Removing
BOTH TANKS
1. Remove the trimmed floorboard.
2. Disconnect the battery earth cable.
3. Remove the spare wheel.
4. Remove the fuel filler caps.
5. Unscrew the drain plug on the left-hand tank approximately three turns and allow the fuel to drain from both tanks.

LEFT-HAND TANK

6. Disconnect the electrical connections from the tank gauge unit.
7. Remove the tank strap securing bolt.
8. Disconnect the flexible fuel pipe and the vent pipe from the tank.
9. Ease the tank to the centre of the luggage compartment and withdraw it.

RIGHT-HAND TANK

10. Disconnect and remove the battery.
11. Carry out instruction 7 and disconnect the flexible hose from the left-hand tank.
12. Move the tank slightly from its mountings, taking care not to damage the flexible fuel pipes. The tank will still retain a small amount of fuel which should be drained off into a small container when the flexible fuel pipe is disconnected.
13. Disconnect the flexible fuel pipe.
14. Release the vent pipe from the tank and withdraw the tank from the luggage compartment.

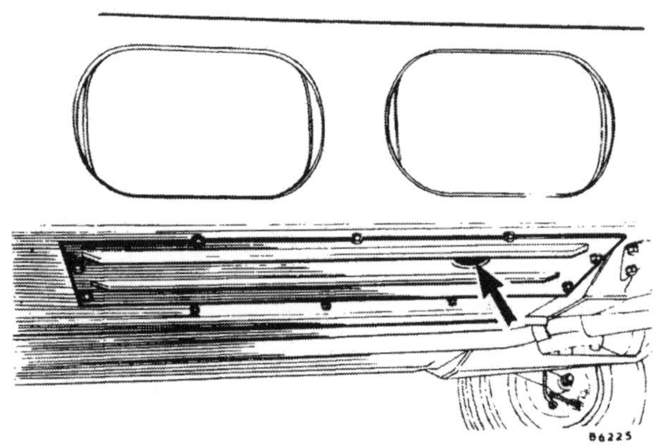

Fig. D.10
The fuel tank drain plug access

Refitting

15. Reverse the removal instructions.
16. Ensure that the seal around the drain plug housing is watertight.

SECTION Da

THE FUEL SYSTEM

The information in this Section refers specifically to engines fitted with automatic transmission and must be used in conjunction with Section D

† These operations must be followed by an exhaust emission check 

Section Da.1

AIR CLEANER 

Cars equipped with automatic transmission are fitted with a larger paper-element-type air cleaner.

Removing

1. Unscrew the wing nuts.
2. Disconnect the breather hose.
3. Lift the air cleaner from the carburetter.

Element replacement

4. Remove the cover from the container and lift out the paper element.
5. Wipe all dust deposit from inside the container.
6. Fit the new element and refit the cover.

Refitting

7. Reverse the removal procedure.

NOTE.–The air cleaner intake should be positioned adjacent to the exhaust manifold during winter operating conditions in order that the possibility of carburetter icing is reduced to the minimum. It is advisable to move the intake away from the manifold in warmer weather.

Section Da.2

 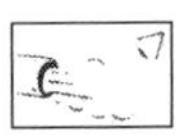

CARBURETTER

(Type HS4)

Description

The HS4 carburetter is fitted to an engine equipped with automatic transmission.

The dismantling and reassembling of the carburetter is as described for the HS2 type in Section D.6.

IMPORTANT.–The instructions given in this section for adjusting, dismantling and reassembling the carburetters applies only to **cars not fitted with exhaust emission control equipment**. Carburetters fitted to **cars with exhaust emission control equipment** must be tuned and serviced in accordance with the instructions given in **Workshop Manual Supplement AKD 4957 A.**

Removing

1. Remove the air cleaner as detailed in Section Da.1.
2. Disconnect the mixture and throttle control cables, the suction advance pipe, and the fuel delivery hose from the carburetter.
3. Disconnect the governor control rod fork end from the throttle lever.

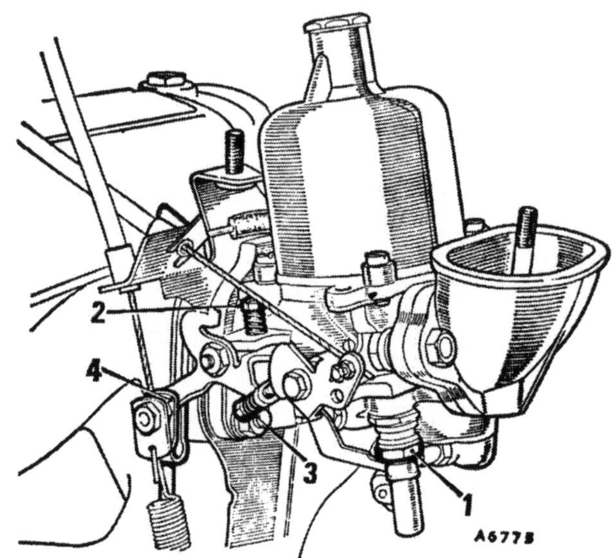

Fig. Da.1
The HS4 carburetter

1. Jet adjusting nut.
2. Throttle adjusting screw.
3. Fast idle adjusting screw.
4. Governor control rod.

4. Remove the securing nuts and spring washers and lift off the carburetter and the cable abutment plate.

Refitting

5. Reverse the removal instructions, fitting new joint washers between the manifold face and the abutment plate and carburetter flange if any have been damaged during removal.

Adjustments

The method of adjusting the jet and slow running is as described in Section D.6 with the following exceptions.

6. Connect a tachometer.
7. Select 'N' on the gear lever quadrant and apply the hand brake.
8. Run the engine until it attains its normal running temperature and adjust the jet as described in Section D.6.
9. With the carburetter correctly tuned, adjust the throttle adjusting screw 2 (Fig. Da.1) until a maximum idling speed of 650 r.p.m. is obtained.
10. Pull out the choke control to the maximum fast idle position. Check, and adjust if necessary, the fast idle adjustment screw 3 (Fig. Da.1), to obtain a maximum fast idle speed of 1,050 r.p.m. Push in the choke control and re-check the idling speed.
11. Adjust the governor control rod as detailed in Section Fa.2.

SECTION Db

THE FUEL SYSTEM

The information contained in this Section refers specifically to new or modified components fitted to the Mini range coincident with the introduction of NEGATIVE earth electrical systems and must be used in conjunction with Sections D and Da.

Section Db.1

MECHANICAL FUEL PUMP (Type AUF 705)

General description and operation

The pump is mounted on the rear left-hand side of the crankcase and is driven from the camshaft. The cam lobe actuates the rocker lever which moves the diaphragm downwards. Fuel is drawn in through the filter, down past the inlet valve flap, and into the diaphragm chamber. When the cam lobe passes the rocker lever the diaphragm moves upwards under the influence of the spring and forces fuel through the outlet valve.

When the float needle valve closes, the diaphragm stays in the down position and the rocker arm idles until the pressure drops.

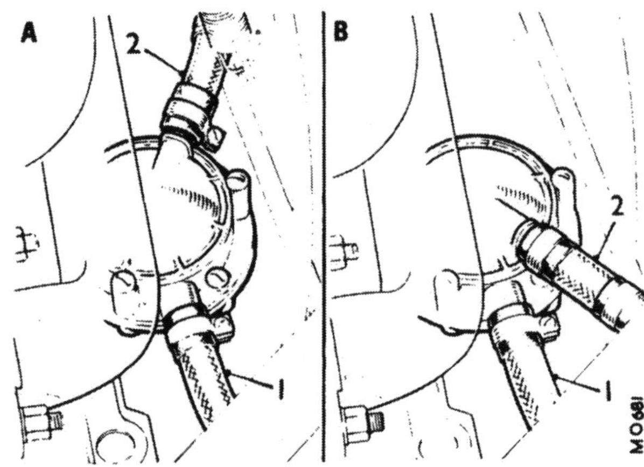

Fig. Db.1
The fuel pump location

A. 1275 GT. B. 850/1000 and Clubman.
1. Inlet connection. 2. Outlet connection.

Maintenance

FILTER CLEANING

1. Clean the outside of the pump and mark the cover and body for alignment when refitting (see Fig. Db.1 for correct positions of the inlet and outlet connections).
2. Remove the outlet cover, sealing washer, and filter.
3. Clean any sediment from the filter chamber and clean the filter (air jet or fuel).
4. Fit a new joint washer (if necessary), refit the outlet cover and tighten the screws evenly.

Fault diagnosis

5. To check the fuel flow, disconnect the fuel hose at the carburetter and put the end into a container. Disconnect the (–) connection from the ignition coil and turn the crankshaft by operating the starter.
   a. Flow normal–examine float needle valve and seating.
   b. Flow normal, but falls off rapidly–check fuel tank venting. Other causes: choked pump or tank filter.
   c. Air bubbles emerge–air leak on suction side.
   d. No flow–dismantle pump, examine valves and diaphragm.

DO NOT PASS COMPRESSED AIR THROUGH THE PUMP.

Removing

6. Disconnect the battery and remove the air cleaner for access.
7. Disconnect and remove the fuel pump to carburetter feed pipe, disconnect the fuel pump feed pipe.
8. Remove the pump securing nuts and partially pull the pump from the engine. Use a screwdriver and separate the insulating block from the pump; pull out the pump followed by the insulating block.
   The total thickness of the insulating block with its two joint washers must not be altered.

Dismantling

REFER TO FIG. Db.2

9. Mark the outlet cover and the upper and lower bodies for alignment (arrowed).
10. Remove the outlet cover, sealing washer and filter.
11. Unscrew the three short securing screws and remove the upper body.
12. Remove the combined inlet/outlet valve.
    NOTE.–The valve is a press fit; take care not to damage the fine edge of the inlet valve.
13. Hold the diaphragm and rocker lever against spring pressure, and tap out the rocker lever pivot pin.
14. Remove the rocker lever and spring.
15. Withdraw the diaphragm and spring, lubricate the crankcase seal to avoid damage as the spindle stirrup is pulled through.
16. Remove the crankcase seal and retaining cup only if the seal is to be replaced.
    Replacing seal. Screw centre of service tool 18G 1119 into the retaining cup and withdraw the cup from the lower body.

Inspection

Examine components for wear and damage, particularly the diaphragm, the fine edge of the inlet/outlet valve, and the insert in the outlet cover.

Reassembling

17. Reverse the dismantling sequence, noting the following:
    a. Press the retaining cup into the lower body using 18G 1119.
    b. Remove any sharp edges from the diaphragm spindle and stirrup, lightly oil, position stirrup slot for engagement by the rocker lever.
    c. Ensure that the inlet/outlet valve groove registers in the housing, and that the fine edge of the inlet valve contacts its seating evenly.

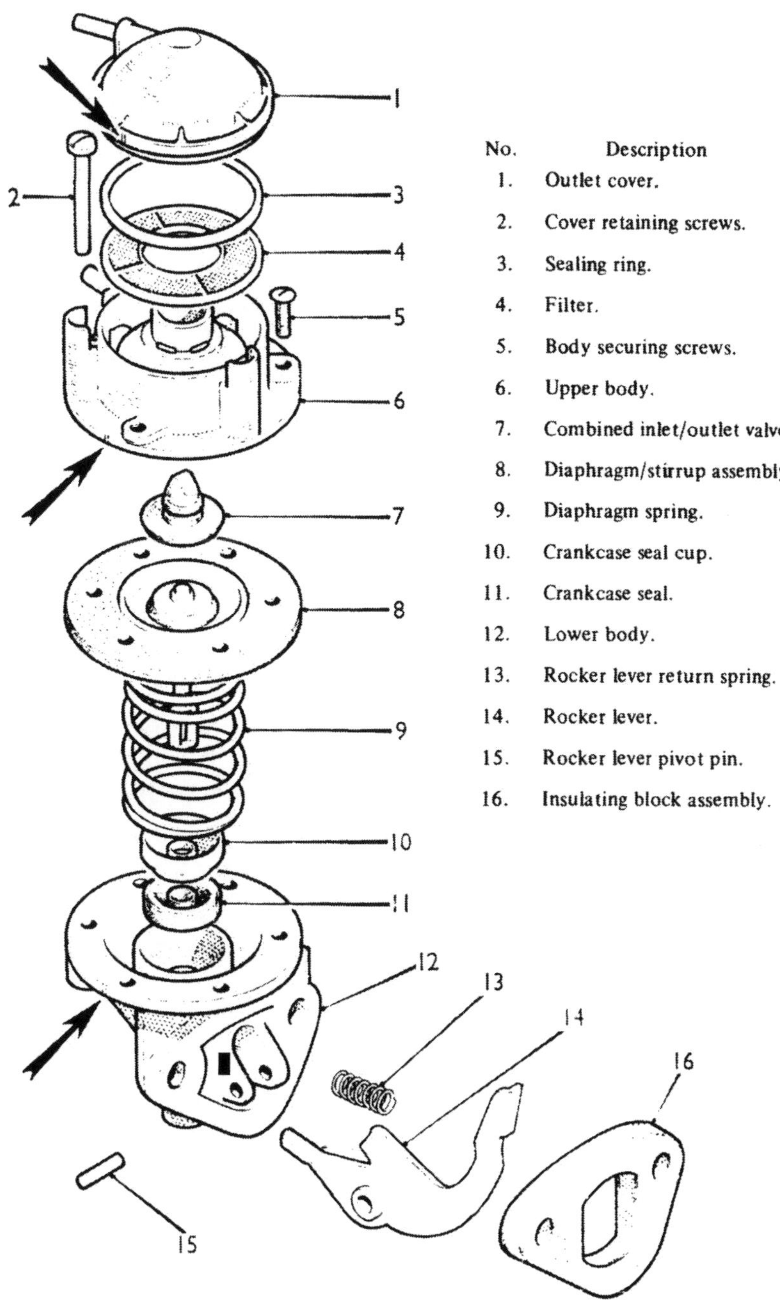

No.	Description
1.	Outlet cover.
2.	Cover retaining screws.
3.	Sealing ring.
4.	Filter.
5.	Body securing screws.
6.	Upper body.
7.	Combined inlet/outlet valve.
8.	Diaphragm/stirrup assembly.
9.	Diaphragm spring.
10.	Crankcase seal cup.
11.	Crankcase seal.
12.	Lower body.
13.	Rocker lever return spring.
14.	Rocker lever.
15.	Rocker lever pivot pin.
16.	Insulating block assembly.

Fig. Db.2
The fuel pump components. Mark the components (arrowed) for correct reassembly.

d. Line up the screw holes in the lower body and the holes in the diaphragm, depress the rocker lever so that the diaphragm lies flat, fit the short screws and leave slack. Fit the filter, sealing washer, and outlet cover; tighten all screws evenly.

e. Test pump–Section Db.2.

Refitting

18. Reverse the removing procedure, using new joints on the fuel pump insulating block.
19. Switch on the ignition and use the starter continuously for 20 seconds to prime the pump.

Section Db.2

TESTING THE FUEL PUMP

Dry test before dismantling a suspect pump and after reassembly (see Fig. Db.3).

Testing using 18G 1116

SUCTION

1. Connect the gauge to the inlet nozzle.
2. Operate the rocker lever, using the extension lever, through three full strokes. Minimum vacuum reading 6 in. (150 mm.) Hg, must not drop more than 2 in. (50 mm.) in 15 seconds.
3. Disconnect the gauge.

DELIVERY

4. Connect the gauge to the outlet nozzle.
5. Operate the rocker lever, using the extension lever, through two full strokes. Minimum pressure reading 3 lb./sq. in. (.2 kg./cm.^{2}), must not drop more than ½ lb./sq. in. (.04 kg./cm.^{2}) in 15 seconds.

Testing without gauge

A reasonable indication of pump condition can be obtained using the following procedure:

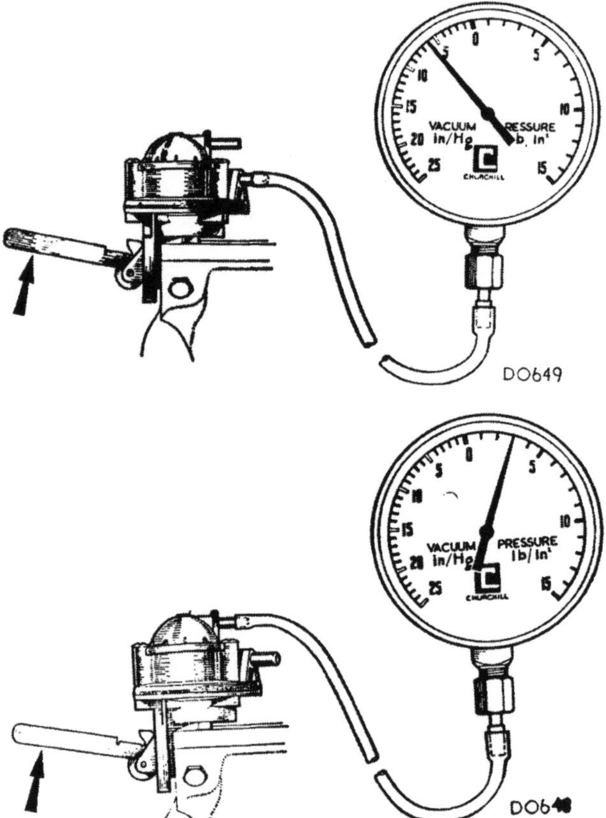

Fig. Db.3
Testing the pump for suction (above) and for pressure (below) using Service tool 18G 1116

SUCTION

1. Hold a finger over the inlet nozzle and operate rocker lever through three full strokes.
2. Release finger; a noise caused by suction should be heard.

DELIVERY

3. Hold a finger over the outlet nozzle and depress the rocker arm fully. Pressure should hold for up to 15 seconds.

SECTION E

THE CLUTCH

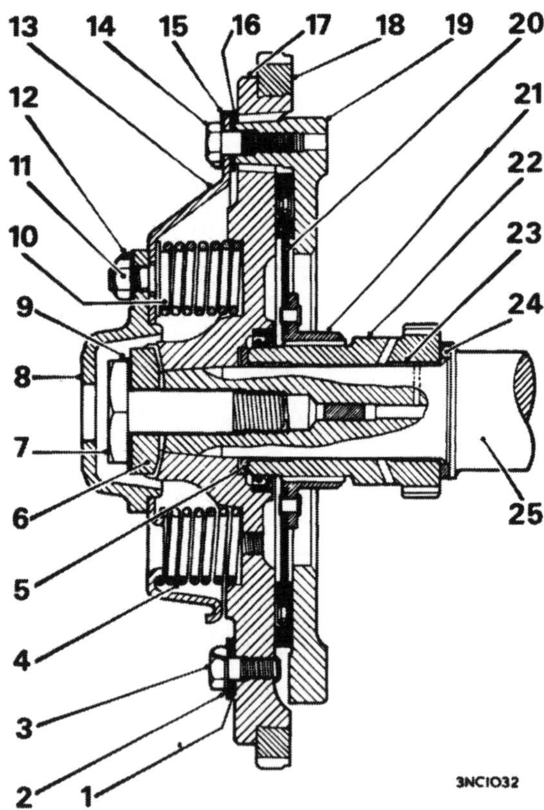

Fig. E.1
A section through the clutch assembly

1. Driving strap.
2. Lock washer.
3. Driving pin.
4. Pressure spring.
5. Circlip.
6. Key plate.
7. Flywheel screw.
8. Thrust plate.
9. Locking washer.
10. Pressure spring guides.
11. Guide nut.
12. Lock washer.
13. Pressure spring housing.
14. Driving pin.
15. Lock washer.
16. Driving strap.
17. Flywheel.
18. Starter ring.
19. Pressure plate.
20. Driven plate.
21. Driven plate hub.
22. Crankshaft primary gear.
23. Primary gear bearing.
24. Thrust washer.
25. Crankshaft.

Section E.1

OVERHAUL
(Coil Pressure Spring Type)

Removing

1. See Section A.11.

Dismantling

2. Mark the driving pins, driving straps, and the housing so that these parts can be refitted in their original positions. Note the clutch balance mark (Fig. E.2).
3. Insert the three screws (Service tool 18G 304 M) through the recessed holes in the pressure spring housing and screw them into the flywheel.
4. Screw the nuts down against the housing with the fingers and then tighten them one turn at a time until the load is off the driving pins.
5. Unscrew the three driving pins.
6. Unscrew the nuts of the Service tool 18G 304 M, gradually releasing the housing. Remove the housing and the springs.

Inspecting

7. Inspect the housing for elongation of the driving pin holes.
8. Inspect the driving pins for ridging and wear; fit three new pins if any are worn.
9. Inspect the driving straps; fit three new ones if any are worn.

Reassembling

NOTE. -When reassembling, fit the pressure plate to the clutch cover with the marks 'A' adjacent to each other and fit the clutch unit to the flywheel as shown in Fig. E.2.

10. Centralize the driven plate and the flywheel hub with Service tool 18G 571.
11. Locate the springs, housing and driving straps, and tighten the nuts evenly (Service tool 18G 304 M).
12. Insert and tighten the driving pins. If the driving straps have been removed from the flywheel, ensure that the spacing washers are refitted between the straps and the flywheel face.

Refitting

13. Reverse the removing instructions (Section A.11).

Section E.2

ADJUSTMENTS

Pedal movement

1. Pull the operating lever outwards until all free movement is taken up, then check the clearance between the lever and the stop.

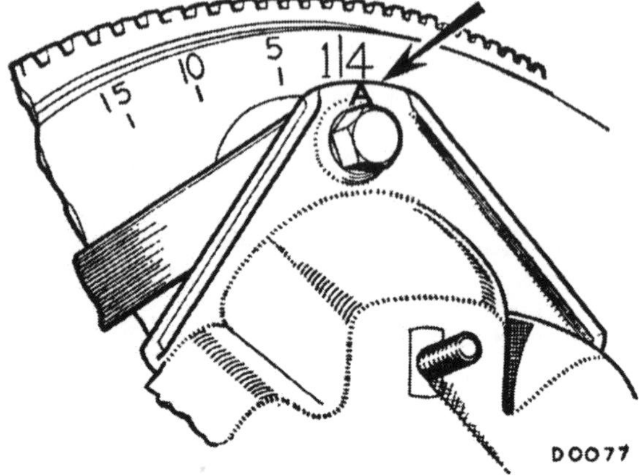

Fig. E.2
The fitted position of the clutch cover, with the balance mark 'A' adjacent the 1/4 timing mark on the flywheel

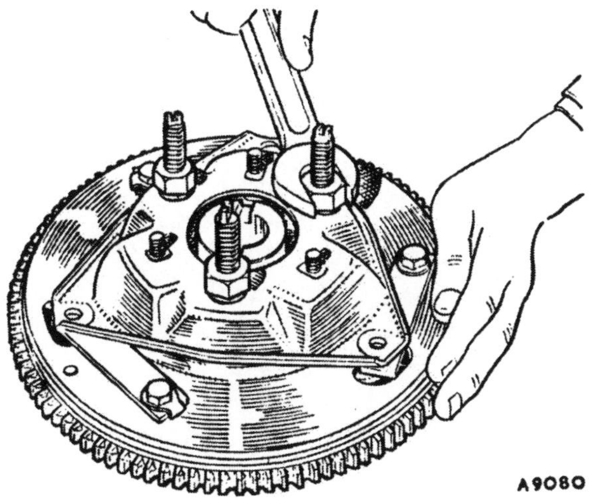

Fig. E.3
The clutch pressure springs being compressed with the aid of Service tool 18G 304 M, with Service tool 18G 571 used to keep the driven plate and flywheel hubs centralized during the operation

2. If necessary, adjust the stop to give a clearance of .060 in. (1.52 mm.). On later models with the throw-out stop, adjust to give a clearance of .020 in. (.50 mm.).

Throw-out stop (later models)

Adjustment is normally only necessary if the stop has been removed during overhaul.

3. Screw the stop and locknut away from the clutch housing to the limit of its travel.
4. Fully depress the pedal.
5. Screw the stop up against the housing, release the pedal and screw up another .007 to .010 in. (.20 to .25 mm.), approximately one flat of the locknut.
   Re-check the pedal movement (items 1 and 2).

Clutch over-throw

TO TEST

7. Run the engine at its normal temperature and at about 500 r.p.m.
8. Depress and release the pedal three or four times; if the engine stalls or slows down appreciably, over-throw is occurring.

TO RECTIFY

9. Check the pedal movement and test for over-throw.
10. Adjust the pedal movement to a maximum of .075 in. (2.0 mm.) and test for over-throw.
11. Fit a stronger lever return spring and test for over-throw.
12. If over-throw persists, fit new pressure springs.

Section E.3

DRAG

With the car stationary, run the engine and hold the clutch out for several seconds; if drag persists, carry out the following test in sequence.

1. Check for air leaks in the hydraulic system.
2. Check the pedal movement.
3. Check the crankshaft end-float (Section A.25).
4. Dismantle the clutch and fit a new flywheel oil seal (if fitted).

Section E.4

MASTER CYLINDER

Removing

1. Disconnect the pedal lever from the push-rod.
2. Unscrew the pipe union from the cylinder.
3. Remove the two bolts securing the unit to the bulkhead.

Dismantling

4. Drain out the fluid.
5. Pull back the rubber dust cover.
6. Extract the circlip, dished washer, and push-rod.
7. Withdraw the piston cups and spring from the barrel.
8. Use only the fingers to remove the secondary cup from the piston.

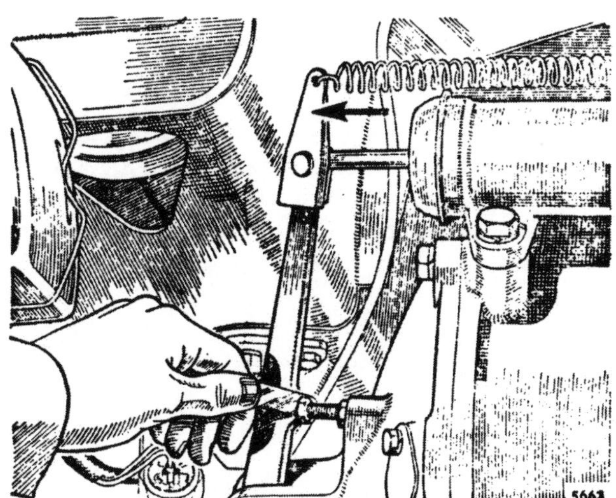

Fig. E.4
A clearance of .060 in. (1.52 mm.) or .020 in. (.50 mm.) on later models must exist between the adjustable clutch return stop and the operating lever

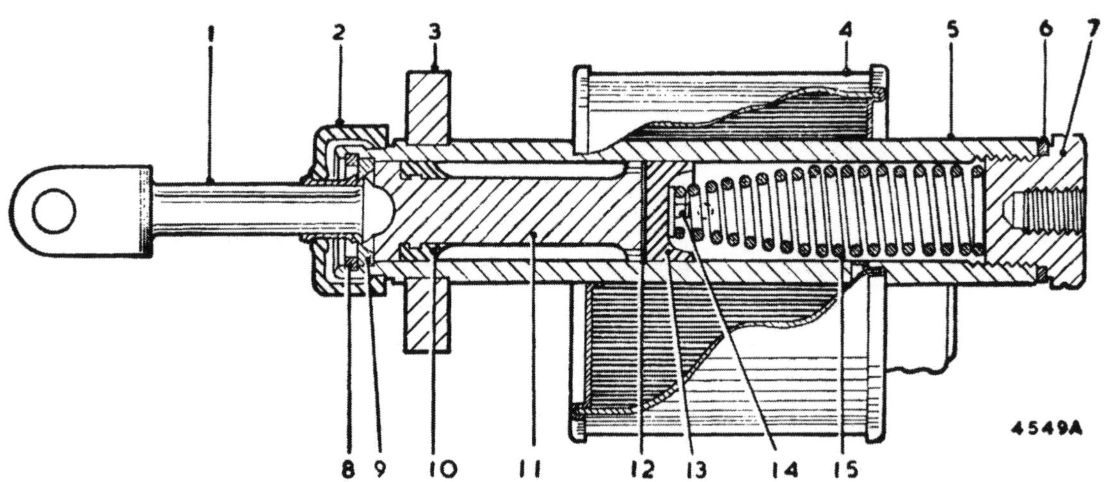

Fig. E.5
A section through the clutch master cylinder

1. Push-rod.
2. Rubber boot.
3. Mounting flange.
4. Supply tank.
5. Body.
6. Washer.
7. End plug.
8. Circlip.
9. Stop washer.
10. Secondary cup.
11. Piston.
12. Piston washer.
13. Main cup.
14. Spring retainer.
15. Return spring.

Reassembling

9. Clean all rubber parts with brake fluid and remove all traces of petrol (fuel), kerosene, and trichlorethylene from the metal parts.
10. Fit new rubbers and assemble the internal components lubricated with brake fluid.
11. Stretch the secondary cup over the end flange of the piston with the lip of the cup towards the opposite end of the piston; work it round to ensure correct sealing.
12. Insert the return spring, largest coils first. Make sure the spring seat is positioned on the small end of the spring.
13. Insert the main cup, lip first, and press it down onto the spring seat.
14. Push the piston down the bore and refit the push-rod, circlip, and rubber dust cover.

Refitting

15. Reverse the removing instructions and fill up with Lockheed Super Heavy Duty Brake Fluid, or (COOPER), Lockheed Disc Brake Fluid. Bleed the system.

Section E.5

SLAVE CYLINDER

Removing

1. Attach a bleed tube to the cylinder bleed nipple and a container, pump the pedal and drain out the fluid.
2. Disconnect the pressure pipe.
3. Disconnect the push-rod from the clutch lever.
4. Unscrew the two securing bolts and remove the cylinder from the housing.

Dismantling

5. Clean the exterior before stripping.
6. Withdraw the rubber boot and push-rod.
7. Remove the circlip, piston, piston cup, cup filler, and return spring.
8. Renew all rubber parts: examine the remainder and renew as required.

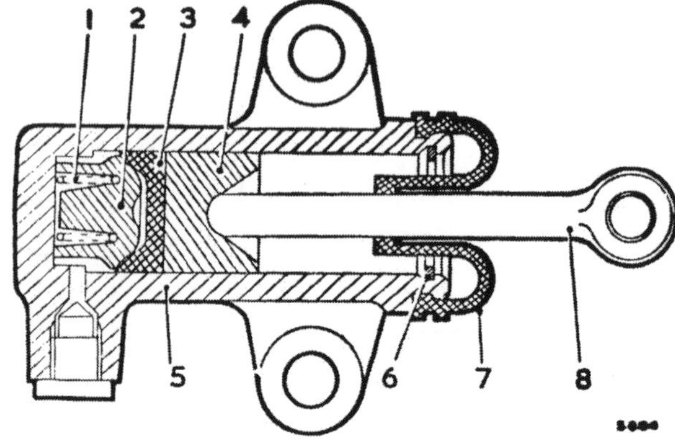

Fig. E.6
A section through a clutch slave cylinder

1. Spring.
2. Cup filler.
3. Cup.
4. Piston.
5. Body.
6. Circlip.
7. Rubber boot.
8. Push-rod.

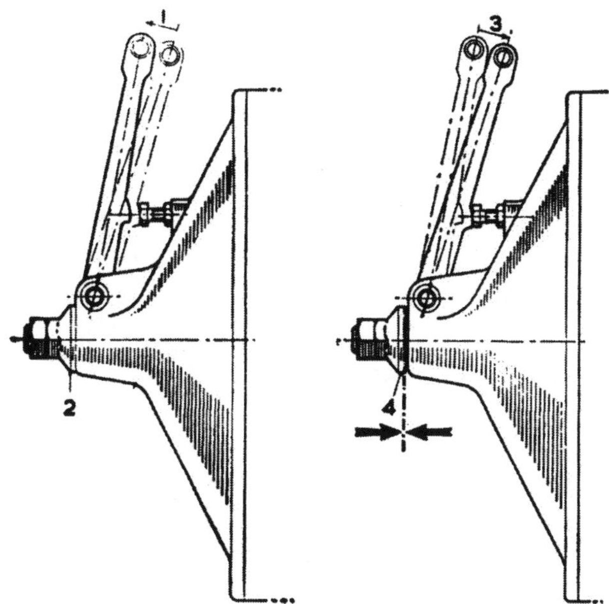

Fig. E.7
(1) The clutch fully released, with (2) the throw-out stop screwed up to the cover boss. (3) The clutch fully engaged and the stop (4) screwed up a further .007 to .010 in. (.178 to .254 mm.) towards the cover boss

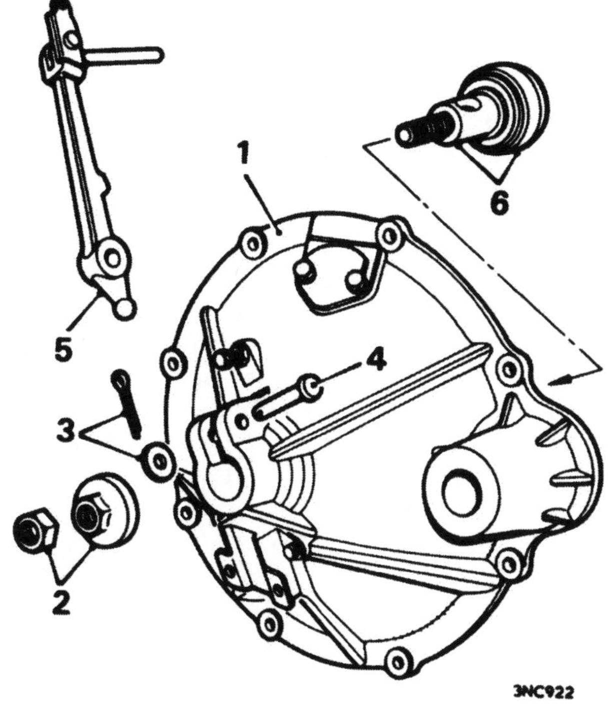

Fig. E.8
Removing the release lever, bearing and plunger assembly from the clutch cover

1. Clutch cover.
2. Plunger stop and locknut.
3. Washer and split pin–clevis pin.
4. Clevis pin–release lever.
5. Release lever.
6. Release bearing assembly.

Reassembling

Carry out items 5 to 8 in the reverse order.

Refitting

Reverse the removal procedure items 1 to 4 and bleed the system.

Section E.6

CLUTCH
(Diaphragm Spring Type)

A diaphragm spring replaces the six conventional coil pressure springs on this clutch assembly.

Remove and refit the flywheel and clutch as detailed in Section A.28.

Section E.7

CLUTCH COVER ALIGNMENT
(Using Service tool 18G 1247)

Removing

1. Remove the engine/transmission assembly from the car, see Section A.13 or A.33 (rod change transmission).
2. Remove the cover retaining screws and pull off the clutch end-cover.
3. Remove the starter motor.
4. Remove the clutch/flywheel assembly, see Section A.28.
5. Remove the split pin and washer and withdraw the release lever clevis pin, Fig. E.8.
6. Pull the release lever out of the release bearing plunger.
7. Unscrew and remove the plunger stop and locknut; pull out the plunger and release bearing assembly.
8. Clean the cover and the crankshaft taper.
9. Apply engineers marking blue or chalk to the clutch cover register.
10. Insert Service tool 18G 1247 into the cover and refit the cover with the tool locating over the crankshaft taper, Fig. E.9.
11. Push the cover up to the flywheel housing to determine the amount of misalignment of the cover with the flywheel housing.
12. Remove the clutch cover and note the subsequent misalignment markings showing on the marking blue. File off the 'high marked' areas of the register as necessary.
13. Repeat the marking and fitting procedure in operations 9 to 12 as necessary; the cover must be able to contact the flywheel housing without any force being used to ensure correct alignment of the cover with the crankshaft.
14. When correct alignment is obtained, secure the cover in position with two retaining bolts.

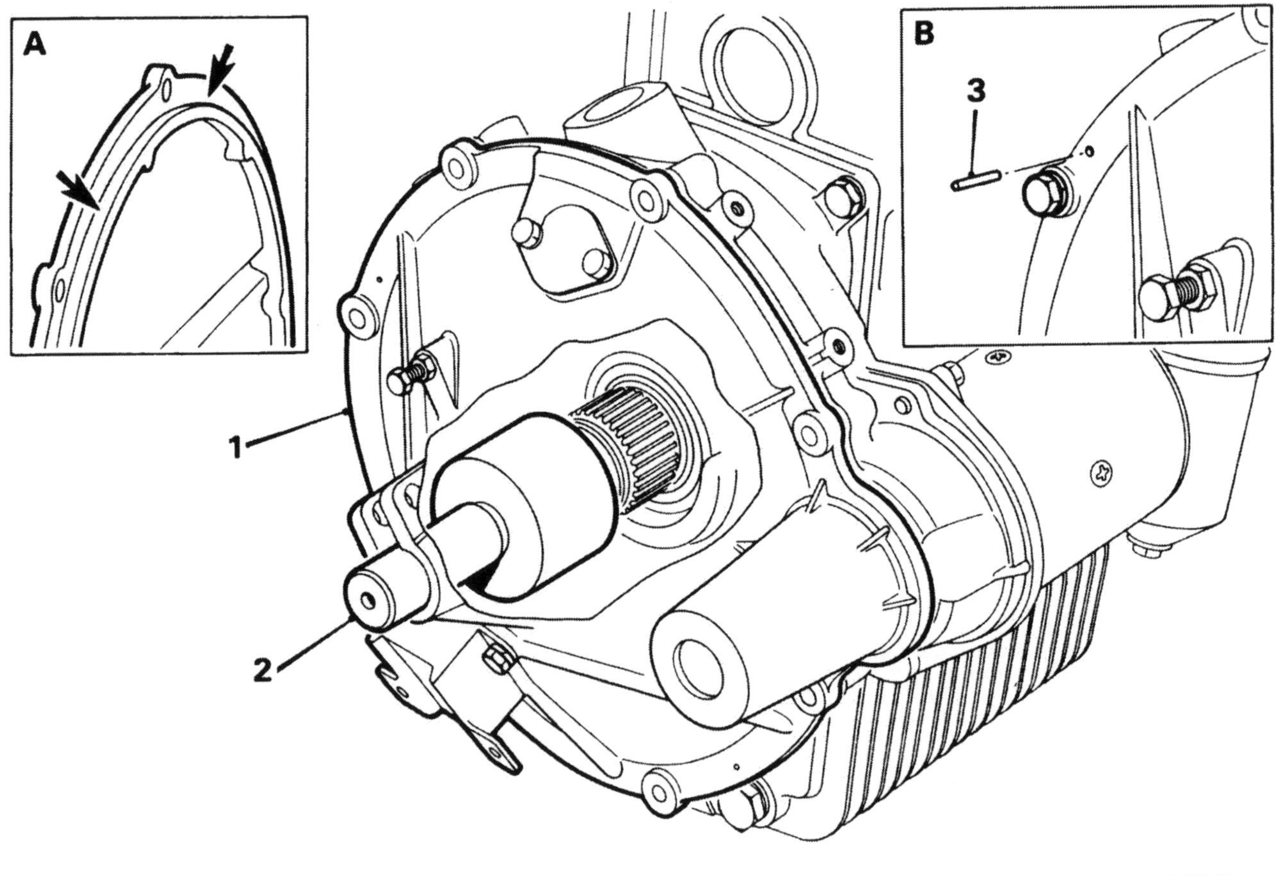

Fig. E.9
Using Service tool 18G 1247 to align the clutch cover with the crankshaft and flywheel housing
Inset 'A': File off the high spots 'arrowed' from the cover register. Inset 'B': Drill cover and housing and fit dowels

1. Clutch cover. 2. Service tool 18G 1247. 3. Dowels.

15. In two diametrically opposite locations, use a No. 40 drill (0.098 in diameter) and drill holes through the end cover and flywheel housing flanges, Fig. E.9.
16. Remove the end-cover and take out Service tool 18G 1247.
17. Lubricate the operating surfaces of the release bearing plunger with a graphite grease and refit the release bearing and plunger assembly into the cover; refit the release lever and clevis pin and secure with a new split-pin, Fig. E.8.
18. Refit the clutch assembly, Section A.28.
19. Refit the clutch cover.
20. Fit the cover retaining bolts loosely.
21. Fit two dowels 2.49 mm dia x 21 mm into the drilled holes to retain the alignment of the end-cover with the flywheel housing.
NOTE: The dowels used are needle-rollers from a bearing; any similar size rollers or dowels may be used provided that the correct size drill is used to ensure an interference fit.
22. Tighten the end cover retaining bolts.
23. Check and adjust if necessary, the clutch throw-out stop adjustment and the return stop adjustment, see Section E.2.
24. Refit the engine/transmission, see Section A.13 or A.33 (rod change transmission) as applicable.

SECTION F

THE TRANSMISSION

NOTE

The gear change remote control shaft lubrication nipple on the differential cover requires attention at major overhaul periods only, when grease should be used.

Not applicable to transmission with rod type gearchange.

Section F.1

TRANSMISSION

Dismantling

1. Remove the transmission casing from the crankcase (Section A.19).
2. Withdraw the idler gear with its thrust washers.
3. Remove the differential assembly (Section F.4).
4. Withdraw the reverse detent plug, plunger, and spring or the reverse light switch and plunger, where fitted.
5. Remove the clamp and key from the inner end of the gear change operating shaft and pull out the shaft.
6. Remove the speedometer pinion bush securing screw and withdraw the bush assembly and pinion.
7. Remove the speedometer gear retaining plate and the gear.
8. Remove the securing nuts and screws, and pull off the front cover.
9. Remove the selector interlocking arm.
10. Disconnect the oil suction pipe from the bracket (where a clip is fitted), and the flange and withdraw the pipe from the strainer.
11. Extract the circlip and withdraw the first motion shaft roller bearing using Service tool 18G 705 and adaptor 18G 705 C.
12. Use the selector shafts and lock first and third gears together.
13. Tap back the locking washers and remove the first motion shaft nut. Use Service tool 18G 587 to remove the final drive gear nut, and withdraw both the input and final drive gears.
14. Tap back the locking plates, remove the four securing screws and the third motion shaft bearing retainer and packing shims.
15. Remove the layshaft and reverse shaft locking plate, push the layshaft from the clutch side of the casing and remove the laygear and thrust washers.
16. Unscrew the plugs from the outside of the casing and withdraw the selector rod interlocking plungers and springs.
17. Remove the first motion shaft bearing circlip and withdraw the bearing and shaft from the casing with Service tools 18G 284 and 18G 284 B.

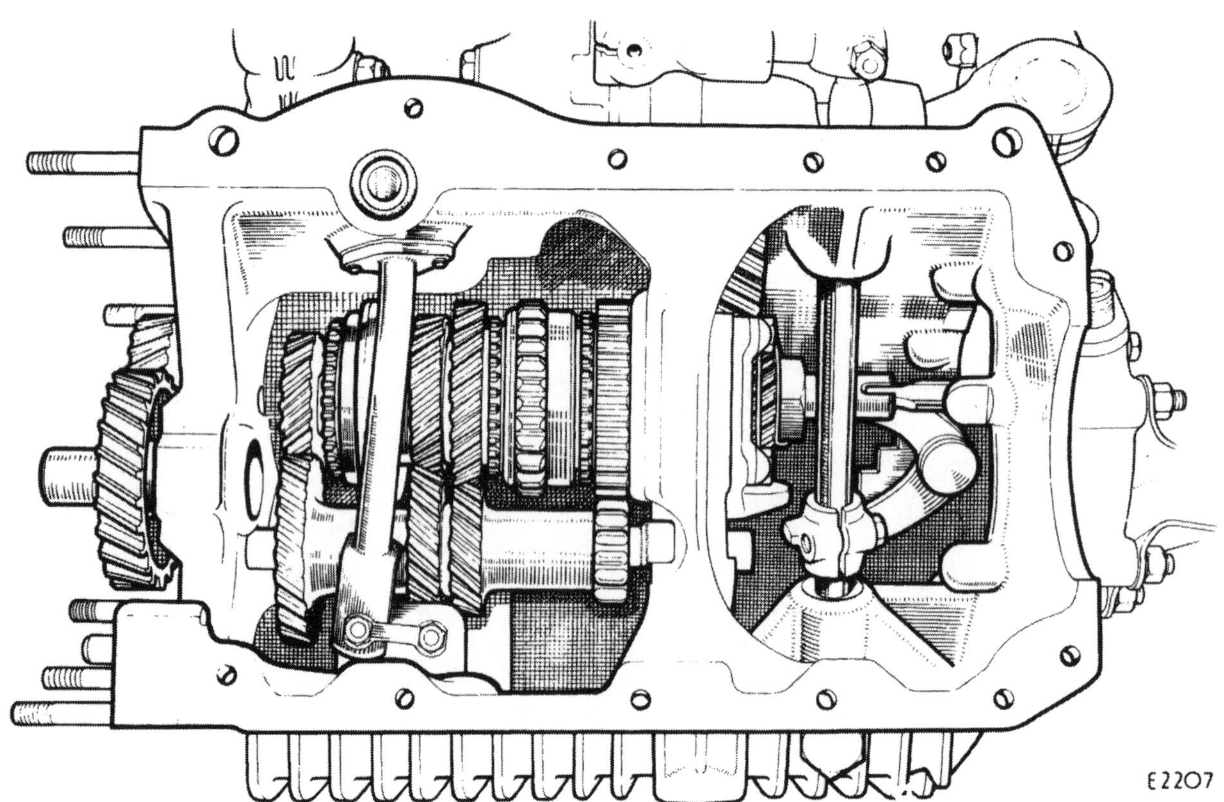

Fig. F.1
The four-speed synchromesh transmission assembly, with all the gears assembled into the casing

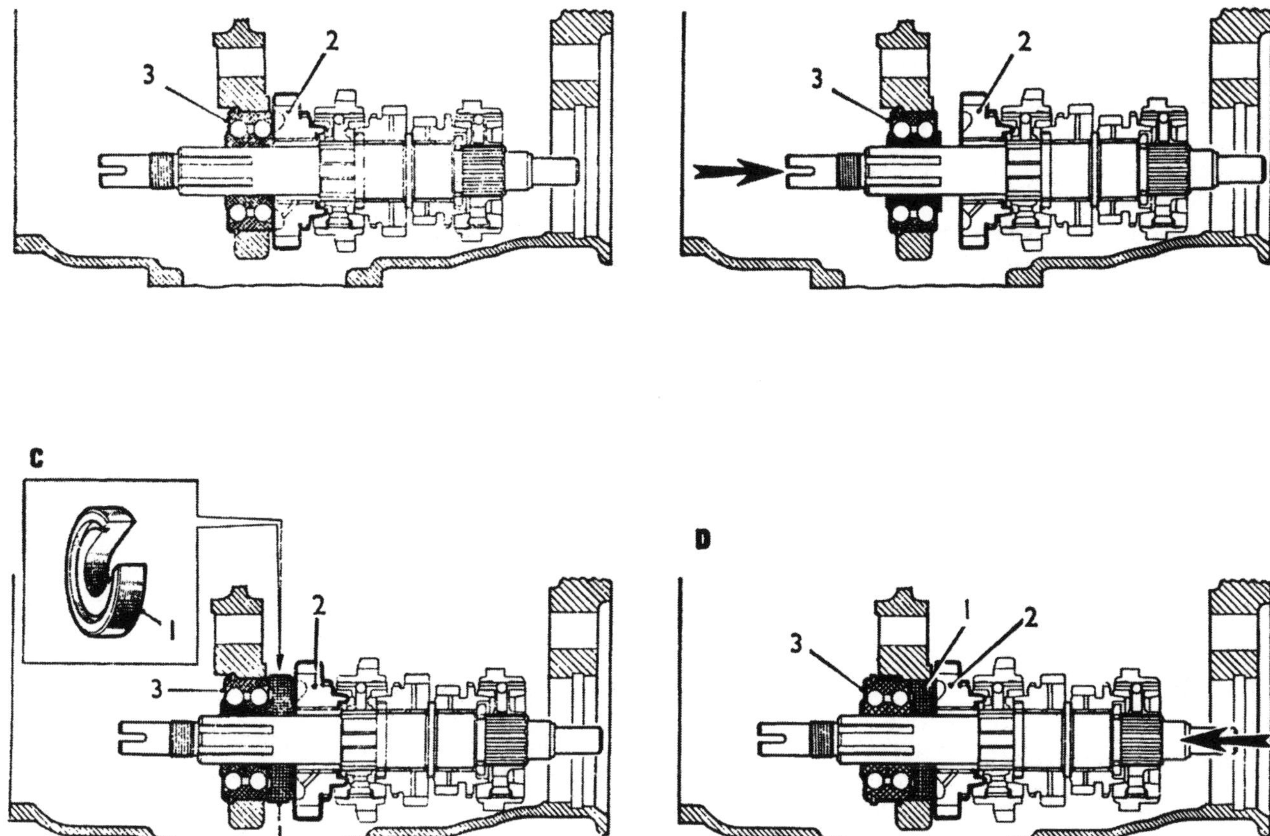

Fig. F.2
Removing the third motion shaft bearing

18. Refer to Fig. F.2. Drift the third motion shaft backwards, as indicated by the arrow in (B), until a special Service tool 1 can be placed between the first speed gear 2 and the bearing 3 as illustrated in (C). On three-speed synchromesh gearboxes use 18G 613, and on four-speed units 18G 1127 with their relieved side towards the bearing. These two tools must not be interchanged, or the bearing or casing will be damaged. Drift the third motion shaft forward as illustrated in (D), to push the bearing 3 from the web, taking care not to damage the selector forks. Pull the bearing from the shaft, and lift the shaft from the casing.
19. Remove the strainer assembly.
20. Withdraw the reverse shaft, gear and selector fork.

The following operations are only necessary if complete stripping of the casing is required.

21. Unscrew the selector shaft/fork locking screws and withdraw the shafts and forks.
22. Remove the circlip from the reverse gear shifter lever pivot pin and remove the lever.

Reassembling

23. If the gearbox has been completely stripped, first refit the reverse gear shifter lever and pivot pin. Push in the selector rods from the front of the casing, engage them with the selector forks, tighten the selector screws, and secure the lock nuts.
24. Position the reverse gear and fork, and refit the reverse shaft, with the plain end foremost.
25. Refit the oil strainer and smear some grease onto the sealing ring to assist when fitting the oil suction pipe.
26. Refer to item 18. Refit the third motion shaft assembly with the slotted end passing through the centre web of the casing. Engage the sliding hubs with the selector forks.
27. Refer to item 17. Drift the first motion shaft and bearing assembly into the casing using Service tool 18G 569 (modified).

    Use Service tool 18G 569 to gauge the correct thickness of circlip required to retain the bearing assembly. Try the thicker side of the gauge first; the two sizes are marked on the handle. Refer to Fig. F.3, which illustrates this operation, and fit the circlip selected from the chart beneath it.

28. Refer to item 18. Drift the third motion shaft bearing into the central web using Service tool 18G 579 modified, together with the spacer washer.

29. Refit the laygear with the standard sized thrust washer at one end, and measure the gap at the other. Refer to the chart (Fig. F.4) to select the correct variable thrust washer, to give an end clearance of between .002 and .006 in. (.05 and .15 mm.). On three-speed synchromesh gearboxes the small thrust washer is of a standard size, the large one selective, and vice versa on four-speed synchromesh gearboxes.

Use the dummy layshaft, Service tool 18G 471 to position the thrust washer, and refit the layshaft from the clutch side, with its slotted end positioned horizontally and towards that of the reverse shaft. Refit the layshaft and reverse shaft locking plate.

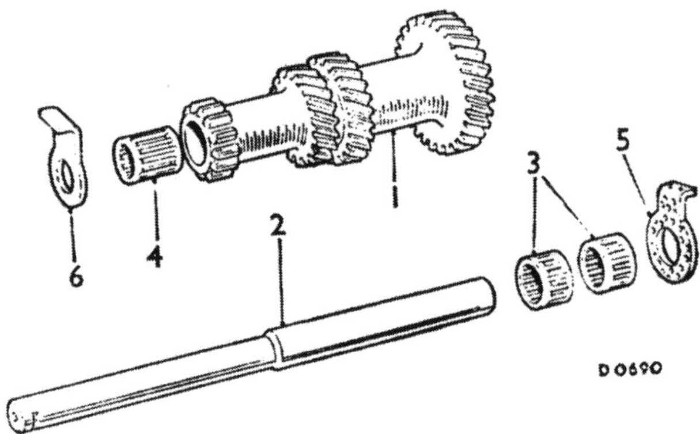

Fig. F.4
The laygear assembly. With the standard-sized thrust washer fitted, use the table below to select the correct size of variable washer. The part numbers of the thrust washers available for the three-speed and four-speed synchromesh gearboxes are given in columns 'A' and 'B' respectively

1. Laygear.
2. Layshaft (un-stepped on three-speed synchromesh units).
3. Needle-roller bearings (one only on three-speed synchromesh units).
4. Needle-roller bearing.
5. Large thrust washer.
6. Small thrust washer.

Early three-speed synchromesh gearboxes were fitted with uncaged needle-roller bearings, with which the later caged type are inter-changeable.

WHEN GAP IS	A	B
.125 to .127 in. (3.18 to 3.22 mm.)	88G 325	22G 856
.128 to .130 in. (3.25 to 3.30 mm.)	88G 326	22G 857
.131 to .133 in. (3.32 to 3.37 mm.)	88G 327	22G 858
.134 in. (3.41 mm.)	88G 328	22G 859

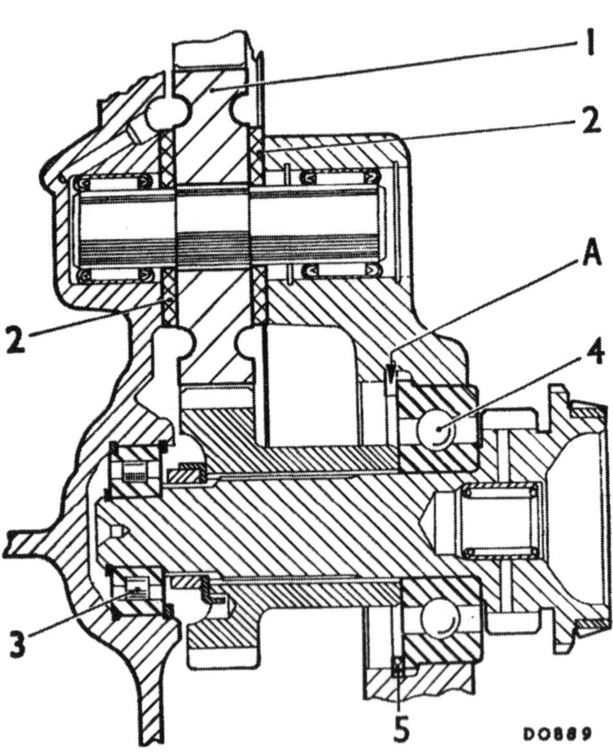

Fig. F.3
A section through the idler gear and first motion shaft. Measure the gap 'A' between the bearing face and register with Service tool 18G 569, and fit the appropriate circlip as indicated by the chart below

1. Idler gear.
2. Idler gear thrust washers.
3. First motion shaft roller bearing.
4. First motion shaft ball bearing.
5. First motion shaft circlip.

WHEN GAP IS	USE CIRCLIP PART No.
.096 to .098 in. (2.43 to 2.48 mm.)	2A 3710
.098 to .100 in. (2.48 to 2.54 mm.)	2A 3711

30. Refit the third motion shaft bearing retainer without any shims, lightly tighten the bolts and measure the gap, see Fig. F.5. Fit the shims required (see chart), ensure that they are fitted under the layshaft and reverse shaft locking plate, and finally tighten the bolts and turn over the tab washers.

31. Refer to item (10). Insert the oil suction pipe into the oil strainer assembly, and tighten first the external flange securing bolts and then the bracket retaining bolts. Take care not to displace the oil seal from the strainer.

32. Fit new idler gear needle-roller bearings if required. Engage the expandable collets of Service tool 18G 581 with each old bearing and screw up the nut on the tool to extract them, after removing the outer circlip (when fitted) from the transmission casing boss.

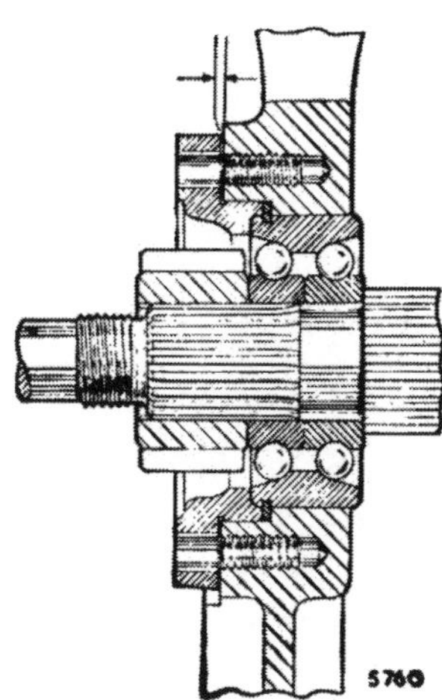

Fig. F.5
A section through the third motion shaft bearing and retainer. Use the following table to ensure that the correct thickness of shim is used

WHEN GAP IS	USE SHIMS TOTALLING
.005 to .006 in. (.13 to .15 mm.)	.005 in. (.13 mm.)
.006 to .008 in. (.15 to .20 mm.)	.007 in. (.18 mm.)
.008 to .010 in. (.20 to .25 mm.)	.009 in. (.23 mm.)
.010 to .012 in. (.25 to .30 mm.)	.011 in. (.28 mm.)
.012 to .014 in. (.30 to .35 mm.)	.013 in. (.33 mm.)
.014 to .015 in. (.35 to .38 mm.)	.015 in. (.38 mm.)

Use Service tool 18G 582 (three-speed synchromesh) or 18G 1126 (four-speed synchromesh) to fit the new bearings. Use the collar supplied with each tool to control the depth to which the bearing is pressed into the flywheel housing, the boss of which must be well supported during this operation. These collars are not required when fitting the transmission casing bearing, since each tool's shoulder governs the depth to which it is pressed. Replace the outer circlip, if fitted.

33. Refer to items 12 and 13. Refit the input and final drive gears, and, using new lock washers tighten the first motion shaft and final drive gear nuts, using Service tool 18G 587 for the latter; the torque figures are given in **'GENERAL DATA'**.

34. Refit the first motion shaft roller bearing and circlip.

35. Reverse the instruction in item 16.

36. Refit the selector interlocking arm, the front cover, the speedometer gear and cover, pinion, bush, and pinion housing. Push in the gear change operating shaft, refit its key and clamp, and replace the reverse detent plunger and spring, or the reverse light switch (if fitted).

37. Refit the differential and check adjustment as given in Section F.4.

38. Refit the idler gear and thrust washers, with the chamferred side of each washer against the gear.

39. Refit the flywheel housing with a new joint washer and tighten to the torque figure given in **'GENERAL DATA'**.

    Check with feeler gauges that the idler gear has an end-float of between .003 and .008 in. (.08 and .2 mm.), see Fig. F.3. Thrust washers ranging in thickness from .132 to .139 in. (3.34 to 3.54 mm.) are available for adjustment.

40. Remove the flywheel housing and gasket, and refit the transmission unit to the engine as detailed in Section A.19, using a new housing gasket to replace the one used for the idler gear end-float check.

Section F.2

THIRD MOTION SHAFT
Three-speed synchromesh transmission

The baulk ring synchromesh is fitted to Mk. I cars from Engine No. 8AM/U/H412992 and to all Mk. II models. The dismantling and reassembling sequences for the early-type transmission are the same as detailed below except that the second and third/top gear synchronizers are not fitted with baulk rings.

Removing

1. Remove the third motion shaft assembly from the transmission as detailed in Section F.1.

Dismantling

2. Remove the first speed gear, hub and baulk ring from the rear of the shaft, and the top and third gear synchromesh hub and baulk rings from the front of the shaft.
3. Remove the front thrust washer by pressing down the spring-loaded locating plunger and rotating the washer until the splines register with those on the shaft. Withdraw the thrust washer and third speed gear, complete with needle-roller bearings on later type gears, and take out the plunger and spring.

    EARLY TYPE GEARS. Withdraw the third gear bush and interlocking ring, followed by the second speed gear and bush and the rear thrust washer.

    LATER TYPE GEARS. Depress the spring loaded pegs, turn and remove the second speed gear locking collar and take out the two split washers. Pull the gear from the rear of the shaft, and remove the needle-roller bearings from their journal.

    If it is necessary to separate the second or third and fourth speed striking dog from its synchromesh hub and cone assembly, press the assembly into Service tool 18G 572, to retain the three balls and springs which are located in each hub.

Reassembling

EARLY TYPE GEARS

4. Fit the rear thrust washer, then the plain half of the split bush with its flat end towards the thrust washer.

5. Fit the second speed gear, with the synchronizer cone facing the rear of the shaft, the interlocking ring and the splined half of the split bush. Engage the dogs of the split bushes with the slots in the interlocking ring. New bushes must be fitted, since the interference fit of the old ones will have been lost when they were removed. Heat the bushes to a temperature of 180 to 200° C. (356 to 392° F.), to allow them to be fitted without force, and to obtain a permanent 'shrink fit' on cooling.

6. Refit and depress the spring and locking plunger, refit the third speed gear, plain side first, and the front thrust washer. Turn the thrust washer until the plunger engages the spline and locks the washer.

LATER TYPE GEARS

7. Slide the second speed gear on from the rear of the shaft, plain side first, after sticking the needle-roller bearings to their journal with grease. Replace the two split washers, depress the two spring loaded locking pegs, and refit the locking collar, turning it until the pegs are heard to engage the splines.

8. From the front of the shaft refit the third speed gear, plain side first, with its needle-roller bearings. Slide on the front thrust washer and turn it until the spring loaded peg is heard to lock it.

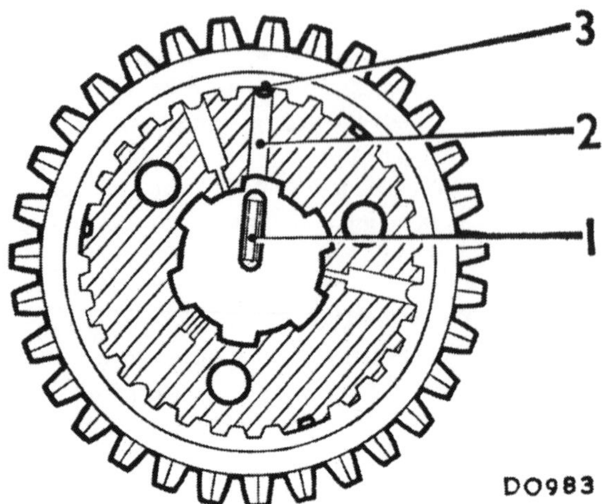

Fig. F.6
The three-speed synchromesh first and second speed gear assembly, showing the plunger (1) in its drilling in the hub (2) aligned with the cut-away tooth (3) in the gear assembly

EARLY AND LATER TYPE GEARS

9. The end-float of both the second and third speed gears when assembled on the third motion shaft must be between .0035 and .0055 in. (.09 and .13 mm.).

10. Refit the top and third speed synchromesh hub and baulk rings, with the plain side of the hub towards the rear of the shaft.

11. Refit the speed gear, hub, and baulk ring, with the cone end of the hub towards the front of the shaft.

Should the first and second speed gear assembly have been dismantled, the gear must be correctly repositioned on the hub, otherwise selection of second gear will be impossible. Ensure that the plunger in the hub aligns with the cut-away tooth in the gear assembly (see Fig. F.6), and that the cone end of the hub and the tapered side of the gear teeth are on opposite sides of the assembly.

Section F.3

THIRD MOTION SHAFT
Four-speed synchromesh transmission

Removing

1. Remove the shaft assembly from the transmission as detailed in Section F.1.

Dismantling

2. Withdraw the top and third gear synchromesh hub and baulk rings from the front end of the shaft.

3. Press the front thrust washer plunger, and turn the washer until its splines register with those on the shaft, enabling it to be removed, complete with plunger and spring. Remove the third speed gear, with its caged needle-roller bearing.

4. Remove the first speed gear, baulk ring, and caged needle-roller bearing from the opposite end of the shaft.

5. Carefully lever the needle-roller bearing journal backwards sufficiently to fit Service tool 18G 2 and pull the journal from the shaft.

6. Remove the reverse mainshaft wheel and first/second speed synchronizer assembly, and the baulk ring.

7. Press in the two plungers securing the rear thrust washer, turn it to align it with the shaft splines and withdraw it from the shaft. Remove the second speed gear, and the split caged needle-roller bearing.

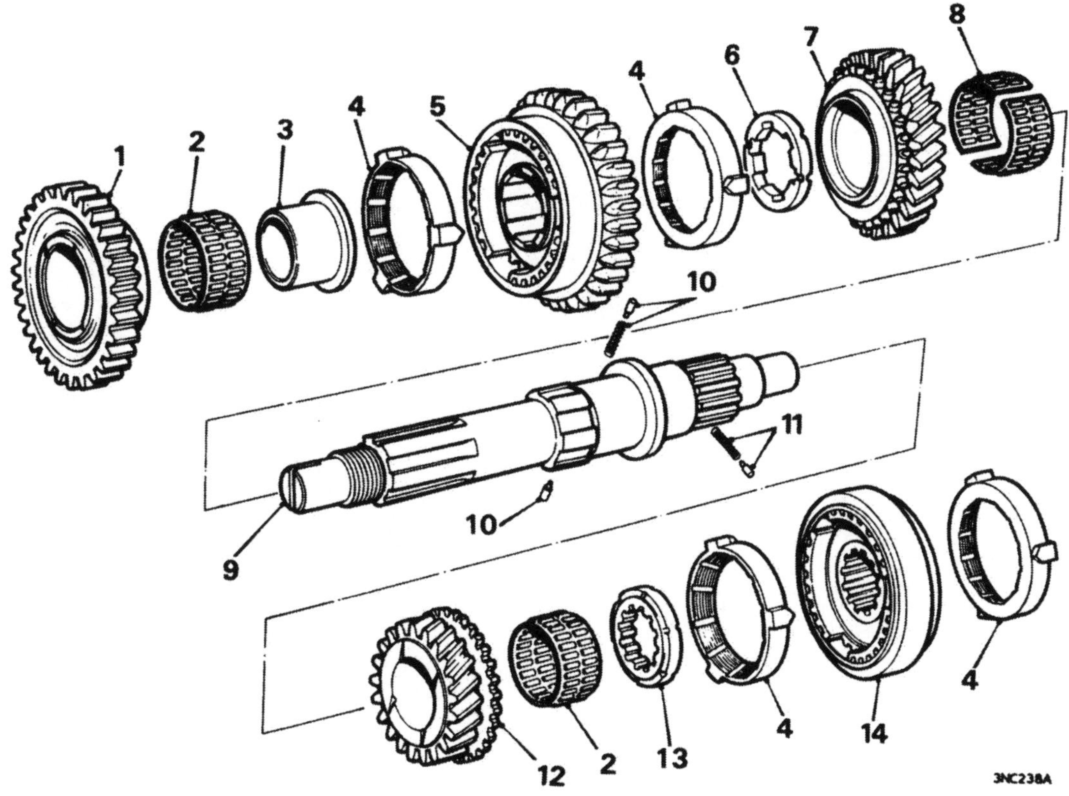

Fig. F.7
The third motion shaft assembly (four-speed synchromesh transmission)

1. First speed gear.
2. Needle roller bearings.
3. Bearing journal–needle roller.
4. Baulk rings.
5. Reverse mainshaft gear and 1st and 2nd speed synchronizer.
6. Rear thrust washer.
7. Second speed gear.
8. Split-caged needle roller bearing– second speed gear.
9. Third motion shaft.
10. Plunger and spring–rear thrust washer.
11. Plunger and spring–front thrust washer.
12. Third speed gear.
13. Front thrust washer.
14. 3rd and 4th speed synchronizer.

Reassembling

8. Carry out the dismantling instructions, but note items 9 to 11 in Section F.2.
9. Use Service tool 18G 572 to prevent the balls and springs from being lost, should it be necessary to separate the striking dogs from the synchromesh hub and cone assemblies. When reassembling the synchronizers, ensure that the long boss on both the sleeve and the hubs are on the same side.
10. When refitting the third and top speed synchronizer assembly, the long boss on the synchronizer sleeve must face the first motion shaft bearing. The first and second speed synchronizer assembly must be fitted with the long boss towards the first speed gear, or second speed synchromesh action will be lost.
11. Use Service tool 18G 186 to drift the first speed gear needle-roller bearing journal onto the third motion shaft.

Section F.4

DIFFERENTIAL ASSEMBLY

Removing

1. Remove the engine and transmission as detailed in Section A.13.
2. Remove the transmission from the engine as detailed in Section A.19 **only** if it is necessary to fit a new final drive pinion into the transmission, or if the differential components have suffered damage with the result that swarf has been introduced into the transmission unit.
3. Remove the gear-change extension bottom cover plate.
4. Release the control shaft lever from the top of the remote control shaft, which can now be withdrawn.
5. Extract the split pin from the slotted nuts securing both right- and left-hand driving flanges to the differential gear shafts, using Service tool 18G 669 to hold each driving flange in turn, remove the nuts and withdraw the flanges. **Do not under any circumstances use the transmission casing as a stop or leverage point when removing the driving flange nuts or other components of the transmission. Serious damage to the casing can easily result from misuse in this way.**
6. Unscrew the five set screws from each of the final drive end covers, and remove them from the differential housing. Note the number of shims fitted between the differential bearing and the housing.
7. Remove the differential housing stud nuts, withdraw the housing from the transmission case and remove the differential assembly.

THE DIFFERENTIAL COMPONENTS

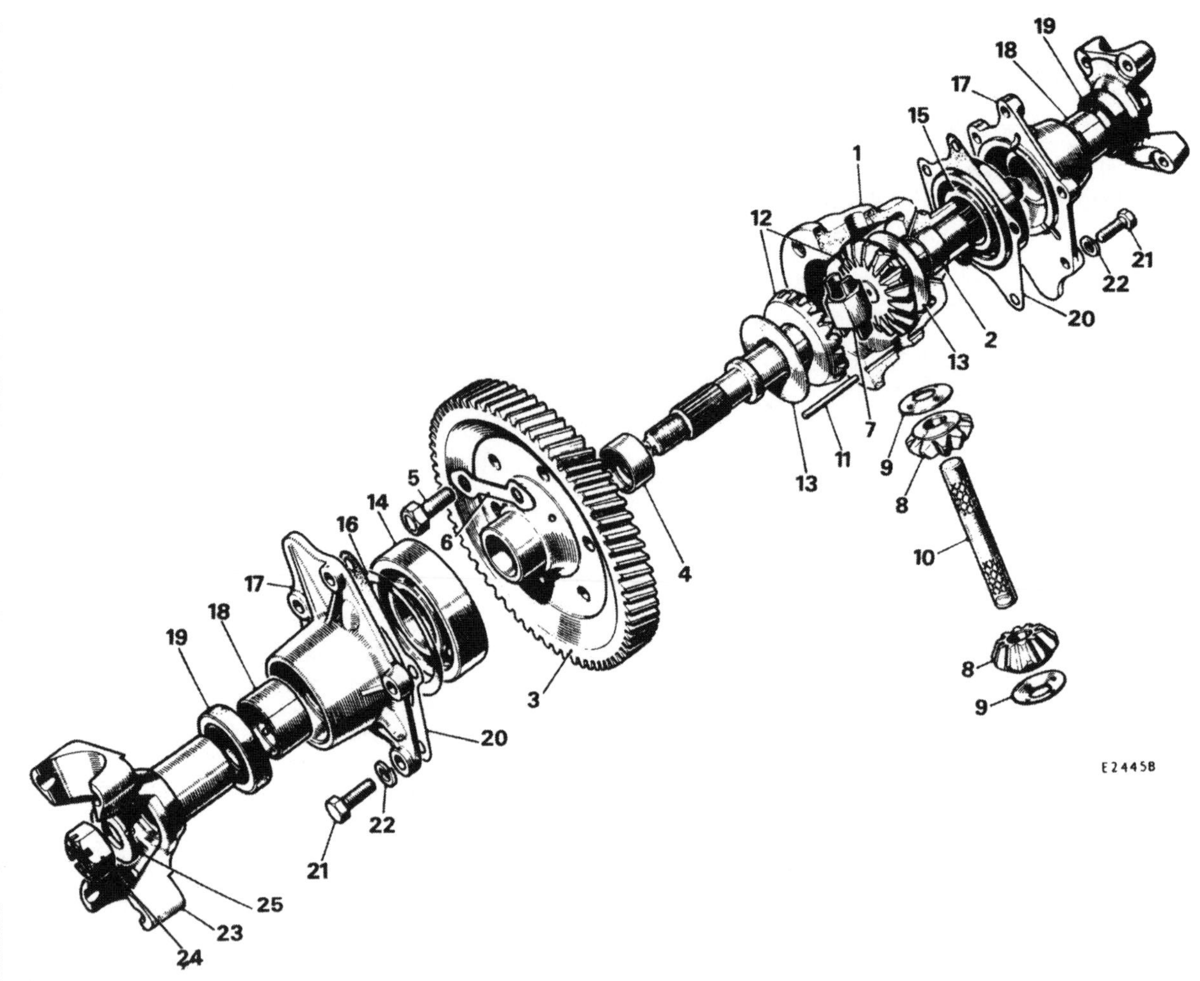

No.	Description
1.	Differential case.
2.	Case bush.
3.	Drive gear.
4.	Gear bush.
5.	Gear bolt.
6.	Lock washer.
7.	Thrust block.
8.	Differential pinion.
9.	Pinion thrust washer.
10.	Centre pin.
11.	Pin peg.
12.	Differential gear.
13.	Gear thrust washer.
14.	Drive gear bearing.
15.	Case bearing.
16.	Bearing shim.
17.	End cover.
18.	Cover bush.
19.	Oil seal.
20.	Cover joint.
21.	End cover screw.
22.	Washer.
23.	Driving flange.
24.	Flange out.
25.	Washer.

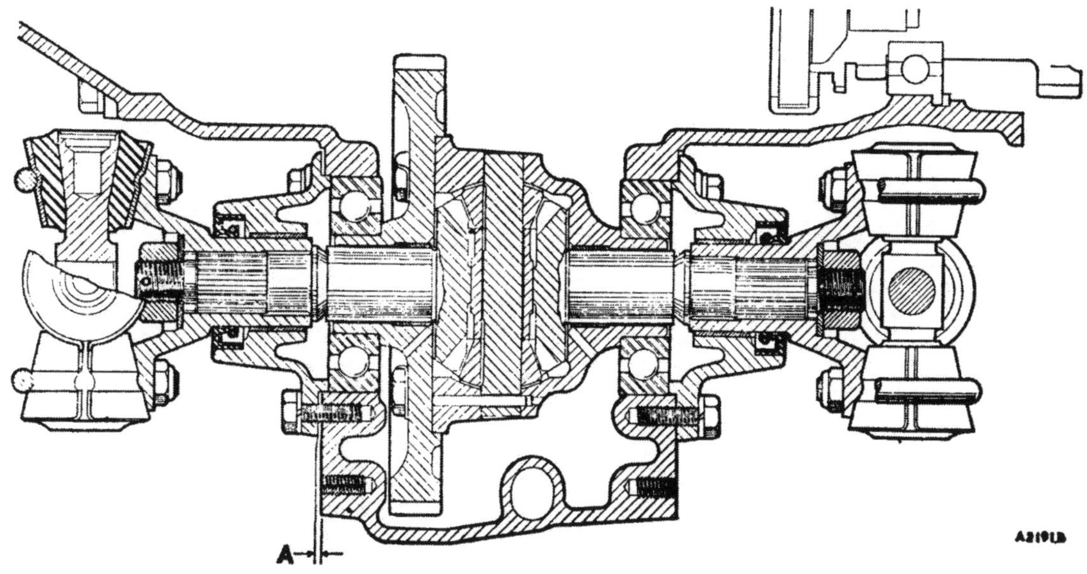

Fig. F.8
With the left-hand drive cover fitted without its joint washer, measure the gap at point 'A', and fit shims between the bearing and cover to obtain the required pre-load

Dismantling

8. Withdraw the two differential bearings, using Service tool 18G 2. Knock back the locking plate tabs and remove the six set bolts securing the driving gear to the cage, which may now be separated after marking them to assist in refitting them in their original positions. Extract the differential gear and thrust washer from the bore of the driving gear.

9. Tap out the taper pin peg to release the pinion centre pin, the thrust block, both differential pinions and thrust washers and the other differential gear and washer.

Reassembling

10. Reverse the dismantling sequence, making sure that the gear thrust washers are refitted with their chamfered bores against the machined face of the differential gears, and that all parts are refitted in their original positions.

Refitting

11. Place the differential assembly in the transmission casing with a slight bias towards the flywheel side. Refit the differential housing with its joint washers, and nip up the nuts sufficiently to hold the bearings, yet still allowing the assembly to be moved sideways.

12. Refit the right-hand drive end cover together with its joint washer. Then carefully and evenly tighten up the set screws, to displace the differential assembly away from the flywheel side and ensuring full contact between the register on the inner face of the cover and the differential bearing.

 Fit the left-hand final drive cover, without its joint washer, the compressed thickness of which is .007 in. (.18 mm.). Tighten the set screws sufficiently for the cover register to nip the bearing outer race; overtightening will distort the cover flange. The required preload on the bearings is .001 to .002 in. (.025 to .05 mm.), hence the gap between the cover flange and the differential housing and transmission casing must be between .008 to .009 in. (.2 to .23 mm.). Measure this gap ('A' in Fig. F.8) with feeler gauges, and correct it as necessary by fitting shims between the bearing and the register on the cover. For example if the gap as measured is .005 in. (.13 mm.) a shim of .003 in. (.076 mm.) is required. Measure the gap in several places: any deviations will indicate that the end cover set screws have not been tightened evenly.

 Remove and refit the end cover with its joint washer and the selected shims, tighten the cover screws and differential housing nuts.

 NOTE.—Later assemblies are fitted with increased thrust capacity bearings, which must be fitted with the identification word 'THRUST' facing the outside, towards the end cover. Since the pre-load is increased to .004 in. (.1 mm.), adjust the gap 'A' (see Fig. F.8) with shims until it is .011 in. (.28 mm.) before the joint washer is fitted.

13. Refit the driving flanges, making reference to item 4. The torque tightening figure is given in **'GENERAL DATA'**.

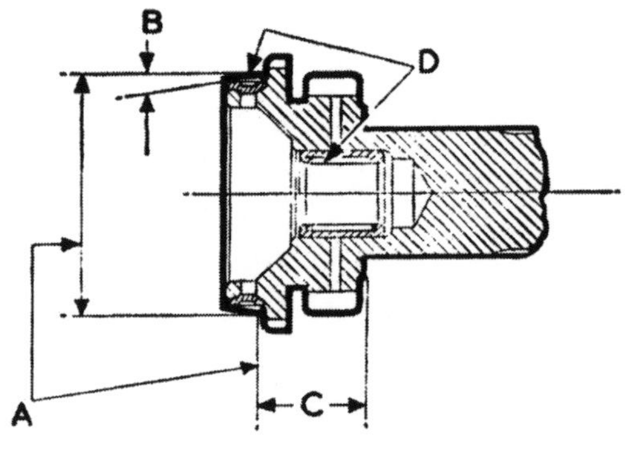

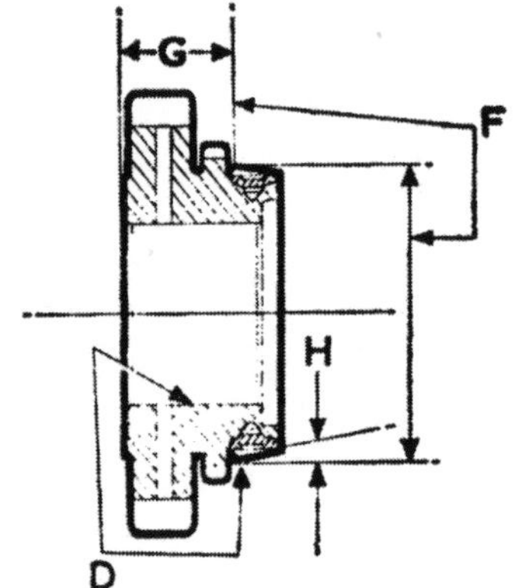

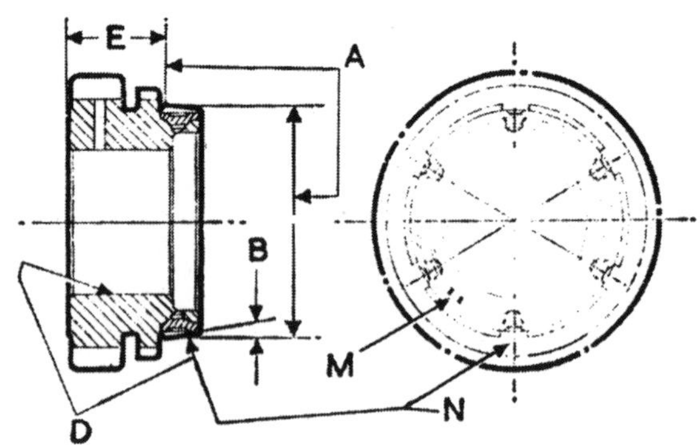

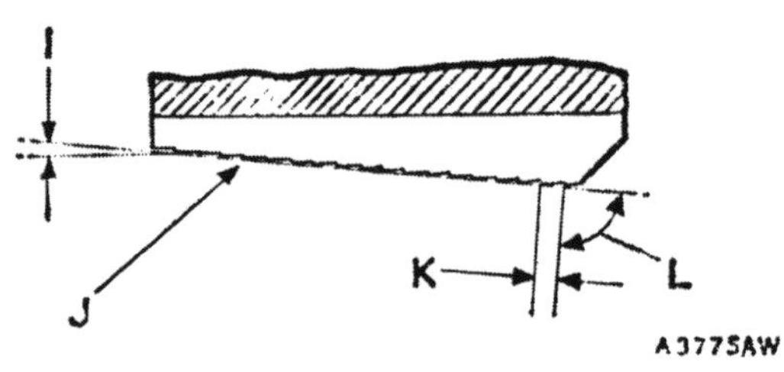

Fig. F.9
Top left: first motion shaft. Lower left: third speed mainshaft gear. Top right: second speed mainshaft gear. Lower right: Cone

DIMENSIONS

A. Taper 2.150 in. (54.61 mm.) dia. at this line to gauge.

B. Taper 10°30', to be true and concentric with bore to .001 in. (.025 mm.).

C. .909/.912 in. (23.09/23.16 mm.).

D. Taper to be true and concentric with bore to .001 in. (.025 mm.).

E. .862/.865 in. (21.8/21.9 mm.).

F. Taper 2.150 in. (54.61 mm.) dia. at this line to gauge.

G. .837/.840 in. (21.254/21.335 mm.).

H. 8°30'.

I. 6°

J. Coarse turning may be either right or left-hand.

K. .015 in. (.38 mm.).

L. 90°

M. One notch to be ground in position shown relative to grooves with indentations.

N. Synchronizing cone to be heated in oil shrunk onto gear, and punched into holes as shown with centre-line of holes and spaces in cone in line.

14. Make certain that both drive shafts are equally free to rotate, otherwise the vehicle's steering may pull to one side.

15. Refer to item 3. Position the remote control shaft lever on the ball end of the operating lever, insert the remote control shaft from underneath and engage it with the splined bore of the former. Insert the set screw after checking that the drilling in the boss and the recess in the shaft are in alignment.

16. Reassemble the transmission, clutch assembly and housing to the engine (if removed, see item 2).

17. Refit the power unit into the car and reassemble the gear-change to the transmission (or refit the remote control assembly).

Section F.5

SYNCHRONIZING CONES
(Non-baulk-ring Transmission)

Cones may be shrunk onto the second, third and fourth gears by heating in oil to 121°C. (250°F.) and quenching in cold water when in position.

See Fig. F.9 for machining dimension.

GEAR CHANGE REMOTE CONTROL COMPONENTS

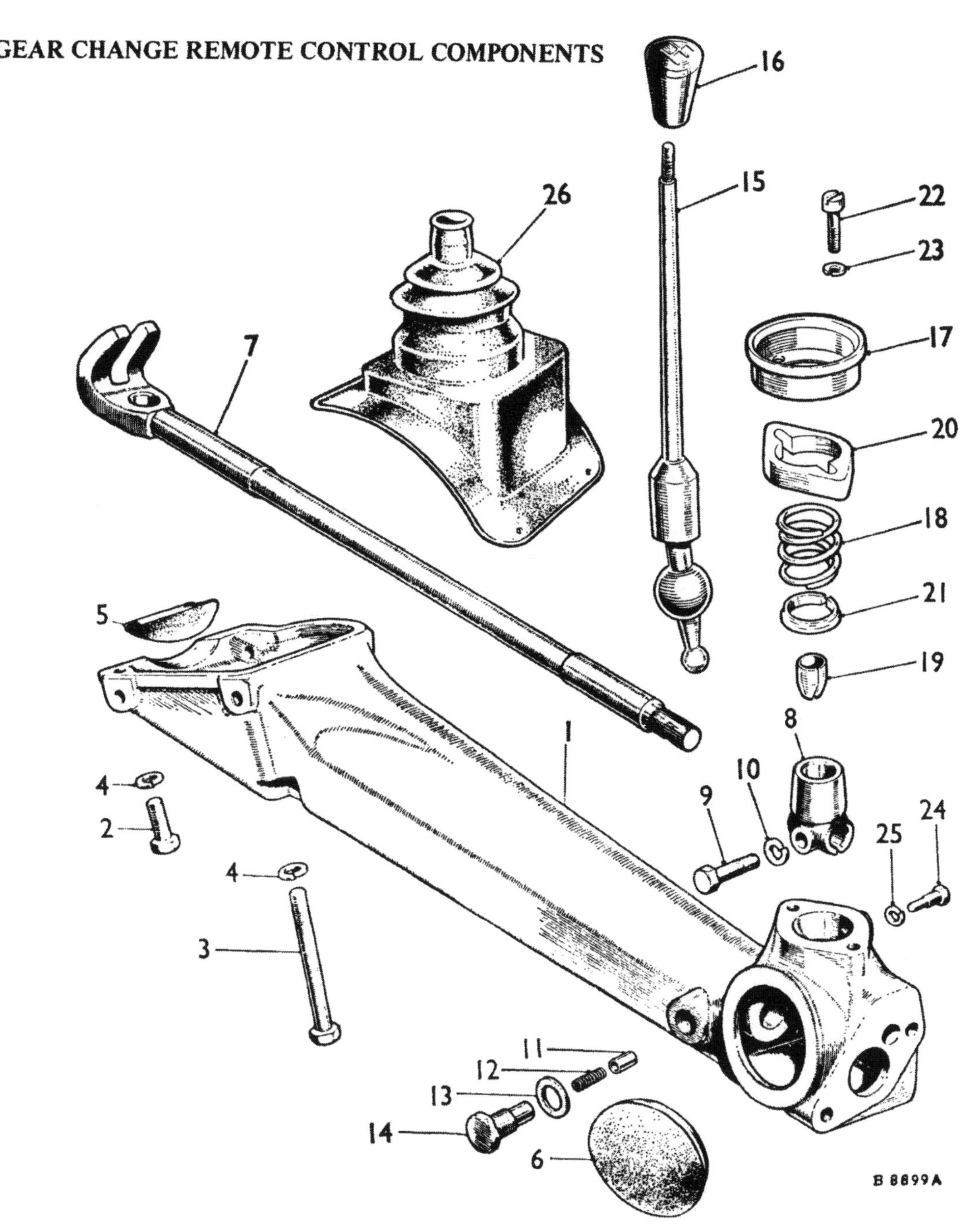

No.	Description	No.	Description
1.	Housing.	14.	Cap nut–spring retainer.
2.	Securing screw–short.	15.	Change speed lever.
3.	Securing screw–long.	16.	Lever knob.
4.	Spring washers.	17.	Retainer.
5.	Rubber plug.	18.	Spring.
6.	Rubber dust cover.	19.	Bush–split.
7.	Primary shaft.	20.	Distance piece.
8.	Primary shaft lever.	21.	Flange.
9.	Lever–screw.	22.	Screw–retainer to housing.
10.	Spring washer.	23.	Spring washer.
11.	Damper plunger.	24.	Locating pin.
12.	Plunger spring.	25.	Spring washer.
13.	Washer.	26.	Gaiter–change speed lever.

Section F.6

GEAR CHANGE REMOTE CONTROL ASSEMBLY

Removing

1. Remove the front floor covering, the gear lever knob, and the rubber gaiter.
2. From beneath the car, remove the securing screws and nuts from the extension rear support bracket (see Fig. A.12).
3. Remove the four bolts securing the extension to the transmission casing and detach the extension.

Dismantling

4. Remove the rubber dust cover, and slacken the lever locating pin.
5. Remove the screws securing the change speed lever retainer and withdraw the lever, retainer, and spring.
6. Lift out the distance piece and spring flange.
7. Remove the remote control shaft damper assembly and the screw securing the remote control shaft to the primary shaft lever. Withdraw the shaft and the lever from the housing.

Inspection

Clean and examine all components for wear, and fit new parts as required.

Reassembling

8. Reassemble all components in the reverse order of dismantling. Lubricate the operating surfaces of all components with grease.

Refitting

9. Reverse the removing procedure, ensuring that the rubber plug is correctly located between the extension and the transmission casing.

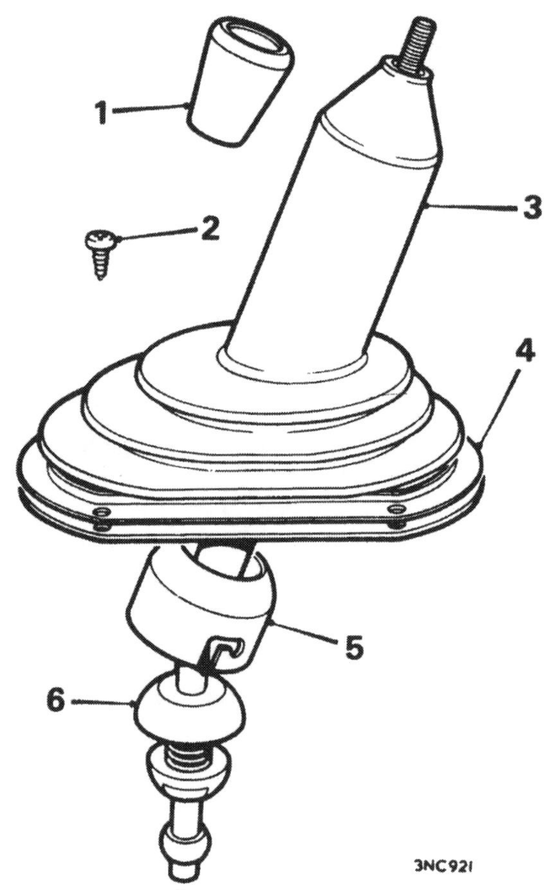

Fig. F.10
Removing the gear change lever assembly

1. Lever knob.
2. Gaiter.
3. Screw–gaiter.
4. Retaining cap –lever assembly.
5. Lever assembly.

Section F.7

GEAR CHANGE LEVER (Rod-change transmission)

Removing

1. Unscrew the knob from gear-change lever.
2. Remove the front floor carpet.
3. Remove the gaiter retaining ring screws and pull the gaiter up the lever.
4. Press down and turn the bayonet cap fixing to release the lever from the remote control assembly.
5. Remove the gear-change lever.

Refitting

6. Reverse the procedure in 1 to 5.

Section F.8

GEAR CHANGE REMOTE CONTROL ASSEMBLY (Rod-change transmission)

Removing

1. Release the gear change lever from the remote control from beneath the car.
2. Drift out the roll-pin retaining the extension rod to the selector rod at the final drive housing, Fig. F.30.
3. Remove the nut and bolt securing the remote control steady rod to the final drive housing on the gearbox.
4. Remove the one nut and bolt securing the remote control housing to the mounting bracket and withdraw the assembly.

Dismantling

5. Hold the assembly in a vice and remove the bottom cover-plate.
6. Remove the steady rod from the housing.
7. Move the extension rod eye rearwards, and remove the roll-pin retaining the extension rod to the rod eye.
8. Withdraw the extension rod.

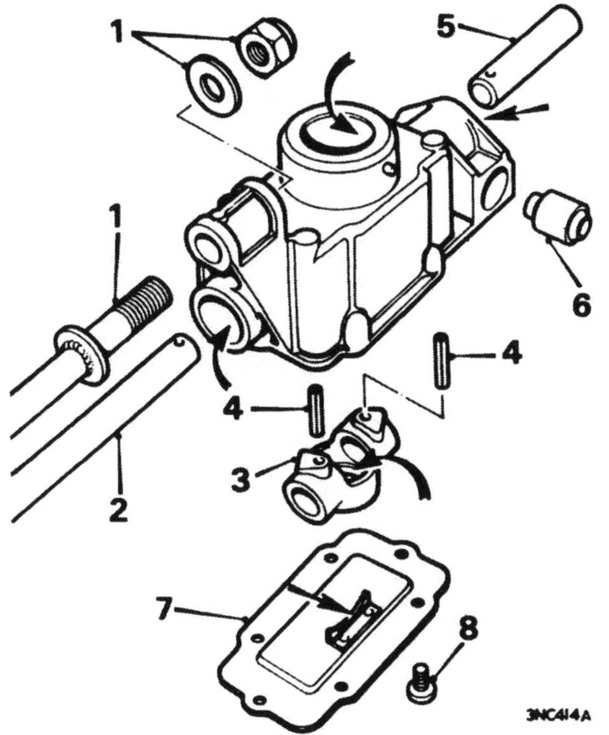

Fig. F.11
A dismantled view of the remote control components, the 'arrows' indicate the areas to be lubricated on assembly

1. Steady rod assembly.
2. Selector rod.
3. Eye–extension rod.
4. Roll pins.
5. Extension rod.
6. Bush–remote housing.
7. Cover plate.
8. Screw–cover plate.

9. Move the extension rod eye forward and remove the roll-pin retaining the support rod to the extension rod eye.
10. Drift out the support rod.
11. Lift out the extension rod eye.

Inspecting

12. Examine all parts for undue wear, and replace as necessary.

Reassembling

13. Use ½ oz (14 g) of Duckhams Laminoid 'O' Grease and apply with a brush onto the following parts and locations (arrowed), see Fig. F.11 when reassembling:
    a. To the hemispherical fulcrum surface in the housing.
    b. Into the selector rod eye.
    c. Into the two selector rod bearing locations.
    d. To the inner surface of the bottom cover-plate and particularly onto the reverse lift plate.
14. Refit the extension rod eye into the housing.
15. Insert the support rod.
16. Reverse the procedure in 7 to 9 to reassemble the support and extension rods to the eye.
17. Reverse the procedure in 5 and 6.

Refitting

18. Reverse the procedure 1 to 4.

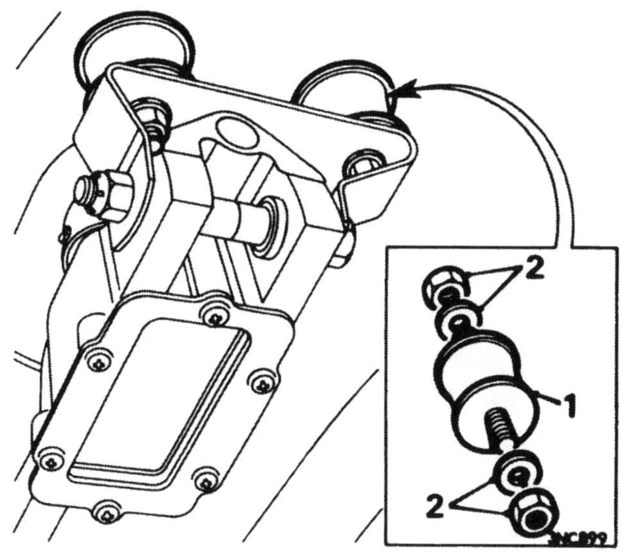

Fig. F.12
Removing the gear change remote control mountings

1. Mounting.
2. Retaining nuts and washers.

Section F.9

REMOTE CONTROL MOUNTINGS
(Rod-change transmission)

Removing

1. Remove the front floor carpet.
2. Remove the nuts and spring washers securing the remote control mountings to the tunnel panel and lower the assembly.
3. Remove the nuts and spring washers securing the mountings to the support bracket.
4. Remove the mountings.

Refitting

5. Reverse the procedure 1 to 4.

Section F.10

TRANSMISSION ASSEMBLY–OVERHAUL
(Rod-change type)

Removing

1. Remove the engine/transmission assembly, Section A.33.
2. Remove the transmission from the engine, Section A.19.

Dismantling

3. Remove the securing screws and detach the final drive end covers.
4. Extract the selector shaft detent spring, sleeve and ball.

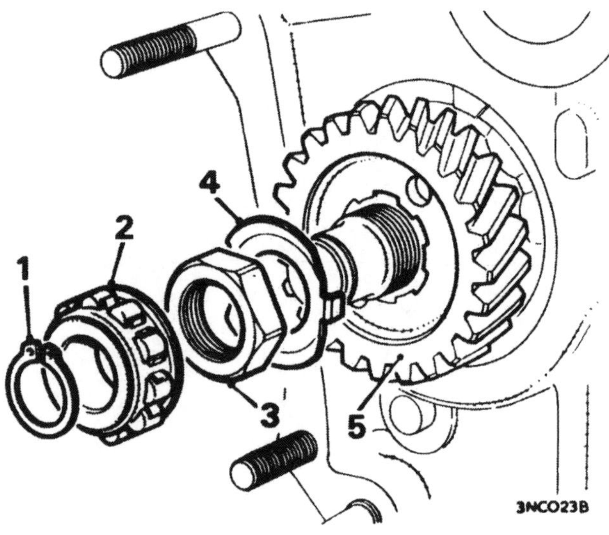

Fig. F.13
Removing the first motion shaft gear

1. Retaining circlip–roller bearing.
2. Roller bearing–first motion shaft.
3. Nut–first motion shaft.
4. Lockwasher.
5. First motion shaft gear.

5. Knock back the lock washer tabs from the final drive housing securing nuts; remove the nuts and lock washers.
6. Locate the oil seal protector sleeve (tool 18G 1236) over the selector shaft.
7. Remove the final drive housing.
8. Remove the final drive gear assembly.
9. Remove the speedometer drive pinion.
10. Remove the engine mounting adaptor housing.
11. Remove the speedometer drive housing.
12. Tap back the lock washer tabs and remove the screws securing the oil suction pipe to the gearbox casing; pull out the pipe.
13. Remove the circlip retaining the first motion shaft roller bearing, using tool 18G 1004.
14. Use tools 18G 705 and 18G 705C to pull off the first motion shaft roller bearing.
15. Knock back the lock washer tab from the first motion shaft securing nut.
16. Knock back the lock washer tab from the third motion shaft final drive gear securing nut.
17. Rotate the selector shaft anti-clockwise to disengage the operating stub and the interlock spool from the bellcrank levers, Fig. F.14.
18. Engage first and fourth gears simultaneously to lock the gear train.
19. Use tool 18G 587 and remove the third motion shaft final drive gear nut.
20. Pull off the lock washer and final drive gear.
21. Remove the first motion shaft gear nut.
22. Pull off the lock washer and the first motion shaft gear.
23. Move first and fourth gears to neutral position.

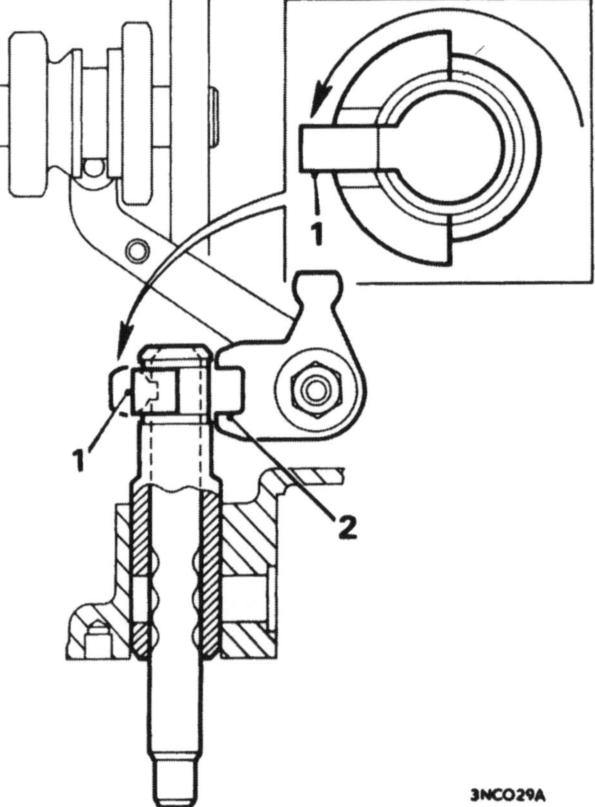

Fig. F.14
Showing the selector shaft (1) rotated out of engagement with the selector bellcrank levers (2)

24. Knock back the lock washer tabs on the third motion shaft bearing retainer bolts and remove the bolts.
25. Remove the retainer complete with the adjustment shim(s).
26. Remove the reverse locking plate.
27. Withdraw the layshaft.

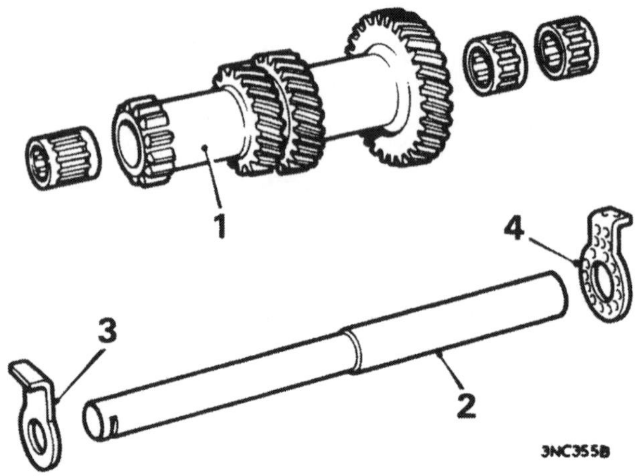

Fig. F.15
An exploded view of the laygear and shaft assembly

1. Laygear and bearings.
2. Layshaft.
3. Thrust washer (selective)–small.
4. Thrust washer–large.

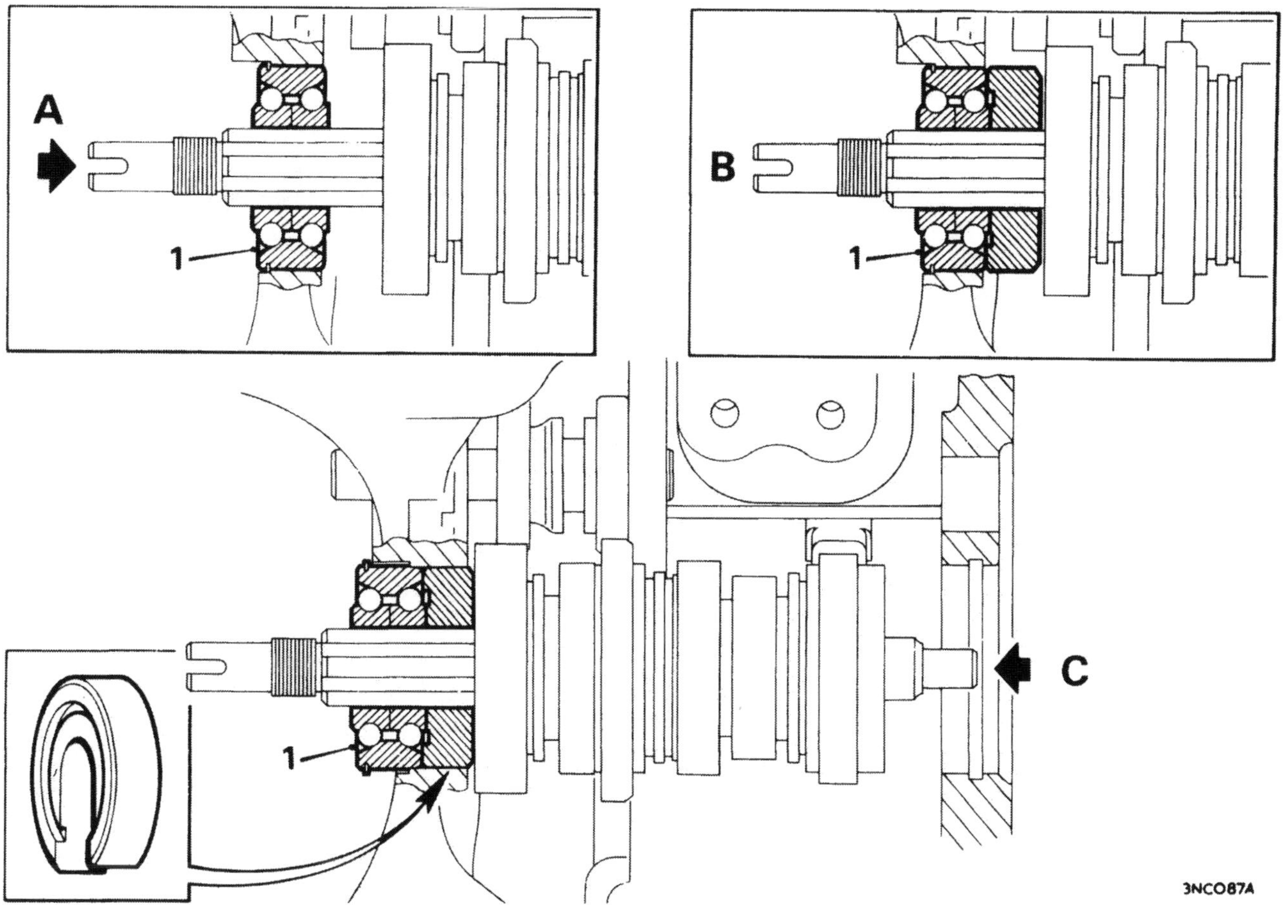

Fig. F.16
Removing the third motion shaft bearing (1)

28. Take out the small thrust washer from the laygear, remove the laygear and the larger thrust washer, Fig. F.15.
29. Use tool 18G 257 to remove the first motion shaft bearing retaining circlip.
30. Use tools 18G 284 and 18G 284B and withdraw the first motion shaft and bearing from the end casing.
31. Refer to removing procedure 'A', 'B' and 'C' on Fig. F.16 to remove the third motion shaft bearing:

    'A': Use a soft drift and drift the third motion shaft towards the clutch end of the gearbox. Take care not to disengage the third/fourth speed synchronizer from its hub and release the balls and springs.

    'B': Insert tool 18G 1127 with its relieved side against the bearing.

    'C': Drift the other end of the third motion shaft in the opposite direction to remove the third motion shaft bearing from the centre web of the casing.

    NOTE: Should the bearing not be completely removed from the centre web by the procedures given, it can be carefully levered out by using a screwdriver between the casing and the bearing circlip.

32. Lift out the third motion shaft assembly.
33. Remove the oil strainer.
34. Withdraw the reverse idler shaft and gear, Fig. F.17.

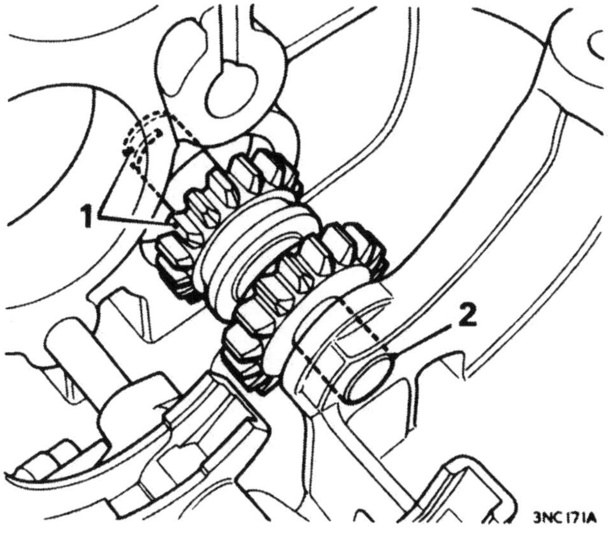

Fig. F.17
Removing the reverse idler gear (1) and shaft (2)

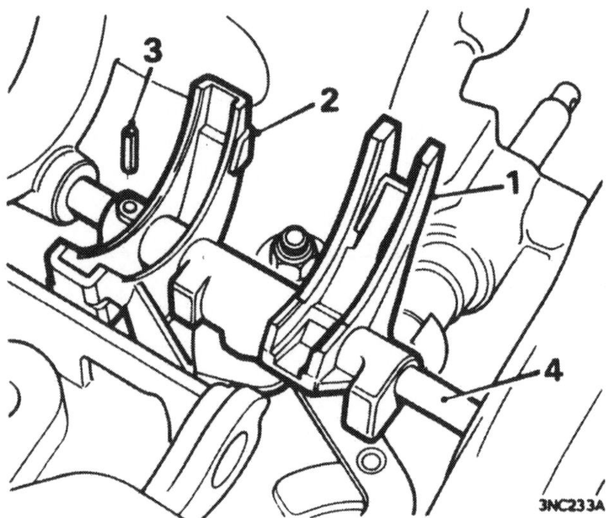

Fig. F.18
The selector shaft and forks.

1. First speed selector fork.
2. Third/fourth speed selector fork.
3. Roll pin.
4. Selector fork shaft.

35. Drift out the roll-pin securing the third/fourth speed selector fork to its shaft, Fig. F.18.
36. Remove the selector shaft and forks, Fig. F.18.

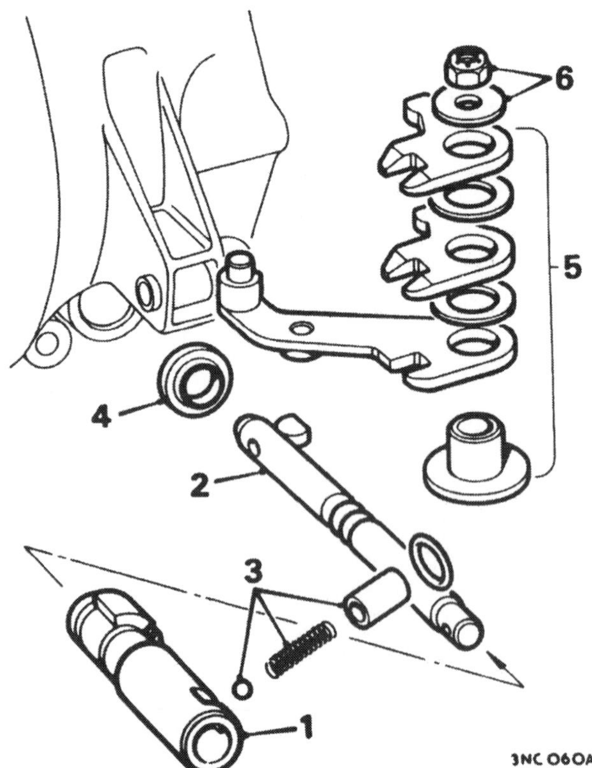

Fig. F.19
An exploded view of the selector shaft and bellcrank lever assemblies

1. Interlock spool.
2. Selector shaft.
3. Detent ball, spring, sleeve and oil seal.
4. Oil seal–selector shaft.
5. Bellcrank lever assembly.
6. Pivot post nut and washer.

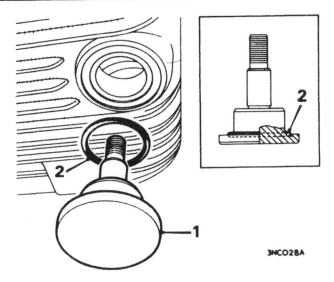

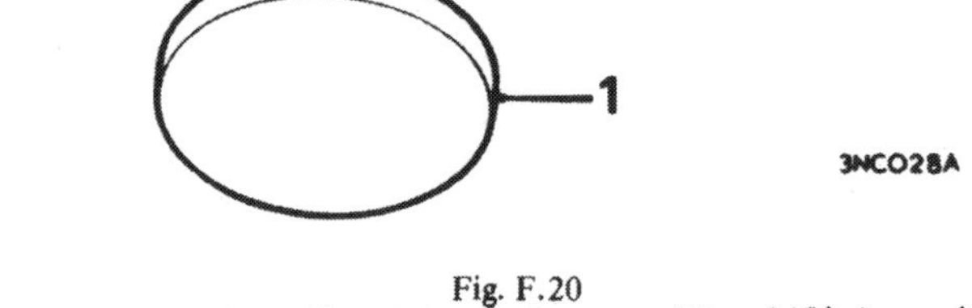

Fig. F.20
Showing the bellcrank lever pivot post (1) and 'O' ring seal (2) drifted out of the transmission casing

37. Remove the bellcrank lever pivot post nut and washer.
38. Lift out the bellcrank levers, washers and pivot sleeve, Fig. F.19. Note the location and markings on the levers for reassembly.
39. Withdraw the interlock spool and selector shaft from inside the casing, Fig. F.19.
40. Drift the bellcrank lever pivot post out of the gearbox casing if the 'O' ring oil seal is to be renewed, Fig. F.20.
41. Remove the two circlips retaining the idler gear needle-roller bearing in the gearbox casing.

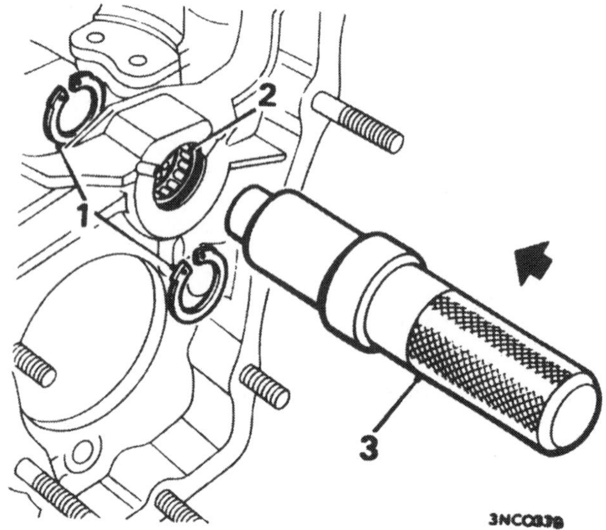

Fig. F.21
Removing the idler gear bearing from the transmission case

1. Retaining circlips.
2. Idler gear bearing.
3. Service tool 18G 1126.

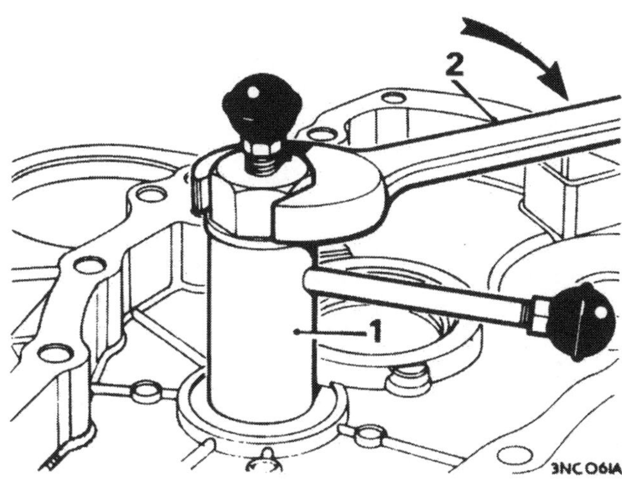

Fig. F.22
Extracting the idler gear bearing from the flywheel housing using (1) Service tool 18G 581. Turn the nut with the spanner (2) in the direction 'arrowed'.

42. Use tool 18G 1126 (without its outer sleeve) and drift out the idler gear bearing, Fig. F.21.
43. Remove the other idler gear bearing from the flywheel housing, using tool 18G 581, Fig. F.22.
44. Extract the circlip retaining the outer race of the first motion shaft spigot bearing in the flywheel housing.
45. Use tool 18G 617A to pull out the outer race (arrowed), Fig. F.23.
46. Remove the primary gear oil seal from the flywheel housing.

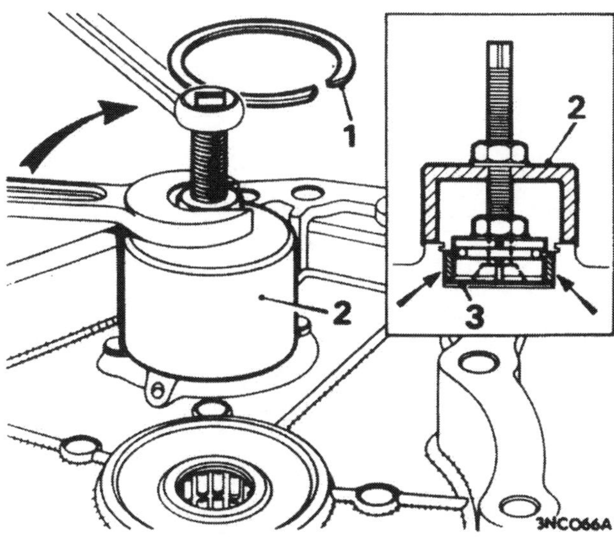

Fig. F.23
Extracting the first motion shaft spigot bearing outer race 'arrowed' from the flywheel housing

1. Retaining circlip. 2. Service tool 18G 617A. 3. Bearing outer race.

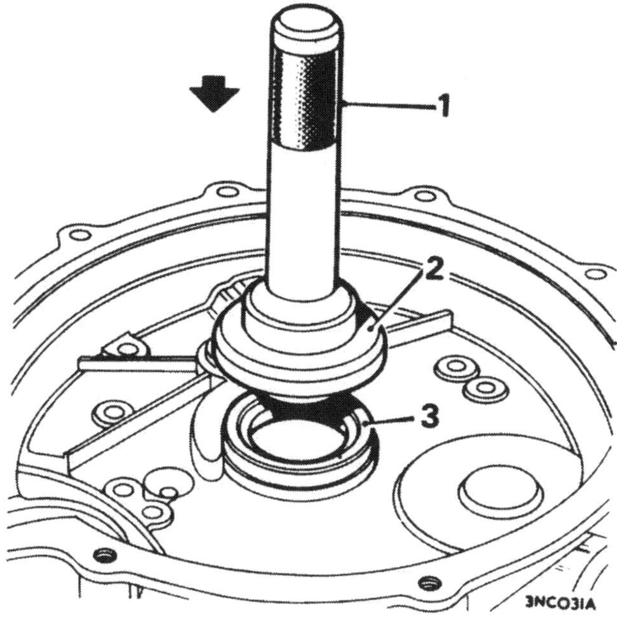

Fig. F.24
Refitting the primary gear oil seal into the flywheel housing

1. Service tool 18G 134. 2. Service tool adaptor 18G 134BC. 3. Primary gear oil seal.

Inspecting

47. Clean all assemblies and examine for wear. Completely dismantle the main assemblies and thoroughly examine their components, refer to the overhaul procedure for each main assembly given in the reassembling procedure.

Reassembling

48. Fit a new primary gear oil seal into the flywheel housing, using tools 18G 134 and 18G 134BC, Fig. F.24.
49. Use the 'replacer' of tool 18G 617A and drift the first motion shaft spigot bearing outer race into the flywheel housing, Fig. F.25.
50. Refit the bearing retaining circlip.
51. Use tool 18G 1126 with its outer sleeve and drift the idler gear bearing into the housing to the depth governed by the outer sleeve of the tool, Fig. F.26.
52. Refit the inner circlip into the gearbox casing, drift in the new idler gear bearing using tool 18G 1126, and refit the outer retaining circlip, Fig. F.21.
53. Lubricate and fit a new 'O' ring oil seal onto the bellcrank lever pivot post and drift it into the gearbox casing, Fig. F.20.
54. Insert the selector shaft into the interlock spool and refit the assembly into the gearbox with the operating stub facing away from the pivot post.
55. Refit the sleeve, bellcrank levers (in their correct order) onto the pivot post and tighten the self-locking nut, Fig. F.19.

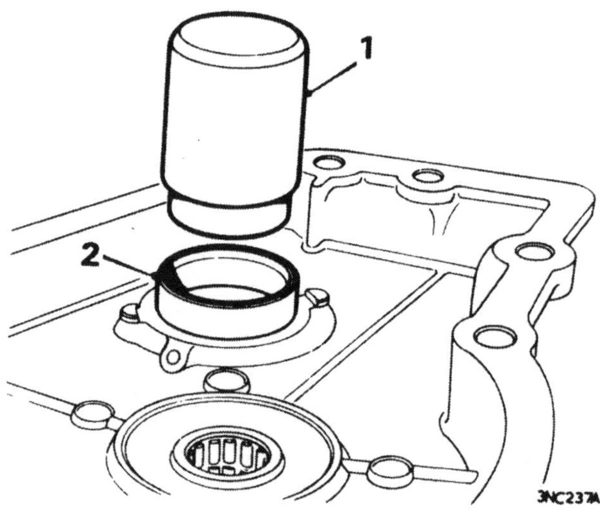

Fig. F.25
Refitting the first motion shaft spigot bearing outer race into the flywheel housing

1. Service tool 18G 617A (replacer). 2. Bearing outer race.

NOTE: DO NOT turn the selector shaft and interlock spool into engagement with the bellcrank levers until the first and third motion shaft gear retaining nuts have been torque-tightened.

56. Refit the third/fourth speed selector fork.
57. Refit the first speed selector fork and drift the selector rod through the casing and forks; align the hole in the shaft with the hole in the third/fourth speed fork, Fig. F.18.
58. Drift in the roll-pin until it is flush with the fork.
59. Refit the reverse idler gear into engagement with the reverse bellcrank lever pivot and refit the shaft, Fig. F.17.
60. Place the oil strainer into its location in the casing.
61. Dismantle and overhaul the third motion shaft assembly, see Section F.3.
62. Dismantle and overhaul the first motion shaft assembly.
63. Insert the third motion shaft assembly into the gearbox assembly and locating in the two selector forks.
64. Use tool 18G 579 and drift the third motion shaft bearing into the centre web of the casing.
65. Insert the first motion shaft needle-roller bearing into its location in the gear.
66. Drift the first motion shaft assembly into the casing, using tool 18G 579.
67. Use tool 18G 569 to gauge the correct thickness circlip required, try the thicker side of the tool first; the sizes are marked on the handle.
68. Select the correct circlip from the chart given below and fit it using tool 18G 257.

When gap is	Use Circlip Part No.
0.096 to 0.098 in (2.43 to 2.48 mm)	2A 3710
0.098 to 0.100 in (2.48 to 2.54 mm)	2A 3711

69. Insert the needle-roller bearings into the laygear.
70. Refit the laygear and shaft with its thrust washers.
71. Use feeler gauges and check the laygear end-float, which should be 0.002 to 0.006 in (0.05 to 0.15 mm). Select and fit the required washer from the chart given below:

Layshaft thrust washer chart

Washer thickness		Part No.
inches	mm.	
0.123 to 0.124	3.12 to 3.14	22G 856
0.125 to 0.126	3.17 to 3.20	22G 857
0.127 to 0.128	3.22 to 3.25	22G 858
0.130 to 0.131	3.30 to 3.32	22G 859

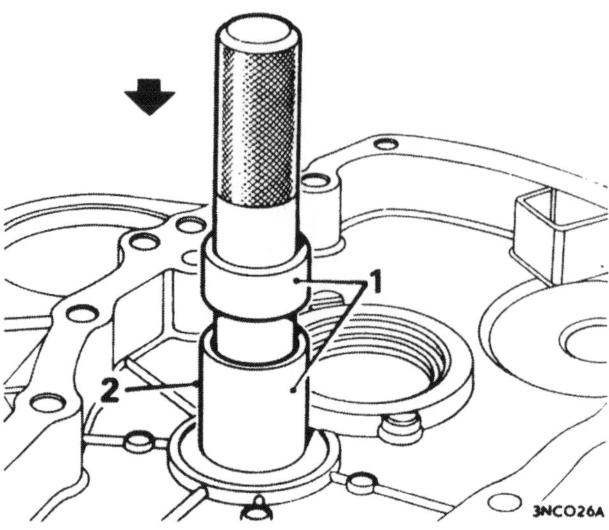

Fig. F.26
Drifting the idler gear bearing into the flywheel housing to the depth governed by the outer sleeve of the tool

1. Service tool 18G 1126. 2. Sleeve.

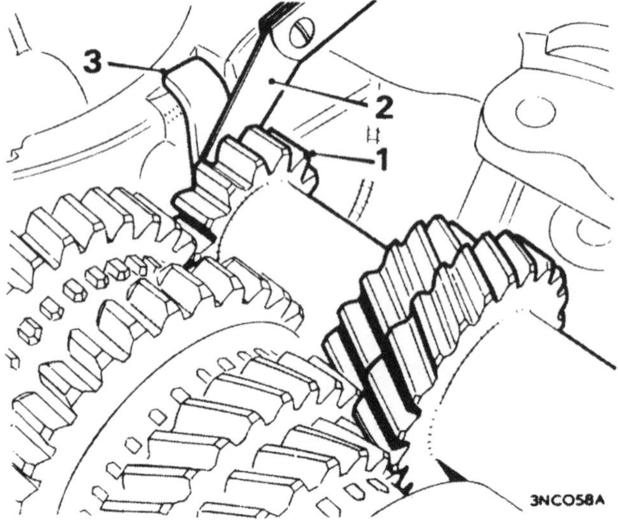

Fig. F.27
Checking the laygear end-float adjustment with feeler gauges

1. Laygear. 2. Feeler gauges.
3. Thrust washer (selective)—small.

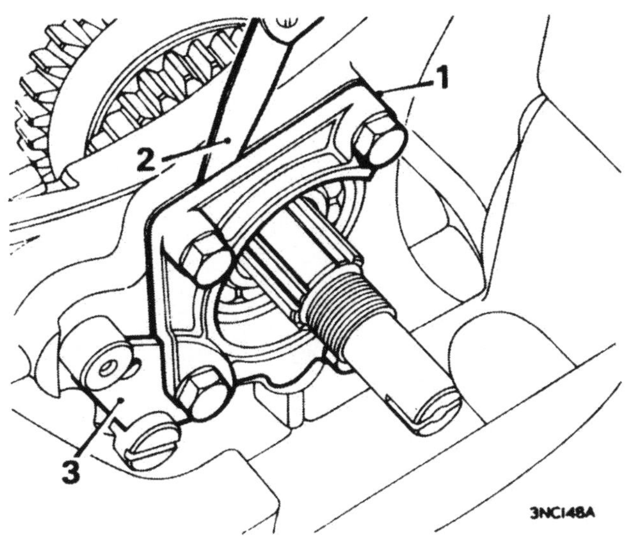

Fig. F.28
Checking the gap between the third motion shaft bearing retainer (1) and housing with feeler gauges (2). Note the location of the reverse and layshaft locking plate (3).

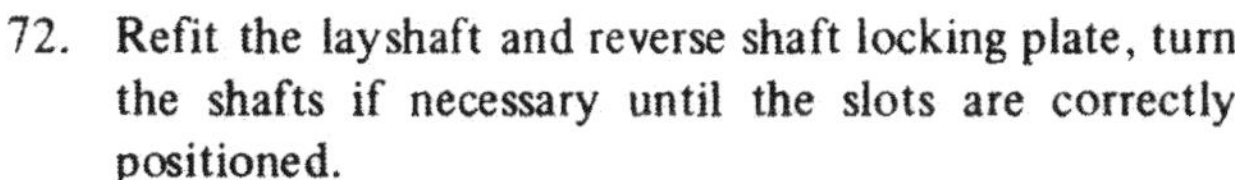

72. Refit the layshaft and reverse shaft locking plate, turn the shafts if necessary until the slots are correctly positioned.
73. Refit the third motion shaft bearing retainer without any shims, lightly and evenly tighten the retainer bolts.
74. Check the gap with feeler gauges, see Fig. F.28; select the required thickness of shims from the chart given below:

When gap is		Use shims totalling	
inches	mm.	inches	mm.
0.005 to 0.006	(0.13 to 0.15)	0.005	(0.13)
0.006 to 0.008	(0.15 to 0.20)	0.007	(0.18)
0.008 to 0.010	(0.20 to 0.25)	0.009	(0.23)
0.010 to 0.012	(0.25 to 0.30)	0.011	(0.28)
0.012 to 0.014	(0.30 to 0.35)	0.013	(0.33)
0.014 to 0.015	(0.35 to 0.38)	0.015	(0.38)

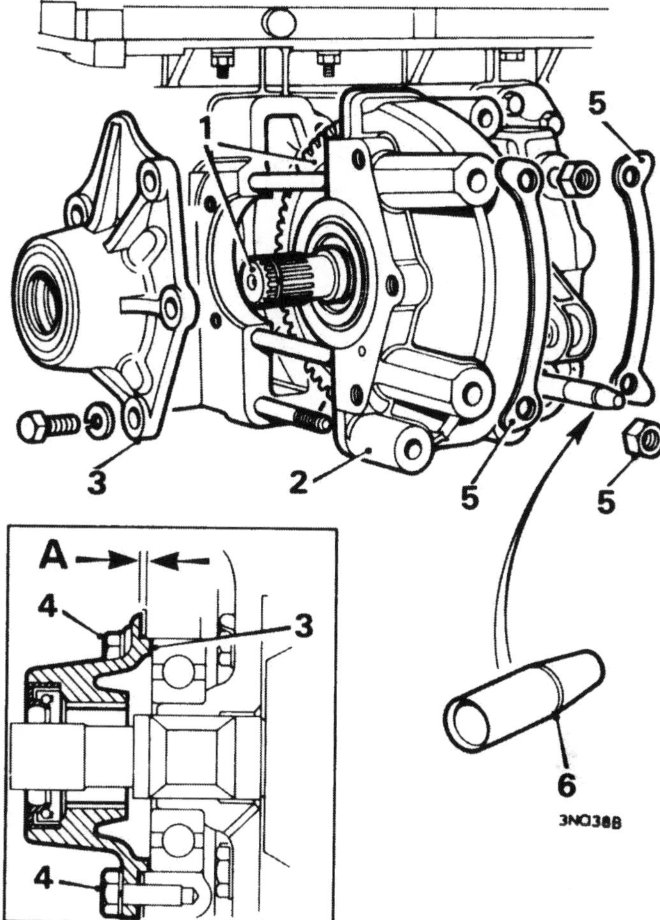

Fig. F.29
Refitting the final drive assembly and carrying out the bearing preload adjustment. Measure the gap 'A', select and fit shims to give the required bearing preload

1. Final drive assembly.
2. Housing.
3. End cover.
4. Screw–end cover.
5. Retaining nuts and lock plates.
6. Service tool 18G 1236–oil seal protector sleeve.

75. Fit the shims under the layshaft and reverse shaft locking plate.
76. Refit the bearing retainer with new lock washers, tighten the securing screws to the torque figure given in **'GENERAL DATA'**. Tap over the lock washer tabs.
77. Engage first and fourth gears simultaneously to lock the gear train.
78. Refit the final drive pinion, a new lock washer and the securing nut onto the third motion shaft.
79. Tighten the final drive gear pinion nut using tool 18G 587 to the torque figure given in **'GENERAL DATA'**. Tap over the lock washer tabs.
80. Refit the first motion shaft gear with a new lock washer. Refit and tighten the securing nut to the torque figure given in **'GENERAL DATA'**. Tap over the lock washer tab.
81. Refit the first motion shaft roller-bearing and refit the retaining circlip with tool 18G 1004.
82. Move first and fourth gears to the neutral position.
83. Rotate the selector shaft and interlock spool into engagement with the bellcrank levers.
84. Insert the oil suction pipe into the strainer.
85. Fit a new joint washer and locking plates, tighten the external flange securing screws first, then the pipe bracket screws. Tap over the locking plate tabs.
86. Refit the speedometer drive housing with a new joint washer to the gearbox casing. Tighten the securing nuts and screws to the torque figure given in **'GENERAL DATA'**.
87. Refit the speedometer drive pinion with a new joint washer.
88. Refit the engine mounting adaptor housing.

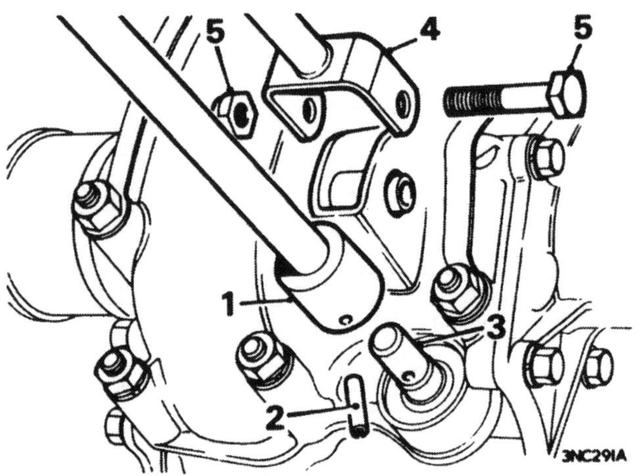

Fig. F.30
Disconnect the rod gear change remote control from the transmission.

1. Extension rod.
2. Roll pin – extension rod.
3. Selector shaft.
4. Steady rod.
5. Nut and bolt – steady rod fork.

89. Fit oil seal protector sleeve (tool 18G 1236) over the selector shaft.
90. Refit and adjust the final drive gear assembly, see Section F.4.
91. Refit the selector shaft sleeve, ball and spring before fitting the final drive end covers.

Refitting

92. Refit the transmission to the engine.
93. Refit the engine/transmission assembly.

Section F.11

GEAR CHANGE SELECTOR SHAFT OIL SEAL

Removing

1. Drain the engine/transmission oil.
2. Raise the front of the vehicle and place supports under the sub-frame side members.

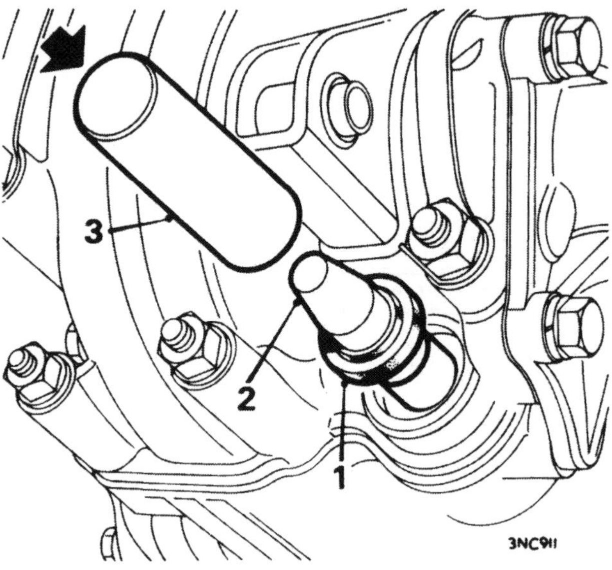

Fig. F.31
Fitting a new gear change selector shaft oil seal

1. Oil seal. 2. Protector sleeve–service tool 18G 1238. 3. Service tool 18G 1236.

3. Drift out roll pin securing the gear change rod to the selector shaft, see Fig. F.30.
4. Remove the nut and bolt securing the steady rod fork to the final drive casing, see Fig. F.30.
5. Lever out the old oil seal.

Refitting

6. Place protector sleeve, Service tool 18G 1238 over the selector shaft, see Fig. F.31.
7. Lubricate the new oil seal and drift it into the casing using Service tool 18G 1236, see Fig. F.31.
8. Remove Service tool 18G 1238 from the selector shaft.
9. Reverse the removing procedure 1 to 4.

SECTION Fa

THE AUTOMATIC TRANSMISSION

GENERAL DESCRIPTION

The automatic transmission incorporates a three-element fluid torque converter with a maximum torque conversion ratio of 2 : 1 coupled to a bevel gear train which provides four forward gears and reverse.

Engine power is transmitted from the crankshaft converter output gear through an idler gear to the input gear which drives the bevel reduction gears in the gear train assembly.

The final drive is transmitted from a drive gear to a conventional-type differential unit (similar to that fitted to a synchromesh transmission unit), which in turn transmits engine power through two flange-type coupling drive shafts employing constant velocity joints to the road wheels.

The complete gear train assembly, including the reduction gear and differential units, runs parallel to, and below, the crankshaft and is housed in the transmission casing which serves also as the engine sump.

The system is controlled by a selector lever within a gated quadrant marked with seven positions, and mounted centrally on the floor of the car. The reverse, neutral, and drive positions are for normal automatic driving, with the first, second, third, and fourth positions used for manual operation or over-ride as required. This allows the system to be used as a fully automatic four-speed transmission, from rest to maximum speed with the gears changing automatically according to throttle position and load. If a lower gear is required to obtain greater acceleration, an instant full throttle position, i.e. 'kick-down' on the accelerator, immediately produces the change.

Complete manual control of all four forward gears by use of the selector lever provides rapid changes. However, it is very important that downward changes are effected at the correct road speeds otherwise serious damage may result to the automatic transmission unit. The second, third, and top gears provide engine braking whether driving automatic or manual; in first gear a free-wheel condition exists when decelerating. Manual selection to third or second gear gives engine braking and also allows the driver to stay in a particular lower gear to suit road conditions or when descending steep hills.

The hydraulic system

Oil is drawn from the transmission casing through the main gauze strainer and pick-up pipe by the main oil pump which has a high potential output and serves both the engine lubrication and transmission systems with a common oil supply. The oil passes through drillings in the cylinder block and a pipe to the external full-flow filter and thence to the valve block.

The valve block assembly controls pressures to the transmission. Separate valves control the converter and engine pressures. The oil passes from the valve block through a long connecting pipe to the converter stator unit. Three short interconnecting pipes take the necessary line pressure to each of the servos which control brake band operation in manual and automatic selector positions.

The power flow through the bevel reduction gears is coupled to the final drive gear pinion by means of two multi-disc clutch assemblies operated hydraulically in manual and the automatic selector positions.

In the event of tow-starting the engine, an auxiliary oil pump of low capacity is employed which is responsive to vehicle speed only; immediately the engine starts the main pump automatically takes over.

The governor system

The governor is driven by auxiliary pump gears and is of the spring-loaded mechanical type, with its bobweights mounted on short links. A rod linkage transfers the movement to the governor valve incorporated in the valve block chest.

A spring-loaded rod connected to the carburetter provides an over-ride device. The spring tends to be compressed by accelerator pedal operation, and transfers this load by levers to the governor. The effect is to delay travel of the governor, which in turn delays gear shifts more as the accelerator is depressed.

The torque converter

This is fitted onto a taper on the rear of the crankshaft. Basically it comprises three elements, i.e. an impeller, a turbine, and a stator, but it is only serviced as a unit.

There is a continuous supply of oil circulating through the unit; this assists in dissipating the heat generated, and the out-flow passes through a low-pressure valve which maintains a 30 lb./sq. in. (2.1 kg./cm.^{2}) pressure within the converter to improve efficiency.

The brake bands and servos

Three brake bands are used. One is for reverse and the others provide second and third speed reactions. The clamping load is applied by three hydraulic servos in a common casing.

The multi-disc clutches

For forward motion a single-piston multi-disc clutch carries the drive and is engaged at all times during forward motion of the car. This forward clutch unit is fitted on one side of the final drive pinion and on the other side is a top and reverse clutch assembly which has a tandem piston arrangement. This feature is necessary because the clutch is also engaged for reverse and since a greater torque capacity is required in this case both pistons are pressurized.

The valve block

Two types of valve block may be fitted, the later type is fitted to the Mk.II B type transmission units and these assemblies can be identified by the prefix to the serial number starting at the letter 'K'.

The later type valve block incorporates an engagement control device which comprises an additional control valve and two shuttle valves and these are located together with the various other valves in the valve chest and pipe chest sections of this unit.

The assembly is constructed of three basic units, i.e. the lid, valve chest, and pipe chest, with a separator plate fitted between the lid and the valve chest on the later assembly.

A linkage arrangement locates the selector valve and this in turn is controlled by the selector rod, externally connected by cable to the gear selector lever in the car. The function of the various valves is as follows:

THE SELECTOR VALVE, directs oil from the main supply to either the governor valve for automatic gear-shifting or alternatively to the appropriate clutch or servo for manual selection.

THE REGULATOR VALVE controls the main line pressure, a secondary piston on the valve boosts this pressure when reverse is selected.

THE GOVERNOR VALVE movement is controlled by the mechanical governor and it directs the oil flow to the appropriate clutch or servo for automatic gear-shifts.

THE RELAY VALVES are used for shifts from second to third and third to top. They enable the clutch or servo required to be supplied either from the selector valve in 'manual' control or the governor valve in 'automatic'. In addition, pistons are fitted in front of the second and third relay valves to ensure that on up-shifts the engagement of the new ratio and release of the old occur simultaneously to prevent engine overspeeding between shifts. A relay valve is not required for the first gear as the torque reaction is controlled mechanically by a one-way clutch.

THE TOW START VALVE is only fitted to the early type valve block; it short-circuits the auxiliary pump under all normal driving conditions but supplies the required line pressure for tow starting. Immediately the engine starts the main pump automatically takes over. TOW STARTING IS NOT POSSIBLE when a transmission is fitted with a later type valve block which incorporates the engagement control valve.

THE ENGAGEMENT CONTROL VALVE has a primary function of eliminating harsh engagement when selecting 'D' or a forward gear from the rest position.

OPERATION OF ENGAGEMENT CONTROL VALVE
When a forward gear is selected, the selector valve in the valve block directs oil to shuttle valves located in the back of the valve block. The oil passes through the shuttle valves and pressurizes the third and reverse gear servos, thus applying the brake bands and bringing the rotating components of the gear train gently to rest. The oil flows simultaneously to the engagement control valve which, at a predetermined pressure, directs oil to the forward clutch; and as there is relatively little movement between the driving and driven members the gear engagement is smooth.
To complete the operating sequence, oil is also fed behind the shuttle valves which move and allow the oil pressure in the third and reverse servos to exhaust, thus releasing the third and reverse gear bands.

The low-pressure valve

This valve controls the pressure in the converter to 30 lb./sq. in. (2.1 kg./cm.^{2}). When the engine is stopped the valve is seated, preventing the converter draining. This avoids difficulties in checking the combined engine/transmission oil level and prevents a noisy and inefficient converter when restarting the engine.

The auxiliary pump

This unit is used for tow-starting. It is of limited capacity and is responsive to road speed only.

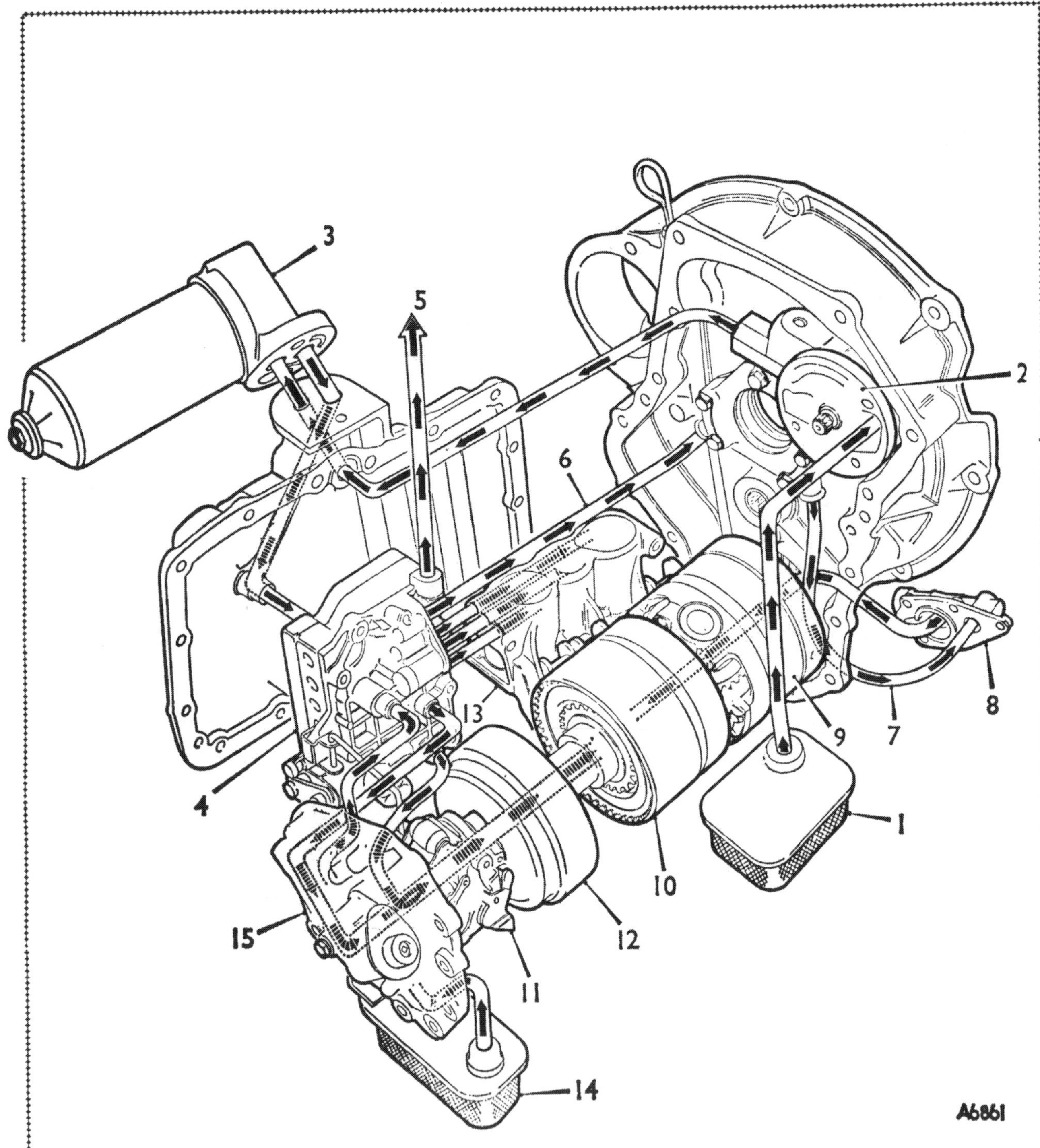

The components of the automatic transmission with the lubrication system and 'power flow' indicated by arrows to the various components

1. Main oil strainer.
2. Oil pump.
3. Oil filter assembly.
4. Valve block.
5. Engine oil feed.
6. Converter feed pipe.
7. Converter to low pressure valve feed.
8. Low pressure valve.
9. Gear train.
10. Top and reverse clutch.
11. Governor.
12. Forward clutch.
13. Servo unit.
14. Auxiliary pump oil strainer.
15. Auxiliary pump.

POWER FLOW DIAGRAMS (MECHANICAL)

The power flow diagrams indicate how the various ratios are obtained. Four speeds and reverse are provided and these are brought into operation by engaging the appropriate friction members.

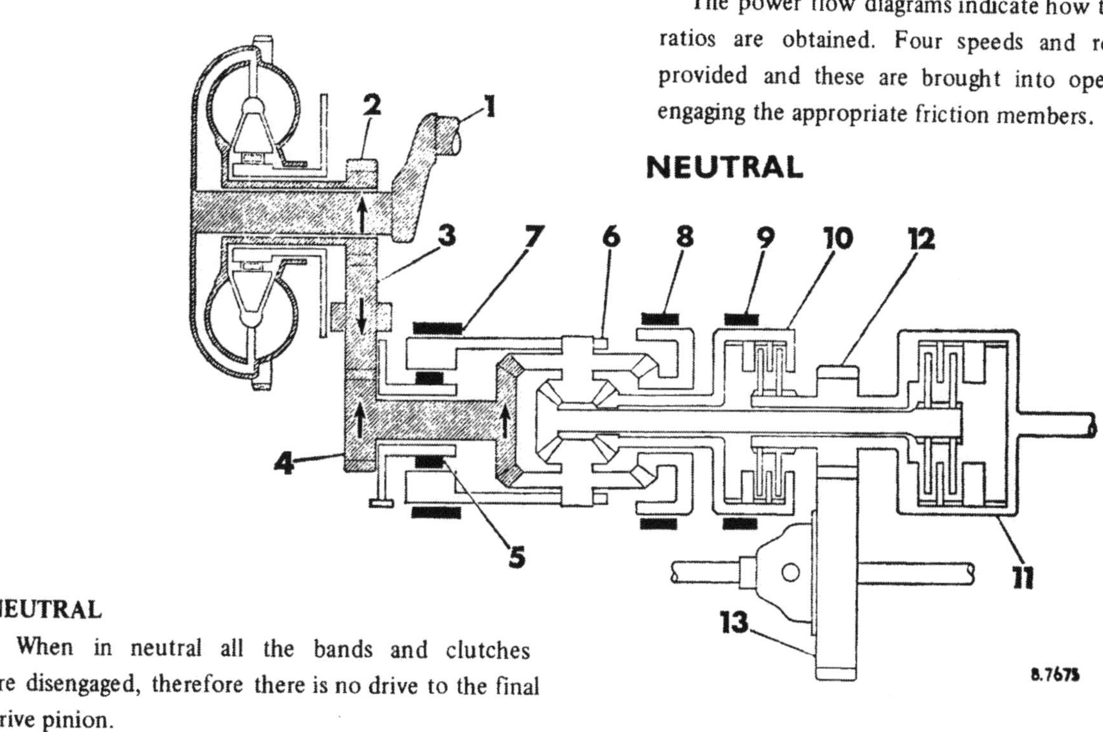

NEUTRAL

When in neutral all the bands and clutches are disengaged, therefore there is no drive to the final drive pinion.

KEY TO COMPONENTS

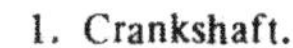

1. Crankshaft.
2. Converter output gear.
3. Idler gear.
4. Input gear.
5. One-way clutch.
6. Gear carrier.
7. Reverse band.
8. Third gear band.
9. Second gear band.
10. Top and reverse clutch.
11. Forward clutch.
12. Final drive pinion.
13. Final drive gear.

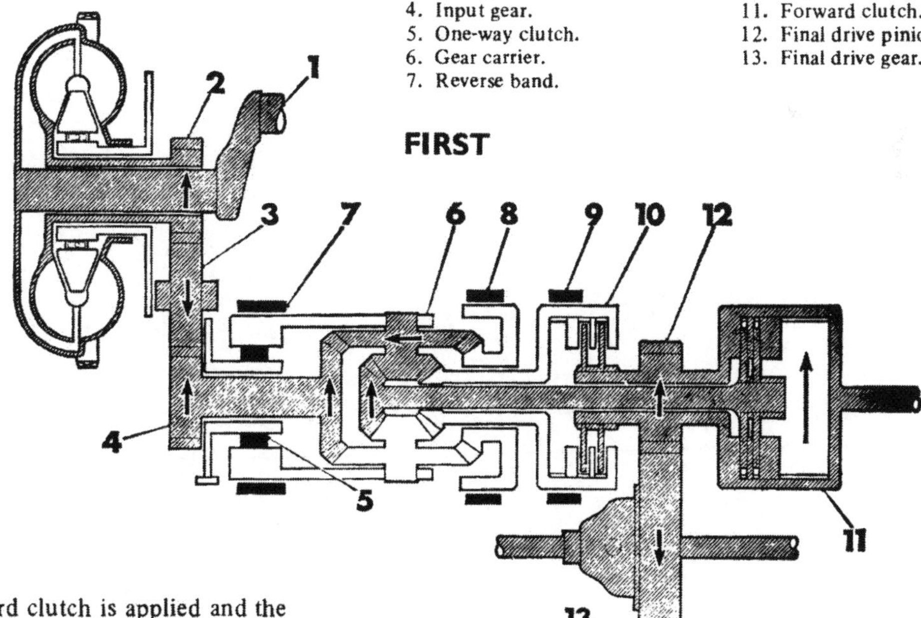

FIRST SPEED

In this ratio the forward clutch is applied and the one-way clutch is operative. The carrier is stationary, its reaction being controlled by the one-way clutch. The input bevel drives the planet wheels and the planet pinions drive the forward output pinion and shaft. Thus power is transferred through the planet assemblies to the mainshaft, forward clutch, and the output gear, providing a ratio of 2.69 : 1.

POWER FLOW DIAGRAMS (MECHANICAL)

SECOND SPEED

As for all forward gears the forward clutch remains engaged, and in addition the second speed brake band applied. This controls the reaction which is imposed on the reverse drive bevel when in this ratio. With the planet cluster orbiting around the reverse drive bevel power is transmitted from the input bevel through the planets to the mainshaft and provides a ratio of 1.845 : 1.

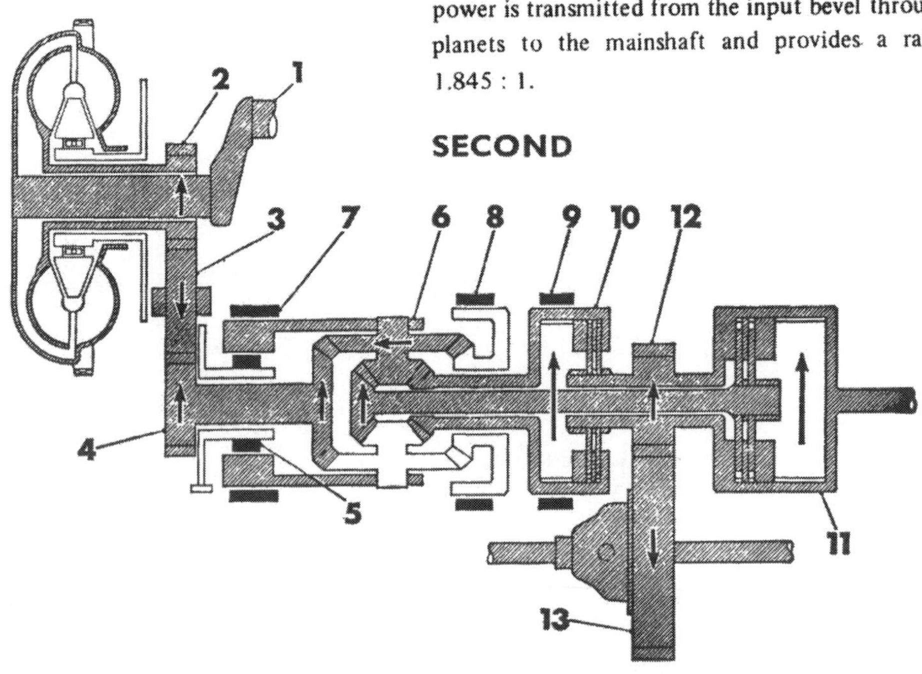

KEY TO COMPONENTS

1. Crankshaft.
2. Converter output gear.
3. Idler gear.
4. Input gear.
5. One-way clutch.
6. Gear carrier.
7. Reverse band.
8. Third gear band.
9. Second gear band.
10. Top and reverse clutch.
11. Forward clutch.
12. Final drive pinion.
13. Final drive gear.

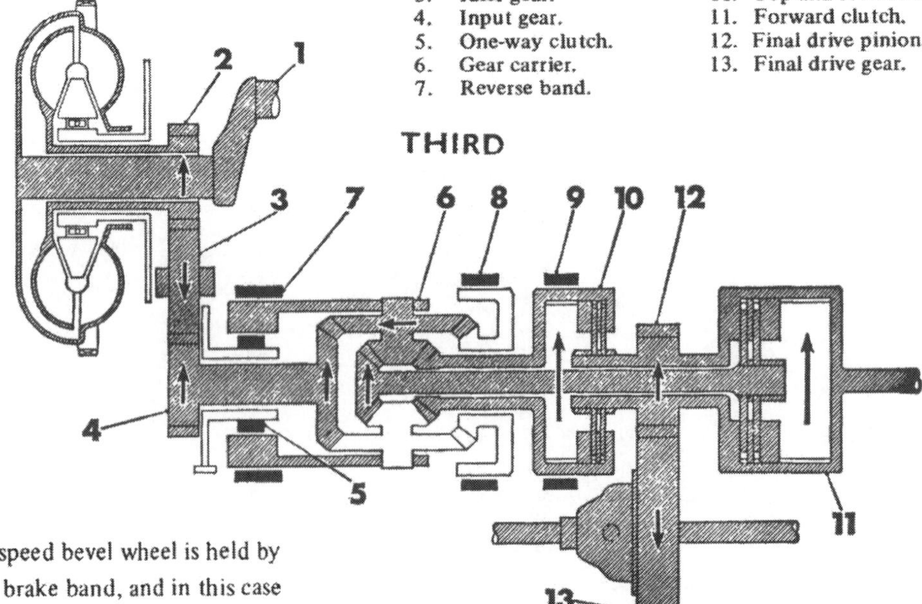

THIRD SPEED

For this ratio the third speed bevel wheel is held by its appropriate drum and brake band, and in this case the planet clusters orbit around this gear. Like second speed, power is transmitted from the input bevel through the planets to the mainshaft and in this case provides a ratio of 1.46 : 1.

POWER FLOW DIAGRAMS (MECHANICAL)

TOP SPEED

In addition to the forward clutch, the top and reverse clutch is engaged. This in effect locks up the bevel gears and the reduction gear assembly then rotates as one unit to provide direct drive.

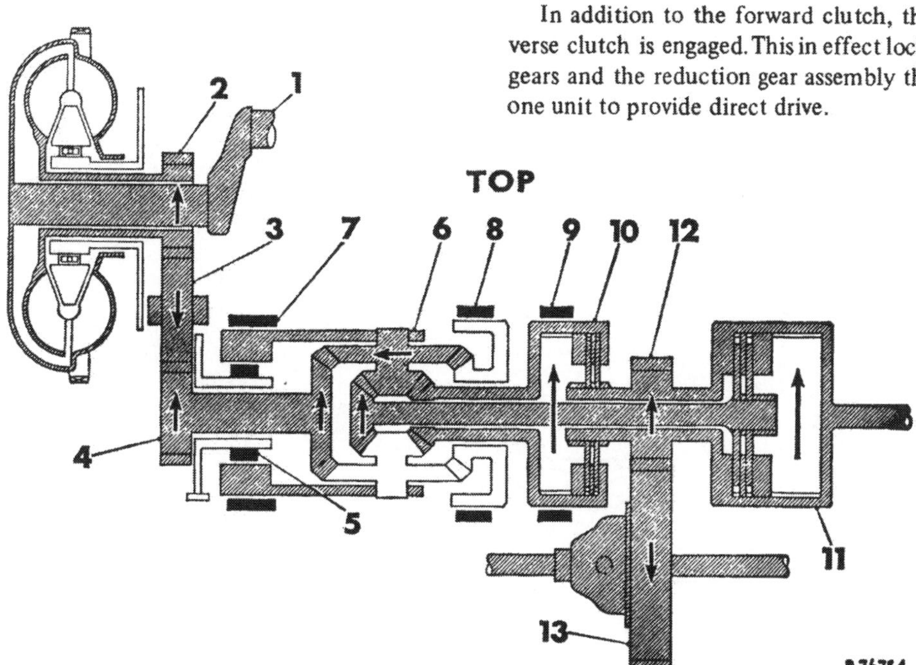

KEY TO COMPONENTS

1. Crankshaft.
2. Converter output gear.
3. Idler gear.
4. Input gear.
5. One-way clutch.
6. Gear carrier.
7. Reverse band.
8. Third gear band.
9. Second gear band.
10. Top and reverse clutch.
11. Forward clutch.
12. Final drive pinion.
13. Final drive gear.

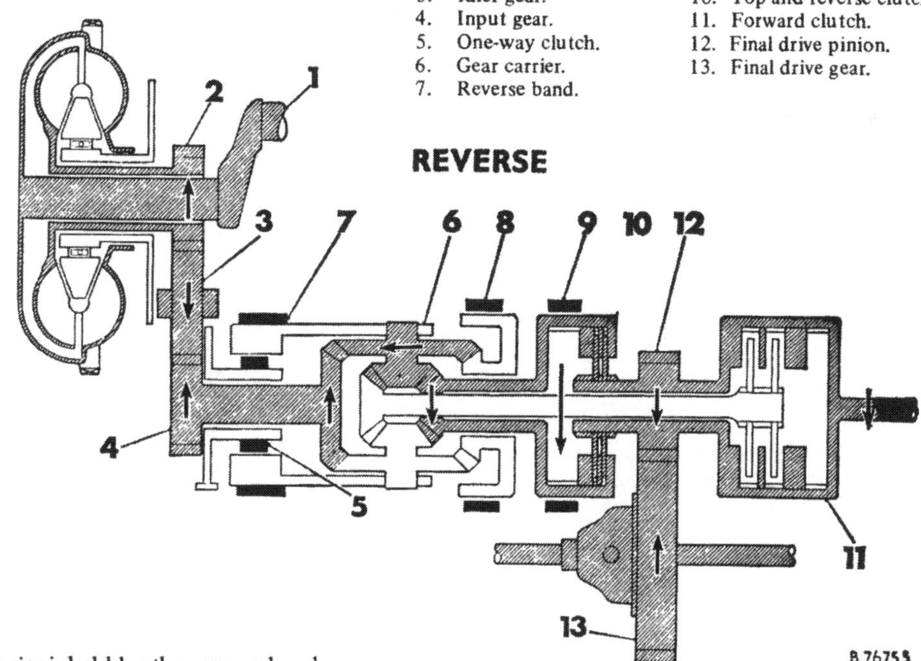

REVERSE

In this ratio the carrier is held by the reverse band – (the one-way clutch being inoperative because the reaction is in the opposite direction to first speed).

In addition the top and reverse clutch is engaged.

The input bevel wheel drives the planet wheel and the planet pinion drives the reverse drive gear. Thus power is transmitted through the planet assemblies to the top and reverse clutch and thence to the final drive pinion to provide a ratio of 2.69 : 1.

LINE PRESSURE AND LUBRICATION DIAGRAMS

MK. I AND II TRANSMISSIONS

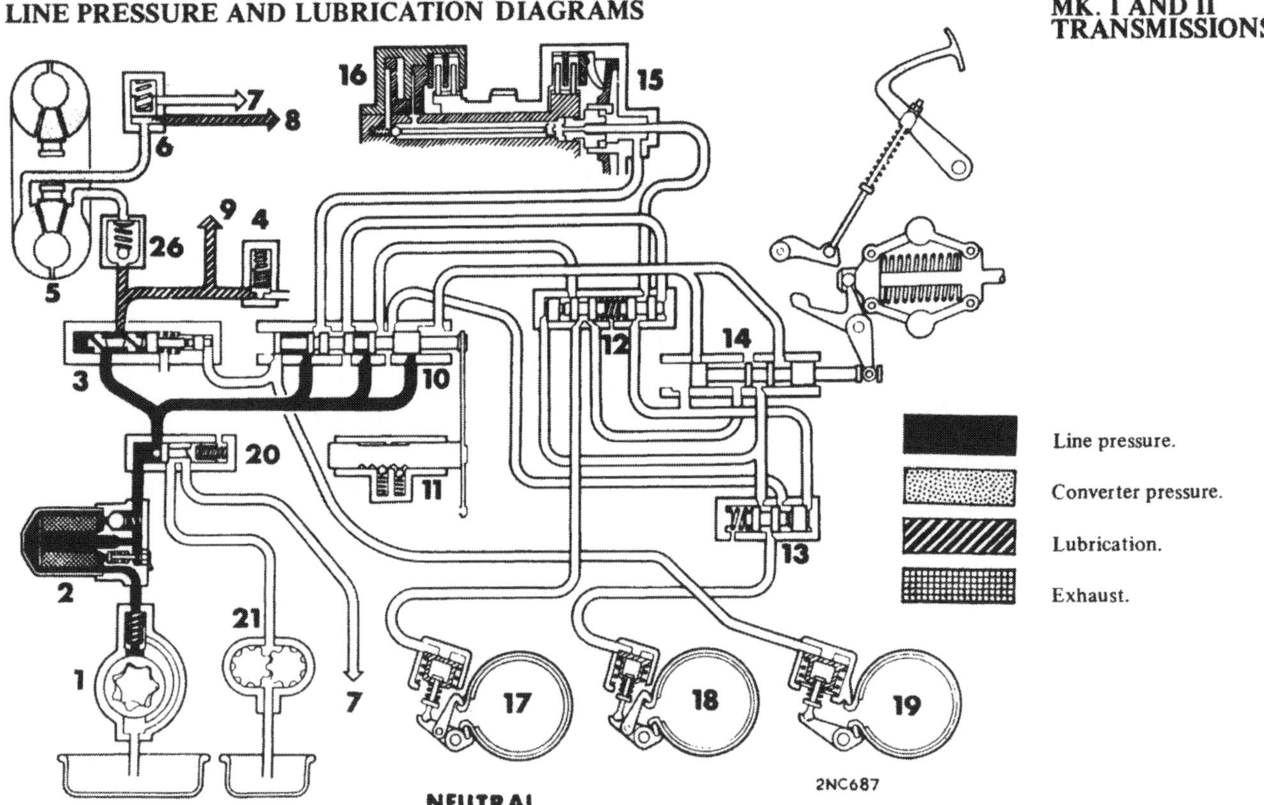

NEUTRAL

KEY TO DIAGRAMS

1. Main oil pump.
2. Oil filter.
3. Regulator valve.
4. Engine lubrication relief valve.
5. Converter.
6. Low pressure valve.
7. To sump.
8. Gear train lubrication.
9. Engine lubrication.
10. Selector valve.
11. Selector valve detent.
12. Second and top gear valves.
13. Third gear valve.
14. Governor valve.
15. Forward clutch.
16. Top and reverse clutch.
17. Second gear brake band.
18. Third gear brake band.
19. Reverse gear brake band.
20. Tow start valve.
21. Auxiliary pump.
26. Restrictor valve (in converter pipe).

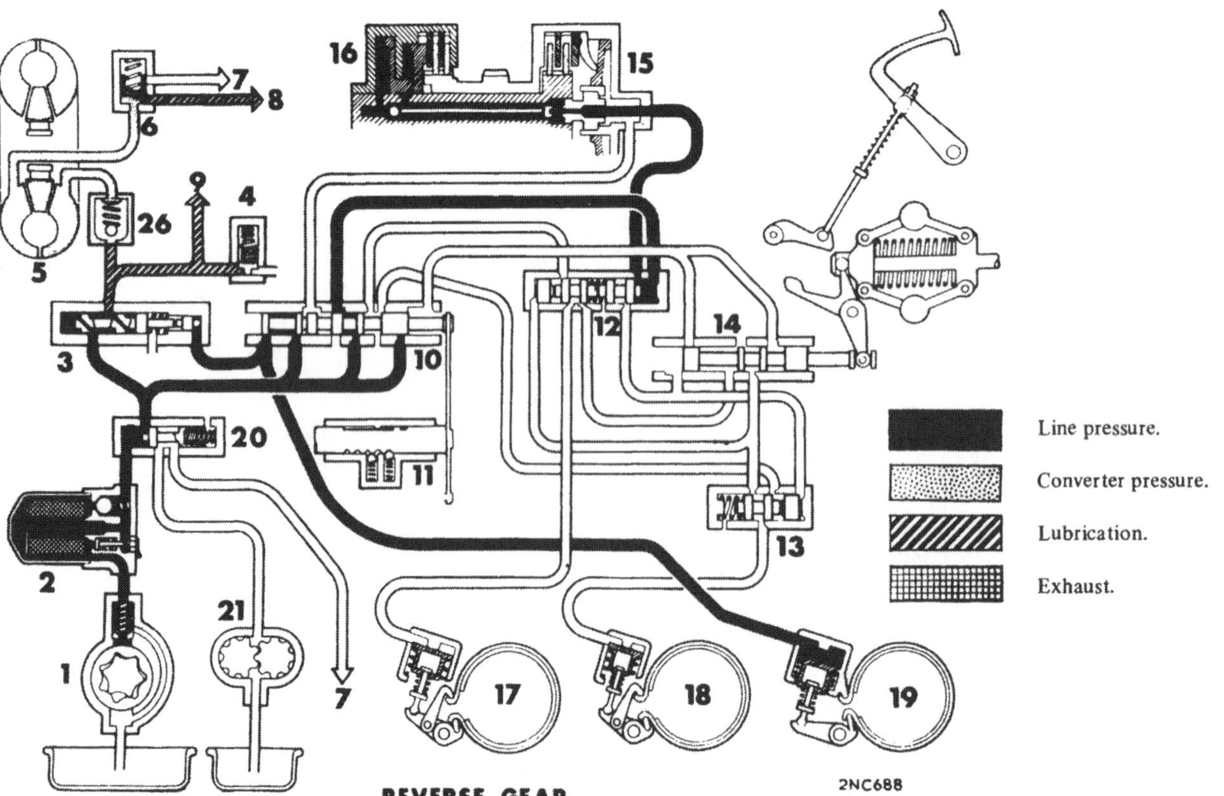

REVERSE GEAR

LINE PRESSURE AND LUBRICATION DIAGRAMS

MK. I AND II TRANSMISSIONS

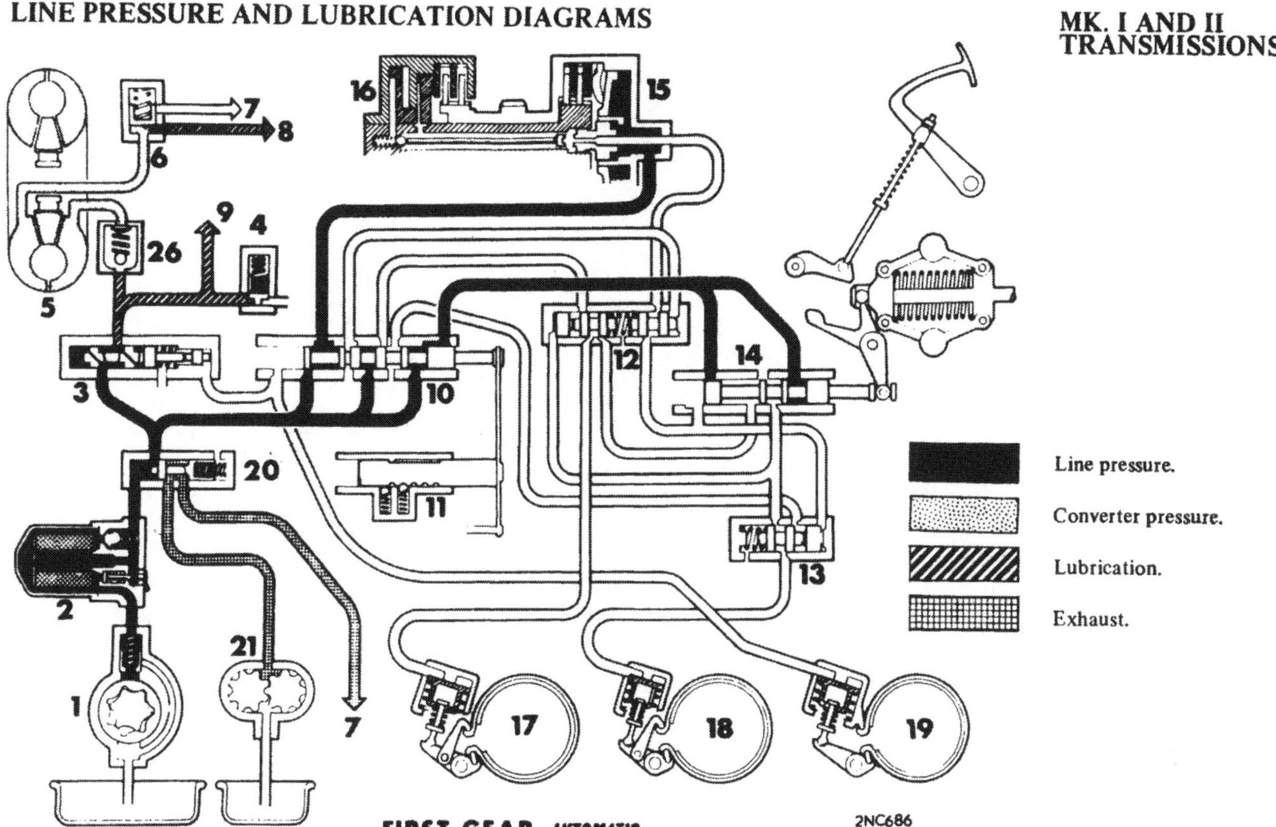

FIRST GEAR *AUTOMATIC*

KEY TO DIAGRAMS

1. Main oil pump.
2. Oil filter.
3. Regulator valve.
4. Engine lubrication relief valve.
5. Converter.
6. Low pressure valve.
7. To sump.
8. Gear train lubrication.
9. Engine lubrication.
10. Selector valve.
11. Selector valve detent.
12. Second and top gear valves.
13. Third gear valve.
14. Governor valve.
15. Forward clutch.
16. Top and reverse clutch.
17. Second gear brake band.
18. Third gear brake band.
19. Reverse gear brake band.
20. Tow start valve.
21. Auxiliary pump.
26. Restrictor valve (in converter pipe).

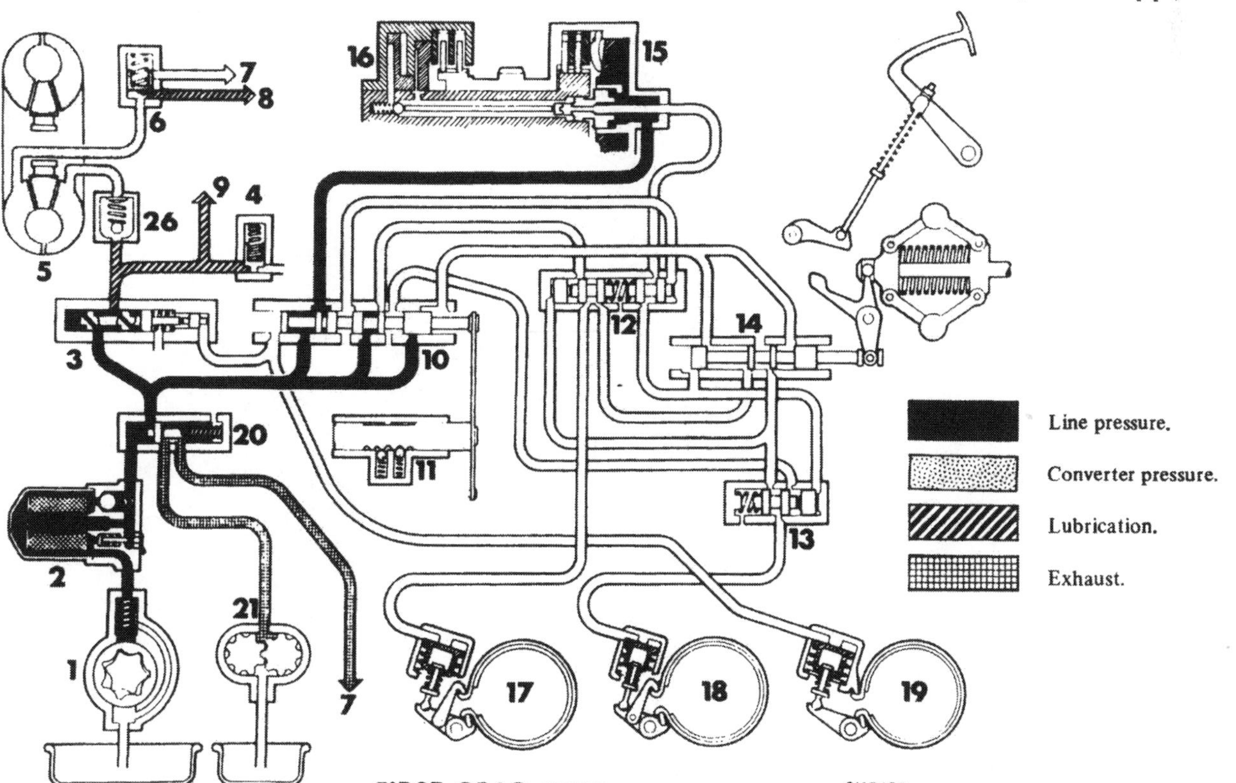

FIRST GEAR *MANUAL*

LINE PRESSURE AND LUBRICATION DIAGRAMS

MK. I AND II TRANSMISSIONS

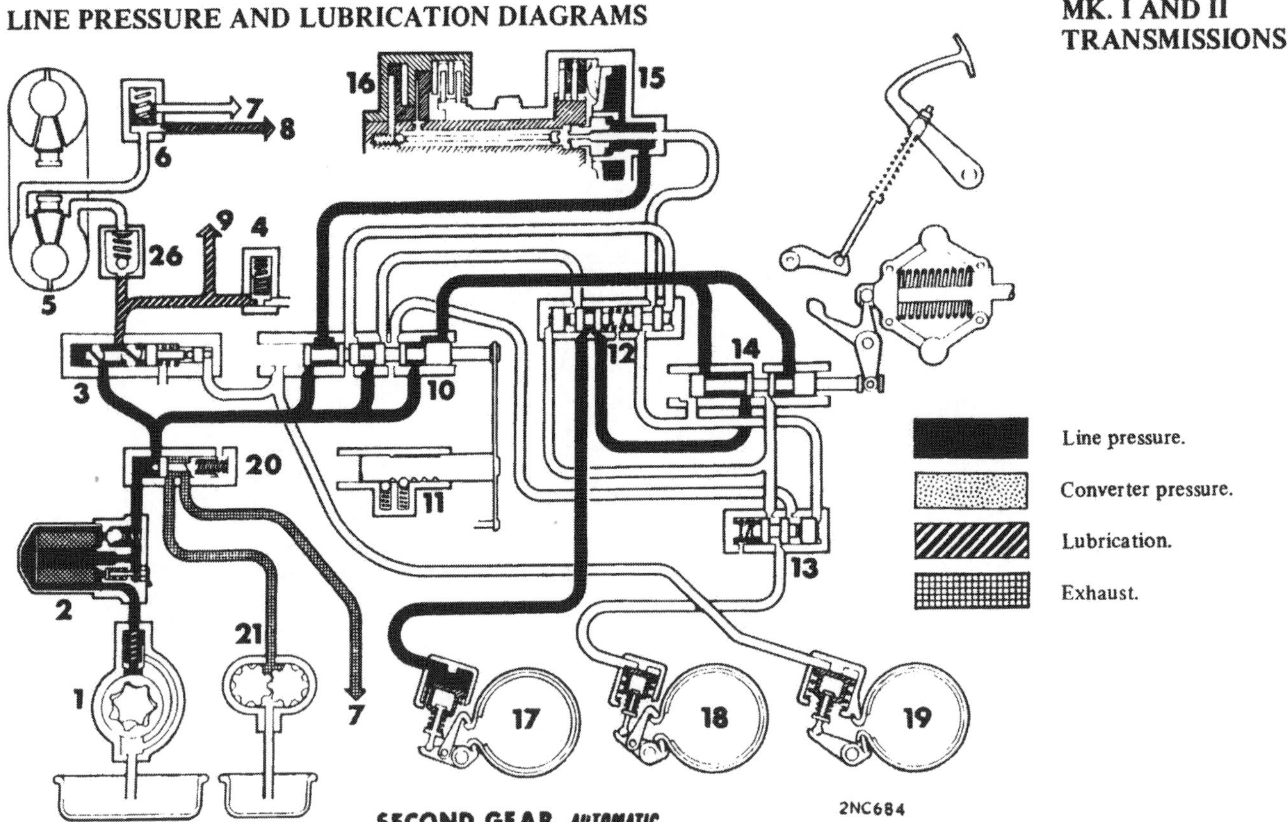

SECOND GEAR *AUTOMATIC*

KEY TO DIAGRAMS

1. Main oil pump.
2. Oil filter.
3. Regulator valve.
4. Engine lubrication relief valve.
5. Converter.
6. Low pressure valve.
7. To sump.
8. Gear train lubrication.
9. Engine lubrication.
10. Selector valve.
11. Selector valve detent.
12. Second and top gear valves.
13. Third gear valve.
14. Governor valve.
15. Forward clutch.
16. Top and reverse clutch.
17. Second gear brake band.
18. Third gear brake band.
19. Reverse gear brake band.
20. Tow start valve.
21. Auxiliary pump.
26. Restrictor valve (in converter pipe).

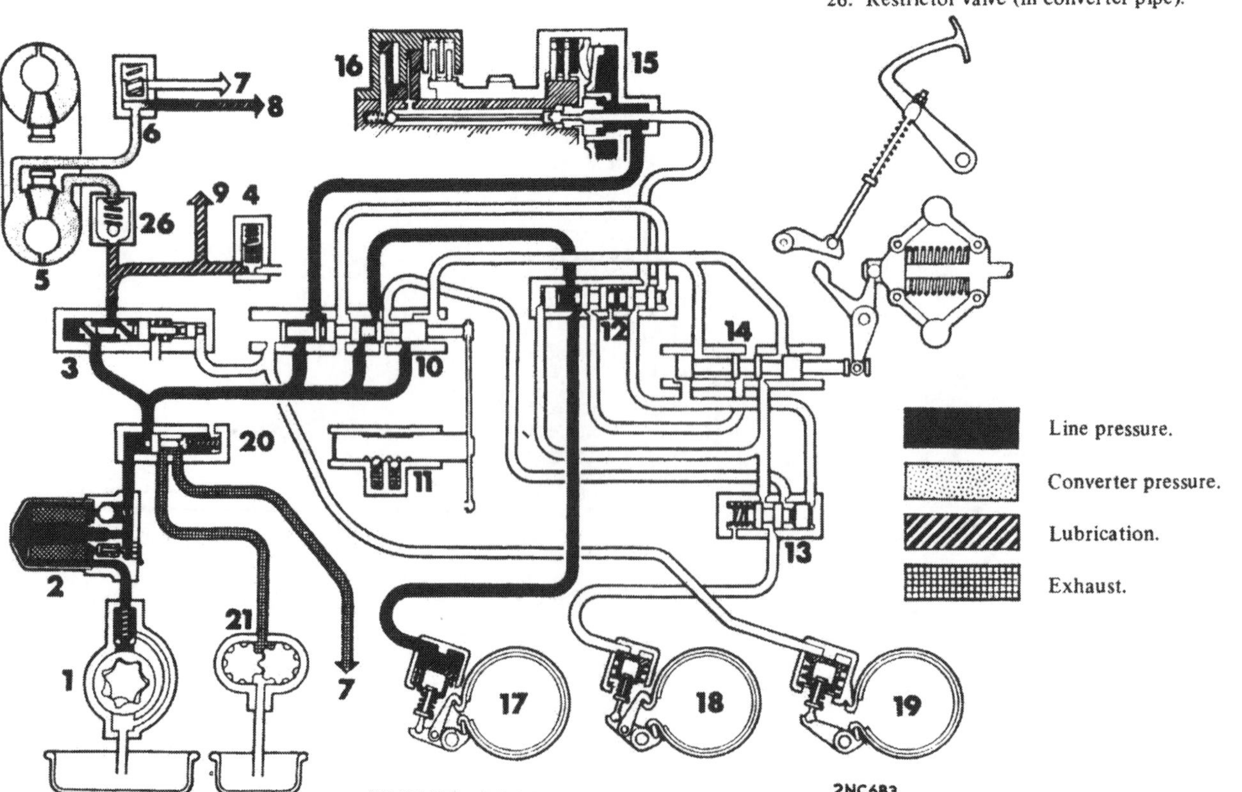

SECOND GEAR *MANUAL*

LINE PRESSURE AND LUBRICATION DIAGRAMS

MK. I AND II TRANSMISSIONS

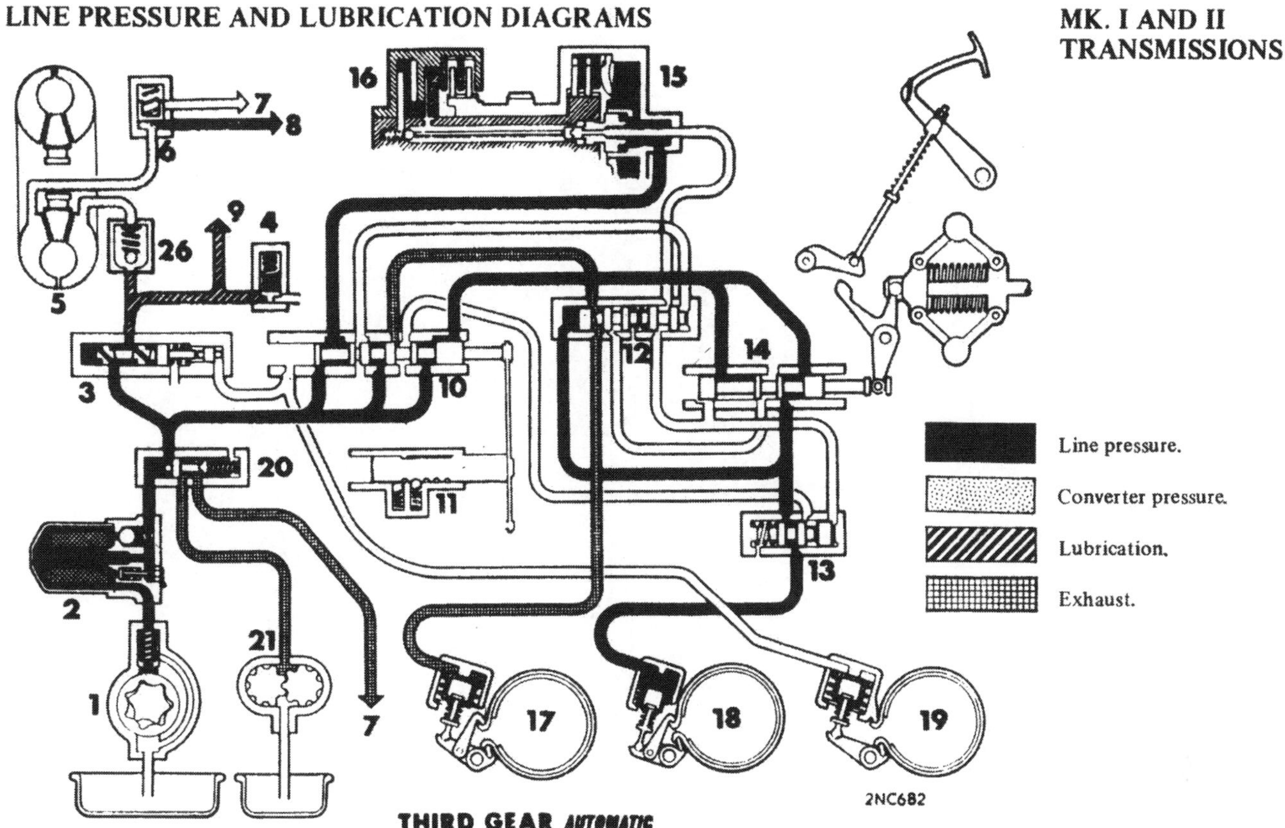

THIRD GEAR AUTOMATIC

KEY TO DIAGRAMS

1. Main oil pump.
2. Oil filter.
3. Regulator valve.
4. Engine lubrication relief valve.
5. Converter.
6. Low pressure valve.
7. To sump.
8. Gear train lubrication.
9. Engine lubrication.
10. Selector valve.
11. Selector valve detent.
12. Second and top gear valves.
13. Third gear valve.
14. Governor valve.
15. Forward clutch.
16. Top and reverse clutch.
17. Second gear brake band.
18. Third gear brake band.
19. Reverse gear brake band.
20. Tow start valve.
21. Auxiliary pump.
26. Restrictor valve (in converter pipe).

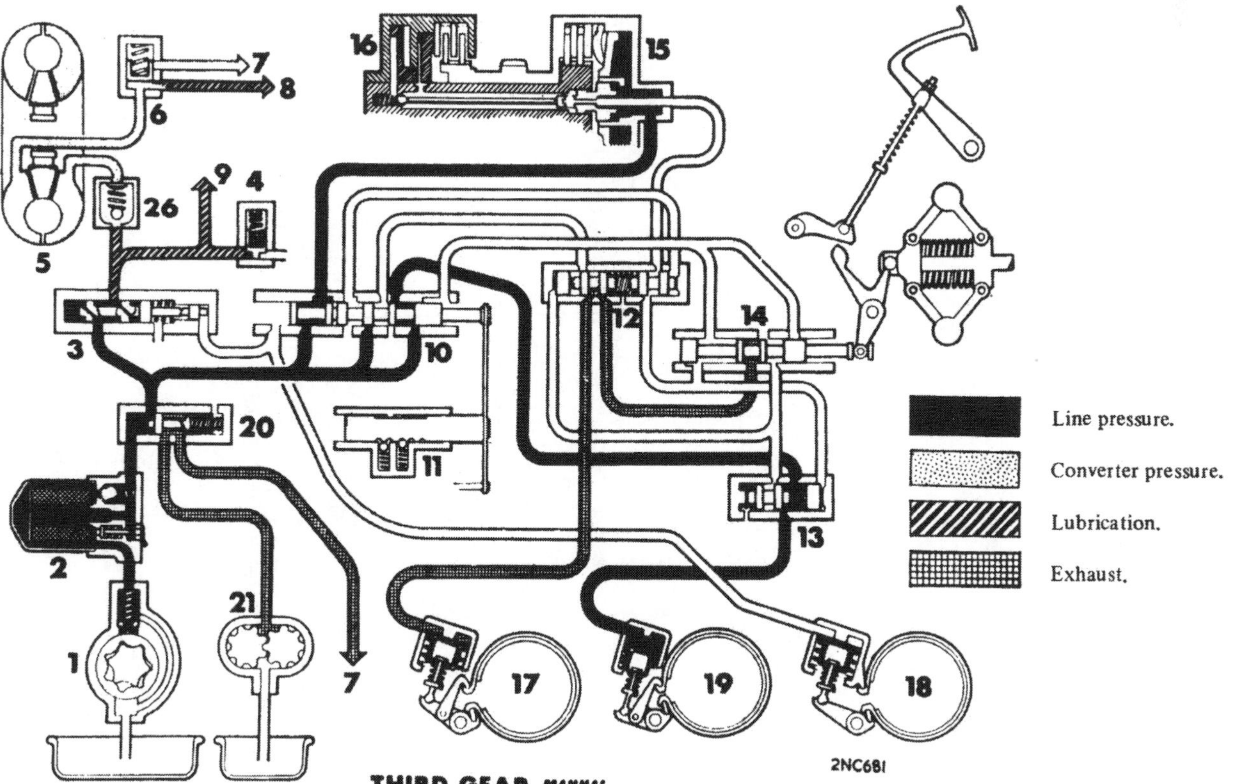

THIRD GEAR MANUAL

LINE PRESSURE AND LUBRICATION DIAGRAMS

MK. I AND II TRANSMISSIONS

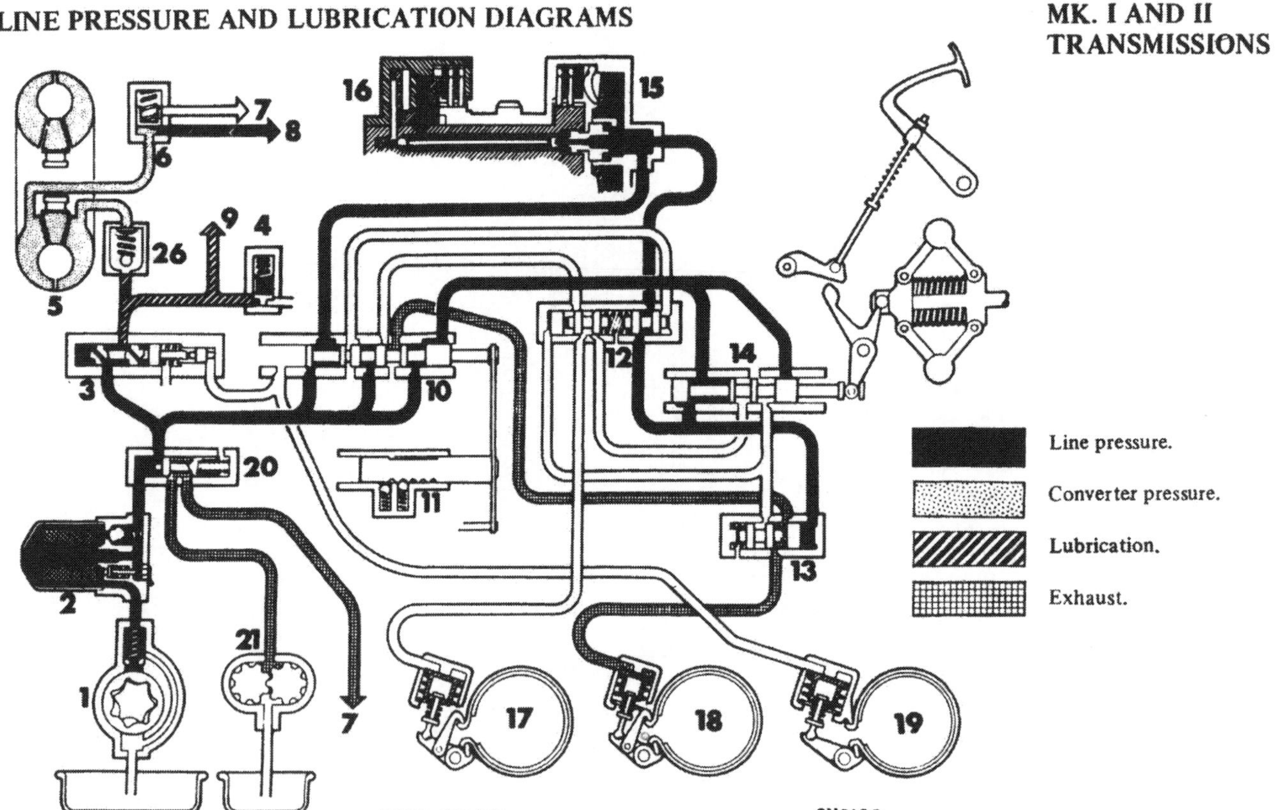

TOP GEAR AUTOMATIC

KEY TO DIAGRAMS

1. Main oil pump.
2. Oil filter.
3. Regulator valve.
4. Engine lubrication relief valve.
5. Converter.
6. Low pressure valve.
7. To sump.
8. Gear train lubrication.
9. Engine lubrication.
10. Selector valve.
11. Selector valve detent.
12. Second and top gear valves.
13. Third gear valve.
14. Governor valve.
15. Forward clutch.
16. Top and reverse clutch.
17. Second gear brake band.
18. Third gear brake band.
19. Reverse gear brake band.
20. Tow start valve.
21. Auxiliary pump.
26. Restrictor valve (in converter pipe).

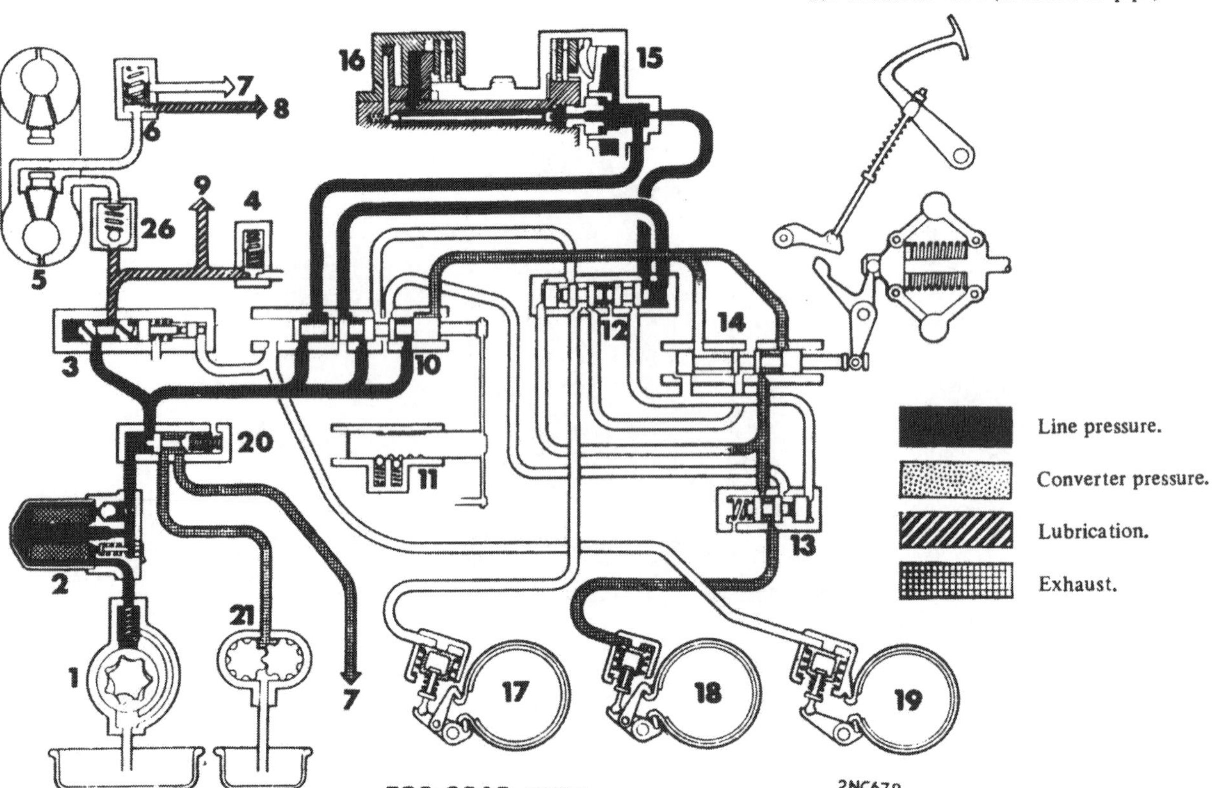

TOP GEAR MANUAL

LINE PRESSURE AND LUBRICATION DIAGRAMS

MK. IIB TRANSMISSIONS

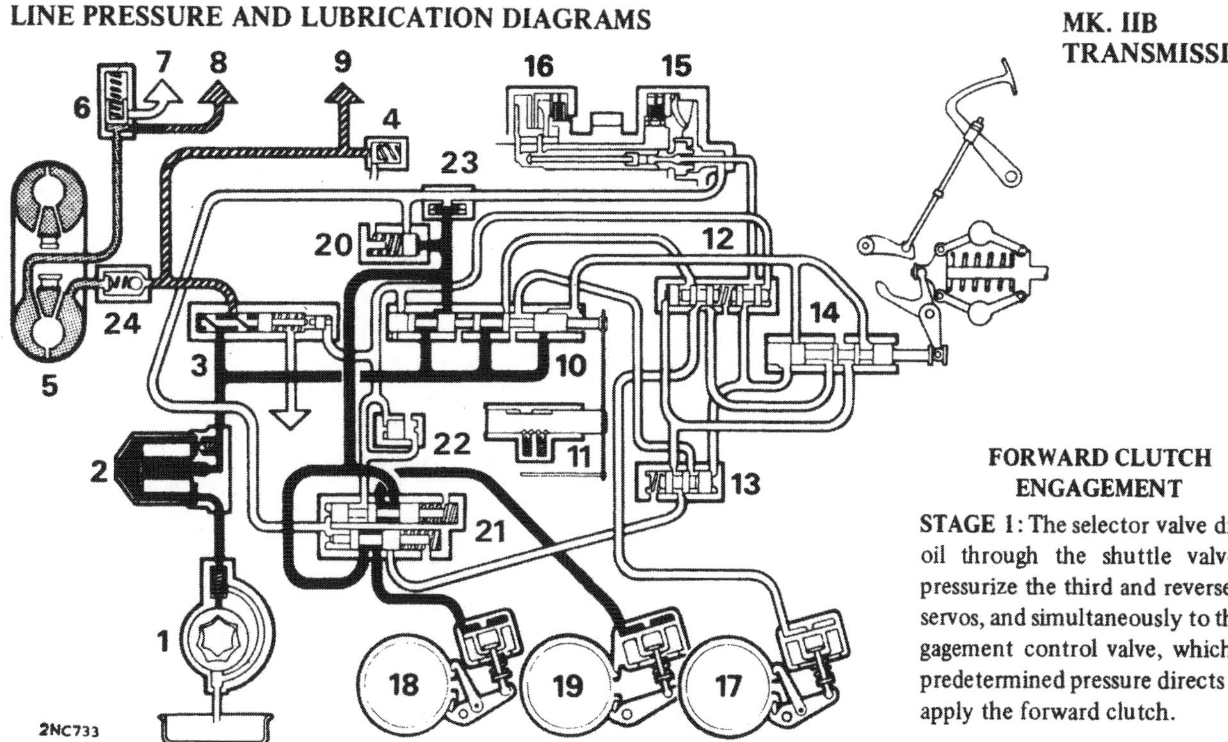

FORWARD CLUTCH ENGAGEMENT

STAGE I: The selector valve directs oil through the shuttle valves to pressurize the third and reverse gear servos, and simultaneously to the engagement control valve, which at a predetermined pressure directs oil to apply the forward clutch.

KEY TO DIAGRAMS

1. Main oil pump.
2. Oil filter.
3. Regulator valve.
4. Engine lubrication relief valve.
5. Converter.
6. Low pressure valve.
7. To sump.
8. Gear train lubrication.
9. Engine lubrication.
10. Selector valve.
11. Selector valve detent.
12. Second and top gear valves.
13. Third gear valve.
14. Governor valve.
15. Forward clutch.
16. Top and reverse clutch.
17. Second gear brake band.
18. Third gear brake band.
19. Reverse gear brake band.
20. Engagement control pressure valve (Mk. II B only).
21. Engagement control shuttle valves (Mk. II B only).
22. One-way dump valve (Mk. II B only).
23. One-way flap valve (Mk. II B only).
24. Restrictor valve (in converter pipe).

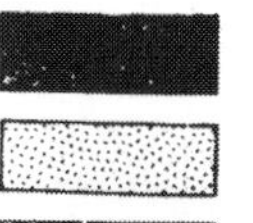

Line pressure.

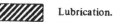

Converter pressure.

Lubrication.

Exhaust.

MK. IIB TRANSMISSION

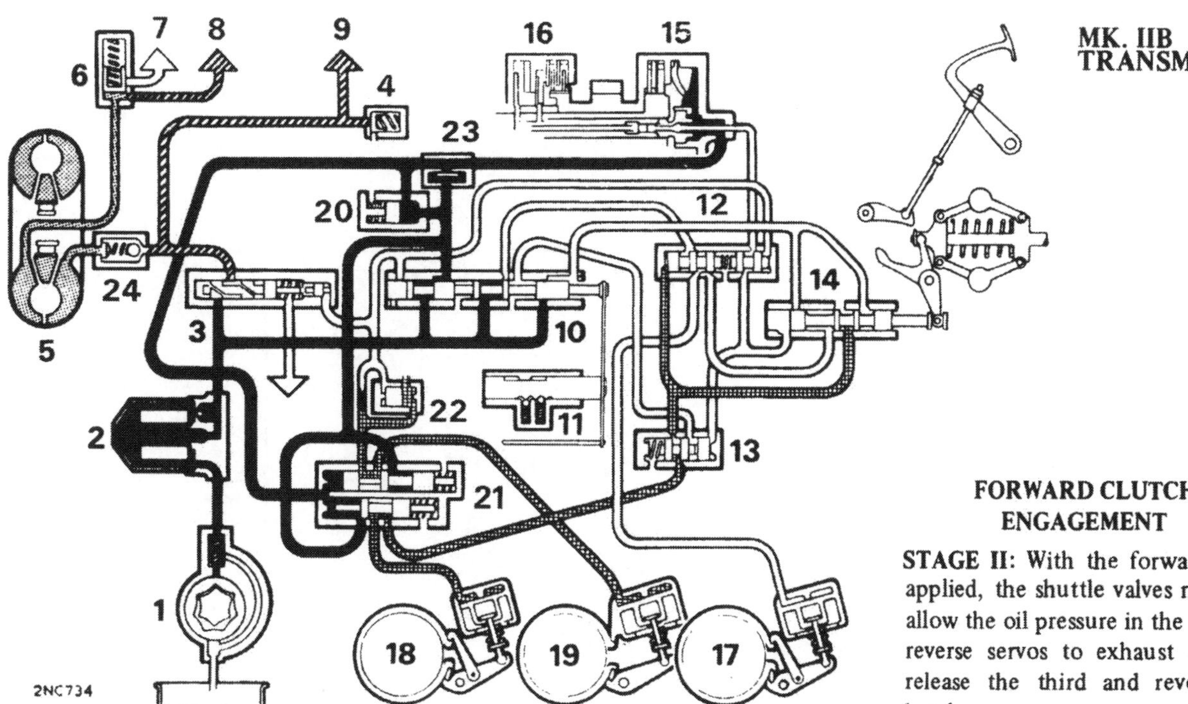

FORWARD CLUTCH ENGAGEMENT

STAGE II: With the forward clutch applied, the shuttle valves move and allow the oil pressure in the third and reverse servos to exhaust and thus release the third and reverse gear bands.

FAULT DIAGNOSIS CHART

FAULTS	RECTIFICATION SEQUENCE
Torque converter	
Excessive creep or engine stalls when selecting gears	2
Poor acceleration and difficulty in starting from rest on hills	5
Severe overheating and reduced maximum speed in all gears	6
Rattle from converter on engagement of gears and frequency increasing with engine speed, particularly when under load	6
Rattle or vibration from converter area in neutral and all gears	11
Rattle or buzz in 'N' up to approximately 1,250 r.p.m. Noise disappears on engagement of any gear	48, 49, 50
Squeal from converter area in neutral and all gears	12, 13
Gear selection and change speeds	
Gear selection faulty	3, 21
Kick-down change speeds incorrect	7, 2
Change speeds incorrect on light throttle driving, possibly no drive in '1' or '4' of automatic 'D' range	22, 23
Erratic change speeds in automatic 'D' range	24, 25
'Tie-up' in 4 automatic 'D' range and/or transmission slip in automatic 1 and 4	3, 22, 23, 4
Clutch slip or 'flare up' on 3 to 4 change in automatic and manual ranges	3, 22, 1, 4, 9, 28, 35, 36, 37, 42, 45
Vehicle moves off in 4 when any of the forward gears are selected and 'ties up' in reverse	41, 42
No automatic gear changes, transmission slip in all forward gears	43
Transmission slip/loss of drive	
Complete loss of drive in all gear positions (transmission oil pressure normal), vehicle attempts to drive in 3 and 4	31, 32
Transmission slip in all gear positions	1, 4, 9, 27, 28, 29, 30
Slip or no drive in reverse 'R'	3, 1, 4, 9, 28, 8, 35 36, 37
Slip or no drive in all forward gears	1, 4, 33, 34
No drive in manual or automatic 1	38
Drive in 1 but 'tie-up' in 2, 3 and 4 manual or automatic	38
Transmission slip in manual and automatic 2 or premature wear of second gear band	3, 22, 28, 8, 39, 40
Transmission slip in 3	3, 8, 28, 39, 40
Slip or 'tie-up' on intermediate gear changes	3, 4, 7, 23, 54
Drag in 4 and 'R' reverse, other gears function normally	42
Pressures	
Excessive transmission pressures when starting from cold, with possible oil leakage from oil filter bowl seal	28, 44
Low engine oil pressure	1, 4
Noise	
Continual whine consistent with road speed but not in top gear	51, 52
Continual whine consistent with engine speed except when car is stationary	53
Noise or vibration with road speed in all gear positions	26, 55
Oil leaks	
Oil leaks from converter area	11, 14, 10, 15, 16 17, 18, 19, 20
Oil leak from filter bowl seal, see **'Pressures'**	44, 28

DIAGNOSIS RECTIFICATION CHART

SEQ.	RECTIFICATION	SECTION
1.	Check oil level.	Aa.1
2.	Thoroughly check engine tune, idle and fast idle speeds, choke operation, also that the throttle opens fully.	Da.2
3.	Check selector lever cable and transverse rod adjustment.	Fa.2
4.	Carry out oil pressure check.	Fa.5
5.	Carry out stall test.	Fa.5
6.	Carry out road test.	Fa.1
7.	Check governor control rod (kick-down) adjustment.	Fa.4
8.	Check band adjustment.	Fa.6
9.	Check location of sealing rings and/or joint washer under oil filter head.	Aa.2
10.	Check tightness of converter drain plugs.	Aa.3
11.	Check if converter retaining bolt or the six hub bolts are loose.	Aa.4
12.	Check converter housing bush for seizure or if loose in housing.	Aa.4
13.	Check converter does not foul converter housing, or housing loose and fouling converter.	Aa.4
14.	Check low pressure valve for flange distortion or core plug leakage.	Aa.4
15.	Check converter housing oil seal for damage or incorrect location.	Aa.15
16.	Check for oil leakage from converter housing oil pump cover.	Aa.4
17.	Examine idler gear closed end bearing for leakage.	Aa.4
18.	Check for oil leakage from the converter hub bolts (6).	Aa.4
19.	Check converter casing seam weld for oil leakage.	Aa.4
20.	Check converter housing for porosity.	Aa.4
21.	Check for correct assembly of the valve block, i.e. that the selector valve is engaged with the selector fork of the pipe chest.	Fa.7
22.	Check setting and alignment of the valve block governor valve with the governor lever (on pipe chest).	Fa.7
23.	Check that correct governor/auxiliary pump assembly is fitted in relationship with valve block (two types of each unit have been used).	Fa.7
24.	Check that the governor and governor valve operate freely; and for correct location of the valve block-governor link with the governor unit.	Fa.7
25.	Check that the governor carrier shaft circlip is correctly positioned.	Fa.10
26.	Check the auxiliary pump gears and the alignment of the pump housing with the end cover.	Fa.10
27.	Remove front cover and check 'O' rings on cover to valve block connection.	Fa.6
28.	Remove and clean valve chest.	Fa.8 or 9
29.	Check main oil pump; joint washer, retaining screws are tight, drive coupling, examine delivery pipe connections (pump to transmission case).	Aa.8, Aa.9
30.	Check oil pump pick-up pipe and oil strainer seals.	Aa.4
31.	Check converter feed pipe for blockage by blowing through with compressed air from the valve block end.	Aa.4, Fa.7
32.	Check the bevel gear train planetary pinions.	Fa.12
33.	Check fit of forward clutch feed pipe, the condition of all sealing rings (clutch feed) and ensure that correct cast iron sealing rings are fitted to forward clutch/auxiliary pump drive shaft.	Fa.6, Fa.11
34.	Check condition of clutch plates and piston in forward clutch. Check and rectify clutch plate end-float.	Fa.11
35.	Check feed pipes and sealing rings to top and reverse clutch and reverse band servo.	Fa.7
36.	Remove the top/reverse clutch from the gear train and check that the bush in the reverse output shaft has not turned and shut off the oil feed to the top/reverse clutch.	Fa.12
37.	Check top and reverse clutch piston ring gaps and fit of rings in the piston grooves; check condition of clutch plates.	Fa.13
38.	Check if free wheel support dowel bolt is loose or sheared; replace if necessary.	Fa.6
39.	Examine servo feed pipes, seals, and servo piston seal.	Fa.11
40.	Examine 2nd gear band and replace if excessively heat darkened or worn. Replace top/reverse clutch if damaged by worn band.	Fa.6, Fa.13
41.	Replace forward clutch.	Fa.11
42.	Check that the gear train thrust washers are correctly positioned, and that the top/reverse clutch circlip is correctly located.	Fa.12, Fa.13
43.	Check the forward clutch–auxiliary pump drive shaft for breakage; also check pump gears, replace forward clutch and auxiliary pump housing assemblies if damaged.	Fa.10, Fa.11
44.	Check torque tightness of filter bowl retaining bolt.	'General Data'
45.	Incorrect re-assembly of gear train; check and replace any damaged clutch plates and refit gear train correctly.	Fa.12
46.	Check that clutch plates are correctly engaged on hub.	Fa.13
47.	Check condition of auxiliary pump gear thrust washer.	Fa.10
48.	Remove valve chest and check that correct regulator valve is fitted.	Fa.8
49.	Check torque tightness of camshaft sprocket retaining nut.	'General Data'
50.	Fit replacement oil pump assembly.	Aa.8
51.	Check the bevel input gear preload.	Aa.3
52.	Check the shim adjustment of the top/reverse clutch-assembly to gear train.	Fa.12
53.	Check the helical input and idler gear adjustment.	Aa.3
54.	Check that the interconnecting feed pipe with the restricted bore is connected between the valve block and reverse servo.	Fa.7
55.	Check condition of final drive gears and for correct pinion bearing preload.	Fa 16, Fa.6

CHANGE SPEED CHART

SELECTOR POSITION	THROTTLE POSITION	GEAR SHIFT	M.P.H.	Km.P.H.
'D'	Light	1–2 2–3 3–4	10–14 15–19 20–24	16–22 24–30 32–39
'D'	Kick-down	1–2 2–3 3–4	25–33 37–45 49–57	40–53 60–72 78–91
'D'	Kick-down	4–3 3–2 2–1	47–39 39–31 26–18	76–64 62–50 41–29
'D'	Closed (roll out)	4–3 3–2 2–1	20–16 14–10 8–4	32–26 22–16 12–6

Section Fa.1

FAULT DIAGNOSIS

It is important to carry out a thorough road test of the vehicle to establish the exact fault symptoms and to confirm which component(s) of the transmission are faulty or require adjustment. **The mechanical power flow diagrams indicate the components in use for each gear.** Always check the engine/transmission oil level and top up if necessary before commencing a road test. It may also be advisable to carry out the other preliminary checks detailed below.

Preliminary checks and tests

a. Check oil level (Section Aa.1).
b. Check engine idling speed (Section Da.1).
c. Carry out oil pressure check (Section Fa.5).
d. Carry out stall test (Section Fa.5).

Road test procedure

GEAR SELECTION

1. Check operation of gear selector in all seven positions as given below:
   'N'. Check that there is key start in this position only, and not in the drive positions.
   '1'. Confirm that there is drive and NO engine braking.
   '2', '3', '4'. Confirm that there is drive WITH engine braking.
   'D'. See 'CHANGE SPEEDS'.
   'R'. Confirm that there is drive WITH engine braking.

CHANGE SPEEDS

2. Check the 'kick-down' up-change speeds in 'D' position, refer to the 'CHANGE SPEED CHART'.

Section Fa.2

SELECTOR LEVER CABLE AND TRANSVERSE ROD ADJUSTMENT

Checking

1. Ensure that the hand brake is applied and start the engine. Move the selector lever to the 'R' position and check that reverse is engaged. Slowly move the lever back towards the 'N' position, checking that the gear is disengaged just before or as soon as the lever drops in the 'N' position on the quadrant. Repeat this procedure in the first gear '1' position. If adjustment is necessary, proceed as detailed below and refer to Fig. Fa.1.

Adjusting

SELECTOR LEVER TRANSVERSE ROD (1st TYPE)

2. Pull back the rubber boot and remove the clevis pin. Ensure that the transverse selector rod is screwed in tightly and pushed fully into the transmission case. **WARNING.–Never start the engine with the transverse selector rod disconnected.**
3. Swivel the bell-crank lever arm clear of the transverse selector rod yoke and refit the clevis pin. Check the measurement 'A' as shown in Fig. Fa.2 and, if necessary, adjust the yoke as described in item 4.
4. Slacken the locknut and turn the yoke until the correct measurement is obtained. Re-tighten the locknut, ensuring that the yoke is set square to the bell-crank.

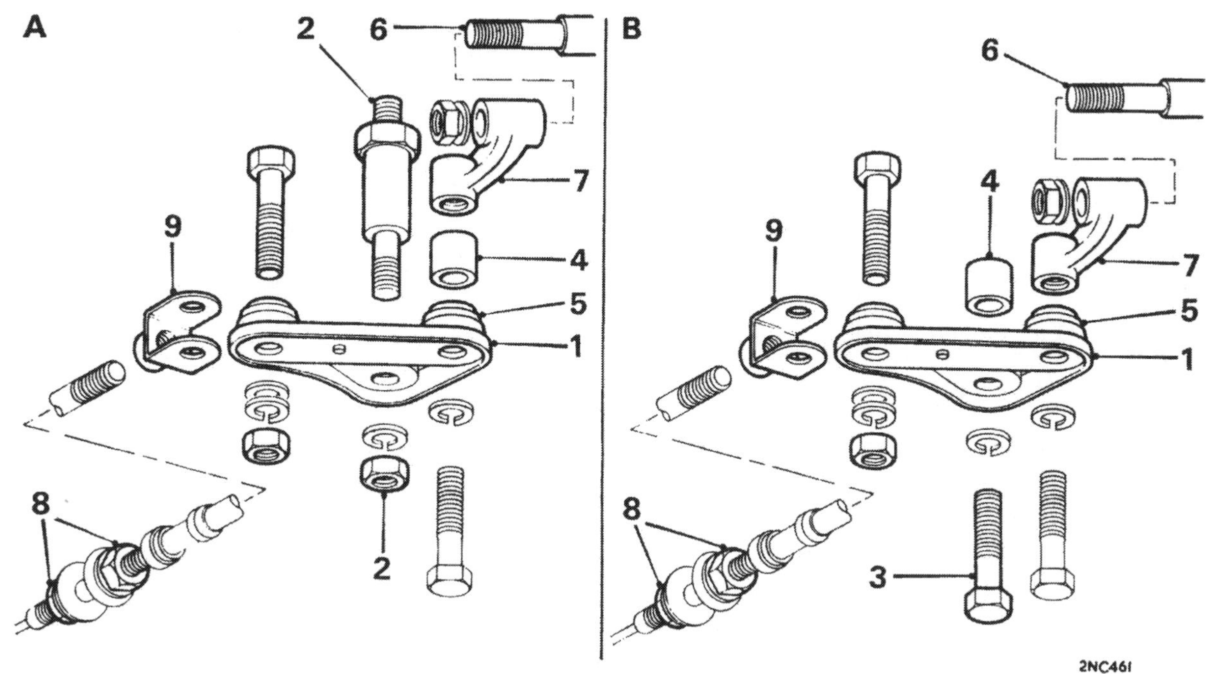

Fig. Fa.1
Both versions of the pressed-type minimum backlash bell-crank lever assembly, showing 'A' the first exposed type and 'B' the second enclosed type

1. Pressed bell-crank lever arm.
2. Bell-crank lever pivot pin and securing nut.
3. Bell-crank lever pivot bolt.
4. Collar.
5. Spherical joint.
6. Transverse rod.
7. Transverse rod bracket (fixed).
8. Cable adjusting nuts.

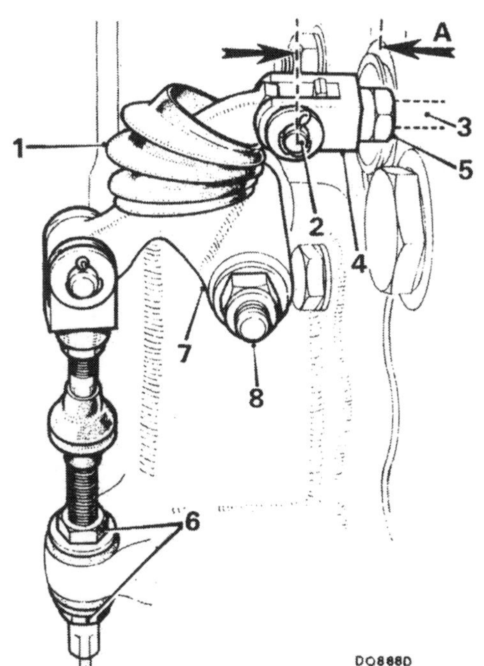

Fig. Fa.2
The gear-change cable and transverse rod adjustment (Forged-type bell-crank)

A = $\frac{25}{32}$ in. (20 mm.) with transverse rod fully in

1. Rubber boot.
2. Clevis pin.
3. Transverse rod (adjustable).
4. Transverse rod yoke.
5. Yoke locknut.
6. Cable adjusting nuts.
7. Forged bell-crank lever arm.
8. Bell-crank lever pivot and securing nut.

SELECTOR LEVER TRANSVERSE ROD (2nd TYPE)

The transverse rod is not adjustable and is fitted on units having the later-type minimum backlash bell-crank lever assembly (see Fig. Fa.1).

Selector lever cable

5. a. **Transmissions with seven selector positions.** Select 'N' in the transmission unit by pulling the transverse rod fully out and then pushing it back in ONE detent.

   b. **Transmissions with six selector positions.** Proceed as above except that the transverse rod must be pushed back in TWO detents.

6. a. EARLY MODELS. Engage 'N' with the selector lever; adjust the selector cable until the hole in the cable fork aligns with the bell-crank lever and the clevis pin can easily be inserted (see Fig. Fa.2).

   b. LATER MODELS. On units fitted with the minimum backlash bell-crank lever, the adjustment procedure is as detailed above except that the cable fork must align with the bore of the spherical joint in the bell-crank lever until the bolt can easily be inserted (see Fig. Fa.1).
   NOTE: Ensure that the yoke end on the selector cable is secured square to the bell-crank lever before reconnecting.

7. Carry out the checking procedure in item 1; slight readjustment may be necessary so that the amount of movement to engage or disengage gears is equalized in both directions.

8. Tighten all adjustment/locking nuts and ensure that the clevis pins (when fitted) are secured. Pack the rubber boots (when fitted) with Duckhams Lammol Grease, refit the boots and the bell-crank lever guard.

   NOTE: The bell-crank lever guard fitted to units having the minimum backlash bell-crank is reshaped, but the earlier-type guard can be modified (see Fig. Fa.3) to use with the later-type bell-crank.

9. Carry out a road test checking the operation in each selector position.

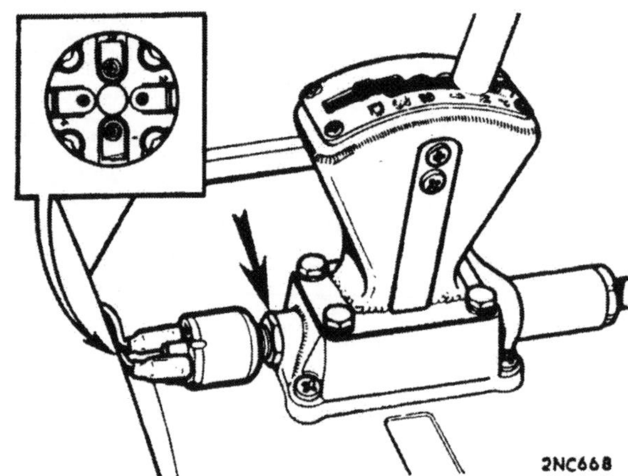

Fig. Fa.4
The later type selector lever housing and two terminal type inhibitor switch. 'Inset' shows the earlier switch with four connections

Section Fa.3

INHIBITOR SWITCH ADJUSTMENT

The switch is located on the rear of the gear selector housing (Fig. Fa.4) and must be adjusted to ensure that the engine can only be started when the selector lever is in the 'N' position on the quadrant.

The earlier-type switches have four terminals, two of which are connected through the ignition/starter circuit; later-type switches have two terminals only.

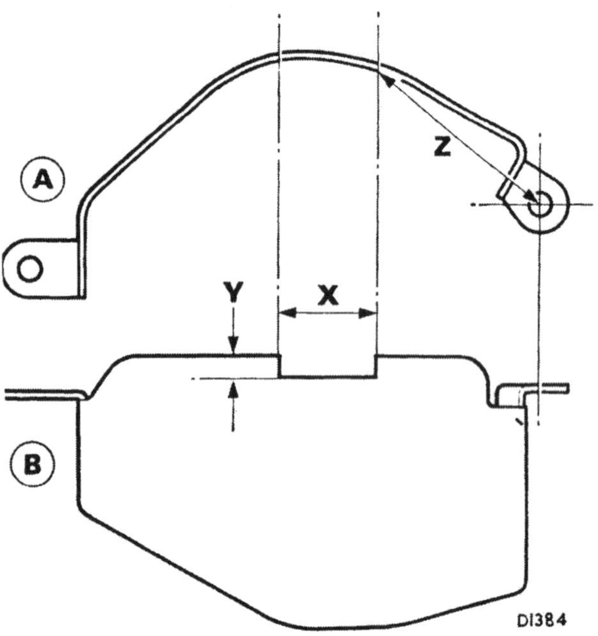

Fig. Fa.3
Reset the original bell-crank lever guard for use with the pressed bell-crank by bending it to the revised shape (view 'A') and adding the cut-out (view 'B')

X=1⅜ in. (35 mm.) Y=⅜ in. (9.5 mm.) Z=2⅝ in. (67 mm.)

ELECTRICAL CONNECTIONS
Ignition/starter circuit: Connect to 2 and 4 (wiring connections are interchangeable).
Reverse light (when fitted): Connect to 1 and 3.
Check the selector lever cable and transverse rod adjustment before adjusting the inhibitor switch.

Checking adjustment

1. Verify that the starter operates only when the selector lever is in the 'N' position, and also that the reversing light (when fitted) operates only when 'R' is selected.

Adjusting

2. Select 'N' and disconnect the electrical connections from the switch.
3. Slacken the locknut (arrowed, see Fig. Fa.4), and unscrew the switch almost out of the housing.
4. Connect a test lamp or meter across the switch terminals 2 and 4. Screw the switch into the housing until the circuit is made, and mark the switch body. Continue screwing in the switch and note the number of turns required until the circuit breaks. Remove the test equipment and unscrew the switch from the housing half the number of turns counted.
5. Tighten the locknut and refit the electrical leads to the appropriate terminals.

NOTE:–If the switch cannot be adjusted to operate correctly it must be renewed.

Section Fa.4

GOVERNOR CONTROL ROD (KICK-DOWN) ADJUSTMENT

Checking

1. Run the engine to its normal working temperature.
2. Check with a tachometer that the carburetter is adjusted to give an engine idling speed of 650 r.p.m.
3. Disconnect the governor control rod at the carburetter, insert a ¼ in. (6.4 mm.) diameter rod through the hole in the intermediate bell-crank lever and locate the hole in the transmission case (Fig. Fa.5).
4. Check if the control rod can now be re-connected to the carburetter with its fulcrum pin an easy sliding fit through the forked end and with the carburetter linkage.
   Adjust if necessary, as detailed below.

Adjusting

5. Slacken the control rod locknut, disconnect the forked end at the carburetter linkage and turn the rod until the correct length is obtained. Connect up at the carburetter end, tighten the locknut and remove the checking rod (see Fig. Fa.5).
6. Road-test the car and check that automatic change speeds corresponds to those given in the '**CHANGE SPEED CHART**'in Section Fa.1.

   If full throttle change speeds are LOW, disconnect the forked end of the rod, slacken the locknut and SHORTEN the rod; conversely, if full throttle change speeds are HIGH, turn the rod anti-clockwise to LENGTHEN it slightly.

   Road-test to ensure correct change speeds can now be obtained.

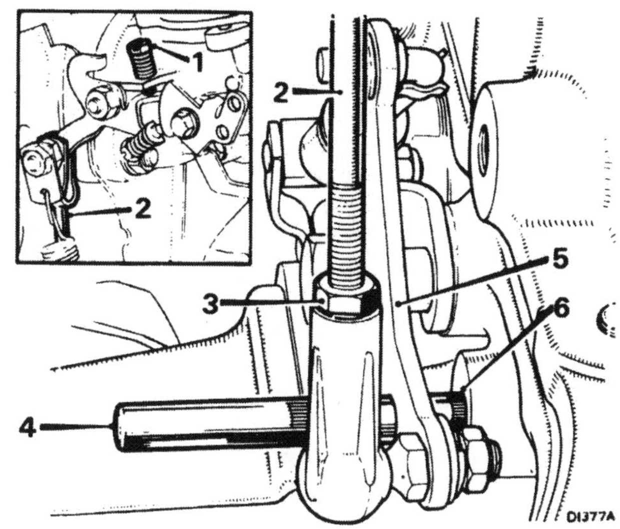

Fig. Fa.5
The governor control rod adjustment

1. Throttle adjustment screw.
2. Governor control rod.
3. Locknut.
4. ¼ in. (6.4 mm.) diameter rod.
5. Intermediate bell-crank lever.
6. Transmission case hole.

Section Fa.5

OIL PRESSURE AND STALL SPEED CHECKS

In suspected cases of slip or poor acceleration a converter stall speed check should be carried out as detailed below. If there is slip in all gears a low oil pressure is indicated which should be confirmed by a pressure check.

Oil pressure check

1. Check and top up the oil level (see Section Aa.1).
2. Remove the pressure point plug on the engine oil filter, fit Service tool adaptor 18G 677 C, and connect Service tool 18G 677 Z (see Fig. Fa.6) or use pressure gauge (Service tool 18G 502 A with pipe and adaptor 18G 502 K).
3. Start and run the engine until the oil temperature is 80° C. (176° F.) (check with a thermometer inserted into the dipstick hole). Re-start and run the engine at 1,000 r.p.m. and check the following approximate pressures:

   a. In all gear positions except 'R' a pressure of between 75 and 85 lb./sq. in. (5.3 and 6 kg./cm.²) should register on the gauge.
   b. In 'R' the pressure should be between 115 and 125 lb./sq. in.(8 and 8.8 kg./cm.²).

NOTE.–Should the approximate pressures given above not be obtainable, see Section Fa.1, 'FAULT DIAGNOSIS'.

4. Remove the pressure test equipment and refit the plug.

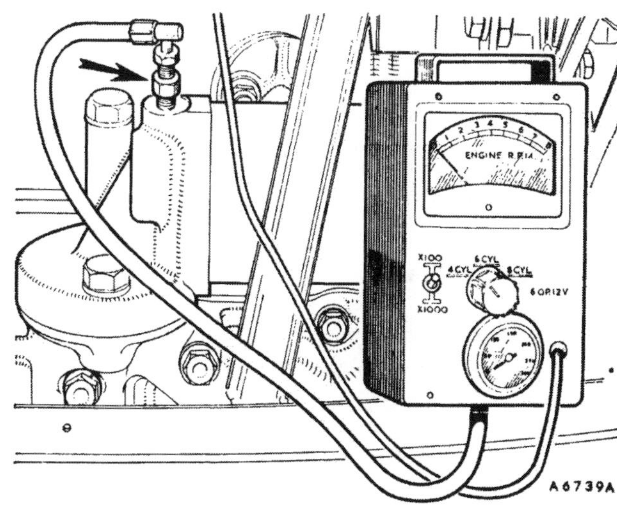

Fig. Fa.6
Checking the pressures and the stall speed with Service tool 18G 677 Z and adaptor 18G 677 C (arrowed)

Stall speed check

5. Start and run the engine until it reaches its normal working temperature and check the oil level.
6. Connect a suitable tachometer or that of Service tool 18G 677 or 18G 677 Z (see Fig. Fa.6).
   Service tool electrical connections:
   18G 677 – Green to ignition coil CB.
   Red to battery positive.
   Black to battery negative.
   18G 677 Z – Red to ignition coil CB.
   Black to earth connection.
7. Apply the hand and foot brakes, select any gear position except 'N' or '1', apply maximum throttle for **not more than 10 seconds** and note the tachometer reading. Compare the figure obtained with the 'Stall speed' chart.

Stall speed chart

8. Disconnect the tachometer.

MODEL	R.P.M.	Condition	Rectification
848 c.c.	1,300–1,400	Satisfactory	Nil
998 c.c.	1,400–1,500	Satisfactory	Nil
848 c.c. and 998 c.c.	Under 1,000	Stator free wheel slip	Change torque converter
	Over 1,500	Transmission slips	Check transmission unit (see Road Test note)
	Under 1,300	Engine down for power	Check engine

Section Fa.6

TRANSMISSION UNIT

Dismantling

1. Remove the engine and transmission from the car, see Section Aa.3.
2a. Remove the transmission from the engine as detailed in Section Aa.4 **only** if fitting a replacement engine, transmission case, or if it is necessary to remove the main oil strainer pick-up pipe and seals.
2b. Remove the converter and converter housing as detailed in Section Aa.4, items 1 to 11 and 13.
3. Unscrew and withdraw the transverse rod and remove the front cover (the connection is pressed into the later-type cover).
4. Remove the governor control assembly from the transmission case and fit Service tool 18G 1097 (see Fig. Fa.19).
5. Remove the securing nuts and pull the auxiliary pump and governor assembly from the transmission case.

NOTE. – For auxiliary pump and governor dismantling and reassembling see Section Fa.10.

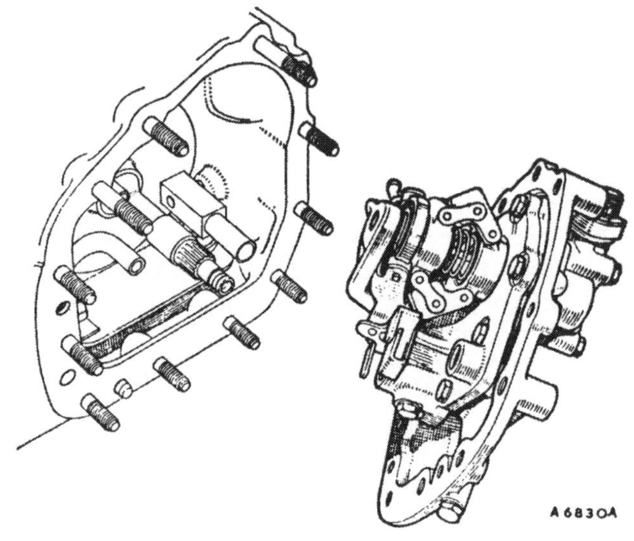

Fig. Fa.7
Removing the auxiliary pump and governor assembly

6. Remove the dowel bolt and pull out the auxiliary pump filter outlet pipe.
7. Pull out the auxiliary pump outlet and the forward clutch apply pipes.
8. Remove the set screw and lift out the auxiliary pump filter.
9. Remove Service tool 18G 1097 and withdraw the forward clutch from the casing.

NOTE.–For forward clutch dismantling and reassembling see Section Fa.11.

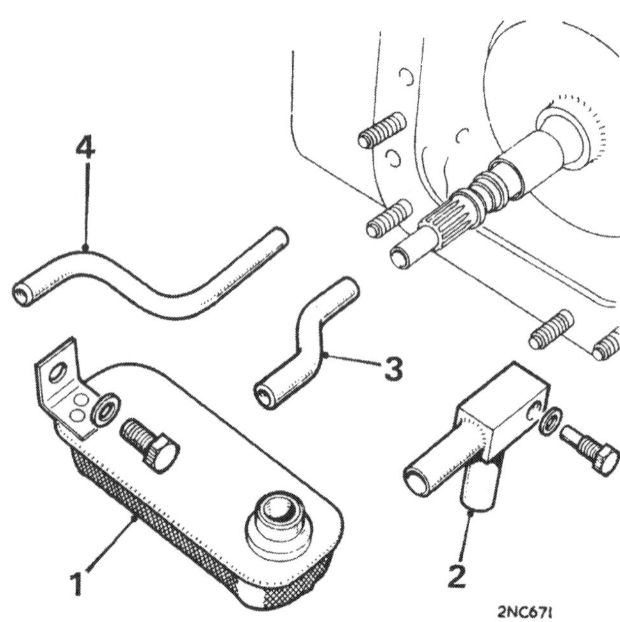

Fig. Fa.8
Removing the auxiliary oil pump strainer 1 and pipe 2, with 3 the outlet pipe, and 4 the forward clutch apply pipe

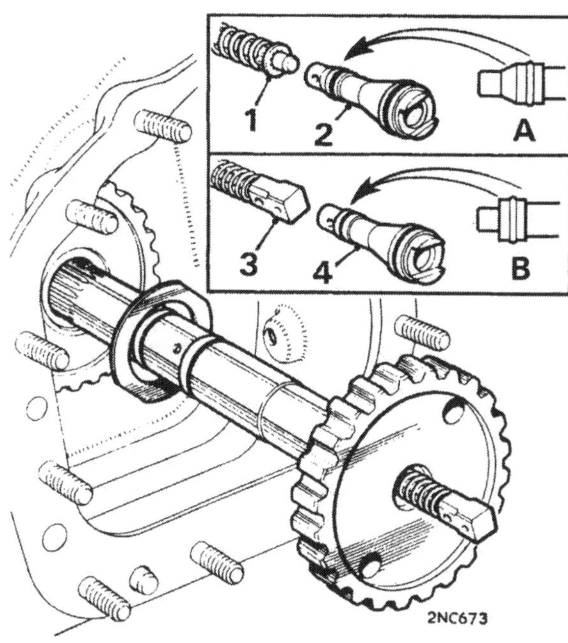

Fig. Fa.9
The forward output shaft and the reverse shut-off valve

Inset 'A'–1. Reverse shut-off valve } early type
2. Shut-off valve piston

Inset 'B'–3. Reverse shut-off valve } later type
4. Shut off valve piston

10. Withdraw the forward output shaft and remove the reverse shut-off valve, which should be identified for reassembly. The Mk. II transmission is fitted with a shut-off valve having a squared bronze thrust pad (see Fig. Fa.9) and a modified valve piston having a square cut shoulder. These can only be interchanged as a pair and the lastest type should be fitted when rebuilding the transmission.
11. Insert the dummy output shaft Service tool 18G 1093 or 18G 1093 A.
12. Slacken off the servo band adjusters.

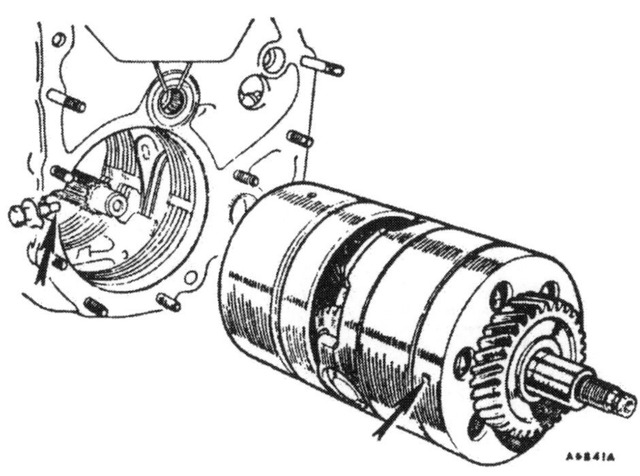

Fig. Fa.10
Removing the gear train assembly. The arrows indicate the dowel bolt and its location in the free-wheel support

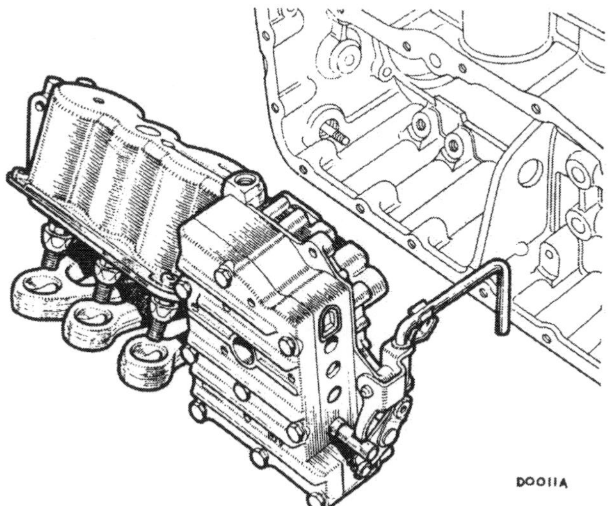

Fig. Fa.11
Removing the valve block and servo unit as an assembly

13. Remove the dowel bolt (Fig. Fa.10) and remove the gear train which includes the top and reverse clutch with its Torrington needle thrust bearing and steel washer, and the first gear free-wheel assembly.
NOTE.–For gear train dismantling and reassembling see Section Fa.12.
14. Remove the engine oil feed pipe as shown in Fig. Aa.9. On later transmissions unscrew the adaptor and withdraw the valve block connecting pipe through the adaptor hole.

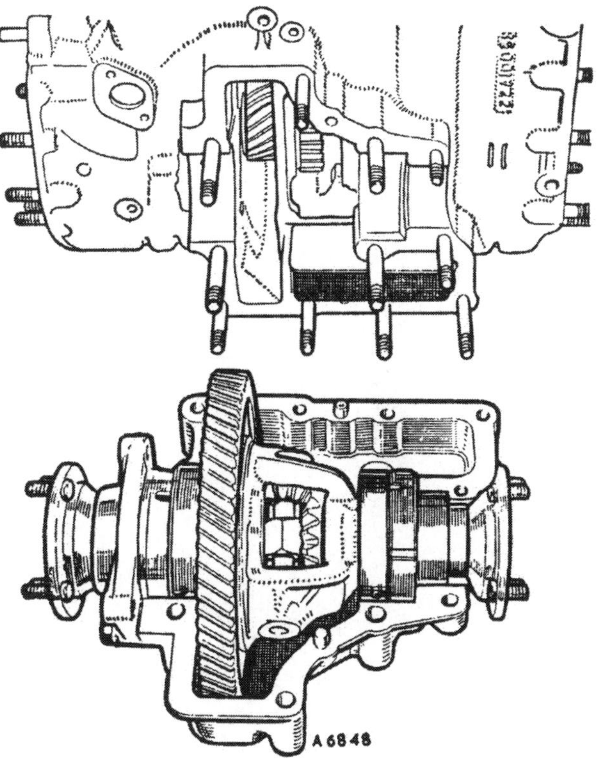

Fig. Fa.12
Removing the differential assembly

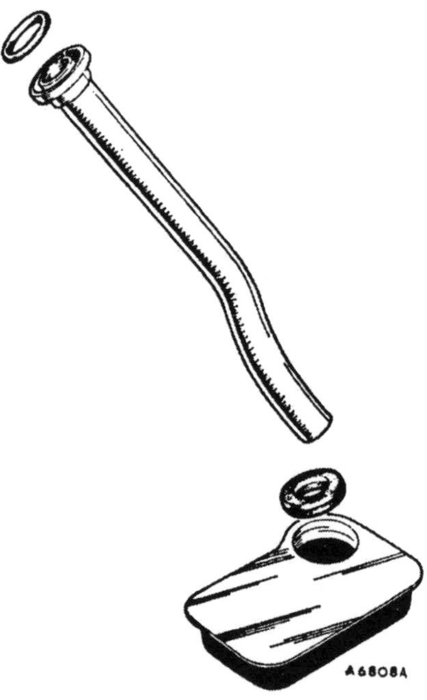

Fig. Fa.13
The main oil strainer, pick-up pipe and seals

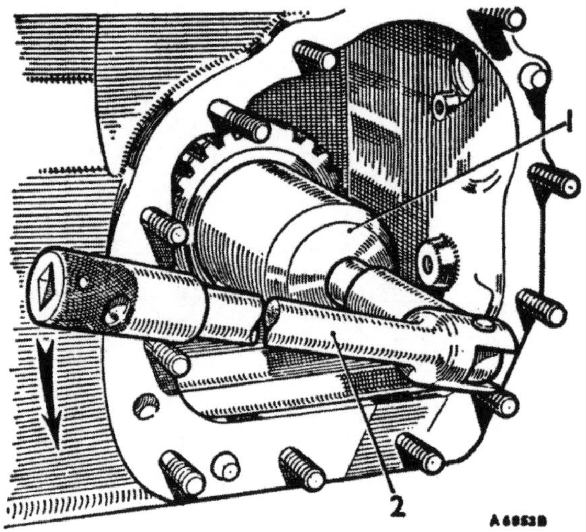

Fig. Fa.15
Removing the forward clutch hub nut

1. Service tool 18G 1096. 2. Socket handle.

15. Remove the valve block and servo unit securing bolts. Depress the tops of the bands and unhook them from the servos and lift out the valve block and servo unit as an assembly (Fig. Fa.11).
NOTE.–For valve block dismantling and reassembling see Section Fa.8, 9. For servo unit dismantling and reassembling see Section Fa.14.
16. Remove the bands from the transmission case.
17. Remove the governor control assembly from the transmission case.
18. Knock back the lock washers and remove the nuts from the differential housing and the differential end cover set screws. Remove the differential and housing assembly.
NOTE.–For differential dismantling and reassembling see Section Fa.16.
19. Remove the main oil feed pipe and strainer (see item 2a).

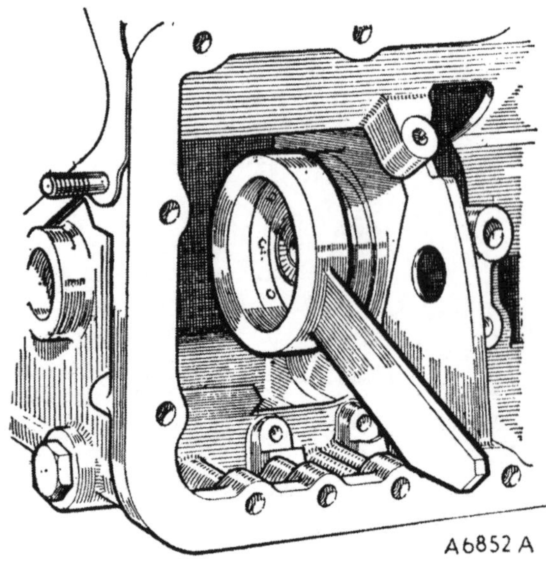

Fig. Fa.14
Using Service tool 18G 1095 to hold the top and reverse splines when removing the forward clutch hub nut

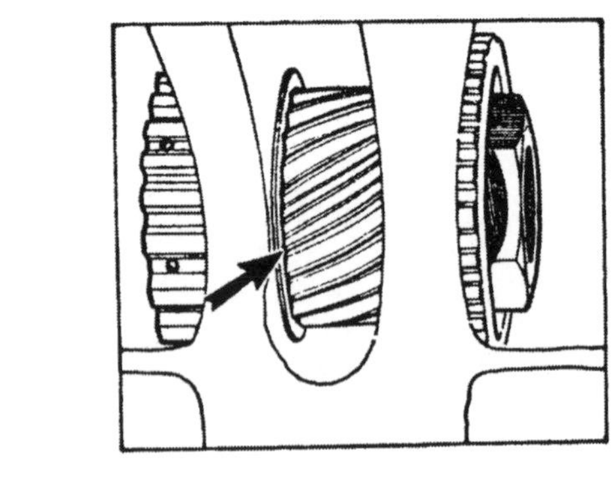

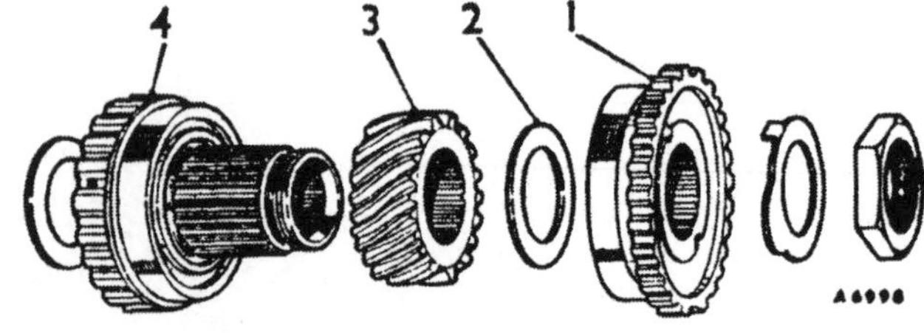

Fig. Fa.16

1. Forward clutch splines.
2. Selective thrust washer.
3. Final drive pinion.
4. Top and reverse splines.

Shown (inset) correctly assembled with the arrow indicating the chamfer on the pinion

20. Knock back the lock washer on the nut on the forward clutch splines and use Service tool 18G 1095 to hold the top and reverse clutch hub (Fig. Fa.14) and remove the nut with 18G 1096 (Fig. Fa.15). Drift out the top and reverse clutch hub and lift out the pinion assembly.
21. Remove both the bearings from the centre webs of the transmission case; each bearing must be drifted out on its outer race and from opposing sides of the webs.

Reassembling the transmission unit

Absolute cleanliness is essential, use fuel (petrol) or paraffin (kerosene) where necessary for cleaning. Dry the components with an air pressure line or use non-fluffy rag.

Clean all joint faces and fit new joint washers and oil seals.

After reassembly of each dismantled unit the complete transmission can now be rebuilt.

Lubricate all components with one of the recommended oils, refer to the **'RECOMMENDED LUBRICANTS'** chart shown in the **'MAINTENANCE'** Section. Ensure that new 'O' rings and seals are well lubricated when reassembling units or rebuilding the transmission assembly.

22. Refit the top and reverse clutch hub bearings to the centre webs of the transmission casing. Drift each bearing on its outer cage into the web until the bearing register contacts the face of the web.
23. Refit the top and reverse clutch hub, together with the final drive gear pinion but without the selective washer. Lightly tighten the forward clutch hub nut until light friction is felt on the bearings when rotating the hub.

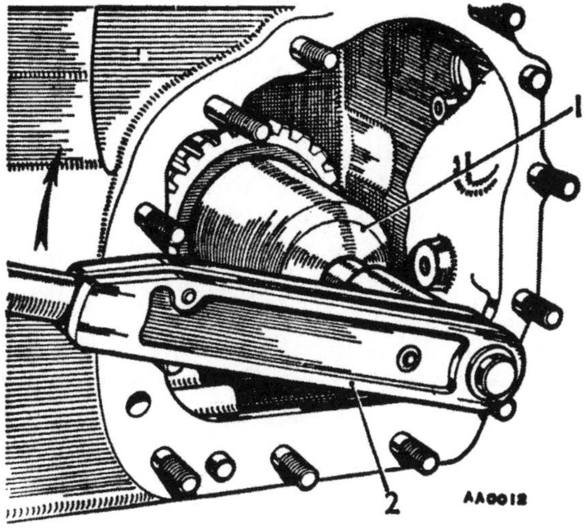

Fig. Fa.18
Tightening the forward clutch hub nut with Service tools 18G 1096 1, and 18G 592, 2

24. Check the gap existing between the final drive gear and the forward clutch hub bearing face.
25. Subtract .002 in. (.05 mm.) from the gap measurement and select a washer of this thickness from the range available.
26. Remove the hub and refit the assembly with the selected washer and with the chamfer on the final drive pinion facing the gear train (see Fig. Fa.16).
27. Use Service tool 18G 1095 to hold the top and reverse clutch splines (see Fig. Fa.17) and tighten the forward clutch hub nut with Service tool 18G 1096 and 18G 592 (see Fig. Fa.18), to the torque figure given in **'GENERAL DATA'**.

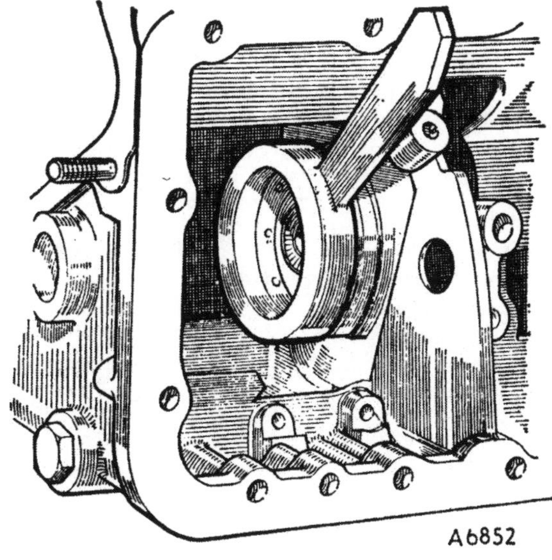

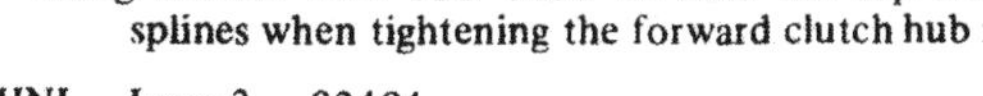

Fig. Fa.17
Using Service tool 18G 1095 to hold the top and reverse splines when tightening the forward clutch hub nut

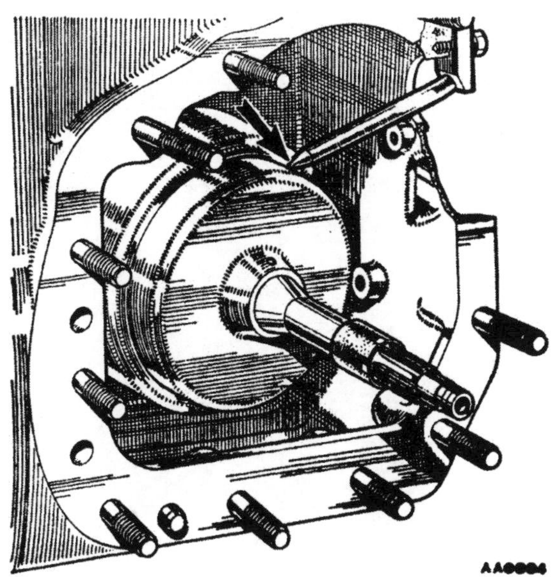

Fig. Fa.19
Holding the forward clutch in position with Service tool 18G 1097

28. Check that there is light friction on the bearings when rotating the hub, i.e. the bearings should have a preload of .002 in. (.05 mm.).
29. Tap up the locking washer.
30. Insert the forward output shaft with its bi-metal washer (see Fig. Fa.9) through the output gear assembly. Ensure that the correct type of reverse shut-off valve is located in the end of the shaft (see item 10), and that the rings on the shaft are in good condition.
31. Position the plastic sleeve over the rings on the forward clutch shaft and refit the forward clutch unit. If an earlier unit is being replaced by one of a later type, the reverse shut-off valve must also be changed (see item 10). Fit Service tool 18G 1097 to retain the correct position of the forward clutch unit (see Fig. Fa.19).
32. Fit new seals to the valve block connections and fit them into their correct locations in the transmission casing.
If a new transmission casing is being fitted, check the distance from the front flange of the transmission to the face of the centre connection inside the case. See that the correct connections are fitted according to the chart below, or else the valve block may later prevent the front cover from seating properly.

DISTANCE	CONNECTIONS
2.25 in. (57.2 mm.)	22A 1336
2.48 in. (62 mm.)	22A 812

33. Reassemble the valve block and servo unit as an assembly, fitting new seals to the inter-connecting pipes.
34. Refit the second, third, and reverse gear bands into the transmission casing.

Fig. Fa.20
Using the positioning fixture Service tool 18G 1094 to ensure correct alignment of the pipes

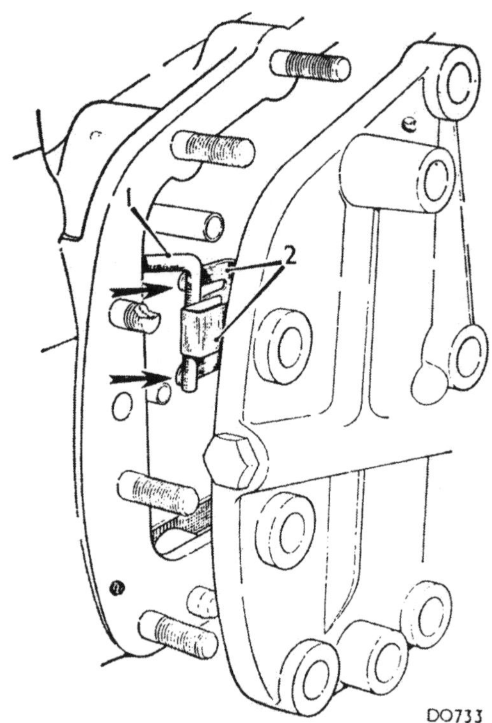

Fig. Fa.21
Engaging the valve block linkage 1 with the spring clip drive mechanism 2 of the later-type governor

35. Refit the valve block and the servo unit as an assembly into the transmission case, ensuring correct location of the valve block with the connections in the case and that the governor linkage is positioned over the web in the transmission casing.
36. Locate the bands on the servo struts.
37. Tighten the valve block and the servo unit securing bolts to the torque figure given in **'GENERAL DATA'**.
38. Refit the forward clutch apply pipe into its location in the transmission casing.
39. Refit the auxiliary pump pick-up strainer and pipe; secure the pipe with the dowel bolt (fitted with a copper sealing washer). Refit and tighten the strainer securing screw.
40. Fit a new joint washer to the transmission casing. Fit Service tool 19G 1094 and align the pipes (Fig. Fa.20) and remove the tool.
41. Refit the auxiliary pump and governor assembly and engage the valve block linkage with the later-type governor unit as shown in Fig. Fa.21, also ensuring correct alignment with the oil pipes and the forward shaft. The plastic sleeve fitted over the rings on the shaft is for assembly purposes, and will become safely displaced along the forward clutch shaft. Tighten the securing nuts to the torque figure given in **'GENERAL DATA'**.
42. Remove the forward clutch retainer—Service tool 18G 1097.

43. Refit the top and reverse clutch hub washer and the Torrington needle thrust bearing into position with grease.
44. Ensure that the top and reverse clutch friction plates are free to drop before refitting the gear train assembly into the transmission. Correctly position the second, third, and reverse gear bands in the case and refit the gear train, using hand pressure only to push it into position. Quick rotation of the input gear will assist in engaging the top and reverse clutch friction plates. When correctly reassembled the dowel bolt will engage easily in the free-wheel support (Fig. Fa.10).
45. Refit the dowel bolt with a new lock washer.
46. Screw the gear change transverse rod fully into the valve block linkage. Check and reset if necessary the transverse rod adjustment (see Section Fa.2).
47. Adjust the second, third and reverse servos (see Fig. Fa.24). Slacken the locknut 1 and turn the spherical adjuster 2 until each brake band 3 is in contact with the transmission casing stops 4 and all slack is just eliminated. Turn back the adjuster nine flats to obtain the clearance 'A' and tighten the locknut, which should give the minimum clearance.
48. Fit a new seal to the front cover connection, and refit the cover using a new joint washer.

    On early units the front cover connection can be removed and therefore requires two oil seals.

    If the front cover fails to mate correctly with the transmission case check that the correct transmission casing to valve block connections have been fitted as described in item 32.
49. Refit the engine oil feed pipe as shown in Fig. Fa.23. On later transmissions refit the valve block connecting pipe through the adaptor hole and screw the adaptor back in.

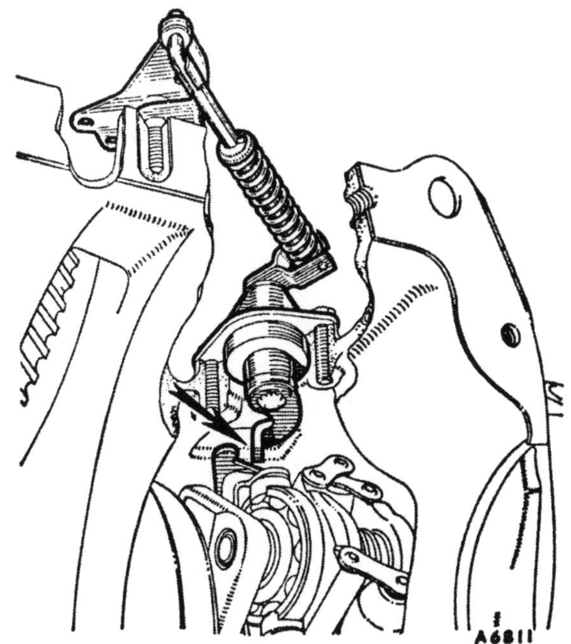

Fig. Fa.22
The correct position of the kick-down rod assembly

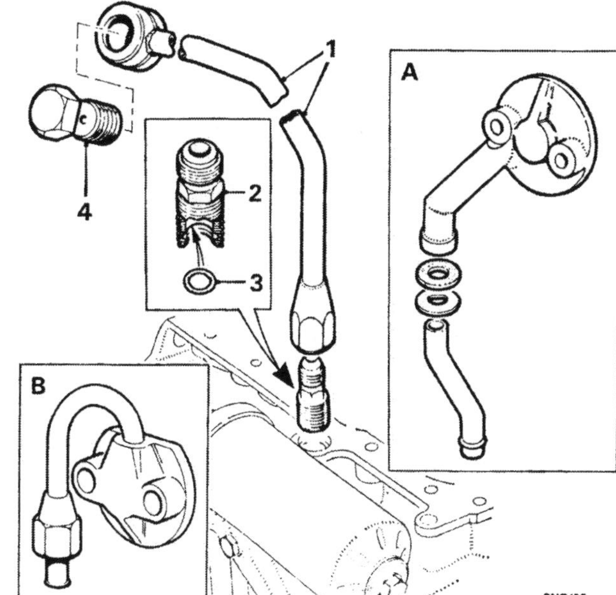

Fig. Fa.23
The engine oil feed pipe assembly. Inset 'A' shows the early type assembly. Inset 'B' shows the adaptor used when a later transmission is fitted to an early type engine

1. Engine oil feed pipe.
2. Adaptor.
3. Adaptor 'O' ring seal.
4. Banjo union screw.

50. Refit the main oil strainer and pick-up pipe using new seals (if these items were removed), see item 2a.
51. Refit the differential assembly as detailed in Section Fa.16.
52. Refit the engine to the transmission as detailed in Section Aa.4 (if removed see item 2a).
53. Refit the converter and components removed in item 2b see Section Aa.4.
54. Refit the engine/transmission unit to the car as detailed in Section Aa.3.

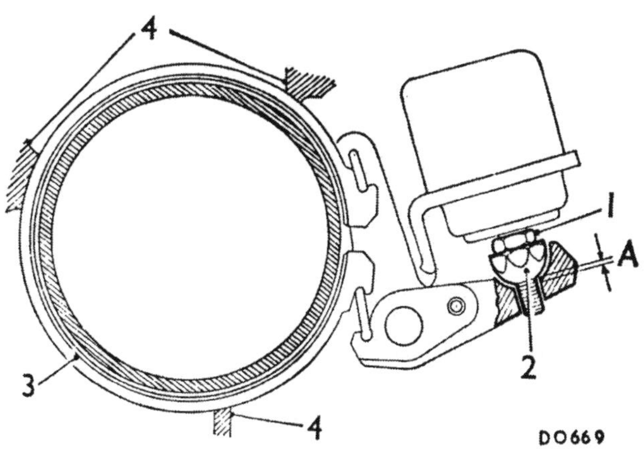

Fig. Fa.24
The servo unit band adjustment
A = .040 to .080 in. (1.02 to 2.03 mm.)

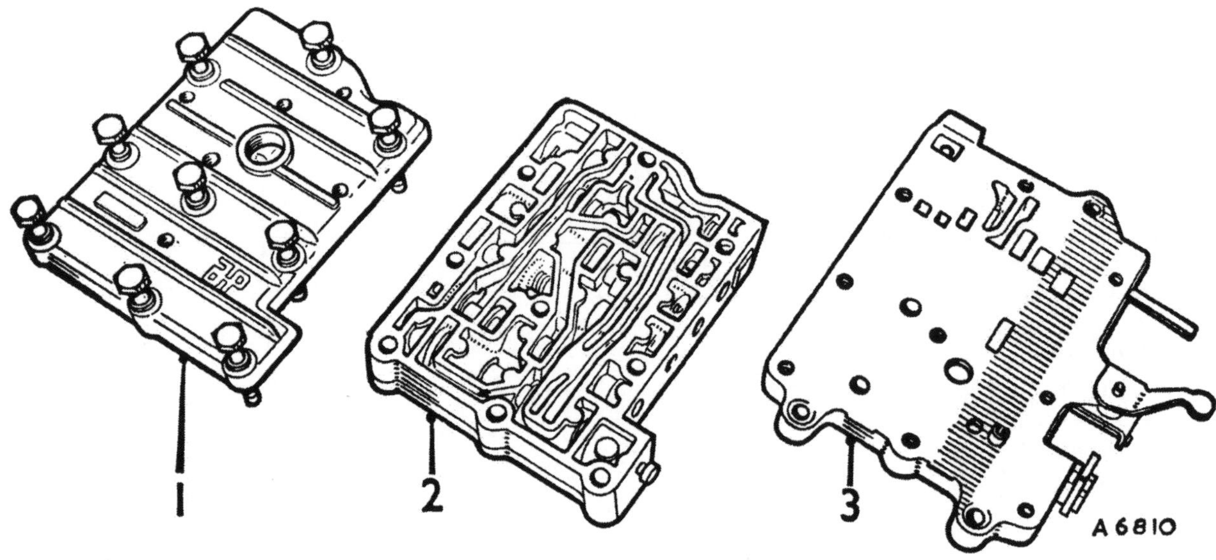

Fig. Fa.25
The valve block assembly (Mk. I and II transmissions)

1. Lid. 2. Valve chest. 3. Pipe chest.

Section Fa.7

VALVE BLOCK
(Removing and Refitting)

Early unit (848 c.c. Up to Engine No. 8AH/A/H9733)
The valve block can be removed from the transmission unit with the power unit IN SITU by removing the unit as three individual sections.
It is necessary to clean thoroughly the area around the transmission front cover before any dismantling is commenced. Absolute cleanliness is essential at all times and especially so whilst servicing this unit.

Later 848-c.c. and 998-c.c. units (From Engine No. 8AH/A/H9734)
The valve block assembly cannot be removed from the transmission unit with the power unit IN SITU but the lid and valve chest can be removed for dismantling and cleaning. If it is necessary to examine and/or fit new seals to the valve block/servo unit interconnecting pipes or to remove the pipe chest, it is necessary to remove the power unit from the car and remove the converter and housing (see items 25 to 32).

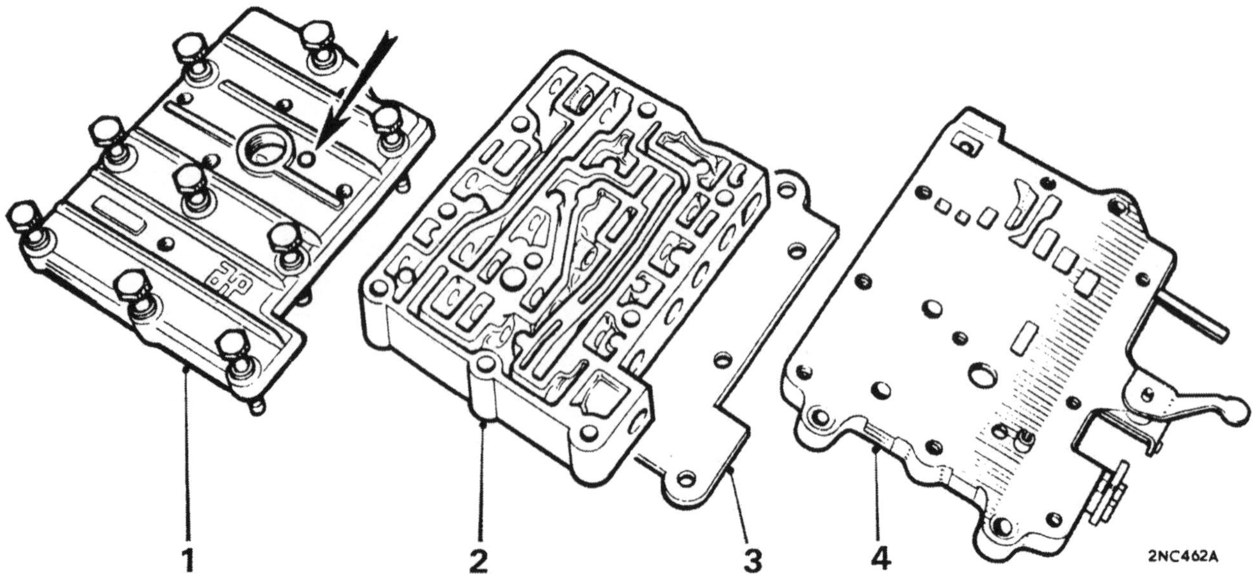

Fig. Fa.26
The valve block (with inbuilt engagement control and shuttle valves) which is fitted to the Mk. II B transmission unit. This unit may be identified by the exhaust hole in the lid (arrowed)

1. Lid. 2. Valve chest. 3. Separator plate. 4. Pipe chest.

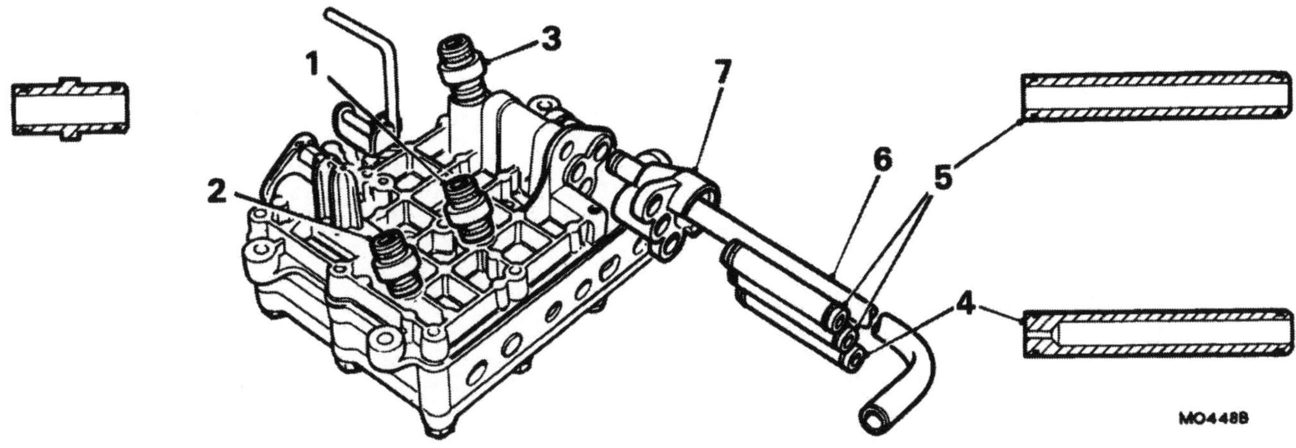

Fig. Fa.27
The valve block connections and pipes. Assemble the pipe 4 with its restricted end in the valve block (Mk. I and II transmissions only)

1. Connection–top/reverse clutch.
2. Connection–forward clutch.
3. Connection–auxiliary pump (not fitted on Mk. II B units).
4. Connecting pipe with restrictor to reverse servo(pipe without restrictor fitted to Mk. II B units).
5. Connecting pipes (to second and third servos).
6. Converter feed pipe.
7. Pipe assembly guide.

Removing (early models)

1. Remove the front grille.
2. Remove the filter assembly as detailed in Section Aa.2.
3. Remove the engine oil feed pipe.
4. Drain the engine/transmission unit.
5. Remove the transmission front cover and valve block connection.
6. Place the gear selector lever in the 'R' position on the quadrant.
7. Remove the bell-crank lever clevis pin. Unscrew and pull out the transverse rod sufficiently to remove the valve block.
8. Loosen the servo unit securing bolts.
9. Remove the valve block assembly as individual components, i.e. the lid, valve chest, and finally (if necessary) the pipe chest (Fig. Fa.25).

The valve block can only be removed as an assembly with the power unit removed from the car.

VALVE CHEST ONLY–'POWER UNIT IN SITU'

Removing (later 848-c.c. and 998-c.c. models)

10. Carry out items 1, 2, and 4.
11. Disconnect the engine oil feed pipe and remove the adaptor. Withdraw the valve block connecting pipe through the adaptor hole.

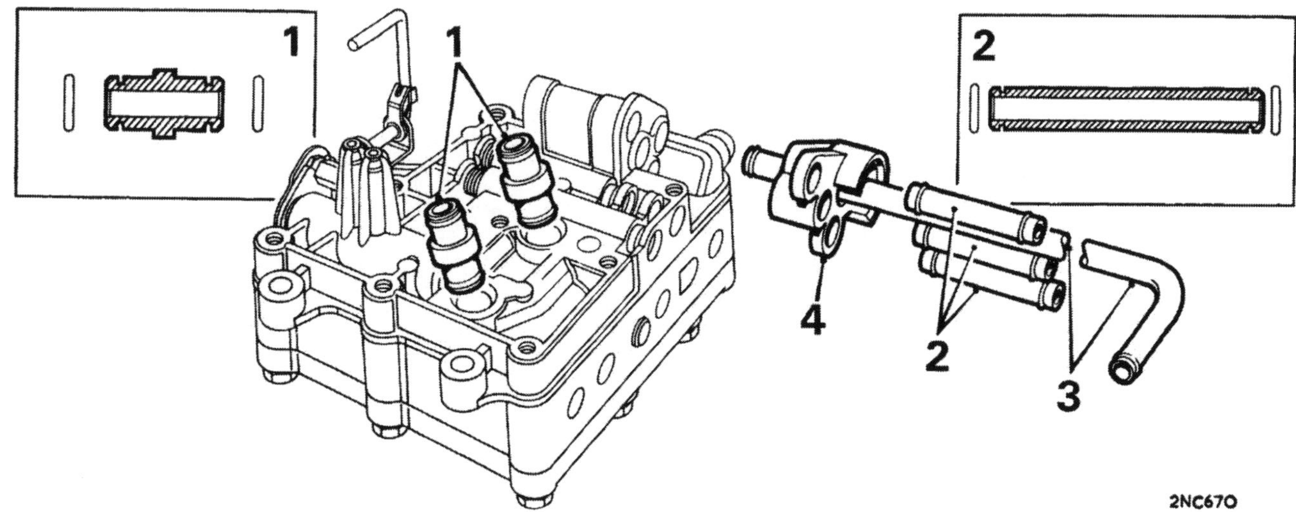

Fig Fa.28
The valve block fitted to Mk. II B transmissions (with engagement control valve incorporated in the valve block assembly)

1. Connections (top/reverse clutch and forward clutch).
2. Connecting pipes (to second, third and reverse servos).
3. Converter feed pipes.
4. Guide–converter feed pipe.

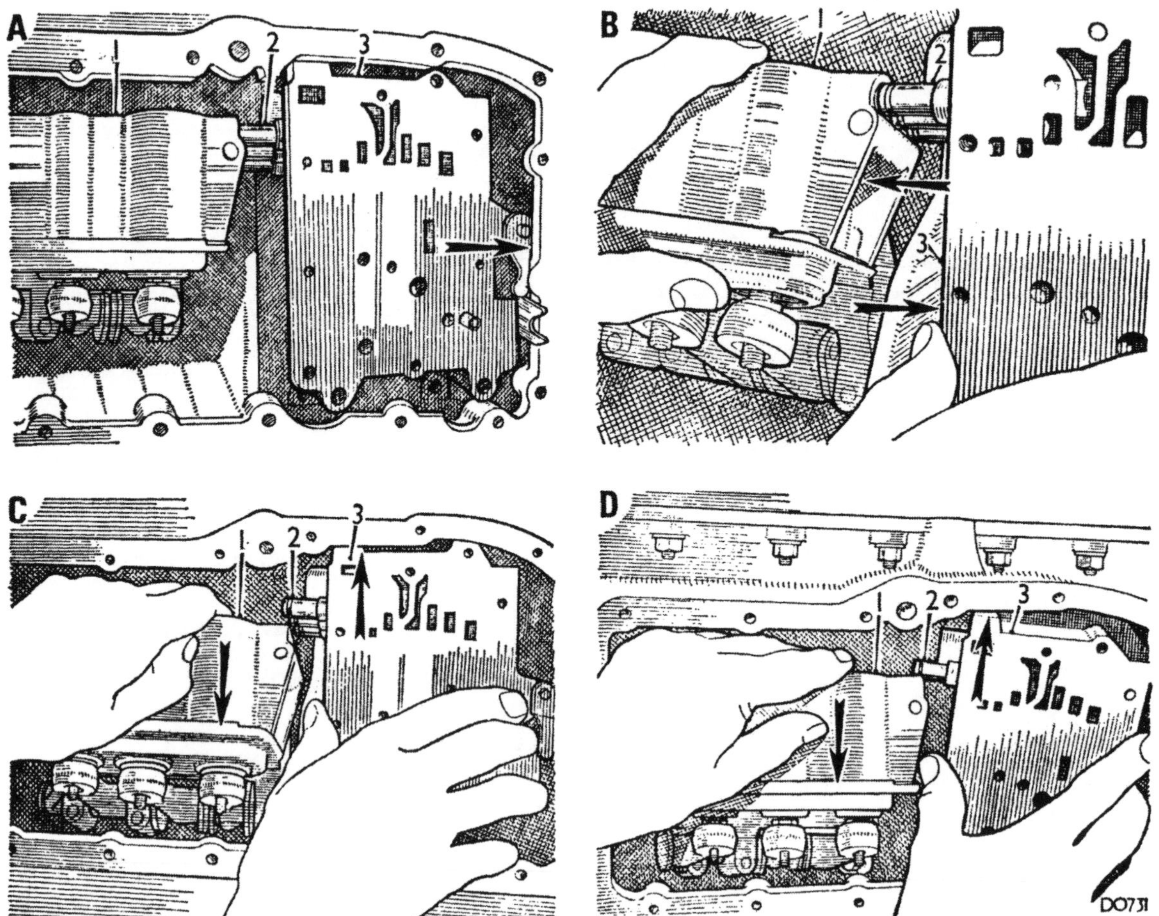

Fig. Fa.29
The removing and refitting sequence of the pipe chest section of the valve block

1. Servo unit. 2. Connecting pipes. 3. Pipe chest.

12. Remove the transmission front cover and manoeuvre the cover upwards and out through the grille aperture.
13. Remove the valve block lid and the valve chest.

Refitting

14. Refitting is a reversal of the removal procedure; take care to locate the selector valve with the linkage and the governor rod with the governor. The flat on the governor valve must face inwards. Tighten all securing bolts to the torque figures given in **'GENERAL DATA'**.
15. Ensure that the new joint washer fitted to the filter head/transmission front cover is correctly fitted.
16. Check the gear change selector lever cable and transverse rod as detailed in Section Fa.2 and adjust if necessary.
17. Refill the engine/transmission unit with one of the recommended oils (see **'RECOMMENDED LUBRICANTS'** chart in **'MAINTENANCE'** Section). Top up to the 'MAX' mark on the dipstick, see the procedure given in Section Aa.1.

VALVE BLOCK ASSEMBLY REPLACEMENT 'POWER UNIT REMOVED'

Removing (later 848-c.c. and 998-c.c. models)

18. Remove the engine/transmission unit from the car (Section Aa.3).
19. Remove the converter cover, converter and converter housing as detailed in Section Aa.4, items 3 to 11.
20. Drain the engine/transmission unit.
21. Remove the complete filter assembly as detailed in Section Aa.2.
22. Disconnect the engine oil feed pipe and remove the adaptor. Withdraw the valve block connecting pipe through the adaptor hole.
23. Remove the front cover.
24. Disconnect, unscrew, and pull out the transverse rod.
25. Remove the governor control assembly from the transmission case and fit Service tool 18G 1097 to hold the forward clutch (see Fig. Fa.19).
26. Remove the securing nuts and withdraw the auxiliary pump and governor assembly from the transmission case.

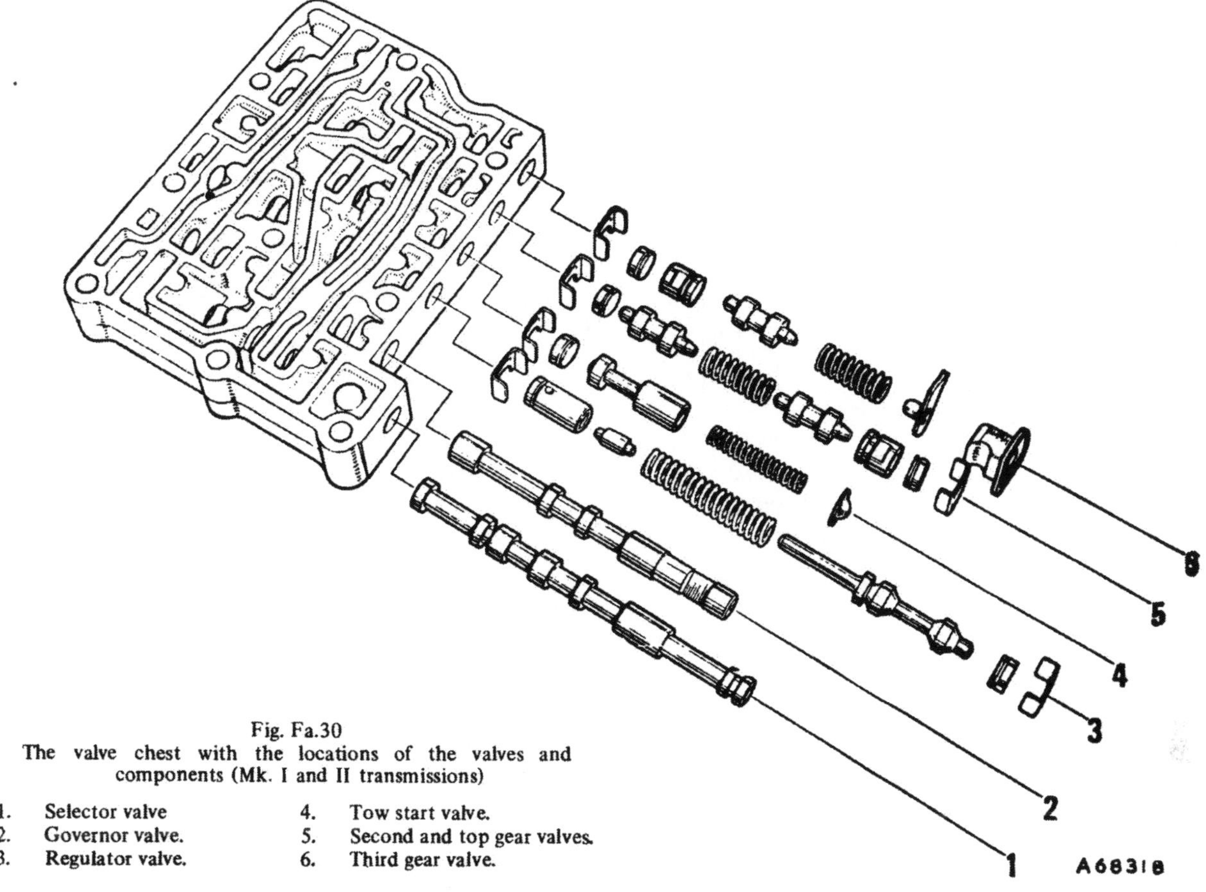

Fig. Fa.30
The valve chest with the locations of the valves and components (Mk. I and II transmissions)

1. Selector valve
2. Governor valve.
3. Regulator valve.
4. Tow start valve.
5. Second and top gear valves.
6. Third gear valve.

27. Remove the valve block lid and valve chest.
28. Remove the pipe chest as shown in the operation sequence in Fig. Fa.29 after pulling it outwards to release it from the connections and to disconnect the governor linkage.
29. Refer to Fig. Fa.29.
    a. Push the pipe chest fully against the casing.
    b. Move the servo unit in the opposite direction until the three pipes are clear of the servo unit.
    c. Pull the servo unit outwards and downwards; lift the pipe chest upwards and (when clear), move it so that the pipes are over the top of the servo and the regulator valve lever is clear of the transmission casing.
    d. Hold the servo unit down and withdraw the pipe chest after lifting the linkage over the web in the casing.

Fitting replacement unit

30. Remove the lid and valve chest from the pipe chest of the new unit. Refit these as individual components in the reverse order of the removing procedure, noting the following points.
31. Fit the connections into their locations in the transmission case.
32. Assemble the three pipes into the pipe chest (together with the nylon guide) before refitting the unit to the transmission casing.
33. Carry out operation 14.
34. Position the plastic sleeve over the rings on the forward clutch shaft.
35. Carry out operations 40 to 42 in Section Fa.6.
36. The remainder is a reversal of the removal procedure.

Section Fa.8

VALVE BLOCK
(Dismantling and Reassembling)

Dismantling

NOTE.– Before dismantling the valve block it must be remembered that the valves are selected for each bore. It is of the utmost importance therefore to reassemble each valve into its original bore and position. Cleanliness is essential at all times.

1. If the valve block has been removed as a complete unit, detach the lid and valve chest from the pipe chest. See Fig. Fa.25.
2. Remove the selector and governor valves.
3. Remove the 'C' clips and the plugs. Remove the regulator valve, spring, and reverse booster piston assembly.
4. Remove the 'C' clip and the plug. Remove the tow-start valve, spring, and spring retainer.

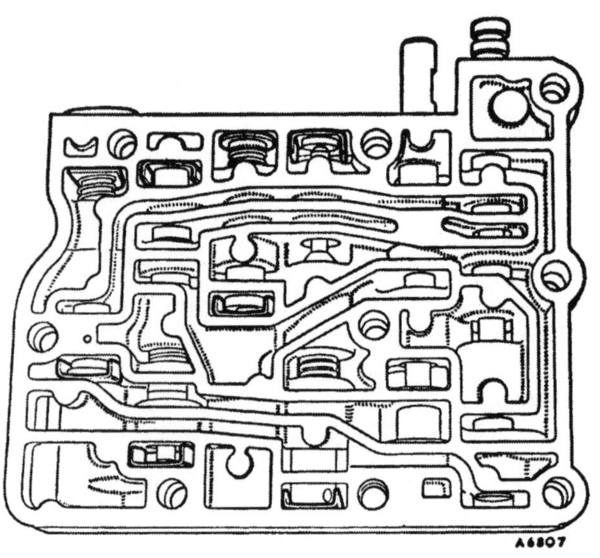

Fig. Fa.31
The valve chest with the 'C' clips correctly positioned (Mk. I and II transmissions)

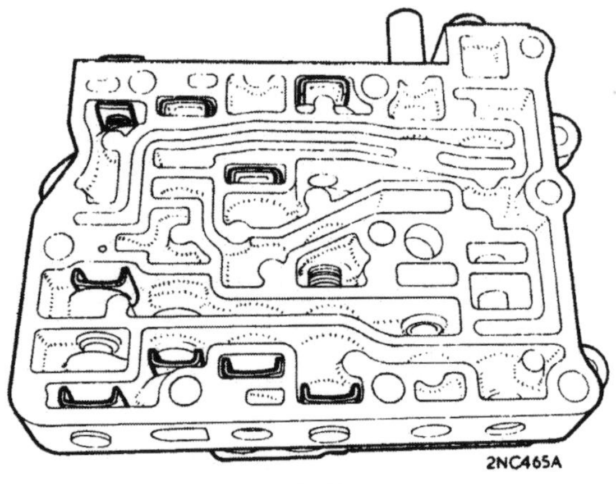

Fig. Fa.33
The locations of the 'C' clips in the valve chest (Mk. II B transmission)

5. Remove the 'C' clips and the plugs. Remove the second and fourth gear valves, spring, and booster piston.
6. Remove the 'C' clip and plug. Remove the third gear valve booster piston, spring, spring retainer and the plastic plug.

Inspecting

Clean all parts thoroughly in clean fuel (petrol) or paraffin (kerosene) and dry off using an air pressure line.

Check for burrs on the valves and valve chest and for sticking valves. Place all components in automatic transmission oil before reassembling to the valve block.

Reassembling

7. Reassemble each valve assembly in the reverse order of dismantling (see Fig. Fa.30). Check that the 'C' clips and plugs are correctly located in the valve chest (see Fig. Fa.31).

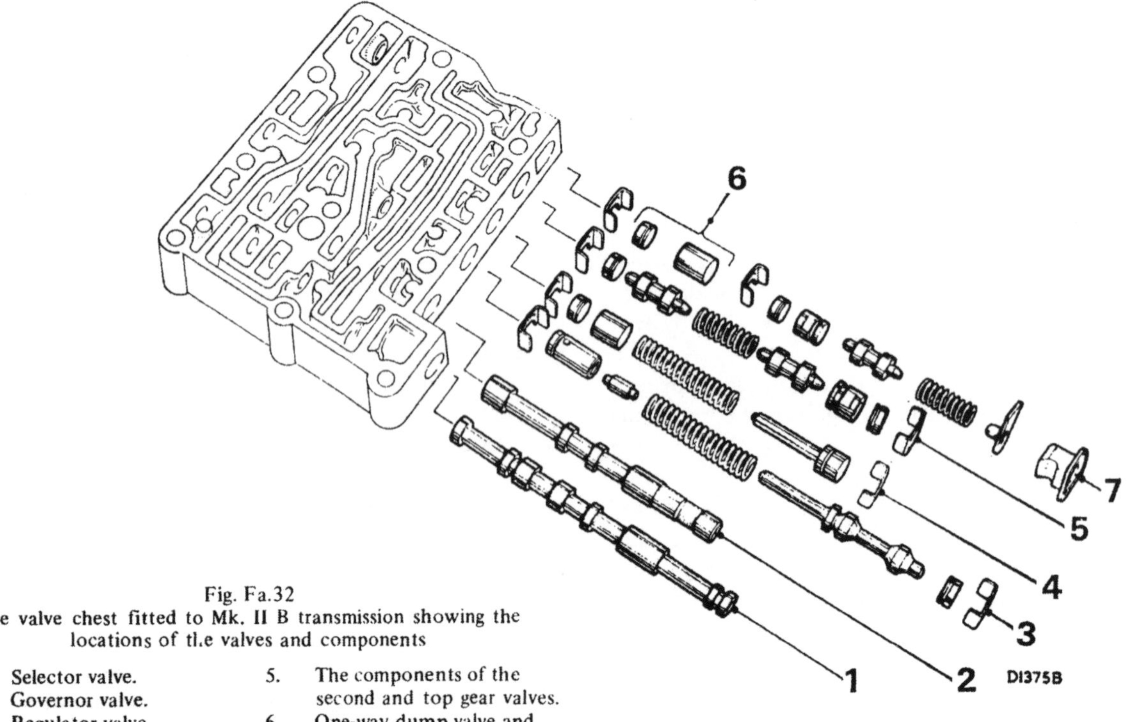

Fig. Fa.32
The valve chest fitted to Mk. II B transmission showing the locations of tl.e valves and components

1. Selector valve.
2. Governor valve.
3. Regulator valve. components.
4. Engagement control valve components.
5. The components of the second and top gear valves.
6. One-way dump valve and stop (plug).
7. Third gear valve components.

Section Fa.9

VALVE BLOCK–WITH INBUILT ENGAGEMENT CONTROL AND SHUTTLE VALVES

(Dismantling and Reassembling)

Dismantling

NOTE.–Before dismantling the valve block it must be remembered that the valves are selected for each bore. It is of the utmost importance therefore to reassemble each valve into its original bore and position. Cleanliness is essential at all times.

1. If the valve block has been removed as a complete unit, which is essential if the shuttle valves are to be dismantled, detach the lid and valve chest from the pipe chest and also take out the separator plate and flap valve.
2. Pull out the selector and governor valves.
3. To remove the regulator valve components, pull out both 'C' clips and extract the plugs, the regulator valve, spring and reverse booster piston.
4. Pull out both the 'C' clips which secure the engagement control valve components, and extract the plain plug, the plug with the extended stop, the spring and the valve.
5. Pull out both the retaining 'C' clips and extract the plugs, second and top gear valves, spring and booster piston.
6. Pull out the end 'C' clip and extract the plug and the one-way dump valve. Withdraw the centre 'C' clip and remove the third gear valve with the booster piston, spring, spring retainer and the plastic plug.

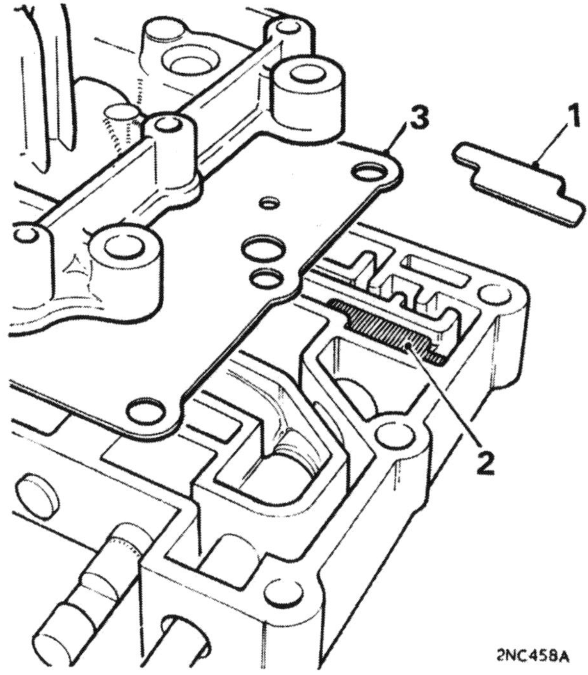

Fig. Fa.35
It is essential that the flap valve 1 is positioned flat on its seatings 2 before the separator plate 3 is located and the valve block is reassembled

ENGAGEMENT CONTROL SHUTTLE VALVES

7. From the back of the pipe chest depress in turn the abutment of each of the shuttle valve components sufficiently to release the retaining washer; then extract the abutment, engagement piston (reverse gear shuttle), shuttle valve and the spring.

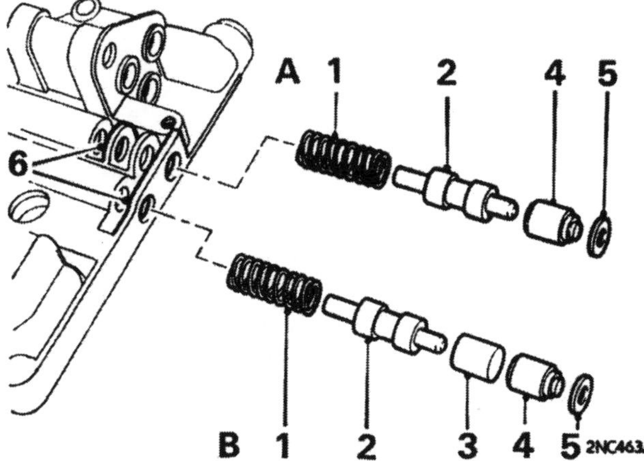

Fig. Fa.34
'A'–Third gear shuttle valve assembly
'B'–Reverse gear shuttle valve assembly

1. Spring.
2. Shuttle valve.
3. Engagement piston.
4. Abutment.
5. Washer.
6. Washer locating ribs.

Inspecting

Clean all parts thoroughly in clean fuel (petrol) or paraffin (kerosene) and dry off using an air pressure line.

Check for burrs on the valves and valve chest and for sticking valves. Place all components in automatic transmission oil before reassembling them into the valve block.

Reassembling

8. Reassemble for each valve assembly into its correct bore in the reverse order of dismantling (see Fig. Fa.32). Check that the 'C' clips and plugs have been correctly located in the valve chest, as shown in Fig. Fa.33, and then the retaining washers of the shuttle valves are properly seated in their correct locations (see Fig. Fa.34).
9. When reassembling the complete valve block see that the flap valve is fitted, lying flat, in its correct location behind the selector valve as shown in Fig. Fa.35, and that the separator plate is fitted between the valve chest and the pipe chest.

Section Fa.10

AUXILIARY PUMP AND GOVERNOR

Removing

1. Remove the engine/transmission unit from the car as detailed in Section Aa.3.
2. Remove the governor control assembly from the transmission case and fit Service tool 18G 1097 (see Fig. Fa.19).
3. Remove the securing nuts and pull the auxiliary pump and governor assembly from the transmission case.

Dismantling

4. Remove the speedometer drive assembly.
5. Remove the set screws and bolt. Pull out the governor centre shaft, and lift away the governor assembly together with one of the auxiliary pump gears.
6. Remove the circlip, lift off the auxiliary pump gear, and remove the governor.
7. Lift out the governor bearing trunnions and washer.
8. Remove the second auxiliary pump gear from the auxiliary pump housing together with its thrust washer; the earlier type cover is fitted with a bi-metal thrust washer with a plain bush fitted in the housing while the later type cover has a flanged bush and a steel thrust washer, see Fig. Fa.37.

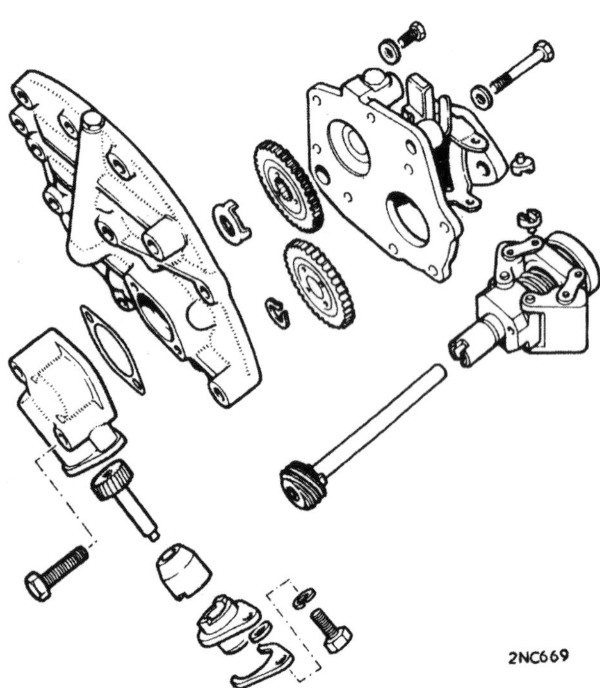

Fig. Fa.36
The speedometer drive, auxiliary pump gears and governor assembly components

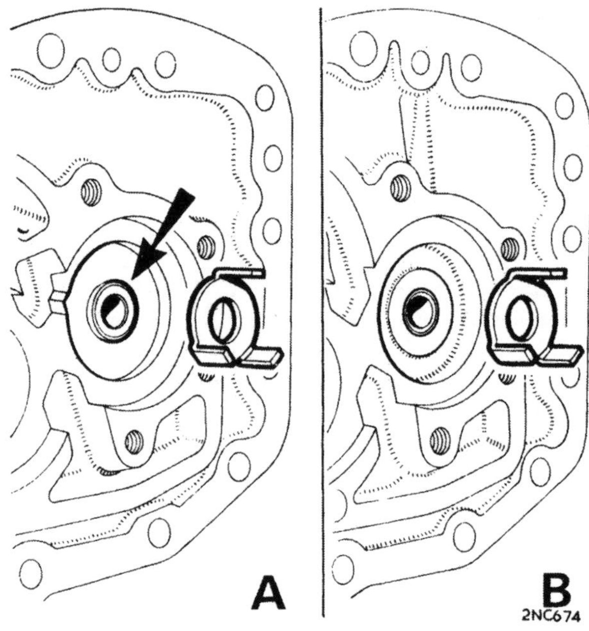

Fig. Fa.37
Both types of auxiliary pump housing. 'A' shows the later type housing with a flanged bush (arrowed) and steel thrust washer. 'B' shows the early type housing with a plain bush and bi-metal thrust washer

Inspecting

Examine all components for wear or damage.

All units except Mk. II B. Check the condition of the bi-metal thrust washer; if it has broken up and caused the bush in the housing to move deeper into its bore, replace the gears and housing assembly with the Mk. II B assembly which has a flanged bush and a steel thrust washer, see Fig. Fa.37.

Reassembling

9. Reassemble the auxiliary pump gear with its thrust washer to the pump casing (see Fig. Fa.37).

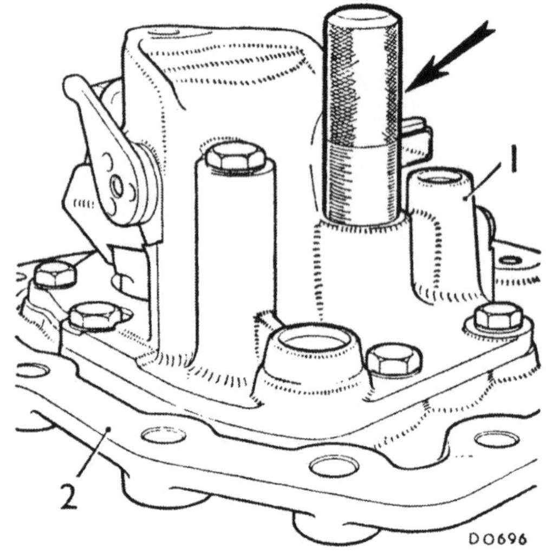

Fig. Fa.38
Centralizing the pump and governor unit 1 with the end cover 2 using Service tool 18G 1106 (arrowed)

10. Refit the governor auxiliary pump gear and circlip. Ensure that both gears are seating correctly and will rotate freely after assembly.
11. Refit the governor assembly to the auxiliary pump and refit the centre shaft.
12. Use Service tool 18G 1106 to centralize the auxiliary pump and governor unit with the end cover, tighten the securing bolts to the torque figure given in **'GENERAL DATA'** and remove the Service tool.
13. Refit the speedometer drive assembly, with a new joint washer.

Refitting

14. Carry out the instructions given in Section Fa.6, items 40 and 42.
    NOTE.–See 'GENERAL DATA' for all torque figures.

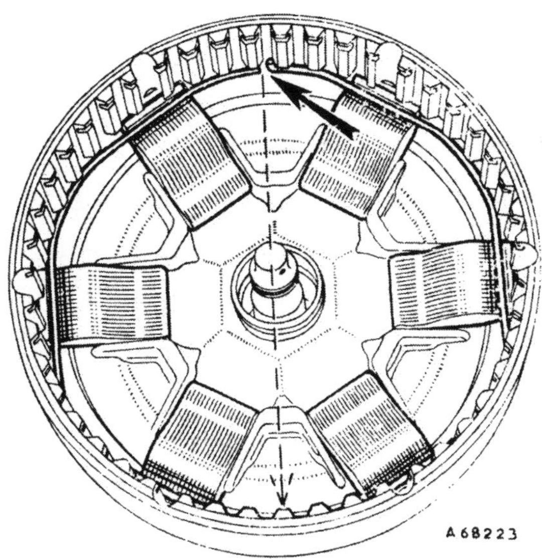

Fig. Fa.40
The fitted position of the toggles and spring ring (fitted to very early units). The arrow indicates location of spring ends exactly opposite the only five tooth section of the clutch unit

Section Fa.11

FORWARD CLUTCH

Two types of clutch assembly have been fitted. The earlier type has 47 teeth and is shown in Fig. Fa.41. This has now been replaced by a clutch having 30 teeth which is shown in Fig. Fa.43. The two clutches are interchangeable as complete assemblies, although the individual components are not.

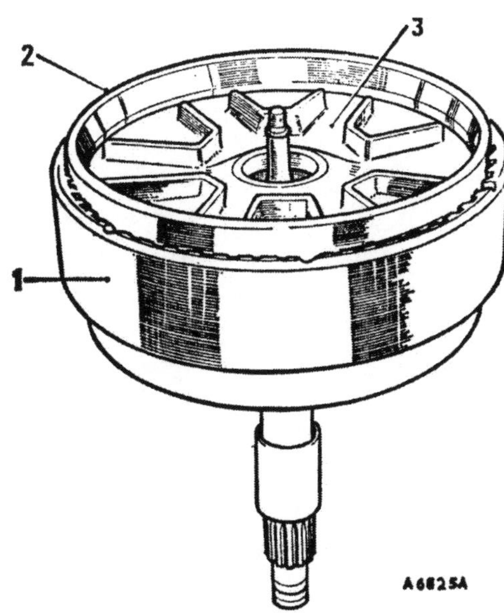

Fig. Fa.39
Fitting the forward clutch piston using Service tool 18G 1102
1. Forward clutch. 2. Service tool 18G 1102.
3. Forward clutch piston.

NOTE.– Later 30 tooth forward clutches are fitted with a modified reverse shut-off valve piston (see item 10, Section Fa.6). If fitting a new clutch having the modified piston, the reverse shut-off valve in the forward output shaft must also be replaced by one of the modified types.

Removing

1. Carry out the operations given in Section Fa.6, items 1 and 4 to 9.

Dismantling

2. Remove the retaining circlip or Spirolox ring.
   NOTE.–Mark the retainer plate and steel clutch plate to assist when reassembling.
3. 30 TOOTH CLUTCH: Remove and discard any shims which have been fitted to rectify clutch plate end-float. A new method of controlling clutch plate end-float using end and intermediate steel plates of varying thicknesses together with a wider section retaining circlip was introduced at the Engine Numbers given below.
   Commencing Engine Numbers: 85H–285E–H347, 99H–285E–H3832, and 99H471E–H1421.
   NOTE.– Whenever a transmission is dismantled prior to the above Engine Numbers, the assembly may be brought up to the latest specification. Always check the specification of a new forward clutch unit taken from stock; fit the relevant parts required and check the end-float adjustment before fitting.
   Refer to '**Adjusting**' and the chart giving the range of plates available.

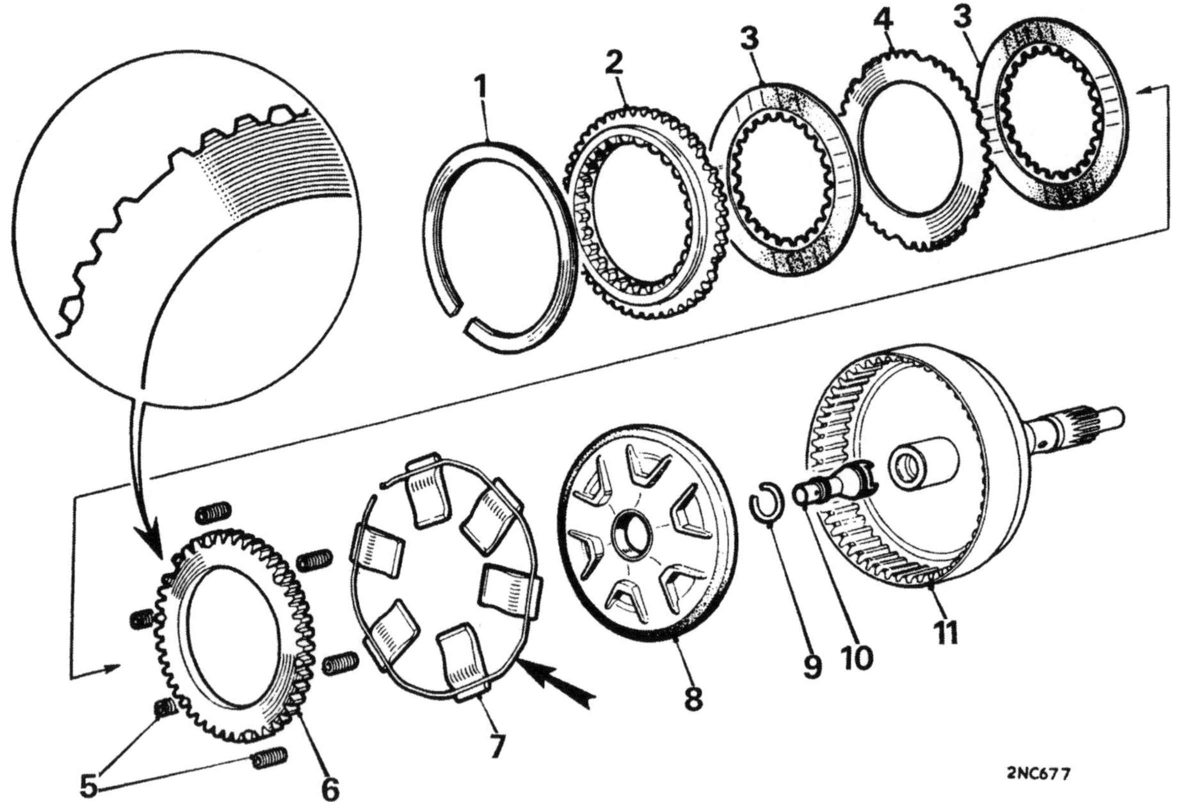

Fig. Fa.41
The early-type (47-tooth) forward clutch components. The arrow indicates the spring ring fitted to very early units only

1. Circlip (replacing Spirolox ring).
2. End plate.
3. Clutch plates (paper faced).
4. Intermediate plate.
5. Piston return springs (6).
6. Pressure plate.
7. Toggles.
8. Piston.
9. Circlip–reverse shut-off valve.
10. Reverse shut-off valve.
11. Forward clutch unit.

4. Lift out the piston return springs and pressure plate.
5. Remove the spring ring (if fitted) and toggles (see Fig. Fa.41).
6. Use an air pressure line to blow out the piston.
7. Remove the circlip and lift out the reverse shut-off valve piston, which should be identified as detailed in item 10 of Section Fa.6, for reassembly.

Inspecting

Check all parts for wear and renew if necessary. Check the reverse shut-off valve oil seals and renew if necessary.

Reassembling

8. Refit the reverse shut-off valve piston of the correct type, and fit a new circlip.
9. Assemble the seal onto the piston with the lips of seal facing inwards and lubricated with one of the recommended oils, see **'RECOMMENDED LUBRICANTS'**.
10. Insert Service tool 18G 1102 into the clutch unit and press the piston through the tool until it is fully into its bore, see Fig. Fa.39.

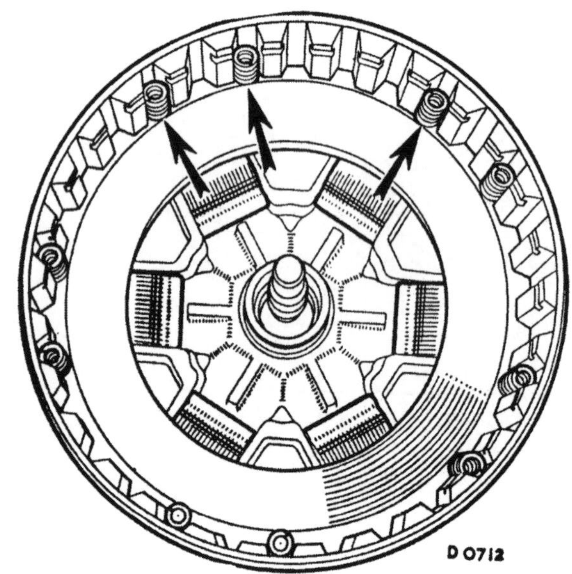

Fig. Fa.42
The fitted position of the toggles and springs of the 30-tooth clutch

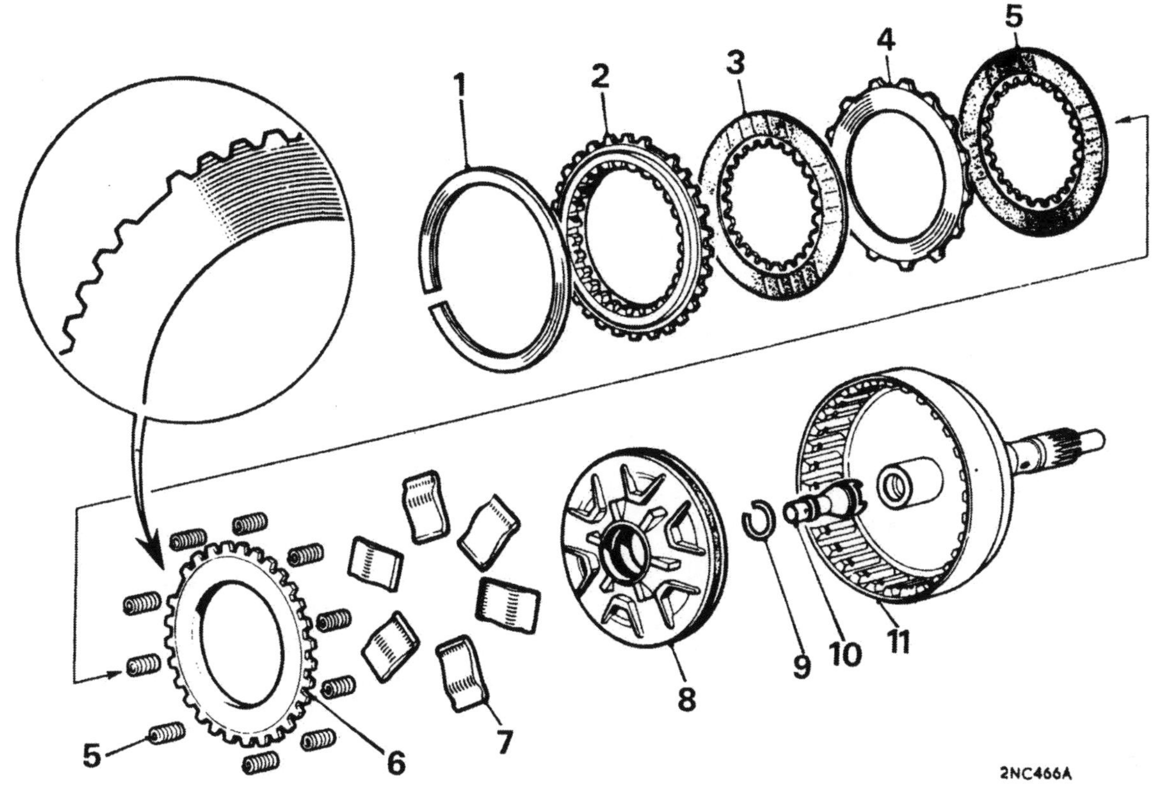

Fig. Fa.43
The (30-tooth) forward clutch components

1. Circlip (replacing Spirolox ring).
2. End plate.
3. Clutch plates (paper faced).
4. Intermediate plate.
5. Piston return springs (10).
6. Pressure plate.
7. Toggles.
8. Piston.
9. Circlip–reverse shut-off valve.
10. Reverse shut-off valve.
11. Forward clutch unit.

11. 47-TOOTH CLUTCH. Assemble the toggles and spring ring (early units) with the end of the spring-ring located as shown in Fig. Fa.40, and with the cut-out tooth on the pressure plate in the relative position to the ends of the spring ring (Fig. Fa.41). Assemble the first friction plate and the piston return springs.
12. 47-TOOTH CLUTCH. Assemble the remainder of the components as shown in Fig. Fa.41 with the six recessed teeth on the end plate positioned relative to the piston return springs.

NOTE.– Since selective end and intermediate plates are not available for the 47 tooth clutch unit, the later type 30 tooth clutch must be fitted as a replacement if the clutch plate end-float is not within the tolerance allowed in the '**Adjusting**' procedures given below.
13. 30-TOOTH CLUTCH. Assemble the toggles, pressure plate and the piston return springs, see Fig. Fa.42.

Fig. Fa.44
Check the clearance between the end and intermediate–plates with feeler gauges
'A' = 0.010 to 0.035 in.
(0.25 to 0.9 mm.)
Arrow 'B' shows the drain hole on later-type clutch unit

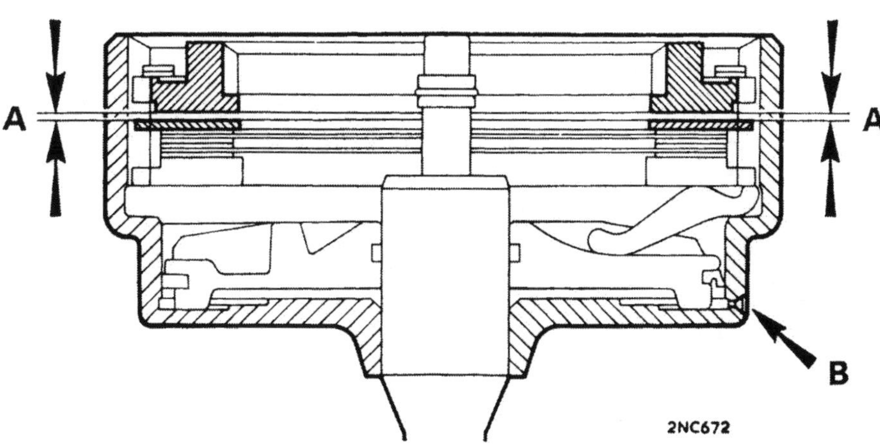

14. Refit the remaining components in the following order for the purpose of CHECKING THE END-FLOAT ADJUSTMENT ONLY.
    a. Refit the two paper-faced plates together.
    b. Refit the intermediate plate, end plate and the retaining circlip.

Adjusting

15. Check with feeler gauges the clearance 'A' between the intermediate plate and the end plate, see Fig. Fa.44. The end-float required is between .010 and .035 in. (.25 and .9 mm.), proceed with item 16 if adjustment is required.
    NOTE.–Shims MUST NOT be fitted to rectify end-float.
16. Measure the thickness of the intermediate and end plates and from this measurement, select from the chart below the correct thickness plate(s) to rectify the end-float to within the tolerance given in item 15.

Intermediate and end plate chart

PLATE	THICKNESS	PART NO.
Intermediate	0.064 in. (1.70 mm.)	27H 7722
Intermediate	0.074 in. (1.88 mm.)	37H 7033
End	0.342 in. (8.22 mm.)	27H 7724
End	0.362 in. (9.21 mm.)	37H 7032

17. Reassemble the components into the clutch unit in the order shown in Figs. Fa.41 and Fa.43. If a Spirolox retaining ring has been fitted, it should be replaced with a solid type circlip, preferably the later (wider section) type, Part No. 37H 7031.

Refitting

18. Carry out the operations given in Section Fa.6 items 30 and 38 to 42.
19. Refit the governor linkage.

Section Fa.12

GEAR TRAIN

Two types of bevel gear train assemblies have been fitted. The later Mk. II type is fitted to all transmission units from Engine Nos. 8AH–A–H10554, 9AG–A–H1603, and the 99H series from outset.
Special equipment is used to obtain the correct backlash for the various gears when assembling the gear train; it is not possible to assemble the gear train with this equipment. The only washer in the gear train that is not selective and can be renewed is the forward output gear bi-metal washer (see Figs. Fa.50 and Fa.52–item 8). In the event of failure of any part of this unit a new gear train assembly must be fitted.

Interchangeability of assemblies

In the event of the Mk. I gear train assembly not being available, the later type Mk. II assembly may be fitted–together with the following components which must be used with the Mk. II unit and replaces similar parts used in the Mk. I transmission unit.

Replacement parts

Freewheel housing.
Forward shaft and thrust washer.
Top/reverse clutch with thrust bearing and washers.*
Top/reverse clutch hub with thrust bearing and washer.

* Only required if prior to Transmission No. E04859.

Removing

1. Carry out the operations given in Section Fa.6, items 1 to 2b and 12.

Dismantling

Dismantling of the gear train is necessary only if the forward output gear bi-metal washer is to be replaced.

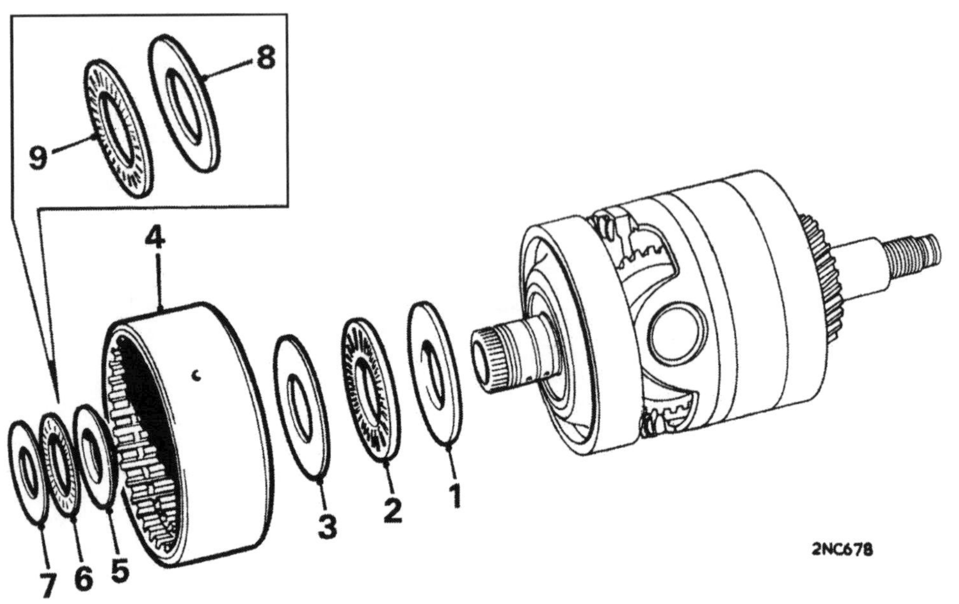

Fig. Fa.45
Removing or refitting the top and reverse clutch

1. Selective washer.
2. Needle thrust bearing.
3. Thrust washer.
4. Top and reverse clutch.
5. Thrust washer (stepped) } later type.
6. Needle thrust bearing. } later type.
7. Thrust washer.
8. Thrust washer.
9. Needle thrust bearing.

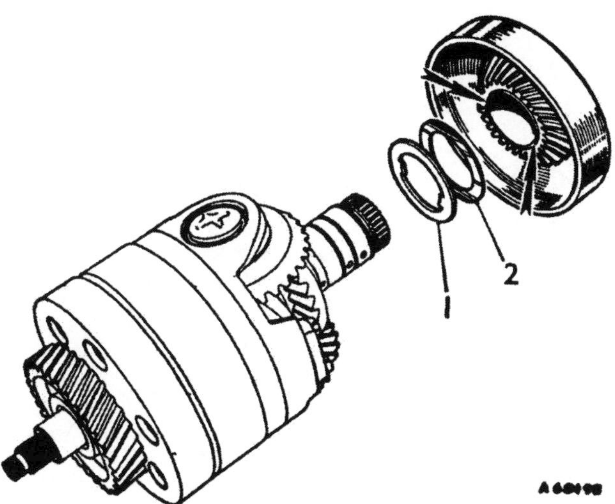

Fig. Fa.46
Removing the third speed reaction gear. The arrows indicate the bi-metal washer locations

1. Bi-metal washer. 2. Shim (if fitted).

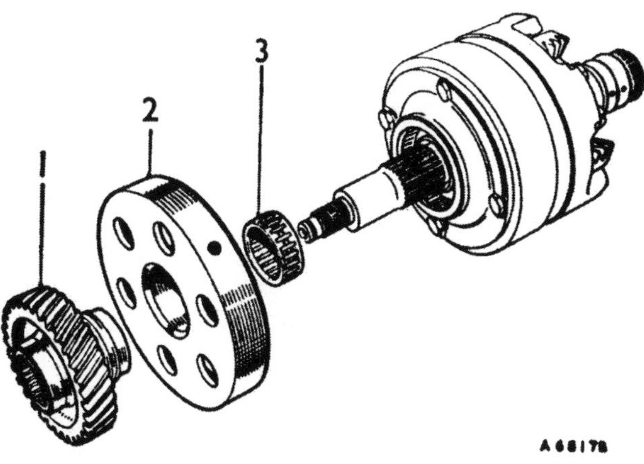

Fig. Fa.47
Removing the input gear 1, the first gear free-wheel reaction member 2, and the needle-roller bearing 3

2. Remove the top and reverse clutch.
   NOTE.–For top and reverse clutch dismantling and reassembling see Section Fa.13.
3. Remove the thrust race and washers (Fig. Fa.45).
4. Remove the third gear reaction member together with its thrust washer and shim (if fitted) (Fig. Fa.46).
5. Remove the input gear, and pull off the first gear free-wheel reaction member and needle-roller bearing (Fig. Fa.47).
6. Knock back the lock washers and remove the first gear free-wheel housing set screws.
7. Pull out the first gear free-wheel assembly, input gear, Torrington thrust race, and washer (Fig. Fa.48).
   NOTE.–For first gear free-wheel assembly dismantling and reassembling see Section Fa.15.
8. a. **Dismantling of the Mk. II gear train assembly is given below in items 9 to 15, with the reassembly sequence in items 20 to 32.**
   b. **To dismantle the Mk. I gear train assembly, as shown in Figs. Fa.49 and Fa.50, refer to items 16 to 19 with the reassembly sequence given in items 33 to 36.**

Dismantling gear train (Mk. II)

9. Remove the spindle end cover circlips and covers; remove the small locking circlip and unscrew the spindle locking screws.
10. Hold the unit on its side until the locking ball rolls out from the hole in the planetary gear spindle. Repeat this operation on the other side.
11. Insert Service tool 18G 1093 A into the forward output gear and through the complete assembly to assist the dismantling procedure.
12. Screw the Service tool adaptor 18G 284 AJ into one of the planetary gear spindles and using Service tool 18G 284 pull the spindle from the gear. Repeat this operation with the other spindle and withdraw the needle-roller bearings.

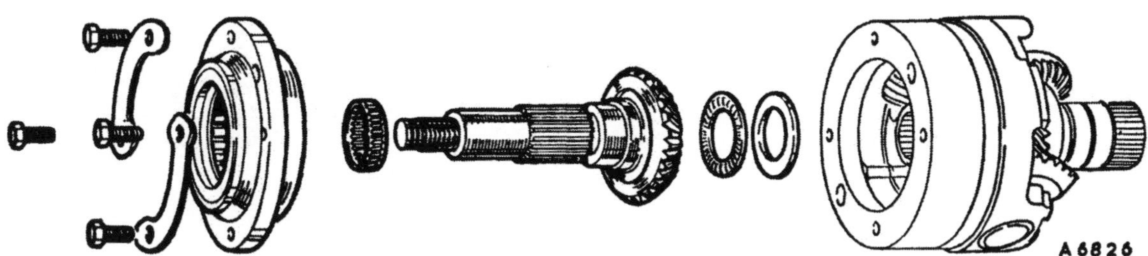

Fig. Fa.48
Removing the one-way clutch and the input gear with its Torrington needle thrust bearing and washer

13. Knock back the locking tabs and remove the strap securing bolts.
14. Ease the strap off the dowels and lift the complete assembly from the carrier.
    Retain the respective positions of each planetary gear thrust washer with the carrier.
15. Dismantle the assembly, ensuring that all components are retained in their respective positions for reassembly (see Fig. Fa.51).

Dismantling gear train (Mk. I)

16. Check the markings on the carrier and the bearing caps, i.e. marked NIL or with the letter 'O'. These are reference marks to fitting dimensions and the caps must be refitted in their original positions as indicated by the markings on reassembly of the unit.
17. Knock back the locking tabs and remove the bearing cap bolts and the strap securing bolts. Lift out the forward output gear, reverse output gear, and the pinions.
18. Lift off the thrust bearings, pinions, and thrust washers.
19. Lift off the forward output gear and thrust washer, the reverse output gear, thrust washer, and thrust race.

Inspecting

Clean and examine all parts for wear. Fit a new bi-metal washer to the forward output gear if required and renew if necessary the Torrington needle-thrust races.

Fit new rubber seals and replace the locking plates.

Check that the internal bush of the reverse output shaft has not turned and shut off the output feed.

NOTE.– Use petroleum jelly when reassembling to secure the various thrust washers and needle thrust races in position.

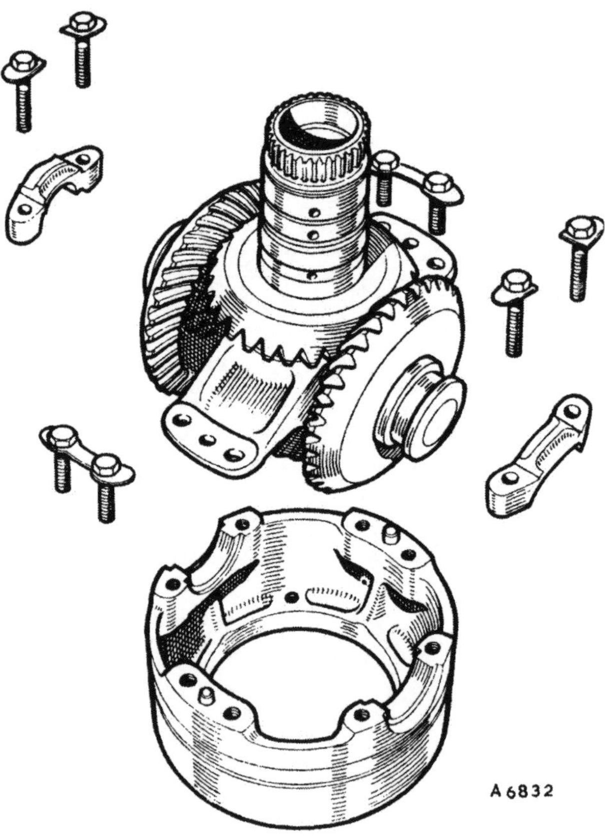

Fig. Fa.49
Removing the forward and reverse output gears, and the planetary gears from the carrier

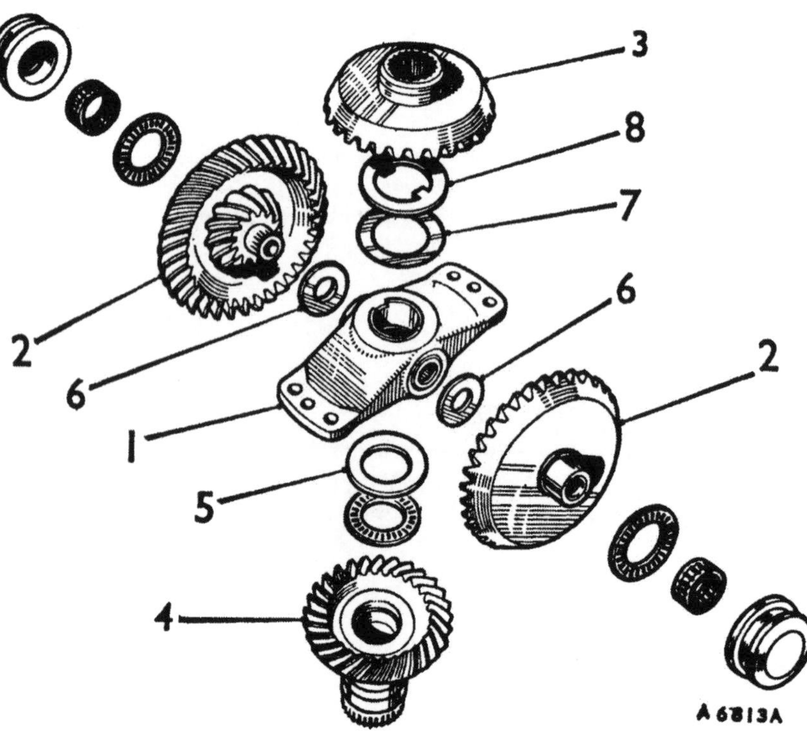

Fig. Fa.50
The early-type gear train completely dismantled

1. Gear carrier.
2. Planetary gears.
3. Forward output gear.
4. Reverse output gear.
5. Steel washer (reverse output gear).
6. Planetary gear washers.
7. Steel shim (forward output gear).
8. Bi-metal washer (forward output gear).

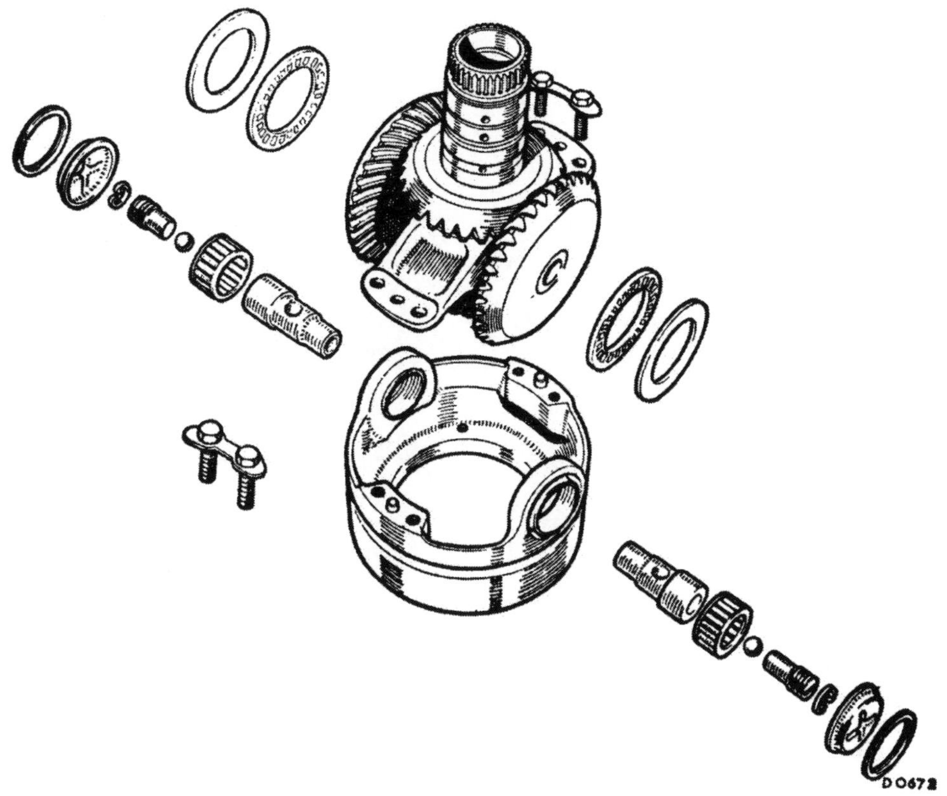

Fig. Fa.51
The later-type gear train, with the forward and reverse output gears and the planetary gears removed from the carrier

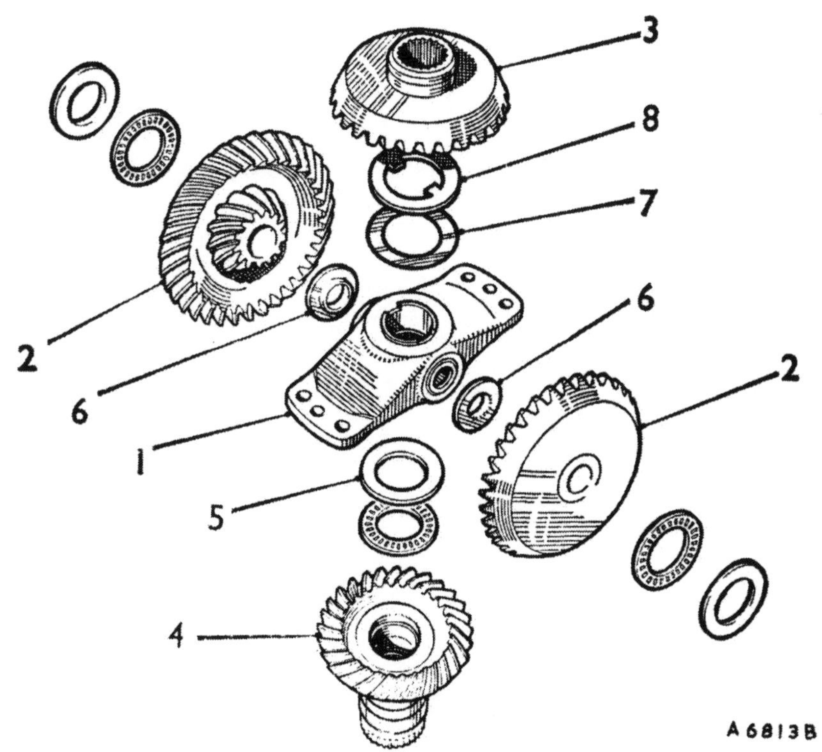

Fig. Fa.52
A dismantled view of the later-type gear train assembly

1. Gear carrier.
2. Planetary gears.
3. Forward output gear.
4. Reverse output gear
5. Steel washer (reverse output gear).
6. Planetary gear washers.
7. Steel shim (forward output gear).
8. Bi-metal washer (forward output gear).

Reassembling gear train (Mk. II)

20. Assemble the forward output gear with its bi-metal washer and the .004 in. (.10 mm.) shim (if fitted) interposed between the bi-metal washer and the carrier (see Fig. Fa.52).
    Assemble the reverse output gear with its Torrington needle thrust bearing and steel washer.
21. Insert Service tool 18G 1093A through the forward output gear and the assembly to ensure correct alignment.
22. Check and reset the timing of the gear train (see Fig. Fa.53) by rotating the planetary gears until the timing marks are in alignment.
23. Retain the timed position of the gear train and refit to the carrier ensuring that both timing marks align with the dowel surface of the carrier.
24. Refit the planetary gear needle-roller bearings and tap in the spindles (with the hole on the centre of the spindle facing downwards).
25. Insert a ball into each spindle and screw in the locking screws. Refit the locking screw circlips, end covers, and the cover circlips.
26. Assemble the third speed reaction gear with its bi-metal washer fitted with the white metal face towards the reverse output gear (see Fig. Fa.54) and with the steel shim(s) located between the bi-metal washer and the gear.
    Retain each washer and shim in position with petroleum jelly and refit the assembly to the gear train (see Fig. Fa.54).

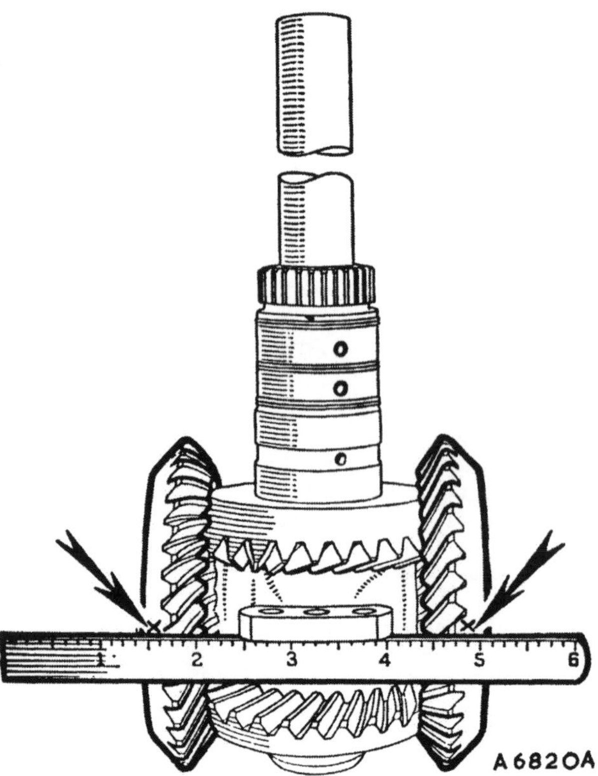

Fig. Fa.53
Timing the gear train

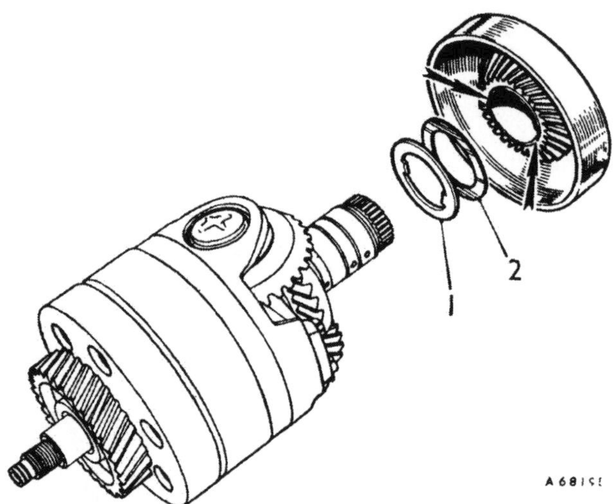

Fig. Fa.54
Refitting the third speed reaction gear with its bi-metal washer, locations indicated by arrows

1. Bi-metal washer. 2. Shim (if fitted).

27. Assemble the bevel input gear with its Torrington needle thrust bearing and selective steel washer (see Fig. Fa.48).
28. Refit the one-way clutch to the gear train housing (Fig. Fa.48), tighten the securing bolts, and tap up the locking plate tabs.
29. Refit the free-wheel support.
30. Refit the input gear and needle-roller bearing (see Fig. Fa.55).
31. Refit the top and reverse clutch with its selective steel washer and needle thrust bearing onto the reverse output shaft. Use the correct diameter thrust washer and needle bearing required for the particular type of clutch and gear train assembly fitted.

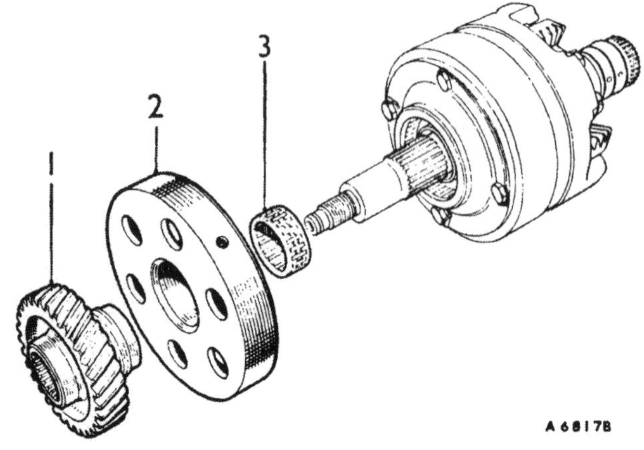

Fig. Fa.55
Refitting the input gear 1, the first gear free-wheel reaction member 2, and the needle-roller bearing 3

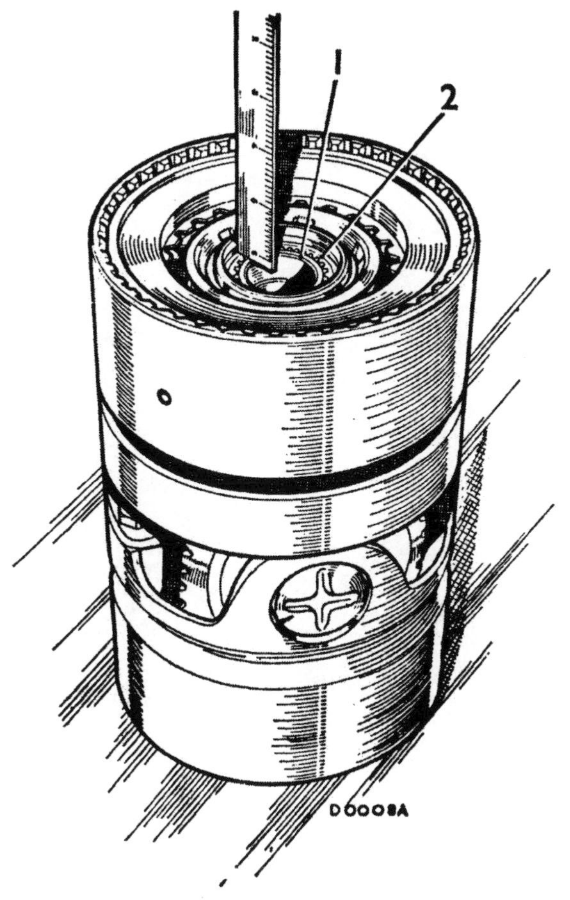

Fig. Fa.56
Checking that the end of the reverse output shaft 1 is level with the internal face of the top and reverse clutch 2

Mk. II GEAR TRAIN ASSEMBLY. When the second type clutch (with annular groove) is fitted, use the larger diameter (stepped type) thrust washer 5 and needle thrust bearing 6, see Fig. Fa.45.

Mk. I GEAR TRAIN ASSEMBLY. When either clutch assembly (first or second type) is fitted, use the small diameter thrust washer 8 and needle thrust bearing 9, see Fig. Fa.45.

32. Check across the splined end of the reverse output shaft and the adjacent face of the top and reverse clutch (Fig. Fa.56). Both faces must be exactly level with no gap, to ensure that the third speed reaction gear has no end-float and the correct backlash is maintained. If both faces are not level, remove and measure the thickness of the selective steel washer fitted in item 31 and fit the correct selective washer from the range available (see washer chart below).

Selective washer sizes	Part Nos.
.076 to .078 in. (1.93 to 1.98 mm.)	22G 748
.072 to .074 in. (1.83 to 1.88 mm.)	22G 749
.068 to .070 in. (1.73 to 1.78 mm.)	22G 750
.064 to .066 in. (1.63 to 1.68 mm.)	22G 751

Reassembling gear train (Mk. I)

33. Carry out items 20 to 23 with the following exceptions: Refer to Fig. Fa.50, and use Service tool 18G 1093 when reassembling this early-type gear train.

34. Refit the bearings caps to their respective positions (see markings) and using new locking plates, refit and tighten the bearing cap and carrier bolts to the torque figure given in '**GENERAL DATA**'.

35. Carry out items 26 to 31.

36. Carry out item 32 to determine whether the splined end of the reverse output shaft and the face of the top and reverse clutch are level (see Fig. Fa.56), if they are not, fit the correct selective washer from the range available (see washer chart below).

    Note that the selective washers for the early units are not interchangeable with those fitted to later units.

Selective washer sizes	Part Nos.
.116 to .118 in. (2.95 to 3.0 mm.)	22A 777
.112 to .114 in. (2.85 to 2.9 mm.)	22A 778
.108 to .110 in. (2.74 to 2.79 mm.)	22A 779
.104 to .106 in. (2.64 to 2.69 mm.)	22A 780

Refitting

37. Carry out the operations given in Section Fa.6, items 44 and 45. The remainder is a reversal of the removal procedure.

38. Refit the power unit to the car as detailed in Section Aa.3.

Section Fa.13

TOP AND REVERSE CLUTCH

Two types of clutch units have been fitted, the later (second type) is identified by the annular groove machined in the clutch drum. This unit has a shortened flange above the piston return spring retaining circlip to enable it to be suitable for fitment to both the Mk. I and II bevel gear train assemblies.

This unit is fitted to all transmissions from Transmission No. E04859 and can be used for replacement on all Mk. I and II gear train assemblies from the following Engine Nos. 9AG–A–H1630 and the 99H engine range from outset.

Fit the first type clutch when replacement is required on Mk. I transmissions prior to the above change points.

Removing

1. Carry out the operations given in Section Fa.6, items 1, 2b, and 12.
2. Remove the top and reverse clutch from the gear train together with the Torrington needle thrust bearing and the steel washer.

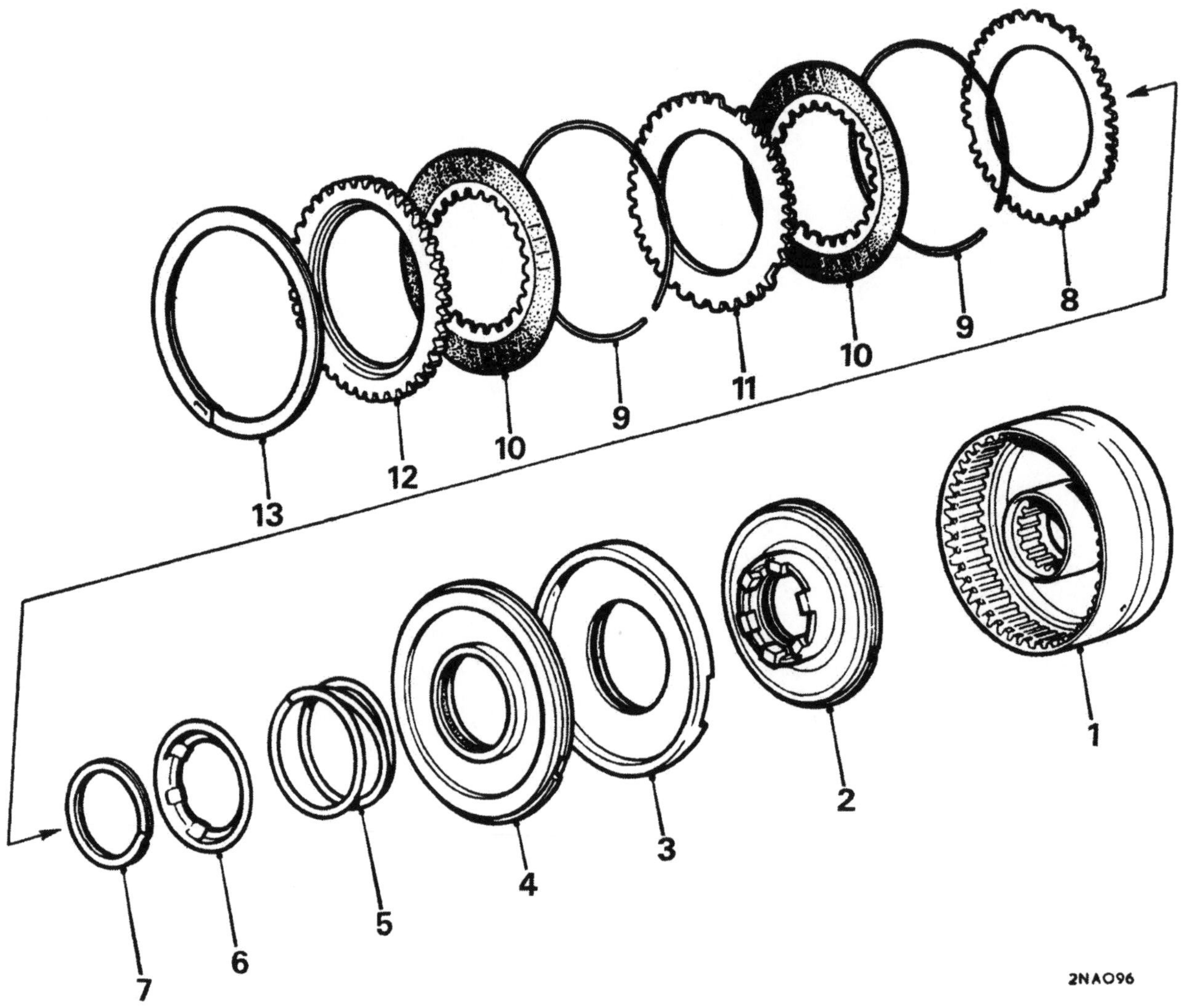

Fig. Fa.57
The top and reverse clutch components

1. Housing.
2. Reverse gear booster piston.
3. Top gear cylinder.
4. Top gear piston.
5. Piston return spring.
6. Spring retainer.
7. Spirolox retaining ring.
8. Pressure plate (thin).
9. Separation spring rings.
10. Clutch plates (paper-faced).
11. Pressure plate (intermediate).
12. End plate.
13. Spirolox retaining ring.

Dismantling

3. Remove the Spirolox retaining ring.
4. Remove the retainer plate.
5. Lift out the paper plate, spring ring, steel plate, paper plate, spring ring, and the thin steel plate.
6. Remove the circlip, spring retainer, and the piston return coil spring.
7. Lightly shock the assembly against a flat surface to remove the top gear piston and cylinder.
8. Refit the reverse (booster) piston into the bore, easing the piston ring into the bore with a screwdriver.
9. Fit Service tool 18G 1103 into the clutch unit and holding these together, lightly shock the assembly against a flat surface to remove the reverse booster piston.

Inspecting

Check all parts for wear and renew if necessary. Renew the oil seals in the pistons. Check the piston ring gap which must be .016 to 0.20 in. (.4 to .51 mm.), for both rings when fitted in their respective bores.

Reassembling

10. Refit the reverse gear booster piston with the boss facing outwards, using Service tool 18G 1103 (see Fig. Fa.58).
11. Refit the top gear piston into its cylinder with the boss facing outwards.
12. Fit the top gear piston and cylinder into the clutch housing, with the cut-aways on the rear outer edge of the cylinder opposite the holes in the clutch housing.

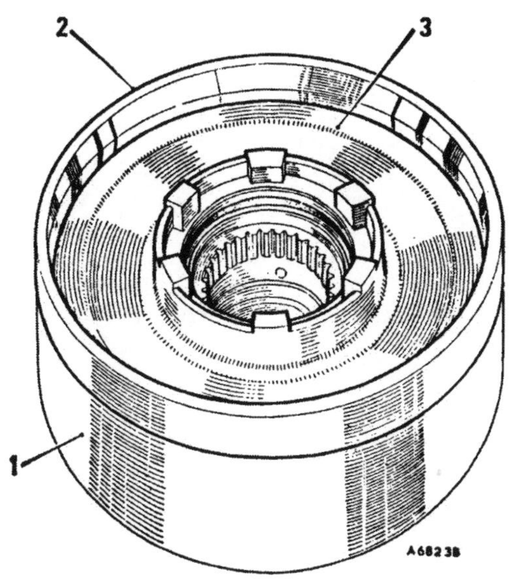

Fig. Fa.58
Using Service tool 18G 1103 (2) to remove or refit the reverse gear piston (3) to the top and reverse clutch unit (1)

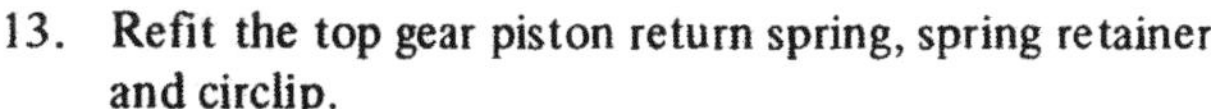

13. Refit the top gear piston return spring, spring retainer, and circlip.
14. Refit the clutch plates in the assembly order shown in Fig. Fa.57, with the cut-away portion of the steel plates in alignment.
15. Refit the retainer plate and circlip.
    NOTE.–Before refitting the clutch unit, ensure that the friction plates are free to drop.

Refitting

16. Carry out the operations given in Section Fa.12, items 31 and 32.
17. The remainder is a reversal of the removal procedure.

Section Fa.14

SERVO ASSEMBLY

Removing

1. Carry out the operations given in Section Fa.6 items 1 to 13.
2. Remove the servo unit from the valve block assembly.

Dismantling

3. Remove the centre shaft and lift out the servo levers, reaction levers, washers, and struts.
4. Hold the servo cover and release the securing screws and the cover.
5. Lift out the springs and pistons.

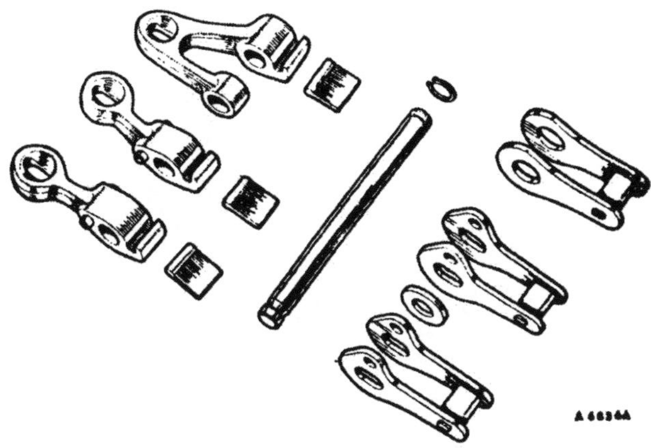

Fig. Fa.59
The fitting relationship of the servo levers with the reaction levers and struts

Inspecting

Check all parts for wear and renew if necessary.

Reassembling

6. Lubricate the seals and fit the pistons into the correct bores (lips of seals facing downwards).
7. Assemble the springs and cover.
8. Hold the cover in position and fit the drive screws.
9. Assemble the struts, washer(s), reaction levers, and servo levers in the reverse order of dismantling (Figs. Fa.59 and 61).
10. Insert the centre shaft with the cutaway in the shaft correctly positioned.

Refitting

11. Carry out the operations detailed in Section Fa.6, items 33 to 48, 53, and 54.

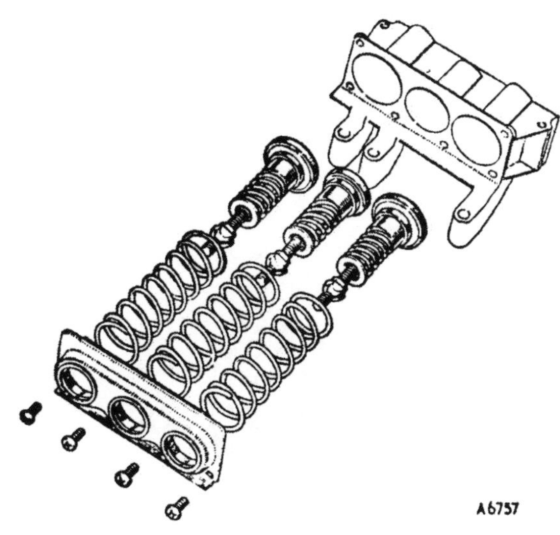

Fig. Fa.60
The servo unit components

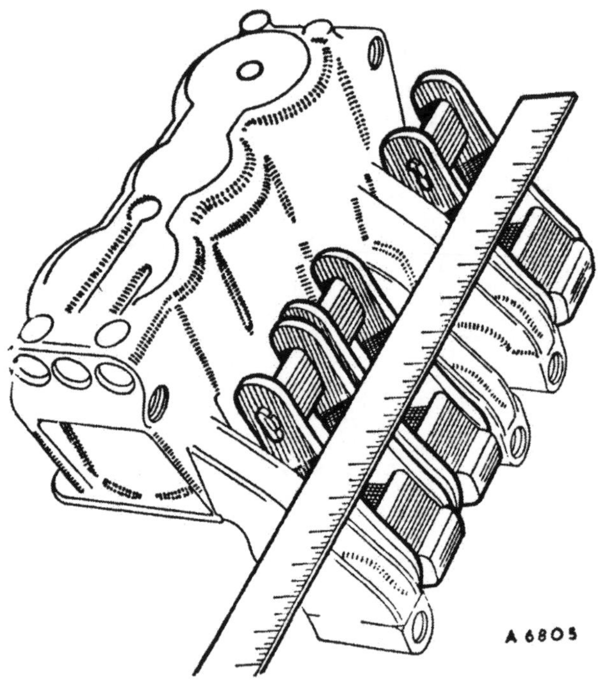

Fig. Fa.61
The brake band and struts correctly positioned

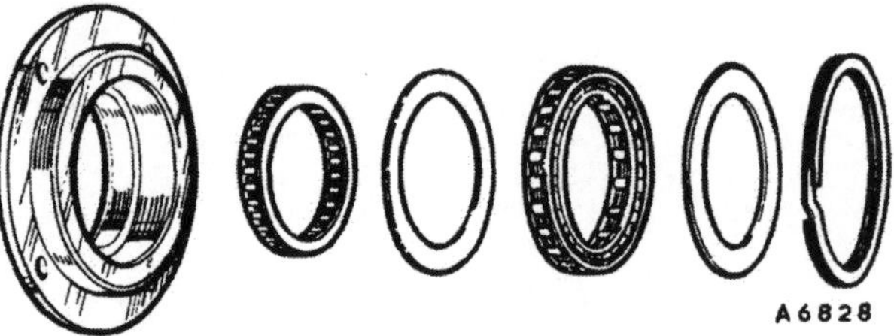

Fig. Fa.63
The components of the new one-way clutch

5. Lift out the spring ring, first gear free-wheel intermediate spring ring, and thrust bearing (see Fig. Fa.63).

Fig. Fa.64
Fitting the one-way clutch with the lip (arrowed) correctly positioned uppermost

Section Fa.15

FIRST GEAR FREE-WHEEL ASSEMBLY (ONE-WAY CLUTCH)

Removing

1. Carry out the operation given in Section Fa.6, items 1, 2b, and 12.
2. Remove the first gear free-wheel reaction member.
3. Knock back the locking plate tabs and remove the retaining bolts and the first gear free-wheel (one-way clutch) from the housing.

Dismantling

4. Remove the circlip.

Inspecting

Check all parts for wear and renew if necessary.

Reassembling

6. Reassemble the thrust bearing, intermediate spring ring, first gear free-wheel (lip facing outwards, see Fig. Fa.64), spring ring, and refit the circlip.

Refitting

7. Refitting is a reversal of the removing procedure.

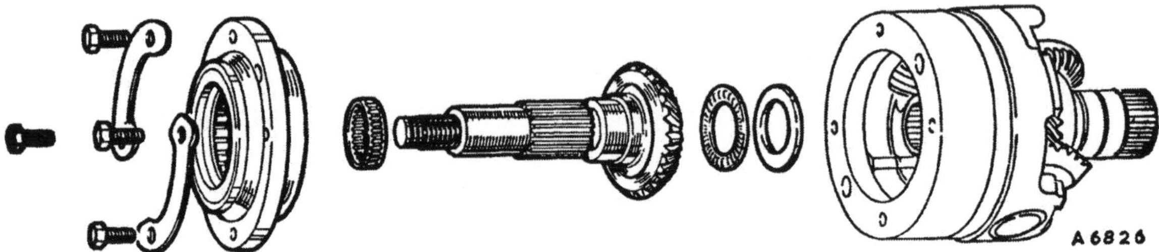

Fig. Fa.62
The one-way clutch removed from the gear train, with the input gear, bearings and thrust washer shown in assembly sequence

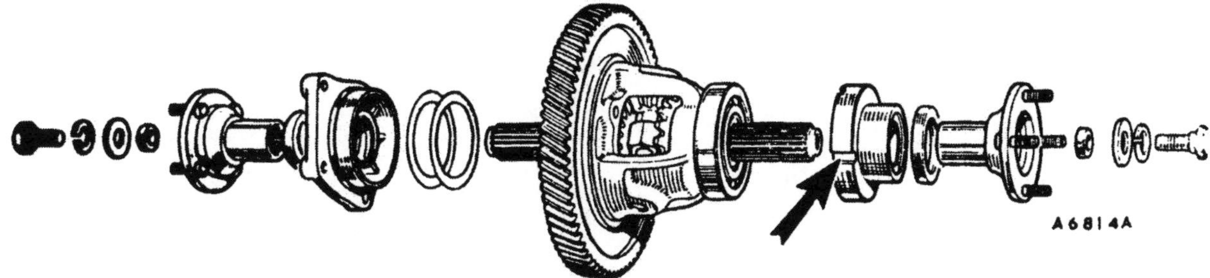

Fig. Fa.65
The differential components with the arrow indicating the alignment slot in the spacer

Section Fa.16

DIFFERENTIAL ASSEMBLY

Removing

1. Remove the engine and transmission from the car (see Section Aa.3).
2. Drain the engine/transmission unit.
3. Use Service tool 18G 1100 to hold the driving flanges and remove the centre securing bolts. Withdraw the flanges from the splined shafts.
4. Knock back the lock washers and remove the nuts from the final drive housing.
5. Remove the securing screws and pull the kick-down linkage assembly clear of the transmission case.
6. Remove the two set screws securing the end cover to the transmission, and remove the final drive and housing assembly (Fig. Fa.12).
7. Remove the remaining securing bolts from the end cover and remove the cover and the adjustment shims.

Dismantling

8. Remove the differential unit from its casing.
9. Withdraw the oil seal housing, remove the bearings using Service tool 18G 2.
10. Knock back the locking plate tabs and remove the bolts securing the driving gear to the cage. Mark the gear and cage so that they can be refitted in their original positions.
11. Separate the driving gear from the cage and remove the differential gear and thrust washer from the driving gear.
12. Tap out the roll pin and remove both pinions and thrust washers, pinion spacer, and the other differential gear and thrust washer.

Inspection

Clean and examine the components for wear and fit new parts as necessary.

NOTE.–If any component has suffered damage with the result that swarf has been introduced into the lubricating system the automatic transmission must be removed (Section Aa.4) and dismantled as detailed in Section Fa.6. This also applies if fitting a replacement drive gear pinion into the transmission unit.
Absolute cleanliness is essential.

Reassembling

13. Reassembly is a reversal of the dismantling procedure. Make sure that the differential gear thrust washers are fitted with their chamfered bores against the machined faces of the differential gears. Refit all components in their original positions.

Refitting

14. Refit the differential unit into the transmission case and push the assembly towards the converter, with the slot in the spacer in alignment with the dowel in the transmission case (Fig. Fa.65). Fit a new joint washer coated with Hylomar jointing compound. Ensure that the oil seal is pressed squarely against the face of the spacer and refit the differential housing, fit new locking plates, and lightly tighten the securing nuts.

ADJUSTMENT

15. Refit the end cover without a joint washer but with the original adjustment shims, tighten the cover bolts evenly and sufficiently only for the cover register to nip the bearing outer race; overtightening will distort the flange.
16. Take a feeler gauge measurement at varying positions between the side cover flange and the differential housing, any variations in measurement will indicate that the cover bolts are not evenly tightened. Adjust the cover bolts accordingly until identical measurements can be obtained. The compressed thickness of a new cover joint washer is .007 in. (.178 mm.) and the required preload on the bearings is .002 in. (.051 mm.). The correct gap is therefore .009 in. (229 mm.), any deviation from this figure must be made up by adding or subtracting shims.

EXAMPLE: If the feeler gauge measurement is .005 in. (.127 mm.), add a shim of .004 in. (.10 mm.) thickness between the bearing and the end cover.

17. Remove the end cover, fit shims as required, and refit the cover with a new joint washer coated with Hylomar jointing compound. Tighten the differential housing nuts and the cover bolts to the torque figures given in 'GENERAL DATA'. Tap up the locking plate tabs, except the nut which accepts the exhaust pipe bracket (fitted when the engine is in the car).
18. Lubricate the driving flange oil seal and refit the flanges making sure that the split collets are correctly located inside the flanges. Fit new rubber seals to and refit the central securing bolts. Hold the flanges with Service tool 18G 1100 and tighten the flange bolts with Service tool 18G 372 to the torque figure given in 'GENERAL DATA'
19. Refit the governor control linkage to the transmission case with a new washer. Ensure the lever is positioned correctly, relative to the governor (see Fig. Fa.22).
20. Carry out the '**Refitting**' instructions given in Section Aa.3.

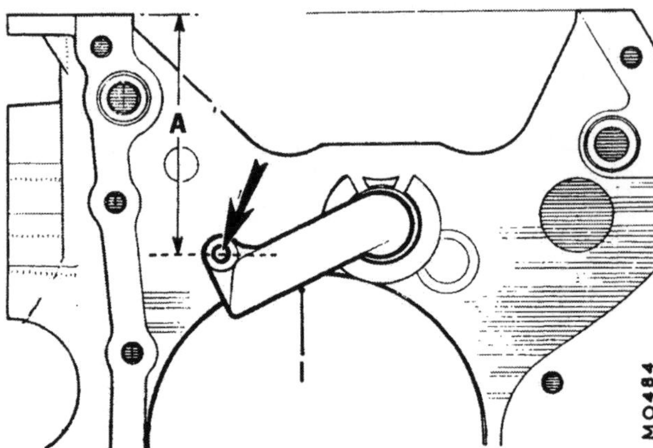

Fig. Fa.66
The reservoir fitted upside-down on the outside of the casing with the marked line shown through the centre of the securing lug. An arrow indicates the drilling location.'A' = $3\frac{19}{32}$ in. (91.3 mm.)

Section Fa.17

LUBRICATION RESERVOIR (IDLER GEAR BEARING)

To provide additional lubrication to the idler gear bearings, a transmission case incorporating a 'cast in' oil reservoir was introduced at the following Engine Nos: 8AH–A–H11338, 99H–143–H5983 and 99H–147–H834.
Earlier units should be modified by fitting a separate reservoir as detailed below.

Fitting

1. Remove the engine/transmission from the car (see Section Aa.3).
2. Remove the transmission unit from the engine (see Section Aa.4).
3. Refer to Fig. Fa.66. Measure down from the joint face on the outside of the casing $3\frac{19}{32}$ in. (91.3 mm.) and from this point mark a horizontal line across the casing as indicated. Place the reservoir upside-down on the outside of the casing with its spigot located in the idler gear bearing bore and with its securing lug positioned centrally over the horizontal marking. Indent this position; remove the reservoir and drill through the casing using a $\frac{9}{32}$ in. (7.14 mm.) drill; place a piece of Plasticine inside the casing where the hole will break through to trap any swarf.
4. If necessary, file the reservoir casting to ensure that it will fit snugly against the transmission casing.
5. Smear the reservoir spigot with Hylomar jointing compound and fit the reservoir as shown in Fig. Fa.67. It may be necessary to fit a flat washer beneath the securing lug to ensure that the spigot is square in the idler gear bearing bore; later reservoirs have a built-up boss around the securing lug. Leave the idler gear bearing circlip in position and tighten the securing bolt.
6. Refit the transmission unit to the engine (see Section Aa.4).
7. Refit the engine/transmission unit into the car (see Section Aa.3).

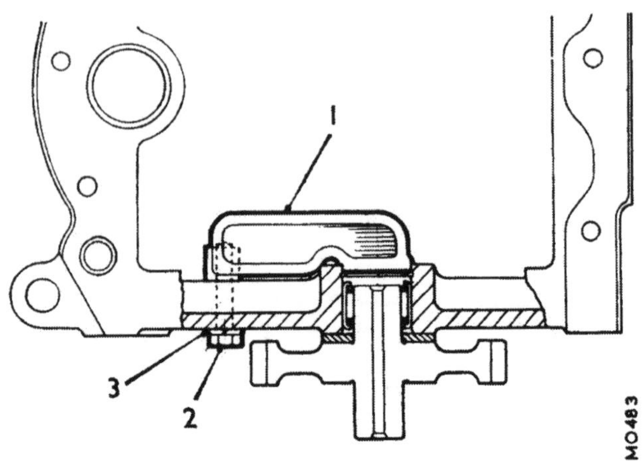

Fig. Fa.67
The fitted position of the idler gear bearing reservoir

1. Reservoir. 2. Securing screw. 3. Spring washer.

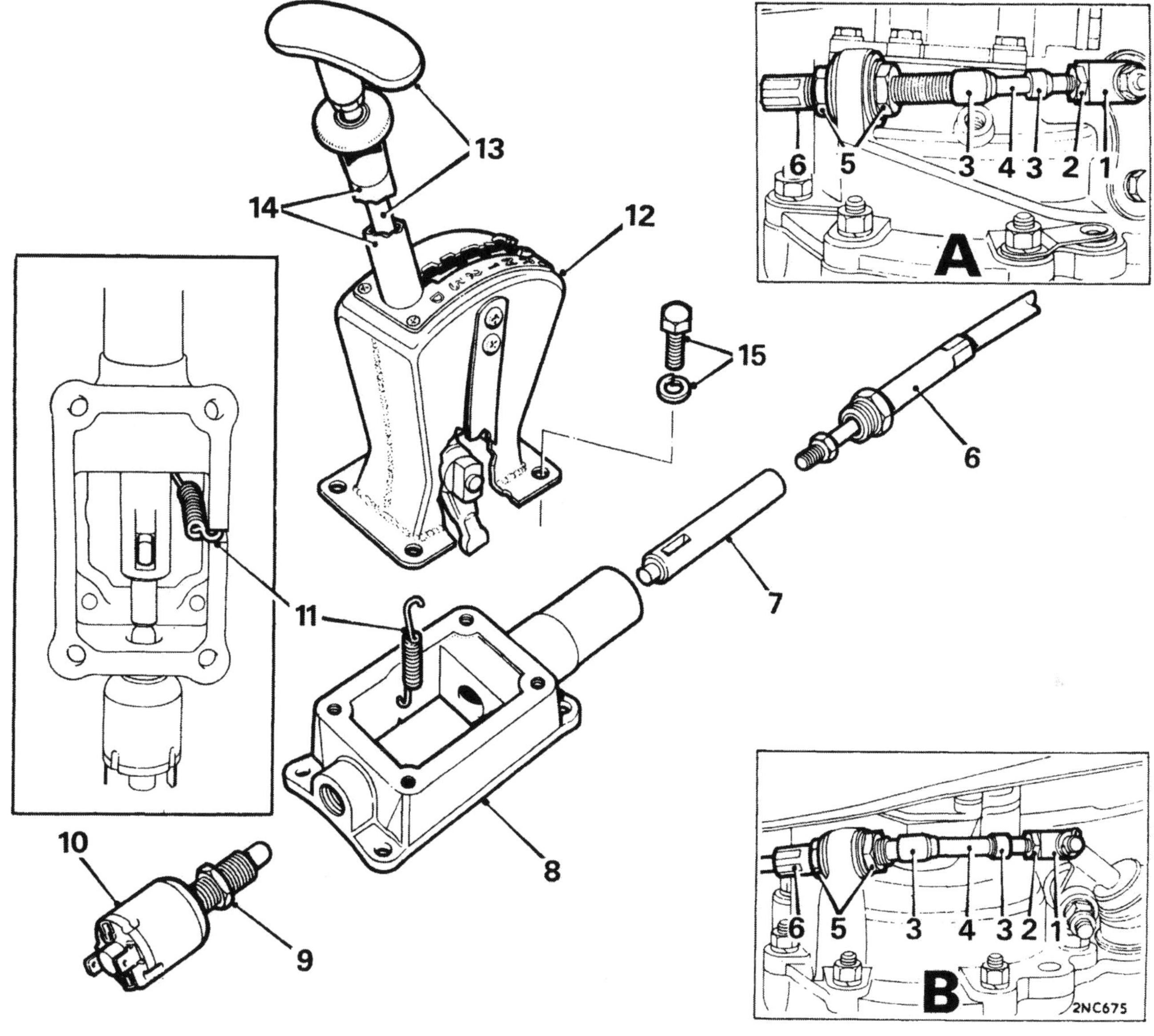

Fig. Fa.68
The selector lever mechanism and cable components. Inset 'A' shows the second type (minimum backlash) assembly. Inset 'B' shows the first type assembly

1. Yoke.
2. Locking nut–yoke.
3. Rubber ferrules.
4. Cable sleeve.
5. Cable adjusting nuts.
6. Cable.
7. Lever plunger.
8. Selector lever housing.
9. Locknut–switch.
10. Inhibitor switch.
11. Reverse return spring.
12. Quadrant.
13. Selector lever.
14. Spring-loaded sleeve.
15. Securing screws and washers.

Section Fa.18

SELECTOR LEVER MECHANISM

Removing

1. 1ST TYPE BELL-CRANK LEVER ASSEMBLY. Remove the bell-crank lever guard (later models) from the converter housing or pull back the rubber sleeve (early models) and disconnect the gear-change cable by removing the clevis pin.

   2ND TYPE BELL-CRANK LEVER ASSEMBLY. Remove the modified bell-crank lever guard from the converter housing and disconnect the gear-change cable by removing the nut and bolt from the yoke.
2. Slacken the yoke locknut and remove the yoke, locknut, both rubber ferrules and the cable sleeve. Remove the front adjusting nut from the outer cable and pull the cable clear of the transmission.
3. Release the cable clip from the floor panel.
4. Remove the front floor covering.

5. Disconnect the electrical leads from the inhibitor switch.
6. Remove the screws securing the gear change housing, carefully pull the cable through the rubber dust excluder, and remove the housing and cable assembly.

Dismantling

7. Hold the assembly in a vice and remove the set screws securing the quadrant to the housing. Release the reverse return spring from the base of the housing and remove the quadrant and lever assembly.
8. Unscrew the cable securing nut from the front of the housing, pull the cable and plunger from the housing and release it from the gear change lever plunger.

Inspection

Clean and inspect moving parts for wear.

Reassembly

9. Lubricate all moving parts with grease.
10. Reassembly is a reversal of the dismantling procedure. Refer to Fig. Fa.68 and ensure that the gear selector lever (13) is re-inserted into the relieved side of the plunger (7).

Refitting

11. Refitting is a reversal of the removing procedure, but note items 12 to 14.
12. a. If seizure of early versions of the first-type bell-crank lever has occurred due to overtightening of the pivot pin nut (see Fig. Fa.1), replace the pivot pin and distance tube with a modified pivot pin having a shoulder.

    b If the backlash on the first type of selector lever mechanism is excessive, fit the minimum backlash bell-crank lever assembly (see Fig. Fa.1). Remove the forged bell-crank lever and its pivot pin, the front cover and the transverse rod. Fit the modified type of pivot pin and clevis, the non-adjustable transverse rod (see item 4, Section Fa.2) and the pressed type of bell-crank lever. Refit the front cover and the bell-crank lever guard, which . ust be reshaped as described in item 8 of Section Fa.2.

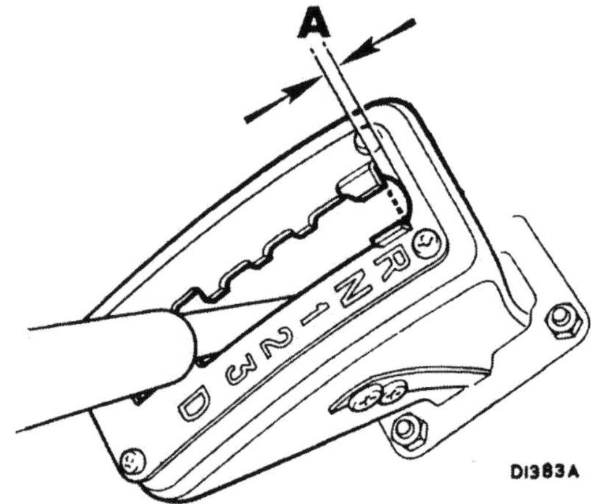

Fig. Fa.69
Modifying the selector lever indicator gate to ensure that the reverse gear position can be fully engaged. 'A' = $\frac{1}{16}$ in. (1.6 mm.)

    c. On transmissions which have been fitted with the minimum backlash bell-crank lever assembly, the reverse position of the selector lever indicator gate should be modified as described below to ensure that the selector valve detent is fully engaged when reverse gear is selected. Unscrew the gear selector handle from its lever and then remove the four screws securing the indicator gate to the quadrant. File a radius $\frac{1}{16}$ in. (1.6 mm.) deep in the end of the gate, as shown in Fig. Fa.69, and reassemble the quadrant components.

    NOTE.– If slip or loss of drive in reverse gear occurs on replacement transmissions which incorporate the minimum backlash bell-crank lever, check that the selector gate has been lengthened. If it has not, and adjusting the selector lever cable as described in Section Fa.2 fails to remedy the fault, carry out the above modification.

13. Adjust the selector lever cable and the transverse rod (1st type only) as detailed in Section Fa.2 and the inhibitor switch as detailed in Section Fa.3.

SECTION G

THE DRIVE SHAFTS

GENERAL DESCRIPTION

Each of the two drive shafts employed has two principle members incorporating a Hardy Spicer constant-velocity bell joint. The hemispherical interior of the bell joint and the exterior of the inner ball race have six grooves machined in line with the shaft axis, and a ball cage carrying six steel balls is interposed between the two. The steel balls engage the grooves of both members to key them together and at the same time allow the members to hinge freely upon each other.

The joint is packed with special grease and the unit is enclosed in a sealed rubber boot. The inner end of the drive shaft is splined and has a pre-lubricated sliding joint sealed with a rubber boot.

Section G.1

DRIVE SHAFTS

Removing

To remove the drive shaft assembly from the vehicle follow the removing instructions given for swivel hubs in Section K.2 or G.5 (offset sphere type).

The constant-velocity bell joint may be removed from the drive shaft for replacement as a unit or to have a Service kit fitted. Under no circumstances must individual components be replaced in the bell joint assembly.

Should a rubber boot enclosing the joint be damaged with a consequent loss of lubricant, it is necessary to remove the joint from the shaft for dismantling and inspection of the components.

If a rubber boot is damaged in the workshop and dirt has not entered the joint, a new boot may be fitted after first repacking the joint with the recommended grease.

To fit a new boot the drive shaft must be removed from the vehicle.

Constant-velocity (bell) joint

The bell joint can be removed from the drive shaft for dismantling and inspection of the components.

Service kits are available which include the required amount of lubricant to service a bell joint.

When servicing of the joint becomes necessary, the procedure given in Section G.2 must be followed.

Sliding joint flange

On later models the sliding joint is prepacked with ¾ oz. (21 gm.) of Duckham's M.B. grease (pack AKF 1457) and sealed with a rubber housing seal, early models were fitted with lubricating nipple. When servicing the sliding joint or fitting a new seal, refer to Section G.2.

Section G.2

DRIVE SHAFT OVERHAUL

Dismantling the shaft assembly

1. Clean the shaft of road dirt and grease and mount the shaft centrally in a vice fitted with soft jaws.
2. Prise off the boot and housing seal clips or cut the soft iron wire, turn back the housing seal and slide off the joint flange. Remove the housing seal and the rubber boot, if they are worn or damaged, replacements must be fitted on reassembly.
3. The bell joint can only be dismantled after removal of the shaft; a round-section spring ring located in a deep groove in the extreme end of the shaft is expanded into the chamfered end of the inner race bore, and for shaft removal this must be contracted into the groove.
4. Hold the shaft and joint vertically, the bell joint downwards, and give the edge of the outer race a sharp tap with a soft faced mallet (see Fig. G.1). This shoud contract the spring ring so that the joint can be drawn off the shaft. It should not be necessary to use heavy blows for this operation.

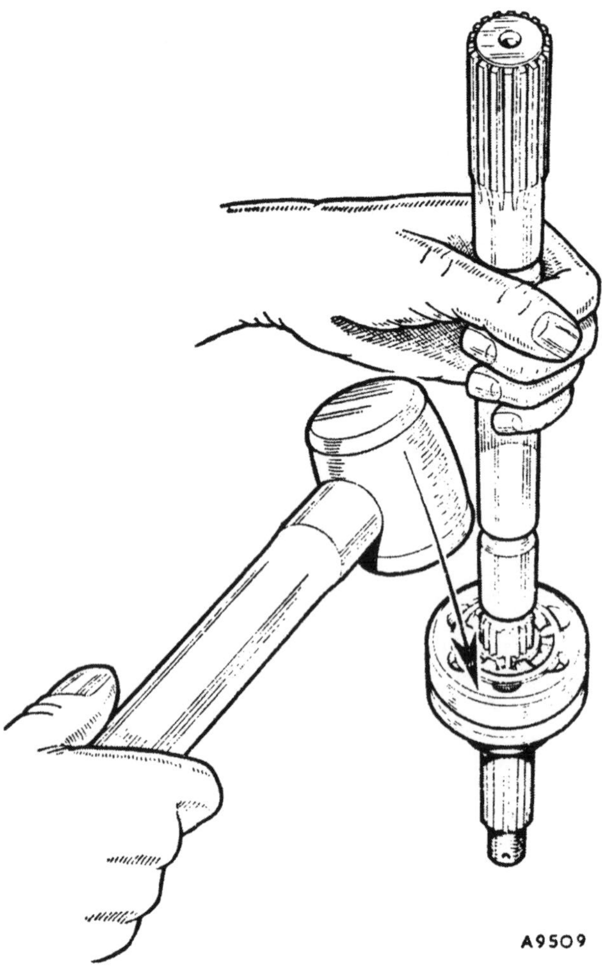

Fig. G.1
Drive the bell joint from the shaft at the point indicated

Dismantling the joint

5. The joint should be dismantled only if there is reason to believe that it is still serviceable.
6. As the components are mated and have operated together, they must be kept in the same mating relationship. The relative positions of the inner and outer races and the cage should be marked with blue marker or a paint which will not wash off when the parts are cleaned.
7. With the shaft withdrawn the inner race can swivel freely, tilt the inner race until one ball is released (Fig. G.2). Note that the cage swivels through half the angle of the inner race. If the joint is sticky with grease each ball may be eased out in turn with a pointed tool.
8. Swivel the cage into line with the axis of the joint and turn it until two opposite elongated windows coincide with two lands of the bell joint. One land will drop into a window, allowing the cage and race assembly to be lifted out (Fig. G.3).
9. Swivel the inner race at right angles to the cage and turn it until two of the lands between the inner race tracks are opposite elongated windows in the cage. One land will drop into a window, allowing the inner race to be extracted from the cage (Fig. G.4).

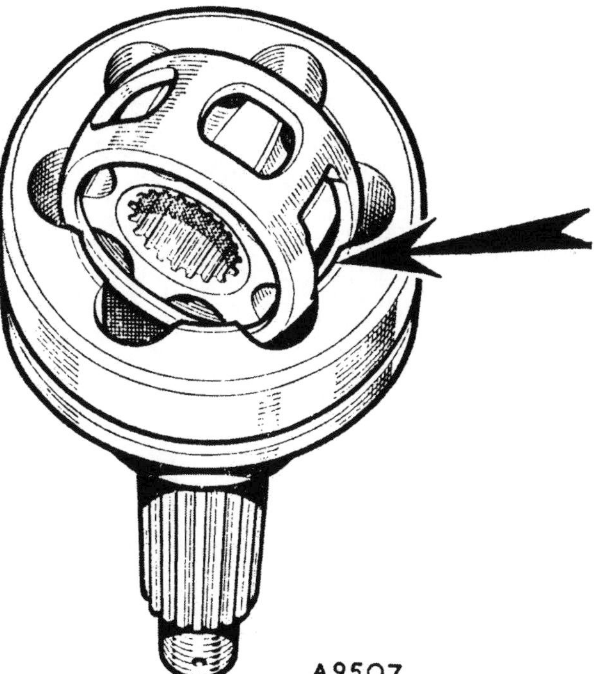

Fig. G.3
Removing the cage and inner race assembly, from the bell joint

Inspecting

10. Clean all parts thoroughly in petrol (fuel), paraffin (kerosene), or white spirit and dry off. In normal service, wear should be distributed fairly evenly over all components and the joint will remain serviceable until the amount of end-float exceeds the acceptable wear maximum of .025 in. (.64 mm.).

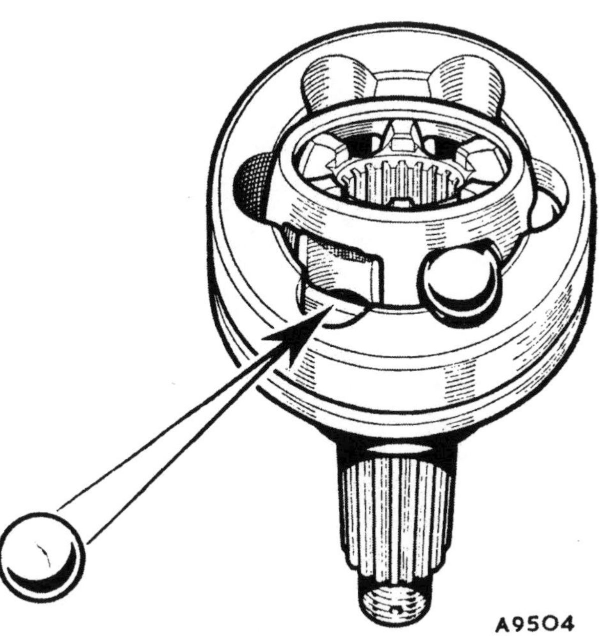

Fig. G.2
Tilt the inner race to remove or replace each ball in turn

11. Examine the six balls and if worn, rust-pitted or bearing evidence of flatting, the joint assembly must be replaced.
12. Inspect the inner and outer race tracks, these will be marked on the flanks where the balls roll, but should be free from indentation and the marking should be consistent.
13. Inspect the inner and outer spherical surfaces of the cage and the corresponding surfaces of the inner and outer races; these will be polished by contact but must be free from any sign of 'picking-up'. The edges of the cage windows may show signs of wear towards the outer side. Wear at these points may cause knocking when the joint is operated at high angles.
14. Carefully examine the shaft for cracks, and ensure that the square-section outer circlip is firmly in its groove.

Replacing the ball cage

The majority of cages used in the original assembly are of a standard size, although on some shafts two other non-standard oversize cages have also been used, and all three may be encountered in Service.

It is important to note that a joint will only accept a replacement cage of the same size as the original.

To effect easy identification of cage sizes use Service tool 18G 1012. The fitting of a Service kit must not be attempted without this tool.

Fig. G.4
Manoeuvre the inner race in the cage to the required position to allow it to be extracted

The three kits available are as follows:

Kit 'A', Part No. 18G 8000 (Standard)
Kit 'B', Part No. 18G 8002 (.004 in. oversize)
Kit 'C', Part No. 18G 8001 (.010 in. oversize)

It is extremely difficult to check the ball cage internal dimensions and a gauge, Service tool 18G 1012, must be used to determine the size of the cage fitted.

15. The small bore of the gauge is a clearance fit over a standard inner race but will not accept an inner race .004 in. (.100 mm.) oversize. The larger bore of the tool is a clearance fit over a standard cage but will not accept a cage .010 in. (.25 mm.) oversize.

A If the inner race passes through the small bore of the gauge, and the cage passes through the larger bore, the joint is size 'A'.

B If the inner race will not pass through the gauge, the joint is size 'B'. The cage should also be checked, but must be accepted by the gauge.

C If the inner race passes through the gauge, but the cage will not pass through, the joint is size 'C'.

NOTE.–Should the gauge 18G 1012 not accept the inner race or cage, the joints must be replaced as a unit.

Reassembling the joint

16. This is an exact reversal of the dismantling procedure. All components should be lightly lubricated with Duckham's M–B grease (BMC pack AKF 1457). The components should go together easily and no force should be required.

17. Insert the inner race into the cage by introducing one of the lands into an elongated window in the cage (Fig. G.4).

18. Insert the cage and inner race assembly into the bell joint by fitting one of the elongated windows over one of the lands in the outer race (Fig. G.3). The three parts can now be turned or swivelled freely in relation to each other.

19. Locate the cage and inner race in their original position relative to the bell joint (as marked before dismantling).

20. Keeping this relationship between the parts, tilt the cage until one ball can be inserted in a window. Repeat this operation with the remaining balls (Fig. G.2).

21. Ensure that the inner race articulates freely with the cage in the bell joint, but care must be taken not to release the balls.

22. The joint should be filled with the remainder of the pack of Duckham's M–B grease, before inserting the shaft.

23. Fit a new rubber boot if necessary, smearing the inside with Duckham's M–B grease, take care when easing the boot over the circlip on the shaft.

Assembling the shaft to the joint

24. Replace the round-section spring ring with a new one (Fig. G.5). If replacing the shaft, fit a new circlip.

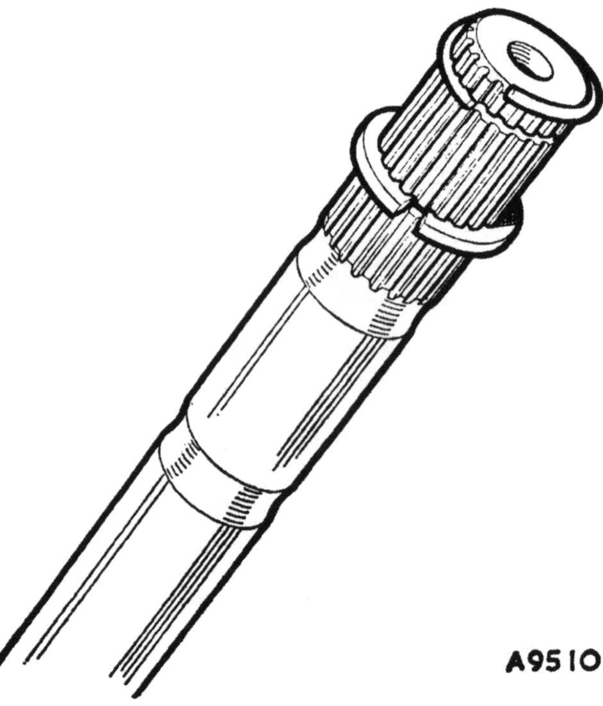

Fig. G.5
The splined bell joint end of the drive shaft showing the circlip and the round-section spring ring

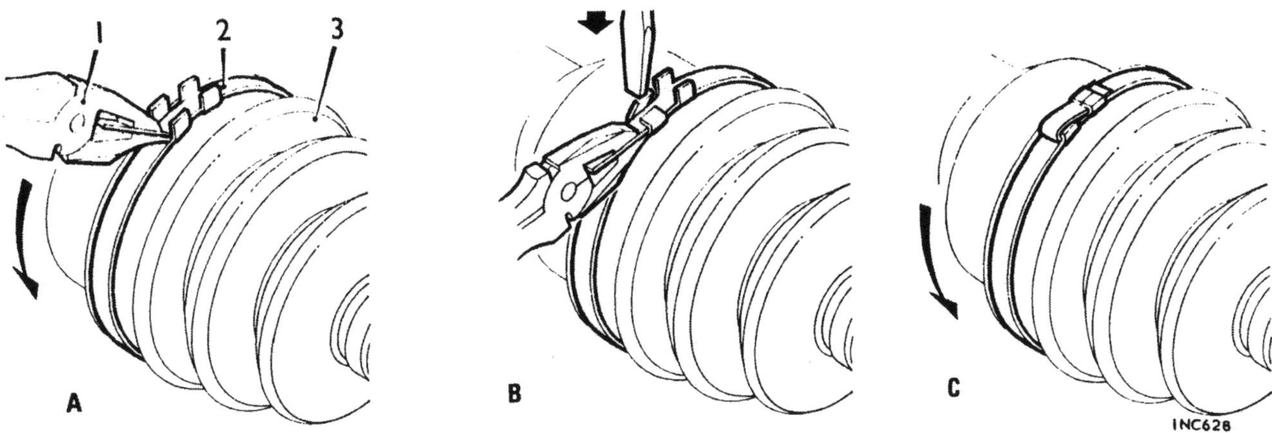

Fig. G.6
Securing the rubber boot to the drive shaft bell joint. 'Arrows' indicate forward rotation of drive shaft

1. Service tool 18G 1099. 2. Clinching clip. 3. Rubber boot (modified type).

25. Hold the shaft in a vice and locate the inner race on the shaft. Press the joint assembly against the spring ring whilst locating the ring centrally and contracting it in the chamfer of the inner race with screwdrivers. With the spring ring centralized, a sharp tap on the end of the stub shaft with a soft faced mallet will close up the ring, and the assembly can then be tapped on to the drive shaft. Make sure that the shaft is fully engaged, with the inner race against the circlip and that the inner ring has expanded inside the joint.

26. Slide the rubber boot over the bell joint until the radiused rib registers in the locating groove, and secure it with the large clinching clip using Service tool 18G 1099 (Fig. G.6). This is fitted with the tab pulled through away from the direction of forward rotation. Locate the other end of the boot in the groove in the drive shaft and secure it with the small clinching clip using pliers 18G 1099.

    NOTE.—A modified rubber boot which has axial convolutions (see Fig. G.6) should be fitted when a replacement is required.

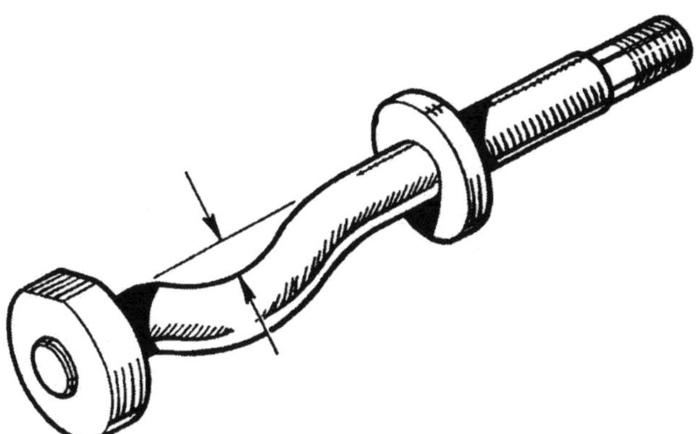

Fig. G.7
The lower arm pivot pin. The measurement at the position indicated must be .312 in. (7.9 mm.) to accommodate the rubber boot of later drive shaft assemblies

27. Lubricate the yoke end of the drive shaft and the inside of the yoke housing seal and slide the seal onto the shaft. Fill the cavity in the sliding joint yoke with ¾ oz. (21 gm.) of Duckham's M—B grease and fit the yoke to the shaft. Locate the seal into the groove on the shaft and the other end over the sleeve location. Push the shaft to the bottom of the yoke so that grease is driven into the seal. Hold outer lip of the seal open to allow air and surplus grease to escape, ensure that the diameter of the bellows does not exceed 1.75 in. (44.5 mm.). Secure the yoke seal with clinching clips using pliers 18G 1099.

Refitting

28. Refitting is a reversal of the removing procedure given in Section K.2.

29. When fitting a replacement drive shaft assembly (of the type fitted with a rubber boot on the sliding joint) to the left hand side of an early model, it will also be necessary to fit a modified lower arm inner pivot pin to ensure sufficient clearance for the rubber boot. Reference should be made to Fig. G.7 for the dimension of the modified pivot pin.

Section G.3

DRIVE SHAFT COUPLING

Removing

1. Jack up the front of the vehicle, place supports under the sub-frame and remove the road wheel.

2. Remove the upper and lower swivel hub ball pin retaining nuts and release the ball pins from the suspension arms using Service tool 18G 1063.

3. Remove the 'U' bolts and nuts securing the drive flange coupling.

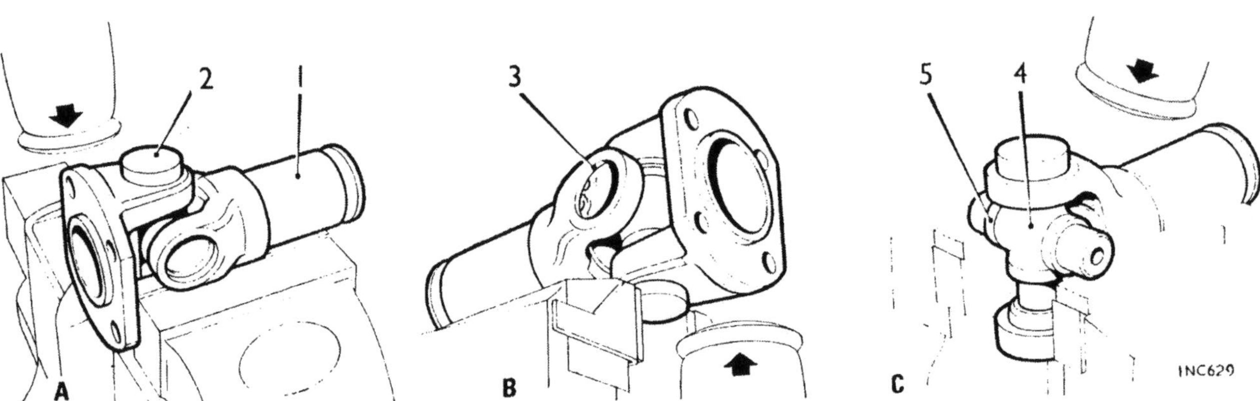

Fig. G.8
The sequence of operations when removing the needle bearings from the universal joint

1. Yoke.
2. Needle bearing race.
3. Retaining circlip.
4. Journal spider.
5. Rubber seal.

4. Disconnect the swivel hub assembly from the suspension arms and pull it out sufficiently to release the rubber coupling.
   NOTE.–Support the swivel hub on a stand or suitable support until it is refitted, do not stretch the hydraulic brake hose.

Refitting

5. Before refitting, check that the coupling 'U' bolts will easily engage the drive shaft yoke. If they have opened, squeeze both threaded ends together in a soft jawed vice until they are in alignment.
   NOTE.–When reassembling, fit new 'U' bolt nuts.
6. Fit the new coupling to the final drive yoke.
7. Refit the swivel hub assembly to the suspension arms and at the same time engage the drive shaft yoke with the new coupling.
8. Tighten the new nuts on the coupling 'U' bolts equally until approximately $\frac{1}{16}$ in. (1.6 mm.) of thread extrudes through the nuts.
9. Tighten the swivel hub ball pin retaining nuts to the torque figure given in **'GENERAL DATA'**.
10. Refit the road wheel and lower the car.

Section G.4

UNIVERSAL JOINT OVERHAUL
(Cooper 'S' and Automatic models)

Removing

1. Remove the drive shaft and swivel hub assembly as detailed in Section K.2, operations 1 to 7.
2. Remove the clinching clip securing the yoke housing seal to the drive shaft and pull the yoke housing assembly off the drive shaft splines.

Dismantling

3. Clean the universal joint assembly.
4. Remove the bearing retaining clips with a pair of thin-nosed pliers and prise them out with a screwdriver. If a retaining clip cannot be removed easily, tap the end of the bearing race to relieve pressure on the clip.
5. Hold the joint in one hand and support the underside of the yoke on the top of a vice. Tap the radius of the yoke lightly with a copper mallet, Fig. G.8, until the bearing race emerges from the yoke.
6. Turn the joint over and grip the bearing race in the vice. Tap the underside of the yoke until the bearing race is extracted, Fig. G.8.
7. Repeat operations 5 and 6 on the opposite bearing.
8. Support the two exposed bearing trunnions on the top of the vice (with wood or soft metal packings between the vice and the bearing trunnions). Tap the top lug of the flange yoke as detailed in operations 5 and 6 to extract the two remaining bearing races, Fig G.8.
9. Withdraw the journal spider from the drive shaft yoke.

Inspecting

10. Wash all parts thoroughly in a cleaning fluid.
11. Check the bearing races and spider for signs of wear or load markings. Fit a new journal repair kit if any components are defective. Check that the bearing races are a light drive fit in the yoke trunnions, if any of the races are a loose fit, replace the complete end assembly.

Reassembling

12. Ensure that each bearing race has a complete set of needle rollers, smear the inside walls of the races and needle roller bearings with grease, with a $\frac{1}{8}$ in. (3 mm.) depth of grease in the end of each race.

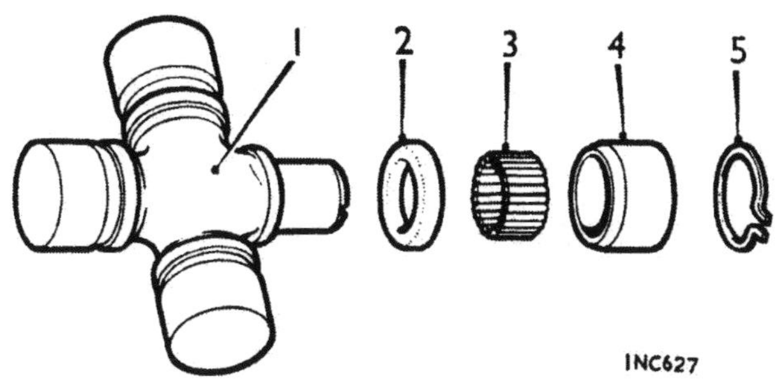

Fig. G.9
The universal joint bearing components

1. Journal spider.
2. Rubber seal.
3. Needle rollers.
4. Bearing race.
5. Retaining circlip.

13. Check that yoke journal bearing apertures are clean and dry and insert the spider into the yoke.
14. Use a soft drift slightly smaller in diameter than the bearing race and tap the race into position; hold the spider into the race as it is drifted into position to retain the needle rollers in position.
15. Repeat the above operation on the opposite side of the yoke.
16. Engage the other journal over the spider and repeat operations 14 and 15.
17. Fit the circlips and ensure that they are firmly located in their grooves. If the joint appears to bind, tap the yoke journals lightly with a wooden mallet to relieve pressure of the bearing races on the ends of the journals.

Refitting

18. Fit a new rubber boot and refill it with the recommended grease as detailed in operation 27 of Section G.2.
19. Refit the drive shaft to the swivel hub and reassemble the complete assembly to the vehicle as detailed in operations 19 to 24 of Section K.2.

Section G.5

DRIVE SHAFT
(Offset sphere inboard joint type)

Removing

1. Remove the one screw retaining the suspension upper arm rebound rubber and place a solid wedge of the same thickness in its place.
2. Remove the wheel trim and slacken the road wheel nuts.
3. Remove the split pin retaining the drive shaft nut and slacken the nut.
4. Jack up the vehicle, place stands under the sub-frame side members and remove the road wheel.
5. Remove the nut retaining the steering tie-rod ball joint and release the joint from the steering lever using Service tool 18G 1063.
6. Remove the upper swivel hub ball pin retaining nut and spring washer. Release the joint using Service tool 18G 1063 and refit the retaining nut loosely.

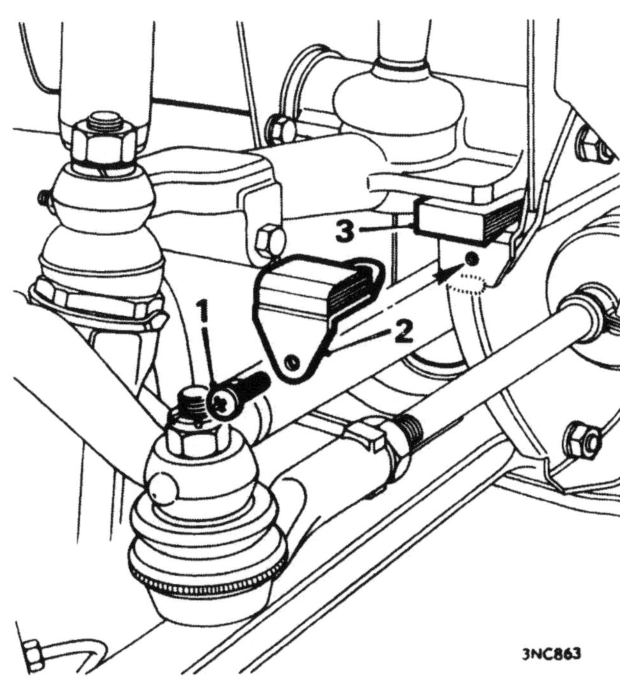

Fig. G.10
Removing the suspension rebound rubber and fitting a solid wedge

1. Retaining screw.
2. Rebound rubber.
3. Wedge.

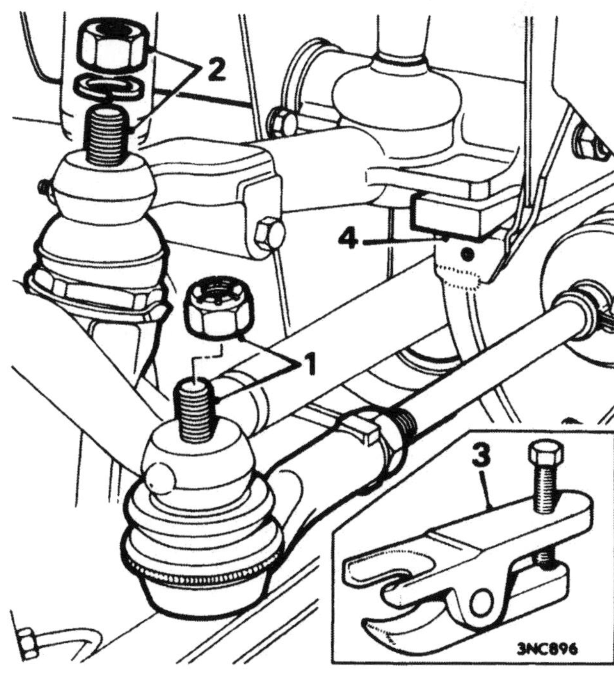

Fig. G.11
Showing Service tool 18G 1063 used to disconnect the ball joints

1. Steering tie-rod ball-joint.
2. Swivel hub ball-joint (upper).
3. Service tool 18G 1063.
4. Wedge.

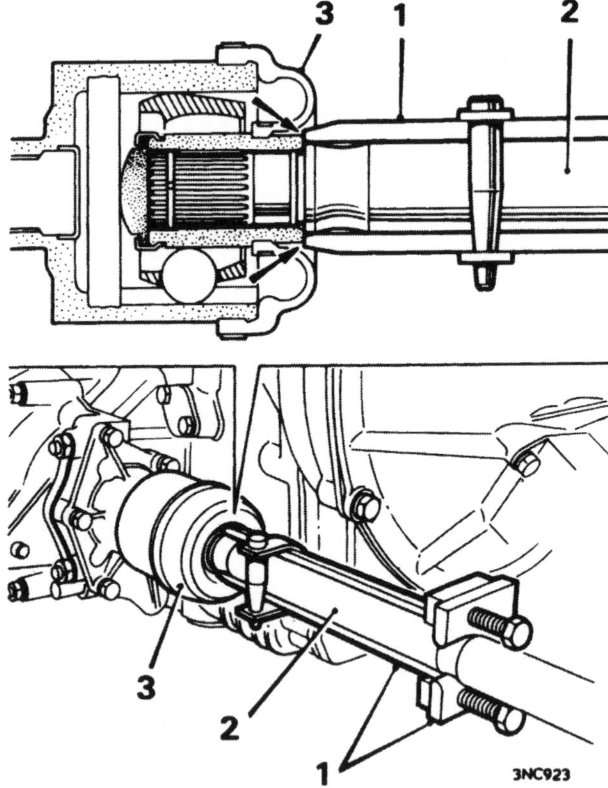

Fig. G.12
Using Service tool 18G 1243 to release the drive shaft from the inboard joint. Inset shows the end of the tool hard against the inboard joint 'arrowed'

1. Service tool 18G 1243.
2. Drive shaft.
3. Inboard joint.

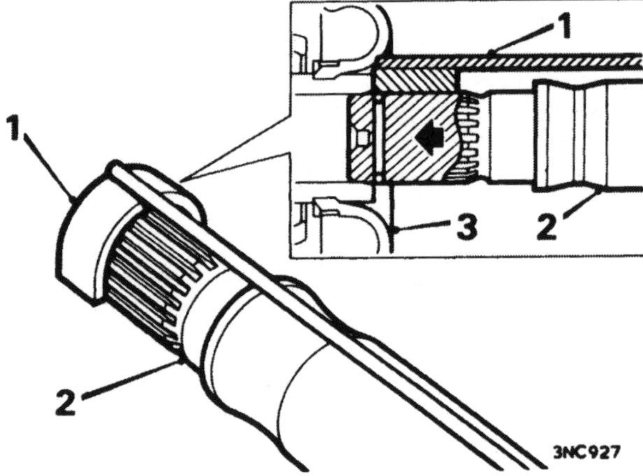

Fig. G.13
Compressing the inboard joint circlip with Service tool 18G 1241

1. Service tool 18G 1241.
2. Drive shaft.
3. Inboard joint.

7. Assemble Service tool 18G 1243 to the drive shaft with the tool hard against the inboard joint before inserting the taper pin, see Fig. G.12. Insert the 'U' shaped part of the tool into the groove on the shaft, tighten the two bolts evenly until the drive shaft is released from the inboard joint. Remove the tool.
8. Remove the nut and disconnect the swivel hub ball pin from the suspension upper arm.
   WARNING. Take care not to stretch the brake hose.
9. Retain the position of the inboard joint boot and at the same time withdraw the shaft out of the joint.
10. Push the shaft inwards and over the top of the final drive assembly; remove the drive-shaft retaining nut and tap the shaft out of the driving flange.
11. Withdraw the drive shaft out of the swivel hub and then outwards away from the vehicle.

Refitting

12. Reverse the removing procedure except that the Service tools previously used are not required also noting the following:
    a. Locate the drive shaft into the swivel hub and screw on the retaining nut.
    b. When assembling the drive shaft into the inboard joint, use Service tool 18G 1241 to compress the inboard joint circlip, see Fig. G.13.
    c. Push the drive shaft smartly into the inboard joint to lock the shaft into the joint.
    d. Tighten the swivel hub ball pin retaining nut to the torque figure given in **'GENERAL DATA'.**
    e. Tighten the drive shaft nut to the correct torque figure, see **'GENERAL DATA'** for the particular model application.

Section G.6

DRIVE SHAFT BOOT REPLACEMENT
(Offset sphere inboard joint type)

Removing

1. Remove the drive shaft, Section G.5.
2. Remove and discard the rings securing the rubber boot to the outer member of the constant velocity joint and the drive shaft.
3. Withdraw the boot off the drive shaft.
4. Thoroughly clean the joint assembly in petrol (fuel) paraffin (kerosene), or white spirit and dry off.

Refitting

5. Slide the new rubber boot up the drive shaft.
6. Pack the joint with 1 oz (30 cm^3) quantity of Duckhams Bentone Grease Q5795.

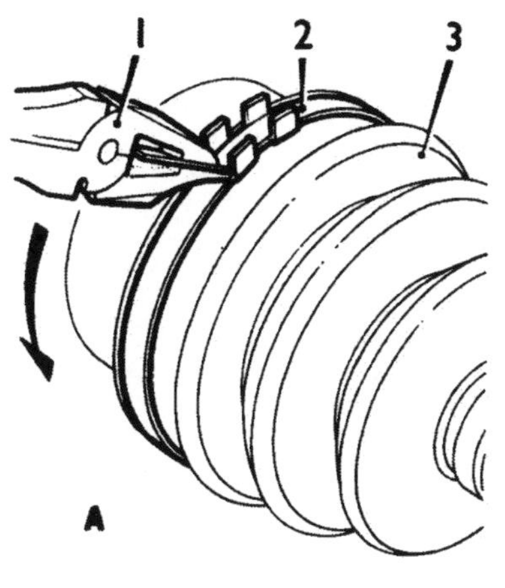

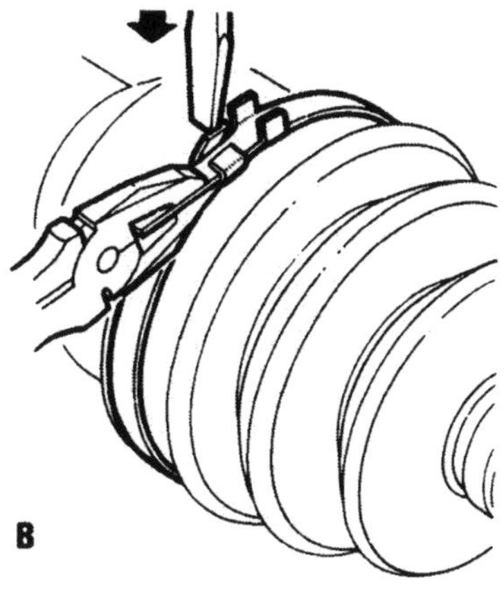

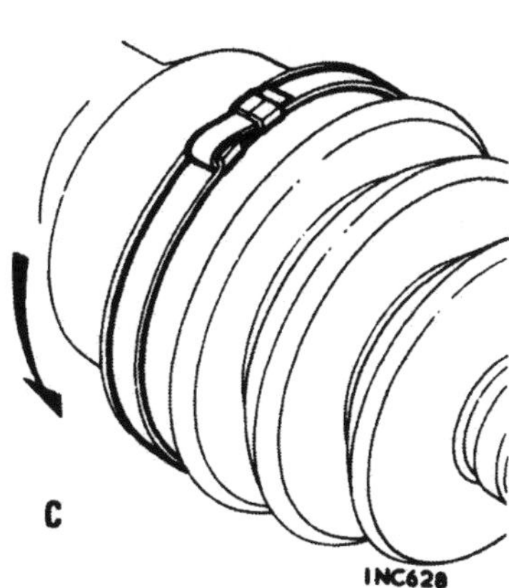

Fig. G.14
Securing the rubber boot to the drive shaft; outboard joint illustrated. 'Arrows' indicate forward rotation of the drive shaft.

1. Service tool 18G 1099. 2. Clinching clip. 3. Rubber boot.

7. Secure the rubber boot to the drive shaft and constant velocity joint with the service clips using Service tool 18G 1099 and following the procedure detailed below and illustrated in Fig. G.14. If the service clips are not available see alternative method in operation 8.
   a. The clip must be fitted with the fold in the clip facing toward the forward rotation of the drive shaft, see Fig. G.14.
   b. Pull the free end of the clip tightly between the front locking tabs of the clip and close the front locking tabs onto the clip.
   c. Fold the clip back over the front locking tabs and close the rear locking tabs to secure the clip end.
8. Alternative method. Secure the boot to the joint using 20 S.W.G. soft iron wire; wind the wire twice around the boot, twist the ends firmly together several turns and bend the ends away from the direction of rotation.
9. Refit the drive shaft, Section G.5.

Section G.7

DRIVE SHAFT INBOARD JOINT
(Offset sphere type)

Removing

1. Drain the engine/transmission oil.
2. Follow the procedure 1, 2 and 4 to 9 in Section G.5 to withdraw the drive shaft out of the inboard joint.
3. Insert Service tool 18G 1240 with its relieved side against the inboard joint and drift it between the joint and the final drive end cover with the block adjacent the end cover bolt, see Fig. G.15.
4. Give the tool a sharp blow on its flat face (arrowed), inwards towards the final drive to release the joint, see Fig. G.15.
5. Pull the inboard joint off the splined final drive shaft.

Refitting

6. Check the condition of the nylon oil flinger on the inboard joint and fit a replacement if it has been damaged in any way.
7. Insert the inboard joint into the final drive and push in until the joint is securely engaged over the retaining circlip on the splined shaft.
8. When refitting the drive shaft into the inboard joint, use Service tool 18G 1241 to compress the inboard joint circlip, see Fig. G.13. Push the shaft smartly into the joint to lock the shaft in the joint.
9. Tighten the swivel hub ball pin retaining nut to the torque figure given in **'GENERAL DATA'**.

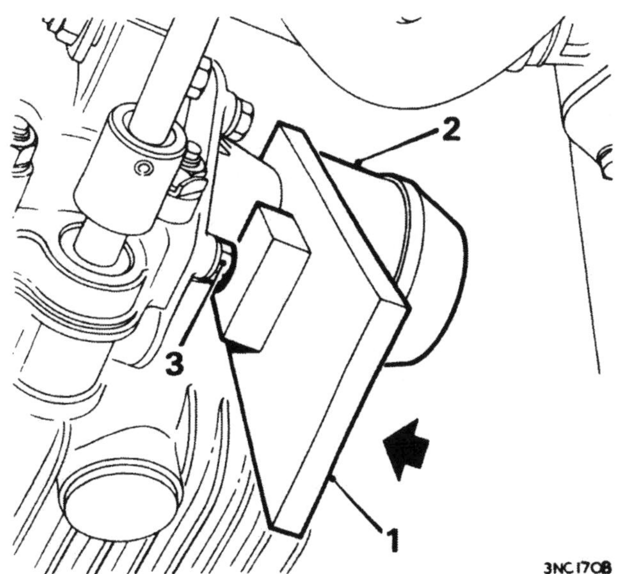

Fig. G.15
Using Service tool 18G 1240 to remove the inboard joint; hit the tool on side 'arrowed'

1. Service tool 18G 1240. 2. Inboard joint.
3. Differential end cover bolt.

Section G.8

DRIVE SHAFT INBOARD JOINT BOOT REPLACEMENT (Offset sphere type)

Removing

1. Remove the drive shaft inboard joint as detailed in Section G.7.
2. Remove and discard the large clip retaining the boot to the joint.
3. Turn the boot inside-out, remove and discard the inner retaining clip and withdraw the boot from the joint.
4. Withdraw the inner joint member and ball cage assembly from the outer member.
5. Prise the balls from the ball cage, then rotate the cage until its internal grooves coincide with the lands on the joint inner member and separate the two, see Fig. G.17.

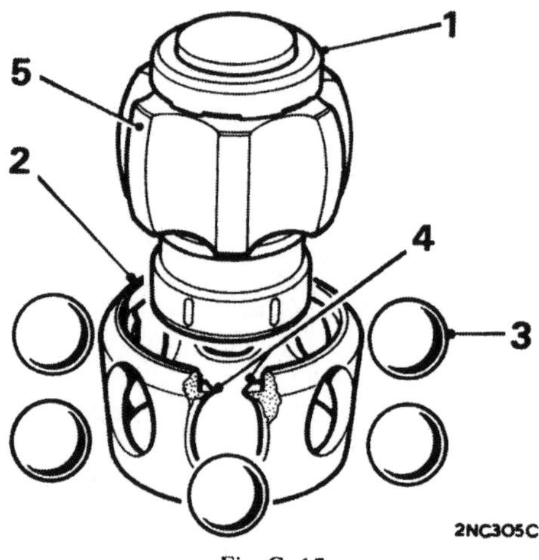

Fig. G.17

1. Inner member
2. Ball cage
3. Balls
4. Internal grooves – ball cage
5. Lands – inner member

Inspecting

6. Clean the joint and components thoroughly in a cleaning solvent, paraffin (kerosene) or white spirit and dry off.
7. Inspect the components for wear or damage, if any component is defective, a new offset sphere joint assembly must be fitted.

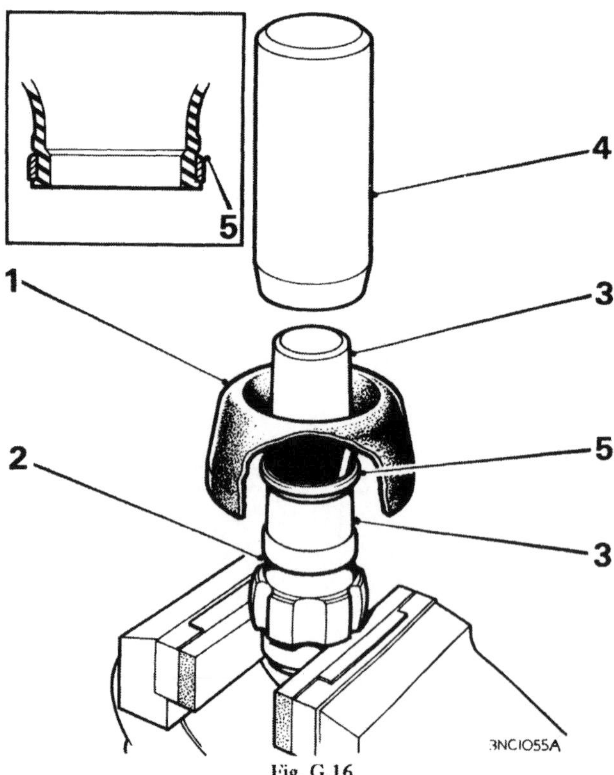

Fig. G.16
Using Service tool 18G 1251 to fit a new rubber boot with endless type retaining clip onto the inner member of the offset sphere inboard joint. Inset shows the correct fitment of the clip on the rubber boot

1. Rubber boot
2. Inner member
3. Mandrel – Service tool 18G 1251
4. Sleeve – Service tool 18G 1251
5. Retaining clip

Refitting

8. Fit a new endless retaining clip over the inner neck of the new rubber boot, with the chamfer of the clip towards the inside of the boot, see Fig. G.16.
9. Refer to Fig. G.16. Support the inner member with its boss uppermost, in a soft-jawed vice and insert the mandrel of Service tool 18G 1251. Apply a liberal coating of 'Teepol' or liquid detergent onto the boss and mandrel also to the inside neck of the rubber boot. Slide the boot down the mandrel and then use the sleeve of Service tool 18G 1251 to push the boot (using hand pressure) fully onto the circlip locating register of the joint boss. Thoroughly clean all traces of the 'Teepol' or liquid detergent from the joint and boot.
10. Reverse the procedure in operation 5 to assemble the inner member and balls into the ball cage, see Fig. G.17.
11. Use Shell S7274 Tivella 'A' Grease (in sachet of 50 c.c. capacity) and pack the joint as follows:
    a. Use half the sachet of grease to load the ball cage.
    b. Pack the remainder into the interior of the outer member of the joint.
12. Install the inner member and ball cage assembly into the outer member, and locate the rib of the rubber boot over the end of the joint.
13. Fit the retaining clip using Service tool 18G 1099 following the procedure detailed below and illustrated in Fig. G.14.
    a. The clip must be fitted with the fold in the clip facing toward the forward rotation of the drive shaft, see Fig. G.14.
    b. Pull the free end of the clip tightly between the front locking tabs of the clip and close the front locking tabs onto the clip.
    c. Fold the clip back over the front locking tabs and close the rear locking tabs to secure the end.
14. Refit the drive shaft inboard joint. Section G.7.

SECTION H

THE REAR SUSPENSION

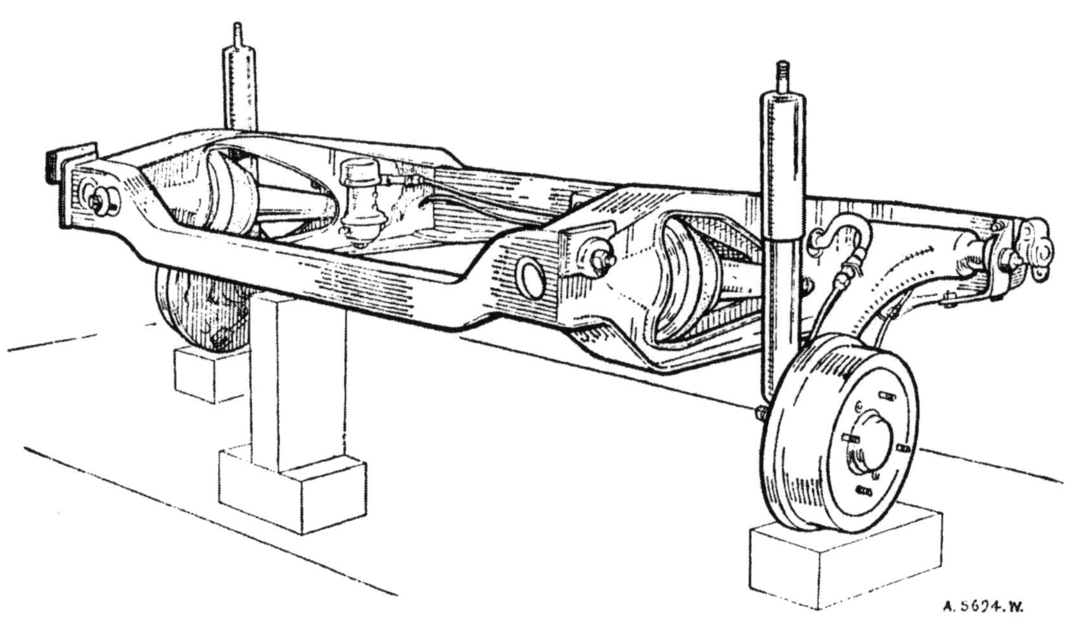

Fig. H.1
The rear sub-frame assembly (rubber suspension)

Section H.1

SUB-FRAME

Removing

1. Disconnect the battery.
2. Remove the exhaust pipe (Section A.3).
3. Disconnect the hydraulic pipe from the pressure regulating valve.
4. Remove the end finishers from the sill panels.
5. Release the rear dampers from inside the luggage compartment as in Section L.1.
6. Release the hand brake cable fairleads and disconnect the cables from the lever trunnion. Pull the cables downwards through the floor.
7. Lift the body with padded hooks under the wings.
8. Unscrew the eight sub-frame mounting bolts and withdraw the sub-frame.

Refitting

Reverse the removing instructions.

Section H.2

RADIUS ARMS

Removing

1. Release the rear damper(s) as in Section L.1.
2. Raise the car and support it under the sub-frame side-member.
3. Remove the road wheel.
4. Disconnect the brake hose from the bracket on the radius arm.
5. Prise out the strut assembly (Fig. H.2). The nylon cup may remain in the boss on the radius arm and, unless damaged, it can be removed with the fingers.
6. Disconnect the hand brake cable from the lever on the backplate, prise the guide tube from the clip on the arm and pull the tube away from the arm.
   On later models remove the nut from the cable sector pivot and withdraw the selector and pivot.
7. Remove the end finisher from the sill panel.
8. Unscrew the nut and remove the washer from the radius arm pivot shaft and lift the arm away from the car.

Dismantling and overhauling

9. Slide the dust seal and washer from the ends of the pivot.
10. If new bearings are necessary, withdraw the outer bronze bush with Service tool 18G 585 and fit the new bush with Service tool 18G 584.
11. Remove the needle-roller bearing from the inner end with Service tools 18G 583 and 18G 583 B and ream the outer bronze bush with Service tools 18G 588 and 18G 588 A.
12. Refit the needle-roller bearing with Service tool 18G 620, the marked end of the bearing faces outwards.
13. Lubricate all parts with grease.

Refitting

14. Reverse the removal instructions, but note:
15. Refers to item 5. Repack the nylon cup and dust seal with Dextragrease Super G.P. Lip the dust seal over the edge of the cup.

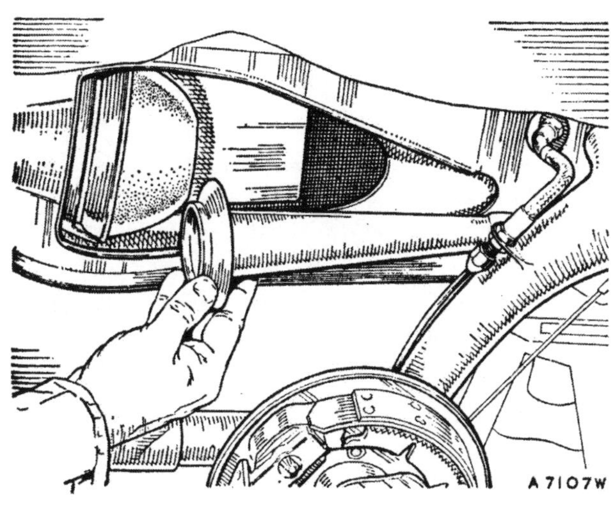

Fig. H.2
Extract the strut from the spring unit and pull it rearwards to disengage the ball end from the radius arm

Section H.3

SPRING UNITS

Removing

1. Carry out instructions 1 to 3 and 5 in Section H.2.
2. Remove the spring unit.
3. Prise out the nylon seating.

Refitting

4. Reverse the removing instructions, but note:
5. Make sure that the spring unit and spring strut are correctly located in their spigots while the radius arm is being raised to connect the upper end of the damper.

Section H.4

SUB-FRAME MOUNTINGS

Removing

1. Jack up the car at a point near the bumper and the rear body panel.

FRONT

2. Remove the radius arm (Section H.2).
3. Unscrew and remove the nut securing the mounting support pin to the sub-frame (Fig. H.3). Withdraw the mounting block to body screws. Prise the body and sub-frame apart sufficiently to allow the support pin, blocks, and rubbers to be extracted.

REAR

4. Jack up the car at a point between the bumper and the rear body panel.
5. Withdraw the mounting block to body screws and remove the nut from the end of the mounting support pin.
6. Prise the body and frame apart sufficiently to allow the block and rubbers to be removed.

Refitting

7. Reverse the removing instructions. Insert the mounting block to body screws before tightening the support pin nut.

Section H.5

HUB

Removing

1. Jack up the car and remove the road wheel and the brake-drum.
2. Prise off the hub cap.
3. Extract the split pin and screw the nut from the end of the stub shaft.
4. Withdraw the hub assembly.

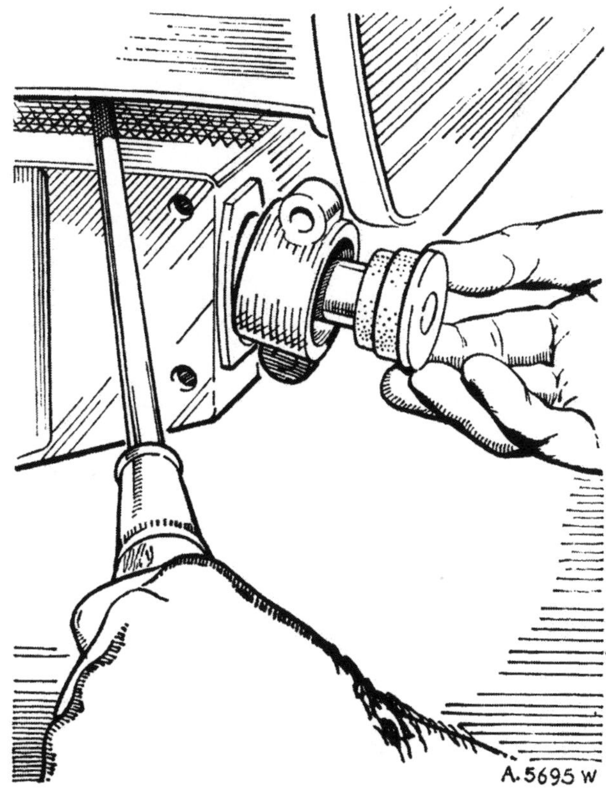

Fig. H.3
Removing the rear sub-frame front mounting support pin assembly

Dismantling

5. Drift the inner races of both bearings from the hub.
6. Remove the seal.
7. Extract the outer bearing races with Service tool 18G 260 and adaptor 18G 260 C.

Reassembling

8. Reverse the dismantling instructions and pack the bearings only with grease.

Refitting

9. Reverse the removing instructions, taking care to fit the chamfered bore of the thrust washer on the stub shaft towards the bearing.

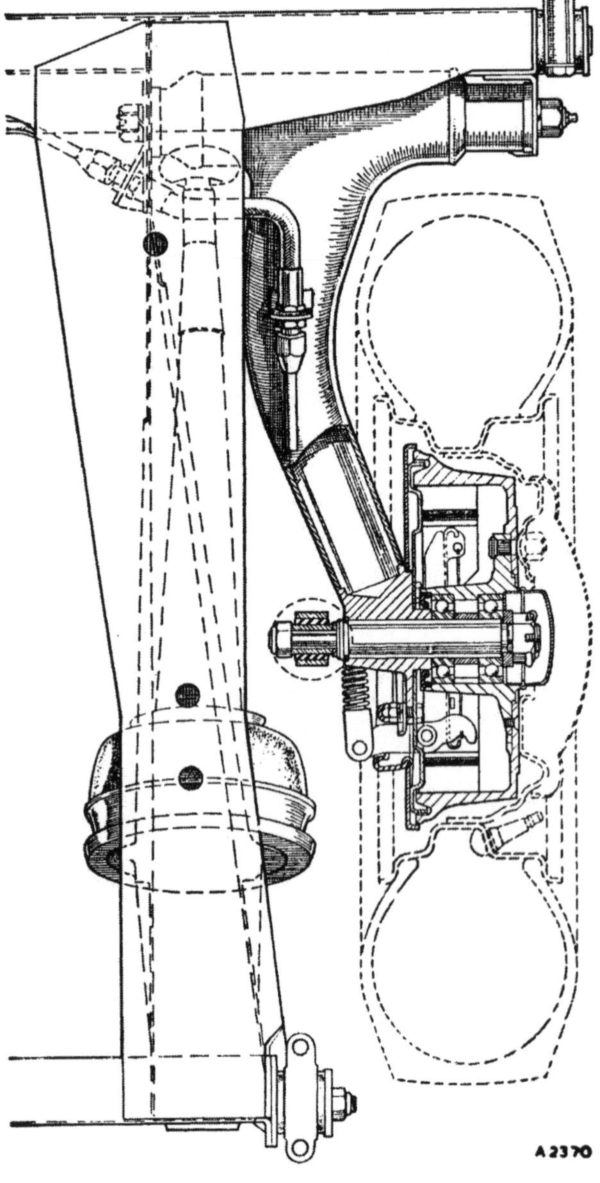

Fig. H.4
The rear radius arm, showing a section through the hub assembly

Section H.6

HYDROLASTIC SUSPENSION

The system consists of two front and two rear displacer units intercoupled longitudinally. Each is made of sheet steel and rubber and consists of a piston, a diaphragm, a lower and upper chamber housing, and a conical spring of compressed rubber.

Contact of the front wheels with a road irregularity forces the piston to push the diaphragm up; increased pressure displaces some of the fluid from the bottom chamber to the top chamber. The rubber springs deflect due to the pressure increase and fluid displacement, and the resultant pressure increase causes fluid to discharge through the interconnecting pipe into the rear displacer unit.

The fluid entering the rear displacer forces the diaphragm to react against the piston, resulting in the car height at the rear being raised. These events are virtually simultaneous and the car therefore rides an obstruction without pitch motion of the body. The action of the suspension is similar when the rear wheels negotiate the irregularity.

The fluid used in the system is a mixture of water and alcohol into which an anti-corrosive agent has been introduced.

The front suspension also comprises upper and lower arms of unequal length located in the side-members of the front sub-frame with their outer ends attached by ball joints to the swivel hubs.

The rear suspension, in addition to the Hydrolastic units, consists of independent trailing arms with auxiliary coil springs.

Section H.7

DEPRESSURIZING, EVACUATING, AND PRESSURIZING THE HYDROLASTIC SYSTEM

Before any major work can be carried out on the suspension and its components the Hydrolastic system must be depressurized and in some cases evacuated. For this operation Service equipment Part No. 18G 703 or 18G 682 must be connected to the pressure valves on the rear sub-frame.

Before using Service equipment 18G 703 check that the pressure/vacuum tank is filled to the level indicated at the rear of the unit. The vacuum and pressure valves are identified by colour only; vacuum (yellow) and pressure (black).

Early Service equipment (18G 682) has separate fillers for the pressure and vacuum tanks and are filled to the level shown on the dipstick. Oneside of the dipstick shows the level in the pressure tank and the other side the level in the vacuum tank.

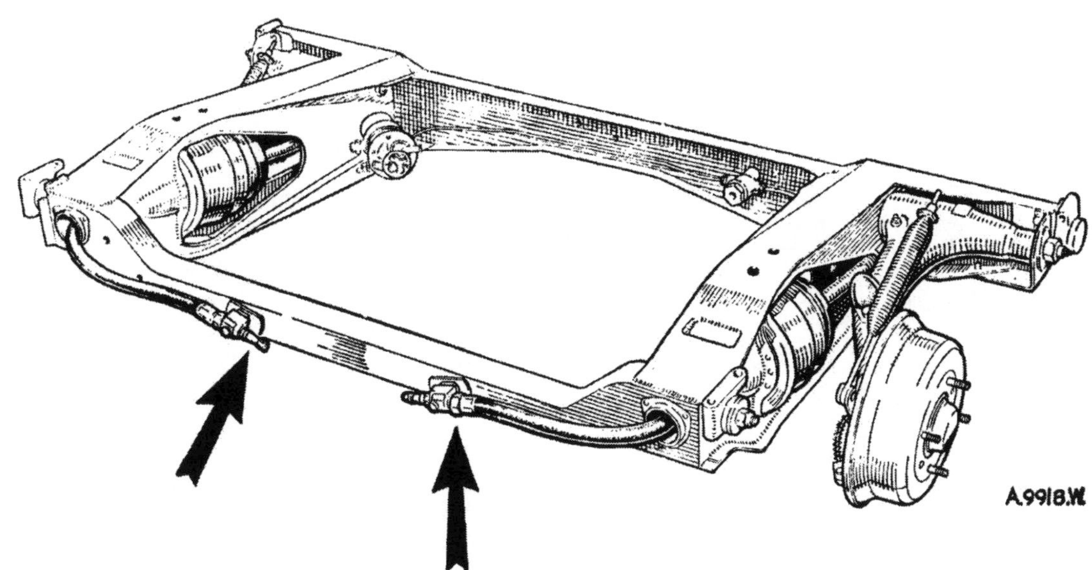

Fig. H.5
The Hydrolastic system pressure valves on the rear sub-frame

Top up to the correct levels with Hydrolastic Fluid, BMC Part No. 97H 2801.

The vacuum and pressure valves are identified by number or colour; vacuum (1) yellow, and pressure (2) black.

Depressurizing

1. Remove the pressure valve dust cap and connect the black connector to the valve with the knurled knob unscrewed.
2. Open the black valve (valve 2) and screw in the knurled knob to release the fluid from the suspension system into the unit's pressure tank.
3. Close the black valve (valve 2). The gauge should read zero if all the pressure has been released.
4. Remove the black connector and replace the pressure valve dust cap, and the plug in the black connector.
5. Repeat the above procedure on the second valve to depressurize the other side of the system.

Evacuating

After fitting new interconnecting pipes or displacer units it is essential that the air is evacuated from the system and a partial vacuum created. Service equipment 18G 703 or 18G 682 must be used for this purpose as follows:

6. Remove the pressure valve dust cap and connect the yellow connector to the valve on the sub-frame.
7. Close the yellow valve (valve 1) on the service unit.
8. Operate the vacuum pump until a reading of 27 in. (68.6 cm.) of mercury is obtained on the vacuum gauge and all movement of fluid in the tube has stopped. Subtract .5 in. (1.27 cm.) of mercury for every 500 ft. (152 m.) above sea-level.
9. Open the yellow valve (valve 1). Wait one or two minutes until any further movement in the tube has stopped and remove the yellow connector.
10. Replace the connector plug.

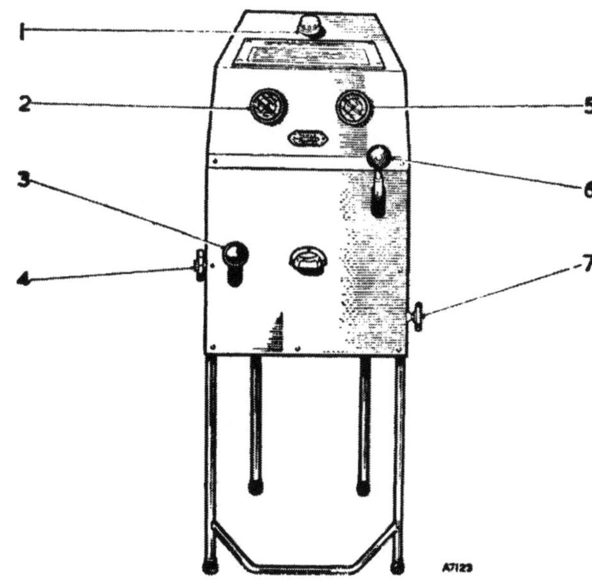

Fig. H.6
The suspension service unit

1. Combined vacuum/pressure tank.
2. Pressure gauge.
3. Pressure pump handle.
4. Black valve (valve 2).
5. Vacuum gauge.
6. Vacuum pump handle.
7. Yellow valve (valve 1).

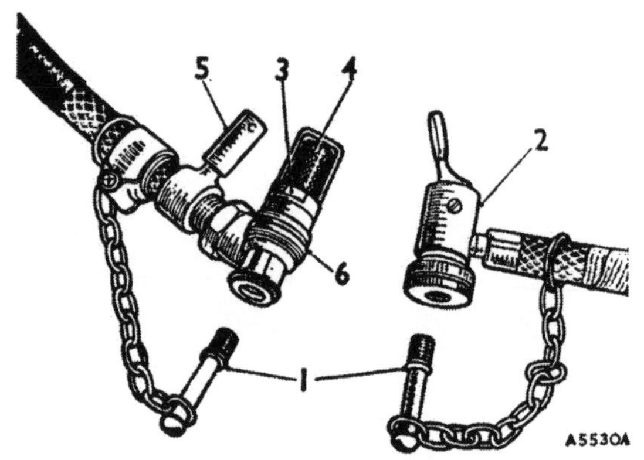

Fig. H.7
The suspension service unit connectors

1. Sealing plugs.
2. Evacuating connector.
3. Depressurizing and pressurizing connector.
4. Knurled knob.
5. Bleeding screw.
6. Locking slide.

Pressurizing

Having carried out repairs and evacuated to ensure that all air is out of the system, the pressurization should be carried out as follows with the car in the condition given in Section H.9 and resting on all four wheels.

11. Connect the servicing unit black connector to the pressure valve on the rear sub-frame with the knurled knob unscrewed.
12. Close the black valve (valve 2) and open the bleed valve.
13. Operate the pressure pump until air is evacuated from the connecting tube and fluid appears at the bleed valve.
14. Close the bleed valve and screw in the knurled knob.
15. Increase the pressure until the normal operating pressure is obtained (see **'GENERAL DATA'**).
    If a new displacer unit has been fitted pressurize to 350 lb./sq. in. (24.6 kg./cm.^{2}).
16. Unscrew the knurled knob and open the black valve (valve 2) to release the pressure in the connecting pipe.
17. Remove the black connector and refit the sealing plug.
18. When pressurizing above the normal pressure as item 15, wait 30 minutes to allow the vehicle to settle. Reconnect the black connector with the knurled knob unscrewed, close black valve (valve 2), screw in the knurled knob, open black valve (valve 2) until the normal pressure is shown on the gauge.
19. Unscrew the knurled knob, open the black valve (valve 2) to release the pressure in the connecting pipe.
20. Remove the black connector, replace the connecting sealing plug and the valve dust cap.

Servicing unit maintenance

Should the service equipment be used continuously, it may be necessary to carry out the following maintenance.

SERVICE TOOL 18G 682

21. Remove the front panel.
22. Remove the drain plug from the vacuum pump, drain the fluid.
23. Refill with the recommended vacuum oil S.A.E. 10 through the top of the pump. Replace the plug immediately the fluid commences to flow from the drain hole.
24. Lubricate the service unit mechanism periodically.

SERVICE TOOL 18G 703

25. Remove the front panel and fill the vacuum pump with the recommended vacuum oil S.A.E. 10 through the filler hole in the top of the pump. Fill only when the level is at the end of its downward stroke.
26. Lubricate the service unit mechanism periodically.
    IMPORTANT.–When the equipment is not in use both valves should be left open.

Section H.8

DISPLACER UNITS

Removal

1. Remove the road wheel and release the helper spring from the radius arm.
2. Raise the car and support it beneath the sub-frame member.

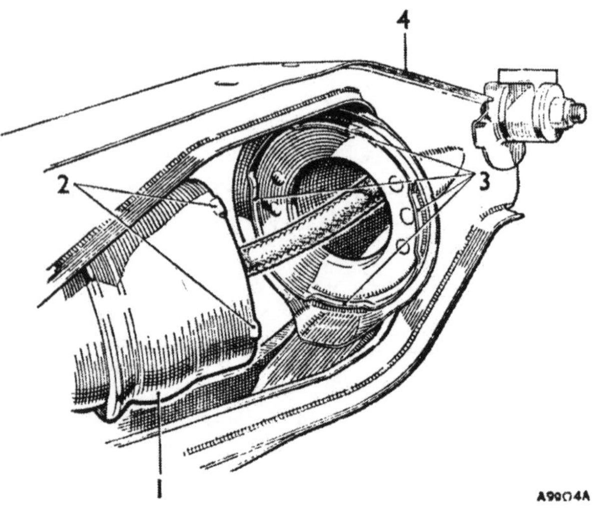

Fig. H.8
A rear displacer unit separated from the locating plate

1. Displacer unit.
2. Locating lugs.
3. Locating plate.
4. Sub-frame.

3. Remove the bump rubber from the sub-frame.
4. Depressurize the Hydrolastic system (see Section H.7).
5. Disconnect the flexible Hydrolastic hose from its union on the rear face of the sub-frame.
6. Remove the displacer strut and turn the unit anti-clockwise and withdraw it from the frame.

Refitting

7. Reverse the removal instructions.
8. Rotate the displacer clockwise to lock it into the registers on the locating plate.
9. Lubricate the strut ball and the nylon seat with Dextragrease G.P. and make sure the dust seal is fitted over the lip of the nylon cup.
10. Evacuate and pressurize the system (Section H.7).

Section H.9

SUSPENSION PRESSURE AND WING HEIGHTS

CONDITION OF CAR

Water; oil; petrol (max.) 4 Imp. gal. (4.8 U.S. gal., 18.2 litres)

Wing heights (early models)		Wing heights (later models)	
A	B	A	B
13±¼ in. (330±6.35 mm.)	13½±¼ in. 343±6.35 mm.)	12⅝±¼ in. (320.7±6.35 mm.)	13⅛±¼ in. (333.4±6.35 mm.)

NOTE.—It is most important that the Hydrolastic suspension system be pressurized to the figures given in 'GENERAL DATA'.

During the initial assembly, or subsequently if a new displacer unit is fitted, the system should be pressurized for a period of 30 minutes to 350 lb./sq. in. (24.6 kg./cm.^{2}) on early models, and to 400 lb./sq. in. (28.1 kg./cm.^{2}) on later models (see chart for commencing car numbers).

On all later cars, modified displacer units, helper springs and rear suspension struts are fitted. These components are not interchangeable individually with those fitted to earlier cars. The suspension pressure is also increased to suit the modified units (see **'GENERAL DATA'**).

Commencing car numbers:

Austin	Morris	R.H.D.	L.H.D.
Mini		830899	832055
	Mini	370004	370197
Cooper		830061	829417
	Cooper	830127	829490
Cooper 'S'		820487	820514
	Cooper 'S'	820705	820706

To check and adjust pressures

1. Ensure that the car is resting on all four wheels and that the load condition is as described above.
2. Use Service equipment 18G 703 and fit the black connector with the knurled knob unscrewed. Close valve 2 (black valve) and open the bleed valve. Use the pressure pump until air is evacuated from the connection tube and fluid appears. Close the bleed valve, operate the pressure pump until the working pressure is reached (see 'GENERAL DATA'), and then screw in the knurled knob. If the pressure reading is low, operate the pressure pump until the correct working pressure is reached (see 'GENERAL DATA'). If the pressure gauge reading is high, adjust to the correct working pressure by opening valve 2 (black valve). When the pressure reading is correct unscrew the knurled knob, open valve 2 (black valve), and remove the black connector. Replace the sealing plug in the black connector and the pressure dust cap on the suspension unit inter-connecting pipe valve.
3. A check can also be made on the suspension pressure, using Service tool 18G 685. The tool must first be adjusted in the following manner. Connect the pump to a pressure gauge fitted with a Schrader valve from which the core has been removed. Fill the tool with Hydrolastic fluid and operate the hand lever of the tool, noting the pressure registered on the gauge. Adjust the valve seat until the working pressure of the system is registered on the gauge (see 'GENERAL DATA'). Tighten the lock screw replace the washer and screw.

   Fit the connector to the suspension unit inter-connecting valve and operate the hand lever until the relief valve in the tool commences to operate. The suspension will now be at its correct working pressure.

Checking wing heights

4. Ensure that the load condition is as described above.
5. Measure the wing heights as illustrated.

NOTE.–Should the Hydrolastic suspension system suffer damage and the fluid be lost, the suspension arms on the damaged side of the vehicle will contact the bump rubbers at both front and rear. In this condition the car may be driven with complete safety at 30 m.p.h. (50 km.p.h.) over metalled roads.

Section H.10

RADIUS ARMS
(Hydrolastic Suspension)

Removing

1. Depressurize the Hydrolastic system (see Section H.7).
2. Remove the road wheel and release the helper spring from the radius arm.
3. Raise the vehicle and support it beneath the sub-frame side-member.
4. Disconnect the brake hose from the radius arm.
5. Disconnect the hand brake cable and release the cable sector from the arm.
6. Remove the bump rubber from the sub-frame and the end finisher from the sill panel.
7. Remove the displacer strut.
8. Remove the nut and washers from the arm pivot shaft and the four set screws to release the outer bracket.
9. Lift the radius arm assembly away from the vehicle, taking care not to lose the thrust washers and rubber seal fitted between the arm and the sub-frame side-member.

   Dismantling is described in Section H.2.

Refitting

10. Reverse the removing instructions.
11. Lubricate the strut ball end and the nylon seat with Dextragrease Super G.P. and make sure the dust seal is fitted over the lip of the nylon cup.
12. Bleed the hydraulic brake system.
13. Pressurize the Hydrolastic system (see Section H.7).

Section H.11

SUB-FRAME
(Hydrolastic Suspension)

Remove and refit the sub-frame as in Section H.1, with the following additional operations:

1. Depressurize and evacuate the Hydrolastic system prior to any dismantling, follow the instructions in Section H.7.
2. Disconnect both helper springs from the radius arms.
3. Disconnect the pressure valves from the sub-frame.
4. Evacuate and re-pressurize the Hydrolastic system when reassembly is complete, following the instructions in Section H.7.

Section H.12

SUB-FRAME
(Moke)

Remove and refit the sub-frame as in Section H.1 with the following exceptions:

Fuel tank and pump removal not necessary.

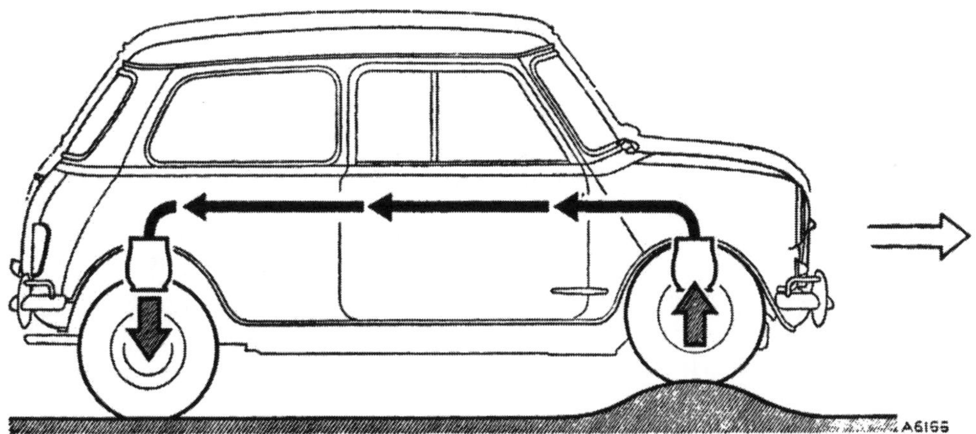

Fig. H.10
The tail rises in response to upward motion of the front wheel

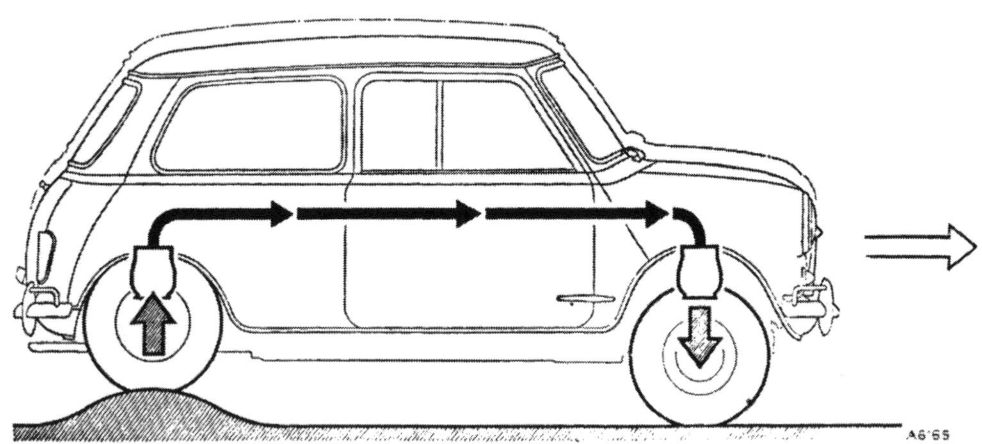

Fig. H.11
The nose rises in response to upward motion of the rear wheel

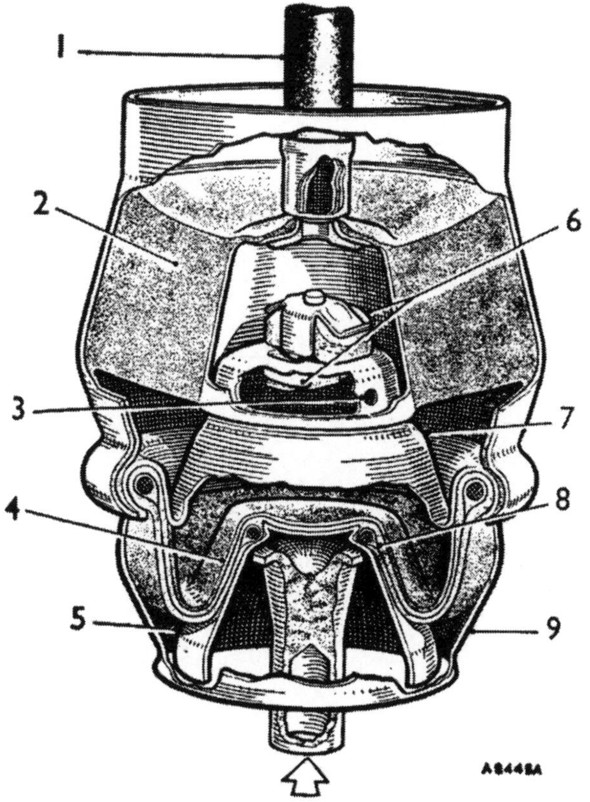

Fig. H.9
The Hydrolastic displacer unit

1. Interconnecting pipe.
2. Rubber spring.
3. Damper bleed.
4. Butyl liner.
5. Tapered piston.
6. Damper valve.
7. Fluid separating member.
8. Rubber diaphragm.
9. Tapered cylinder.

Section H.13

RADIUS ARMS
(Moke)

Remove and refit as in Section H.2 with the following exceptions:

Fuel tank and pump removal not necessary.

Section H.14

SCHRADER VALVE EXTENSION HOUSING
(Hydrolastic Suspension)

To rectify fluid leakage from the Schrader valve extension housing to the pipe elbow:

1. Depressurize the Hydrolastic system (see Section H.7).
2. Remove the Schrader valve extension housing from the pipe elbow and clean the threads of both the valve extension housing and the elbow.
3. The threads of the valve extension housing must be lightly coated with Loctite Grade A after the housing has been re-started on its threads in the elbow. Under no circumstances must Loctite be applied to the valve extension housing before inserting it in the elbow.
4. Tighten the valve extension housing to a torque of 16 to 20 lb. ft. (2.2 to 2.8 kg.m.) and leave for 24 hours at room temperature before pressurizing the system.
5. Evacuate and pressurize the system (see Section H.7).

SECTION J

THE STEERING

Section J.1

STEERING-WHEEL

Removal

1. Disconnect the battery.
2. EARLY MODELS. Withdraw the grub screw in the wheel hub and lift up the horn switch.
3. MK. II MODELS. Carefully prise off the wheel hub centre cover.
4. Unscrew the wheel retaining nut and pull off the wheel.

Refitting

Reverse the above removing instructions. Tighten the nut to the recommended torque (see **'GENERAL DATA'**).

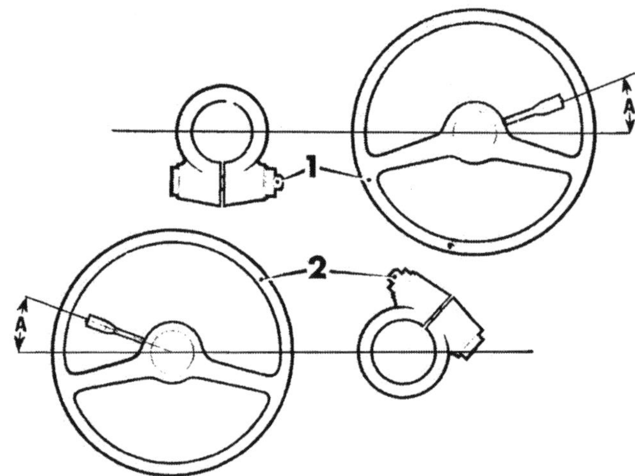

Fig. J.2
The position of the clamp bolt and direction indicator lever, A = 20°
1. Right-hand-drive models. 2. Left-hand-drive models.

Section J.2

STEERING-COLUMN

Removing

1. Disconnect the column switch wiring connectors located below the parcel shelf.
2. Remove the bolt from the lower column clamp/ steering rack pinion shaft.
3. Remove the column upper support clamp bolt.
4. Mark the fitted position of the outer column with the upper support bracket.
5. Pull the column assembly upwards and out of the car.

Dismantling

6. Remove the steering-wheel as described in Section J.1.
7. Remove both halves of the column cowl.
8. Remove the direction indicator switch and screw out the cancelling stud from the column.
9. EARLY MODELS. Remove the horn connection slip-ring assembly.

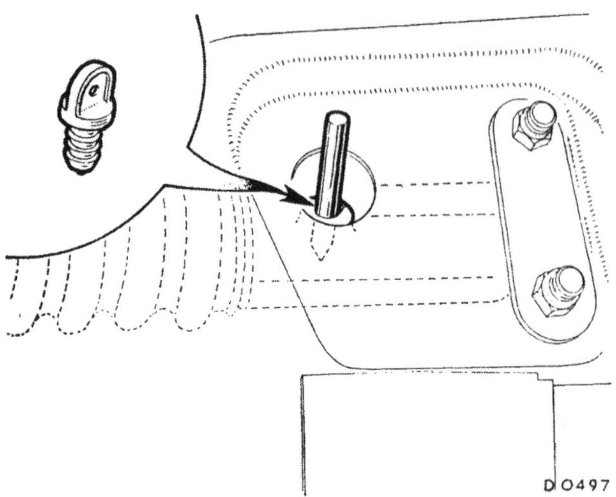

Fig. J.1
Using a locator pin to centralize the rack, with (inset) the plastic plug

10. Withdraw the inner column from the lower end of the outer column tube.
11. Extract the upper and lower bushes from the outer column tube.

Inspection

12. Check the inner column alignment and rectify if required to ensure that when rotated the upper bearing face does not exceed $\frac{1}{8}$ in. (3 mm.) run-out.
13. Examine the upper and lower felt bushes and use replacements if necessary. Cylindrical polythene upper bushes are now fitted to all later models.

Reassembling

14. Soak the lower felt bush in oil.
15. Lubricate the polythene bush with a graphite-based grease and insert it fully into the upper end of the outer column tube.
16. Insert the inner column into the outer column, and at the same time roll the lower felt bush around its fitted position on the inner column until both joint faces butt together, then carefully enter the assembly into the outer column.
17. Reverse the removing procedure for the other components.
18. Before refitting the assembly to the car ensure that the inner column turns freely (see instruction 12).

Refitting

19. Slacken the rack 'U' bolts to allow the rack pinion to align with the column.
20. Slacken the column fascia bracket bolts to allow sideways movement.
21. Align the road wheels to the straight-ahead position and refit the assembly to the car.
22. EARLY MODELS. Engage the marked spline of the pinion shaft with the split portion of the inner column clamp. Push down the assembly until the clamp bolt can be easily inserted. The clamp must be positioned as follows:

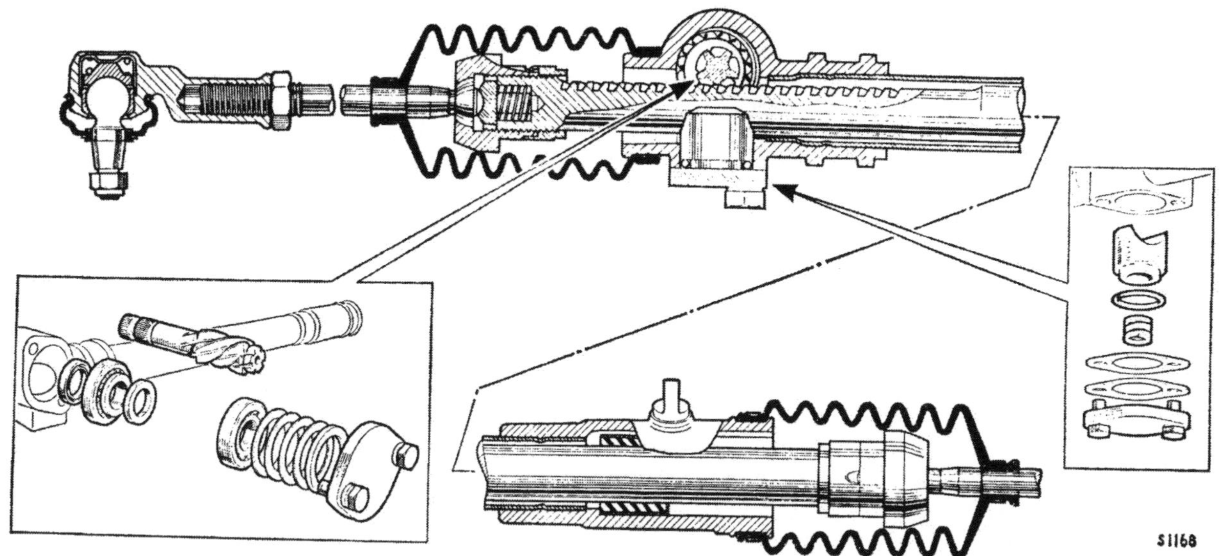

Fig. J.3
A section through the Mk. II steering-rack assembly, with the damper and pinion components shown inset

LEFT-HAND-DRIVE. The clamping bolt axis must be above the steering-column at an angle of 16° to the rack housing.

RIGHT-HAND-DRIVE. The clamping bolt axis must be below and parallel to the rack axis.

Tighten the clamping bolt to the correct torque figure (see **'GENERAL DATA'**).

23. MK. II MODELS. Pull out the plastic plug from the rack casing and insert a locator pin, i.e. a ¼ in. (6 mm.) diameter bolt approximately 2 in. (50 mm.) long into the hole. Centralize the rack until the locator pin fully engages in the rack shaft to lock the centralized assembly in position (see Fig. J.1).
24. MK. II MODELS. Refit the column onto the pinion with the clamp bolt positioned as shown in Fig. J.2, and tighten to the torque figure given in **'GENERAL DATA'**.
25. Lift the column and insert the clip into the support bracket, moving the bracket to meet the clip and **not** vice versa, so that the column remains free of load. Tighten the bracket to fascia rail securing bolts.
26. Refit and adjust the indicator trip stud until the combined measurement of the column and the stud is between 1.176 and 1.195 in. (29.87 and 30.35 mm.). Ensure that the longitudinal head of the stud is parallel to the column and tighten the locknut. Tighten the column clip to the fascia bracket.
27. Ensure that the outer column and direction indicator lever is positioned as shown in Fig. J.2, i.e. with the indicator trip stud exactly between the two cancelling mechanisms of the switch.
28. Tighten each of the rack 'U' Bolts nuts as a pair, turning each nut alternately a half-turn at a time until secure.
29. MK. II MODELS. Remove the locator pin and refit the plastic plug.
30. The remainder is a reversal of the removing procedure.

Section J.3

STEERING RACK ASSEMBLY

The rack fitted to the Mk. II models is not inter-changeable as a unit or as individual components with those racks fitted to earlier vehicles. Together with the new rack, modified steering levers are fitted and combine to provide the vehicle with a smaller turning circle. Correct wheel alignment is vitally important (see Section J.4).

Removing

1. Remove the air cleaner(s).
2. Slacken the column clamp bolt.
3. Remove the nut, bolt, and spring washer securing the column to the pinion shaft.
4. Mark the lower edge of the column shroud at the clamp bracket so that they can be refitted in line.
5. Pull the column upwards to free it from the pinion shaft.
6. Jack up the front sub-frame and remove the wheels and dampers. Remove the rack ball end retaining nuts and release the ball ends with Service tool 18G 1063.
7. Unscrew the four nuts and bolts securing the rear of the sub-frame to the body.
8. Remove the four bolts securing the sub-frame towers to the bulkhead cross-member.
9. Disconnect the exhaust pipe from the manifold and gear-change extension.
10. Disconnect the engine tie-rod.
11. Slacken the front sub-frame mounting bolts.
12. Remove the nuts from the steering rack 'U' bolts.
13. Support the body and remove the jack from the sub-frame; allow the sub-frame to drop and give clearance for the removal of the steering rack.
14. MK. II MODELS. Disconnect the remote-control gear lever extension from the floor (see Fig. A.12).

COOPER

Carry out the instructions detailed above and also:

15. Disconnect the gear lever extension from the floor.
16. Remove the exhaust pipe and silencer (Section A.3).

Dismantling

17. Disconnect the tie-rods from the steering-arms.
18. Remove the rubber gaiters.
19. Remove the damper cover plate, yoke, and spring(s).
20. Remove the pinion shaft tail bearing retaining plate, shims, thrust washer, bearing and bearing race, and withdraw the pinion. Extract the top bearing race, bearing, and thrust washer from behind the rack teeth.
21. Extract the pinion shaft oil seal.
22. Use Service tool 18G 707 to unscrew the ball housing and release the tie-rod, ball seat and tension spring. Remove the second tie-rod.
23. Withdraw the rack from the pinion end of the rack housing to obviate damage to the felt or 'Vulkollan' bush fitted in the opposite end of the rack housing.
24. Remove the bush securing screw from the rack housing, lever the felt bush at its joint and extract it. The felt bush metal sleeve must be removed if a plastic ('Vulkollan') bush is to be fitted as a replacement for the felt bush.

Inspecting

25. Clean all parts and examine for wear, particularly the rack and pinion teeth, and the rubber gaiters. Fit new parts where necessary.

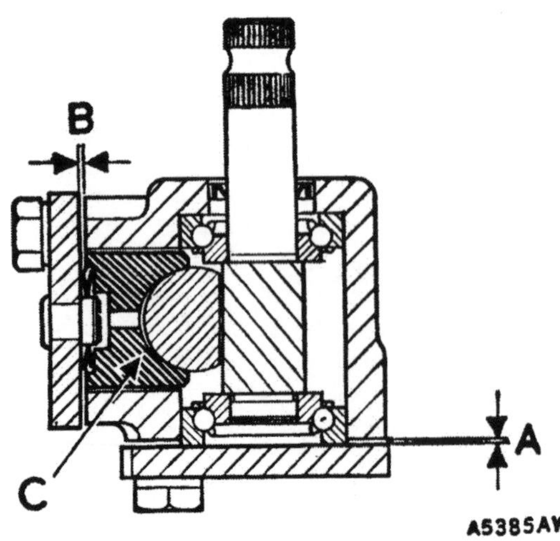

Fig. J.4
A section through the steering pinion and rack damper (1st type)

A. Take a feeler gauge measurement and fit the pinion end cover with shims to the value of the measurement minus .001 to .003 in. (.025 to .076 mm.) before fitting the damper yoke (C).
B. Measure the gap and fit shims.
C. Damper yoke.

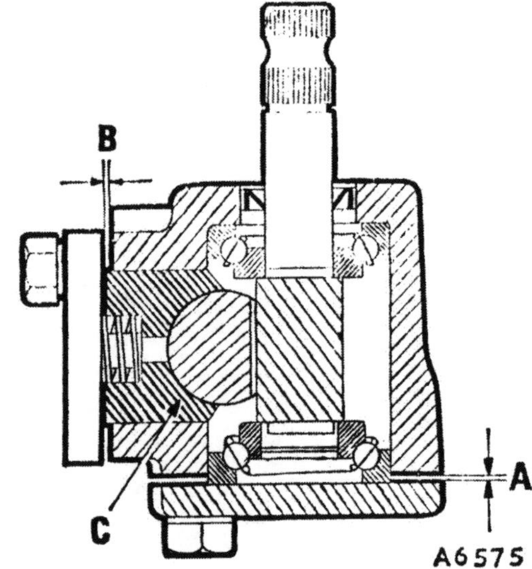

Fig. J.5
A section through the steering pinion and rack damper (2nd type)

A. Take a feeler gauge measurement and fit the pinion end cover with shims to the value of the measurement minus .001 to .003 in. (.025 to .076 mm.) before fitting the damper yoke (C).
B. Measure the gap and fit shims.
C. Damper yoke.

Reassembling

26. Reverse the dismantling sequence but note: If fitting a new felt bush (early models), soak the bush in E.P. S.A.E. 140 oil.
27. The plastic bush may be used as a replacement for the felt bush and is used together with a steel sleeved bush and spacer. Insert the spacer (plain end first) into the rack housing. Fit the plastic bush into the steel sleeve and insert it into the rack housing (plain end first), with the flats on the plastic bush positioned offset to the retaining screw hole in the rack housing. Ensure that the spacer and bush are correctly positioned and drill through the retaining screw hole and the bush with a $\frac{7}{64}$ in. (.27 mm.) drill.

    Remove all swarf; coat the retaining screw with a jointing compound and refit to secure the bush. Check that the screw does not project into the bore of the plastic bush.
28. PINION ADJUSTMENT (EARLY MODELS). Refit the cover without the shims, but do not over-tighten the screws. Measure the gap between the cover and the housing. Remove the cover and add shims to the thickness of the measurement minus .002 in. (.05 mm.). Refit the cover with jointing compound.
29. PINION ADJUSTMENT (MK. II MODELS). Refit the pinion and bearings as shown in Fig. J.3. Add sufficient shims together with the spacer washer to provide a clearance of approximately .010 in. (.25 mm.) between the rack housing and the cover plate. Fit and lightly tighten the cover plate. Take a feeler gauge measurement of the clearance (A) and reduce the shimming by the measurement taken, less .002 to .005 in. (.05 to .13 mm.), to give the required pre-load.

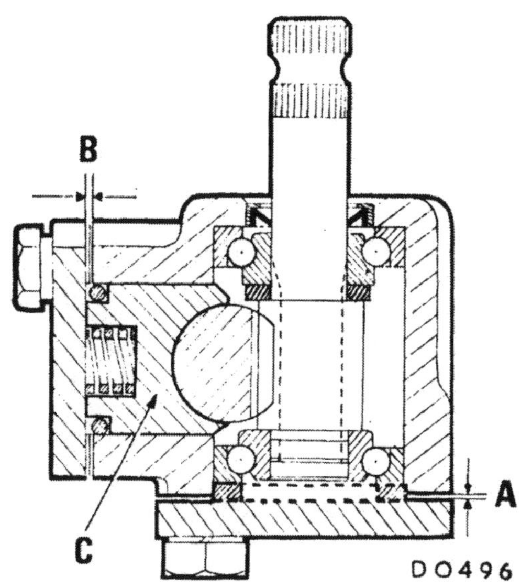

Fig. J.6
A section through the steering pinion and rack damper (Mk. II models)

A. Take a feeler gauge measurement and fit the pinion end cover with shims to the value of the measurement minus .002 to .005 in. (.05 to .13 mm.) before fitting the damper yoke (C).
B. Measure the gap and fit shims.
C. Damper yoke.

30. Refers to item 22. Screw the ball housing locking ring onto the rack end as far as it will go and refit the lock washer. On models not fitted with a lock washer, fit a new locking ring. Refit the seat spring, seat, tie-rod and ball housing, and tighten up until the tie-rod is pinched. Slacken the housing one-eighth of a turn and tighten the locking ring to the recommended torque. Punch the lock washer into the slots of the housing and locking ring. If no lock washer is fitted, punch the lips of the locking ring into the slots of the ball housing and rack.
31. DAMPER ADJUSTMENT (1ST TYPE). Refit the yoke with the disc springs but without the packing shims.

    With the rack in the straight-ahead position, tighten the cover screws until it is just possible to rotate the pinion with the pre-load gauge, 18G 207 and 18G 207 A set at 15 lb. in. (.17 kg. m.). Measure the gap between the damper housing flange and the rack housing. Remove, and then refit the damper with shims to the thickness of the measurement minus .002 in. (.05 mm.).
32. DAMPER ADJUSTMENT (2ND TYPE AND MK. II MODELS). Refit the yoke and cover plate without the spring.

    Follow the measurement checking procedure given in item 31 and refit the yoke with its 'O' ring seal (Mk. II models), together with the spring and cover plate, with shims to the value of the measurement plus .002 in. to .005 in. (.05 to .13 mm.).
33. Refit the rubber gaiters to the housing and the tie-rods. Before securing the gaiter clip on the tie-rod at the pinion end, stand the assembly upright and pour in approximately $\frac{1}{3}$ pint (.4 U.S. pint, .19 litre) of Extreme Pressure S.A.E. 90 oil through the end of the gaiter. Refit and tighten the gaiter clip.
34. Check that the tie-rods have an equal number of threads visible behind each locknut, i.e. approximately eight threads on early racks and 11 threads on the Mk. II racks.
35. EARLY MODELS. Centralize the rack in the housing. The full travel of the rack in each direction is 1.75 in. (44.5 mm.).

Refitting

ALL MODELS

Reverse the removal instructions, but note:

36. Refit the rack to the body with the 'U' bolts lightly tightened to allow the pinion to accept the column alignment.
37. Align the road wheels to the straight-ahead position.
38. Carry out the operations 20, and 22 to 30 in Section J.2.
39. Check and reset the wheel alignment (see Section J.4).

Section J.4

FRONT WHEEL ALIGNMENT

Checking

When checking or adjusting the front wheel alignment it is essential to use equipment designed to work at the specified height and diameter, and preferably a gauge which measures the angles involved rather than the difference in distance between the wheels in front of and behind the centres.

With the car unladen, tyres at the correct pressures, and the steering in the straight-ahead position, each wheel should make an angle of 70' 30 " with the longitudinal axis

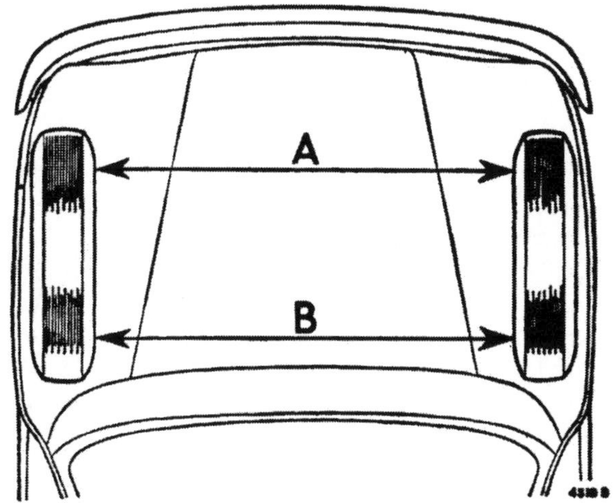

Fig. J.7
The front wheel alignment check must be taken with the front wheel in the straight-ahead position. Dimension (A) must be $\frac{1}{16}$ in. (1.6 mm.) greater than (B)

of the car. When this angle is correct the distance between the front of the wheels will be $\frac{1}{16}$ in. (1.6 mm.) greater than that at the rear (see Fig. J.7).

When measuring distances rather than angles the measurements must be made on a 14½ in. (368.3 mm.) diameter on the side wall of the tyre at a distance of 9.4 in. (239 mm.) above the ground.

If a base-bar alignment gauge is used, take two measurements; take a measurement at the front, mark the point on the tyres with chalk, push the car forward half a road wheel revolution and take the second measurement at the same points on the tyres and behind the centres.

With an optical gauge, take two readings with the car moved forward 180° and three with it moved forward 120°. The average figure should then be calculated.

Adjustment (Early models)

To adjust the track, slacken the tie-rod ball joint locknuts and the rubber gaiter clips, and turn each tie-rod the same number of turns until the adjustment is correct.

The tie-rods must be exactly the same length.

MK. II MODELS

The later steering-rack provides a smaller turning circle and it is vitally important that the wheel alignment is checked, and adjusted if necessary, following the correct procedure. Incorrect adjustment could result in excess articulation of the drive shaft constant velocity joints, and subsequent fouling of the suspension tie-rods by the road wheels when on full lock. Checking and adjustment must only be carried out when the vehicle is at 'kerbside' trim, i.e. fully equipped but without occupants or excess luggage.

Checking

1. With the vehicle resting on its wheels, turn the steering on each lock and check the clearance between the road wheel and the suspension tie-rod. The minimum clearance should not be less than ¾ in. (19 mm.), or with the suspension at full rebound, not less than ¼ in. (6.5 mm.).

   Correct adjustment on each tie-rod will be indicated by the clearance figures given above being approximately the same on each side. Check the wheel alignment with an optical gauge, see item 6.

Adjustment

2. Slacken the rack tie-rod locknuts and the gaiter clips. Disconnect the ball joints from the steering levers, using Service tool 18G 1063.
3. Lift the floor covering and remove the rubber grommet from the floor panel (opposite side to the rack pinion).
4. Pull out the plastic plug from the rack body and insert a locator pin, i.e. ¼ in. (6 mm.) diameter bolt into the hole (see Fig. J.1).
5. Centralize the rack until the locator pin fully engages with the rack, to lock the centralized assembly.
6. Use an optical setting gauge and align the road wheels to the straight-ahead position, i.e. $\frac{1}{16}$ in. (1.6 mm.) toe out, and in alignment with the centre line of the car.
7. Adjust the tie-rods until each ball pin will correctly locate its steering lever without disturbing the alignment given in item 6, and secure in position.
8. Recheck the setting and adjust equally each tie-rod until the setting is obtained and tighten the locknuts. Ensure that the rubber gaiters are not under stress from twist and tighten the securing clips.
9. Remove the locator pin and refit the plastic plug.
10. Recheck the adjustment as detailed in item 1.
11. Refit the floor grommet and covering.

    NOTE.–The hole in the rack from which the plastic plug was removed MUST NOT be utilized for the purpose of 'topping up' with lubricant.

Section J.5

STEERING RACK LUBRICATION

Lubricating nipples are not provided and rack lubrication is only necessary if leakage is evident from the rack housing or the rubber gaiters.

The following procedure should be followed provided the leakage can be rectified without the assembly being removed.

1. Centralize the steering rack.
2. Remove the gaiter retaining clip on the driver's side.
3. Inject $\frac{1}{3}$ pint (.2 litre) of E.P. S.A.E. 90 oil into the rubber gaiter.
4. Refit the gaiter clip and turn the steering from side to side to distribute the oil through the housing.

WARNING.–If the vehicle is hoisted with its front wheels clear of the ground care should be taken to avoid forceful movement of the wheels from lock to lock, otherwise damage may occur within the steering mechanism.

Section J.6

NYLON TIE-ROD BALL ENDS

Later ball joints have nylon seats sealed for life and protected by rubber boots; no lubrication is required.

The rubber boots must be maintained in good condition, and if it is found that a boot has become damaged in service both boot and joint must be renewed. However, if a boot is damaged in the workshop during the removal of a joint which has therefore not become contaminated by road dirt, the boot alone may be renewed.

Before fitting a new boot smear the area adjacent to the joint with a little De.:tragrease Super G.P. lubricant.

SECTION K

THE FRONT SUSPENSION

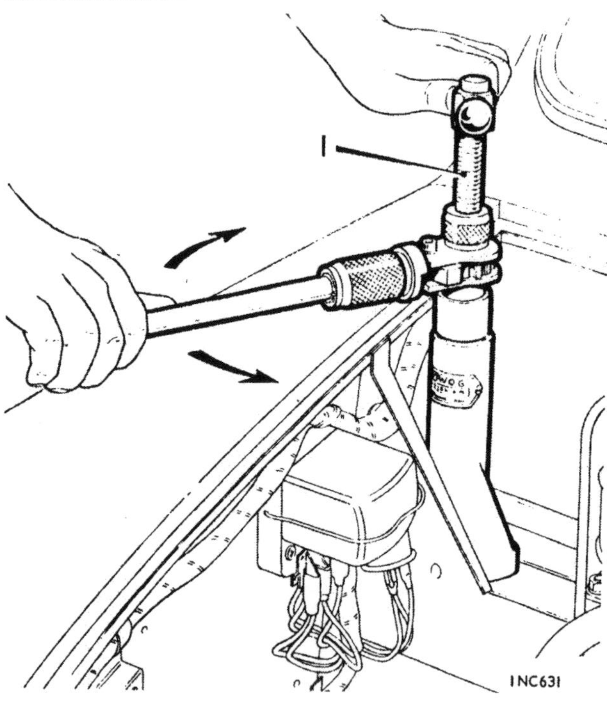

Fig. K.1
Compressing the spring unit
1. Service tool 18G 574 B

Section K.1

SPRING UNITS
(Rubber Suspension)

Compressing

1. Slacken one bolt (or nut) and remove the other securing the sub-frame towers to the engine bulkhead cross-member.
2. Move the locking plate to one side to expose the access hole in the cross-member. Refit the bolt (or nut) and tighten both.
3. Insert Service tool 18G 574 B through the cross-member, locate the body of the tool over the two sub-frame bolts (or nuts), and screw the centre of the tool nine complete turns into the spring unit. Use the ratchet handle to turn the centre nut and make contact with the body of the tool. Hold the centre screw to prevent further rotation and then turn the ratchet handle clockwise to compress the spring sufficiently to allow removal of the spring strut from the tower. Do not over-compress the spring.

Removing

4. Jack up the car after compressing the spring, and remove the road wheel.
5. Remove the bump rubber from the tower.
6. Remove the retaining nut and release the upper suspension arm with Service tool 18G 1063.
7. With the spring unit compressed, lever the strut from the spring unit, see Fig. K.4.
8. Detach the hydraulic damper, dismantle the upper arm pivot and remove the upper arm.
9. Hold the centre screw of the tool to prevent it turning, screw the ratchet handle upwards to release the spring compression, remove the tool, and extract the spring unit from the tower.

Refitting

10. Reverse the removing instructions.

Section K.2

SWIVEL HUBS

Removing

1. Jack up the front of the vehicle, place supports under the sub-frame and remove the road wheel.
2. Remove the steering lever ball joint retaining nut and release the ball joint using Service tool 18G 1063.
3. Mark the drive shaft flange for correct reassembly and disconnect the inner flexible joint by removing the four outer 'U' bolts.
   On models which have a universal joint flange, remove the four retaining nuts.
4. Slacken the front brake pipe union from its hose connection and unscrew the nut securing the hose to the anchor bracket. Unscrew the hose from the backplate (it will still remain attached to the anchor bracket and pipe union).
   Disc brake models. Remove the brake calliper and support it; **do not** allow it to hang on the hydraulic hose.
5. Disconnect the tie-rod from the lower suspension arm.
6. Remove the upper and lower swivel hub ball pin retaining nuts and release the ball pins from the suspension arms using Service tool 18G 1063.
7. Withdraw the swivel hub and drive shaft from the vehicle.

Dismantling

8. Remove the brake-drum (except disc brake models).
9. Extract the split pin and remove the nut, and distance washer (outer taper collar on Disc brake models).
10. Drift the drive shaft from the flange and hub. Drift the driving flange from the hub using Service tool 18G 575.
    Disc brake models. Tap the end of the drive shaft with a hide mallet and pull off the driving flange and disc assembly. Remove the drive shaft, the inner and outer bearing and distance ring from the hub.
11. Remove the bearing to flange distance piece and outer seal, the inner seal with water shield (if fitted) and spacer.

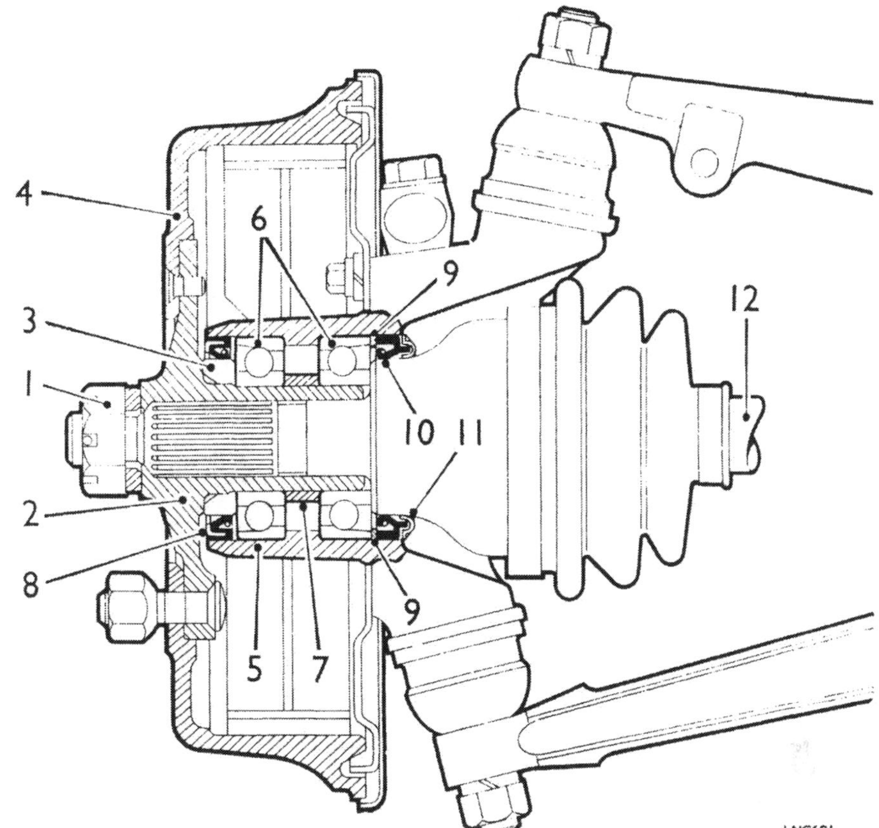

Fig. K.2

The swivel hub assembly

(Mini range with front drum brakes)

1. Drive shaft nut.
2. Driving flange.
3. Distance piece.
4. Brake-drum.
5. Hub assembly.
6. Hub bearings.
7. Bearing distance ring.
8. Outer oil seal.
9. Spacer for oil seal.
10. Inner oil seal.
11. Water shield.
12. Drive shaft.

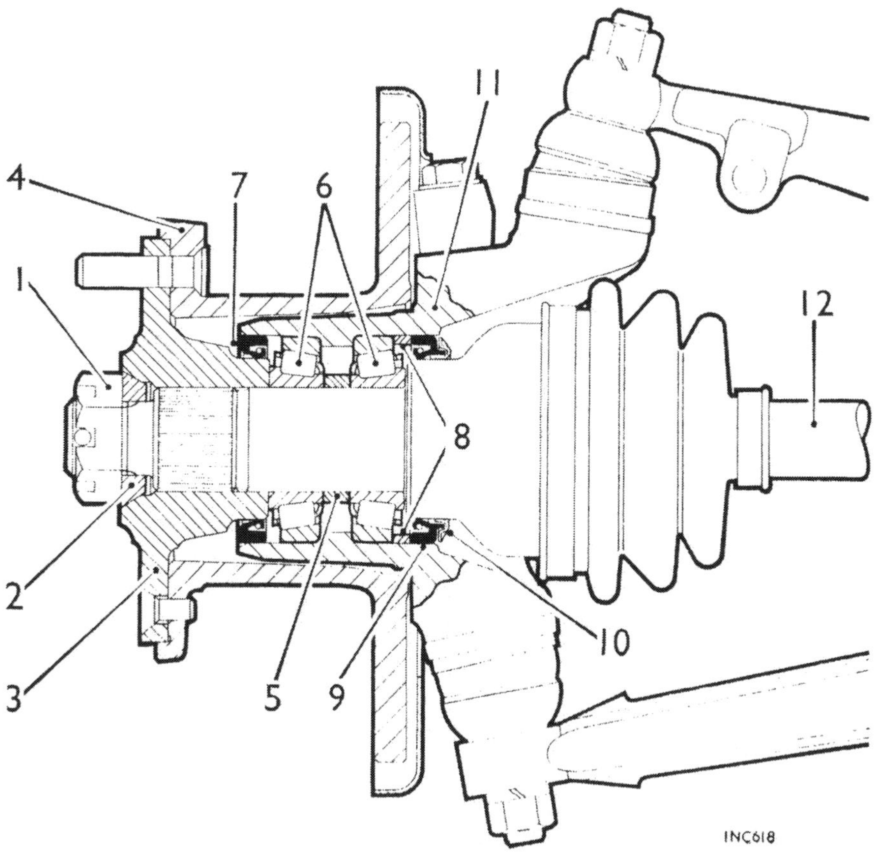

Fig. K.3

The swivel hub assembly

(Cooper 'S' and 1275 GT)

1. Drive shaft nut.
2. Outer tapered collar.
3. Driving flange.
4. Hub and disc assembly.
5. Bearing distance rings.
6. Taper roller bearings.
7. Outer oil seal.
8. Spacer (inner bearing to seal).
9. Inner oil seal.
10. Water shield.
11. Swivel hub.
12. Drive shaft.

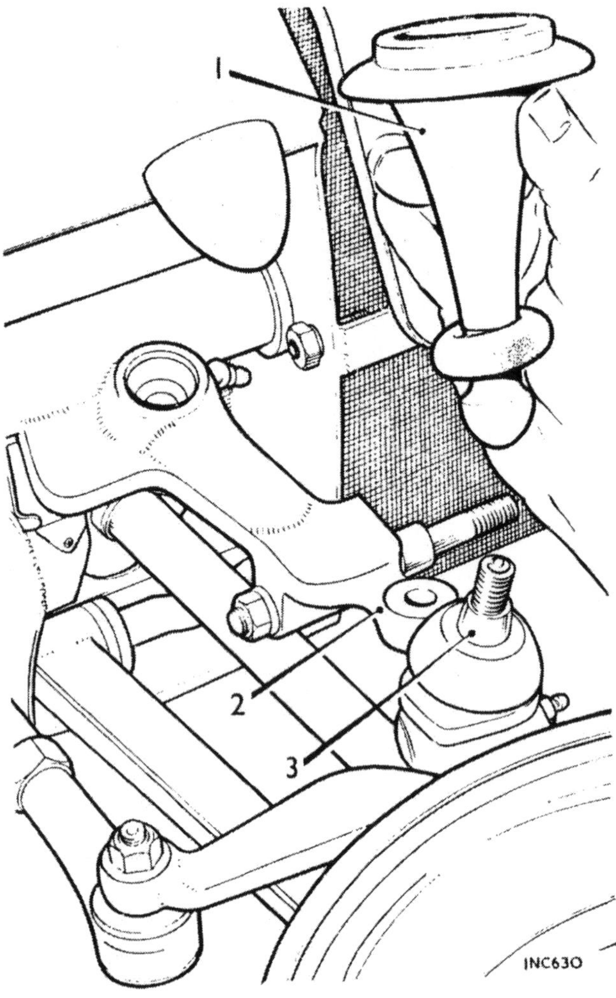

Fig. K.4
Removing the spring strut (1) with the spring unit compressed and the upper support arm (2) removed from the hub ball pin (3)

12. Drift out the inner race of each bearing and remove the distance ring. Use Service tool 18G 260 H to withdraw the outer races.

13. **Disc brake models.** Substitute for operations 11 and 12. Remove the outer seal and the inner seal with water shield (if fitted), drive out the inner and outer bearing cups with a brass drift, note that the hub has recesses for this but take care not to damage the hub bore.

Reassembling

14. Reassembling is a reversal of the dismantling procedure but note the following points:

    a. Pack the bearings only with a high-melting point grease, e.g. (Duckhams L.B.10).

    b. When refitting 'thrust type' bearings, ensure that the sides marked 'THRUST' are facing each other, with the distance ring between them.

    c. When replacing the inner oil seal, ensure that the later type single lipped seal together with its plastic water shield is used. This seal and water shield must be fitted as a pair and replaces all seals previously used for the various models.

    d. Use Service tool 18G 134 and adaptor 18G 134 DO to fit both new seals to the hub. Ensure that the water shield is fitted to the drive shaft as shown in Fig. K.5.

Refitting

15. Reverse the removing procedure noting the following points:

    a. Tighten the ball pin retaining nuts to the torque figure given in 'GENERAL DATA'.

    b. Tighten the drive shaft nut to the correct torque figure, see **'GENERAL DATA'** for the particular model application.

    c. **Disc brake models.** Check the run-out on the periphery of the disc. If this exceeds .006 in. (.15 mm.) reposition the driving flange assembly on the drive shaft splines until the run-out is within this limit.

    d. Use a new split pin to lock the drive shaft nut, refit the brake drum or calliper as applicable.

    e. Bleed the braking system (Section M.8) if the brake pipe has been disconnected.

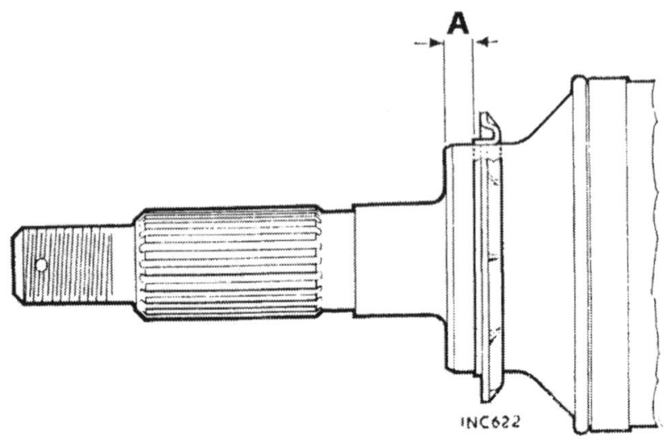

Fig. K.5
The fitted location of the water shield on the drive shaft before the hub is refitted
'A' = ¼ in. (6.4 mm.)

Section K.3

SWIVEL HUB BALL JOINTS

Removing

1. Compress the rubber spring unit as detailed in Section K.1 or depressurize the Hydrolastic system, see Section H.7.
2. Carry out operations 1, 2 and 4 in Section K.2.
3. Fit Service tool 18G 304 with adaptor bolts 18G 304 F to the wheel hub studs, ensure that the swivel hub is free of the upper and lower suspension arms and extract the hub from the drive shaft.

Dismantling

4. Remove the Service tool and secure the swivel hub assembly firmly in a vice.
5. Remove the ball housing dust seal and lubricator.
6. Tap back the lock washer and unscrew the upper ball pin retainer using Service tool 18G 587.
7. Repeat operation 6 on the lower ball joint noting the spring fitted under the ball pin seat.
8. Clean and examine the components and fit replacements as necessary.

Adjusting

9. Reassemble the upper ball pin assembly; refit the ball pin seat, pin and retainer without the packing shims and locking washer.
10. Screw down the ball pin retainer until there is no free movement between the ball pin and its seating. Measure the gap between the retainer and the swivel hub, see Fig. K.6.
11. Note that the thickness of a new locking washer is .036 in. (.9 mm.); deduct this figure from the gap measurement taken in operation 10 to obtain the correct thickness of shims required.
    The final assembly must have no nip to .003 in. (.7 mm.) end-float, add a further shim if necessary to obtain the correct adjustment.
12. Pack the joint with grease and refit the assembly complete with shims and a new locking washer to the hub.
13. Tighten the ball pin retainer with Service tool 18G 372 and adaptor 18G 587 to the torque figure given in **'GENERAL DATA'.**
14. Repeat operations 9 to 13 for the lower ball pin, except that the spring fitted in the lower assembly must be removed when taking the gap measurement as detailed in operation 10 and refitted under the ball pin seating on final assembly.
15. Tap up the locking washer against three flats of the ball pin retainer (one flat must be adjacent to the brake disc on disc brake models).
16. Fit new ball pin dust seals if required.

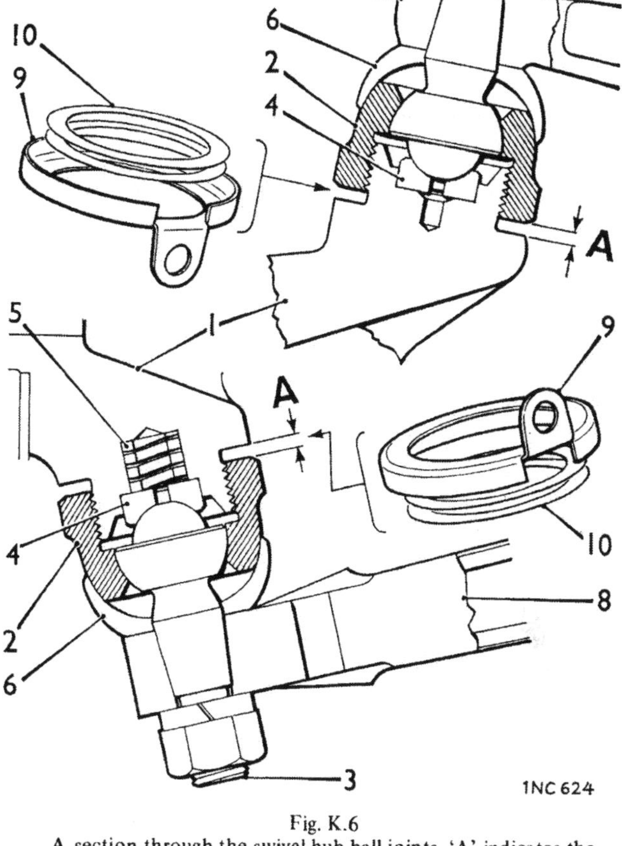

Fig. K.6
A section through the swivel hub ball joints. 'A' indicates the gap measured for shim adjustment

1. Hub assembly.
2. Ball pin retainer.
3. Ball pin.
4. Ball pin seat.
5. Seat spring (lower assembly only).
6. Dust seal.
7. Suspension upper arm.
8. Suspension lower arm.
9. Locking washer } fitted on final assembly.
10. Shims } fitted on final assembly.

Refitting

17. Refitting is a reversal of the removing procedure, tighten the upper and lower ball pin nuts to the torque figure given in **'GENERAL DATA'**.
18. Tighten the drive shaft nut to the correct torque figure, see **'GENERAL DATA'** for the particular model application.
19. Release the rubber spring unit from compression as detailed in Section K.1, operation 9; or pressurize the Hydrolastic system as detailed in Section H.7.
20. Tighten the brake pipe connection and bleed the braking system (Section M.8).
21. **Disc brake models.** Refit the brake calliper.
22. Refit the road wheel and lower the car.

Section K.4

UPPER ARM
(Rubber Suspension)

Removing

1. Compress the spring as in Section K.1.
2. Jack up the vehicle and remove the road wheel and damper.
3. Remove the ball-pin retaining nut, release the upper suspension arm with Service tool 18G 1063 and withdraw the strut, see Fig. K.4.
4. Remove the nut and washer from each end of the shaft.
5. Remove the front thrust collar retaining plate, the collar and the seal and push the shaft forward.
6. Remove the rear thrust washer and seal and manoeuvre the arm from the frame.
7. Extract the needle-roller bearings from the arm with Service tool 18G 581.

Refitting

Reverse the removing instructions, but note:

8. Lubricate all parts with grease.
9. Fit the needle-roller bearings with the marked ends outwards, using Service tool 18G 582 and adaptor 18G 582 A to push them into position.
10. Lubricate the spring unit strut nylon cup with Dextragrease Super G.P.

Section K.5

LOWER ARM

Removing

1. Jack up and remove the road wheel and damper.
2. Support the suspension with a jack under the brake-drum.
3. Disconnect the tie-rod from the lower arm.
4. Release the lower arm from the swivel hub with Service tool 18G 1063.
5. Remove the nut and washer from the rear end of the shaft and withdraw the shaft.

NOTE.—Later vehicles are fitted with modified lower arms and these are fitted with composite steel/rubber bushes. These new parts can be fitted to earlier vehicles but only as complete sets.

6. Refitting is a reversal of the removing instructions but note the following:

   Tighten the shaft securing nut when the vehicle is resting on the road wheels—to prevent pre-loading of the rubber bushes.

Section K.6

SUSPENSION STRUTS
(Rubber Suspension)

Some cars have been fitted with struts having a circular-section washer between the body of the suspension strut and the knuckle end. When fitting a new strut to these vehicles, make sure the washer is included.

Section K.7

DISPLACER UNITS
(Hydrolastic Suspension)

Removing

1. Jack up the car and remove the road wheel.
2. Depressurize and evacuate the Hydrolastic system (see Section H.7).
3. Release the displacer strut dust seal from the nylon seat and extract the strut from the displacer unit.
4. Disconnect the displacer hose from the union on the engine bulkhead.
5. Remove the suspension upper arm (see Section K.4).
6. Push the displacer upwards and remove two screws to release the displacer bracket from inside the sub-frame tower.
7. Rotate the displacer anti-clockwise and withdraw it from the sub-frame.

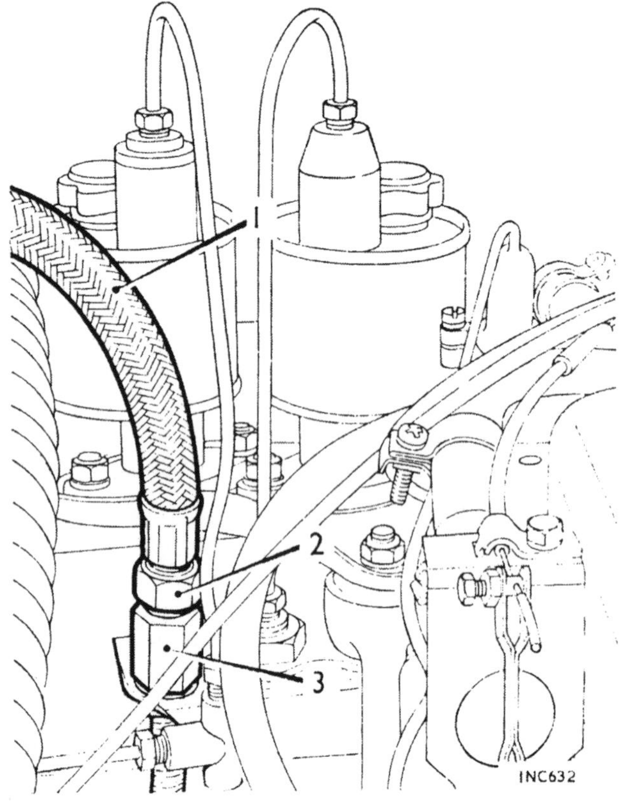

Fig. K.7
The right-hand front displacer hose connector

1. Displacer hose. 2. Hose nut.
3. Connector.

Refitting

8. Reverse the removing instructions.
9. Rotate the displacer clockwise to lock it into the registers on the locating plate.
10. Lubricate the strut ball end and the nylon seat with Dextragrease Super G.P. and make sure the dust seal is fitted over the lip of the nylon cup.
11. Evacuate and pressurize the system (see Section H.7).

Section K.8

UPPER SUSPENSION ARMS (Hydrolastic Suspension)

Removal

Depressurize the Hydrolastic system as in Section H.7 and follow the instruction in K.4 for arm removal.

Section K.9

SWIVEL HUB OUTER OIL SEAL

The following instructions will permit a leaking outer seal to be replaced when the driving flange is removed.

NOTE.—**A bearing overhaul will still require swivel hub removal as in Section K.2.**

Removing

1. Remove the hub cover, extract the split pin, and slacken the drive shaft nut.
2. Slacken the wheel nuts and jack up the vehicle.
3. Take off the road wheel and remove the brake-drum.
4. Remove the drive shaft nut and assemble the Service tool 18G 304 and 18G 304 F to the drive flange.
5. Replace the Service tool centre screw with adaptor 18G 304 P and use the impulse extractor 18G 284 to remove the flange.
6. Should the outer bearing inner race come away with the driving flange, it can be removed with Service tool 18G 705 and adaptor 18G 705 B.

Refitting

7. Refit the inner bearing race (if extracted).
8. Fit the new seal and apply a suitable amount of lubricant to the lip to prevent burning.
9. Insert the outer bearing distance piece into the seal with the chamfered bore to the outside.
10. Assemble the drive flange to the hub, drifting it into position gently, turning the flange 180 degrees several times to align the bearing distance piece with the flange boss.
11. Refit the brake-drum.
12. Refit the drive shaft washer, chamfered bore facing inward and refit the nut.
13. Tighten the drive shaft nut to the torque figure given in 'GENERAL DATA' and secure with the split pin.

SECTION L

THE HYDRAULIC DAMPERS

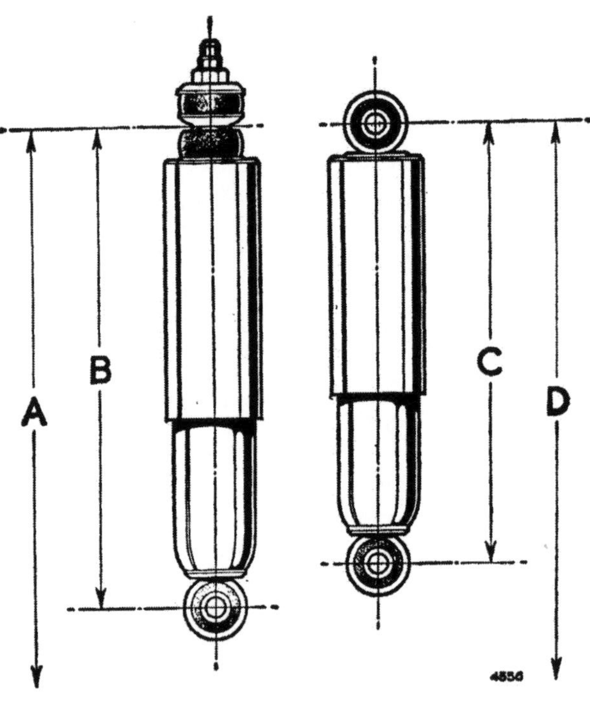

Fig. L.1
The hydraulic dampers

REAR
A. Extended length $15\frac{3}{16}$ in. (385.76 mm.).
Van only $16\frac{1}{8}$ in. (409.6 mm.).

B. Compressed length $9\frac{9}{16}$ in. (242.89 mm.).
Van only 10 in. (254 mm.).

FRONT
C. Compressed length 8½ in. (215.90 mm.).
D. Extended length 12¾ in. (323.85 mm.).

Section L.1

REMOVAL AND REFITTING

Front

1. Jack up and remove the road wheel.
2. Support the suspension under the brake-drum.
3. Remove the upper and lower securing nuts and pull the damper from the mounting spigots.
4. Hold the damper upright in a vice and compress and extend it six times to expel air. Retain the damper upright until refitted.
5. Fit new rubber bushes as required.
6. Refit.

Right-hand damper (rear)

7. Remove the upper damper mounting nuts from inside the luggage boot.
8. Jack up the vehicle and remove the road wheel. Take off the lower mounting nut and washer collapse the damper, and remove it from its anchorage point on the radius arm.
9. Retain the damper in an upright position after removal from the car.
10. Make certain that the rubber bushes are in good condition; fit new bushes if they are worn or damaged.
11. Before refitting a damper to the vehicle it must be primed (see Section L.2).
12. When refitting the rear dampers make certain that the rubber cone spring and the spring strut are correctly located on their individual spigots whilst the radius arm is being raised to reconnect the upper end of the damper.

Left-hand damper (rear)

Access to the damper upper fixing nuts can only be obtained after the fuel tank has either been completely removed, or (as on most cars) it is only necessary to release the tank from its mounting position. On cars produced having a fuel tank with a rigid tube the tank must be drained and removed (see Section D.1).

TO RELEASE THE FUEL TANK

13. Remove the fuel filler cap and release the tank securing strap.
14. Pivot the tank around the tank front hose connection, taking care not to damage the hose, and lift the rear of the tank towards the centre-line of the car until access to the damper is obtained.
15. Remove and refit a damper as operation sequence 7 to 12 for right-hand damper.

Section L.2

PRIMING

If air is suspected in a hydraulic damper, remove the damper from the vehicle and stand it in a vertical position for approximately five hours, then prime as follows.

Armstrong

Hold the damper vertically, extend to its full travel and then compress slowly. Continue to extend and compress until there is no free travel when changing direction of stroke.

Girling

Hold the damper, with the dust shield uppermost, at an angle of 15° to 20° to the vertical. Extend the damper about 76 mm. very slowly and then compress fully. Rotate the dust shield at the same time. Repeat until all free play has disappeared. Do not fully extend the damper during this process.

New dampers need only be held in their vertical position for a few minutes before priming. After priming, always store dampers in a vertical position.

Section L.3

REAR DAMPERS
(Moke)

Removing

1. Jack up and remove the road wheel.
2. Remove the cover from the upper mounting point inside the vehicle.
3. Remove the nuts from the upper and lower mounting points, collapse the damper, and pull it from its anchorage on the radius arm.

SECTION M

THE BRAKING SYSTEM

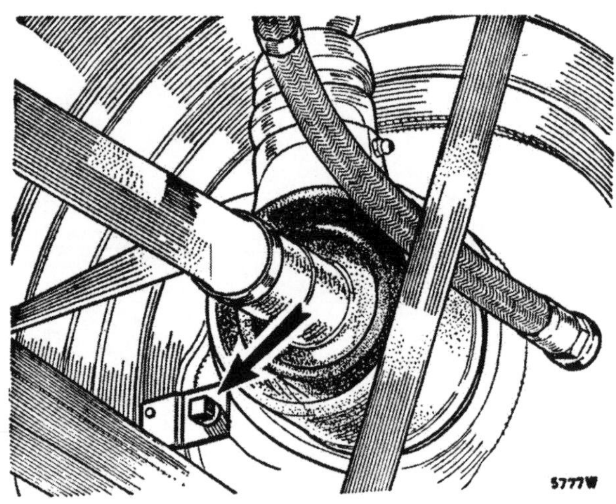

Fig. M.1
The front brake-shoe adjuster. One square-headed adjuster is provided on each of the four brake back-plates

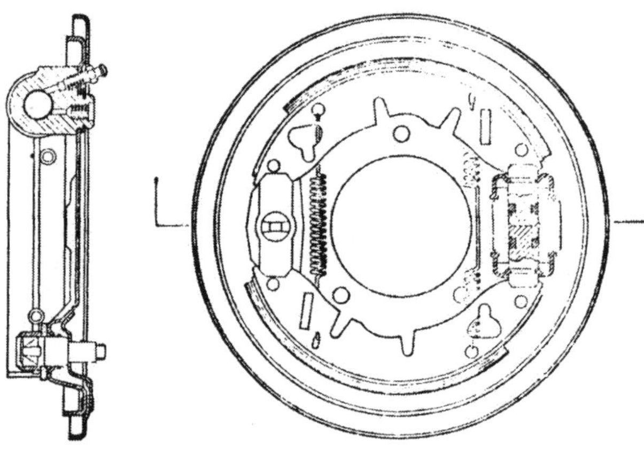

Fig. M.2
The right-hand front brake assembly, showing the fitted positions of the leading and trailing brake-shoes, with the pull-off springs anchored in the correct holes in the shoe web

Section M.1

MASTER CYLINDER

See Section E.4, but note the non-return valve fitted in this cylinder.

Section M.2

ADJUSTMENT

Early models have one square-headed adjuster screw projecting from each brake backplate. For adjustment on cars having two-leading-shoe brakes see Section M.10.

Jack up the car and turn the adjuster in a clockwise direction until the wheel is locked and then slacken the screw until the shoes are just free of the drum.

COOPER

Front disc brakes are not adjustable.

The rear brakes are adjusted as above.

Hand brake

ALL MODELS

1. Adjust the brake-shoes as detailed above.
2. Apply the hand brake to the third notch on the ratchet.
3. Take up excessive cable movement, turning the nuts at the lever trunnion until the wheels can only just be turned by heavy hand pressure.
4. Ensure that the wheels rotate freely when the hand brake is released.

Section M.3

SHOE ASSEMBLIES

Removing (front)

1. Jack up and remove the road wheel.
2. Unscrew the two retaining screws and pull off the drum.
3. Note the position of each spring; release them from the shoe webs and remove the springs and shoes.

   NOTE.—Do not press the pedal when the shoes and springs have been removed.

Removing (rear)

As for the front shoes.

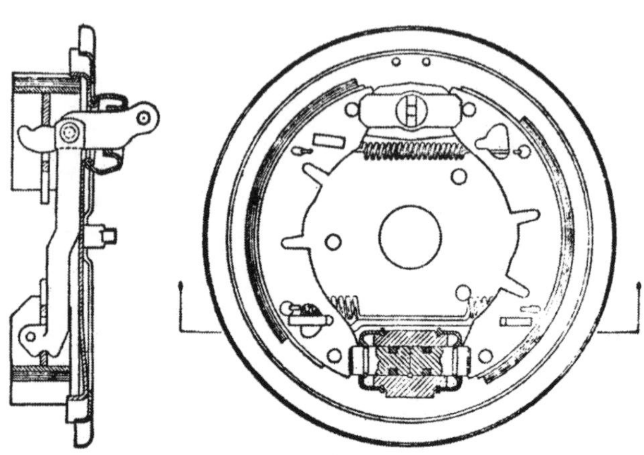

Fig. M.3
The right-hand rear brake assembly, showing the pull-off springs anchored in the correct holes in the shoe web

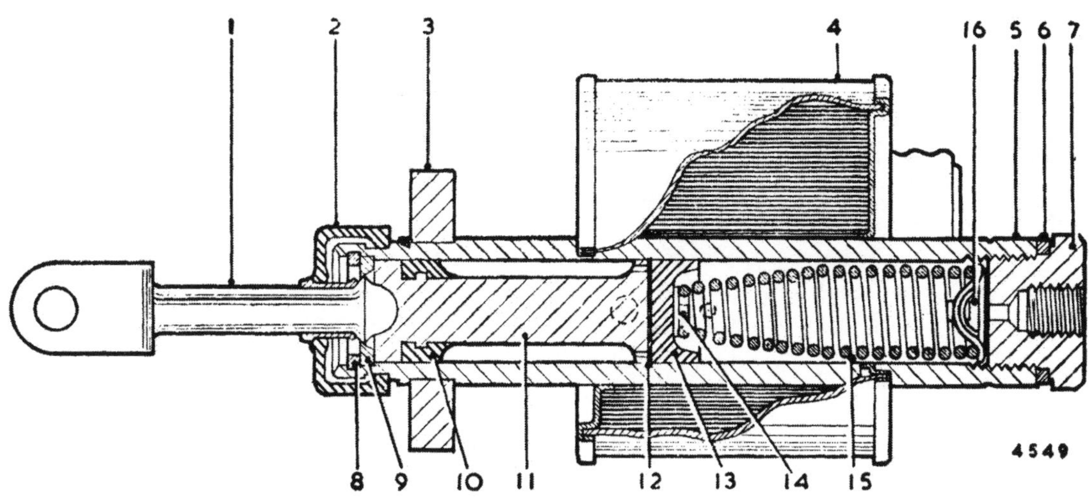

Fig. M.4
A section through the brake master cylinder

1.	Push-rod.	7.	End plug.	12.	Piston washer.
2.	Rubber boot.	8.	Circlip.	13.	Main cup.
3.	Mounting flange.	9.	Stop washer.	14.	Spring retainer.
4.	Supply tank.	10.	Secondary cup.	15.	Return spring.
5.	Body.	11.	Piston.	16.	Non-return valve.
6.	Washer.				

Refitting (front and rear)

Reverse the removing instructions.

COOPER **Removing disc brake friction pads**

1. Jack up, remove the wheel.
2. Depress the pad retaining spring and withdraw the split pins (Fig. M.6).
3. Remove the spring and withdraw the pads from the calliper.
4. Thoroughly clean the exposed face of each piston and the recesses in the calliper.

On later cars the pads are retained in the callipers by means of split pins only. The pins pass through the calliper body and the pads, and no pad retaining springs are fitted. To remove the pads, it is only necessary to remove the split pins and extract the pads with a direct pull. Pads for the earlier- and later-type callipers are NOT INTERCHANGEABLE.

Refitting

5. Press the pistons back into the calliper with Service tool 18G 672.
6. Check that the cut-away edge of each piston is facing upwards and that anti-squeak shims are correctly placed.
7. Insert the new pads and check that they move easily in the calliper.
8. Remove any high spots from the pressure plate by careful filing.
9. Refit the spring, press it down and insert the split pins.
10. Press the pedal several times to adjust the brakes.

Section M.4

WHEEL CYLINDERS

Removing front and rear

1. Carry out instructions 1, 2, and 3 in Section M.3.
2. Thoroughly clean the backplate.
3. Disconnect the flexible hose.
4. Unscrew and remove the bleed screw.
5. Remove the circlip and dished washer from the cylinder boss protruding through the backplate and withdraw the cylinder.

COOPER **Removing (rear only)**

As instructions 1 to 5 above.

Dismantling

6. Remove the dust seals from the ends of the cylinder and extract both pistons.
7. Remove the piston seals with the fingers only.
8. Clean all parts with brake fluid.

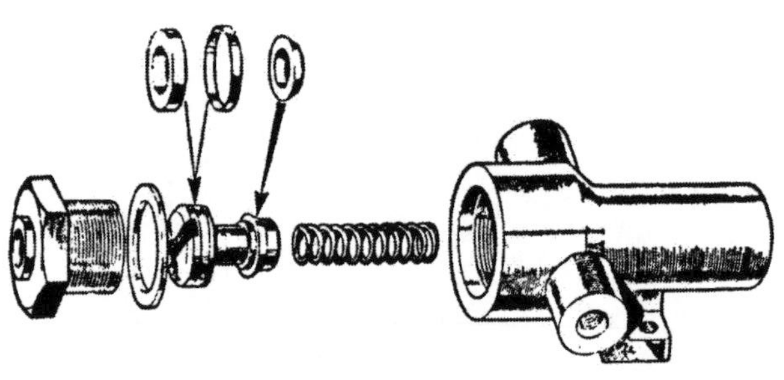

Fig. M.5
The hydraulic pressure regulating valve components

Reassembling

9. Fit new parts as required and then reverse the dismantling procedure.

Refitting

Reverse the removal instructions and bleed the system.

Section M.5

PRESSURE REGULATING VALVE

Removing

1. Disconnect the three pressure lines, unscrew the securing nut and withdraw the assembly from the rear sub-frame cross-member.

Overhauling

2. Clean the exterior.
3. Remove the end plug and sealing washer.
4. Extract the valve assembly and return spring.
5. If the rubber seals are not in good condition, fit a new piston and seal assembly.
6. Clean all parts with brake fluid, reassemble and refit.

Section M.6

INTENSIFIER

COOPER (Early models)

The brake intensifier is only fitted on early models. Later models have a pressure regulating valve incorporated in the system (see Section M.5).

Removing

1. Slacken the top pipe union, remove the nuts and washers and take out the mounting bolts.
2. Completely unscrew the tip union and withdraw the pipe and union.
3. Unscrew the bottom pipe union and withdraw the pipe and union.
4. Remove the intensifier.

Dismantling

5. Hold the intensifier in a vice and unscrew the large hexagon plug.
   NOTE.–The plug is under spring pressure.
6. Extract the piston assembly and springs.
7. Thoroughly clean all parts with brake fluid and examine for wear.

Reassembling

8. Renew all worn or damaged parts. If the rubber seals have deteriorated, renew the piston assembly.

Refitting

Reverse the removing instructions.
Bleed the system.

Section M.7

DISC BRAKE CALLIPER

COOPER

Removing and dismantling

Do not separate the two halves of the calliper; each piston assembly must be dealt with individually.

1. Disconnect the tie-rod from the steering-arm.
2. Remove the locking plate from the dust cover.

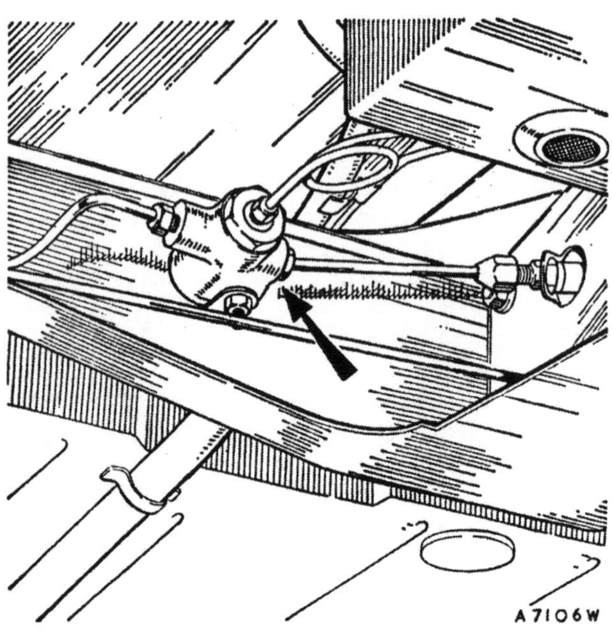

Fig. M.6
The hydraulic pressure regulating valve

3. Unscrew the two bolts securing the calliper to the hub, detach both parts of the dust cover and remove the calliper without disconnecting the brake pipe.
4. Withdraw the pads.
5. Clean the outside of the calliper.
6. Clamp the piston in the mounting half of the calliper.
7. Apply the brake pedal gently to force the other piston from the calliper.
8. Withdraw the fluid seal and the dust seal.

Reassembling

9. Coat a new fluid seal with Lockheed Disc Brake Lubricant and then ease it into its groove.
10. Slacken the bleeder screw one complete turn.
11. Coat the piston with Lockheed Disc Brake Lubricant, insert it into the bore with the cut-away face facing upwards and press it in with Service tool 18G 672 until about $\frac{5}{16}$ in. (8 mm.) remains protruding.
12. Coat a new, dry dust seal with Lockheed Disc Brake Lubricant, fit it to the retainer and position the seal and retainer on the protruding part of the piston with the seal innermost.
13. Press home the piston and seal.
14. Retighten the bleeder screw.
15. Clamp the piston in the rim half of the calliper and then repeat instructions 7 to 12.
16. Disconnect the hose and then repeat 13 and 14.
17. Reconnect the hose and refit the calliper and the two parts of the dust cover to the hub.

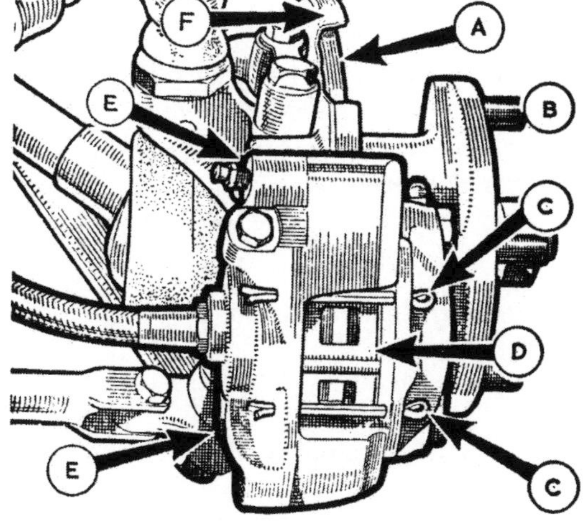

Fig. M.7
The disc brake assembly

A. Brake disc. D. Pad retaining spring.
C. Split pins. E. Calliper mounting bolts.
F. Dust cover.

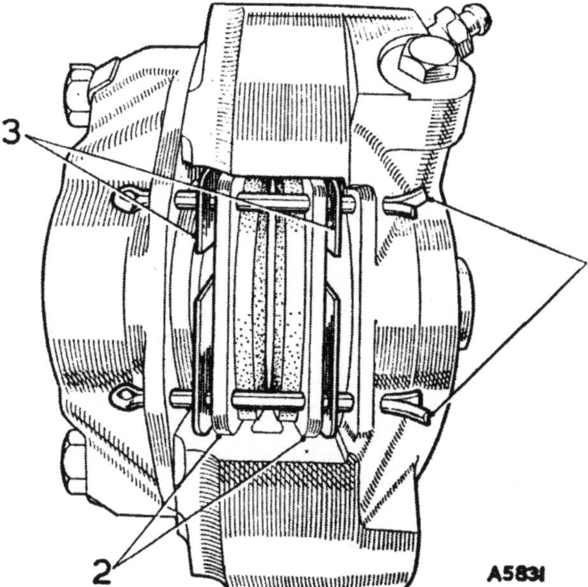

Fig. M.8
The modified calliper assembly

1. Pad-retaining split pins. 2. Brake pads.
3. Anti-squeak shims.

18. Refit the dust cover locking plate.
19. Reconnect the tie-rod.
20. Tighten the calliper mounting bolts.
21. Fit the pads.
22. Bleed the brakes.
23. Apply the brakes several times to adjust.

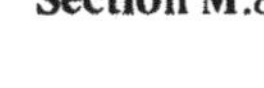

Section M.8

BLEEDING

1. Adjust the brakes.
2. Slacken the bleeder screw on the intensifier (COOPER, when fitted) and pump the pedal until fluid comes out free from air.
3. Tighten the bleeder screw and top up the master cylinder.
4. Bleed the wheel cylinders. (Remove the front wheels—early COOPER.)

Section M.9

VACUUM SERVO (Cooper 'S')

Removing

1. Disconnect the heater hose from the grille, release the clip retaining the hose to the slave cylinder and secure the hose out of the way.
2. Disconnect the hydraulic pipes from the slave cylinder, and plug the open ends of the pipes.

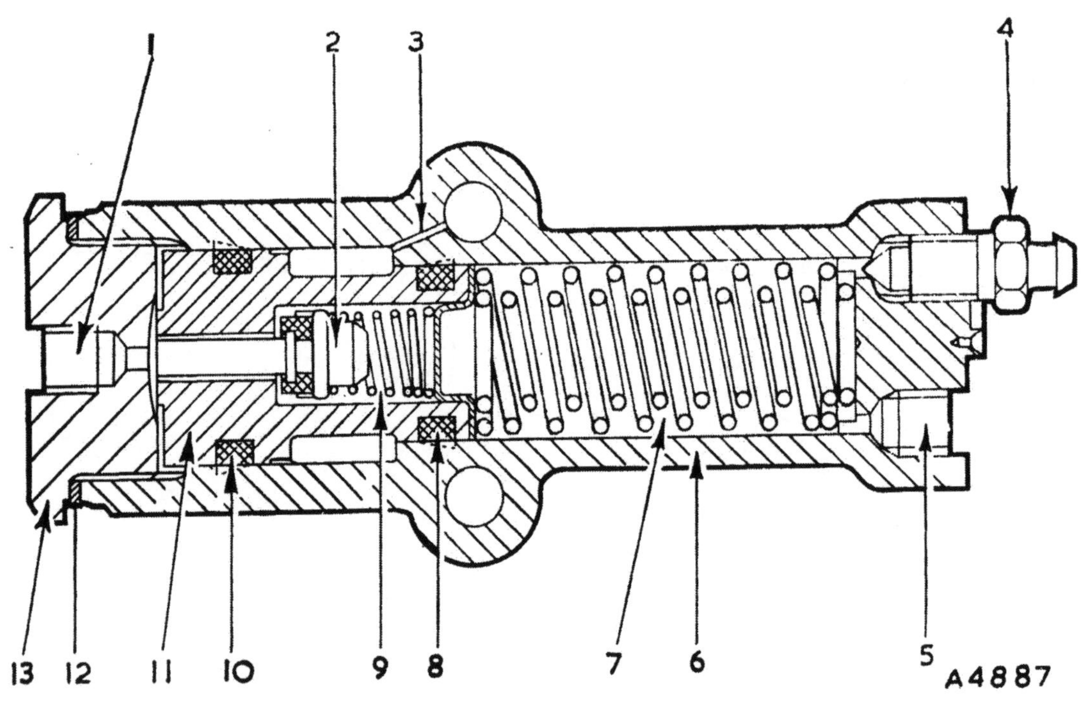

Fig. M.9
The brake cylinder intensifier

1. Fluid inlet.
2. Valve.
3. Air relief passage.
4. Bleed screw.
5. Fluid outlet.
6. Intensifier cylinder body.
7. Piston return springs.
8. Piston seal (small).
9. Valve return spring.
10. Piston seal (large).
11. Piston.
12. Copper gasket.
13. Hexagon end plug.

3. Release the rubber vacuum pipe from the slave cylinder.
4. Remove the two retaining nuts and spring washers from the rear mounting bracket, release the servo unit from the front mounting bracket, and lift the unit from the vehicle.
5. Refitting is a reversal of removing. Bleed the brakes as described in Section M.8.

Dismantling

6. Remove the five screws and detach the air valve cover, disengaging the pipe from the rubber elbow. Pull the elbow off the pipe in the end cover, and lift out the control valve diaphragm.
7. Remove the four screws and lift off the valve housing and gasket. Expel the valve piston by closing the end connection with the thumb and applying a low air pressure at the smaller connection on the side of the cylinder. Ease the rubber cup off the piston.
8. Remove the bolts from the clamping ring, remove the end cover and diaphragm assembly, and disengage the return spring from the locking plates. Hold the push-rod by its hexagon centre-piece, ease off the rubber buffer and unscrew the nut to dismantle the diaphragm assembly.
9. Bend back the locking tabs, remove the four securing bolts, and detach the vacuum shell from the slave cylinder. Extract the guide piece, push-rod cup, cup spreader and spring from the cylinder. Depress the piston with a suitable brass rod and extract the circlip. Gradually release the spring pressure on the piston, and remove the remaining components from the slave cylinder bore.
10. Unscrew the non-return valve from the side of the slave cylinder.

Cleaning

11. Wash all parts in industrial methylated spirit (not the air valve cover). Blow compressed air at a low pressure past the air valve and into the filter chamber. Dry all components thoroughly.

Reassembling

Reassembly is a reversal of the dismantling procedure, noting the following points.

12. Renew all metal parts showing signs of damage or wear.
13. New rubber seals, cups, and diaphragm should be used throughout.
14. Make an assembly sleeve to the following dimensions: length: 1.61 to 1.62 in. (40.89 to 41.15 mm.); outer diameter: .746 to .748 in. (18.95 to 19.00 mm.); inner diameter: .625 to .627 in. (15.87 to 15.92 mm.). Insert this sleeve in the end of the slave cylinder bore to refit the cap and piston.

15. Take extreme care not to damage the surface finish of the push-rod when reassembling the diaphragm. Lock the securing nut by punching the threads in two opposed places.
16. Do not tighten the end cover clamp bolt fully until the air valve cover has been fitted and the pipe in the end cover is lined up with the pipe and rubber elbow on the air valve cover.
17. Check that the diaphragm spring has its smaller end engaged under the locking plate tabs.

Section M.10

TWO-LEADING-SHOE FRONT BRAKES

Each front brake has two squared adjusters projecting from the rear face of the backplate, one adjuster for each brake-shoe.

Adjusting

1. Jack up the car and deal with one adjuster at a time.
2. Turn the adjuster in the same direction as the forward rotation of the front wheel until the drum is locked, then back off the adjuster the minimum amount necessary to allow the drum to rotate freely.
3. Spin the wheel and apply the foot brake firmly to centralize the shoe.
4. Re-check the adjustment, and repeat the complete operation with the other adjuster.
5. Carry out the same sequence on the other front wheel.

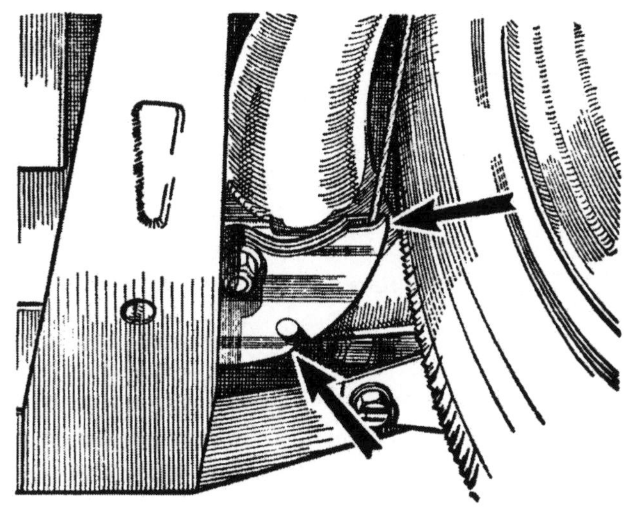

Fig. M.11
The hand brake cable sector mounted on the rear radius arms. Only the corners indicated must be 'nipped' to position the cable

Dismantling

6. Jack up the car and remove the front road wheel.
7. Back off both adjusters completely, extract the two retaining screws, and remove the brake-drum.
8. The tips of the brake shoes are retained on the wheel cylinder pistons by spring-loaded hooks, one to each shoe. Withdraw the hooks from their registers in the pistons and turn them to one side.

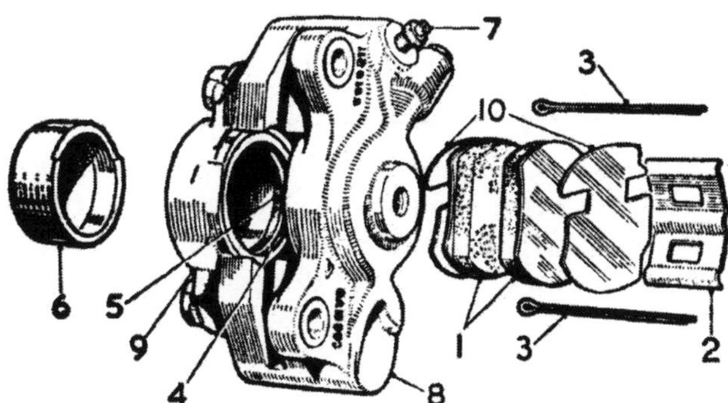

Fig. M.10
The calliper components

1. Friction pads.
2. Pad retaining spring.
3. Retaining split pins.
4. Piston dust seal.
5. Piston fluid seal.
6. Piston, showing cut-away at top.
7. Bleeder screw.
8. Mounting half calliper.
9. Rim half calliper.
10. Anti-squeak shim.

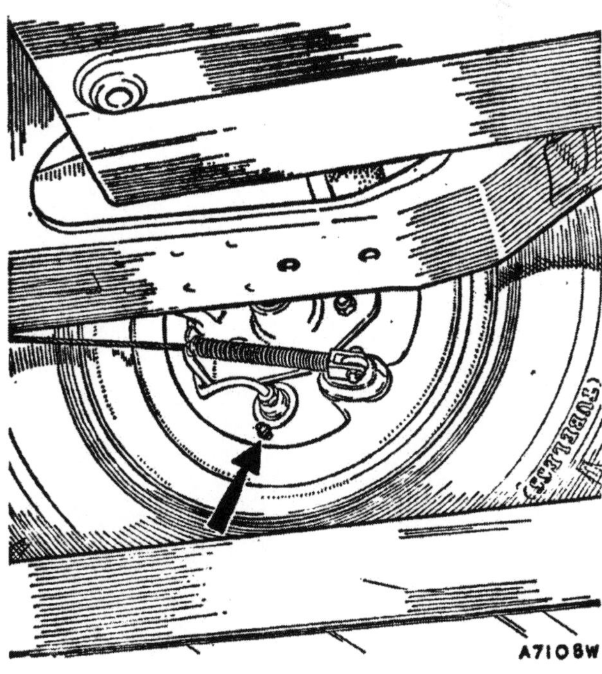

Fig. M.12
A rear wheel cylinder bleeder screw. One bleeder screw is provided on each of the four brake back-plates

9. Mark the position of the shoe return springs in the shoes, and note which end of the shoe is fitted to the wheel cylinder.
10. Lift out one shoe from the recesses in the wheel cylinder, and pivot against the pressure of the return spring. Manoeuvre the assembly of the shoes and springs over the front hub.
11. Wire the pistons to the wheel cylinder castings to prevent them from being accidentally pushed out.

Reassembling

12. Reassembly is a reversal of the dismantling procedure.
13. Ensure that the shoes are replaced the correct way round and the return springs are fitted in their correct positions.
14. The shoes must register correctly in the grooves in the pistons and pivot points.

Wheel cylinder removal

15. Remove the brake-shoes as described under **'Dismantling'**.
16. Disconnect the flexible brake hose from the front wheel cylinder. Unscrew the two union nuts and detach the pipe bridging the two wheel cylinders.
17. Remove the two hexagon screws retaining each wheel cylinder to the backplate and detach the wheel cylinders.
18. Note, on replacement, that the position of the wheel cylinder faces in the same direction as the forward rotation of the brake-drum and that the bleed screw is fitted to the rearmost wheel cylinder.

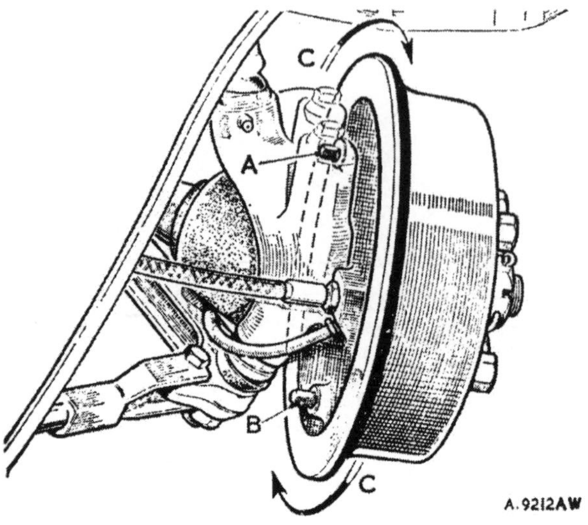

Fig. M.13
The adjusters for the two-leading-shoe front brakes

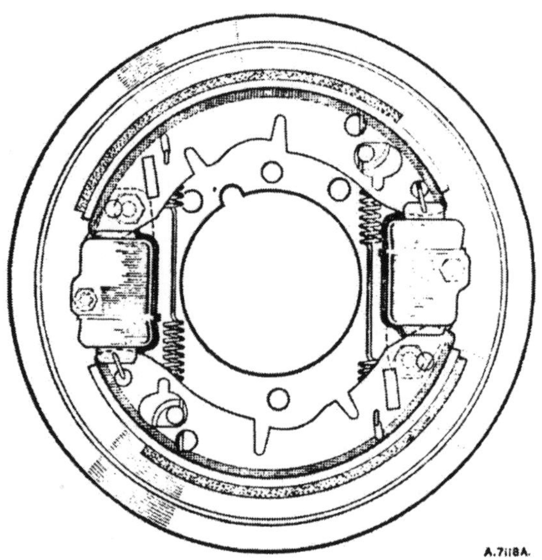

Fig. M.14
The left-hand front brake assembly, showing the fitted position of the shoes and pull-off springs

Section M.11

PREVENTIVE MAINTENANCE

To safeguard against the possible effects of wear, or deterioration, it is recommended that:

1. Disc brake pads, drum brake linings, hoses, and pipes should be examined at intervals no greater than those laid down in the Passport to Service.
2. Brake fluid should be changed completely every 18 months or 24,000 miles (40000 km.) whichever is the sooner.
3. All fluid seals in the hydraulic system and all flexible hoses should be examined and renewed if necessary every 3 years or 40,000 miles (65000 km.) whichever is the sooner. At the same time the working surface of the pistons and of the bores of the master cylinder, wheel cylinders, and other slave cylinders should be examined and new parts fitted where necessary.

Care must be taken always to observe the following points:

a. At all times use the recommended brake fluid.
b. Never leave fluid in unsealed containers. It absorbs moisture quickly and this can be dangerous.
c. Fluid drained from the system or used for bleeding is best discarded.
d. The necessity for absolute cleanliness throughout cannot be over-emphasized.

THE VACUUM SERVO COMPONENTS

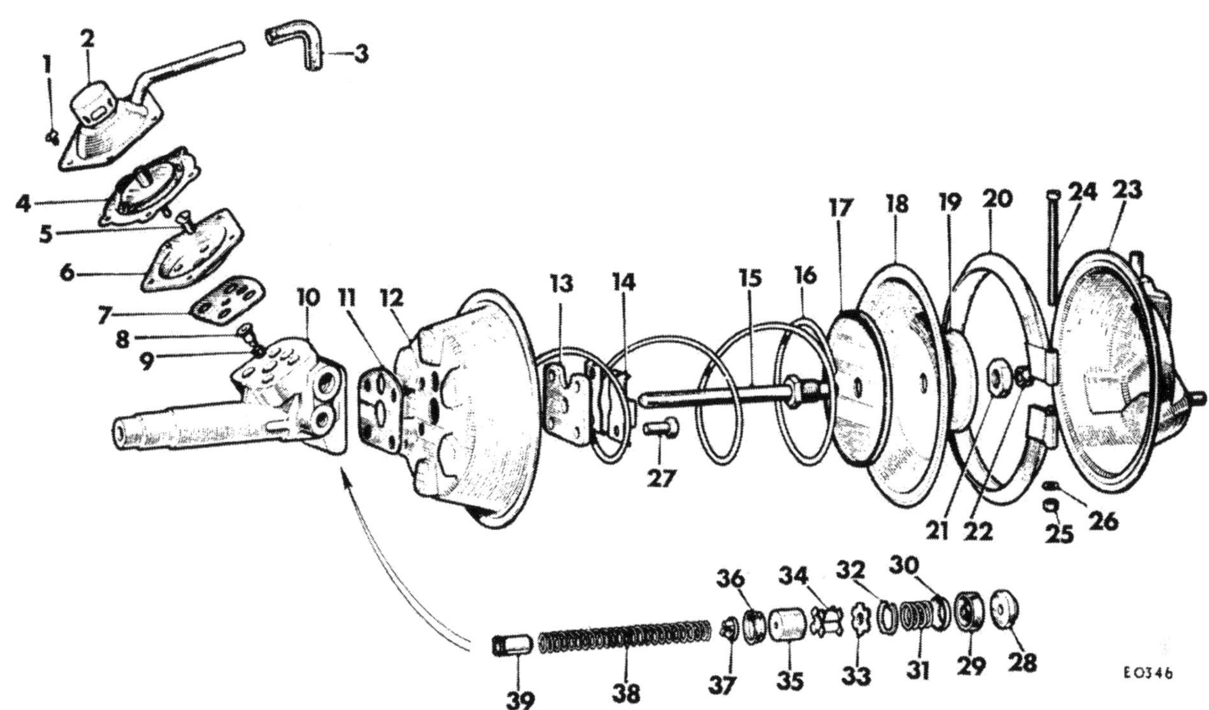

No.	Description	No.	Description
1.	Screw for air valve cover.	21.	Nut for diaphragm assembly.
2.	Air valve cover.	22.	Rubber buffer.
3.	Rubber elbow.	23.	End cover.
4.	Control valve diaphragm.	24.	Clamping bolt.
5.	Screw for valve housing.	25.	Nut for clamping bolt.
6.	Valve housing.	26.	Washer for nut.
7.	Housing gasket.	27.	Screw–vacuum shell to slave cylinder.
8.	Valve piston.	28.	Guide piece.
9.	Rubber cup for piston.	29.	Push-rod cup.
10.	Slave cylinder body.	30.	Cup spreader.
11.	Gasket–slave cylinder to vacuum shell.	31.	Spring.
12.	Vacuum shell.	32.	Circlip.
13.	Abutment plate.	33.	Washer.
14.	Locking plates.	34.	Distance piece.
15.	Push-rod.	35.	Piston.
16.	Return spring.	36.	Cup.
17.	Plate (large) for diaphragm.	37.	Spring guide.
18.	Diaphragm.	38.	Spring.
19.	Plate (small) for diaphragm.	39.	Spring retainer.
20.	Clamping ring.		

SECTION Mb

THE BRAKING SYSTEM

The information contained in this Section refers specifically to new or modified components fitted to the Mini range coincident with the introduction of NEGATIVE earth electrical systems and must be used in conjunction with Section M.

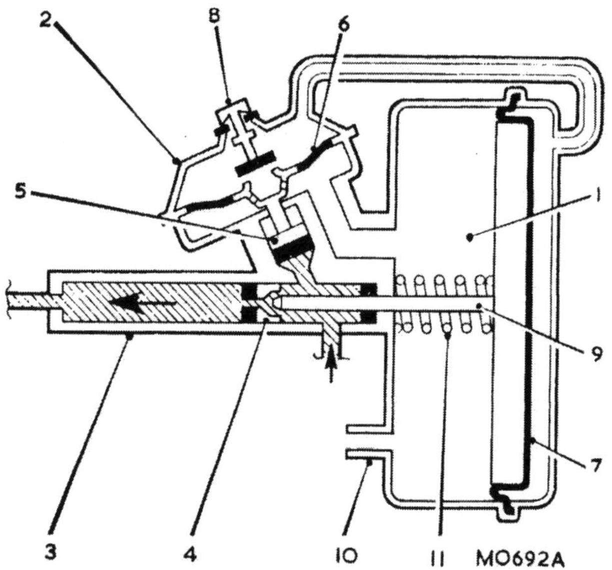

Fig. Mb.1
A schematic diagram showing the principle of operation and the main components of the vacuum servo unit. The shaded area represents brake fluid

Section Mb.1

SERVO UNIT
(Lockheed Type 6)

Operation

Refer to Fig. Mb.1. The vacuum-operated servo unit consists of three main components, namely the vacuum cylinder (1), the air valve assembly (2), and the slave cylinder (3) which is connected in the hydraulic circuit between the main master cylinder and the wheel cylinders. Under light braking, fluid is allowed to pass directly to the wheel cylinders via the hollow centre of the slave piston (4) and no braking assistance is obtained; fluid pressure acting on the air valve piston (5) closes the diaphragm (6), thus separating the chamber behind the main servo diaphragm (7) from the one in front. Under heavier braking, further movement of the air valve pistons opens the air valve and allows air to enter the chamber behind the main diaphragm, destroying the vacuum. The central rod (9) is thus pushed to the left, sealing the hollow centre of the slave piston and pushing it down its bore, so increasing the fluid pressure at the wheel cylinders. When the brake pedal is released, the pressure beneath the air valve piston is destroyed, the diaphragm (6) re-opens and the air valve closes. Via the non-return valve (10), a suspended vacuum is recreated around the main diaphragm. Under the action of the spring (11), the diaphragm and push-rod, and thus the slave piston, are returned to their original positions, and the pressure in the wheel cylinders is lost.

Removing

1. From beneath the right-hand front wing, pull the heater hose off the intake unit, and then withdraw the intake unit from inside the engine compartment.
2. Disconnect the vacuum pipe from the servo unit.
3. Remove the securing bracket from the end of the servo unit, disconnect the brake pipes and plug the holes.
4. Remove the nuts securing the servo to the bracket and withdraw the unit.

Dismantling

AIR VALVE ASSEMBLY (FIG. Mb.2)

5. Grip the slave cylinder in a soft-jawed vice with the air valve uppermost and disconnect the rubber pipe from the connection on the end cover.
6. Remove the screws securing the plastic air valve cover to the valve housing, lift off the cover complete with the air valve sub-assembly. Suspect functioning of the air valve must be remedied by fitting a replacement air valve cover assembly comprising cover, filter, and air valve as an assembled part of the relevant repair kit.
7. Remove the rubber diaphragm and its plastic support to obtain access to valve housing securing screws. Remove the three screws and take off the housing and joint washer.
8. Seal one of the slave cylinder fluid ports with a finger, apply a low-pressure air-line to the remaining port and blow the air control valve piston from its bore. Remove the rubber cup from the valve piston.

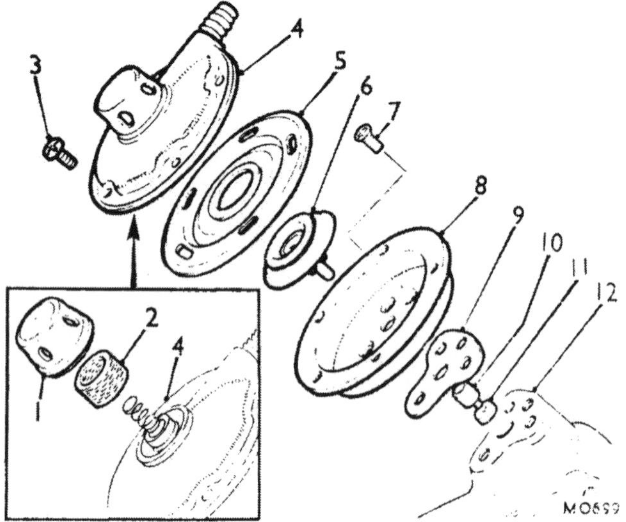

Fig. Mb.2
The air valve assembly components and piston

1. Domed cover for filter.
2. Air filter.
3. Air valve cover securing screws.
4. Air valve cover.
5. Diaphragm.
6. Diaphragm support.
7. Valve housing securing screws.
8. Valve housing.
9. Joint washer.
10. Piston.
11. Piston cup.
12. Slave cylinder.

SERVO CYLINDER ASSEMBLY

9. Use thumb pressure to prise the non-return valve from the servo shell and extract the rubber valve mounting.

10. Remove the clamping ring securing the end cover to the servo shell and lift off the cover.

 EARLY UNITS. To remove the end cover from the servo shell fit Service tool C2030* as shown in Fig. Mb.3. Turn the tool anti-clockwise with a ½ in. (13 mm.) square drive socket 'T' bar as far as the stops on the cover will allow and lift off the end cover.

11. Turn the diaphragm support so that the push-rod retaining key faces downwards. Apply light fluctuating hand pressure on the support into the shell; this will allow the retaining key to drop out, releasing the support from the push-rod under pressure of the main return spring. Extract the spring from the servo shell.

12. Bend back the locking tabs of the servo shell to slave cylinder securing bolts; remove the bolts, together with the locking and abutment plates. Lift off the servo shell and retrieve the joint washer from the mounting face of the slave cylinder.

SLAVE CYLINDER ASSEMBLY

13. Pull the servo push-rod and the piston assembly attached to it from the slave cylinder bore. Slide off the plastic bearing, rubber cup and plastic spacer, noting their relative positions for refitting.

14. Prise off the rubber seal from the head of the slave piston. Open the retaining clip with a small screwdriver to expose the connecting pin, which may then be driven out to separate the piston from the rod (see Fig. Mb.4).

Inspecting

Examine all parts for faults and wear and be prepared to fit new rubber parts throughout. If the air valve is faulty, a replacement kit must be fitted. Dust deposits on the air

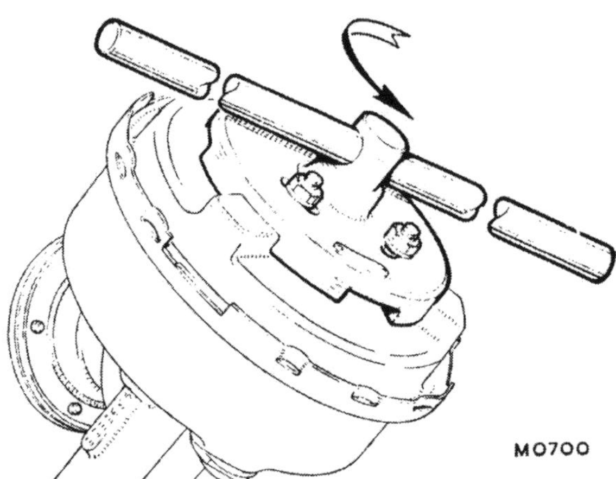

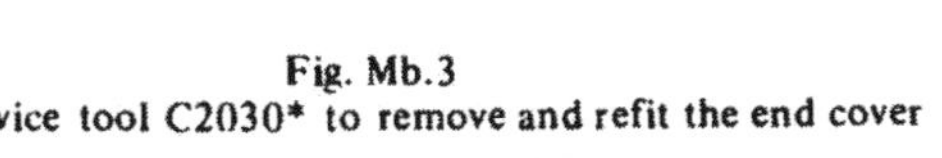
Fig. Mb.3
Using Service tool C2030* to remove and refit the end cover

* Obtainable from V. L. Churchill & Co. Ltd.

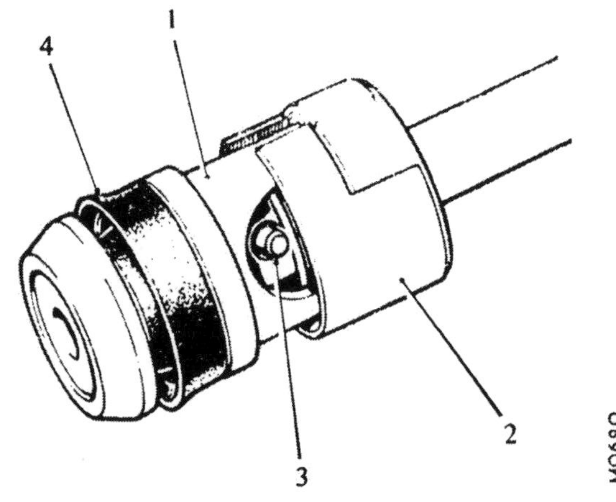

Fig. Mb.4
The slave piston, with the retaining clip withdrawn to expose the connecting pin

1. Piston body.
2. Retaining clip.
3. Connecting pin.
4. Piston seal.

filter, which is otherwise in good condition, can be removed by blowing through with a low-pressure air-line. Do not use a cleaning fluid or lubricant of any description on the filter.

Wash all original components of the slave cylinder assembly and remove light deposits from the cylinder bore with clean brake fluid. If the slave cylinder bore is scored, a replacement unit will be required.

Reassembling

Scrupulous cleanliness of all parts of the servo unit is essential. Lay out all parts to be assembled on a clean sheet of paper. Use clean brake fluid as a lubricant when reassembling the hydraulic components of the servo unit.

SLAVE CYLINDER ASSEMBLY

15. If the piston and push-rod were separated in item 14, a new retaining clip and connecting pin will be required. Insert the chamfered end of the push-rod into the rear of the piston and depress the spring inside it to uncover the hole in the end of the rod. Fit the pin, followed by its retaining clip; see that this is a snug fit, and does not protrude beyond its groove, otherwise the bore will become scored.

 Using only the fingers, bed the rubber seal evenly into the groove on the head of the piston, with the lips of the seal pointing away from the push-rod.

16. Insert the piston into the lubricated bore of the slave cylinder, then, one by one, slide the spacer, the rubber cup, and the bearing over the push-rod into the mouth of the bore. Take care not to bend back the lips of either the seal or the cup, and bed in each part individually.

THE VACUUM SERVO COMPONENTS

(Lockheed Type 6)

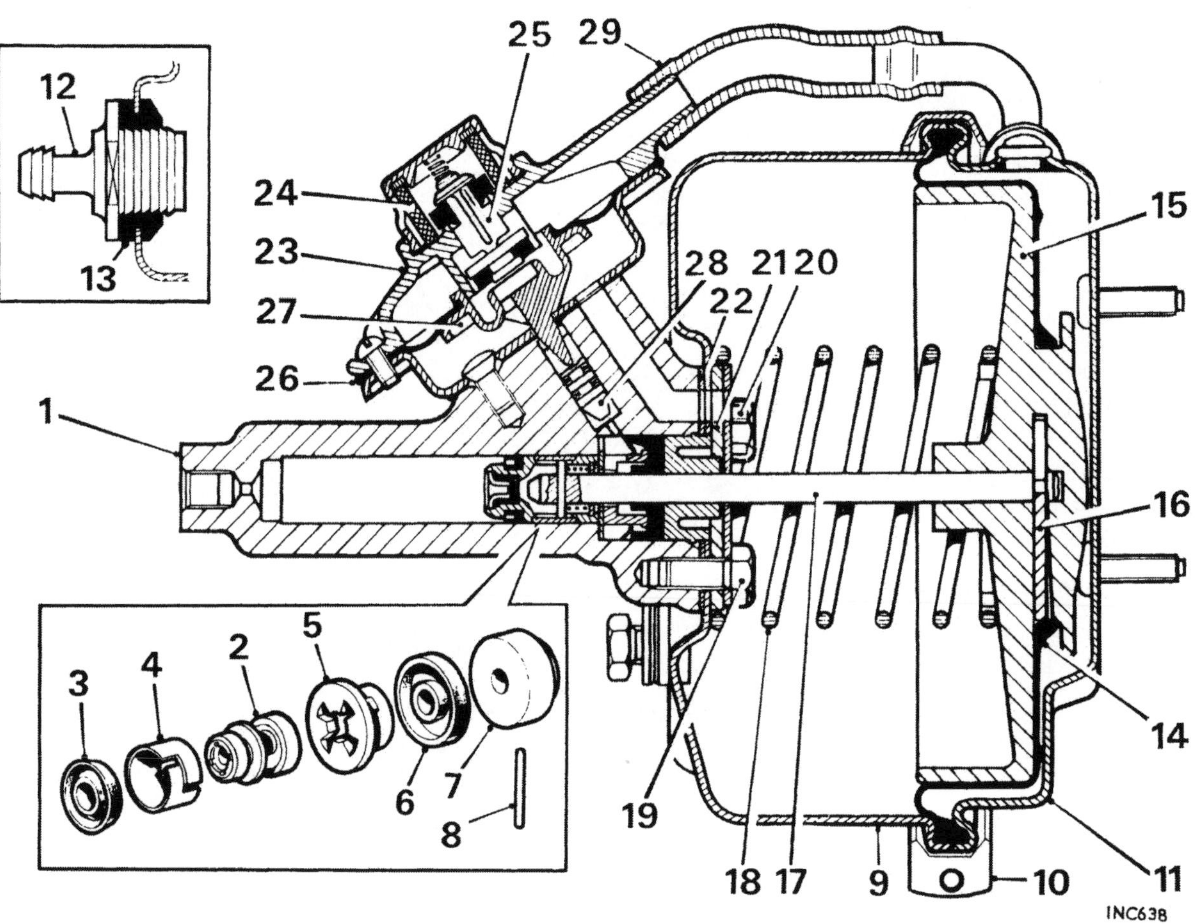

No.	Description		No.	Description	No.	Description
1.	Slave cylinder.		11.	End cover.	21.	Abutment plate.
2.	Slave piston.	Shown inset.	12.	Non-return valve.	22.	Joint washer.
3.	Piston seal.	Shown inset.	13.	Rubber mounting.	23.	Air valve cover.
4.	Retaining clip.	Shown inset.	14.	Main servo diaphragm.	24.	Air filter.
5.	Spacer.	Shown inset.	15.	Diaphragm support.	25.	Air valve.
6.	Cup.	Shown inset.	16.	Retaining key.	26.	Air valve diaphragm.
7.	Bearing.	Shown inset.	17.	Push-rod.	27.	Diaphragm support.
8.	Connecting pin.	Shown inset.	18.	Main return spring.	28.	Air valve piston.
9.	Servo shell.		19.	Servo shell retaining bolts.	29.	Rubber pipe.
10.	Retaining clip.		20.	Locking plate.		

SERVO CYLINDER ASSEMBLY

17. Grip the slave cylinder in a soft-jawed vice, position the mounting face joint washer and refit the servo shell. After correctly positioning the abutment plate and locking plate, which must be renewed if it has been used more than once previously, tighten the three bolts evenly to the torque figure given in **'GENERAL DATA'** and tap up the locking plate tabs.

18. Pull out the push-rod to its limit, fit the main return spring followed by the diaphragm support, with its key slot facing upwards. Make sure that the two end coils are located round the abutment plate and support boss respectively. Press the support into the shell until the groove in the end of the push-rod aligns with the key slot, and insert the key.

    Ensure that both the rubber diaphragm and its support are perfectly dry and then fit the diaphragm to the support. Gently stretch the diaphragm to seat its inner edge in the groove of the support.

19. Smear the outer edge of the rubber diaphragm with Lockheed Disc Brake Lubricant where it will contact the rim of the end cover and of the shell, and position the diaphragm evenly around the rim of the shell.

20. Position the end cover with the shell so that the elbow is in alignment with the air valve and secure the two parts with the clamping ring.

    EARLY UNITS. Using Service tool C 2030* secured to the end cover, turn it clockwise as far as the stops will allow whilst maintaining downward pressure on the end cover. Take care not to trap the edge of the rubber diaphragm; remove the Service tool.

21. Push in the non-return valve with its rubber mounting.

AIR VALVE ASSEMBLY (FIG. Mb.2)

22. Using only the fingers, fit the rubber cup to the spigot of the air valve piston, with the lips pointing away from the drilled head, and insert the piston into its bore, spigot end first. Do not bend over the lips of the cup.

23. Fit the valve housing, with its joint washer, to the mounting face of the slave cylinder and tighten the three securing screws to the torque figure given in **'GENERAL DATA'**.

24. Insert the spigot of the diaphragm support into the drilled head of the air valve piston, and then fit the inner edge of the air valve diaphragm into the groove of its support and align the screw hole slots. Do not use any lubricant.

25. Refit or replace the filter and snap-fit the dome cover if these have been removed in item 6. Place the valve cover over the diaphragm making sure that the projections on the under surface of the cover engage in the slots of the diaphragm. Tighten the five securing screws firmly, progressively and diametrically; do not overtighten, since the smallest air leakage into the air valve assembly will impair the action of the servo.

26. Refit the rubber pipe to join the end cover elbow to the valve cover port.

Refitting

27. Reverse the removing procedure, items 1 to 4.

28. Bleed the braking system (Section Mb.5), using a recommended brake fluid, see **'GENERAL DATA'**.

    Fluid drained from the system or that used for bleeding should be discarded.

Section Mb.2

INERTIA VALVE
(Split braking system)

An inertia valve is fitted in the fluid line to the rear brakes; it replaces the pressure regulating valve described in Section M.5 and is similarly located on the rear sub-frame cross-member.

The angle at which the assembly is mounted allows the steel ball inside the body to hold the valve in the open position, so that fluid may pass to the rear brakes. When braking heavily, the weight transfer to the front of the vehicle causes the ball to move away from the valve, which is then closed by a light spring. Thus further pressure is prevented from reaching the rear brakes, and all additional pressure is transferred to the front brakes.

Removing

1. Remove, and then plug the ends of, the hydraulic brake pipes.

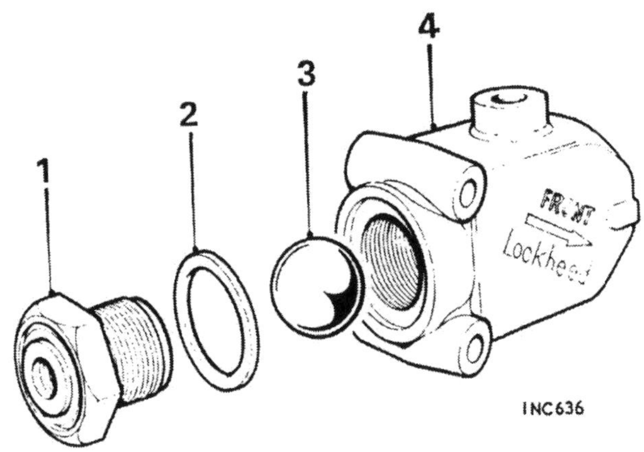

Fig. Mb.5
The inertia valve assembly components

1. Valve sub-assembly.
2. Copper washer.
3. Steel ball.
4. Valve body.

* Obtainable from V. L. Churchill & Co. Ltd.

2. Remove the two fixing bolts and lift the inertia valve assembly from its location on the rear sub-frame cross-member.

Dismantling and examining

3. Remove the end plug and washer from the inertia valve body, and extract the steel ball.
4. Clean the body and steel ball with clean brake fluid or industrial methylated spirit and dry thoroughly.
5. Carefully examine all the components, which must be in perfect condition if they are to be re-used.

Reassembling

6. Insert the steel ball into the body.
7. Screw in a new valve and end-plug sub-assembly, fitting a new copper washer. See that the seating faces of both the body assembly and end plug are clean and undamaged, and tighten to the torque figure given in '**GENERAL DATA**'.

Refitting

8. Reverse the removing procedure noting the marking 'FRONT' on the inertia valve body.
9. Refill the master cylinder reservoir with the recommended brake fluid, see'**GENERAL DATA**'.
10. Bleed the braking system as in Section Mb.5. Then inspect the inertia valve for fluid leaks with the foot brake pedal fully depressed and also with the system at rest.

NOTE.–Brake fluid can have a detrimental effect on paintwork; ensure that fluid is not allowed to contact paint-finished surfaces.

Section Mb.3

TANDEM MASTER CYLINDER
(Split braking system)

Removing

1. Disconnect the hydraulic pipes from the master cylinder, and plug the pipe ends to prevent loss of fluid and the entry of dirt.
2. Unscrew the two nuts securing the master cylinder to the bulkhead, and lift it off, leaving the push-rod attached to the brake pedal.

Dismantling

3. Drain the fluid from the reservoir and refit the cap.
4. Plug the pipe connections, thoroughly clean the exterior of the assembly and remove the rubber boot.
5. Grip the cylinder body in a soft-jawed vice with the mouth of the bore uppermost.

Refer to Fig. Mb.6.

6. Compress the return spring and remove the Spirolox ring from its groove in the primary piston, taking care not to distort the coils of the ring or score the bore of the cylinder.
7. Using Service tool 18G 1112, remove the piston retaining circlip. A slight radiusing of the sides of the tool may be necessary for ease of use on this master cylinder.
8. Move the piston up and down in the bore to free the nylon guide bearing and cap seal; remove the guide bearing and seal.
10. Using Service tool 18G 1112, remove the inner circlip.
11. Withdraw the primary and secondary piston assembly complete with stop washer.
12. Remove the stop washer.
13. Compress the spring separating the two pistons and drive out the roll-pin retaining the piston link.
14. Note the positions of the rubber cups by their moulded indentations and remove the cups and washers from the pistons.
15. Unscrew the four bolts securing the plastic reservoir to the body and remove the reservoir.
16. Remove the two reservoir sealing rings.
17. Unscrew the connection adaptors, discard the copper gaskets, and remove the spring and trap valves.

Inspecting

18. Clean all parts thoroughly in brake fluid and dry them with lint-free cloth.
19. Examine all metal components for wear and damage and renew all worn, damaged, or suspect parts.

Reassembling

20. Reverse the dismantling procedure, with special attention to the following points.
21. Use a complete set of new rubber seals when reassembling.
22. Immerse all internal components in a recommended brake fluid as in item 26, and assemble them while wet.
23. Locate the piston washer 5 over the head of the secondary piston, convex surface first; carefully ease the secondary cup over the piston and seat it with its flat surface against the washer, see Fig. Mb.6.
24. The remainder is a reversal of the dismantling procedure 5 to 17. Fit new copper gaskets to the connection adaptors and tighten the connections to the torque figure given in '**GENERAL DATA**'.

Refitting

25. Refit the unit, taking care to guide the push-rod into the opening in the rubber boot; re-connect and tighten pipe connections.

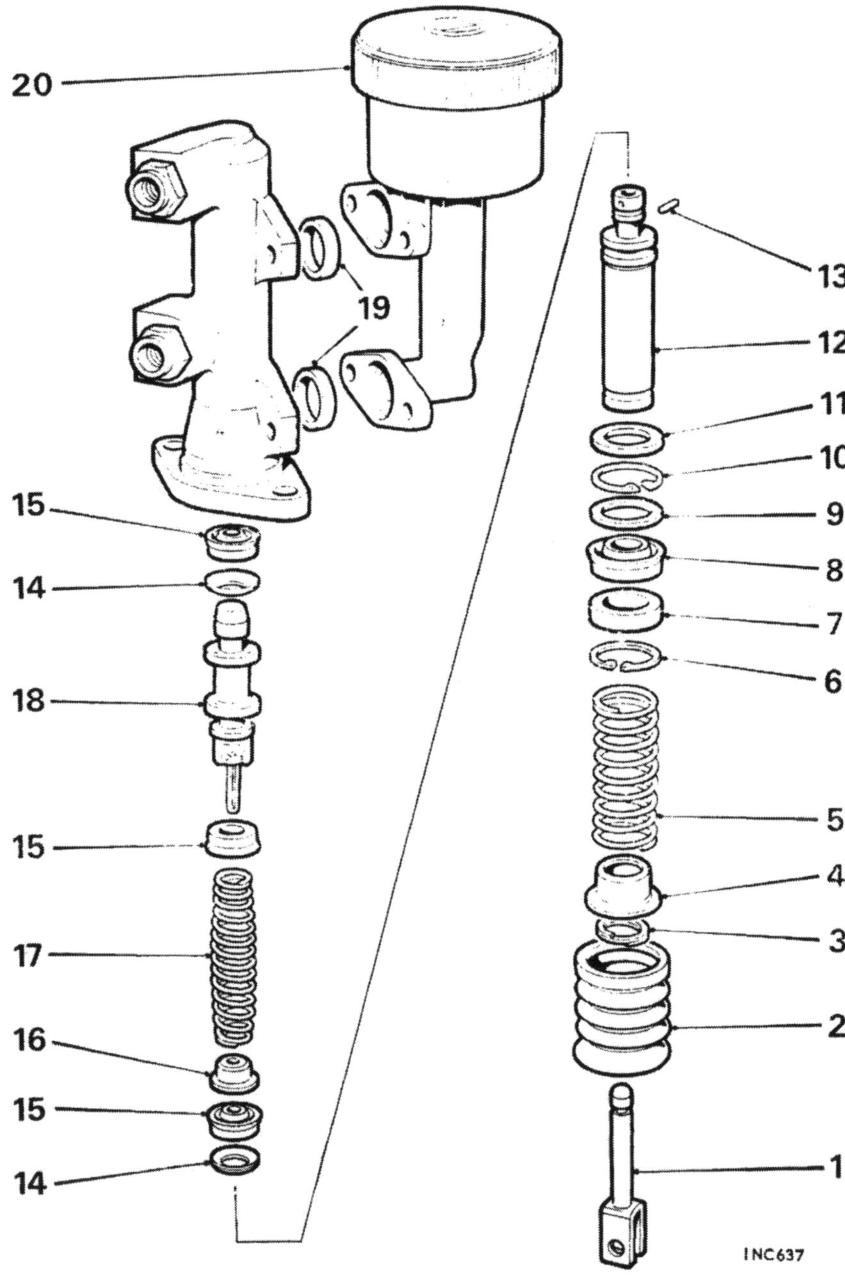

Fig. Mb.6
An exploded view of the tandem master cylinder components

1. Push-rod.
2. Rubber boot.
3. Spirolox ring.
4. Spring retainer.
5. Spring.
6. Circlip.
7. Nylon guide bearing.
8. Secondary cup.
9. Washer.
10. Circlip.
11. Stop washer.
12. Primary piston.
13. Roll pin.
14. Piston washer.
15. Main cup.
16. Pin retainer.
17. Spring.
18. Secondary piston.
19. Reservoir seals.
20. Fluid reservoir.

26. Refill the cylinder reservoir with the recommended brake fluid, see **'GENERAL DATA'**.
27. Bleed the braking system, see Section Mb.5.

NOTE.–Brake fluid can have a detrimental effect on paintwork; ensure that fluid is not allowed to contact paint-finished surfaces.

Section Mb.4.

PRESSURE FAILURE SWITCH ASSEMBLY
(Split braking system)

This switch replaces the three-way brake pipe connector located on the right-hand side of the engine bulkhead cross-member.

Removing

1. Pull the electrical connector off the nylon switch.
2. Clean the switch assembly and its surroundings, particularly the pipe connections.
3. Disconnect and plug the hydraulic pipes.
4. Unscrew the retaining bolt and remove the assembly.

Dismantling

5. Refer to Fig. Mb.7. Remove the end plug and discard the copper washer.
6. Unscrew the nylon switch.
7. Withdraw the shuttle valve piston assembly from the bore; use a low-pressure air line to free the piston if necessary.
8. Remove and discard the two piston seals.

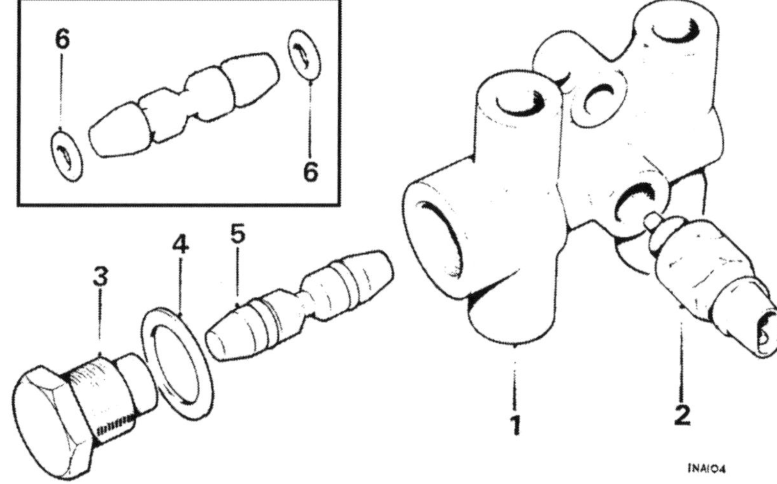

Fig. Mb.7
The pressure failure switch components; inset shows an exploded view of the shuttle valve piston

1. Switch body.
2. Nylon switch.
3. End plug.
4. Copper washer.
5. Shuttle valve piston.
6. Piston seals.

Inspection

9. Thoroughly clean all the components using methylated spirit (denatured alcohol) or the recommended brake fluid, and dry with a lint-free cloth.
10. Inspect the bore of the casing for scoring and damage. The complete assembly must be renewed if the bore is not in perfect condition.
11. Reconnect the wiring to the switch and actuate the switch plunger to test the switch operation and warning light circuit.

Reassembling

12. Refer to Fig. Mb.7. Fit two new seals to the piston.
13. Lubricate the piston assembly with Lockheed Disc Brake Lubricant and fit the piston into the bore.
14. Fit a new copper washer to the end plug, screw in and tighten the plug to the torque figure given in '**GENERAL DATA**'.
15. Screw in the switch and carefully tighten it to the torque figure given in '**GENERAL DATA**'.

Refitting

16. Reverse the removing procedure in 1 to 4.
17. Refill the cylinder reservoir with the recommended brake fluid, see '**GENERAL DATA**'.
18. Bleed the braking system, see Section Mb.5.

Section Mb.5.

BLEEDING THE SYSTEM
(Split braking system)

1. Top up the hydraulic fluid reservoir to the correct level with the recommended brake fluid, see '**GENERAL DATA**'. Do not allow the fluid level to drop more than ½ in. (1.25 cm.) throughout the following operations.
2. Attach bleed tubes to the front and rear bleed screws on the driver's side of the car.
3. Submerge the open end of each tube in a small quantity of clean brake fluid in a transparent container.
4. Open both bleed screws half a turn.
5. Fully depress the brake pedal and hold it down.
6. Close both bleed screws and then allow the pedal to return.
7. Repeat operations 4, 5 and 6 until clean fluid, free from air, issues from both tubes. Having achieved this condition, repeat operations 4, 5 and 6 four more times.
8. Keep the brake pedal depressed and tighten both bleed screws to the correct torque.
9. Attach bleed tubes to the front and rear bleed screws on the opposite side of the car.
10. Carry out operations 3 to 8.

NOTE. Fluid from the system must be discarded.

SECTION N

THE ELECTRICAL SYSTEM

WIRING DIAGRAM

Super, Super De-luxe, Countryman, Traveller and Cooper (up to 1964)

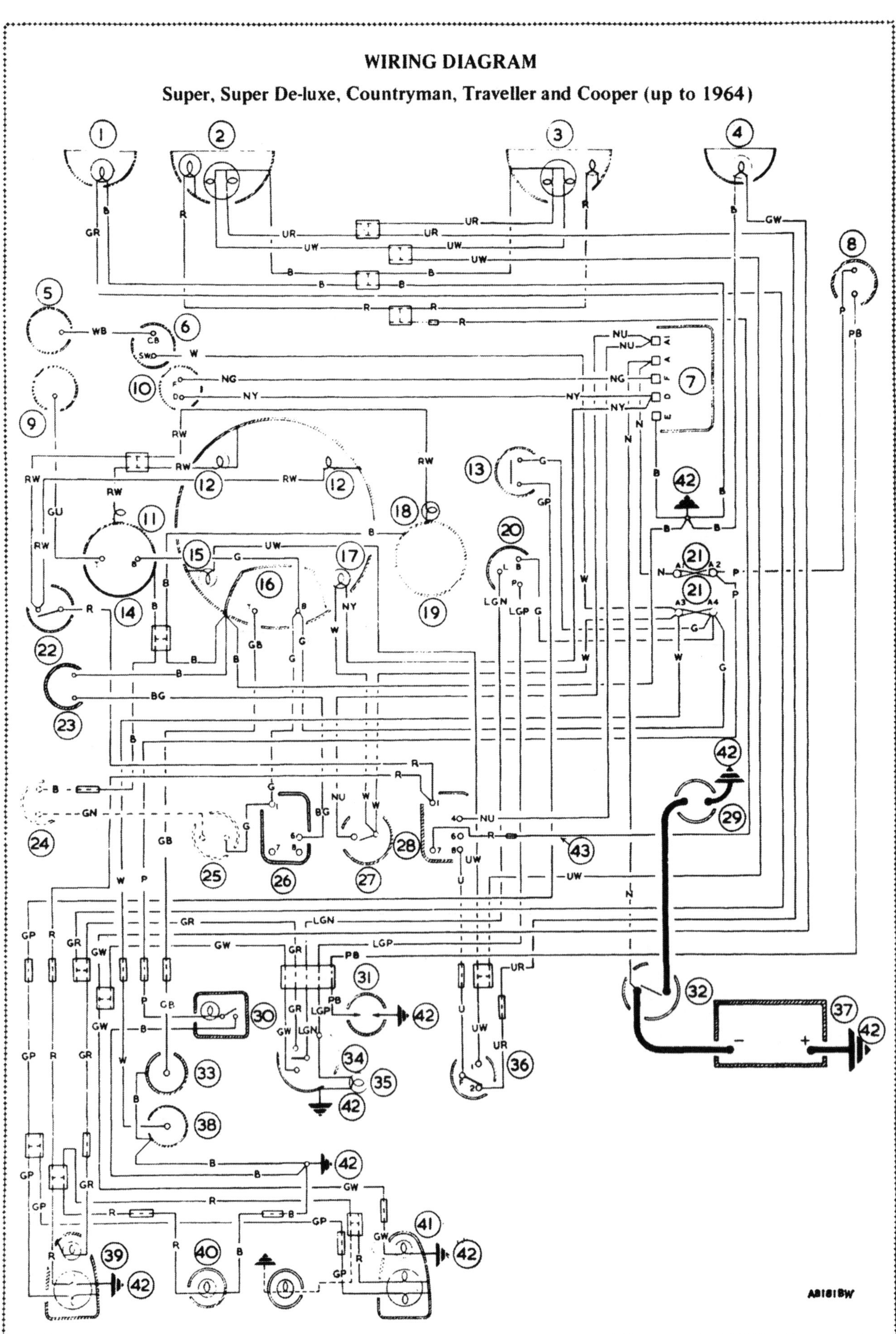

KEY TO WIRING DIAGRAM

No.	Description	No.	Description
1.	L.H. flasher lamp.	23.	Wiper motor.
2.	L.H. headlamp and pilot lamp.	24.	Heater motor.
3.	R.H. headlamp and pilot lamp.	25.	Heater switch.
4.	R.H. flasher lamp.	26.	Wiper switch.
5.	Distributor.	27.	Ignition and starter switch.
6.	Ignition coil.	28.	Lighting switch.
7.	Voltage regulator and cut-out.	29.	Starter motor.
8.	Horn.	30.	Interior lamp.
9.	Thermo element.	31.	Horn-push.
10.	Dynamo.	32.	Starter solenoid.
11.	Thermo gauge illumination light.	33.	Tank unit.
12.	Panel illumination lights.	34.	Direction indicator switch.
13.	Stop lamp switch.	35.	Direction indicator warning light.
14.	Thermo gauge.	36.	Dipper switch.
15.	Main-beam warning light.	37.	12-volt battery.
16.	Fuel gauge.	38.	Fuel pump.
17.	Ignition warning light.	39.	L.H. stop, tail, and flasher lamp.
18.	Oil gauge illumination light.	40.	Number-plate illumination lamp.
19.	Oil gauge.	41.	R.H. stop, tail, and flasher lamp.
20.	Flasher unit.	42.	Earth connection.
21.	35-amp. fuses.	43.	Connect to terminal 6 for North America.
22.	Panel lights switch.		

NOTE.–On Export models the pilot lamps are combined with the flasher lamps.

CABLE COLOUR CODE

B. Black.	P. Purple.	Y. Yellow.
U. Blue.	R. Red.	L. Light.
N. Brown.	S. Slate.	M. Medium.
G. Green.	W. White.	D. Dark.

When a cable has two colour code letters the first denotes the main colour and the second denotes the tracer colour.

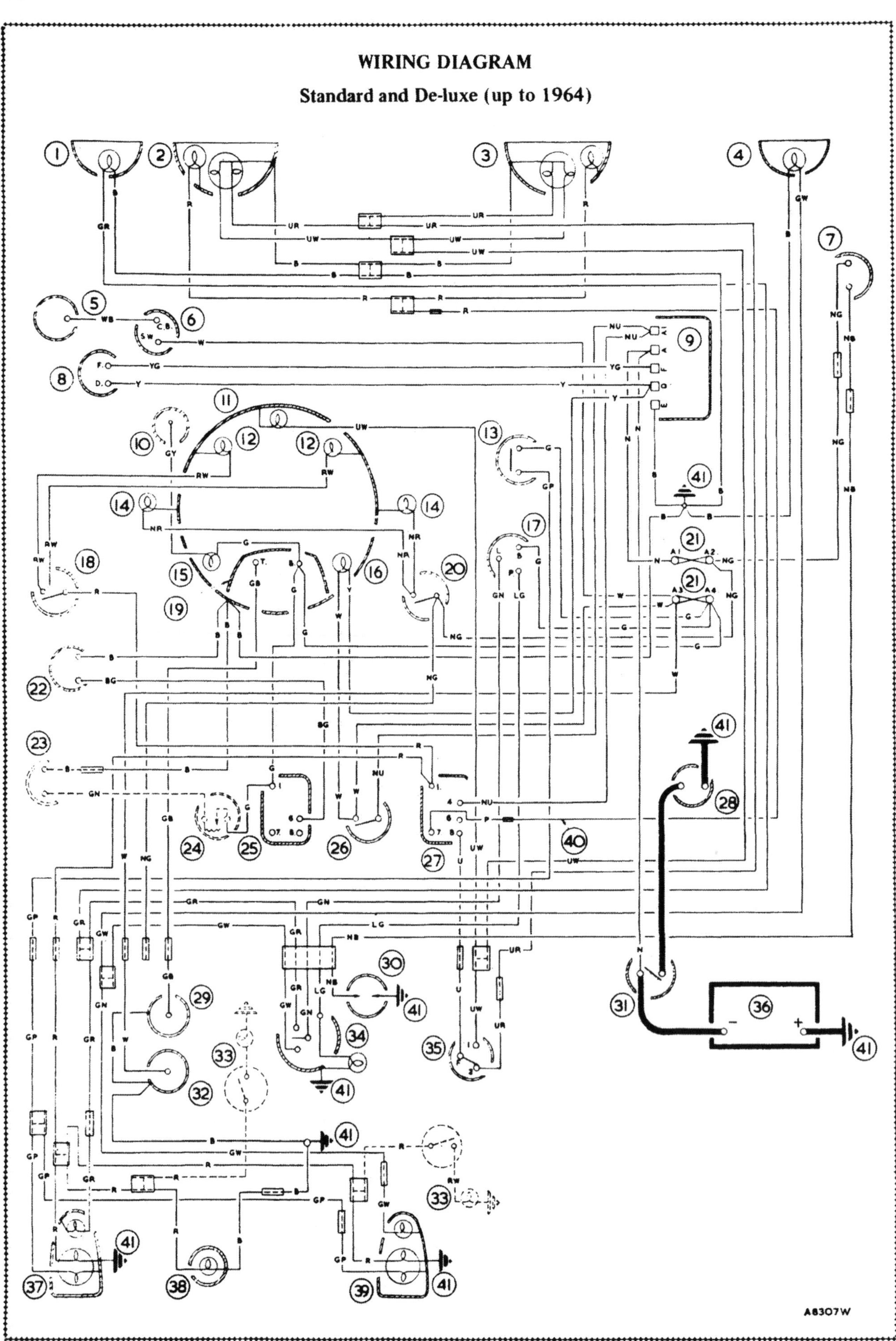
WIRING DIAGRAM
Standard and De-luxe (up to 1964)
A8307W

KEY TO WIRING DIAGRAM

No.	Description
1.	L.H. flasher lamp.
2.	L.H. headlamp and pilot lamp.
3.	R.H. headlamp and pilot lamp.
4.	R.H. flasher lamp.
5.	Distributor.
6.	Ignition coil.
7.	Horn.
8.	Dynamo.
9.	Voltage regulator and cut-out.
10.	Oil pressure switch.
11.	Main-beam warning light.
12.	Panel illumination light.
13.	Stop light switch.
14.	Parcel shelf illumination lamp.
15.	Oil pressure warning light.
16.	Ignition warning light.
17.	Flasher unit.
18.	Panel illumination switch.
19.	Fuel gauge.
20.	Parcel shelf illumination switch.
21.	35-amp. fuse.
22.	Wiper motor.
23.	Heater motor.
24.	Heater switch.
25.	Wiper switch.
26.	Ignition switch.
27.	Lighting switch.
28.	Starter motor.
29.	Tank unit.
30.	Horn-push.
31.	Starter switch.
32.	Fuel pump.
33.	Companion box switch and lamp.
34.	Direction indicator switch and warning light.
35.	Dipper switch.
36.	12-volt battery.
37.	L.H. stop, tail, and flasher lamp.
38.	Number-plate illumination lamp.
39.	R.H. stop, tail, and flasher lamp.
40.	Connect to No. 6 terminal for U.S.A.
41.	Earth connection.

CABLE COLOUR CODE

B. Black.	P. Purple.	L. Light.
U. Blue.	R. Red.	D. Dark.
N. Brown.	W. White.	M. Medium.
G. Green.	Y. Yellow.	

When a cable has two colour code letters the first denotes the main colour and the second denotes the tracer colour.

WIRING DIAGRAM

Saloon, Van, and Pick-up (1964 to 1967)

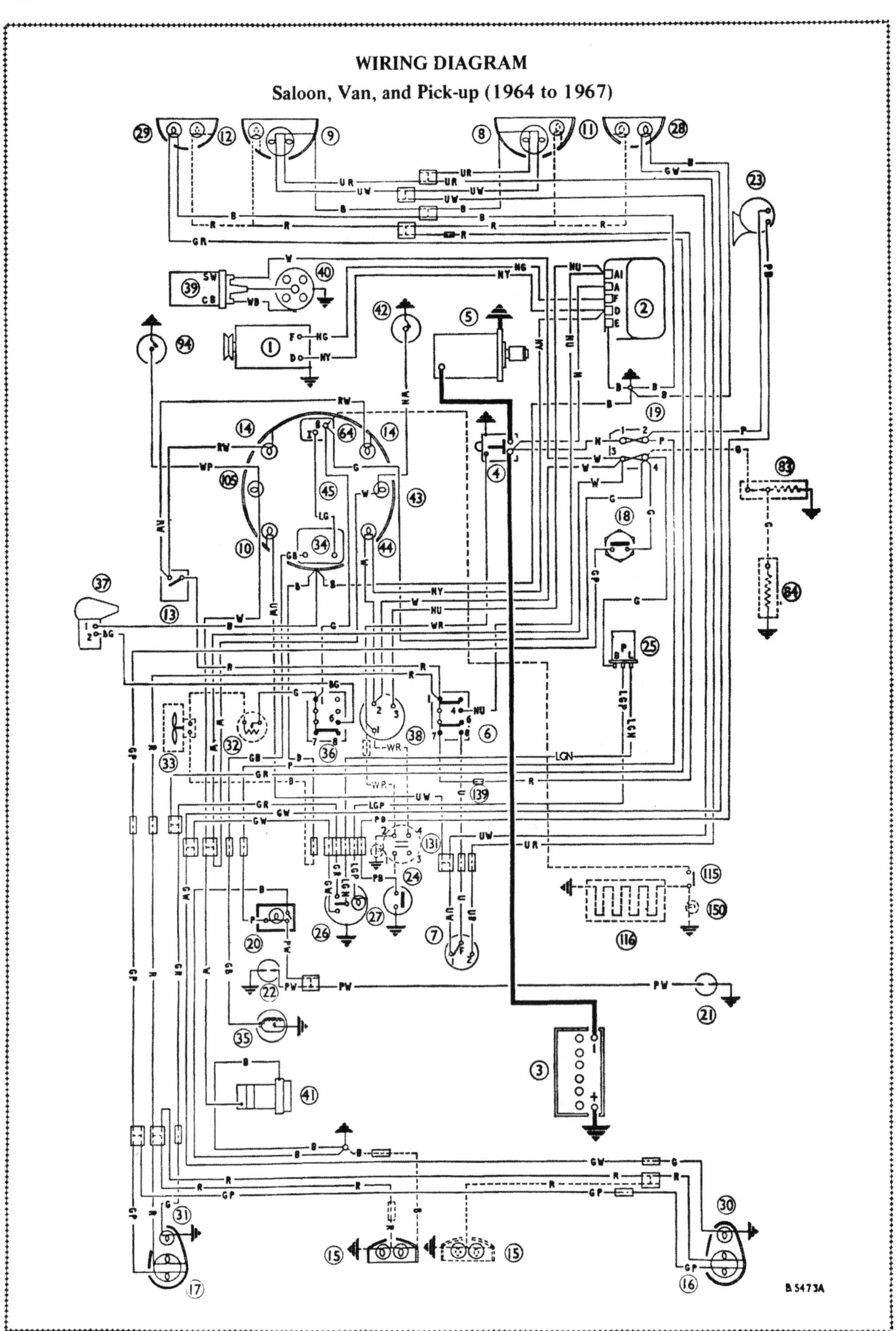

KEY TO WIRING DIAGRAM

No.	Description
1.	Dynamo.
2.	Control box.
3.	12-volt battery.
4.	Starter solenoid.
5.	Starter motor.
6.	Lighting switch.
7.	Headlamp dip switch.
8.	R.H. headlamp.
9.	L.H. headlamp.
10.	Main-beam warning lamp.
11.	R.H. sidelamp (in headlamp or flasher) lamp.
12.	L.H. sidelamp (in headlamp or flasher) lamp.
13.	Panel lamps switch
14.	Panel lamps.
15.	Number-plate lamp (two for Van).
16.	R.H. stop and tail lamp.
17.	L.H. stop and tail lamp.
18.	Stop lamp switch.
19.	Fuse unit: 1-2, 35 amp.; 3-4, 35 amp.
20.	Interior light.
21.	R.H. door switch.
22.	L.H. door switch.
23.	Horn.
24.	Horn-push.
25.	Flasher unit.
26.	Direction indicator switch.
27.	Direction indicator warning lamp.
28.	R.H. front flasher lamp.

No.	Description
29.	L.H. front flasher lamp.
30.	R.H. rear flasher lamp.
31.	L.H. rear flasher lamp.
32.	Heater switch } when fitted.
33.	Heater motor } when fitted.
34.	Fuel gauge.
35.	Fuel gauge tank unit.
36.	Windscreen wiper switch.
37.	Windscreen wiper motor.
38.	Ignition/starter switch.
39.	Ignition coil.
40.	Distributor.
41.	Fuel pump.
42.	Oil pressure switch.
43.	Oil pressure warning lamp.
44.	Ignition warning lamp.
45.	Speedometer.
64.	Bi-metal instrument voltage stabilizer.
83.	Induction heater and thermostat (when fitted).
84.	Suction chamber heater (when fitted).
94.	Oil filter switch.
105.	Oil filter warning lamp.
115.	Rear window demister switch (when fitted).
116.	Rear window demister unit (when fitted).
131.	Combined reverse switch/automatic gearbox switch (when fitted).
139.	Connect to No. 6 for U.S.A. (alternative connection).
150.	Rear window demister warning light (when fitted).

CABLE COLOUR CODE

B. Black.	G. Green.	W. White.
U. Blue.	P. Purple.	Y. Yellow.
N. Brown.	R. Red.	L.G Light Green.

When a cable has two colour code letters the first denotes the main colour and the second denotes the tracer colour.

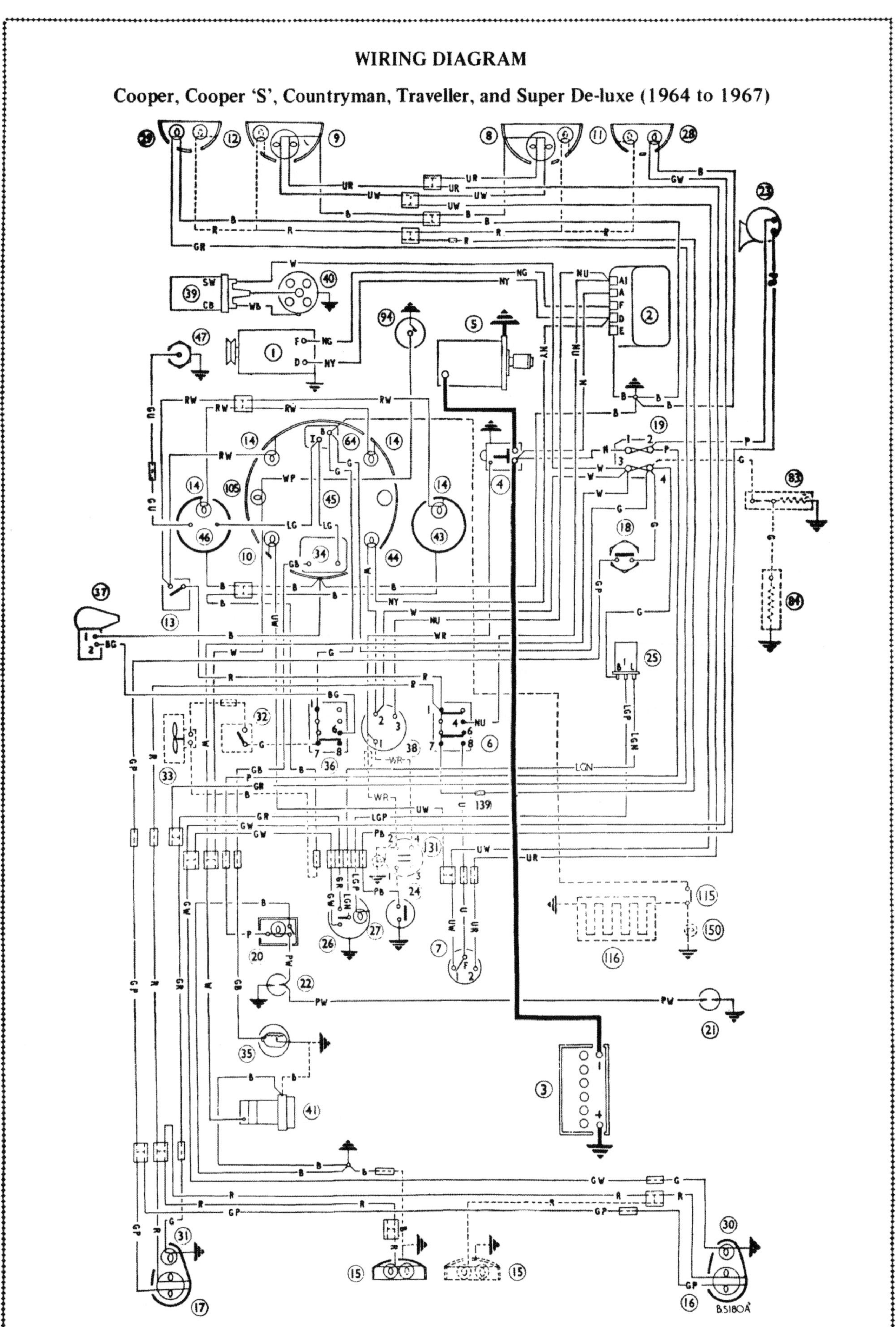

WIRING DIAGRAM

Cooper, Cooper 'S', Countryman, Traveller, and Super De-luxe (1964 to 1967)

KEY TO WIRING DIAGRAM

No.	Description
1.	Dynamo.
2.	Control box.
3.	12-volt battery.
4.	Starter solenoid.
5.	Starter motor.
6.	Lighting switch.
7.	Headlamp dip switch.
8.	R.H. headlamp.
9.	L.H. headlamp.
10.	Main-beam warning lamp.
11.	R.H. sidelamp (in headlamp or flasher) lamp.
12.	L.H. sidelamp (in headlamp or flasher) lamp.
13.	Panel lamps switch.
14.	Panel lamps.
15.	Number-plate lamp (two for Countryman and Traveller).
16.	R.H. stop and tail lamp.
17.	L.H. stop and tail lamp.
18.	Stop lamp switch.
19.	Fuse unit: 1-2, 35 amp.; 3-4, 35 amp.
20.	Interior light.
21.	R.H. door switch.
22.	L.H. door switch.
23.	Horn.
24.	Horn-push.
25.	Flasher unit.
26.	Direction indicator switch.
27.	Direction indicator warning lamp.
28.	R.H. front flasher lamp.
29.	L.H. front flasher lamp.
30.	R.H. rear flasher lamp.
31.	L.H. rear flasher lamp.
32.	Heater switch (when fitted).
33.	Heater motor (when fitted).
34.	Fuel gauge.
35.	Fuel gauge tank unit.
36.	Windscreen wiper switch.
37.	Windscreen wiper motor.
38.	Ignition/starter switch.
39.	Ignition coil.
40.	Distributor.
41.	Fuel pump.
42.	Oil pressure switch.
43.	Oil pressure warning lamp.
44.	Ignition warning lamp.
45.	Speedometer.
46.	Temperature gauge.
47.	Temperature gauge transmitter.
64.	Bi-metal instrument voltage stabilizer.
83.	Induction heater and thermostat (when fitted).
84.	Suction chamber heater (when fitted).
94.	Oil filter switch.
105.	Oil filter warning lamp.
115.	Rear window demister switch (when fitted).
116.	Rear window demister unit (when fitted).
131.	Combined reverse switch/automatic gearbox switch (when fitted).
139.	Connect to No. 6 for U.S.A. (alternative connection).
150.	Rear window demister warning light (when fitted).

CABLE COLOUR CODE

B.	Black.	G.	Green.	W.	White.
U.	Blue.	P.	Purple.	Y.	Yellow.
N.	Brown.	R.	Red.	L.G.	Light Green.

WIRING DIAGRAM

Mini-Moke (up to 1967)

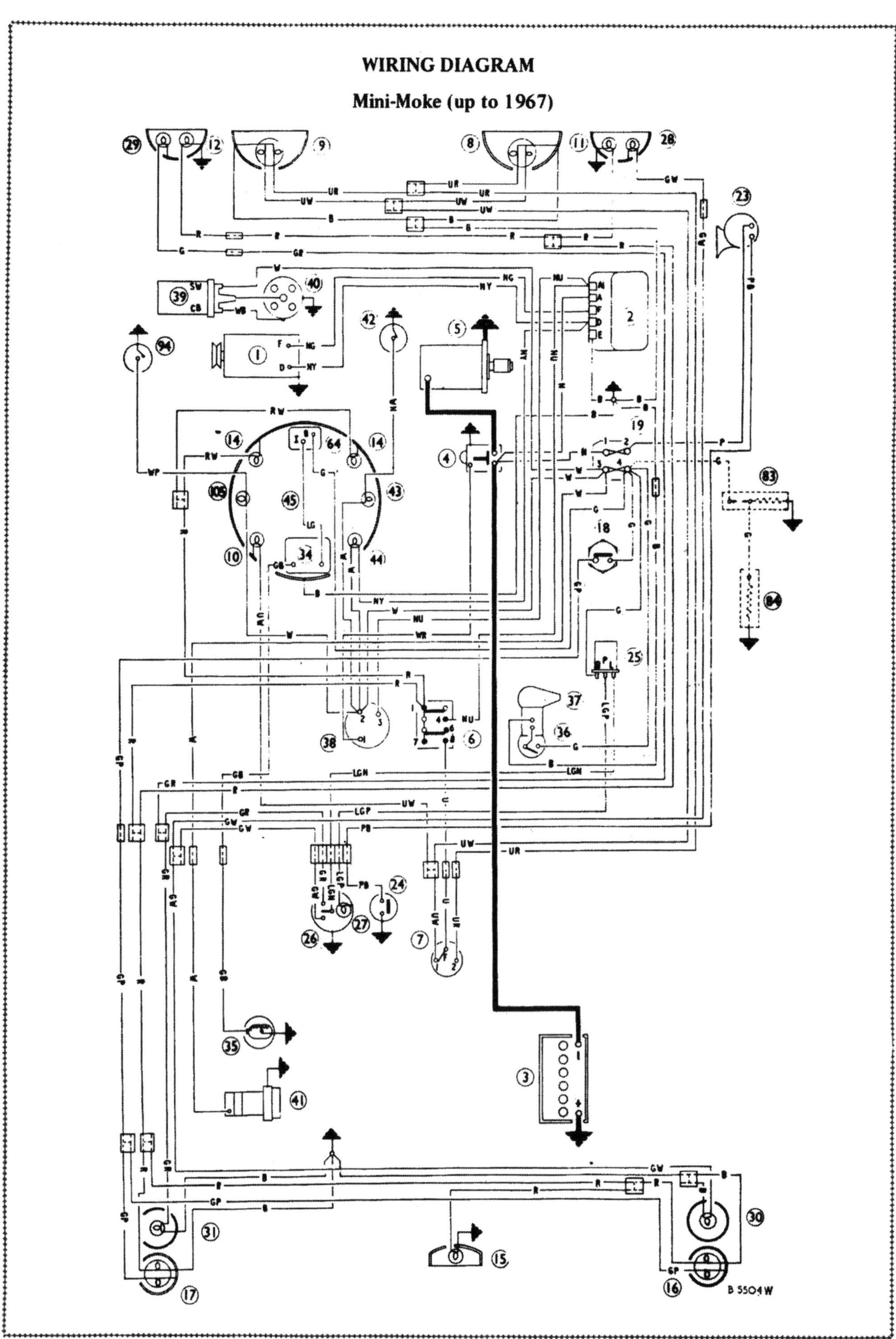

KEY TO WIRING DIAGRAM

No.	Description	No.	Description
1.	Dynamo.	27.	Direction indicator warning lamp.
2.	Control box.	28.	R.H. front flasher lamp.
3.	12-volt battery.	29.	L.H. front flasher lamp.
4.	Starter solenoid.	30.	R.H. rear flasher lamp.
5.	Starter motor.	31.	L.H. rear flasher lamp
6.	Lighting switch.	34.	Fuel gauge.
7.	Headlamp dip switch.	35.	Fuel gauge tank unit.
8.	R.H. headlamp.	36.	Windscreen wiper switch.
9.	L.H. headlamp.	37.	Windscreen wiper motor.
10.	Main-beam warning lamp.	38.	Ignition starter switch.
11.	R.H. sidelamp.	39.	Ignition coil.
12.	L.H. sidelamp.	40.	Distributor.
14.	Panel lamps.	41.	Fuel pump.
15.	Number-plate illumination lamp.	42.	Oil pressure switch.
16.	R.H. stop and tail lamp.	43.	Oil pressure warning lamp.
17.	L.H. stop and tail lamp.	44.	Ignition warning lamp.
18.	Stop lamp switch.	45.	Speedometer.
19.	Two-way fuse unit: 1-2, 35 amp.; 3-4, 35 amp.	64.	Bi-metal instrument voltage stabilizer.
23.	Horn.	83.	Induction heater and thermostat.
24.	Horn-push.	84.	Suction chamber heater.
25.	Flasher unit.	94.	Oil filter switch.
26.	Direction indicator switch.	105.	Oil filter warning lamp.

CABLE COLOUR CODE

B.	Black.	G.	Green.	W.	White.
U.	Blue.	P.	Purple.	Y.	Yellow.
N.	Brown.	R.	Red.	L.G.	Light Green.

When a cable has two colour code letters the first denotes the main colour and the second denotes the tracer colour.

WIRING DIAGRAM

Super De-luxe, Countryman, Traveller, Cooper, and Cooper 'S' Mark II

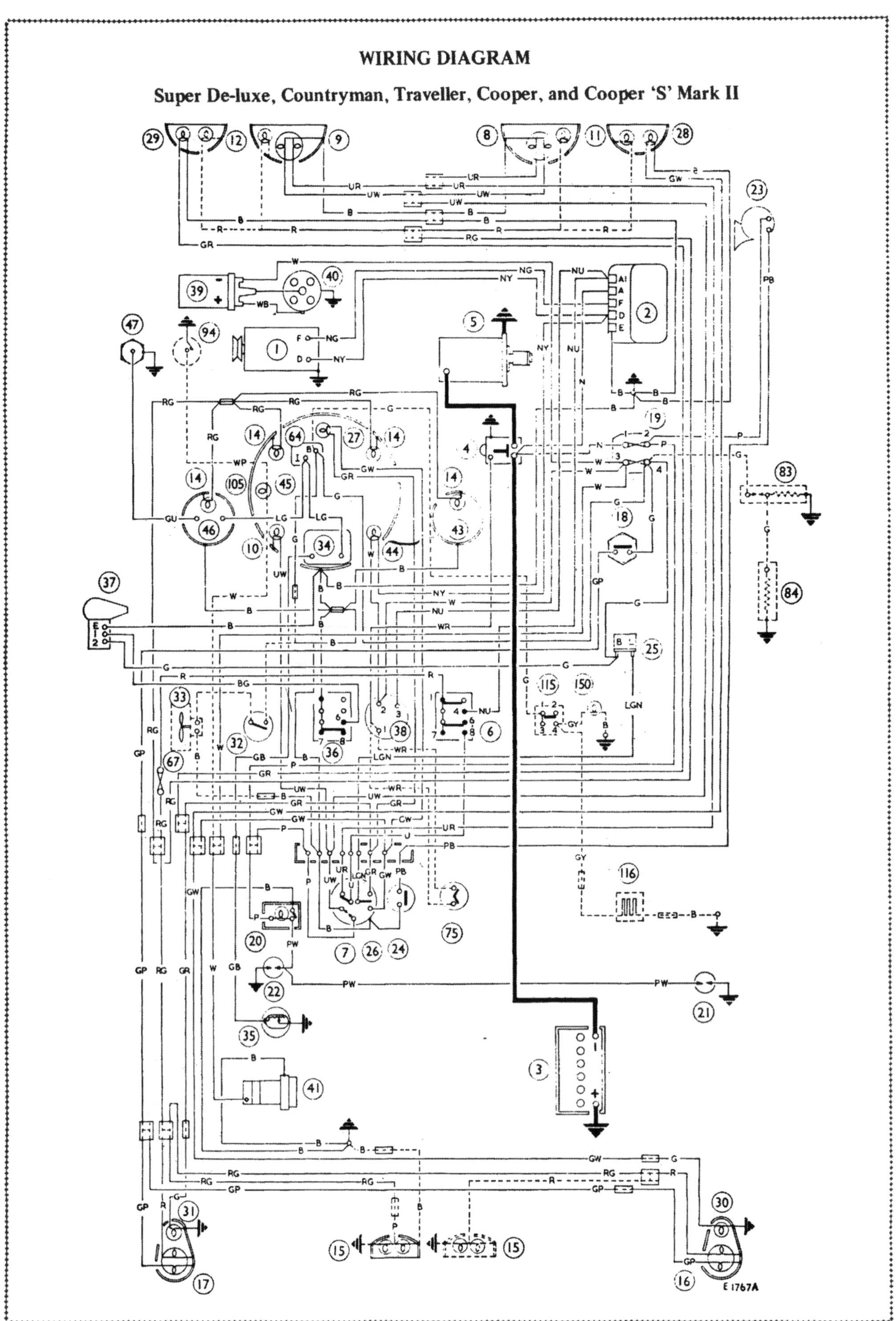

KEY TO WIRING DIAGRAM

No.	Description
1.	Dynamo.
2.	Control box.
3.	12-volt battery.
4.	Starter solenoid.
5.	Starter motor.
6.	Lighting switch.
7.	Headlamp dip switch.
8.	R.H. headlamp.
9.	L.H. headlamp.
10.	Main-beam warning lamp.
11.	R.H. sidelamp (in headlamp or flasher) lamp.
12.	L.H. sidelamp (in headlamp or flasher) lamp.
14.	Panel lamps.
15.	Number-plate lamp (two for Countryman and Traveller).
16.	R.H. stop and tail lamp.
17.	L.H. stop and tail lamp.
18.	Stop lamp switch.
19.	Fuse unit; 1-2, 35 amp.; 3-4, 35 amp.
20.	Interior light.
21.	R.H. door switch.
22.	L.H. door switch.
23.	Horn.
24.	Horn-push.
25.	Flasher unit.
26.	Direction indicator and headlamp flasher switch.
27.	Direction indicator warning lamp.
28.	R.H. front flasher lamp.
29.	L.H. front flasher lamp.

No.	Description
30.	R.H. rear flasher lamp.
31.	L.H. rear flasher lamp.
32.	Heater switch } when fitted.
33.	Heater motor } when fitted.
34.	Fuel gauge.
35.	Fuel gauge tank unit.
36.	Windscreen wiper switch.
37.	Windscreen wiper motor.
38.	Ignition/starter switch.
39.	Ignition coil.
40.	Distributor.
41.	Fuel pump.
42.	Oil pressure switch.
43.	Oil pressure warning lamp.
44.	Ignition warning lamp.
45.	Speedometer.
46.	Temperature gauge.
47.	Temperature gauge transmitter.
64.	Bi-metal instrument voltage stabilizer.
67.	Line fuse, 35 amp.
75.	Automatic gearbox safety switch (when fitted).
83.	Induction heater and thermostat (when fitted).
84.	Suction chamber heater (when fitted).
94.	Oil filter switch. } Not fitted on Automatic.
105.	Oil filter warning lamp. } Not fitted on Automatic.
115.	Rear window demister switch (when fitted).
116.	Rear window demister unit (when fitted).
150.	Rear window demister warning light (when fitted).

CABLE COLOUR CODE

B.	Black.	G.	Green.	W.	White.
U.	Blue.	P.	Purple.	Y.	Yellow.
N.	Brown.	R.	Red.	L.G.	Light Green.

When a cable has two colour code letters the first denotes the main colour and the second denotes the tracer colour.

WIRING DIAGRAM

Standard Saloon, Van, and Pick-up Mark II

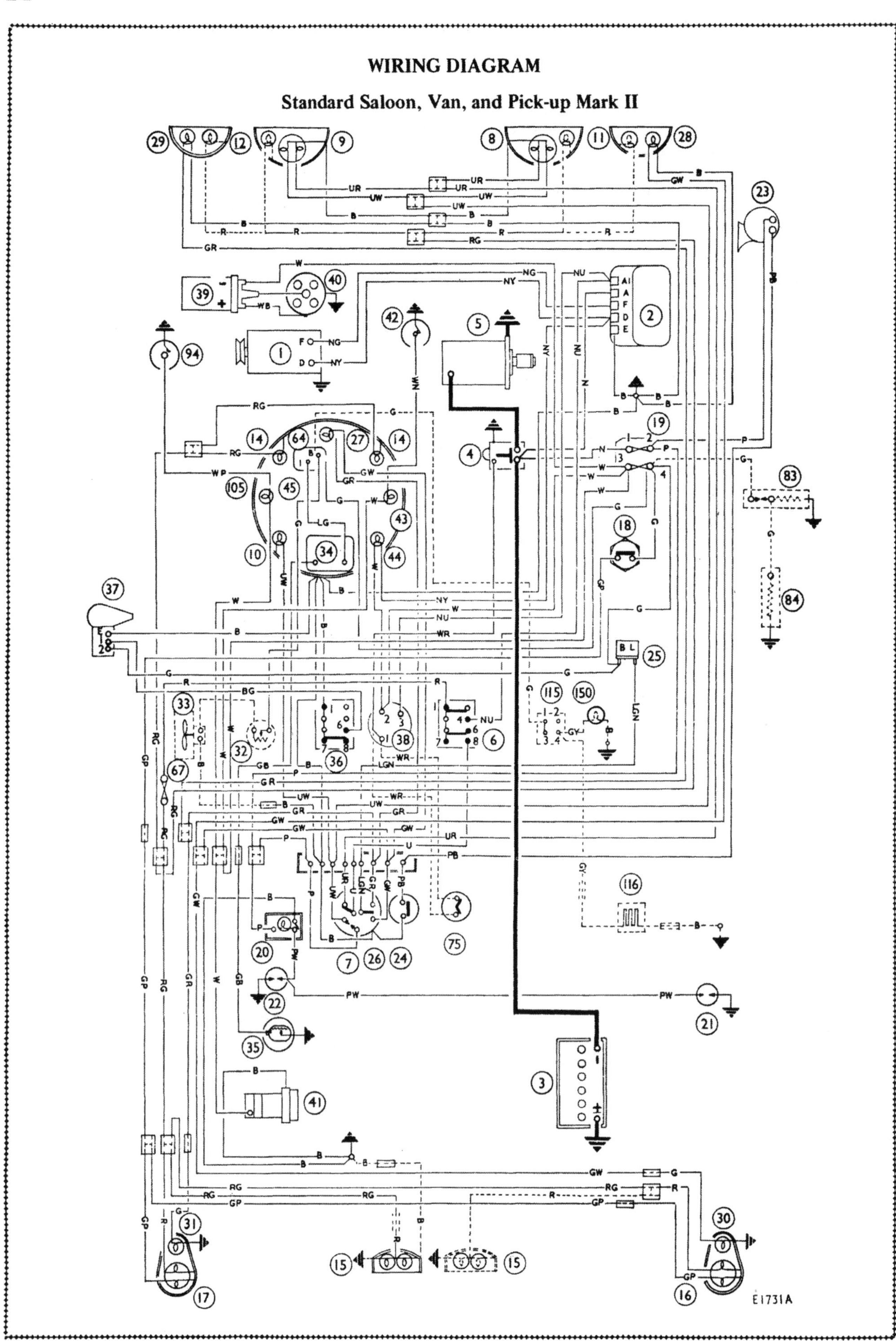

KEY TO WIRING DIAGRAM

No.	Description
1.	Dynamo.
2.	Control box.
3.	12-volt battery.
4.	Starter solenoid.
5.	Starter motor.
6.	Lighting switch.
7.	Headlamp dip switch.
8.	R.H. headlamp.
9.	L.H. headlamp.
10.	Main-beam warning lamp.
11.	R.H. sidelamp (in headlamp or flasher) lamp.
12.	L.H. sidelamp (in headlamp or flasher) lamp.
14.	Panel lamps.
15.	Number-plate lamp (two for Van).
16.	R.H. stop and tail lamp.
17.	L.H. stop and tail lamp.
18.	Stop lamp switch.
19.	Fuse unit: 1-2, 35 amp.; 3-4, 35 amp.
20.	Interior light.
21.	R.H. door switch.
22.	L.H. door switch.
23.	Horn.
24.	Horn-push.
25.	Flasher unit.
26.	Direction indicator and headlamp flasher switch.
27.	Direction indicator warning lamp.
28.	R.H. front flasher lamp.

No.	Description
29.	L.H. front flasher lamp.
30.	R.H. rear flasher lamp.
31.	L.H. rear flasher lamp.
32.	Heater switch. } when fitted.
33.	Heater motor. } when fitted.
34.	Fuel gauge.
35.	Fuel gauge tank unit.
36.	Windscreen wiper switch.
37.	Windscreen wiper motor.
38.	Ignition/starter switch.
39.	Ignition coil.
40.	Distributor.
41.	Fuel pump.
42.	Oil pressure switch.
43.	Oil pressure warning lamp.
44.	Ignition warning lamp.
45.	Speedometer.
64.	Bi-metal instrument voltage stabilizer.
76.	Line fuse, 35-amp.
75.	Automatic gearbox safety switch (when fitted).
83.	Induction heater and thermostat (when fitted).
84.	Suction chamber heater (when fitted).
94.	Oil filter switch. } Not fitted on Automatic.
105.	Oil filter warning lamp. } Not fitted on Automatic.
115.	Rear window demister switch (when fitted).
116.	Rear window demister unit (when fitted).
150.	Rear window demister warning light (when fitted).

CABLE COLOUR CODE

B.	Black.	G.	Green.	W.	White.
U.	Blue.	P.	Purple.	Y.	Yellow.
N.	Brown.	R.	Red.	L.G.	Light Green

When a cable has two colour code letters the first denotes the main colour and the second denotes the tracer colour.

WIRING DIAGRAM

Mini-Moke Mark II

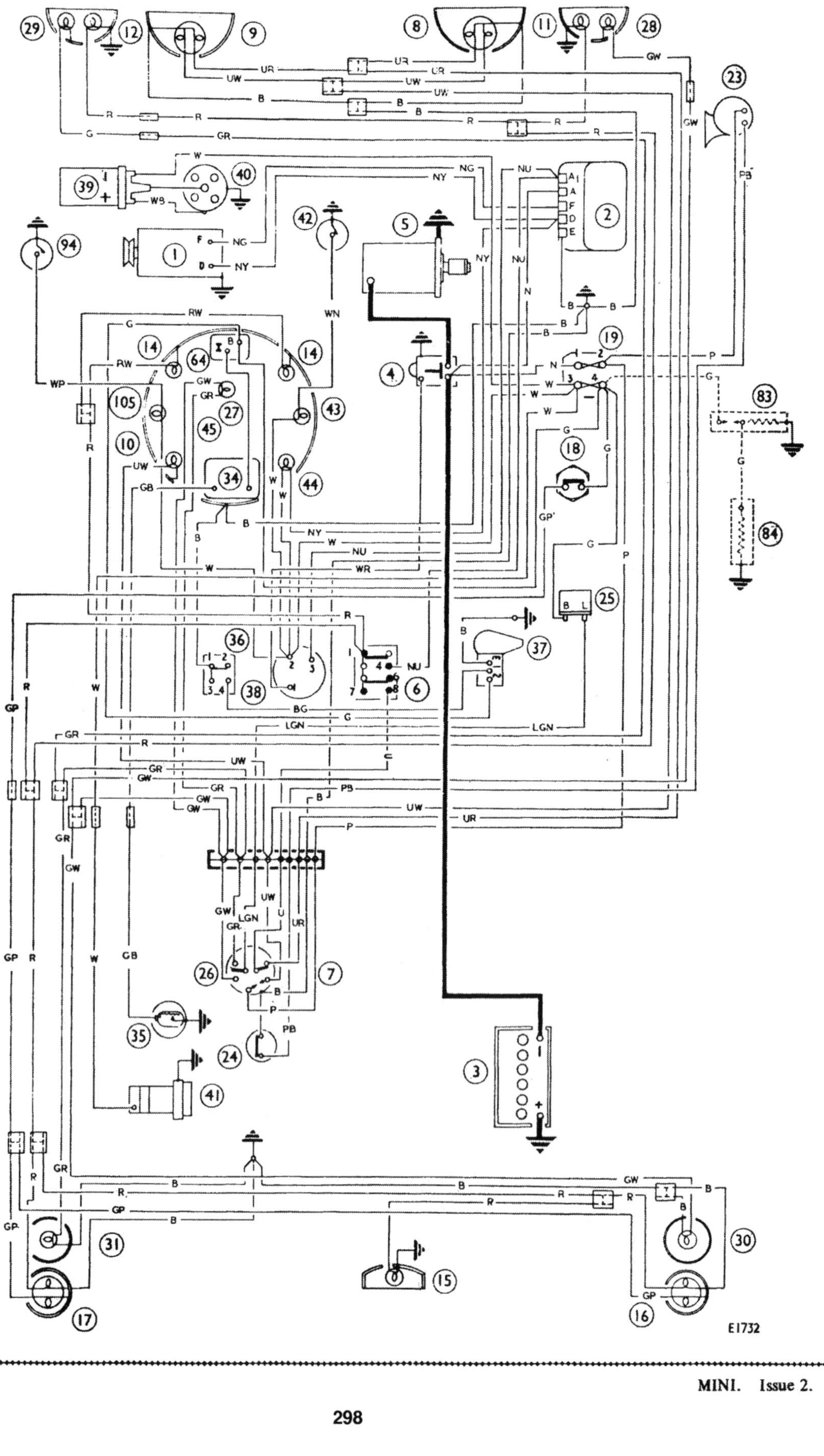

KEY TO WIRING DIAGRAM

No.	Description	No.	Description
1.	Dynamo.	27.	Direction indicator warning lamp.
2.	Control box.	28.	R.H. front flasher lamp.
3.	12-volt battery.	29.	L.H. front flasher lamp.
4.	Starter solenoid.	30.	R.H. rear flasher lamp.
5.	Starter motor.	31.	L.H. rear flasher lamp.
6.	Lighting switch.	34.	Fuel gauge.
7.	Headlamp dip switch.	35.	Fuel gauge tank unit.
8.	R.H. headlamp.	36.	Windscreen wiper switch.
9.	L.H. headlamp.	37.	Windscreen wiper motor.
10.	Main-beam warning lamp.	38.	Ignition starter switch.
11.	R.H. sidelamp.	39.	Ignition coil.
12.	L.H. sidelamp.	40.	Distributor.
14.	Panel lamps.	41.	Fuel pump.
15.	Number-plate illumination lamp.	42.	Oil pressure switch.
16.	R.H. stop and tail lamp.	43.	Oil pressure warning lamp.
17.	L.H. stop and tail lamp.	44.	Ignition warning lamp.
18.	Stop lamp switch.	45.	Speedometer.
19.	Two-way fuse unit; 1-2, 35 amp.; 3-4, 35 amp.	64.	Bi-metal instrument voltage stabilizer.
23.	Horn.	83.	Induction heater and thermostat.
24.	Horn-push.	84.	Suction chamber heater.
25.	Flasher unit.	94.	Oil filter switch.
26.	Direction indicator switch.	105.	Oil filter warning lamp.

CABLE COLOUR CODE

B.	Black.	G.	Green.	W.	White.
U.	Blue.	P.	Purple.	Y.	Yellow.
N.	Brown.	R.	Red.	L.G.	Light Green.

When a cable has two colour code letters the first denotes the main colour and the second denotes the tracer colour.

Section N.1

BATTERY

Maintenance

1. Keep the battery clean and the vent holes in the caps free.
2. Clean corroded terminals with diluted ammonia and smear them with petroleum jelly.
3. Maintain the level of the electrolyte just above the tops of the separators.

   NOTE.–Disconnect the battery earth cable before boost-charging the battery or using arc welding equipment on the body. Considerable damage to the electrical components will result if the ignition is switched on while the battery remains connected to the car electrical system.

Checking

4. The state of charge of the battery is indicated by hydrometer reading as follows:

FOR CLIMATES BELOW 27 °C. (80 °F.)

Cell fully charged	1.270 to 1.290
Cell about half-charged	1.190 to 1.210
Cell completely discharged	1.110 to 1.130

FOR CLIMATES ABOVE 27 °C. (80 °F.)

Cell fully charged	1.210 to 1.230
Cell about half-charged	1.130 to 1.150
Cell completely discharged	1.050 to 1.070

These figures are given assuming an electrolyte temperature of 16 °C. (60 °F.). If the temperature of the electrolyte exceeds this .002 must be added to hydrometer readings for each 3 °C. (5 °F.) rise to give the true specific gravity. Similarly, .002 must be subtracted from hydrometer readings for every 3°C. (5°F.) below 16°C. (60°F.).

Charging (used battery)

5. Charge at 3.0 amps. until all cells are gassing freely and hydrometer readings of each cell have not risen in four hours. Do not allow the temperature of the electrolyte to exceed the following maximum:
   For climates below 27 °C. (80 °F.) 30 °C. (100 °F.)
   For climates above 27 °C. (80 °F.) 49 °C. (120 °F.)

Dry-charged batteries

Dry-charged batteries are supplied without electrolyte but with the plates in a charged condition. No initial charging is required.

6. Fill with electrolyte obtained as follows:

For climates	To obtain specific gravity (corrected to 16°C. (60° F.)) of	Add 1 vol. of acid of 1.840 S.G (corrected to 16°C. (60°F.)) to
Below 27 °C. (80° F.)	1.260	3.2 volumes of water
Above 27 °C. (80° F.)	1.210	4.3 volumes of water

Batteries filled in this way are capable of giving a starting discharge **one hour after filling.** When time permits, however, a short freshening charge at the normal recharge rate (3.0 amps.) will ensure that the battery is fully charged.

During the charge the electrolyte must be kept level with the top edge of the separators by addition of distilled water. Check the specific gravity of the acid at the end of the charge; if 1.260 acid was used to fill the battery, the specific gravity should now be between 1.270 and 1.290. If 1.210 acid was used the specific gravity should now be between 1.210 and 1.230. After filling, a dry-charged battery needs only the attention normally given to a lead-acid battery.

New, unfilled, uncharged battery

7. Half fill each cell with electrolyte prepared as in item 6 above and allow it to stand for six hours, fill each cell to the correct level and allow a further standing period of two hours.
8. Charge at 2 amps. until five successive hourly hydrometer checks show no increase in the reading; this will take from 48 to 80 hours, depending on the length of time the battery has been stored before charging. **This charge should not be broken by long rest periods.**
9. If the temperature of any cell rises above the maximum given in 5, the charge must be interrupted until the temperature has fallen at least 5.5 °C. (10 °F.) below that figure.
10. Maintain the level of the electrolyte during the charge.
11. At the end of the charge carefully check the specific gravity in each cell to ensure that, when corrected to 16 °C. (60° F.) it lies between the specified limits. If any cell requires adjustment some of the electrolyte must be siphoned off and replaced either by distilled water or by acid of strength originally used for filling in, depending on whether the specific gravity is too high or too low. Continue the charge for an hour or so to ensure adequate mixing of the electrolyte and again check the specific gravity readings. If necessary, repeat the adjustment process until the desired reading is obtained in each cell.
12. Finally, allow the battery to cool, and siphon off any surplus electrolyte.

Section N.2

DYNAMO

Removing

1. Disconnect the leads, slacken the four mounting bolts, remove the fan belt from the pulley, take out the two upper and one lower mounting bolts and lift off the dynamo.

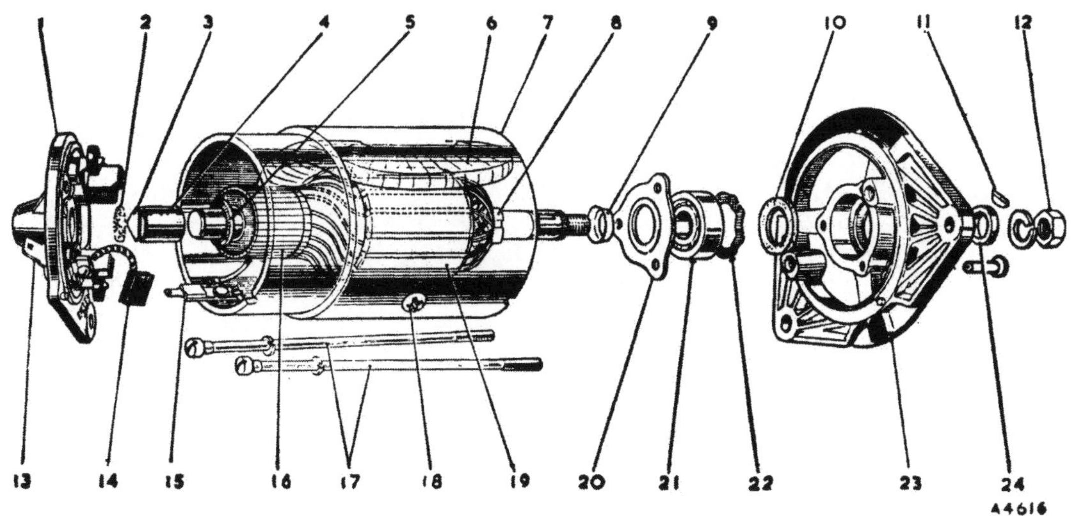

Fig. N.1
The C40/1 type dynamo

1.	Commutator end bracket.	9.	Shaft collar retaining cup.	17.	Through-bolts.
2.	Felt ring.	10.	Felt ring.	18.	Pole-shoe securing screws.
3.	Felt ring retainer.	11.	Shaft key.	19.	Armature.
4.	Bronze bush.	12.	Shaft nut.	20.	Bearing retaining plate.
5.	Thrust washer.	13.	Output terminal 'D'.	21.	Ball bearing.
6.	Field coils.	14.	Brushes.	22.	Corrugated washer.
7.	Yoke.	15.	Field Terminal 'F'.	23.	Driving end bracket.
8.	Shaft collar.	16.	Commutator.	24.	Pulley spacer.

Dismantling

2. Unscrew the nut and take off the pulley.
3. Extract the key from the shaft.
4. Withdraw the two through-bolts and remove the commutator end bracket.
5. Lift the driving end bracket with the armature and bearing out of the yoke.
6. To remove the bearing, press off the end bracket.

Servicing

BRUSHES

7. Clean the brushes with petrol (fuel) and, if sticking, polish them lightly with a smooth file.
8. Test the spring tension (**'GENERAL DATA'**).
9. Fit new brushes if the existing ones are worn to a length of less than ¼ in. (6.5 mm.).

COMMUTATOR

10. Clean with petrol (fuel) and cloth or polish with fine glass-paper. If it is in very poor condition it may be skimmed to a minimum diameter of 1.450 in (.37 mm.). The undercut must have the following dimensions:

    Width .. .. .040 in. (1.02 mm.).
    Depth .. .. .020 to .035 in. (.51 to .89 mm.).

    Clean the insulating material from the sides of the undercut to a minimum depth of .015 in. (.38 mm.).

FIELD COIL REPLACEMENT

11. Mark the position of the pole-shoes relative to the yoke.
12. Withdraw the pole-shoe securing screws (Fig. N.1), draw the shoes and coils from the yoke and remove the coils from the shoes.
13. Fit new coils to the shoes and refit them to the yoke with the shoes in their original positions. Refit the insulating piece at the junction of the coil windings, insert the screws, press the shoes in place with an expander, and tighten the screws (Fig. N.1).

ARMATURE

14. If special equipment is not available, test the armature by substitution.

BEARINGS

15. Screw a ⅝ in. (15.8 mm.) tap into the bush at the commutator end, pull out the bush and fit a new one, using a shouldered mandrel.

    NOTE.–Soak the new bush in thin engine oil for 24 hours before fitting.

16. Renew the bearing at the driving end as follows:
17. Knock out the rivets and remove the bearing retaining plate.
18. Press the bearing out of the bracket and remove the corrugated and felt washers.
19. Pack the new bearing with grease before pressing it in.

Reassembling and refitting

20. Reverse the removing and dismantling instructions.
21. The two upper fixing bolts must be fitted with a flat washer under the head of each bolt to register against the dynamo attachment points.

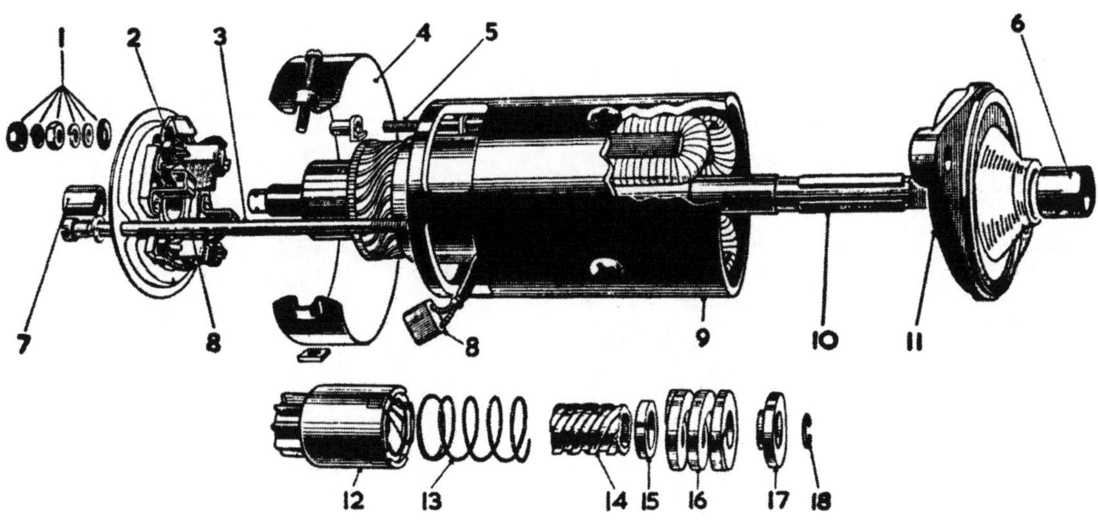

Fig. N.2
An exploded view of the starter motor and drive

1. Terminal nuts and washers.
2. Brush spring.
3. Through-bolt.
4. Band cover.
5. Terminal post.
6. Bearing bush.
7. Bearing.
8. Brushes.
9. Yoke.
10. Armature shaft.
11. Driving-end bracket.
12. Pinion assembly.
13. Restraining spring.
14. Sleeve.
15. Impact washer.
16. Main spring.
17. Locating washer.
18. Circlip.

Section N.3

STARTER

Removing

1. Disconnect the cable, unscrew the three bolts and lift away.

Dismantling

2. Remove the cover band, withdraw the brushes, unscrew the through-bolts and take out the armature complete with drive.

Servicing

BRUSHES

See Section N.2, items 7 to 9.

DRIVE

3. If the pinion is tight on the sleeve, wash it in kerosene.
4. To dismantle, remove the shaft nut and withdraw the main spring and collar. On later types, compress the spring and remove the ciiclip.
5. Rotate the barrel, push out the sleeve and remove the barrel and pinion.
6. The barrel and pinion are supplied as an assembly.

COMMUTATOR

7. If cleaning is not effective, skim lightly removing the absolute minimum amount of metal. Do not undercut the mica.

FIELD COILS

See Section N.2, items 11, 12, and 13.

BEARINGS

See Section N.2, item 15.

ARMATURE

See Section N.2, item 14.

Reassembling and refitting

Reverse the removal and dismantling instructions.

Section N.4

VOLTAGE REGULATOR

Adjusting (cold unit)

ELECTRICAL

1. Disconnect the cables from the control box terminals 'A' and 'A1' and join them together.
2. Connect the negative lead from a voltmeter (0–20 volts) to control box terminal 'D' and the positive lead to terminal 'E'.
3. Slowly increase engine speed until the voltmeter needle flicks and then steadies. This should occur between 15.8 and 16.7 volts, depending on the ambient temperature.
4. If adjustment is required, switch off the engine and remove the control box cover.

5. Turn the voltage adjustment screw (1) (Fig. N.3), in a clockwise direction to raise the voltage and anti-clockwise to lower it. Turn only a fraction of a turn at a time. This adjustment should be completed within 30 seconds or the settings will be affected by heat. Do not run the dynamo at a higher speed than is necessary for the adjustment to be made.

MECHANICAL

6. Slacken the fixed contact and voltage adjusting screws until they are clear of the moving contact and the tension spring respectively. Slacken the two armature assembly securing screws.
7. Insert .021 in. (.53 mm.) feeler gauge between the armature and the core shim. Press the armature squarely down against the gauge and tighten the armature assembly securing screws.
8. With the gauge still in position, screw the adjustable contact down until it just touches the armature contact. Tighten the locking nut.
9. Reset the voltage adjusting screw as in item 5.

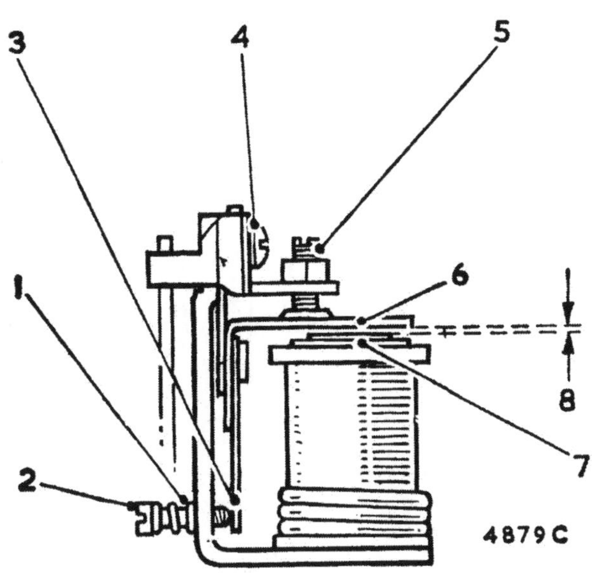

Fig. N.4
Mechanical setting of the regulator

1. Locknut.
2. Voltage adjusting screw.
3. Armature tension spring.
4. Armature securing screws.
5. Fixed contact adjustment screw.
6. Armature.
7. Core face and shim.
8. .021 in. (.533 mm.).

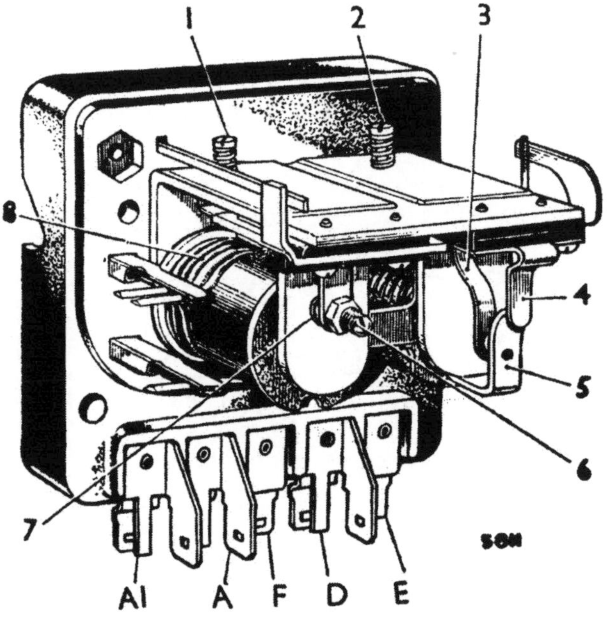

Fig. N.3
The control box

1. Regulator adjusting screw.
2. Cut-out adjusting screw.
3. Fixed contact blade.
4. Stop arm.
5. Armature tongue and moving contact.
6. Regulator fixed contact screw.
7. Regulator moving contact.
8. Regulator series windings.

Section N.5

CUT-OUT

Adjustment

ELECTRICAL

1. To check, connect the voltmeter between terminals 'D' and 'E'. Start the engine and slowly increase the speed until the contacts close; this should occur at 12.7 to 13.3 volts.
2. To adjust, turn the adjusting screw clockwise to raise the voltage and anti-clockwise to reduce it. Turn only a fraction at a time. Make the adjustments as quickly as possible to avoid temperature effects.

MECHANICAL

3. Unscrew the cut-out adjusting screw until it is clear of the armature tension spring. Slacken the armature securing screws.
4. Press the armature down against the copper-sprayed core and tighten the securing screws.
5. Bend the armature stop arm until the gap between it and the tongue is .030 in. (.76 mm.) when the armature is pressed squarely against the core face 8 (Fig. N.6).
6. Bend the fixed contact blade so that there is a gap of .010 to .020 in. (.25 to .30 mm.) between the contact points when the armature is free.
7. Reset the cut-out adjusting screw.

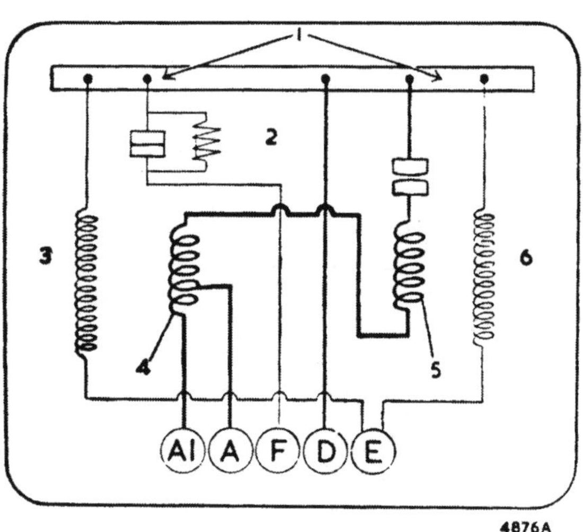

Fig. N.5
The control box (regulator and cut-out) internal connections

1. Regulator and cut-out frame.
2. Field resistance.
3. Shunt coil.
4. Tapped series coil.
5. Series coil.
6. Shunt coil.

Section N.6

LAMPS

Full details of the lamps, bulbs, warning lights, etc., are given in the Driver's Handbook.

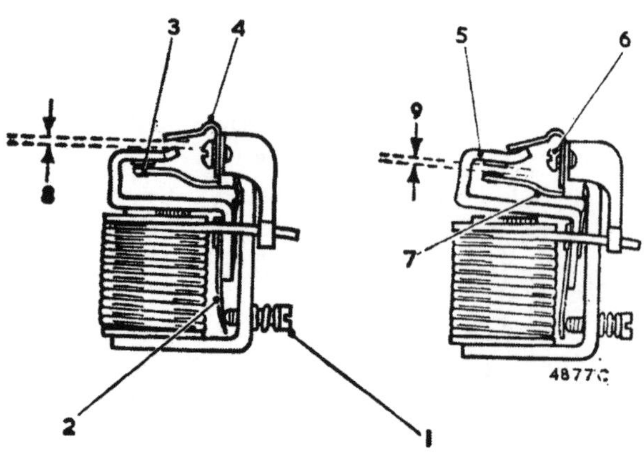

Fig. N.6
Mechanical setting of the cut-out

1. Cut-out adjusting screw.
2. Armature tension spring.
3. 'Follow through'–.010 to .020 in. (.25 to .51 mm.).
4. Stop arm.
5. Armature tongue and moving contact.
6. Armature securing screws.
7. Fixed contact blade.
8. .030 in. (.76 mm.).
9. .010 to .020 in. (.25 to .51 mm.).

Section N.7

BI-METAL RESISTANCE INSTRUMENTATION

General description

The bi-metal resistance equipment for fuel and temperature gauges consists of an indicator head and transmitter unit connected to a common voltage stabilizer. In both applications the indicator head operates on a thermal principle, using a bi-metal strip surrounded by a heated winding, and the transmitter unit is of a resistance type. The system by which the equipment functions is voltage-sensitive and the voltage stabilizer, which serves one or more gauges, is necessary to ensure a constant supply of a pre-determined voltage to the equipment.

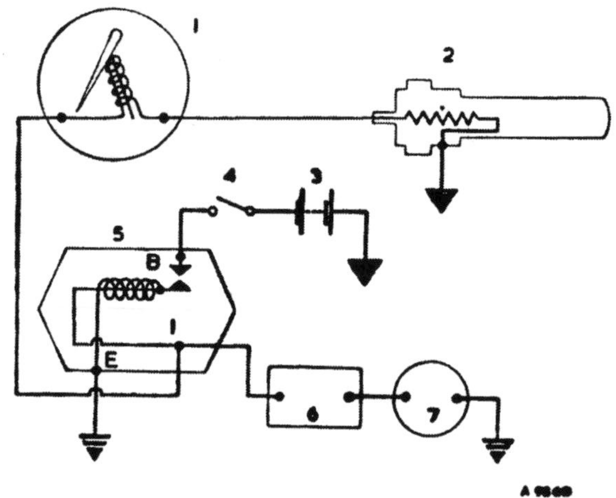

Fig. N.7
The bi-metal resistance instrumentation circuit

1. Temperature gauge.
2. Temperature gauge transmitter.
3. Battery.
4. Ignition switch.
5. Voltage stabilizer.
6. Fuel gauge.
7. Fuel gauge transmitter.

Fault analysis

VOLTAGE STABILIZER

Check the mean voltage between the output terminal 'I' and earth, which should be 10 volts.

Substitute voltage stabilizer if faulty.

GAUGES

Check for continuity between the terminals with the wiring disconnected. The gauges must not be checked by short circuiting to earth.

Substitute the gauge if faulty.

TRANSMITTER

Check for continuity between terminal and case with lead disconnected.

Substitute transmitter if faulty.

WIRING

Check for continuity between each unit. Check for leak to earth. Check for short circuits to earth on wiring to each transmitter. Check terminal wiring for security, earth connections, and wiring continuity. Check that the voltage stabilizer and relating transmitters are earthed.

NOTE.–If the voltage stabilizer is removed it is essential to ensure that, when replacing, B and E are uppermost and not exceeding 20 degrees from the vertical.

Section N.8

WINDSCREEN WIPER MOTOR (Moke)

The wiper motor fitted to early models of this vehicle operated a single wiping blade on the driver's side only.

Later vehicles are equipped with a motor which operates twin wiper blades, and this motor will be referred to below as the (later type).

Removing (early type)

1. Slacken the hexagon screw and pull the blade and arm from the drive spindle.
2. Remove the nuts, locknuts, washers, and seals securing the motor to the scuttle.
3. Disconnect the leads from inside the vehicle and withdraw the motor.

   NOTE.–A rubber flange with steel inserts is fitted between the wiper motor and the scuttle to prevent the insulating flange being over-compressed.

Refitting

4. Reverse the removal sequence.

Removing (later type)

5. Remove the four nuts securing the rack to the wheelboxes.
6. Disconnect the electrical connections from the motor.
7. Remove the three screws securing the motor to the bracket and remove the assembly.
8. Remove the gearbox cover and withdraw the retaining circlip from the cross-head connecting link pin and lift off the connecting link and rack cable assembly.

Dismantling the motor (later type)

9. Remove the through-bolts and the commutator housing.
10. Lift the brush unit clear of the commutator and withdraw it. Note the position occupied by each brush so that it may be refitted in its original setting on the commutator.
11. Access to the armature and field coils is obtained by withdrawing the yoke.
12. Clean the commutator and brushes, replacing any that are worn. Ensure that the commutator segments are clean; short-circuiting of adjacent segments will cause excessive current consumption. The resistance between segments should be .29 to .35 ohms.

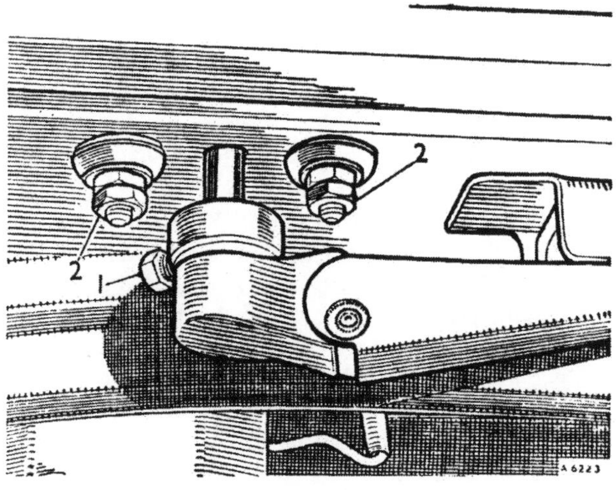

Fig. N.8
The windscreen wiper (Moke)

1. Arm-locating screw. 2. Motor mountings.

Dismantling the gearbox

13. Carry out instruction 8.
14. Remove the circlip and washer from the final drive gear shaft located underneath the gearbox casing, and lift out the final drive gear.
15. The armature can now be withdrawn for cleaning or replacement.
16. Examine the worm drive of the armature and the teeth of the final drive gear and fit replacements if either are damaged or excessively worn.

Reassembling

17. Reverse the dismantling procedures, using the following lubricants:

    Use Ragosine Listate grease liberally on the cross-head, guide channel, connecting rod assembly, worm drive, and on the rack cable and wheelbox assemblies.

    Use S.A.E. 20 oil sparingly on the armature and final drive gear bearings.
18. Ensure that the plain steel washer is placed beneath the connecting rod when assembling the final drive gear crankpin.
19. The armature end-float adjusting screw should be set to allow an end-float of .008 to .012 in. (.2 to .3 mm.); this is approximately a quarter of a turn clear of the armature thrust pad.

Refitting

20. Reverse the removing procedure, but before switching on the motor remove the wiper arms from the spindles. Switch on the motor and stop it at the end of the stroke; refit the arms so that they are in the correct parking position.

Section N.9

WINDSCREEN WIPER WHEELBOXES

Removing

1. Withdraw the wiper arms from the wheelbox spindles, and remove the external securing nuts.
2. ALL MODELS EXCEPT MOKE. From under the bonnet, slacken the nut securing the rack to the motor. Swivel the wheelboxes through into the engine compartment sufficiently to enable the securing nuts to be removed and release the wheelbox from the rack and cable. Note the location of the flared ends of the Bundy tubing with each wheelbox.
3. MOKE. Removing is similar to item 2 except that the wheelboxes are located inside the vehicle.

Refitting

4. Reverse the removing procedure and fit new external sealing grommets if required. Tighten the rack securing nut on the motor.
5. Switch on the motor and stop it at the end of the stroke. Ensure that the arms are correctly positioned to give maximum wipe area and park at the end of the stroke.

Section N.10

ALTERNATOR SERVICE PRECAUTIONS

The following precautions must be observed when dealing with vehicles fitted with an alternator.

1. When fitting a replacement alternator ensure that it is of the same polarity as the original. Terminal polarity is clearly marked.
2. Do not reverse the battery connections. This will damage the alternator rectifiers. Connect up the earth terminal of the battery first.
3. If a high-rate battery charger is used to charge the battery in position in the vehicle, damage will occur to the regulator if the ignition/starter switch is switched on to the auxiliary position. Detach the connectors from the regulator as a safety measure before boost-charging. Re-connect after charging.
4. When starting an engine with the aid of a high-rate charger, detach the connectors from the regulator prior to using the charger. Do not re-connect the regulator until the charger is disconnected, and the engine is running at idling speed.
5. The battery must never be disconnected while the engine is running, nor must the alternator be run with the main output cable disconnected either at the alternator end or the battery end.
6. The cable connecting the battery and alternator is 'live' even when the engine is not running. Take care not to earth the alternator terminal or the cable end if removed from the terminal.

   Do not make or break any connections in the alternator circuit while the engine is running.
7. Disconnect the alternator and regulator as a safety precaution when arc-welding on the vehicle.

Section N.11

TESTING THE ALTERNATOR CHARGING CIRCUIT IN POSITION

Before commencing the charging circuit tests given below carry out the '**Maintenance**' instructions.

Maintenance

The driving belt must be tensioned so that a deflection of ½ in. (13 mm.) can be obtained under finger pressure at the mid-point of the longest run of the belt.

DO NOT apply leverage to any point of the alternator other than the drive end bracket, or run the engine with the battery or alternator disconnected.

Keep the ventilating holes in the slip-ring end cover clean.

Alternator charging circuit

The following procedure should be adopted to locate a fault in the charging circuit using the test equipment recommended below.

TEST EQUIPMENT REQUIRED

a. Moving-coil D.C. ammeter, accurate up to at least 60 amps.
b. Moving-coil D.C. voltmeter, scale 0–30 volts (plus one of low range if possible).
c. Ohmmeter–battery powered. Hand-driven generator type must never be used for testing diodes.

Testing

1. Check the driving belt for wear and tension (see '**Maintenance**').
2. Check that the battery voltage is reaching the brush gear by disconnecting the two cables from the alternator field terminals, connect a voltmeter between the two cables and run the engine. The voltmeter should register battery voltage. If no reading is obtained, check the field circuit wiring.
3. Check the alternator output.

   Stop the engine and disconnect the battery earth cable (+). If an ammeter is not fitted, disconnect both connectors from the alternator main output terminal 'B' and connect up a moving-coil ammeter between the terminal and the connectors.

   Withdraw the cables from the alternator field terminals and connect a pair of auxiliary cables direct between these terminals and the battery (Fig. N.9).

   Re-connect the battery earth lead (+). Start the engine and gradually increase speed until the alternator is rotating at 4,000 r.p.m. At this speed the ammeter reading should be approximately 40 amps.

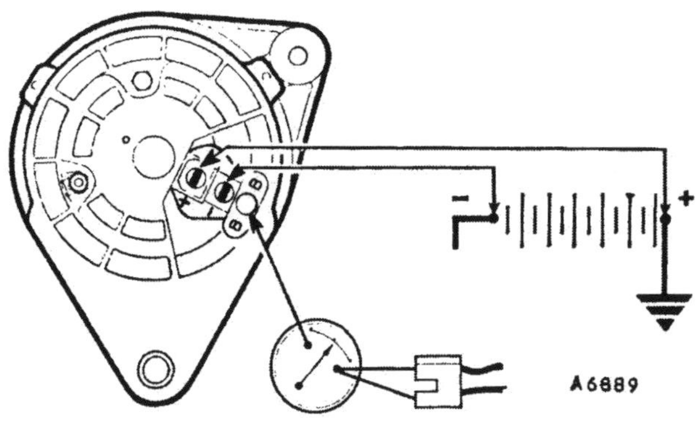

Fig. N.9
Alternator output test connections

a. Zero reading: Stop the engine. Remove and inspect the brush gear (see **'Inspection'**). Fit new brush gear if necessary and retest. If zero reading persists, remove and dismantle the alternator for detailed inspection.

b. Low reading: Indicates either a faulty alternator or poor wiring circuit connections.

Stop the engine and check the wiring connections. Connect a voltmeter (low range) between the alternator output terminal 'B' and the battery negative (–) terminal, restart the engine and note the reading. Transfer the voltmeter connections to the alternator frame and the battery earth (+) terminal and note the reading.

If either reading exceeds .5 volt there is high resistance in the charging circuit which must be traced and remedied. Should the test show no undue resistance (although output is low) proceed to dismantle and inspect the alternator.

Section N.12

DISMANTLING AND OVERHAULING THE 11AC ALTERNATOR

Removing

1. Disconnect the battery and detach the electrical leads from the alternator.
2. Slacken the alternator securing bolts, push the alternator towards the engine and detach the driving belt from the alternator pulley. Remove the securing bolts and detach the alternator from the engine.

Dismantling

3. Remove the securing nut and detach the drive pulley, fan, and key from the armature shaft.
4. Mark the relative positions of the drive end bracket, the stator lamination pack, and the slip-ring end bracket for correct reassembly.
5. Remove the through-bolts and detach the drive end bracket and rotor.

   The drive end bracket and rotor need not be separated unless the drive end bearing requires examination or the rotor is to be replaced. Remove the rotor from the drive end bracket by means of a hand press having first removed the shaft key and bearing collar.
6. Remove the terminal nuts, brush box retaining screws, and the heat sink bolt. Withdraw the stator and heat sink from the slip-ring end bracket.
7. Close the retaining tongues on the brush terminal blades and withdraw the terminals from the brush box.

Inspection

BRUSH GEAR

Brushes worn below $\frac{5}{16}$ in. (8 mm.) should be replaced.

a. The new brush complete with spring and 'Lucar' terminal blade is pushed into the holder until the tongue registers. To retain the terminal, carefully lever up the retaining tongue with a thin blade.

b. Check that the brushes move freely in their holders. If sluggish, clean brush sides with a petrol-moistened cloth or, if ineffective, lightly polish brush sides with a smooth file. Clean off and re-house.

SLIP-RINGS

Surfaces should be smooth and free of oil or other foreign matter. Clean the surfaces if necessary, using a petrol-moistened cloth or, if there is evidence of burning, very fine glass-paper.

NOTE.–Do not attempt to machine the slip-rings.

Testing

TEST EQUIPMENT REQUIRED:

a. Moving-coil D.C. ammeter, accurate up to 60 amps.

b. Moving-coil D.C. voltmeter, scale 0–30 volts.

c. Ohmmeter–battery-powered. Do not use a hand-driven generator type for testing diodes.

d. Mains test lamp, 110-volt A.C., 15-watt.

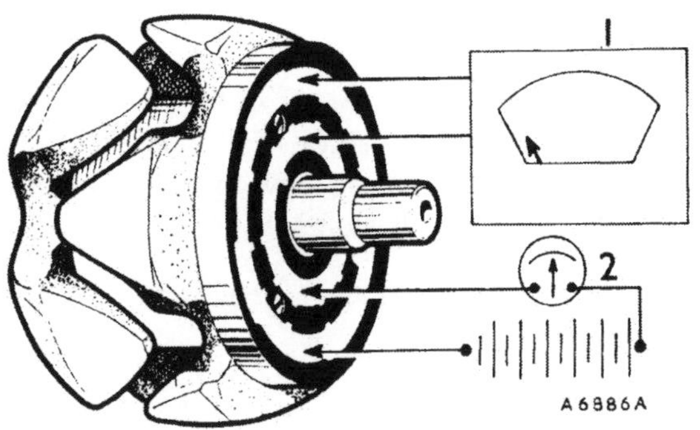

Fig. N.10
Using an ohmmeter (1) or a battery and ammeter (2) to test the resistance or current flow of the field winding

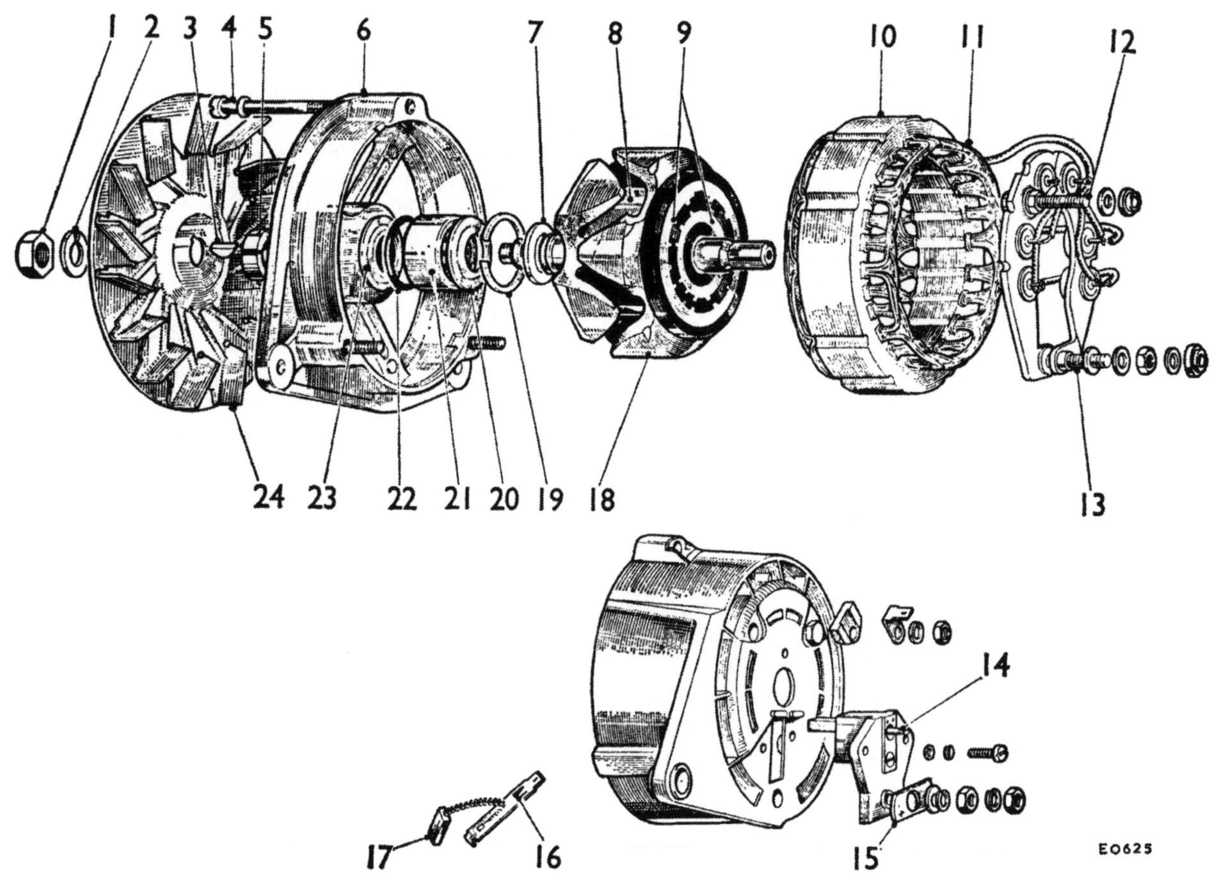

Fig. N.11
Alternator components

1. Shaft nut.
2. Spring washer.
3. Key.
4. Through-bolt.
5. Distance collar.
6. Drive end bracket.
7. Jump ring shroud.
8. Rotor (field) winding.
9. Slip rings.
10. Stator laminations.
11. Stator windings.
12. Warning light terminal.
13. Output terminal.
14. Field terminal blade.
15. Output terminal plastic strip.
16. Terminal blade retaining tongue.
17. Brush.
18. Rotor.
19. Bearing circlip.
20. Bearing retaining plate.
21. Ball bearing.
22. 'O' ring oil seal.
23. 'O' ring retaining washer.
24. Fan.

Rotor

a. Test the rotor windings by connecting an ohmmeter, or a 12-volt battery supply and ammeter in series, between the slip-rings (Fig. N.10). The resistance or current of the field coils should be as given in **'GENERAL DATA'**.

b. Defective insulation between the slip-rings and one of the rotor poles. Use a mains test lamp (110-volt A.C., 15-watt), connect it between one of the slip-rings and rotor poles; if the lamp lights, the coil is earthing. Replace the rotor assembly.

NOTE.–Do not attempt to machine the rotor poles or true a distorted shaft.

Stator

a. Check for continuity of the stator windings. Unsolder the three stator cables from the heat sink assembly (see **'Replacing diode heat sink'**). Connect any two of the three stator cables in series with a 1.5-watt test lamp and a 12-volt battery. Repeat the test, replacing one of the two cables by a third. Failure of the test lamp to light in either test indicates that the stator windings are open circuit. Replace the stator.

b. Test insulation between stator coils and lamination pack with the mains test lamp. Connect the test probes between any of the three cable ends and the lamination pack. If the lamp lights, the stator coils are earthing. Replace the stator.

Carry out the following test before resoldering the stator cables.

Diodes

Test each diode by connecting a 12-volt D.C. supply and a 1.5-watt test lamp in series with each diode in turn as shown in Fig. N.12, and then reversing the connections. Current should flow in one direction only.

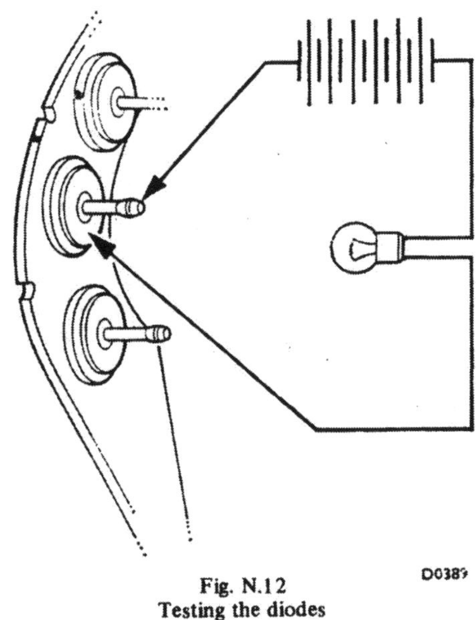

Fig. N.12
Testing the diodes

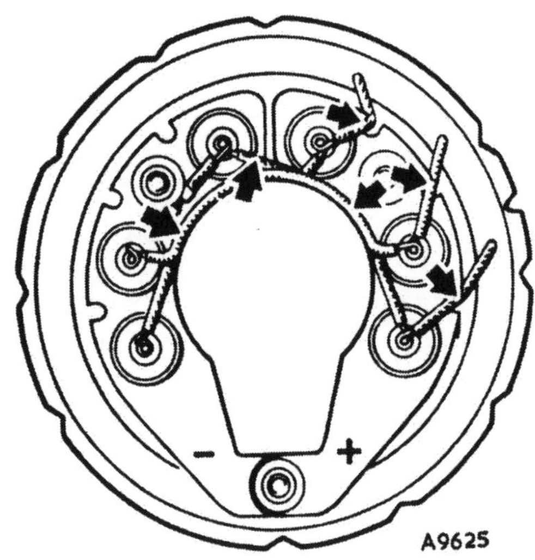

Fig. N.13
The heat sink diode internal connections

Should the bulb light up, or not light at all, in both tests the diode is defective. Replace the appropriate heat sink assembly.

The above procedure is adequate for testing. If, however, a battery-ohmmeter is used, it should be understood that no realistic readings can be obtained. A good diode will yield 'Infinity' in one direction, and a much lower, indefinite reading in the other.

Replacing diode heat sink

The heat sink assembly comprises two mutually insulated portions, one of positive polarity carries cathode-based diodes (marked red), and the other, negative, carries anode-based diodes (marked black).

a. Make the interconnection with 'M' grade 45-55 tin-lead solder.
b. Take great care to avoid overheating the diodes. Lightly grip the diode pins with a pair of long-nosed pliers, which will act as a thermal shunt, and carry out the soldering as quickly as possible.
c. Arrange the connections neatly around the heat sinks to ensure adequate clearance for the rotor, and secure with a suitable heat-resistant adhesive (Fig. N.13). The three stator connections must pass through the appropriate notches at the edge of the heat sink.

Bearings

Renew bearings which allow excessive side play of the rotor shaft.

BEARING–SLIP-RING END-COVER

The needle-roller bearing and slip-ring end cover should be renewed as an assembly; if however a new bearing is to be fitted, follow the procedure below.

a. Check the depth to which the original bearing is pressed into its housing so that the new bearing may be positioned likewise.
b. Support the bearing boss, and press the bearing to the required depth. Pack with high-melting-point grease.

BEARING–DRIVE-END BRACKET

a. Withdraw the rotor shaft from the drive-end bracket.
b. The bearing retaining plate is secured by either screws, rivets or a circlip.

   File away the rivet heads and punch out the rivets; withdraw the screws or extract the circlip.
c. Press the bearing from the bracket.
d. Ensure that the new bearing is clean and pack it with high-melting-point grease. Locate the bearing and press fully into the housing.
e. Refit the bearing retaining plate. When circlip retained, press in enough to allow the circlip to be located.

Re-assembling

8. Reverse the dismantling procedure, bending the retaining tongues of the field terminal blades out at an angle of 30 degrees before fitting.
9. Align the marks on the drive-end bracket, stator lamination pack and the slip-ring end-bracket.
10. Support the inner journal of the drive-end bearing on a suitable tube and press the rotor home. Do not use the drive-end bracket as a support for the bearing while fitting the rotor. Tighten the through-bolts, brushbox fixing screws, and diode heat sink fixings to the correct torque figures (see 'GENERAL DATA').

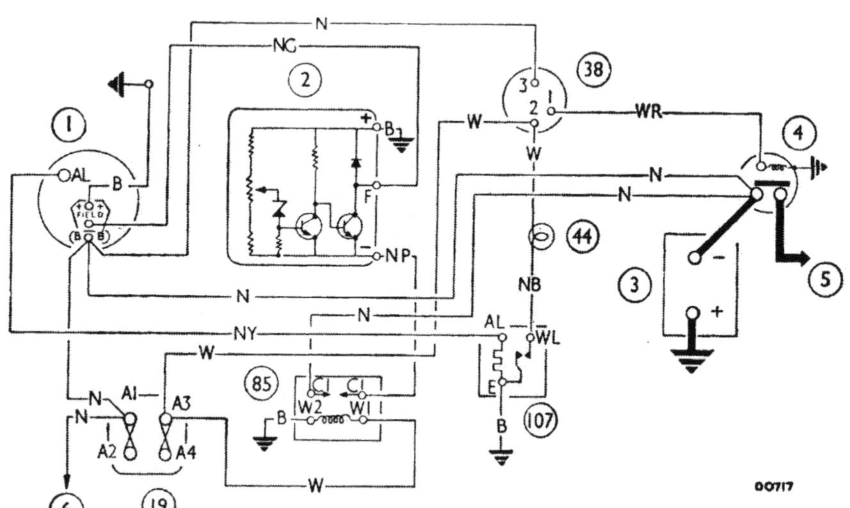

Fig. N.14
The alternator charging circuit

1. Alternator.
2. 4TR control unit.
3. 12-volt battery.
4. Starter solenoid.
5. Starter motor.
6. Lighting switch.
19. Fuse unit; 1-2, 35-amp.; 3-4, 35-amp.
38. Ignition/starter switch.
44. Ignition warning lamp.
85. Alternator field isolating relay.
107. Alternator charge indicator unit 3AW.

Section N.13

CONTROL UNIT (4TR)

Testing

1. Check the resistance of the wiring circuits of the alternator, control unit and battery to control unit, including the relay unit. The resistance should not exceed .1 ohm.
   NOTE.–Do not use an ohmmeter of the type which incorporates a hand-driven generator when checking the rectifiers or transistors.
2. Check that the battery is fully charged.
3. Check the voltage output as follows:
   a. Connect an accurate voltmeter across the battery terminals and note the reading.
   b. Connect an ammeter between the alternator main cable and its terminal 'B' on the alternator.
   c. Switch on enough lights to give a load of 2 amps.
   d. Start the engine and run for at least eight minutes at an alternator speed of 3,000 r.p.m. until the ammeter reads 10 amps.
   e. The voltmeter reading should then be between 13.9 and 14.3 volts. If the reading is unstable or has not risen above the battery voltage, renew the control unit. If the reading is stable but outside the correct limits, adjust the control unit.
4. If adjustment is needed, proceed as follows:
   a. Stop the engine and detach the control unit from its mountings.
   b. Scrape out the compound sealing the potentiometer adjustment at the back of the unit.
   c. Ensure the connections on the unit are secure and re-start the engine.
   d. Run the engine to give an alternator speed of 3,000 r.p.m., with the conditions of test as in 3.

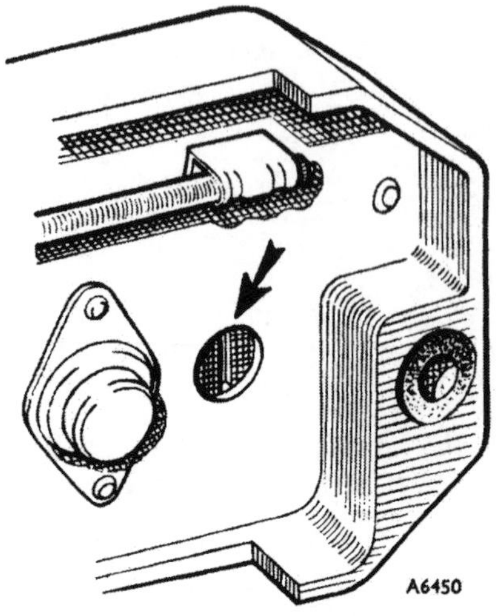

Fig. N.15
The 4TR control unit potentiometer adjuster. Turn clockwise to increase the voltage reading

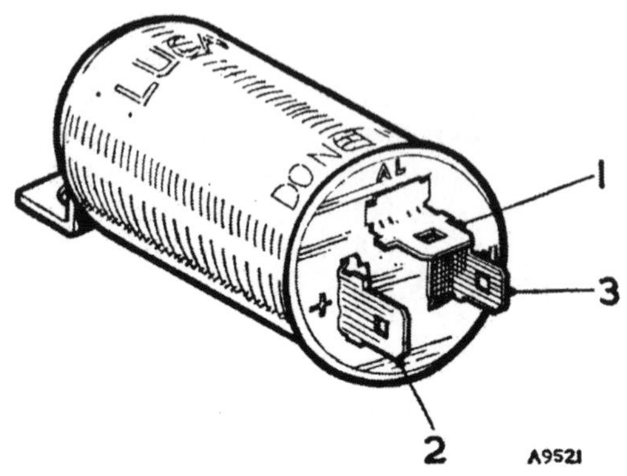

Fig. N.16
Warning light control terminals

1. Alternator 'AL'. 2. Positive '+'. 3. Warning light 'WL'.

e. Turn the adjuster slot gradually until the voltmeter registers a stable reading within the correct voltage limits (see Fig. N.15). Only a small adjuster movement is needed to effect an appreciable difference in the voltmeter reading.

f. Re-check by stopping the engine, re-starting it and running the alternator at 3,000 r.p.m. Check the voltmeter reading, and when it is correct, refit the control unit and remove the voltmeter and ammeter. Do not attempt to re-seal the adjuster hole. Application of undue heat will damage the control unit.

Section N.14

RELAY

Description

The relay de-energizes the alternator rotor field winding when the engine is stationary by disconnecting the supply from the rotor field immediately the ignition is switched 'off'. This allows contact 'C1' and 'C2' to part and open-circuit the rotor field winding. The alternator will not generate if the contacts fail to close when the ignition is switched 'on'.

Testing

1. Connect an ammeter as detailed in Section N.11, item 3.
2. Remove the lead from terminal 'C2' and temporarily join to the 'C1' terminal, ensuring good electrical contact.
3. If the alternator generates its specified output with the leads connected (as above), the relay is faulty and must be replaced.

   Check the continuity of relay operating winding, relay circuit wiring, and earth. If the relay and circuit are satisfactory (with cables 'C1' and 'C2' still joined), but no output from the alternator, check the alternator and control unit.

Section N.15

WARNING LIGHT CONTROL

The control is electrically connected to the centre point of one pair of diodes in the alternator and enables a warning light to be used to indicate that the alternator is charging when the engine is running at normal speed.

If proved faulty, replace the unit.

SECTION Nb

THE ELECTRICAL SYSTEM

The information contained in this section refers specifically to new or modified components fitted to the Mini range coincident with the introduction of NEGATIVE earth electrical systems and must be used in conjunction with Section N.

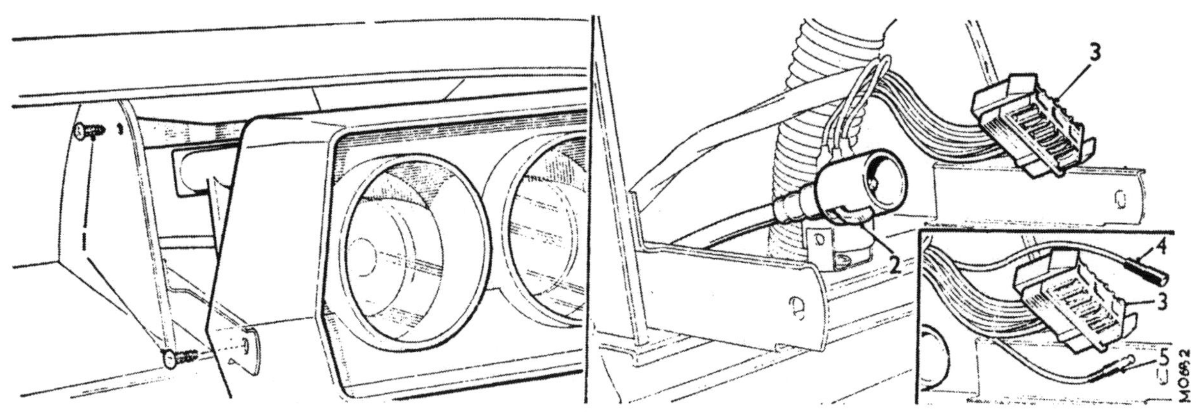

Fig. Nb.1
Removing the instrument panel (Mini Clubman and 1275 GT)

1. Panel securing screws.
2. Speedometer cable release lever.
3. Multi-plug wiring connector.
4. Tachometer connection } 1275 GT.
5. Tachometer connection } 1275 GT.

Section Nb.1

INSTRUMENT PANEL
(Clubman and 1275 GT)

Removing

1. Disconnect the battery earth cable (NEGATIVE).
2. Remove the air ventilation louvre adjacent to the instrument panel (see Section Rb.4).
3. Release the portion of the door seal securing the fascia trim liner, withdraw the liner from behind the side of the panel and remove it.
4. Release the trim liner on the other side of the instrument panel in a similar manner but do not remove it; the instrument panel securing screws are now accessible (see Fig. Nb.1).
5. Remove the four securing screws (1) and partially withdraw the panel; press in the release lever (2) on the speedometer cable and pull the cable out of the instrument. Pull out the multi-plug wiring connector (3) from the rear of the panel and remove the assembly (see Fig. Nb.1).
   1275 GT. In addition to the above instructions also disconnect the tachometer connections (4) and (5) (see Fig. Nb.1).

Refitting

6. Reverse the removing instructions but note that the connector plug will fit one way only and make sure the speedometer cable is fully engaged in the instrument. Carefully refit the trim liners and use adhesive when refitting the door seal.

Section Nb.2

INSTRUMENTS
(Clubman and 1275 GT)

Removing

1. Remove the instrument panel (see Section Nb.1).

Removal of the instruments for replacement is as follows:

SPEEDOMETER (CLUBMAN)

2. Remove the screws securing the complete instrument unit to the panel, and lift off the unit.
3. Remove the three clips (1) and withdraw the lens assembly (2) (see Fig. Nb.2).
4. Unscrew the retaining screws (3) and withdraw the speedometer unit (4) (see Fig. Nb.2).

SPEEDOMETER (1275 GT)

5. Before removing the complete instrument unit as detailed in item 2, disconnect the printed circuit earth connection (arrowed) and remove the illuminating light bulb holder (5) from the tachometer (see Fig. Nb.2).
6. Carry out instructions 3 and 4.

FUEL AND TEMPERATURE GAUGES

7. Remove the clips (1), withdraw the lens assembly (6) from the instrument unit and lift out the instrument sub-dial (7). Unscrew the appropriate securing screws (8) and remove the instrument(s) (9), (10) for replacement (see Fig. Nb.2).

TACHOMETER (1275 GT)

8. Disconnect the printed circuit earth connection (arrowed) and withdraw the illuminating bulb holder (5). Remove the screws securing the tachometer unit to the panel and lift out the complete assembly.
   The tachometer is replaceable as a complete unit (12) (see Fig. Nb.2). Do not remove the unit from its casing.

Refitting

INSTRUMENTS AND GAUGES

9. Reverse the removing procedure for all units.

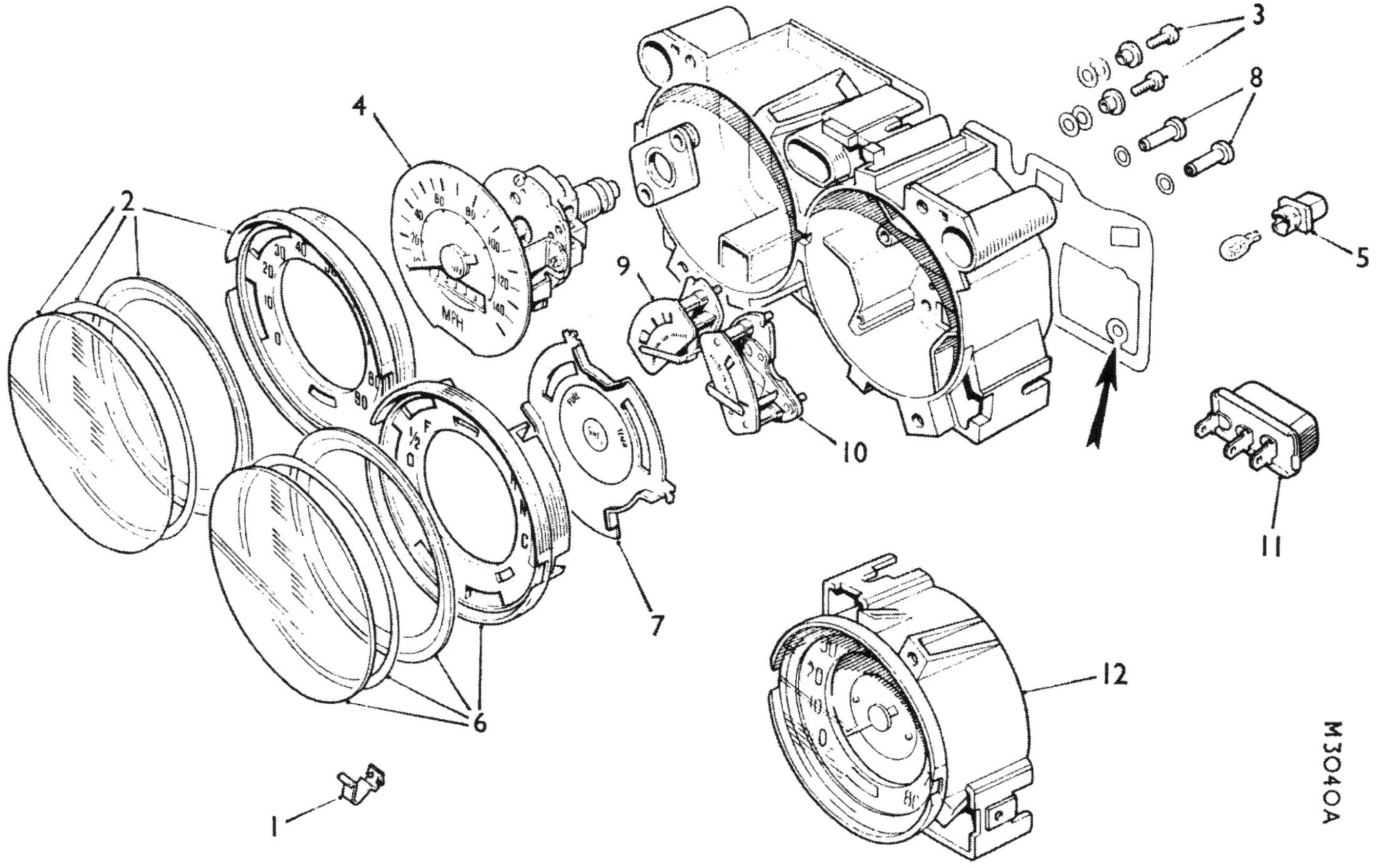

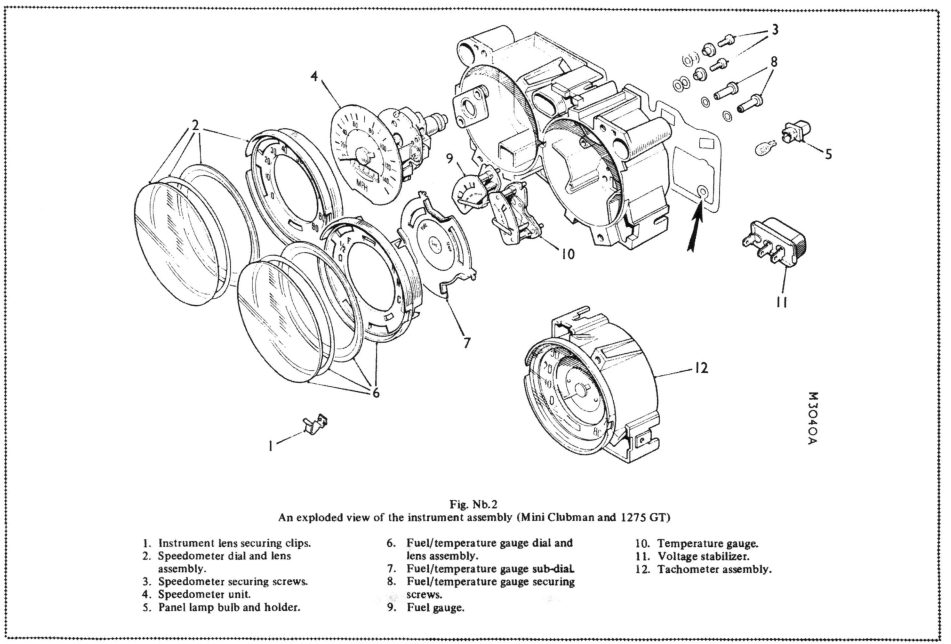

M3040A

Fig. Nb.2

An exploded view of the instrument assembly (Mini Clubman and 1275 GT)

1. Instrument lens securing clips.
2. Speedometer dial and lens assembly.
3. Speedometer securing screws.
4. Speedometer unit.
5. Panel lamp bulb and holder.
6. Fuel/temperature gauge dial and lens assembly.
7. Fuel/temperature gauge sub-dial.
8. Fuel/temperature gauge securing screws.
9. Fuel gauge.
10. Temperature gauge.
11. Voltage stabilizer.
12. Tachometer assembly.

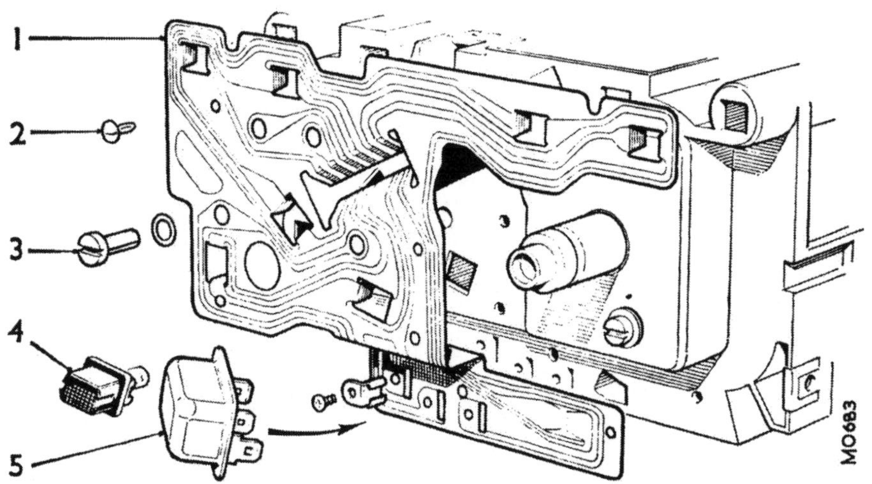

Fig. Nb.3
Removing the printed circuit

1. Printed circuit.
2. Printed circuit securing stud.
3. Fuel and temperature gauge securing screws.
4. Panel and warning lamp bulb holders.
5. Voltage stabilizer.

Section Nb.3

INSTRUMENT PANEL PRINTED CIRCUIT
(Clubman and 1275 GT)

Removing

1. Remove the instrument panel (Section Nb.1).
2. Withdraw all the panel and warning light bulb holders (4) and pull off the voltage stabilizer (5) (see Fig. Nb.3).
3. Remove the three voltage stabilizer terminals.
4. To avoid damaging the fuel and temperature gauge indicators, remove these instruments from their holder as detailed in Section Nb.2.
5. 1275 GT. In addition to the above instructions disconnect the connections to the tachometer and withdraw the additional bulb holder(s).
6. Ease out the pins (2) securing the printed circuit and remove the circuit (1).

Replacing

7. Fit the replacement circuit, bending the bulb contacts into each respective holder recess. The remainder is a reversal of the removing procedure.

Section Nb.4

VOLTAGE STABILIZER

The voltage stabilizer is a push-fit into the rear of the instrument panel. For testing or replacement of the unit the panel must be withdrawn.

Testing

To carry out a rapid diagnosis of the voltage stabilizer, fuel and temperature gauges and their electrical circuits use a Smiths Automotive Instrument Tester (which incorporates a thermal-sensitive voltmeter).

1. Withdraw the instrument panel for access to the voltage stabilizer and gauges (see Section Nb.1), but leave the battery connected and do not disturb the wiring connector plug on the rear of the panel.

BATTERY VOLTAGE

1. Connect a voltmeter to the '2' terminal of the fuse block and earth. With the ignition switched off, check the voltage, it should be approximately 12 volts.
2. Start the engine and run it at approximately 1,000 r.p.m., and ensure that the ignition warning light is out. Check the voltage, which should be 12 to 13 volts.

WIRING

3. Check for continuity between each unit and for short-circuits in the wiring to the temperature gauge transmitter.
4. Ensure that the voltage stabilizer, gauges and transmitter are earthed.

VOLTAGE STABILIZER

5. Switch the ignition on. After a pause of two minutes, check the main voltage between the output terminal 'I' and earth; it should be 10 volts.
6. Substitute the voltage stabilizer if faulty.

GAUGES

7. Check for continuity between the terminals with the wiring disconnected. **DO NOT short-circuit a gauge to earth.**
8. Substitute a gauge if faulty.

TRANSMITTER

9. Check for continuity between the terminal and outer casing with the lead disconnected.
10. Substitute the transmitter if faulty.

Refitting

11. Refit the instrument panel as detailed in Section Nb.1.

Section Nb.5

SPEEDOMETER DRIVE CABLE

Removing

1. Remove the instrument panel (see Section Nb.1).
2. Press in the release lever (2) on the cable and pull the cable out of the instrument (see Fig. Nb.1). Withdraw the cable into the engine compartment.
3. From beneath the car, disconnect the cable through the aperture above the left-hand drive shaft. If the cable securing nut is too tight to turn by hand, use a suitable tool, or, remove the set screw securing the speedometer drive and withdraw the cable complete with the drive assembly and then remove the cable.

Refitting

4. Reverse the removing procedure, fitting a new joint washer if the speedometer drive has been removed. Tighten the lower securing nut by hand.

Lubrication

5. Withdraw the inner cable and lightly grease it except for 8 in. (200 mm.) at the speedometer end, re-insert it in the outer casing and wipe away surplus grease. Check that there is approximately in. (10 mm.) projection of the inner cable beyond the outer casing at the speedometer end.

Section Nb.6.

DIRECTION INDICATOR FLASHER UNIT

Removing

1. Access to the unit is through an aperture in the fascia parcel shelf. Pull the flasher unit from its spring clip holder and through the access hole; pull off the wiring connections.

Replacing

2. Connect the wiring to the new unit and refit it into the holder.

Section Nb.7

STARTER
(Type M35J–Inertia Drive)

Removing

1. Disconnect the battery earth cable.
2. Disconnect the cable at the starter motor, remove the two bolts securing the starter motor to the flywheel housing and manoeuvre the starter away from the engine.

Dismantling

3. Remove the screws securing the drive-end bracket.
4. Withdraw the drive-end bracket complete with the armature and drive.
5. Remove the thrust washer from the commutator end of the armature.
6. Remove the screws securing the commutator end bracket.
7. Detach the bracket from the yoke, disengage the field brushes from the brush gear and remove the bracket.
8. If necessary the drive assembly can be removed by compressing the spring, removing the jump ring and withdrawing the drive from the shaft.

Inspecting and testing

BRUSH GEAR

9. Check the brush spring tension; fit a new brush into each holder in turn, and press on top of the brush with a push-type spring gauge until the brush protrudes approximately in. (1.5 mm.) from the holder. At this point check the gauge, which should read approximately 28 oz. (794 gm.): renew the commutator-end bracket if the tension is incorrect.
10. Check the brushes for wear, and renew any brush worn to or approaching the minimum length of in. (9.5 mm.).
11. To renew the end-bracket brushes, cut the brush leads from the terminal post, slot the head of the post sufficiently deep to accomodate the new brush leads and solder the new leads to the post.
12. To renew the field winding brushes, cut the brush lead approximately ½ in. (6.4 mm.) from the field winding junction, solder the new brush leads to the stumps of the old ones ensuring that the insulation sleeves provide adequate coverage.

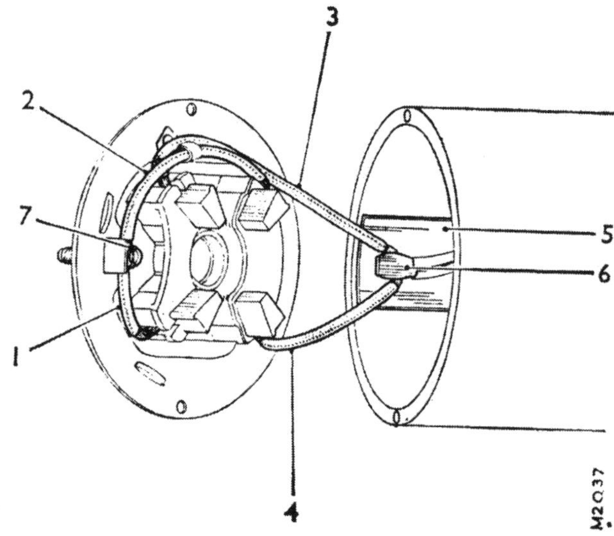

Fig. Nb.4
Commutator end bracket assembly

1. Short brush-flexible, commutator end bracket.
2. Long brush-flexible commutator end bracket.
3. Long brush-flexible, field winding.
4. Short brush-flexible, field winding.
5. Yoke insulation piece.
6. Field winding junction.
7. Terminal post.

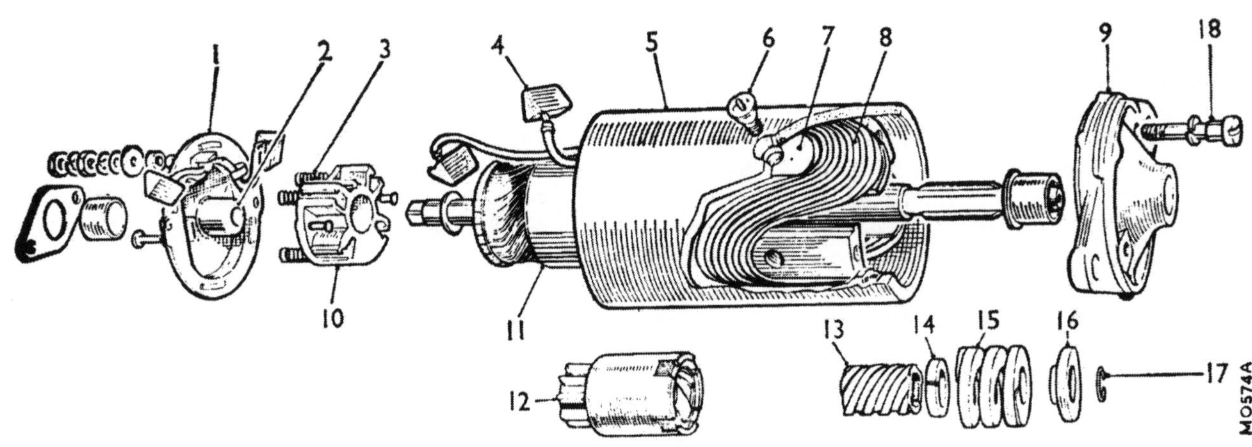

Fig. Nb.5
The M35J-type starter motor components

1.	Commutator end bracket.	7.	Pole shoe.	13.	Screwed sleeve.
2.	Bush housing.	8.	Field coils.	14.	Buffer washer.
3.	Brush springs.	9.	Drive end bracket.	15.	Main spring.
4.	Brushes.	10.	Brush box mouldings.	16.	Spring cup.
5.	Yoke.	11.	Armature.	17.	Circlip.
6.	Pole screw.	12.	Pinion and barrel.	18.	Drive end bracket bolt.

COMMUTATOR

13. Clean the commutator with a cloth moistened with fuel and examine it for burrs, pitting and excessive wear; provided that the amount of metal removed does not reduce the thickness of the commutator beyond the minimum thickness, the commutator may be reconditioned as follows:

a. Skim the commutator at high speed using a very sharp tool and removing the minimum amount of metal necessary to restore the surface.

b. Polish the commutator with very fine sandpaper.

c. Using an air-blast, clean any copper residue from the armature.

IMPORTANT.–The commutator segment insulators must not be undercut.

ARMATURE

14. Test the insulation of the armature windings with a 110-volt A.C., 15-watt test lamp connected between the armature shaft and the commutator; if the lamp lights the armature must be renewed.

15. Check the windings at their connections with the commutator for signs of melted solder or lifted conductors.

16. Check the shaft for distortion, and if it is bent or distorted the armature must be renewed; do not attempt to straighten the shaft or machine the armature core laminations.

FIELD WINDINGS

17. Connect a 12-volt battery-operated test lamp between each of the field brushes and a clean part of the yoke; the lamp will light if continuity is satisfactory between the brushes, windings and yoke connection.

18. Disconnect the field windings from their riveted connection with the yoke, and using a 110-volt A.C., 15-watt test lamp connected between the yoke and each of the brushes in turn, check the insulation of the field windings; if the lamp lights the windings must be renewed.

19. The field windings may be renewed as follows:

a. Disconnect the windings from their connection with the yoke.

b. Slacken the four pole-shoe retaining screws using a wheel-operated screwdriver.

c. Remove the retaining screws from one pair of diametrically opposite pole-shoes and remove them from the yoke.

d. Slide the windings from beneath the remaining pair of pole-shoes and withdraw them from the yoke.

e. Clean the inside of the yoke, the pole-shoes, and the insulation piece.

f. Loosely fit the new windings and the pole-shoes and position the insulation piece between the yoke and the brush connections to the windings.

g. Tighten the pole-shoe screws evenly using a wheel-operated screwdriver.

h. Re-connect the winding junction connector to the yoke.

COMMUTATOR END BRACKET

20. Check the insulation of the springs and terminal post by connecting a 110-volt A.C., 15-watt test lamp between a clean part of the end bracket and, in turn, each spring and the terminal; the lamp will light if the insulation is unsatisfactory.

BEARINGS

21. If a bearing is worn sufficiently to allow excessive side play of the armature shaft, the bearing bush must be renewed as follows:

Commutator-end bracket

a. Drill out the rivets securing the brush box moulding and remove the moulding, bearing seal retaining plate and felt washer seal.

b. Screw a ½-in. tap a few turns into the bush and withdraw the bush with the tap.

Drive-end bracket

c. Support the bracket and press out the bush.

NOTE.–New bushes must be immersed in S.A.E. 30/40 engine oil for 24 hours or in oil heated to 100° C. (212°F.) for two hours prior to fitting. The bushes must not be reamed after fitting.

Commutator- and drive-end brackets

d. Using a polished, shouldered mandrel, the same diameter as the shaft bearing journal press the new bushes into the brackets.

DRIVE

22. Wash the drive with paraffin (kerosene) and dry using an air blast.

23. Check the components for damage and excessive wear; renew worn or damaged parts.

Reassembling and refitting

24. Carry out items 3 to 8 in reverse order, and refit the starter by reversing the removal sequence items 1 and 2.

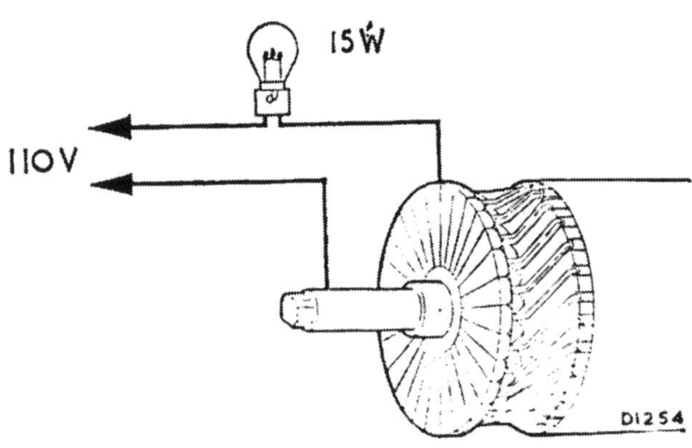

Fig. Nb.6
Armature insulation test

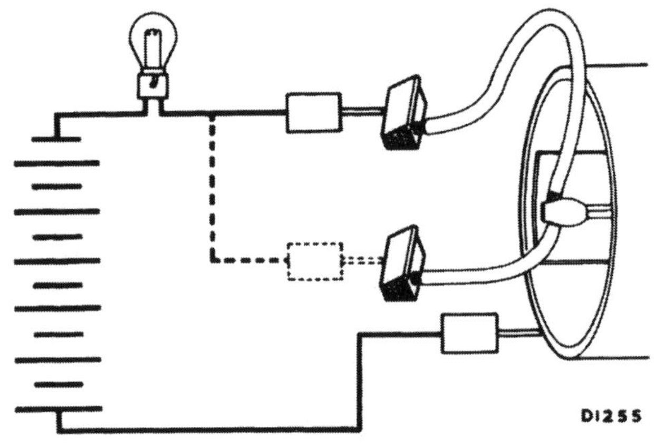

Fig. Nb.7
Field winding continuity test

Bench testing

LIGHT RUNNING CURRENT

25. Clamp the starter firmly in a vice.

26. Connect a starter switch, a 0–600 amp. ammeter and a 12-volt battery in series, to the starter, using the lug as the earth connection.

27. Operate the switch and check the speed of the motor with a tachometer while noting the ammeter readings.

28. Check the readings obtained in item 27 against the figures given for light running speed and current in **'GENERAL DATA'**.

LOCK TORQUE AND CURRENT

29. With the starter connected and clamped as for the light running check, secure an arm to the driving pinion.

30. Connect a spring balance to the free end of the arm.

31. Operate the switch and note the ammeter and spring balance readings. Calculate the lock torque by multiplying the reading of the spring balance in pounds by the length of the arm in feet.

32. Check the readings obtained in item 31 against the figures given for lock torque and current in **'GENERAL DATA'**.

Section Nb.8

WINDSCREEN WIPER
(Lucas Type 14W–Permanent Magnet)

Operation

This windscreen wiper, which is produced in either single- or two-speed form, has two permanent field magnets incorporated in a cylindrical yoke. The two-speed type is fitted with a third brush, to which the positive feed is transferred when a faster wiper speed is required.

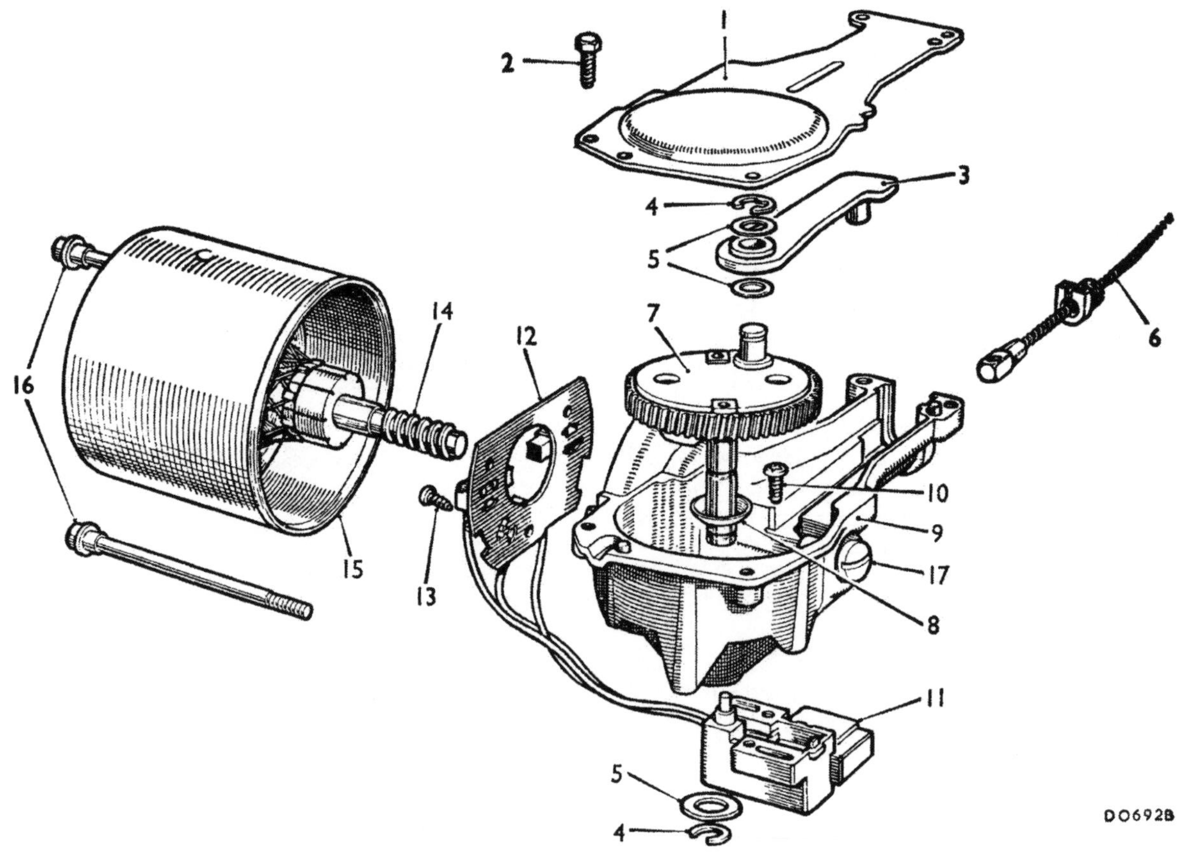

Fig. Nb.8
The two-speed windscreen wiper motor components

1. Gearbox cover.
2. Screw for cover.
3. Connecting rod.
4. Circlip.
5. Plain washers.
6. Cross-head and rack.
7. Shaft and gear.
8. Dished washer.
9. Gearbox.
10. Screw for limit switch.
11. Limit switch assembly.
12. Brush gear.
13. Screw for brush gear.
14. Armature.
15. Yoke assembly.
16. Yoke bolts.
17. Armature thrust screw.

A self-switching limit switch is incorporated in the terminal assembly. A cam on the underside of the gear wheel operates the two-stage switch via a plunger. When switched off, the motor continues under control of the limit switch until the wipers reach park position, the first stage contacts open and the motor is switched off. A period of no contact by the switch follows, then the second-stage contacts close to brake the armature and park the blades in the same position each time.

Testing

If the wiper fails to operate, or the wiper speed is slow or irregular, first locate the fault. Start by checking that the battery is fully charged, and that the wiper blades are in good condition and are not sticking.

1. Check the voltage at the motor connector plug; if the fuse (35/17 amp.) connecting '3' and '4' has blown, replace it, but before continuing make certain that this has not been caused by a fault in another circuit or by poor insulation.
2. Remove the motor, disconnect the cable rack at the gearbox (see '**Dismantling**' items 13 to 15), connect a 0-15 moving-coil ammeter to the supply cable, and switch on the wiper. If the current consumption of the motor and the operating speeds of the drive gear are not as given in '**GENERAL DATA**', carry out the electrical tests; if the operation is now satisfactory, the fault is mechanical.

ELECTRICAL

3. If the wiper takes no current and the fuse is intact, check the electrical circuit for continuity, including the fascia switch. If the fuse had blown, (item 1) check the wiring insulation, and if in order carry out the electrical test, 5.
4. If the wiper takes an abnormally low current, the motor must be dismantled and an examination made of the brush gear and commutator (see '**Inspecting**').

5. If the wiper takes an abnormally high current, adjust the armature end-float if necessary (see item 25). If the current consumption is still abnormal with the correct end-float, remove and test the armature (see '**Inspecting**', item 22).

NOTE.–If the motor is run other than from the vehicle's own connector, connect up as follows: negative–terminal 1, positive– terminal 5 for normal speed or terminal 3 for fast speed (two-speed type).

MECHANICAL

6. See that the wiper arm spindles rotate freely; replace seized or damaged wheelboxes.
7. Use a spring balance to measure the force required to pull the cable rack out of the casing from the fully-in position. This force must not exceed 6 lb. (2.7 kg.). Reform any bends of less than 9 in. (230 mm.) radius and replace any kinked or damaged tubes. Inspect the drive cable rack for damage.
8. Check the wheelboxes and connector tubes for alignment.

Removing

MOTOR AND GEARBOX ASSEMBLY

9. Disconnect the battery, withdraw the terminal connector from the motor, and release the earth wire from the valance.
10. Remove the wiper arms.
11. Unscrew the union on the Bundy tube at the gearbox and release the strap from the mounting bracket. Withdraw the assembly, pulling the cable rack from the Bundy tube.

WHEELBOXES

12. Remove the wheelboxes, as described in Section N.9.

Dismantling

MOTOR AND GEARBOX ASSEMBLY (WHEN REMOVED)

13. Unscrew the four gearbox cover retaining screws and remove the cover.
14. Remove the circlip and flat washer securing the connecting rod to the crankpin.
15. Withdraw the connecting rod, noting the flat washer fitted under it.
16. Remove the circlip and washer securing the shaft and gear.
17. Clean any burrs from the gear shaft and withdraw the gear, noting the dished washer fitted under it.
18. After marking the motor yoke and gearbox to ensure that they are reassembled the original way round, unscrew the two fixing bolts and remove the yoke and armature assembly. Keep the yoke clear of metallic particles which will be attracted to the pole pieces.
19. Remove the screws securing the brush gear and the terminal and switch assembly, which are connected by cables, and remove both of them.

Inspecting

MOTOR AND GEARBOX ASSEMBLY

20. Examine the brush gear assembly, which must be replaced before either of the main brushes is worn to the minimum length of $\frac{3}{16}$ in. (5 mm.), or the narrow section of the third brush (two-speed models) is worn down to the full width of the brush (see Fig. Nb.9).
21. Check that the brushes move freely in the boxes and test the brush spring pressure with a push-type gauge. The gauge reading should be 5 to 7 oz. (140 to 200 gm.) when the bottom of the brush is level with the end of the slot in the brush box (see Fig. Nb.9). Renew the brush gear assembly if the springs are unsatisfactory.
22. Test the armature for open- or short-circuits. Use a mains test lamp of 110 volts and 15 watts and renew the armature if faulty.
23. Examine the gear wheel for damage or excessive wear. Renew if necessary.

Reassembling

MOTOR AND GEARBOX ASSEMBLY

24. Reverse the dismantling procedure in 13 to 19, noting the following points.
    a. If either the brush gear or switch assembly requires replacing, unsolder the motor supply leads at the brush boxes. If a new switch is to be fitted to a single-speed motor remove the third wire, yellow and green, at the switch terminal. Use high-melting-point solder to reconnect the leads to the brush boxes, in the order shown in Fig. Nb.9, when refitting the new assembly(ies); ensure that the leads are inside the recess in the switch unit moulding when refitting it to the gearbox.

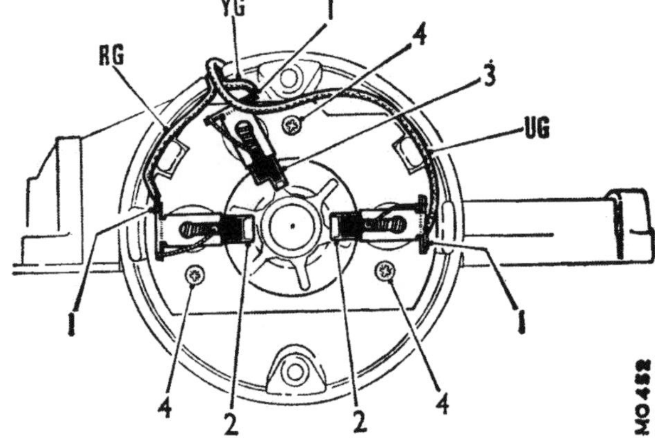

Fig. Nb.9
The brush gear assembly components

1. Soldered brush box connections.
2. Main brushes.
3. Fast speed brush (where fitted).
4. Brush gear assembly securing screws.

RG–Red with green. YG–Yellow with green. UG–Blue with green.

b. Use Ragosine Listate Grease to lubricate the gear wheel teeth and cam, armature shaft worm gear, connecting rod and connecting pin, crosshead slide, cable rack and wheelbox gear wheels.

c. Use Shell Turbo 41 oil to lubricate the bearing bushes, armature shaft bearing journals (sparingly), gear wheel shaft and crankpin, felt washer in the yoke bearing (thoroughly soak), and the wheelbox spindles.

d. If a replacement armature is being fitted, slacken the thrust screw to provide end float for fitting the yoke.

e. Tighten the yoke fixing bolts to a torque figure of 14 lb. in. (0.16 kg. m.).

f. Fit the dished washer beneath the gear wheel with its concave side towards the gear wheel.

IMPORTANT.– If a new gear wheel is being fitted, ensure that the type obtained has the correct relationship between the crankpin and ramp to give the parking position required for either right- or left-hand-drive vehicles (see Fig. Nb.10).

g. When fitting the connecting rod to the crankpin ensure that the larger of the two flat washers is fitted under the connecting rod with the smaller one on top beneath the circlip.

ARMATURE END-FLOAT ADJUSTING

25. Tighten the thrust screw until the end-float is just eliminated, and then turn back one-quarter turn to give an end-float within the limits of .002 to .008 in. (.05 to .2 mm.). Measure the gap under the head of the thrust screw with a feeler gauge, fit a suitable shim beneath it and fully tighten it.

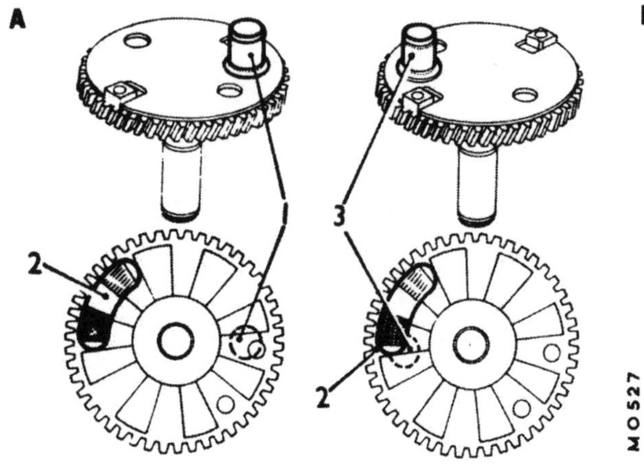

Fig. Nb.10
The gear wheel showing the alternative positions of the crankpin

(A) R.H.D. cars: cable rack retracted with the crankpin (1) opposite the ramp (2).

(B) L.H.D. cars: cable rack extended with the crankpin (3) adjacent to the ramp (2).

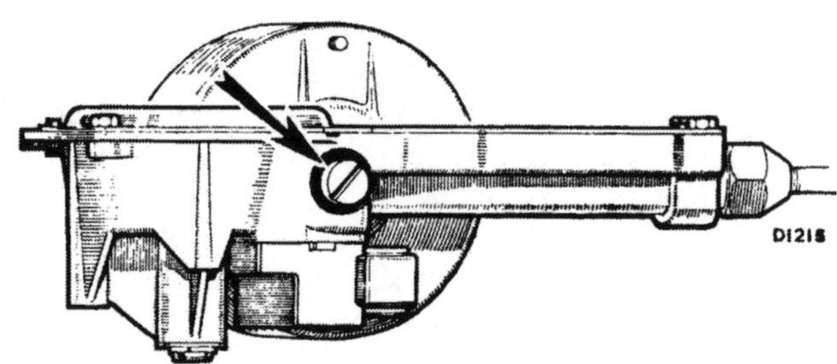

Fig. Nb.11
The armature end-float adjusting screw

Refitting

26. Reverse the procedure 9 to 12, leaving the wheelbox covers slack until after the cable rack has been inserted and the motor secured. Do not re-fit the wiper blades until after the action of the wheelboxes has been checked.

Section Nb.9

ALTERNATOR
(Lucas type 16ACR)

The model 16ACR alternator is similar in basic construction to that of the type 11AC as described in Section N.12, except that the slip-rings are mounted behind the rear rotor shaft bearing outside the slip-ring end bracket, and no separate control unit is fitted. Instead, a voltage regulator, of micro-circuit construction is incorporated on the slip-ring end bracket, inside the alternator cover.

Precautions

The alternator service precautions given in Section N.10 must be observed. Note that the battery polarity is **NEGATIVE EARTH**, which must be maintained at all times. The field connector block, which has three blades and is marked 'B+' and 'IND', has an offset moulded stop and must be removed before the main output connector block, which has two blades and is marked '+' and '–'. Since the B+ connector blade, although shrouded, is always live, disconnect the battery earth before removing the field connector block.

Testing in position

OUTPUT TEST

1. Check that the fan belt is correctly tensioned and that all charging circuit electrical connections are secure.
2. Run the engine at fast idle speed until its normal operating temperature is reached, and see that the battery is fully-charged.
3. Diconnect both connector blocks from the alternator.

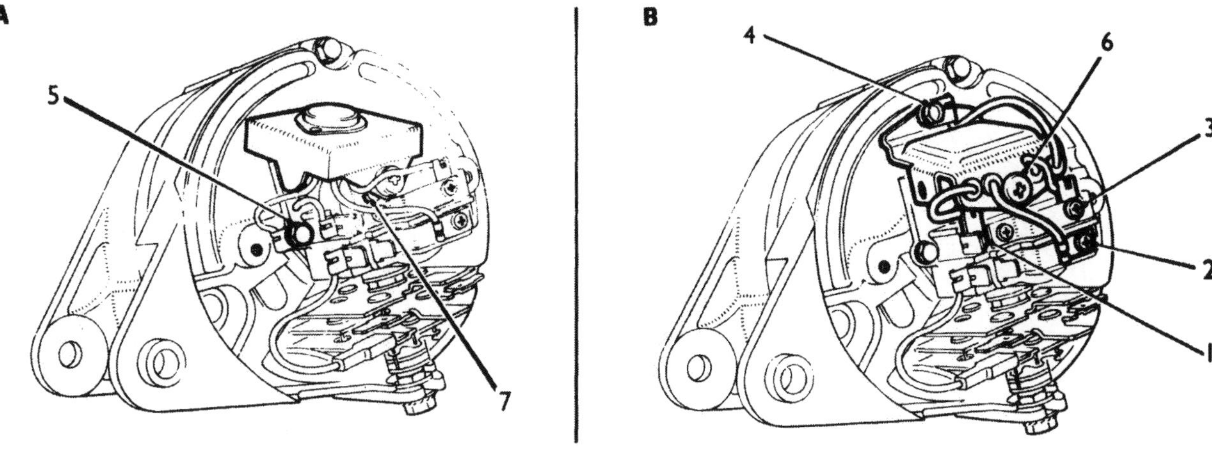

Fig. Nb.12
The in-built regulator connections, showing 'A' the 11TR and 'B' the 8TR type of regulator unit

1. B+.
2. Positive (+).
3. Field (F).
4. Earth (–)–8TR.
5. Earth (–)–11TR.
6. Mounting screw–8TR.
7. Long mounting screw and spacer–11TR.

4. Switch on the ignition and connect up a voltmeter with its negative lead to earth and with its positive lead to each cable connector blade of the two connector blocks in turn. If battery voltage is not available at any cable, locate and remedy the fault.
5. Remove the alternator end cover.
6. The leads from the in-built regulator to the alternator are unmarked. Refer to Fig. Nb.12 and then bridge the regulator field connector to a suitable earth, such as the earth-lead tag.
7. Refit the three-way connector block to the alternator. Do not refit the two-way connector block, instead, connect an ammeter in series with its positive blade and the main positive output terminal of the alternator. Do not make any connection to the inner (negative) main terminal.
8. Start the engine and run it at 2,800 r.p.m. The ammeter should read 34 amps. nominal. If the correct alternator output cannot be obtained, repair or replace the alternator.

REGULATOR TEST

9. Disconnect the lead which was connected up in item 6 to bridge the regulator field connector to earth.
10. Connect a voltmeter across the battery terminals. Start the engine and run it at 2,800 r.p.m. If the ammeter which was connected for item 7 of the output test reads zero, the regulator pack must be replaced.
11. Adjust the engine speed until the ammeter reading falls below 10 amps. The voltmeter should read between 14.0 and 14.4 volts. If it does not, either the regulator is faulty or there is a high resistance in the charging circuit cables; restore the original connections to the alternator and then check the charging circuit resistance.

CHARGING CIRCUIT RESISTANCE TEST

12. Connect a voltmeter between the positive terminal of the alternator and the positive terminal of the battery. Start the engine, switch on the headlamps, and run the engine at 2,800 r.p.m. The voltmeter reading should not exceed .5 volt.
13. Transfer the voltmeter connections to the negative terminals of the alternator and battery. With the engine running at 2,800 r.p.m. the voltmeter reading should not exceed .25 volt.
14. If either of the readings in 12 and 13 exceed the voltage stated, the charging circuit has developed a high-resistance fault, which must be traced and remedied.

If this test is satisfactory, then the incorrect voltage reading obtained in 11 would have been caused by a faulty regulator pack, so the alternator must either be replaced or removed for overhaul.

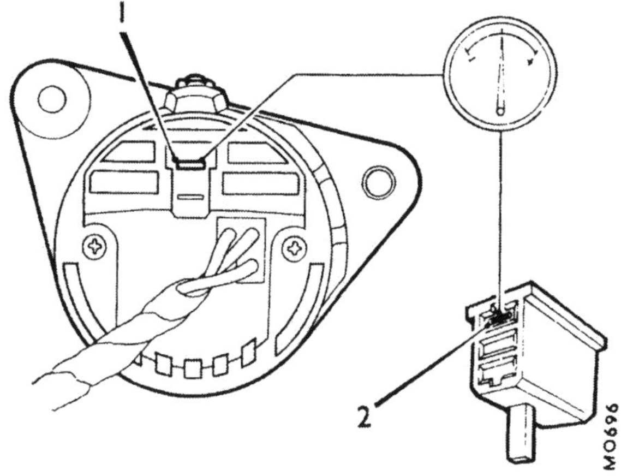

Fig. Nb.13
Alternator output test
1. Positive terminal of alternator.
2. Positive blade of two-way connector block.

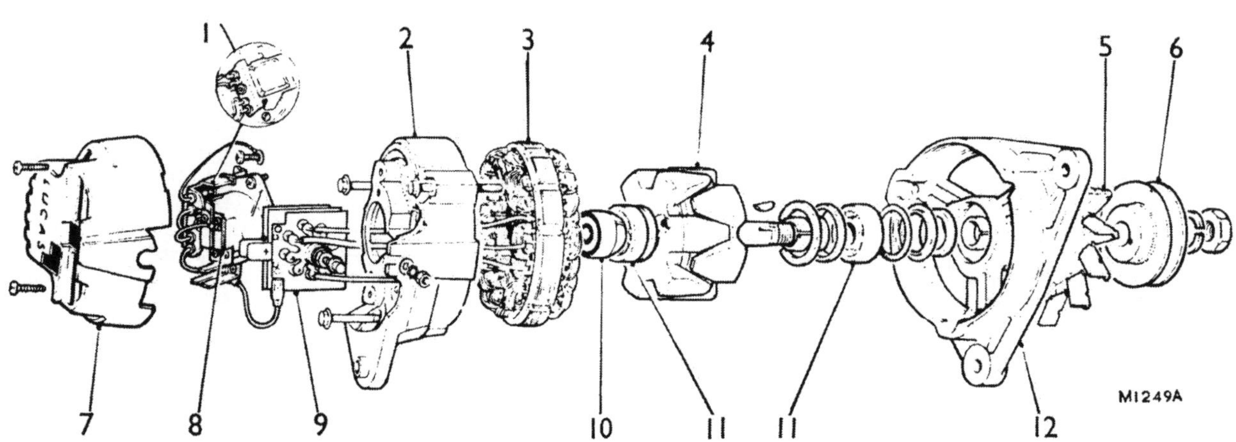

Fig. Nb.14
The 16ACR alternator components

1. Regulator pack.
2. Slip-ring end bracket.
3. Stator.
4. Rotor.
5. Fan.
6. Pulley.
7. End cover.
8. Brush box moulding.
9. Rectifier pack.
10. Slip-rings.
11. Rotor bearings.
12. Drive end bracket.

Removing the regulator pack

15. Remove the alternator as described in items 17 to 20.
16. Remove the moulded end cover, and identify the type of regulator pack fitted; the 8TR type has two short mounting screws at each end, while the 11TR type has a single longer one, with a spacer, screwed into the top lug of the brush box moulding only. Both types have two legs which locate in the brush box moulding.

    Disconnect the coloured tag lead connectors from the brush box, and detach the black (earth) lead after removing the lower mounting screw (8TR) or one of the brush box retaining screws (11TR). Remove the remaining screw securing the regulator pack.

Removing the alternator

17. Withdraw the terminal block from the alternator.
18. Remove the adjusting link bolt from the alternator.
19. Slacken the alternator mounting bolts, lower the alternator and slip the fan belt from the alternator pulley.
20. Unscrew the alternator mounting bolts and remove the alternator.

Testing–alternator removed

21. Unscrew the cover retaining screws and remove the cover if this has not already been done in item 16.
22. Unsolder the three stator connections from the rectifier pack, noting the connection positions.

IMPORTANT.–When soldering or unsoldering connections to the diodes great care must be taken not to overheat the diodes or bend the pins. During the soldering operations the diode pins should be gripped lightly with a pair of long-nosed pliers which will then act as a thermal shunt, see Fig. Nb.15.

23. Unscrew the two brush moulding securing screws, and, if necessary, the lower regulator pack securing screw.

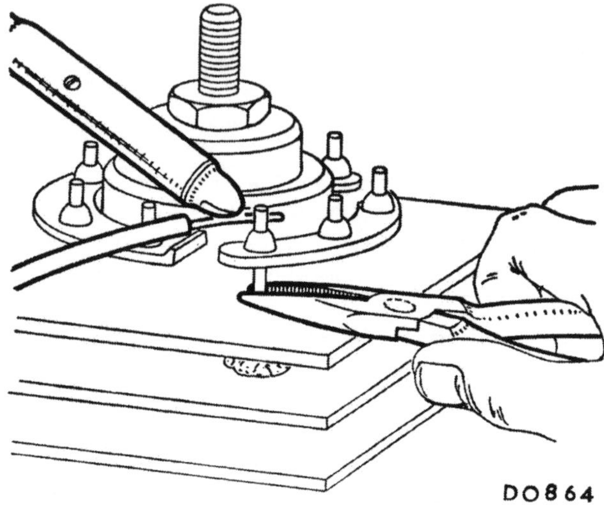

Fig. Nb.15
Using pliers as a thermal shunt when soldering the alternator diodes

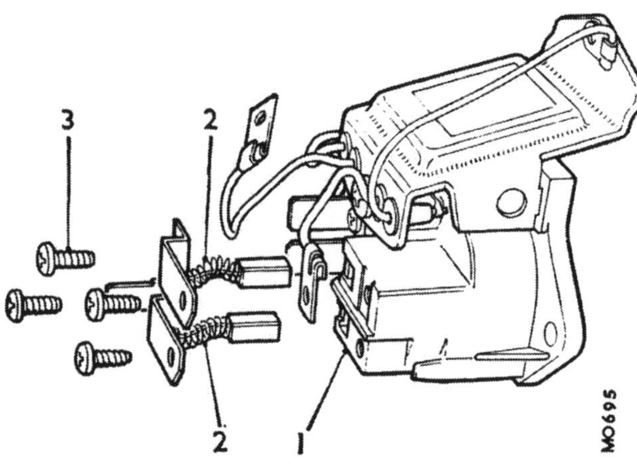

Fig. Nb.16
To renew a brush and spring assembly, remove the appropriate pair of screws and extract the brush assembly from its housing

1. Brush box moulding.
2. Brush and spring assembly.
3. Retaining screws (4).

24. Slacken the rectifier pack retaining nuts and withdraw both the brush moulding, with or without the regulator pack, and the rectifier pack.

BRUSHES

25. Check the brushes for wear by measuring the length of brush protruding beyond the brushbox moulding. If the length protruding is .2 in. (5 mm.) or less, the brush must be renewed.
26. Check that the brushes move freely in their holders. If a brush shows a tendency to stick, clean it with a petrol- (gasoline-) moistened cloth or, if necessary polish the sides of the brush with a fine file.
27. Check the brush spring pressure using a push-type spring gauge. The gauge should register 7 to 10 oz. (198 to 283 gm.) when the brush is pushed back until its face is flush with the housing. If the gauge reading is outside the limits given, renew the brush assembly, as shown in Fig. Nb.16.

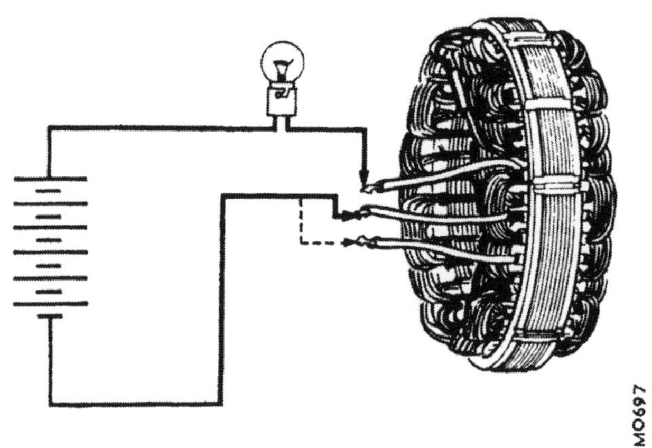

Fig. Nb.17
The stator winding continuity test

SLIP-RINGS

28. Clean the surfaces of the slip-rings using a petrol- (gasoline-)moistened cloth.
29. Inspect the slip-ring surfaces for signs of burning; remove burn marks using very fine sand paper. On no account must emery-cloth or similar abrasives be used or any attempt made to machine the slip-rings.

ROTOR

30. Connect an ohmmeter, or a 12-volt battery and an ammeter, to the slip-rings. An ohmmeter reading of 4.3 ohms or an ammeter reading of 3 amps. should be recorded.
31. Using a 110-volt A.C. supply and a 15-watt test lamp, test for insulation between one of the slip-rings and one of the rotor poles. If the test lamp lights, the rotor must be renewed.

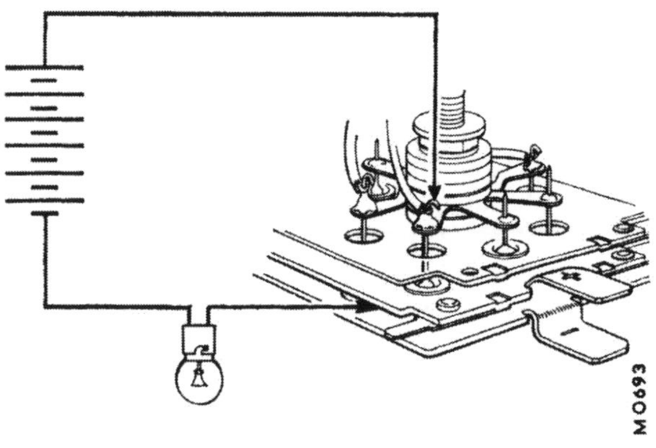

Fig. Nb.18
Testing the diodes

STATOR

32. Connect a 12-volt battery and a 36-watt test lamp to two of the stator connections. Repeat the test, replacing one of the two stator connections with the third. If the test lamp fails to light in either of the tests, the stator must be renewed (see Fig. Nb.17).
33. Using a 110-volt A.C. supply and a 15-watt test lamp, test for insulation between any one of the three stator connections and the stator laminations. If the test lamp lights, the stator must be renewed.

DIODES

34. Connect a 12-volt battery and a 1.5-watt test lamp in turn to each of the nine diode pins and its corresponding heatsink on the rectifier pack, then reverse the connections. The lamp should light with the current flowing in one direction only. If the lamp lights in both directions or fails to light in either, the rectifier pack must be renewed (see Fig. Nb.18).

IMPORTANT.– See notes on soldering the diodes given in item 22.

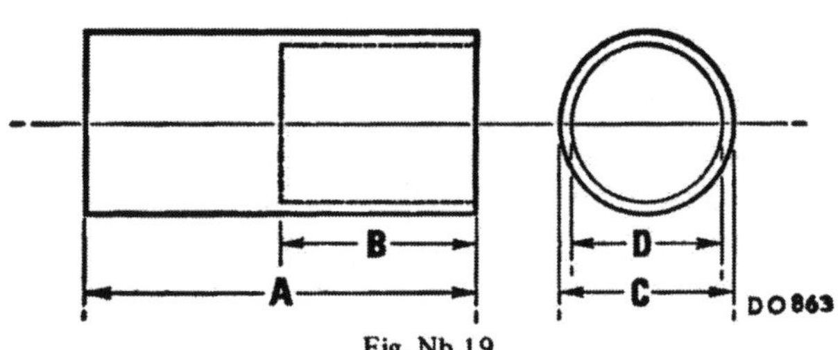

Fig. Nb.19
Dimensions of the rotor removing tool

A. 3 in. (76 mm.).
B. 1.5 in. (38 mm.).
C. 1.32 in. (33.5 mm.).
D. 1.24 in. (31.5 mm.).

Dismantling

35. Carry out the operations detailed in 21 to 24.
36. Remove the three through-bolts.
37. Fit a tube of the dimensions given in Fig. Nb.19 over the slip-ring moulding so that it registers against the outer track of the slip-ring end bearing and carefully drive the bearing from its housing.
38. Remove the shaft nut, washer, pulley, fan, and shaft key.
39. Press the rotor from the drive end bracket.
40. Remove the circlip retaining the drive end bearing and remove the bearing.
41. Unsolder the field connections from the slip-ring assembly and withdraw the assembly from the rotor shaft.
42. Remove the slip-ring end bearing.

Reassembling

43. Reverse the dismantling procedure in 35 to 42 and 21 to 24, noting the following points.
    a. Use Shell Alvania 'RA' to lubricate the bearings where necessary.
    b. When refitting the slip-ring end bearing, ensure that it is fitted with its open side facing towards the rotor and is pressed onto the rotor shaft as far as it will go.
    c. Re-solder the field connections to the slip-rings using Fry's H.T.3 solder.
    d. When refitting the rotor to the drive end bracket, support the inner track of the bearing with a suitable piece of tube. Do not use the drive end bracket as the only support for the bearing when fitting the rotor.
    e. Tighten the through-bolts evenly.
    f. Check that the brushes are enterd in their housings before fitting the brush moulding.
    g. Tighten the shaft nut to the torque figure given in **'GENERAL DATA'**.
    h. Refit the regulator pack to the brush moulding if it had been removed separately. See that the correct number and size of securing screws are used for the type being refitted, which need not be the same as the original, using the spacer if required. Refer to item 16.

Refitting the alternator

Reverse the removal procedure in 17 to 21, and ensure that the drive belt is correctly tensioned.

FAULT DIAGNOSIS

Alternator			Probable fault and associated damage
Temperature	**Noise**	**Output**	
High	Normal	Higher than normal—40 amps. approximately at 2,800 r.p.m.	Live side output diode open-circuit. (May damage rotor windings and regulator output stage, overheat brush boxes, and blow warning light).
High	Excessive	Very low—10 amps. approximately at 2,800 r.p.m.	Live side output diode short-circuit. (May cause failure of associated field diode.)
Normal	Excessive	Poor at low speed, slightly below normal at 2,800 r.p.m.—32 amps. approximately.	Earth side output diode open-circuit.
Normal	Excessive	Very low at all speeds above 850 r.p.m.—7 amps. approximately.	Earth side output diode short-circuit. or one phase winding shorted to earth.
Normal	Normal	Lower than normal—29 amps. approximately at 2,800 r.p.m.	Field diode open-circuit.
Normal	Excessive	Very low—7 amps. approximately at 2,800 r.p.m.	Field diode short-circuit.

THE ELECTRICAL SYSTEM

WIRING DIAGRAMS

MASTER KEY TO WIRING DIAGRAMS

Several of the components listed in this key may not be fitted to individual models. Some are a special fitment to vehicles exported to certain countries or territories to conform to the mandatory requirements or legislation of those countries.

No.	Description
1.	Alternator or dynamo.
2.	Control box.
3.	Battery (12 volt).
4.	Starter solenoid.
5.	Starter motor.
6.	Lighting switch.
7.	Headlamp dip switch.
8.	R.H. headlamp.
9.	L.H. headlamp.
10.	Main-beam warning lamp.
11.	R.H. sidelamp/parking lamp.
12.	L.H. sidelamp/parking lamp.
14.	Panel lamps.
15.	Number-plate lamp(s).
16.	R.H. stop and tail lamps.
17.	L.H. stop and tail lamps.
18.	Stop lamp switch.
19.	Fuse block.
20.	Interior light.
21.	R.H. door switch (and buzzer) } when fitted.
22.	L.H. door switch (and buzzer) } when fitted.
23.	Horn(s).
24.	Horn-push.
25.	Flasher unit.
26.	Direction indicator, headlamp flasher and dip switch.
27.	Direction indicator warning lamp(s).
28.	R.H. front direction indicator lamp.
29.	L.H. front direction indicator lamp.
30.	R.H. rear direction indicator lamp.
31.	L.H. rear direction indicator lamp.
32.	Heater or fresh air blower switch.
33.	Heater or fresh air blower.
34.	Fuel gauge.
35.	Fuel gauge tank unit.
36.	Windscreen wiper switch.
37.	Windscreen wiper motor.
38.	Ignition/starter switch.
39.	Ignition coil.
40.	Distributor.

No.	Description
41.	Fuel pump.
42.	Oil pressure switch.
43.	Oil pressure gauge or warning lamp.
44.	Ignition warning lamp.
45.	Headlamp flasher switch (Mini 1000 Canada).
46.	Coolant temperature gauge.
47.	Coolant temperature transmitter.
49.	Reverse lamp switch.
50.	Reverse lamp.
64.	Bi-metal instrument voltage stabilizer.
67.	Line fuse.
75.	Automatic transmission safety switch (when fitted).
83.	Induction heater and thermostat.
84.	Suction chamber heater.
95.	Tachometer.
110.	R.H. direction indicator repeater lamp. } when fitted.
111.	L.H. direction indicator repeater lamp. } when fitted.
115.	Rear window demister switch.
116.	Rear window demister unit.
139.	Alternative connection for two-speed wiper motor and switch.
150.	Rear window demist warning lamp.
153.	Hazard warning switch.
154.	Hazard warning flasher unit.
158.	Printed circuit instrument panel.
159.	Brake pressure warning lamp and lamp test switch.
160.	Brake pressure differential switch.
164.	Ballast resistor.
168.	Ignition key audible warning buzzer.
170.	R.H. front side-marker lamp.
171.	L.H. front side-marker lamp.
172.	R.H. rear side-marker lamp.
173.	L.H. rear side-marker lamp.
198.	Driver's seat belt switch.
199.	Passenger's seat belt switch.
200.	Passenger's seat switch.
201.	Seat belt warning gearbox switch.
202.	Seat belt warning lamp.
203.	Seat belt warning diode.

CABLE COLOUR CODE

B.	Black.	N.	Brown.	U.	Blue.
G.	Green.	O.	Orange.	W.	White.
K.	Pink.	P.	Purple.	Y.	Yellow.
L.G.	Light Green.	R.	Red.		

When a cable has two colour code letters the first denotes the main colour and the second denotes the tracer colour.

Mini Cooper 'S' Mk. III

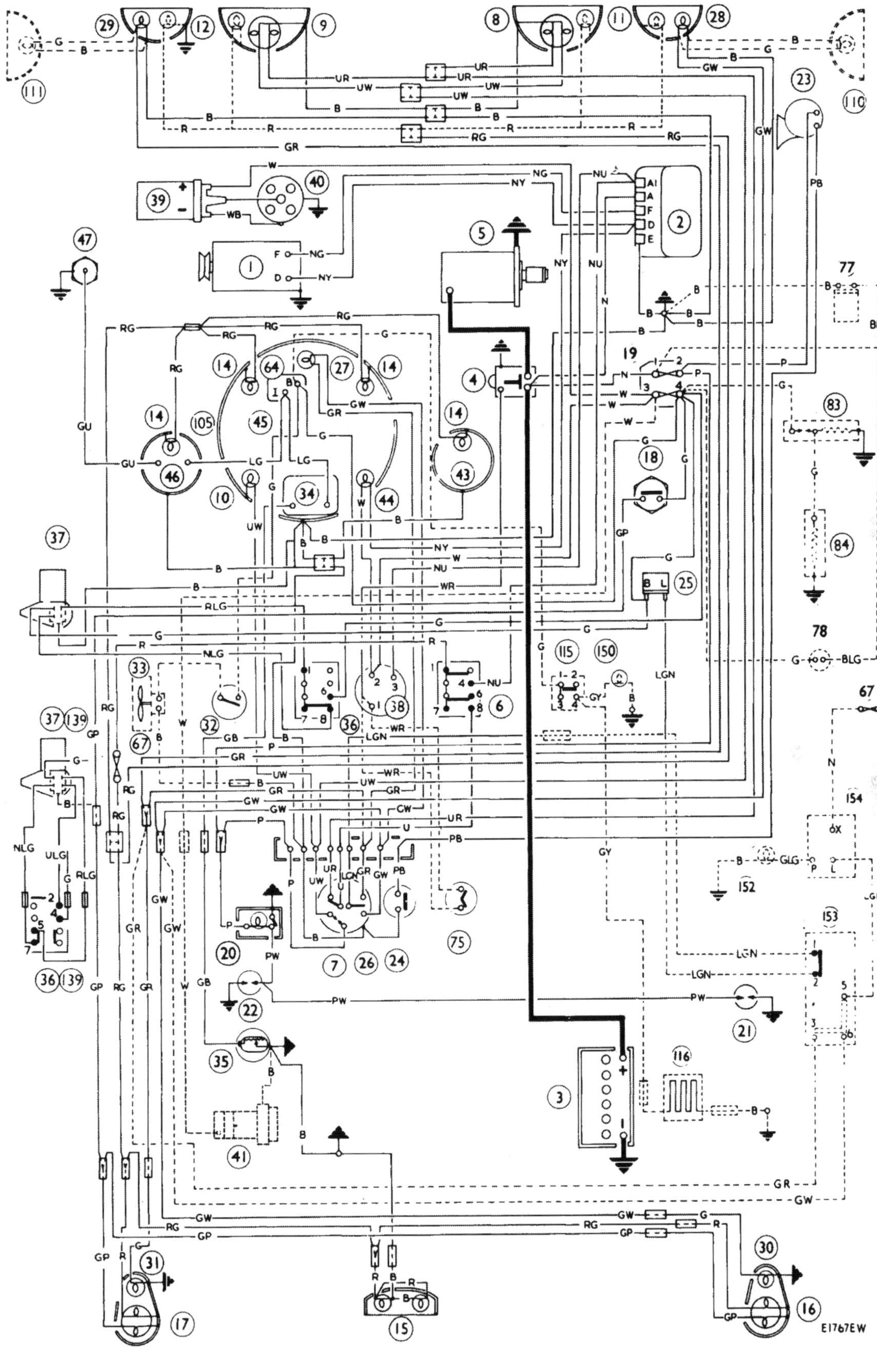

E1767EW

Mini 850 De-luxe Saloon, Van and Pick-up (with dynamo and toggle type switches)

E3169W

Mini 850 De-luxe Saloon, Van and Pick-up (with alternator and rocker type switches)

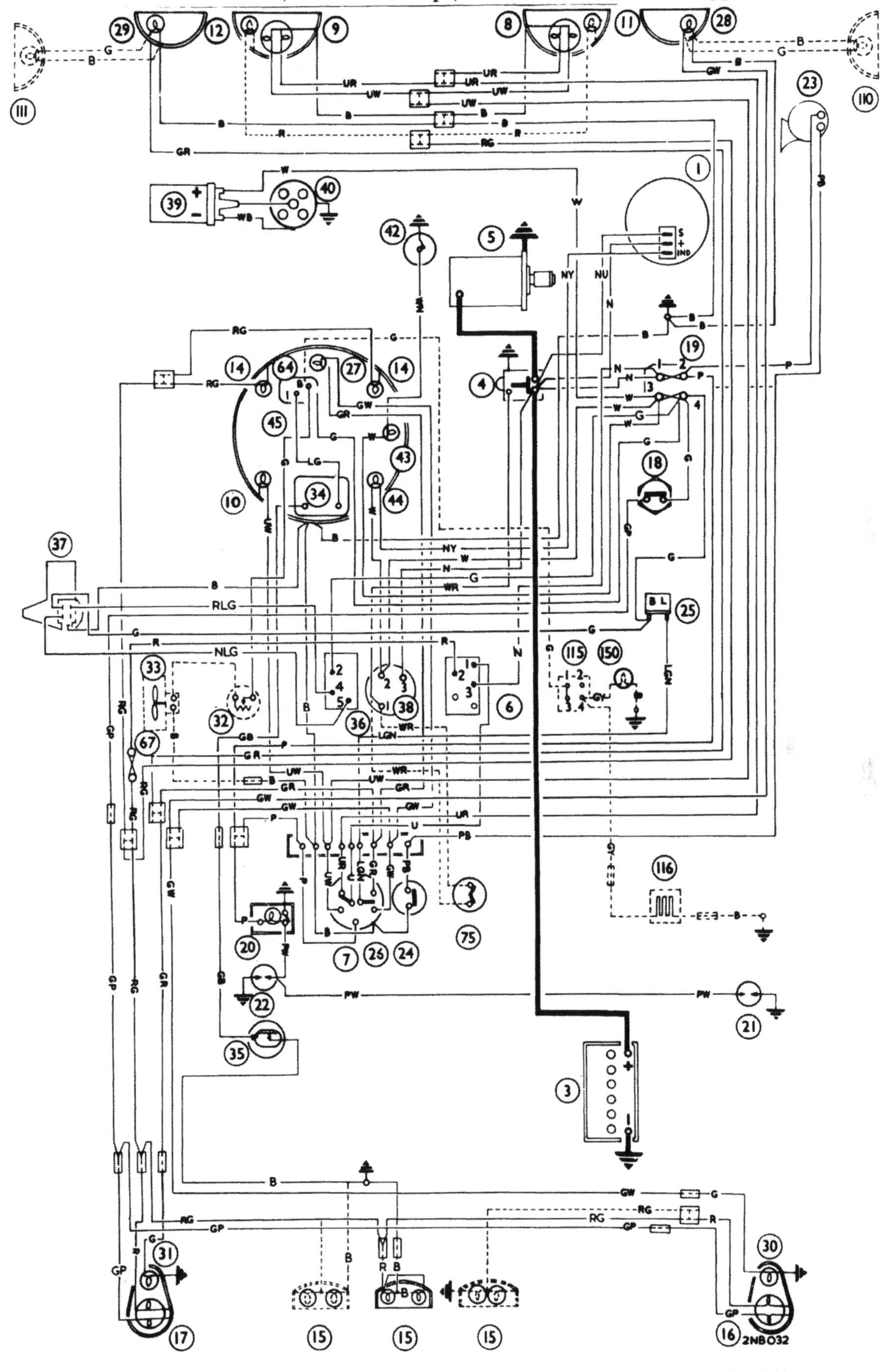

Mini 1000 Special De-luxe Saloon (with dynamo and toggle type switches)

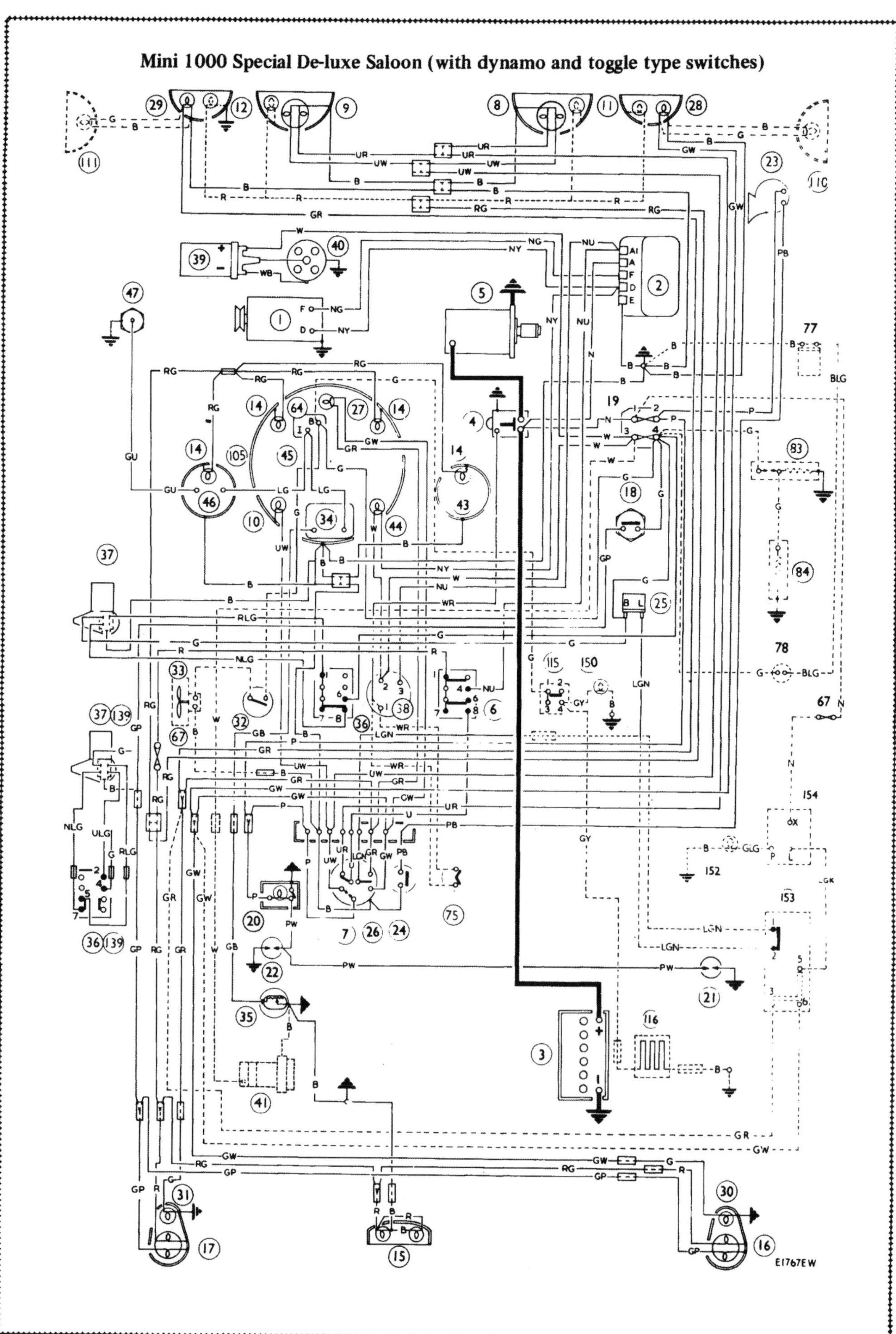

Mini 1000 Special De-luxe Saloon (with alternator and rocker type switches)

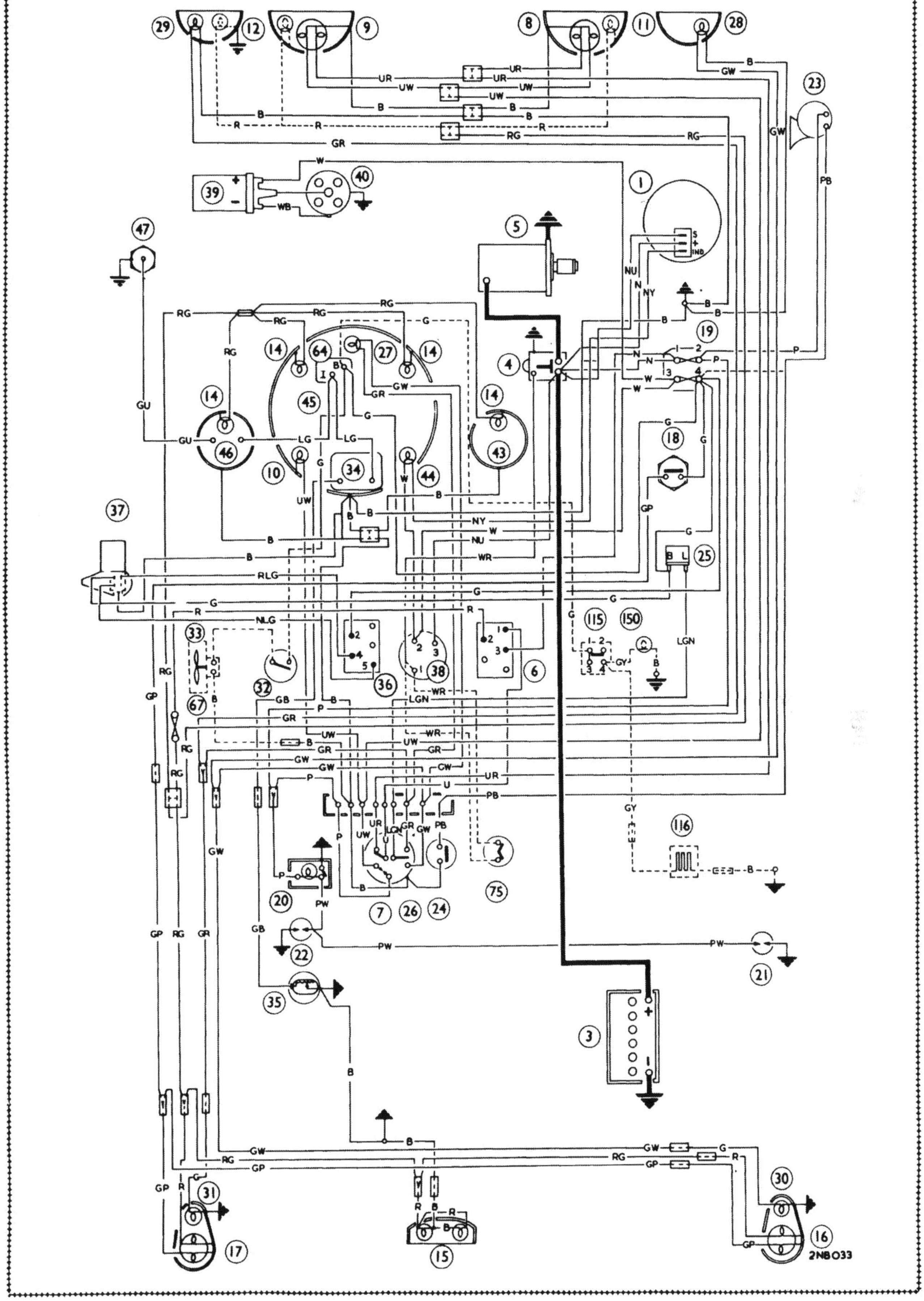

2NB033

Mini Clubman Saloon and Estate (with dynamo and toggle type switches)

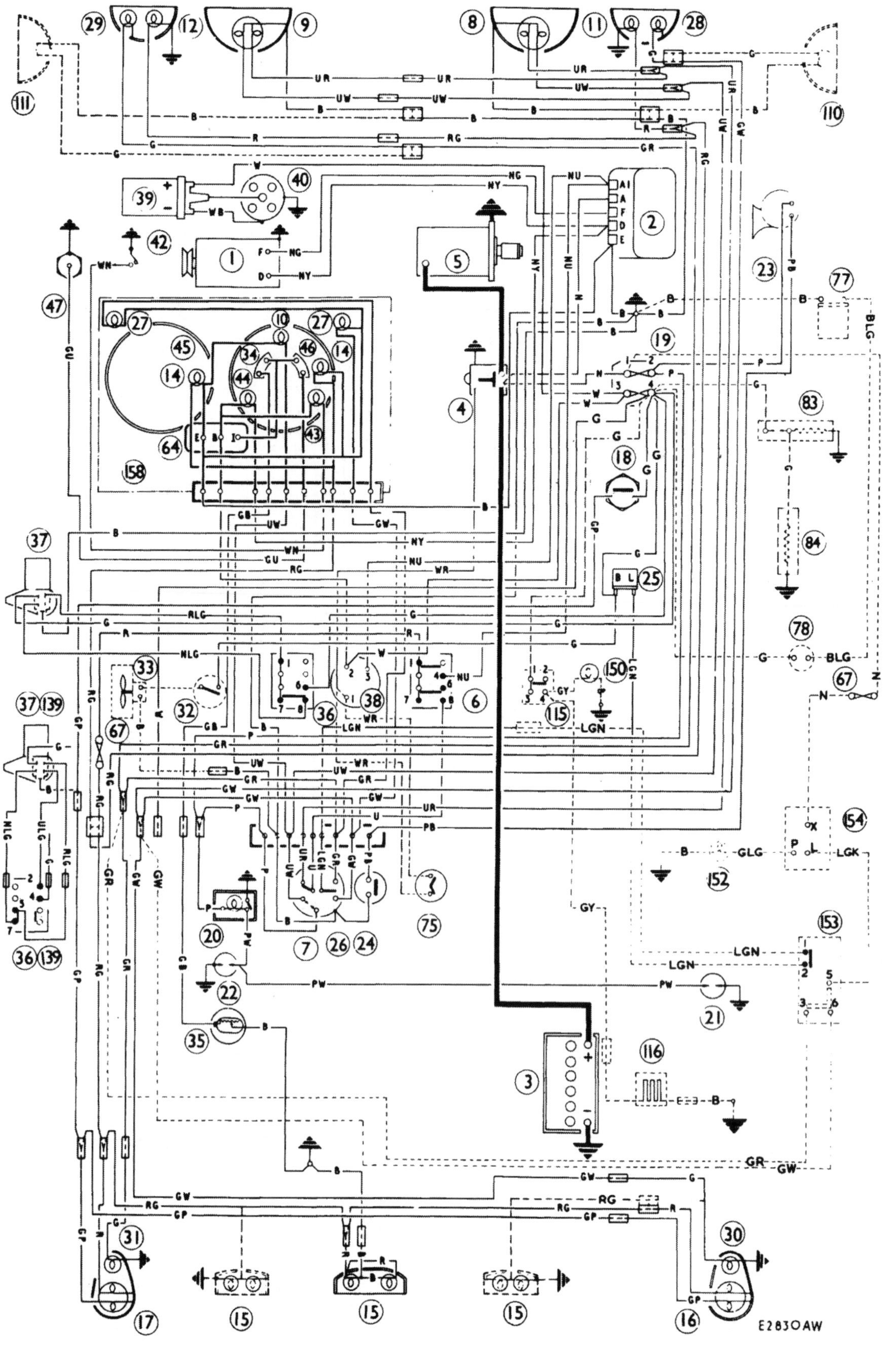

E2830AW

Mini Clubman Saloon and Estate (with alternator and rocker type switches)

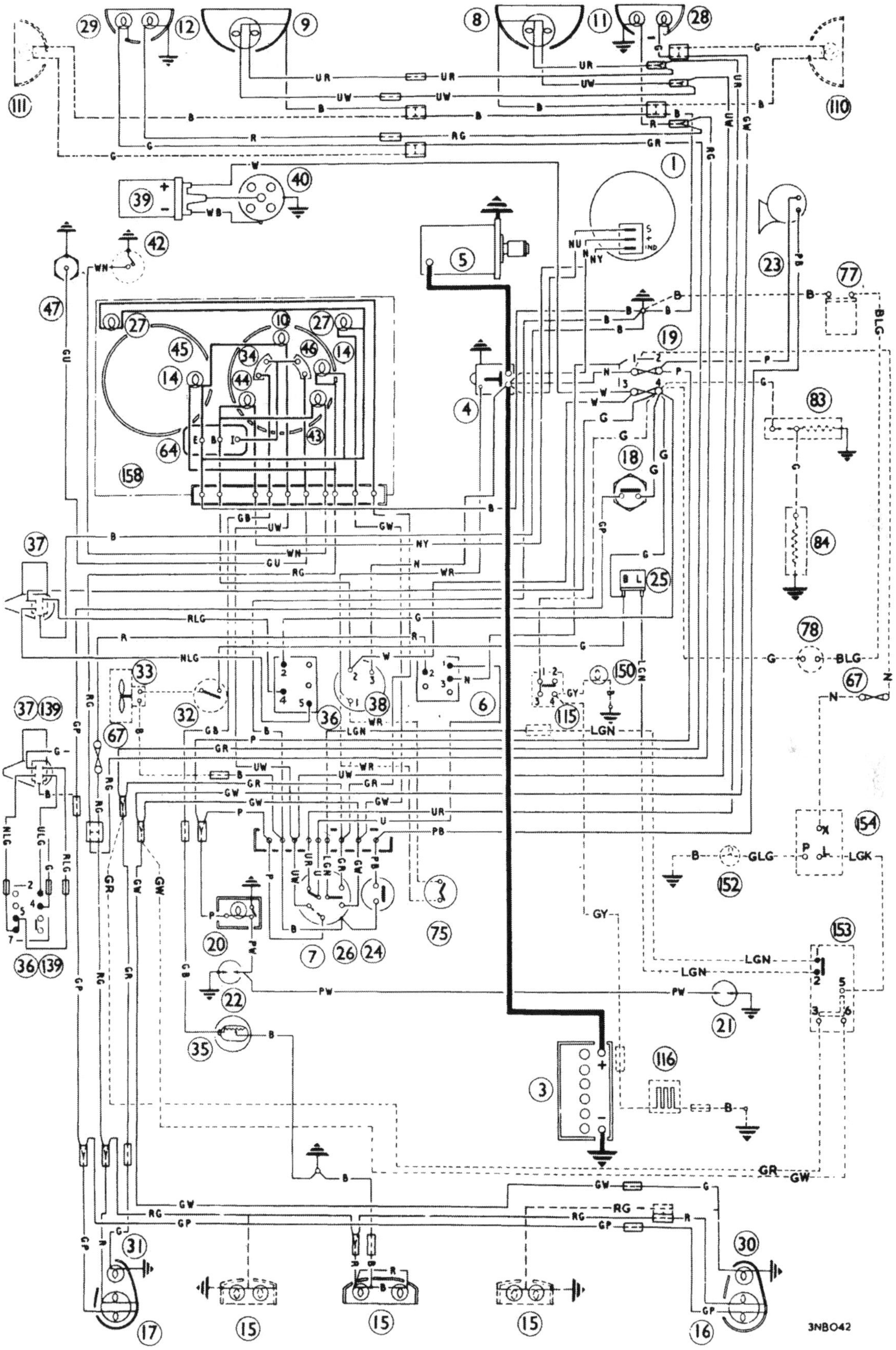

3NBO42

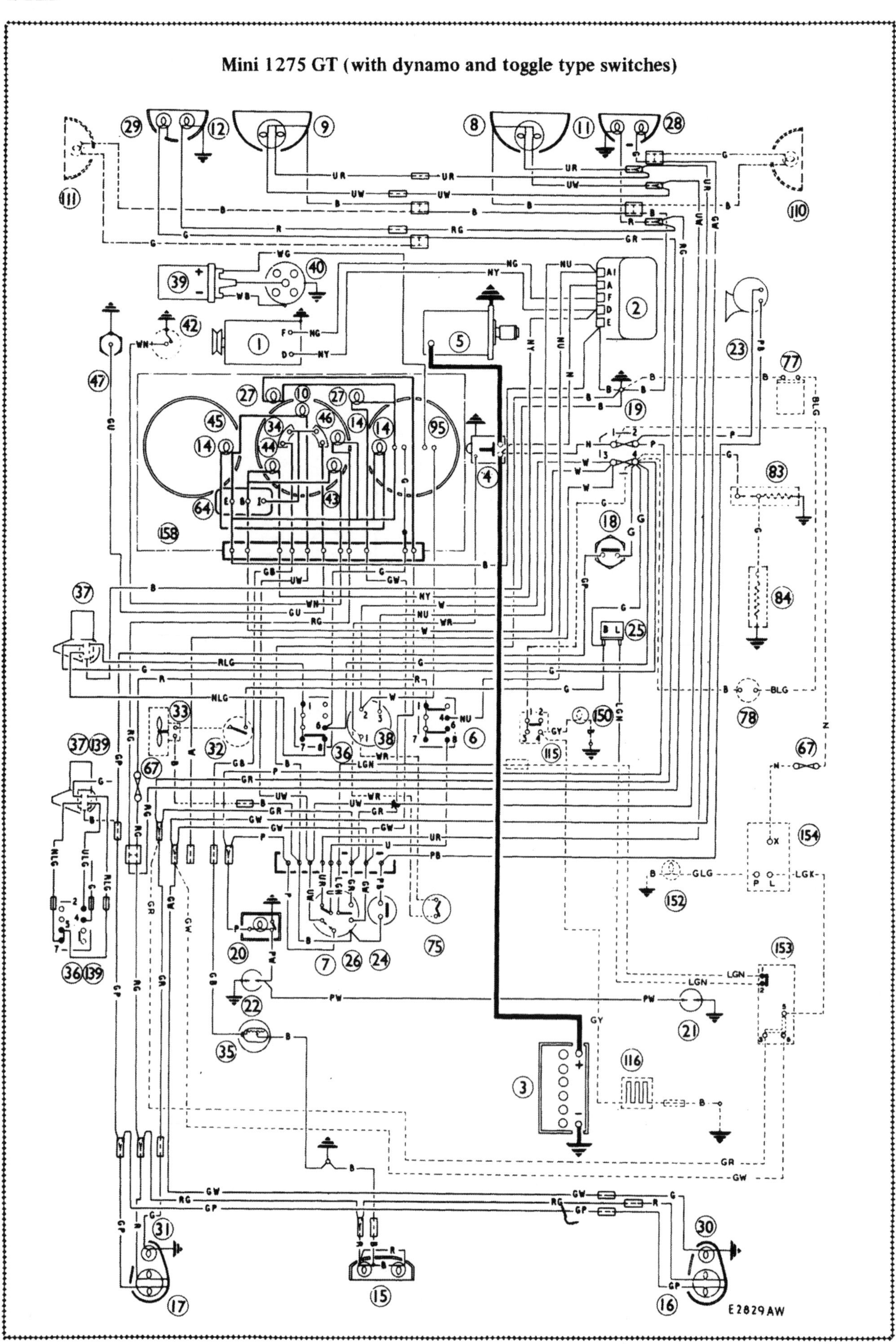
Mini 1275 GT (with dynamo and toggle type switches)
E2829AW

Mini 1275 GT (with alternator and rocker type switches)

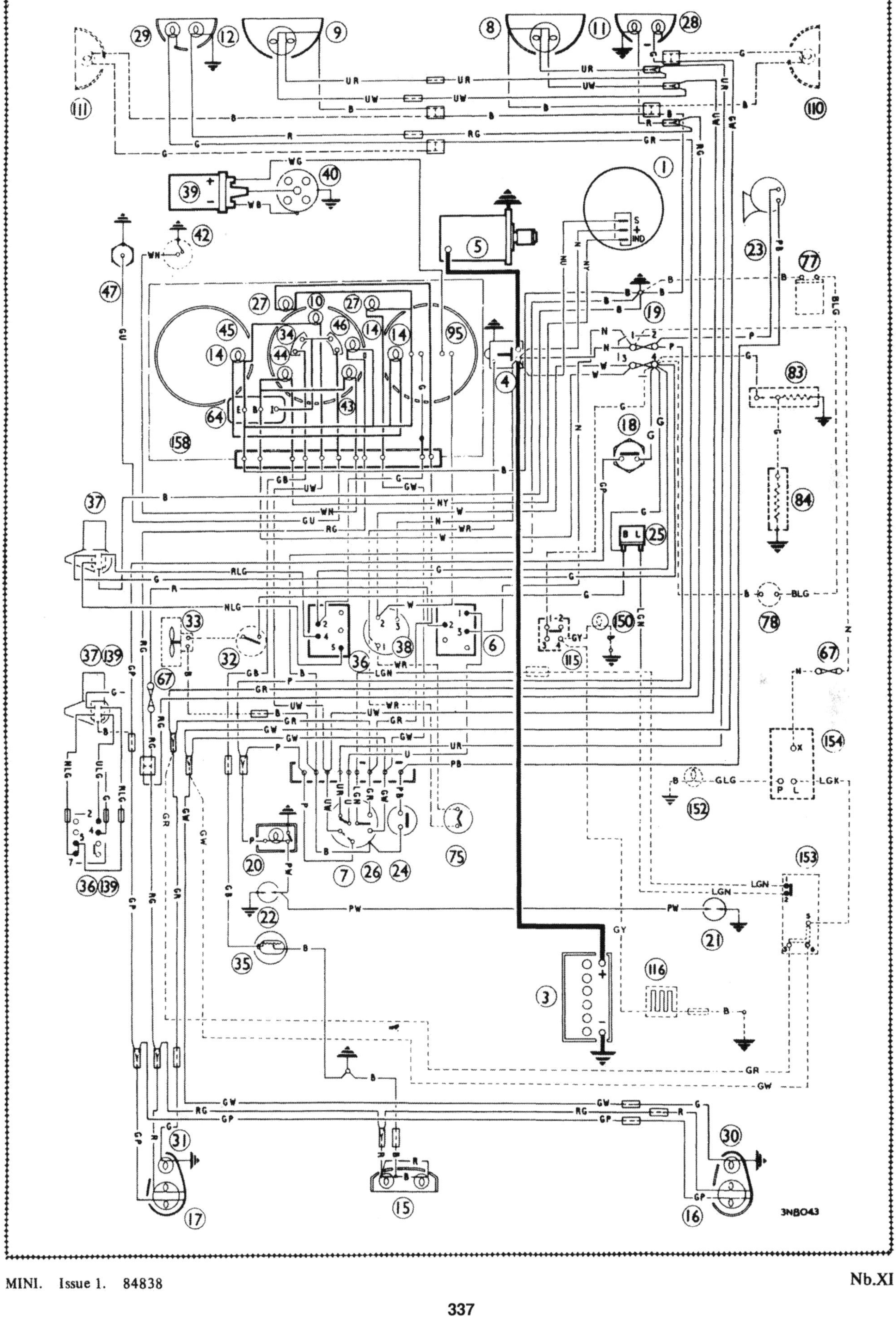

3NB043

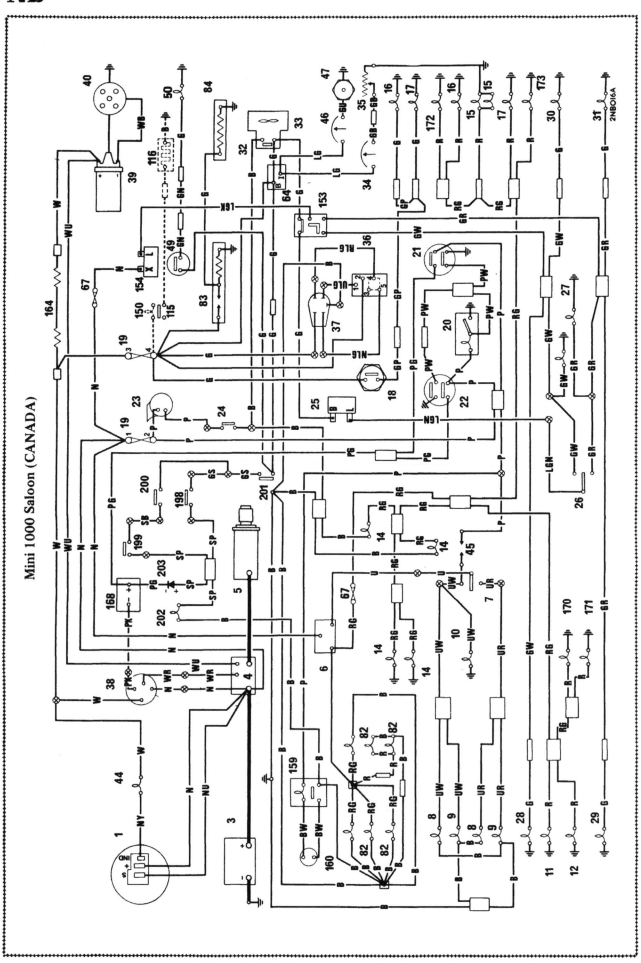

Mini 1000 Saloon (CANADA)

2NB016A

SECTION R

THE BODY

Section R.1

WINDSCREEN GLASS

Removing

1. Lift the wiper blades from the glass.
2. Prise up the end of the locking filler and pull it from the rubber channel.
3. Push the glass from inside the car and ease the rubber surround from the body.

Refitting

4. Fit the rubber surround to the body and lubricate with soap and water.
5. Fit the glass into the lower channel of the rubber and lift the lip of the surround with the short peg of Service tool 18G 468, starting at one corner and working round.
6. Thread the locking filler through the handle and eye of the tool, insert the tool into the filler strip channel and draw the tool along the channel, feeding the filler through the tool. When cutting the filler, allow a small overlap and then force the ends into position.

Section R.2

BACK-LIGHT GLASS

As items 2 to 6 in '**Windscreen Glass**'.

Section R.3

DOOR GLASSES

Removing and refitting

Take out the screws from the lower channel and remove the glass and channel. Reverse to refit.

Section R.4

QUARTER-LIGHT GLASSES

Removing (Fixed type)

1. Support the outside of the glass and hit it with the palm of the hand inside at the top, then remove the glass and rubber.

Refitting

2. Fit the surround rubber to the glass.
3. Pass a length of thin cord round the outer channel of the surround, leaving the ends hanging down on the inside of the glass.

Fig. R.1
Use Service tool 18G 468 to ease the channel lip over the windscreen glass

4. Lubricate the body edge with soap and water, hold the glass in position, press lightly and pull the cord from inside the car to draw the lip of the rubber over the edge of the body.

Removing (Hinged type)

5. Remove the catch from the body.
6. Open the quarter-light, ease up the seal on the body, unscrew the exposed screws securing the hinge and detach the window assembly.
7. Remove the frame from the glass after unscrewing the hinge screws at top and bottom.

Refitting

Reverse the removal instructions.

Section R.5

HEATER ASSEMBLY
(Recirculatory Type)

Initial fitting

Full instructions for fitting are contained in the heater kit.

Removing

1. Disconnect the battery.
2. Drain the cooling system.
3. Disconnect the motor leads.
4. Slacken the demister and water hose clips.
5. Withdraw the screws securing the unit to the parcel shelf and remove.

Refitting

6. Reverse the removal instructions.
7. Open the heater tap on the rear of the engine and refill the cooling system.
8. Test the heater; if the water return hose does not warm up in a few minutes, there may be an airlock.
9. To clear, disconnect the return hose from the lower radiator hose and plug the hole.
10. Extend the return hose to reach the radiator filler.
11. Start up and note the flow of water from the return hose; when it is free from bubbles, switch off and reconnect.

Section R.6

ROOF LINER

Removal

1. Disconnect the battery and remove the roof light.
2. Mark the position of the rear edge of the front liner on the cant rail.
3. Grip the outer edges of the liner and pull it backwards and inwards.
4. Mark the position of the front edge of the rear liner and pull it forwards and inwards.

Refitting

Reverse the removal instructions.

Section R.7

DOOR LOCKS

Removing

1. Withdraw the screw securing the lock to the inner panel and the screw from the end of the locking handle spindle.
2. Slacken the screw clamping the inner lever and remove the handle and escutcheon.

Refitting

Reverse the removal instructions. Ensure that the inner control cable lever is fitted upright.

Section R.8

DOOR FRAME–REAR (Countryman and Traveller)

Removing

The wood frame is a complete assembly.

1. Remove the rear door and take off the lock.
2. Remove the two screws from the centre of the inner door panel.
3. Remove the door sealing rubber and retaining clips.

Fig. R.2
The use of the glazing tool and eye to thread the locking filler strip into the rubber channel

4. Extract the self-tapping screws from the edge of the door and remove the frame assembly from the panel.

Refitting

5. Clean off sealing compound and remake the joints.
6. Refit the frame; locate all the screws before tightening any.

Section R.9

SLIDING GLASSES (Countryman and Traveller)

Removing

1. Remove the trim panel from above the sliding windows.
2. Remove the upper channels, support the inside and push the glass from the outside.

Refitting

3. Reverse the removal instructions.

Section R.10

TILT FRAME AND COVER (Pick-up)

The tilt frame and cover are supplied as a separate kit; the centre and rear hoop sockets, and the front attachment bracket for the struts, are fitted to the vehicle as original equipment.

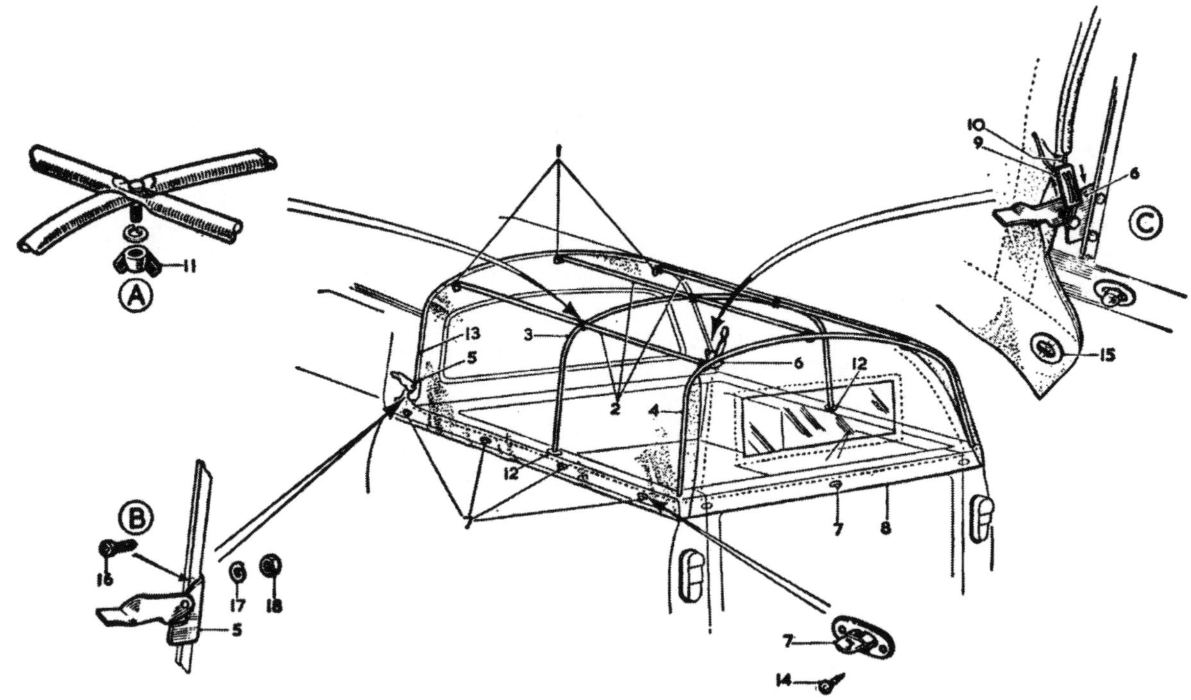

Fig. R.3
The tilt frame and cover assembly

1. Front fixing brackets.
2. Strut.
3. Front hoop.
4. Rear hoop.
5. L.H. lever bracket.
6. R.H. lever bracket
7. Turn-button.
8. Cover assembly.
9. Adjuster plate–cable.
10. Cover fixing cable.
11. Wing nut–strut to hoop.
12. Hoop housing assembly.
13. Cover retaining channel.
14. Screw–turn-button to body side.
15. Eyelet–tilt cover.
16. Screw–lever bracket to body.
17. Spring washer.
18. Nut for screw.

Fitting

1. Fit the rear hoop ends into the sockets at either side of the rear end of the body. Ensure that the three brackets attached to the top of the hoop face forwards.
2. Fit the centre hoop ends into the sockets at the centre position.
3. Engage the studs of one of the struts of the hole in the centre bracket at the top of the rear hoop, the centre hole pierced in the top of the centre hoop, and the hole in the centre bracket attached to the rear of the cab at the top (see Fig. R.3). Fit a spring washer and wing nut to each stud and tighten fully (inset (A) of Fig. R.3).
4. Repeat this operation with the other two struts, using the fixing holes in the brackets and centre hoop either side of the central fixing points.
5. Place the R.H. lever bracket assembly on the rear face of the channel fixed around the rear of the cab with the drilled face of the bracket against the channel, its lower edge approximately in line with the top edge of the seam (body cross-member to cab). The lever attached to the bracket must face outwards and the lever pin must face forwards.

   Mark off the position of the two holes in the drilled face of the bracket onto the body and drill two holes $\frac{13}{64}$ in. (5.16 mm.) diameter. Fix the bracket to the channel with two of the No. 10 panhead screws, nuts, and spring washers, the heads of the screws facing outwards (see inset (B) of Fig. R.3). Repeat this operation with the L.H. bracket on the L.H. side of the channel.
6. Lay the tilt cover, smooth face upwards, over the tilt frame with the fixing cable at the front.

   Arrange the centre longitudinal seam to run centrally along the central strut and the centre transverse seam to be central about the centre hoop.

   Lift the levers on the bracket to their fullest extent and hook the fixed loop in one end of the fixing cable over the pin of the corresponding lever.

   Ensure that the cable running through the tilt cover is forwards of the rear edge of the channel round the outer edge of the cab for its full length. Adjust the loop at the other end of the cable until it will engage over the pin on its lever without undue slackness in the cable. The adjuster consists of a rectangular plate pierced with four holes. The cable is fed up through one hole from the rear of the plate, and then passed down through the hole below and in line along the length of the plate. The loop is formed below the plate, and the free end of the cable is then threaded through the lower vacant hole from the bottom face of the plate, and returns down through the corresponding hole at the top. By adjusting the position of the cable in the plate the length of the cable can be varied as necessary (see inset [C] of Fig. R.3).

With both loops engaged over their respective lever pins, press down each lever in turn until it toggles over into its locked position. The cable should now be holding the front of the tilt cover firmly, and must fit snugly down in the retaining channel throughout its length.

When the adjustment of the cable is satisfactory and the cable and tilt cover are seating correctly in the channel, tuck the free end of the cable back into the tilt cover alongside the cable.

7. Arrange the tilt cover so that it lies evenly and smoothly over the tilt frame. The fixing position of the turn-buttons can be marked off, using the eyelets in the lower edges of the cover as templates.

   Beginning with the extreme front eyelets, adjust the cover so that it takes its natural position and mark around the inside of the eyelet on the vertical face of the body. Hold the base of the turn-button against the body in the position so marked and mark and drill the two fixing holes, using a $\frac{7}{64}$ in. (2.78 mm.) diameter drill. Attach the turn-button to the body with two of the No. 6 countersunk self-tapping screws provided.

   Repeat this operation on the remaining turn-button positions, working from front to rear, attaching the cover to the body as the work proceeds. Repeat on the opposite side of the body, then lower the rear flap and mark off, fit the turn-button in the centre of the tailboard in the same manner.

8. Loop the short centre strap attached to the under side of the top of the cover around the central strut, and fasten the ends together with the turn-button and eyelet provided. Attach the corners of the rear flap to the side of the cover by means of the turn-buttons and eyelets provided. The two long straps at the top of the cover are for securing the rear flap when it is rolled and out of use.

Section R.11

INSTRUMENT PANEL
(Super De-luxe, Traveller, and Countryman)

COOPER

Removing

1. Remove four screws from the front face of the shroud.
2. Withdraw the shroud and disconnect the panel light switch wires.
3. Disconnect the oil gauge pipe and the temperature gauge wires.
4. Remove four screws and withdraw the panel with oil and temperature gauges.
5. Unscrew the knurled nuts and remove the gauges.

Refitting

Reverse the removal instructions.

Section R.12

SPEEDOMETER
(Super De-luxe and Cooper)

Removing

1. Remove the panel.
2. Unscrew two screws and remove the speedometer instrument panel brackets and distance pieces.
3. Disconnect the cable from the speedometer.
4. Disconnect the fuel gauge cable.
5. Pull out the bulb holders from the speedometer.
6. Withdraw the speedometer into the engine compartment.

Section R.13

CHECKING BODY ALIGNMENT
(Without Checking Jig)

1. Raise the vehicle and support it parallel to a level floor using the comparative measurements given on page R.11 (vertical alignment check).
2. Check the relative heights of all the intermediate points for distortion of the vehicle in the vertical plane.
3. Chalk the floor below the points shown on page R.12 (horizontal alignment check).
4. With a plumb-line, project the checking points from the vehicle onto the floor and mark the position with a pencil.
5. Mark the central points between each pair of checking points on the floor.
6. Mark the diagonals between any two pairs of points and intersections.
7. Stretch a length of chalk-covered cord so that it passes through as many of the marked central points and intersections as possible.
8. While the cord is held taut by two operators, a third should raise the cord and allow it to spring back and leave a white line on the floor. Any points through which the resulting white line does not pass will indicate the point where the underframe is out of alignment.

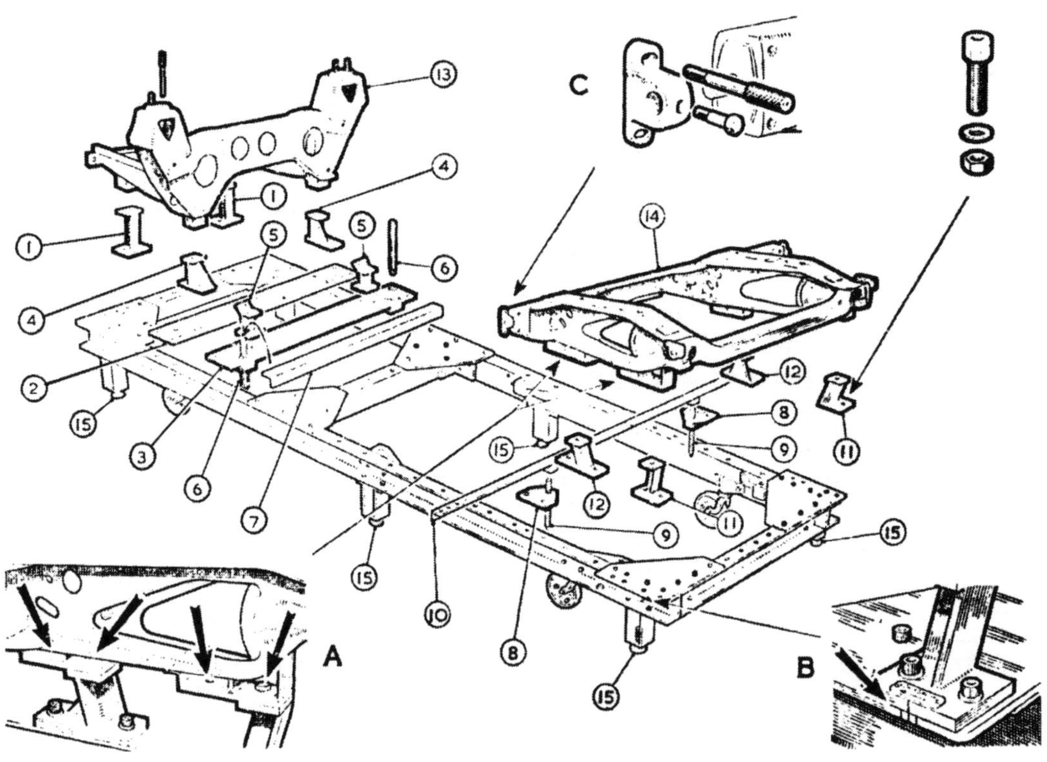

Fig. R.4
The assembly of the jig components

9. Considerable deviations in the measurements given on pages R.11 and R.12 confirm body misalignment. Allowance must be made for normal manufacturing tolerances and a reasonable departure from nominal dimensions can be permitted without detriment to performance.

Section R.14

CHECKING BODY ALIGNMENT
(With Checking Jig)

The equipment required for checking the body alignment consists of the basic body checking jig Service tool 18G 560, and adaptor set 18G 560 E used in conjunction with basic adaptor set 18G 560 A.

This equipment is intended to be used solely as a checking fixture, and under no circumstances must any welding or repair work be carried out on the body while it is still in position on the jig.

Assembling the jig

Where item numbers are quoted in this sub-section refer to Fig. R.4.

Remove the two inner socket screws from each corner plate on the front cross-member of the basic jig. Attach the two tall support pedestals (1) from adaptor set 18G 560 E to the cross-member at these points. Each pedestal is clearly labelled to show its correct location directionally. Fit the plate marked 'Forward 1' (2) from the basic adaptor set 18G 560 A and the plate marked 'Forward 2' (3) from the adaptor set 18G 560 E to the basic jig at the points indicated on the inside of the left hand side-member.

Attach the shorter pair of support pedestals (4) from adaptor set 18G 560 E to the rear of the front checking frame (13). Mount the frame with the rear pedestals on plate 1 (2) and attach the frame to the front pedestals and the rear pedestals to the plate.

Fit the two checking adaptors (5) and the two jacking screws (6) from 18G 560 E to plate 2 (3). Place the short jacking bar (7) from adaptor set 18G 560 in position on the jacking screws.

Attach the two jacking screw brackets (8) from 18G 560E to the side-member of the basic jig at the position marked 'OX' on the top of the left-hand side-member and at the corresponding position on the right-hand side-member.

Screw in the two longer jacking screws (9) from adaptor set 18G 560 A. Assemble the long jacking bar (10) from 18G 560 A and place in position on the screws.

Fit the two support pedestals (11) from 18G 560 E to the rear of the jig corner plates.

Attach the other pair of pedestals (12) from 18G 560 E to the front of the rear checking frame (14) and mount the checking frame on the rear pedestals and the side-member

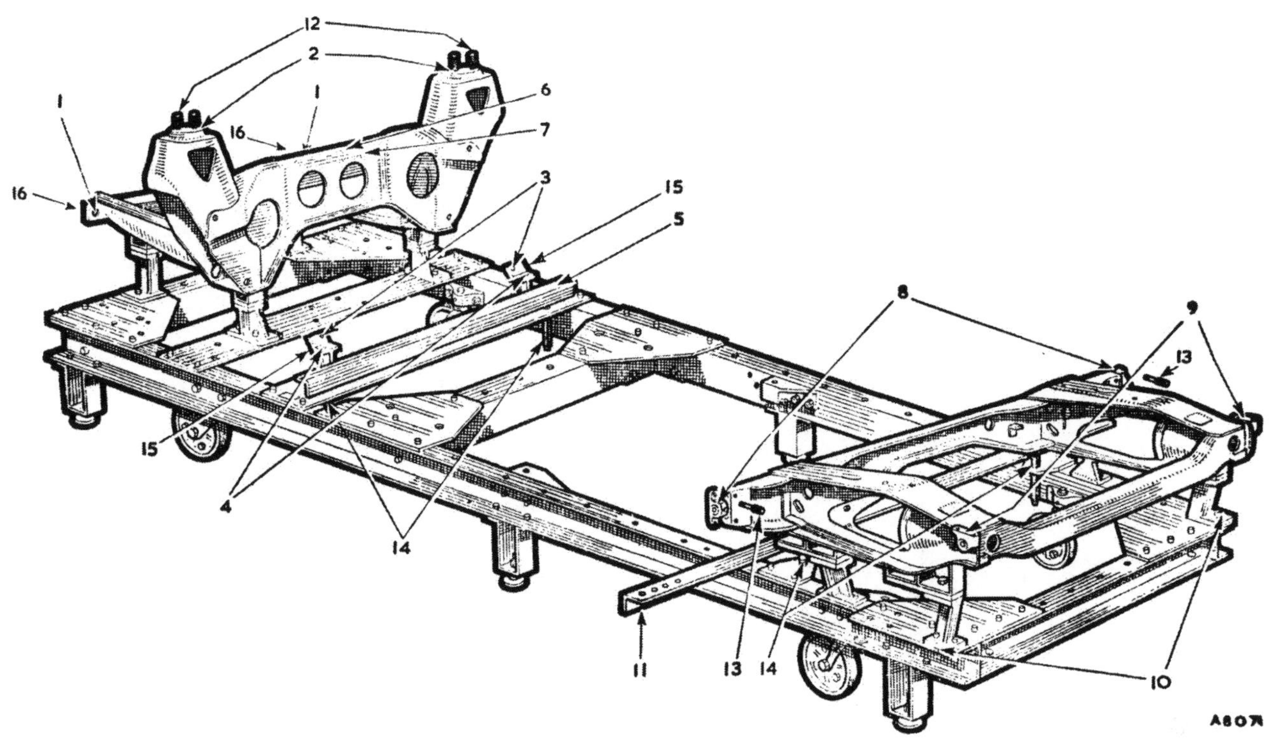

Fig. R.5
The jig checking points

of the basic jig. Do not tighten completely the pedestal to jig fixing bolts.

NOTE.–The rear checking frame has two alternative pairs of holes each side for attachment to the pedestals. The forward pair are for use when checking the body of a Van, Countryman or Traveller, the pair are for use when checking a Saloon body (see inset [A]).

When the assembly of the jig and adaptor sets is complete, adjust the basic jig by means of its six adjustable feet (15) (one at each corner, one on each side) until the weight is taken from the castors and the jig is level. Levelling indicators are provided, one on each side-member and one on the front cross-member.

If a fixed-position hoist is to be used to lift the body onto the jig, the jig must be levelled up in a central position under the hoist with the body already raised.

Checking alignment

All item numbers quoted in the following description refer to Fig. R.5.

Remove the four pins with knurled heads (12) from the top checking faces (2) of the front checking frame.

Move the rear checking frame to its most rearward position by means of the slotted holes in the base of the pedestal supports.

Lower the body squarely over the checking frames until it rests on the jacking bars.

At no time must the weight of the body be taken by the checking frames.

Lower the jacking bars equally, keeping the body square with the jig, until the body is lightly in contact with the top faces (2) of the front checking frame.

Insert the four pins (12) through the holes in the body and into the holes in the top faces of the front checking frame. Check the relation of the holes in the body to the plain shank of the checking pins. The ideal position is when each of the holes in the body is concentric with the shank of its checking pin (see Fig. R.6). Adjust the body on the jig until this position, or the nearest possible approach to it, has been attained.

Line up the top holes in the front checking brackets (8) of the rear checking frame with the corresponding holes in the body. Insert one of the threaded checking pins (13) in each side to check the alignment.

Move the rear checking frame forward until a parallel clearance of $\frac{1}{8}$ in. (3.18 mm.) is obtained between the forward faces of the front checking brackets (8) and the body (a drill shank is a convenient gauge to use when checking these clearances).

Tighten down the pedestal fixing bolts, and check the relative positions of the lines scribed on the outer edge of each rear pedestal and the lines scribed on either outer edge of the jig rear corner plates (10). The ideal position is when the lines on the pedestals coincide with the central lines on the corner plates (see inset [B], Fig. R.4). The lines scribed either side of each central line show the maximum permissible limits of adjustment, and the correct clearance between the checking bracket and the body must be obtained with the adjustment set within these limits.

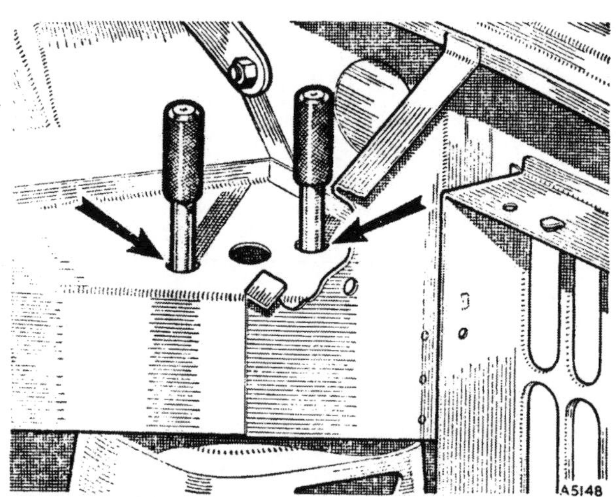

Fig. R.6
Showing an equal clearance around the checking pins with the body correctly aligned

Should the body be damaged in such a way that it is impossible to lower the body on the checking jig with all of the checking brackets on the rear checking frame in position, it is possible to detach either bracket by removing the hexagon-headed dowel bolt passing through the bracket, which can then be pulled off its mounting point.

After the correct location of the body on the jig has been established at the top checking faces on the front frame (2), and at the top holes of the front checking brackets (8) on the rear frame, the remaining alignment points and clearances can be checked.

The two checking holes (1) on the front member of the front checking frame, the four holes on the checking adaptors (3 and 4), and the eight holes in the front and rear checking brackets (8 and 9) on the rear checking frame should all line up by sight with their corresponding holes in the body.

A parallel clearance of ¼ in. (6.35 mm.) must exist between the checking faces (16) on the front member of the checking frame and the body and between both faces of each checking adaptor (15) and the under side of the body floor.

Examine the clearance between the body and the front checking frame at all points, including around the sides of the frame towers. If there is a foul at any point, the body must be dressed back until a clearance is obtained.

The face of the cross-member at the rear of the front frame must have a clearance to the body on its top vertical face (6) of ⅛ in. (3.18 mm.). and $\frac{1}{16}$ in. (1.6 mm.) clearance at the inclined face (7). Should these clearances not be present, the body must be dressed back until the requisite clearance is obtained.

A parallel clearance of ⅛ in. (3.18 mm.) must exist between the body and the checking faces of the four checking brackets (8 and 9) on the rear checking frame.

Section R.15

WINDSCREEN
(Moke)

Removal

1. Remove the windscreen wiper arm and blade.
2. Remove four nuts and screws.
3. Slacken the bottom retaining screws.
4. Lift the frame and glass from the vehicle.
5. Remove two screws, detach the bottom channel, and remove the glass from the frame.

Section R.16

HEATER ASSEMBLY
(Fresh-air Type)

Removing

1. Disconnect the battery and drain the cooling system.
2. Remove the front floor covering to avoid damage by coolant when removing the heater pipes.
3. Disconnect the two electrical snap connectors below the parcel shelf and the blower switch connection from the ignition switch.
4. Remove the demister tube covers, pull off the demister tubes and release the fresh-air intake hose.
5. Release the heater water hose clips and pull the hoses from the heater unit.
6. Slacken the nut securing the rear of the unit to the bracket, and remove the two screws beneath the parcel shelf securing the front of the heater (Fig. R.7). Lift the unit from the slotted rear brackets, hold the fingers over the matrix pipes and lift the unit out of the car. Drain the coolant from the unit.

   On early models the heater unit is secured by four nuts. Lift the parcel shelf trimming and remove the nuts to withdraw the unit; distance pieces are fitted on the mounting studs.

Heater matrix replacement

7. Slacken the screws securing the control panel, remove the end cover screws and lift off the cover complete with the blower motor.
8. Lift out the heater matrix and fit the replacement unit.
9. Reverse the procedure given in item (7).

Heater motor replacement

10. Carry out operations 1 to 7.
11. Drill out the three Pop rivets securing the motor unit to the end cover and remove the motor.
12. Locate the replacement motor in the end cover with the wiring positioned to the top of the heater box when reassembled, and Pop rivet in position.

13. Refitting the end cover is a reversal of the removal procedure. Ensure that the flap valve is located on the end cover pivot and operated correctly before refitting the heater to the car.

Blower switch replacement

14. Remove the heater control panel and the switch securing nut. Pull the flap valve outwards, withdraw the switch and pull off the wiring connections.
15. Fitting a replacement switch is a reversal of item 14.

Refitting

16 Reverse the removal procedure and refill the radiator with coolant. Start and warm up the engine, check for leaks and correct operation of the heater assembly. Top up the coolant in the radiator to the correct level.

Section R.17

INSTRUMENTS
(Mk. II Models)

It is not necessary to withdraw the instrument nacelle to remove the instruments, access to these being from under the bonnet behind the carburetter.

Removing

SPEEDOMETER

1. Remove the carburetter air cleaner and pull back the sound blanket from the speedometer aperture.
2. Disconnect the speedometer cable and pull off the electrical connections from the rear of the instrument. Remove the two securing screws and withdraw the instrument through the aperture into the engine compartment.

FUEL GAUGE

3. Carry out instructions 1 and 2; remove the two securing screws and lift out the fuel gauge.

OIL AND TEMPERATURE GAUGES

4. Carry out instruction 1.
5. Disconnect the electrical connections and the oil pressure gauge pipe, unscrew the knurled securing nuts and withdraw the gauges through the nacelle into the car interior.

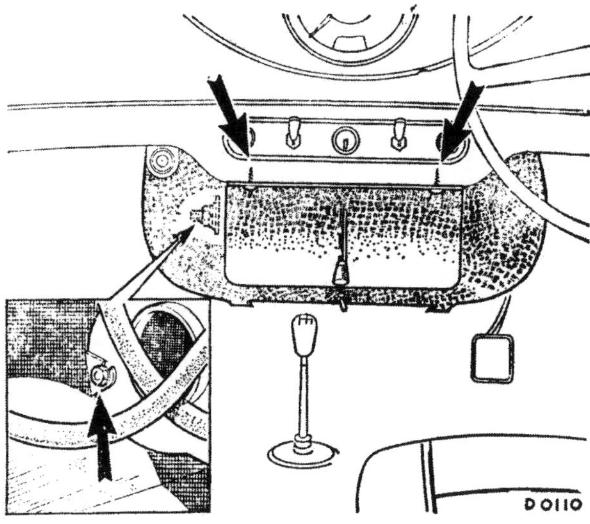

Fig. R.7
The fresh-air heater assembly securing points (arrowed)

Refitting

6. Refitting or replacing all units is a reversal of the removing procedure.

Section R.18

INSTRUMENT NACELLE
(Mk. II Models)

Removing

1. Remove the fascia ashtray and bend up the retaining tab.
2. Release the portion of the door seal covering the fascia trim liner and carefully lift the liner which is fixed by adhesive solution to the body. Ease the liner from the fascia sufficiently to gain access to the instrument nacelle securing screws.
3. Remove the nacelle securing screws and lift off the nacelle complete with instruments after disconnecting the speedometer cable, oil gauge pipe and the electrical connections (see Section R.17).

Refitting

4. Reverse the removing procedure.

THE HEATER ASSEMBLY COMPONENTS
(Fresh-air Heater)

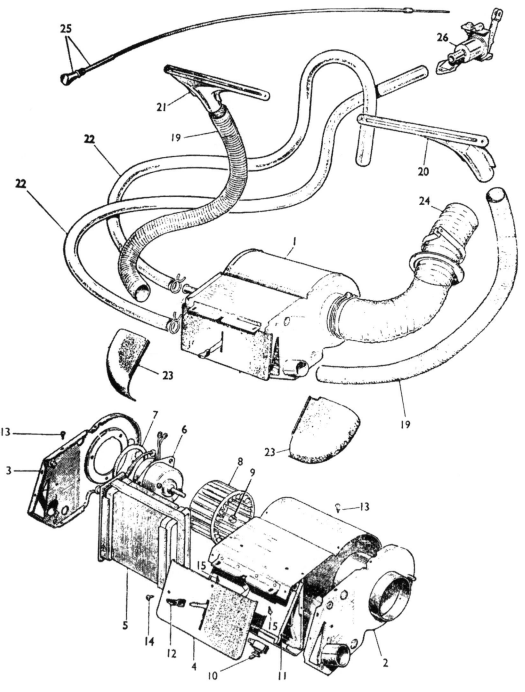

No.	Description	No.	Description	No.	Description
1.	Heater unit.	10.	Blower switch.	19.	Demister tubes.
2.	Cover–air intake side.	11.	Flap valve.	20.	Demister duct–R.H.
3.	Cover–motor side.	12.	Control knob.	21.	Demister duct–L.H.
4.	Control panel.	13.	Securing screws–side cover.	22.	Water hoses.
5.	Matrix.	14.	Securing screws–control panel.	23.	Covers–demister tube.
6.	Motor.	15.	Securing screws–heater assembly.	24.	Air intake hose.
7.	Seal.	16.	Securing nut–heater assembly.	25.	'Heat' control cable.
8.	Rotor (fan).	17.	Plain washer.	26.	Valve–water control.
9.	Rotor securing ring.	18.	Spring washer.		

VERTICAL ALIGNMENT CHECK

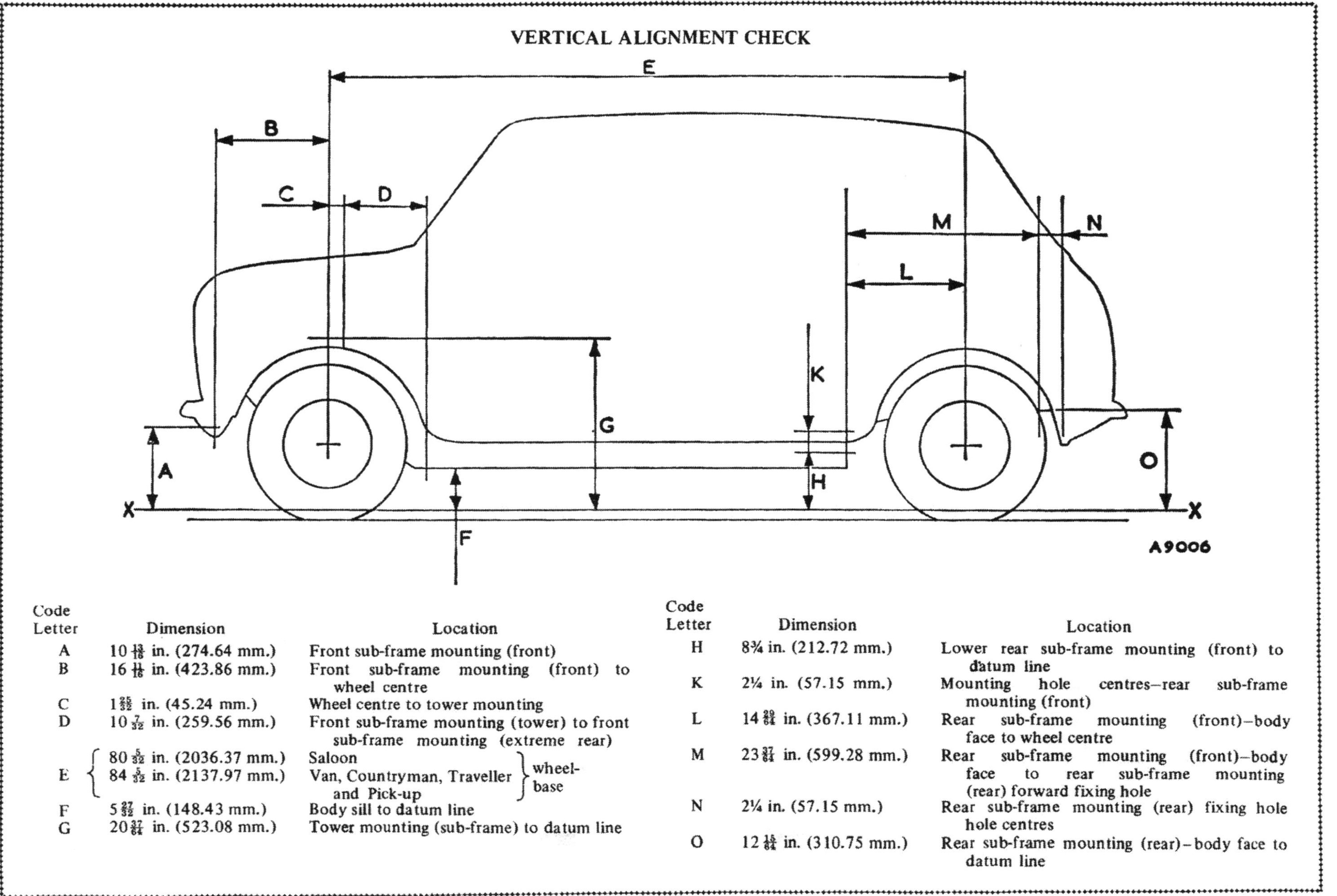

Code Letter	Dimension	Location
A	10 13/16 in. (274.64 mm.)	Front sub-frame mounting (front)
B	16 11/16 in. (423.86 mm.)	Front sub-frame mounting (front) to wheel centre
C	1 25/32 in. (45.24 mm.)	Wheel centre to tower mounting
D	10 7/32 in. (259.56 mm.)	Front sub-frame mounting (tower) to front sub-frame mounting (extreme rear)
E	80 5/32 in. (2036.37 mm.)	Saloon } wheel-base
	84 5/32 in. (2137.97 mm.)	Van, Countryman, Traveller and Pick-up } wheel-base
F	5 27/32 in. (148.43 mm.)	Body sill to datum line
G	20 37/64 in. (523.08 mm.)	Tower mounting (sub-frame) to datum line

Code Letter	Dimension	Location
H	8¾ in. (212.72 mm.)	Lower rear sub-frame mounting (front) to datum line
K	2¼ in. (57.15 mm.)	Mounting hole centres—rear sub-frame mounting (front)
L	14 29/64 in. (367.11 mm.)	Rear sub-frame mounting (front)—body face to wheel centre
M	23 37/64 in. (599.28 mm.)	Rear sub-frame mounting (front)—body face to rear sub-frame mounting (rear) forward fixing hole
N	2¼ in. (57.15 mm.)	Rear sub-frame mounting (rear) fixing hole hole centres
O	12 15/64 in. (310.75 mm.)	Rear sub-frame mounting (rear)—body face to datum line

HORIZONTAL ALIGNMENT CHECK

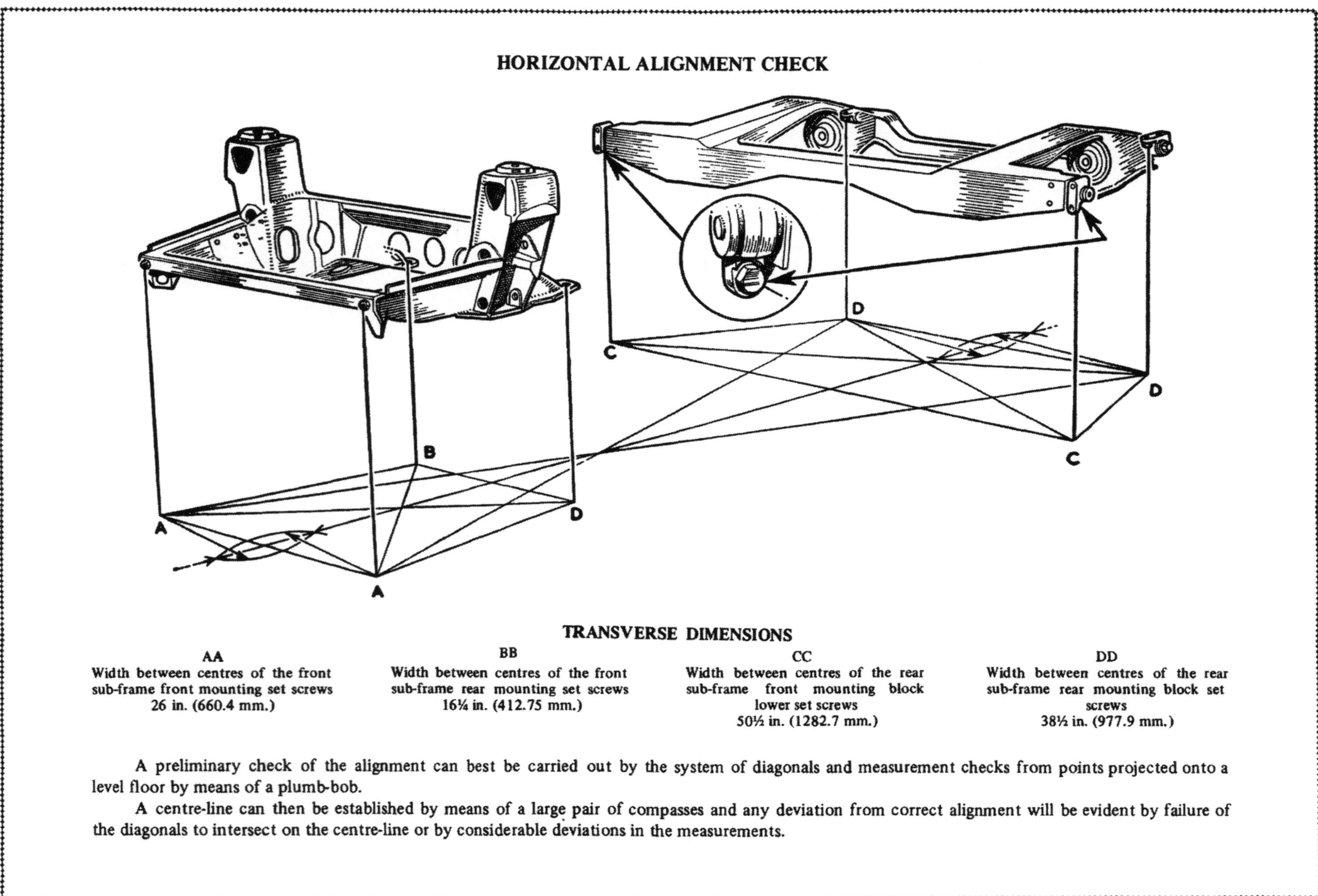

TRANSVERSE DIMENSIONS

AA	BB	CC	DD
Width between centres of the front sub-frame front mounting set screws 26 in. (660.4 mm.)	Width between centres of the front sub-frame rear mounting set screws 16¼ in. (412.75 mm.)	Width between centres of the rear sub-frame front mounting block lower set screws 50½ in. (1282.7 mm.)	Width between centres of the rear sub-frame rear mounting block set screws 38½ in. (977.9 mm.)

A preliminary check of the alignment can best be carried out by the system of diagonals and measurement checks from points projected onto a level floor by means of a plumb-bob.

A centre-line can then be established by means of a large pair of compasses and any deviation from correct alignment will be evident by failure of the diagonals to intersect on the centre-line or by considerable deviations in the measurements.

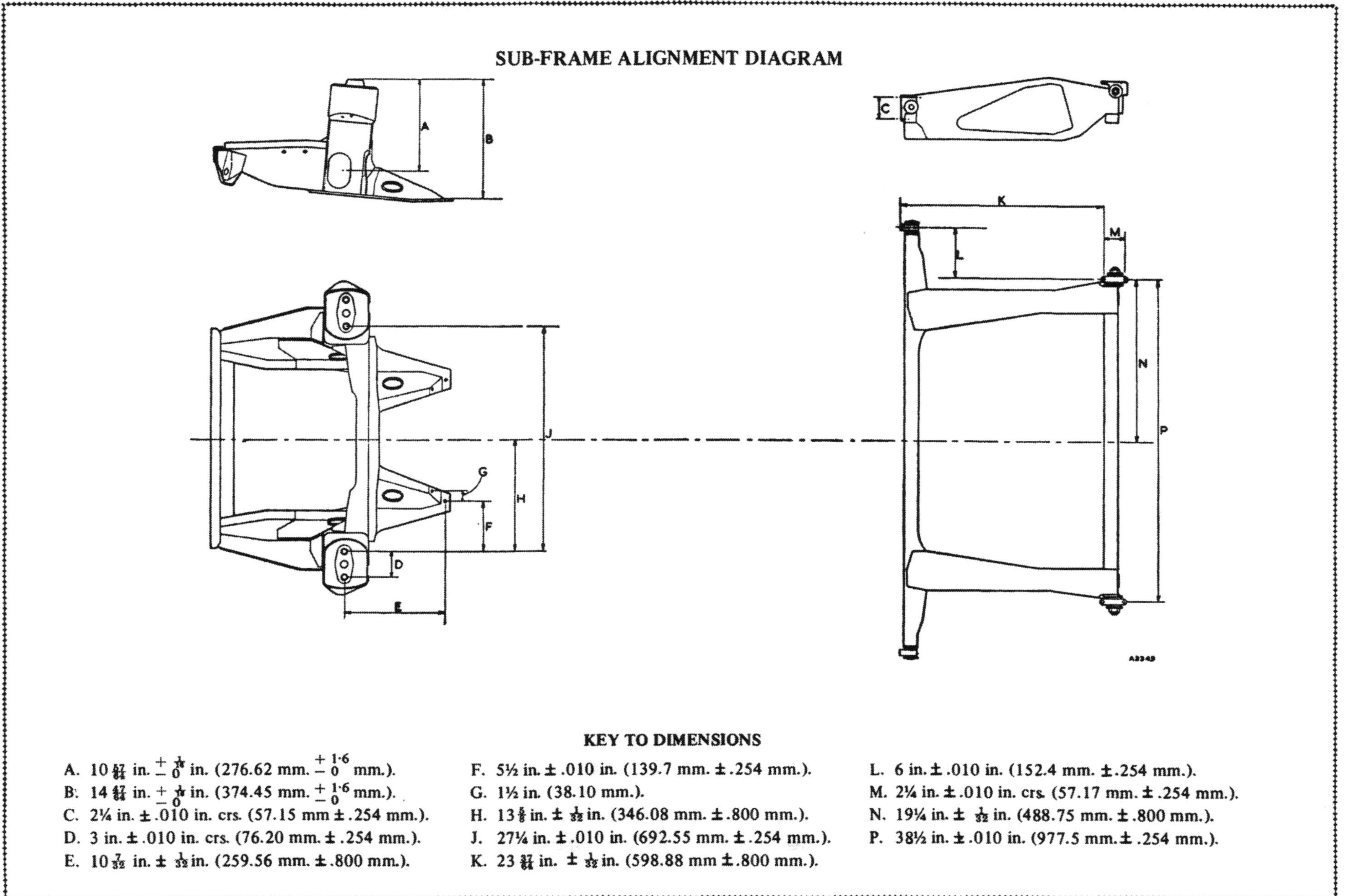

KEY TO DIMENSIONS

A. 10 $\frac{57}{64}$ in. $^{+\frac{1}{16}}_{-0}$ in. (276.62 mm. $^{+1\cdot6}_{-0}$ mm.).

B. 14 $\frac{47}{64}$ in. $^{+\frac{1}{16}}_{-0}$ in. (374.45 mm. $^{+1\cdot6}_{-0}$ mm.).

C. 2¼ in. ± .010 in. crs. (57.15 mm ± .254 mm.).

D. 3 in. ± .010 in. crs. (76.20 mm. ± .254 mm.).

E. 10 $\frac{7}{32}$ in. ± $\frac{1}{32}$ in. (259.56 mm. ± .800 mm.).

F. 5½ in. ± .010 in. (139.7 mm. ± .254 mm.).

G. 1½ in. (38.10 mm.).

H. 13 $\frac{5}{8}$ in. ± $\frac{1}{32}$ in. (346.08 mm. ± .800 mm.).

J. 27¼ in. ± .010 in. (692.55 mm. ± .254 mm.).

K. 23 $\frac{37}{64}$ in. ± $\frac{1}{32}$ in. (598.88 mm ± .800 mm.).

L. 6 in. ± .010 in. (152.4 mm. ± .254 mm.).

M. 2¼ in. ± .010 in. crs. (57.17 mm. ± .254 mm.).

N. 19¼ in. ± $\frac{1}{32}$ in. (488.75 mm. ± .800 mm.).

P. 38½ in. ± .010 in. (977.5 mm. ± .254 mm.).

SECTION Rb

THE BODY

The information contained in this Section refers specifically to new or modified components fitted to the Mini range coincident with the introduction of NEGATIVE earth electrical systems and must be used in conjunction with Section R.

Section Rb.1

BUMPERS

Removing

FRONT

1. From beneath the wings, remove the two bolts securing each end of the bumper.
2. Remove the under-riders (secured by four bolts inside the front valance). Unscrew the remaining two bumper securing bolts and remove the bumper.

REAR

3. Remove the four securing screws from the under side of the bumper and remove it.

Refitting

FRONT AND REAR

4. Reverse the removing instructions.

Section Rb.2

FRONT GRILLE

Removing

1. Remove the headlamp/grille extension panels (four screws securing each panel).
2. Remove the grille panel securing screws and lift the panel out of the locating holes in the lower grille panel assembly.

Refitting

3. Engage the lower attachment strips on the panel into the locating holes in the lower grille panel; the remainder is a reversal of the removing procedure.

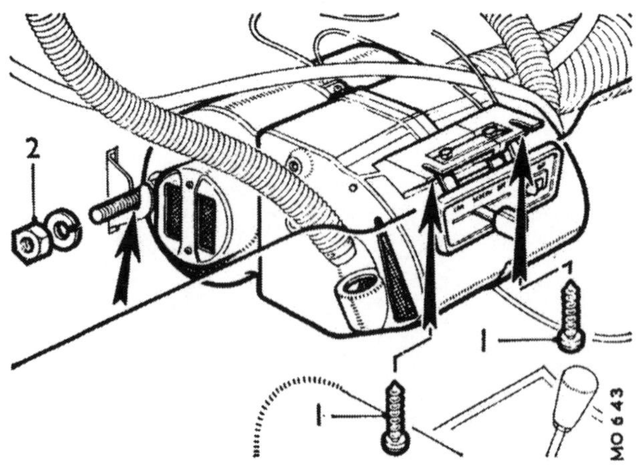

Fig. Rb.1
The heater unit securing points (arrowed)

Section Rb.3

HEATER ASSEMBLY

Removing

1. Drain the cooling system (Section C.1).
2. Remove the front floor covering to avoid damage by coolant when disconnecting the heater pipes.
3. Pull the demister and air intake tubes out of the heater unit.
4. Remove the two screws (1) securing the front of the heater and slacken the nut (2) securing the rear of the unit (Fig. Rb.1).
5. Disconnect the electrical connections from the blower motor and switch.
6. Disconnect the heater water hoses, hold the fingers over the matrix pipes and lift the heater from the slotted rear bracket and out of the car. Drain the coolant from the heater.

Dismantling

HEATER MATRIX REPLACEMENT

7. Remove the blower switch/air distribution panel (two screws), lever off the clips securing the twin casings and separate the unit (see page Rb.3).
8. Withdraw the matrix, clean the casings and fit the replacement unit.

BLOWER MOTOR REPLACEMENT

9. Carry out operations 1 to 7.
10. Remove the motor assembly, withdraw each rotor from the unit and fit them to the replacement motor. Remove and connect the electrical wiring to the new unit.
11. Refit the unit into the heater casing.

BLOWER SWITCH REPLACEMENT

12. The blower switch can be removed without removing the heater unit as follows:
    From behind the blower switch/air distribution panel, pull off the electrical connections, and using a pair of pliers, press in the retainers on each side of the switch and manoeuvre the switch through the face of the panel.
13. Press in the replacement switch and refit the electrical connections.

Refitting the heater

14. Reverse the removing procedure and refill the cooling system. Start and warm up the engine, check for leaks and correct operation of the heater. Top up the coolant in the radiator to the correct level.

THE HEATER UNIT COMPONENTS

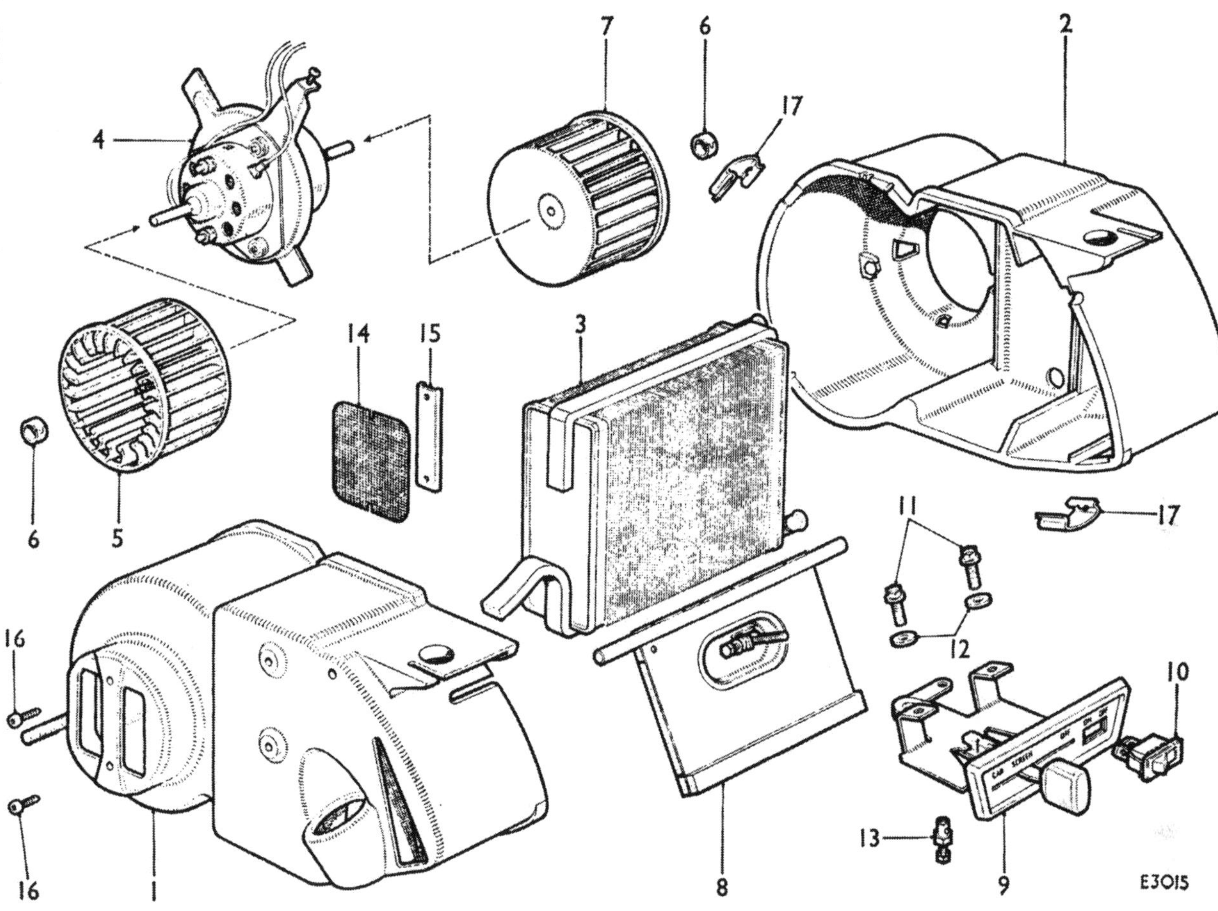

No.	Description
1.	Heater casing.
2.	Heater casing.
3.	Matrix.
4.	Blower motor.
5.	Rotor (recirculatory).
6.	Rotor securing clips.
7.	Rotor (air intake).
8.	Air distribution flap.
9.	Heater control panel.
10.	Blower switch.
11.	Securing screws–control panel to casing.
12.	Washers for item (11).
13.	Trunnion and screw–control lever to flap.
14.	One-way valve.
15.	Valve securing plate.
16.	Valve securing screws.
17.	Heater casing joining clips.

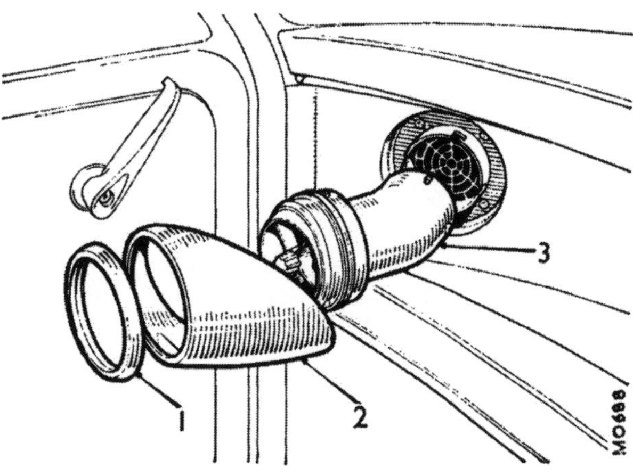

Fig. Rb.2
Removing a fresh-air ventilating louvre

1. Retaining ring. 2. Moulding. 3. Louvre.

Section Rb.4

FRESH-AIR VENTILATION
(Fascia Louvres)

Removing

LOUVRES

1. Unscrew the louvre moulding retaining ring and remove the moulding (Fig. Rb.2). Turn the ventilation louvre anti-clockwise and withdraw it.

INTAKE HOSES

2. From beneath the wing, pull off both ends of the hose(s) from their respective units and remove the hose(s).

Refitting

3. Reverse the removing procedures.

Section Rb.5

DOOR LOCKS
(Operation, Adjustments, Lubrication)

Before attempting to remove any part of the mechanism because of faulty operation first check that the condition is not caused by bad installation.

Operation

1. Wind the window down and close the door.
2. Move the interior locking latch rearwards to the locked position. Check that the exterior handle push-button is inoperative and that the door is locked.
3. To unlock the door, insert the key and turn it one-quarter of a turn towards the rear of the car; open the door by depressing the exterior handle push-button.
4. Close the door and re-open it using the interior release lever.

NOTE.–The interior locking latch cannot be set in the locked position while the door is open.

Adjustments

PUSH-BUTTON PLUNGER

This is preset during manufacture to provide free button movement before the latch contactor 1 begins to operate and release from the striker before full depression (see Fig. Rb.3). However, if further adjustment of the plunger screw is required proceed as detailed below:

5. Remove the exterior door handle (see Section Rb.6).
6. Adjust the plunger screw and ensure that when the handle is refitted there is a clearance of approximately $\frac{1}{32}$ to $\frac{1}{16}$ in. (1 to 1.5 mm.) between the head of the screw and the contactor mechanism.

IMPORTANT.–The plastic bush immediately under the head of the screw must not be screwed in fully against the plastic push-button stem or the lock link cannot be operated.

STRIKER UNIT

Before attempting to close the door ensure that the latch disc is in the open position; if not, 'fire' the latch (using the push-button) and pull the latch disc back to the open position using a screwdriver. Do not slam the door while making adjustments as the mechanism may be strained. The striker screws (1) (see Fig. Rb.4) should be tightened sufficiently to allow the door to be closed to the fully

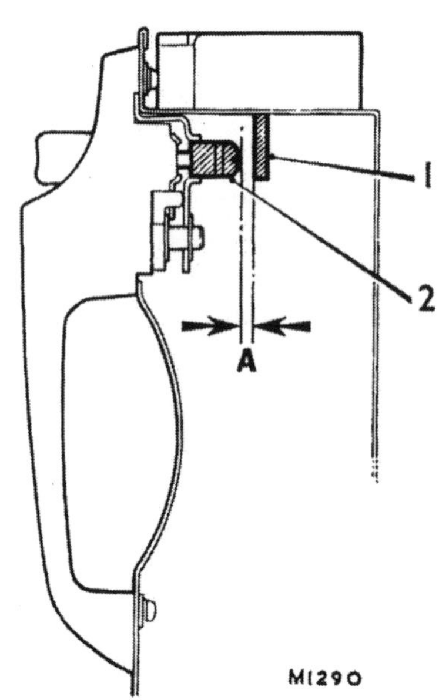

Fig. Rb.3
Door handle push-button plunger adjustment

1. Latch contactor. 2. Push-button plunger screw.
'A' = $\frac{1}{32}$ to $\frac{1}{16}$ in. (1 to 1.5 mm.)

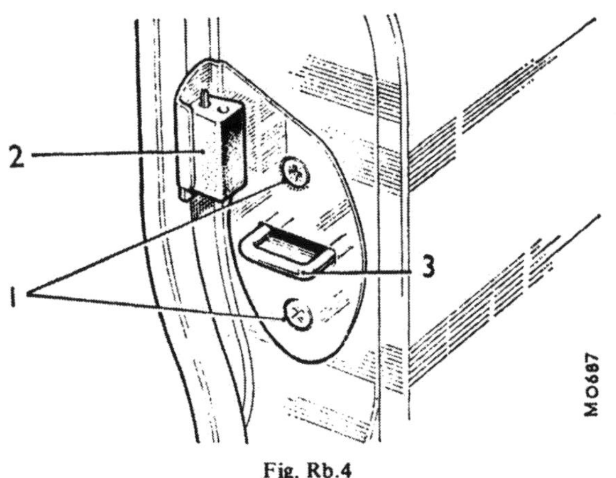

Fig. Rb.4
The door striker unit

1. Securing screws. 2. Over-travel stop.
3. Striker loop.

Positioning is carried out by a process of trial and error, until the door can be closed easily without rattling and no lifting or dropping of the door is apparent. When the door is closed it should be possible to press it in fractionally against its seals beyond the latched position thus ensuring that the striker is not set too far in.

Lubrication

The latching elements are enclosed and apart from initial lubrication during manufacture will need no further attention.

11. Smear with grease any moving parts of the door latch locking and release mechanism connecting points.
12. After assembly, introduce a few drops of 'Loclùbe' or a thin machine oil into the key slots.

latched position, but will allow the striker to move with the door as the door is aligned with the body.

7. Pull the door outwards or press it inwards (without using the press-button) until the door is in alignment with the body.
8. Use the push-button to open the door and pencil a line around the striker cover-plate to establish its new horizontal position.
9. Remove the striker plate over-travel rubber stop (2) as this tends to twist the striker during adjustment (see Fig. Rb.4).
10. Set the striker loop (3) at right angles to the door hinge plane before finally tightening the screws (1) (see Fig. Rb.4). The door can then be checked for 'drop' or 'lift' and if necessary the striker screws slackened again while the striker is moved vertically as required.

Section Rb.6

DOOR LOCKS

Removing

1. Remove the interior release handle, window regulator handle, and the door trim panel. Pull back the adhesive strip adjacent to the lock.
2. Remove the screws securing the latch unit and the lock remote control (Fig. Rb.5).
3. Remove the interior locking control securing screws (Fig. Rb.5).
4. Pull or carefully prise the bottom of the key-operated lock link (3) off the latch locking rod (4) (see Fig. Rb.6).
5. Ease the latch outwards, remove the circlips securing the remote control (1) and the interior locking lever (2) to the latch (see Fig. Rb.6) and withdraw both units and the latch from the door frame.

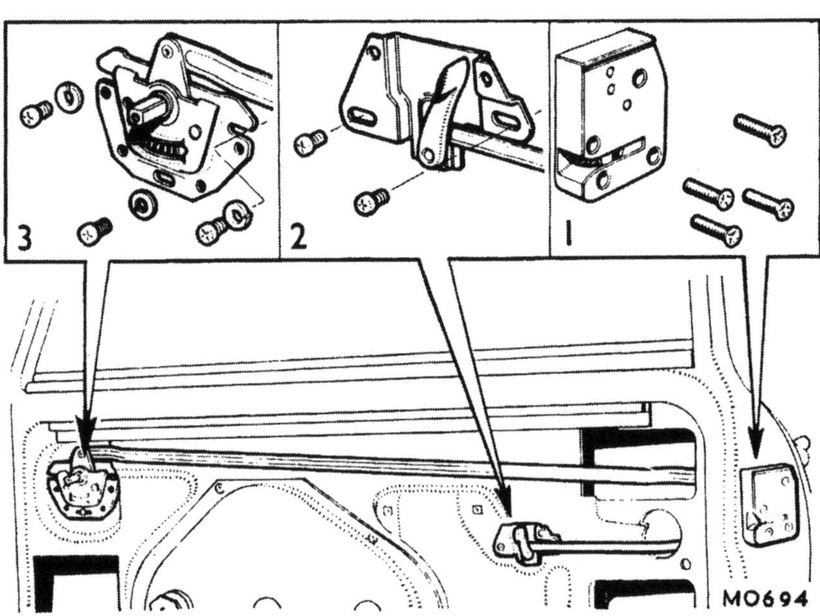

Fig. Rb.5
Removing the latch (1), interior locking control (2), and remote control (3)

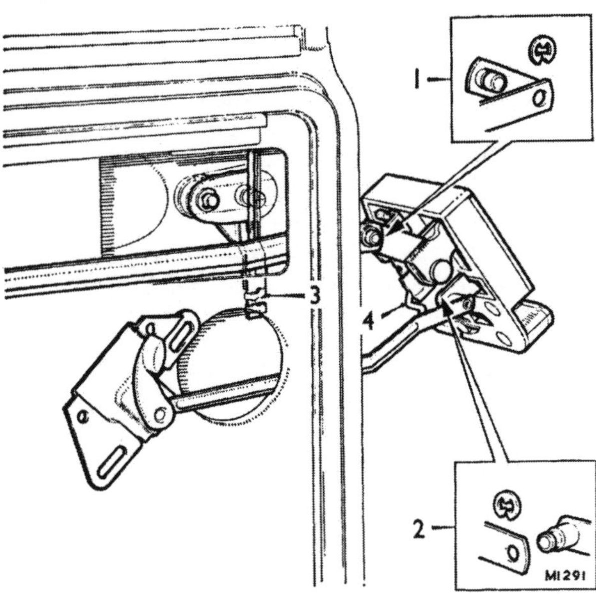

Fig. Rb.6
Showing the locking latch connections

1. Remote control.
2. Interior locking control.
3. Exterior handle lock link.
4. Latch locking rod.

Refitting

6. Reverse the removing procedure, with particular attention to the following instructions.
7. Refer to Fig. Rb.6. Ensure that the circlip securing the remote control lever (1) and the interior lock control lever (2) are correctly located, and that the latch locking rod (4) is engaged in the spring clip of the exterior handle lock link (3).
8. Check the adjustment of the push-button plunger; see '**Adjustments**' in Section Rb.5.
9. Refit or fit new adhesive sealing strips to the door panel. Check the door lock operation before refitting the trim panel.
10. The door striker-plate can be repositioned if required, see '**Adjustments**' in Section Rb.5.

Section Rb.7

EXTERIOR DOOR HANDLES

Removing

1. Remove the interior handles, door trim, and latch assembly–Section Rb.6, operations 1 to 5.
2. Wind up the window, remove the exterior handle securing screws (Fig. Rb.7), and withdraw the handle from the door.

Refitting

3. Reverse the removing procedure, with particular attention to instructions 7 and 8 as detailed in Section Rb.6.

Section Rb.8

DOOR GLASS

Removing

1. Remove the interior release handle, the window regulator handle, and the door trim panel. Pull off the adhesive sealing strips where necessary.
2. Remove the outer and inner waist rail finishers (Fig. Rb.8).
3. Remove the regulator assembly securing screws and use the regulator handle to raise the door glass approximately one-half of its travel (Fig. Rb.8), and use a wooden wedge or block to maintain this position whilst removing the regulator.
4. Lever the regulator assembly slightly away from the door panel and turn the regulator handle until the arms are in the vertical position (see Fig. Rb.8). The regulator arms can now be disengaged from the glazing channel by moving the regulator towards the front of the door until the rear arm is free and then moving it rearwards to release the other arm.
5. Release the wedge on the door glass, turn the glass as shown in Fig. Rb.8 and remove it from the door.

Refitting

6. Reverse the removing procedure, with particular attention to the following instructions.
7. When refitting the door glass, ensure that it is located in the glazing channels and wedge it in the position shown in Fig. Rb.8 to facilitate engagement of the regulator arms. Apply sealer around the edge of the regulator plate.
8. Ensure that the waist rail securing clips are equally spaced before refitting the finishers.
9. When refitting the inner waist rail finisher, butt the forward end against the glazing channel rubber seal before attempting to refit the remainder in position.
10. Refit or fit new adhesive sealing strips.

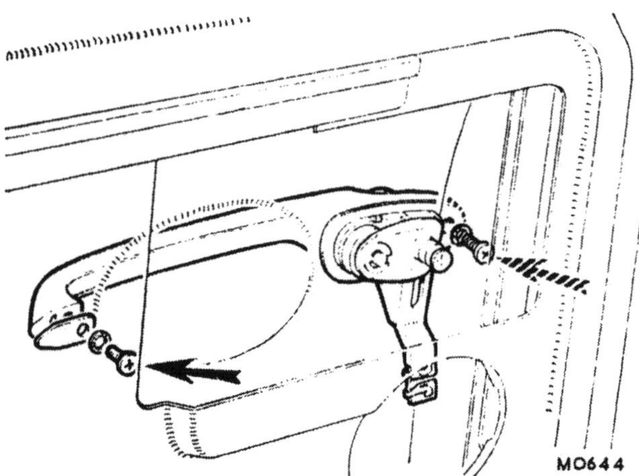

Fig. Rb.7
The exterior handle securing screws (arrowed)

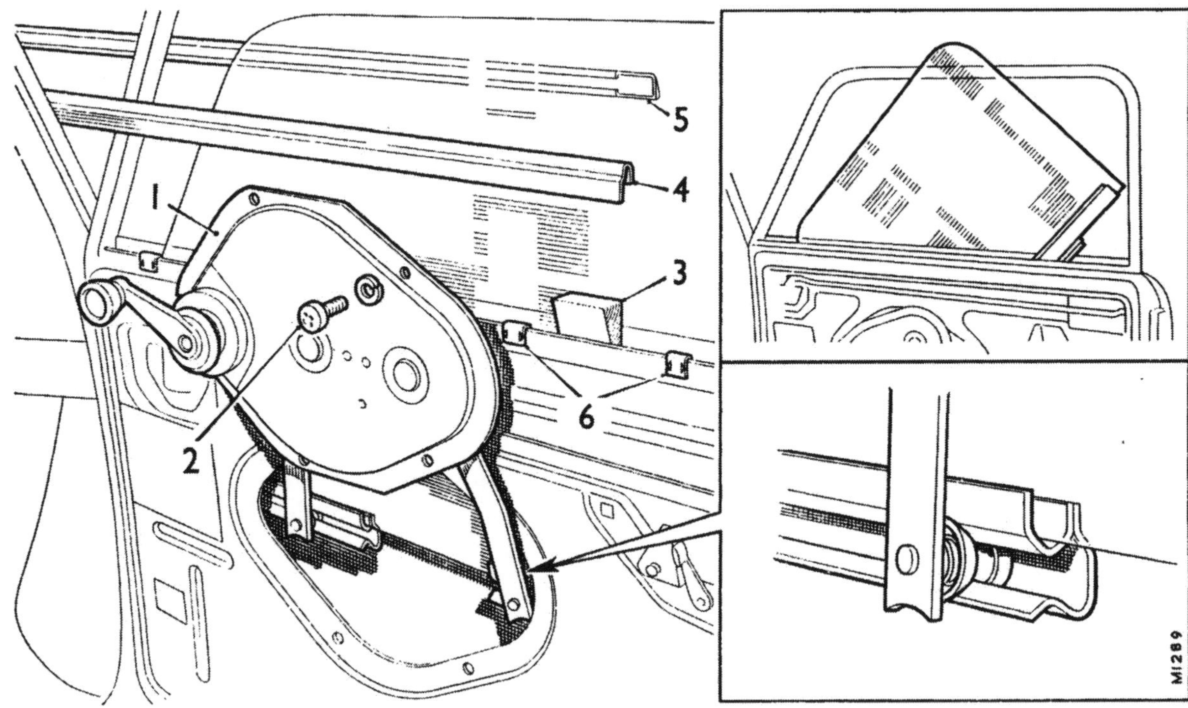

Fig. Rb.8
Removing the door glass regulator, with insets showing the regulator arms and position of the door glass for removal

1. Regulator unit.
2. Regulator securing screws.
3. Wedge (to secure glass).
4. Waist rail finisher (inner).
5. Waist rail finisher (outer).
6. Securing clips for finishers.

Section Rb.9

DOOR GLASS REGULATOR

Removing

1. Remove the interior handles, door trim, and regulator assembly—see Section Rb.8, operations 1, 3, and 4.

Refitting

2. Apply sealer around the edge of the regulator plate. Ensure that the lip on the front edge of the regulator is engaged inside the door frame. The remainder is a reversal of the removing procedure.

Section Rb.10

DOOR GLASS CHANNEL

Removing

1. Follow the instructions given in Section Rb.8 for door glass removal.
2. Remove the glazing channel rubber strip and pull the channel from the door frame.

Refitting

3. Fit a new glazing channel into the door frame and refit the rubber securing strip.
4. The remainder is a reversal of the removal procedure as detailed in Section Rb.8, items 6 to 10.

Section Rb.11

ROOF LINING
(Mini Saloon range)

Removing

1. Disconnect the battery earth cable.
2. Disconnect and remove the roof lamp.
3. Remove both front seats and the rear seat squab (to give increased access).
4. Remove the sun visors and driving mirror.
5. Remove the front and rear screens as detailed in Sections R.1 and R.2.
6. Remove the rear quarter-light glass assemblies (hinged or fixed type).
7. Release the door seals from around the top of the door apertures.
8. The roof lining is secured with adhesive to the roof cant-rail and on the outside flanges of the front and rear screens, door and quarter-light apertures. Release the stuck down areas of the lining, pull the lining towards the front and disengage the lining support rails from the roof cant-rails.
9. Before refitting or replacing the liner remove surplus adhesive from the body using white spirit.

Refitting

10. If fitting a new roof liner, remove the support rails from the old liner and insert them into the new liner;

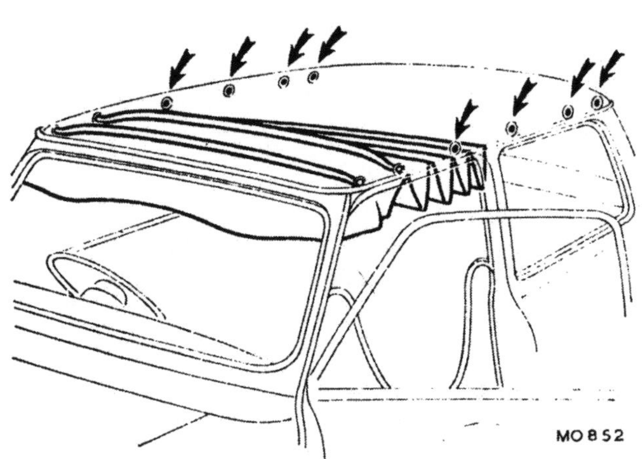

Fig. Rb.9
Fitting the liner support rails into the plastic locators (arrowed) of the roof cant rails

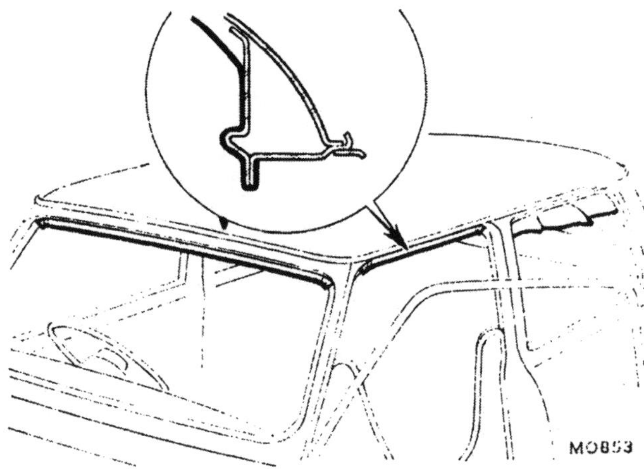

Fig. Rb.10
Cutting and sticking the liner around the screen, door and quarter light exterior flanges

the rails are colour coded and should be fitted in the following order commencing at the front: Nos. 1 (Red), 2, 3 (White), 4 (Black), 5 (Blue), and 6 (Yellow).
On earlier cars the support rails are also colour coded and are fitted from front to rear as follows: Nos. 1 (Red), 2 and 3 (Green), 4 (Blue), and 5 (Yellow).

11. Lay out the lining and apply a 4 in. (100 mm.) wide strip of Dunlop adhesive (S914 or S1022) around the edge of the lining.
12. Apply the above adhesive to the roof cant rails and to all exterior aperture flanges to which the lining is to be secured.
13. Start at the front and engage the liner support rails into the plastic locators in the roof cant rails (see Fig. Rb.9).
14. Stretch out the lining front to rear and keeping the lining taut, commence sticking the lining to the front and rear screen aperture flanges and then simultaneously to both roof cant rails.
15. Continue cutting and sticking the lining to the door and quarter light exterior flanges and trim off excess material as required.
16. Use adhesive when refitting the door seals. The remainder is a reversal of the removing procedure.
17. Water test the front screen, back-light, and the rear quarter-light ventilators.

Section Rb.12

ROOF LINERS
(Mini Clubman Estate)

Removing

1. Disconnect the battery and remove the roof light.
2. Mark the position of the rear edge of the front liner on the roof cant rail.
3. Grip the outer edges of the liner and pull it backwards and inwards to withdraw it.
4. Remove the trim liner from over the rear doors.
5. Mark the position of the front edge of the rear liner and pull it forward and inwards to withdraw it.

Refitting

6. Reverse the removing procedure items 1 to 5.

Section Rb.13

AUTOMATIC SEAT BELTS
(Central Console Type)

Removing

REEL ASSEMBLY–BRITAX BELTS

1. Before removing any belt fixings, attach a clip (1) to the belt just above the reel assembly to prevent the belt retracting during removal and storage. The clip (1) must not be removed until the belt assembly has been refitted, see Fig. Rb.11.
2. Withdraw most of the belt webbing from the reel and remove the locking unit retaining screw (3). Lift up the locking unit (4) to expose the reel retaining screw (2). Remove the screw (2) and detach the reel and locating bracket (5), see Fig. Rb.11.
3. Remove the screws retaining the belt brackets to the door pillar and sill. Note the assembly sequence of the distance pieces and anti-rattle washers, also the individual lengths of the fixing screws, see Figs. Rb.11 and Rb.12.

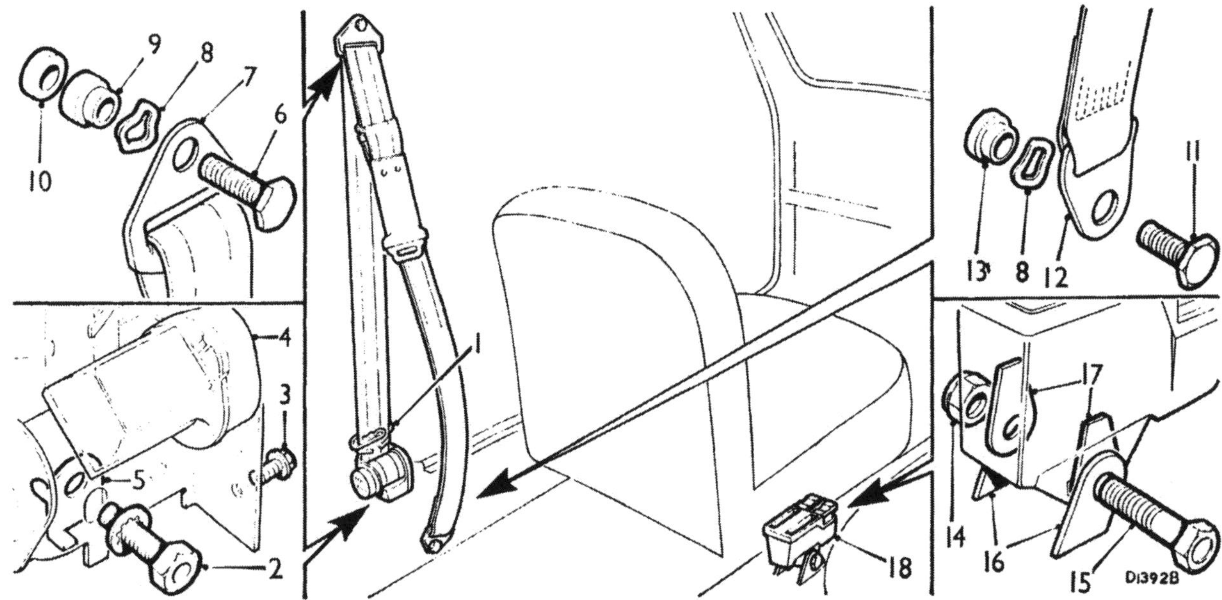

Fig. Rb.11
The Britax 'automatic type' seat belt

1. Belt restraining clip.
2. Reel retaining screw.
3. Locking unit retaining screw.
4. Locking unit.
5. Reel locating bracket.
6. Upper belt bracket retaining screw.
7. Upper belt bracket.
8. Anti-rattle washers.
9. Deep shouldered distance piece.
10. Plain distance piece.
11. Lower belt bracket retaining screw.
12. Lower belt bracket.
13. Shallow shouldered distance piece.
14. Self-locking nut.
15. Centre console retaining bolt.
16. Centre console mounting straps.
17. Fibre washers.
18. Centre console.

REEL ASSEMBLY–KANGOL BELTS

4. Remove the reel retaining screw (1) with the plain washer (2) and detach the reel assembly, see Fig. Rb.12.
5. Carry out operation 3.

CENTRAL CONSOLE

6. Remove the nut and bolt retaining the central console to its mounting straps and detach the console unit.
   Britax: Note that a fibre washer (17) is fitted on either side of the console and is located between the central console and the mounting strap, see Fig. Rb.11.

MOUNTING BRACKETS–CENTRAL CONSOLE

7. Remove the carpet to obtain access to the bracket securing screws. Unscrew and remove the two securing screws (1) (with their spring washers) and detach the mounting straps (3), see Fig. Rb.15.

Refitting

8. Reverse the order of the removing procedure, noting the following:
   a. On the Britax belt use the short retaining screw (11) with the shallow shouldered distance piece (13) when attaching the belt bracket to the sill mounting point.
   b. Ensure that the reel locking plate is not distorted and that the threaded hole in the anchor plate is in perfect condition.
   c. The reel must be mounted at an angle of 6½° from the vertical. This is attained by the reel being mounted onto the locating bracket which has two legs and these engage the holes in the companion box.
      KANGOL. Check that the 'arrow' on the side of the reel is pointing vertically. To adjust, slacken the screw (15) adjacent to the arrow, turn the arrow (16) to the vertical position and retighten the screw, see Fig. Rb.12.
   d. The reel assembly, belt brackets and central console must be refitted with the relevant component parts assembled in the order shown in Figs. Rb.11, Rb.12, Rb.13, and Rb.14.
   e. All distance pieces must make metal-to-metal contact with the body fixing points.
   f. Tighten the bolt and nut securing the central console until the unit is **lightly gripped** between the mounting straps, but can be pivoted with resistance.
   g. Tighten all belt bracket securing screws to a torque figure of 25 lb. ft. (3.5 kg. m.).
   h. Tighten the reel locking unit retaining screw (3) Fig. Rb.11 to a torque figure of 5 lb. in. (.06 kg. m.).

NOTE.–If the seat belts were being used whilst the car was involved in a severe impact, the complete belt assemblies must be renewed including the central console, its mounting straps and the reel-to-companion box locating bracket.

Testing

9. With the belts being worn, drive the car at 5 m.p.h. (8 km.p.h.) and brake sharply; the automatic locking device should operate and lock the reel.

Section Rb.14

STATIC SEAT BELTS
(Central Console Type)

Removing

BELT FIXING BRACKETS

1. Remove the hexagon screw (1) retaining the belt bracket (2) to the sill mounting point; note the anti-rattle washer (3) and the shouldered distance piece (4), see Figs. Rb.13 and Rb.14.
2. Prise out the protective cap (5) covering the hexagon screw (6) at the pillar fixing point. Remove the screw and detach the belt bracket noting the plain washer, parking device, anti-rattle washer and shouldered distance piece on the 'Kangol' belt, and the parking device and shouldered distance piece on the 'Britax' belt, see Figs. Rb.13 and Rb.14.

CENTRAL CONSOLE

3. Remove the nut (10) and bolt (11) retaining the central console to its mounting straps (14) and detach the console unit.

   BRITAX. Note that a fibre washer (12) is fitted on either side of the console and is located between the central console and the mounting strap, see Fig. Rb.13.

MOUNTING STRAPS–CENTRAL CONSOLE

4. Remove the carpet to obtain access to the strap securing screws. Unscrew and remove the two securing screws (1) (with their spring washers) and detach the mounting straps (3), see Fig. Rb.15.

Refitting

5. Reverse the order of the removing procedure, noting the following:
   a. All distance pieces must make metal-to-metal contact with the body fixing points.
   b. The belt brackets must be refitted with their relevant component parts assembled in the order shown in Fig. Rb.13.

      Tighten the bracket securing screws to a torque figure of 25 lb. ft. (3.5 kg. m.).
   c. Tighten the central console until the unit is **lightly gripped** between the mounting straps, but can be pivoted with resistance.

NOTE.–If the seat belts were being used whilst the car was involved in a severe impact, the complete belt assemblies must be renewed including the central console and its mounting straps.

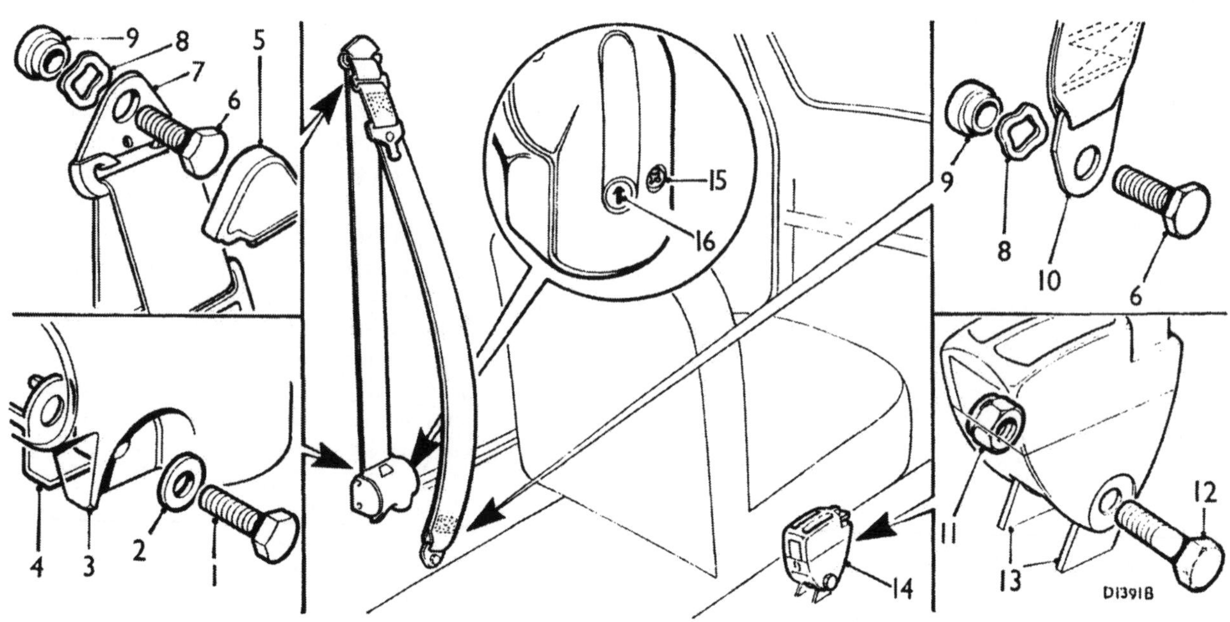

Fig. Rb.12
The Kangol 'automatic type' seat belt

1. Reel retaining screw.
2. Plain washer.
3. Reel assembly
4. Reel locating bracket.
5. Plastic cover for upper fixing.
6. Belt bracket retaining screws.
7. Upper belt bracket.
8. Anti-rattle washer.
9. Distance piece–upper and lower fixing.
10. Lower belt bracket.
11. Self-locking nut.
12. Centre console retaining bolt.
13. Centre console mounting straps.
14. Centre console.
15. Screw–(slacken for arrow adjustment).
16. Vertical adjustment arrow.

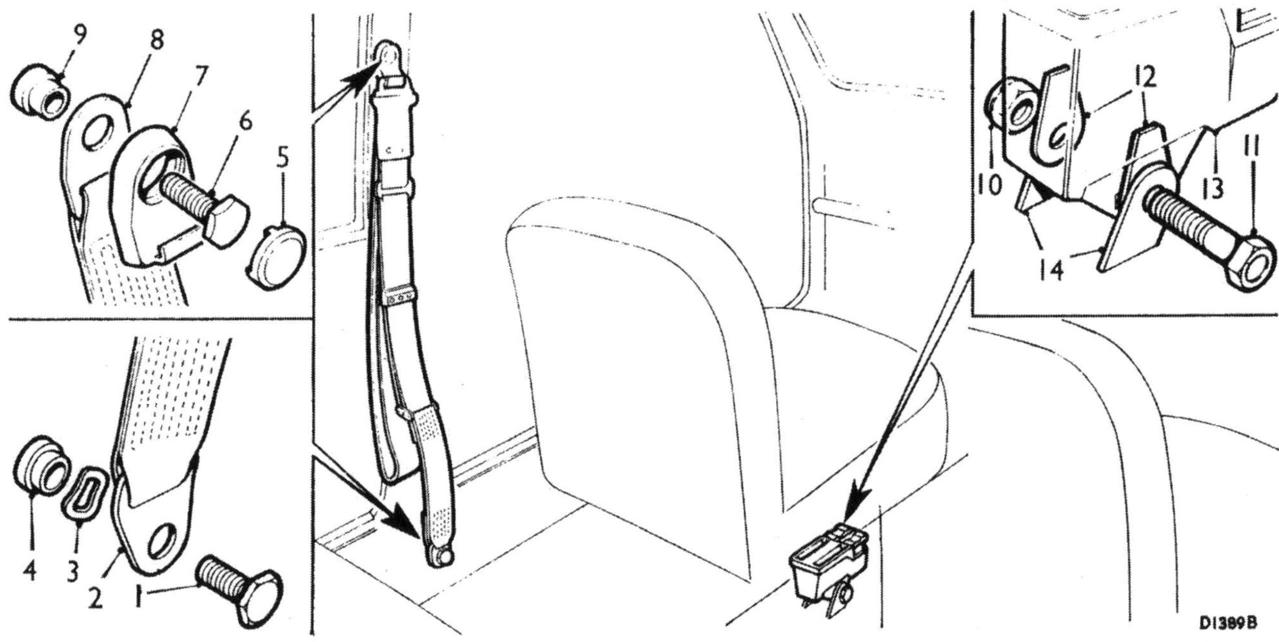

Fig. Rb.13
The Britax 'static type' seat belt

1. Lower belt bracket retaining screw.
2. Lower belt bracket.
3. Anti-rattle washer.
4. Distance piece.
5. Protective cap.
6. Upper belt bracket retaining screw.
7. Parking device.
8. Upper belt bracket.
9. Distance piece–upper fixing.
10. Self-locking nut.
11. Centre console retaining bolt.
12. Fibre washers.
13. Centre console.
14. Centre console mounting straps.

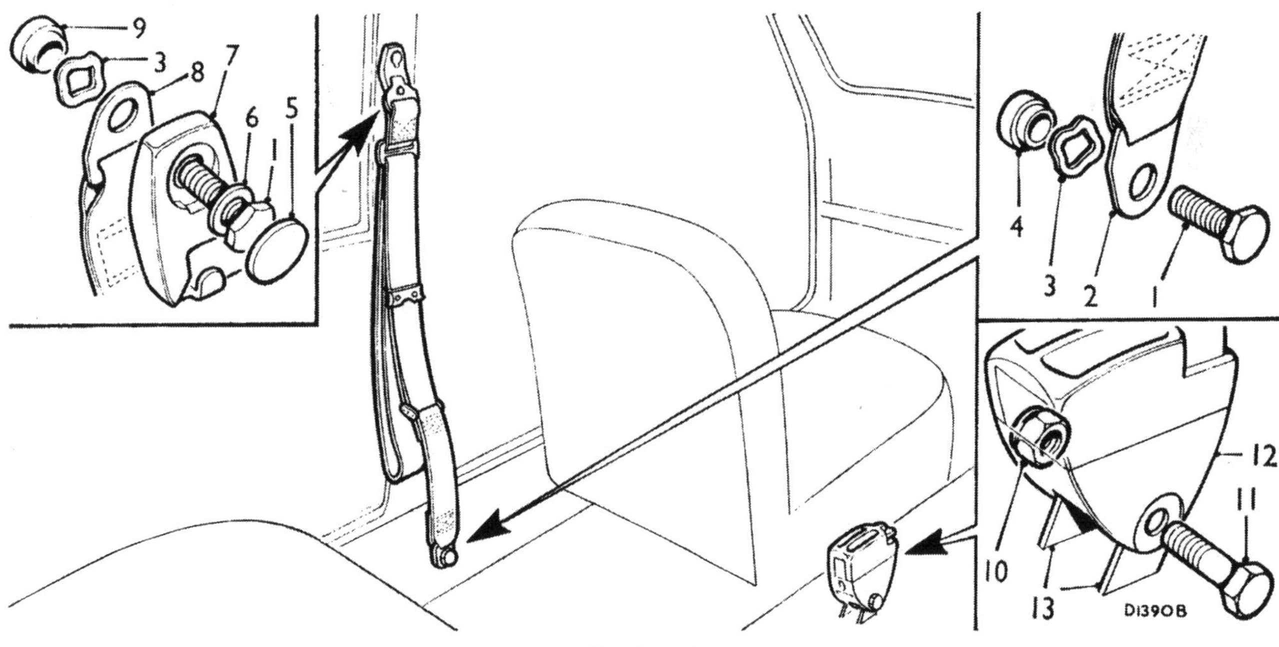

Fig. Rb.14
The Kangol 'static type' seat belt

1. Belt bracket retaining screws.
2. Lower belt bracket.
3. Anti-rattle washers.
4. Distance piece.
5. Protective cap.
6. Plain washer.
7. Parking device.
8. Upper belt bracket.
9. Distance piece–upper fixing.
10. Self-locking nut.
11. Centre console retaining bolt.
12. Centre console.
13. Centre console mounting straps.

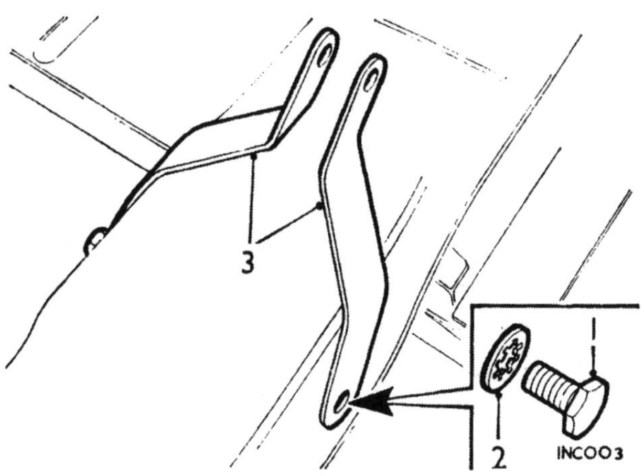

Fig. Rb.15
The centre console mounting straps

1. Securing screw.
2. Lock washer.
3. Mounting straps.

Section Rb.15

REAR SEAT BELTS
(When fitted)

Removing

1. Remove the rear seat cushion and squab.
2. Remove the belt bracket retaining screws (1) with their spring washers (2), see Fig. Rb.16.

Refitting

3. Reverse the order of the removing procedure, noting that the longer section of the belt is fitted to the fixing point nearest to the centre line of the car, see Fig. Rb.16.
4. Ensure that a spring washer is fitted under the head of each bracket retaining screw; align the brackets as shown in Fig. Rb.16 and tighten the retaining screws to a torque figure of 25 lb. ft. (3.5 kg. m.).

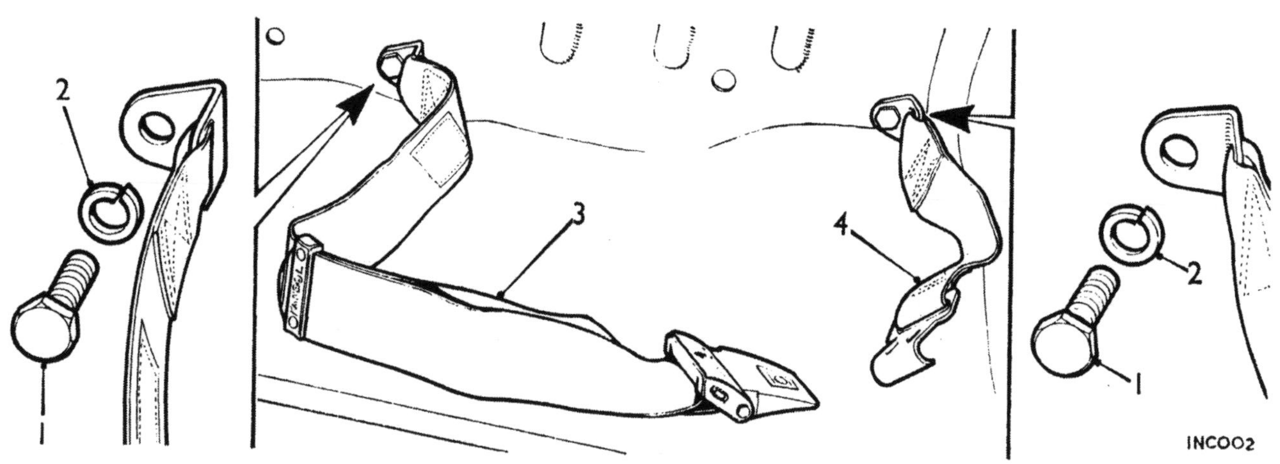

Fig. Rb.16
The rear seat belt mounting points and the belt components

1. Securing screws.
2. Spring washers.
3. Belt with buckle fixing (adjustable).
4. Short belt.

SECTION S

SERVICE TOOLS

All Service tools mentioned in this Manual are only obtainable from the tool manufacturer:

Messrs. V. L. Churchill & Co. Ltd.
P.O. Box No. 3,
London Road, Daventry
Northants, England

This Section includes all Service tools for the Mini range of vehicles including the Mini-Cooper, Mini-Cooper 'S' and the 1275 GT. The tools which are only applicable to these models are shown in brackets after the 'Operation' description.

OPERATION	TOOL No.	PAGE No.
ENGINE		
Camshaft liner reaming	18G 123 A	S.7
	18G 123 AH	S.8
	18G 123 AJ	S.8
	18G 123 AN	S.8
Camshaft liner reaming (Cooper and Cooper 'S')	18G 123 A	S.7
	18G 123 B	S.8
	18G 123 AN	S.8
	18G 123 AP	S.8
	18G 123 AT	S.8
	18G 123 AQ	S.8
	18G 123 BA	S.8
	18G 123 BB	S.8
	18G 123 BC	S.8
Camshaft liner removing and replacing	18G 124 A	S.8
	18G 124 K	S.9
Camshaft liner removing and replacing (Cooper, Cooper 'S' and 1275 GT)	18G 124 A	S.8
	18G 124 B	S.9
	18G 124 K	S.9
	18G 124 M	S.9
Circlip removing and refitting	18G 257	S.10
	18G 1004	S.17
Crankshaft and camshaft gear removing	18G 2	S.7
	18G 98	S.7
Crankshaft primary gear oil seal removing and replacing	18G 134	S.9
	18G 134 BC	S.9
	18G 1043	S.18
	18G 1068	S.18
Flywheel and clutch removal (coil spring clutch)	18G 304	S.11
	18G 304 M	S.11
	18G 587	S.15
Flywheel and clutch removal (diaphragm spring clutch)	18G 304	S.11
	18G 304 N	S.11
	18G 587	S.15
Flywheel housing bearing removing and replacing	18G 617 A	S.16

OPERATION	TOOL No.	PAGE No.
Flywheel oil seal replacing	18G 134	S.9
	18G 134 BH	S.9
Oil pump relief valve seat grinding	18G 69	S.7
Piston refitting	18G 55 A	S.7
Piston refitting (Cooper, Cooper 'S' and 1275 GT)	18G 55 A	S.7
	18G 1150	
	18G 1150 A or	S.21
	18G 1002	S.17
Timing cover oil seal replacing	18G 134	S.9
	18G 134 BD	S.9
Timing cover refitting	18G 138	S.9
	18G 1044	S.18
Torque setting nuts and bolts	18G 372	S.11
	18G 536	S.12
	18G 537	S.12
	18G 592	S.15
Valve removing and refitting	18G 45	S.7
Valve grinding-in	18G 29	S.7
Valve seat cutting	18G 27	S.7
	18G 167	S.9
	18G 167 A	S.9
	18G 167 B	S.10
	18G 167 C	S.10
	18G 167 D	S.10
FUEL SYSTEM		
Fuel tank gauge unit removing and refitting	18G 1001	S.17
Mechanical fuel pump testing	18G 1116	S.20
Mechanical fuel pump oil seal removing and replacing	18G 1119	S.21
CLUTCH		
Clutch dismantling and reassembling (coil spring clutch)	18G 304 M	S.11
	18G 571	S.12
Clutch dismantling and reassembling (coil spring clutch–Cooper) ..	18G 304 M	S.11
	18G 684	S.16
Clutch dismantling and reassembling (diaphragm spring clutch) ..	18G 304 N	S.11
	18G 571	S.12
Clutch dismantling and reassembling (diaphragm spring clutch–Cooper, Cooper 'S' and 1275 GT)	18G 304 N	S.11
	18G 684	S.16
Clutch housing cover – alignment	18G 1247	S.22

OPERATION	TOOL No.	PAGE No.
TRANSMISSION UNIT		
Change speed shaft oil seal replacement	18G 573	S.13
Circlip removing and refitting	18G 257 18G 1004	S.10 S.18
Final drive gear removing and refitting	18G 586 18G 587	S.15 S.15
First and third motion shaft bearing replacement	18G 579	S.14
First motion shaft and bearing removing	18G 284 18G 284 B	S.11 S.11
First motion shaft bearing circlip—checking for correct thickness circlip	18G 569	S.12
First motion shaft needle-roller bearing removing and replacing	18G 581 18G 581 B 18G 589	S.14 S.14 S.15
Idler gear bearing removing and replacing (3-speed synchromesh)	18G 581 18G 582	S.14 S.14
Idler gear bearing removing and replacing (4-speed synchromesh)	18G 1126	S.21
Laygear needle-roller bearing replacement	18G 194	S.10
Layshaft reassembly	18G 471	S.12
Synchromesh unit assembling	18G 572	S.13
Third motion shaft bearing removing (3-speed synchromesh)	18G 613	S.15
Third motion shaft bearing removing (4-speed synchromesh)	18G 1127	S.20
Torque setting nuts and bolts	18G 372 18G 536 18G 537	S.11 S.12 S.12
DIFFERENTIAL UNIT		
Differential bearing removing and replacement	18G 2 18G 2 G 18G 578	S.7 S.7 S.14
Differential assembly removing and refitting (Rod change type transmission)	18G 1236	S.21
Differential end cover oil seal replacement (Rod change type transmission)	18G 1238	S.22
Drive shaft coupling flange removing and refitting	18G 669	S.16
Torque setting nuts and bolts	18G 372 18G 537	S.11 S.12
AUTOMATIC TRANSMISSION		
Auxiliary pump and governor assembly removing and refitting	18G 1094 18G 1097 18G 1106	S.19 S.20 S.20
Converter housing oil seal replacing	18G 1068 18G 1068 A 18G 1087	S.18 S.18 S.19

OPERATION	TOOL No.	PAGE No.
Converter housing removing and refitting	18G 1088 18G 1098	S.19 S.20
Converter removing and refitting	18G 587 18G 1086	S.15 S.19
Differential drive shaft coupling removing	18G 1100	S.20
Forward clutch dismantling and reassembling	18G 1102	S.20
Forward clutch hub nut removing and refitting	18G 1095 18G 1096	S.19 S.19
Gear carrier assembly dismantling and reassembling (early-type units)	18G 1093	S.19
Gear carrier assembly dismantling and reassembling (later-type units)	18G 284 AJ 18G 1093 A	S.11 S.19
Idler and input gears—checking adjustment	18G 1089 18G 1089 A	S.19 S.19
Pressure and stall checks	18G 677 C 18G 677 Z	S.16 S.16
Converter output gear oil seal removing and replacing	18G 134 18G 134 CN	S.9 S.9
Top and reverse clutch dismantling and reassembling	18G 1103	S.20
Top and reverse clutch hub removing and refitting	18G 1095 18G 1096	S.19 S.19
Torque setting	18G 372 18G 537 18G 592	S.11 S.12 S.15
DRIVE SHAFTS		
Constant velocity joint—checking ball cage and inner race	18G 1012 18G 1099	S.18 S.20
Drive shaft removing and refitting	18G 1063 18G 304 or 18G 304 Z 18G 304 F	S.18 S.11 S.11 S.11
● Drive shaft or offset sphere inboard joint removing and refitting	18G 1240 18G 1241 18G 1243	S.22 S.22 S.22
Offset sphere inboard joint rubber boot replacement (fitting the small endless clip)	18G 1251	S.22 ●
Torque setting	18G 372	S.11
REAR SUSPENSION		
Displacer unit or strut removing and refitting	18G 703	S.17
Hub bearing outer race removing	18G 260 18G 260 C	S.10 S.10
Hub removing	18G 304 or 18G 304 Z 18G 304 F	S.11 S.11 S.11

OPERATION	TOOL No.	PAGE No.
Hydrolastic suspension–checking pressure	18G 685 18G 703	S.17 S.17
Hydrolastic suspension–depressurizing, evacuating, and pressurizing	18G 703	S.17
Radius arm bush reaming	18G 588 18G 588 A	S.15 S.15
Radius arm bushes removing and replacing	18G 583 18G 584	S.14 S.15
Radius arm needle bearing removing and replacing	18G 583 18G 583 B 18G 620	S.14 S.15 S.16
Radius arm (Hydrolastic suspension) removing and refitting	18G 703	S.17
Sub-frame (Hydrolastic models) removing and refitting	18G 703	S.17
STEERING GEAR		
Steering-column bush (upper) removing and replacing	18G 1191	S.21
Steering rack dismantling and reassembling	18G 207 18G 207 A 18G 707	S.10 S.10 S.17
Steering rack tie-rod ball joint removal	18G 1063	S.18
Torque setting	18G 372 18G 537	S.11 S.12
FRONT SUSPENSION		
Displacer unit or strut removing and refitting	18G 703	S.17
Hydrolastic suspension–checking pressure	18G 685 18G 703	S.17 S.17
Hydrolastic suspension–depressurizing, evacuating, and pressurizing	18G 703	S.17
Lower arm removal	18G 1063	S.18
Spring unit or strut (Rubber suspension models) removing and refitting	18G 574 B 18G 1063	S.13 S.18
Swivel hub joint removing and replacing	18G 587 18G 1063	S.15 S.18
Swivel hub dismantling, fitting bearings, and reassembling	18G 304 or 18G 304 Z 18G 304 F 18G 575 18G 260 18G 260 H	S.11 S.11 S.11 S.14 S.10 S.10

OPERATION	TOOL No.	PAGE No.
Swivel hub driving flange removing (without dismantling the swivel hub)	18G 284	S.11
	18G 304 or	S.11
	18G 304 Z	S.11
	18G 304 F	S.11
	18G 304 P	S.11
Swivel hub oil seal (inner), replacing	18G 134 DO	S.9
Swivel hub outer oil seal replacing	18G 284	S.11
	18G 304 or	S.11
	18G 304 Z	S.11
	18G 304 F	S.11
	18G 304 P	S.11
	18G 705	S.17
	18G 705 B	S.17
Swivel hub removing and refitting	18G 1063	S.18
Torque setting nuts and bolts	18G 372	S.11
	18G 537	S.12
Upper arm (Hydrolastic suspension models) removing, dismantling and reassembling	18G 581	S.14
	18G 582	S.14
	18G 582 A	S.14
	18G 703	S.17
	18G 1063	S.18
Upper arm (rubber suspension models) removing, dismantling, and re-assembling	18G 574 B	S.13
	18G 581	S.14
	18G 582	S.14
	18G 582 A	S.14
	18G 1063	S.18
BRAKING SYSTEM		
Brake adjusting	18G 619 A	S.16
Disc brake piston seal replacing (Cooper, Cooper 'S' and 1275 GT) ..	18G 672	S.16
BODY		
Body alignment checking .. .. Existing alternative to 7-700 range.	18G 560	S.13
	18G 560 A	S.13
	18G 560 E	S.13
Body alignment checking (not illustrated) .. .. This jig is available with various adaptors for model ranges. The operating notes supplied with the jig adaptors must be used instead of the instructions given in Section R.14, which refer to the existing jig 18G 560 only.	Churchill 7-700	
Door hinge screws removing and refitting (doors with wind-up windows) ..	18G 1188	S.21
Windscreen and back-light glass refitting	18G 468	S.12
	18G 468 A	S.12

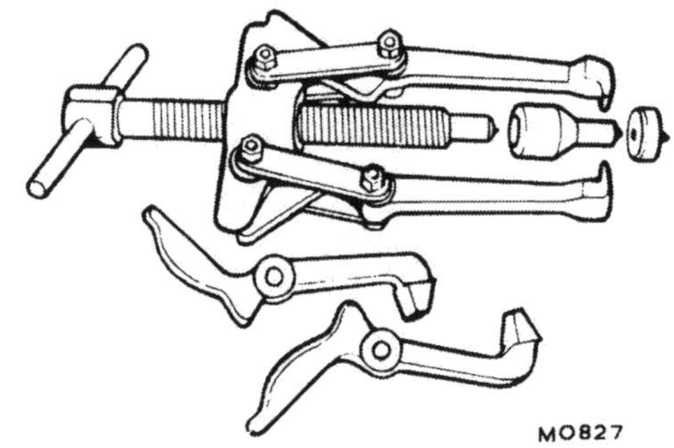

18G 2. Crankshaft Gear and Pulley Remover

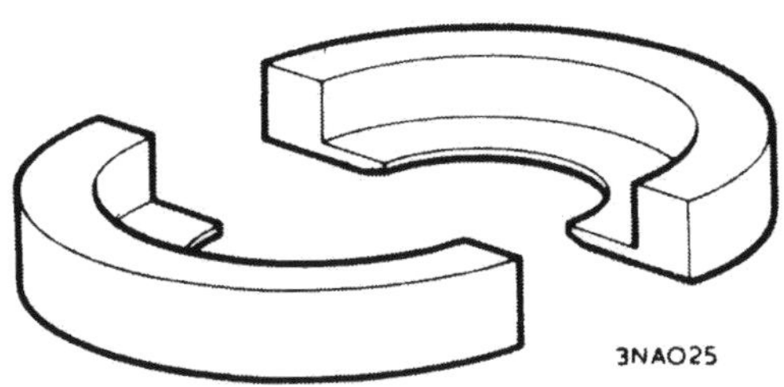

18G 2 G. Differential Shaft Bearings Remover – Adaptor

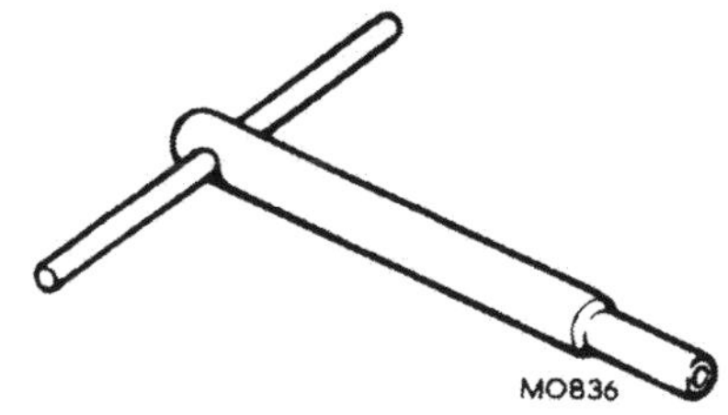

18G 27. Valve Seat Cutter Handle

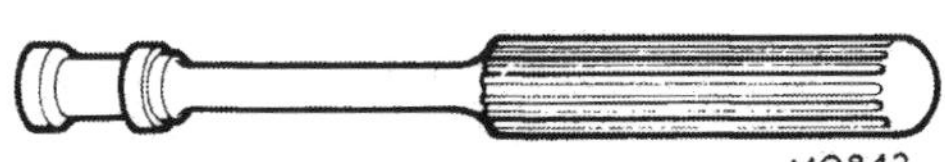

18G 29. Valve Suction Grinder

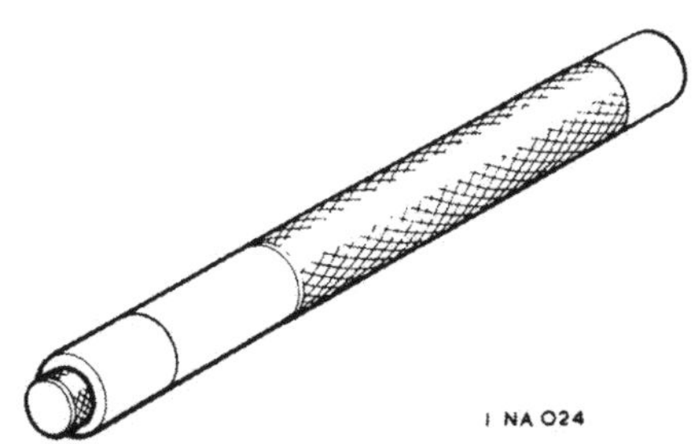

18G 69. Oil Pump Release Valve Grinding-in Tool

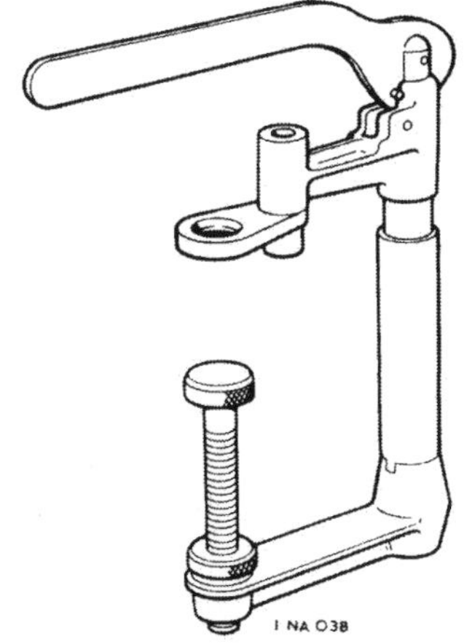

18G 45. Valve Spring Compressor

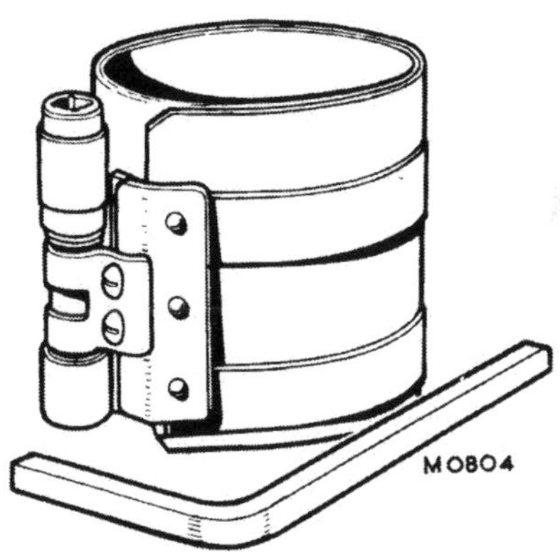

18G 55 A. Piston Ring Compressor

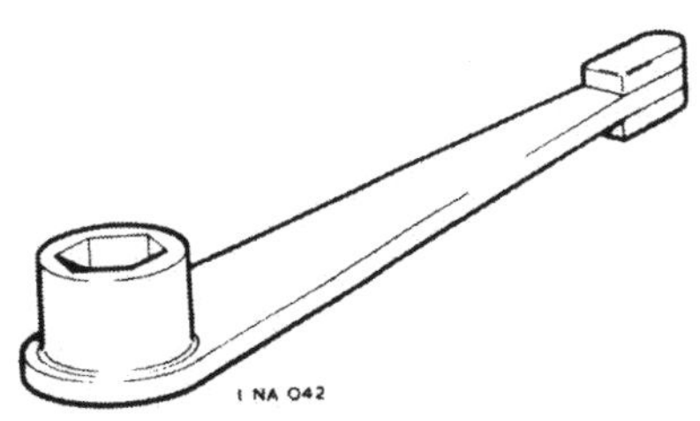

18G 98 A. Crankshaft Nut Spanner

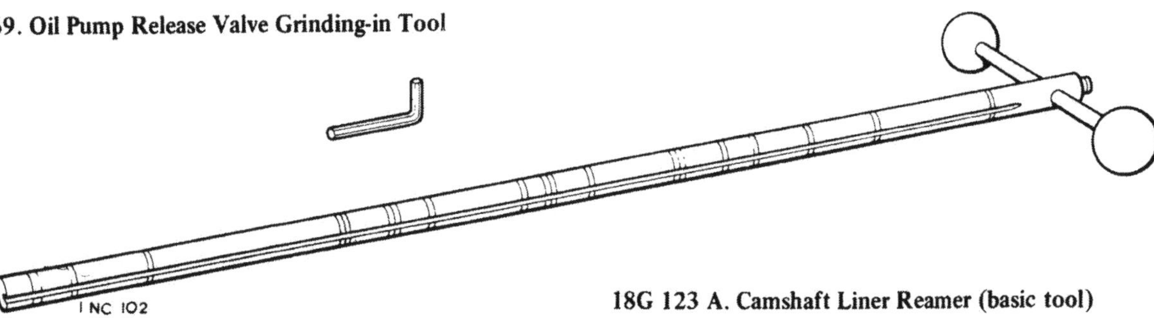

18G 123 A. Camshaft Liner Reamer (basic tool)

18G 123 AH. Camshaft Liner Reamer Pilot–Centre

18G 123 AJ. Camshaft Liner Reamer Pilot–Rear

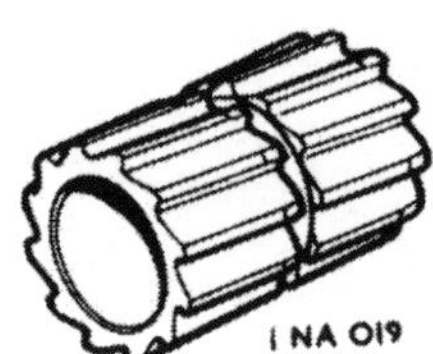

18G 123 AN. Camshaft Liner Reamer Cutter–Front

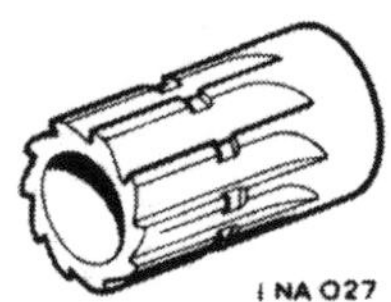

18G 123 AP. Camshaft Liner Reamer Cutter–Rear

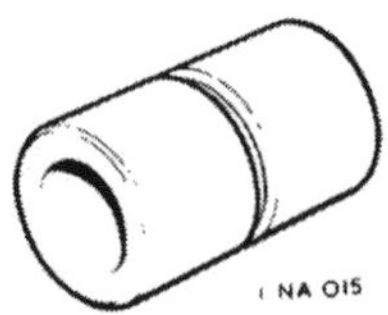

18G 123 AQ. Camshaft Liner Reamer Pilot–Front

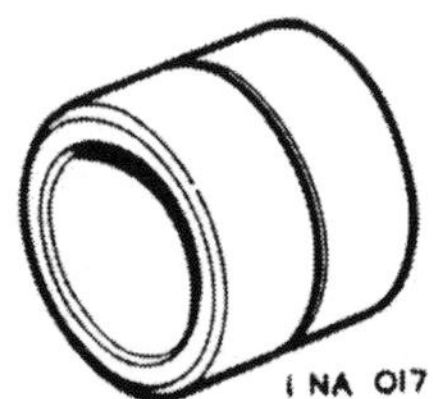

18G 123 AT. Camshaft Liner Reamer Pilot–Centre

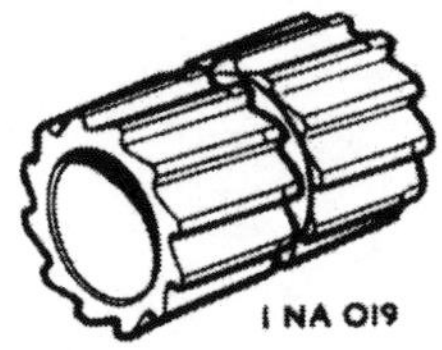

18G 123 B. Camshaft Liner Reamer Cutter

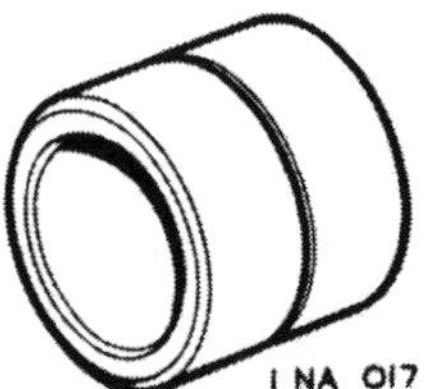

18G 123 BA. Camshaft Liner Reamer Pilot–Rear

18G 123 BB. Camshaft Liner Reamer Pilot–Rear

18G 123 BC. Camshaft Liner Reamer Pilot–Front

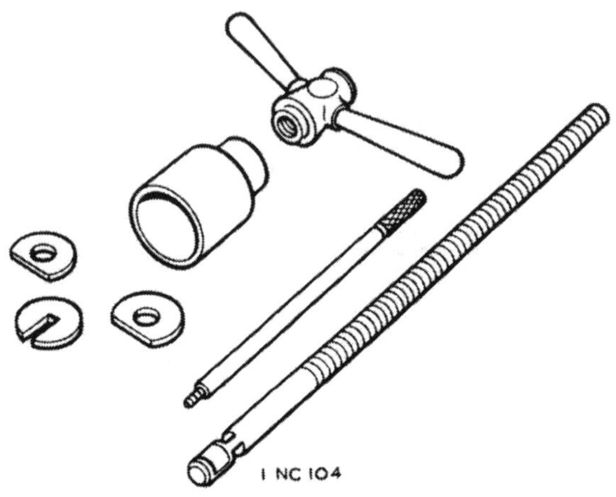

18G 124 A. Camshaft Liner Remover and Replacer (basic tool)

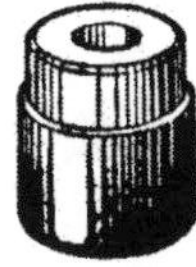

18G 124 B. Camshaft Liner Remover Adaptor

18G 124 K. Camshaft Liner Remover Adaptor

18G 124 M. Camshaft Liner Remover Adaptor

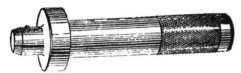

18G 134. Bearing and Oil Seal Replacer (basic tool)

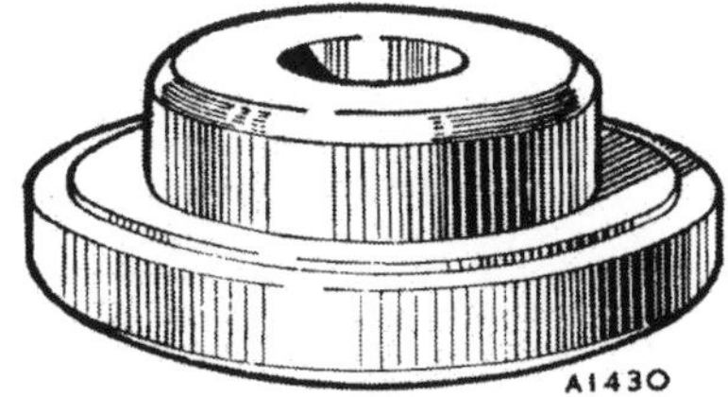

18G 134 BC. Crankshaft Primary Gear Oil Seal Replacer Adaptor

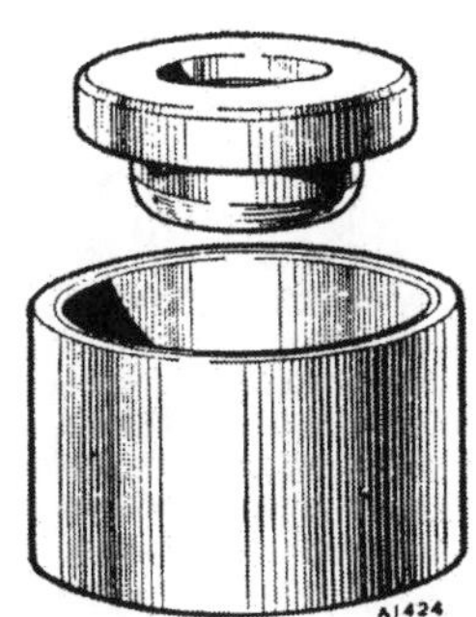

18G 134 BD. Timing Case Oil Seal Replacer Adaptor

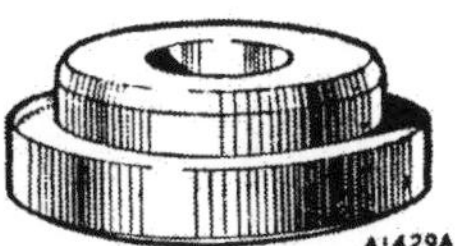

18G 134 BH. Flywheel and Front Hub Oil Seal Replacer Adaptor

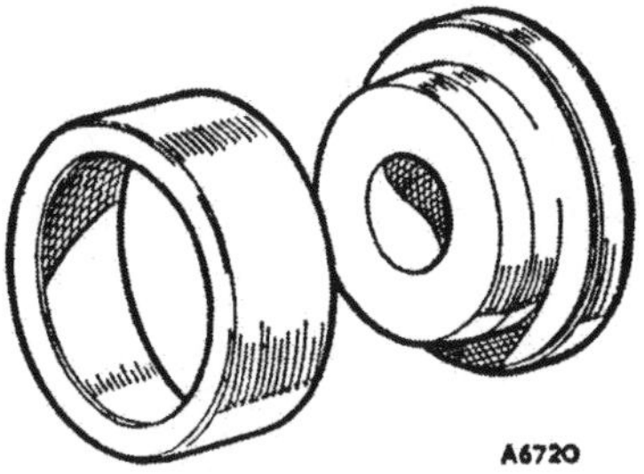

18G 134 CN. Replacer Oil Seal Stator Carrier

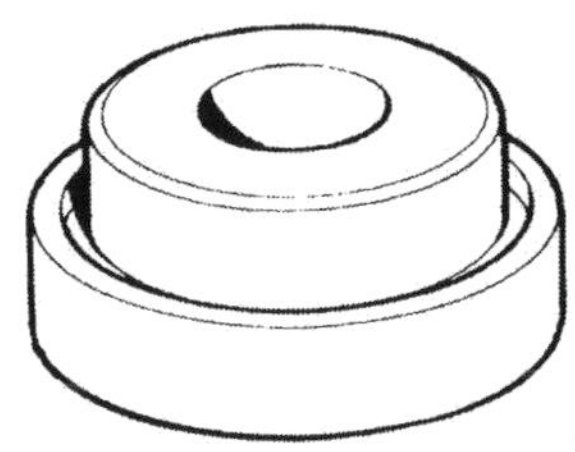

18G 134 DO. Swivel Hub Oil Seal Replacer
(Inner oil seal with water shield.)

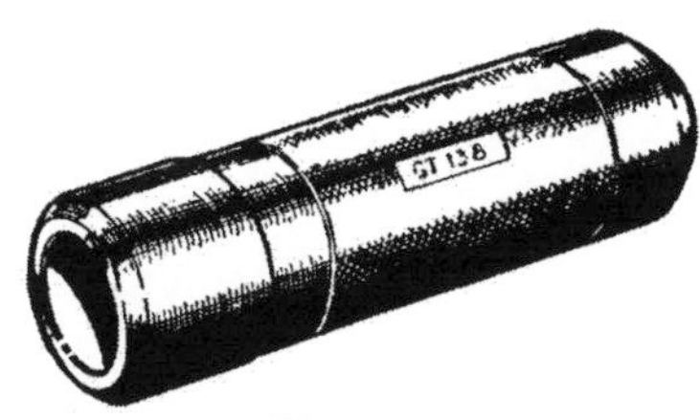

18G 138. Crankshaft Gear and Pulley Replacer

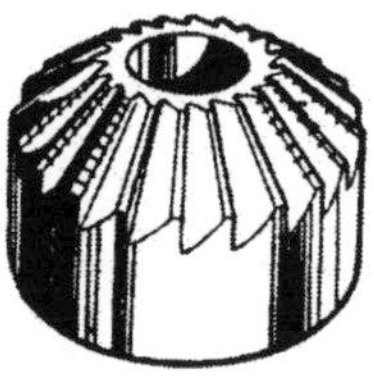

18G 167. Valve Seat Finishing Cutter

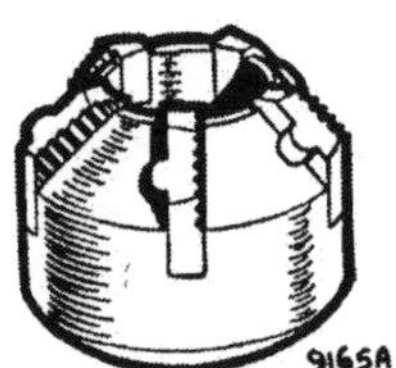

18G 167 A. Valve Seat Glaze Breaker

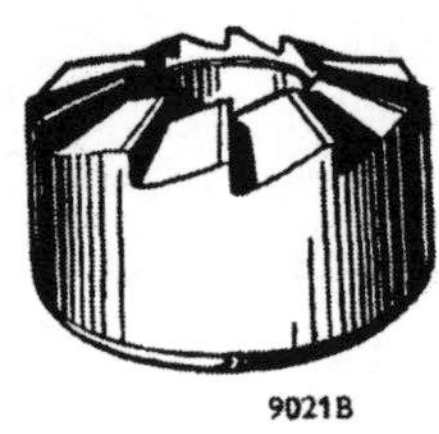

18G 167 B. Valve Seat Narrowing Cutter–Top

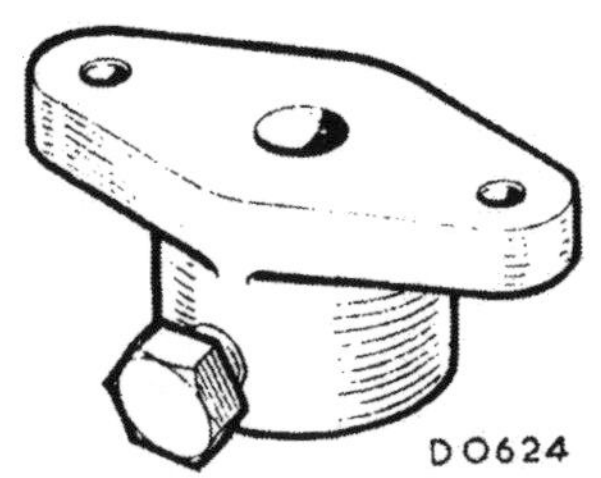

18G 207 A. Steering Rack Pinion Preload Adaptor

18G 167 C. Valve Seat Narrowing Cutter–Bottom

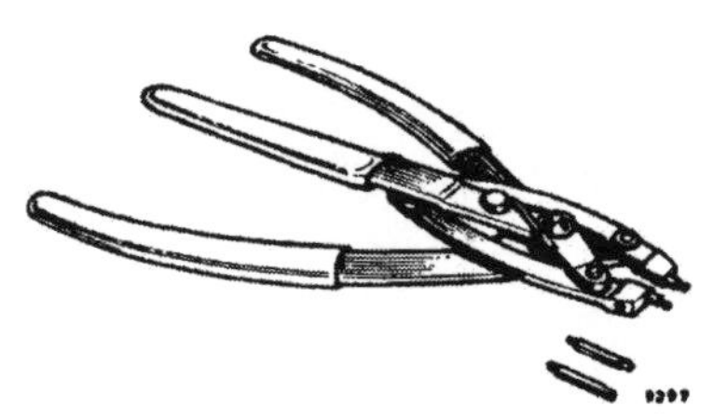

18G 257. Circlip Pliers–Large

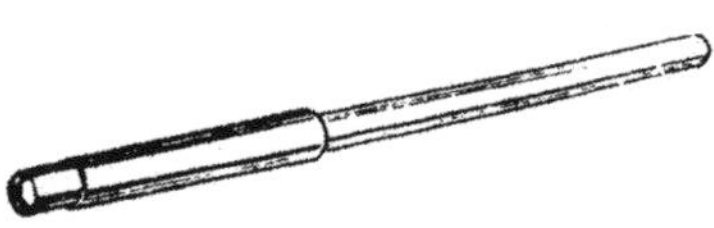

18G 167 D. Valve Seat Cutter Pilot

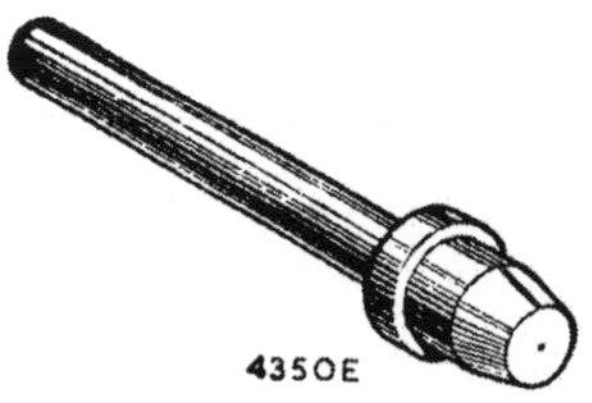

18G 260. Hub Bearing Outer Race Remover (basic tool)

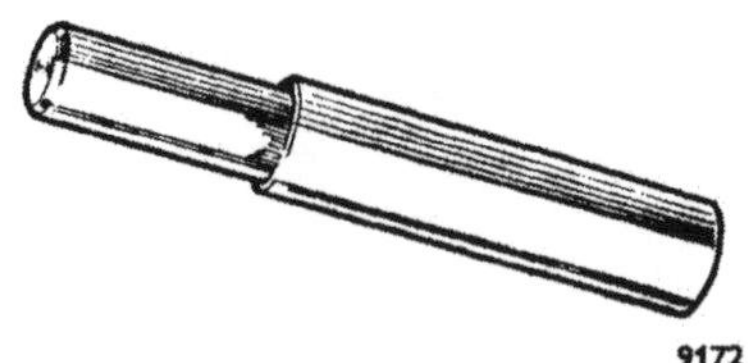

18G 194. Laygear Needle-roller Bearing Replacer

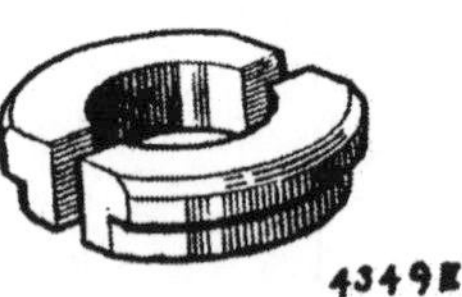

18G 260 C. Hub Bearing Outer Race Remover Adaptor

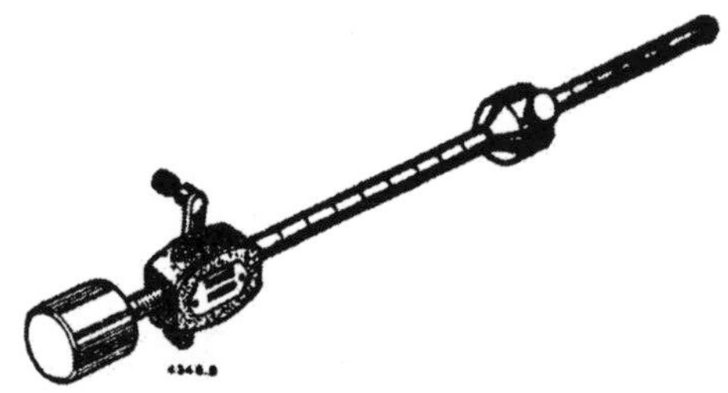

18G 207. Bearing Preload Gauge

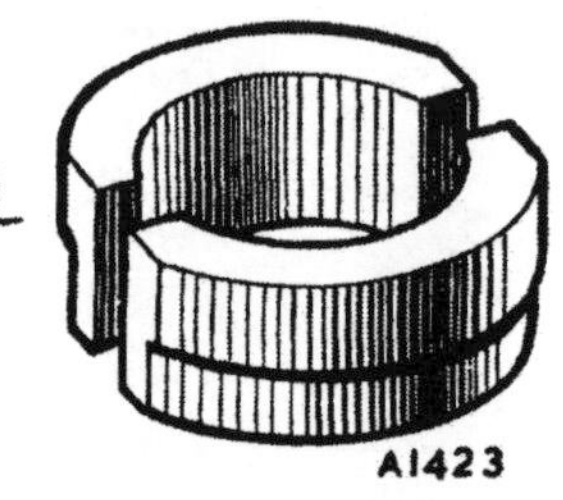

18G 260 H. Front Hub Drive Flange Bearing Outer Race Remover Adaptor

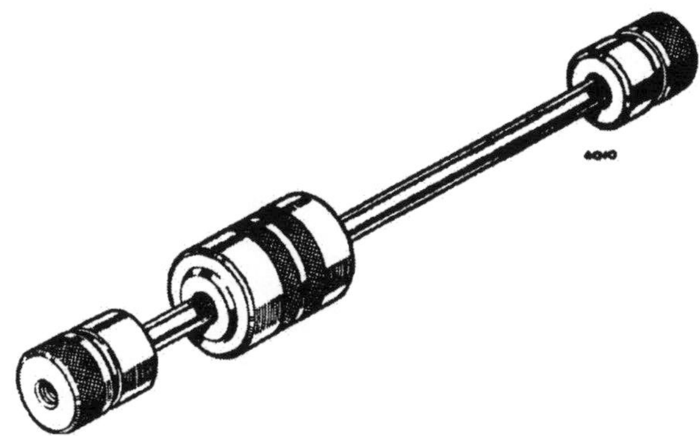

18G 284. Impulse Extractor (basic tool)

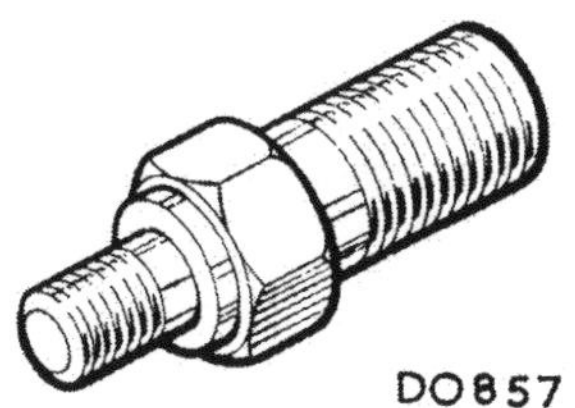

18G 284 AJ. Planetary Gear Spindles Remover Adaptor

18G 284 B. First Motion Shaft Remover Adaptor

18G 304. Front and Rear Hub Remover (basic tool)

18G 304 F. Front and Rear Hub Remover Bolt Adaptor

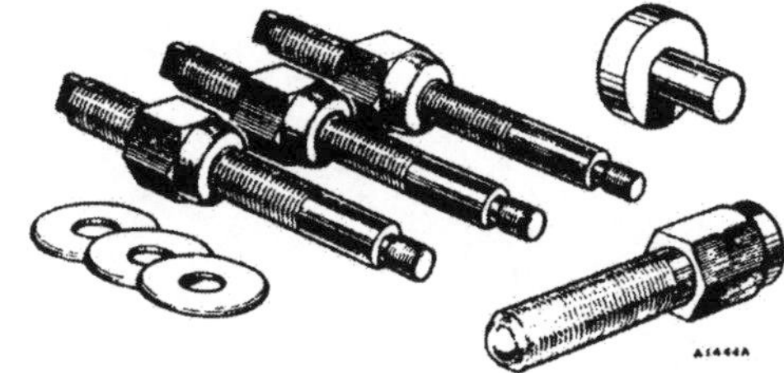

18G 304 M. Flywheel and Clutch Remover Adaptor

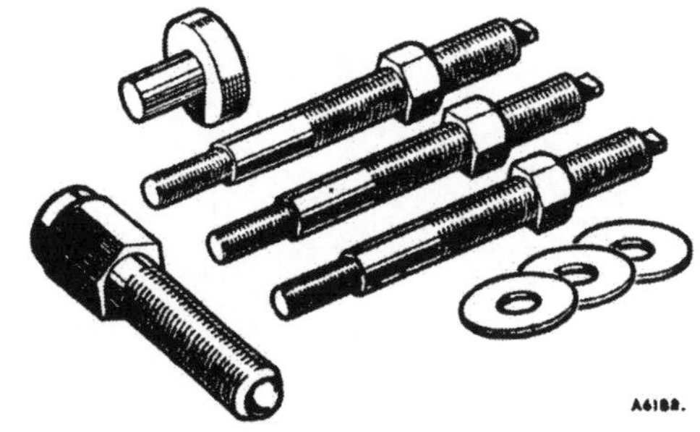

18G 304 N. Flywheel and Clutch Remover Adaptors

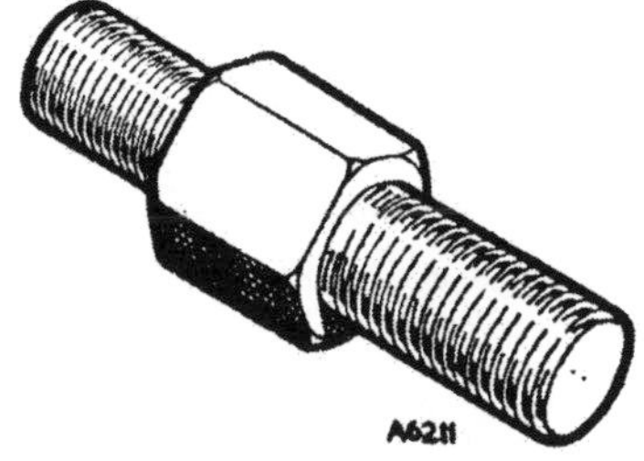

18G 304 P. Drive Flange Remover Adaptor

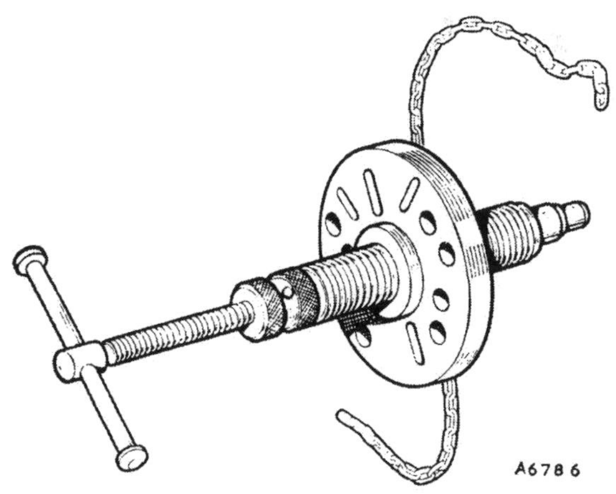

18G 304 Z. Hub Remover–Hydraulic (basic tool)

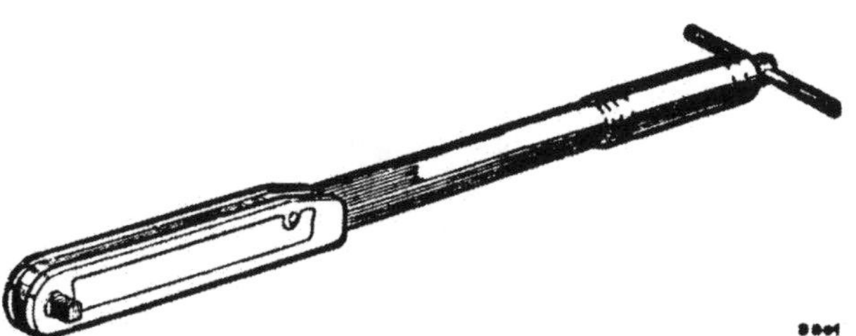

18G 372. Torque Wrench–30 to 140 lb. ft. (4 to 20 kg.m.)

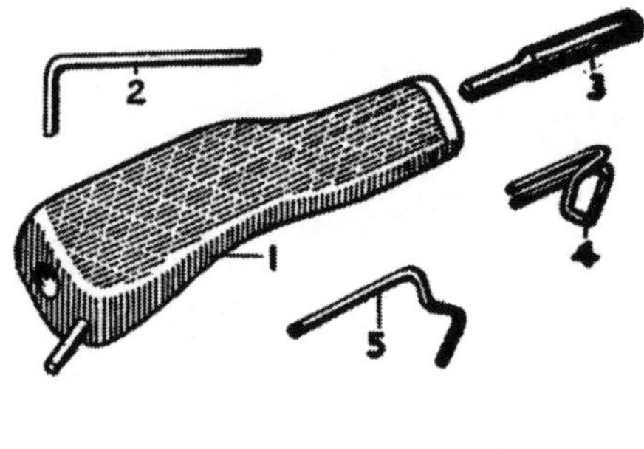

18G 468. Rubber Moulding Glazing Tool

The tool comprises:

1. Handle.	3. Post.	5. Hook.
2. Key.	4. Eye.	

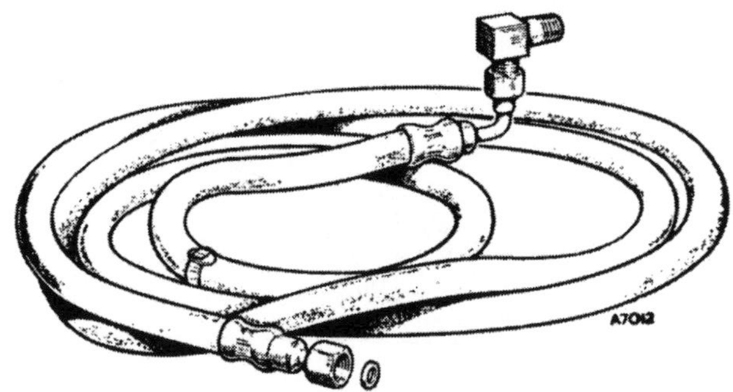

18G 502 K. Pressure Hose (8 ft.) with Adaptor

18G 468 A. Rubber Moulding Glazing Tool Adaptor

18G 536. Torque Wrench—20 to 100 lb. in. (2 to 8 lb. ft.) (300 to 1200 gm.m.)

18G 537. Torque Wrench—10 to 50 lb. ft. (2 to 7 kg. m.)

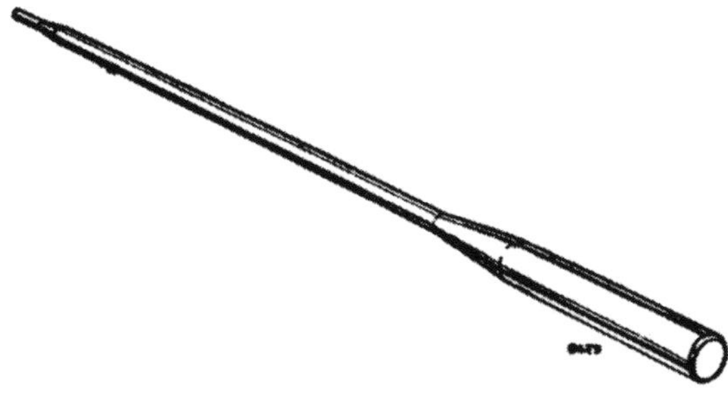

18G 471. Dummy Layshaft

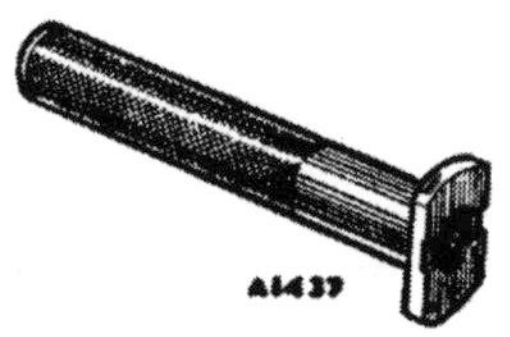

18G 569. First Motion Shaft Bearing Circlip Gauge

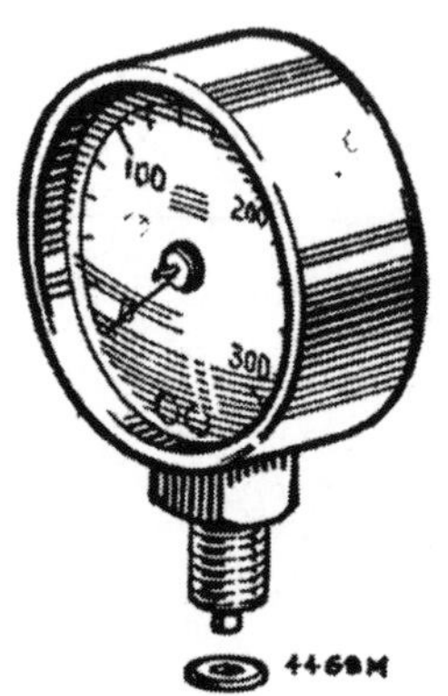

18G 502 A. Hydraulic Pressure Gauge

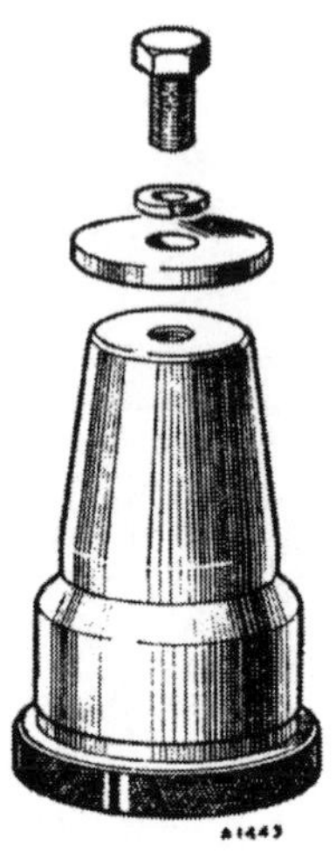

18G 571. Clutch Centralizer

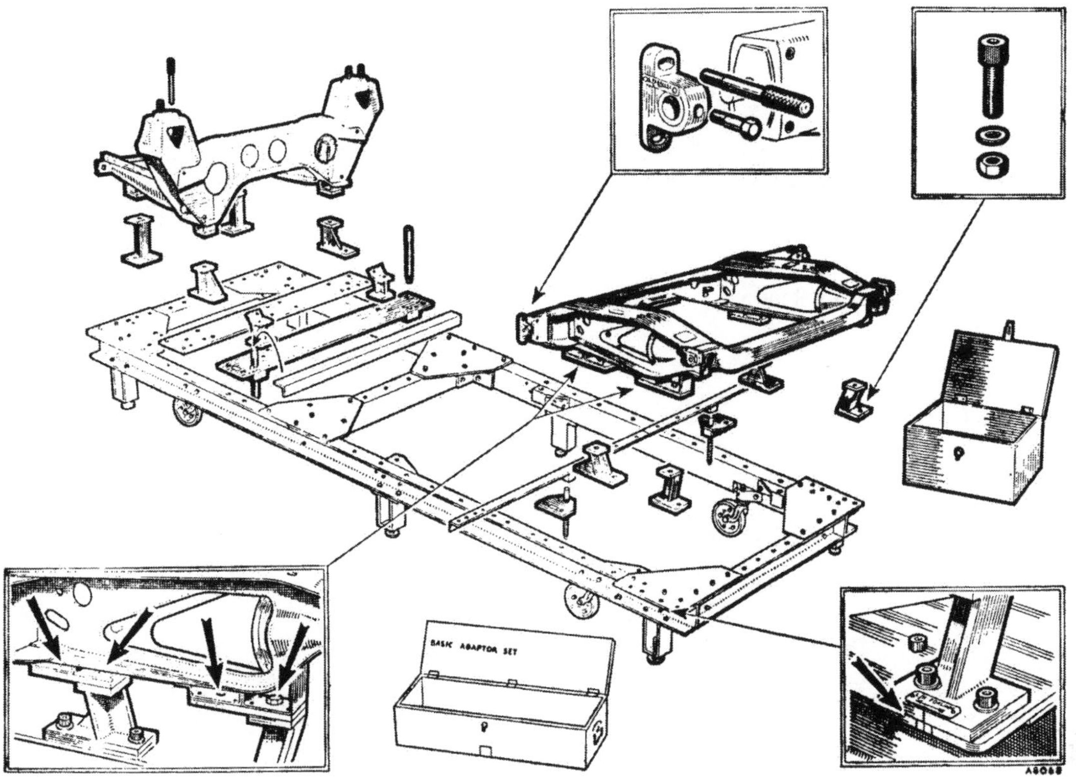

18G 560 E. Body Checking Jig Adaptor Set

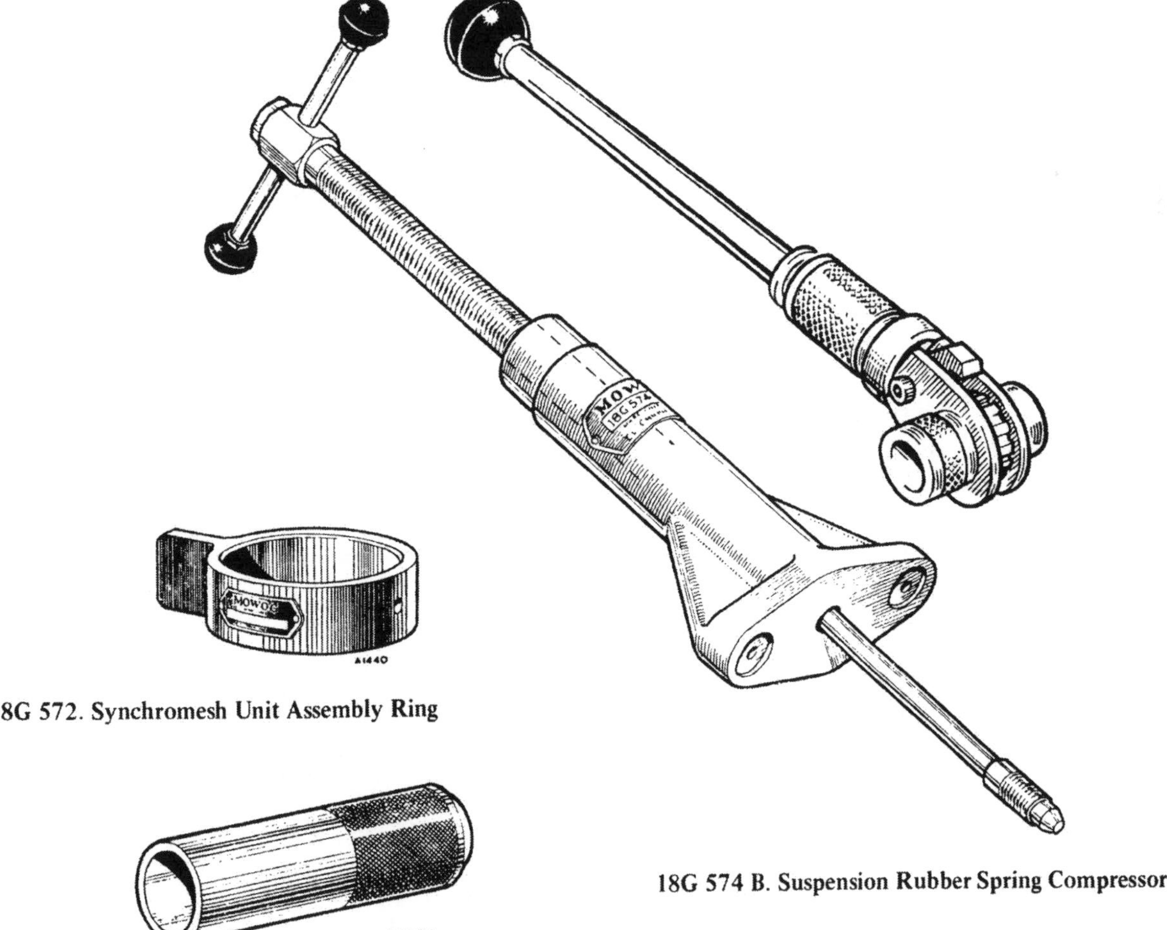

18G 572. Synchromesh Unit Assembly Ring

18G 574 B. Suspension Rubber Spring Compressor

18G 573. Change Speed Shaft Oil Seal Replacer

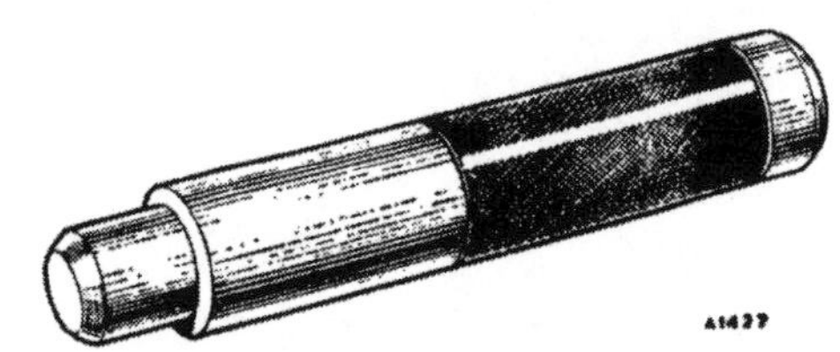

18G 575. Front Hub Drive Flange Remover

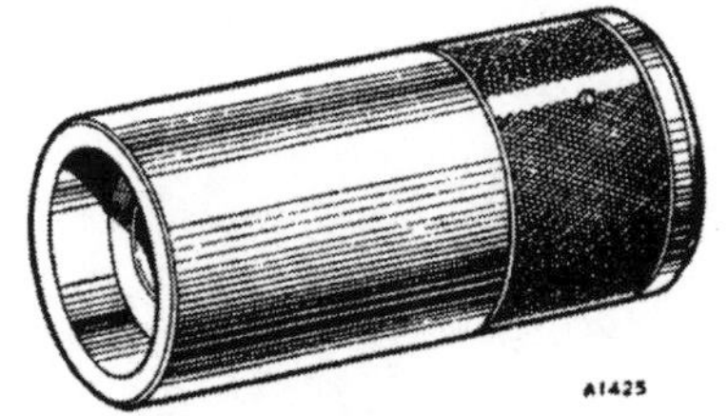

18G 578. Differential Bearing Replacer

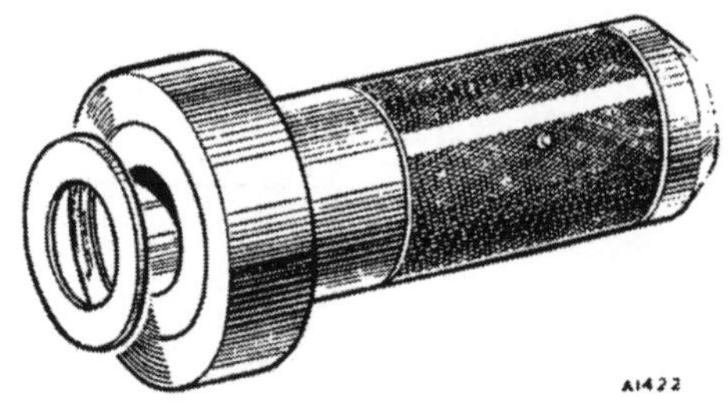

18G 579. First and Third Motion Shaft Bearing Replacer

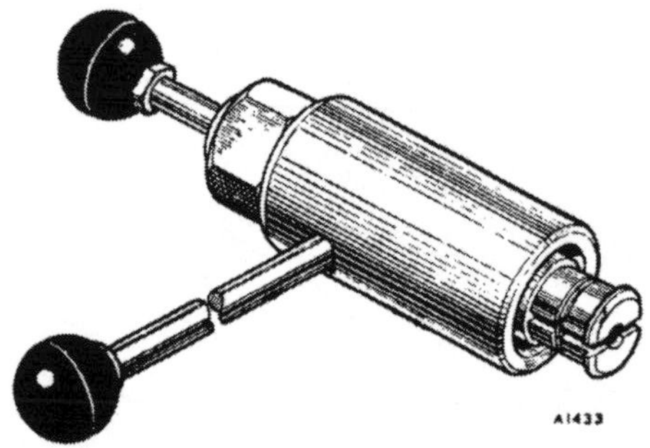

18G 581. Front Suspension and Idler Gear Needle-bearing Remover

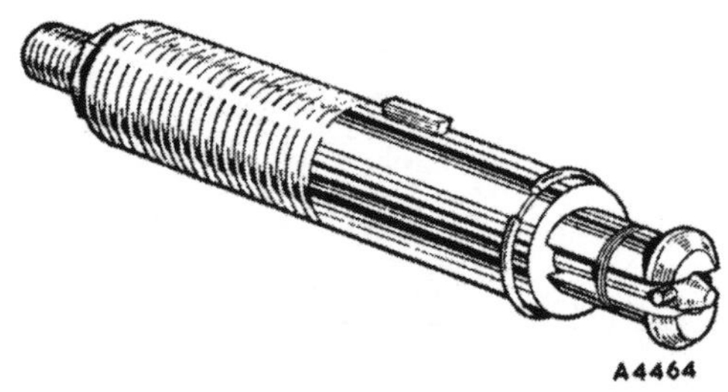

18G 581 B. First Motion Shaft Spigot Bearing Remover Adaptor

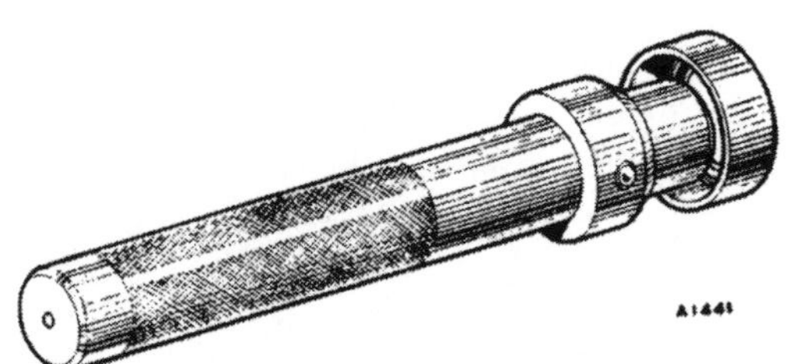

18G 582. Front Suspension and Idler Gear Bearing Replacer

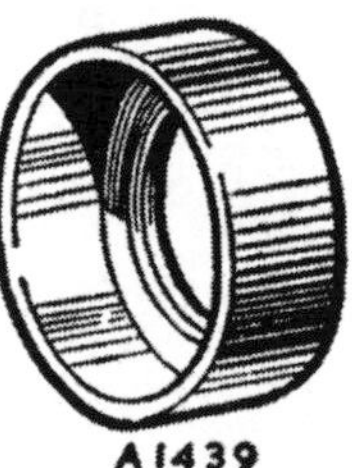

18G 582 A. Front Suspension and Idler Gear Needle Bearing Replacer Adaptor

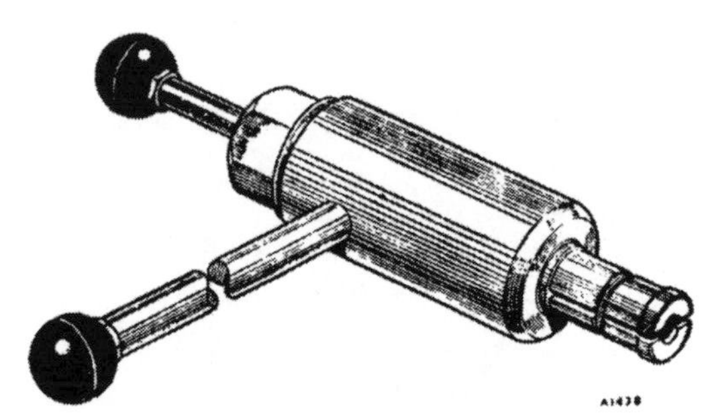

18G 583. Rear Radius Arm Bush Remover.

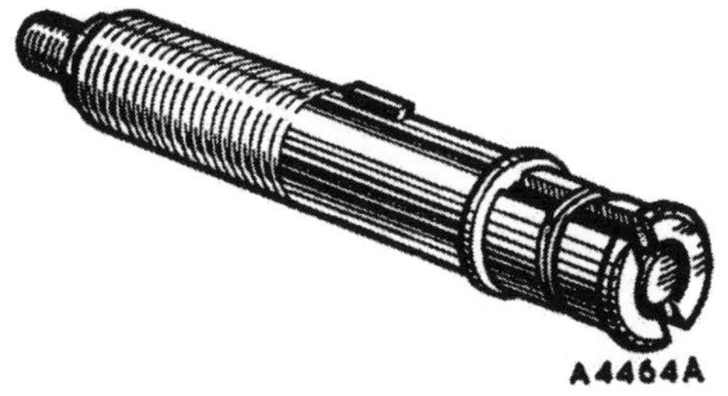

18G 583 B. Rear Radius Arm Needle Bearing Remover Adaptor

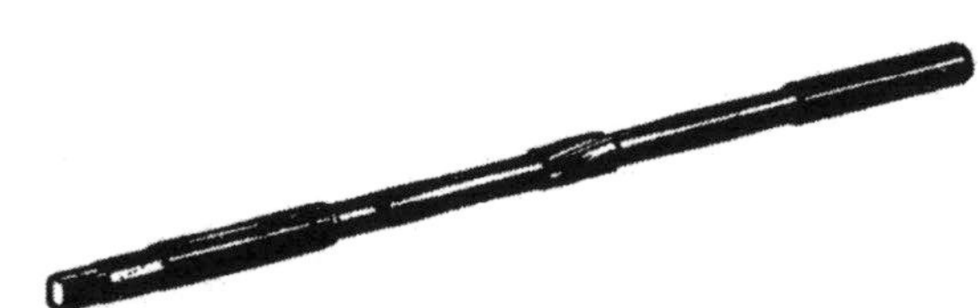

18G 588. Rear Radius Arm Bush Reamer

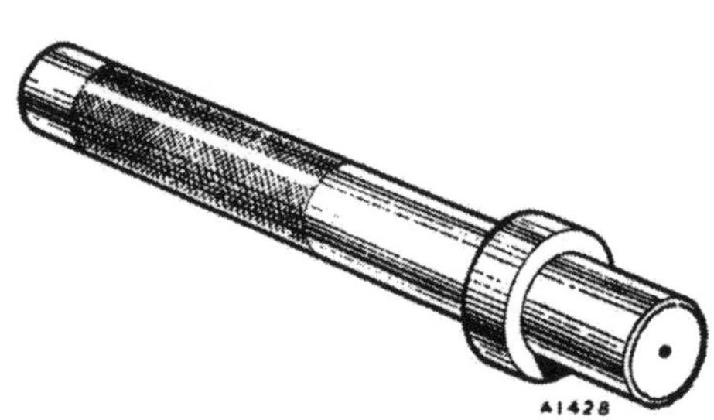

18G 584. Rear Radius Arm Bush Replacer

18G 588 A. Reamer Guide Bush

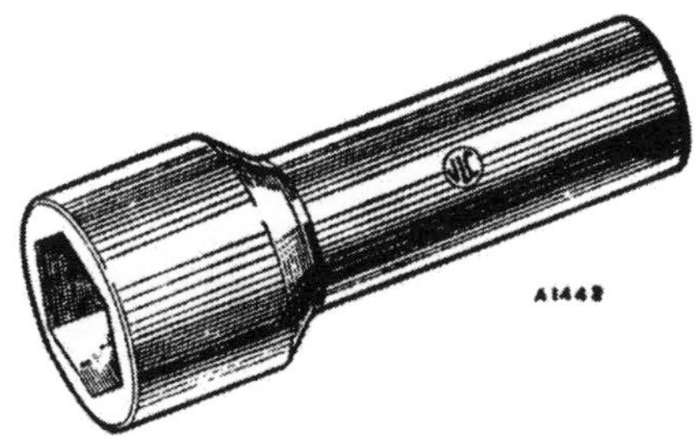

18G 586. Final Drive Gear Nut Spanner

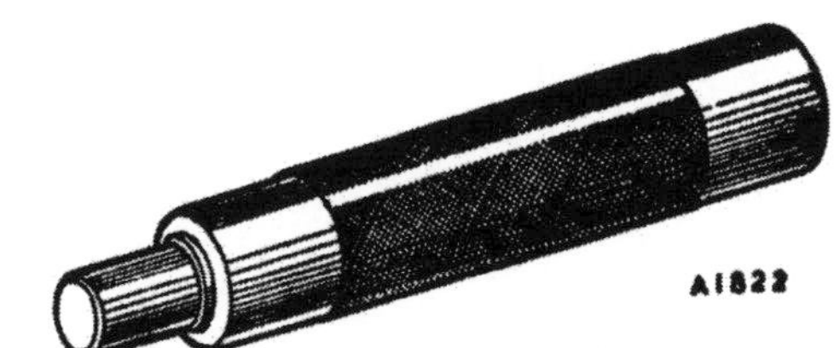

18G 589. First Motion Shaft Spigot Bearing Replacer

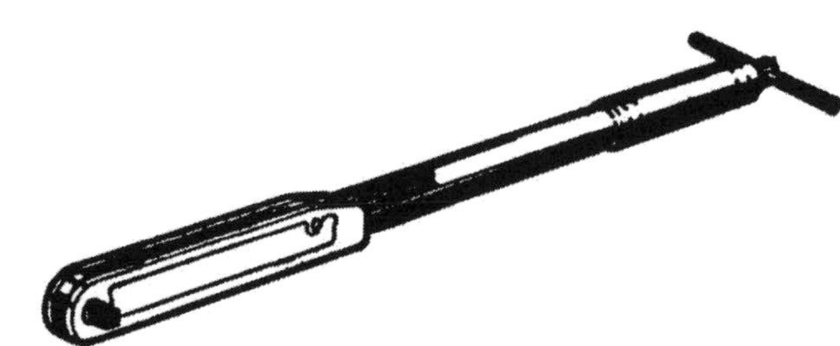

18G 592. Torque Wrench–50 to 225 lb. ft. (5 to 30 kg. m.)

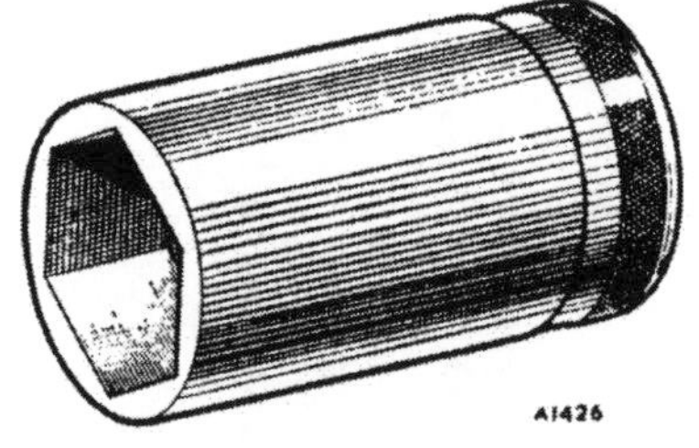

18G 587. Swivel Hub Ball Pin Nut Spanner

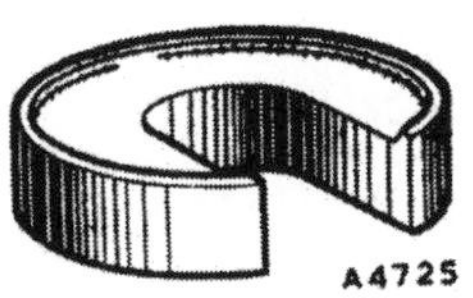

18G 613. Third Motion Shaft Bearing Remover

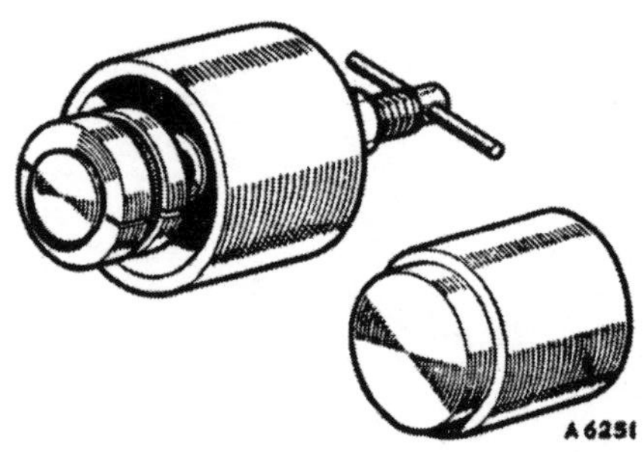

18G 617 A. Flywheel Housing Bearing (First Mo. on Shaft) Outer Race Remover/Replacer

18G 672. Disc Brake Piston Seal Replacer

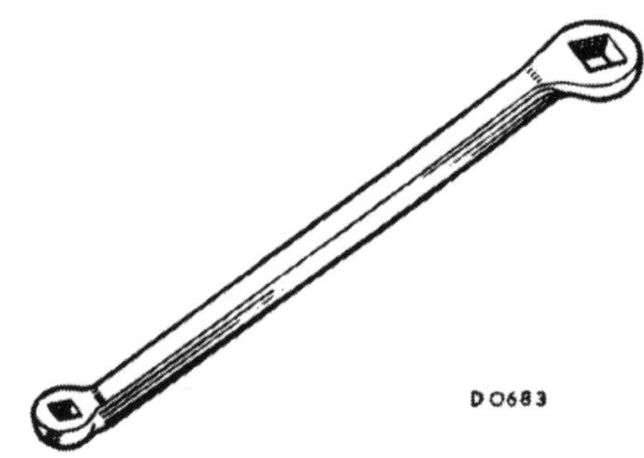

18G 619 A. Brake Adjusting Spanner

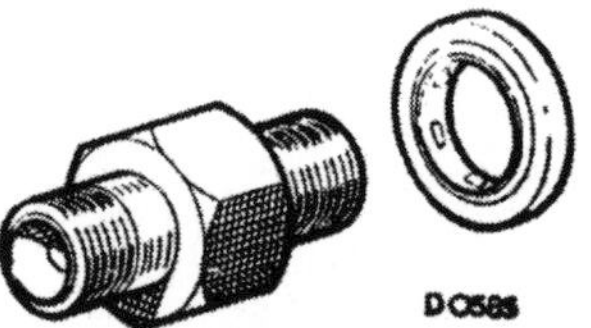

18G 677 C. Pressure Test Equipment Adaptor

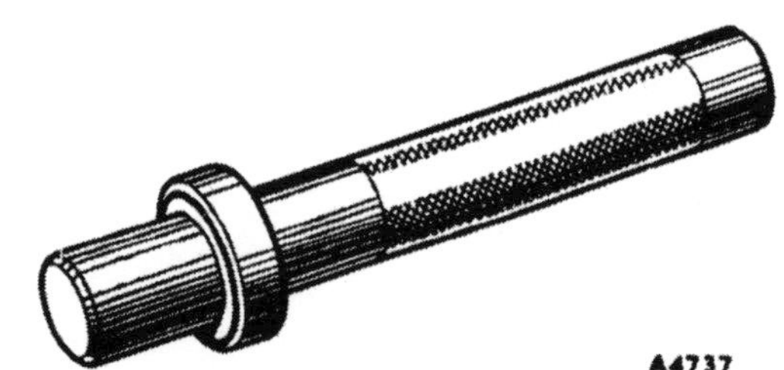

18G 620. Rear Radius Arm Needle Bearing Replacer

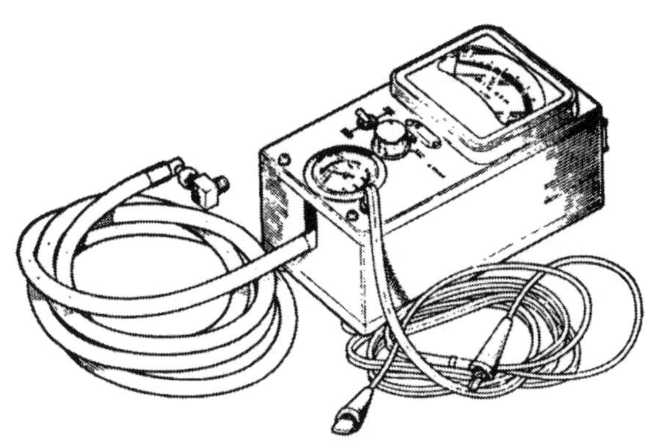

18G 677 Z. Pressure Test and Tachometer Equipment

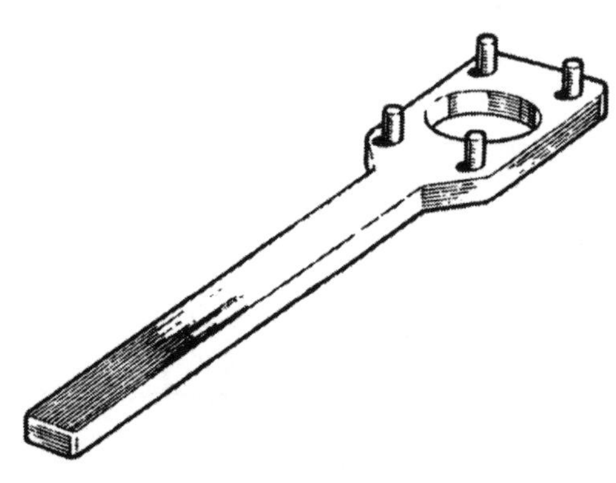

18G 669. Drive Shaft Coupling Flange Wrench

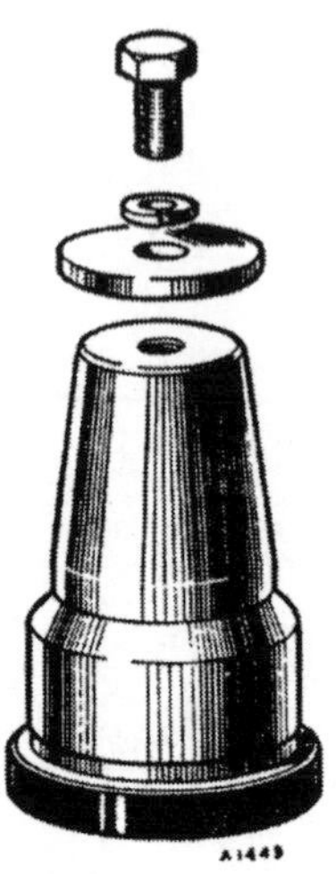

18G 684. Clutch Centralizer

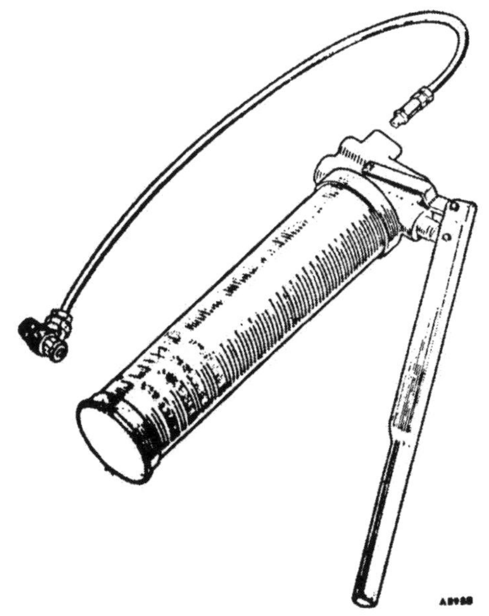

18G 685. The Hydrolastic Hand Pump

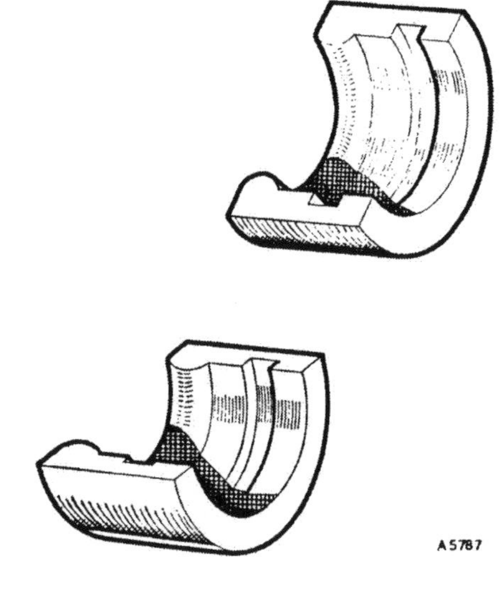

18G 705 B. Bearing Centre Race Remover Adaptor

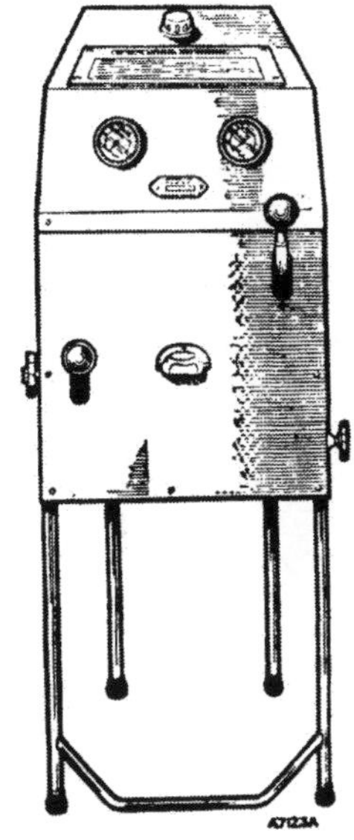

18G 703. The Hydrolastic Suspension Service Unit

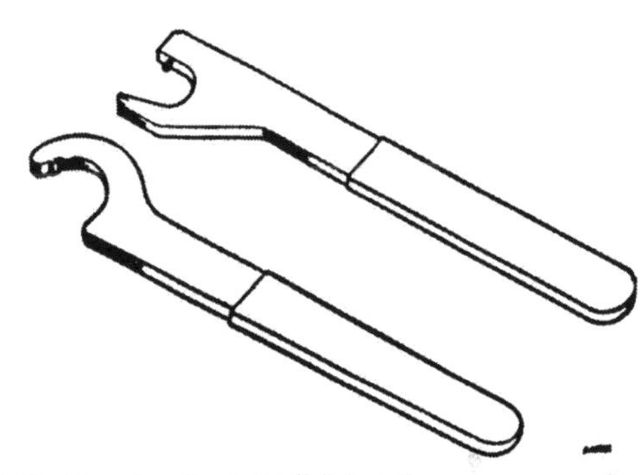

18G 707. Steering Rack Ball Joint Spanners

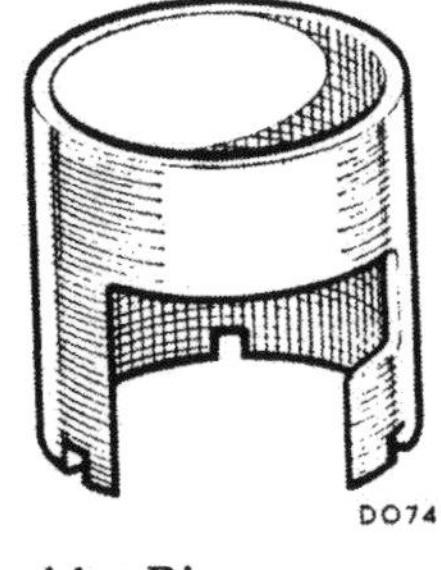

18G 1001. Gauge Locking Ring

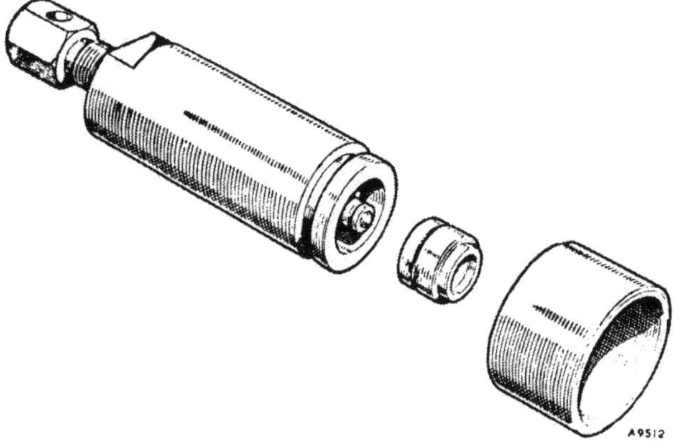

18G 705. Bearing Centre Race Remover (basic tool)

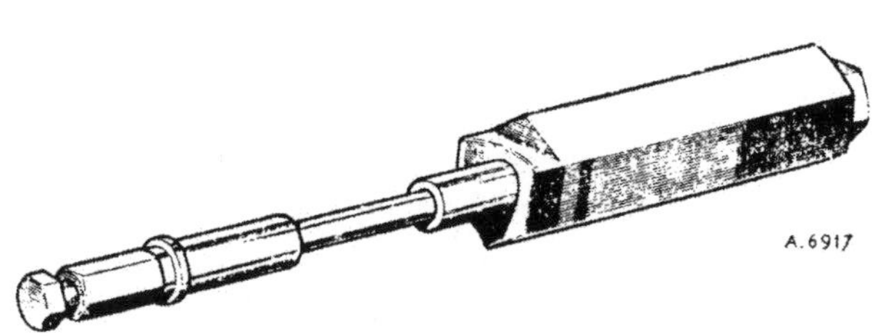

18G 1002. Gudgeon Pin Removing and Replacing Tool
Existing alternative to 18G 1150.

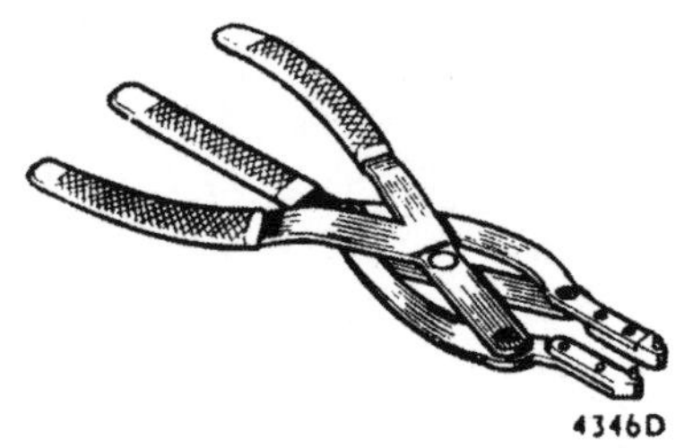

18G 1004. Circlip Pliers

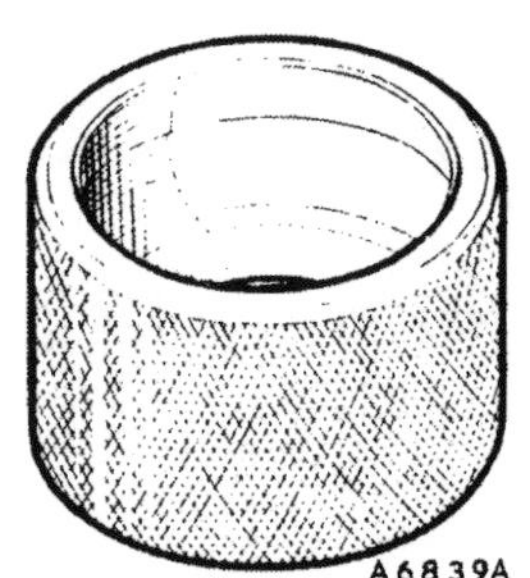

18G 1012. Selection Gauge–Constant Velocity Joint

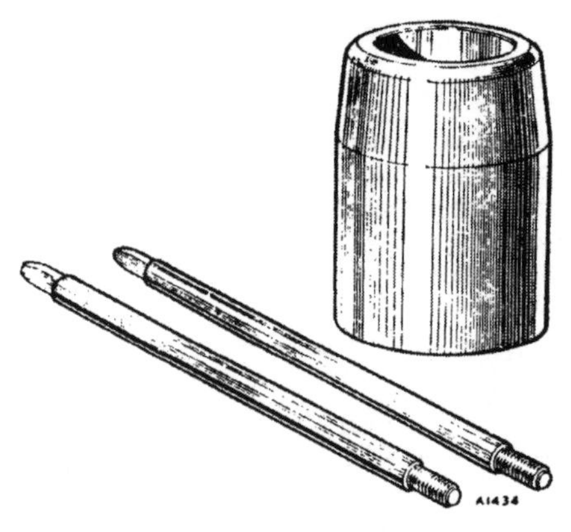

18G 1043. Crankshaft Primary Gear Oil Seal Protector Sleeve

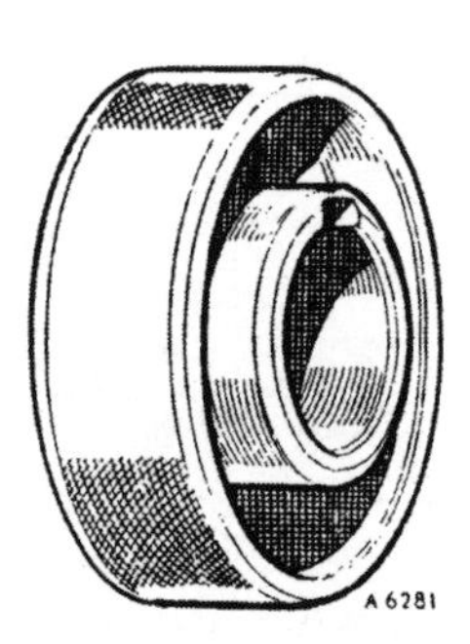

18G 1044. Engine Front Cover Centralizer

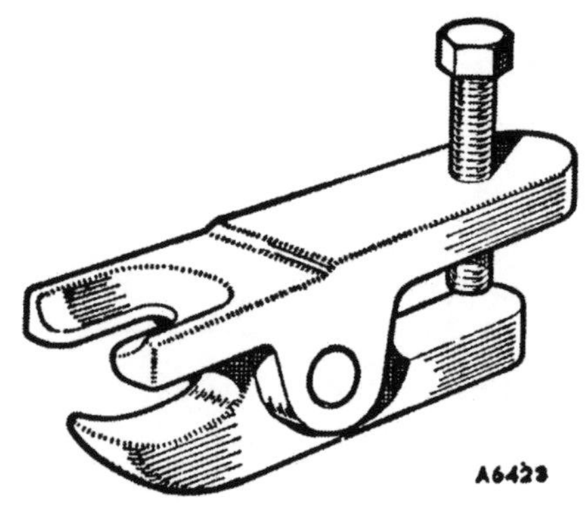

18G 1063. Steering Arm and Swivel Hub Ball Pin Remover

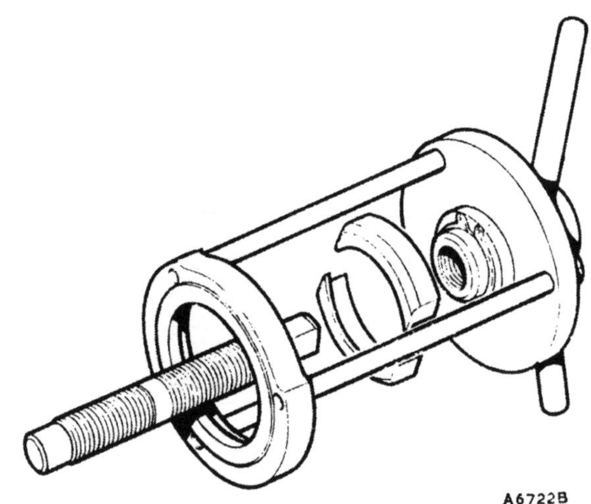

18G 1068 B. Remover and Replacer (basic tool)

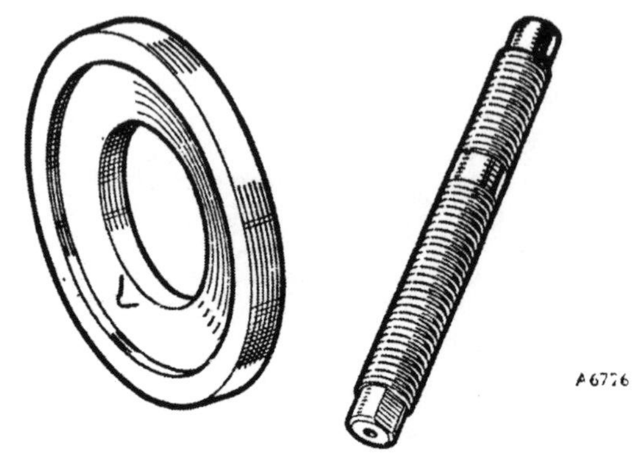

18G 1068 A. Adaptor Set–Replacer Converter Housing Oil Seal. Use with 18G 1068

18G 1086. Converter Remover

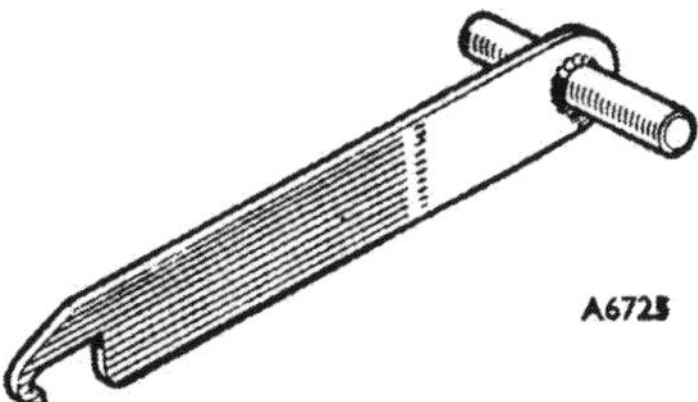

18G 1087. Converter Housing Oil Seal Remover

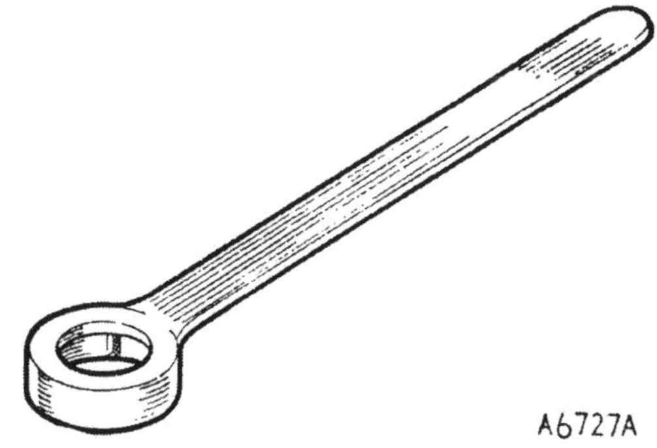

18G 1088. Converter Output Gear Holding Tool

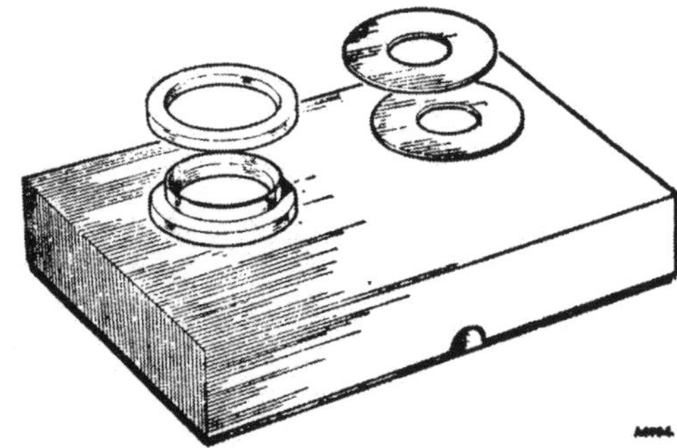

18G 1089. Idler and Input Gear Gauge Kit

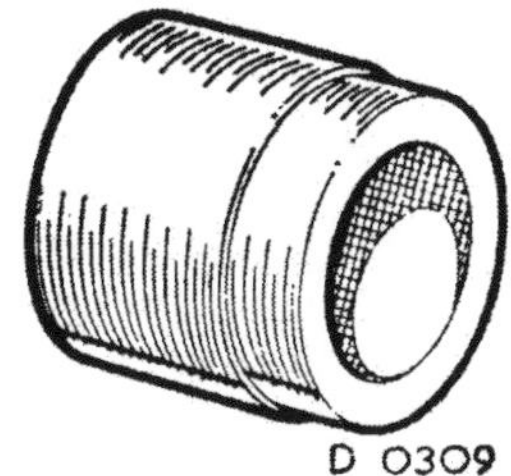

18G 1089 A. Input Gear Gauge Kit Adaptor

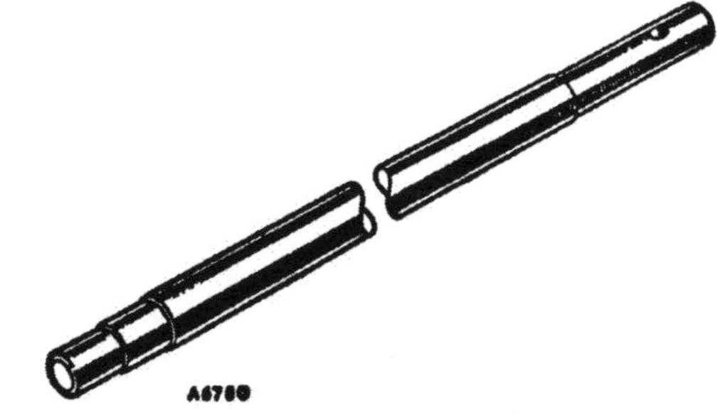

18G 1093. Dummy Shaft–Forward Gear Carrier Assembly

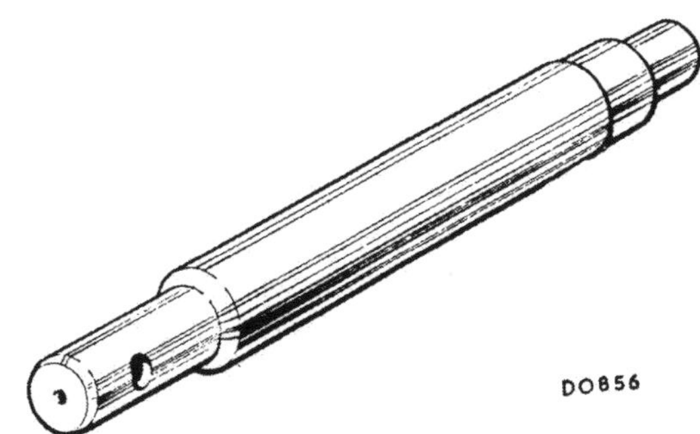

18G 1093 A. Dummy Shaft–Forward Gear Carrier

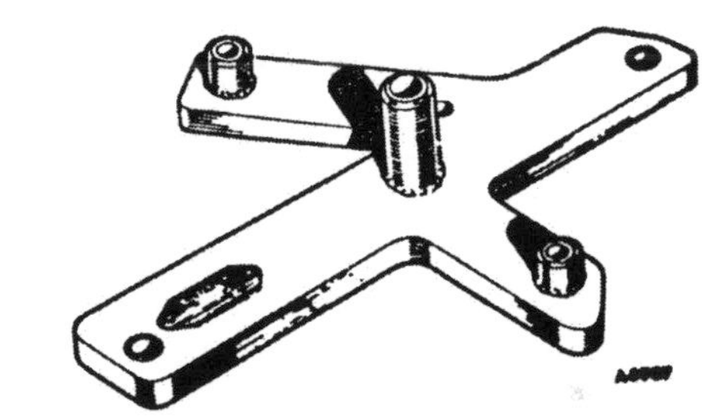

18G 1094. Positioning Fixture–Oil Pump Pipes

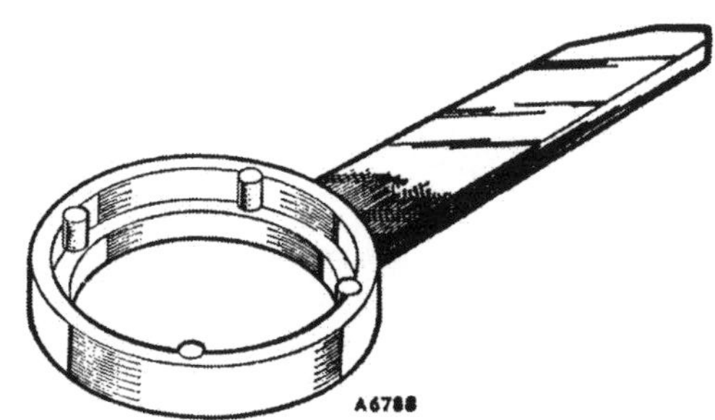

18G 1095. Holder–Top and Reverse Clutch Hub

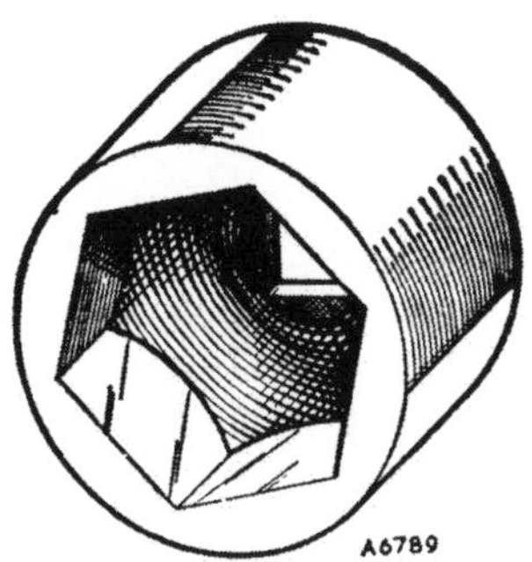

18G 1096. Socket Spanner–Forward Clutch Hub Nut

18G 1097. Retainer–Forward Clutch

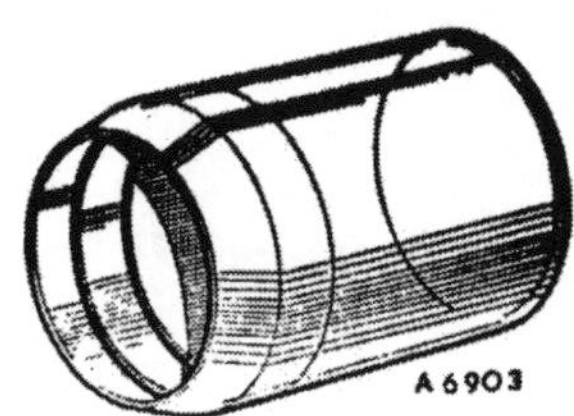

18G 1098. Protector Sleeve–Converter Output Gear Oil Seal

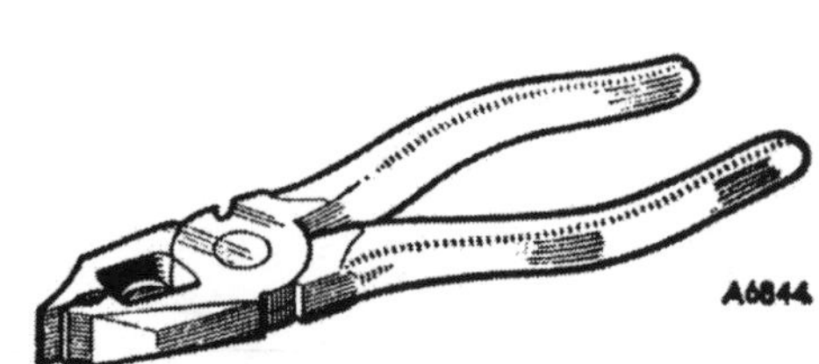

18G 1099. Pliers–Retaining Clip–Drive Shaft Boots

18G 1100. Wrench–Drive Shaft Coupling Flange

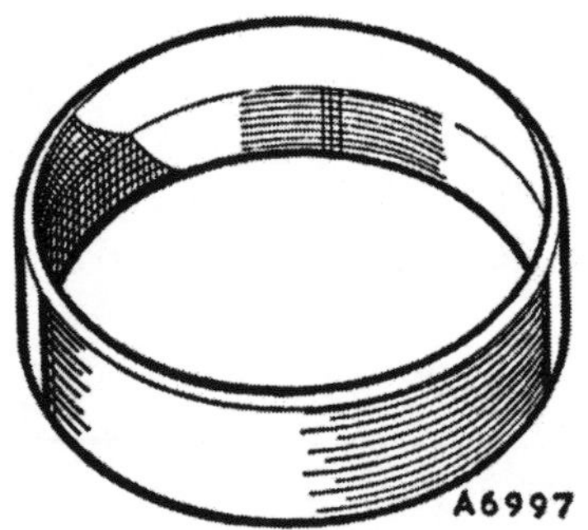

18G 1102. Replacer–Forward Clutch Piston Seal

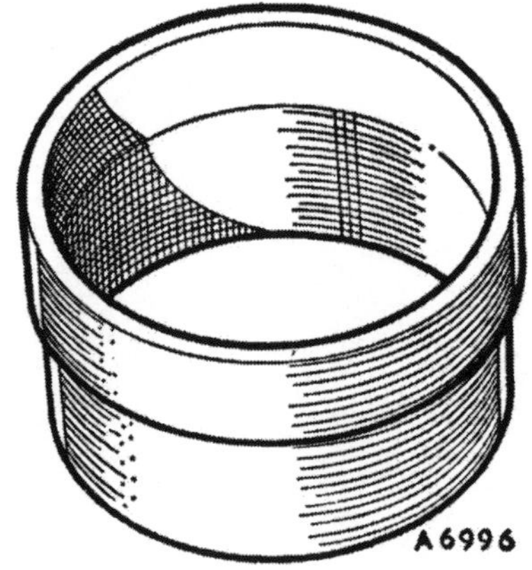

18G 1103. Replacer–Reverse Clutch Piston Seal

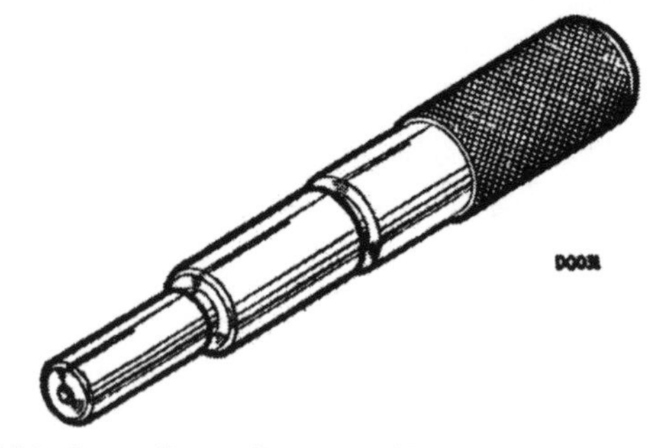

18G 1106. Centralizer–Governor Housing

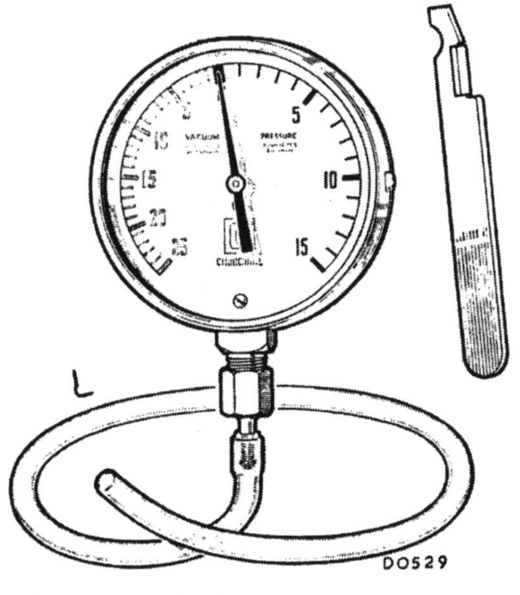

18G 1116. Test Gauge–Mechanical Fuel Pump.

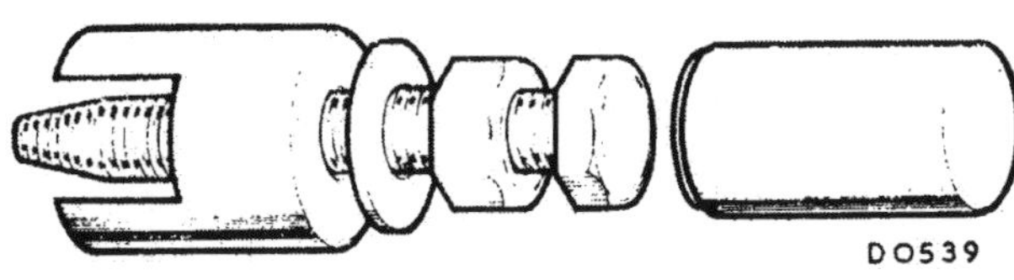

18G 1119. Mechanical Fuel Pump Oil Seal Retainer—Remover/Replacer

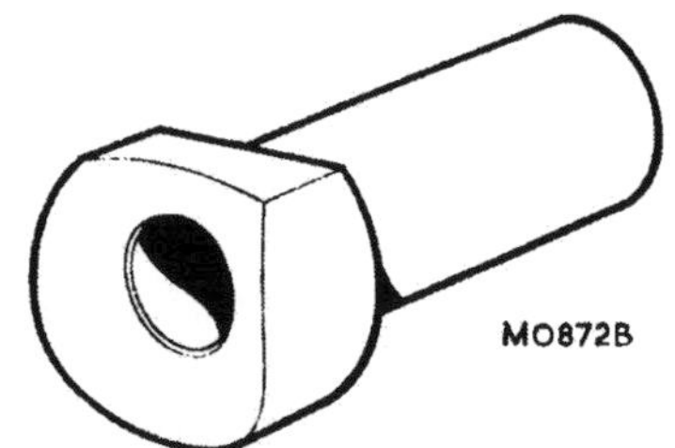

18G 1150 A. Gudgeon Pin Remover/Replacer Adaptor

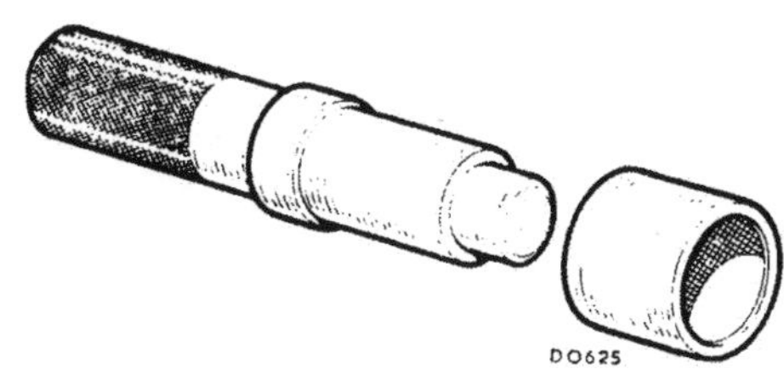

18G 1126. Idler Gear Bearing Remover/Replacer
(Four-speed synchromesh transmission only.)

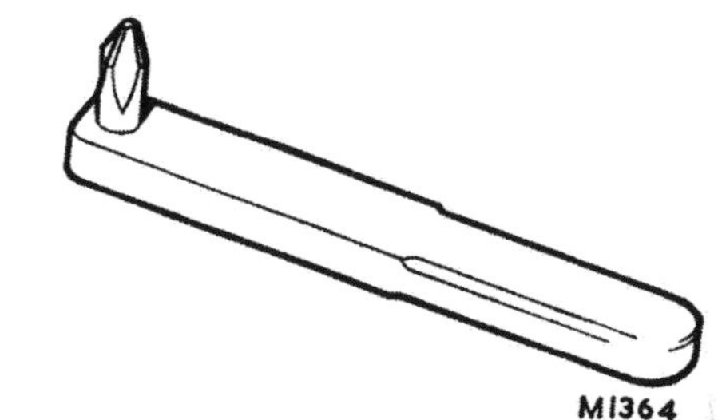

18G 1188. Door Hinge Screws Remover/Replacer

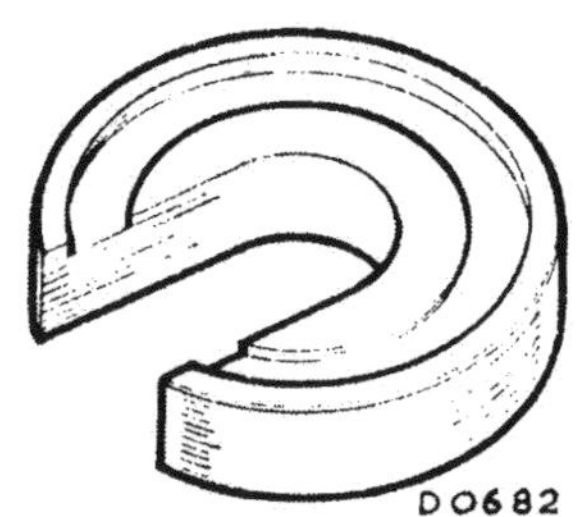

18G 1127. Third Motion Shaft Bearing Remover
(Use on four-speed synchromesh transmission.)

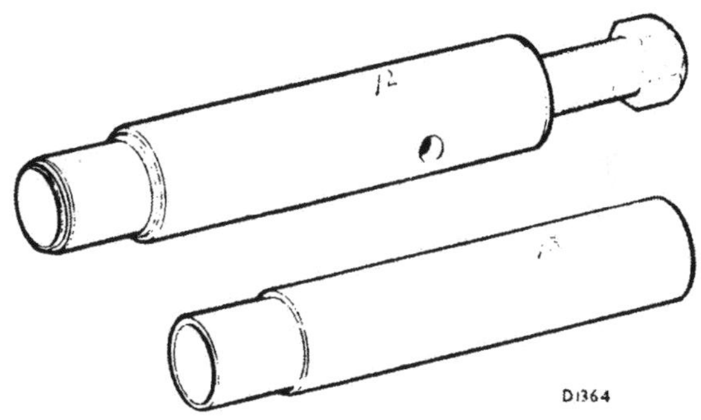

18G 1191. Steering-column Bush (Upper) Remover/Replacer

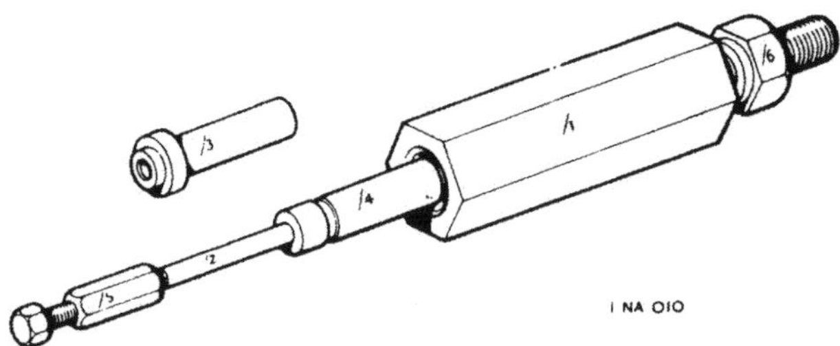

18G 1150. Gudgeon Pin Remover/Replacer (basic tool)
(18G 1002 existing alternative.)

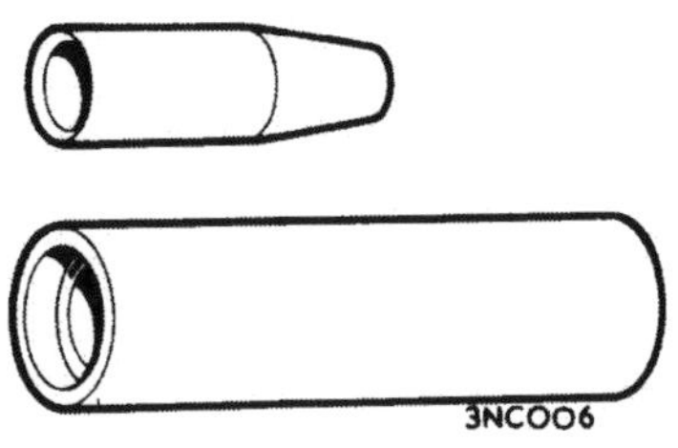

18G 1236. Selector Shaft Seal Protector and Replacer

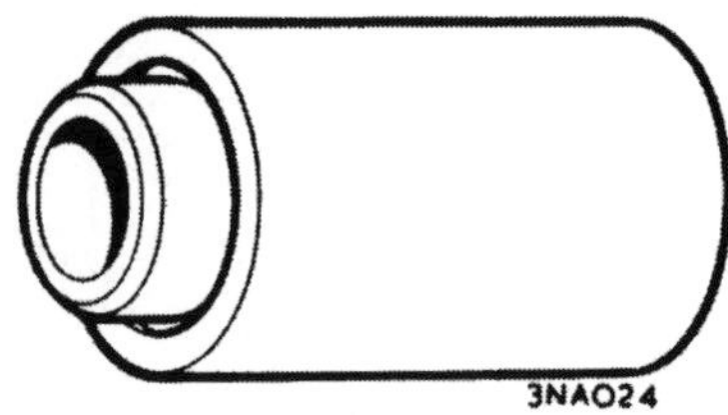

18G 1238. Differential End-cover Seal Replacer

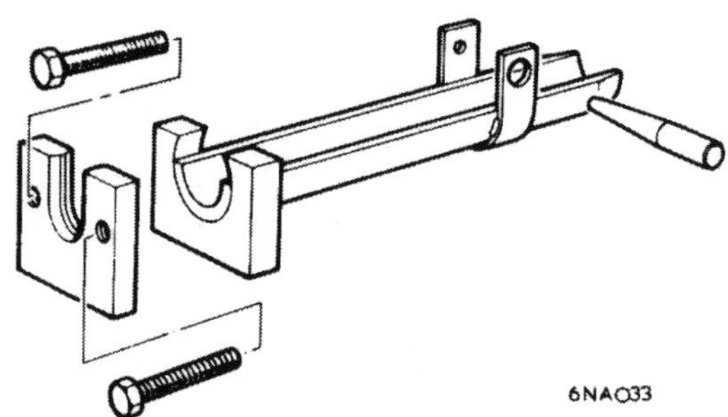

18G 1243. Separator Drive Shaft from Inboard Joint

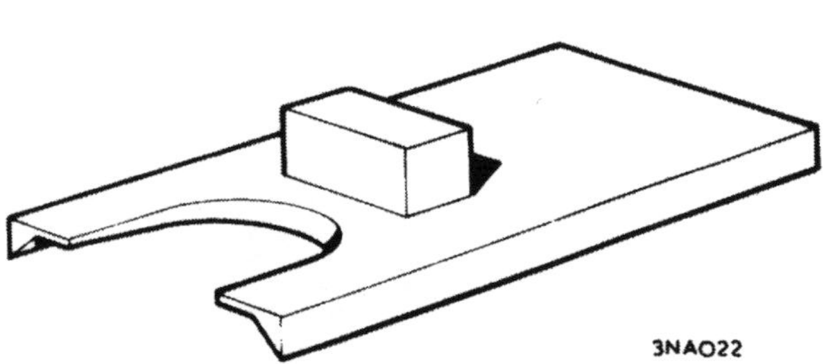

18G 1240. Drive Shaft Assembly Remover

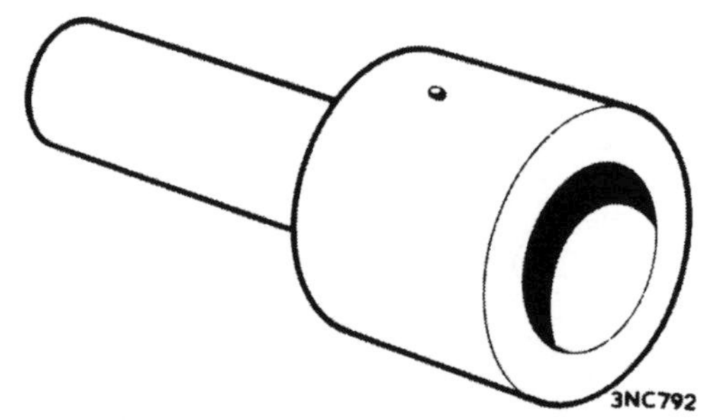

18G 1247. Clutch Housing Cover Alignment Gauge

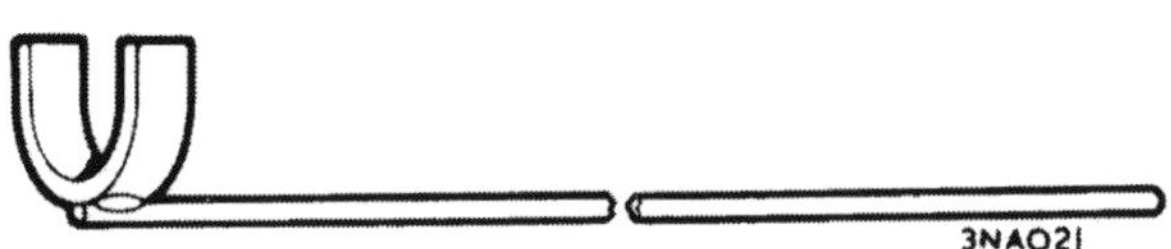

18G 1241. Drive Shaft Circlip Compressor

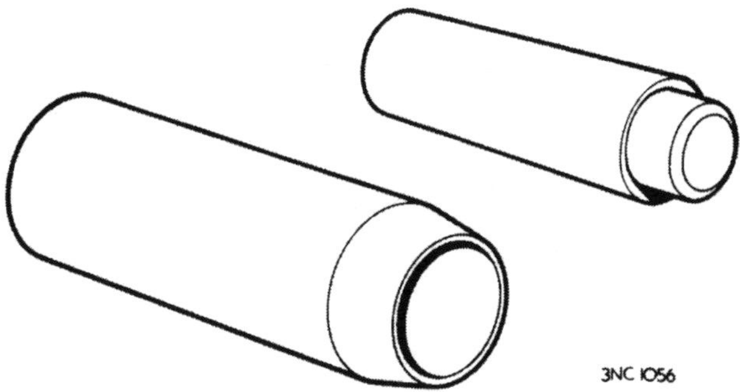

18G 1251. Inboard Joint Boot Retaining Clip Fitting Tool

SECTION T

EMISSION CONTROL

This section contains information and servicing instructions for the exhaust emission, crankcase emission, and evaporative loss control systems fitted to 1975 vehicles onwards, to conform with the Canadian Federal Motor Vehicle Safety Act.

The sequence numbers in each Section identifies the components numbered in the appropriate illustration.

Section T.1

SERVICE OPERATIONS SUMMARY

The maintenance summary on this and the following pages is the minimum service required to maintain your vehicle under normal driving conditions. For other than normal driving conditions, and those caused by seasonal changes, we recommend that you consult your Dealer.

NOTE: The service intervals are based on an annual mileage of approximately 12,500 miles. Should the vehicle complete substantially less miles than this per annum, it is recommended that a 'C' service is completed at six-month intervals, and a 'D' service at twelve-month intervals.

Service	Mileage x 1000	Monthly intervals
A	1	After Sales Service
B	3, 9, 16, 22, 28, 34, 41, 47	3
C	6, 19, 31, 44	6
D	12.5, 37.5	12
E	25, 50	24

† These items are emission related 

	A	B	C	D	E
LUBRICATION					
Lubricate all grease points including hand brake mechanical linkage and cable guides	X	X	X	X	X
Renew engine oil filter			X	X	X
Renew engine oil	X		X	X	X
Check/top up engine oil	X	X	X	X	X
Lubricate all locks and hinges except steering lock	X		X	X	X
†Lubricate accelerator control linkage and pedal pivot; check operation	X		X	X	X
ENGINE					
Check/top up cooling system	X	X	X	X	X
Check cooling and heater systems for leaks, hoses and pipes for security and condition	X		X	X	X
†Check all driving belts; adjust or renew	X	X	X	X	X
†Check exhaust system for leaks and security	X	X	X	X	X
Check security of engine bolts and mountings	X				
†Check/adjust torque of cylinder head nuts	X				
†Check/adjust valve clearances	X			X	X
†Check/adjust air injection system hoses for security	X				
†Check air injection hoses/pipes for condition and security; rectify if necessary				X	X
†Check gulp valve, check valve and air diverter valve operations; rectify/renew if necessary				X	X
†Check crankcase breathing and evaporative loss systems, check hoses/pipes and restrictor for security, condition and blockage; rectify if necessary				X	X
Check/adjust clutch return stop clearance		X	X	X	X
IGNITION SYSTEM					
†Check ignition wiring for fraying, chafing and deterioration; rectify if necessary	X			X	X
†Check/adjust ignition timing and dwell angle using electronic equipment	X		X	X	X
†Check distributor cap, check for cracks and tracking				X	X

	A	B	C	D	E
IGNITION SYSTEM – continued					
†Lubricate distributor	X		X	X	X
†Renew contact breaker points				X	X
†Clean and adjust spark plugs			X		
†Renew spark plugs				X	X
†Check coil performance on oscilloscope				X	X
FUEL SYSTEM					
†Check fuel system for leaks	X	X	X	X	X
†Top up carburetter piston damper	X			X	X
†Check condition of fuel filler cap seal				X	X
†Renew fuel line filter				X	X
†Renew carburetter air filter element				X	X
†Check air intake temperature control system				X	X
†Renew adsorption canister					X
†Check/adjust crankcase breathing and evaporative loss system hoses for security	X				
†Check/adjust carburetter idle settings	X			X	X
SAFETY					
Check all fluid reservoirs; brake, clutch, battery and windscreen washer	X	X	X	X	X
Check visually hydraulic pipes and unions for chafing, leaks and corrosion	X	X	X	X	X
Check brake linings for wear and drums for condition; rectify/renew if necessary				X	X
Check/adjust foot and hand brakes	X	X	X	X	X
Check condition and security of steering unit, joints and gaiters	X	X	X	X	X
Check suspension dampers and steering rack for oil leaks	X	X	X	X	X
Check/adjust tightness of steering-column clamp bolt			X	X	X
Check/adjust security of suspension fixings	X		X	X	X
Check/adjust tyre pressures, including spare	X	X	X	X	X
Check/adjust front wheel alignment	X		X	X	X
Check tightness of road wheel fastenings	X	X	X	X	X
Check tyres comply with manufacturer's specification		X	X	X	X
Check tyres for tread depth, visually for cuts in tyre fabric, exposure of ply or cord structure, lumps or bulges	X	X	X	X	X
Check output of charging system	X		X	X	X
Check function of original equipment, i.e. interior and exterior lamps, horns, warning indicators, wipers and washers	X	X	X	X	X
Check instrumentation	X		X	X	X
Check, if necessary renew, wiper blades		X	X	X	X
Check/adjust headlamp alignment	X	X	X	X	X
Check operation of all door locks and window controls	X			X	X
Check condition and security of seats, seat belts, and seat belt warning system			X	X	X
TEST					
Road/roller test and check operation of all instrumentation; report additional work required	X		X	X	X

SUPPLEMENT

Brakes

Every 19,000 miles or 1½ years, whichever is the sooner, renew the brake fluid.

Every 37,500 miles or 3 years, whichever is the sooner, renew all fluid seals and flexible hoses in the brake and clutch systems. Examine working surfaces of pistons and bores in master, slave and wheel cylinders and renew parts where necessary.

Section T.2

ENGINE TUNING DATA

Model: **MINI 1000 (CANADA)** Year: **1975 on**

ENGINE	
Type	99H 834 V.
Capacity	998 c.c. (60.96 cu.in.).
Compression ratio	8.3 : 1.
Firing order	1, 3, 4, 2.
Compression pressure (cranking)	120 lb/sq. in. (8.44 kg./cm^2.).
Idling speed	850 ± 100 r.p.m.
Fast idle speed	1,250 ± 100 r.p.m.
Ignition tuning:	
Stroboscopic at 1,500 r.p.m. *	8°B.T.D.C.
Timing marks	Dimples on timing wheels, marks on flywheel.
Valve rocker clearance (warm)	.012 in. (.30 mm.).
DISTRIBUTOR	
Make/type	Lucas 43D4.
Rotation of rotor	Anti-clockwise.
Dwell angle	51° ± 5°
Contact breaker gap	.014 to .016 in. (.35 to .40 mm.).
Condenser capacity	.18 to .24 mF.
Serial No.	41404.
Centrifugal advance	
Decelerating check*	18° to 22° at 4,000 r.p.m.
	11° to 15° at 2,800 r.p.m.
	4° to 8° at 1,600 r.p.m.
	0° to 3° at 800 r.p.m.
No advance below	300 r.p.m.

* Crankshaft degrees and r.p.m.

SPARK PLUGS	
Make/type	Champion N-9 Y.
Gap	.025 in. (.65 mm.).
IGNITION COIL	
Make/type	A.C. Delco or Lucas 11C 12.
Primary resistance at 20°C (68°F)	1.43 to 1.58 ohms.
Consumption–ignition on	4.5 to 5 amps.
Ballast resistance	1.3 to 1.4 ohms.
CARBURETTER	
Make/type	S.U. HS4.
Type specification	FZX 1016.
Choke diameter	1½ in. (38 mm.).
Jet size	.090 in. (3 mm.).
Needle	ADD.
Piston spring	Red.
Initial jet adjustment	11 flats from bridge
Throttle to damper	.080 in. (2.0 mm.).
Fuel minimum octane setting	91.
EXHAUST EMISSION	
Exhaust gas content (carbon monoxide) at engine idle speed	5% ± ½%.

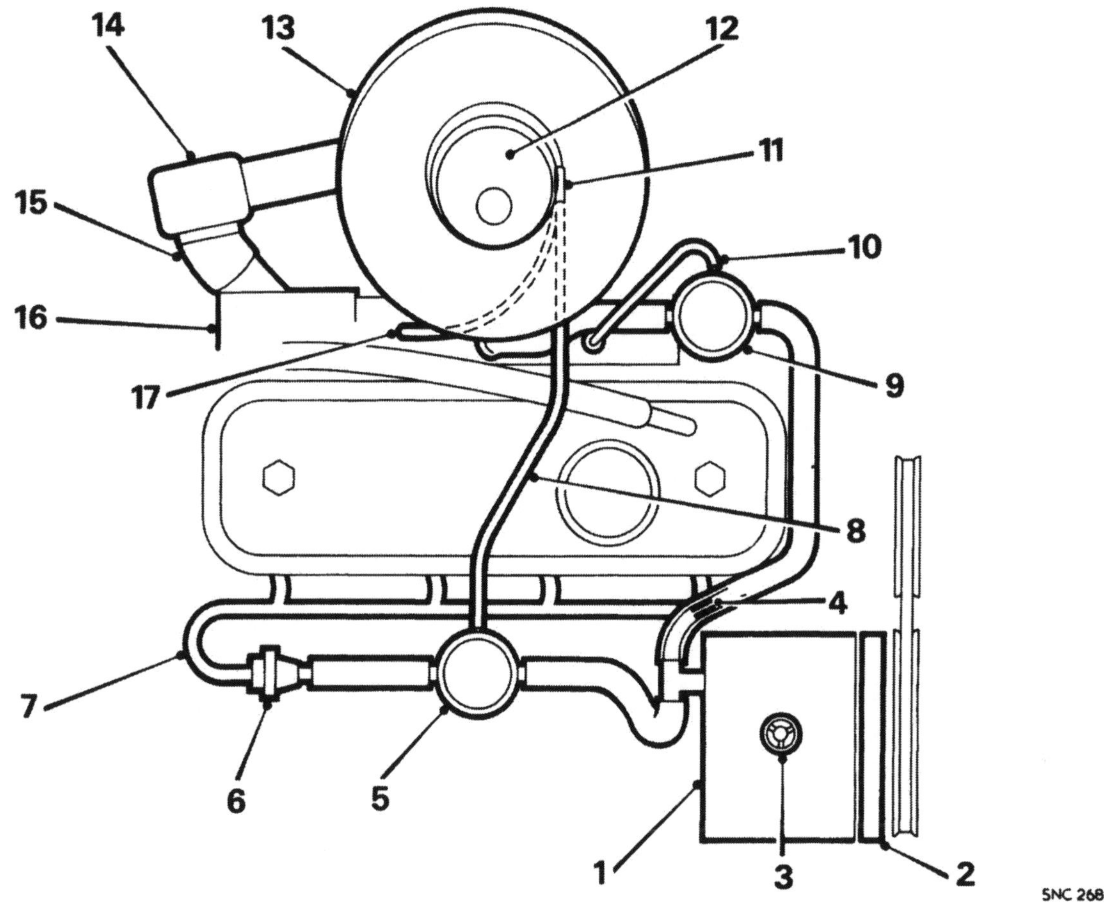

THE EMISSION CONTROL COMPONENTS

1. Air pump
2. Air pump filter
3. Air pump relief valve
4. Restrictor (gulp valve line)
5. Air diverter valve
6. Check valve
7. Air manifold
8. Air diverter valve signal pipe (from carburetter)
9. Gulp valve
10. Gulp valve signal pipe
11. Air diverter control valve
12. Carburetter
13. Carburetter air cleaner
14. Air temperature control device
15. Hot air duct
16. Shroud (hot air duct)
17. Manifold vacuum pipe to air diverter control valve

Section T.3

EMISSION CONTROL SYSTEMS

EXHAUST EMISSION

Air is pressure-fed from an air pump via an injection manifold to the cylinder head exhaust port of each cylinder. A check valve in the air delivery pipe prevents blow-back from high pressure exhaust gases. The pump also supplies air through a gulp valve to the inlet manifold to provide air during conditions of deceleration and engine over-run.

IMPORTANT: The efficient operation of the system is dependent on the engine being correctly tuned. The ignition and spark plug settings, valve clearances, and carburetter adjustments given for a particular engine (see **'ENGINE TUNING DATA'**) must be strictly adhered to at all times.

Air pump

The rotary vane type air pump is mounted on the front of the cylinder head and is belt driven from the water pump pulley. Provision is made for tensioning the belt.

Air is drawn into the pump through an extraction filter. A relief valve in the pump discharge port allows excessive air pressure at high engine speeds to discharge to the atmosphere.

Diverter valve

The vacuum operated diverter valve, fitted between the pump and the check valve, is actuated by a vacuum switch operated by the mixture control (choke) mechanism. During choke operation the air injection is cut off and air pressure is diverted to atmosphere.

Check valve

The check valve, fitted in the pump discharge line to the injection manifold, protects the pump from the back-flow of exhaust gases.

The valve shuts if the air pressure ceases while the engine is running; for example, if the pump drive belt should break.

Gulp valve

The gulp valve, fitted in the pump discharge line to the inlet manifold, controls the flow of air for leaning-off the rich air/fuel mixture present in the inlet manifold immediately following throttle closure after running at full throttle opening (i.e. engine over-run)

A sensing pipe connected between the inlet manifold and the gulp valve maintains manifold depression directly to the underside of the diaphragm and through a bleed hole to the upper side. Sudden increases in manifold depression which occur immediately following throttle closure act on the underside of the diaphragm which opens the valve and admits air to the inlet manifold. The bleed hole allows the differences in depression acting on the diaphragm to equalize and the valve closes.

A restrictor is fitted in the air pump discharge connection to the gulp valve, to prevent surging when the gulp valve is operating.

Carburetter

The carburetter is manufactured to a special exhaust emission control specification and is tuned to give optimum engine performance with maximum emission control.

The metering needle is arranged in such a manner that it is always lightly spring-loaded against the side of the jet to ensure consistency of fuel metering.

The throttle by-pass valve limits the inlet manifold depression and ensures that during conditions of engine over-run the air/fuel mixture enters the engine cylinders in a burnable condition consistent with low emission levels.

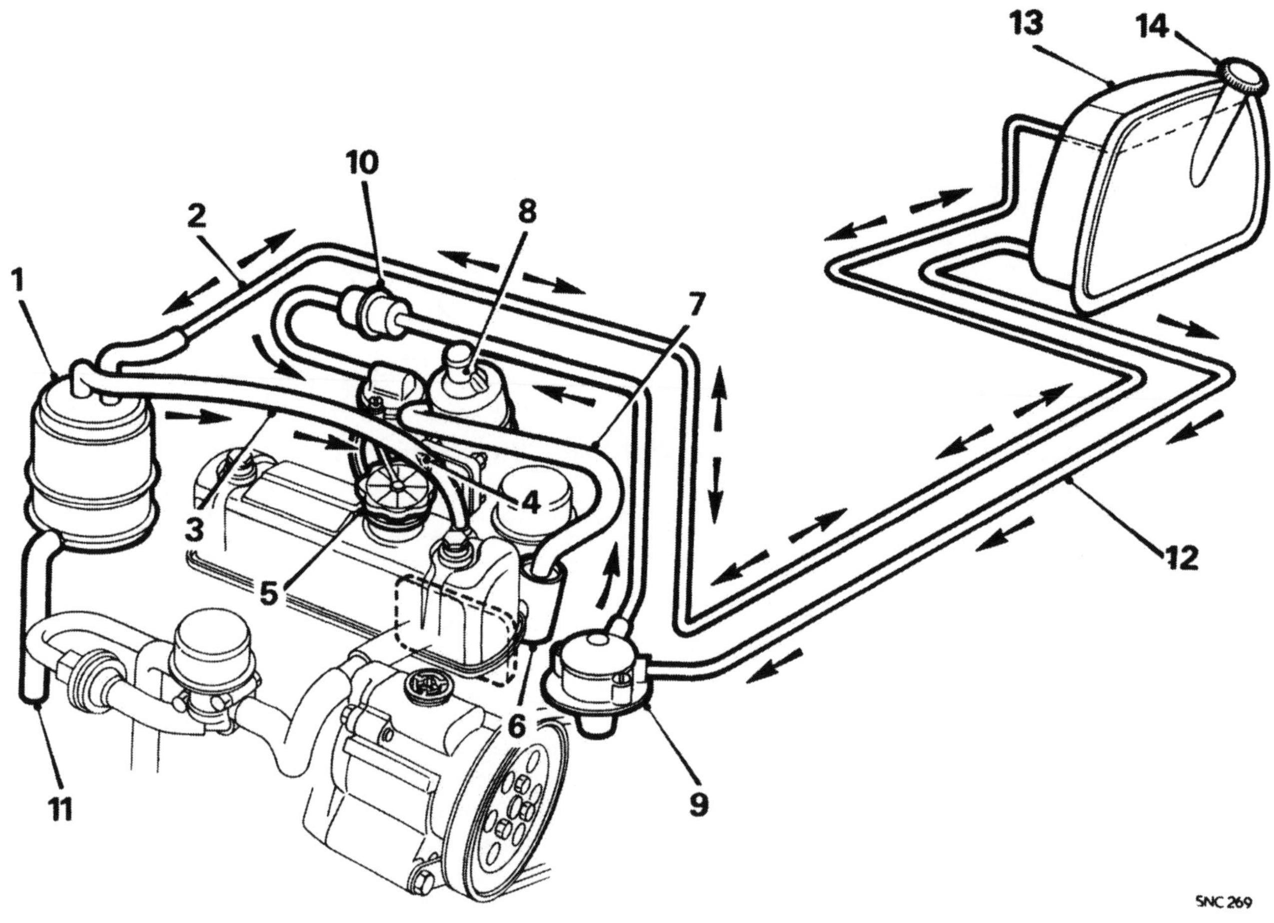

THE LAYOUT OF THE FUEL EVAPORATIVE LOSS CONTROL SYSTEM

1. Charcoal adsorption canister
2. Vapour lines
3. Purge line
4. Restricted connection
5. Sealed oil filler cap
6. Oil separator/flame trap (arrester)
7. Crankcase purge pipe
8. Carburetter
9. Fuel pump
10. Fuel filter
11. Air vent hose
12. Fuel pipe
13. Fuel tank
14. Sealed fuel filler cap

CRANKCASE EMISSION CONTROL

The engine crankcase breather outlet incorporates an oil separator flame-trap (arrester) attached to the cylinder block side cover which is connected by a hose to the controlled depression chamber between the piston and the throttle disc of the carburetter. Piston blow-by fumes are drawn into the depression chamber of the carburetter from the side cover and are joined by purged air from the charcoal canister of the fuel evaporative loss system. These fumes combine with the inlet charge for combustion in the normal way.

FUEL EVAPORATIVE LOSS CONTROL

To prevent air pollution by vapours from the fuel tank, the control equipment stores the vapour in a charcoal-filled canister while the engine is stopped and disposes of it via the engine crankcase emission control system when the engine is running.

The fuel tank venting is designed to ensure that no liquid fuel is carried to the storage canister with the vapours and that vapours are vented through the control system.

The capacity of the fuel tank is limited by the position of the filler tube which ensures sufficient volume is available after filling to accommodate fuel which would otherwise be displaced as a result of a high temperature rise.

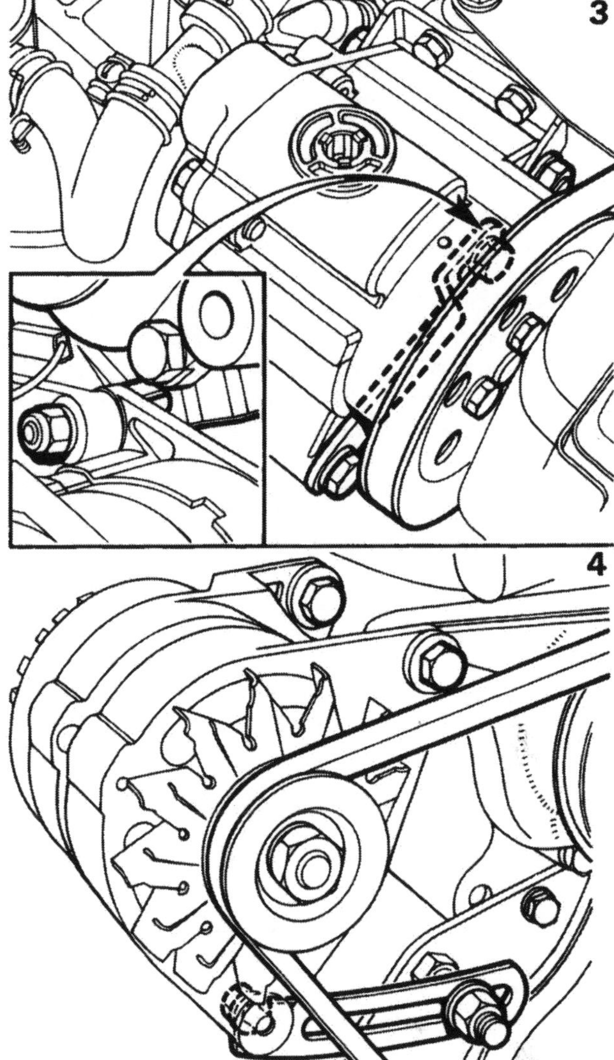

Section T.4

DRIVE BELTS

Removing

1. Remove the two screws securing the radiator to the top mounting bracket.
2. Slacken the top hose to radiator clip and pull the radiator against the valance.
3. Slacken the pump pivot and adjusting link bolts.
4. Slacken the alternator pivot and adjusting link bolts. Press the alternator against the engine.
5. PUMP: Remove the drive belt from the pulleys and feed the belt between the fan blades and the radiator cowling at the top as the blades are rotated. Pull the belt out from between the fan and radiator.
6. ALTERNATOR: Release the drive belt from the pulleys and remove the belt in the same way as for the pump belt.

Refitting

7. Fit the belts onto the pulleys.
8. Adjust the tension of the alternator drive belt and then the pump drive belt. Total deflection: ½ in under thumb pressure at mid-point between pulleys.
9. Reconnect radiator and top hose. Top up the cooling system.

Section T.5

AIR PUMP

Removing

1. Disconnect the outlet hoses from the pump adaptor.
2. Remove the No. 1 cylinder spark plug.
3. Slacken the pump adjusting bracket and the alternator pivot bolt securing the pump.
4. Remove the screw securing the adjusting bracket to the pump.
5. Remove the pump pivot bolt.
6. Release the drive belt and remove the pump assembly.
7. Remove the pump pulley.

Refitting

8. Reverse the procedure in 1 to 7.
9. Adjust the drive belt tension; total deflection of ½ in under thumb pressure at mid-point between pulleys.

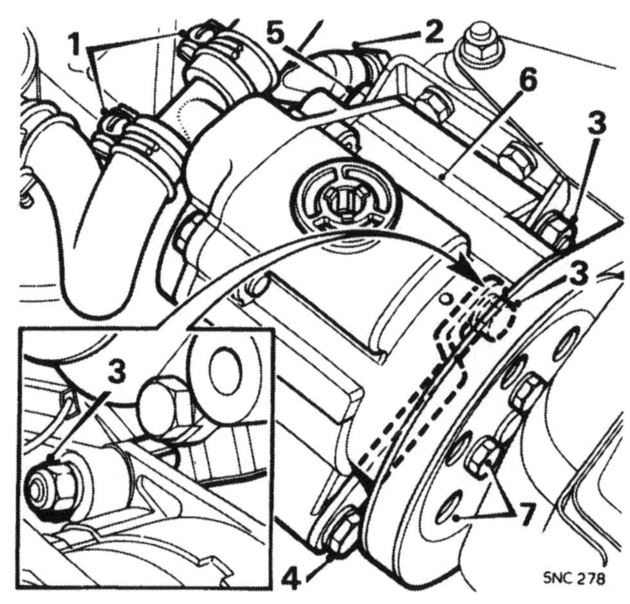

Section T.6

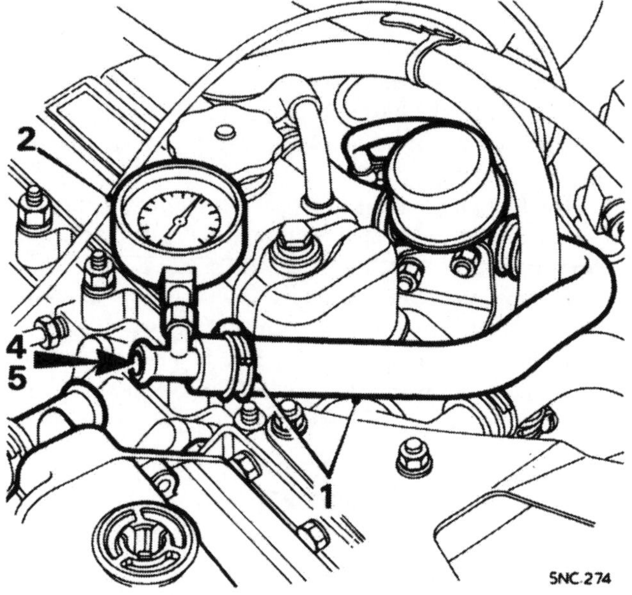

GULP VALVE

Testing

1. Slacken the clip and disconnect the gulp valve air supply hose at the air pump.
2. Connect a vacuum gauge, with a 'T' (tee) adaptor to the gulp valve hose.
3. Start the engine and run it at idle speed.
4. The engine must remain at idle during this test. Seal the end of the 'T' (tee) adaptor and check that the gauge reads zero for approximately 15 seconds. If a vacuum is registered, renew the gulp valve.
5. Seal the end of the 'T' (tee) adaptor and open the throttle rapidly; the gauge should register a vacuum. Unseal the adaptor. Repeat the test several times. If a vacuum is not registered, renew the gulp valve.
6. Reconnect the supply hose and tighten the hose clips securely.

Section T.7

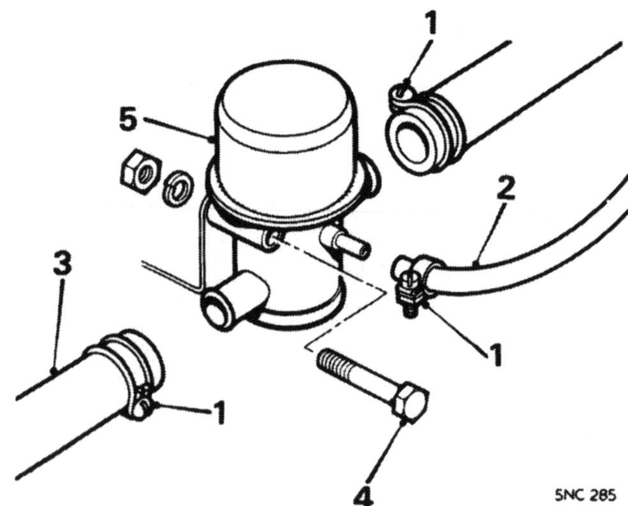

GULP VALVE

Removing

1. Slacken all the hose to valve clips.
2. Pull the vacuum hose from the valve adaptor.
3. Pull the pump hose from the valve.
4. Remove the two bolts securing the valve to the bracket.
5. Pull the gulp valve from the manifold hose.

Refitting

6. Reverse the procedure in 1 to 5.

Section T.8

DIVERTER VALVE

Checking

1. Slacken the clip securing the hose to the check valve.
2. Remove the two bolts securing the valve to the bracket.
3. Pull the diverter valve and hose from the check valve.
4. Start the engine and allow it to idle. Air pressure should be felt at the hose end.
5. Operate the mixture control (choke); the air supply should be cut off completely. If air pressure is felt at the hose, renew the diverter valve.

Removing

6. Slacken all the hose to valve clips.
7. Pull the vacuum hose from the valve adaptor.
8. Pull the pump hose from the valve.
9. Remove the two bolts securing the valve to the bracket.
10. Pull the valve from the check valve hose.
11. Remove the air vent hose from the diverter valve.

Refitting

12. Reverse the procedure in 6 to 11.

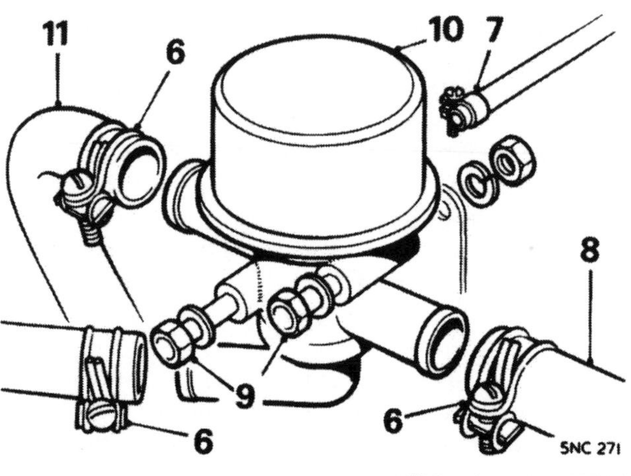

Section T.9

CHECK VALVE

Removing

1. Release the clip securing the hose to the check valve. Move the clip along the hose and free the hose on the valve adaptor.
2. Hold the air manifold union to prevent it twisting and unscrew the check valve.
3. Pull the check valve from the hose.

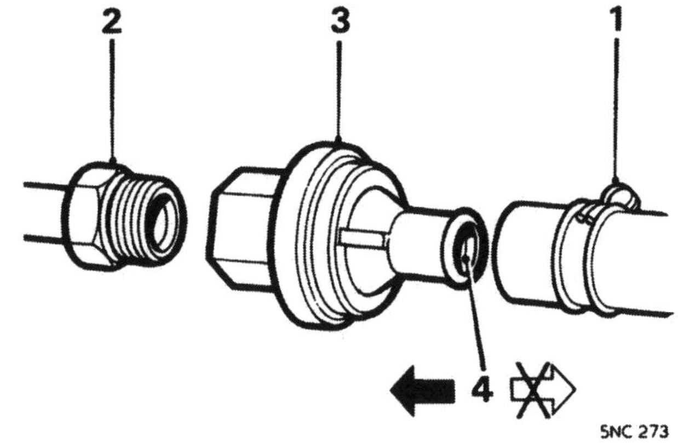

Testing

4. Using the mouth; blow into the valve from each end in turn. Air should only pass through the valve from the air supply end. If air passes through from the air manifold end, renew the check valve.
   CAUTION: DO NOT APPLY AIR LINE PRESSURE TO THE VALVE.

Refitting

5. Reverse the procedure in 1 to 3.

Section T.10

AIR MANIFOLD

Removing

1. Release the clip securing the hose to the check valve and move the clip along the hose.
2. Disconnect the lead from No. 1 spark plug.
3. Unscrew the four unions from the cylinder head, pull the check valve from the hose and remove the air manifold assembly.
4. Hold the air manifold union and unscrew the check valve.

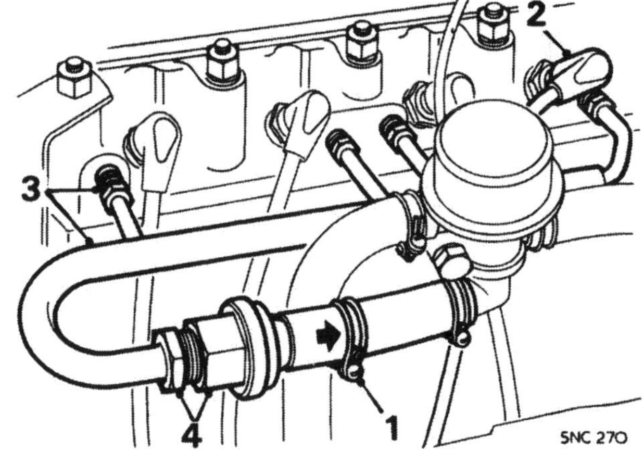

Refitting

5. Reverse the procedure in 1 to 4.

Section T.11

AIR TEMPERATURE CONTROL VALVE

Checking

1. Note the position of the valve plate (when the engine is cold or warm), depress the plate and release it. The plate should return to its original position.
2. Inspect the valve seal for signs of deterioration.

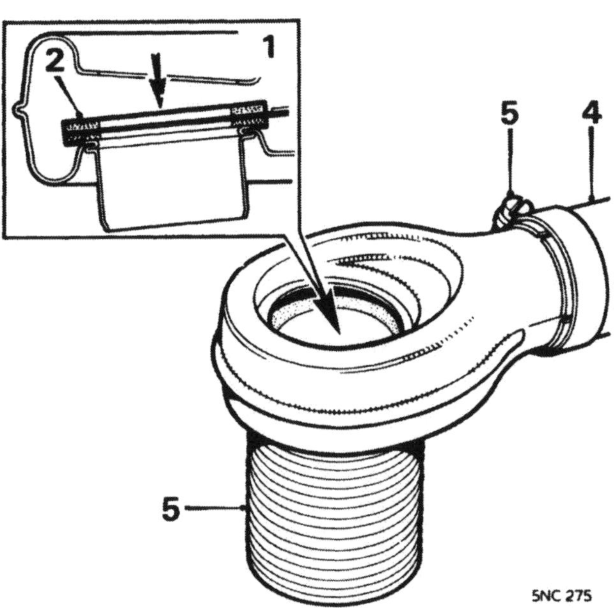

Removing

3. Slacken the clip securing the control valve adaptor to the air cleaner.
4. Pull the control valve assembly from the air cleaner and hot air box tube.
5. Remove the adaptor from the control valve.

Refitting

6. Reverse the procedure in 1 to 5; ensure the valve is aligned correctly.

Section T.12
THROTTLE DAMPER

NOTE: The engine idle speed must be set before checking and adjusting.

Checking
1. Remove the air cleaner and air temperature control valve assembly.
2. Insert a 0.080 in (2.03 mm) feeler gauge between the lever pad and the damper plunger.
3. Depress the lever, the idle adjusting screw should contact and the damper plunger should be fully depressed.

Adjusting
4. Slacken the damper lever clamp.
5. Insert a 0.080 in (2.03 mm) feeler gauge between the lever pad and the damper plunger.
6. Depress the lever and hold the plunger at the bottom of its stroke. Ensure the throttle is closed and that a clearance exists between the lever clamp and the carburetter body.
7. Tighten the lever clamp nut. Check the action of the throttle linkage.
8. Refit the air cleaner and air temperature control valve assembly.

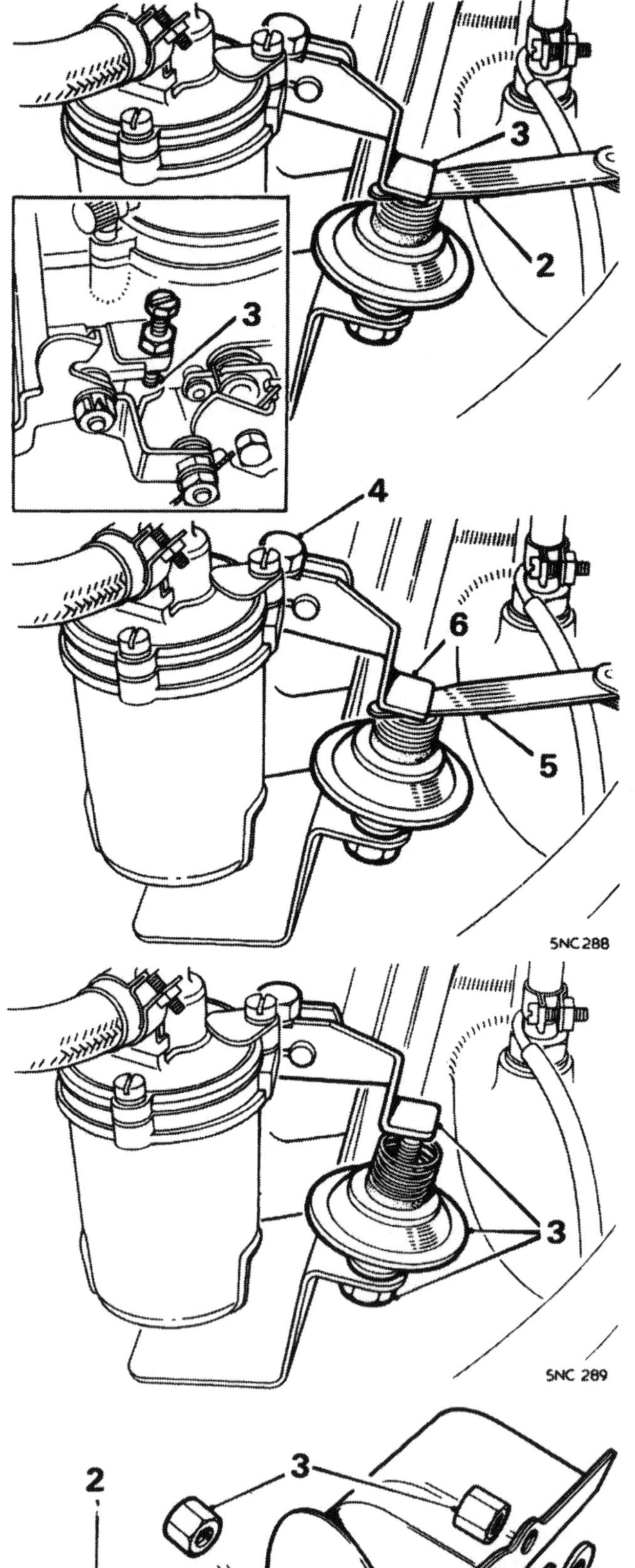

Section T.13
THROTTLE DAMPER

Removing
1. Remove the air cleaner and air temperature control valve assembly.
2. Remove the hot air duct, see Section T.14.
3. Release the nut, hold the throttle open and unscrew the throttle damper.

Refitting
4. Fit the damper and adjust the lever, see Section T.12.
5. Refit the hot air duct, see Section T.14.
6. Refit the air cleaner and air temperature control valve.

Section T.14
HOT AIR DUCT

Removing
1. Remove the air temperature control valve assembly.
2. Remove the flexible tube from the hot air duct.
3. Remove the two nuts securing the duct to the manifold.
4. Extract the hot air duct.

Refitting
5. Ensure the two plain washers are on the outside stud.
6. Ensure the large washer bridging the manifold flanges is in place.
7. Reverse the procedure in 1 to 4.

Section T.15

FUEL LINE FILTER

Removing

1. Slacken the clip and disconnect the inlet hose.
2. Slacken the clip and pull the fuel filter from the outlet hose.

Refitting

3. Ensure the filter is fitted with the flow arrow towards the carburetter.
   Alternative filter: Inlet hose to connector marked 'IN'.

Section T.16

ADSORPTION CANISTER

Removing

1. Disconnect the air vent hose from the bottom of the canister.
2. Disconnect the vapour and purge hoses from the top of the canister.
3. Remove the retaining screw, open the the bracket sufficiently to withdraw the canister.

Refitting

4. Reverse the procedure in 1 to 3.
5. Disconnect the purge hose from the rocker cover elbow.
6. Examine the restrictor orifice, clear any dirt or deposits using a length of soft wire.
7. Reconnect the purge hose.

Section T.17

CARBURETTER

Tuning

Adjustments should only be undertaken if an accurate tachometer, and exhaust gas analyser (CO meter) are available for use.

The tuning of the carburetter is confined to topping-up the damper, setting idle and fast idle speeds, mixture strength (CO percentage), and adjusting the throttle damper.

The efficient operation of the engine and exhaust emission equipment depends not only on correct carburetter settings but is also affected by:

Ignition timing
Spark plug condition
Contact breaker condition (dwell angle)
Valve rocker clearances
Presence of air leaks in the induction system

Also; check for good seals at oil filler cap, rocker cover to cylinder head, engine oil dipstick to block.

Refer to **'ENGINE TUNING DATA'** or to the **'Vehicle Emission Control Information'** label attached to the vehicle.

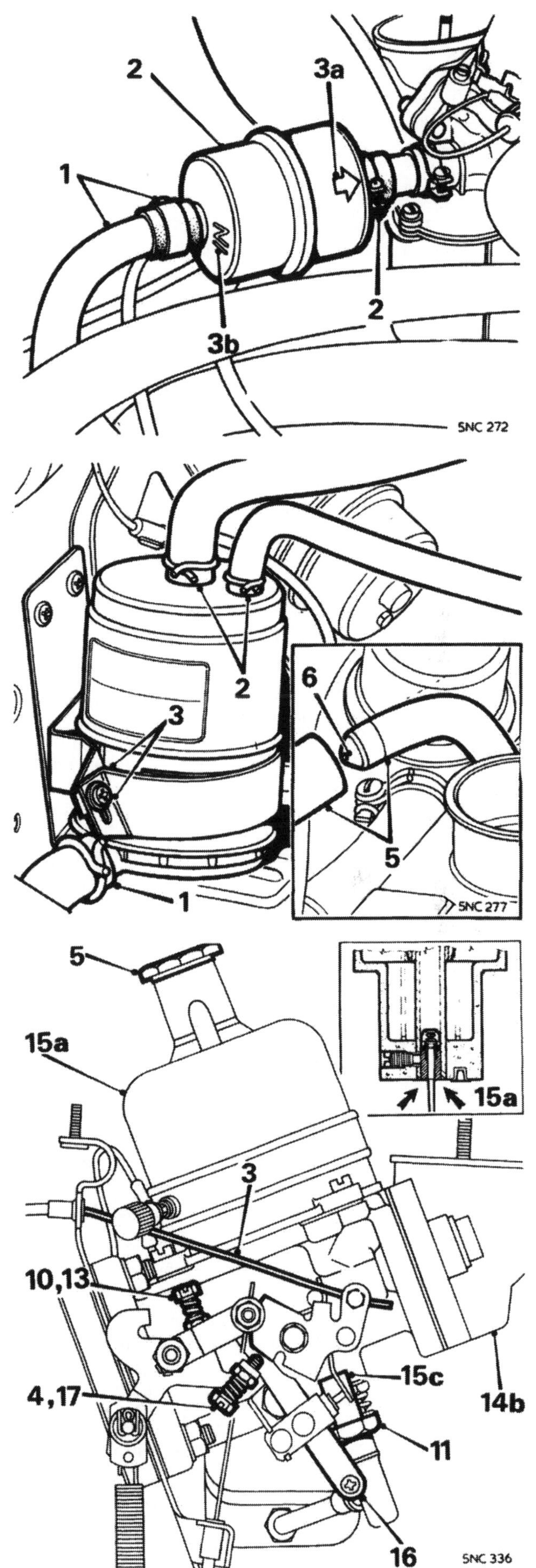

1. Remove the air cleaner assembly.
2. Check that the throttle functions correctly.
3. Ensure the mixture control (choke) is fully returned, that the cable has $\frac{1}{16}$ in free movement before it starts to pull on the lever.
4. The fast idle screw must be well clear of the cam, unscrew if necessary.
5. Top up the carburetter piston damper.
6. Start the engine and run it at fast idle speed until it attains normal running temperature, and then drive the vehicle for five minutes on the road.
7. Connect a tachometer.
8. Disconnect the diverter valve hose at the pump and plug the hose.
   DO NOT restrict the pump outlet.
9. Increase the engine speed to 2,500 r.p.m. for 30 seconds.

NOTE: Tuning must commence immediately the car reaches normal running temperature. If delay prevents the adjustment being complete within three minutes, increase the engine speed to 2,500 r.p.m. for 30 seconds and then continue tuning. Repeat this clearing procedure at three minute intervals until tuning is completed.

10. Set the engine idle speed by turning the throttle adjusting screw, see **'ENGINE TUNING DATA'**.
11. Connect an exhaust gas analyser. In accordance with the manufacturer's instructions check the percentage CO at idle. If the reading falls outside the limits (see **'ENGINE TUNING DATA'**) turn the jet adjusting nut by the **minimum** amount to bring the reading within the limits.
    NOTE: If adjustment cannot be obtained within the limits of the restrictor see item 15.
12. Unplug and reconnect the diverter valve hose to the pump.
13. Run the engine at 2,500 r.p.m. for 30 seconds and then reset the idle speed.
14. Adjust the throttle damper, see Section T.12.
15. If a smooth idle at the correct speed and CO reading is not obtainable and all other engine adjustments are correct, check the needle and piston as follows and then readjust:
    a. Remove the suction chamber and piston assembly. Check that the correct needle is fitted. Refit, ensure the needle guide mark is towards the piston transfer ports and the shoulder of the needle **must be flush** with the face of the piston. Refit the suction chamber assembly. Top up the damper with oil.
    b Raise the piston slowly up and down through its full travel using a finger, remove the intake elbow if necessary.
    The piston movement must be free and smooth.
    c. Repeat operations 9 to 11. If the CO reading is still outside the limits, bend the restrictor tab clear of the jet adjusting nut and turn the nut by the minimum amount necessary to bring the CO reading within the limits.
    Centralize the restrictor and bend the tab down against the nut.
    e. Carry out operations 13 to 15.

FAST IDLE

16. Pull out the mixture control knob until the jet linkage is just about to move the carburetter jet, and lock the control.
17. Turn the fast idle adjusting screw to give the correct fast idle speed, see **'ENGINE TUNING DATA'**.
18. Unlock and return the mixture control fully. Stop the engine.
19. Refit the air cleaner assembly.

Section T.18

CYLINDER HEAD ASSEMBLY

Removing

1. Drain the cooling system and refit the cylinder block drain plug.
2. Remove the air cleaner and air temperature control valve assembly.
3. Remove the bolts securing the diverter valve to the bracket.
4. Disconnect the hose at the check valve, the vacuum hose from the diverter valve and the pump hose from the gulp valve.
5. Disconnect the leads from the spark plugs.
6. Remove the No. 1 spark plug.
7. Slacken the bolt, alternator pivot and air pump adjusting link.
8. Remove the screw securing the adjusting bracket to the air pump.
9. Remove the air pump pivot bolt, release the drive belt and remove the air pump and diverter valve assembly.
10. Slacken the top hose clips, remove the two screws securing the radiator to the top mounting bracket and remove the top hose.
11. Remove the rocker cover nuts. Position the heater hoses clear.
12. Pull the purge pipe from the rocker cover pipe and remove the rocker cover and gasket.
13. Release the heater water control valve from the cylinder head and position it clear.
14. Disconnect the lead from the manifold heater.
15. Remove the two nuts securing the carburetter to the manifold. Withdraw the carburetter assembly, induction heater and mounting bracket from the studs and position them clear.
16. Remove the hot air duct.
17. Remove the exhaust manifold pipe clamp.
18. Progressively slacken the cylinder head and rocker shaft nuts in the reverse order of the tightening sequence.
19. Remove the rocker assembly.
20. Remove the push-rods, **keeping them in their installed order.**
21. Remove the coil and position it clear.
22. Slacken the clip securing the by-pass hose to the cylinder head.
23. Remove the four remaining nuts and lift the cylinder head assembly squarely off the studs. Lift the gasket from the studs.
    NOTE: If the head will not release from the gasket, tap each side of the head with a soft faced mallet.

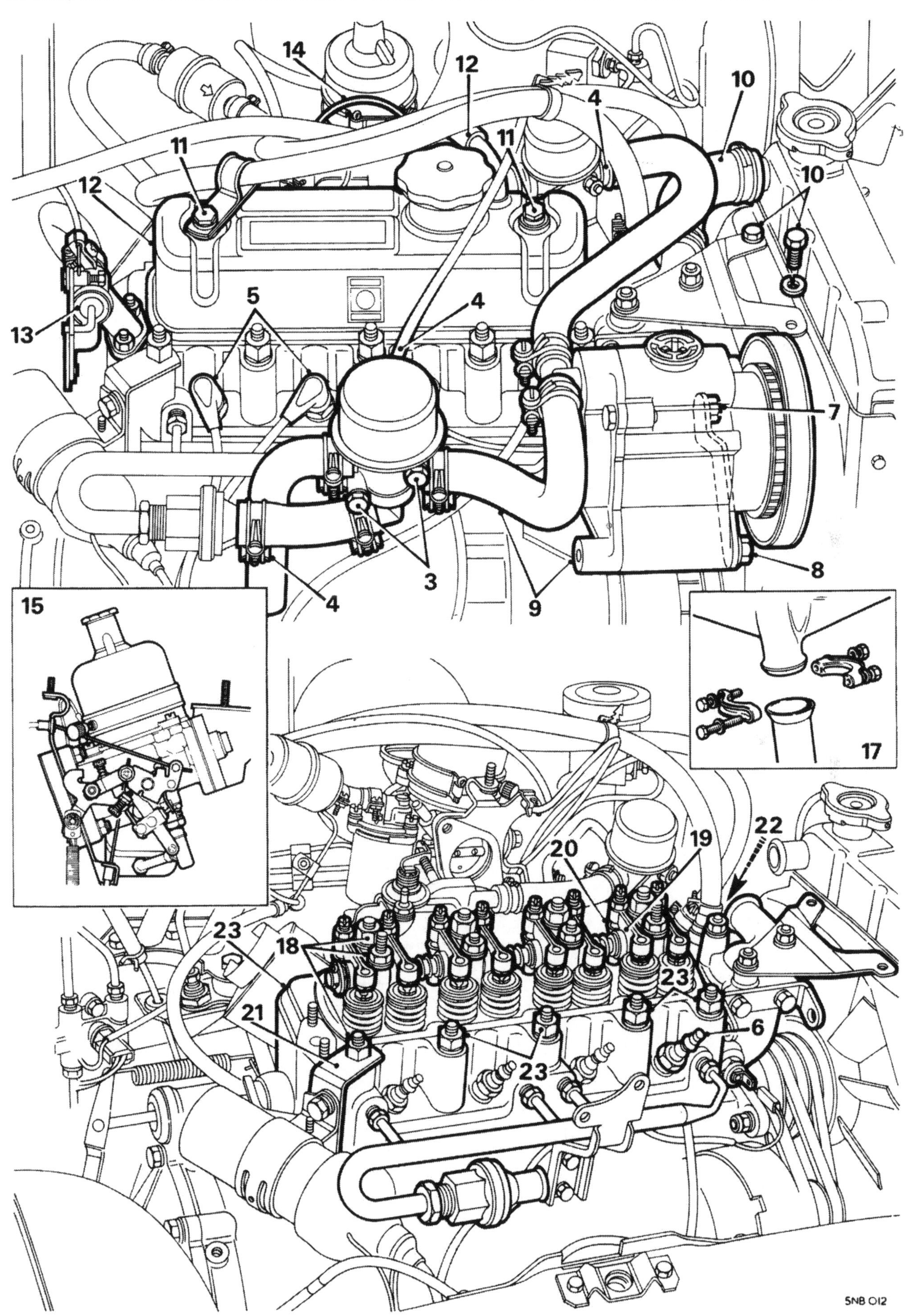
14
12
10
4
11
11
12
10
13
5
4
7
3
4
9
8
15
17
22
19
20
23
18
23
21
6
23
5NB 012

WIRING DIAGRAM–1975 model year on

4NB 019A

Refitting

24. Reverse the procedure in 1 to 23, noting:
    a. Thoroughly clean the joint faces of the cylinder block and head.
    b. Fit a new gasket dry, with the end marked 'FRONT' to the water pump and the face marked 'TOP' upwards.
    c. Progressively tighten the cylinder head and rocker bracket nuts in sequence illustrated.

Cylinder head nuts	40 lbf ft	5.5 kg m
Rocker bracket nuts	25 lbf ft	3.5 kg m

    d. Check the carburetter throttle damper, see Section T.12.
    e. Check and adjust the valve rocker clearances, see **'MAINTENANCE'**.
    f. Refill the cooling system.
    g. Check and adjust the carburetter setting, see Section T.17.
    h. Adjust the tension of the drive belts, see Section T.4.

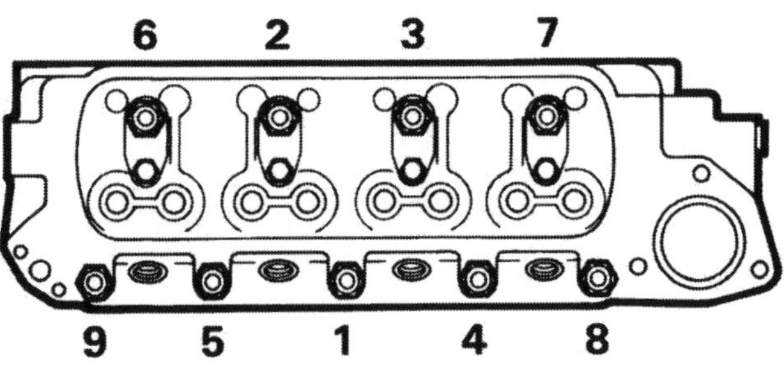

KEY TO THE WIRING DIAGRAM

1. Alternator
3. Battery
4. Starter solenoid
5. Starter motor
6. Lighting switch
7. Headlamp dip switch
8. R.H. headlamp
9. L.H. headlamp
10. High-beam warning lamp
11. R.H. parking lamp
12. L.H. parking lamp
14. Panel lamps
15. Number-plate illumination lamp
16. R.H. stop and tail lamp
17. L.H. stop and tail lamp
18. Stop lamp switch
19. Fuse unit
20. Interior lamp
21. R.H. door switch light and buzzer
22. L.H. door switch light and buzzer
23. Horn
24. Horn-push
25. Flasher unit
26. Direction indicator switch
27. Direction indicator warning lamp
28. R.H. front direction indicator lamp
29. L.H. front direction indicator lamp
30. R.H. rear direction indicator lamp
31. L.H. rear direction indicator lamp
32. Heater motor switch
33. Heater motor
34. Fuel gauge
35. Fuel gauge tank unit
36. Windscreen wiper switch
37. Windscreen wiper motor
38. Ignition/starter switch
39. Ignition coil
40. Distributor
44. Ignition warning lamp
45. Headlamp flasher switch
46. Coolant temperature gauge
47. Coolant temperature transmitter
49. Reverse lamp switch
50. Reverse lamp
59. Interior light switch
60. Radio (when fitted)
64. Bi-metal instrument voltage stabilizer
67. Line fuse
77. Windscreen washer motor
78. Windscreen washer switch
82. Switch illumination lamp
83. Induction heater and thermostat
84. Suction chamber heater
115. Heated rear window demist switch
116. Heated rear window demist unit
150. Heated rear window warning light
153. Hazard warning switch
154. Hazard warning flasher unit
159. Brake failure warning lamp and test switch
160. Brake pressure differential switch
164. Ballast resistor
169. Buzzer–door switch
170. R.H. front side-marker lamp
171. L.H. front side-marker lamp
172. R.H. rear side-marker lamp
173. L.H. rear side-marker lamp
198. Driver's seat belt switch
199. Passenger seat belt switch
200. Passenger's seat switch
201. Seat belt warning gearbox switch
202. Seat belt warning lamp
203. Seat belt warning diode
210. Panel light rheostat
211. Heater control illumination

CABLE COLOUR CODE

B. Black	N. Brown	S. Slate
G. Green	O. Orange	U. Blue
K. Pink	P. Purple	W. White
L.G. Light Green	R. Red	Y. Yellow

When a cable has two colour code letters the first denotes the main colour and the second denotes the tracer colour.

Published by Brooklands Books Ltd., PO Box 146,
Cobham, Surrey KT11 1LG, England
Phone: +44 (0) 1932 865051
e-mail: info@brooklands-books.com web-site: www.brooklands-books.com

Part No. AKD 4935 (9th Edition)

AUSTRALIAN SUPPLEMENT

MANUAL ARRANGEMENT

The Manual and Supplement is divided into Sections, and each Section carries a reference letter that identifies the Section with an assembly or a major component.

The contents page at the front of the manual includes a Section Index which list the reference letters for each Section.

Sections identified by a small letter (a, h, k, etc.) contain supplementary information for vehicles manufactured in Australia.

Taking the Fuel System as an example of this arrangement, it will be seen that it is divided into D, Da, Db, Dc, and d. The later two being found in the Supplement.

Section D is the basic text.
Section Da is supplementary information for automatic transmission vehicles.
Section Db is supplementary information for vehicles with negative earth electrical systems.
Section Dc is supplementary information for vehicles fitted with engine emission control equipment.
Section d is supplementary information for vehicles manufactured in Australia.

Complete vehicle specifications and data are grouped in two sections. One at the front of the Manual and the other at the front of the Supplement.

IMPORTANT 

On cars fitted with exhaust emission control equipment (Exhaust Port Air Injection) service operations and adjustments showing this symbol must be followed by an exhaust emission check.

Servicing and adjusting engine emission control equipment must be carried out in accordance with the instructions given in the appropriate sections.

AUSTRALIAN SUPPLEMENT

Identification Plate

The car identification will be found stamped on a plate secured to various panels within the engine compartment such as, the Right hand or Left hand side of the bulkhead, on top of the radiator cowl or on the bonnet locking platform.

This plate is stamped with a combination of letters representing in code the name and type of vehicle, the car or serial number, the engine number and the paint colour of the vehicle.

Commercial vehicles have a similar identification plate which includes the Gross Vehicle Weight (G.V.W.).

The identification plate was deleted from some Saloon Models in June 1969, the car identification code being stamped on the top of the engine radiator cowl. This coding can be located by lifting the rubber radiator surround.

On these cars the paint colour name is shown on a pressure sensitive label affixed to the Right hand side of the bulkhead above the master cylinder.

Engine Prefix and Number

The engine number prefix comprises a series of numbers and letters presenting in code details relating to engine cubic capacity, type of engine, the country of manufacture, type of transmission and ancillaries, and compression ratio. The engine number follows this prefix.

The prefix and engine number are stamped directly onto the front Left hand side of the cylinder block, just below the cylinder head gasket.

Compliance Plate

Some countries have legislated that a compliance plate be fitted to every type of vehicle. This plate is coded with the various Motor Vehicle Safety Design Standards, together with the vehicle identification code and the date the vehicle was manufactured.

This plate is secured to the flitch plate on the Right hand side of the engine compartment bulkhead.

On vehicles supplied to countries whose regulations require Exhaust Emission Control Equipment, the compliance plate is secured to the dash panel on the driver's side of the vehicle and a pressure sensitive label is affixed to the Right hand valance in the engine compartment. This label contains technical specifications for tuning to meet the emission control regulations.

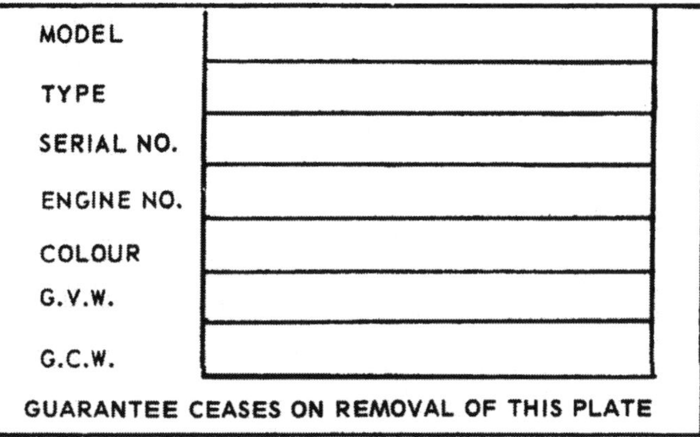

MODEL
TYPE
SERIAL NO.
ENGINE NO.
COLOUR
G.V.W.
G.C.W.
GUARANTEE CEASES ON REMOVAL OF THIS PLATE

A typical identification plate.

Automatic Transmission Number

This number is located on a small plate secured to the final drive housing as illustrated below.

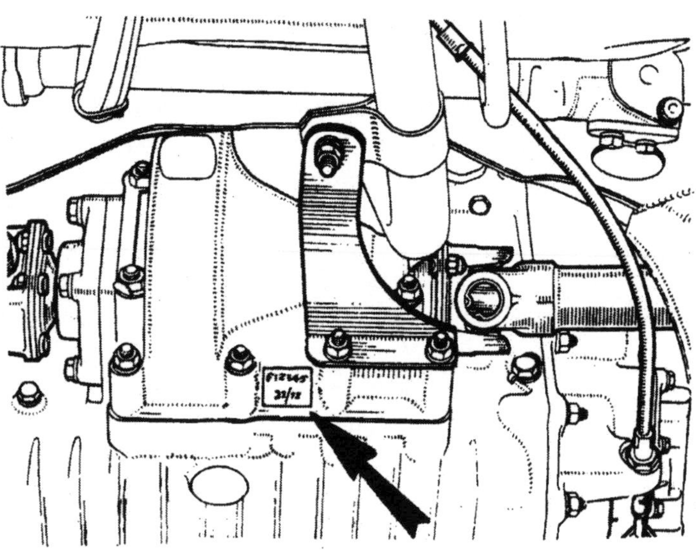

Ordering Replacement Parts

When ordering replacement parts it is essential to quote the appropriate prefix together with the car, vehicle, engine or automatic transmission numbers.

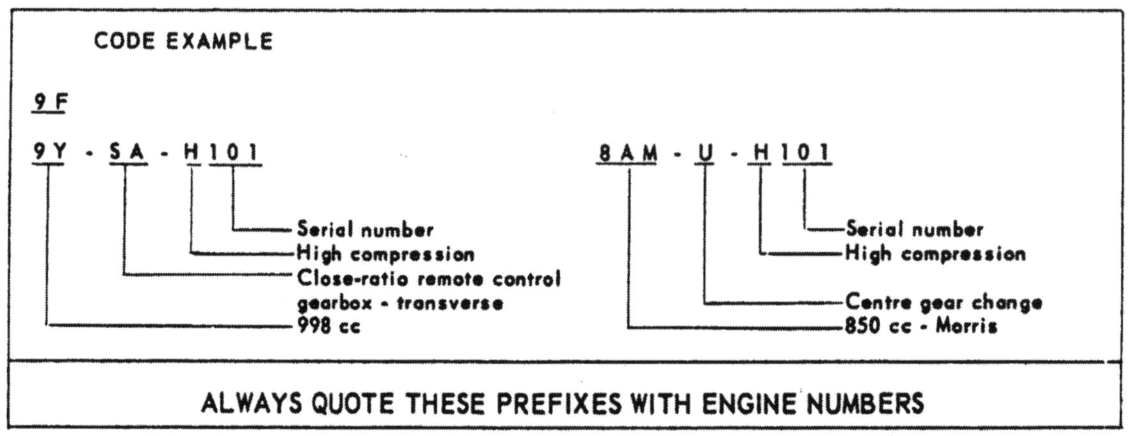

CONTENTS

GENERAL DATA

The following figures are taken from the latest manufacturing specifications and drawings available at the time of publication, but the manufacturers, in accordance with their policy of constant product improvement, reserve the right to vary the specifications contained in this manual without notice. Where tolerances are not shown, the figure quoted must be regarded as nominal.

	848 cc. 850 Saloon and Van	998 cc. Mini Minor, Deluxe, Mini Matic, Van, Moke, BMC Moke and Cooper	997 c.c. Cooper	1098 cc. Mini 1100 Saloons and Vans, BMC Moke, Clubman Saloon	1275 cc. Cooper 'S', Moke, Clubman 'G.T.'
ENGINE					
Type symbol	8AM and 8Y Saloon and Van	9YE — Saloon and Van, 9YA — Deluxe, 9AN—99H—Mini Matic, 9FA and 9Y — Cooper, 9YB — Moke, 9YH — BMC Moke.	9F	10Y 10YJ—Std. Saloon & Van 10YC and 10YM — Saloon 10YF — BMC Moke 10YN — Mini K 1000—1100 Saloon & Van 1001 — Clubman Saloon	9F/SA/Y Cooper 'S' 1200 — Clubman G.T. 12Y — G.T. or Moke 1204 Moke
Number of cylinders and valve operation	4 cylinder OHV pushrod operated.	= = =	= = =	= = =	= = =
Bore	2.478" (62.94 mm)	2.543" (64.588 mm)	2.458" (62.43 mm)	2.543" (64.588 mm)	2.780" (70.60 mm)
Stroke	2.687" (68.26 mm)	3.00" (76.20 mm)	3.20" (81.33 mm)	3.296" (83.72 mm)	3.20" (81.33 mm)
Capacity	51.7 cu. in. (848 cc)	60.96 cu in (998 cc)	60.87 cu. in. (997 cc)	67 cu in (1098 cc)	77.9 cu. in. (1275 cc)
Firing order	.. 3. 4. 2.	= = =	= = =	= = =	= = =
Compression ratio — high compression	8.3 : 1	8.3 : 1, 9.0 : 1 Cooper & Mini Matic	9.0 : 1	8.5 : 1	9.75 : 1 Cooper 'S' and Clubman G.T.
— low compression	7.8 : 1	7.8 : 1 Cooper, 7.6 : 1 Moke	8.3 : 1	7.5 : 1	8.8 : 1 Moke
Capacity of combustion chambers	24.5 cc	24.5 cc, 22.4 cc Mini Matic, 28.3 c.c. Cooper	26.1 cc.	1.59 cu. in. (26.1 c.c.)	1.306 cu. in. (21.4 cc)
Torque	44 lb. ft. (6.08 kg.m) @ 2900 r.p.m.	52 lb. ft. (7.27 kg. m) @ 2700 r.p.m. 57 lb. ft. (7.88 kg. m) @ 3000 r.p.m. H.C. Cooper 56 lb. ft. (7.74 kg. m) @ 2900 r.p.m. L.C. Cooper	54 lb. ft. (7.65 kg.m) @ 3600 r.p.m. (H.C.) 53 lb. ft. (7.32 kg.m) @ 3500 r.p.m. (L.C.)	60 lb. ft. (8.29 kg.m) @ 2500 r.p.m.	79 lb. ft. (10.9 kg.m) @ 3000 r.p.m. Cooper 'S' and Clubman G.T. 69 lb. ft. (9.6 kg.m) @ 2500 r.p.m. Moke
Brake horse power	34 @ 5500 r.p.m.	40 & 42 Mini Matic @ 5250 r.p.m. 55 @ 5800 r.p.m. Cooper H.C. 52 @ 6100 r.p.m. Cooper L.C.	55 @ 6000 r.p.m. (H.C.) 52 @ 6000 r.p.m. (L.C.)	50 @ 5100 r.p.m.	78 @ 5800 r.p.m. Cooper 'S' and Clubman G.T. 65 @ 5250 r.p.m. Moke
R.A.C. rating	9.8 h.p.	10.3 h.p.	9.64 h.p.	10.3 h.p.	12.4 h.p.
Engine idle speed (approx.)	500 r.p.m.	500 r.p.m. (650 r.p.m. in Neutral — Mini Matic)	500 r.p.m.	= = =	= = =
Oversize bore: first	+ .010" (0.254 mm)	+ .010" (.254 mm)	+ .010" (0.254 mm)	+ .010" (.254 mm)	+ .010" (.254 mm)
maximum	+ .040" (1.016 mm)	+ .020" (.508 mm)	+ .040" (1.016 mm)	+ .020" (.508 mm)	+ .020" (.508 mm)

= = = denotes common to model listed in preceding column.

	848 cc 850 Saloon and Van	998 cc Mini Minor, Deluxe, Mini Matic, Van, Moke, BMC Moke and Cooper	997 cc Cooper	1098 cc Mini 1100 Saloons & Vans BMC Moke Clubman Saloon	1275 cc Cooper 'S' Moke Clubman G.T.
CRANKSHAFT					
Main journal diameter	1.750" — 1.751" (44.6 — 44.7 mm)	===	===	1.7505" — 1.751" (44.46 — 44.47 mm.)	2.0005" — 2.0010" (50.81 — 50.82 mm)
Minimum regrind diameter	1.7105" — 1.711" (43.45 — 43.46 mm)	===	===	1.7105" — 1.711" (43.45 — 43.46 mm)	1.9805" — 1.9810" (50.30 — 50.31 mm)
Crankpin journal diameter	1.6254" — 1.6259" (41.28 — 41.29 mm)	===	===	1.6254" — 1.6259" (41.28 — 41.29 mm)	===
Crankpin minimum regrind diameter	1.5854" — 1.5859" (40.27 — 40.28 mm)	===	===	1.5854" — 1.5859" (40.27 — 40.28 mm)	===
MAIN BEARINGS: Shell type all models.					
Material	Steel backed — white metal	Steel backed — copper lead — thin wall	===	===	===
Length	1.187" (30.16 mm)	1.0625" (26.99 mm)	===	1:0625" (27 mm)	1.00" (25.40 mm)
End clearance	.002" — .003" (:051 — .076 mm)	===	===	===	===
Running clearance	.0005" — .002" (.013 — .051 mm)	.001" — .0027" (.025 — .069 mm)	===	===	===
BIG END BEARINGS: Common to all models.	Material: Steel backed copper-lead; lead-bronze or aluminium-tin; thin wall. Side clearance: .008" — .012" (.203 — .305 mm). Diametral clearance: .001" — .0025" (.025 — .063 mm).				
PISTONS					
Ref. (1) Early models. To engine numbers: 9YA/Ta/H 17754, 9YB/U/H 1873, 9FA/Sa/H 2486, 9Y/SB/H 1552.	Split skirt	Solid skirt — 4 ring piston	===	Solid skirt — 3 ring piston	===
Ref. (2) Late models. From engine numbers: 9YA/Ta/H 17755, 9YB/U/H 1874, 9YE/U/H 1001, 9YH/U/H 1001 onward.		Solid skirt — 3 ring piston (Australian design)			
Clearance: bottom skirt	.0006" — .0012" (.015 — .030 mm)		.0016" — .0022" (.048 — .063 mm)		.0019" — .0025" (.048 — .063 mm)
Early models, refer (1)		.0006" — .0012" (.015 — .030 mm)			
Late models, refer (2)		.0005" — .0012" (.013 — .030 mm)			
Oversizes	.010" — .020" — .030" — .040" (.254 — .508 — .762 — 1.016 mm)	.010" — .020" (.254 — .508 mm)	.010" — .020" — .030" — .040" (.254 — .508 — .762 — 1.016 mm)	.010" — .020" (.254 — .508 mm)	.010" — .020" (.254 — .508 mm)
PISTON RINGS					
Compression — top Early models — ref. (1) piston section	Plain	Plain chrome faced	===	Torsional Molybdenum	===
Late models — ref. (2) piston section		Chrome torsional			
Compression — second and third Early models — ref. (1) — 2nd and 3rd	Tapered	===	===		Tapered
Late models — ref. (2) — 2nd only		Ferrox torsion		Plain Multoseal	

PISTON RINGS (continued)					
Compression — width	.069" — .070" (1.75 — 1.78 mm)		.0615" — .0625" (1.583 — 1.588 mm)	Top: .0620" — .0625" (1.574 — 1.588 mm) 2nd: .0780" — .0775" (1.981 — 1.963 mm)	.0459" — .0469" (1.16 — 1.19 mm)
width — early model, ref. (1)		.0620" — .0625" (1.574 — 1.588 mm)			
width — late models, ref. (2)		.0780" — .0775" (1.981 — 1.968 mm)			
Compression — thickness	.095" — .101" (2.41 — 2.56 mm)		.095" — .101" (2.41 — 2.56 mm)	Top: .100" — .110" (2.54 — 2.79 mm) 2nd: .105" — .115" (2.66 — 2.92 mm)	.116" — .122" (2.94 — 3.09 mm)
thickness — early models, ref. (1)		.106" — .112" (2.692 — 2.835 mm)			
thickness — late models, ref. (2)		.106" — .116" (2.692 — 2.94 mm)			
Compression — fitted gap	.007" — .012" (.178 — .305 mm)		.007" — .012" (.178 — .305 mm.)	.007" — .014" (.171 — .355 mm)	.008" — .013" (.20 — .33 mm)
fitted gap — early models, ref. (1)		.007" — .012" (.178 — .305 mm)			
fitted gap — late models, ref. (2)		.007" — .017" (.178 — .431 mm)			
Compression — clearance in grooves	.0015" — .0035" (.038 — .089 mm)		.0015" — .0035" (.038 — .089 mm.)	Top: .002" — .0035" (.050 — .089 mm) 2nd: .0015" — .0035" (.038 — .089 mm)	= = =
clearance in grooves — early, ref. (1)		.0015" — .0035" (.038 — .089 mm)			
clearance in grooves — late, ref. (2)		.002" — .0035" (.050 — .089 mm)			
Oil control	Slotted scraper		Slotted scraper	Chrome faced twin rail with circumferential expander	Slotted scraper
oil control — early models, ref. (1)		Chrome faced twin rail with expander.			
oil control — late models, ref. (2)		Chrome faced twin rail with spacer and expander spring.			
Oil control — width	.124" — .125" (3.15 — 3.175 mm)		.124" — .125" (3.15 — 3.175 mm.)	= = =	.1153" — .1563" (2.94 — 2.86 mm)
— thickness	.095" — .101" (2.41 — 2.56 mm)		.095" — .101" (2.41 — 2.56 mm.)	= = =	.116" — .122" (2.94 — 2.96 mm.)
— fitted gap	.007" — .012" (.178 — .305 mm)		.007" — .012" (.178 — .305 mm.)	= = =	.008" — .013" (.20 — .33 mm)
— clearance in grooves	.0015" — .0035" (.038 — .089 mm.)		.0015" — .0035" (.038 — .089 mm.)	= = =	= = =

GUDGEON PINS					
Type	Clamped in con. rod.		Clamped in con. rod	Fully floating with circlip location	Pressed in con. rod
early, ref. (1) piston section		Fully floating with circlip location			
late, ref. (2) piston section		Pressed in con rod			

= = = denotes common to model listed in preceding column.

	848 cc 850 Saloon and Van	998 cc Mini Minor, Deluxe, Mini Matic, Van, Moke, BMC Moke and Cooper	997 cc Cooper	1098 cc Mini 1100 Saloons and Vans BMC Moke Clubman Saloon	1275 cc Cooper 'S' Moke Clubman G.T.
GUDGEON PINS (continued)					
Fit in piston	Hand push fit		Hand push fit	= = =	= = =
early, ref. (1) piston section		.0001" — .0035" (.0025 — .0089 mm)		.0001" — .0003" (.0025 — .0075 mm)	
late, ref. (2) piston section		.0001" — .0003" (.0025 — .0075 mm)			
Outer diameter	.6244" — .6247" (15.86 — 15.87 mm)		.6244 — .6247" (15.86 — 15.87 mm)	Production Colour Code (.6243" — .6244" Yellow (15.857 — 15.8598 mm) (.6244" — .6245" Green (15.598 — 15.8623 mm) (.6245" — .6246" White (15.8623 — 15.8648 mm)	.8123" — .8125" (20.63 — 20.64 mm.)
early, ref. (1) piston section		.6244" — .6247" (15.86 — 15.87 mm)			
late, ref. (2) piston section		.7567" — .7569" (19.2199 — 19.2249 mm)			
Fit in connecting rod	Clamped		Clamped		.0008" — .0015" (.020 — .038 mm) interference
early, ref. (1) piston section		.0002" (.00508 mm) slack		.0001" — .0003" (.0025 — .0075 mm)	
late, ref. (2) piston section		.0009" — .0012" (.0225 — .0305 mm.) interference			
VALVES AND VALVE GEAR					
Valves — Head diameter: Inlet	1.093" — 1.098" (27.76 — 27.89 mm)	= = = Cooper 1.213" — 1.218" (30.81 — 30.94 mm)	1.156" — 1.565" (29.4 — 29.5 mm)	1.151" — 1.156" (29.23 — 29.26 mm)	1.402" — 1.406" (35.58 — 35.71 mm)
Exhaust	1.000" — 1.005" (25.40 — 25.53 mm)	= = =	= = =	= = =	1.214" — 1.219" (30.83 — 30.96 mm)
	Valve seat angle inlet and exhaust: 45°. Valve stem diameter — Inlet: .2793" — .2798" (7.096 — 7.109 mm) — Exhaust: .2788" — .2793' (7.081 — 7.096 mm). Valve stem to guide clearance — Inlet: .0015 — .0025" (.038 — .064 mm) — Exhaust: .002" — .003" (.051 — .076 mm.). Valve rocker clearance: .012" (.305 mm.) cold. (Cooper 'S' set hot.) Valve guides: Length inlet and exhaust: 1.689" (42.68 mm). Outside diameter: .469" (11.91 mm). Inside diameter: .2813" — .2818" (7.143 — 7.25 mm). Rocker bush bore: .5630" (14.300 mm.).				
Valve lift	.285" (7.24 mm)	.285" (7.24 mm) Cooper .312" (7.92 mm)	.312" (7.92 mm)	.312" (7.92 mm)	.318" nominal (8.08 mm)

VALVE TIMING

	848 cc	998 cc	998 cc Cooper	997 cc	1098 cc	1275 cc (1) *	1275 cc (2) **
Inlet valve: opens: — B.T.D.C.	5°	5°	5°	16°	5°	5°	10°
closes: — A.B.D.C.	45°	45°	45°	56°	45°	45°	50°
Exhaust valve: opens: — B.B.D.C.	40°	40°	51°	51°	51°	51°	51°
closes: — A.T.D.C.	10°	10°	21°	21°	21°	21°	21°

* (1) To Eng. No. 9F/SA/Y 40005.
** (2) Eng. No. 9F/SA/Y 40006 on.

VALVE SPRINGS

			Cooper			
Free length: inlet and exhaust — inner	1.625" (41.27 mm)	1.625" (41.27 mm)	1.672" (42.47 mm)	1.750" (44.55 mm)	1.750" (44.45 mm.)	1.705" (43.31 mm)
— outer			1.750" (44.45 mm)			1.740" (44.19 mm)
Number of working coils — inner	4½	4½	6½	4½	4½	6½
— outer			4½			4½
Pressure: inlet and exhaust valve open — inner	70 lb (31.8 kg)	70 lb. (31.8 kg)	30 lb. (13.6 kg)	85 lb (36.6 kg)	85 lb (38.6 kg)	46 lb. (20.865 kg)
valve closed — inner	37.5 lb (17.02 kg)	37.5 lb. (17.02 kg)	18 lb. (8.17 kg)	52.5 lb (23.8 kg)	52.5 lb (23.8 kg)	26.6 lb. (12.065 kg)
valve open — outer			88 lb. (39.9 kg)			94 lb. (42.638 kg)
valve closed — outer			55½ lb. (25.13 kg)			49.6 lb. (22.498 kg)

NOTE: 998 cc. engines from Eng. Nos. — 9YH/U/H 1001 — 9YB/U/H 4237 — 9YE/U/H 1894. Use valve spring specification for Mini 1100.

TAPPETS

Common to all models. Barrell type with an outside diameter of 0.812" (20.64 mm) and a length of 1.5" (38.10 mm).

CAMSHAFT

3 Bearing — Journal diameters: Front: 1.6655" — 1.666" (42.30 — 42.31 mm). Centre: 1.6227" — 1.6232" (41.21 — 41.23 mm).
Rear: 1.3725" — 1.3735" (34.86 — 34.88 mm). End float: .003" — .007" (.076 — .078 mm.).

Bearings — type: front	White metal lined steel backed	= = =	= = =	= = =	= = =
centre	Plain running in block	White metal lined steel backed	= = =	= = =	= = =
rear	Plain running in block	White metal lined steel backed	= = =	= = =	= = =
Inside dimeter — reamed: front	1.667" — 1.6675" (42.342 — 42.355 mm.)	= = =	= = =	= = =	= = =
centre		1.6245" — 1.6255" (41.261 — 41.287 mm)	= = =	1.6245" — 1.6255" (41.261 — 41.287 mm)	= = =
rear		1.3748" — 1.3755" (34.914 — 34.937 mm)	= = =	1.3748" — 1.3755" (34.914 — 34.937 mm)	1.3745" — 1.3750" (34.091 — 34.92 mm)
Running clearance: front	.001" — .002" (.025 — .051 mm)	= = =	= = =	= = =	= = =
centre) rear)	.00125" — .00275" (.0347 — .0698 mm)	.001" — .002" (.025 — .051 mm)	= = =	.001" — .002" (.025 — .051 mm)	.001 — 00225" (.025 — .057 mm)

COOLING SYSTEM

Type

All models: Pressurised thermo-syphon; pump and fan assisted. Thermostat opening temperature: 82°C (180°F).
Radiator pressure cap (except 850 cc): 13 p.s.i. (0.90 Kg/cm²). 850 cc: 7 p.s.i (0.49 Kg/cm²).

= = = denotes common to model listed in preceding column.

	848 cc 850 Saloon and Van	998 cc Mini Minor, Deluxe, Mini Matic, Van, Moke, BMC Moke and Cooper	997 cc Cooper	1098 cc Mini 1100 Saloons & Vans BMC Moke Clubman Saloon	1275 cc Cooper "S" Moke Clubman GT
ENGINE LUBRICATION SYSTEM					
Oil pump	All models — Hobourn Eaton or Concentric, Rotor type.				
Oil filter	All models — External full flow type.				
Oil relief valve opening pressure	60 p.s.i. (4.22 kg/cm²)	60 p.s.i. (4.22 kg/cm²) Cooper: 70 p.s.i. (4.92 kg/cm²)	70 p.s.i. (4.92 kg/cm²)	= = =	60 p.s.i. 4.22 kg/cm²)
Oil pressure — Idle	15 p.s.i. (1.05 kg/cm²)	= = =	= = =	= = =	= = =
Oil pressure relief valve spring — Free length	2$\frac{55}{64}$" (72.63 mm)	2$\frac{55}{64}$" (72.63 mm) Cooper: 2$\frac{39}{64}$" (66.28 mm)	2$\frac{39}{64}$" (66.28 mm)	= = =	2$\frac{55}{64}$" (72.63 mm)
IGNITION SYSTEM					
Coil	Lucas LA12	= = = Cooper HA12	Lucas HA12	Lucas LA12	Lucas HA12
Distributor Serial No. *Early Model H.C.	Lucas DM2 — 40768 A	Manual Models except Cooper Lucas 25D4 — 41045	Lucas 25D4 — 40774A	1100 Saloons and Vans Lucas 29D4—62941053A or Lucas 29D4—AYG1056	Cooper "S" Model Lucas 23D4 — 40819I B
· Early Model L.C.	Lucas DM2 — 40707D		Lucas 25D4 — 40873	Lucas 25D4 — 40899	
· **Late Model H.C.	Lucas 25D4 — 40941 or Lucas 29D4 — AYA0192	Lucas 25D4 — 41057 or Lucas 29D4 — AYA0194			Lucas 23D4—40819H or AYG 0175
· Late Model L.C.	Lucas 25D4 — 62941051A				
* Ref (1) Piston Section ** Ref (2) Piston Section		Mini Matic Model Lucas 29D4 — 62941052A or Lucas 29D4 — AYA0200			Moke Model (H.C.) Lucas 25D4 — 41271B
H.C.		Cooper Model Lucas 25D4 — 40955A		Clubman Model HC Lucas 29D4 — AYG1056	Clubman GT Model (H.C.) Lucas 29D4 — AYG0175
L.C.		Lucas 25D4 — 40958A			
Contact point gap — Cam dwell angle — Sparking plugs and gap — Condenser capacity	Contact gap: .014" — .016" (.35 — .40 mm). Cam dwell angle: 60° ± 3°. Sparking plugs: Champion N5 (Coopers — N9Y). Gap: .025" (.625 mm). Condenser capacity: .18 — .24 m.f.d. REFER APPENDIX I				
DISTRIBUTOR TEST DATA					
Stroboscopic ignition timing — with vacuum line disconnected	3° B.T.D.C. @ 500 r.p.m.	= = =	= = =	5° B.T.D.C. @ 500 r.p.m.	Cooper "S" Mk I 3° A.T.D.C. @ 600 r.p.m. After Eng. No. 4006:— 2° B.T.D.C. @ 600 r.p.m.
L.C.	10° B.T.D.C. @ 500 r.p.m.	Moke 10° B.T.D.C. @ 500 r.p.m.		6° B.T.D.C. @ 600 r.p.m.	Cooper "S" Mk. II and Clubman GT 2° B.T.D.C. @ 600 r.p.m. (100 Octane Fuel)
H. & L.C.		Cooper 7° B.T.D.C. @ 600 r.p.m.			3° A.T.D.C. @ 600 r.p.m. (97 Octane Fuel) Moke 3° B.T.D.C. @ 1000 r.p.m.
FUEL SYSTEM					
Air Cleaner — Type	All models: Paper element except early Cooper — oil wetted gauze.				
Carburettor — Number, make and type	Single S.U. HS2	= = = Mini Matic Single S.U. HS4 Cooper Twin S.U. HS2	Twin S.U. HS2	Single S.U. HS2	Cooper "S" & Clubman G.T. Twin S.U. HS2 Moke Single S.U. HS4
— Diameter	1$\frac{1}{4}$" (31.75 mm)	= = = HS4 — 1$\frac{1}{2}$" (38.1 mm)	= = =	= = =	= = =

FUEL SYSTEM (continued)

			Mini Matic	Cooper			Cooper 'S'	Clubman GT	Moke
Carburettor — Jet diameter	.090" (2.29 mm)	===			===	===	===		
— Needle type — Std.	EB	GX	AC	GY	GZ	AN	M	===	AAG
" — Rich	M	M	MI	M	AH2	H6	AH2	===	—
" — Weak	GG	GG	H6	GG	EB	EB	EB	===	—
— Spring colour	Red	Red	Blue	Blue	Blue	Red	Blue	Red	===
Fuel Pump — Make and type	S.U. — P.D. or — S.U. — S.P. electrical	Goss YD mechanical Cooper — S.U. — S.P. electrical			S.U. — S.P. electrical	Goss YD mechanical	===	===	===
— Working pressure	S.U. pump: 2 to 3 p.s.i. (.14 to .21 Kg/cm²).					Goss pump: 1½ to 2½ p.s.i. (.105 to .175 Kg/cm²).			

EXHAUST EMISSION

Exhaust gas analyser reading:
At engine idle speed (850 r.p.m.) — 2 to 2.5% CO (provisional)
Air pump test speed — 1,200 r.p.m. (engine)

CLUTCH

Type	BMC Helical coil spring, single dry plate, to Eng. No. 8Y/U/H 25503 Borg & Beck diaphragm spring, single dry plate from Engine Number: 8Y/U/H 25504	Borg & Beck diaphragm spring, single dry plate Cooper — as 997 cc to Eng. No. 9Y/Sa/H 1061, then as above	BMC helical spring, single dry plate	Borg & Beck diaphragm spring, single dry plate	===
Diameter	7⅛" (180.9 mm)	===	===	===	===
Pressure springs — Helical coil only	6	6	6	—	—
Colour code — Helical coil springs	Red spot	Black enamel with white spot	===	—	—
— Diaphragm spring	Brown	Brown Cooper — Light green or dark blue	—	Dark blue	Light green

GEARBOX

	850 Mini Minor, Deluxe, Vans, (all models)	Mini Moke	BMC Moke (998 cc)	Mini Matic	Cooper 997 and 998 cc	Cooper "S" Clubman GT	Mini 1100 Saloon and Van (Early models)	BMC Moke (1098 cc) 10" wheels	Moke (1098 and 1275 cc) 13" wheels	Mini 1100 Saloon and Van (late models) Clubman
Number of forward speeds	4		===		===		===		===	
Synchromesh	2nd, 3rd, 4th		===		===		1st, 2nd, 3rd, 4th		===	
Ratios: top	1.0 : 1			1.0 : 1	1.0 : 1		1.0 : 1			
third	1.412 : 1			1.460 : 1	1.357 : 1		1.430 : 1			
second	2.172 : 1	===	===	1.845 : 1	1.916 : 1	===	2.218 : 1	===	===	===
first	3.628 : 1			2.690 : 1	3.200 : 1		3.526 : 1			
reverse	3.628 : 1			2.690 : 1	3.200 : 1		3.545 : 1			
Overall Ratios: top	3.765 : 1	4.130 : 1	4.270 : 1	3.760 : 1	3.765 : 1	3.440 : 1	3.765 : 1	4.130 : 1	4.270 : 1	3.650 : 1
third	5.317 : 1	5.840 : 1	6.020 : 1	5.480 : 1	5.110 : 1	4.670 : 1	5.400 : 1	5.918 : 1	6.130 : 1	5.280 : 1
second	8.176 : 1	8.980 : 1	9.270 : 1	6.930 : 1	7.213 : 1	6.600 : 1	8.350 : 1	9.160 : 1	9.471 : 1	8.090 : 1
first	13.657 : 1	14.990 : 1	15.480 : 1	10.120 : 1	12.050 : 1	11.020 : 1	13.280 : 1	14.562 : 1	15.056 : 1	12.860 : 1
reverse	13.657 : 1	14.990 : 1	15.480 : 1	10.120 : 1	12.050 : 1	11.020 : 1	13.350 : 1	14.641 : 1	15.129 : 1	11.410 : 1
Converter max. torque multiplication:				2.000 : 1						
Converter output gear ratio:				1.150 : 1						
Differential ratio:	3.765 : 1	4.130 : 1	4.270 : 1	3.270 : 1	3.765 : 1	3.440 : 1	3.765 : 1	4.130 : 1	4.270 : 1	3.650 : 1
Road speed per 1000 r.p.m. in top gear	14.82 m.p.h. (23.7 Km/hr.)	13.50 m.p.h. (21.5 Km/hr.)	16.0 m.p.h. (25.6 Km/hr.)	14.9 m.p.h. (23.8 Km/hr.)	14.82 m.p.h. (23.7 Km/hr.)	16.07 m.p.h. (25.7 Km/hr.)	14.82 m.p.h. (23.7 Km/hr.)	13.50 m.p.h. (21:5 Km/hr.)	16.00 m.p.h. (25.6 Km/hr.)	15.39 m.p.h. (24.78 Km/hr.)

	848 cc 850 Saloon & Van	998 cc Mini Minor, Deluxe, Mini Matic, Van, Moke, BMC Moke and Cooper	997 cc Cooper	1098 cc Mini 1100 Saloons & Vans BMC Moke Clubman	1275 cc Cooper 'S' Moke Clubman 'G.T.'
DRIVE SHAFTS					
Make & type	Solid shaft reverse spline Hardy Spicer constant velocity	= = = = = = BMC Moke: Hardy Spicer constant velocity with rubber protector on front hub	= = = = = =	= = = = = = BMC Moke: Hardy Spicer constant velocity with rubber protector on front hubs	= = = = = = Moke = = =
UNIVERSAL JOINTS					
Inner	Dunlop rubber coupling	= = = Mini Matic: Hardy Spicer flanged mechanical	= = =	= = = BMC Moke: Harly Spicer flanged mechanical	= = = From Eng. No. 1918 (Cooper 'S') Hardy Spicer flanged mechanical Clubman G.T.: Hardy Spicer flanged mechanical
STEERING					
Steering wheel turns lock to lock	2⅓	= = = BMC Moke: 2¹⁄₁₆	= = =	= = = BMC Moke: 2¹⁄₁₆	= = =
Lock angle — outer wheel 20° — inner wheel	21½° ± 1½°	= = =	= = =	= = =	= = =
Total lock angle		BMC Moke: Left wheel 50° Right wheel 48°		BMC Moke: Left wheel 50° Right wheel 48°	
Type	Rack & pinion	= = =	= = =	= = =	= = =
Camber angle	2° ± 1°	= = =	= = =	= = =	= = =
Castor angle	3° ± 1°	= = =	= = =	= = =	= = =
King pin (swivel hub) inclination	9½° ± 1°	= = =	= = =	= = =	= = =
Toe out	¹⁄₁₆" (1.6 mm)	= = =	= = =	= = =	= = =
FRONT SUSPENSION					
Type	Rubber cone	Deluxe & Mini Matic: Hydrolastic Mini, Cooper, Van and Mokes: Rubber cone	Rubber cone	Mini-K & Clubman Hydrolastic Mini 1100, Moke & Van: Rubber cone	Cooper 'S' & Clubman G.T. Hydrolastic Moke Rubber cone
Hydrolastic capacity (each side)		4 pints (5 US pts — 2.27 litres)		4 pints (5 US pts — 2.27 litres)	4 pints (5 US pts — 2.27 litres)
Hydrolastic displacer units — colour code (band around rubber pipe or unit)	Deluxe and Mini Matic: Deluxe — plain to Car No. 16755 — orange to Car No. 30543 — green from Car No. 30544 onward. Mini Matic — orange to Car No. 511 — green from Car No. 512 onward.			Cooper 'S' — double orange to Car No. 1917 — blue to Car No. 3715 — silver from Car No. 3716 Clubman G.T. — silver Mini 1100 & Clubman — green	

REAR SUSPENSION					
Type	Rubber cone	Deluxe & Mini Matic: Hydrolastic Mini, Cooper, Van & Mokes: Rubber cone	Rubber cone	= = = Mini 1100 Std., Moke & Van: Rubber cone	Hydrolastic Moke: rubber cone
Toe in	$\frac{1}{8}$" (3.18 mm)	= = =	= = =	= = =	= = =
Camber	1° — 3° positive	1° positive	= = =	= = =	= = =
HYDRAULIC DAMPERS	Applicable only to vehicles with rubber cone suspension				
Type — front & rear	Tubular Telescopic	= = =	= = =	= = =	= = =
BRAKES					
System	Lockheed Hydraulic	= = =	= = =	= = =	= = =
Type — Front	Drum — single leading shoe	Drum — two leading shoe, except: Mini Minor to 2317 — as 848 cc Cooper — Disc	Disc	Drum — two leading shoe	Disc Moke Drum — two leading shoe
— Rear	Drum — single leading shoe	= = =	= = =	= = =	= = =
Drum size (Front and/or rear)	7" (17.78 cm)	= = =	= = =	= = =	= = =
Disc diameter		7" (17.78 cm)	= = =		7.5" (19.05 cm)
Lining dimensions — Front	6.75" × 1.25" (17.14 cm. × 3.17 cm)	6.75" × 1.50" (17.14 cm. × 3.18 cm) Mini Minor to Car No. Car No. 2317 — as 848 cc	—	6.75" × 1.50" (17.14 cm × 3.18 cm)	—
— Rear	6.75" × 1.25" (17.14 cm × 3.17 cm)	= = =	= = =	= = =	Moke = = =
Lining material	DON 202	DON 202 or Hardie Ferodo E501	DON 202	Hardie Ferodo E501	DON 202 or Hardie Ferodo E501
Disc pad material		Hardie Ferodo DA 3	= = =		Hardie Ferodo DA 6 or DS 11
Colour code	202 — Three red stripes. E 501 — One red, one blue stripe. DA3 — Three yellow, two blue dots. DA 6 — Two yellow, two blue dots. DS 11 — Two yellow, three blue dots.				
Front wheel cylinder size	$\frac{3}{4}$" dia (19.05 mm) — early models $\frac{5}{8}$" dia (15.87 mm) — later models	Deluxe — 80" dia (20.32 mm) to Car No. 14271 1" dia (25.4 mm) onward Mini Minor — $\frac{5}{8}$" dia (15.87 mm) to Car No. 2317. 1" dia (25.4 mm) onward Mini Matic, Moke & Van — 1" dia ((25.4 mm)	—	1" dia (25.4 mm)	Moke 1" dia (25.4 mm)
Rear wheel cylinder size	$\frac{3}{4}$" dia (19.05 mm) to Car No. 28044 $\frac{5}{8}$" dia (15.87 mm) onward	(See below)*	$\frac{3}{4}$" dia. (19.05 mm) to Car No. 2056 $\frac{5}{8}$" dia. (15.87 mm) from Car No. 2057	$\frac{3}{4}$" dia (19.05 mm)	Cooper 'S' & Clubman G.T. $\frac{5}{8}$" dia (15.87 mm) Moke $\frac{3}{4}$" dia (19.05 mm)
	* Deluxe — $\frac{5}{8}$" dia. (15.87 mm) to Car No. 14271. $\frac{3}{4}$" dia. (19.05 mm) onward. Mini Minor: $\frac{5}{8}$" dia. (15.87 mm) to Car No. 2317. $\frac{3}{4}$" dia. (19.05 mm) onward. Mini Matic, Moke and Van: $\frac{3}{4}$" dia. (19.05 mm). Cooper: $\frac{5}{8}$" dia. (15.87 mm).				

= = = denotes common to model listed in preceding column.

	848 cc 850 Saloon & Van	998 cc Mini Minor, Deluxe, Mini Matic, Van, Moke, BMC Moke and Cooper	997 cc Cooper	1098 cc Mini 1100 Saloons & Vans BMC Moke Clubman	1275 cc Cooper 'S' Moke Clubman G.T.
BRAKES (Cont'd.)					
Limiting valve shut-off pressure	250 — 300 p.s.i. (17.6 — 21.1 Kg/cm²) to Car No. 170653. 450 p.s.i. (31.6 Kg/cm²) onward Van — 450 p.s.i. (31.6 Kg/cm²)	Deluxe — 370 p.s.i. (26 Kg/cm²) to Car No. 12117. 390 p.s.i. (27.4 Kg/cm²) onward Mini Minor — 450 p.s.i. (31.6 Kg/cm²) to Car No. 2317. 390 p.s.i. (27.4 Kg/cm²) onward Mini Matic, Moke & Van — 390 p.s.i. (27.4 Kg/cm²) Cooper — 450 p.s.i. (31.6 Kg/cm²)	250 — 300 p.s.i. (17.6 — 21.1 Kg/cm²) early models. 450 p.s.i. (31.6 Kg/cm²) later models	390 p.s.i. (27.4 Kg/cm²)	370 p.s.i. (26 kg./cm.²) to Car No. 1322. 340 p.s.i. (23.9 kg/cm.²) onward Moke 390 p.s.i. (27.4 Kg/cm²)
Master cylinder bore diameter	¾" (29.05 mm) to Car No. 28044 70" (17.78 mm) onward	70" (17.78 mm) Cooper — ⅝" (15.87 mm)	.70" (17.78 mm) to Car No. 2056 ⅝" (15.87 mm) onward	= = =	.70" (17.78 mm)
WHEELS					
Type	Ventilated disc, 4 stud, ⅜" U.N.F. fixing	= = =	= = =	= = =	= = =
Size	3.50 B × 10	= = = BMC Moke — 4.50 J × 13	= = =	3.50 B × 10 Moke — 4.50 J × 13	= = = Moke — 4.50 J × 10 Cooper 'S' & Clubman G.T. 4.50 J × 13
TYRES					
Type	Tubeless cross-ply	= = =	= = =	Tubeless cross ply Moke — All weather tread, 4 ply (tubed) 5.20 × 10	Radial ply with tubes Moke 5.60 × 13 Standard tread — tubed
Size	5.20 × 10	Mokes — All weather tread, 4 ply (tubed)			Cooper 'S' & Clubman G.T. 145 mm. ×10"

TYRE PRESSURES

(p.s.i.) (Kg/cm²)

		850, Mini Std. & Mini 1100 Vans — all models	Mini Matic Deluxe Mini K & Clubman	Mini Moke	Moke 1275 cc BMC Moke	Cooper (except 'S')	Clubman G.T. Cooper 'S'
Front	Normal load	24 — 1.7	22 — 1.55	24 — 1.7	22 — 1.55	24 — 1.7	28 — 1.97
Rear	Normal load	22 — 1.55	24 — 1.7	22 — 1.55	20 — 1.4	22 — 1.55	26 — 1.83
Front	Full load	24 — 1.7	22 — 1.55	24 — 1.7	22 — 1.55	24 — 1.7	28 — 1.97
Rear	Full load	22 — 1.55	26 — 1.83	24 — 1.7	20 — 1.4	24 — 1.7	26 — 1.83
High speed driving		Increase pressures by 4 to 6 p.s.i. (.3 to .42 Kg/cm²).					

ELECTRICAL EQUIPMENT					
Voltage & polarity	12 volt POSITIVE earth	= = =	= = =	12 volt NEGATIVE earth	Cooper 'S' Mk. I 12 volt POSITIVE earth Cooper 'S' Mk. II Clubman G.T. & Moke 12 volt NEGATIVE earth
Battery	Lucas 12BST 38	Lucas 12BST 38	Lucas 12BT 48	Lucas 12BST 38 or Lucas 'Alert' 3619	Lucas 12BT 48 or Lucas 'Albert' 3623
Capacity — amp/hr at 20 hr rate	38	BST 38 — 38, BT 48 — 48	48	BST 38 — 38, 3619 — 40	BT 48 — 48, 3623 — 46
Method of charge	Lucas C40 Generator	= = =	= = =	Lucas 15 AC Alternator	Cooper 'S' Mk. I Lucas C40 Generator Cooper 'S' Mk. II Clubman G.T. Lucas 15 AC Alternator Moke Lucas 16 ACR Alternator
Control box	Lucas RB 106/2	= = =	= = =	Lucas 8 TR	Cooper 'S' Mk. I Lucas RB 106/2 Cooper 'S' Mk. II Clubman G.T. & Moke Lucas 8TR
Adjustment & settings (refer Sections N. Nb. n)					
Starter Motor	Lucas M 35 G	= = =	= = =	= = =	= = =
Windscreen Wiper Motor	Lucas DR Type	Lucas DR Type or Permag. Mokes — Preslite	Lucas DR Type	Lucas Permag. (single or twin speed) Moke — Preslite	Lucas DR Type or Permag. (single or twin speed)

GENERAL DIMENSIONS		Metric		Metric		Metric		Metric		Metric
Wheel base	6' 8"	2.03 m.	= = =		7' 0"	2.13 m.	6' 8" MOKE 13" WHEELS 6' 11"	2.03 m. 2.10 m.	= = = MOKE (1275 cc) 6' 10½"	 2.06 m.
Track — front	3' 11 $\frac{15}{16}$"	1.20 m.	= = =		= = =		3' 11¾" MOKE 13" WHEELS 4' 0⅛"	1.21 m. 1.22 m.	4' 1¼"	1.25 m.
— rear	3' 9⅞"	1.64 m.	= = =		= = =		3' 10⅞" MOKE 13" WHEELS 4' 1¼"	1.82 m. 1.24 m.	3' 11 $\frac{21}{32}$" MOKE (1275 cc) 4' 1¾"	1.19 m. 1.27 m.
Overall length	10' 0¼" LATE MINI 1100 10' 5¼"	3.05 m. 3.176 m.	= = =		10' 9⅞" LATE MODEL 11.2⅞"	3.259 m. 3.314 m.	10' 7¼	3.22 m.	10' 0¼" MOKE (1275 cc) 10' 4¼"	3.05 m. 3.15 m.
Overall width	4' 7½"	1.41 m.	= = =		= = =		4' 3½" MOKE 13" WHEELS 4' 9"	1.36 m. 1.44 m.	4' 7½" MOKE (1275 cc) 4' 9" CLUBMAN G.T. 4' 8⅜"	1.41 m. 1.44 m. 1.58 m.
Overall height	4' 5"	1.35 m.	= = =		4' 6½"	1.38 m.	4' 10" (Hood up) 4' 5" (Hood down) MOKE 13" WHEELS 5' 00" (Hood up) 4' 7" (Hood down)	1.47 m. 1.32 m. 1.53 m. 1.39 m.	4' 5" MOKE (1275 cc) = = = = = =	1.35 m.
Ground clearance	6½"	162 mm.	= = =		= = =		6¼" MOKE 13" WHEELS 8¼"	158.7 mm. 206.2 mm.	5⅛" MOKE (1275 cc) = = =	130.2 mm.

= = = denotes common to model listed in preceding column.

	850, Mini Minor, Cooper 997 cc 998 cc Mini 1100 all models	Mini Matic Deluxe Mini 'K' Clubman	Mini Vans all models	Mini Moke BMC Moke Moke (1098 cc)	Cooper 'S' MK. I and II Moke (1275 cc) Clubman G.T.
WEIGHTS (approximately)					
Kerbside weight (full fuel tank)	1390 lb. 630 kg. COOPER MODELS 1400 lb. 635 kg. LATE MINI 1100 1381 lb 626.45 kg.	1437 lb. 652.4 kg. MINI MATIC 1491 lb. 676.9 kg. CLUBMAN 1449 lb. 657.3 kg.	1350 lb. 597.5 kg. LATE MODEL 1100 1341 lb. 610 kg.	1283 lb. 582.48 kg. MOKE 13" WHEELS 1367 lb. 620.6 kg.	1576 lb. 716.36 kg. MOKE (1275 cc) 1367 lb. 620.6 kg. CLUBMAN G.T. 1564 lb. 709.8 kg.
Registration weight (2 gallons fuel)	1362 lb. 618.35 kg. COOPER MODELS 1370 lb. 622 kg. LATE MINI 1100 1352 lb. 612.21 kg.	1406 lb. 638.32 kg. MINI MATIC 1458 lb. 661.93 kg. CLUBMAN 1418 lb. 643.23 kg.	1318 lb. 592.1 kg. LATE MODEL 1100 1312 lb. 596 kg.	1251 lb. 567.95 kg. MOKE 13" WHEELS 1335 lb. 606.09 kg.	1513 lb. 663.63 kg. MOKE (1275 cc) 1335 lb. 606.09 kg. CLUBMAN G.T. 1496 lb. 678.5 kg.
G.V.W.*			2044 lb. 919.8 kg.	1867 lb. 847.6 kg.	
*NOTE: This G.V.W. is not applicable for vehicles operating over rough terrain				MOKE 13" WHEELS 2000 lb. 908 kg.	MOKE (1275 cc) 2000 lb. 908 kg.
Maximum towing weight	8 cwt. 406.4 kg.	= = =	6 cwt. 304.7 kg.	8 cwt. 406.4 kg.	= = =

CAPACITIES	Imp.	U.S.	litres	Imp.	U.S.	litres	Imp.	U.S.	litres	Imp.	U.S.	litres	Imp.	U.S.	litres
Engine/transmission oil incl. filter	8½ pt	10.2	4.83	= = =	= = =	= = =	= = =	= = =	= = =	= = =	= = =	= = =	= = =	= = =	= = =
Eng./trans. oil, incl. filter and oil cooler (automatic)		—		9¼	11.2	5.2									
—initial fill		—		13	15.6	7.4									
—oil change				9	11	5									
Cooling system—less heater	5¼ pt	6.3	3	= = =	= = =	= = =	= = =	= = =	= = =	= = =	= = =	= = =	= = =	= = =	= = =
Cooling system—with heater	6¼ pt	7.5	3.55	= = =	= = =	= = =	= = =	= = =	= = =	= = =	= = =	= = =	= = =	= = =	= = =
Fuel tank — single	5½ gl	6.6	25	= = =	= = =	= = =	6 gl	7.2	27.3	6¼ gl	7½	28.4	= = =	= = =	= = =
— twin				11 gl	13.2	50							MOKE (1275 cc) 6 gl	7.2	27.3

= = = denotes common to model listed in preceding column.

TORQUE WRENCH SETTINGS

	All models where applicable	
	lb/ft.	kg/m.
Cylinder head stud nuts	40	5.5
Cylinder head stud nuts — Cooper 'S' (10 nuts)	42	5.8
Cylinder head bolt — Front one only — Cooper 'S'	25	3.4
Connecting rod big-end bolts	35	4.8
Connecting rod big-end bolts — Cooper 'S'	46	6.2
Main bearing set screws	60	8.3
Main bearing nuts — early Cooper 'S' only	67	9.2
— late Cooper 'S' only	57	7.8
Flywheel centre bolt	110 — 115	15.2 — 15.9
Gudgeon pin clamp screws	25	3.4
Rocker shaft bracket nuts	25	3.4
Transmission case to crankcase	6	0.8
Transmission drain plug	40 — 50	5.5 — 6.9
Cylinder side cover	2	.28
Second type — deep pressed cover	5	0.7
Timing cover — ¼" U.N.F. bolts	6	0.8
Timing cover — 5⁄16" U.N.F. bolts	14	1.9
Water pump	17	2.3
Water outlet elbow	8	1.1
Oil filter	10 — 15	1.4 — 2
Oil pump	9	1.2
Manifold to cylinder head	15	2.1
Rocker cover	4	0.56
Crankshaft pulley nut	70	9.6
Transmission case studs — ⅜" dia U.N.C.	8	1.1
— 5⁄16" dia U.N.C.	6	0.8
Transmission case stud nuts — ⅜" U.N.F.	25	3.45
— 5⁄16" U.N.F.	18	2.5
Bottom cover set screw — ¼" dia U.N.C. (change speed tower)	6	0.8
First & Third motion shaft nut	150	20.7
Flywheel housing bolts and stud nuts	18	2.5
Set screw, driving strap to flywheel	16	2.2
Set screw, clutch spring housing to pressure plate	16	2.2
Distributor clamp bolt: fixed nut type	50(lb./in.)	0.576
fixed bolt type	30(lb./in.)	0.345
Alternator drive pulley nut	25 — 30	3.46 — 4.15

	All models where applicable	
	lb/ft.	kg/m.
Final Drive:		
Driven gear to differential cage	60	8.3
Nut, driving flange to differential (tighten to specified figure and align to next split pin hole)	70	9.6
End cover bolts (differential housing)	18	2.5
Automatic Transmission:		
Governor to auxiliary pump housing bolts	10 — 15	1.4 — 2
Converter centre bolt	110 — 115	15.2 — 15.9
Converter (six central bolts)	22 — 24	3.04 — 3.32
Converter drain plugs	18 — 20	2.5 — 2.77
Converter housing bolts	18	2.55
Differential driving flange securing bolts	40 — 45	5.53 — 6.62
Gear train bearing caps	12	1.66
Gear train carrier strap	12	1.66
Input shaft nut	70	9.6
Servo unit securing bolts	17	2.35
Top and reverse clutch hub nut	150	20.7
Transmission to engine securing nut	12	1.66
Valve block securing bolts	10	1.4
Valve block bolts (securing three sections)	7	.97
5⁄16" U.N.F. bolts	18 — 20	2.5 — 2.77
⅜" U.N.F. bolts	30	4.15
Suspension and Steering:		
Steering — column/rack pinion clamp bolt	8 — 9	1 — 1.2
Steering lever to hub bolts	35	4.8
Steering lever ball joint nut	25 — 30	3.46 — 4.15
Steering knuckle ball pin bottom nut	35 — 40	4.8 — 5.5
Steering knuckle ball pin retainer	70	9.6
Front hub nut (drive shaft)	60	8.3
Front hub nut (drive shaft) — Cooper	150	20.74
Rear suspension stub axle nut (tighten to specified figure and align to next slot)	60	8.3
Rear suspension pivot arm (Nyloc) nut	50	6.9
Front suspension upper arm pivot pin nut	26 — 28	3.6 — 3.87
Steering wheel nut	41	5.76
Road wheel nuts	42	5.8
Brake caliper retaining bolts	35 — 40	4.84 — 5.53

Additional information for vehicles of U.K. manufacture

	848 cc Mini Mk. I & Mk. II, Mini Automatic, Mini Van, Mini Pickup, Traveller, Countryman, Moke	998 cc Mini Mk. II, Mini Automatic, Mini Van, Mini Pickup, Traveller, Countryman, Moke, Clubman Saloon, Clubman Estate	997 cc & 998 cc Mini Cooper	970 cc & 1071 cc Mini Cooper 'S'	1275 cc Mini Cooper 'S' Mk. I, Mk. II, Mk. III, Mini 1275 G.T.
ENGINE					
Type	8MB, 8AH, 85H.	9AG, 99H	9F, 9FA	9FC, 10F	12 FA, 12 H,
Bore	2.478 in. (62.94 mm.)	2.543 in. (64.588 mm.)	997 c.c. MODEL 2.458 in. (62.43 mm.) 998 c.c. MODEL 2.543 in. (64.588 mm.)	2.780 in. (70.6 mm.)	= = =
Stroke	2.687 in. (68.26 mm.)	3.00 in. (76.2 mm.)	997 c.c. MODEL 3.20 in. (81.28 mm.) 998 c.c. MODEL 3.00 in. (76.2 mm.)	970 cc MODEL 2.437 in. (61.91 mm.) 1071 cc MODEL 2.687 in. (68.26 mm.)	3.2 in. (81.33 mm.)
Cubic capacity	51.7 cu. ins.	60.96 cu. ins.	997 c.c. MODEL 60.87 cu. ins. 998 c.c. MODEL 60.96 cu. ins.	970 cc MODEL 59.1 cu. in. 1071 cc MODEL 63.35 cu. in.	77.9 cu. in,
Compression ratio	8.3:1 (H.C.) 7.6:1 (L.C.) AUTOMATIC MODEL 8.9 : 1	= = = = = =	997 cc 9 : 1 8.3 : 1 998 cc 9 : 1 (H.C.) 7.8 : 1 (L.C.)	970 cc MODEL 10 : 1 1071 cc MODEL 9 : 1	COOPER 'S' ALL MODELS 9.75 : 1 1275 G.T. 8.8 : 1 (H.C.) 8.0 : 1 (L.C.)
Torque	44 lb. ft. (6.08 kg.m.) @ 2900 r.p.m. AUTOMATIC MODEL 44 lb. ft. (6.08 kg. m) at 2500 r.p.m.	52 lb. ft. (7.18 kg.m.) @ 2700 r.p.m. AUTOMATIC MODEL 52 lb. ft. (7.18 kg.m.) at 2750 r.p.m.	997 c.c. MODEL 54 lb. ft. (7.46 kg.m.) @ 3600 r.p.m. (H.C.) 53 lb. ft. (7.32 kg.m.) @ 3500 r.p.m. (L.C.) 998 c.c. MODEL 57 lb. ft. (7.88 kg.m.) @ 3000 r.p.m. (H.C.) 56 lb. ft. (7.74 kg.m.) @ 2900 r.p.m. (L.C.)	970 cc MODEL 57 lb/ft (7.88 kg/m) @ 5000 r.p.m. 1071 cc MODEL 62 lb/ft (8.58 kg/m) @ 4500 r.p.m.	79 lb/ft (10.92 kg/m) @ 3000 r.p.m. 1275 G.T. 69 lb/ft (9.55 kg/m) @ 3500 r.p.m.
Oversize bores	+.010 in. (.254 mm.) +.020 in. (.508 mm.)	= = = = = =	= = = = = =	= = = = = =	= = = = = =
Idling speed	500 r.p.m. AUTOMATIC MODEL 650 r.p.m. (N)	= = =		600 r.p.m.	= = = 1275 G.T. 650 r.p.m.
Fast idle speed	900 r.p.m. AUTOMATIC MODEL 1050 r.p.m. (N)	= = = = = =	= = =	1000 r.p.m.	= = = 1275 G.T. 1050 r.p.m.
CRANKSHAFT					
Main journal diameter	1.7505 to 1.751 in. (44.46 to 44.47 mm.)	= = =	= = =	2.0005 to 2.001 in. (50.81 to 50.82 mm.)	= = =
Minimum regrind diameter	1.7105 in. (43.45 mm.)	= = =	= = =	1.9805 to 1.9810 in. (50.30 to 50.31 mm.)	= = =
Crankpin journal diameter	1.6254 to 1.6259 in. (41.28 to 41.29 mm.)	= = =	= = =	1.7504 to 1.7509 in. (44.45 to 44.47 mm.)	= = =
Crankpin minimum regrind diameter	1.5848 in. (40.27 mm.)	= = =	= = =		

MAIN BEARINGS					
Material	Steel backed, white metal	Steel backed, copper-lead; thin wall.	Steel backed, copper-lead or aluminium-tin; thin wall.	Steel backed, copper-lead; thin wall.	Steel backed, copper-lead-indium; thin wall.
Diametral clearance	.0005 to 002 in. (.013 to .051 mm.)	.001 to .0027 in. (.025 to .069 mm.)	= = =	= = =	= = =
Length	1.187 in. (30.16 mm.)	= = =	1.0625 in. (26.99 mm.)	1.00 in. (25.4 mm.)	COOPER 'S' 1.000 in. (25.4 mm.) MINI 1275 G.T. .975 to .985 in. (24.76 to 25.02 mm.)

CONNECTING RODS					
Length between centres	5.75 in. (14.6 cms.)	= = =	= = =	= = =	= = =
Big end bearing diametral clearance	.001 to .0025 in. (0.25 to .063 mm.)	= = =	= = =	= = =	= = =
Big end bearing side clearance	.008 to .012 in. (.203 to .305 mm.)	= = =	= = =	.006 to .010 in. (.15 to .25 mm.)	= = =
Big end bearing length	.875 in. (22.22 mm.)	= = =	= = =	.840 — .850 in. (21.33 — 29.59 mm.)	= = =

PISTONS					
Type	Split skirt	Solid skirt	= = =	= = =	= = =
Clearance in cylinder: Top of skirt	0026 to .0032 in. (.066 to .081 mm.)	= = =		.025 to .0283 in. (.630 to .72 mm.)	1275 G.T. .0029 to .0037 in. (.07 to .09 mm.)
Bottom of skirt	.0006 to .0012 (.015 to .030 mm.)	.0005 to .0011 in. (.013 to .028 mm.)	997 c.c. MODEL .0016 to .0022 in. (.041 to .056 mm.) 998 c.c. MODEL .0005 to .0011 in. (.013 to .028 mm.)	.0019 to .0025 in. (.048 to .063 mm.)	.0019 to .0025 in. (.048 to .063 mm.) Bottom .0015 to .0021 in. (.04 to .05 mm.)
Oversizes	+.010, +.020, +.030, +.040 in. (+.254, +.508, +.762, +.1.016 mm.)	+.010, +.020 in. +.254, +.508 mm.)	= = =	= = =	= = =

PISTON RINGS					
Type: Top	Plain compression	Chrome faced compression	= = =	= = =	= = =
Second	tapered compression	= = =	= = =	= = =	= = =
Third	tapered compression	= = =	= = =	= = =	= = =
Oil control	slotted scraper	= = =		slotted oil control	= = = 1275 G.T. Duaflex 61
Width: compression rings	.069 to .070 in. (1.75 to 1.78 mm.)	.0620 to .0625 in. (1.574 to 1.588 mm.)	= = =	.0459 to .0469 in. (1.16 to 1.19 mm.)	= = = 1275 G.T. .0615 to .0625 (1.57 to 1.60 mm.)
Fitted gap: compression rings	.007 to .012 in. (.178 to .305 mm.)	= = =	= = =	.008 to .013 in. (.20 to .33 mm.)	= = = 1275 G.T. Top: .011 to .016 in. (0.28 to 0.35 mm.) Second and third: .008 to .013 in. (.20 to .33 mm.)

= = = denotes common to model listed in preceding column.

Additional information for vehicles of U.K. manufacture

	848 cc Mini Mk. I & Mk. II, Mini Automatic, Mini Van, Mini Pickup, Traveller, Countryman, Moke	998 cc Mini Mk. II, Mini Automatic, Mini Van, Mini Pickup, Traveller, Countryman, Moke, Clubman Saloon, Clubman Estate	997 cc & 998 cc Mini Cooper	970 cc & 1071 cc Mini Cooper 'S'	1275 cc Mini Cooper 'S' Mk. I, Mk. II, Mk. III, Mini 1275 G.T.
PISTON RINGS (continued)					
Clearance in groove: compression rings	.0015 to .0035 in. (.038 to .089 mm.)	= = =	= = =	= = =	= = =
Width: oil control ring	.124 to .125 in. (3.15 to 3.175 mm.)	= = =		.1553 to .1563 in. (3.94 to 3.96 mm.)	= = =
Fitted gap: oil control ring	.007 to .012 in. (.178 to .305 mm.)	= = =	= = =	.008 to .013 in. (.20 to .33 mm.)	= = = 1275 G.T. Rails and side spring .012 to .028 in. (.30 to .70 mm.)
Clearance in groove: oil control ring	.0015 to .0035 in. (.038 to .089 mm.)	= = =	= = =	= = =	= = =
GUDGEON PINS					
Type	Clamped in small end	Fully floating (circlips)	= = =	Pressed in connecting rod	= = =
Fit in piston	Hand push fit	= = =	.0001 in. (.0025 mm.) tight to .00035 in. (.0089 mm.) slack	Hand push fit	= = =
Diameter — outer	.624 in. (15.86 mm.)	= = =	.6244 to .6247 in. (15.86 to 15.867 mm.)	.8123 to .8125 in. (20.63 to 20.64 mm.)	= = =
Interference fit in connecting rod				.0008 to .0015 in. (.020 to .038 mm.) interference	= = =
VALVES & VALVE GEAR					
Head diameter: Inlet	1.093 to 1.098 in. (27.76 to 27.89 mm.)	= = =	997 c.c. MODEL 1.156 in. (29.4 mm.) 998 c.c. MODEL 1.219 in. (30.86 mm.)	1.401 to 1.406 in. (35.58 to 35.71 mm.)	= = = 1275 G.T. 1.307 to 1.312 in. (33.2 to 33.21 mm.)
Exhaust	1.000 to 1.005 in. (25.4 to 25.53 mm.)	= = =	1.00 in. (25.4 mm.)	1.214 to 1.219 in. (30.83 to 30.76 mm.)	= = = 1275 G.T. 1.1515 to 1.1565 in. (29.24 to 29.37 mm.)
Stem diameter: Inlet	.2793 to .2798 in. (7.096 to 7.109 mm.)	= = =	= = =	= = =	= = =
Exhaust	.2788 to .2793 in. (7.081 to 7.096 mm.)	= = =	= = =	= = =	= = =
Valve lift	.285 in. (7.24 mm.)	.280 in. (7.14 mm.)	.312 in. (7.92 mm.)	.318 in. (8.08 mm.)	= = =
Valve stem to guide celarance: Inlet	.0015 to .0025 in. (.038 to .064 mm.)	= = =	= = =	= = =	= = =
Exhaust	.002 to .003 in. (.051 to .076 mm.)	= = =	= = =	= = =	= = = 1275 G.T. .0015 to .0025 in. (.04 to .08 mm.)

Valve rocker clearance	.012 in. (.305 mm.) COLD	= = =	= = =	Std. .012 in. (.30 mm.) COLD Competition .015 in. (.38 mm.) COLD	= = =
Inlet valve: opens:	5° B.T.D.C.	= = =	997 c.c. 16° B.T.D.C. 998 c.c. 5° B.T.D.C.	5° B.T.D.C.	= = =
closes:	45° A.B.D.C.	= = =	997 c.c. 56° A.B.D.C. 998 c.c. 45° A.B.D.C.	45° A.B.D.C.	= = =
Exhaust valve: opens:	40° B.B.D.C.	= = =	997 c.c. 51° B.B.D.C. 998 c.c. 51° B.B.D.C.	51° B.B.D.C.	= = =
closes:	10° A.T.D.C.	= = =	997 c.c. 21° A.T.D.C. 998 c.c. 21° A.T.D.C.	21° A.T.D.C.	= = =
VALVE SPRINGS					
Free length (outer)	1.625 in. (41.27 mm.)	= = =	1.75 in. (44.45 mm.)	1.740 in. (44.19 mm.)	= = = 1275 G.T. 1.95 in. (49.13 mm.)
(inner)			1.672 in. (42.47 mm.)	1.705 in. (43.31 mm.)	= = = 1275 G.T.—not fitted
Number of working coils — inner				6¼	
— outer	4½	= = =		4½	= = =
Pressure (outer): valve open	70 lb. (31.8 kg.)	= = =	997 c.c. MODEL 90 lb. (40.8 kg.) 998 c.c. MODEL 88 lb. (39.9 kg.)	94 lb. (42.6 kg.)	= = = 1275 G.T. 124 lb. (56.3 kg.)
valve closed	37.5 lb. (17.03 kg.)	= = =	997 c.c. MODEL 55 lb. (24.9 kg.) 998 c.c. MODEL 55½ lb. (25.1 kg.)	49.6 lb. (22.49 kg.)	= = = 1275 G.T. 79.5 lb. (36.03 kg.)
(inner): valve open			30 lb. (13.6 kg.)	46 lb. (20.865 kg.)	= = =
valve closed			18 lb. (8.17 kg.)	26.6 lb. (12.065 kg.)	= = =
ENGINE LUBRICATION SYSTEM					
Oil pump					
Type	Concentric or Hobourn-Eaton	= = =	= = =	= = =	1275 G.T. Internal gear
Relief valve spring: Free length	2 55/64 in. (72.63 mm.)	2 39/64 in. (66.28 mm.)	= = =	= = =	= = =
Fitted length	2 5/32 in (54.77 mm)	= = =	= = =	= = =	= = =
Oil pressure					
Running	60 lb/sq in (4.22 kg/cm²)	= = =	= = =	70 lb/sq in (4.92 kg/cm²)	70 lb/sq in (4.92 kg/cm²) approx.
Idling	15 lb/sq in (1.05 kg/cm²)	= = =	= = =	= = =	= = =
FUEL SYSTEM					
Fuel pump					
Make & type: Early saloons	S.U. electric PD	= = =		= = =	= = =
Later vehicles	S.U. electric SP	S.U. electric SP & AUF 201 type CLUBMAN S.U. Mechanical AUF 700 (AUF 705 model)	= = = = = =	= = = = = =	= = = 1275 G.T. S.U. Mechanical AUF 700 (AUF 705 model)
Delivery rate: PD type	45 pints/hr. (25.5 litres/hr.)	= = =	= = =	= = =	= = =
SP and AUF 201 type	56 pints/hr. (32 litres/hr.)	= = =	= = =	= = =	= = =
Suction (min.) SU Mechanical		6 in (152 mm) Hg			6 in. (152 mm.) Hg.
Pressure (min.) SU Mechanical		3 lb/sq in (.21 kg/cm²)			3 lb./sq. in. (.21 kg./cm.²)

= = = denotes common to model listed in preceding column.

Additional information for vehicles of U.K. manufacture

	848 cc Mini Mk. I & Mk. II, Mini Automatic, Mini Van, Mini Pickup, Traveller, Countryman, Moke	998 cc Mini Mk. II, Mini Automatic, Mini Van, Mini Pickup, Traveller, Countryman, Moke, Clubman Saloon, Clubman Estate	997 cc & 998 cc Mini Cooper	970 cc & 1071 cc Mini Cooper 'S'	1275 cc Mini Cooper 'S' Mk. I, Mk. II, Mk. III, Mini 1275 G.T.
CARBURETTOR					
Type	Single HS2	= = = AUTOMATIC MODEL S.U. Single HS4	Twin S.U. type HS2	= = =	= = =
Needle: Standard	EB AUTOMATIC MODEL AN	GX AUTOMATIC MODEL AC	997 c.c.: GZ 998 c.c.: GY	970 c.c.: AN 1071 c.c.: H6	COOPER 'S' M 1275 G.T. GX
Rich	M AUTOMATIC MODEL H6	M AUTOMATIC MODEL M1	997 c.c.: — 998 c.c.: M		COOPER 'S' AH2 1275 G.T. M
Weak	GG AUTOMATIC MODEL EB	GG AUTOMATIC MODEL HA	997 c.c.: — 998 c.c.: GG		COOPER 'S' EB 1275 G.T. GG
Piston spring	RED	= = =	997 c.c. RED, 998 c.c. BLUE	Red	= = =
Jet size	.090 in. (2.29 mm.)	= = =	= = =	= = =	= = =
IGNITION SYSTEM					
Coil	Lucas LA12	= = =	Lucas HA 12	= = =	= = = 1275 G.T. Lucas LA12
Spark plugs: make & type	Champion N5	= = =	= = =	Champion N9Y	= = =
gap	.025 in. (.625 mm.)	= = =	= = =	= = =	= = =
DISTRIBUTOR					
Make/Type:	Lucas DM2 (early) Lucas 25D4 (later)	= = =	= = =	Lucas 23D4	= = =
Serial number:	40768, 41026 (Premium fuel) 40767, 41007 (Regular fuel)	40931, 41030 Automatics: 41134, 41242, 41251	997 c.c.: 40774 (H.C.) 40873 (L.C.) 998 c.c.: 40955 (H.C.) 40958 (L.C.) 41032 (H.C.) 41031 (L.C.)	40819	COOPER 'S' 40819, 41033 1275 G.T. 41257
Dwell angle	60° ± 3°	= = =	= = =	= = =	= = =
Contact breaker gap	.014 to .016 in. (.35 to .40 mm.)	= = =	= = =	= = =	= = =
Condenser capacity	.18 to .24 mF.	= = =	= = =	= = =	= = =

DISTRIBUTOR TEST DATA	REFER APPENDIX				
IGNITION TIMING Static	T.D.C. (Premium fuel distributor) 7° B.T.D.C. (Regular fuel distributor) 3° B.T.D.C. (Automatic models)	5° B.T.D.C. 4° B.T.D.C. (Automatic models)	997 c.c.: 7° B.T.D.C. (H.C.) 5° B.T.D.C. (L.C.) 998 c.c.: 5° B.T.D.C. (H.C.) 5° B.T.D.C. (L.C.)	970 c.c.: 12° B.T.D.C. 1071 c.c.: 3° B.T.D.C.	2° B.T.D.C.
Stroboscopic at 600 r.p.m.	3° B.T.D.C. (Premium fuel distributor) 10° B.T.D.C. (Regular fuel distributor) 6° B.T.D.C. (Automatic models)	8° B.T.D.C. 6° B.T.D.C. (Automatic models)	997 c.c.: 9° B.T.D.C. (H.C.) 7° B.T.D.C. (L.C.)	970 c.c.: 14° B.T.D.C. 1071 c.c.: 5° B.T.D.C.	4° B.T.D.C. 1275 G.T.: 5° B.T.D.C.
COOLING SYSTEM					
Type	Pressurized radiator, thermo-syphon, pump and fan assisted	= = =	= = =	= = =	= = =
Pressure cap	13 p.s.i. (.91 kg/cm²)	= = =	= = =	= = =	= = =
Thermostat setting (Std.)	82° (180°F)	= = =	= = =	= = =	= = =
— Cold climates	88° (188°F)	= = =	= = =	= = =	= = =
— Hot climates	74° (165°F)	= = =	= = =	= = =	= = =
CLUTCH					
Type	BLMC single dry plate diaphragm or coil spring	= = =	= = =	= = =	= = = 1275 G.T. Borg and Beck Diaphragm spring type
Diameter and facing type	7¼" (180 mm.) Woven yarn	= = =	= = =	= = =	= = =
Coil or diaphragm spring colour code — Coil:	Red spot	= = =	Black/white spot	(Inner) green spot (Outer) white spot	= = =
Diaphragm:	Brown	light green	= = =	Green/blue	= = =
TRANSMISSION					
Number of forward speeds	4	= = =	= = =	= = =	= = =
				= = = / Optional (close ratio)	
Gearbox Ratios: Top	1.0 : 1	= = =	= = =	= = = / = = =	= = =
Third	1.412 : 1	= = =	1.357 : 1	1.357 : 1 / 1.242 : 1	= = =
Second	2.172 : 1	= = =	1.916 : 1	1.916 : 1 / 1.78 : 1	= = =
First	3.627 : 1	= = =	3.200 : 1	3.200 : 1 / 2.57 : 1	= = =
Reverse	3.627 : 1	= = =	3.200 : 1	3.200 : 1 / 2.57 : 1	= = =
Final drive Ratio:	3.765 : 1 (17/64)	3.44 : 1 (18/62) Van & Pick-up: 3.76 : 1 (17/64)	3.765 : 1 standard 3.444 : 1 optional	3.765 (17/64) 3.444 (18/62) 3.939 (16/63) 4.133 (15/62)	= = = = = = = = = = = = 1275 G.T. 3.65 : 1 (17/62)

= = = denotes common to model listed in preceding column.

Additional information for vehicles of U.K. manufacture

	848 cc Mini Mk. 1 & Mk. II, Mini Automatic, Mini Van, Mini Pickup, Traveller, Countryman, Moke	998 cc Mini Mk. II, Mini Automatic, Mini Van, Mini Pickup, Traveller, Countryman, Moke, Clubman Saloon, Clubman Estate		997 cc & 998 cc Mini Cooper		970 cc & 1071 cc Mini Cooper 'S'		1275 cc Mini Cooper 'S' Mk. I, Mk. II, Mk. III, Mini 1275 G.T.	
		Saloon	Van & Pick-up	Standard	Optional	Options		1275 G.T. 3.65 (17/62)	
Overall ratios: Top	3.765 : 1	3.44 : 1	3.76 : 1	3.765 : 1	3.444 : 1	3.765 : 1	3.444 : 1	= = =	= = =
Third	5.317 : 1	4.93 : 1	5.40 : 1	5.11 : 1	4.674 : 1	5.11 : 1	4.67 : 1	= = =	= = =
Second	8.176 : 1	7.63 : 1	8.32 : 1	7.213 : 1	6.598 : 1	7.21 : 1	6.60 : 1	= = =	= = =
First	13.657 : 1	12.13 : 1	13.25 : 1	12.05 : 1	11.03 : 1	12.05 : 1	11.02 : 1	= = =	= = =
Reverse	13.657 : 1	12.19 : 1	13.30 : 1	12.05 : 1	11.03 : 1	12.05 : 1	11.02 : 1	= = =	= = =
						3.939 : 1	4.133 : 1	= = =	= = =
						5.34 : 1	5.61 : 1	= = =	= = =
						7.54 : 1	7.92 : 1	= = =	= = =
						12.06 : 1	13.27 : 1	= = =	= = =
						12.06 : 1	13.27 : 1	= = =	= = =
						4.267 : 1		= = =	
						5.79 : 1		= = =	
						8.18 : 1		= = =	
						13.65 : 1		= = =	
						13.65 : 1		= = =	

TRANSMISSION (all synchromesh)

	848 cc	998 cc		997 cc & 998 cc	970 cc & 1071 cc	1275 cc
Number of forward speeds	(From Engine No. 8AM—WE—H101) 4	(From Engine Nos. 99H—159—H101 and 99H—251—H101) 4		Not applicable = = =	= = = = = =	All 9FXE Cooper "S" power units and 1275 G.T. = = =
					Standard (close ratio)	Standard (close ratio)
Gearbox Ratios: Top	1.00 : 1	1.00 : 1			1.00 : 1	1.00 : 1
Third	1.43 : 1	1.43 : 1			1.35 : 1	= = =
Second	2.21 : 1	2.21 : 1			2.07 : 1	= = =
First	3.52 : 1	3.52 : 1			3.30 : 1	= = =
Reverse	3.54 : 1	3.54 : 1			3.35 : 1	= = =
Final drive ratios	3.76 : 1 (17/64)	Saloon 3.44 : 1 (18/62) Van & Pick-up 3.76 : 1 (17/64)			3.65 : 1 (17/62)	= = =
		Saloon	Van & Pick-up			
Overall ratios: Top	3.76 : 1	3.44 : 1	3.76 : 1		3.65 : 1	= = =
Third	5.40 : 1	4.93 : 1	5.40 : 1		4.93 : 1	= = =
Second	8.32 : 1	7.63 : 1	7.63 : 1		7.56 : 1	= = =
First	13.25 : 1	12.13 : 1	12.13 : 1		12.04 : 1	= = =
Reverse	13.30 : 1	12.19 : 1	12.19 : 1		12.21 : 1	= = =

DRIVE SHAFTS					
Make	Hardy Spicer	= = =	= = =	= = =	= = =
Type of shaft	Solid shaft, reverse spline	= = =	= = =	= = =	= = =
Joint at wheel end	Constant velocity hemispherical joint	= = =	= = =	= = =	= = =
Coupling at inner end	Rubber coupling AUTOMATIC MODEL Hardy Spicer flange joint	= = = AUTOMATIC MODEL = = =	= = =	= = =	Needle roller universal joint

AUTOMATIC TRANSMISSION					
Ratios: top	1.00 : 1	= = =			
3rd	1.46 : 1	= = =			
2nd	1.845 : 1	= = =			
1st	2.69 : 1	= = =			
reverse	2.69 : 1	= = =			
Differential ratio:	3.27 : 1	= = =			
Overall ratios: top	3.76 : 1	= = =			
3rd	5.49 : 1	= = =			
2nd	6.94 : 1	= = =			
1st	10.11 : 1	= = =			
reverse	10.11 : 1	= = =			
Torque converter: max. torque multiplication	2.00 : 1	= = =			
Output gear ratio	1.15 : 1	= = =			

STEERING					
Type	Rack and pinion	= = =	= = =	= = =	= = =
Camber angle	1° pos. to 3° pos.	= = =	= = =	= = =	= = =
Caster angle	3° (With vehicle in unladen condition)	= = =	= = =	= = =	= = =
King pin (swivel hub) inclination	9° 30′ (With vehicle in unladen condition)	= = =	= = =	= = =	= = =
Toe-out	1/16″ (1.6 mm.) (With vehicle in unladen condition)	= = =	= = =	= = =	= = =
Lock angle (outer wheel at 20°) Inner wheel	23° (With vehicle in unladen condition)	= = =	= = =	= = =	= = =

SUSPENSION					
Type	Rubber cone spring (early) Hydrolastic (late)	= = =	= = =	= = =	= = = Cooper "S" & 1275 G.T. Hydrolastic
Fluid capacity (Hydrolastic models)	4 pts. (5 U.S. pts. 2.27 litres)	= = =	= = =	= = =	= = =
Fluid pressure	263 lb./sq. in. 18.49 kg./sq. cm.) (early)	= = =	= = =	= = =	= = =
	282 lb./sq. in. (19.74 kg./sq. cm.) (late)	= = =	= = =	= = =	1275 G.T. 292 lb./sq. in. (20.6 kg./cm.²)
Rear suspension: camber	1° pos.	= = =	= = =	= = =	= = =
Rear suspension: toe-in	⅛″ (3.18 mm.)	= = =	= = =	= = =	= = =
Radius arm bushes: Reamed bore	.8125 to .8130 in. (20.63 to 20.65 mm.)	= = =	= = =	= = =	= = =

= = = denotes common to model listed in preceding column.

Additional information for vehicles of U.K. manufacture

	848 cc Mini Mk. I & Mk. II, Mini Automatic, Mini Van, Mini Pickup, Traveller, Countryman, Moke	998 cc Mini Mk. II, Mini Automatic, Mini Van, Mini Pickup, Traveller, Countryman, Moke, Clubman Saloon, Clubman Estate	997 cc & 998 cc Mini Cooper	970 cc & 1071 cc Mini Cooper 'S'	1275 cc Mini Cooper 'S' Mk. I, Mk. II, Mk. III, Mini 1275 G.T.
BRAKES					
Type	Lockheed hydraulic	= = =	= = =	Lockheed hydraulic with vacuum servo	= = =
Servo unit				Lockheed 5½ in. (140 mm.)	MK. I and MK. II Lockheed 5½ in. (140 mm.) MK. III and 1275 G.T. Lockheed type 6
Front brakes: type	Single leading shoe (early) Two leading shoe (late)	= = = = = =	Disc	= = =	= = =
Drum or disc diameter	7 in. (178 mm.)	= = =	= = =	7½ in. (190.5 mm.)	= = =
Lining dimensions	6.75 in. × 1.25 in. (17.14 × 3.17 cm.) (early) 6.75 in. × 1.50 in. (17.14 × 3.80 cm.) (late)	= = = = = =			
Lining or pad area	33.75 sq. in. (217.7 cm²) (early) 41.0 sq. in. (264 cm.²) (late)	= = = = = =	13.8 sq. in. (89 cm.²) Total Swept area 101 sq. in. (651 cm²)	17.3 sq. in. (111.4 cm²) Total Swept area 122 sq. in. (787 cm.²)	= = =
Lining or pad material	Don 202	= = =	M 78 Red/green/red/green/red	Ferodo DA6 (early) Mintex M78 red/green/red/green/red	= = =
Wheel cylinder bore diameter	13/16 in. (20.64 mm.) (early) 15/16 in. (23.81 mm.) (late)				
Minimum pad thickness			1/16 in. (1.6 mm.)	= = =	= = =
Rear Brakes: Drum diameter	7 in. (178 mm.)	= = =	= = =	= = =	= = =
Lining dimensions	6.75 × 1.25 in. (17.14 × 3.17 cm.) (early) 6.75 × 1.50 in. (17.14 × 3.80 cm.) (late)	= = = = = =	= = = = = =	= = =	= = =
Lining area	33.75 sq. in. (217 cm.²) (early) 34.2 sq. in. (221 cm.²) (late)	= = = = = =	40 sq. in. (261.29 cm²)	= = =	= = =
Lining material	Don 202	= = =	= = =	= = =	= = =
wheel cylinder bore diameter	⅝ in. (15.87 mm.) (early) ¾ in. (19.05 mm.) (late)	= = = = = =	= = =	= = =	= = =
Master cylinder bore diameter	¾ in. (19.05 mm.)	= = =	= = =	= = =	= = =
Brake fluid	To S.A.E. spec. 70R3	= = =	Lockheed 329	= = =	= = =

= = = denotes common to model listed in preceding column.

DISTRIBUTOR — TEST DATA

Distributor centrifugal advance (vacuum pipe disconnected). Check readings at decelerating **Distributor** r.p.m.

SERIAL No. 40768 A

CENTRIFUGAL ADVANCE

Dist. r.p.m.	Dist. Advance
2200	17° MAX.
1250	12° — 14°
350	½° — 2½°
250	No advance

VACUUM ADVANCE
7 Hg 13 Hg 5°

SERIAL No. 41057

CENTRIFUGAL ADVANCE

Dist. r.p.m.	Dist. Advance
2800	13° — 15°
1150	8° — 10°
450	½° — 2½°
200	No advance

VACUUM ADVANCE
4 Hg 7 Hg 8°

SERIAL No. 40941

CENTRIFUGAL ADVANCE

Dist. r.p.m.	Dist. Advance
2500	12° — 14°
2000	12° — 14°
1600	10° — 12°
700	6° — 8°
500	2½° — 4½°
400	½° — 2½°

VACUUM ADVANCE
4 Hg 15 Hg 11°

SERIAL No. 62941051 A or AYA 0192

CENTRIFUGAL ADVANCE

Dist. r.p.m.	Dist. Advance
2500	12° — 14°
2000	12° — 14°
1360	9° — 11°
700	6° — 8°
530	3° — 5°
360	0° — 2°

VACUUM ADVANCE
4 Hg 15 Hg 11°

SERIAL No. 62941053 A or AYG 0156

CENTRIFUGAL ADVANCE

Dist. r.p.m.	Dist. Advance
2200	12° — 14°
1800	12° — 14°
1300	10° — 12°
900	8½ — 10½°
680	4° — 6°
480	0° — 2°

VACUUM ADVANCE
3 Hg 9 Hg 8°

SERIAL No. 41271 B

CENTRIFUGAL ADVANCE

Dist. r.p.m.	Dist. Advance
2000	9° — 11°
1400	5½° — 7½°
800	2° — 4°
400	0° — 1½°
150	No advance

VACUUM ADVANCE
3 Hg 10 Hg 10°

SERIAL No. 62941052 A

CENTRIFUGAL ADVANCE

Dist. r.p.m.	Dist. Advance
2800	13° — 15°
2500	13° — 15°
1400	9° — 11°
850	7° — 9°
600	3° — 5°
400	0° — 2°
200	No advance

VACUUM ADVANCE
7 Hg 13 Hg 8°

SERIAL No. 41045 or AYA 0194

CENTRIFUGAL ADVANCE

Dist. r.p.m.	Dist. Advance
2830	13° — 15°
2500	13° — 15°
1400	9° — 11°
850	7° — 9°
600	3° — 5°
400	0° — 2°
300	No advance

VACUUM ADVANCE
7 Hg 13 Hg 8°

SERIAL No. 62941069 A or AYA 0200

CENTRIFUGAL ADVANCE

Dist. r.p.m.	Dist. Advance
2000	11° — 13°
1600	11° — 13°
1150	8½° — 10½°
700	6° — 8°
570	3° — 5°
440	0° — 2°
325	No advance

VACUUM ADVANCE
3 Hg 10 Hg 7°

SERIAL No. 40955 A

CENTRIFUGAL ADVANCE

Dist. r.p.m.	Dist. Advance
3300	15° — 17°
2000	10° — 12°
900	6° — 8°
400	½° — 2½°
200	No advance

VACUUM ADVANCE
3 Hg 8 Hg 7°

SERIAL No. 40958 A

CENTRIFUGAL ADVANCE

Dist. r.p.m.	Dist. Advance
3300	16° MAX.
2000	11° — 13°
900	8° — 10°
500	1½° — 4½°
200	No advance

VACUUM ADVANCE
3 Hg 8 Hg 7°

SERIAL No. 40774 A

CENTRIFUGAL ADVANCE

Dist. r.p.m.	Dist. Advance
1200	9° — 11°
500	1° — 4°
400	0° — 1½°
300	No advance

VACUUM ADVANCE
3 Hg 8 Hg 7°

SERIAL No. 40873

CENTRIFUGAL ADVANCE

Dist. r.p.m.	Dist. Advance
1300	13° — 15°
600	7½° — 9½°
450	4° — 6°
300	0° — 2½°
150	No advance

VACUUM ADVANCE
4 Hg 7 Hg 7°

SERIAL No. 40899

CENTRIFUGAL ADVANCE

Dist. r.p.m.	Dist. Advance
2800	16° — 18°
1900	14° — 16°
1250	7° — 9°
600	½° — 2½°
350	0° — ½°
250	No advance

VACUUM ADVANCE
5 Hg 17 Hg 10°

SERIAL No. 40819 B

CENTRIFUGAL ADVANCE

Dist. r.p.m.	Dist. Advance
3800	14° — 16°
3500	14° — 16°
2600	11° — 13°
800	5° — 7°
500	3° — 6°
300	0° — 1½°
225	No advance

NO VACUUM ADVANCE

SERIAL No. 40819H or AYG 0175

CENTRIFUGAL ADVANCE

Dist. r.p.m.	Dist. Advance
3800	14° — 16°
3500	14° — 16°
2000	9° — 11°
500	4° — 6°
415	2° — 4°
325	0° — 2°
225	No advance

NO VACUUM ADVANCE

SERIAL No. 40931, 41030

CENTRIFUGAL ADVANCE

Eng. r.p.m.	Eng. Advance
5000	22° — 26°
3400	16° — 20°
1600	9° — 13°
1300	6° — 10°
900	0° — 4°
600	No advance

VACUUM ADVANCE
5 in. (12.7 cm.) Hg.
11 in. (27.9 cm.) Hg. 14°

SERIAL No. 41033

CENTRIFUGAL ADVANCE

Eng. r.p.m.	Eng. Advance
7000	28° — 32°
5200	22° — 26°
1600	10° — 14°
1000	6° — 12°
600	0° — 3°
450	No advance

NO VACUUM ADVANCE

SERIAL No. 41030

CENTRIFUGAL ADVANCE

Eng. r.p.m.	Eng. Advance
5000	22° — 26°
3400	16° — 20°
1600	9° — 13°
1300	6° — 10°
900	0° — 4°
600	No advance

VACUUM ADVANCE
5 in. (12.7 cm.) Hg.
11 in. (27.9 cm.) Hg. 14°

SERIAL No. 41257

CENTRIFUGAL ADVANCE

Eng. r.p.m.	Eng. Advance
4000	18° — 22°
2800	11° — 15°
2000	6° — 10°
1600	4° — 8°
800	0° — 3°
300	No advance

VACUUM ADVANCE
3 in. (7.62 cm.) Hg.
10 in. (25.4 cm.) 18°

SERIAL No. 40955, 41032

CENTRIFUGAL ADVANCE

Eng. r.p.m.	Eng. Advance
6000	30° — 34°
5400	28° — 32°
4200	24° — 28°
2300	18° — 22°
1800	12° — 16°
800	1° — 5°
300	No advance

VACUUM ADVANCE
3 in. (7.62 cm.) Hg.
8 in. (20.32 cm.) Hg. 14°

SERIAL No. 40958, 41031

CENTRIFUGAL ADVANCE

Eng. r.p.m.	Eng. Advance
5500	28° — 32°
4400	26° — 30°
2200	22° — 26°
1800	16° — 20°
1000	3° — 9°
600	0° — 3°
400	No advance

VACUUM ADVANCE
3 in. (7.62 cm.) Hg.
7 in. (17.7 cm.) Hg. 16°

SERIAL No. 41134, 41242, 41251

CENTRIFUGAL ADVANCE

Eng. r.p.m.	Eng. Advance
5500	26° — 30°
4800	24° — 28°
1800	15° — 19°
1600	12° — 16°
800	0° — 4°
600	No advance

VACUUM ADVANCE
3 in. (7.62 cm.) Hg.
15 in. (38.1 cm.) Hg. 18°

SERIAL No. 40768, 41026

CENTRIFUGAL ADVANCE

Eng. r.p.m.	Eng. Advance
3400	30° — 34°
2500	24° — 28°
1300	16° — 20°
900	9° — 15°
700	1° — 7°
500	No advance

VACUUM ADVANCE
7 in. (17.7 cm.) Hg.
13 in. (33 cm.) Hg. 10°

SERIAL No. 40767, 41007

CENTRIFUGAL ADVANCE

Eng. r.p.m.	Eng. Advance
5000	22° — 26°
3900	15° — 19°
1700	1° — 5°
850	No advance

VACUUM ADVANCE
5 in. (12.7 cm.) Hg.
11 in. (27.9 cm.) Hg. 16°

SECTION Ac
ENGINE
CRANKCASE EMISSION CONTROL

This section deals with the maintenance and servicing of the Exhaust Emission Control System fitted to MOKE engines in accordance with various territorial motor vehicle regulations.

Section Ac-1

CRANKCASE EMISSION CONTROL

Description

With this system the engine breather outlet is connected by hoses to the controlled depression chamber; the chamber between the piston and the throttle disc valve, of the carburetter. Engine fumes and blow by gases are drawn from the crankcase by the depression in this chamber, through an oil separator incorporated in the engine outlet connection, and from there to the inlet manifold. Fresh air is supplied to the engine through the combined oil filler cap and filter.

Servicing

The oil filler cap must be renewed every 12,000 miles (20000 km.) or 12 months; no other service is required.

Section Ac-2

DESCRIPTION
— EXHAUST PORT AIR INJECTION

Air is pressure-fed from an air pump via an injection manifold to the cylinder head exhaust port of each cylinder. A check valve in the air delivery pipe prevents blow-back from high pressure exhaust gases. The pump also supplies air through a gulp valve to the inlet manifold to provide air during conditions of deceleration and engine over-run.

IMPORTANT. The efficient operation of the system is dependent on the engine being correctly tuned. The ignition and spark plug settings, valve clearances, and carburetter adjustments given for a particular engine (see **GENERAL DATA**) must be strictly adhered to at all times.

Air pump

The rotary vane type air pump is mounted on the front of the cylinder head and is belt driven from the water pump pulley. Provision is made for tensioning the belt.

Air is drawn into the pump through a dry-type renewable element filter. A relief valve in the pump discharge port allows excessive air pressure at high engine speeds to discharge to the atmosphere.

Check valve

The check valve, fitted in the pump discharge line to the injection manifold, protects the pump from the back-

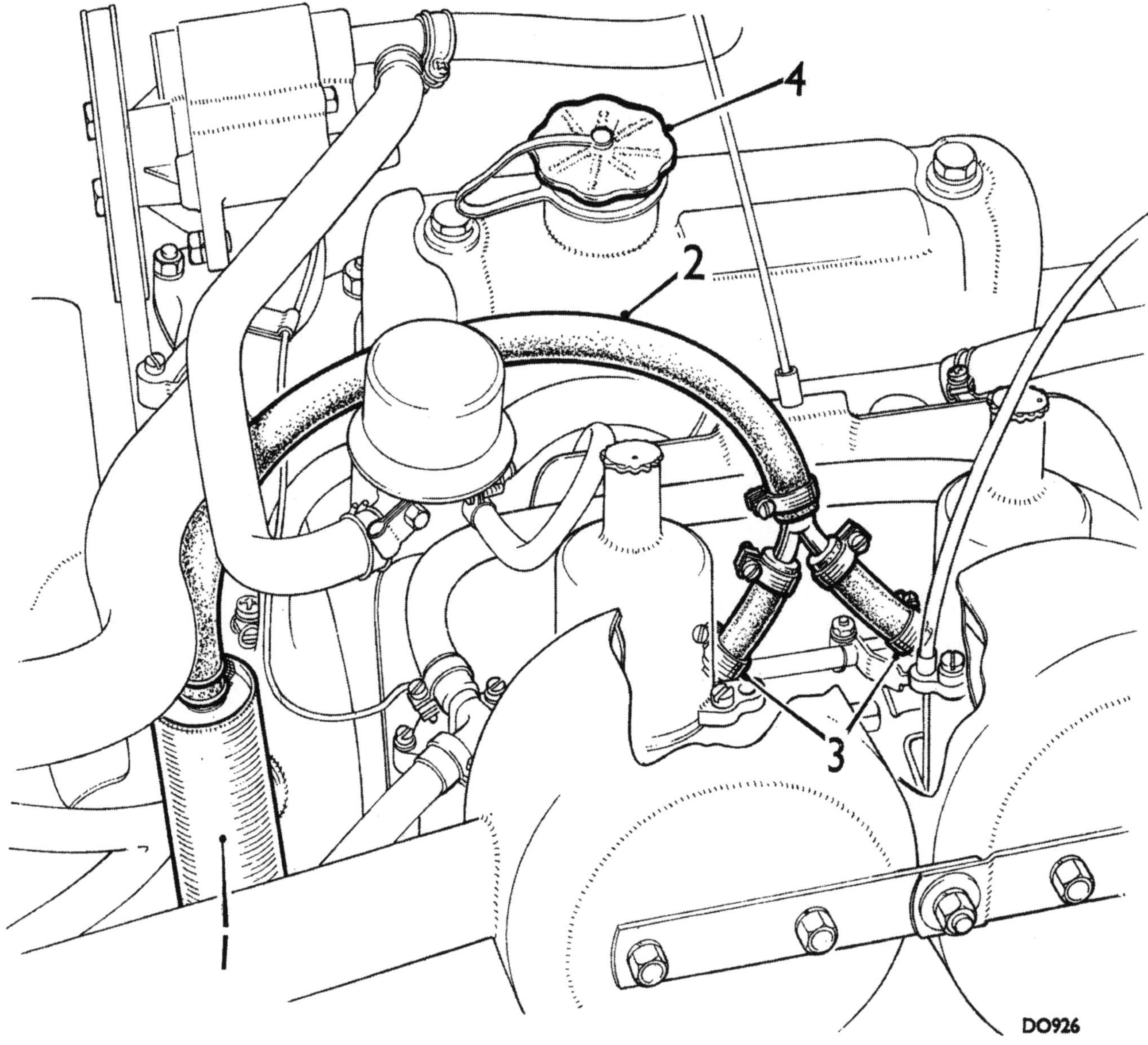

Fig. 2
A later-type crankcase emission control system ***twin carburettor installation shown.***

1. Oil separator.
2. Breather hose.
3. Carburetter chamber connection.
4. Filtered filler cap.

flow of exhaust gases.

The valve shuts if the air pressure ceases while the engine is running; for example, if the pump drive belt should break.

Gulp valve

The gulp valve, fitted in the pump discharge line to the inlet manifold, controls the flow of air for leaning-off the rich air/fuel mixture present in the inlet manifold immediately following throttle closure after running at full throttle opening (i.e. engine over-run).

A sensing pipe connected between the inlet manifold and the gulp valve maintains manifold depression directly to the underside of the diaphragm and through a bleed hole to the upper side. Sudden increases in manifold depression which occur immediately following throttle closure act on the underside of the diaphragm which opens the valve and admits air to the inlet manifold. The bleed hole allows the differences in depression acting on the diaphragm to equalize and the valve closes.

On some engines a restrictor is fitted in the air pump discharge connection to the gulp valve, to prevent surging when the gulp valve is operating.

Carburetter

The carburetters are manufactured to a special exhaust emission control specification and are tuned to give optimum engine performance with maximum emission control.

A limit valve is incorporated in the carburetter throttle disc which limits the inlet manifold depression ensuring that under conditions of high inlet-manifold depression

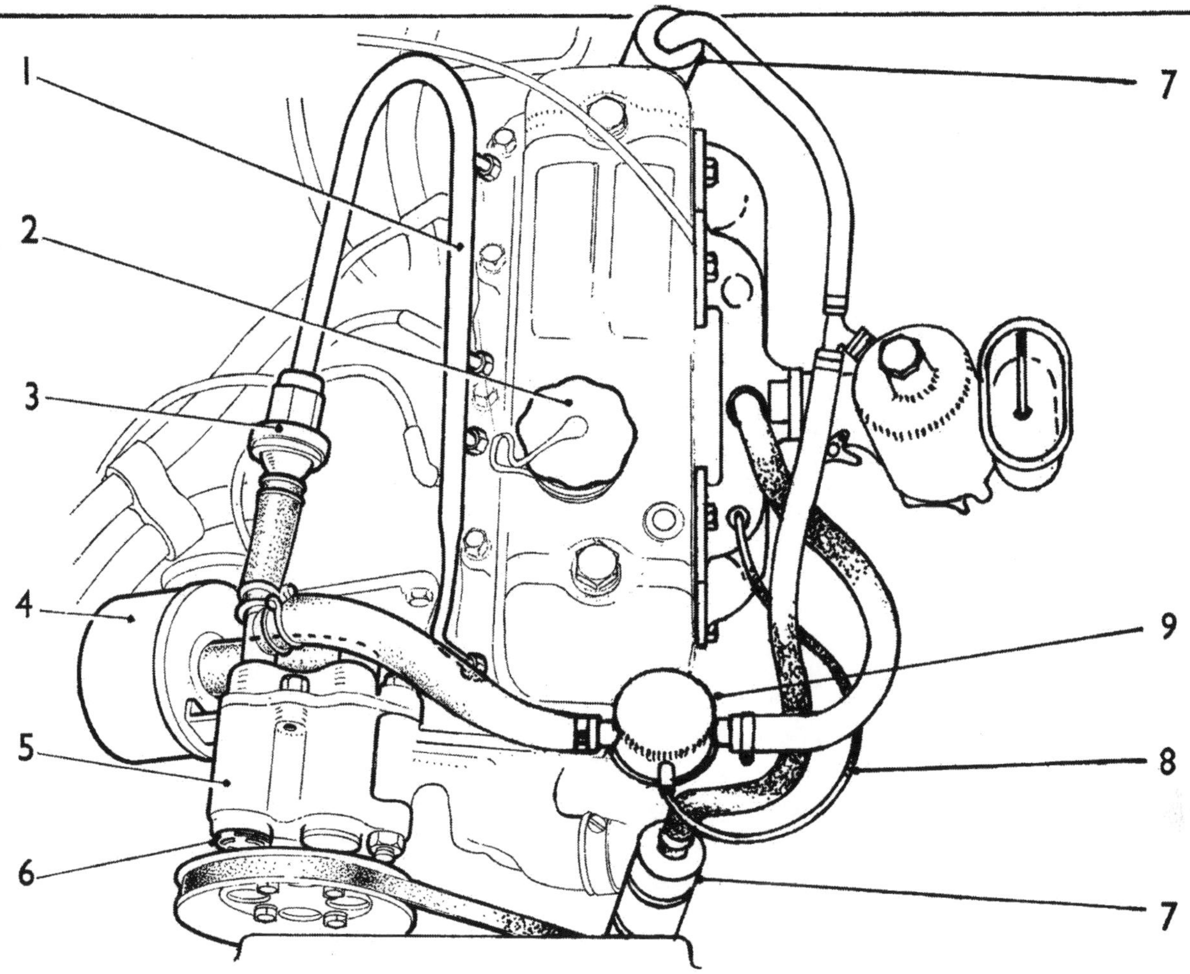

Fig. 1

A typical engine emission control system layout (Single carburettor installation.)

1. Air manifold.
2. Oil filler cap.
3. Check valve.
4. Emission air cleaner.
5. Air pump.
6. Relief valve.
7. Oil separator.
8. Vacuum sensing tube.
9. Gulp valve.

the mixture entering the cylinders is at a combustible ratio.

Section Ac-3

AIR PUMP

Drive belt tension

When correctly tensioned, a total deflection of $\frac{1}{2}$ in., under moderate hand pressure, should be possible at the midway point of the longest belt run between the pulleys.

To tension the belt:

(1) Slacken the air pump mounting bolt and adjusting link bolts (see Fig. 3).

(2) Using hand pressure only, move the pump in the required direction until the correct tension is obtained.

(3) Tighten the mounting and adjusting bolts to a torque figure of 10 lb. ft.

Testing

(1) Check the drive belt for correct tensioning.

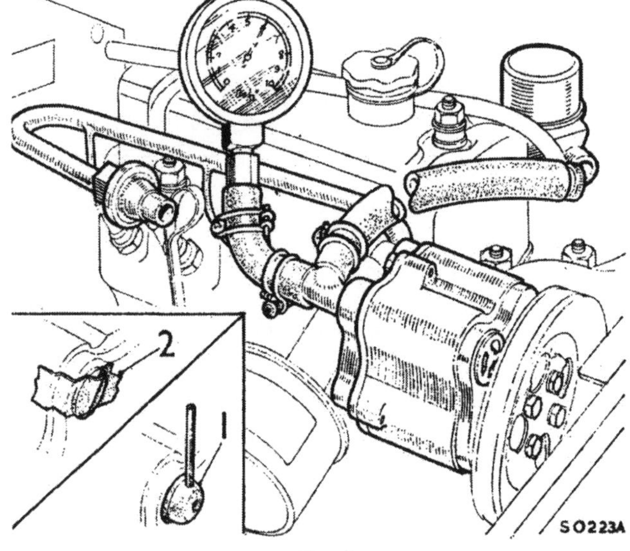

Fig. 2

The pressure gauge connected (four-cylinder engines)

1. Relief valve test tool. 2. Tape used to duct air.

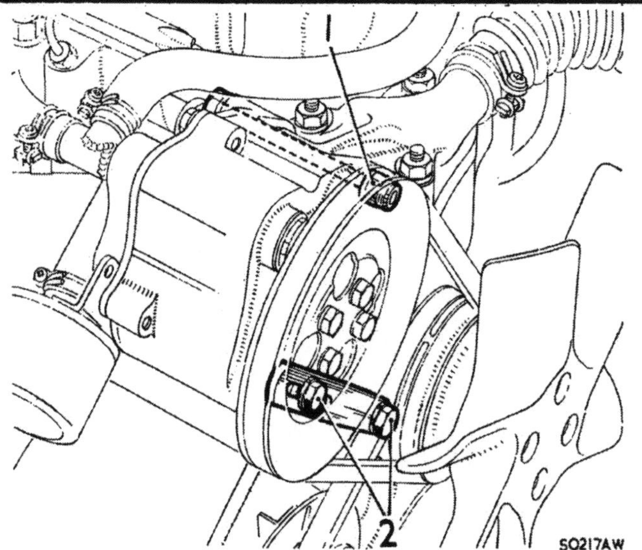

Fig. 3

Air pump (four-cylinder engines)

1. Pump mounting bolt. 2. Adjusting link bolts.

(2) Connect a tachometer to the engine in accordance with the instrument-maker's instructions.

(3) Disconnect the gulp valve air supply hose at the gulp valve and securely plug the hose.

(4) Disconnect the air manifold supply hose at the check valve, and connect a pressure gauge to the hose (see Fig. 2).

(5) Run the engine at the air pump test speed given in **'GENERAL DATA':** a gauge reading of not less than 2·75 lb./sq. in. should be registered.

(*a*) If a lower reading is obtained, remove, dismantle and clean the pump air cleaner. Reassemble using a new element, refit the air cleaner and repeat the test.

(*b*) If the reading is still unsatisfactory, temporarily blank off the relief valve and repeat the test; if the reading is now correct, renew the relief valve.

(*c*) If a satisfactory reading is still unobtainable. remove and service the air pump.

(6) Stop the engine and fit a temporary air duct over the face of the relief valve. Two methods of doing this are shown in Fig. 2. The tool (1) may be fabricated from grommet (Part No. 1B 1735) and a short length of metal brake tube, or (2) by using a piece of adhesive tape to form the duct.

DO NOT ATTEMPT TO CHECK AIR FLOW FROM THE RELIEF VALVE BY PLACING A FINGER BETWEEN THE VALVE AND THE DRIVING PULLEY.

(*a*) Start the engine and slowly increase the speed until air flow from the relief valve duct is detected, when a gauge reading of 4·5 to 6·5 lb./sq. in. should be registered.

(*b*) If the relief valve fails to operate correctly, remove the pump and renew the valve.

Removing

(1) Disconnect the air hoses from the pump connections and remove the air cleaner.

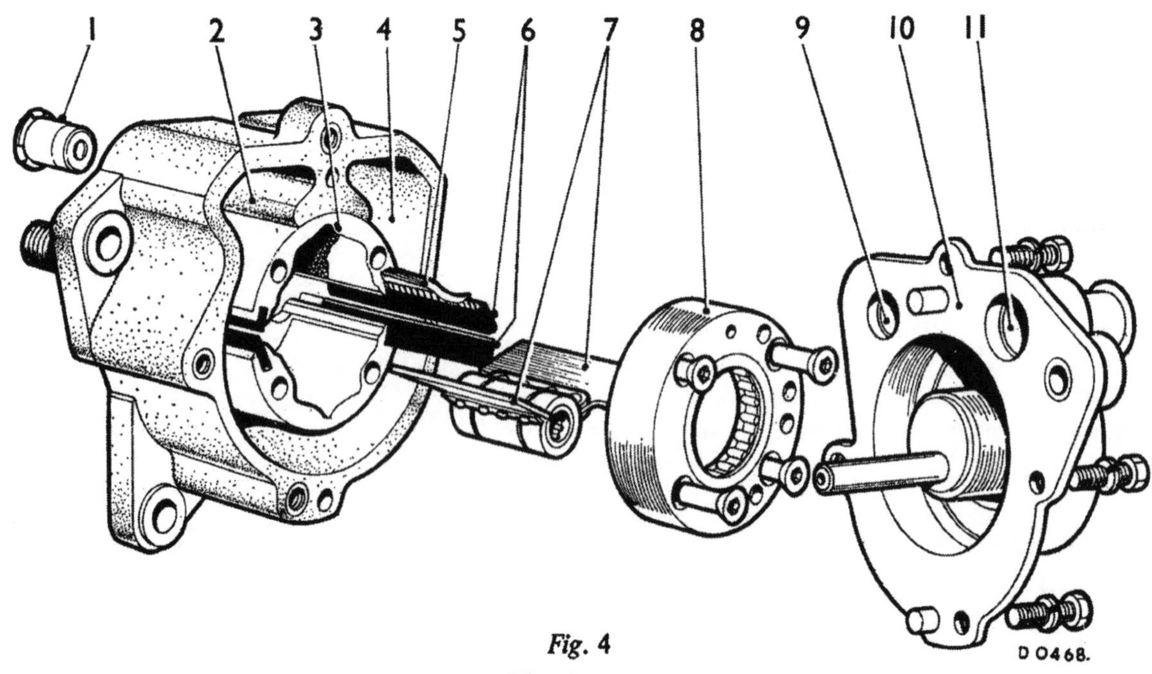

Fig. 4

The air pump

1. Relief valve.
2. Inlet chamber.
3. Rotor.
4. Outlet chamber.
5. Spring.
6. Carbons.
7. Vane assemblies.
8. Rotor bearing end plate.
9. Outlet port.
10. Port-end cover.
11. Inlet port.

(2) Slacken the mounting and adjusting link bolts and slip the drive belt from the pump pulley.
(3) Remove the top adjusting link bolt and the nut securing the pump mounting bolt.
(4) Support the pump, withdraw the mounting bolt and lift the pump from the engine.

Dismantling

(1) Remove the four port-end cover retaining bolts and withdraw the cover.
(2) Remove the four screws securing the rotor bearing end plate to the rotor and remove the end plate.
(3) Lift out the vane assemblies.
(4) Remove the carbon and spring assemblies from the rotor.

Servicing

(1) Wipe the interior and components of the pump clean, using a lint-free cloth.

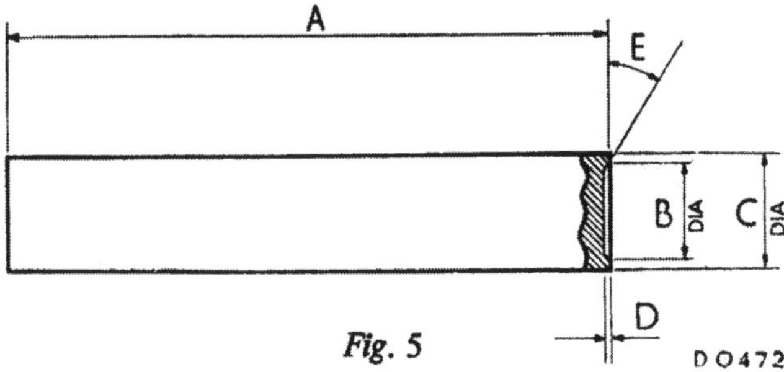

Fig. 5

The dimensions of the relief valve replacing tool

A = 5 in. B = ·986 in. C = 1·062 in.
D = ·05 in. E = 30°.

(2) Clean the vane carrier roller bearings and the rotor end plate bearing and repack the bearings with Esso 'Andok' 260 lubricant.
(3) Inspect the vane assemblies for signs of having fouled the pump wall, and for grooving in area of contact with the carbons. Renew worn or damaged vanes.
(4) Fit new carbons (the original springs may be re-used if serviceable). Note that the slots which carry the carbon and springs are the deeper ones, and the carbons are all fitted with the chamfered edge to the inside.

Reassembling

(1) Reassemble the pump by reversing the dismantling procedure and noting that the underside of the heads of the rotor bearing end plate screws must be smeared with 'Locktite' before tightening.

Refitting

(1) Position the pump in the mounting bracket and fit, but do not tighten, the pump mounting bolt.
(2) Screw in, but do not tighten, the adjusting link bolt.
(3) Fit and tension the drive belt.
(4) Reconnect the hoses and refit the air cleaner.

Relief valve—replacing

(1) Remove the air pump.
(2) Remove the pump pulley.
(3) Pass a ½-in. diameter soft metal drift through the pump discharge connection so that it registers against the relief valve, and drive the valve from the pump.
(4) Fit a new copper seating washer to the new relief valve and enter the valve into the pump body.
(5) Using a tool made to the dimensions shown in Fig. 5, drive the valve into the pump until the copper seating washer is held firmly, but not compressed, between the valve and the pump.
(6) Refit the pulley and refit the air pump.

Section Ac-4

CHECK VALVE

Removing

(1) Disconnect the air supply hose from the check valve connection.
(2) Hold the air manifold connection to prevent it twisting and unscrew the check valve.

Testing

(1) Blow through the valve, orally, in turn from each connection. Air should only pass through the valve when blown from the air supply hose connection. If air passes through when blown from the air manifold connection, renew the check valve.
On no account may an air blast be used for this test.

Refitting

(1) Hold the air manifold connection to prevent it twisting, screw in and tighten the check valve.
(2) Reconnect the air supply hose to the check valve.

Section Ac-5

AIR MANIFOLD AND INJECTORS

Testing

(1) Disconnect the air manifold from the cylinder head connections.
(2) Slacken the air supply hose clip at the check valve connection.
(3) Rotate the manifold about its connection axis until the injector connections are accessible.
(4) Tighten the air supply hose clip.
(5) Run the engine at idle speed and observe the flow of air from each of the manifold connection tubes. Should the flow of air from any of the connections be restricted, remove the manifold and clear the obstruction using an air blast.
(6) With the engine running at idle speed, check that exhaust gases blow from each of the cylinder head injectors.

IMPORTANT.—The injectors may be free in the cylinder head and care must be taken to ensure that they are not displaced during this test.

To clear a restricted injector:

(*a*) Crank engine until the exhaust valve below the injector is closed.

(*b*) Using a hand drill (not power-driven), pass a ⅛-in. drill through the injector bore, taking care that the drill does not contact the exhaust valve stem after passing through the injector. Damage may result if a power-driven drill is used.

(*c*) Insert an air-blast nozzle into the injector connection to clear carbon dust from the exhaust port.

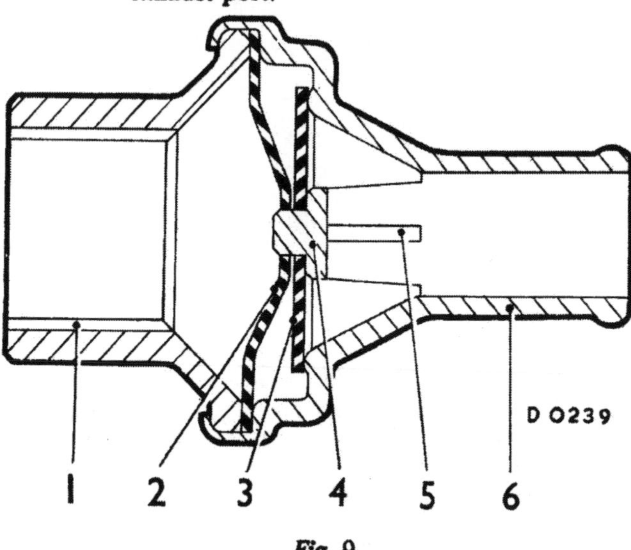

Fig. 9

A section through the check valve

1. Air manifold connection.
2. Diaphragm.
3. Valve.
4. Valve pilot.
5. Guides.
6. Air supply connection.

Section Ac-6

GULP VALVE

Testing

(1) Disconnect the gulp valve air supply hose from the air pump connection.

(2) Connect a vacuum gauge, with a tee connection to the disconnected end of the gulp valve air hose.

(3) Start the engine and run it at idle speed.

(4) Temporarily seal the open connection on the gauge tee and check that a zero gauge reading is maintained for approximately 15 seconds; if a vacuum is registered, renew the gulp valve. It is most important that the engine speed is not increased above idling during this test.

(5) With the gauge tee connection temporarily sealed, operate the throttle rapidly from closed to open; the gauge should then register a vacuum. Repeat the test several times, temporarily unsealing the tee piece connection to destroy the vacuum before each operation of the throttle. If the gauge fails to register a vacuum, renew the gulp valve.

Removing

(1) Disconnect the air hoses.

(2) Unscrew the mounting screw and remove the gulp valve.

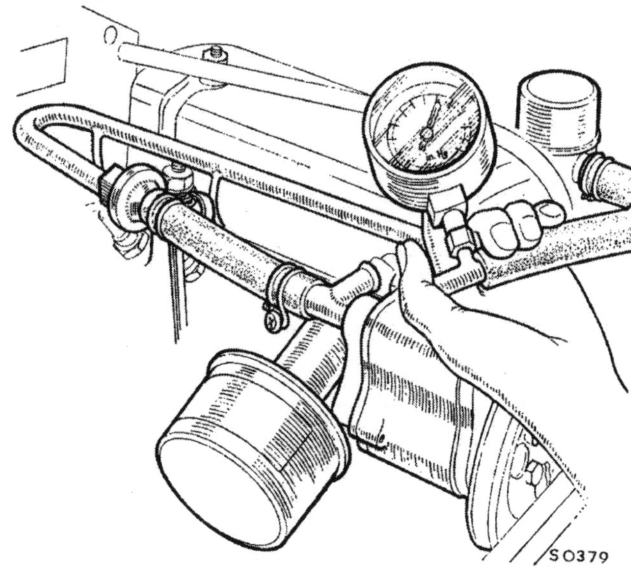

Fig. 10

The vacuum gauge connected for testing the gulp valve

Refitting

(1) Reverse the removing procedure.

Section Ac-7

LIMIT VALVE (INLET MANIFOLD DEPRESSION)

Testing

(1) Disconnect the gulp valve sensing pipe from the inlet manifold.

(2) Connect a vacuum gauge to the sensing pipe connection on the inlet manifold.

(3) Connect a tachometer in accordance with the instrument maker's instructions.

(4) Warm the engine at fast idle speed until normal operating temperature is reached.

(5) Increase the engine speed to 3,000 r.p.m. then release the throttle quickly; the vacuum gauge reading should immediately rise to between 20·5 and 22 in. Hg. If the gauge reading falls outside these limits the carburetter must be removed and the throttle disc and limit valve assembly renewed. After refitting, the carburetter must be tuned as described in Section 4-A.

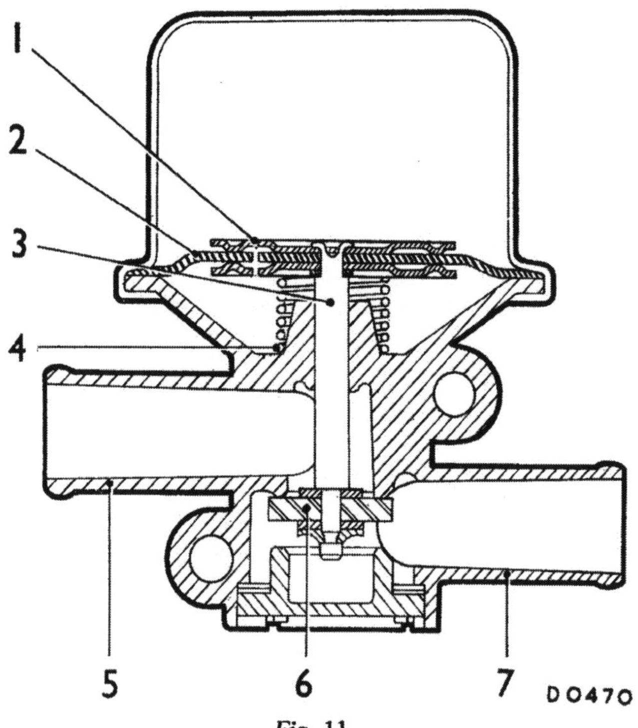

Fig. 11
A section through the gulp valve

1. Metering balance orifice.
2. Diaphragm.
3. Valve spindle.
4. Return spring.
5. Inlet manifold hose connection.
6. Valve.
7. Air pump hose connection.

SECTION a

ENGINE

The information contained in this Section refers to Australian produced vehicles. It does not supersede the previous Sections but should be used in conjunction with them.

(MANUAL MODELS)

(AUTOMATIC TRANSMISSION MODELS)

ENGINE AND TRANSMISSION ASSEMBLY
(Alternative method for removing and refitting)

Section a.1

Removing

1. Disconnect battery.
2. Drain water.
3. Remove bonnet.
4. Disconnect expansion tank hose, heater hoses and remove heater.
5. *Emission Control models*. Remove air pump filter and evaporative loss absorption canister together with connecting hoses.
6. *Cooper, Cooper "S" and Clubman G.T.* Disconnect brake booster vacuum hose and hydraulic brake lines. Remove the booster and mounting bracket.
7. Remove engine steady(s).
8. Disconnect clutch slave cylinder and lay aside — do not break hydraulic line.
9. *Cooper and Cooper "S"*. Disconnect oil pressure line from engine.
10. Remove air cleaner and adaptor(s), accelerator and choke cable. Disconnect fuel line, vacuum line, breather hose and return spring where applicable.
11. *Mini Matic*. Disconnect kickdown rod from carburettor.
12. Remove carburettor and cables from engine and lay aside.
13. *Single Carburettor Models*. Disconnect exhaust pipe from manifold.
14. *Cooper "S" and Clubman G.T.* Remove grille and disconnect oil cooler from engine.
15. *Cooper "S"*. Remove oil cooler.
16. Remove windscreen washer bottle and bracket (where necessary), remove distributor cap and disconnect all electrical wiring from engine including the earth strap.
17. Remove horn and bracket (where necessary).
18. Fit suitable hardwood spacers under both front suspension upper control arms so that the drive shafts remain horizontal when front of vehicle is raised.
19. Jack vehicle and place on stands.
20. *850, Early Model Van/Moke*. Lift the floor mat (where fitted) and remove rubber gear lever boot. Remove gear lever retaining plate and withdraw lever complete.
21. Disconnect exhaust pipe from transmission.
22. *Cooper and Cooper "S" and Clubman G.T.* Disconnect exhaust pipe clamp from extractor manifold, remove exhaust pipe mounting clips and release assembly from the extractor manifold.
23. Remove four set screws retaining either the gear lever remote control housing or steel cover plate. (Cover plate fitted to later model *Moke* and *Van*.) Removal releases gear lever from the transmission.
24. *Moke and Mini Matic*. Remove sump guard.
25. *Mini Matic*. Release the gear selector cable front adjusting nut from outer cable; disconnect inner cable from the bell crank lever and withdraw cable assembly through the adjusting lug on the transmission housing.
26. *Cooper "S", Mini Matic, Moke* — (Hardy Spicer universal joints). Remove drive shaft nuts and lever shaft from the transmission drive flange.
27. Disconnect both drive shaft rubber couplings leaving couplings attached to the transmission drive flanges.
28. Disconnect both engine mountings.
29. Lift engine using the "hole" position in the lifting bracket 18GA 498A.
30. Move engine forward and up until the drive shafts can be disconnected from couplings.
    NOTE: In some cases the operator may have difficulty in releasing drive shafts from the transmission. In this case remove the left hand road wheel, release the top suspension ball joint, allowing drive shaft to move outward. This enables the engine to be moved laterally, allowing drive shafts to be disconnected.
31. Raise the power unit approximately ten inches and release the speedometer cable from speedometer pinion bush assembly. Care should be taken that surrounding components are not damaged.

Refitting

Reverse the above procedure with particular attention to the following points:—

1. Use the "hook" position of the engine lifting bracket when lowering the power unit into position.
2. It is necessary to line up the drive flanges with the drive shafts before the engine mounts are resting on the sub-frame.
3. *Mini Matic*. Before starting the engine, ensure that the gear selector cable and kickdown linkage are correctly adjusted. Check the operation of the starter inhibitor switch.
4. When fitting the exhaust pipe it is essential that the mating flanges are clean, undamaged and accurately positioned to ensure a good seal.
5. *Cooper "S" and Clubman G.T.* The brake system must be bled as described in Section M.8. Use only approved fluids to specification. (See Maintenance and Lubrication Section.)

Section a.2

FLYWHEEL AND CLUTCH ASSEMBLY
(Removing and refitting)

The flywheel and clutch assembly can be removed without taking the power unit out of the vehicle. The following method is recommended:—

Removing

1. Disconnect the battery.
2. Remove components, where applicable, such as heater unit, brake booster, battery lead, screen washer and bracket from the clutch end of the engine compartment.
3. Remove the air cleaner, distributor cap and rotor arm.
4. Disconnect the starter cable from the solenoid.
5. Remove the radiator upper support bracket.
6. Remove the clutch withdrawal lever return spring and slave cylinder retaining bolts.
7. Secure the slave cylinder on the bulkhead, but do not disconnect the flexible hose.

8. Remove all the accessible flywheel cover set screws.
9. Raise the front of the vehicle and place on stands.
10. Remove the sump guard if fitted.
11. Disconnect engine steady from the engine (Moke — clutch end only).
12. Disconnect the rear engine mounting from the sub-frame.
13. Raise the clutch end of the engine with a suitable lifting jack sufficient to allow removal of the remaining flywheel cover set screws.
14. Remove the flywheel cover.
15. Withdraw the starter motor.
16. Remove the clutch diaphragm spring housing complete with release plate. Do not attempt to remove the flywheel with the clutch diaphragm spring housing in position, as damage may be caused to the cover resulting in thrust plate run out. (Diaphragm type clutch.)
    Remove the clutch thrust plate. (Coil spring type clutch.)
17. Remove the flywheel bolt, lockwasher and key, using socket 18G 587.
18. Ensure that the crankshaft keyway is horizontal. This will prevent the primary gear retaining washer from falling into the flywheel recess.
19. Fit extractor 18GA 304LX and remove flywheel being careful not to allow the flywheel to rotate so that the keyway loses its horizontal position.

Refitting

1. Clean all parts before reassembly.
2. Ensure that the clutch plate moves freely along the primary gear splines.
3. Align crankshaft keyway to the horizontal position and refit the flywheel.
4. Replace the remaining components in the reverse order of removal.
5. Replenish water if the heater has been removed.
6. Replenish brake fluid and bleed system if the brake booster has been removed.

Section a.3

STARTER RING GEAR

Australian manufactured replacement ring gears are now painted with a strip of scarlet-coloured temperature indicating paint.

When fitting these ring gears, they should be heated evenly until the paint colour changes from SCARLET to GREY-BROWN, indicating a temperature range of 575° to 752° F. (300° to 400°C.).

If the ring gear is heated beyond this temperature range, the colour will change to YELLOW. This colour or temperature range must be avoided, as softening of the gear will occur.

NOTE: Should the ring gear not bear the strip of indicating paint, follow the procedure outlined in Section A.11.

Section a.4

CRANKSHAFT PRIMARY GEAR OIL SEALS

To replace the primary gear oil seal without removing the power unit from the vehicle, the following procedure should be adopted:—

Removing

1. Remove the flywheel and clutch as detailed in Section a.2.
2. Remove the primary gear retaining washer and backing ring.
3. Fit the primary gear puller 18GAO1 and crankshaft thrust pad and extract the primary gear and seal.

Refitting

1. Clean the flywheel housing seal aperture and parts for refitting.
2. Ensure that the clutch plate moves freely along the primary gear splines.
3. Test fit the primary gear with thrust washers, backing ring and retainer and select the correct thrust washer to provide an end float of .0035 in. to .0065 in. (0.09mm. to 0.16mm.).
4. Remove the primary gear, thrust washers, backing ring and retainer.
5. Replace the primary gear thrust washer, using a smear of grease to retain the thrust washer against the crankshaft shoulder. (Chamfer to radius.)
6. Fit the nylon protector sleeve 18GA1043 over the primary gear splines. Liberally lubricate the protector sleeve and primary gear oil seal and slide the seal fully on to the primary gear. Remove the protector sleeve.
7. Offer up the primary gear and seal to the crankshaft and place the gear in mesh with the idler gear. Do not allow the seal to move off the ground surface of the gear.
8. Using the flywheel bolt and the replacer 18GAO2, push the seal until it contacts the register in the flywheel housing recess. **Do not overtighten.**
9. Remove the crankshaft bolt and seal replacer and assemble the primary gear backing ring and retainer.
10. Replace flywheel and clutch as detailed in Section a.2.

Section a.5

CRANKSHAFT PRIMARY GEAR (modified type)

To further assist the oil seal in preventing oil passing into the flywheel housing, an oil slinger has been fitted to the primary gear.

As the oil slinger is not serviced separately, a complete primary gear assembly will be required if it is desired to incorporate this design improvement.

The new gear will interchange with the previous gear.

Section a.6

CRANKSHAFT PRIMARY GEAR BUSHES

Fitting replacement bushes

When fitting bushes to the primary gear, they must NOT be machine pressed or drifted into position These methods will cause cracking of the sintered bronze, resulting in loss of the necessary interference fit of the bush to the primary gear which will cause early bush failure.

(a) When replacing bushes, pack them in dry ice for at least 10 mins. This will cause the outside diameter to contract by .002" to .005" (0.05 - 0.13mm.). Quickly insert the bushes into the primary gear bore, and push them home by hand pressure.

(b) Machine the bushes to obtain a running clearance of .003" to .0045" (0.08 - 0.11mm.). Refer Figs. a.1 and a.2.

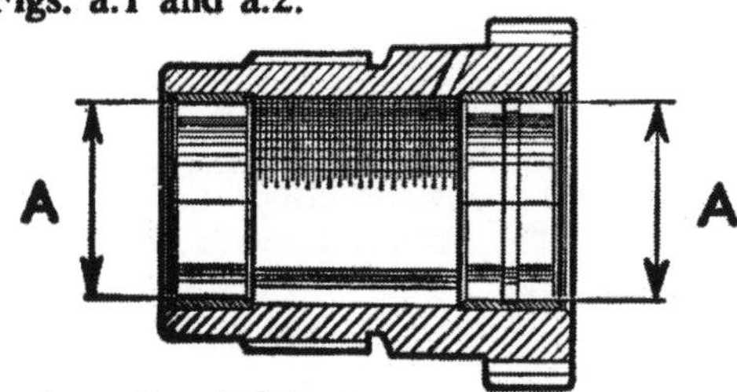

Fig. a.1 — Parallel Bore
Mini Models
Machine A to 1.503" - 1.504".
(38.17 - 38.2mm.)

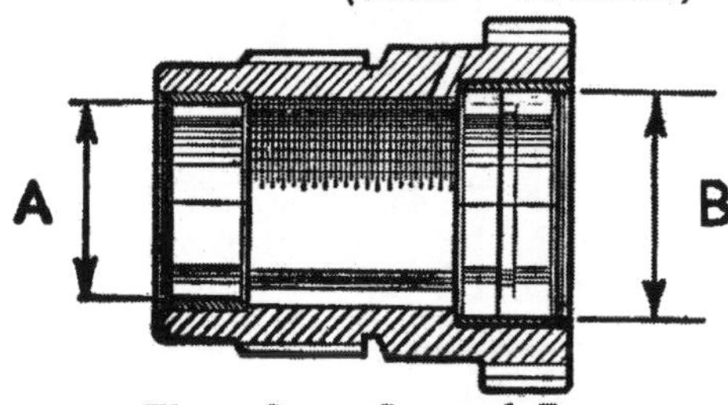

Fig. a.2 — Stepped Bore
Cooper "S" and Clubman G.T.
Machine A to 1.503" - 1.504".
(38.17 - 38.2mm.)
Machine B to 1.628" - 1.629".
(41.35 - 41.37mm.)

Section a.7

TRANSMISSION CASE
FLYWHEEL HOUSING AND IDLER GEAR REPLACEMENT

The external diameter of the needle roller bearings for the idler gear has been increased from 1 in. (25.4 mm.) to 1 1/16 in. (25.46 mm.) necessitating a larger bore size in the transmission case and the clutch housing.

The bearing journal on the transmission case side of the idler gear has been increased in length by approximately 3/8" (9.52 mm.) without increase in diameter.

Interchangeability

Flywheel housings are interchangeable, but the correct outside diameter needle roller bearing must be fitted.

When fitting the lengthened journal type idler gear to earlier transmission cases, remove the existing circlip which prevents the bearing being pushed through into the gearbox. Replace it with a new circlip to accommodate the longer shaft.

New transmission cases have the new circlip each side of the bearing, which is positioned in the centre of the bearing bore. It is essential that only the lengthened journal idler gear be used for replacement.

Note: Some early idler gears have an identification spigot machined on the end of the journal which fits into the transmission case. This type must not be confused with the lengthened journal type, and should only be used with the earlier transmission cases.

Early type gears which may be fitted either way must be marked during dismantling to ensure that gear teeth loading is not altered.

Section a.8

ROCKER SHAFT

Later engines have the cast-iron rocker shaft brackets replaced with brackets of sintered material together with longer locating studs. The oil feed to the rocker shaft remains in No. 1 rocker bracket, but the shaft locating hole has been transferred to No. 2 rocker bracket.

Section a.9

FRONT ENGINE STEADY

On some Australian-produced vehicles an additional engine steady is fitted between the cylinder head and bulkhead. When removing the power unit or cylinder head, the following additional procedure is necessary for removal of this component:—

Removing

1. Remove the rear pivot bolt and nut.
2. Slacken off the head bracket pivot bolt.
3. Remove the thermostat housing.
4. Remove the steady rod and head bracket by pressing the rear end of the steady rod down and around the bulkhead bracket.

Refitting

Reassembly is a reversal of the above.

Section a.10

TIMING COVER

An Australian produced timing cover and double lip seal were introduced at the following engine numbers:—

B.M.C. Moke	1278
Mini Minor	24562
Mini Deluxe	15508
Mini 1100	1st Production
Clubman	1st Production

The timing cover can be identified by strengthening swages and a gasket retaining rib. This seal cannot be used with the earlier type timing covers.

Section a.11

TIMING GEARS

When aligning the two gears, the following procedure should be used:—

1. Move both the camshaft and crankshaft sprocket gears away from the cylinder block face until all end float has been eliminated.
2. Check alignment of the timing gears, by the use of a straight edge and a feeler gauge.
3. If misalignment exceeds 0.003" (0.076 mm.) adjust the crankshaft gear by fitting the necessary shims behind the crankshaft gear to obtain this measurement.

Section a.12

OIL FILTERS

A "Ryco" oil filter assembly was introduced to the Mini Deluxe from engine number 9YA/Ta/H 5439 and 9YB, 9YH and 9YE engines at numbers commencing at 1001 — Mini 1100 and Clubman series engines were fitted with this filter from first production.

This filter assembly has a larger oil capacity, and some versions of it incorporated a pressure differential switch. The switch operates a warning lamp in the instrument panel to give an indication that the filter element should be changed. If the warning lamp continues to glow when the engine is running, the filter element must be changed as soon as possible within the maximum of 300 miles (500 Km.). The pressure differential switch was ultimately deleted.

NOTE: The "Ryco" oil filter assembly does not supersede previous oil filter assemblies, and its element is not interchangeable with the earlier elements.

The following procedure is recommended when removing and refitting the oil filter.

Removing

1. Remove the sump guard where fitted.
2. Unscrew the central retaining bolt of the filter and remove the bowl and element assembly.
3. Remove the filter element and discard.
4. Wash the bowl assembly and dry the components.
5. Remove the filter bowl sealing washers and clean the groove in the filter head.

Refitting

1. Fit new sealing washers. (Refer Fig. a.3.)
2. Place a new element in the filter bowl and reassemble, taking care to ensure that the components are correctly positioned and the filter bowl is square with the filter head.
3. Tighten the retaining bolt to the torque figure shown in the General Data.

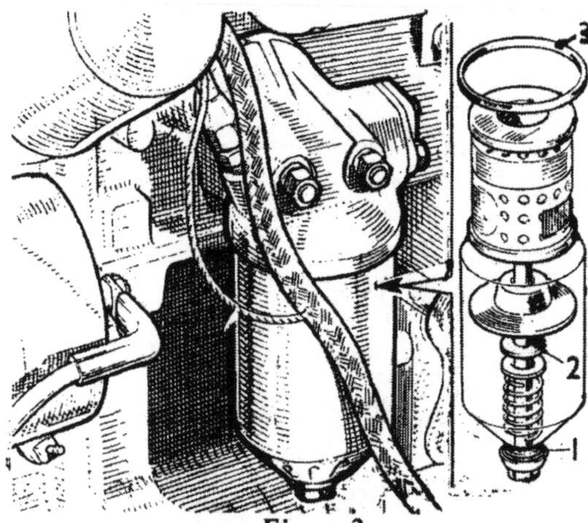

Fig. a.3
The oil filter components
Note the location of the three seals.

Section a.13

CLOSED CIRCUIT BREATHING SYSTEM
(Mini Series, except Mini Matic, Cooper "S", Clubman GT)

The crankcase breathing system fitted to these models consists of

1. A front side cover containing a gauze separator, vented to the atmosphere through a .020" (0.508 mm.) slot in the tube.
2. A rocker cover containing a gauze separator and hose outlet.
3. A non-vented oil filler cap.
4. An adaptor fitted between the carburettor body and the air filter adaptor.
5. A hose connecting (2) and (4).

On later models the rocker cover outlet pipe is connected to the carburettor body.

This breather system does not require periodic servicing.

Section a.14

OIL PUMP

An Australian designed oil pump which has five lobes was introduced at the following engine numbers.

Mini Minor	24462
Mini Deluxe	15316
B.M.C. Moke	1108
Mini 1100	1st Production
Mini Clubman	1st Production

This pump is interchangeable with pumps of English manufacture.

Section a.15

PISTON AND CONNECTING ROD ASSEMBLIES
(Australian 998 c.c. engines, Cooper "S" and Clubman GT)

Reference should be made to Section A.24 for general instruction with regard to the procedures for removing and refitting pistons to connecting rods.

Service tool No. 18GA05 is made available in place of the English tool 18G1002 recommended for use with Cooper "S". A similar tool, 18GA06, is used for 998 c.c. engines having gudgeon pins with an interference fit in the connecting rod.

Note: Extreme care should be taken to avoid piston damage when carrying out this operation. Refit the pin to the same side of the piston from which it was removed.

Section a.16

FRONT MAIN BEARING SEAL

When fitting the rubber-cork type seal, the following procedure should be employed:—

1. Thoroughly degrease the surface of the transmission case in the seal area with a solvent which drives rapidly and leaves no residue, e.g., Toluol or Shell X60.
2. Allow the solvent to evaporate.
3. Apply a rubber base contact adhesive to the transmission case and to the seal.
4. Allow a few minutes for the adhesive to become tacky.
5. Carefully push the seal into place.

Section a.17

FIRST MOTION SHAFT OUTER RACE

Removing

To remove the outer race of the first motion shaft roller bearing from the flywheel housing, remove the large circlip from its groove and immerse the flywheel housing in very hot water for several minutes to expand the bearing housing. Do not use other methods of heating the housing, as permanent distortion may result.

Using service tool 18GA617, grip together the spring handle of the split collet, place the collet inside the race till the lips of the collet register evenly under the lower edge of the race, and release the handles. Place the outer cover of the tool squarely on the bearing boss, run back the nut and flat washer to the head of the screw. Fit the screw through the outer cover and engage the threaded centre of the collet until the nut and washer reach the top of the outer cover. Hold the hexagon of the screw and continue screwing down the nut until the race is withdrawn.

Refitting

When refitting an outer race, expand the flywheel housing as previously described, lubricate the bore, and position the race squarely in the mouth of the bore of the housing. Support the face of the housing directly behind the bearing bore on a flat piece of hardwood to prevent distortion. Using the plug portion of service tool 18GA617, press in the race until the top edge is just sufficiently clear of the ring groove to enable the circlip to be refitted.

Section a.18

VALVES (modified type)

Referring to Fig. A.5, it should be noted that on later Mini — 1100, Moke engines and all Clubman models, the spring clip and the shrouds have been deleted.

Section a.19

VALVE SEAT (machining dimensions)

Refer to Fig. A.7 and Page A7.

The following table has additional information to that shown in table on Page A.

Section a.20

TORQUE CONVERTER

The torque converter may be removed without removing the power unit from the vehicle. The following method is recommended:—

Removing

1. Disconnect the battery.
2. Remove the heater unit.
3. Remove the air cleaner, distributor cap and rotor arm.
4. Disconnect the starter cable from the solenoid.
5. Remove the radiator upper support bracket.
6. Remove from the top the accessible converter cover setscrews.
7. Disconnect the engine steady from the engine.
8. Raise the front of the vehicle and place on stands.
9. Remove the sump protector.

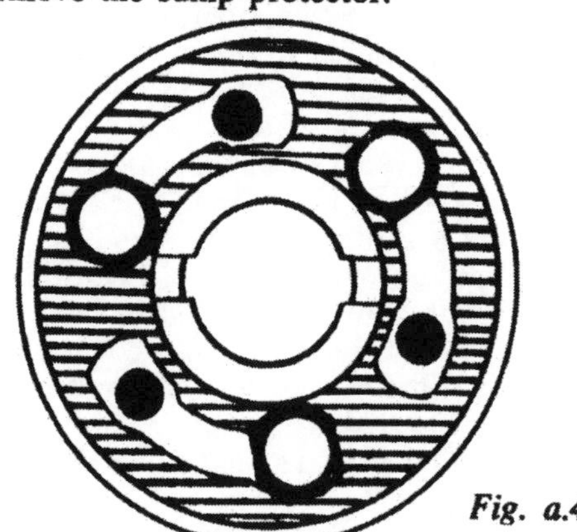

Fig. a.4

The converter centre with the retaining bolt removed, showing:—

1. 3 set screws removed.

2. Keyway horizontal.

10. Disconnect the rear engine mounting from the sub frame.
11. Raise the converter end of the engine with a suitable lifting jack.
12. Remove the remaining converter cover setscrews.
13. Remove the converter cover.
14. Drain the converter.
15. Remove the starter motor.
16. Remove the large converter centre bolt, lockwasher and key using socket spanner 18G 587.
17. Ensure that the crankshaft keyway is horizontal. (This will prevent the converter output gear retaining washer falling into the recess, preventing removal of the converter.)
18. Remove three of the setscrews and fit Service Tool 18GA 304LX. Remove the converter, being careful not to allow the converter to rotate so that the keyway loses its horizontal position. Refer Fig. a.4.

It is important that the six bolts mounted through the reinforcement plate in the centre of the unit are not all removed at one time.

Failure to observe this recommendation could result in any swarf within the converter finding its way between the central tapered hub and converter casing, causing oil leakage between the reinforcement plate and converter casing or incorrect balance of the assembly.

Refitting

1. Renew the three tab washers in the converter centre.
   Note: Do not remove the six bolts at any one time. Remove one of the three remaining bolts only, fit a new tab washer and replace both bolts. Tighten to 22 to 24 lb. ft. (3.0 to 3.3 Kg.m) before repeating the operation on the next bolt and tab washer.
2. Replace the remaining components in the reverse order of removal from item 17.

Section a.21

STARTER RING GEAR

Removing

1. Remove the converter assy. as detailed in Section a.20.
2. Drain the converter assembly, carefully masking the holes in the centre of the unit to prevent ingress of dirt after removal.
3. Using soft jaws in the vice, **lightly** hold the converter assembly and hacksaw through the ring gear in seven positions as shown in Fig. a.5. Ensure that the depth of the hacksaw cuts does not extend into the converter body pressing.
4. Clamp the ring gear between the two sawcuts which are 1.25 in. (31.75 mm.) apart — refer Fig. a.6 — and by carefully pushing and pulling the converter alternately, fatigue the weld metal. **Take care not to distort the converter pressing during this operation.**
   Repeat this procedure for the remaining six sections, finally carefully dressing off the fractured weld metal. **Do not remove any other welds, otherwise balance of the unit will be affected.**

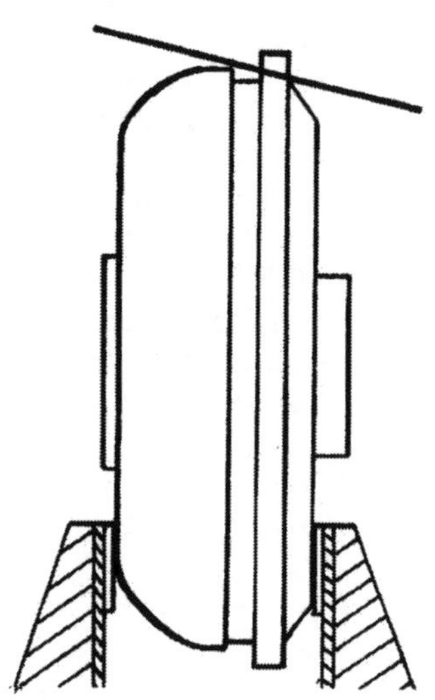

Fig. a.5

Refitting

1. The replacement starter ring must be heated to 200°C. (390°F.) by either of the following methods:—
   (a) Suspend the ring gear in a bath of oil to to ensure even heating. To prevent possible ignition of oil fumes, the oil bath should be covered and it should be ensured that thermometers do not touch the bottom of the bath.
   (b) The foregoing method is preferable, but if circumstances do not permit its use the ring may be heated carefully with a welding torch until 60/40 solder will just melt when applied to the ring.

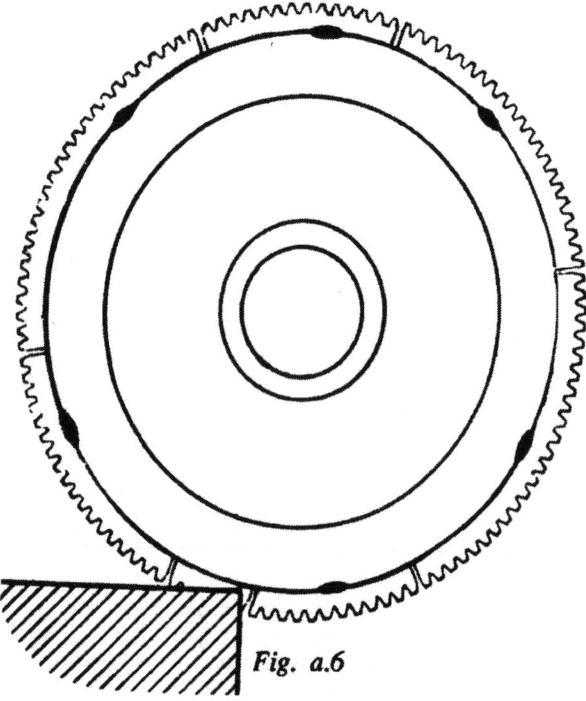

Fig. a.6

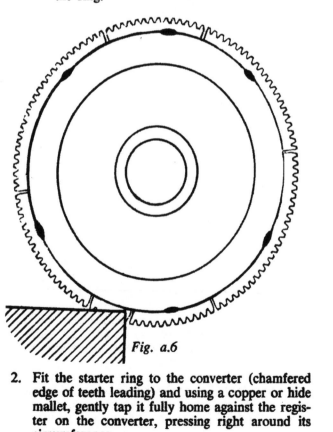

2. Fit the starter ring to the converter (chamfered edge of teeth leading) and using a copper or hide mallet, gently tap it fully home against the register on the converter, pressing right around its circumference.
3. Using arc welding equipment, weld the ring gear to the converter in the six positions originally used. Work diagonally to minimise distortion and ensure that the weld length is kept equal. It must not exceed ½ in. to ¾ in. (12.7 mm. to 17.78 mm.) in length.
   IMPORTANT: The positioning and lengths of the weld are of the utmost importance if converter balance is to be preserved.
4. Ensure that none of the weld metal will foul the converter housing on re-assembly.
5. Carefully clean the converter externally and remove the masking.
6. Refit the drain plug using a new sealing washer.
7. Refit the converter assembly as detailed in Section a.20.

Section a.22

TORQUE CONVERTER HOUSING OIL SEAL

Removing

1. Remove the converter as detailed in Section a.20.
2. Remove the converter output gear oil seal, using tool 18G 1087 and a suitable lever.

Refitting

1. Clean the components before re-assembly, with particular attention to the oil seal aperture.
2. Refer to Section Aa.15 and calculate measurement "A" for seal depth.
   NOTE: The replacement seal must be fitted to the correct depth in order that the oil drain hole behind the seal remains fully open.
3. Lubricate the replacement oil seal, offer it up to the aperture. Place the replacer 18G 08 against the seal and, using the torque converter retaining bolt, push the seal in to the calculated depth.
4. Remove the seal replacer.
5. Refit converter as detailed in Section a.20.

Section .23

INPUT GEAR ADJUSTMENT
(Later models)

The following method of input gear adjustment is an alternative to the method listed in Section Aa.4, items 30 to 38, and is applicable to transmissions where adjustment is effected by shims instead of thrust washers (Fig. Aa.19).

1. Carry out item 23.
2. Clean the outer end face of the input gear boss and the mating face of the converter housing bearing with a solvent, such as Shell X60, and fit the gear on to the transmission input shaft.
3. Clean all the existing shims with solvent and refit all but one of these shims on to the shaft against the input gear. If no shims were previously fitted, install a .003 in. (.076 mm.) shim.
4. Place a strip of "Plastigage" of suitable size against the shim and refit the converter housing as detailed in item 25, Section Aa.4. "Plastigage" is available in three size ranges, these being .001 in. - .003 in. (0.25 mm.) - .075 mm), .002 in - .006 in. (.051 mm. - 15 mm.), .004 in - .009 in. (.102 mm. - 230 mm.).
5. Remove the converter housing and measure the Plastigage strip. If the strip is not compressed or is excessively compressed, it will be necessary to add or remove a shim to obtain a reading.
6. After ascertaining the shim thickness required to eliminate end float, add shims to the value of .001 in. to .003 in. (.025 mm. to .076 mm.) to give the required input bearing preload.
7. Carry out item 37, Section Aa.4.
   NOTE: "Plastigage" is a plastic strip measuring material manufactured by Perfect Circle of Indiana, U.S.A., and is frequently used when checking bearing clearances.

Section a.24

OIL FILTER ASSEMBLY

A larger capacity oil filter element has been used, being $\frac{3}{8}$in. (9.53 mm.) longer than the original, and the support spring $\frac{5}{8}$ in. (15.88 mm.) shorter. The new spring is copper-plated, and the filter container is unchanged.

When a replacement filter of the larger capacity is purchased, it will be supplied with the shorter copper-plated spring. The smaller filter element is not supplied with a spring.

A physical check must be made to ensure that only the short element and assembly is used in the early engines. If this precaution is neglected, passage of unfiltered oil could occur.

Reassembling the remote control assembly

Lubricate the operating surfaces of all components and reassemble by reversing the dismantling procedure, paying particular attention to the positioning of the primary shaft lever. When fitting the lever to the shaft ensure that the lever is positioned in the same vertical plane as the primary shaft.

Should the lever be incorrectly fitted, it is possible for the gear lever to dislodge the split bush when selecting reverse gear thereby causing loose gear lever action and difficult gear selection.

Section a.25

MODIFICATIONS AND ASSEMBLY NOTES

Design changes

There have been major changes associated with the change speed lever (30) which was originally retained by a die cast block (27) with separate nylon seat bearing on the large sphere of the change speed lever. Vibration damping was effected by a spring-loaded nylon cup (28) bearing UPWARD against the small lower sphere of the lever. The Morris Cooper incorporated dual springs (29) to improve damping, refer Fig. f.9.

1st Change: The retaining block (27) was replaced by a spacer block (20). The lever was retained by a spring-loaded nylon seat (21) bearing DOWN on the large sphere, and the spring (18) was retained by an additional pressed steel retaining plate (17) fitted above the spacer (20). One convolution of the change speed lever rubber boot is located in this retaining plate to improve water and dust sealing. The nylon cup was replaced by a nylon split bush (19). Refer Fig. f.9.

2nd Change: A secondary rubber boot was introduced to improve sealing around change speed lever. This change necessitated the replacement of the pressed steel retainer (17) with a flat, circular plate which incorporates a change speed lever stop. The secondary boot fits over the lever and locates around this plate, the large boot is retained to seal the body aperture. A small rubber ring is fitted to the upper portion of the change speed lever to separate and prevent contact between the two boots. Refer Fig. f.9.

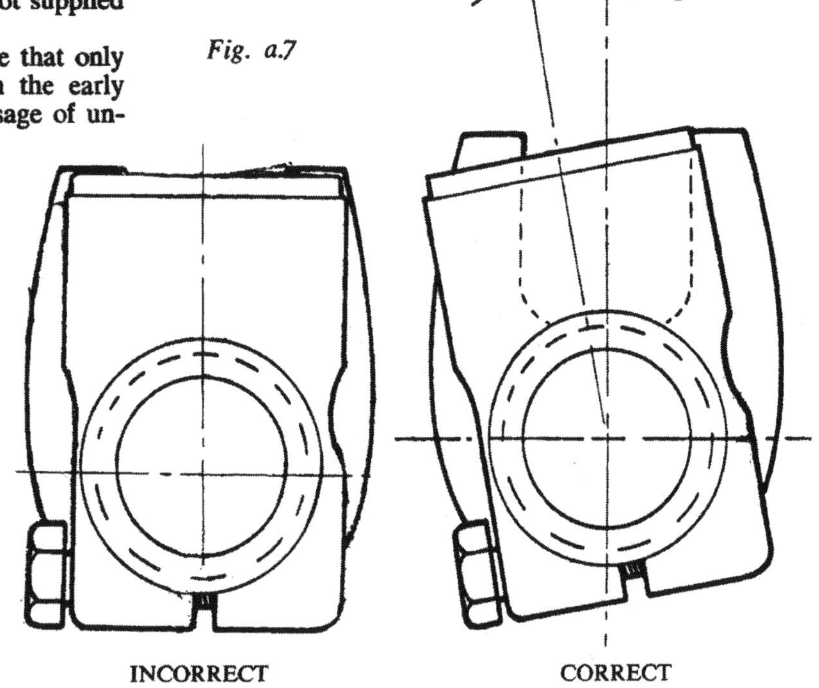

Fig. a.7

GEAR CHANGE REMOTE CONTROL COMPONENTS

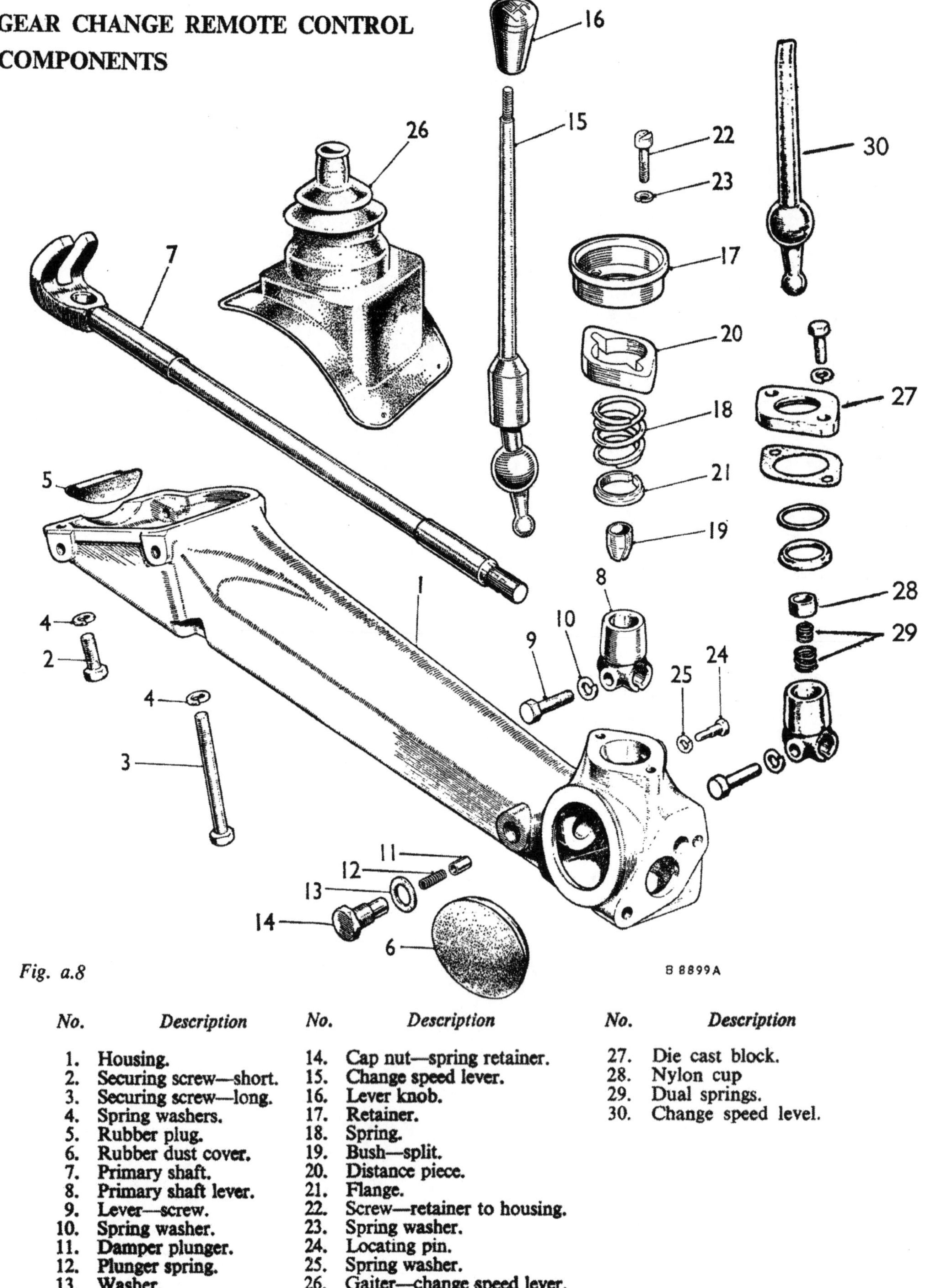

Fig. a.8

No.	*Description*
1.	Housing.
2.	Securing screw—short.
3.	Securing screw—long.
4.	Spring washers.
5.	Rubber plug.
6.	Rubber dust cover.
7.	Primary shaft.
8.	Primary shaft lever.
9.	Lever—screw.
10.	Spring washer.
11.	Damper plunger.
12.	Plunger spring.
13.	Washer.
14.	Cap nut—spring retainer.
15.	Change speed lever.
16.	Lever knob.
17.	Retainer.
18.	Spring.
19.	Bush—split.
20.	Distance piece.
21.	Flange.
22.	Screw—retainer to housing.
23.	Spring washer.
24.	Locating pin.
25.	Spring washer.
26.	Gaiter—change speed lever.
27.	Die cast block.
28.	Nylon cup
29.	Dual springs.
30.	Change speed level.

SECTION Dc

CARBURETTER

This section deals with the maintenance and servicing of the Exhaust Emission Control System fitted to MOKE engines in accordance with various territorial motor vehicle regulations.

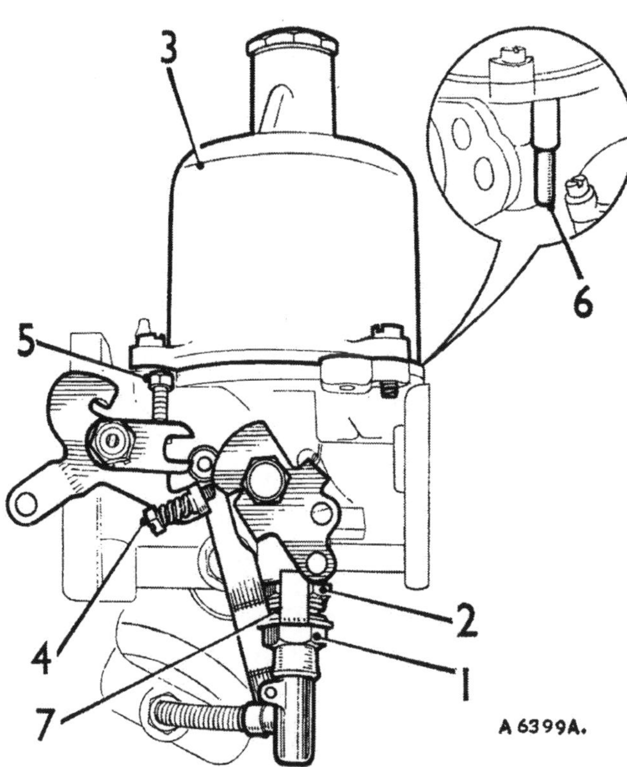

The type HS carburetter

1. Jet adjusting nut.
2. Jet locking nut.
3. Piston suction chamber.
4. Fast-idle adjusting screw.
5. Throttle adjusting screw.
6. Piston lifting pin.
7. Jet adjustment restrictor.

Section Dc-1

CARBURETTER TUNING—BASIC

GENERAL

The carburetters fitted to cars equipped with engine emission control systems are balanced to provide maximum performance with maximum pollution control. Under no circumstances may they be interchanged, or parts substituted.

Tuning must be carried out with the engine emission control equipment connected and operating, and is confined to the following procedure. If the required settings cannot be obtained, the service procedure detailed under **'CARBURETTER SERVICING'** must be carried out and then the carburetter tuned in accordance with the procedure given in **'CARBURETTER TUNING —COMPLETE'**.

Tuning conditions

To ensure that the engine temperature and mixture requirements are stabilized, tuning must be carried out in accordance with the following setting cycle.

(1) Connect a tachometer in accordance with the instrument-maker's instructions.

(2) Warm the engine at a fast idle to normal operating temperature, preferably with the car standing in an ambient temperature of between 16 and 27° C. (60 to 80° F.). Run the engine for at least five minutes after the thermostat has opened; the thermostat opening point can be detected by the sudden rise in temperature of the radiator header tank.

(3) Set the engine speed at 2,500 r.p.m., at no load, and run for one minute.

(4) Tuning operations may now be commenced and must be carried out in the shortest possible time. If the time for settings exceeds a three-minute period, open the throttle and run the engine at 2,500 r.p.m. for one minute then resume tuning. Repeat this clearing operation if further periods of three minutes are exceeded.

NOTE.—In no case should the jet adjustment restrictor be removed or repositioned. Only mixture adjustments within the limits of the restrictor are available for tuning. If satisfactory adjustment is not obtainable within the limits of the jet adjustment restrictor refer to **'CARBURETTER SERVICING'**.

(1) Top up the piston damper with the recommended engine oil until the level is ½-in. above the top of the hollow piston rod.

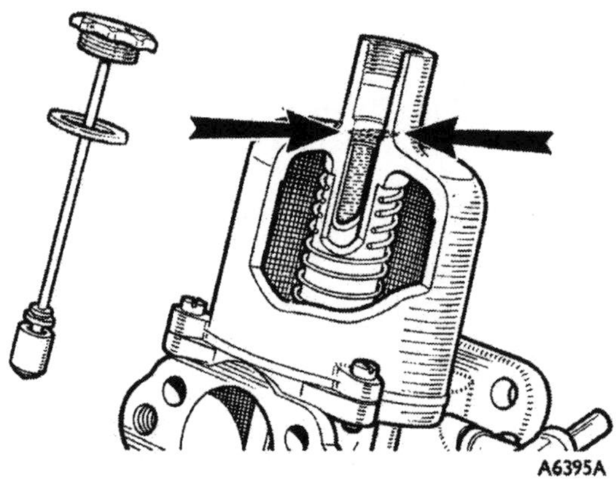
A6395A

NOTE.—On dust-proofed carburetters, identified by a transverse hole drilled in the neck of the suction chambers and no vent hole in the damper cap, the oil level must be ½-in. below the top of the hollow piston rod.

(2) Check throttle control action for signs of sticking.

(3) Check the idling speed (Tachometer) against the figure given in **'GENERAL DATA'**

(*a*) If the reading is correct and the engine runs smoothly, proceed to operations (7) and (8).

(*b*) If the reading is not correct, adjust the speed by turning the throttle adjusting screw in the required direction until the correct speed consistent with smooth running is obtained, then proceed to operations (7) and (8).

(*c*) If a smooth idle at the correct speed is not obtainable by turning the throttle adjusting screw, carry out operations (4) to (8).

(4) With the engine stopped, check that the piston falls freely onto the bridge, indicated by a distinct metallic click, when the lifting pin (6) is released. If not refer to **'CARBURETTER SERVICING'**.

(5) Turn the jet adjusting nut (1) to cover the full range of adjustment available within the limits of the restrictor, selecting the setting where maximum speed is recorded on the tachometer consistent with smooth running.

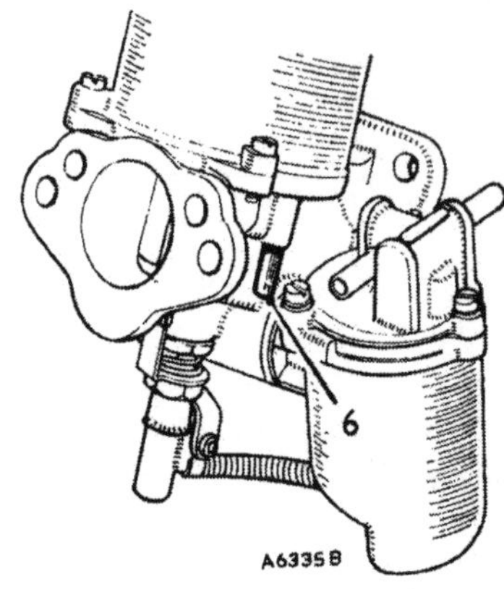

A6335B

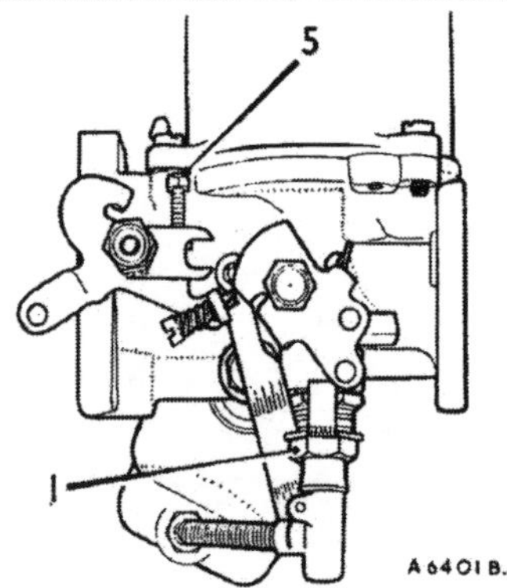

A6401B.

(6) Readjust the throttle adjusting screw (5) to give the correct idling speed if necessary.

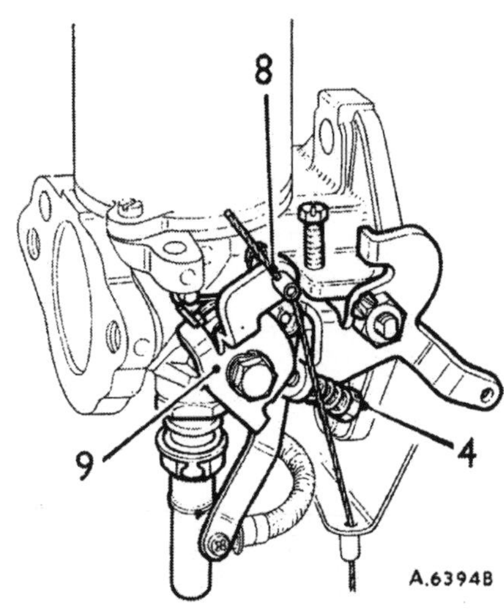

A.6394B

(7) Check, and if necessary adjust, the mixture control wire (8) to give a free movement of approximately $\frac{1}{16}$-in. before it starts to pull on the jet lever (9).

(8) Pull the mixture control knob until the linkage is about to move the carburetter jet and adjust the fast-idle screw (4) to give the engine fast-idle speed (Tachometer) given in **'GENERAL DATA'**

Section Dc-2

CARBURETTER SERVICING

Dismantling

Carburetters—all types

(1) Thoroughly clean the outside of the carburetter.

(2) Mark the relative position (12) of the suction chamber (3) and the carburetter body (13).

(3) Remove the damper (14) and its washer (15). Unscrew the chamber retaining screws (16).

(4) Lift off the chamber in the direction of arrow (17) without tilting.

(5) Remove the piston spring (18).

(6) Carefully lift out the piston assembly (19) and empty the damper oil from the piston rod (20).

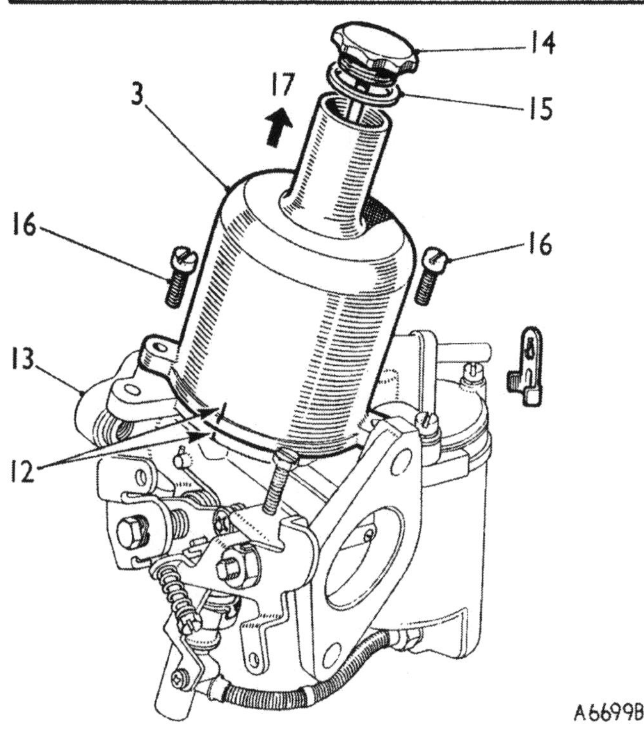

Carburetters—fixed needle type

(7) Remove the needle locking screw (21) and withdraw the needle (22). If it cannot easily be removed, tap the needle inwards first and then pull outwards. Do not bend the needle.

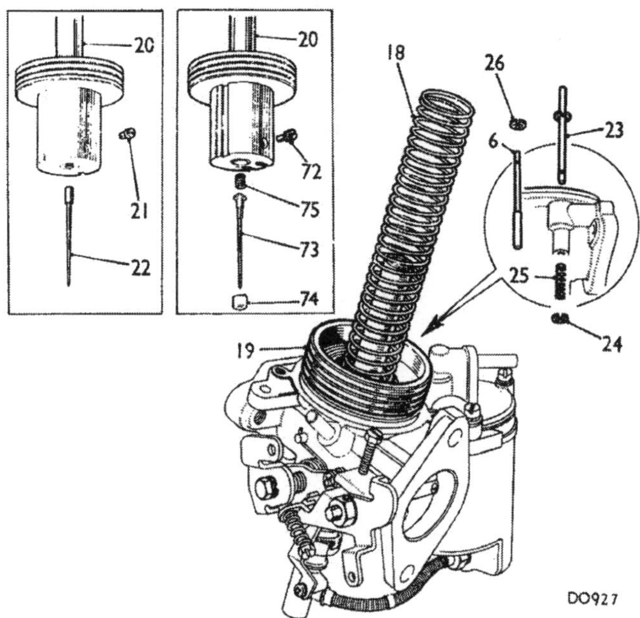

Carburetters—spring-loaded needle type

(8) Remove the guide locking screw (72), withdraw the needle assembly (73), needle support guide (74) and spring (75), taking care not to bend the needle.

(9) Withdraw the needle from the guide and remove the spring from the needle assembly.

Carburetters—all types

(10) If a piston lifting pin (23) with an external spring is fitted, remove the spring retaining circlip (24) and spring (25), then push the lifting pin upwards to remove it from its guide. With the concealed spring type (6) press the pin upwards, detach the circlip (26) from its upper end, and withdraw the pin and spring downwards.

(11) Support the moulded base of the jet (26) and slacken the screw (27) retaining the jet pick-up link (28).

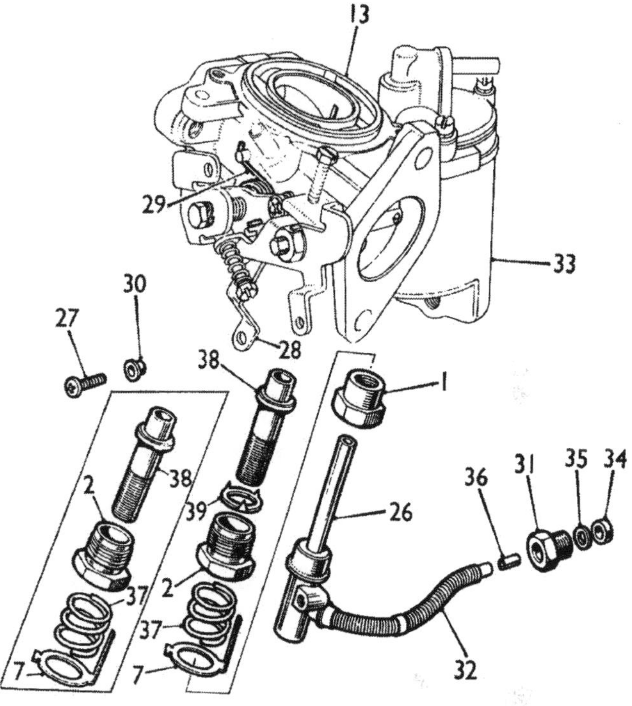

(12) Relieve the tension of the pick-up lever return spring (29) from the screw and remove screw and brass bush (30) (when fitted).

(13) Unscrew the brass sleeve nut (31) retaining the flexible jet tube (32) to the float-chamber (33) and withdraw the jet assembly (26) from the carburetter body (13). Note the gland (34), washer (35), and ferrule (36) at the end of the jet tube.

(14) Bend back the small tag on the restrictor (7) to clear the jet adjusting nut, and remove the jet adjusting nut (1), restrictor (7), and spring (37). Unscrew the jet locking nut (2) and detach the nut and jet bearing (38). Withdraw the bearing from the nut, noting, on fixed needle carburetters only, the locking washer (39) under the shoulder of the bearing.

(15) Note the location points (see inset, 40) of the two ends of the pick-up lever return spring (41). Unscrew the lever pivot bolt (42) together with its double-coil spring washer (43), or spacer (44).

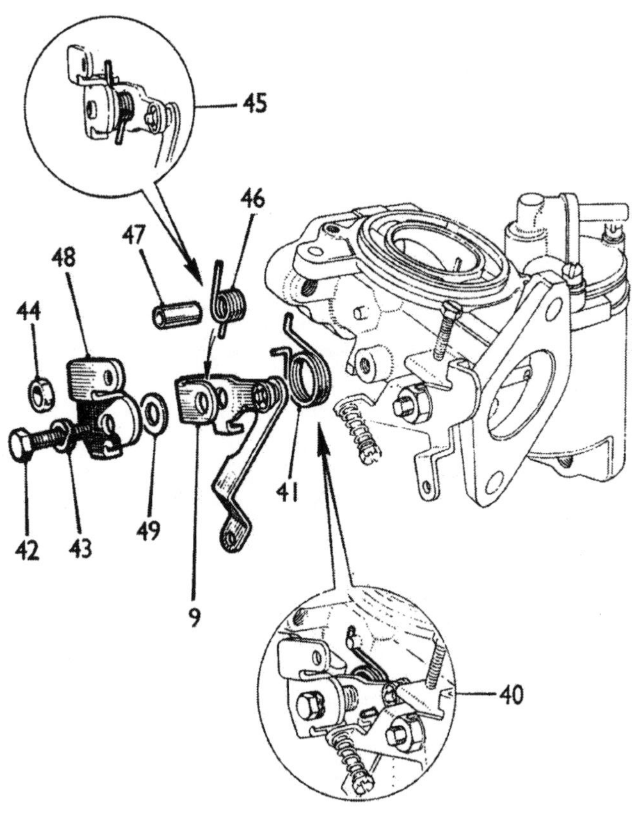

Detach the lever assembly (9) and return spring.

(16) Note the location (see inset, 45) of the two ends of the cam lever spring (46) and push out the pivot bolt tube (47) (or tubes), taking care not to lose the spring. Lift off the cam lever (48), noting the skid washer (49) between the two levers.

(17) Slacken and remove the bolt (50) retaining the float-chamber (33) to the carburetter body. Note the component sequence of the flexibly mounted chambers (33) and (51).

(18) Mark (52) the location of the float-chamber lid (53). Unscrew the lid retaining screws (54) and detach the lid and its gasket (55) complete with float assembly (56).

(19) Push out the float hinge pin (57) from the end opposite its serrations and detach the float.

(20) Extract the float needle (58) from its seating (59) and unscrew the seating from the lid, using a wrench ·338 in. across the flats. Do not distort the seating.

(21) Close the throttle and mark (60) the relative positions of the throttle disc (61) and the carburetter flange (62). **Do not mark the throttle disc in the vicinity of the limit valve** (63).

(22) Unscrew the two disc retaining screws (64). Open the throttle and ease out the disc from its slot in the throttle spindle (65). The disc is oval and will jam if care is not taken; store the disc in a safe place until required for reassembly.

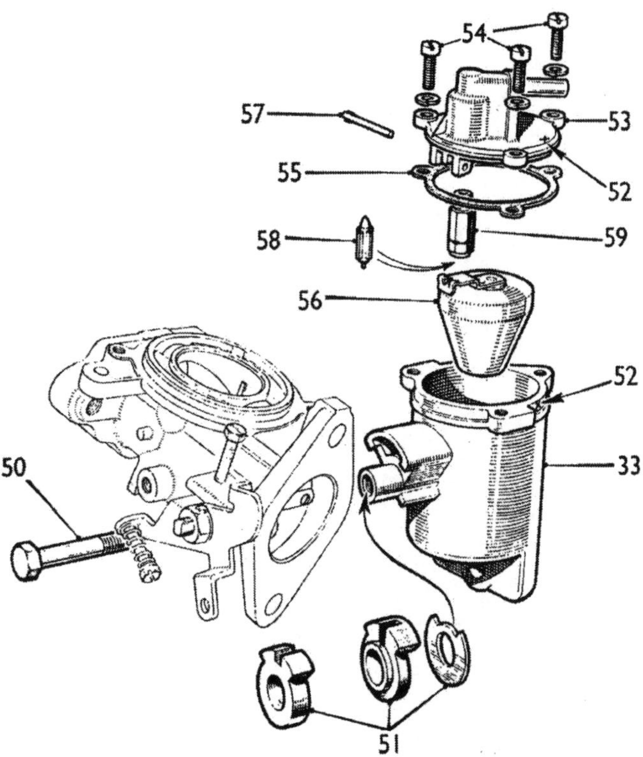

(23) Tap back the tabs of the tab washer (66) securing the spindle nut (67). Note the location of the lever arm (68) in relation to the spindle and carburetter body; remove the nut and detach the arm.

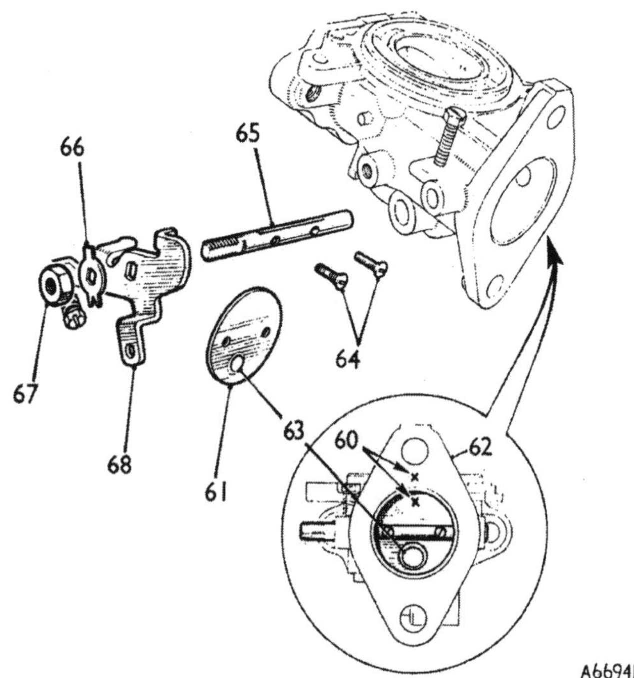

Reassembling

Carburetters—all types

NOTE.—Before reassembling, examine all components for wear and damage. Renew unserviceable components, ensuring that only parts to the correct specification (see 'GENERAL DATA') are used.

(1) Examine the throttle spindle and its bearings in the carburetter body. Check for excessive play. Renew parts as necessary.

(2) Refit the spindle to the body. Assemble the operating lever with tab washer and spindle nut, to the spindle. Ensure that when the stop on the lever is against the abutment on the carburetter body (i.e. throttle closed position) the countersunk ends of the holes in the spindle face outwards. Tighten the spindle nut and lock with the tab washer.

(3) Insert the throttle disc in the slot in the spindle in its original position as marked. Manœuvre the disc in its slot until the throttle can be closed, snap the throttle open and shut to centralize it in the bore of the carburetter, taking care not to damage the throttle limit valve. When assembled, the valve must be positioned at the bottom of the disc with the head of the valve towards the engine. Fit two new disc retaining screws but do not fully tighten. Check visually that the disc closes fully, and adjust

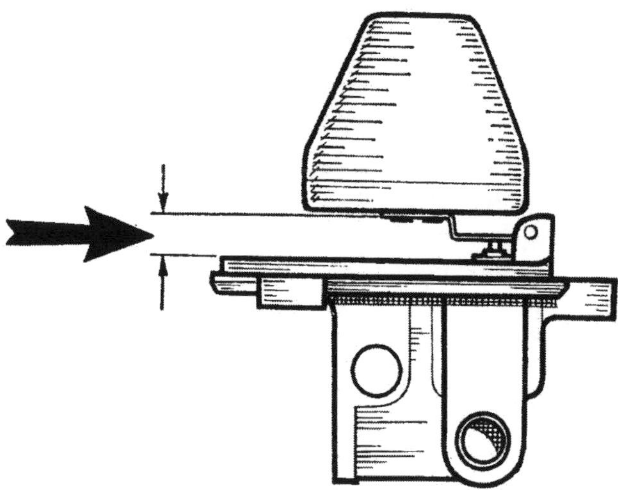

its position as necessary. With the throttle closed there must be clearance between the throttle lever and the carburetter body. Tighten the screws fully and spread their split ends just enough to prevent turning.

(4) Examine the float needle and seating for damage. Check that the spring-loaded plunger in the end of the plastic-bodied needle operates freely.

(5) Screw the seating into the float-chamber carefully. Do not overtighten. Replace the needle in the seating, coned end first. Test the assembly for leakage with air pressure.

(6) Refit the float and lever to the lid and insert the hinge pin and invert the float-chamber lid. With the needle valve held in the shut-off position by the weight of the float only, there should be a $\frac{1}{8}$ to $\frac{3}{16}$ in. gap (arrowed) between the float lever and the rim of the float-chamber lid.

(7) Examine the lid gasket for re-use. Assemble the gasket on the lid and refit the lid to the float-chamber in the position marked on dismantling. Tighten the securing screws evenly.

(8) Refit the float-chamber assembly to the carburetter body and tighten the retaining bolt fully, making sure that the registers on the body and the chamber engage correctly.

(9) Refit the piston lifting pin, spring and circlip.

(10) Examine the piston assembly for damage on the piston rod and the outside surface of the piston. The piston assembly must be scrupulously clean. Use gasoline or methylated spirit (denatured alcohol) as a cleaning agent. **Do not use abrasives.** Wipe dry, using a clean dry cloth.

(11) Clean inside the suction chamber and piston rod guide using gasoline or methylated spirit (denatured alcohol) and wipe dry. Refit the damper and washer. Temporarily plug the piston transfer holes (69) and fit the piston into the suction chamber. Fit a nut and screw, with a large flat washer under the head of the screw into one of the suction

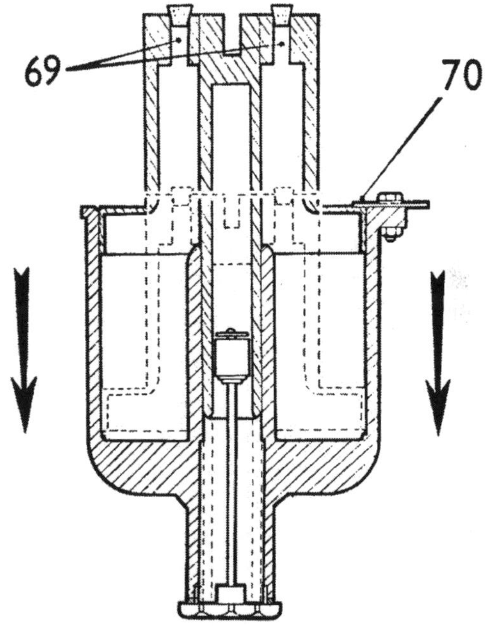

chamber fixing holes, positioning the washer (70) so that it overlaps the suction chamber bore (see illustration). Check that the piston is fully home in the suction chamber and invert the assembly to allow the chamber to fall away from the piston until the piston contacts the flat washer. Check the time taken for the suction chamber to fall the full extent of the piston travel. For HS2-type carburetters of $1\frac{1}{4}$ in. bore the time taken should be 3 to 5 seconds, and for larger carburetters 5 to 7 seconds. If these times are exceeded check the piston and suction chamber for cleanliness and mechanical damage. If after rechecking the time taken is still not within these limits, renew the suction chamber and piston assembly.

Carburetters—fixed needle type

(12) Refit the needle to the piston assembly (19). The lower edge of the needle shoulder (22) must be level with the bottom face of the piston rod (20).

(13) Fit a new needle locking screw (21) and tighten. Invert the suction chamber and spin the piston assembly inside it to check for concentricity of the needle.

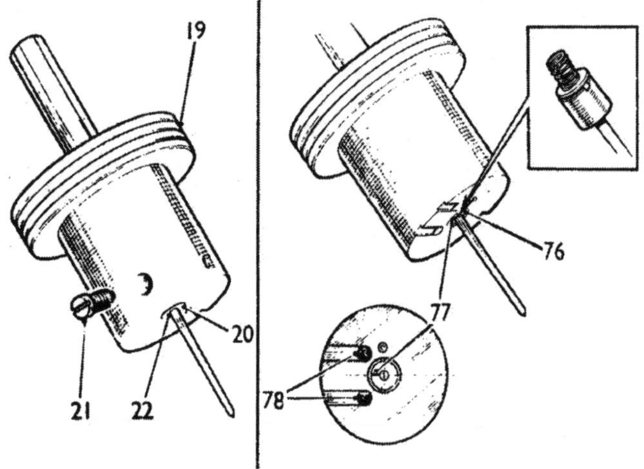

(14) Check the piston key for security in the carburetter body. Refit the piston assembly to the body and replace the piston spring over the piston rod.

(15) Fit the suction chamber and retaining screws, taking care not to wind up the spring; tighten the securing screws evenly.

(16) Refit the jet bearing, a new locking washer, and the locking nut; do not tighten the nut.

(17) Centralize the jet as follows:

(*a*) Enter the end of the nylon feed tube into the base of the float-chamber, without the gland or washer fitted. Loosely secure with the retaining nut.

(*b*) Feed the jet into the jet bearing; do not fit the jet nut spring, jet adjustment restrictor, or adjusting nut at this stage.

(*c*) With the carburetter positioned with its inlet flange downwards, insert the piston loading tool into damper tube at the top of the suction chamber and screw in until fully home. Screw the tool back until the arrow, on the tool, points towards the inlet flange of the carburetter. **The tool and carburetter must remain in this position throughout the centering operation.**

(*d*) With the piston at the bottom of its travel (on the bridge), and the jet hard up against the jet bearing, slowly tighten the jet locking nut. During the tightening process ensure that the jet is not binding in its bearing when drawn in and out. If any tightness between the jet and bearing is detected, the jet locking nut must be slackened and the process repeated.

(*e*) Remove the jet loading tool.

(18) Withdraw the jet and tube; refit the spring, restrictor and jet adjusting nut. Fit the gland and washer to the flexible tube. The end of the tube should project a minimum of $\frac{3}{16}$ in. beyond the gland. Refit the jet and tube. Tighten the sleeve nut until the neoprene gland is compressed. Overtightening can cause leakage.

Carburetters—spring-loaded needle type

(19) Refit the jet bearing, fit and tighten the jet locking nut. No jet centering is required with the spring-loaded type jet needle.

(20) Fit the jet nut spring and adjustment restrictor. Fit the jet adjusting nut and screw it up as far as possible.

(21) Feed the jet into the jet bearing. Fit the sleeve nut, washer and gland to the end of the flexible tube. The tube must project a minimum of $\frac{3}{16}$ in. (4·8 mm.) beyond the gland. Tighten the sleeve nut until the gland is compressed. Overtightening can cause leakage.

(22) Refit the spring to the jet needle assembly, ensuring that it locates completely in the groove of the needle support.

(23) **IMPORTANT.** Spring-loaded needles are supplied complete with shouldered spring seats; no attempt should be made to alter the position of the spring seat or convert a fixed-type needle to spring- loaded application. The raised 'pip' formed in the needle guide ensures that the needle is correctly centralized. Under no circumstances must the 'pip' be removed or repositioned.

Fit the needle assembly into its guide and fit the assembly into the piston. The lower edge of the guide (76) must be flush with the face of the piston and the guide positioned so that the etched locating mark (77) on its lower face is adjacent to and in line with the midway point between the two piston transfer holes as illustrated.

Alternative needle guides have a flat machined on the guide which must be positioned so that the guide locking screw tightens down onto the flat. If the guide is incorrectly positioned so that the locking screw has not tightened down on the flat, the head of the screw will protrude from the piston.

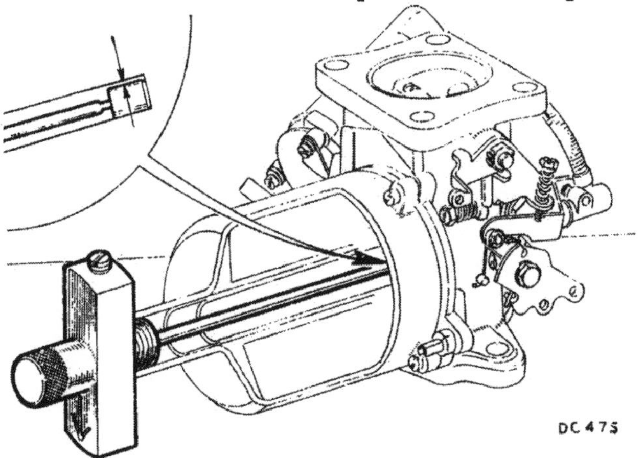

(24) Fit a new guide locking screw. **NOTE.**—Guide locking screws for spring-loaded needles are shorter than the needle locking screws used with fixed needles.
(25) Check the piston key for security in the carburetter body. Refit the piston assembly to the body and place the piston spring over the piston rod.
(26) Fit the suction chamber and retaining screws, taking care not to wind up the spring; tighten the securing screws evenly.

Carburetters—all types
(27) Refit the damper and washer.
(28) Reassemble the pick-up lever, cam lever, cam lever spring, skid washer, and pivot bolt tube or tubes in the positions noted on dismantling.
(29) Place the pick-up lever return spring in position over its boss and secure the lever assembly to the carburetter body with the pivot bolt. Ensure that the double-coil spring washer or spacer fits over the projecting end of the pivot bolt tube.
(30) Register the angled end of the return spring in the groove in the pick-up lever, and hook the other end of the spring around the moulded peg on the carburetter body.
(31) Fit the brass ferrule to the hole in the end of the pick-up link. Relieve the tension of the return spring and fit the link to the jet with its retaining screw. When finally tightening the screw, support the moulded end of the jet.
(32) Without removing the suction chamber, screw the jet adjusting nut until the top face of the jet is flush with the bridge of the carburetter.
(33) Turn down the jet adjusting nut to the initial jet setting given in **'GENERAL DATA'**
(34) Refit the carburetter(s) to the engine,

Tune the carburetters in accordance with the instructions given in **'CARBURETTER TUNING —COMPLETE'**.

Section Dc-3

CARBURETTER TUNING—COMPLETE

The following instructions apply only to new carburetters or carburetters which have been serviced as described in **'CARBURETTER SERVICING'**.

The tuning must be carried out with the engine emission control equipment connected and operating.

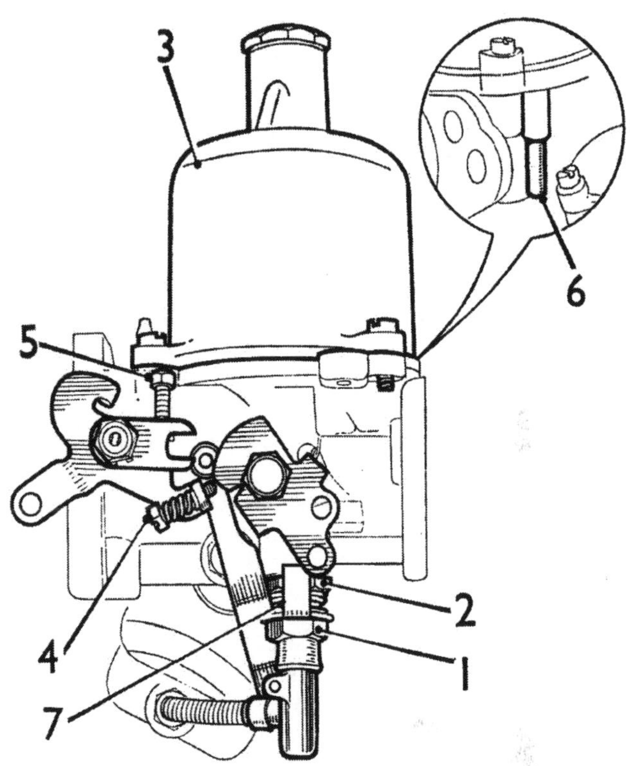

The type HS carburetter

1. Jet adjusting nut.
2. Jet locking nut.
3. Piston suction chamber.
4. Fast-idle adjusting screw.
5. Throttle adjusting screw.
6. Piston lifting pin.
7. Jet adjustment restrictor.

Initial setting

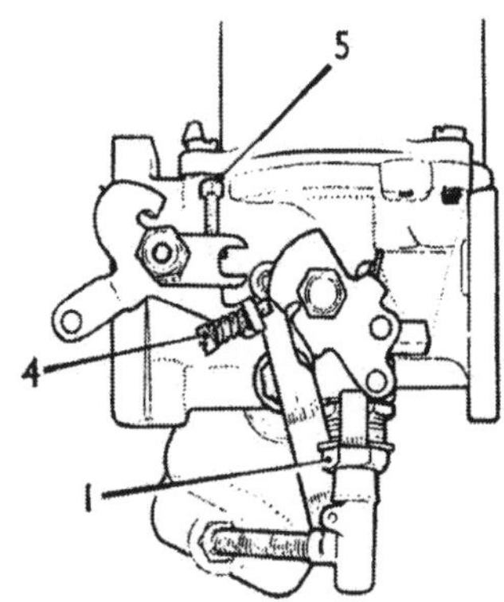

(1) Disconnect the mixture control (choke) wire if fitted.

(2) Unscrew the fast-idle screw (4) until it is well clear of the cam.

(3) Unscrew the throttle adjusting screw (5) until it is just clear of its stop and the throttle is closed.

(4) Set the throttle adjusting screw one full turn open.

(5) The jet adjusting nut must not be altered at this stage as it will be initially set to a datum setting at the factory or during the carburetter servicing procedure.

Tuning conditions

To ensure that the engine temperature and mixture requirements are stabilized, tuning must be carried out in accordance with the following setting cycle.

(1) Connect a tachometer and an approved exhaust gas analyser in accordance with the instrument-maker's instructions.

(2) Warm the engine at a fast idle to normal operating temperature preferably with the car standing in an ambient temperature of between 16 and 27° C. (60 to 80° F.). Run the engine for at least five minutes after the thermostat has opened; the thermostat opening point can be detected by the sudden rise in temperature of the radiator header tank.

(3) Set the engine speed at 2,500 r.p.m., at no load, and run for one minute.

(4) Tuning operations may now be commenced and must be carried out in the shortest possible time. If the time for settings exceeds a three-minute period, open the throttle and run the engine at 2,500 r.p.m. for one minute then resume tuning.

Tuning procedure

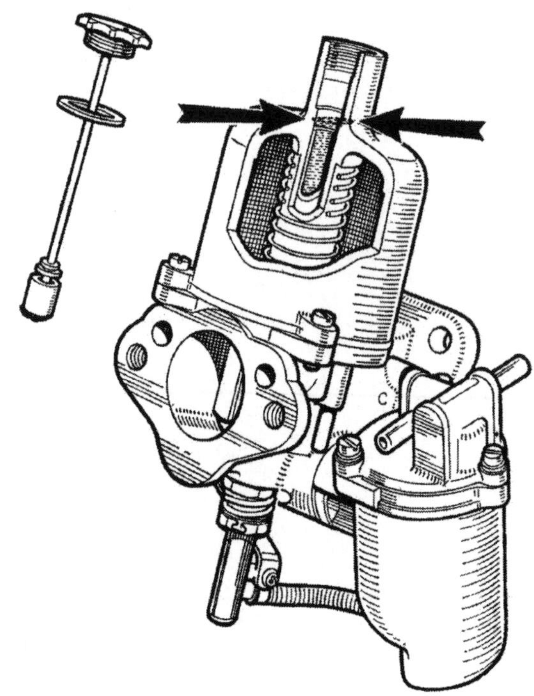

Repeat this clearing operation if further periods of three minutes are exceeded.

(1) Top up the piston damper with the recommended engine oil until the level is ½ in. above the top of the hollow piston rod.

NOTE.—On dust-proofed carburetters, identified by a transverse hole drilled in the neck of the suction chambers and no vent hole in the damper cap, the oil level must be ½ in. below the top of the hollow piston rod.

(2) Warm up the engine as described in **'Tuning conditions'**.

Turn the throttle adjusting screw until the idling speed given in **'GENERAL DATA'** is obtained.

(3) During the following procedure, just before the readings of the tachometer and exhaust gas analyser are taken gently tap the neck of the suction chamber with a light non-metallic instrument (e.g. a screwdriver handle).

Turn the jet adjusting nut up to weaken, down to richen, until the fastest speed is recorded on the tachometer. Turn the jet adjusting nut very slowly up (weaken) until the engine speed just commences to fall, then turn the nut one flat down (rich). Check the idling speed against the figure given in **'GENERAL DATA'** and adjust if necessary using the throttle adjusting screw.

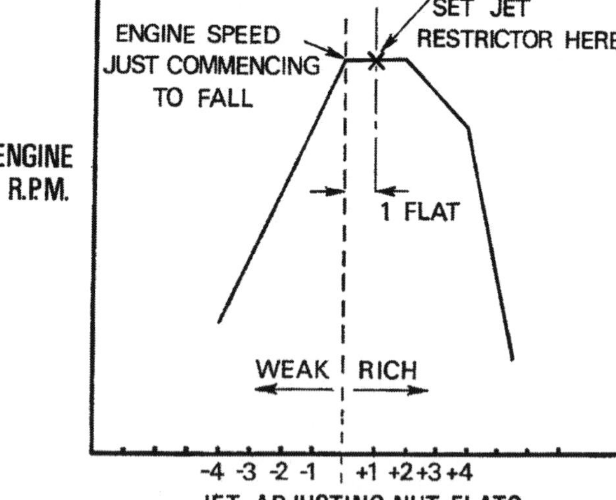

(4) Using the exhaust gas analyser, check that the percentage CO reading is within the limits given in **'GENERAL DATA'**

If the reading falls outside the limits given, reset the jet adjusting nut by the minimum amount necessary to bring the reading just within the limits. If an adjustment exceeding two flats is required to achieve this the test equipment should be checked for correct calibration.

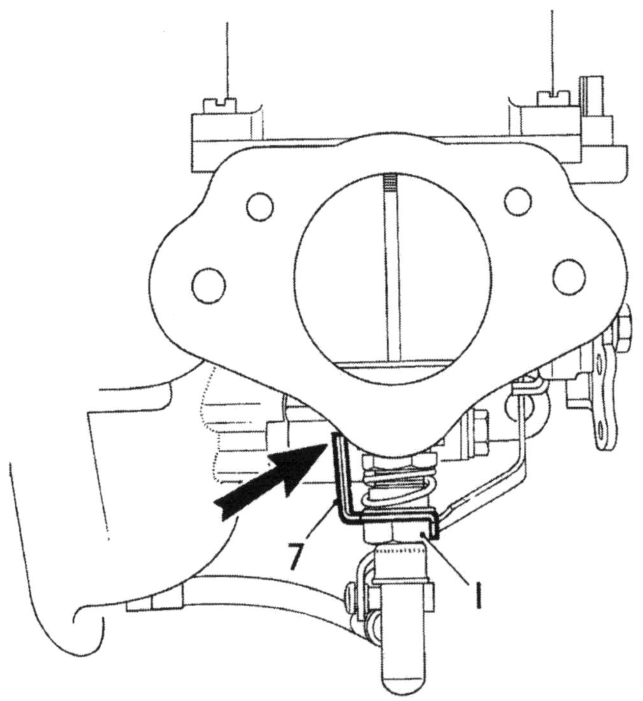

(5) Hold the jet adjusting nut (1) to prevent it turning, and rotate the adjustment restrictor (7) round the nut until the vertical tag contacts the carburetter body on the left-hand side when viewed from the air cleaner flange (see illustration). In this position, bend the small tag on the adjustment restrictor down so that the restrictor locks to the nut and will follow its movements.

(6) Paint the small tag of the jet adjusting nut restrictor and the adjacent flat of the jet nut to identify the locking position.

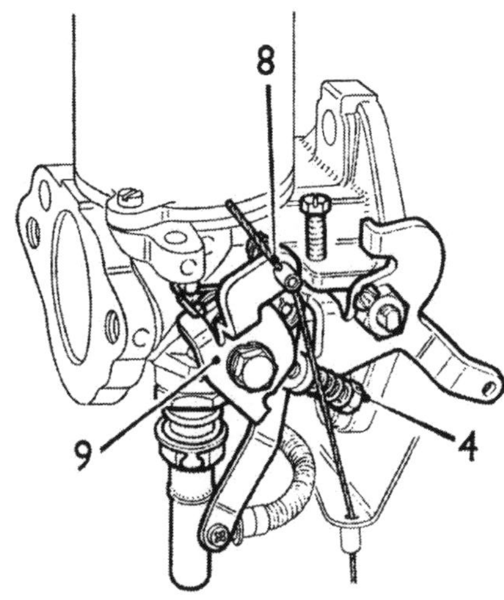

(7) Reconnect the mixture control wire (8) with approximately $\frac{1}{16}$ in. free movement before it starts to pull on the jet lever (9).

(8) Pull the mixture control knob until the linkage is about to move the carburetter jet and adjust the fast-idle screw (4) to give the engine fast-idle speed given in 'GENERAL DATA'

Section Dc-4

EVAPORATIVE LOSS CONTROL

General description

The function of the control system is to prevent fuel system hydrocarbon vapours from entering the atmosphere. Vapours normally lost from the fuel tank, and in some instances the carburettor, while the vehicle is stationary are absorbed and stored in a small canister containing a bed of activated charcoal. These vapours are desorbed or purged from the charcoal by means of the crankcase ventilation air, which is drawn through the charcoal bed by the action of the crankcase emission control system, and together with the piston blowby gases are consumed by the engine during operation. Vapours normally lost while the engine is running are consumed directly by the engine via the crankcase emission control system.

The venting of the fuel tank has also been designed to ensure that the tank is effectively vented, even when the vehicle is parked at a fairly severe attitude.

Charcoal canister

The nylon canister is mounted in the engine compartment and contains approximately 300 grams of activated charcoal.

Air filter pads are fitted below and above the charcoal bed to prevent the ingress of foreign matter into the charcoal, or the passage of charcoal granules into the purgeline.

Vapours emitted from the fuel tank, and in certain installations, from the carburettor, enter the top of the canister through separate connections such that the vapours cannot come into contact with the atmosphere. The purging air enters the bottom of the canister and passes through the charcoal bed to the separate purge outlet at the top of the canister.

Fuel expansion and tank venting

As vehicles equipped with evaporative loss control systems have no external fuel tank breather system, other than through the charcoal canister, it is necessary to protect the canister from flooding with liquid fuel resulting from an expansion due to an increase in temperature of the fuel within the tank, particularly when full.

The fuel tank is vented from the centre of the top of the fuel tank. The vent pipe rises and connects to the bottom of a small liquid-vapour separator located above the main fuel tank. The vent pipe continues on from the top of the separator to connect to the vapour inlet on the charcoal canister.

Vapours condensed in the separator automatically drain back into the fuel tank.

As it is not feasible due to space limitations on these particular models to have an external expansion tank, it has been necessary to incorporate means for preventing the fuel tank from being filled to capacity. The fuel tank is designed to ensure that a dead volume always exists above the liquid level, such that it can be utilised when the fuel is expanded.

The fuel tank is prevented from completely filling by means of a small tank of approximately 5% of the fuel tank volume. This small tank is situated within the fuel tank and contains large holes in the bottom and a small bleed orifice in the top. As the tank is refueled, the fuel is prevented from entering the inner tank by the entrapped vapour which can only escape slowly through the orifice. The orifice size is selected to ensure that the vapour in the inner tank takes a considerably longer time to escape than it normally takes to refuel the main tank, therefore, during a normal refueling operation in which the tank is filled to capacity (or near) the effect of the inner tank is to displace a volume of fuel almost equal to its own volume. As the entrapped vapour is gradually expelled from the inner tank and consequently is replaced with liquid fuel, the level of the fuel tank falls accordingly, to provide the necessary dead volume above the surface of the liquid, to accommodate any subsequent expansion of the fuel.

The dead volume above the fuel also acts to ensure that the fuel tank vent pipe is prevented from becoming covered with fuel when the vehicle is parked on a severe incline.

Fuel Tank. The fuel tank is fitted with a sealed cap on the fuel filler neck. The cap is designed to provide a complete seal against fuel vapour leakage.

For safety reasons, in the event of the vent pipe becoming blocked, a 2.5 p.s.i. pressure relief valve is incorporated in the filler cap. As previously described, the only vent to the tank under normal operating conditions is through the charcoal canister system.

Carburettor float chamber

As the hydrocarbon vapour from the float chamber of this model is negligible, no evaporative control is necessary.

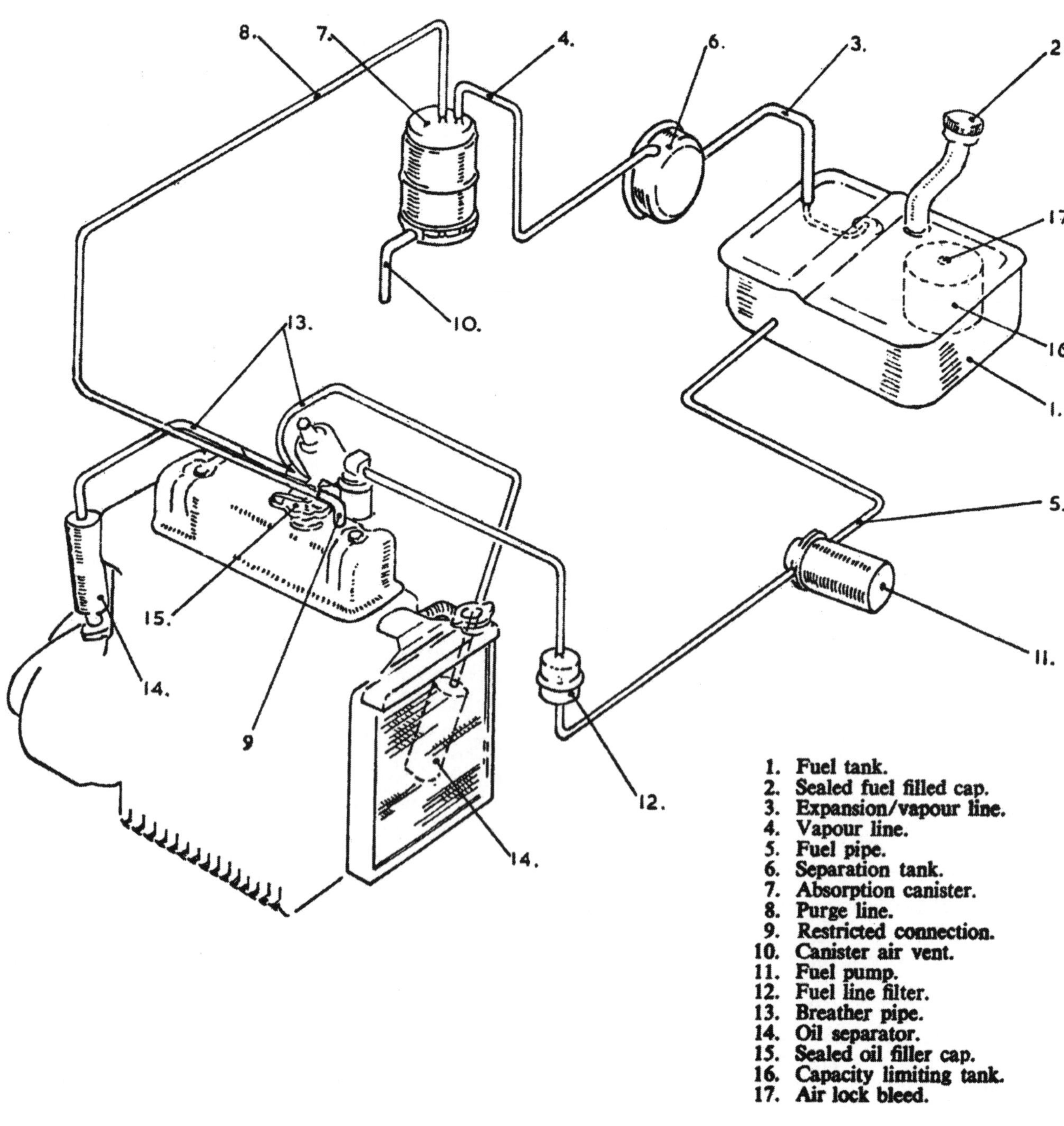

1. Fuel tank.
2. Sealed fuel filled cap.
3. Expansion/vapour line.
4. Vapour line.
5. Fuel pipe.
6. Separation tank.
7. Absorption canister.
8. Purge line.
9. Restricted connection.
10. Canister air vent.
11. Fuel pump.
12. Fuel line filter.
13. Breather pipe.
14. Oil separator.
15. Sealed oil filler cap.
16. Capacity limiting tank.
17. Air lock bleed.

SECTION d

FUEL SYSTEM

The information contained in this Section refers to Australian produced vehicles and it does not supersede the previous Section, but should be used in conjunction with it.

Section d.1

MECHANICAL FUEL PUMP
(Goss Type YD)

Description

The mechanical type pump fitted to all models except Cooper "S", is operated by an eccentric on the engine camshaft, which lifts the pump rocker arm and link, moving the pull rod together with the diaphragm, downward against the spring pressure, thus creating a vacuum in the pump chamber.

Petrol is drawn from the tank and enters into the sediment chamber through the filter gauze and into the pump chamber. On the return stroke the spring pressure pushes the diaphragm upwards, forcing petrol from the chamber to the carburettor.

Section d2

TESTING THE FUEL PUMP
(in position)

Disconnect the fuel line at the carburettor. Remove the H.T. lead from the coil. Crank the engine with the starter. A well defined flow of fuel should be evident at each working stroke of the pump. Delivery pressure should be between 1½ and 2½ p.s.i. (.105 to .176 $Kg.cm^2$).

If no fuel is delivered, disconnect the inlet line at the fuel pump and test for fuel flow from the tank to the pump. If fuel is delivered to the pump, do not overlook the following points before removing the pump for overhaul.

(a) Check the domed filter cover retaining screw for looseness.
(b) Check the condition of the cover gasket and the fibre washer under the head of the retaining screw.
(c) Check for foreign material in the bowl under the filter.

Section d.3

OVERHAULING THE FUEL PUMP

Removing

NOTE: To facilitate removing and refitting, the use of a ⅜" or ¼" square drive, ½" A.F. socket and ratchet handle is advised.

1. Disconnect the left hand engine steady at the bulkhead bracket where applicable.
2. Remove the fuel supply line between carburettor and fuel pump.
3. Disconnect plug and the flexible line from pump to fuel tank line.
4. Remove the accelerator return spring.
5. Remove the nut from the fuel pump stud closest to the timing cover.
6. Remove the remaining nut and the engine breather pipe bracket (when fitted).
7. Remove the pump from the engine block.

Clean the exterior of the pump and mark the two flanges to indicate the position of the inlet and outlet when reassembling. Separate the two main castings. The diaphragm and pull rod assembly can be withdrawn by turning it either way through 90°. Remove the rocker arm pin.

All parts must be thoroughly cleaned to ascertain their condition.

The diaphragm and pull rod assemblies should normally be renewed, unless in entirely sound condition, without signs of cracking or hardening.

The upper and lower castings should be examined for cracks or damage and if the diaphragm or flanges are distorted, they should be re-faced.

All worn or corroded parts should be renewed. (No more than .010 in. wear is permissible on the cam contact face.) The rocker arm spring and all gaskets should be replaced. Minor or major repair kits are available.

Incorrect fitting of diaphragm (Fig. d.1)

It is possible to insert the diaphragm pull rod too far through the slot in the link so that the latter — instead of engaging in the two small slots in the pull rod — rides on the pull rod shoulder, at the top of its stroke.

Correct fitting of diaphragm (Fig. d.2)

When correctly fitted, the slot in the link should engage with the two slots in the diaphragm pull rod so that when the diaphragm is subsequently turned 90° it is positively located in the link.

Refitting

Refitting is the reversal of the removing procedure.

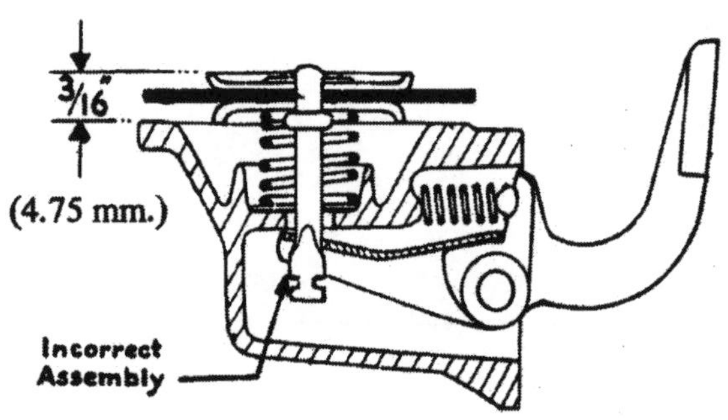

Fig. d.1

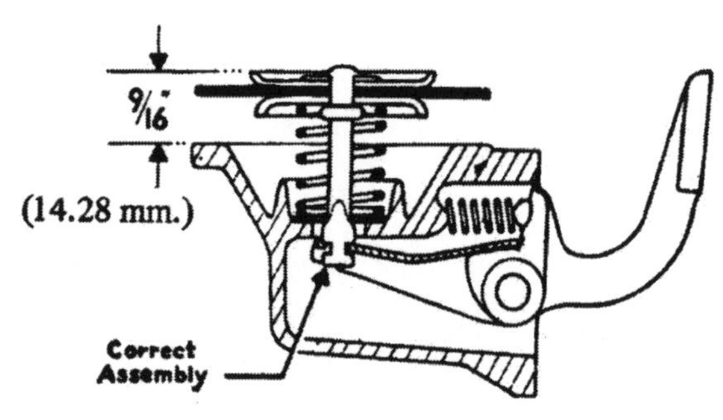

Fig. d.2

Section D.4
THE FUEL TANK UNIT
(Moke)

Removing

Remove the fuel tank as in Section D.9.

(1) Release the tank unit locking ring and remove.

(2) Lift out the tank unit and sealing ring.

Refitting

(3) Reverse the removal procedure, ensuring that the float is located correctly and that it is away from the tank fuel pick-up pipe and be certain that the sealing ring is in good condition.

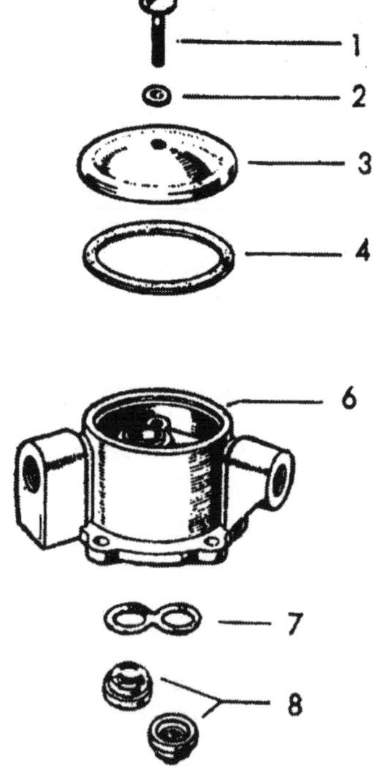

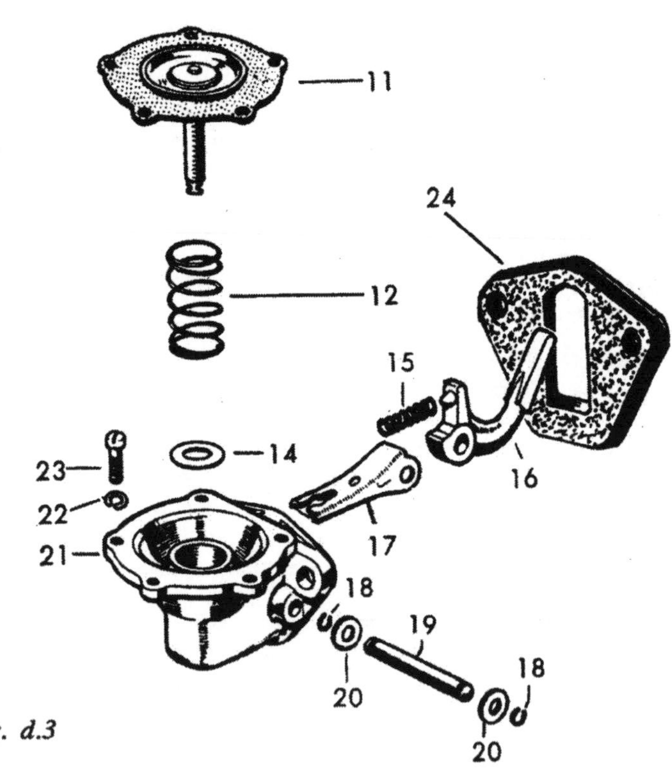

Fig. d.3

Fuel Pump (Type YD) — Exploded view (typical only)

1. Screw, filter cover.
2. Gasket, screw.
3. Filter cover.
4. Gasket, filter cover.
5. Gauze, filter.
6. Upper casting.
*7. Gasket, valve and cage.
8. Valve and cage assembly.
*9. Retainer, valve and cage.
10. Screw, valve and cage retainer.
11. Diaphragm and pull rod assembly.
12. Spring, diaphragm.
*13. Washer, oil seal (metal).
*14. Washer, oil seal (fabric).
15. Spring, rocker arm.
16. Rocker arm.
17. Link.
18. Clip, rocker arm pin.
19. Pin, rocker arm.
20. Washer, rocker arm spacer.
21. Lower body.
22. Lockwasher, casting screw.
23. Screw, upper casting.
24. Heat insulator block.

*Late type YE pumps modified.

SECTION e

CLUTCH

The information contained in this Section refers to Australian produced vehicles. It does not supersede the previous Section, but should be used in conjunction with it.

Section e.1

CLUTCH MASTER CYLINDER
(Late models)

The clutch master cylinder is mounted on the bulkhead behind the right-hand end of the power unit. Attached to the body of the cylinder is a translucent reservoir incorporating a rubber diaphragm under the filler cap.

The master cylinder piston is backed by a rubber cup and is normally held in the "off" position by a return spring. Immediately in front of the cup, when it is in the "off" position, is a compensating orifice connecting the cylinder with the fluid supply. This port allows free compensation for any expansion or contraction of fluid, thus ensuring that the system is constantly filled; it also serves as a release for additional fluid drawn into the cylinder during clutch applications.

Pressure is applied to the piston by means of the push-rod attached to the clutch pedal.

The reduced skirt of the piston forms an annular space which is filled with fluid from the supply tank via the feed hole. Leakage of fluid from the open end of the cylinder is prevented by the secondary cup fitted to the flange end of the piston.

By releasing the clutch pedal after application the piston is returned quickly to its stop by the return spring, thus creating a vacuum in the cylinder; this vacuum causes the main cup to collapse and pass fluid through the small holes in the piston head from the annular space formed by the piston skirt. This additional fluid finds its way back to the reserve supply through the compensating orifice.

No pressure is maintained in the clutch line when the pedal is released.

Removing

1. Attach a bleed tube to the slave cylinder bleed screw, open the screw and pump out the fluid in the master and slave cylinders into a container.
2. Withdraw the clevis pin securing the master cylinder push-rod to the clutch pedal lever.
3. Disconnect the pressure pipe union from the top of the cylinder.
4. Remove the two nuts securing the cylinder to the bulkhead, and withdraw the assembly complete from the car.

Dismantling

1. Remove the filler cap and drain out the remaining fluid.
2. Pull back the rubber dust cover and remove the circlip with a pair of long-nosed pliers.
3. Remove the push-rod assembly.
4. Withdraw the remaining parts from the cylinder barrel.
5. To remove the secondary cup from the piston carefully stretch the cup over the end flange of the piston, using only the fingers.

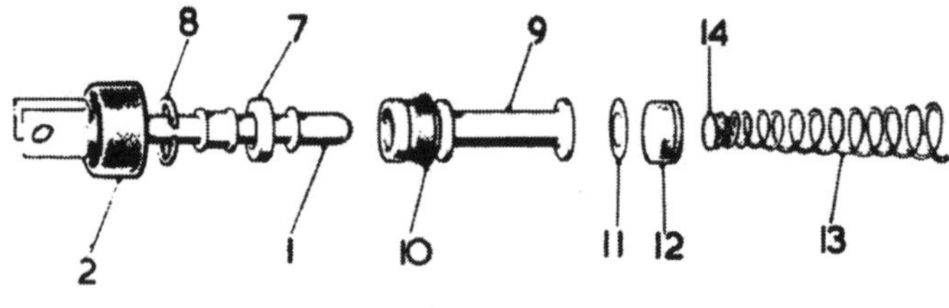

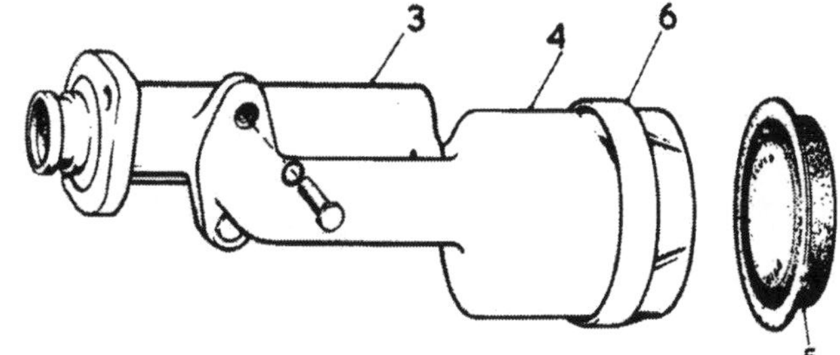

Fig. e.1
A section through the clutch master cylinder

1. Push rod.
2. Rubber boot.
3. Master cylinder body.
4. Reservoir.
5. Reservoir diaphragm.
6. Filler cap.
7. Washer.
8. Circlip.
9. Piston.
10. Secondary cup.
11. Washer.
12. Main cup.
13. Return spring.
14. Spring retainer.

Inspecting

Wash all parts thoroughly only in clean methylated spirits. Do not use mineral fluids as these will destroy the rubber parts.

Blow out all passages and orifices with compressed air. Air dry all parts and place on clean paper or lint-free cloth. **Do not** use wire to clean out or check parts.

Examine all rubber parts for damage or distortion. It is advisable to renew the rubbers when reassembling the cylinder.

Inspect the bore of the cylinder for wear or pitting and renew the cylinder body if necessary.

Reassembling

NOTE: Dip all the internal parts in recommended hydraulic fluid (HBF6) and assemble them wet.

1. Stretch the secondary cup over the end flange of the piston with the lip of the cup facing towards the opposite end of the piston. When the cup is in its groove work it round gently with the fingers to ensure correct seating.
2. Insert the return spring, largest-diameter coils first, into the barrel, ensuring that the spring seat is positioned on the small diameter end of the spring.
3. Insert the master cup, lip first, taking care not to damage or turn back the lip, and press it down onto the spring seat.
4. Insert the piston, taking care not to damage or turn back the lip of the secondary cup.
5. Push the piston down the bore and replace the push-rod, retaining circlip, and rubber dust cover.
6. Test the master cylinder by filling the reservoir with hydraulic fluid and pushing the piston down the bore and allowing it to return, after one or two applications fluid should flow from the outlet.

Replacing

1. Fit the master cylinder to the bulkhead, lining up the push-rod yoke on the pedal.
2. Connect the pressure pipe to the master cylinder.
3. Fit the clevis pin to the push-rod yoke and pedal and secure.
4. Refill the reservoir with the correct hydraulic fluid and bleed the system.

Bleeding the system

Fill the master cylinder reservoir with the recommended fluid (HBF6) and attach a rubber tube to the slave cylinder bleed valve; immerse the open end of the tube in a clean receptacle containing a small amount of clean fluid.

With a second operator to pump the clutch pedal, open the bleed screw on the slave cylinder approximately three-quarters of a turn and depress the clutch pedal slowly; at the end of the down stroke on the clutch pedal close the bleed screw before allowing the pedal to return to the "off" position.

Continue this series of operations until clear fluid free from air bubbles is delivered into the container, ensuring that the reservoir does not drain completely whilst bleeding.

Note: Hydraulic fluid bled out during the bleeding operation should not be used again.

Section e.2

CLUTCH SHUDDER (Diaphragm Spring Clutches)

(Removing and refitting clutch assembly. Refer Section a-2.)

Shudder may be caused by incorrect assembly of the driving straps "A" (Fig. e.2). It is essential when fitting the straps to the flywheel and pressure plate that the dowel portion of the fixing screws "B" (Fig. e.2) enters both holes "C" (Fig. e.2) in each pair of driving straps before being finally tightened down.

If this method of assembly is not followed, the holes could be out of line and subsequent tightening down of the screws would cause the straps to buckle and, in effect, shorten. This in turn puts the pressure plate out of centre, resulting in shudder.

When investigating conditions of shudder, the above condition is identifiable by a thread form cut into the dowel portion of the cover screws, caused by forcing the straps into alignment. Additionally, the "out of line" condition of the straps would be noticeable after the removal of the short flywheel dowel screws.

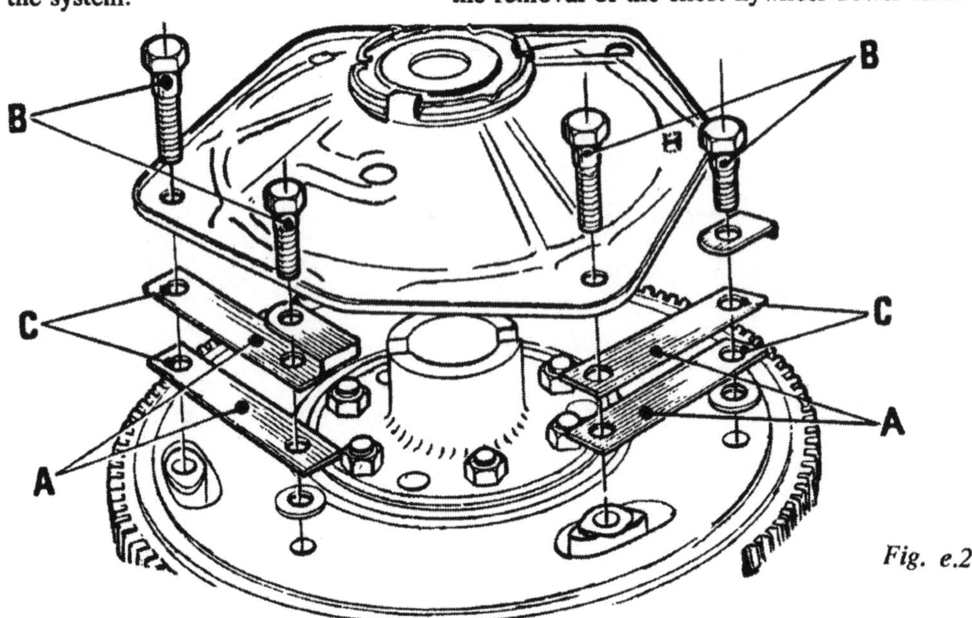

Fig. e.2

SECTION f

SYNCHROMESH TRANSMISSION

The information contained in this Section refers to Australian produced vehicles. It does not supersede the previous Section, but should be used in conjunction with it.

GENERAL

Section f.1

Since the introduction of the Mini range of vehicles, the gear train has undergone various design improvements and modifications. Many of these apply to U.K. vehicles, whilst some apply to Australian produced vehicles only.

The following is a brief summary of the changes, but it is stressed that it is absolutely essential to refer to the appropriate (U.K. or Australian) Parts List and quote Engine and Chassis numbers on every occasion.

Section f.2

DESIGN CHANGES—THREE SPEED SYNCHROMESH TRANSMISSIONS

Original Production

Constant pressure synchromesh with bronze bushed 3rd motion shaft gears, together with force feed lubrication through drillings between the helical teeth to bushes was fitted from first production.

Housings for transmissions fitted with constant pressure synchromesh can be identified by the raised casting numbers (22A 145 or 22A 363) located behind the oil filter.

First Major Design Change

Baulk ring synchronisation replaced constant pressure synchronisation. To convert the earlier transmission to baulk ring synchronisation, Service Kits were introduced.

The above conversion kits were developed to utilise the existing transmission case, third motion shaft ball bearing, and a spacing washer was added to the gear train on the third motion shaft.

Note: If renewal of the third motion shaft ball bearing is necessary in the constant pressure type transmission case, the smaller diameter ball bearing 22A 575 *only* can be fitted, whether the synchromesh is original constant pressure type or has been modified to baulk ring type.

Second Major Design Change

Positive lubrication of the third motion shaft bushes was introduced at Engine Numbers: –

Mini 850 (U.K.) 8AM/U/H 711640
Mini 850 (Australian) 8Y/U/H 5312

Lubrication to the third motion shaft bushes and the caged needle rollers retained in the first motion shaft was obtained by deleting the oil hole drillings between the gear teeth and adding a machined recess in the gear bores and an axial drilling of the first motion shaft.

Note: On assembly always smear a molybdenum disulphide grease such as "Molybond" G10 on the bronze bushes and apply engine oil to the grooves in the gears. **Do not pack the grooves with grease.**

Third Major Design Change

Twenty-Six needle rollers were fitted to the second and third speed gears by introducing the following changes:

a. Inside diameter of the second and third gears increased by 1/8 in. (3.175 mm.) to 1 19/64 in. (32.94 mm.).
b. Roller bearings retained in position by locking devices.
c. New third motion shaft with integral steel spacer and involute splines for the third and fourth speed coupling.
d. End float non-adjustable—now .003 in. to .007 in. (.076 mm. to .177 mm.).
e. Re-introduction of force feed lubrication through oil holes in second and third gears.

Fourth Major Design Change

The fourth change is applicable *only* to the Morris Cooper and commenced at Engine Numbers: –

Cooper 997 c.c.
(U.K.) 9F/Sa/L 28576 to 28950
Cooper 998 c.c.
(U.K.) 9FA/Sa/L 101
Cooper 998 c.c.
(Australian) 9Y/Sa/H 1001 to 9H/Sa/ 1267
Cooper 'S' 1071 c.c.
(U.K.) 9FA/Sa/H 20249 to 20410
plus 26501 to 26772

The design change consists of strengthening the spur gear teeth by adopting the heavier 'B' series tooth form. The gears are identified as follows: –

Laygear—Machined groove in face of top gear, and/or Part No. 22G 204 stamped on the gear. Refer B, Fig. f.3.

First Speed Gear—Machined identification on the edge of the ground surface on the gear body. Refer C, Fig. f.3.

Reverse Idler Gear—Forged identification groove on gear face. Refer A, Fig. f.3.

'B' form gears cannot be used except in complete sets.

Fifth Major Design Change

The stronger 'B' series gear tooth form was introduced to the helical gears as well as the spur gears at the following Engine Numbers:

Mini 850 c.c.	(U.K.)	8AM/U/H 803601
Mini 850 c.c.	(Australian)	8Y/U/20020
Mini Deluxe	(Australian)	9YA/U/H 1001
Cooper 998 c.c.	(U.K.)	9FD/Sa/L 645
Cooper 998 c.c.	(Australian)	9Y/Sa/L 1268
Cooper 'S' 1275 c.c.	(U.K.)	9F/Sa/Y 31001

The gears are identified as follows:

Laygear—Part No. 22G 231 (or 22G 232 Cooper 'S') stamped on the gear. Refer B, Fig. f.3.

Third Speed Gear—Dished oil recess on rear face of gear plus 90° oil grooves. Refer D, Fig. f.3.

Where individual gears cannot be identified, place the gear in mesh with a laygear of known form and, if the lines projected through the bores are parallel, they are of a similar helical tooth form. Refer Fig. F.1.

If the projected lines are not parallel, the gears are of a different form. Refer Fig. f.2.

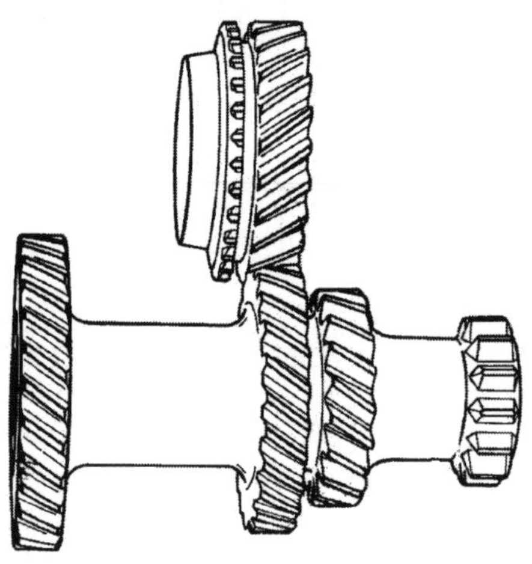

Fig. f.1 Correct helix angles

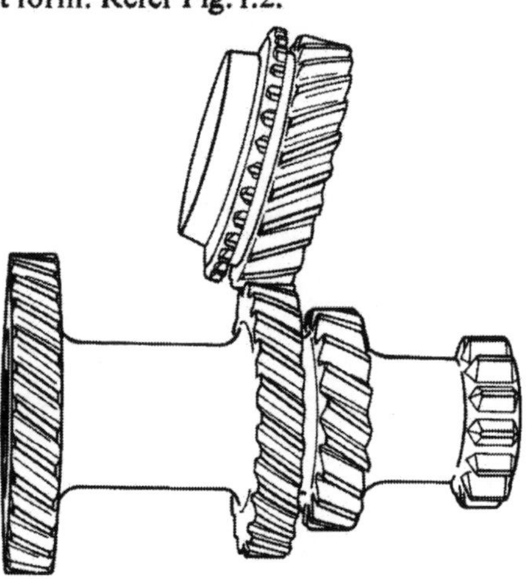

Fig. f.2 Incorrect helix angles

Sixth Major Design Change

Introduction of synchromesh on first gear. This design improvement coincided with the introduction of the 1098 c.c. engine into the Mini Range. Refer Section f.3.

Section f.3

DESIGN CHANGES—FOUR SPEED SYNCHROMESH TRANSMISSIONS

The transmission fitted to the Mini 'K' and 1100 c.c. models is externally similar to earlier models, but internally it has been redesigned for use with the higher output engines and incorporates synchromesh on first gear.

Servicing procedures are basically similar to earlier models and are covered in Section F and f, but the following points should be noted. The numbers in brackets refer to Fig. f.4.

Gearbox Casing

This has been completely redesigned to provide space for the new gear train assembly and clearance for the crankshaft of 1275 c.c. engines. The main difference

1. Reverse shaft
2. Reverse gear bush
3. Reverse idler gear
4. Thrust washer (small)
5. Caged needle bearing
6. Bearing distance piece
7. Laygear
8. Spring ring
9. Needle roller bearing with spacer (alternative)
10. Thrust washer (large)
11. Layshaft
12. Pinion nut
13. Lock washer
14. Final drive pinion
15. Setscrew
16. Lock washer
17. Bearing retainer
18. Locating plate
19. Adjusting shim
20. Circlip
21. Third motion shaft bearing
22. First/Second speed synchronizer hub
23. First speed gear
24. Synchronizer ball
25. Synchronizer spring
26. Plunger
27. Baulk ring
28. Locking collar
29. Locking collar split washer
30. Locking collar peg
31. Peg spring
32. Needle roller bearing
33. Second speed gear
34. Third motion shaft
35. Third speed gear
36. Needle roller bearing
37. Peg spring
38. Peg-locking collar
39. Locking collar for third speed gear
40. Third/Fourth speed synchronizer assembly
41. Synchronizer ball
42. Synchronizer spring
43. First motion shaft
44. First motion shaft bearing
45. First motion shaft circlip
46. Input gear
47. Lock washer
48. Input gear nut
49. Spigot bearing

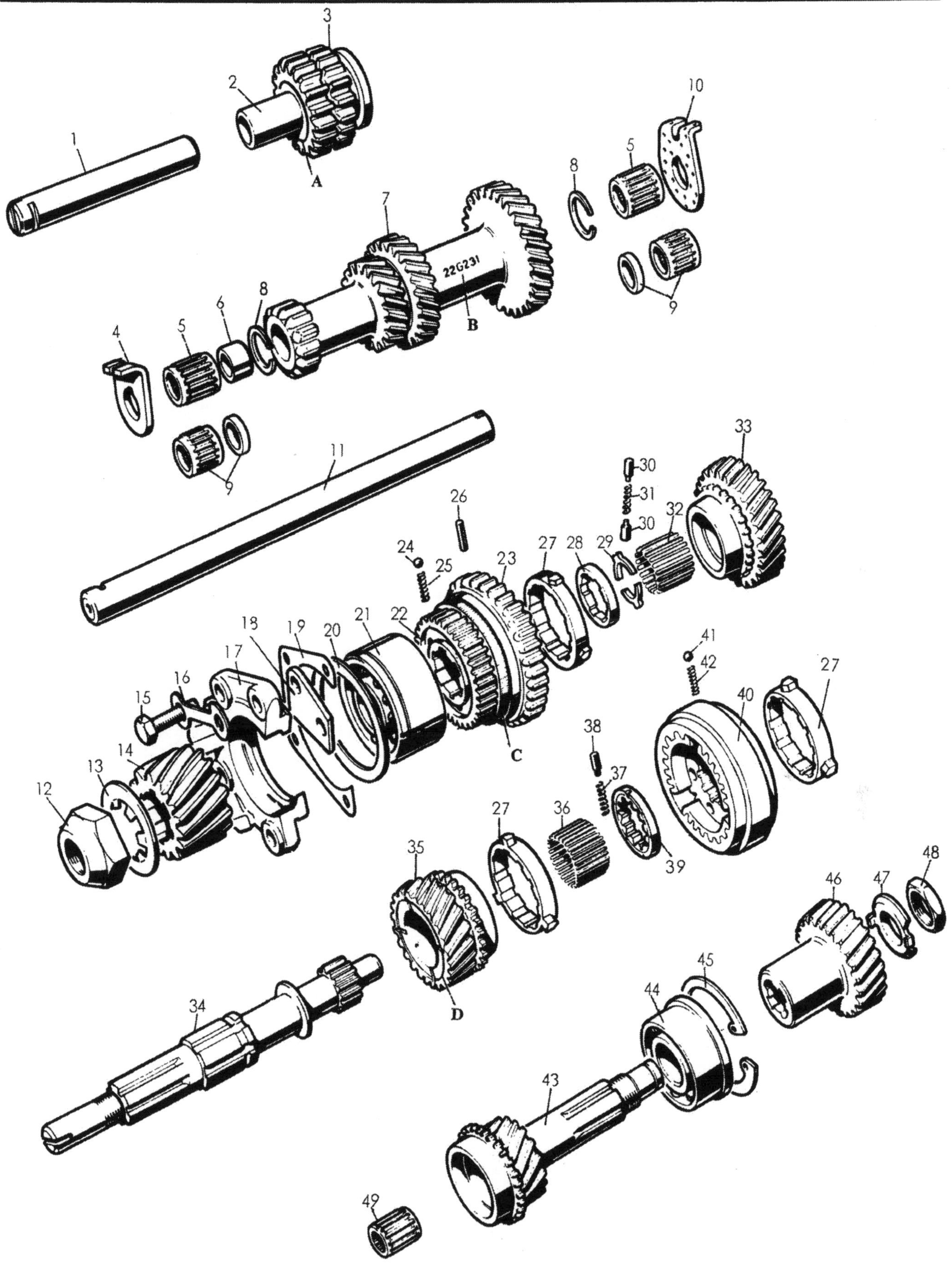

FIG. f.3 THREE SPEED SYNCHROMESH TRANSMISSION COMPONENTS

being that the side of the casing nearest the flywheel housing has been redesigned to allow the new gear train to be fitted. The first motion shaft bearing boss has been deleted and the bearing tunnel bore has been enlarged. Circlip grooves are now fitted to both sides of the idler gear bearing. The centre web of the casing is thinner in the area of the laygear to accommodate the new gear.

Clutch Housing

The idler gear bearing bore diameter has been increased from 1.00 in. (25.4 mm.) to 1 1/16 in. (26.98 mm.).

Idler Gear

A modified idler gear having a larger spigot on the transmission case side is now being fitted in conjunction with larger diameter bearings.

Input Gear

The splined boss on the inner end of the input gear has been shortened by 9/16 in. (14.28 mm.) as the input bearing position has been moved outward.

First Motion Shaft

The shaft diameter has been increased to accept the larger first motion shaft bearing.

Layshaft Removal

The stepped layshaft (10) is lengthened by 7/8 in. (22.22 mm.) and can only be removed from the clutch end of the transmission case.

Lay Gear

A 1 in. longer laygear is supported by three caged needle roller bearings, the two larger bearings being fitted at the clutch housing end. Both thrust washers have single tabs, the smaller washer being available in selective sizes.

After removal of the lay shaft, the lay gear (11) should be dropped out of mesh with the main gear train. The first motion shaft cannot be removed from the box until the main shaft assembly has been removed.

Third Motion Shaft Bearing

The third motion shaft bearing (40) steel cage (was brass) stands proud of the bearing and faces inwards. A new bearing remover 18G 1127 is required to avoid damaging the steel cage.

Second and Third Gear Bearings

Second gear (30) is supported by a split caged needle roller bearing (31). Third gear (25) is supported by a similar one piece bearing (26).

First Gear

First gear (36) is supported by a caged needle roller bearing (38) running on a sleeve (39) which is a push fit on the shaft. This sleeve must be fitted with its collar facing the first gear synchromesh assembly, otherwise the first and second speed gears and synchronizer assembly will be over-stressed causing possible damage to the baulk rings.

First and Second Gear Synchromesh Assembly

The hub has shaft bosses of unequal length. The long boss must be fitted toward the first speed gear (36) to prevent loss of second speed synchromesh action. The reverse gear (37) also has bosses of unequal length, the long boss being fitted toward the first speed gear (36).

Third and Fourth Gear Synchromesh Assembly

The synchromesh hub has bosses of unequal length. The long boss is fitted toward the first motion shaft bearing (5). The third speed hub has 12 splines, while the three speed synchromesh transmission has 11.

Third Motion Shaft

This is longer to accomodate the first speed synchronizer assembly.

Selector Fork and Rods

The first and second speed selector fork has a reduced arc to provide clearance for the reverse idler gear when reverse is selected. The first and second speed selector rod is different, having equally spaced detents and the selector fork is repositioned on the rod to suit the first speed gear.

The third and fourth speed selector fork is repositioned on the rod to suit the third and fourth speed synchronizer assembly.

Reverse Idler Gear

When reverse gear is engaged, the spur teeth of the lay gear (11) are meshed with the reverse idler gear (16) which drives the mainshaft reverse gear (37). The selector fork is machined on one side to provide a running clearance for the reverse idler gear, and the centre line of the fork pivot is offset from the centre line of the gear with the large offset facing the differential assembly. The operating arm is also offset.

Differential Bearings

Thrust bearings are fitted to the differential assembly. These bearings are fitted with the THRUST mark facing out. Adjustment is the same as that described in Section F. 4.

Oil pick-up pipe

The pick-up is slightly cranked to clear the layshaft third gear, also the mounting bracket has been repositioned to suit.

1. Idler gear
2. Idler gear thrust washer
3. First motion shaft
4. Spigot bearing
5. First motion shaft bearing
6. Circlip
7. Input gear
8. Lock washer
9. Nut
10. Layshaft
11. Laygear
12. Needle roller bearing
13. Needle roller bearing
14. Thrust washer (small)
15. Thrust washer (large)
16. Reverse idler gear
17. Reverse gear bush
18. Reverse shaft
19. Third motion shaft
20. Baulk ring
21. Third/Fourth speed synchronizer
22. Synchronizer ball
23. Synchronizer spring
24. Baulk ring
25. Third speed gear
26. Needle roller bearing
27. Thrust washer
28. Peg
29. Spring
30. Second speed gear
31. Needle roller bearing (split)
32. Thrust washer
32. Thrust washer
33. Peg
34. Spring
35. Baulk ring
36. First speed gear
37. Reverse gear
38. Needle roller bearing
39. First speed gear sleeve
40. Third motion shaft bearing
41. Circlip
42. Adjusting shim
43. Locating plate
44. Bearing retainer
45. Lock washer
46. Set screw
47. Final drive pinion
48. Lock washer
49. Pinion nut

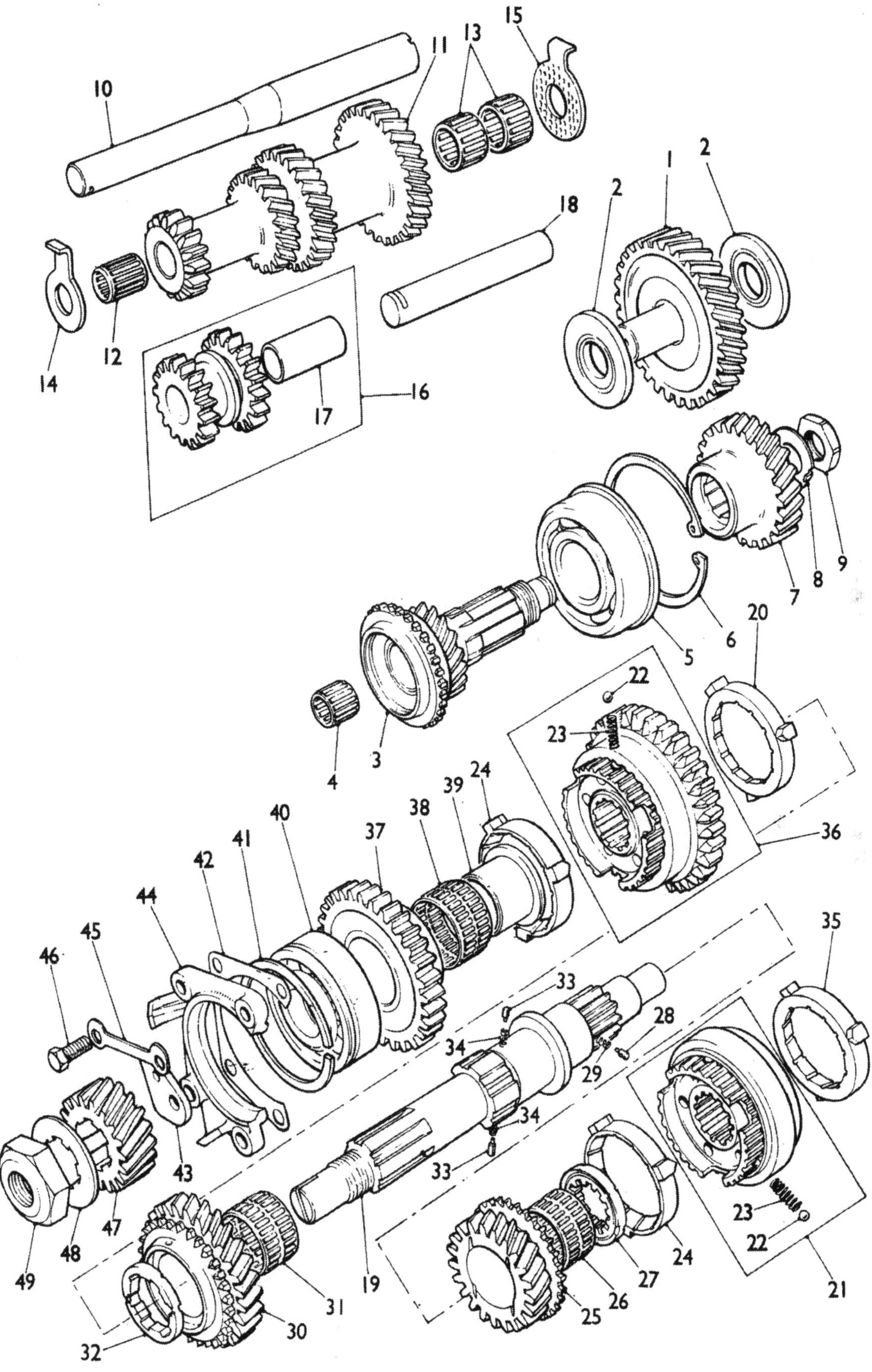

FIG. f.4 FOUR SPEED SYNCHROMESH TRANSMISSION COMPONENTS

Interchangeability of Transmission Assemblies

The new transmission assemblies complete may be used to replace the three speed synchromesh type, but the latter cannot be converted by fitting modified parts.

Section f.4

PRE ASSEMBLY CHECKS AND PRECAUTIONS

The following list of precautions is to be read in conjunction with the methods described in section F.

Gear Train

When loosening or tightening the pinion or input gear nuts the transmission should never be locked by jamming the drive flanges against the case as the case may be severely damaged. In early transmissions wihth 'A' form gears the drive flanges must be locked using a suitable jig. Locking the transmission in two gears is not recommended except on late type transmissions with 'B' form gears. In these transmissions lock 1st and 4th gears together.

First Motion Shaft

When removing the first motion shaft assembly, it is important to use special tools 18G 284 impulse extractor and 18G 248B adaptor. The first motion shaft must not be driven out dy drifting the 3rd motion shaft forward, as this will cause damage to the 3rd motion shaft spigot bearing.

First Motion Shaft Bearing Circlip

The circlip has two tapered hole which engage the dowels on circlip pliers 18G 257. When refitting, the smaller end of those holes must face the operator.

Change Speed Forks

The clearance between the running faces of the forks and synchromesh assemblies should not exceed 0.015 in. (.381 mm.).

First Speed Gear

Backlash between the first gear and the hub must not exceed 0.006 in. (.152 mm.). To check this figure clamp the hub to a steel plate placed on the edge of a flat bench. Refer Fig. f.5. Position a dial indicator as shown in Fig. f.5 so that the finger points directly to the centre of the gear, making a point of contact on a pitch circle diameter of the tooth. This will ensure that movement of the gear on the hub will not allow the finger to ride the contour of the tooth.

With the gear held firmly in an anti-clockwise direction set the dial gauge to zero. Using firm downward pressure on each thumb, rotate the gear back and forth on the hub. The measurement indicated on the gauge will be the backlash of the gear on its hub. Rotate the gear one-half turn and repeat the operation to ascertain a mean reading.

Second and Third Speed Gears

End float of these gears must be 0.0035 in. (0.089 mm.) to 0.0055 in. (1.397 mm.) and is achieved by selective assembly of gears and shafts.

Selector Shafts

It is essential that a degree of gear overshoot exist in the movement of the selector rods. This should be between a minimum of 0.012 in. and a maximum of 0.020 in. (.30 mm. to .50 mm.), as a figure in excess of 0.020 in. (.30 mm.) will cause permanent locking in gear due to exposure of the three synchromesh balls whilst insufficient overshoot may cause auto-disengagement of the gear. The overshoot should be measured on each selector rod with a feeler gauge between the end of the rod and the gate stop.

General

1. When assembling, particular care must be taken not to damage the oil pick-up strainer. If the gauze is distorted it may allow the small metal disc at the base of the strainer to move up against the pick-up pipe and subsequently restrict the oil flow at high engine revolutions.
2. When lubricating the gear change remote control shaft bushes, note that high pressure or excessive lubrication may dislodge the shaft bushes.
3. When assembling the transmission case, jointing compound should be used on all gaskets.
4. It is recommended that all detent springs be replaced with Part No. 2A3647 or 22G 253 which gives an increase in plunger pressure.
5. Remote control assembly. Refer engine section.

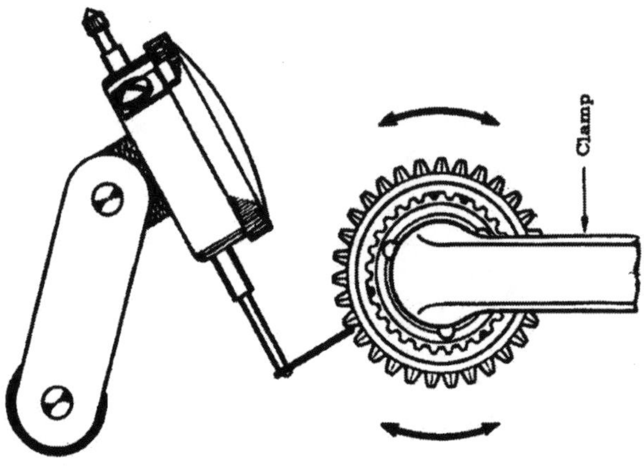

Fig. f.5 Checking the backlash of 1st speed gear

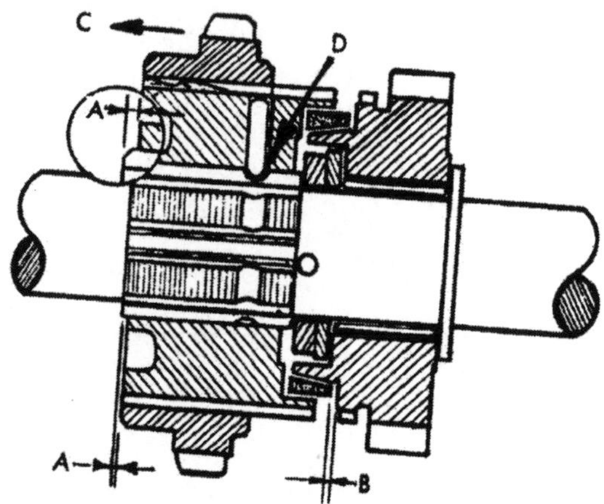

Fig. f.6 Checking baulk ring and hub clearances
Dimension A—Splines standing proud.
Dimension B—Baulk ring back clearance 0.030 in. (.76mm).

Synchromesh Assemblies

The synchromesh balls and springs must have freedom of movement in their respective hub bores. If necessary deburr the bores.

Baulk Rings

The synchromesh baulk rings should be checked for back clearance. Refer Fig. f.6. Push the baulk ring onto its gear cone. A minimum clearance of 0.030 in. (.76 mm.) should exist between the back face of the baulk ring and the gear engagement dogs (Refer dimension B, Fig. f.6). Normally the clearance is in excess of 0.030 in. (.76 mm.). This check should be made prior to the baulk ring being placed in a sub-assembly. It is not related to dimension A.

First Gear Hub Clearance

Prior to refitting the assembled third motion shaft to the transmission case, check the relationship of the first and second gear assembly to the shaft. Referring to Fig. f.6 slide the first speed gear (23) Fig. f.3 close up onto the hub (22) Fig. f.3, in the direction of arrow 'C' and align the end faces of the hub and gear. The hub locking plunger (26) Fig. f.3 will now be located in the shaft groove as shown by arrow 'D' in Fig. f.6. Push the hub assembly in the direction of second gear. In this position the shaft splines must stand proud of the hub centre shown by dimension A (Fig. f.6), otherwise a binding condition will exist between the hub, the baulk ring and second gear.

SECTION

AUTOMATIC TRANSMISSION

The information contained in this section refers to Australian produced vehicles and is additional to that included in Section Fa.

Section fa.1

ADJUSTMENTS

Idle speed adjustment

Correct idling speed adjustment is essential to avoid stalling in traffic or an excessive thump on engagement of gear from "N". A high idling speed will cause excessive "creep". Set to 650 r.p.m. when at operating temperature, using an electric tachometer. The selector must be in "N" when the setting is made. It is normal for the idle speed to drop 50-100 r.p.m. when a gear is selected.

Selector cable and rod adjustment

It is most important to carry out the adjustment procedure detailed below and refer to Fig. fa.1.

1. Pull back the rubber boot (1) and remove clevis pin (2). Ensure that the selector rod (3) is screwed in tightly and push it fully into the transmission case.
   Note: Never start the engine with the selector rod disconnected.
2. Refit the clevis pin (2) into the selector rod yoke (4) and check the measurement indicated in Fig. fa.1, noting that the dimension is measured from the machined face of the transmission housing.
3. Slacken the locknut (5) behind the selector rod yoke and turn the yoke (4) until the correct measurement of 25/32" (20 mm.) is effected — tighten the locknut (5), ensuring that the yoke is set squarely to the bell-crank lever arm.
4. Select "D" in the transmission unit by pushing the selector rod fully in.
5. Insert a 3/16" rod in the selector gate behind the gear lever and pull the gear lever right back into the "D" position so as to trap the rod in the quadrant. (Refer Fig. fa.2.) Secure the lever in this position.
6. Adjust the cable so that the clevis pin can be refitted freely.

3/16" rod.

7. Check this adjustment with the gear lever in "R" and the selector rod pulled out to its utmost position. This check will also verify the condition of the cable, clevis pins, and forks.
8. Check that the starter inhibitor switch adjustment is still correct.

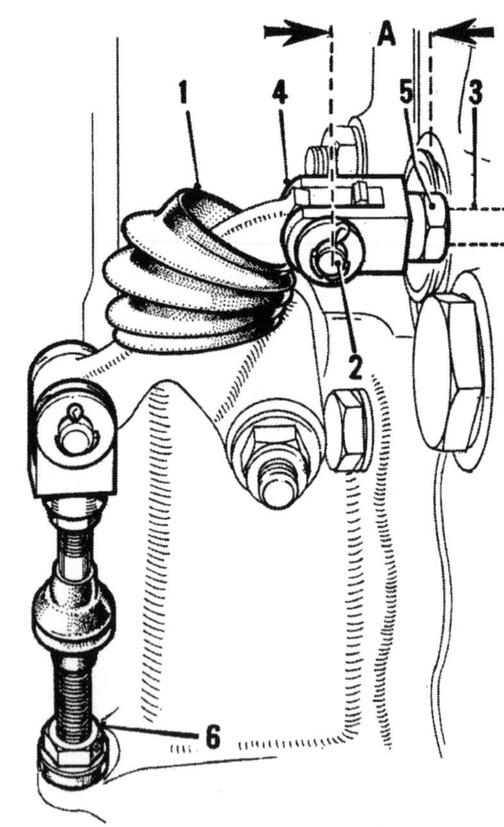

Fig. fa.1

The gear-change cable and selector rod adjustment

1. Rubber boot.
2. Clevis pin.
3. Selector rod.
4. Selector rod yoke.
5. Selector rod yoke locknut.
6. Cable adjusting nuts.

A = 25/32" (20 mm.) selector rod checking dimension.

NOTE: Ensure that the forked ends on the selector cable and rod are square to the bell-crank lever, before reconnecting.

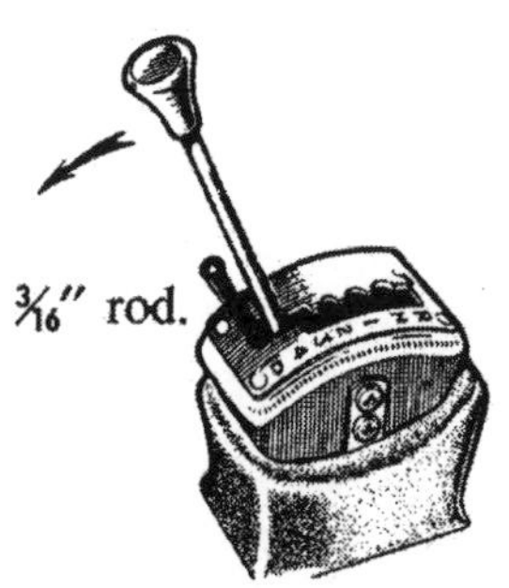

Fig. fa.2

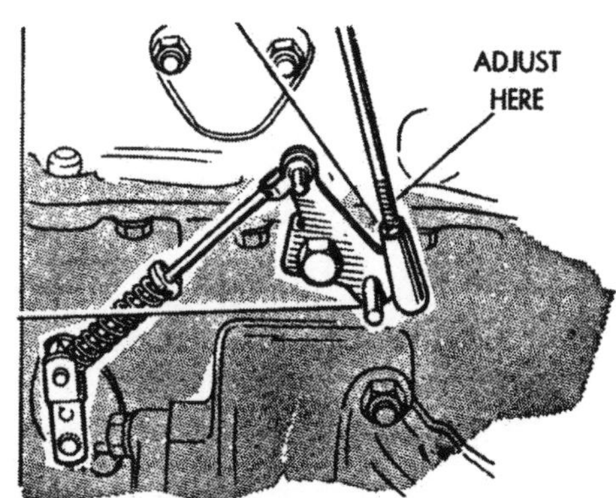

Fig. fa.3

Testing the adjustment

1. Apply the hand and foot brakes, and ensure that the starter operates only in the "N" position; if this is not correct, adjust the inhibitor switch as detailed in Section fa.2.
2. Start the engine, and move the gear lever to the "R" position and check that reverse is engaged. Slowly move the lever back towards the "N" position, checking that the gear is engaged just before or as soon as the lever drops into the "N" position on the quadrant. Repeat this procedure in the first gear "1" position. Re-adjust the outer cable slightly if necessary to obtain the above conditions.
3. Ensure that all adjustment/locking nuts are tight and the clevis pins are secured. Pack the rubber boots with Zinc Oxide grease. Refit the boots and the weather protection shield, (if fitted).
4. Carry out a road-test, checking the operation in each gear lever position.

Throttle linkage adjustment

The operation and adjustment of the throttle cable should be checked prior to adjusting the transmission throttle control rod. It will not be possible to obtain correct shift speeds at full throttle unless the accelerator does, in fact, open the throttle completely.

1. Run the engine to its normal working temperature.
2. Disconnect the governor control rod at the carburettor.
3. With the carburettor correctly tuned, adjust the throttle adjusting screw to give a tachometer reading of 650 r.p.m. at tickover in "N".
4. Insert a ¼" (6.4 mm.) diameter rod through the hole in the governor control rod bell-crank lever and into the hole in the transmission case (Fig. fa.3).
5. Slacken the locknut and adjust the length of the rod to suit the carburettor linkage in the tickover position.
6. Reconnect the governor control rod to the carburettor. Tighten the ball joint locknut and remove the checking rod from the bell-crank lever.
7. Road-test the vehicle.
   Should it be found that full throttle upshift speeds are excessively low or high, despite correct adjustment of the governor control rod, the following procedure should be followed:—

(a) Disconnect the governor control rod from the carburettor spindle.

(b) Slacken the lock nut at the lower end of the rod and turn the rod to SHORTEN if full throttle change speeds are HIGH. Turn the rod to LENGTHEN if full throttle change speeds are LOW.

(c) Tighten the lock nut and replace the clevis pin. Ensure that full throttle opening has NOT been restricted.

NOTE: It may be necessary to increase the length of the thread at the ball joint end of the throttle rod and to shorten the threaded end of the rod by up to ¼" (6.4 mm.). The thread is No. 10 U.N.F.

Band adjustments

The bands do not require periodical adjustment, in fact they should never require resetting due to normal wear and tear.

Access to the adjustments can be obtained without removal of the power unit, but with some difficulty.

To gain access to the bands, remove the sump guard, oil filter complete, distributor and starter motor. The transmission front cover can now be removed from the top. Referring to Fig. fa.4 the adjustment procedure is as follows:—

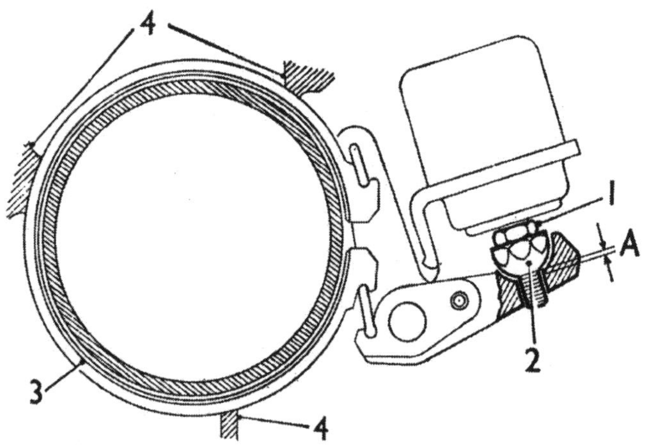

Fig. fa.4
The servo unit band adjustment

A = .040 to .080 in. (1.02 to 2.03 mm.)

1. Ensure that the bands are resting against the stops (4) machined in the transmission case. If necessary slacken lock nut (1) and screw the spherical adjusting nut (2) away from the lever.
2. Adjust the spherical nut (2) to provide .040 in. - .080 in. (1.02 mm. - 2.03 mm.) clearance between the nut and its spherical seating in the lever. This may best be achieved by screwing the nut by hand into the lever until no free play exists (taking care not to move the band off the stops in the transmission case). In this position the bands are in the "off" position and they are sprung against the stops machined within the housing.
   Screw back the spherical nut 1½ to 2 turns to obtain the clearance of 0.040 in. to 0.080 in. (1.02 mm. to 2.03 mm.).
   It will be noticed that with this setting the amount of total travel necessary to apply the bands fully will be greater on the reverse band than on either of the 2nd or 3rd gear bands.
3. Replace front cover and filter, ensuring that the filter head to front cover "O" rings and/or gasket are renewed.

Section fa.2

STALL SPEED CHECK

The instructions in Section Fa.2 should be followed but substituting the chart figures below.

1600 - 1700 r.p.m. Satisfactory.
Under 1000 r.p.m. Stator Free Wheel Slip.
Under 1300 r.p.m. Engine Down on Power.
Over 1800 r.p.m. Transmission Slip.

Section fa.3

REFITTING THE GEAR LEVER

In addition to the instructions contained in Section Fa.12, it is important to ensure that the gear lever is correctly engaged with the gear lever plunger (9), Fig. Fa.60. The slot in the gear lever plunger (9) is recessed on one side only. The recessed side must face upwards when the gear lever is engaged with it.

Section fa.4

LOCATION OF THRUST WASHERS

Refer pages fa.4 and fa.5.

Section fa.5

MODIFICATIONS AND ASSEMBLY NOTES

The modifications as detailed in Section Fa.5 also apply to Australian produced vehicles.

Section fa.4 LOCATION OF THRUST WASHERS

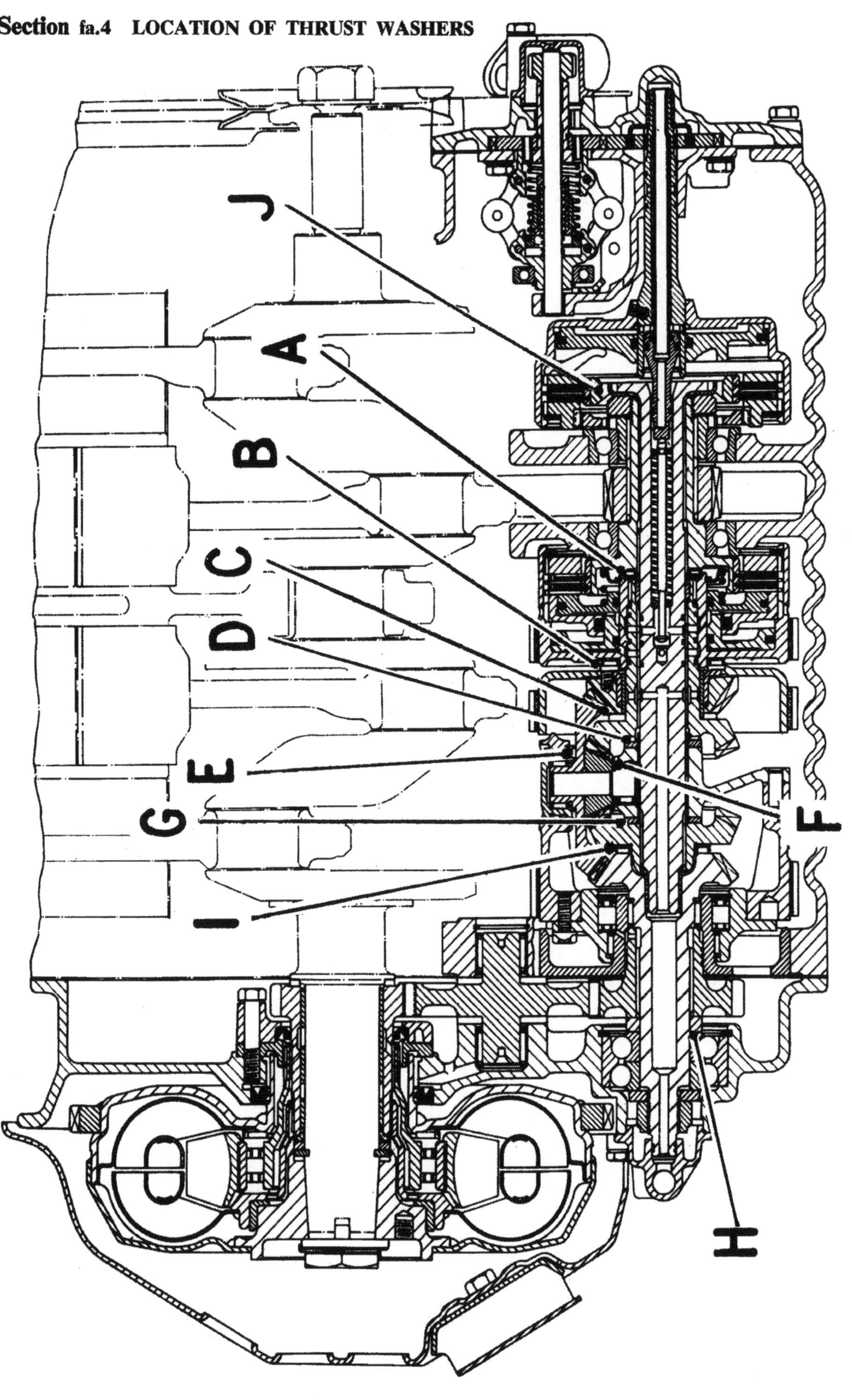

Fig. fa.5

THRUST WASHER IDENTIFICATION

The thrust washers whose locations are set out in Fig. fa.5 can be identified from the FULL SCALE illustrations below.

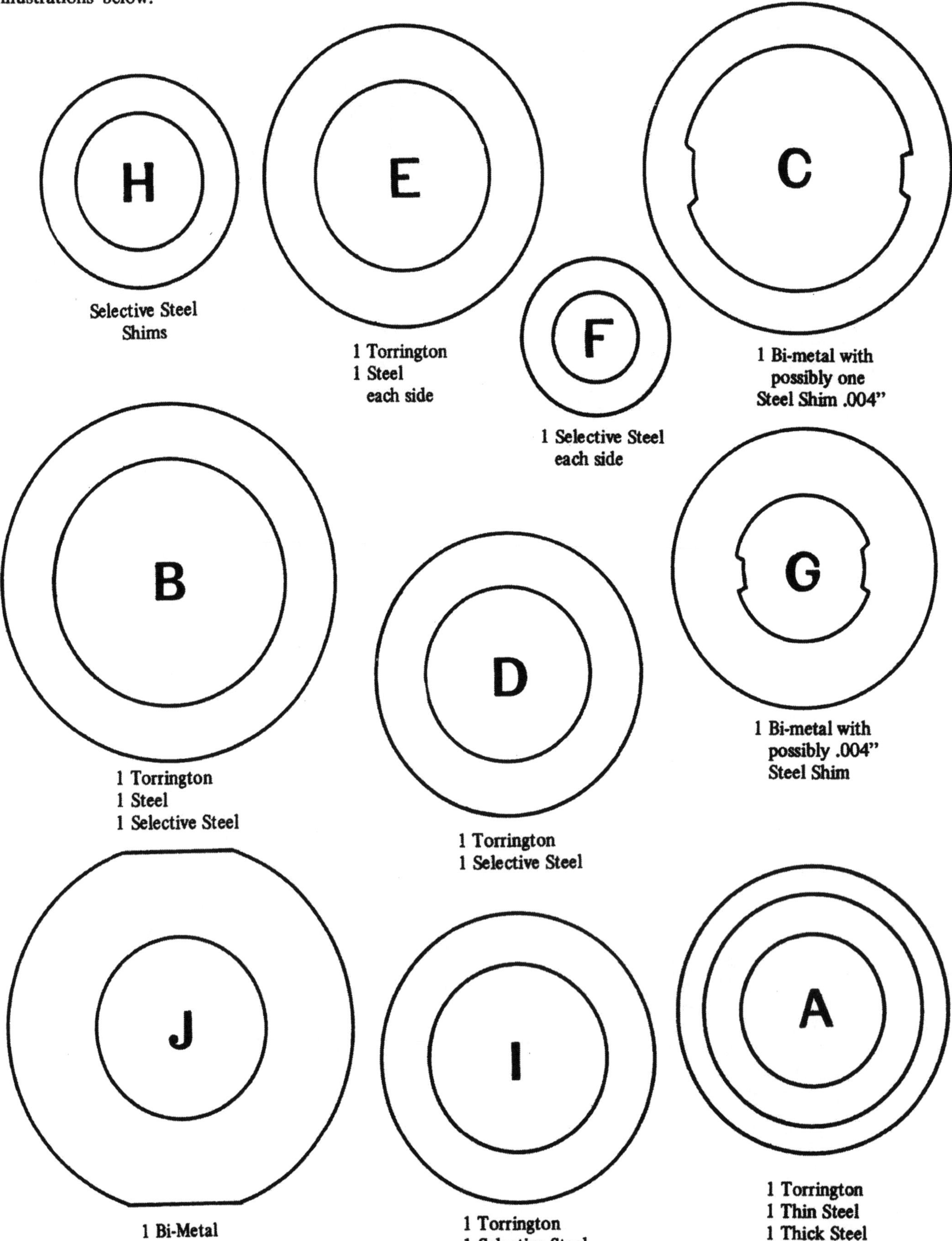

SECTION g

DRIVE SHAFTS

Section g.1

General

The information contained in Section G is applicable to all Australian vehicles with drive shafts incorporating sliding inner joints for use with rubber drive couplings.

Later model Mokes, Cooper, "S", Mini-matic and Clubman G.T. are fitted with drive shafts incorporating sliding inner joints for use with Hookes type needle roller universal couplings.

Major servicing of the Constant Velocity joints on both shafts is the same as detailed in Section G with the exception that in Australia grease under BLMC Part No. HYL3434 is used for lubricating components.

Regular maintenance attention: Lubricate constant velocity joints at each 12,000 mile service.

Section g.2

RUBBER DRIVE COUPLINGS

The service life of rubber drive couplings is greatly reduced if they are continually contaminated by oil and grease or the U-bolt nuts over tightened.

Prior to fitting a new coupling ensure the drive flanges are tight and seals in good condition.

Drive couplings

Removing

1. Fit a suitable wedge between suspension upper support arm and rebound rubber.
2. Jack up car to give suitable working clearance under the car and allow front wheel removal.
3. Remove road wheel.
4. Disconnect steering tie rod end.
5. Disconnect lower suspension arm from swivel hub.
6. Remove 4 U-bolt nuts facing swivel hub.
7. Remove 4 U-bolt nuts from drive flange and remove the U-bolts.
8. Push sliding joint toward outside of car and remove coupling.

Refitting

Refitting is the reversal of the removal procedure. See General Data for Suspension and U-bolt nut torque figures.

Section g.3

SLIDING JOINT AND UNIVERSAL ASSEMBLY

Removing sliding joint

1. Remove drive shaft assembly. Section K.2.
2. Clean off dirt and grease from the flange area.
3. Prise off the housing sealing clips and pull the housing from the flange.
4. Mark drive shaft and flange sleeve for refitting in their original positions.
5. Close ends of circlip together and release from groove (use two screwdrivers). Pull shaft from flange.

Inspection

6. Clean the splines thoroughly.
7. If the housing has been damaged, check the splines for excessive clearance. Also check spline clearance when a new shaft is to be fitted to a used flange; and vice-versa.

Refitting

8. Each joint should contain 2 oz. (56.7 gm.) of grease (refer Section g.1).
9. Grease the spline end of the shaft and the inside of the housing seal, and slide the housing onto the shaft followed by the circlip. Fill the flange sleeve with the remainder of the grease.
10. Locate the shaft spring, push the shaft into the flange, and fit the circlip (Fig. g.1). Fit the housing into the shaft and sleeve grooves.
11. Force the shaft to the bottom of the splines, holding the outer lip of the housing open to allow air and surplus grease to escape.
12. Check the diameter of the rubber housing with the shaft in the closed position. If exceeding 2 in. 51 mm.) (Fig. g.1), squeeze by hand until reduced as required.
13. Partially withdraw the shaft and fit and secure the retaining clips (see Fig. g.1).

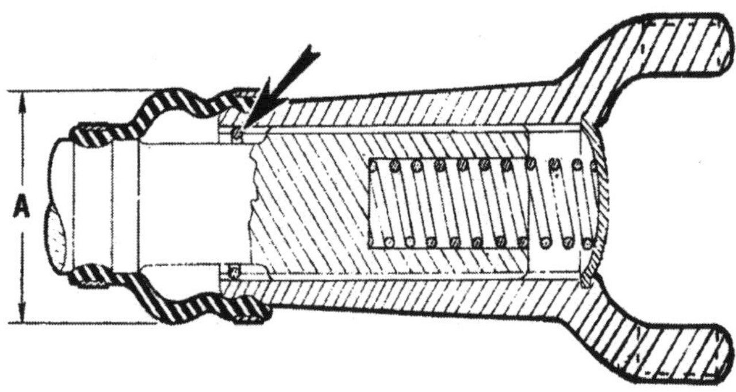

Fig. g.1

Sliding joint assembly. The rubber housing must not exceed 2 in. (51 mm.), diameter "A". Shaft securing circlip arrowed.

The Universal Assembly

Dismantling

1. Remove the drive shaft assembly complete.
2. Thoroughly clean the assembly and remove paint from the snap-rings and bearing faces.
3. Remove the snap-rings; if a snap-ring will not snap out, tap the end of the bearing to relieve pressure.
4. Hold the joint and lightly tap the yoke; the opposite bearing should begin to emerge; remove with the fingers. If necessary, tap the bearing race from inside the joint (Fig. g.2). Repeat this operation for opposite bearing.
5. Rest the exposed trunnions on a soft surface, and tap the lug of the yoke to remove the two remaining races.

Inspecting

6. Wash the flanges in fuel and check the cross-holes for wear. The new bearings must be a good push-fit at least; replace the joint if suspect.

Reassembling

7. Fill the holes in the journal spider with Molybdenumized grease, taking care to exclude all air. Fill each bearing with grease to a depth of ⅛ in. (3 mm.).
8. Fit the seals to the spider journals and insert spider into the flanges, tilting to engage the bores.
9. Fit a bearing race into the bore in the bottom position, using a soft drift, tap it down the yoke bore until it is just possible to fit the circlip.
10. Repeat this operation for the other bearings, starting opposite the bearing first fitted.
11. Remove all surplus grease. Check for free movement of the journals; tap lightly with mallet to relieve any bearing pressure on the journals.

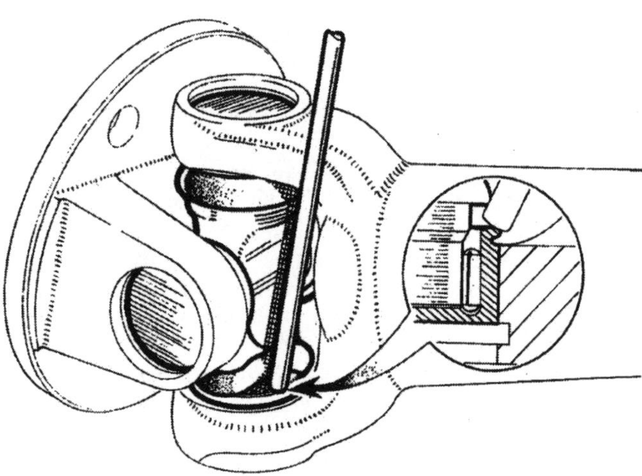

Fig. g.2

Tap the bearings from the universal joint with a small-diameter rod.

SECTION h

REAR SUSPENSION

The information contained in this section refers to Australian produced vehicles. It does not supersede the previous section, but should be used in conjunction with it.

Section h.1

REAR WHEEL TOE-IN

The rear wheels must conform to the toe-in specifications as shown in the General Data. Allowance for adjustment of toe-in has not been provided in the vehicle design, but some correction of excessive toe-in is possible by the use of non-standard shims or spacers interposed between the sub-frame and the outer radius arm brackets, to a limit of .120" (30 mm.). Spacers may be made up from the dimensions shown in Fig. h.1. A spacer of approximately .040" (10 mm.) will reduce the rear wheel toe-in approximately ¼° or 1/16" (1.58 mm.).

The toe-in of each rear wheel must be considered singly and not as an overall figure between the two.

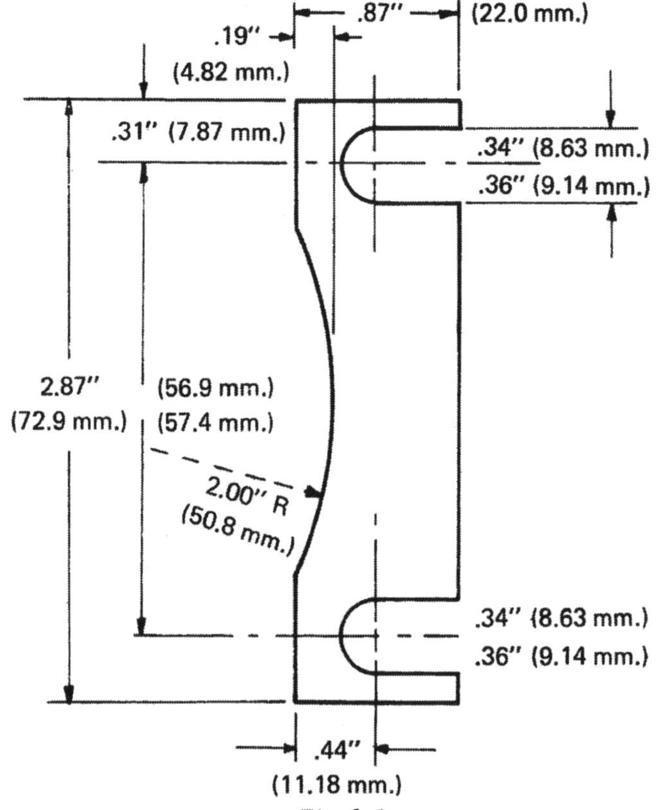

Fig. h.1

Section h.2

REAR RADIUS ARM BEARINGS
(Moke)

Needle roller bearings are fitted to both the inner and outer ends of the arm.

The instructions given in Section H.2 should be followed, except item 10, which should be disregarded and items 11 and 12 repeated on the outer needle roller bearing.

Section h.3

REAR HUB BEARINGS
(Cooper "S")

In late model vehicles, taper roller bearings have replaced the ball bearings in the rear hubs. The bearing spacer is ground to a predetermined length to provide correct bearing fit. Should the taper roller bearings be replaced, the new spacer supplied with the bearing kit must be used.

NOTE: With taper bearings, the seal is fitted with its spring facing OUTWARD.

Section h.4

BUMP STOP
(Moke)

Late model 13" wheel vehicles are fitted with a rear suspension "bump stop" in the form of a steel button mounted in the centre of the spring seat.

The button is secured by a press on spring steel retainer.

It is advisable that all early vehicles be modified to accept the new bump stop and when fitted, it is essential that it be correctly retained in the frame, or major suspension damage may result.

SECTION j

STEERING

The information contained in this Section refers to Australian produced vehicles and it does not supersede the previous Section, but should be used in conjunction with it.

Section j.1

OVERHAULING THE STEERING RACK

Steering rack assemblies used in Australian built vehicles may be of either English or Australian manufacture, and under no circumstances should relevant components be inter-mixed when overhauling these assemblies.

English steering racks are 13/16" dia. (20.638 mm.) and the ball housing carries a milled axial slot for a "C" spanner, while the Australian rack is ⅞" diam. (22.225 mm.) and has two blind drillings in the ball housing.

If tie rods and ball housings are inter-mixed, a dangerously low contact area between the ball and housing will result.

If it is suspected that a steering rack has been incorrectly overhauled and components inter-mixed, the following checking procedure should be followed:—

1. Remove the rubber boot from the rack housing.
2. Disconnect the steering knuckle joint from the steering arm and move the tie rod downwards to the extremity of its travel.

Where English and Australian components have been intermixed, a large gap will exist between the tie rod ball and the ball housing at the top of the seat area. Should this condition be found, the correct parts must be fitted to enable the vehicle to be operated with safety. Refit the rubber boot and replace any oil that has been lost by operating a pressure type oil can with its nozzle slipped under the outer end of the boot before the clip is refitted. Reconnect the knuckle joint to the steering arm.

The English rack assembly complete and the Australian rack assembly complete will interchange for service requirements, except on early model BMC Moke. The rack for this model is fitted with internal lock stops to suit 13" wheels.

On later models the lock stops were deleted, making the rack interchangeable with the later saloons and vans. Vehicles fitted with the commonised rack have a reduced turning circle and may be identified by their wider front track produced by commonisation of the front brake drums and wheel studs with those of the rear.

Section j2

STEERING RACK PINION

An improved steering rack pinion was introduced, in which the undercut on the pinion shank is omitted, and this area increased in diameter by 0.010 in. (0.25 mm.). To ensure positive location of the pinion in the rack, a ¼ in. (6.35 mm.) spacer is fitted. The overall length of the pinion has not been increased, but the pinion housing boss is raised by ¼ in. (6.35 mm.) in height.

The earlier pinion is no longer available, but the rack assembly may be brought up to date by fitting this pinion and spacer together with a new housing, and spacers between the clamping "V" bolts between the rack and the toe-board.

The new type pinion must UNDER NO CIRCUMSTANCES be machined to suit the old housing.

Old and new complete rack assemblies are completely interchangeable, and the method of identification is as follows—

On early type assemblies the pinion stand proud of the rack housing by approximately 1 5/16 in. (33.34 mm.).

On the later racks, the pinion stand proud by approximately 1 in. (25.4 mm.).

Section j.3

WHEEL ALIGNMENT

Set the total toe-out to 1/16 in. (1.59 mm.) or to 7 minutes 30 seconds per wheel.

Distances must be measured on a 14½ in. (36.8 cm.) diameter, at a height of 9.4 in. (23.8 cm.) above the ground on the side wall of the tyre.

The car should be on an absolutely level surface, the tyres set at their recommended pressures, car at registration weight, and the suspension heights correct.

To obviate unnecessary adjustments to the rack, up to ¼ in. (6.35 mm.) difference in the exposed thread lengths is permitted.

If this difference is less than ⅛ in. (3.18 mm.), adjustment may be made to one side only. If the difference is more than ⅛ in. adjustment must be made to both steering tie-rods.

NOTE: The above heights and diameters are for vehicles with 10 in. wheels. Vehicles with 13 in. wheels should be measured on a 17½ in. (44.4 cm.) diameter at a height of 11¼ in. (28.5 cm.).

SECTION k

FRONT SUSPENSION

The information contained in this Section refers to Australian produced vehicles and it does not supersede the previous Section, but should be used in conjunction with it.

Section k.1

HYDROLASTIC SUSPENSION HEIGHTS

When Hydrolastic suspension heights are to be checked, the following points must receive attention before proceeding:—

1. Tyre pressures must be correct. (Refer to General Data.)
2. Vehicle kerb weight must be correct. The kerb weight of a standard vehicle is assessed with 5 gls. (22.73 litres) of fuel, and water and oil levels brought to the "full" mark. The spare wheel should be housed in its original position and the standard tool kit stowed in the boot. (Refer General Data for kerb weight.)
3. The Hydrolastic system should be at ambient temperature before checking suspension heights and pressures. Ensure sufficient time is allowed for cooling where this is necessary.
4. The suspension must have mechanical freedom. Mechanical freedom may be assured by rocking the vehicle from side to side with the hand brake released.

Suspension height measurements

The Hydrolastic system pressures must conform with the figures given below and the heights should be measured as described in Section H.9.

After adjustment and with the hand brake released, the vehicle may be rocked from side to side to settle the suspension. The trim height should then be rechecked. A 10 p.s.i. (.7 Kg.cm^2) difference in pressure between sides is permissible to equalise the trim heights.

Fitting packing washers

To overcome the condition where correct suspension heights cannot be obtained before reaching maximum pressure, it is permissible to fit one packing washer only between the front strut and the shoulder of the knuckle joint assembly.

The washers are supplied in two thicknesses: Part No. 21A463 — .080″ (2.03 mm.), and Part. No. AJH 3322 — .100″ (2.54 mm.) which will give an increased trim height of approximately 5/16″ (7.94 mm.) and 7/16″ (11.11 mm.) respectively. (Refer Fig. k.1.)

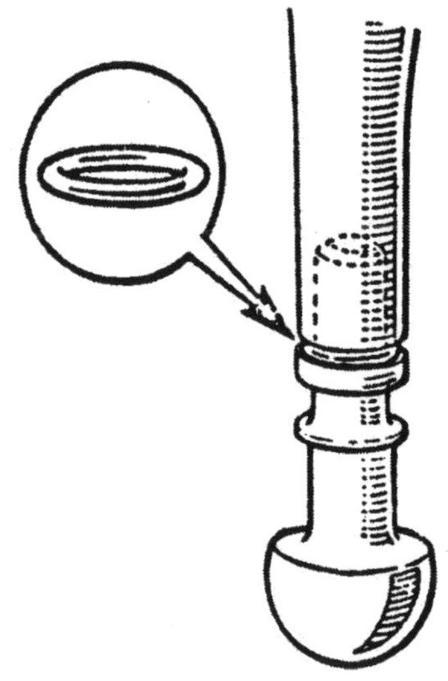

Fig. k.1

Section k.2

DISPLACER UNITS

Displacer units are colour-coded to enable identification. Coloured bands have been attached to the hose section or painted on the body of the displacer. Commencing car numbers for various design changes are shown in the General Data under "Suspension". A replacement unit must match with the colour-coding of the original part.

After fitting a new displacer unit, it is necessary to "scrag" or stretch the unit by pressurising the appropriate side of the suspension. A pressure of 350 ± 20

Model	Normal Suspension Pressure	Front Wing Height "A"
Mini 1100	275 ± 10 p.s.i. (19.3 ± .7 Kg.cm^2)	13¼″ ± ¼″ (336.54 ± 6.4 mm.)
Mini Deluxe and Clubman	275 ± 10 p.s.i. (19.3 ± 7 kg.cm^2)	13¼″ ± ¼″ (336.54 ± 6.4 mm.)
Cooper "S" and G.T.	275 ± 10 p.s.i. (19.3 ± 7 kg.cm^2)	12 5/16″ ± ¼″ (312.7 ± 6.4 mm.)

p.s.i. (24.6 ± 1.4 Kg.cm²) is required to be held for a minimum period of 60 minutes.

Before reducing the pressure to normal, the system should be checked for possible leaks.

Adverse handling characteristics of the vehicle can be expected if pressures are increased or decreased from the recommended limits quoted in Section k.1. Operating the vehicle under minimum pressure limits will cause premature failure of bump rubbers. **Pressures in excess of recommendations will lead to premature failure of displacer units.**

Under extreme conditions of terrain where above-normal ground clearance is required for temporary operation only, a high limit of 300 p.s.i. (21.1 Kg.cm²) is permissible. In this case, light loads only should be carried.

Section k.3

HYDROLASTIC FLUID

When recharging or topping up the Hydrolastic system, only fluid supplied by an authorised B.M.C. dealer should be used, and all are compatible irrespective of specification or part number.

Section k.4

LOWER CONTROL ARM AND BUSHES

To extend the life of the inner bushes of the lower control arm, composite steel and rubber bushes have been introduced to replace the all-rubber type. The control arms have been modified to suit.

The new bushes may be fitted to earlier cars, if the lower control arms are changed.

SECTION m

BRAKING SYSTEM

The information contained in this Section refers to Australian produced vehicles. It does not supersede the previous Section, but should be used in conjunction with it.

Section m.1

HAND BRAKE ADJUSTMENT

If excessive hand brake lever travel is present with linings in good condition, it is permissible to take up the excess travel at the brake hand lever trunnion, provided the following procedure is strictly adhered to.

First make sure that the shoes are properly adjusted by means of the shoe adjusters as explained in Section M.2 and M.10. This is most important.

Apply the hand brake until the pawl engages with the first notch on the ratchet, and adjust the nuts at the hand brake lever until it is just possible to rotate the wheel.

Section m.2

BRAKE LININGS

Two types of brake linings have been fitted to Australian manufactured vehicles.

(1) Don 2oz. Identification, 3 red stripes.

(2) Hardie Ferodo E.501 — Identification one red and 1 blue stripe.

These brake linings are interchangeable only in complete car sets.

Section m.3

THE HYDROPOWER SERVO UNIT
(P.B.R. Model VH-44 JA)

Description

The Hydropower servo unit is composed of the following major assemblies:

1. Vacuum Power Chamber.
2. Hydraulic Slave Cylinder.
3. Hydraulically Actuated Control Valve.

The Vacuum Power Chamber comprises two steel pressings held together at their rims by a clamp ring (11). Refer *Fig. m.1* and *m.2*. The rear or control half (1) is isolated from the front or vacuum half (12) by the diaphragm (10) and push rod assembly. The diaphragm (10) is clamped at its outer edge between the rims of the vacuum power chamber valves.

The diaphragm spring (9) holds the diaphragm and push rod assembly in the released position.

The check valve (43) is fitted directly into the vacuum half. An important feature is the large volume of the power chamber vacuum half (12). This chamber acts as a reserve vacuum supply and eliminates the

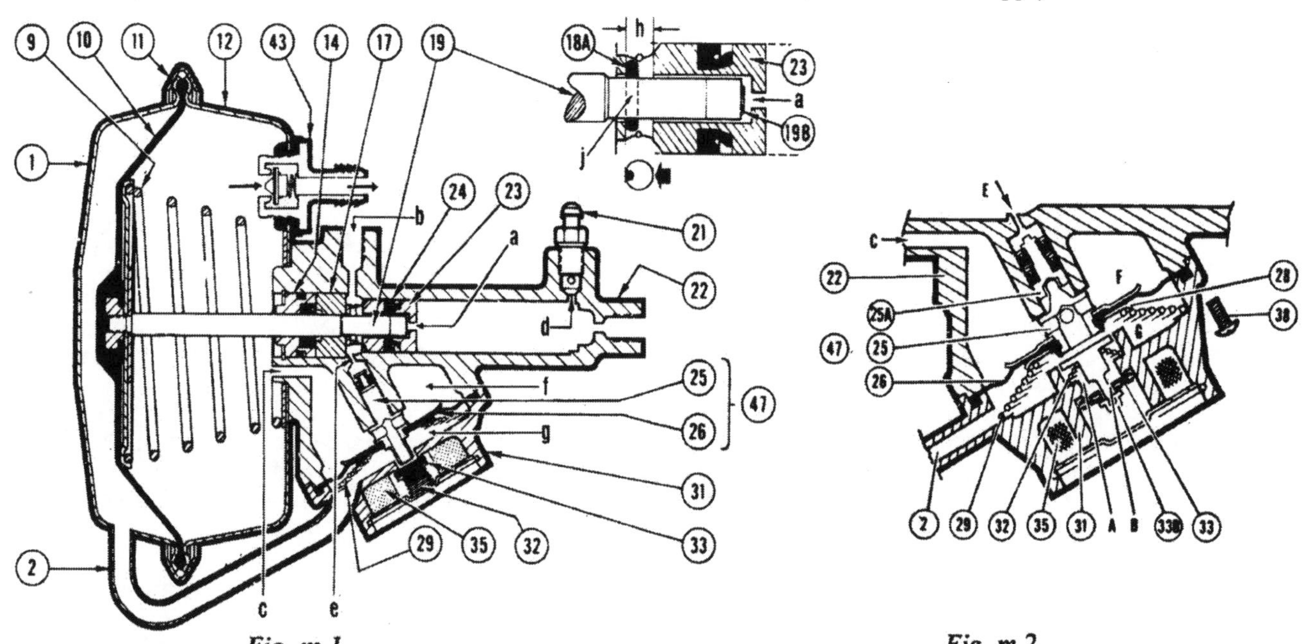

Fig. m.1
Servo — released position.

Fig. m.2
Control Valve Assembly

necessity for a separate vacuum reserve tank. Since the unit consumes vacuum only when power is released, a small manifold fitting will provide sufficient volume. The hydraulic slave cylinder (22) is an aluminium casting and is attached to the vacuum chamber front half.

The slave cylinder design is such that with the unit mounted correctly, i.e. with the slave cylinder pointing slightly upward (approximately ¼ in.), air will collect at the entrance of the bleeder port (d) and be expelled through the bleeder valve (21) during bleeding.

The slave cylinder components are: a bush (14) with vacuum and hydraulic seals, and spacer (17) through which the push rod (19) passes to actuate the slave cylinder piston (23) and cup assembly (24).

The hydraulically actuated control valve (47) consists of a hydraulic piston (25) and diaphragm assembly (26). The control valve body contains a poppet valve (33), poppet return spring (32), and an air filter (35).

Compound control valve

The "Compound Control" Hydropower is basically identical to all other models, and varies only in the hydraulically actuated control valve and poppet assembly.

Principle of operation

The brake fluid from the master cylinder enters the unit at the inlet port (b) and passes through port (a) in slave cylinder piston (23) into the slave cylinder. At the same time it is directed to the upper side of the control valve piston (25) via restrictor (e).

Vacuum from the intake manifold is transmitted through vacuum check valve (43) to power chamber (12). Vacuum enters valve chambers (f) through passage (c) and passes through the centre of the control valve and diaphragm assembly (47) to valve chamber (g).

Valve chamber (g) is connected to vacuum power chamber controller rear half (1) by tube (2) thus transmitting manifold vacuum to both sides of power diaphragm (10). The unit is therefore described as "vacuum suspended".

Hydropower in released position — Fig. m 1

In the released position, the power diaphragm (10) is held to the left in the power chamber by return spring (9). The slave cylinder piston (23) is held against spacer (17) by the pin (18A) which passes through hole (h) in slave cylinder piston (23) and hole (j) in push rod (19). The hole (h) in slave cylinder piston (23) is considerably larger than pin (18A) allowing the push rod (19) to move axially in relation to the slave cylinder piston (23).

In the released position the pin (18A) is at its rearmost position in relation to the slave cylinder piston (23). The push rod seal (19B) is thus held clear of port (a) in the slave cylinder piston (23). The control valve piston (25) is held at the innermost position by the action of the control valve return spring (29). In this position, the hollow stem of the control valve (47) is held clear of the poppet valve (33).

As a result, vacuum is equal in power chambers (1) and (12) and valve chambers (g) and (f).

Operation of compound control valve with hydropower on released position — Refer Fig. m.2

The control valve assembly (47) is held at its innermost position by return spring (29). In this position the hollow centre of push rod (25) is held clear of poppet valve stem (33A). Chambers "F" and "G" are therefore open to each other, and vacuum is equal on each side of the diaphragm. Valve seal (33) is seated on atmospheric port (A) in control valve body (31) and poppet retainer (33B) is seated on small atmospheric port (b) in the centre of valve seat (33) thus isolating chamber "G" from atmosphere.

Hydropower applying — Refer Fig. m.3

Application of pressure to the brake pedal causes fluid from the master cylinder to enter the slave cylinder at inlet port (b) pass through port (a) in slave cylinder piston (23) and through outlet port (k) to wheel cylinders via brake lines.

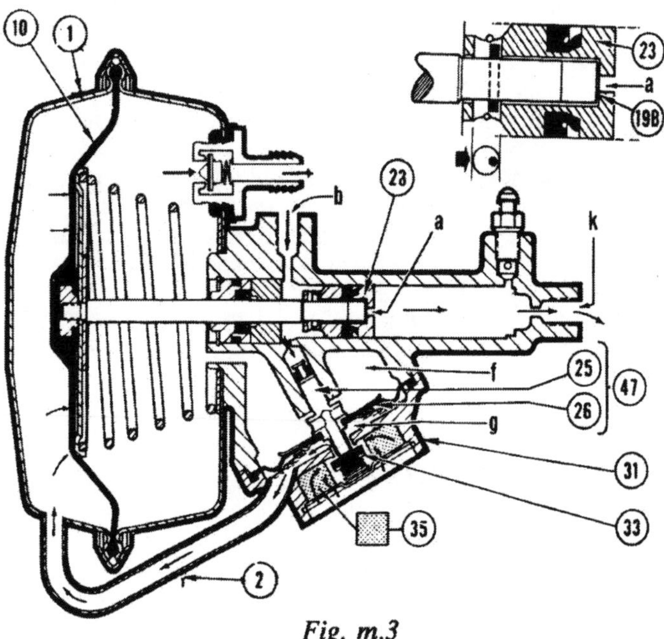

Fig. m.3
Servo — applying position.

Simultaneously, pressure is built up on the top of the control valve piston (25) moving the control valve and diaphragm assembly (47) so that the hollow stem seats on the poppet valve (33) thus isolating valve chamber (f) from valve chamber (g). Further movement lifts poppet valve (33) from its seat admitting air at atmospheric pressure through air cleaner (35) to valve chamber (g) and control chamber (1) via tube (2).

Pressure differential moves power diaphragm (10) forward causing push rod seal (19B) to close port (a) in slave cylinder piston (23), trapping fluid in the slave cylinder (m). Hydraulic fluid under pressure is transmitted to the wheel cylinders through outlet port (k), thus applying the brakes.

The pressure differential across the control valve diaphragm (26) is balanced by master cylinder hydraulic input pressure on upper side of control valve piston (25). In this way the hydraulic output pressure in the slave cylinder (m) is in proportion to the master cylinder input pressure.

The fluid displacement in front of the slave cylinder piston (23) is approximately equal to that at the rear of the piston, giving the driver pedal position as well as pressure control. The volume of fluid at the rear of the piston is actually slightly less than that in front of the piston, due to the displacement of fluid by the push rod (19).

The hydraulic output pressure transmitted to the wheel cylinders is the sum of the pressure developed by the Hydropower plus the pressure from the master cylinder.

Operation of compound control valve with hydropower applying — Refer Fig. m.2

When hydraulic pressure is built up through port "E" on to the control valve piston, (25A) the following sequence is introduced.

First Stage: Refer Fig. m.4

Initial movement of the control valve piston (25A) seals the hollow centre of push rod (25) on to poppet valve stem (33A) thus isolating chamber "F" from chamber "G".

Second Stage: Refer Fig. m.5

Further movement of the control valve piston (25A) lifts the poppet retainer (33B) away from the small atmospheric port "B" to admit air through the centre of valve seal (33) resulting in lower crack pressure. (See specification.)

Third Stage: Refer Fig. m.6

Further movement of the control valve piston (25A) lifts the valve seal (33) away from port "A" opening the main atmospheric port. Admitting air in two stages through first a small and then a large atmospheric port gives a smooth operation of the unit.

Hydropower holding — Refer Fig. m.7

After the required degree of brake applications has been obtained and pressure on the brake pedal is held constant the control valve of the Hydropower will reach a "lap" or holding position. The hydraulic pressure

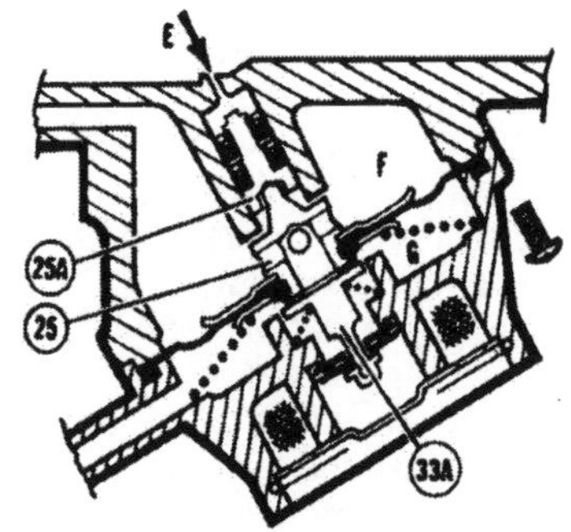

Fig. m.4
First stage.

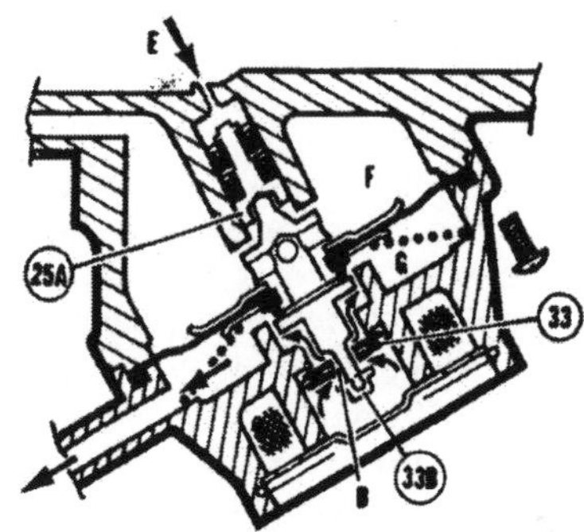

Fig. m.5
Second stage.

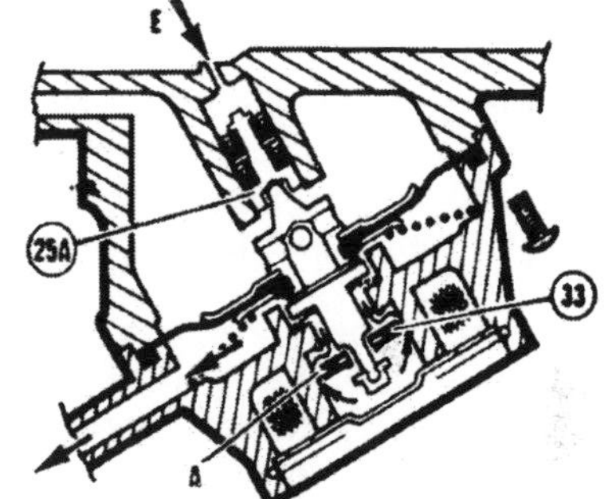

Fig. m.6
Third stage.

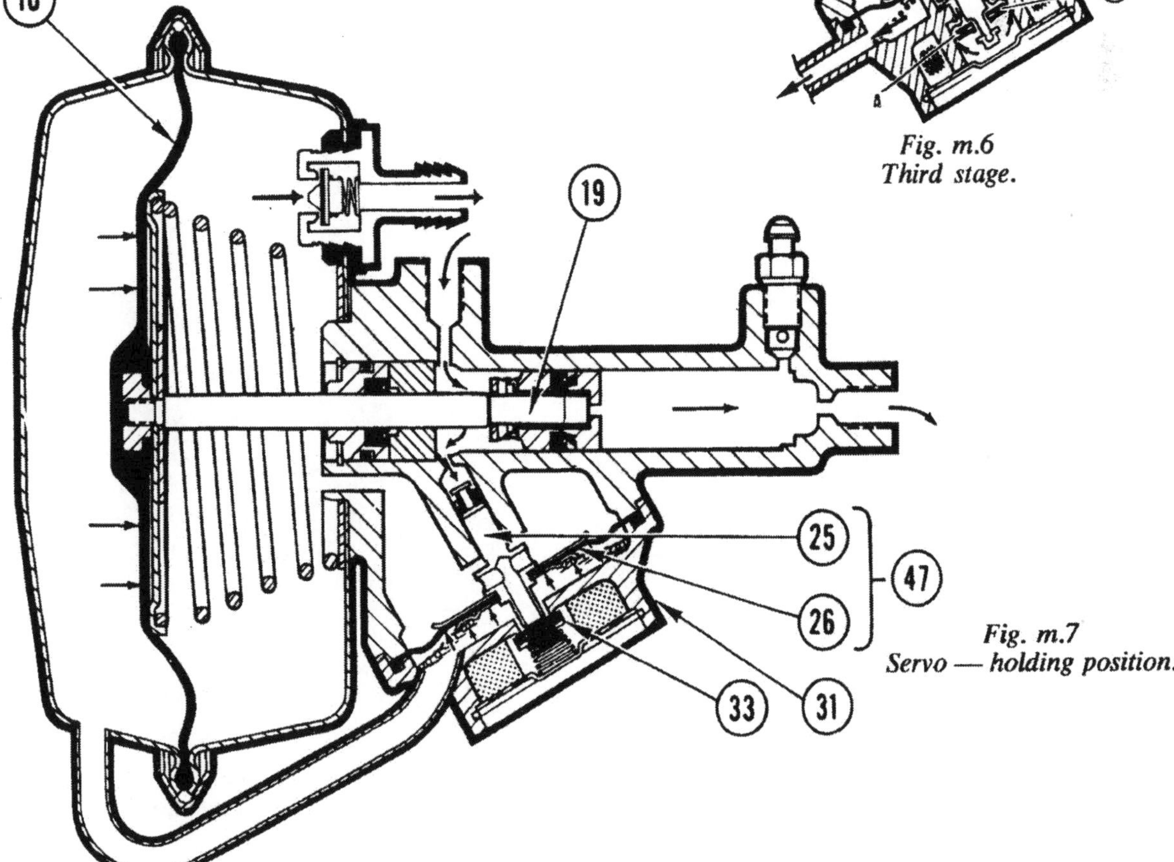

Fig. m.7
Servo — holding position.

above the control valve piston (25) is balanced by the vacuum differential across the control valve diaphragm (26) and the poppet valve (33) is seated on the control valve body (31) and hollow stem of control valve (47).

No further air is admitted to the rear side of the power diaphragm (10) and movement of the diaphragm (10) and push rod (19) ceases.

In the holding position, the output of hydraulic pressure remains constant and in proportion to the pressure applied to the brake pedal. Any increase or decrease in hydraulic input pressure will cause a corresponding increase or decrease in vacuum differential and a consequent variation in hydraulic output pressure.

Hydropower fully applied — Refer Fig. m.7

When the Hydropower is fully applied, the control, valve (47) has moved completely down against its stop on the control valve body (31) and the poppet valve (33) is lifted from its seat. Therefore, control half (1) of vacuum power chamber is completely exposed to atmospheric pressure, and maximum possible differential exists across the power diaphragm (10). Any further increase in hydraulic output is supplied by master cylinder pressure only.

Hydropower releasing — Refer Fig. m.1

When hydraulic pressure is removed from above the control valve piston (25), the control valve assembly (47) is returned to its released position by the action of the control valve return spring (29).

Poppet valve (33) is returned to its seat on the control valve body (31) by the action of the return spring (32) isolating valve chamber (g) and vacuum power chamber control half (1) from atmosphere Chamber (f) of control valve body is placed in communication with chamber (g) via port and hollow stem of control valve (47).

Since vacuum power chamber control half (1) is connected to chamber (g) by tube (2) air contained in these chambers is exhausted through hollow stem of control valve (47) to chambers (f) and (12) and thence via vacuum check valve (43) to engine manifold. Vacuum in both halves of the vacuum power chamber is equalized and power diaphragm (10) push rod (19) and slave cylinder piston (23) are returned to their released positions by the action of return spring (9). Hydraulic port (a) in slave cylinder piston (23) is open, permitting the master cylinder to compensate for any variations in fluid volume in the brake lines caused by expansion or contraction of the fluid. The safety feature provided by the Hydropower, is the fact that the brakes can be applied in the conventional manner in the remote possibility of vacuum power failure. In this case, fluid under master cylinder pressure passes directly through port (a) through the lines to the wheel cylinders.

Removing the Hydropower Servo Unit

The servo unit is mounted on brackets attached to the right hand valance panel.

1. Disconnect battery under bonnet.
2. Disconnect and remove heater air intake hoses.
3. Disconnect the vacuum hose from the non-return valve on the servo unit.
4. Disconnect brake line from master cylinder to servo and output line from servo.
5. Slacken the three nuts securing the servo to the bracket and slide out the unit.

Refitting

Refitting is a reversal of the removing procedure.

The braking system must then be bled as described in this section.

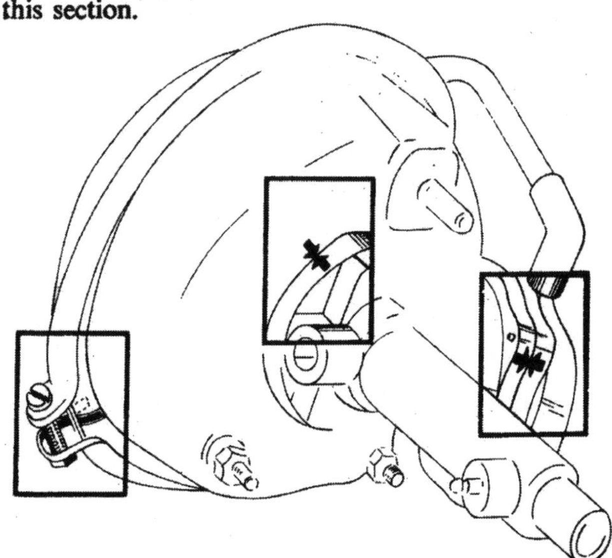

Ensure this area is clear of Alternator control box plug when servo is mounted to brackets.
Fig. m.8

Marking the relative position prior to dismantling.

Dismantling the Servo Unit

1. Clean outside of unit — Do not permit oil or grease to come into contact with rubber parts of this unit.
2. Before disassembly of any section of unit mark relative positions as *Fig. m.8.*
3. Hold unit inverted by cylinder barrel in jaws of vice with wood between vice jaws and cylinder. Refer *Fig. m.9.*
   Caution: Do not distort cylinder with excessive pressure.
4. Remove screw (45) and nut (46) from clamp ring and remove clamp ring (11).
5. Remove vacuum chamber rear half (1), disen-

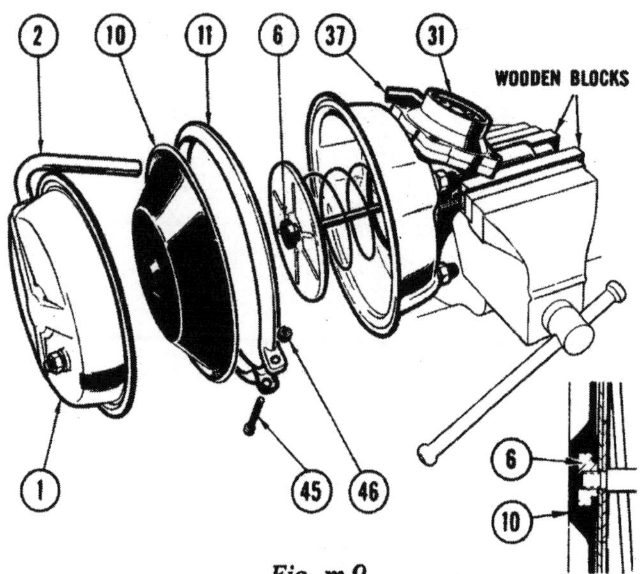

Fig. m.9
The servo unit held in a vice.

gaging vacuum pipe (2) from rubber elbow (37) at control valve body (31).

6. Remove power diaphragm (10) from diaphragm collar (6) at rear of push rod. Refer insert *Fig. m.9.*

Push rod and seal removing — Refer Fig. m.10

1. Using bent nose snap ring pliers inserted between coils of return spring (9) remove Seegar circlip (13) from rear of main body (22).
2. Grasp diaphragm plate (8) and remove diaphragm plate and push rod assembly and return spring (9).

Push rod and seal dismantling

1. Remove wire snap ring (19) from groove in slave cylinder piston (23) and remove pin (18A).
2. Remove slave cylinder piston (23) and remove slave cylinder piston seal (24) from piston.

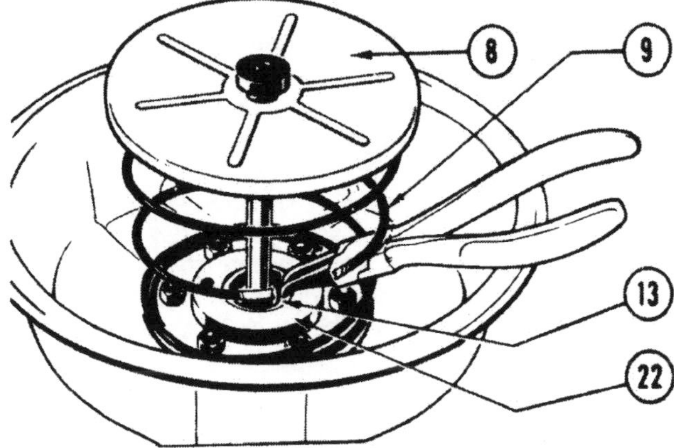

Fig. m.10
Removing push rod and seal

3. Remove from push rod (19A) spacing collar (17) bush (14) and Seegar circlip (13).
4. Remove seal (16) and "O" ring (15) from bush (14).
   Caution: Do not attempt to dismantle push rod and diaphragm plate unless it is to replace any of these parts. The round collar (6) at rear of push rod (19A) is staked in place to prevent loosening, and removal will result in damage to the threads of the collar and push rod.
5. To remove push rod seal assembly (19B) from push rod (19A), grip seal body in jaws of vice, grasp diaphragm plate (8) by hand, and with twisting motion remove push rod from stem of seal.
   Caution: Do not grip push rod (19A) in vice. Do not use pliers, wrench, or similar tools on push rod, as damage to push rod will result.

Power chamber and main body dismantling

1. Mark relative position of vacuum power chamber front shell (12) and main body (22). Refer *Fig. m 8.*
2. Remove six hexagon headed self-tapping screws (42) holding vacuum power chamber front shell (12) to main body (22) and remove support washer (41), front shell (12) and gasket (40).

Check valve removing

Remove vacuum check valve (43) from vacuum power chamber front shell (12) by pressing on rear of valve. Remove rubber grommet (44) from power chamber front shell.

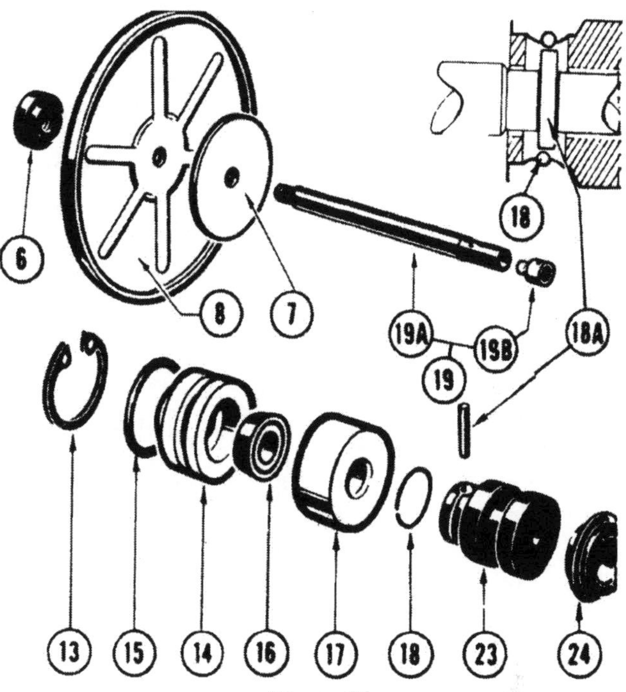

Fig. m.11
Push rod and seal components.

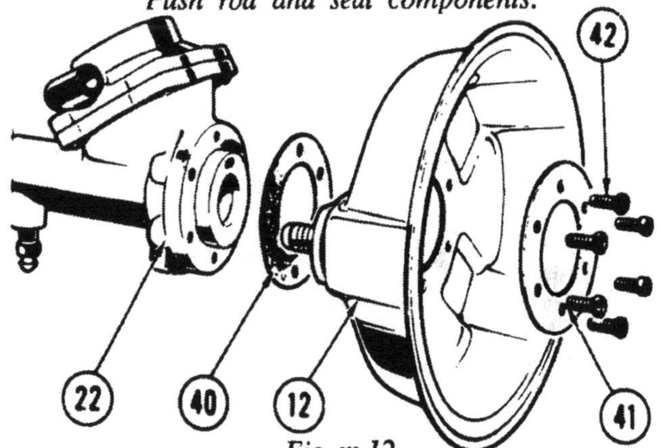

Fig. m.12
Power chamber and main body.

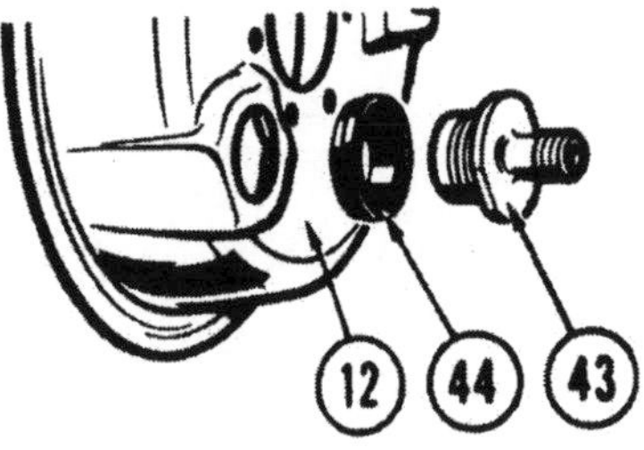

Fig. m.13
Vacuum check valve.

Dismantling compound type control valve — Refer Fig. m 14 and m 15

1. Remove snap ring (36) cover plate (34) and filter (35) from control valve body.
2. Mark relative positions of control valve body. Refer *Fig. m 8.*
3. Remove four "Phillips Head" screws (38) holding

control body (31) to main body (22).

4. Remove control valve return spring (29) and diaphragm assembly (57) leaving control valve piston (25A) in the bore.
5. Hold a clean cloth over end of control piston bore, and slowly apply air pressure to hydraulic inlet port (b) control valve piston (25A) will be ejected into the cloth.
Caution: Ensure no water or oil can be blown from air line into the unit.

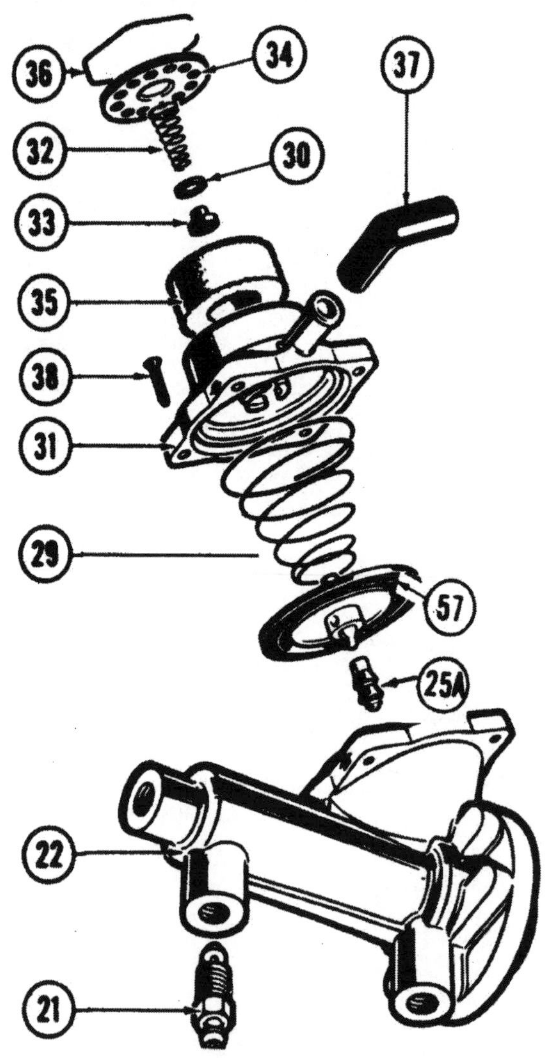

Fig. m.14
Control valve components.

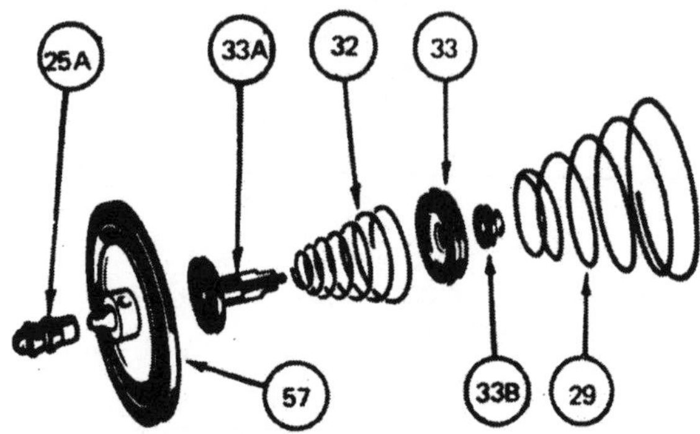

Fig. m.15
Compound control valve.

6. From forward end of control valve body (31) remove—
   (a) Poppet retainer (33B). Use slight leverage to snap off retainer.
   (b) Remove valve seal (33) and valve stem (33A) together with poppet spring (32).

Cleaning procedure

When disassembly is complete, wash all metal parts in clean methylated spirit.

Mineral base cleaning solvents must not be used, as contact with rubber parts will cause swelling and distortion of rubber parts, resulting in erratic operation or failure of unit.

With air hose, blow out all internal passages after washing and ensure that restrictor to control valve cylinder passage is free from dirt.

Using clean piece of lint-free cloth, dry the bores of slave cylinder and control valve cylinder.

Any cleaning fluid remaining in unit will cause dilution of brake fluid and subsequent reduction of boiling point of brake fluid. After drying, place all parts on a clean sheet of paper or cloth.

Examination

The following inspection procedure will be a guide to check parts which are not included in the Hydropower repair kit and therefore, would not normally be replaced during re-assembly. If, after checking, any of the following parts prove to be defective, they must be replaced.

Main Body

1. Check bores of slave cylinder and control valve cylinder for scores and excessive wear. Do not attempt to reclaim cylinder by honing. If slightly marked it may be lightly polished using 400 grit wet and dry rubbing paper.
   Note: Main body should be replaced when slave cylinder bore measures 0.007 in. (0.1178 mm.) oversize or control valve cylinder bore measure 0.004 in. (0.1016 mm.) oversize.

Slave cylinder bore — VH.44J 0.625 in. (15.87 mm.)
Control valve cylinder bore — .312 in. (7.92 mm.)

2. Check for damage threads or seats in hydraulic ports. Check for damaged circlip grooves. Replace cylinder if necessary.

Slave cylinder piston

1. Check control valve piston for scores on outer surface.
2. Check that hole for retainer pin is not elongated.
3. Check seat for push rod seal at port in slave cylinder piston for wear and damage; replace piston if necessary.

Control valve

1. Check control valve piston for scores on outer surface.
2. Check control valve diaphragm for cracks or tears. If the diaphragm is swollen, it indicates that petrol or oil is entering the control section of the unit.
3. Check the air valve seat in control valve body for excessive wear, distortion, nicks or burrs.
4. Check control valve body for worn snap ring grooves, nicks, burrs or warping and distortion at mating surfaces.

Vacuum power chamber

1. Check all pressed metal parts for dents, holes or distortion. Any damaged parts should be replaced. Do not attempt to straighten distorted parts as this practice may result in vacuum leaks and erratic operation of unit.
2. Check mounting studs for damaged threads or looseness in halves of vaccum power chamber.
3. Check that vacuum transfer tube is not loose in rear half. Looseness at this point will result in erratic operation.
4. Check clamp ring for distortion.
5. Check diaphragm for cracks and worn spots where it contacts the rim of the pressure plate. If diaphragm is swollen it indicates that petrol or oil is entering the power chamber.

Push rod — Refer Fig. m.11

1. Check bush and spacer for wear in the bores where push rod operates.
2. Check diaphragm pressure plate (8) for nicks or burrs at the rim which would result in damage to the power diaphragm.
3. Check diaphragm pressure plate (8) for distortion or looseness on push rod and replace where necessary.
4. Check push rod for wear and scores where it operates through the bush and spacer at the rear of the slave cylinder. Check that the push rod is not bent. Do not attempt to straighten the push rod — it should be replaced.

Reassembling

Clean hands thoroughly before commencing assembly of this unit. The slightest trace of mineral oil or grease on rubber parts will cause swelling and distortion of the rubber, resulting in erratic operation or failure of the unit. If the unit is to be installed on a vehicle immediately, brake fluid may be used for assembly purposes, but, if the unit is to be retained as part of a stock, a brake cylinder assembly fluid should be used.

To simplify assembly, the procedure adopted should be to assemble parts into sub-assemblies, and then combine these sub-assemblies to form the completed unit.

Main body and vacuum power chamber front shell — Refer Fig. m.12

1. Place the main body (22) (inverted) in vice. Use wooden blocks between vice jaws and cylinder. **Caution:** Excessive pressure will cause distortion of the cylinder.
2. Place gasket (40) in position on rear of main body (22).
3. Align index marks on main body (22) and vacuum power chamber front shell (12) to ensure correct assembly position.
4. Assemble support washer (41) and install the six hexagon headed screws (42) holding vacuum power chamber front shell (12) to main body (22). Tighten screws to 50-70 lb. in. torque.

Compound type control valve — Refer Figs. m.14 and m.15

Assemble parts into control valve body (31) in the following sequence:

1. (a) From joint face side of body assemble valve stem (33A) and poppet spring (32).
   Note: Small diameter of spring to valve stem (33A).
   (b) From air inlet side of body, valve seal (33) fits on to valve stem (33A).
   Note: Centre recess in seal goes to valve stem.
   (c) Snap poppet retainer (33B) on to end of valve stem (33A).
2. Replace filter (35) cover plate (34) and retain in position with snap ring (36). Into the main body (22) assemble in following order:
   (a) Smear seals of control valve piston (25A) with rubber lubricant, assemble into bore, seals end first. Ensure that lips of seals enter correctly into bore.
   (b) Assemble diaphragm assembly (57), ensure that push rod (25) enters in recess in piston (25A).
   (c) Place control valve return spring (29) in position, i.e. small diameter coil on diaphragm pressure plate (28).
   (d) Reverse dis-assembly procedure 1, 2, 3, to complete operations.

Push rod — Refer Fig. m.11

1. Push stem of push rod seal (19B) into recess in end of push rod (19A). Use hand pressure only on end of push rod. Do not use hammer or similar means as damage to seal will result. Seal should be a firm fit in end of rod or erratic operation of unit may result. If seal is not retained tightly enough, it may be necessary to use selective assembly or alternatively "Loctite" compound, to achieve the required result.

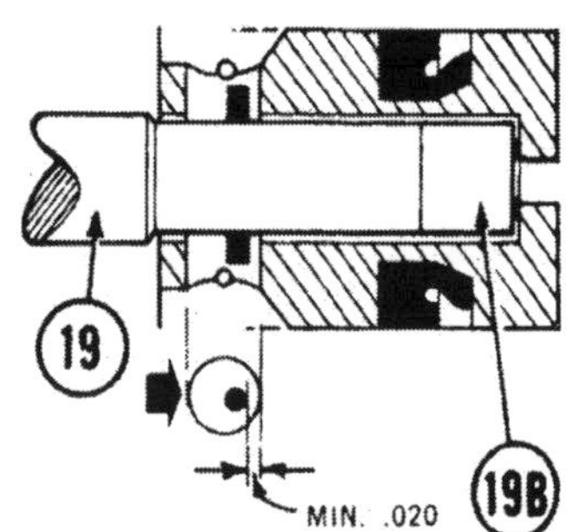

Fig. m.16
The push rod seal.

2. Place slave cylinder (23) temporarily in position on push rod (19) and insert pin (18A). With push rod seal (19B) pressed against seat in slave cylinder piston (23) a minimum clearance of .020 in. (5.159 mm.) should exist between pin (18A) and hole (h) in slave cylinder piston (23). Refer Fig. *m.16*
3. Assemble back-up washer (7) and pressure plate (8) on push rod (19). Tighten diaphragm collar (6) to 50-60 lbs. in. (0.58 to 0.7 kg.m.) torque and stake in three places to prevent loosening.
4. Place "O" Ring (15) in groove and push rod seal (16) in recess in front of bush (14). Lips of seal (16) must face outwards.
5. Using P.B.R. loading tool, place wire snap ring (18) on slave cylinder piston but do not snap into groove. Temporarily leave snap ring on land of piston adjacent to groove.

6. Using correct loading tool for particular model Hydropower place slave cylinder seal (24) in position on slave cylinder piston (23).
7. Assemble parts on push rod in the following sequence.
   (a) Seegar circlip (13).
   (b) Bush (14) with seal (16) facing out.
   (c) Spacer (17) with large recess facing toward bush (14).
   (d) Slave cylinder piston (23).
8. Pass pin (18A) through holes (h) in slave cylinder piston and hole in push rod (19).
9. Place snap ring (18) in position in groove in slave cylinder piston (23) to retain pin (18A). Gap at ends of wire of snap ring (18) should be 90° from holes (h) in slave cylinder piston. Check that push rod (19) is free to move slightly in and out of the slave cylinder piston (23).
10. Place diaphragm return spring (9) in position with small diameter coil on support washer (41).
11. Lubricate slave cylinder and slave cylinder piston (23) with assembly fluid and install slave cylinder piston in slave cylinder, followed in turn by spacer (17) and bush (14).
12. Using bent nose snap-ring pliers passed between the coils of return spring (9), compress Seegar circlip (13) and place in groove at rear of slave cylinder. Check that the circlip is correctly installed in the groove.
13. Assemble power diaphragm (10) to rear of push rod assembly by stretching recess in centre of diaphragm collar (6). After installing, rotate diaphragm several times to ensure that it is fitted correctly over collar (6).
14. Check that the rim of the diaphragm (10) is correctly seated in rim of the vacuum power chamber front shell (12).
15. Place rear, or control half, (1) over diaphragm (10) aligning index marks to maintain correct assembly location. Check that rim of rear half (1) is correctly seated on roll of diaphragm.
16. Place clamp ring (11) in position with gap at index mark. Install screw (45) and nut (46) and tighten to 20-25 lbs. in. (.23 to .286 kg.m.) torque.
17. Lubricate vacuum check valve grommet (44) with methylated spirit and install in port in vacuum power chamber front shell (12).
18. Lubricate vacuum check valve (43) with methylated spirit and install in position in grommet.
19. Assemble connecting elbow (37) to stem of control valve body (31) and vacuum tube (2).
20. Install bleeder valve (21) in bleeder port (d).
21. Install bleeder valve cover (20) on bleeder valve (21), and plug all ports to prevent the entry of foreign matter prior to refitting the unit to the vehicle.

Fig. m.17
P.B.R. loading tool.

SECTION n

ELECTRICAL & INSTRUMENTS

The information contained in this section refers to Australian produced vehicles. It does not supersede the previous section, but should be used in conjunction with it.

Section n.1

VOLTAGE REGULATOR SETTINGS

The instructions given in Section N.4 should be followed substituting the following data at item (3): 15.5 to 16.0 volts at an ambient temperature of 20°C. (68°F.), then add 0.2 volt for every 10°C. (18°F.) below this temperature, or reduce the setting by 0.2 volts for every 10°C. (18°F.) above it.

Section n.2

VOLTAGE/CURRENT REGULATOR
Lucas type 6GC

General description

This unit is fitted to the Australian production of the Moke prior to the introduction of an alternator.

The control box is of the three bobbin type, i.e., voltage regulator, current regulator and cut-out. These are shown respectively from left to right in the illustration (Fig. n.1).

For replacement purposes the R.B.340 control box is interchangeable; the external connections being the same as the 6 GC. Although the internal electrical circuits differ, the electrical settings are the same.

Servicing

The control box should not require periodical adjustment, but should this be necessary it is important to check fan belt tension and have the generator and regulator at operating temperature before any checks are carried out.

Two types of adjustments are provided — electrical and mechanical. Mechanical adjustment is usually only required when contacts have been cleaned or the electrical setting is found to be unobtainable.

Electrical settings

If the electrical settings are to be checked, the following sequence should be followed:—

(1) Voltage regulator setting.
(2) Current regulator setting.
(3) Cut-out setting.

Voltage regulator setting

1. Disconnect wires from both "B" terminals (as indicated on the cover of the regulator) and join them together (for ignition). The charging system is now isolated from battery circuit.
2. Connect voltmeter between "D" or W.L. and earth.

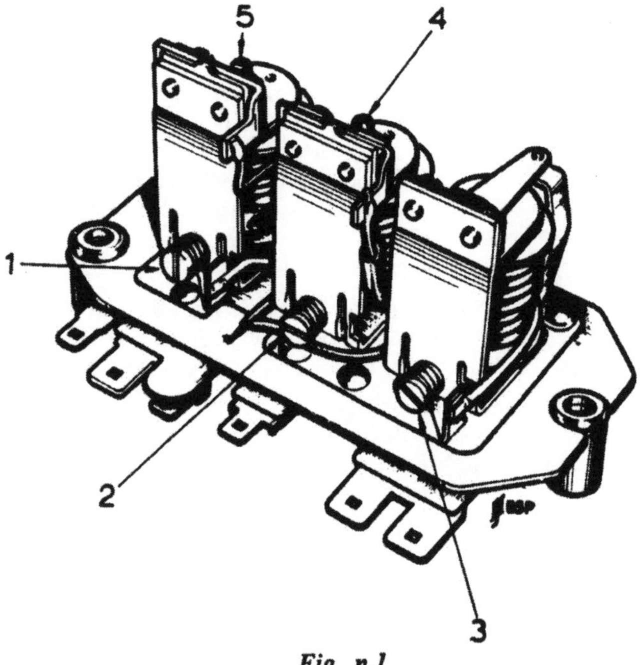

Fig. n.1

Control box type 6 G.C. showing screwdriver adjusting points numbered 1 to 5.

3. As the engine speed is increased, the voltage will rise until regulation is achieved (meter steadies). This occurs about 2000 engine r.p.m.
4. Adjust screw 1 (Fig. n.1) as necessary to obtain the following setting:—
   15.0 volts maximum at an ambient temperature of 20°C. (68°F.), then add 0.2 volt for every 10°C (18°F.) below this temperature, or reduce the setting by 0.2 volt for every 10°C. (18°F.) above it.
   Unsteady readings may be due to dirty contacts.

Current regulator setting

The generator must be made to develop its maximum rated output, which is 22 amperes, whatever the state of charge of the battery. The voltage regulator must therefore be rendered inoperative.

1. Connect ammeter between "B" terminal and the wires that were previously removed from "B" terminal.
2. Put voltage regulator out of action by packing up armature so that regulator contacts cannot open.
3. Switch on lights and accessories.
4. Ammeter will read charge rate increasing with engine speed until a point of regulation is obtained (meter steadies). This occurs about 2000 engine r.p.m.
5. Using adjusting screw 2 (Fig. n.1), set the maximum current to 22 amps. ±1 which is the maximum continuous safe operating current that can be drawn from a C40 generator.

Cut-out setting

Connect a voltmeter and an ammeter as for the voltage regulator and current regular settings.

Observing the voltmeter, the reading should rise steadily with slowly increasing engine r.p.m. (just above idle) and then drop slightly at the instant of contact point closure. The cut-out contact points should close at 12.7-13.3 volts. Increase engine speed to approximately 2000 engine r.p.m. Slowly decelerate and observe the voltmeter.

Cut-out points should open when the generator voltage falls to 10 to 11 volts. The adjustments for these settings are obtained at screw 3 (Fig. n.1).

Cut-out contacts. To clean the cut-out relay contacts use a strip of fine glass paper, never carborundum stone or emery cloth.

Mechanical settings

Alterations to the mechanical settings are not normally required unless these have been disturbed for the purpose of cleaning of contacts or otherwise.

Voltage and current regulator

1. Loosen the two armature securing screws. Screw out adjustable contact until it is well clear of the armature contact.
2. Insert a .018″ (0.46 mm.) gauge between armature and copper disc. Press the armature down on to the gauge squarely and tighten the two securing screws.
3. With the gauge still in position between the armature and copper disc, screw in adjustable contact until it just touches the armature contact.

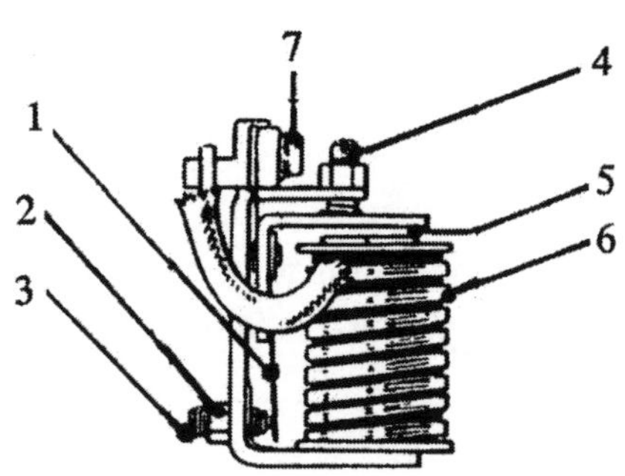

Fig. n.2

Voltage regulator

1. *Bi-metal tension spring.*
2. *Lock nut.*
3. *Voltage regulator adjustment screw.*
4. *Fixer contact adjustment screw.*
5. *Armature.*
6. *0.18 in. (.46 mm.).*
7. *Armature securing screws.*

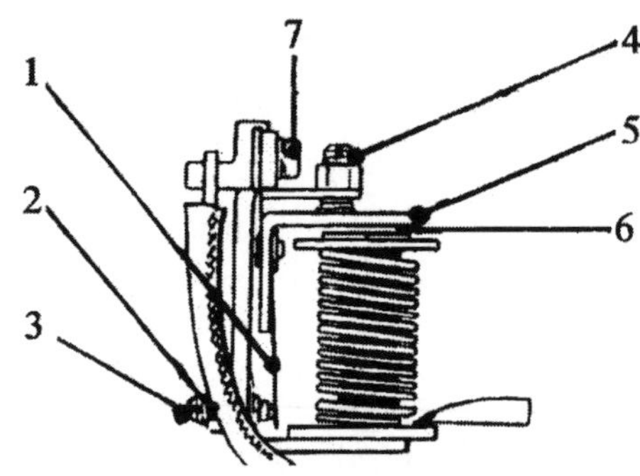

Fig. n.3

Current regulator

1. *Bi-metal tension spring.*
2. *Lock nut.*
3. *Current regulator adjustment screw.*
4. *Fixed contact adjustment screw.*
5. *Armature.*
6. *0.18 in (.46 mm.).*
7. *Armature securing screw.*

Cut-out

1. Loosen the armature securing screw. Screw out adjusting screw until it is well clear of the tension spring.
2. Press the armature squarely down on to the core face, no gauge is necessary, and tighten the securing screw.
3. Press the armature down against the core face and adjust the armature backstop so that a 0.18″ (0.46 mm.) gap is obtained between the tip of the backstop and the contact blade.
4. Insert a .010″ (0.26 mm.) gauge between the underside of the armature and core face. The gauge should be inserted from the side of the core nearest the fixed contact post. The leading edge of the gauge should not be inserted beyond the centre line of the core face. Press the armature down against the gauge (taking care not to press on the contact blade) and check the contacts. These should be just touching. If necessary adjust the height of the fixed contact by carefully blending the legs of the fixed contact posts.

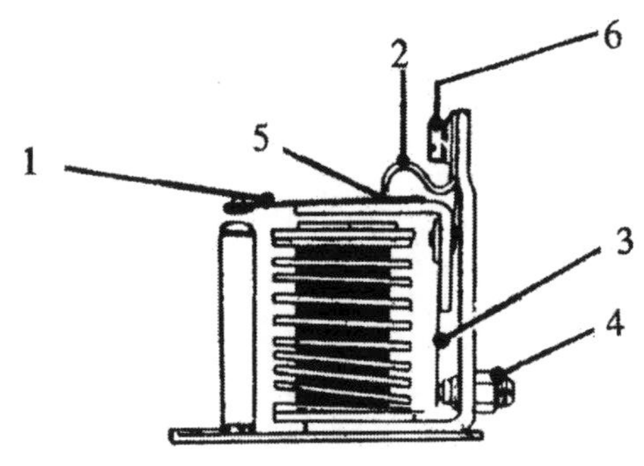

Fig. n.4
Cut-out

1. *Cut-out contact blade.*
2. *Armature back stop.*
3. *Bi-metal tension spring.*
4. *Cut-out adjustment screw.*
5. *0.18 in. (.46 mm.).*
6. *Armature securing screw.*

Section n.3

WINDSCREEN WIPER MOTOR

Lucas model 12AUW, single speed, self-switching permanent magnet wiper motor was introduced on late Mini saloons and vans.

The new unit is not interchangeable with the previously fitted wiper motors.

Description

The two-pole motor has a permanent field consisting of two ceramic magnets housed in a cylindrical yoke.

A worm gear formed on the extended armature shaft drives a moulded gear wheel. Motion is imparted to the cable rack by a connecting rod and crosshead actuated by a crank pin carried on the gear wheel.

Associated with the terminal assembly positioned below the gear box are three fixed contacts, running on an insulated brass slip-ring secured to the underside of the gear wheel.

One of these fulfils the function of providing contact for a self-switching limit switch, whilst the others, in conjunction with the control switch, provide regenerative braking of the armature to give immediate deceleration and constant blade parking when the motor is switched off.

Principle of regenerative braking

If the armature of a permanent magnet field motor is rotated by mechanical means, electrical energy will be generated in the armature.

Should the armature be heavily loaded electrically, and the mechanical drive to the armature shaft discontinued, the armature will quickly come to rest.

During the parking cycle — after the armature is disconnected from the battery by contact, inertia will cause the armature to continue rotation in the strong permanent magnet field and electricity will be generated. The energy thus created by the armature rotation will be rapidly used up when it is short-circuited by contacts in the limiting switch bringing it quickly to rest.

Test specification (no load test)

Single speed

With 13.5v. at motor terminals, speed should be between 50 and 56 r.p.m.

Current draw — 1.8 amps. max.

Motor should start and run when a voltage of 3 volts is applied to the motor terminals.

Resistance between commutator bars 0.20-0.30 ohms.

Brush spring tension 5-7 ozs. (156-219 grams).

Angle of wipe — 110°.

The Clubman and Clubman G.T. models are equipped with a Lucas model 12 AUW two-speed, self-switching permanent magnet wiper motor. The principles of operation, etc., are as for the 12 AUW single-speed motor, except that a third brush is brought in for use when high-speed operation is required.

For testing and overhauling refer to Section Nb.8.

Test specification — (no load test)

Two speed

With 13.5v. at motor terminals speed should be:
46-52 cycles per minute (normal speed).
60-70 cycles per minute (high speed).
Current draw — 1.5 amps. (normal speed).
— 2.0 amps. (high speed).
Motor should start and run at three volts.

Resistance between commutator bars 0.23 to 0.35 ohms. at 16°C. (60°F.).

Brush spring tension — 5 to 7 ozs. (156 to 218 g.).

Angle of wipe — 105°.

Section n.4

WINDSCREEN WIPER

The Australian produced Moke is fitted with a "Pres-lite" windscreen wiper assembly.

Removing

Wiper motor

Remove:

1. Battery lead.
2. Bonnet.
3. The cover over the wiper mechanism (one securing screw is located under the cover of the fuse box).
4. The spring clip from the operating rod near the right-hand wiper spindle.
5. The four screws securing the wiper motor bracket to the body.
6. Motor, complete with bracket.
7. Mounting bracket from the motor by removing the ⅜" A.F. nut and loosening the ⁹⁄₁₆" A.F. nut on the driving spindle. The mounting bracket may then be slipped off over the lever on the driving spindle.

Refitting

Refitting is a reversal of the above procedure.

Servicing

Fitting new brushes

1. Remove cover from wiper motor.
2. Carefully slip brush tension spring off the brush holders.
3. Prise old brushes out of their holders with pliers.
4. Carefully press new brushes fully into holders by hand pressure only.
5. Replace brush tension spring.
6. Refit cover.

Fitting new gears
Remove:
1. Wiper motor.
2. Mounting bracket from motor.
3. The four screws retaining the gear cover.

Clean and replace gears as necessary, carefully lubricating all moving parts with a light general-purpose grease.

Removing and refitting armature
1. Remove wiper motor cover.
2. Unhook brush tension spring.
3. Unscrew brush holder and end bearing assembly.
4. The armature may now be withdrawn.

Reassembly is a reversal of the above.

Section n.5

ALTERNATOR CHARGING SYSTEM

Description

The 12-volt NEGATIVE EARTH charging system consists of a Lucas alternator model 15 AC and a Lucas model 8 TR integrated electronic control unit, supplying current to the 12-volt battery.

The nine diodes contained within the alternator provide rectification of its output current for battery charging, and also prevent reverse current flow. These and other design features overcome the necessity of a cut-out and current regulator and permit the use of a simple charge indicator lamp.

Service Precautions

It is important to observe the following precautions when servicing vehicles fitted with alternator charging systems.
1. Observe **correct polarity** when fitting batteries (positive to positive and negative to negative).
2. Bank batteries must be connected so that the nominal voltage is 12 and the connecting leads, to the vehicle's connected battery, must be in parallel (positive to positive and negative to negative).
3. Battery charger polarity must agree. It is imperative that the negative (—) battery terminal be removed.

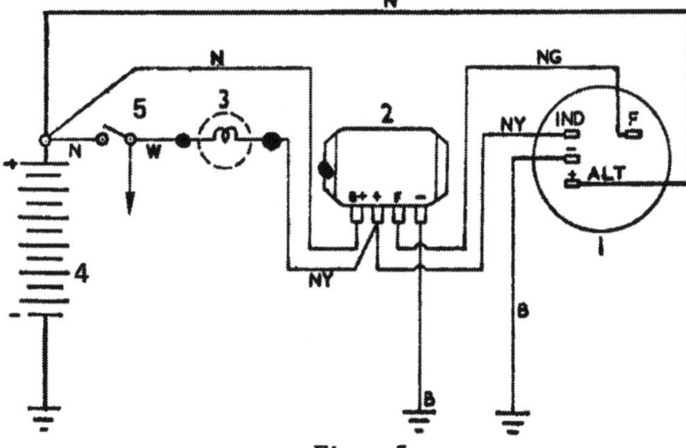

Fig. n.5
1. Alternator. 2. Control box. 3. Warning light. 4. Battery. 5. Ignition switch.

4. **Do not** short across or ground any terminal connected in the charging circuit.
5. **Do not** disconnect battery terminals or make and break connections in the charging circuit while the engine is running.
6. **Remove** control unit and alternator connections prior to carrying out electric arc welding on the vehicle.

Maintenance
1. *Belt adjustment.* The driving belt must be tensioned so that a deflection of ½" (13 mm.) can be obtained under finger pressure at the mid-point of the longest run of the belt. When adjusting the belt, DO NOT apply leverage to any other point than the alternator drive end bracket.
2. *Connections:* All electrical connections in the charging circuit must be kept tight at all times, since quite heavy current flow can take place.

NOTE: Lucas-type 16 ACR alternator incorporating an 11TR control unit is used on some vehicle applications. For details of this unit see Seciton Nb.9.

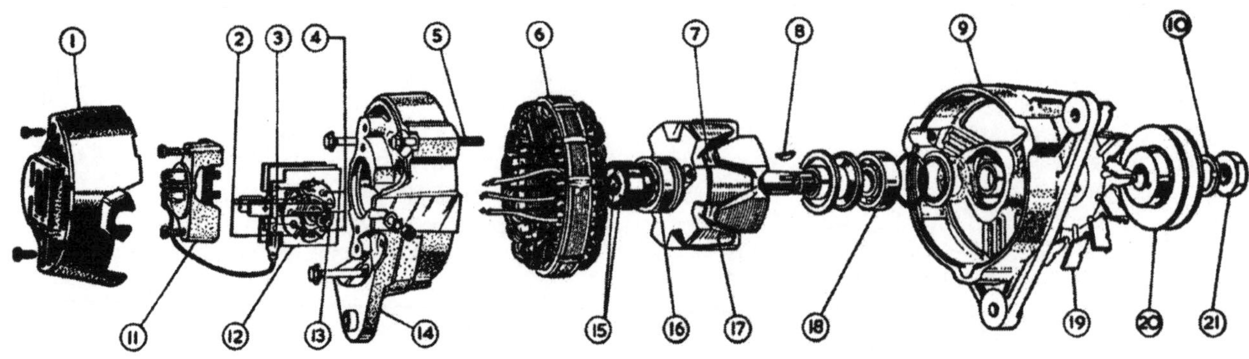

Fig. n.6

LUCAS 15 AC ALTERNATOR COMPONENTS

1. Cover.
2. Live side output diodes.
3. Earth side output diodes.
4. Field diodes.
5. Through bolts.
6. Stator.
7. Field winding.
8. Shaft key.
9. Drive end bracket.
10. Spring washer.
11. Brush box moulding.
12. Rectifier pack.
13. Rectifier assembly bolt.
14. Slip ring end bracket.
15. Slip rings.
16. Slip ring bearing.
17. Rotor.
18. Drive end bearing.
19. Fan.
20. Pulley.

Alternator (Lucas-stype 15 AC)

Testing in position

1. Carry out maintenance instructions.
2. Run the engine at fast idle speed until normal operating temperature is reached.
3. Stop the engine and withdraw the moulded terminal connector block from the alternator.
4. Connect an 0-15 ohm. 35 amp. variable resistance to the alternator terminals as shown in Fig. n.7. The variable resistance must only be connected across the battery for the amount of time necessary to carry out the tests.
   This type of variable resistance (usually of the compressible carbon pile type) is often used in heavy-duty battery testing equipment. As an alternative, a lamp bank, as in Fig. n.8, may be used.

IMPORTANT: Ensure that the correct battery and alternator polarity is preserved. Serious damage to the alternator will result if the polarity is reversed.

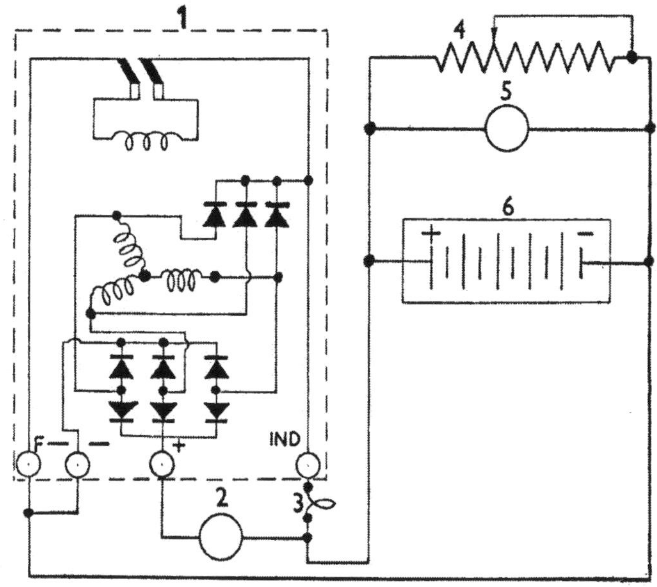

Fig. n.7
15 AC alternator output test circuit.

1. Alternator,
2. 0-40 amp. ammeter.
3. 12 volt, 2.2 watt bulb.
4. 0-15 ohm., 35 amp. variable resistance.
5. 0-20 volt voltmeter.
6. 12 volt battery.
NOTE: The alternator internal circuitry is shown in the dotted rectangle.

5. Start the engine and check the alternator output.
   (a) Run the engine at approx. 750 r.p.m. and observe the charge indicator bulb; the bulb should be extinguished.
   (b) Increase the engine speed to approx. 3000 r.p.m. and adjust the variable resistance until a reading of 14 volts is registered on the voltmeter; at these settings the ammeter should register a reading of approximately 28 amps.

If the charge indicator bulb does not extinguish or its brilliance fluctuates or if the ammeter reading varies considerably from the correct reading, a fault on the alternator is indicated and the alternator must be removed for further tests. Failure of one or more of the diodes will affect the alternator output and in some instances raise the alternator temperature and noise level. The table overleaf indicates the effects that diode failure may have on test results.

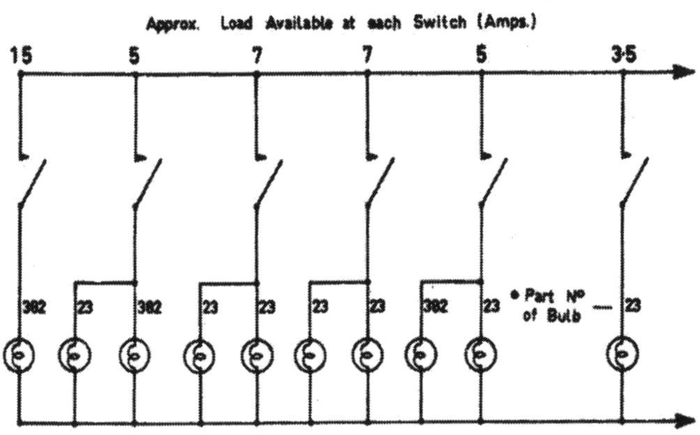

Fig. n.8
Circuit of lamp bank used to provide load for output testing. Bulbs: 7-12v., 36 W., S/C; 3-12v., 21 W., E/C.

NOTE: All circuitry including lamp bases must be insulated from case or adaptor metal work.

6. If the tests in (5) show the alternator to be operating satisfactorily, disconnect the test circuit and reconnect the alternator terminal connector.
7. Connect a 0-20 voltmeter between the positive terminals of the alternator and battery (Fig. n.9).
8. Switch on the headlamps, start the engine and check the voltage drop in the charging circuit as follows:—
   (a) Run the engine at approx. 3000 r.p.m. and note the voltmeter reading.
   (b) Transfer the voltmeter connections to the negative terminals of the alternator and battery, and repeat the test in (a). (Fig. n.10.)

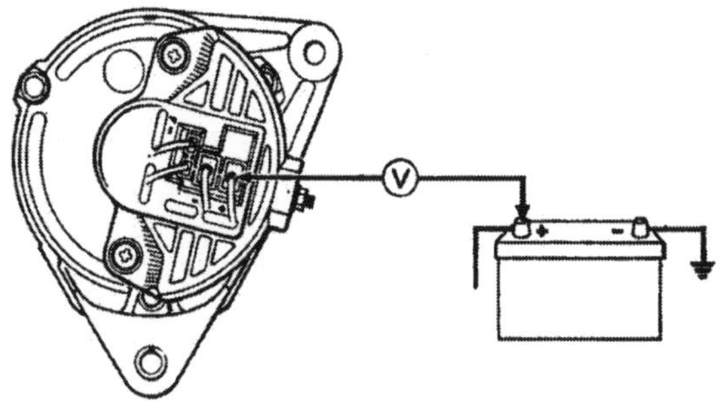

Fig. n.9
Charging circuit voltage drop test (live side)

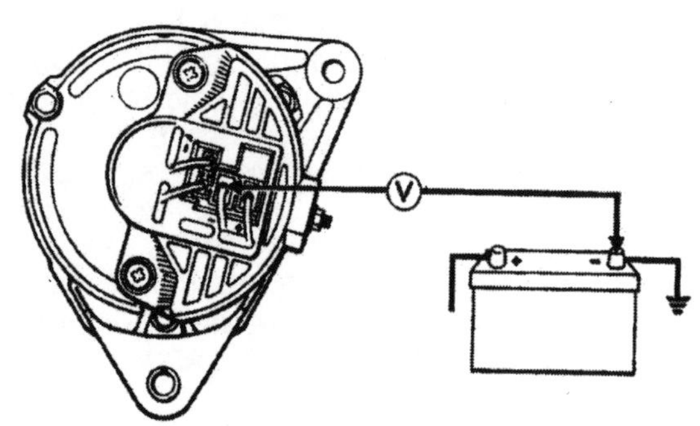

Fig. n.10
Charging circuit voltage drop test (earth side)

Removing the alternator

9. Withdraw the terminal connectors from the alternator and note the positions.
10. Remove the adjusting link bolt from the alternator.
11. Slacken the alternator mounting bolts, lower the alternator and slip the fan belt from the alternator pulley.
12. Unscrew the alternator mounting bolts and remove.

Dismantling and testing — alternator removed

13. Unscrew the cover retaining screws and remove the cover.
14. Unsolder the three stator connections from the rectifier pack, noting the connecting positions.

IMPORTANT: When soldering or unsoldering connections to the diodes, great care must be taken not to overheat the diodes or bend the pins. During the soldering operations the diode pins should be gripped lightly with a pair of long-nosed pliers, which will then act as a thermal shunt. Use 45-55 Tin-Lead Solder.

15. Unscrew the two brush moulding securing screws.
16. Slacken the rectifier pack retaining nuts and withdraw the brush moulding and rectifier pack.

Brushes

17. Check the brushes for wear by measuring the length of brush protruding beyond the brushbox moulding. If the length protruding is .2 in. (5 mm.) or less, the brush must be renewed.
18. Check that brushes move freely in their holders. If a brush shows a tendency to stick, clean it with a petrol (gasoline) moistened cloth or, if necessary, polish the sides of the brush with a fine file.

SYMPTOMS				
	Alternator			
Warning light	*Temperature*	*Noise*	*Output*	*Probable fault and associated damage*
Normal at stand-still, goes out at cut-in speed but then glows progressively brighter as speed increases.	High	Normal	Higher than normal at 3000 engine r.p.m. 15 AC. 35 amp. approx.	Live side output diode open-circuit. (May damage rotor winding and reg. output stage, overheat brushboxes and blow warning light.)
Light out under all conditions.	High	Excessive	very low at 3000 engine r.p.m. 10 amp. approx.	Live side output diode short-circuit. (May cause failure of associated "field" diode.)
Normal at stand-still, dims appreciably at cut-in and gets progressively dimmer at higher speeds.	Normal	Excessive	Poor at slow speed. Slightly below normal at 3000 engine r.p.m. 15 AC. 26 amp. approx.	Earth side output diode open-circuit.
Normal at stand-still, dims slightly at cut-in and remains so throughout speed range.	Normal	Excessive	Very low at all speeds above cut-in. 7 amp. approx.	Earthside output diode short-circuit. (The same symptoms would be apparent if one phase winding was shorted to earth.)
Normal at stand-still, dims slightly at cut-in and remains so throughout speed range.	Normal	Normal	Lower than normal at 3000 engine r.p.m. 15 AC. 23 amp. approx.	"Field" diode open-circuit.
Normal at stand-still, dims appreciably at cut-in and remains so throughout speed range.	Normal	Excessive	Very low at 3000 engine r.p.m. 7 amp. approx.	"Field" diode short-circuit.

Fig. n.11
Use of thermal shunt when soldering diode connections

19. Check the brush spring pressure using a push-type spring gauge. The gauge should register 7 to 10 oz. (198 to 283 gm.) when the brush is pushed back until its face is flush with the housing. If the gauge reading is outside the limits given, renew the brush assembly.

Slip-rings

20. Clean the surfaces of the slip-rings, using a petrol (gasoline) moistened cloth.
21. Inspect the slip-ring surfaces for signs of burning; remove burn marks using very fine sandpaper. On no account must emery-cloth or similar abrasives be used or any attempt made to machine the slip-rings.

Rotor

22. Connect an ohmmeter or a 12-volt battery and and an ammeter to the slip-rings. An ohmmeter reading of 4.3 ohms or an ammeter reading of 3 amps. should be recorded. (Fig. n.12.)

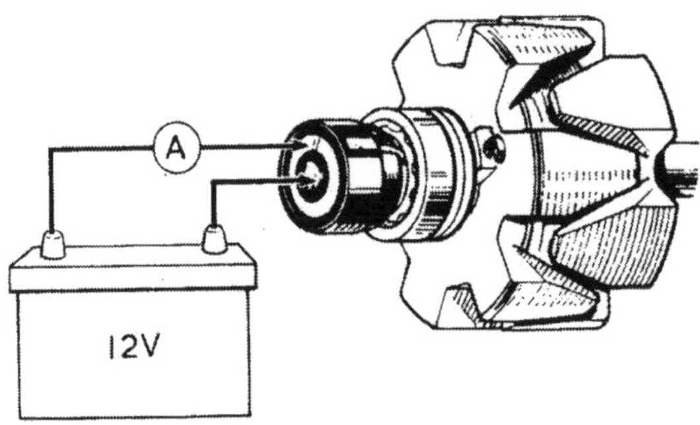

Fig. n.12
Measuring rotor winding resistance with battery and ammeter (alternator dismantled)

23. Using a 110-volt A.C. supply and a 15-watt test lamp, test for insulation between one of the slip-rings and one of the rotor poles. If the test lamp lights, the rotor must be renewed. (Fig. n.13.)

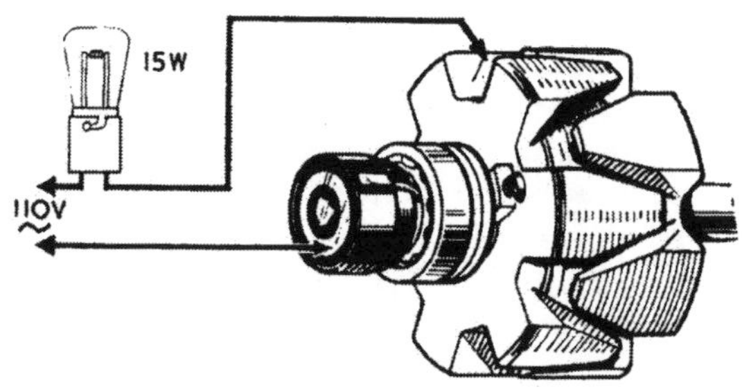

Fig. n.13
Insulation test of rotor winding

Stator

24. Connect a 12-volt battery and a 36-watt test lamp to two of the stator connections. Repeat the test replacing one of the two stator connections with the third. If the test lamp fails to light in either of the tests the stator must be renewed. (Fig. n.14.)

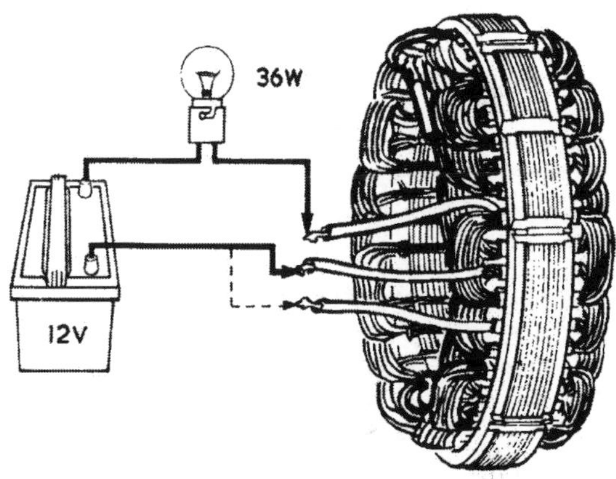

Fig. n.14
Stator winding continuity test

25. Using a 110-volt A.C. supply and a 15-watt test lamp, test for insulation between any one of the three stator connections and the stator laminations. If the test lamp lights, the stator must be renewed. (Fig. n.15.)

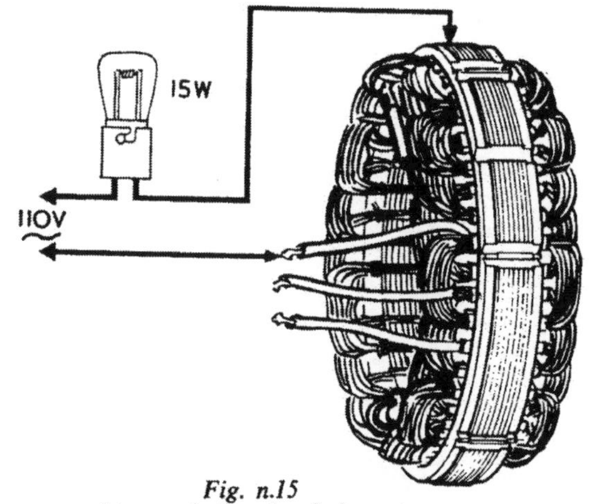

Fig. n.15
Stator winding insulation test

Diodes

26. Connect a 12-volt battery and a 1.5 watt test lamp in turn to each of the nine diode pins and its corresponding heat sink on the rectifier pack, then reverse the connections. The lamp should light with the current flowing in one direction only. If the lamp lights in both directions or fails to light in either, the rectifier pack must be renewed. (Fig. n.16.)

Refer to important notes on soldering the diodes, described in item (14).

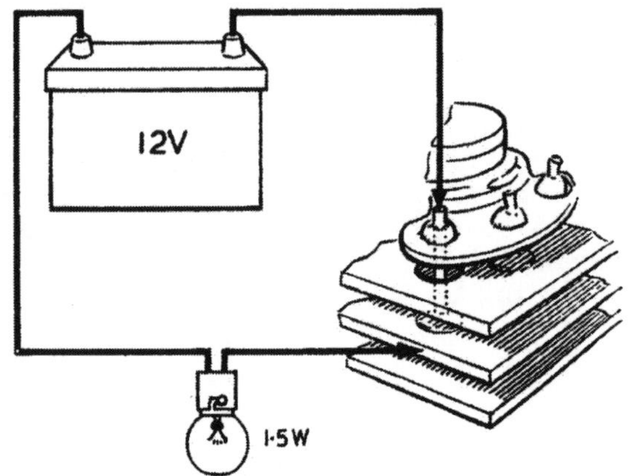

Fig. n.16
Simple test of diodes

Dismantling the alternator

27. Carry out the operations detailed in (13) to (16).
28. Remove the three through-bolts.
29. Fit a tube of the dimensions given in Fig. n.17 over the slip-ring moulding so that it registers against the outer track of the slip-ring end bearing and carefully drive the bearing from its housing.
30. Remove the shaft nut, washer, pulley, fan, and shaft key.
31. Press the rotor from the drive end bracket.
32. Remove the circlip retaining the drive end bearing and remove the bearing.
33. Unsolder the field connections from the slip-ring assembly and withdraw the assembly from the rotor shaft.
34. Remove the slip-ring end bearing.

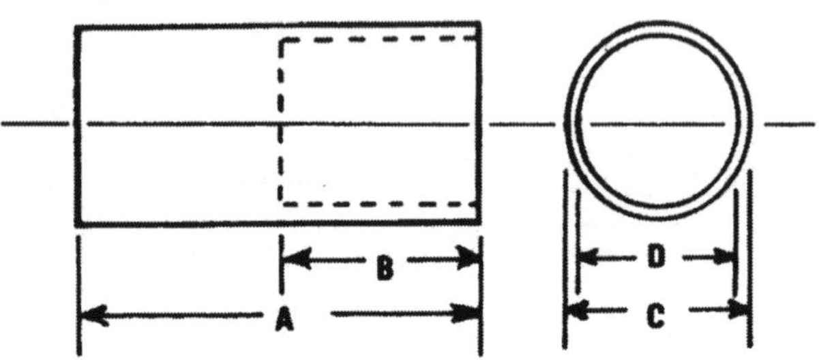

Fig. n.17
Dimensions of the rotor removing tool

A=3 in. (76 mm.) B=1.5 in. (38 mm.)
C=1.32 in. (33.5 mm.) D=1.24 in. (31.5 mm.)

Re-assembling

35. Reverse the dismantling procedure in (28) to (34) and (13) to (16), noting the following points:
    (a) Use Shell Alvania "RA", or equivalent, to lubricate the bearings where necessary.
    (b) When refitting the slip-ring end bearing, ensure that it is fitted with its open side facing towards the rotor and is pressed on to the rotor shaft as far as it will go.
    (c) Re-solder the field connections to the slip-rings.
    (d) When refitting the rotor to the drive end bracket, support the inner track of the bearing with a suitable piece of tube. Do not use the drive end bracket as the only support for the bearing when fitting the rotor.
    (e) Tighten the through-bolts evenly.
    (f) Check that the brushes are entered in their housings before fitting the brush moulding.
    (g) Tighten the shaft nut to 25-30 lb. ft. (3.46 - 4.15 Kg.m.)

Alternator integrated electronic control — Lucas Model 8 TR

Description

The 8 TR control unit used with the 15 AC alternator is of a different design to the 4 TR unit used with the 11 AC alternator fitted to U.K. models.

This unit carries a fourth terminal by means of which battery voltage is sensed directly from the battery connection at the solenoid. This avoids the necessity of having an external ignition relay switch and ensures more accurate sensing of battery voltage.

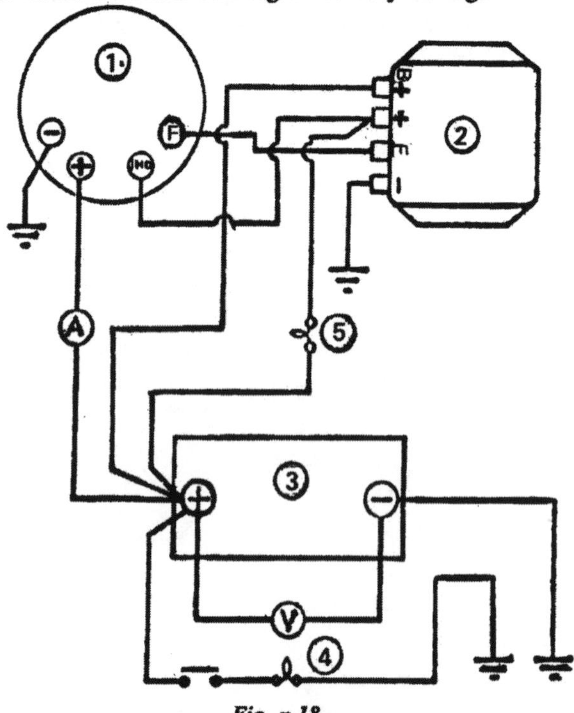

Fig. n.18
Four-terminal 8 TR control test circuit

1 Alternator
2 Output control unit
3 12 V. 9-plate battery
4 Side and tail lighting (if required)
5 Warning light

Checking the voltage setting in position

1. Observe service precautions as indicated in Section n.6(b) and carry out maintenance as in Section n.6(c).
2. Check that the alternator is functioning correctly.
3. Check that the battery is in a fully charged state.
4. Connect a voltmeter across the battery terminals.
5. Connect a 60 amp. ammeter in series with the alternator positive cable.
6. Start the engine and run it at approximately 3000 r.p.m. until a steady reading of not more than 5 amps is obtained. If the charging rate is below this figure, apply a light external load, e.g., side and tail lamps. The voltmeter should now give a reading of 14.3 to 14.7 volts.

   Should the reading fall outside these limits, or is unstable, the control unit is faulty and a replacement unit must be fitted. The component parts are not serviced individually.

Section n.6

SMITH'S ELECTRICAL INSTRUMENT TEST UNIT (Type "M")

This test unit has been designed to enable quick diagnosis of fuel and temperature gauge faults in both bi-metal thermal or semi-conductor indicators.

The test unit consists of a small panel containing a two-way switch to which is attached a long and a short lead with crocodile clips.

The vehicle battery must be in a charged condition to enable these tests to be carried out satisfactorily.

Testing fuel and temperature gauges

With the ignition switched off, disconnect the lead at the tank unit or thermal transmitter and connect the long test lead to it. Connect the short lead to earth.

1. With the switch of the test unit in No. 1 position, switch ignition on. After two minutes the gauge should read EMPTY or COLD.
2. Switch test unit over to No. 2 position. The gauge should move SLOWLY to FULL or HOT.

If, with the test unit installed the gauge reads correctly, the transmitter will be at fault and should be replaced. If the gauge reads incorrectly it should be replaced.

Should the gauge consistently under-record or over-record both on the vehicle and with the test unit, the voltage stabilizer unit to which the instrument(s) are connected could be faulty.

If wiring leads are suspect, the tester may be connected directly to the indicator, making sure the correct terminal is used. If the indicator now reads correctly, the wiring is faulty.

Section n.7

ELECTRIC SCREEN WASHER

A "Tudor" electric screen washer is fitted to later models, it is situated on the forward face of the radiator fan cowling.

Water is forced from the washer bottle by an electrically-driven impeller through plastic tubes connected to two jets which are mounted in front of the windscreen. The water is directed onto the windscreen when the hold-down switch in the facia panel is operated. The jets can be adjusted for height and angle of operation.

Testing

If the windscreen washer fails to operate, check the following:

1. Check that the windscreen washer switch is operative, and that power is being supplied to the electric motor in the base of the washer bottle.
2. Remove the plastic tubes from the washer bottle. Disconnect the electric leads from the electric motor.
3. Supply alternative power to the electric motor. If the electric motor does not function, replace the windscreen bottle assembly.

   Note: The windscreen washer bottle and electric motor are serviced as a complete assembly.
4. Ensure that the holes in the jets are not blocked or corroded.
5. Ensure that all electric leads and tubing are correctly positioned.

Removing

1. Disconnect the battery and the electric lead to the electric motor, which is fitted into the base of the washer bottle.
2. Withdraw the plastic tube from the base of the washer bottle.
3. Remove the screw retaining the windscreen bottle strap.
4. Withdraw the strap and remove the windscreen washer bottle assembly.

Refitting

Refitting is the reversal of the removing procedure.

Section n.8

FLASHER SWITCH OR HORN PUSH

On the Mini 1100 range a direction indicator switch incorporating a horn push was introduced. On later models where a floor-mounted heater is fitted the foot-operated head lamp dip switch is deleted; as the dipping mechanism is incorporated in the direction indicator switch - horn push unit.

Section n.9

HAZARD WARNING LIGHTS (MOKE SPECIAL EXPORT)

In case of emergency, all four direction indicator lamps can be operated simultaneously to provide a hazard warning.

Operation of the system is by a special switch incorporating a repeater lamp and a modulator which works in conjunction with the flasher unit. The flasher unit is mounted on the left-hand inner side face of the instrument panel. It is a two-pin unit fitted to a three-pin base. The unit is reversible and can therefore be fitted incorrectly. When correctly fitted the unit will be distinctly audible in operation.

The system is protected by a 25 amp. line fuse located alongside the switch, which is mounted below and to the right of the main instrument panel.

Section n.10

LAMPS

(1) Headlamp units

Sealed beam or renewable bulb light units are used with alternative types of bulb holders, the type fitted being dependent on the lighting regulations existing in the country for which the vehicle was produced.

(2) Headlamps (R.H.D. and L.H.D. except Europe)

Unscrew the securing screw at the bottom of the lamp rim and lift off the rim. Remove the dust-excluding rubber, which will reveal three spring-loaded screws. Press the light unit inwards against the tension of the springs and turn it in anti-clockwise direction until the heads of the screws can pass through the enlarged ends of the keyhole slots in the rim.

Withdrawal of the light unit gives immediate access to the bulb carrier for replacement. Twist the back-shell anti-clockwise and pull it off. The bulb can then be withdrawn from its holder.

Fit the replacement bulb in the holder with the slot in its disc in engagement with the projections in the holder. Engage the projections on the back-shell with the holder slots, press on, and twist to the right until its catch engages.

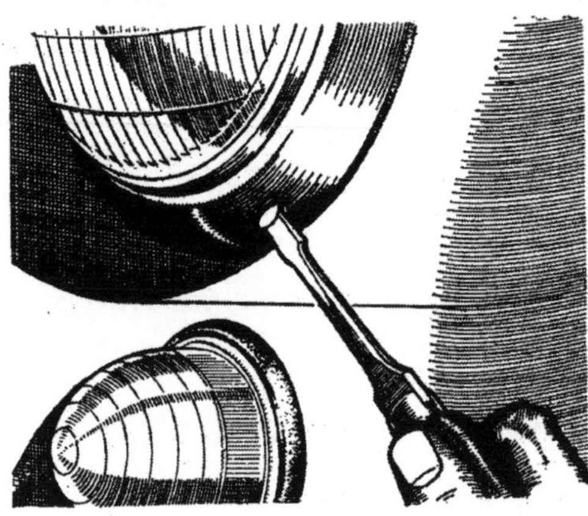

Fig. n.19

The headlamp rim securing screw is located at the bottom of the rim.

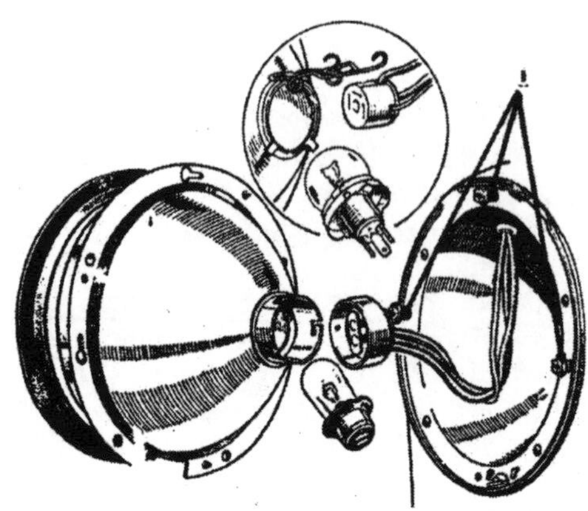

Fig. n.20

The headlamp light unit removed, showing the bulb holder and back-shell, etc., wtih the European-type lamp inset.

(3) Headlamps (European type)

Access to the light unit is obtained in the same manner as that described in item (2) for right-hand-drive cars, but the bulb is released from the reflector by withdrawing the three-pin socket and pinching the two ends of the wire retaining clip to clear the bulb flange. When replacing the bulb care must be taken to see that the rectangular pip on the bulb flange engages the slot in the reflector seating. Replace the spring clip with its coils resting in the base of the bulb flange and engaging the two retaining lugs on the reflector seating for the bulb.

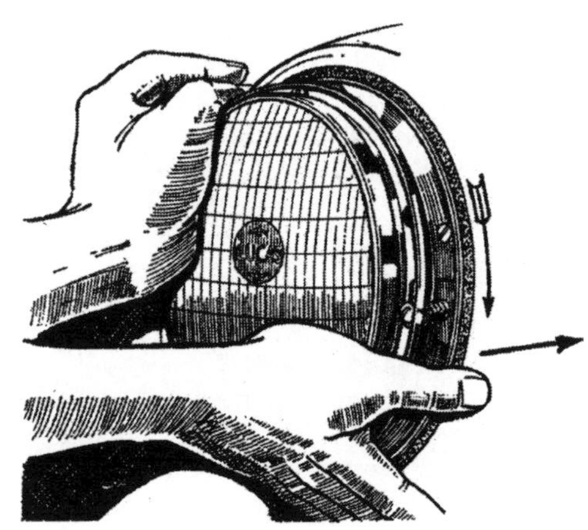

Fig. n.21

Replacing the light unit

(4) Headlamps (sealed-beam type)

To gain access to the sealed-beam light unit, remove the rim retaining screw and lift the rim off the locating lugs at the top of the headlamp shell. Remove the three screws (1) securing the lamp unit retaining plate and remove the plate from the lamp unit. Withdraw the lamp unit from the shell and disengage the plug.

Note: If European-type bulb is fitted remove as previously described.

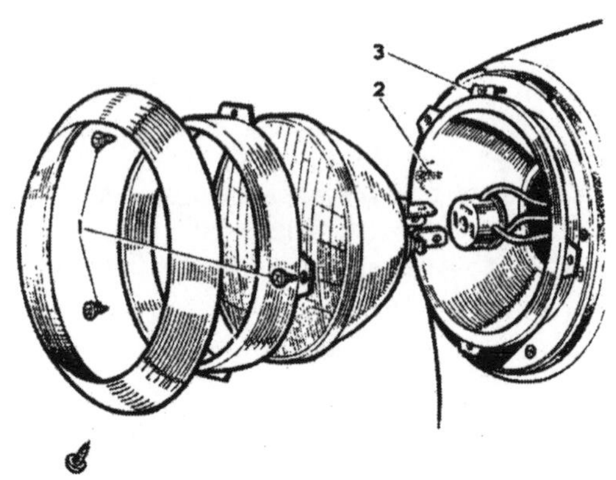

Fig. n.22

Sealed-beam headlamp, showing:

1. Retaining plate screws.
2. Horizontal adjustment screw.
3. Vertical adjustment screw.

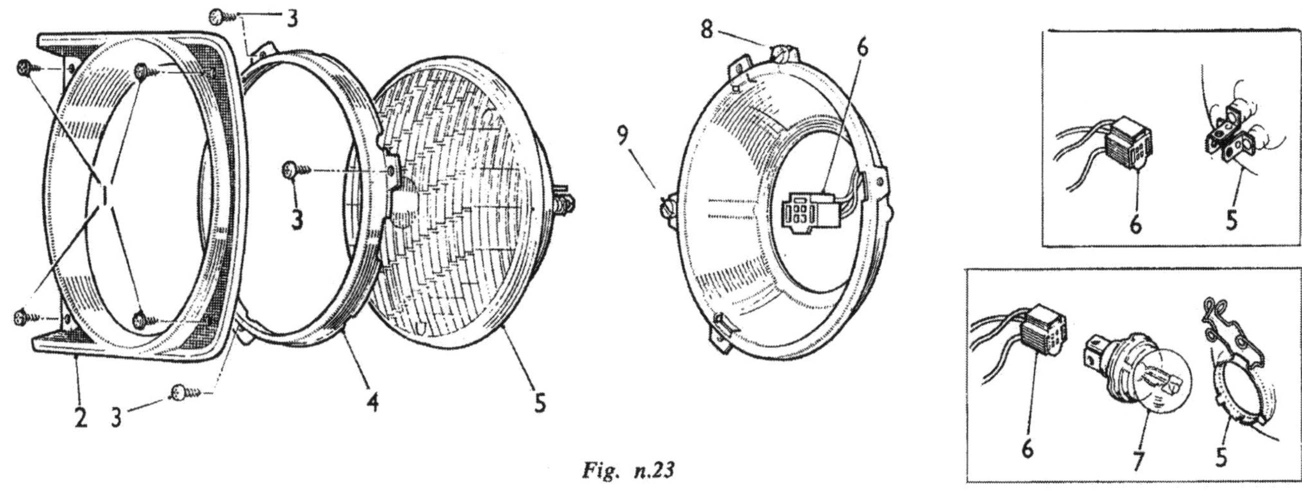

Fig. n.23

(5) Headlamps (late models recessed grille fitment) Fig. n.23

The method of gaining access to the light unit or bulb (7) is as described in the previous paragraph.

With the exception that the grille panel extension (2) held by 4 screws (1), replaces the previous lamp rim.

(6) Beam setting (early models) Fig. n.20

The three spring-loaded screws (1) which retain the light unit are used for vertical and horizontal adjustment.

Late Models using the sealed beam type carrier two separate screws are used, (8) Fig. n.23 for vertical adjustment and (9) for horizontal adjustment. The beams should be set parallel to each other in the straight ahead position and $\frac{1}{2}^\circ \pm \frac{1}{4}^\circ$ below horizontal or in accordance with the local regulations.

(7) Stop tail and direction indicator lamps (saloon and van). (Figs. n.24, n.25.)

To renew a bulb, remove the three screws (3) and withdraw the lamp lenses.

The direction indicator bulb (1) 21W. is fitted in the top and the stop/tail lamp bulb (2) 21/6W. in the lower compartment. The latter is of the double-filament type, giving a marked increase in illumination on brake application to provide a stop warning.

This bulb also has offset locating pins to ensure correct replacement.

Note: Some vehicles incorporate reversing light in the top compartment (amber lens), with these lamps the bulb (1) is a double filament 21/21W., with locating pins suitably set to prevent fitment to lower compartment.

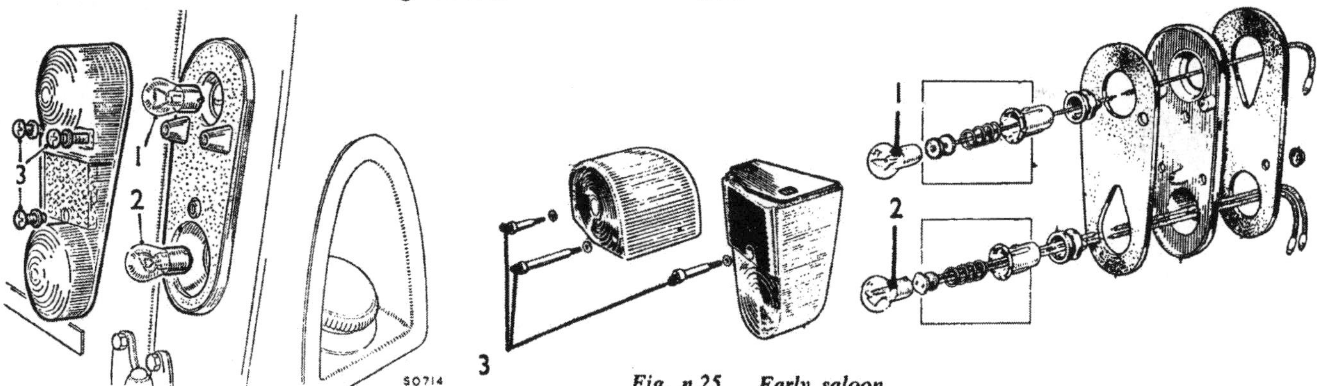

Fig. n.24 Van

Fig. n.25 Early saloon

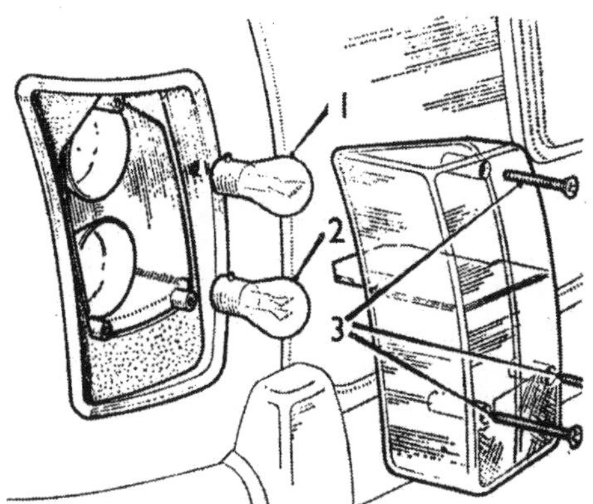

Fig. n.26 Late saloon

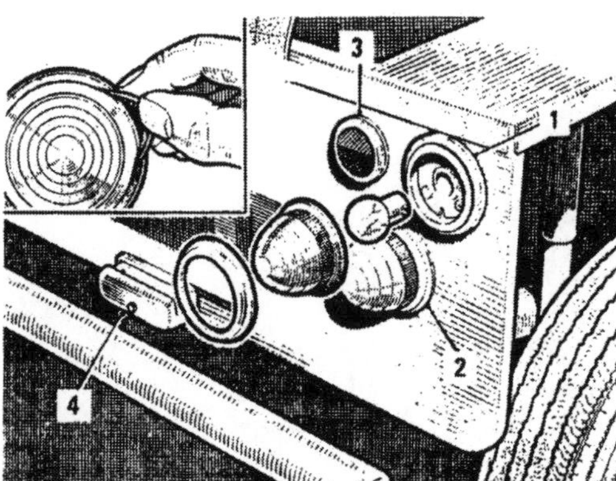

Fig. n.27

MINI MOKE (early models)
1. Stop and tail lamp. 6/21W.
2. Flashing indicator. 21W.
3. Reflex reflector. 21W.
4. Number-plate lamp. 2 x 4W.

(8) Combined stop/tail and direction indicator lamps — Moke (late models)

Three festoon-type bulbs are fitted to late models.

To replace a bulb, remove the two screws (1) retaining the lamp rim and detach the rim complete with lens. The direction indicator bulb, 21W., is fitted to the outside clips, the tailight bulb, 5W., is fitted to centre clips, and the stop light bulb, 21W., to the inside clips.

Fig. n.28

(9) Side and direction indicator lamps, saloon and van (early models). Fig. n.29

All saloons and vans use a combined round lamp assembly with a clear lens, and incorporating a single double filament 6/21W., offset pin bulb.

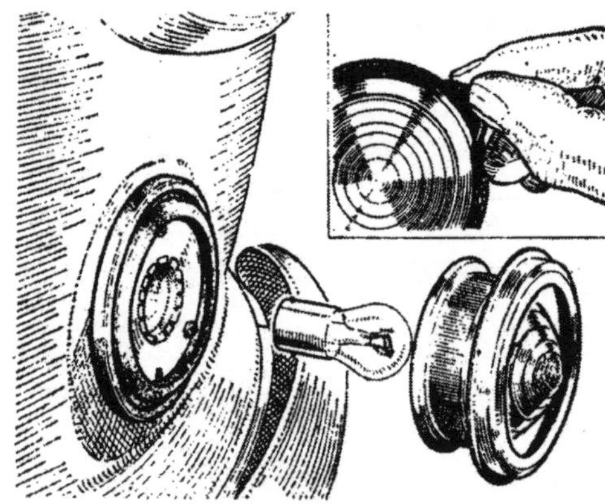

Fig. n.29

(10) To gain access to the bulb. Turn back the outer rubber flange (inset) and remove the lamp rim. Similarly turn back the inner rubber lip and remove the lens.

To refit. Insert the edge of the lens flange under the inner rubber lip. With the aid of a small lever, progressively work the inner rubber lip over the lens flange. Turn lens to ensure it is correctly seated.

Refit rim over the lens and seat it firmly over the outer face of the inner rubber lip. With the aid of a small lever, refit the outer rubber lip over the rim.

(11) Side and direction indicator lamps. Saloon and van (late models). Fig. n.30

Late model vehicles use a combined rectangular lamp assembly incorporating a one-piece amber and clear lens (2), a 5W. single contact side lamp bulb (4), and a single contact 21W. direction indicator bulb (3). To gain access to the bulbs remove the two screws (1).

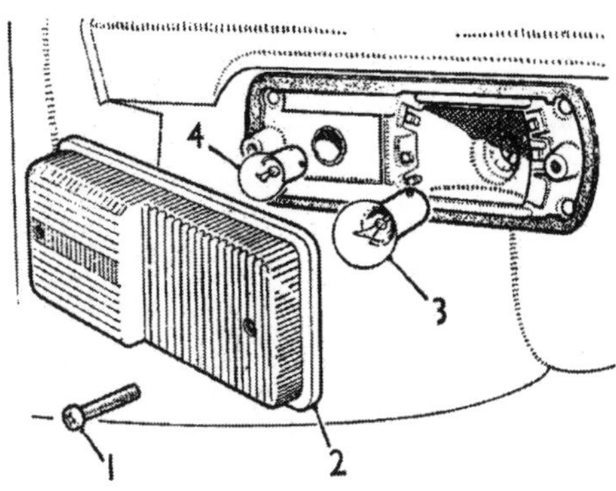

Fig. n.30

(12) Side and direction indicator lamps. Moke (early models). Fig. n.31

The combined lamps fitted to early mokes is of the similar two-bulb design to the late saloons except that the lamp (1) is round and the lens rim assembly (2) wedge locks to the base (3).

Fig. n.31

(13) To gain access to the 21W. direction indicator bulb in the top compartment and the 6W. side bulb in the lower compartment, press in the lens assembly firmly and squarely with both hands and turn in an anti-clockwise direction to release.

(14) Side and direction indicator lamps. Moke (late models) Fig. n.31a

Combined side and direction indicator lamps incorporating two festoon-type bulbs are fitted to late models. Access to the bulb is the same as previously described for late rear lamps. The direction indicator bulb 21W. outside clips, side lamp bulb 5W. inside clips.

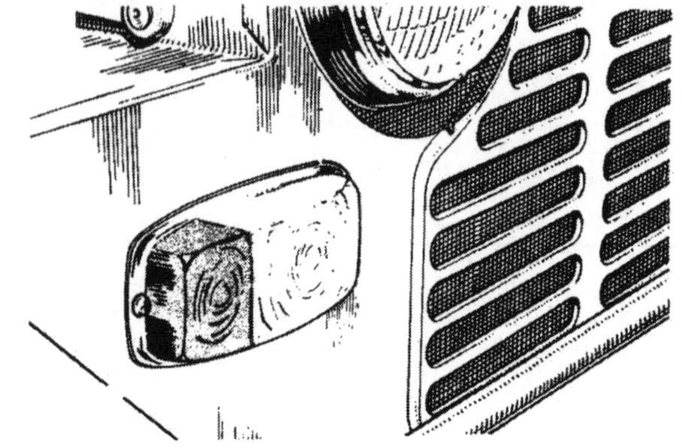

Fig. n.31a

(15) Number plate lamps (all models)
Unscrew the centre screw, remove the cover.

Saloon—1 lamp —2 bulbs 6W.
Van —2 lamps—4 bulbs 6W.
Moke —1 lamp —2 bulbs 6W.

Fig. n.32

(16) Interior lamps. Saloons and vans

To remove the plastic cover, squeeze the sides of the cover together and withdraw. The 6W. festoon-type bulb may then be pulled from its clips.

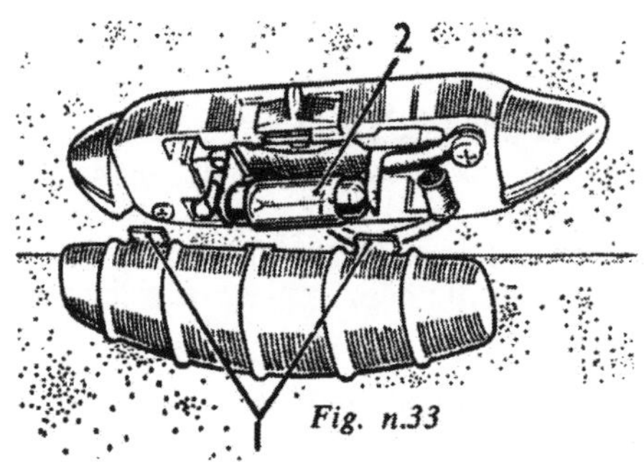

Fig. n.33

(17) Panel and warning lamp bulbs (Early model saloons and vans)

The warning light bulbs for ignition, headlight beam, and oil filter indicators are removed from under the bonnet by withdrawing the push-in type holders from the rear of the central instrument.

Fig. n.34
Typical instrument panel from under the bonnet showing the push-in bulb holders.

The bulbs are screwed in to their respective holders.

Mini 1100 saloon and van

As described for early models.

Cooper and Mini K Models

Access to the bulbs indicated is obtained from behind the panel and is similar for each model. Remove the air cleaner, pull down the felted panel behind the air cleaner area and uncover the aperture in the bulkhead panel. Withdraw the push-in type bulb holder from the rear of the instrument. The bulbs may be removed by pressing and turning anti-clockwise.

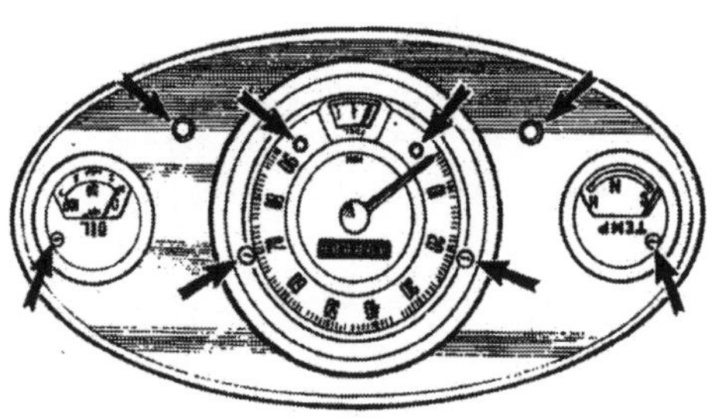

Fig. n.35

Moke

The lower bulbs are directly accessible from behind the instrument panel. Where difficulty is found in reaching the remaining bulbs, it will be necessary to remove the dash panel assembly. To remove, unscrew the six screws retaining the windshield wiper drive cover and the six remaining screws holding the panel assembly. Move the panel outwards slightly and disconnect the speedometer drive cable by unscrewing the milled nut before lifting the panel clear.

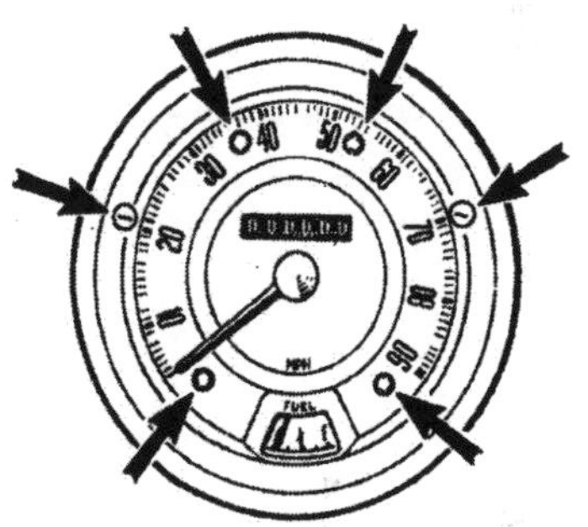

Fig. n.36

Clubman and G.T. Saloons
(Printed circuit instrument panel assembly)

For access to bulb holders see Section Nb.1. To fit replacement bulb, withdraw the respective holder (1) Fig. n.37 and pull out the capless type 2.2W. bulb.

G.T. models use a three instrument panel incorporating-tachometer. The tachometer is fitted with a capless 2.2W. illumination lamp

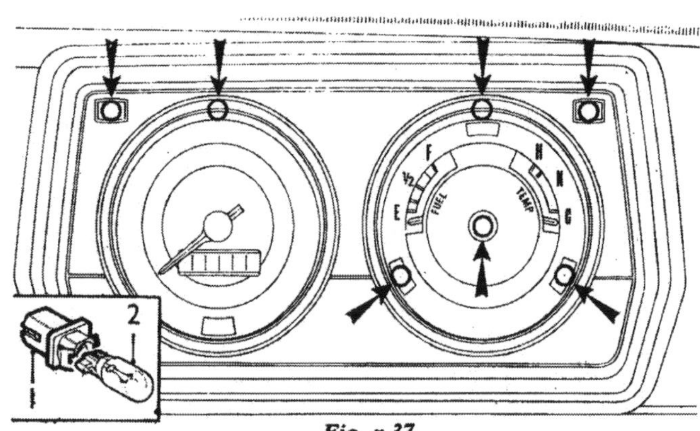

Fig. n.37

LAMPS. MOKE SPECIAL EXPORT

(18) Headlamps

Conventional sealed beam lamps as previously described are used.

(19) Stop and tail lamp (1). Fig. n.38

Remove two lens screws to gain access to the 21/6W. double filament offset pin bulb.

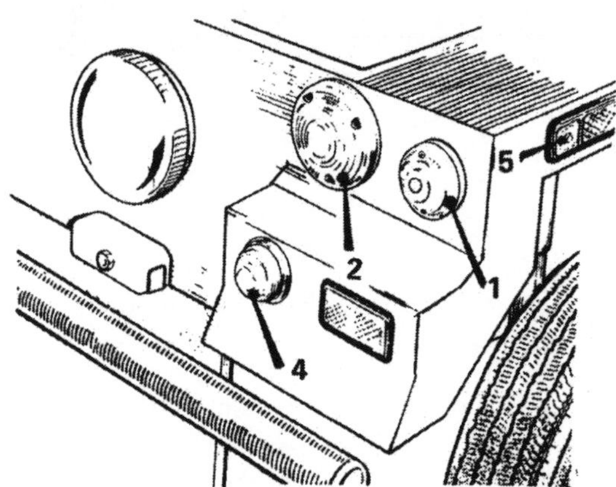

Fig. n.38

(20) Direction indicator lamps (2). Figs. n.38 and n.39.

Remove the three screws from the amber lens to gain access to the single filament 21W. bulb of both front and rear lamps.

(21) Side lamps (3). Fig. n.39. Amber lens and back-up lamps (4). Fig. n.38. Clear lens.

These lamps are identical to the rear direction indicator lamps fitted to early Mini Mokes. To gain access to the 21W. bulb refer item (10).

Fig. n.39

(22) Side marker lamps (5). Fig. n.38 and n.39.

Combination 4W. side lamp with detachable reflex reflector and lens assembly. Rear marker lamp assemblies use red lens and reflex, front amber.

To gain access to a bulb or replace a reflector proceed as Item 10.

(23) Repeater lamp hazard warning

This lamp is built into the red control knob of the hazard warning switch mounted below main fascia panel. To gain access to the bulb screw the switch control knob off anti-clockwise, taking care not to lose the small spring which tensions the 2W. keybase, type bulb to its holder.

(24) Fuses. Refer Owner's Handbook.

Section n.11

WIRING DIAGRAMS

WIRE COLOUR CODE

No.	Colour	No.	Colour	No.	Colour	No.	Colour	No.	Colour
1	Brown	16	Blue with white	37	Green	45	Green with black	59	White with purple
2	Brown with blue	19	Red	38	Green with brown	47	Light green wtih brown	63	White with black
5	Brown with green	25	Red with white	39	Green with blue	50	Light green with purple	73	Black
8	Brown with yellow	28	Purple	40	Green with red	55	White	78	Black with green
10	Blue	34	Purple with white	41	Green with purple	56	White with brown		
12	Blue with red	36	Purple with black	43	Green with white	58	White with red		

WIRING DIAGRAM
MINI STANDARD SALOON AND VAN

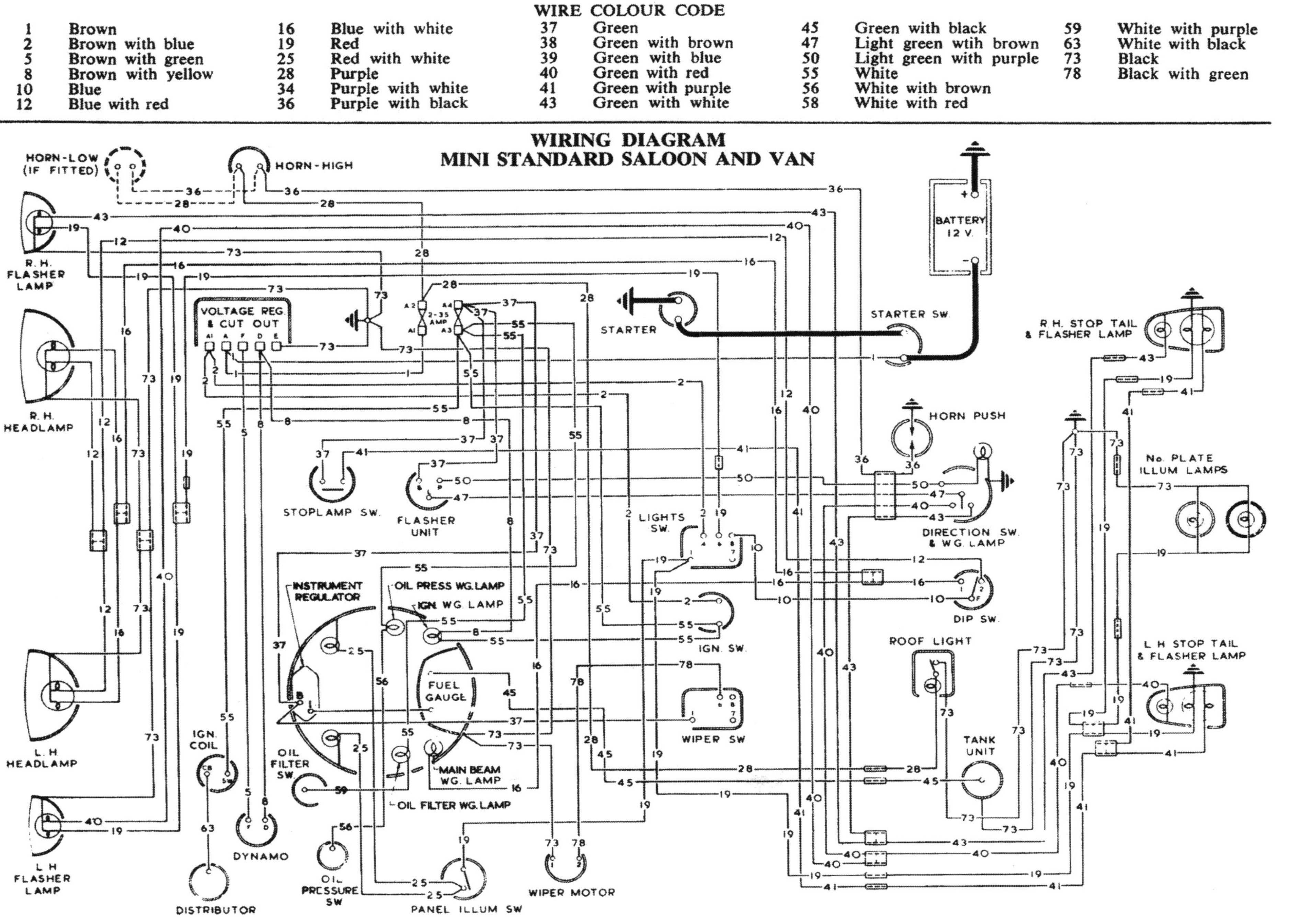

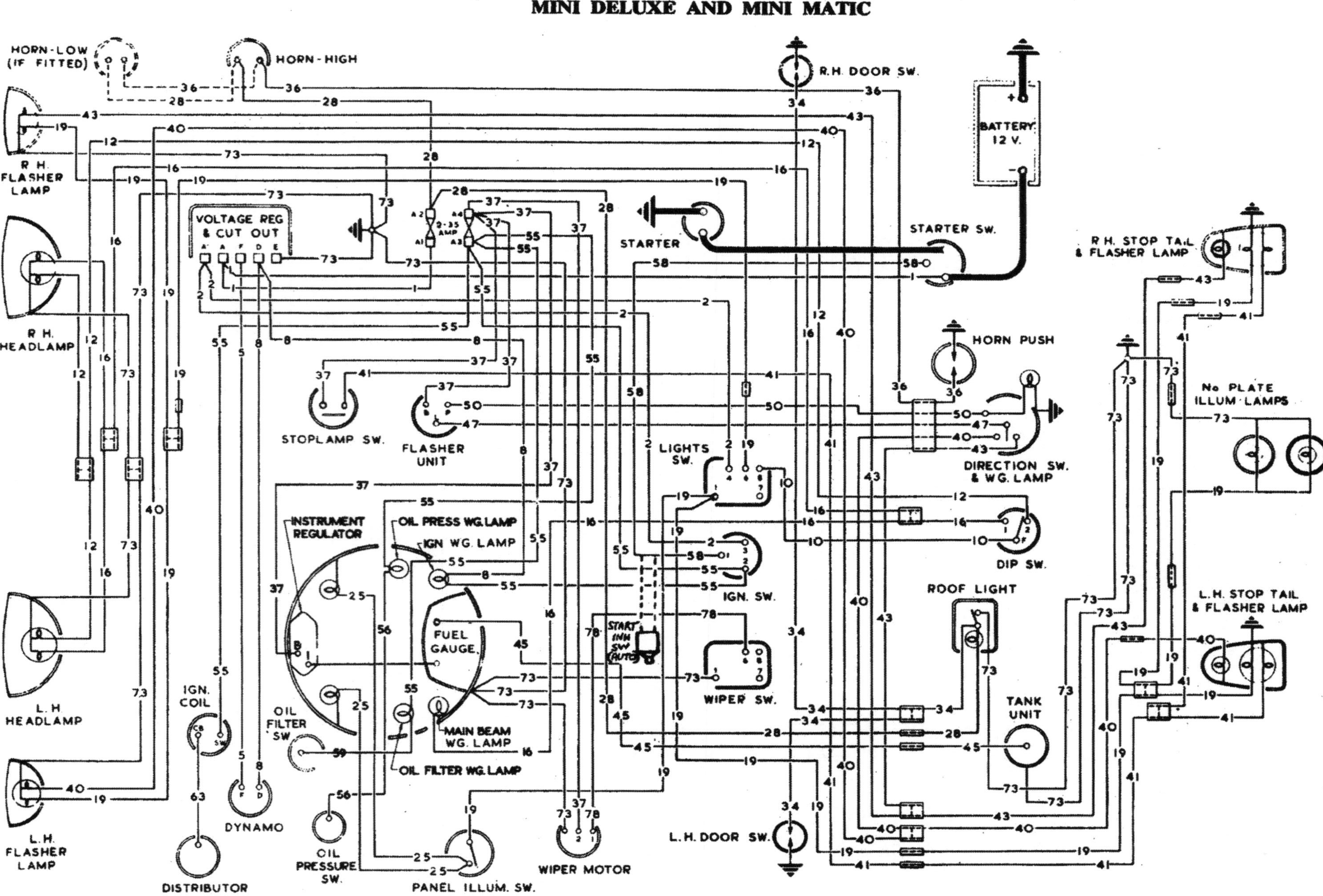
MINI DELUXE AND MINI MATIC
HORN-LOW (IF FITTED)
HORN-HIGH
R.H. DOOR SW.
BATTERY 12 V.
R.H. FLASHER LAMP
VOLTAGE REG & CUT OUT
STARTER
STARTER SW.
R.H. STOP TAIL & FLASHER LAMP
R.H. HEADLAMP
HORN PUSH
No PLATE ILLUM. LAMPS
STOPLAMP SW.
FLASHER UNIT
DIRECTION SW. & W.G. LAMP
LIGHTS SW.
INSTRUMENT REGULATOR
OIL PRESS WG.LAMP
IGN WG. LAMP
DIP SW.
IGN. SW.
ROOF LIGHT
L.H. STOP TAIL & FLASHER LAMP
FUEL GAUGE
START INH SW (AUTO)
L.H HEADLAMP
IGN. COIL
OIL FILTER SW
MAIN BEAM WG. LAMP
WIPER SW.
TANK UNIT
OIL FILTER WG.LAMP
L.H. FLASHER LAMP
DYNAMO
OIL PRESSURE SW.
WIPER MOTOR
L.H. DOOR SW.
DISTRIBUTOR
PANEL ILLUM. SW.

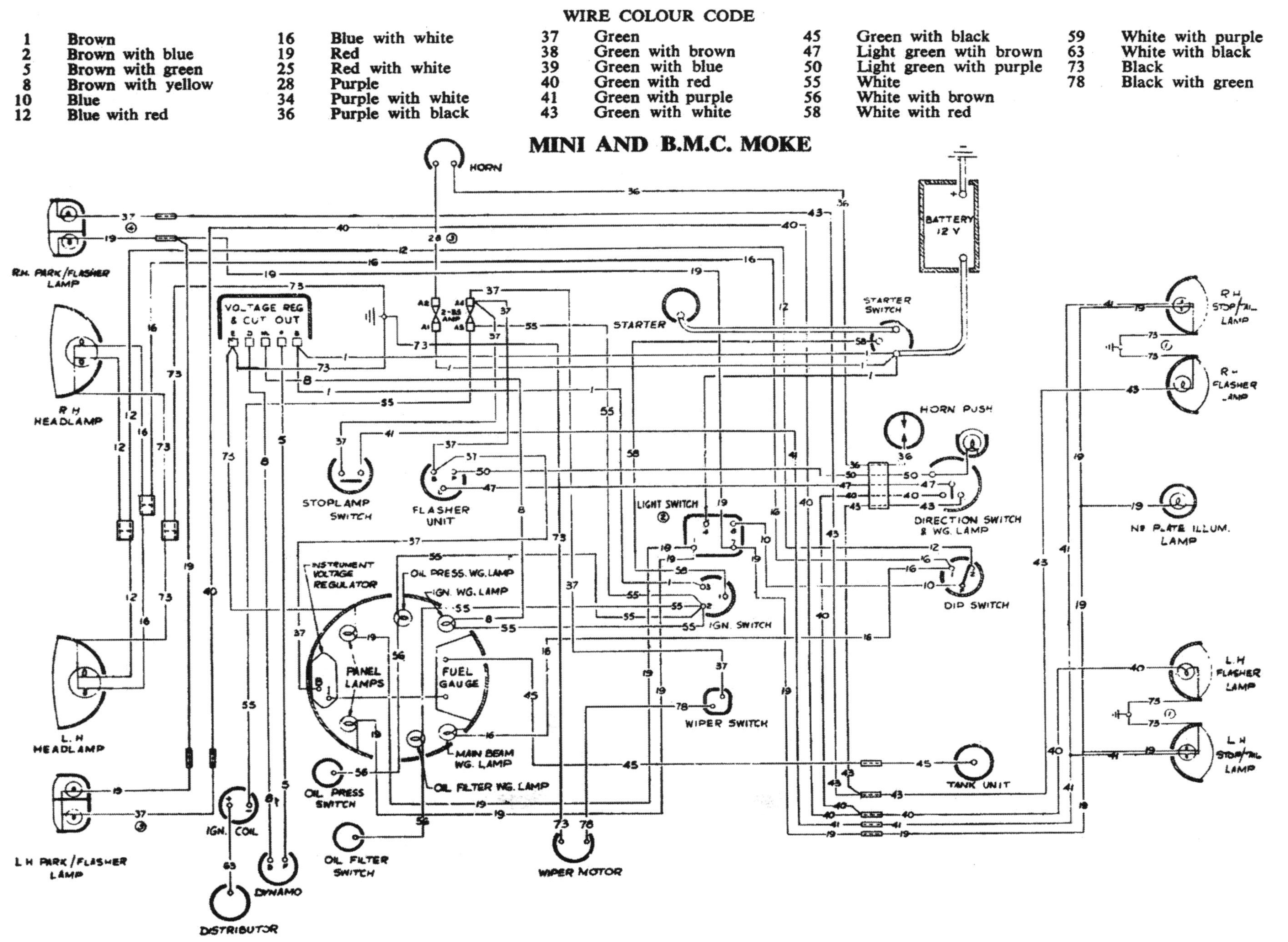
WIRE COLOUR CODE
1 Brown
2 Brown with blue
5 Brown with green
8 Brown with yellow
10 Blue
12 Blue with red
16 Blue with white
19 Red
25 Red with white
28 Purple
34 Purple with white
36 Purple with black
37 Green
38 Green with brown
39 Green with blue
40 Green with red
41 Green with purple
43 Green with white
45 Green with black
47 Light green wtih brown
50 Light green with purple
55 White
56 White with brown
58 White with red
59 White with purple
63 White with black
73 Black
78 Black with green
MINI AND B.M.C. MOKE
HORN
BATTERY 12 V
R.H. PARK/FLASHER LAMP
R H HEADLAMP
L. H HEADLAMP
L H PARK/FLASHER LAMP
VOLTAGE REG & CUT OUT
STARTER
STARTER SWITCH
R H STOP/TAIL LAMP
R - FLASHER LAMP
HORN PUSH
STOPLAMP SWITCH
FLASHER UNIT
DIRECTION SWITCH & WG. LAMP
No PLATE ILLUM. LAMP
LIGHT SWITCH
DIP SWITCH
IGN. SWITCH
INSTRUMENT VOLTAGE REGULATOR
OIL PRESS. WG. LAMP
IGN. WG. LAMP
PANEL LAMPS
FUEL GAUGE
MAIN BEAM WG. LAMP
OIL FILTER WG. LAMP
WIPER SWITCH
L. H FLASHER LAMP
L. H STOP/TAIL LAMP
OIL PRESS SWITCH
IGN. COIL
OIL FILTER SWITCH
DYNAMO
DISTRIBUTOR
WIPER MOTOR
TANK UNIT

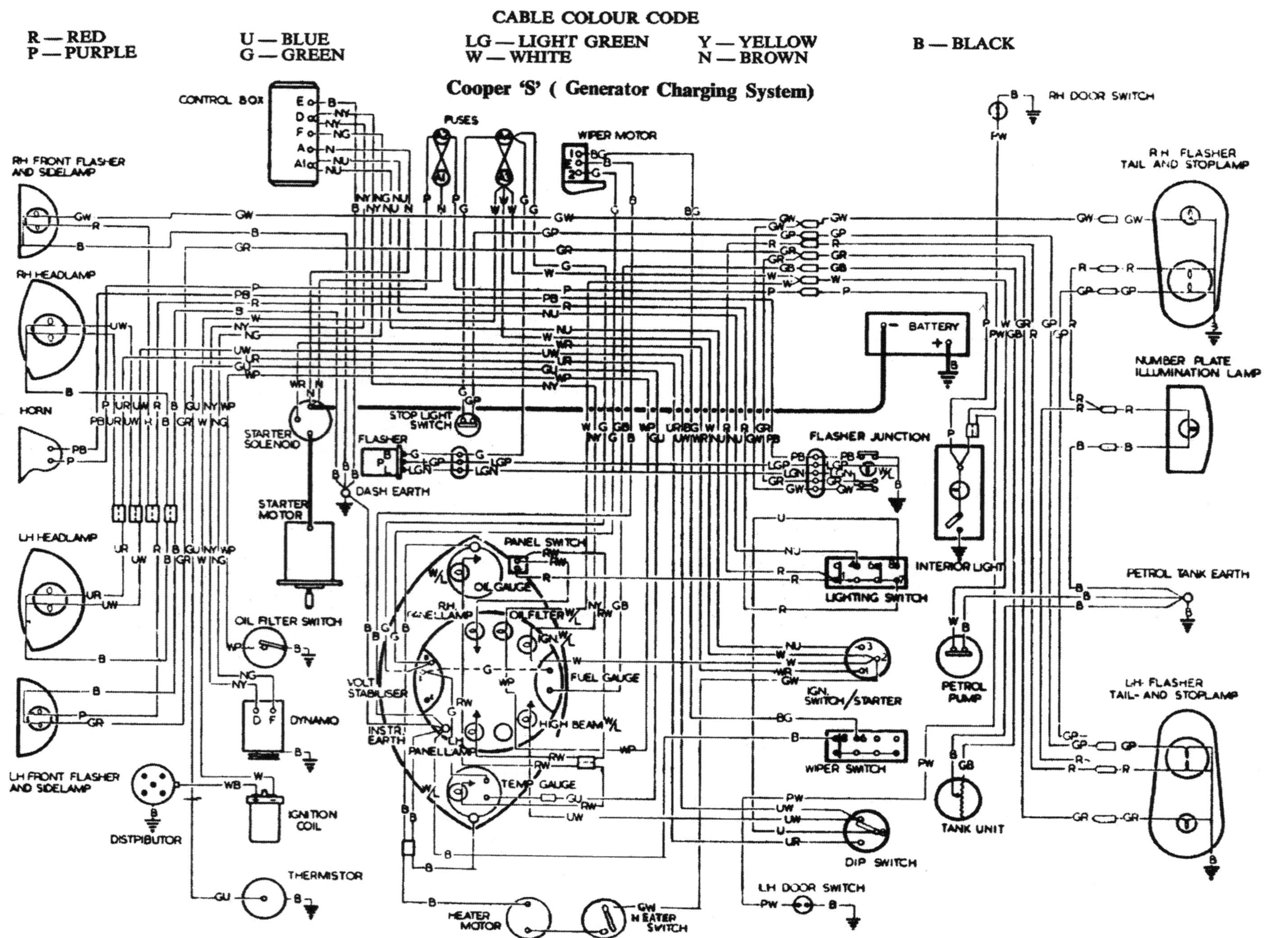
CABLE COLOUR CODE
R — RED
P — PURPLE
U — BLUE
G — GREEN
LG — LIGHT GREEN
W — WHITE
Y — YELLOW
N — BROWN
B — BLACK
Cooper 'S' (Generator Charging System)
CONTROL BOX
FUSES
WIPER MOTOR
RH DOOR SWITCH
RH FRONT FLASHER AND SIDELAMP
RH HEADLAMP
HORN
LH HEADLAMP
LH FRONT FLASHER AND SIDELAMP
DISTPIBUTOR
IGNITION COIL
THERMISTOR
OIL FILTER SWITCH
DYNAMO
STARTER SOLENOID
STARTER MOTOR
STOP LIGHT SWITCH
FLASHER
DASH EARTH
PANEL SWITCH
OIL GAUGE
RH PANEL LAMP
OIL FILTER W/L
IGN W/L
FUEL GAUGE
VOLT STABILISER
INSTR. EARTH
LH PANEL LAMP
HIGH BEAM W/L
TEMP GAUGE
HEATER MOTOR
HEATER SWITCH
BATTERY
FLASHER JUNCTION
INTERIOR LIGHT
LIGHTING SWITCH
IGN. SWITCH/STARTER
WIPER SWITCH
PETROL PUMP
TANK UNIT
DIP SWITCH
LH DOOR SWITCH
RH FLASHER TAIL AND STOPLAMP
NUMBER PLATE ILLUMINATION LAMP
PETROL TANK EARTH
LH FLASHER TAIL- AND STOPLAMP

CLUBMAN AND CLUBMAN G.T.

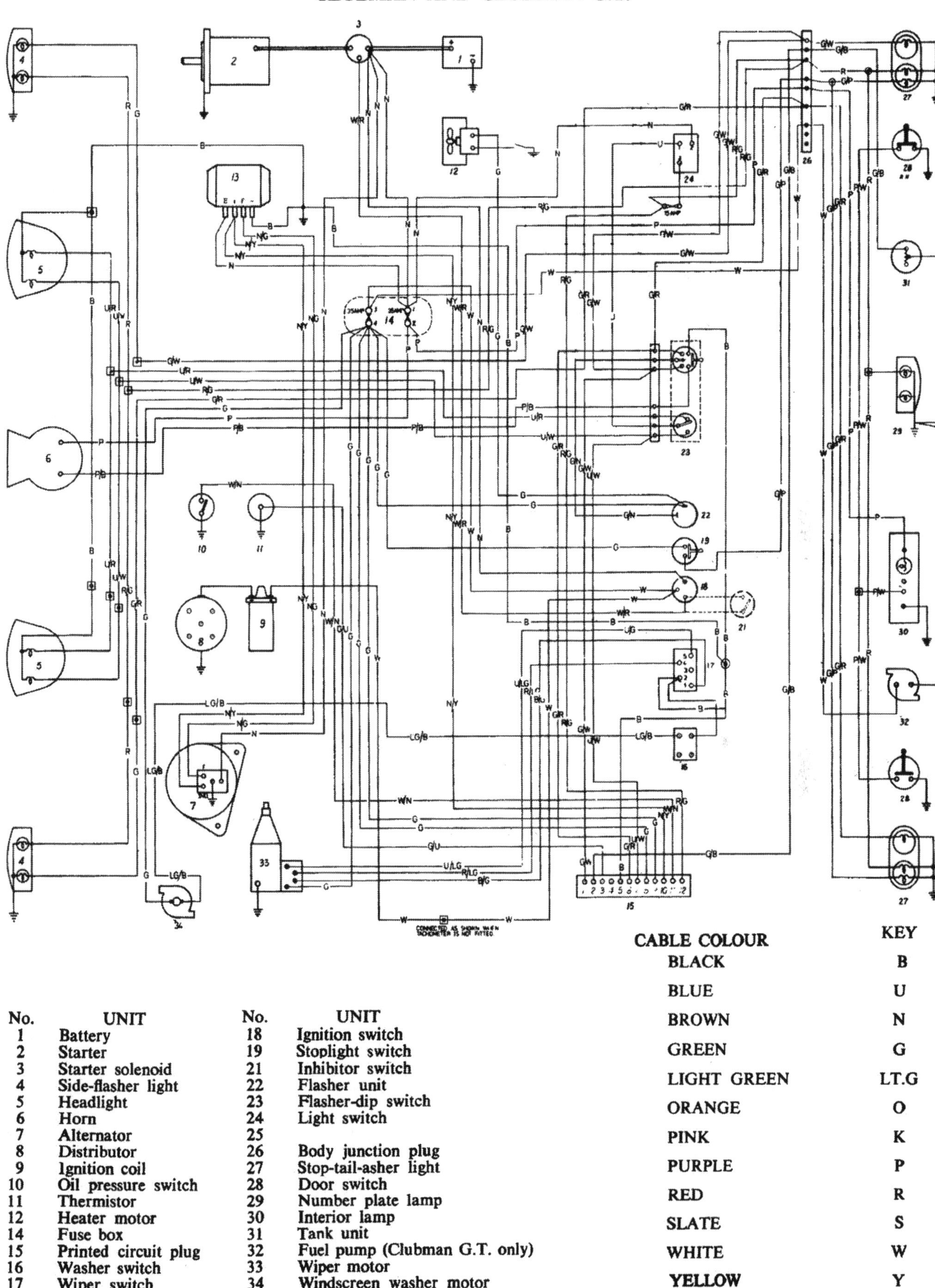

No.	UNIT	No.	UNIT
1	Battery	18	Ignition switch
2	Starter	19	Stoplight switch
3	Starter solenoid	21	Inhibitor switch
4	Side-flasher light	22	Flasher unit
5	Headlight	23	Flasher-dip switch
6	Horn	24	Light switch
7	Alternator	25	
8	Distributor	26	Body junction plug
9	Ignition coil	27	Stop-tail-asher light
10	Oil pressure switch	28	Door switch
11	Thermistor	29	Number plate lamp
12	Heater motor	30	Interior lamp
14	Fuse box	31	Tank unit
15	Printed circuit plug	32	Fuel pump (Clubman G.T. only)
16	Washer switch	33	Wiper motor
17	Wiper switch	34	Windscreen washer motor

CABLE COLOUR	KEY
BLACK	B
BLUE	U
BROWN	N
GREEN	G
LIGHT GREEN	LT.G
ORANGE	O
PINK	K
PURPLE	P
RED	R
SLATE	S
WHITE	W
YELLOW	Y

Mini 1100 K, Mini 1100 Std., Mini Van 1100, Mini Matic, Cooper 'S' (Alternator Charging System)

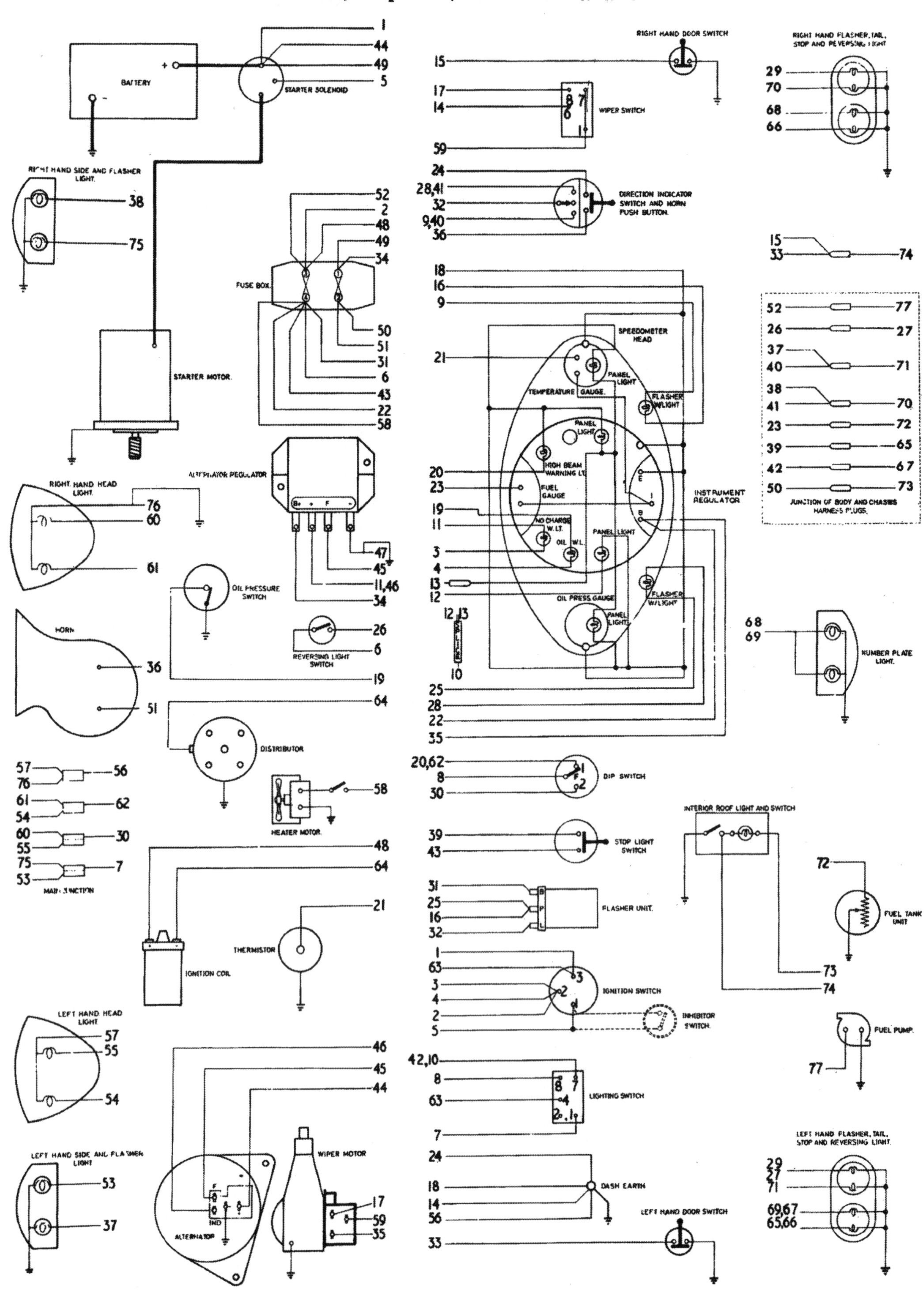

KEY TO WIRING DIAGRAM Mini 1100 K, Mini 1100 Std., Mini Van 1100, Mini Matic, Cooper 'S' (Alternator Charging System)

Wire No.	Service	Colour Main	Colour Trace	Wire No.	Service	Colour Main	Colour Trace
1	Solenoid to ignition switch	Brown		40	Flasher junction left-hand to body junction	Green	Red
2	Ignition switch to fuse A3	White		41	Flasher junction right-hand to body junction	Green	White
3	Ignition switch to no charge warning light	White		42	Body junction to lighting switch	Red	
4	Ignition switch to oil pressure warning light	White		43	Fuse A4 to stop light switch	Green	
5	Ignition switch to starter solenoid	White	Red	44	Starter solenoid to alternator	Brown	
6	Fuse A4 to reversing light switch	Green		45	Regulator F to alternator field (F)	Brown	Green
7	Lighting switch to main junction	Red		46	Regulator + to alternator indicator (ind.)	Brown	Yellow
8	Lighting switch to dip switch	Blue		47	Regulator to valence earth	Black	
9	Flasher warning light left-hand to flasher switch	Green	Red	48	Fuse A3 to ignition coil	White	
10	Lighting switch to splice 1	Red		49	Fuse A1 to solenoid	Brown	
11	Regulator + to no charge warning light	Brown	Yellow	50	Fuse A2 to body junction	Purple	
12	Splice 1 to panel light speedo	Red	White	51	Fuse A2 to horn	Purple	
13	Splice 1 to connector	Red	White	52	Fuse A3 to body junction	White	
14	Dash earth to wiper switch	Black		53	Left-hand side light to main junction	Red	Green
15	Connector to right-hand door switch	Purple	White	54	Left-hand headlight to main junction	Blue	White
16	Flasher warning light right-hand to flasher P	Lt. Green	Purple	55	Left-hand headlight to main junction	Lt. green	Purple
17	Wiper motor to wiper switch	Green	Yellow	56	Dash earth to main junction	Black	
18	Dash earth to instrument earth	Black		57	Left-hand head light to main junction	Black	
19	Oil pressure warning light to oil pressure switch	White	Brown	58	Heater motor to fuse A4	Green	
20	Main beam warning light to dip switch	Blue	White	59	Wiper switch to wiper motor	Black	Green
21	Temperature gauge to thermostat	Green	Blue	60	Main junction to right-hand head light	Blue	Red
22	Instrument regulator to fuse A4	Green		61	Main junction to right-hand head light	Blue	White
23	Body junction to fuel gauge	Green	Black	62	Junction right-hand to dip switch	Blue	White
24	Dash earth to flasher junction	Black		63	Lighting switch to ignition switch	Brown	
25	Flasher P to left-hand flasher warning light	Lt. green	Purple	64	Ignition coil to distributor	White	Black
26	Reversing light switch to body junction	Lt. green	Brown	65	Stop light left-hand to body junction	Green	Purple
27	Reversing light left-hand to body junction	Lt. green	Brown	66	Stop light right-hand to stop light left-hand	Green	Purple
28	Flasher warning light right-hand to flasher switch	Green	White	67	Tail light left-hand to body junction	Red	Green
29	Reversing light right-hand to reversing light l.h.	Green	Brown	68	Tail light right-hand to number plate light	Red	Green
30	Dip switch to head light main junction	Blue	Red	69	Tail light left-hand to number plate light	Red	Green
31	Fuse A4 to flasher B	Green		70	Rear flasher right-hand to body junction	Green	White
32	Flasher junction to flasher 1.	Lt. Green	Brown	71	Rear flasher left-hand to body junction	Green	Red
33	Door switch left-hand to connector	Purple	White	72	Fuel tank to body junction	Green	Black
34	Regulator + to fuse A1	Brown		73	Interior light to body junction	Purple	
35	Wiper motor to instrument regulator	Green		74	Interior light to connector	Purple	White
36	Horn to flasher junction	Purple	Black	75	Main junction to right-hand side light	Red	
37	Body junction to flasher left-hand front	Green	Red	76	Main junction to right-hand head light	Black	
38	Body junction to flasher right-hand front	Green	White	77	Body junction to fuel pump	White	
39	Stop light switch to body junction	Green	Purple				

NOTES

1. Oil pressure and temperature gauges fitted to Mini 1100 K, Cooper 'S', Mini Matic only.
2. Oil pressure warning light and switch fitted to Mini 1100 Std. and van only.
3. One only flasher warning light located in speedometer head fitted to Mini 1100 Std. and van only.
4. Electric fuel pump fitted to Cooper 'S' only.
5. Electric heater motor fitted to Mini K 1100. Supply for some models taken from ignition switch.
6. Inhibitor switch fitted to Mini Matic only.
7. Reversing lights fitted to special order only.

BMC MOKE
(Alternator Charging System)

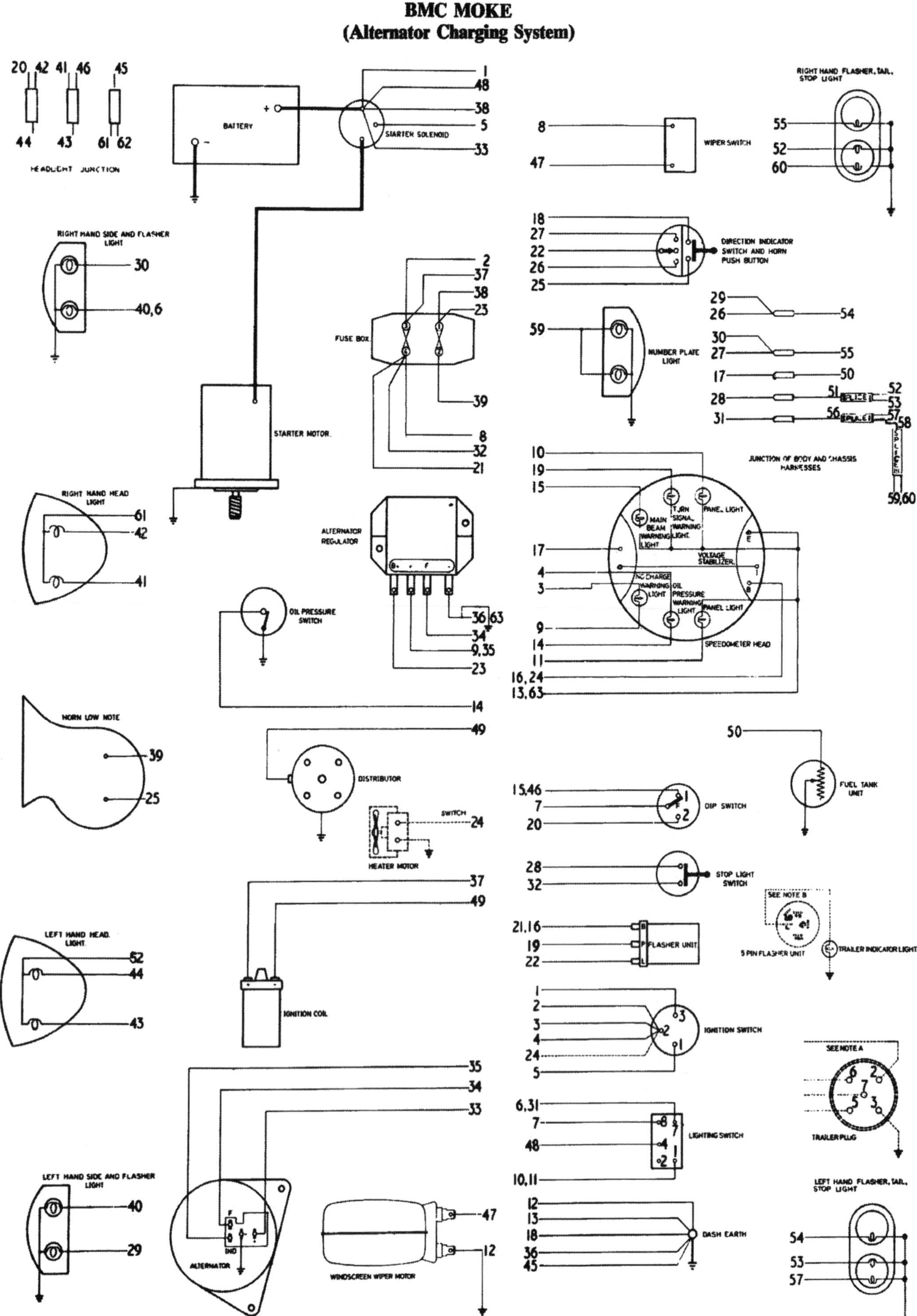

KEY TO WIRING DIAGRAM — B.M.C. MOKE
(Alternator Charging System)

Wire No.	Service	Colour Main	Colour Trace	Wire No.	Service	Colour Main	Colour Trace
1	Solenoid to ignition switch	Brown		33	Starter solenoid to alternator	Brown	
2	Ignition switch to fuse A3	White		34	Regulator F to alternator F	Brown	Green
3	Ignition switch to no charge warning light	White		35	Regulator + to alternator ind.	Brown	Yellow
4	Ignition switch to oil pressure warning light	White		36	Regulator — to valance earth	Black	
5	Ignition switch to starter solenoid	White	Red	37	Fuse A3 to ignition coil	White	
6	Lighting switch to front side lights	Red		38	Fuse A1 to solenoid	Brown	
7	Lighting switch to dip switch	Blue		39	Fuse A2 to horn	Purple	
8	Fuse A4 to wiper switch	Green		40	R/H. flasher junction to l/h. flasher junction	Red	
9	Regulator + to no charge warning light	Brown	Yellow	41	H/light junction to r/h. headlight	Blue	White
10	Light switch to panel light r/h.	Red	White	42	H/light junction to r/h. headlight	Blue	Red
11	Light switch to panel light l/h.	Red	White	43	H/light junction to l/h. headlight	Blue	White
12	H/light junction to l/h. headlight	Black		44	H/light junction to l/h. headlight	Blue	Red
13	Dash earth to instrument earth	Black		45	H/light junction to earth	Black	
14	Oil pressure switch to oil pressure warning light	White	Brown	46	H/light junction to dip switch	Blue	White
15	Main beam warning light to dip switch	Blue	White	47	Wiper motor to wiper switch	Black	Green
16	Voltage stabilizer to flasher unit	Green		48	Lighting switch to solenoid	Brown	
17	Body junction to fuel gauge	Green	Black	49	Ignition coil to distributor	White	Black
18	Dash earth to flasher junction	Black		50	Tank unit to body junction	Green	Black
19	Flasher P to flasher warning light	Lt. Green	Purple	51	Body junction to splice 1	Green	Purple
20	Dip switch to headlight junction	Blue	Red	52	R/H. stop light to splice 1	Green	Purple
21	Fuse A4 to flasher B	Green		53	L/H. stop light to splice 1	Green	Purple
22	Flasher junction to flasher l.	Lt. Green	Brown	54	L/H. flasher lamp to body junction	Green	Red
23	Regulator B+ to fuse A1	Brown		55	R/H. flasher lamp to body junction	Green	White
24	Ignition switch to heater	Green		56	Splice II to body junction	Red	
25	Horn to flasher junction	Purple	Black	57	Splice II lamp to left-hand tail light	Red	
26	Body junction to flasher switch junction	Green	Red	58	Splice II to splice III	Red	
27	Body junction to flasher switch junction	Green	White	59	Number plate light to splice III	Red	
28	Body junction to stop light switch	Green	Purple	60	R/H. lamp to splice III	Red	
29	Body junction to left-hand flasher	Green	Red	61	R/H. h/lamp to headlight junction	Black	
30	Body junction to right-hand flasher	Green	White	62	L/H. h/lamp to headlight junction	Black	
31	Body junction to lighting switch	Red		63	Alternator regulator to dash	Black	
32	Fuse A4 to stop light switch	Green					

WHEN TRAILER PLUG FITTED — WIRED AS SHOWN
7 to tail lights
2 Left turn indicator
5 Right turn indicator
6 Stop light
3 Earth

WHEN 5-PIN FLASHER UNIT (HELLA TYPE) FITTED — WIRED AS SHOWN
C to trailer warning light
49A to flasher switch
49 to Fuse A4
CO to fuse A4
C2 to vehicle warning light

MINI 1100 SALOON AND VAN (Late Models)

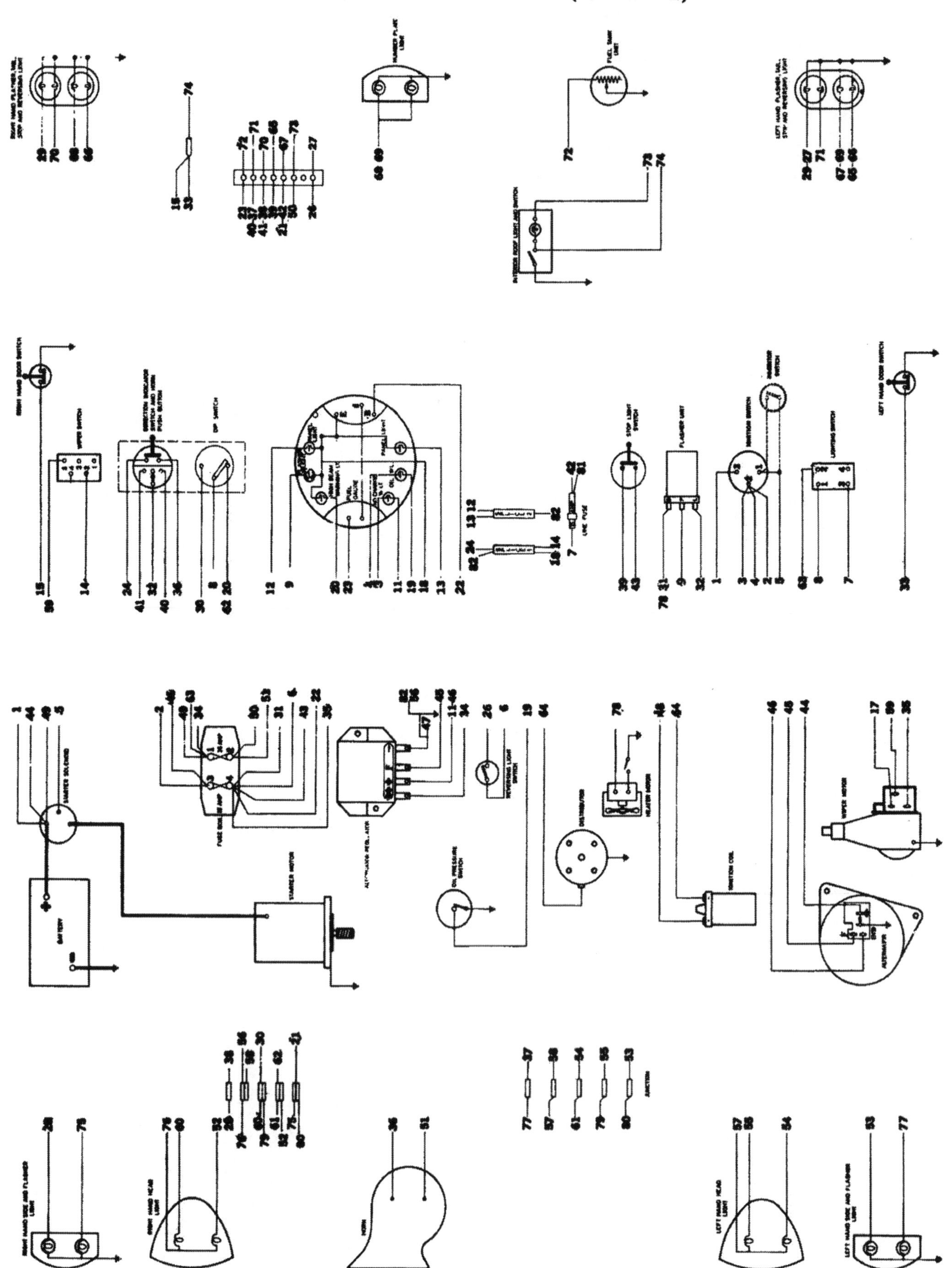

KEY TO WIRING DIAGRAM
MINI 1100 SALOON AND VAN (Late Models)

Wire No.	Service	Colour Main	Colour Trace	Wire No.	Service	Colour Main	Colour Trace
1	Solenoid to ignition switch	Brown		44	Starter solenoid to alternator	Brown	
2	Ignition switch to fuse A3	White		45	Regulator F to alternator field (F)	Brown	Green
3	Ignition switch to no charge warning light	White		46	Regulator+ to alternator indicator (ind.)	Brown	Yellow
4	Ignition switch to oil pressure warning light	White		47	Regulator to valence earth	Black	
5	Ignition switch to starter solenoid	White	Red	48	Fuse A3 to ignition coil	White	
6	Fuse A4 to reversing light switch	Green		49	Fuse A1 to solenoid	Brown	
7	Lighting switch to line fuse	Red		50	Fuse A2 to body junction	Purple	
8	Lighting switch to dip switch	Blue		51	Fuse A2 to horn	Purple	
9	Flasher warning light to flasher unit	Lt. Green	Purple	52	Right hand headlight to junction	Blue	White
11	Regulator + to no charge warning light	Brown	Yellow	53	Left hand side light to junction	Red	Green
12	Splice 2 to panel light speedo	Red	Green	54	Left hand head light to junction	Blue	White
13	Splice 2 to panel light speedo	Red	Green	55	Left hand headlight to junction	Blue	Red
14	Splice 1 to wiper switch	Black		56	Dash earth to main junction	Black	
15	Connector to right-hand door switch	Purple	White	57	Left hand head light to junction	Black	
17	Wiper motor to wiper switch	Red	Green	58	R.H. light junction to L.H. light junction	Black	
18	Splice 1 to instrument earth	Black		59	Wiper switch to wiper motor	Black	Green
19	Oil pressure warning light to oil pressure switch	White	Brown	60	Main junction to right hand head light	Blue	Red
20	Main beam warning light to dip switch	Blue	White	61	Main junction to right hand head light	Blue	White
21	Body junction to R.H. light junction	Red	Green	62	Junction right hand to dip switch	Blue	White
22	Instrument regulator to fuse A4	Green		63	Lighting switch to fuse A1	Brown	
23	Body junction to fuel gauge	Green	Black	64	Ignition coil to distributor	White	Black
24	Dash earth to flasher junction	Black		65	Stop light left hand to body junction	Green	Purple
26	Reversing light switch to body junction	Lt. Green	Brown	66	Stop light right hand to stop light left hand	Green	Purple
27	Reversing light left hand to body junction	Lt. Green	Brown	67	Tail light left hand to body junction	Red	Green
28	R.H. flasher to junction	Green	White	68	Tail light right hand to number plate light	Red	Green
29	Reversing light right hand to reversing light L.H.	Green	Brown	69	Tail light left hand to number plate light	Red	Green
30	Dip switch to head light main junction	Blue	Red	70	Rear flasher right hand to body junction	Green	White
31	Fuse A4 to flasher B	Green		71	Rear flasher left hand to body junction	Green	Red
32	Flasher junction to flasher L.	Lt. Green	Brown	72	Fuel tank to body junction	Green	Black
33	Door switch left hand to connector	Purple	White	73	Interior light to body junction	Purple	
34	Regulator B+ to fuse A1	Brown		74	Interior light to connector	Purple	White
35	Wiper motor to fuse A4	Green		75	Main junction to right hand side light	Red	
36	Horn to flasher junction	Purple	Black	76	Main junction to right hand head light	Black	
37	Body junction to flasher left hand front	Green	Red	77	Left hand flasher to junction	Green	Red
38	Body junction to flasher right hand front	Green	White	78	Heater motor to flasher	Green	
39	Stop light switch to body junction	Green	Purple	79	Right hand headlight to left hand headlight	Blue	Red
40	Flasher junction left hand to body junction	Green	Red	80	R.H. junction to L.H. junction	Red	Green
41	Flasher junction right hand to body junction	Green	White	81	Line fuse to splice 2	Red	Green
42	Body junction to line fuse	Red	Green	82	Splice 1 to panel earth	Black	
43	Fuse A4 to stop light switch	Green					

MOKE-SPECIAL EXPORT U.S.A.

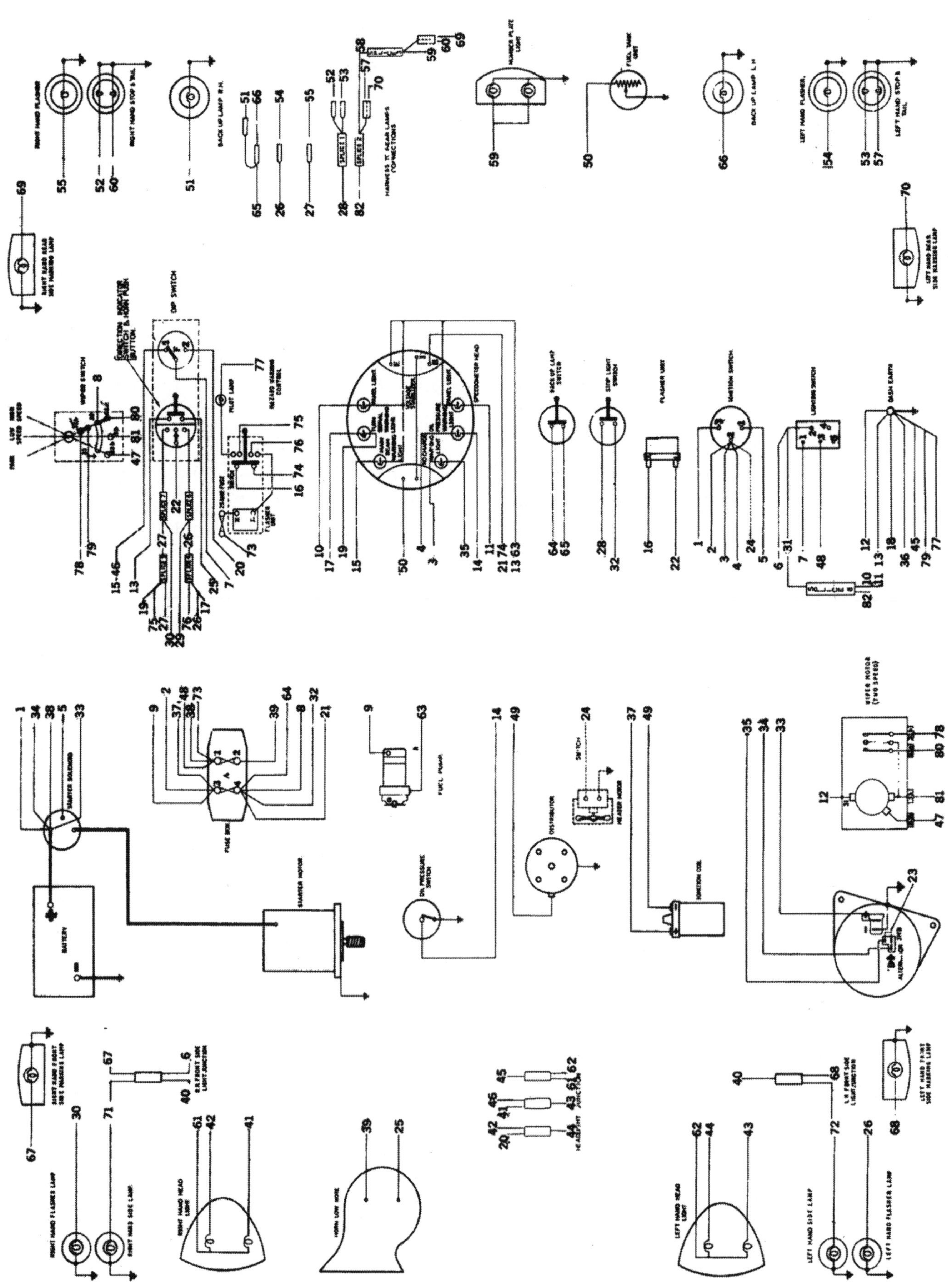

KEY TO WIRING DIAGRAM
MOKE SPECIAL EXPORT U.S.A.

Wire No.	Service	Colour Main	Colour Trace
1	Solenoid to ignition switch	Brown	
2	Ignition switch to fuse A3	White	
3	Ignition switch to no charge warning light	White	
4	Ignition switch to oil pressure warning light	White	
5	Ignition switch to starter solenoid	White	Red
6	Lighting switch to front side lights junction	Red	
7	Lighting switch to dip switch	Blue	
8	Fuse A4 to wiper switch 30	Green	
9	Fuse box A3 to fuel pump	White	
10	Splice 8 to panel light R/H	Red	White
11	Splice 8 to panel light L/H	Red	White
12	Dash earth to wiper motor	Black	
13	Dash earth to instrument earth	Black	
14	Oil pressure switch to oil pressure warning light	White	Brown
15	Main beam warning light to dip switch	Blue	White
16	Flasher unit to hazard control	Green	Brown
17	Splice 4 to flasher warning light	Green	Red
18	Dash earth to flasher junction	Black	
19	Splice 5 to flasher warning light	Lt. Green	White
20	Dip switch to headlight junction	Blue	Red
21	Fuse A4 to voltage stabilizer	Green	
22	Flasher junction to flasher L.	Lt. Green	Brown
23	Alternator indicator link	Brown	Yellow
24	Ignition switch to heater	Green	
25	Horn to flasher junction	Purple	Black
26	Splice 4 to flasher lamp connect. L.H.	Green	Red
27	Splice 5 to flasher lamp connect. R.H.	Green	White
28	Stop lamp switch to splice I	Green	Purple
29	Splice 6 to left hand flasher front	Green	Red
30	Splice 7 to right hand flasher front	Green	White
31	Splice 8 to light switch	Red	
32	Fuse A4 to stoplight switch	Green	
33	Starter solenoid to alternator positive	Brown	
34	Starter solenoid to alternator B÷	Brown	
35	Warning light to alternator ind.	Brown	Yellow
36			
37	Fuse A3 to ignition coil	White	
38	Fuse A1 to solenoid	Brown	
39	Fuse A2 to horn	Purple	
40	R/H side lamp junct. to L/H side lamp junct.	Red	
41	H/light junction to R/H headlight	Blue	White

Wire No.	Service	Colour Main	Colour Trace
42	H/light junction to R/H headlight	Blue	Red
43	H/light junction to L/H headlight	Blue	White
44	H/light junction to L/H headlight	Blue	Red
45	H/light junction to earth	Black	
46	H/light junction to dip switch	Blue	White
47	Wiper switch 53b to wiper motor 53b	Black	Green
48	Lighting switch to fuse A1	Brown	
49	Ignition coil to distributor	White	Black
50	Tank unit to fuel gauge	Red	Black
51	Harness connector to back-up lamp R/H	Green	Brown
52	R/H stoplight to splice 1	Green	Purple
53	L/H stoplight to splice 1	Green	Purple
54	L/H flasher lamp rear to connector	Green	Red
55	R/H flasher lamp rear to connector	Green	White
56			
57	Connector to left hand taillight	Red	
58	Splice II to Splice III	Red	
59	Number plate light to splice III	Red	
60	R/H tail lamp to connector	Red	
61	R/H headlamp to headlight junction	Black	
62	L/H headlamp to headlight junction	Black	
63	Fuel pump to mounting bracket earth	Black	
64	Fuse A4 to back-up lamp switch	Green	
65	Back-up light switch to connector	Green	Brown
66	Harness connec. to back-up lamp L.H.	Green	Brown
67	unction to R.H. front side marking lamp	Red	
68	Junction to L.H. front side marking lamp	Red	
69	R.H. rear side marking lamp to connector	Red	
70	L.H. rear side marking lamp to connector	Red	
71	Junction to R.H. front side lamp	Red	
72	Junction to L.H. front side lamp	Red	
73	Fuse A1 to hazard control	Purple	
74	Voltage stabilizer to hazard control	Green	Brown
75	Hazard control to splice 5	Green	White
76	Hazard control to splice 4	Green	Red
77	Hazard control to dash earth	Black	
78	Wiper switch 31b to wiper motor 31b	Black	Red
79	Wiper switch 31 to dash earth	Black	
80	Wiper switch 53a to wiper motor 53a	Blue	L/Green
81	Wiper switch 53 to wiper motor 53	Red	L/Green
82	Splice 8 to splice 2	Red	

SECTION r

BODY

The information contained in this section refers to Australian produced vehicles and it does not supersede Section R but should be used in conjunction with it.

Section r.1

DOORS AND HARDWARE

General

Early production Morris 850 vehicles were fitted with doors incorporating sliding window glasses and "slam-type" door locks. For details of these refer Section R.

Wind-up windows designed in Australia were introduced with the Mini Deluxe range and subsequently on all saloons and vans. Up to December, 1970, doors with wind-up windows incorporated "slam type" locks with remote control for inner handle.

With the introduction of vehicle design legislation "burst-proof" locks were designed. These are of the "disc type" and are fitted to all vehicles produced after December, 1970. Therefore, the information contained in Section Rb on locks and window mechanisms is not applicable.

Section r.2

INTERIOR DOOR FITTINGS

(Early models)

Removing

Remove the retaining screws and withdraw the door and window handles together with the fibre washers.

Refitting

To refit, reverse the above procedure. For maximum safety the door handles must be positioned pointing diagonally toward the rear lower door corner.

Section r3.

DOOR TRIM

(Early models)

Removing

1. Remove the door pocket trim by withdrawing the two retaining screws and then tilting and lifting the trim.
2. Remove the interior fittings as in Section r.1.
3. Remove the two screws and cup washers at the rear edge of the trim and release the two push-in clips at the forward end of the trim.

NOTE: Inner door panel apertures must be resealed with waterproof sealing tape, refer Section r.15.

During most operations, it is advisable to take precautionary measures to prevent parts falling into the door well.

Late models

Removing

1. Remove the window handle and washer.
2. Depress trim around the interior handle, and remove the two halves of the retainer from around the handle body.
3. Remove the P.K. screw from the rear of the panel.
4. Ease the two nylon snap clips out of their cups at the front of the panel.
5. Very carefully ease the trim out of the top channel and lift the base of the panel out of the tray.

Refitting

Refitting is a reversal of the above procedure.

Section r.4

DOOR LOCKING REMOTE CONTROL

Early models

Removing

1. Remove interior door fittings and door trim as in previous sections.
2. Remove the four screws retaining the remote control to the door panel and the two screws retaining the forward window channel.
3. Push the remote control into the door. Rotate 90° (forward and upward) to release it from the the remote control link. Remove assembly through vertical aperture in the forward section of door panel. Refer fig. r.1.

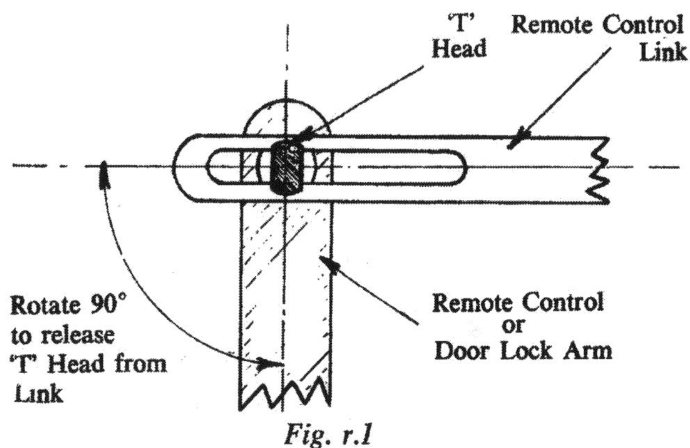

Fig. r.1

Showing method of releasing the remote control from the remote control link.

Refitting

To refit, reverse the above procedure.

Section r.5

INTERIOR DOOR HANDLES

Late models

Removing

1. Remove trim panel.
2. Remove the sealing tape at the door lock.
3. Disconnect the remote control rods by removing the rearmost nuts, and ensuring that the forward nuts do not move, thus retaining the adjustment positions.
4. Remove the screws securing the handle assembly and lift the assembly off.

Refitting

Refitting is a reversal of the above procedure. Retape.

Section r.6

VENTILATOR AND DROP GLASS

Removing

1. Wind down door drop glass. Remove interior door fittings and door trim as in previous sections.
2. Remove the two screws holding the window channel and the three screws holding the ventilator window in the top and forward section of the door.
3. Remove the rubber strip and bottom Bailey channel.

4. Sufficient Bailey channel must be removed from the top channel to allow the assembly to be tilted rearward before it can be lifted from the door.

   NOTE: Place strip of masking tape along top door channel to prevent damage to paint work.
5. The door drop glass may now be removed by tilting and lifting.

Refitting

To refit, reverse the above procedure.

Section r.7

VENTILATOR WINDOW (Inner frame assembly)

Removing

1. Remove the two P.K. screws securing the top pivot to the frame and the lower pivot nut, noting the position of the washers.
2. Lift out the inner frame assembly.

Refitting

To refit, reverse the above procedure.

Section r.8

WINDOW REGULATOR ASSEMBLY

Removing

1. Remove door drop glass as in previous sections.
2. Remove the four screws retaining the regulator to the door panel and the three screws retaining the auxiliary plate and lower assembly into door well.
3. Remove the window regulator assembly through the large vertical aperture in the forward section of the door panel. The regulator assembly should be in the folded position, i.e., to tooth stop.

Refitting

To refit, reverse the above procedure.

Section r.9

DOOR LOCKS

Early models

Removing

1. Remove interior fittings and trim pads as in previous sections.
2. Remove door drop glass as in Section r.4.
3. Using an Allen key, unscrew the interior lock button (left hand side only).
4. Drill out the pop rivets holding the reinforcing plate (early models) and remove sealing tape to gain access to the door lock assembly area.

   NOTE: Do NOT replace the pop rivetted reinforcing plate on early models. Seal aperature with sealing tape.
5. Withdraw the chrome plug. Remove the screw and tap out the lock shaft.
6. Remove the three door lock retaining screws. Push lock into door clear of the lock linkage and remove lock.

Refitting

To refit, reverse the above procedure.

Late models

Removing

1. Remove the trim panel.
2. Window should be right up.
3. Remove sealing tape around lock mechanism aperture.
4. Disconnect the return spring.
6. Remove the lock assembly.

Refitting

Refitting is a reversal of the above procedure. It will be necessary to adjust the lock on reassembly. (See Section r.14.)

Section r.10

EXTERIOR DOOR HANDLES

Early models

Removing

1. Remove door lock as in previous section.
2. Remove circlip retaining the lock linkage to the door handle shaft — insert a screwdriver through the lock shaft hole in the linkage, place under the circlip and twist.
3. Lever the linkage off the shaft and remove the waved washer and handle return spring.
4. Remove the three retaining screws and remove the handle assembly.

Refitting

Reverse the above procedure making sure that the door handle return spring arm is in the downward vertical position. Pre-load the spring by moving the spring arm through 90° to locate on the spacer under the forward securing screw.

To replace the circlip, steady the door (second operator assisting), insert screwdriver as before and press the lock linkage against the waved washer; fit ciclip.

NOTE: Door handle stop position — if this is other than horizontal slacken remote control retaining screws and turn the assembly until the handle assumes the correct stop position (it may be necessary to elongate holes in door panel).

Late models

Removing

1. Remove the trim panel.
2. Wind up the window and remove sealing tape.
3. Disconnect the lever from the outer handle to the bellcrank.
4. Remove the two nuts securing the handle assembly and lift the assembly off.

Refitting

Refitting is a reversal of the above procedure. In addition, a suitable sealer should be applied around the inner edge of the handle where it fits on to the door, and also after refitting the handle, the door lock adjustment should be checked and reset if necessary. Retape.

Section r.11

LOCKING BARRELS

Early models

Removing

1. Remove the door handle as in previous sections.

DISC DOOR LOCK ASSEMBLY

1. *Locking rod — door handle.*
2. *Bellcrank lever.*
3. *Handle assembly.*
4. *Bellcrank rod.*
5. *Bellcrank bracket.*
6. *Bolt, washer, nut.*
7. *Remote control rod — upper.*
8. *Slider.*
9. *Lock device.*
10. *Return spring.*
11. *Nut — rod adjusting.*
12. *Remote control case assembly.*
13. *Grommet.*
14. *Spring.*
16. *Lock assembly.*
17. *Screw — lock retaining.*
18. *Detail of clip to slider only.*
19. *Clip — to rod.*
20. *Plastic sleeve.*

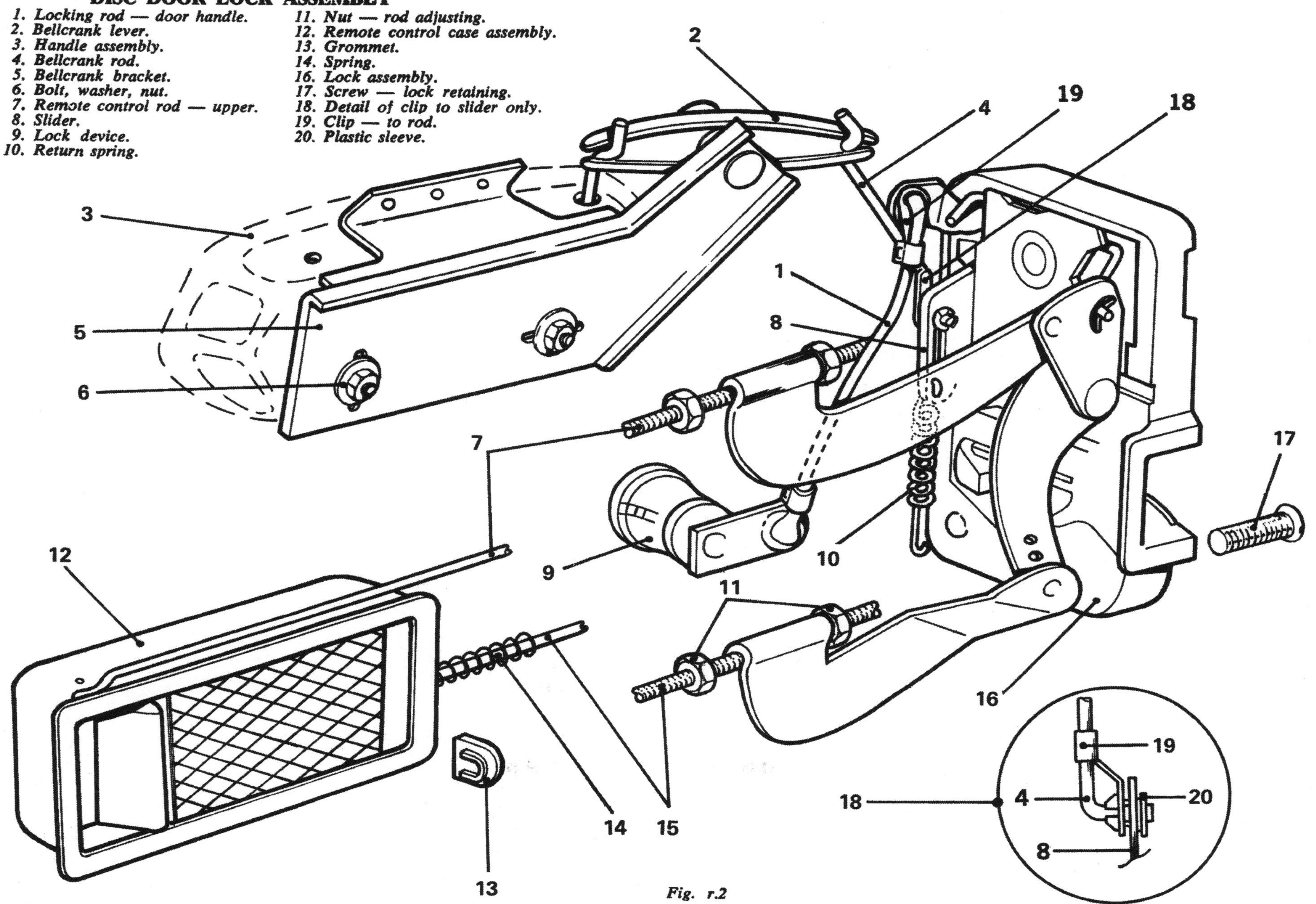

Fig. r.2

2. Remove door handle circlip (later models are fitted with a split pin) and waved washer. Withdraw the escutcheon.

Refitting

To refit, reverse the above procedure.

NOTE: If end float of the door handle is evident on early models, drill the shaft and fit a split pin to replace the circlip.

Late models

Removing

1. Remove the trim panel.
2. Remove sealing tape, wind windows right up.
3. Disconnect the rod from the exterior lock by slipping off the clip and easing the rod from the lever.
4. Compress the two spring clips retaining the lock and lift out.

Refitting

Refitting is a reversal of the above procedure but care should be taken to note that the rubber seal is in good order and in position. Retape.

Section r.12

DOORS

Removing

1. The doors may be removed either by releasing the hinge at forward or rear ends and disconnecting the door straps. The four front hinge nuts are accessible from underneath the front mudguard.
2. To remove the door without the hinges, remove the interior door fittings and the door trim pad.
3. Remove the rubber plug blanking the access hole for the bottom inner nut.
4. Remove the door remote control lock as in previous section and release top inner nut.
5. Remove the two outer hinge screws.

Refitting

To refit, reverse the above procedure.

Section r.13

DOOR ADJUSTMENTS

1. The door hinge mounting holes are elongated to provide adjustment of the door margins.
2. The correct door closing action can be obtained by vertical and lateral adjustment of the door buffer and striker plate.

Section r.14

ADUSTMENT OF DOOR LOCKS (Disc type)

Remove interior door fittings and trim.

Loosen the upper and lower remote connecting rod adjusting nuts to allow sufficient free play of all operating levers.

Rotate the disc to the door closed position and locate the bell crank bracket so that there is slight free play between the end of the vertical slot on the lock slide and the door handle locking rod to operating lever securing pin. **NOTE:** When tightening the two nuts securing the bracket and handle, ensure that the bracket does not move from the optimum adjustment position.

To check the adjustment, position the latch in the locked position and operate the outer handle to its maximum position. If the bellcrank rod jumps out of the end of the bellcrank, refit and adjust the bellcrank lever to allow more free play. Recheck the operation.

Attach the lower hook of the return spring into the tag provided in the lock reinforcement of the door panel.

With the disc still rotated to the door closed position, adjust the nuts on the lower remote control rod to grip the link while held hard towards the lock. Move the top link forward to the unlocked position, move the locking flap on the remote control to its forward position, adjust and tighten the nuts to grip the link in this position.

Operate the exterior handle and rotate the disc to the "door open" position and slam the door. Recheck all controls and adjust striker.

Refit the interior door fittings and trim.

Section r.15

WATER AND DUST SEALING

1. Rubber flap valves are fitted to the bottom of the door with the loose end facing rearward. (Fig. r.3). These valves operate by a difference in air pressure and close to prevent dust entry when the car is moving. Fig. r.3 also shows drain hole (B) for the door pocket. Early models only.

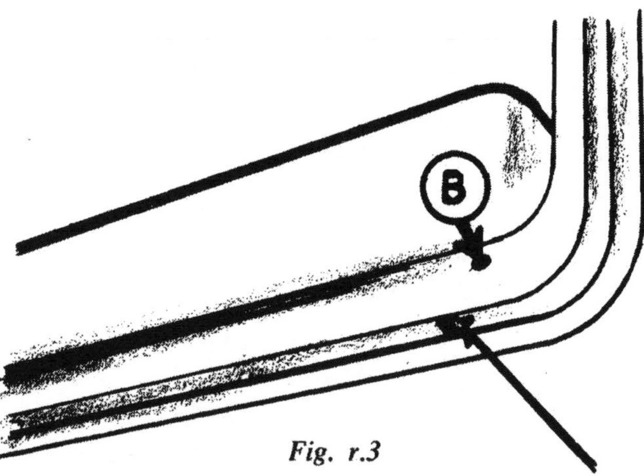

Fig. r.3

2. Water drain holes for the ventilator window are drilled at points "A" (Fig. r.3).
3. Apply 4" wide packaging tape (3M No. 250) to the inner door panel apertures to prevent water and dust entry (Fig. r.5).

NOTE: Should water or dust be apparent at the front and/or rear door pocket drain holes (refer Fig. r.3) the condition of the sealing tape should be checked.

Section r.16

WINDOW APERTURE DOOR FINISHERS

Removing

1. Lever off aperture finisher capping.
2. Tap along the top edge of the door aperture finisher with a rubber hammer until it springs off its locating edge.

Refitting

Apply a smear of Dri-lube to the window aperature frame and press the finisher home. Refit capping.

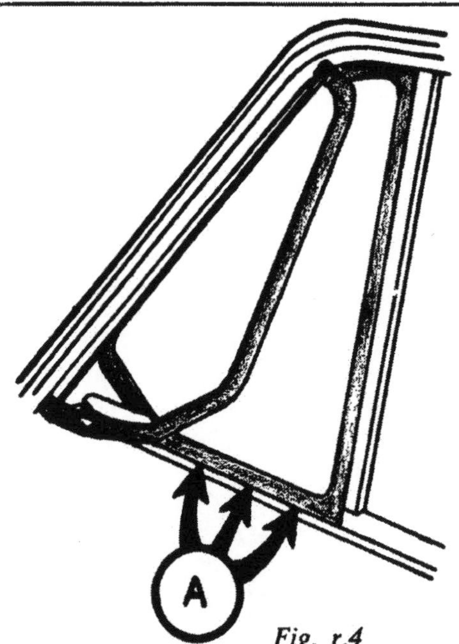

Fig. r.4
Arrows indicate water drainage holes drilled in vent window assembly.

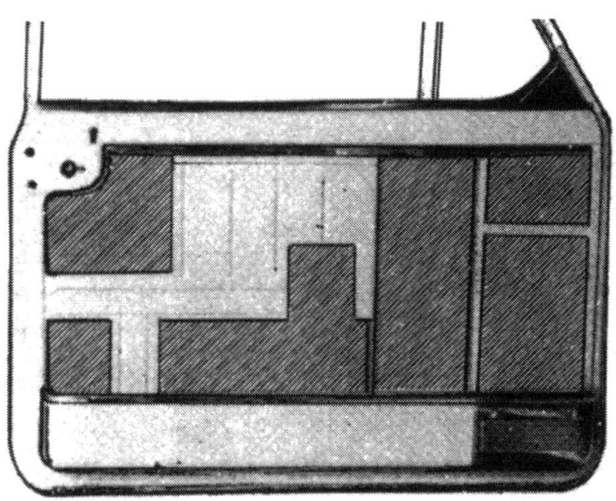

Fig. r.5
Shaded areas show sealing tape covering inner door panel apertures.

Section r.17

FRESH AIR HEATER (Mini Matic)

The heater fitted to the Mini Matic is an integral part of the cooling system. It is emphasised that the heater radiator continues to assist the normal radiator to dissipate engine heat, even when the heater control is in the "O" position. This vehicle, therefore, should not be operated with the heater disconnected from the cooling system.

Removing the heater

1. Disconnect the battery lead.
2. Drain the cooling system.
3. Disconnect the air supply base.
4. Disconnect the operating cable.
5. Disconnect the heater water hoses.
6. Remove the upper and lower bolts securing the the unit to the valance.
7. Remove the heater.

Removing the matrix from the heater

1. Remove the four self-tapping screws from the side cover and lift off the cover with the matrix attached.
2. Remove the grommets from the matrix tubes and lift out the matrix.

Refitting

To refit the unit is a reversal of the above procedure. Ensure that the cable length is adjusted to allow the control knob to be fully "home" when the heater control arm is at the end of the stroke.

Section r.18

FRESH AIR HEATER AND DEMISTER (1971 models)

Removing

1. Disconnect the battery.
2. Disconnect the heater hoses, collecting the water in a suitable drain tin.
3. Remove the front mats or carpets.
4. Release the control panel to gain access to the heater mounting bolts (where applicable).
5. Disconnect the heater electric wires and control cables.
6. Remove the heater unit.

Dismantling

7. Separate the two halves of the casing.
8. Remove the matrix.
9. Slide off the snap ring and remove the impellor.
10. Remove the motor.
11. Open the retaining tag on the heater control tap and remove the tap.

Refitting

Refitting is a reversal of the above procedure.

Section r.19

REAR SEAT BELT ANCHORAGE POINTS (Moke)

Provision has been made for the fitting of rear seat belts. The tapped attachment holes, fitted with screwed plastic blanking plugs, are located on the side walls of the body near the shock absorber upper mountings.

Section r.20

FASCIA TRIM PAD

Removing

1. Remove the trim panels either side of the instrument panel.
2. Remove the four nuts securing the panel of the body, and carefully remove the panel.

Refitting is a reversal of the above procedure.

Section r.21

WINDSCREEN GLASS AND SEALING RUBBERS (Mini Range and Cooper "S")

Two types of windscreen glasses are fitted to the Mini range of vehicles.

A laminated glass ¼" (6.35 mm.) thick is fitted to the Cooper range and a toughened glass 3/16" (4.76 mm.) thick is fitted to the balance of the range (except Moke). Different sealing rubbers are required for each type.

The glasses are interchangeable provided the appropriate sealing rubber is used. Replacement glasses should always be checked against the original before fitting is attempted.

Section r.22

VERTICAL ALIGNMENT CHECK DIAGRAM
(B.M.C. Moke 1098 c.c.)

(10" and 13" wheels unless otherwise stated.)

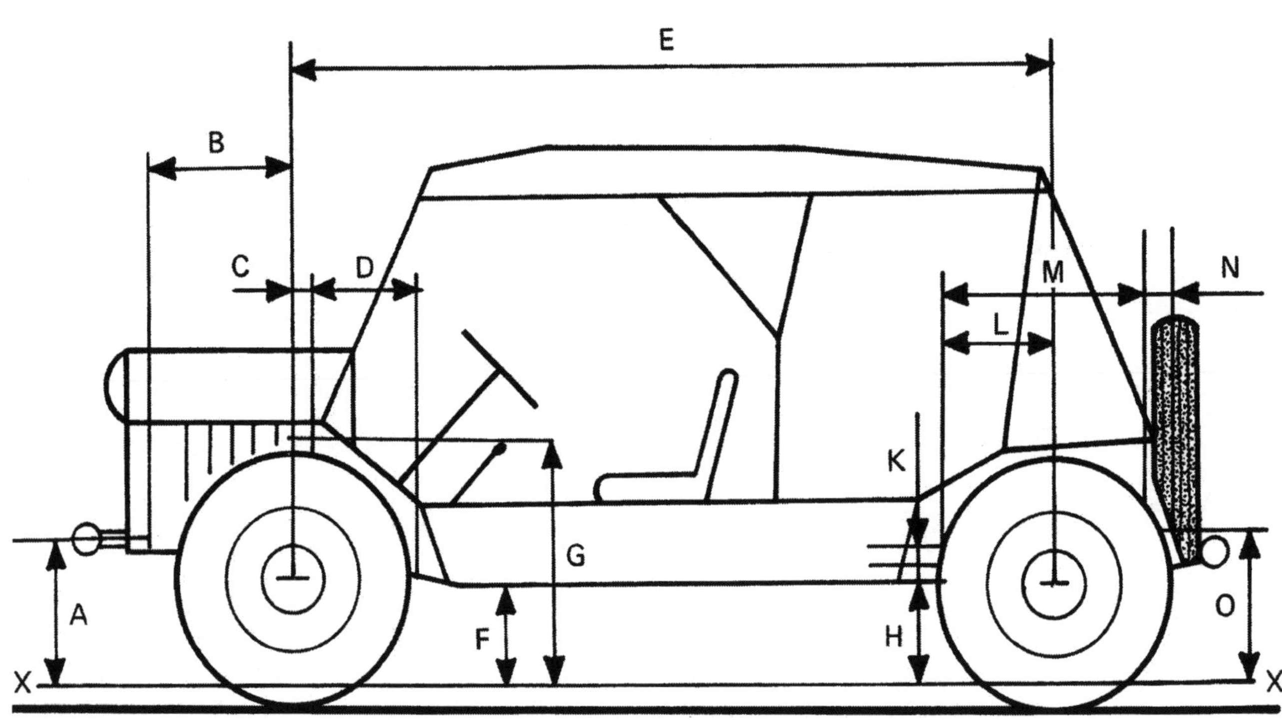

A. Front sub-frame mounting (front) from datum line "X". 10.81" (274.57 mm.)

B. Front sub-frame mounting (front) to wheel centre. 14.66" (372.36 mm.)

C. Wheel centre to tower mounting. 1.71" (45.97 mm.)

D. Front sub-frame mounting (tower) to front sub-frame mounting (extreme rear). 10.19" (258.80 mm.)

E. Wheel base.
- 10" wheels 80.00" (2030.00 mm.)
- 13" wheels 83.00" (2108.00 mm.)

F. Body sill to datum line "X". 6.83" (173.48 mm.)

G. Tower mounting (sub-frame) to datum line "X". 20.60" (66.04 mm.)

H. Lower rear sub-frame mounting (front) to datum line "X". 8.37" (212.59 mm.)

K. Mounting hole centres — rear sub-frame mounting (front). 2.25" (57.15 mm.)

L. Rear sub-frame mounting (front) — body face to wheel centre.
- 10" wheels. 14.37" (364.99 mm.)
- 13" wheels. 17.37" (441.19 mm.)

M. Rear sub-frame mounting (front) — body face to rear sub-frame mounting (rear) forward fixing hole. 23.50" (596.90 mm.)

N. Rear sub-frame mounting (rear) fixing hole centres. 2.25" (57.15 mm.)

O. Rear sub-frame mounting (rear) — body face to datum line "X". 12.89" (327.40 mm.)

SECTION s

SERVICE TOOLS

The Service Tools listed in this section have been developed to suit the methods for servicing vehicles as outlined in the Australian sections of the manual.

To assist in tool identification, the following is an explanation of tool number prefixes:

18G	Original tool (Section S).
18GA	Australian modified original tool.
18GAO	Australian designed tool.

The following list is supplementary to that shown in Section S and reference is made to the equivalent tool where applicable.

INDEX

	Part No.	Description	Page
Power unit	18GA 498	Engine lifting bracket	s-4
Engine	18GA 03	Crankshaft thread tap	s-2
	18GA 05	Gudgeon pin remover/replacer	s-2
	18GA 06	Gudgeon pin remover/replacer	s-2
Primary/Idler Gears/Clutch	18GA 01	Primary gear oil seal remover	s-2
	18GA 02	Primary gear oil seal replacer	s-2
	18GA 1043	Primary gear oil seal protector sleeve	s-2
	18GA 021	Idler gear bearing replacer	s-3
	18GA 304LX	Flywheel clutch and converter remover	s-4
Transmission and Final Drive	18GA 284	Impulse extractor	s-3
	18GA 613	Third motion shaft bearing remover	s-4
Automatic Transmission	18GA 08	Converter housing oil seal replacer	s-2
	18GA 010	Planetary pinion shaft extractor	s-3
	18GA 134 CN	Stator gear carrier oil seal replacer	s-3
Suspension	18GA 574	Front suspension rubber compressor	s-4
	18GA 146	Front and rear hub remover	s-3
Steering	18GA 580	Steering rack spanner and clamp	s-4

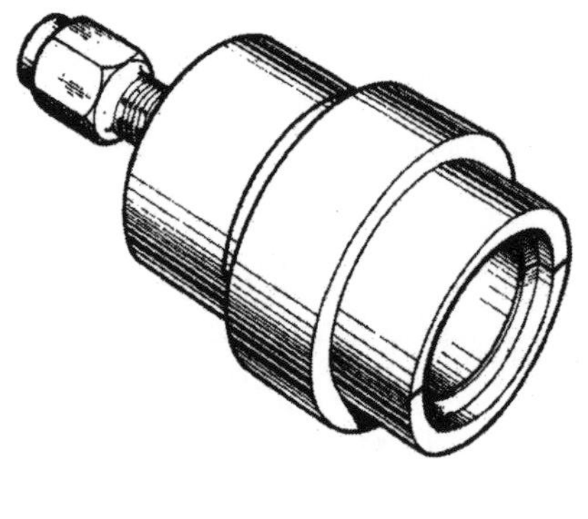

18GA01 — Primary gear oil seal remover
Used to withdraw the primary gear and oil seal with the power unit "in situ" as detailed in Section a.4, or with the power unit removed. Tool 18G1068 (Section S) can only be used with the power unit removed.

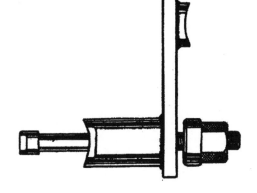

18GA05 — Gudgeon pin remover/replacer
Cooper 'S' only. Equivalent tool is 18G 1002. (Section S).

18GA02 — Primary gear oil seal replacer
This tool is used in conjunction with the flywheel screw to refit the oil seal with the power unit "in situ" or removed. Tools 18G 134 and 18G 134BC (Section S) cannot be used to replace the seal with the power unit "in situ".

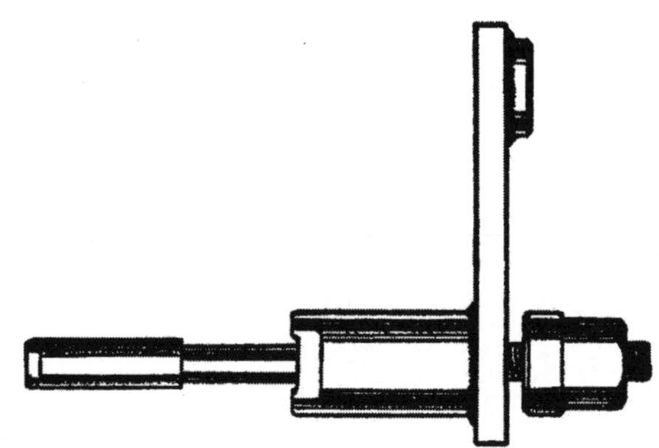

18GA06 — Gudgeon pin remover/replacer
This tool is necessary when removing and replacing press fit gudgeon pins installed in later Australian 998 c.c. engines as detailed in Section a.17.

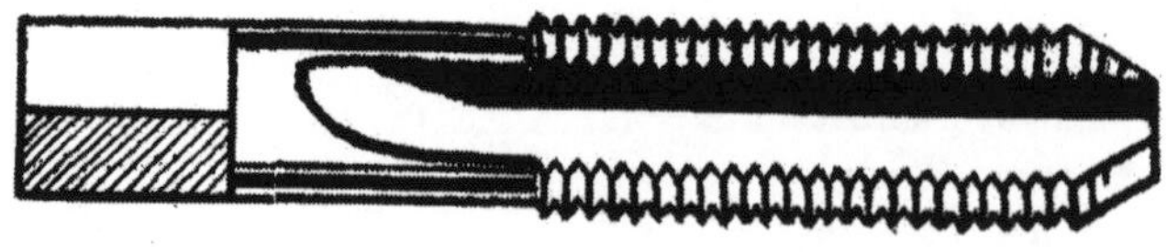

18GA03 — Crankshaft thread tap
Due to the non-standard thread in the flywheel end of the crankshaft, this tap is necessary to rectify slight thread damage.

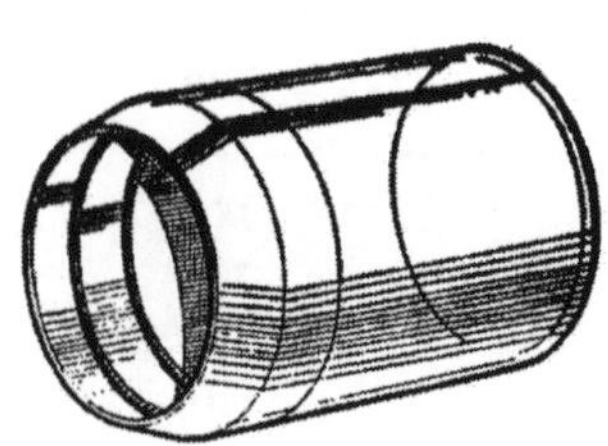

18GA 1043 — Primary gear oil seal protector sleeve

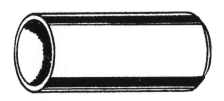

18GA 010 -- Planetary pinion shaft extractor

This tool is used in conjunction with one bolt from 18GA 304 LX to withdraw the planetary gear spindle from the gear train assembly. The equivalent tool 18G 284 AJ (Section S) is used with the impulse extractor 18GA 284 or 18G 284 (Section S).

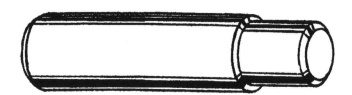

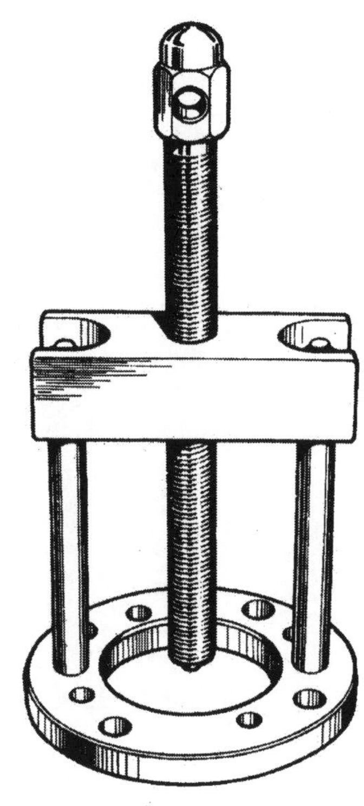

18GA 146 — Front and rear hub remover

18GA021 — Idler gear bearing-replacer

This tool can be used with both the 1 in. (25.4 mm.) and 1-1/16 in. (27.00 mm.) diameter idlear gear bearings and will replace the bearing in the flywheel or converter housing. The equivalent tool 18G 1126 (Section S) is used to replace only the 1-1/16 in. (27.00 mm.) diameter bearing.

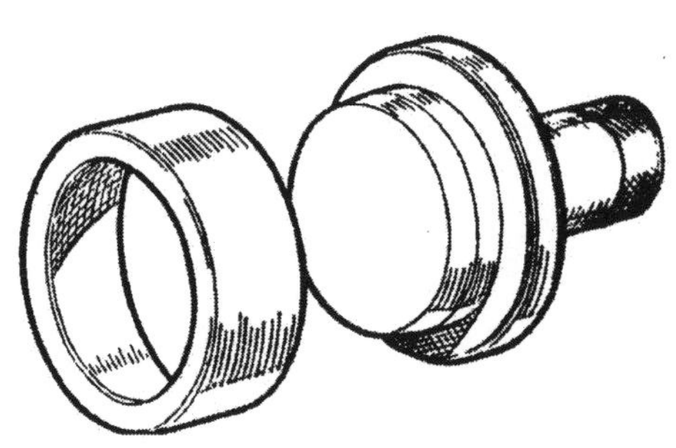

18GA 134 CN — Stator oil seal carrier replacer

18GA 284 — Impulse extractor

Includes heavy weight 18G 284 D.

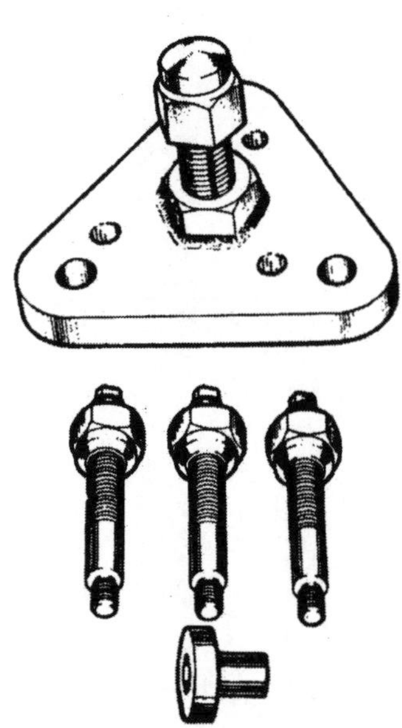

18GA 304 LX — Flywheel, clutch and converter remover

This tool can be used to remove the flywheel or torque converter with the power unit "in situ". 18G 304 and 18G 304M (Section S) are for manual transmission models and can only be used with the power unit removed.

This special peg spanner is essential for turning the locknuts on the steering rack ball joints. These locknuts have a ⅛" (3.18 mm.) dia. hole, but the spanner has been made stronger and more durable by incorporating a $\frac{3}{16}$" (4.77 mm.) peg. It will be necessary therefore to drill out the hole to $\frac{3}{16}$" (4.77 mm.) before using the spanner.

18GA 498 B — Engine lifting bracket

This tool is used to remove and replace the power unit.

18GA613 — Third motion shaft bearing remover
For use on three-speed synchromesh transmission only.

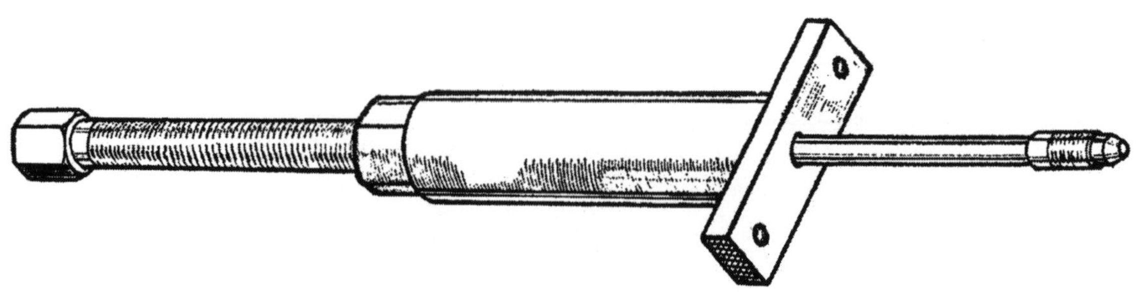

18GA 574 — Front suspension rubber compressor

SECTION T

EXHAUST EMISSION CONTROL — TESTING

This section deals with the testing of the Emission Control System fitted to MOKE engines in accordance with various territorial motor vehicle regulations.

Section T-1

EQUIPMENT

The recommended equipment for servicing should include at least the following:

Ignition Analyser Oscilloscope
Ohmmeter
Voltmeter
Tachometer
Vacuum Gauge
Pressure Gauge (0–10 lb./sq. in.)
Carburetter Balance Meter
Cam Angle Dwell Meter
Ignition Timing Light
Engine Exhaust Combustion Analyser
Cylinder Leak Tester
Distributor Advance Tester
Carburetter Piston Loading Tool

It is important that your test equipment has regular maintenance and calibration.

Section T-2

SERVICING

General

The efficient operation of the exhaust emission control system is dependent on the engine being in good mechanical condition and correctly tuned to the settings given in '**GENERAL DATA**'

Tuning and test procedure for the carburetters, ignition system, and engine are given at the end of the manual. These procedures are the quickest and surest way of locating engine faults or maladjustments and are the only methods that should be used for engine tuning.

Fault diagnosis

After tuning the engine to the correct settings, check for indications of the following symptoms:

Symptoms	Causes	Cure
Backfire in exhaust system	1. Leak in exhaust system	Locate and rectify leak
	2. Leaks in hoses or connections to gulp valve or vacuum sensing pipe	Locate and rectify leak
	3. Faulty gulp valve	Test gulp valve, and renew if faulty
	4. Leak in intake system	Locate and rectify leak
	5. High inlet manifold depression on over-run—faulty carburetter limit valve	Fit new throttle disc and limit valve assembly
Hesitation to accelerate after sudden throttle closure	1. Leaks in hoses or connections to gulp valve or vacuum sensing pipe	Locate and rectify leak
	2. Faulty gulp valve	Test gulp valve, and renew if faulty
	3. Leak in intake system	Locate and rectify leak
Engine surges (erratic operation at varying throttle openings)	1. Leaks in hoses or connections to gulp valve or vacuum sensing	Locate and rectify leak
	2. Faulty gulp valve	Test gulp valve, and renew if faulty
Erratic idling or stalling	1. Leaks in hoses or connections to gulp valve or vacuum sensing pipe	Locate and rectify leak
	2. Faulty gulp valve	Test gulp valve, and renew if faulty
	3. Carburetter limit valve not seating	Fit new throttle disc and limit valve assembly
Burned or baked hose between air pump and check valve	1. Faulty check valve	Test check valve, and renew if faulty
	2. Air pump not pumping	Test air pump, service or renew if faulty
Noisy air pump	1. Incorrect belt tension	Adjust belt tension
	2. Pulleys damaged, loose or misaligned	Tighten loose pulleys, renew damaged pulleys
	3. Air pump failing or seizing	Test air pump, service or renew if faulty

Symptom	Possible cause	Remedy
Excessive exhaust system temperature	1. Incorrect ignition timing	Recheck timing against **'GENERAL DATA'**
	2. Air injector missing	Remove air manifold and check injectors
	3. Air pump relief valve inoperative	Test relief valve and renew if faultv
Mixture requires enriching to obtain correct exhaust emission readings	1. Air leak into crankcase	Locate and rectify leak
	2. Early cars—Diaphragm of crankcase control valve perforated or not correctly seated	Locate and rectify leak or control valve
	Later cars—Crankcase breather hose or connections to carburetter leaking	Locate and rectify leak

EXHAUST EMISSION CONTROL — TESTING

ENGINE SPEED	TEST	COMPONENT CONDITION	READ/OBSERVE
START (cranking)	Cranking voltage	Battery; starting system	Voltmeter
	Cranking coil output	Coil and ignition circuit	Scope trace
	Positive crankcase ventilation/ cranking vacuum	Crankcase emission equipment	Vacuum gauge
IDLING (see 'GENERAL DATA')	Idle speed	Carburetter idle setting	Tachometer
	Dwell	Distributor/drive; points	Dwell meter; scope
	Initial timing	Spark timing setting	Timing light
	Fuel mixture	Carburetter setting	Exhaust gas analyser
	Manifold vacuum	Engine idle efficiency	Vacuum gauge
FAST IDLE (see 'GENERAL DATA')	Dwell variation	Distributor mechanical	Dwell meter
	Coil polarity	Ignition circuit polarity	Scope trace
	Cam lobe accuracy	Distributor cam	Scope trace
	Secondary circuit	Plugs; leads; cap; rotor	Scope trace
	Coil and condenser condition	Coil windings; condenser	Scope trace
	Breaker point condition	Points closing/opening/bounce	Scope trace
	Spark plug firing voltage	Fuel mixture; compression; plug/ rotor gaps	Scope trace
ACCELERATE—DECELERATE	Spark plugs under load	Spark plugs	Scope trace
	Carburetter open/close action	Carburetter	Exhaust gas analyser and vacuum gauge
TURNPIKE (Maximum ignition advance speed see 'GENERAL DATA'	Timing advance	Distributor mech./vacuum advance	Timing light/advance meter
	Maximum coil output	Coil; condenser; ignition primary	Scope trace
	Secondary circuit insulation	H.T. cables, cap, rotor	Scope trace
	Charging voltage	Regulator; cut-out	Voltmeter
	Fuel mixture	Air cleaner, carburetter	Exhaust gas analyser
	Exhaust restriction	Exhaust system	Vacuum gauge

READINGS	CHECK SEQUENCE—FAULT LOCATION
9·6 volts minimum at the battery	Battery—connections/cables—starter motor—dynamo/alternator—regulator
17 KV. minimum	Ignition coil
6—10 in. Hg (crankcase ventilation operating) 8—15 in. Hg (crankcase ventilation blanked)	Hoses and connections—Oil filler cap—Valve rocker clearance—Emission valve—Gulp valve—Oil separator—Servo (if fitted)—Inlet manifold leaks—Valves or seats—Piston rings—Any air leak to crankcase
See **'GENERAL DATA'**	Carburetter adjustment—Hoses and connections—Gulp valve—Servo (if fitted)—Carburetter limit valve or mechanical condition
4-cyl. : 57 to 63°; 6-cyl. : 34 to 37° See Pattern 1 (see inset A)	Breaker points—Distributor and drive mechanical condition
See **'GENERAL DATA'**	Distributor adjustment
See **'GENERAL DATA'**	Carburetter adjustment—Hoses and connections—Gulp valve—Crankcase emission valve—Servo (if fitted)—Carburetter limit valve or mechanical condition—Air pump—Check valve—Spark plugs
12 in. Hg minimum (engine fully run in)	Hoses and connections—Gulp valve—Inlet manifold leaks—carburetter limit valve—Valves or seats—Piston rings
Variation of 2° maximum	Distributor and drive mechanical condition
See Pattern 2 (Trace inverted)	Ignition circuit connections—Ignition coil
3° max. variation. See Pattern 3 (inset A correct; inset B—overlap indicates cam error)	Distributor mechanical condition (cam)
Standard pattern	Spark plugs and leads—Breaker points—Carburetter adjustment—Hoses and connections—Gulp valve—Servo (if fitted)
See Pattern 4 (lack of oscillations indicate fault)	Ignition coil—Condenser
See Pattern 1 (inset B)	Breaker points—Condenser
See Pattern 5; voltage 6—9 kV	Spark plugs and leads—Distributor cap and rotor—Carburetter adjustment (multi-carburetters)
See Pattern 6; acceptable voltage rise 6 to 10 kV	Spark plugs and leads
Initial rich, lean off at throttle closure	Carburetter limit valve and mechanical condition—Hoses and connections—Gulp valve—Air pump
See **'GENERAL DATA'**	Distributor mechanical condition, vacuum unit, centrifugal weights and springs
Standard pattern; minimum reserve $\frac{2}{3}$ more than requirement	Ignition coil—H.T. circuit insulation
Standard pattern	H.T. leads—Distributor cap and rotor
14·5 volts; steady reading	Cut-out—Voltage regulator—Dynamo/Alternator
Leaning off following peak when test speed is reached	Hoses and connections—Carburetter adjustment—Air cleaners—Gulp valve—Air pump—Check valve—Injectors
No variation in reading at constant speed for 10 sec.	Exhaust system

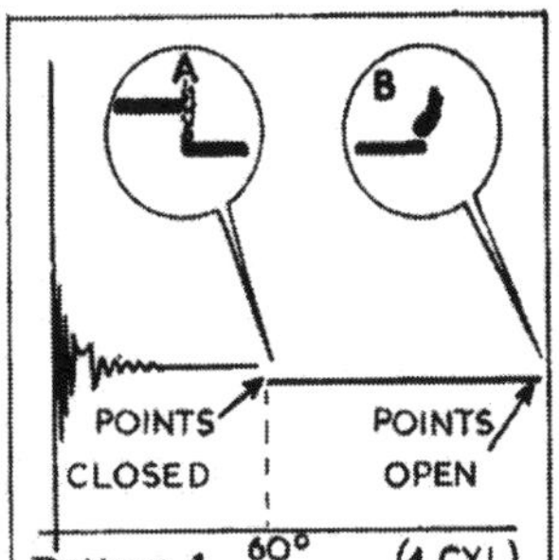

Pattern 1

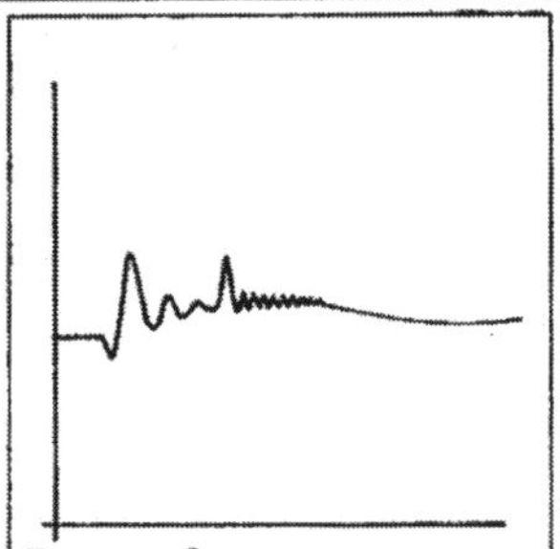

Pattern 2

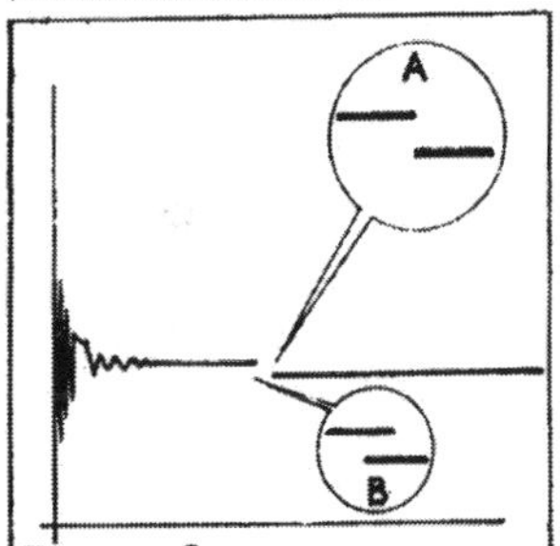

Pattern 3

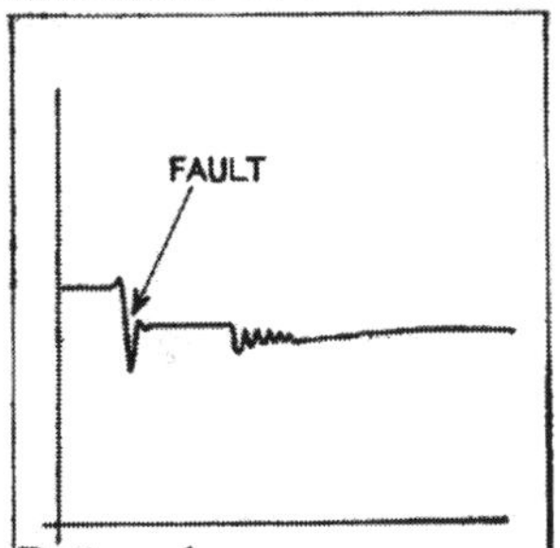

Pattern 4

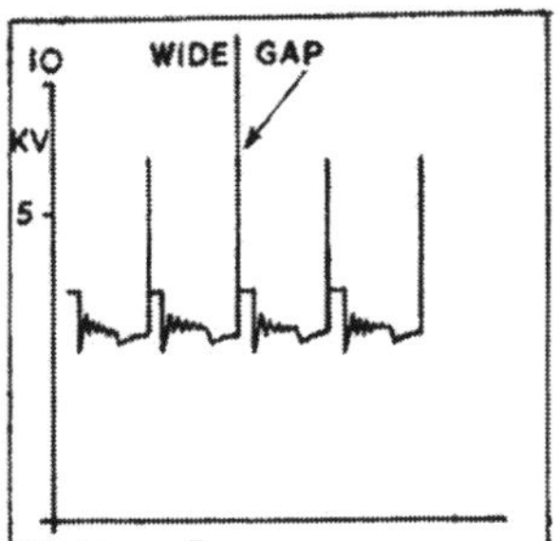

Pattern 5

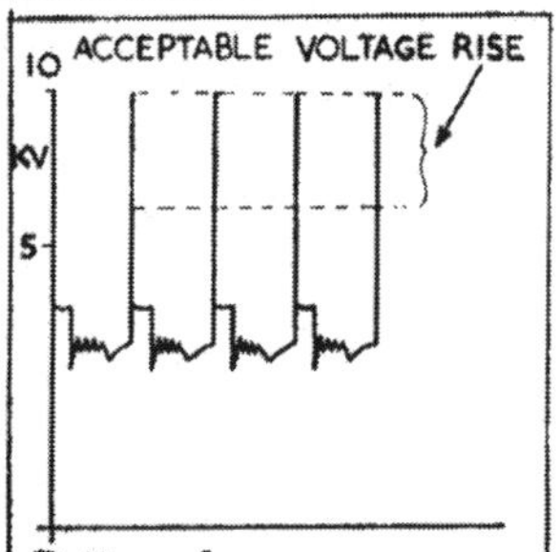

Pattern 6

D0478B

GENERAL DATA

The following specifications are for the Leyland 998cc Mini range of vehicles and more comprehensive information can be obtained by referring to the earlier General Data Section.

	EMISSION CONTROL (ADR 27A) MODELS	LEYLAND MINI	LEYLAND MINI 'S'	MINI VAN	MOKE	MOKE PICK-UP
ENGINE						
Engine type	99H	99H	—	—	—	—
Bore	64.58 mm	64.58 mm (2.543 in)	—	—	—	—
Stroke	76.2 mm	76.2 mm (3.00 in)	—	—	—	—
No. of cylinders	4	4	—	—	—	—
Capacity	.998 Litre	.998 litres (60.96 in³)	—	—	—	—
Compression ratio	8.3:1	8.2:1	—	—	—	—
R.A.C. Rating	7.7 kw	7.7 kW (10.3 H.P.)	—	—	—	—
Max. power Gross	30 kW @ 5100 rpm	30 kw (40 bhp) @ 5100 rpm	—	—	—	—
Torque Gross	69 Nm @ 2600 rpm	69 Nm (51 lbf.ft) @ 2600 rpm	—	—	—	—
Firing order	1.3.4.2.	1.3.4.2.	—	—	—	—
Valve rocker clearance	.30 mm	.305 mm (.012 in)	—	—	—	—
Oil pressure - Normal	2.8 to 4.2 kg/cm²					
Idling	1.0 to 4.2 kg/cm²					
IGNITION						
Contract breaker gap	.36 to .40 mm	.35 to .40 mm (.014 to .016 in)	—	—	—	—
Dwell angle	51° ± 5°	51° ± 5°	—	—	—	—
Spark plugs	Champion N9Y	Champion N9Y	—	—	—	—
Spark plug gap	.60 mm	.65 mm (.025 in)	—	—	—	—
Timing Stroboscopic **Vacuum line disconnected**	8° BTDC @ 1500 rpm	7° BTDC @ 1000 rpm	—	—	—	—
FUEL SYSTEM						
Pump	SU Mechanical	SU Mechanical	—	—	—	—
Carburetter	SU Type HS4	SU Type HS4	—	—	—	—
Needle (Std)	ADF	ABX	—	—	—	—
Spring	Red	Red	—	—	—	—
Idle Speed	750 - 950 rpm	750 rpm	—	—	—	—
CO at idle with air injection disconnected	5½% ± 1%	4%	—	—	—	—
Recommended fuel octane rating	98	98				
TRANSMISSION						
Overall gear ratios:						
First	12.13:1	12.13:1	—	—	15.0:1	—
Second	7.63:1	7.63:1	—	—	9.41:1	—
Third	4.93:1	4.93:1	—	—	6.09:1	—
Fourth	3.44:1	3.44:1	—	—	4.26:1	—
Reverse	12.19:1	12.19:1	—	—	15.08:1	—
Road speed at 1000 rpm in top gear	26.5 km/h	25.7 km/h (16 mph)	—	—		—

— **Denotes common to model listed in preceding column**

	LEYLAND MINI	LEYLAND MINI 'S'	MINI VAN	MOKE	MOKE PICK-UP
WHEELS AND TYRES					
Wheel size	3.50 Bx10	4.50 jx10	3.50 Bx10	4.50J x 13	--
Tyre size	5.95 L10 Cross Ply	145-R-10 Radial Ply	5.95 L10 Cross Ply	5.60 x 13 x 4 ply	--
Tyre pressures					
Normal conditions: Front	165 kPa (24 psi)	192 kPa (28 psi)	165 kPa (24 psi)	152 kPa (22 psi)	--
Rear	165 kPa (24 psi)	180 kPa (26 psi)	165 kPa (24 psi)	138 kPa (20 psi)	--
Full load: Front	165 kPa (24 psi)	192 kPa (28 psi)	165 kPa (24 psi)		
Rear	180 kPa (26 psi)	180 kPa (26 psi)	180 kPa (26 psi)		
ELECTRICAL					
Battery: Type	Lucas 12V-40 Ah 20 hour rate	--	--	--	--
Polarity	Negative earth	--	--	--	--
Fuse: Main	35 Amp blow rating	--	--	--	--
Line	15 Amp blow rating	--	--	--	--
DIMENSIONS					
Track: Front	1.205 m (47 7/16 in)	1.45 m (49¼ in)	1.205 m (47 7/16 in)	1.447 m (49 in)	--
Rear	1.164 m (45⅝ in)	1.210 m (47 11/16 in)	1.164 m (45⅞ in)	1.466 m (49¾ in)	--
Turning circle	9.45 m (31 ft)	9.45 m (31 ft)	9.98 m (32 ft 9 in)	9.754 m (32 ft)	--
Front Wheel Alignment	1.16 mm 1/16 in (toe out)	--	--	--	--
Wheelbase	2.03 m (6 ft 8 in)	2.03 m (6 ft 8 in)	2.138 m (7 ft 0 5/32 in)	2.095 m (6 ft 10½ in)	--
Overall length	3.13 m (10ft 5¼ in)	3.13 m (10 ft 5¼ in)	3.426 m (11 ft 2⅞ in)	3.232 m (10 ft 7¼ in)	3.663 m (12 ft)
width	1.41 m (4 ft 7½ in)	1.538 m (4 ft 8⅝ in)	1.41 m (4 ft 7½ in)	1.45 m (4 ft 9 in)	1.511 m (5 ft)
height	1.35 m (4 ft 5 in)	1.35 m (4 ft 5 in)	1.38 m (4 ft 6½ in)	1.60 m (5 ft 3 in)	1.739 m (5 ft 8 in)
Ground clearance	165 mm (6½ in)	--	--	203 mm (8 in)	--
CAPACITIES					
Fuel tank	24 litres (5¼ gals)	--	26 litres (5¾ gals)	28.4 litres (6¼ gals)	--
Engine including filter	4.83 litres (8½ pts)	--	--	--	--
Filter	0.42 litre (¾ pt)	--	--	--	--
Cooling system	3.55 litres (6¼ pts)	--	--	--	--
WEIGHTS					
Registration weight including 9.1 litre (2 gals) fuel	643 kg (1414 lbs)	668 kg (1470 lbs)	637 kg (1401 lbs)	611 kg (1344 lbs)	696 kg (1531 lbs)
G.V.W.	975 kg (2145 lbs)	1000 kg (2200 lbs)	996 kg (2191 lbs)	991 kg (2180 lbs)	996 kg (2191 lbs)
G.C.W. gross combination	1200 kg (2640 lbs)	--	--	--	--
Roof rack load	25 kg (55 lbs)	--	--		
Towing weight Max.	400 kg (880 lbs)	--	--	--	--
Trailer hitch load	30-50 kg (66-110 lbs)	--	--	--	--
Rated pay load				300 kg (660 lbs)	220 kg (484 lbs)

-- Denotes common to model listed in preceding column

EVAPORATIVE LOSS CONTROL

(To be read in conjunction with Section Dc-4)

MAINTENANCE

Vapour Storage Canister

It is recommended that the air filter fitted in the bottom section of the canister be renewed every 20,000 km (12,000 miles) or more frequently in dusty conditions.

Method

1. Disconnect the air vent tube from the bottom of the canister.
2. Unscrew the securing clip screw and lift out the canister.
3. Unscrew the lower end cap of the canister.
4. Remove and discard the filter pad.
5. Clean any dirt from the cap.
6. Fit the new filter pad and refit the cap.
7. Refit the canister ensuring that the purge pipe (from the engine rocker cover) is connected to the large centre connection on the top of the canister.

NOTE: DO NOT attempt to remove the retainer and gauze, as this causes spillage of the loose granules. The filter pad at the top of the canister is non-serviceable.

The complete canister must be renewed every 40,000 km (24,000 miles) or sooner should it inadvertently become saturated with liquid.

Leak Testing

Should a fault in the operation of the system be suspected or components other than the air filters or canister have been removed and refitted, the Evaporative Loss Control system must be pressure tested for leaks using the following procedure:

1. Check that there is at least 1 gallon of fuel in the tank.
2. Disconnect the underbody vapour pipe hose from the canister and connect a low pressure air supply and manometer.
3. Very slowly apply pressure to the system until 12 in of water is shown on the manometer. Check that the reading does not fall below 7 in of water in 10 seconds. If the reading is not maintained, check the system starting with the fuel tank filler cap and seal.
4. Remove the fuel filler cap and check that the pressure gauge returns to zero.

WARNING: The air pressure required for leak testing is extremely low and should be preferably supplied by a hand pump producing no more than approximately 7 kPa (1 psi). The 12 in of water shown in the manometer is the equivalent of 2.983 kPa (0.433 psi).

CAUTION: Should it become necessary to clear a blocked fuel line between the fuel pump and fuel tank, by using air pressure, it is essential to remove the sealed fuel tank filler cap to avoid pressurising the Evaporative Loss Control system.

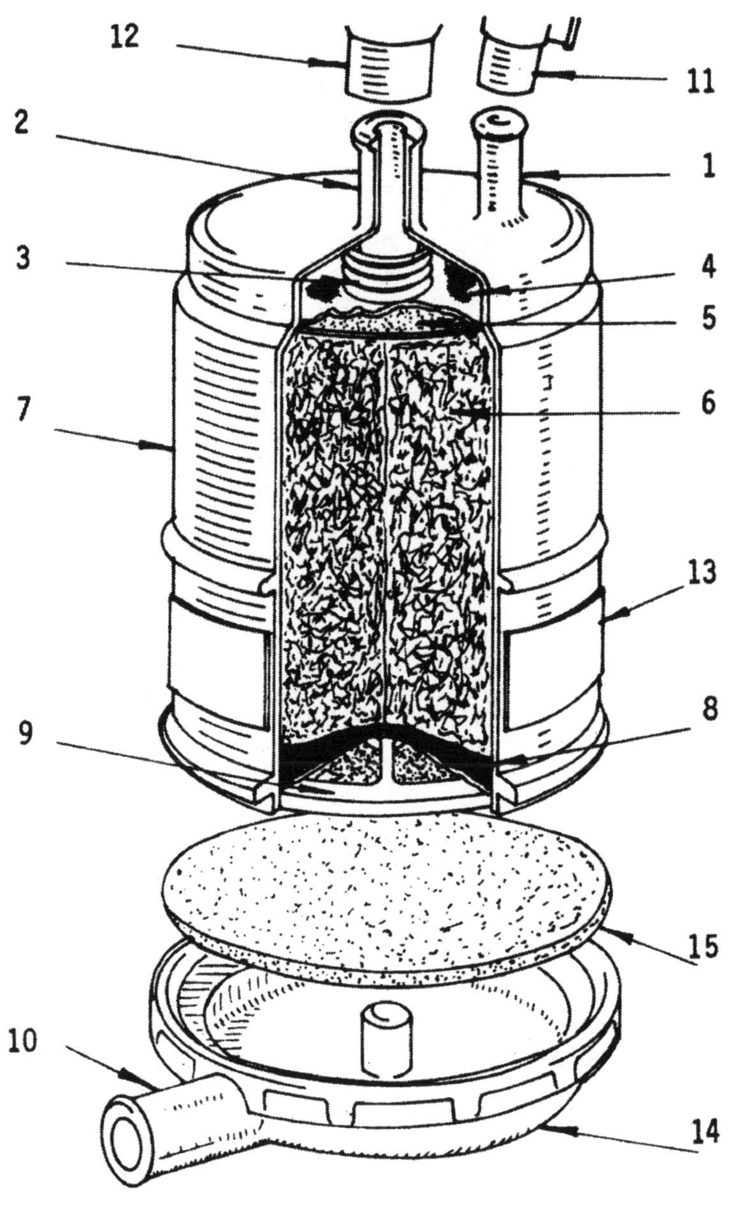

Fig. 1

VAPOUR STORAGE CANISTER & CONNECTIONS:

1. Vapour Pipe Connection
2. Purge Pipe Connection
3. Spring
4. Gauze
5. Filter Pad
6. Charcoal Granules
7. Canister
8. Gauze
9. Retainer
10. Air Vent Connection
11. Vapour Pipe
12. Purge Pipe
13. Canister Securing Clip
14. End Cap
15. Air Filter Pad

WIRING DIAGRAM
Leyland Moke and Pick-up

Wire No.	Service	Colour Main	Colour Trace
1	Starter solenoid to ignition switch	Brown	
2	Splice 1 to l.h. rear flasher	Green	Red
3	Splice 2 to r.h. rear flasher	Green	White
4	Starter solenoid to alternator	Brown	
5	Alternator to no charge warning light	Brown	Yellow
6	Fuse box to back up lamp switch	Green	
7	Ignition switch to starter solenoid	White	Red
8	Splice 7 to no charge warning light	White	
9	Splice 7 to ignition coil	White	
10	Flasher junction to earth	Black	
11	Splice 7 to oil pressure warning light	White	
12	Oil pressure warning light to oil pressure sw.	White	Brown
13	Reverse lamp switch to reverse lamp	Green	Brown
14	Alternator sensing lead	Brown	Blue
15	Ignition switch to fuse A3	White	
16	Starter solenoid to fuse A1	Brown	
17	Fuse A4 to wiper switch	Green	
18	Wiper motor to wiper switch	Black	Green
19	Wiper motor to earth	Black	
20	Fuse A4 to stop light switch	Green	
21	Fuse A4 to flasher unit B	Green	
22	Flasher unit B to instrument voltage stabilizer	Green	
23	Fuel gauge to tank unit	Green	Black
24	Stop light switch to splice 6	Green	Purple
25	Flasher unit L to flasher switch	Lt. Green	Brown
26	Flasher unit P to flasher warning light	Lt. Green	Purple
27	Flasher switch to splice 1	Green	Red
28	Flasher switch to splice 2	Green	White
29	Splice 1 to flasher light left-hand	Green	Red
30	Splice 2 to flasher light right-hand	Green	White
31	Starter solenoid to lighting switch	Brown	
32	Lighting switch to dip switch	Blue	
33	Dip switch to main beam warning light	Blue	White
34	Dip switch to headlight	Blue	White
35	Dip switch to headlight	Blue	Red
36	Headlight to earth	Black	
37	Splice 5 to panel light left-hand	Red	
38	Splice 5 to panel light right-hand	Red	
39	Lighting switch to parking light right-hand	Red	
40	Lighting switch to splice 5	Red	
41	Park light right hand to park light left-hand	Red	
42	Fuse A2 to horn	Purple	
43	Horn to flasher switch junction	Purple	Black
44	Splice 5 to splice 3	Red	
45	Splice 4 to tail light right-hand	Red	
46	Splice 4 to number plate light	Red	
47	Splice 3 to splice 4	Red	
48	Splice 6 to stop light left-hand	Green	Purple
49	Splice 6 to stop light right-hand	Green	Purple
50	Splice 3 to tail light left-hand	Red	
52	Splice 7 to ignition switch	White	Orange
53	Head lamp l.h. to junction	Blue	Red
54	Head lamp r.h. to junction	Blue	White
55	Head lamp l.h. to junction	Blue	White
56	Head lamp r.h. to earth	Black	
57	Head lamp l.h. to earth	Black	
58	Distributor to ign. coil	Black	
59	Ign. switch to heater switch	Green	
60	Headlamp r.h. to junction	Blue	Red
61	Wiper sw. 31B to wiper motor 31B	Black	Red
62	Wiper sw. 53A to wiper motor 53A	Blue	Lt. Green
63	Wiper sw. 53 to wiper motor 53	Red	Lt. Green
64	Wiper sw. 31 to body earth	Black	
65	Fuse box to washer motor	Green	
66	Washer motor to washer sw.	Lt. Green	Black
67	Wiper sw. to washer sw.	Black	

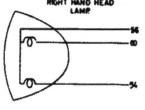

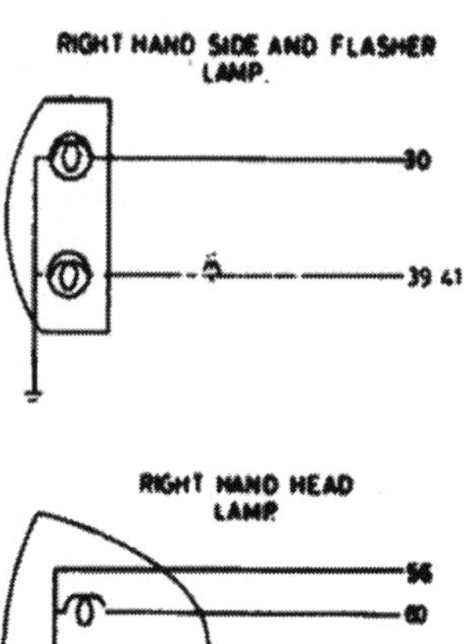

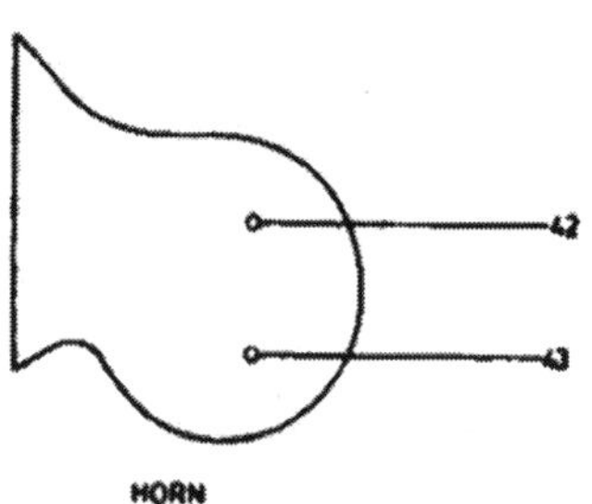

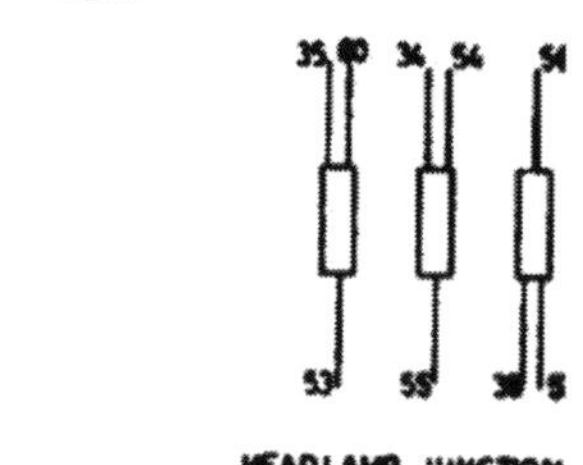

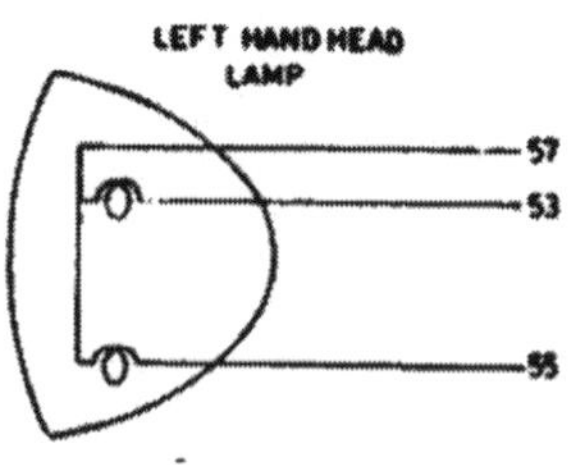

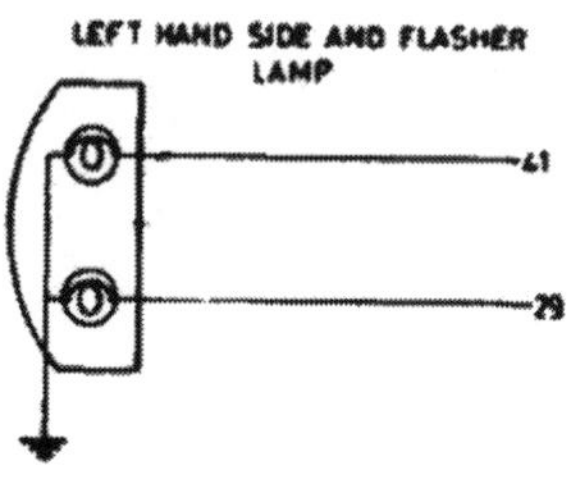

ELECTRICAL

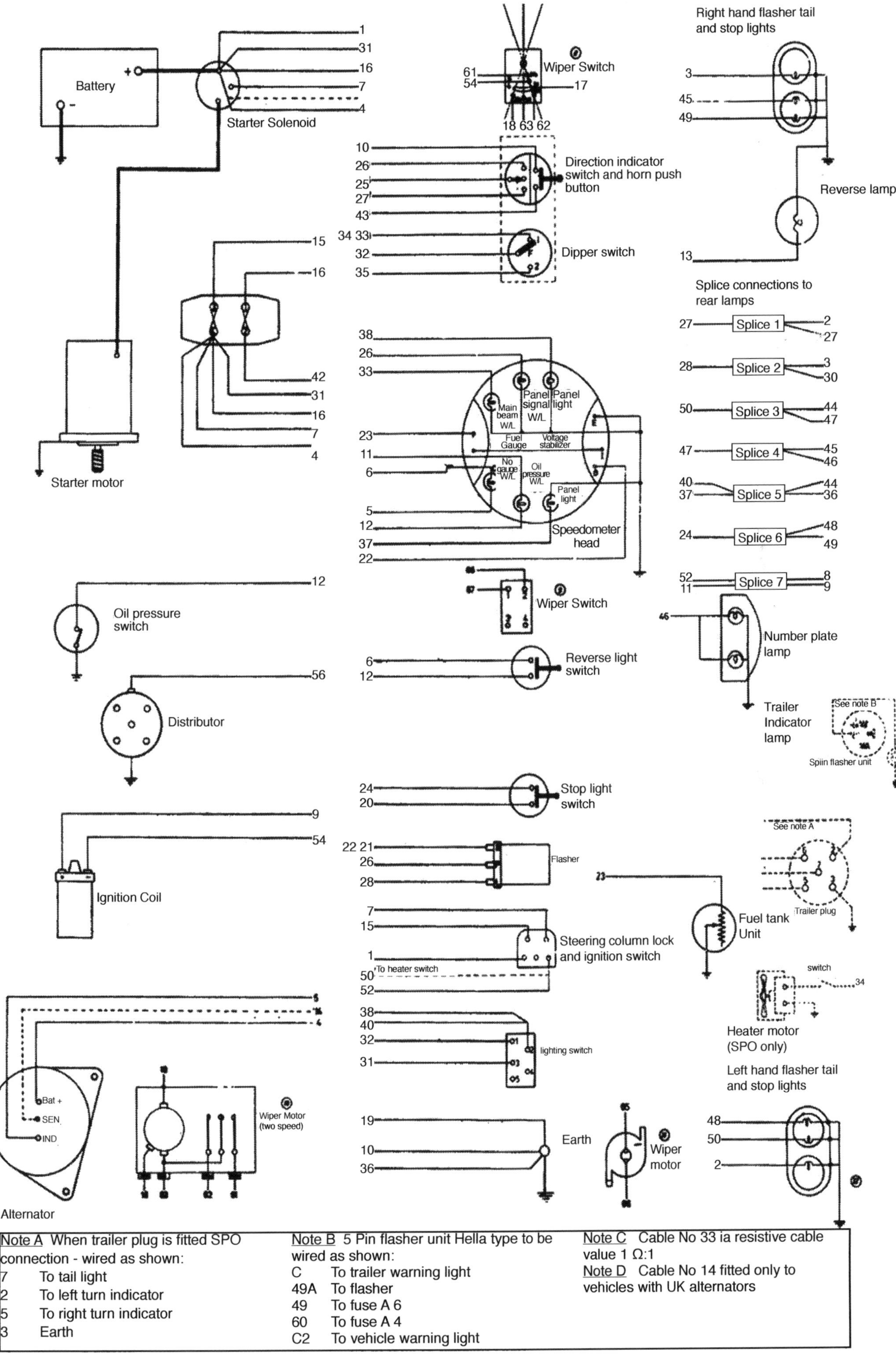

Note A When trailer plug is fitted SPO connection - wired as shown:
7 To tail light
2 To left turn indicator
5 To right turn indicator
3 Earth

Note B 5 Pin flasher unit Hella type to be wired as shown:
C To trailer warning light
49A To flasher
49 To fuse A 6
60 To fuse A 4
C2 To vehicle warning light

Note C Cable No 33 ia resistive cable value 1 Ω:1

Note D Cable No 14 fitted only to vehicles with UK alternators

GENERAL DESCRIPTION

This section gives a general description of the crankcase, exhaust and fuel evaporative emission control systems fitted to this vehicle and the function of their individual components. It must be emphasized that correct carburetter adjustment and ignition timing which have been pre-set at the factory are essential for the efficient functioning of the exhaust emission controls. Should it become necessary to check or adjust these settings this work should be carried out by an authorised Dealer who has the specialist equipment and training to undertake these adjustments.

Crankcase Emission Control

The engine crankcase breather outlet incorporates an oil separator flame-trap (arrester) attached to the cylinder block side cover which is connected by hose to the controlled depression chamber between the piston and the throttle disc of the carburetter. Piston blow-by fumes are drawn into the depression chamber of the carburetter from the side cover and are joined by purged air from the charcoal canister of the fuel evaporative loss system. These fumes combine with the inlet charge for combustion in the normal way.

Mini Saloon

The capacity of the fuel tank is limited by the position of the filler tube which ensures sufficient volume is available after filling to accommodate fuel which would otherwise be displaced as a result of a high temperature rise.

Mini Van

A capacity limiter, with open bottom and a restricted bleedhole in the top, is fitted within the main tank. After the tank has been apparently filled, air and vapour trapped in the capacity limiter can slowly escape through the bleedhole into the top of the main tank, lowering the fuel level so that the outlet of the tank vent is not submerged after thermal expansion has taken place. The separator removes liquid fuel trapped in the vapour line during filling operations etc. for return to the tank under gravity during normal running conditions. The fuel tank filler, is sealed by a non-vented pressure cap.

Fuel Evaporative Loss Control

To prevent air pollution by vapours from the fuel tank and float chamber the control equipment stores the vapour in a charcoal-filled canister while the engine is stopped and disposes of it via the engine crankcase èmission control system when the engine is running. The fuel tank venting is designed to ensure that no liquid fuel is carried to the storage canister with the vapours and that vapours are vented through the control system.

THE LAYOUT OF THE FUEL EVAPORATIVE LOSS CONTROL SYSTEM
Car and Van (Inset)

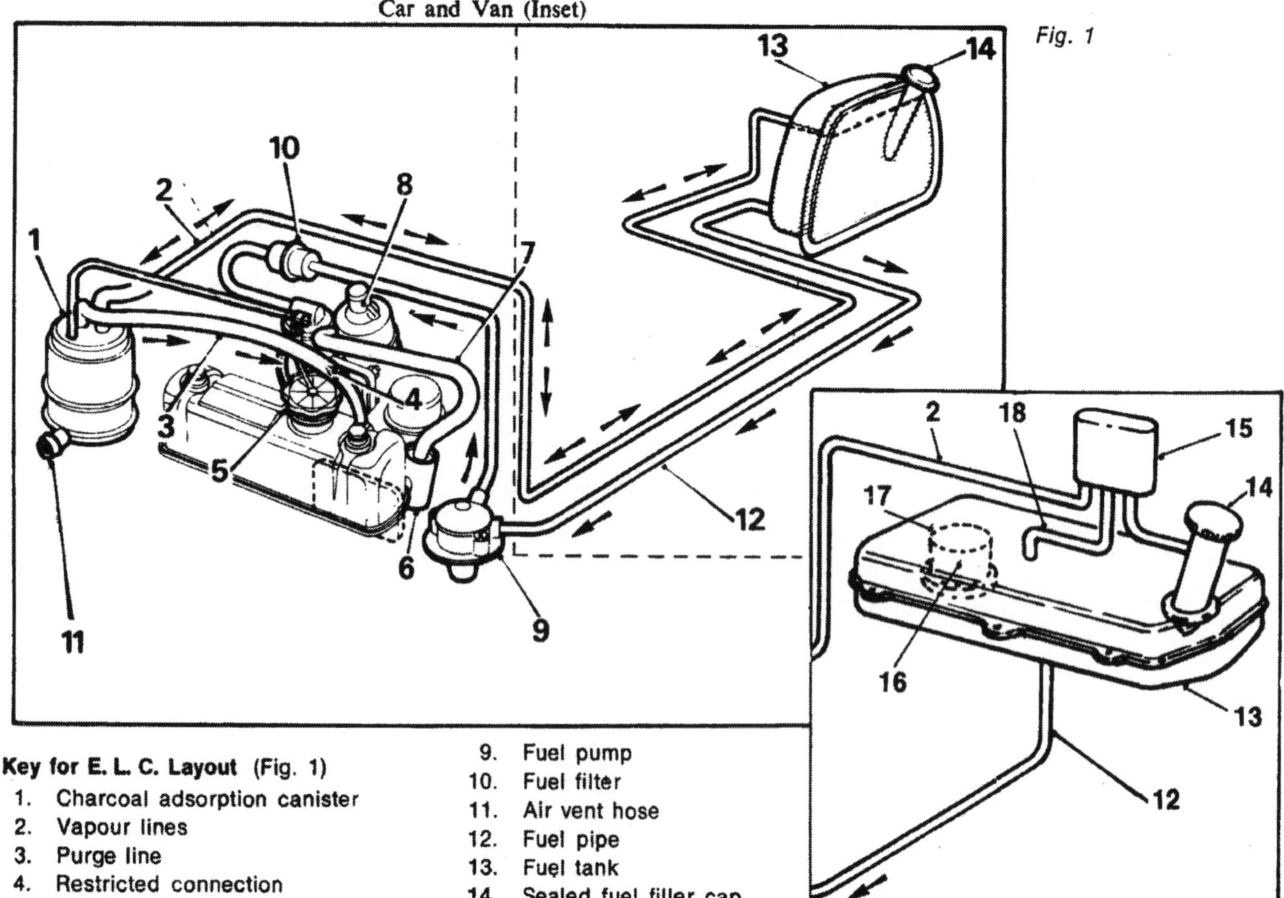

Fig. 1

Key for E. L. C. Layout (Fig. 1)

1. Charcoal adsorption canister
2. Vapour lines
3. Purge line
4. Restricted connection
5. Sealed oil filler cap
6. Oil seperator/flame trap (arrester)
7. Crankcase purge pipe
8. Carburetter
9. Fuel pump
10. Fuel filter
11. Air vent hose
12. Fuel pipe
13. Fuel tank
14. Sealed fuel filler cap
15. Vapour seperator (Van)
16. Capacity limiter (Van)
17. Capacity limiter bleed hole (Van)
18. Tank vent to vapour seperator pipe (Van)

APPENDIX - EMISSION CONTROL (ADR 27A)

THE EMISSION CONTROL COMPONENTS

Fig. 2

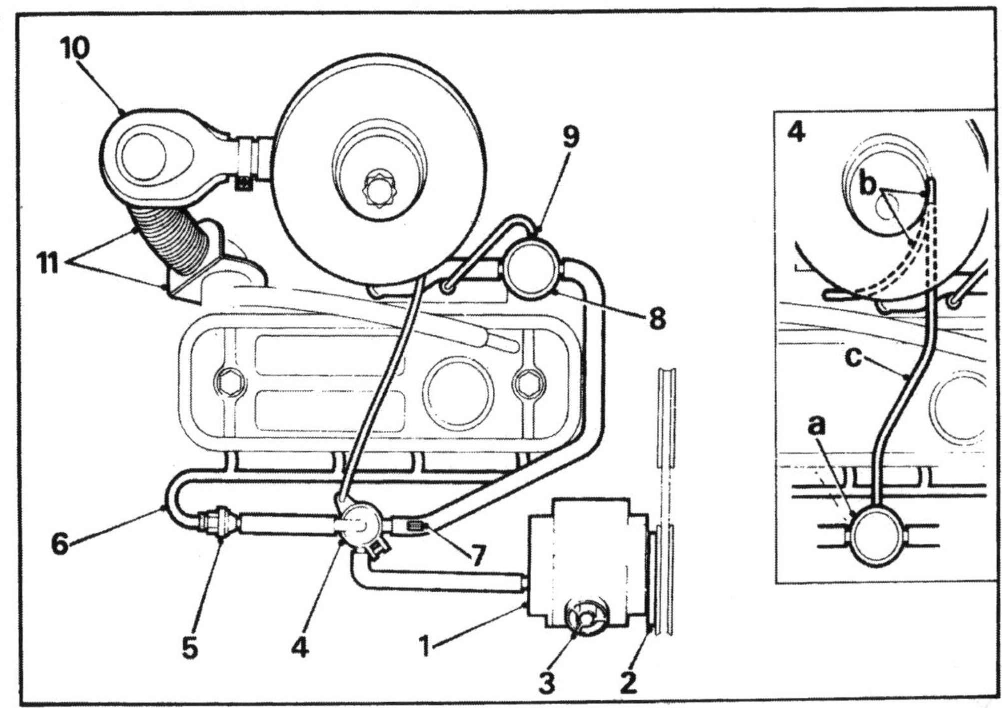

1. Air pump
2. Air pump filter
3. Air pump relief valve
4. Air diverter valve (cable operated)

Inset —
   a. Air diverter valve operated by vacuum
   b. Signal hose and control valve
   c. Vacuum pipe

5. Check valve
6. Air manifold
7. Restrictors (gulp valve line)
8. Gulp valve
9. Gulp valve signal pipe
10. Air temperature control device
11. Hot air duct and shroud
12. Operating cable

Exhaust Emission Control

The exhaust emission control system is designed to give the required degree of control of the carbon monoxide, unburnt hydrocarbons and oxides of nitrogen content of exhaust gases. The quantity of air-polluting elements in the gases leaving the exhaust pipe is reduced by adding air to the hot gases immediately they leave the combustion chambers of the engine. The injection of air into the exhaust gases promotes a continued conversion of the undesirable hydrocarbon and carbon monoxide components of the exhaust gases to relatively harmless carbon dioxides and water.

The emission control system is a combination of engine components and air injection techniques and consists of a special carburetter and air injection into the exhaust ports. An air pump mounted on the front of the engine, and belt driven from the water pump pulley, supplies air under pressure through hoses, a diverter valve, a check valve, and distribution manifold to injectors in each exhaust port in the engine cylinder head. The diverter valve mechanical or vacuum operated redirects the supply of air pressure to atmosphere when the mixture control (choke) is in operation. The check valve prevents high pressure exhaust gases from blowing back into the air pump due to, for example, pump drive failure. When the gulp valve opens, a small quantity of air is admitted directly into the inlet manifold to lean off the rich air/fuel mixture which is present in the manifold under conditions immediately following throttle closure. This mixture, having been reduced to a burnable condition, combines with engine inlet charge for combustion in the engine cylinders in the normal way.

Constant Depression SU Type Carburetter

The carburetter is manufactured to a special exhaust emission specification and is tuned to give the maximum emission control consistent with retaining vehicle performance and driveability. The metering needle is arranged in such a manner that it is always light spring loaded against the side of the jet to ensure consistency of fuel metering. A throttle disc by-pass valve limits the inlet manifold depression and ensures that during conditions of engine overrun the air/fuel mixture enters the engine cylinders in a burnable condition consistent with low emission levels.

Intake Air Temperature Control System

The temperature of the air drawn into the engine is controlled by a Bi-metal operated two-way flap valve. The Bi-metal blade is mounted in the air stream to the air cleaner and senses the temperature of the intake air. The Bi-metal blade controls the position of the two-way valve and admits either cool air from the engine compartment or hot air via the hot air duct from the shroud around part of the exhaust manifold, or a mixture of the two.

At intake temperatures below 18°C, only hot air from the exhaust manifold shroud is drawn, into the air cleaner; at intake temperatures above 33°C, only cool air from the engine compartment is drawn into the air cleaner.

Malfunction Identification
Check the following items regularly for visual signs of a malfunction and also if any of the driving symptoms listed should persistently occur. IF YOU ARE UNABLE TO LOCATE AND/OR CORRECT THE MALFUNCTION YOU ARE ADVISED TO CONTACT YOUR AUTHORISED DEALER OR SERVICE CENTRE IMMEDIATELY.

CHECK LIST — E.E.C. MALFUNCTION

Visual Checks

1. Condition and adjustment of drive belts
2. Baked or overheated hose between air pump, diverter valve and check valve.
3. All hoses for security, damage and deterioration
4. Fuel leakage
5. Oil filler cap for sealing

Driving Symptoms

1. Violent backfire in exhaust system
2. Hesitation to accelerate on re-opening the throttle after sudden throttle closure
3. Engine idles erratically or stalls
4. Noisy air pump
5. Ignition warning light on above idle speed (slack or broken fan belt)
6. Smell of fuel vapours
7. Engine stops after short running periods (fuel starvation)
8. Loss of power
9. High fuel consumption
10. Engine misfire
11. High temperature indicated (overheating of coolant).

Maintenance Operations
All items marked * in the 'MAINTENANCE SCHEDULE' are emission control related.

ENGINE TUNING & SERVICING PROCEDURES

Carburetter Mixture Adjustment (CO%)
Run engine until normal operating temperature is attained. Operate vehicle for five minutes on road. Disconnect air manifold hose from air pump and plug hose. Remove air cleaner. Disconnect float chamber vent pipe. Run engine at 2500 rpm for 30 seconds. Adjust idle screw to give required idle speed.
Adjust mixture nut to give required idle CO.
Unplug air manifold hose and refit hose to pump.
Re-adjust idle screw to give required idle speed.
If this cannot be achieved within 3 minutes repeat procedure. Refit vent pipe and air cleaner.

Valve Rocker Clearance Adjustment
Adjustment must be made with the tappet on the back of the cam, therefore the crankshaft must be rotated to bring each valve in turn to its checking position.

Checking Fig. 3
Unscrew the rocker cover retaining nuts, remove the rocker cover and insert a .305 mm feeler gauge between the valve rocker arm and valve stems (inset). The gauge should be a sliding fit when the engine is cold. To rotate the crankshaft remove the sparking plugs, engage top gear and push the car forward.
Check each clearance in the following order:
Check No. 1 valve with No. 8 fully open. Check No. 8 valve with No. 1 fully open.
Check No. 3 valve with No. 6 fully open. Check No. 6 valve with No. 3 fully open.
Check No. 5 valve with No. 4 fully open. Check No. 4 valve with No. 5 fully open.
Check No. 2 valve with No. 7 fully open. Check No. 7 valve with No. 2 fully open.

Adjusting
Slacken the adjusting screw locknut on the opposite end of the rocker arm and rotate the screw clockwise to reduce the clearance or anti-clockwise to increase it. Retighten the locknut when the clearance is correct, holding the screw against rotation with a screwdriver.

Fig. 3

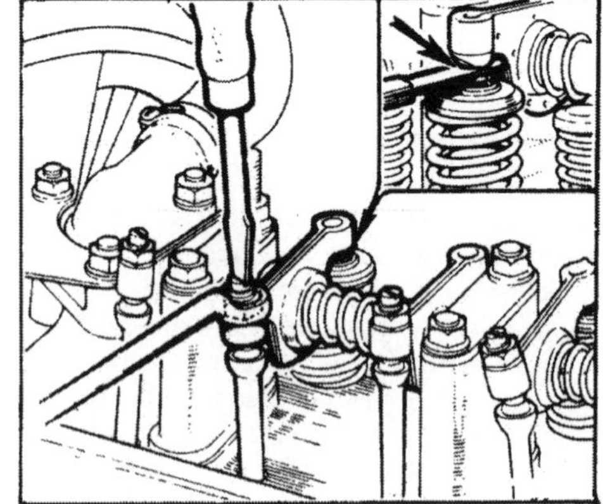

Spark Plugs
The spark plugs should be cleaned, preferably with an air-blast service unit, and the gaps reset to 0.6 mm.
Use a special spark plug gauge and setting tool and move the side electrode on the plug, never the centre one.
When fitting new spark plugs ensure that only the recommended type (see 'GENERAL DATA') is used and that they are set to the correct gap before installation.

Ignition Timing

The ignition timing is set dynamically to give optimum engine performance with efficient engine emission control. Adjustments to the ignition timing setting must be carried out by your approved Dealer or Service Centre.

Distributor Fig. 4

Contact breaker

Release the retaining clips and remove the distributor cover. Remove the rotor arm (1) and turn the crankshaft until the contacts are fully open.

Cleaning contacts

Inspect the contact points (2), and if burned, clean with fine emery cloth or a fine carborundum stone. Wipe the contacts clean with a fuel-moistened cloth. Renew the contact set if the points are pitted or worn.

Contact gap

Turn the crankshaft until the points are fully open. Check the contact gap (2) with a feeler gauge (see 'GENERAL DATA'); the gauge should be a sliding fit. If a gap varies appreciably from the gauge thickness, slacken the contact set securing screw (8) and adjust the gap by inserting a screwdriver between the slot at the end of the plate and the pipe turn anti-clockwise (9) to increase and clockwise (10) to decrease the gap. Retighten the securing screw.

Refit the rotor arm, engage the slot in the spindle and push down firmly. Wipe the inside and outside of the distributor cover clean, particularly between the electrodes, and refit the cover.

Lubrication

Very lightly smear the cam (3) and pivot post (4) with grease. Add a few drops of oil to the felt pad (5) in the top of the cam spindle and through the gap (6) between the contact plate and the cam spindle to lubricate the centrifugal weights. DO NOT OIL THE FELT PAD which contacts the cam face.

Every 40,000 km in addition to the routine maintenance lubricate the contact breaker assembly centre bearing with a drop of oil in each of the two holes (7) in the base plate. Carefully wipe away all surplus lubricant and see that the contact breaker points are perfectly clean and dry.

Contact set renewing

Remove the securing screw (11) with its spring and flat washer, lift the contact set (12), press the spring and release the terminal plate (13) from the end of the spring. Before fitting the new contact set, wipe the points clean with fuel or methylated spirit and very lightly grease the pivot post (4). Reconnect the terminal plate (3) to the end of the contact breaker spring, position the contact set on the distributor base plate and lightly tighten securing screw (11). Ensure that the contact breaker spring is firmly in its register on the insulator and set the contact gap.

Whenever a new contact set has been fitted, re-check the gap after the first 800 km. During this period the heel of the contact will have bedded-in and reduced the gap.

Fig. 4

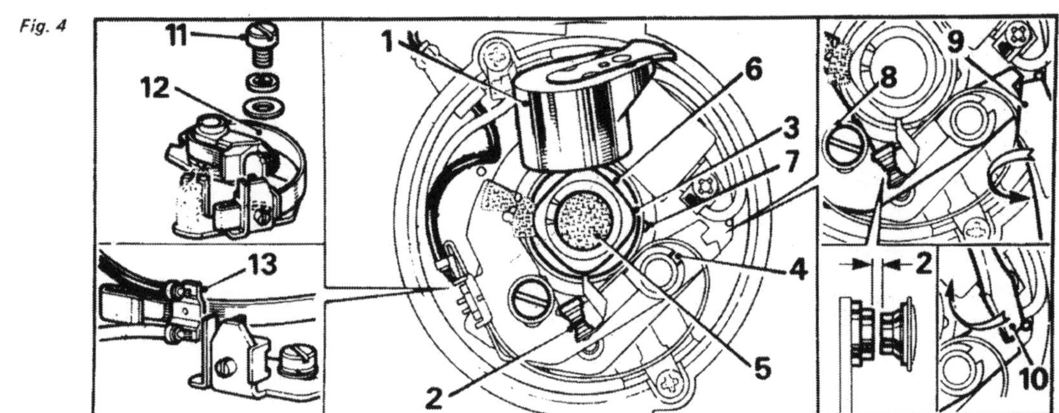

EMISSION CONTROL EQUIPMENT SERVICING

Carburetter

LUBRICATION Fig. 5

Unscrew the oil cap at the top of the carburetter suction chamber and withdraw the cap with its attached plunger. Top up with oil to bring the level 13 mm above the top of the hollow piston rod. In no circumstances should a heavy-bodied lubricant be used.

Failure to lubricate the piston damper will cause the piston to flutter and reduce acceleration.

Tuning

The carburetter is adjusted and tuned to give optimum engine performance with efficient engine emission control. Adjustment to the carburetter settings must only be carried out by your Dealer.

Fig. 5

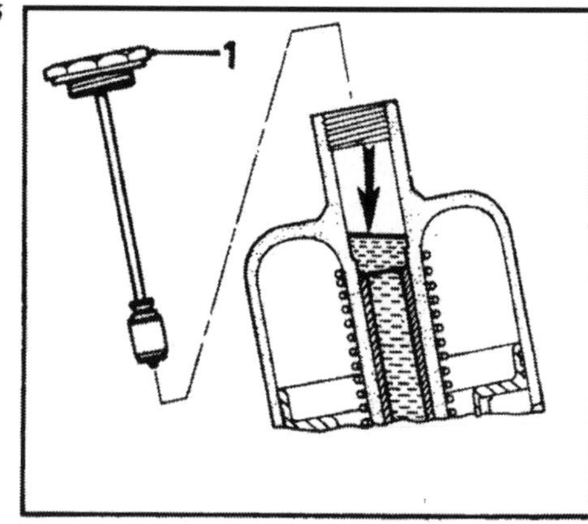

The efficient operation of the engine and exhaust emission control equipment depends not only on correct carburetter setting but also on correct ignition timing, and contact breaker, spark plug and valve rocker clearances. It is essential that these items are checked before adjusting the carburetter. Tuning of the carburetter is confined to setting the idle and fast idle speeds and the mixture setting at idle speed. Adjustments should only be undertaken on cars required to conform with exhaust emission control regulations if a reliable tachometer and an exhaust gas analyser (CO meter) is available.

Air Temperature Control

An air temperature control is fitted to the air cleaner intake. When the engine is cold, air is drawn from the shrouded area of the exhaust manifold. As the temperature of the air entering the air cleaner rises, the control valve will open and admit cooler air to maintain a constant temperature.

INSPECTING Fig. 6

Every 20,000 km or 12 months, note the position of the valve when the engine is cold, depress the valve indicated and release it. The valve should return to its original position. Inspect the valve seat for signs of damage or deterioration.

Air Cleaner Element Renewal Fig. 6

A new air cleaner element must be fitted every 20,000 km or 12 months, or earlier in dusty operating conditions.

Unscrew the two wing nuts (1) securing the air cleaner to the carburetter air manifold, pull the connector (2) off the air temperature control flange and lift off the air cleaner assembly.

Remove the top cover (3) by prising it off with a screwdriver placed beneath the slots on the underside of the cover. Discard the old element (4), thoroughly clean the container and fit the new element. Ensure that the rubber '0' ring is correctly positioned in the groove on the underside of the top cover. Refit the top cover (3) align the arrow on the cover with the location lug (5) of the container. Refit the air cleaner assembly and tighten the wing nuts.

Do not disturb the element at any other time.

Fuel Line Filter Fig. 7

The fuel line filter assembly must be renewed every 20,000 km or 12 months.

Release the hose clips (1), remove the filter (2). Fit a new filter ensuring the flow arrow (3a) is towards the carburetter. Alternative type: connect the end marked''IN' to the inlet hose.

Fig. 7

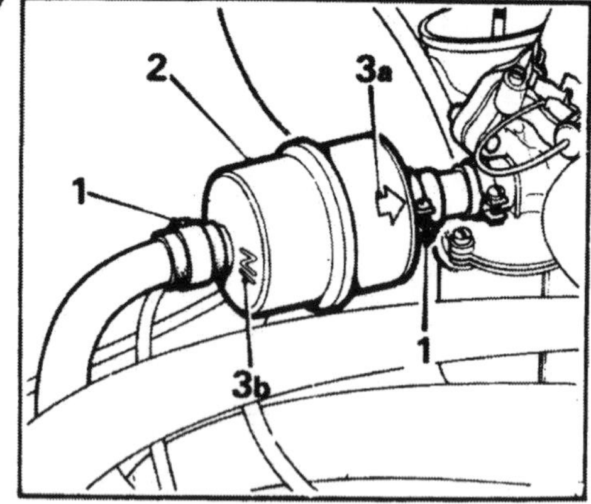

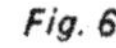
Fig. 6

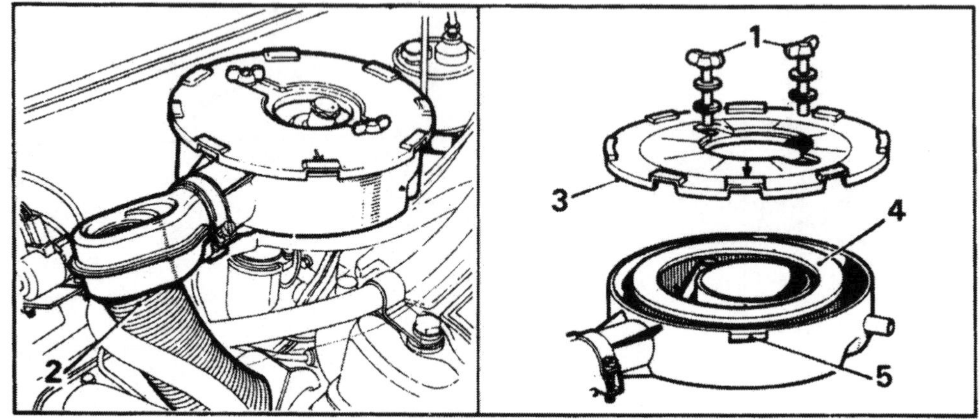

Adsorption Canister Fig. 8
The air for engine breathing is drawn through the adsorption canister and into the engine valve rocker cover.
The adsorption canister must be renewed every 40,000 km or 24 months.
To renew the canister, disconnect the air vent pipe (1) vapour pipes (2) and purge pipe (3) from their connections on the canister. Remove the retaining screw (4), open the bracket clamp sufficiently to withdraw the canister.
When fitting, ensure that all connections to the canister are secure.

Fig. 8

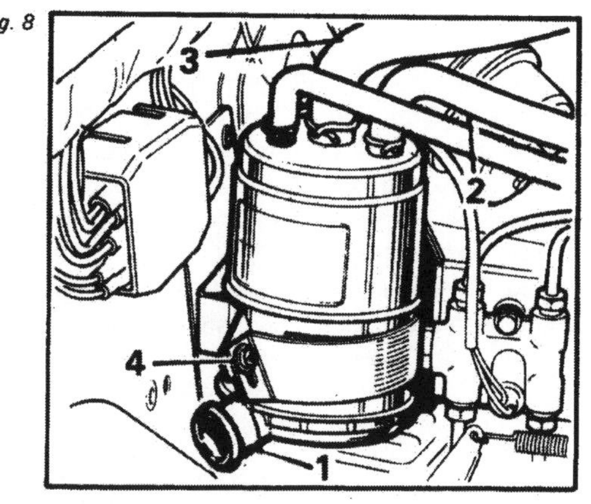

Filler Cap Fig. 9
Both the fuel tank filler cap (1) and the engine oil filler cap (2) are non-venting and form a seal on the filling apertures. IT IS ESSENTIAL TO THE SATISFACTORY OPERATION OF THE EVAPORATIVE LOSS SYSTEM THAT BOTH CAPS ARE ALWAYS REFITTED CORRECTLY AND TIGHTENED FULLY. A DEFECTIVE CAP OR CAP SEAL MUST BE REPLACED.

Purge Line Restrictor Fig. 9
To check, disconnect the purge line (3) from the rocker cover elbow (4). Examine the orifice of the restriction formed in the elbow for obstruction. Clear any dirt or deposits from the restrictor orifice, using a length of soft wire.

Fig. 9

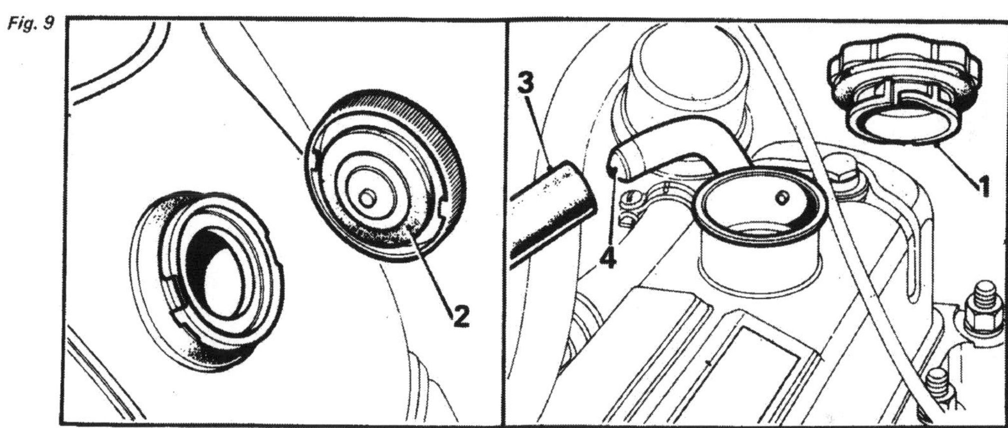

Air Pump Drive Belt Fig. 11
TENSION. When correctly tensioned, a total deflection of 13 mm under moderate hand pressure should be possible at the midway point of the longest belt run between the pulleys.
ADJUSTING. To adjust the belt tension, slacken the securing bolt and nut (1), and the link securing screw (2). Also slacken the bolt and nut (3 — shown inset) retaining the alternator and the air pump drive belt adjusting link. Move the air pump to the required position, tighten the retaining bolts and nuts and re-check the belt tension. DO NOT OVERTIGHTEN.

Gulp Valve Fig. 10
To renew, disconnect the hoses (1) and sensing pipe (1) from the gulp valve. Unscrew the mounting screws and nuts (2) and remove the gulp valve (3). Fit the new valve, reconnect the hoses and sensing pipe ensuring that all joints are made secure and airtight.

Fig. 10

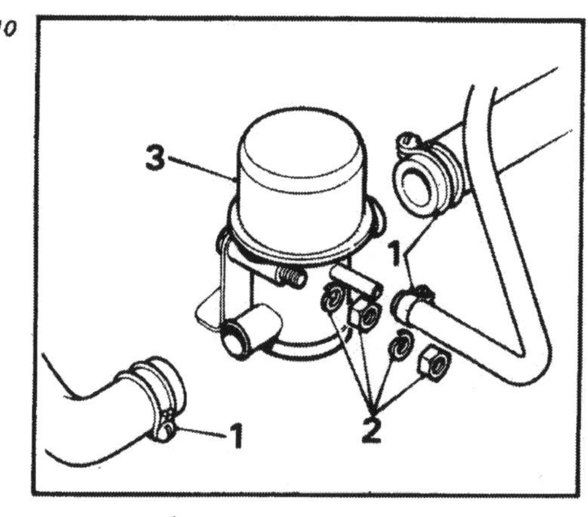

Fig. 11

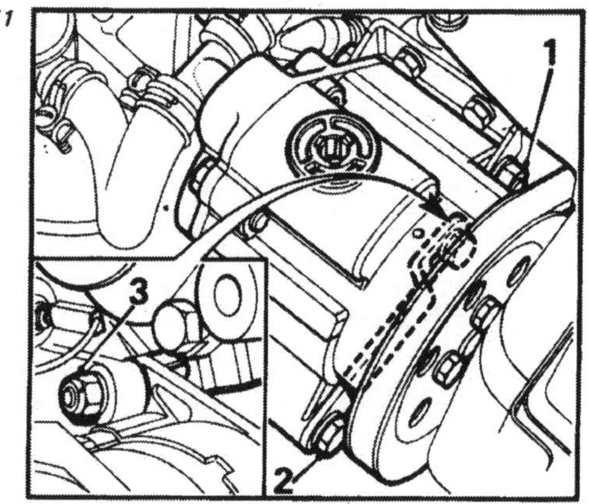

Lubrication
The lubrication system of your new car is filled with a high quality oil. You should always use a high quality oil of the correct viscosity range in the engine/transmission during subsequent maintenance operations or when topping up. The use of oils not to the correct specifications can lead to high oil and fuel consumption and ultimately to damage to the engine or gearbox components. Fig. 12
Oils to the correct specification contain additives which disperse the corrosive acids formed by combustion and also prevent the formation of sludge which can block oilways. Additional oil additives should not be used. Servicing intervals must be adhered to.

Engine Transmission Unit
Use a well-known brand of oil to B.L.S. 01.02 or MIL-L-210 B or A.P.I., SE quality with a viscosity band spanning the temperature range of your locality.

Steering Rack
Use E.P. 90 (MIL-L-2150) above—10°C.
Use E.P. 80 (MIL-L-2105) below —10°C.

Grease Points
Use Multipurpose Lithium Grease N.L.G.I, Consistency No. 2.

Fig. 12

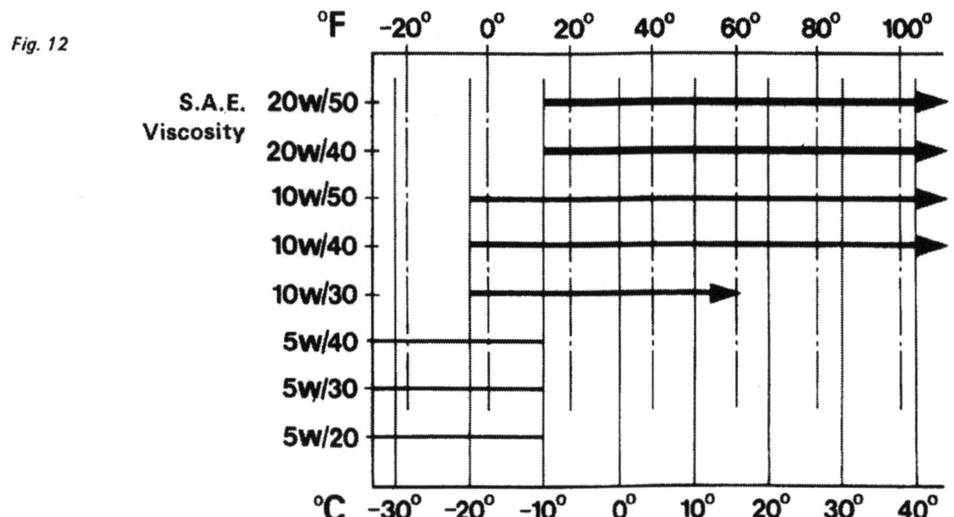

SEATS AND SEAT BELTS

WARNING: Seat Belts must be worn in accordance with the Australian Design Rules and the following instructions must be adhered to if the belts are to provide maximum protection. The belts are designed to bear upon the boney structure of the body and should be worn low across the front of the pelvis or the pelvis, chest and shoulders as applicable. Wearing the belt across the abdominal area must be avoided. Adjust the belt as firmly as possible consistent with comfort. A slack belt will greatly reduce the protection afforded the wearer. Each belt assembly must only be used by one occupant. It is dangerous to put a belt around a child being carried on the occupant's lap. Belts should not be worn with twisted straps.
Care should be taken to avoid contamination of the belt webbing with polishes, oil and chemicals, particularly battery acid. Cleaning may safely be carried out using mild soap and water. The belts must be replaced if they become contaminated or damaged; they must also be replaced after a collision regardless of whether damage is obvious or not. No modifications or additions should be made by the user which will either prevent the seat belt adjusting devices from operating to remove slack, or prevent the seat belt assembly from being adjusted to remove slack.
Seat Belts and anchorages are checked each passport service.

WARNING: Child restraint anchorages are designed to withstand only those loads imposed by correctly fitted child restraints. Under no circumstances are they to be used for adult seat belts or harnesses.

CHILD RESTRAINT ANCHORAGE POINTS

Two sets of anchorage points are provided to allow fitment of suitable approved child restraint harnesses. Fig. 13
They are located in the rear window shelf adjacent to the existing anchorage for rear passenger safety belts and are easily recognised by the plugs (A) fitted to protect the threads. Before fitment of the harness anchorage bolts (B) the plugs must be removed by inserting a screwdriver into the slot in the head and turning in an anti-clockwise direction, at the same time carefully prising the plug from the threads.

Fig. 13

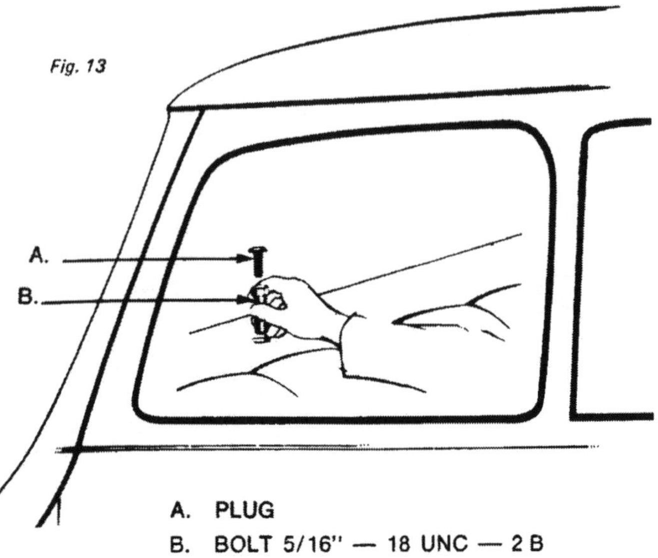

A. PLUG
B. BOLT 5/16" — 18 UNC — 2 B

MAINTENANCE SUMMARY

The maintenance summary on this and the following pages is the minimum service required to maintain your vehicle under normal driving conditions. For other than normal driving conditions, and those caused by seasonal changes, we recommend that you consult your Dealer.

NOTE: The service intervals are based on an annual mileage of approximately 20,000 km and should the vehicle complete substantially less miles than this per annum, it is recommended that a 'C' service is completed at six months intervals, and a 'D' service at twelve-month intervals.

In addition to the periodic maintenance the following checks should be made weekly;

Check/top up engine oil
Check/top up brake fluid reservoir
Check/top up battery electrolyte
Check/top up cooling system
Check/top up washer reservoir
Check function of original equipment, i.e. exterior lamps, wipers and warning indicators. Check tyres for tread depth, visually for external cuts in fabric, exposure of ply or cord structure, lumps and bulges.
Check/adjust tyre pressures, including spare
Check tightness of wheelfastenings.

Maintenance Intervals

Service	km x 1000	Monthly intervals
A	1.6	After Sales Service
B	5-15-25-35-45-55-65-75	Three
C	10-30-50-70	Six
D	20-40-60-80	Twelve
40	40-80	Twenty four

Maintenance Operations

All items marked * in the MAINTENANCE SCHEDULE' are emission control related.

	A	B	C	D
Lubrication				
Lubricate all grease points, including hand brake mechanical linkage and cable guides	•	•	•	•
*Renew engine oil filter			•	•
*Renew engine oil	•		•	•
Check/top up engine oil		•		
Lubricate all locks and hinges except steering lock	•		•	•
*Lubricate accelerator control linkage and pedal pivot. check operation	•		•	•
Engine				
Check/top up cooling system	•	•	•	•
Check cooling and heater systems for leaks, hoses and pipes for security and condition	•		•	•
*Check all driving belts, adjust or renew	•	•	•	•
*Check exhaust system for leaks and security	•	•	•	•
Check security of engine bolts and mountings	•			
*Check/adjust torque of cylinder head nuts	•			
*Check/adjust valve clearances	•			•
*Check/adjust air injection system hoses for security	•			
*Check air injection hoses/pipes for condition and security if necessary	•			•
*Check gulp valve, check valve and air diverter valve operations; rectify/renew if necessary				•
*Check crankcase breathing and evaporative loss systems, check hoses/pipes and restrictor for security, condition and blockage, rectify if necessary	•			•
Check/adjust clutch return stop clearance		•	•	•
Ignition System				
*Check ignition wiring for fraying, chafing and deterioration; rectify if necessary	•			•
*Check/adjust ignition timing and dwell angle, using electronic equipment.	•		•	•
*Check distributor cap, check for cracks and tracking				•
*Lubricate distributor	•		•	•
*Renew contact breaker points				•
*Clean and adjust spark plugs			•	
*Renew spark plugs				•
*Check coil performance on oscilloscope	•			•
Fuel System				
*Check fuel system for leaks	•	•	•	•
*Top up carburetter piston damper	•			•
*Check condition of fuel filler cap seal				•
*Renew fuel line filter				•
*Renew carburetter air filter element				•
*Check air intake temperature control system				•
*Renew adsorption canister				40
*Check/Adjust carburetter idle settings	•			•
*Check/adjust choke settings	•			•
*Check/adjust CO at idle	•			•
Safety				
Check all fluid reservoirs; clutch, battery and windscreen washer	•	•	•	•
Check visually hydraulic pipes and unions for chafing, leaks and corrosion	•	•	•	•
Check brake linings for wear and drums for conditions; rectify/renew if necessary				•
Check/adjust foot and hand brake	•	•	•	•
Check condition and security of steering unit, joints and gaiters	•	•	•	•
Check suspension dampers and steering rack for oil leaks	•	•	•	•
Check/adjust tightness of steering-column clamp bolt			•	•
Check/adjust security of suspension fixings	•		•	•
Check/adjust tyre pressures, including spare	•	•	•	•
Check/adjust front wheel alignment	•		•	•
Check tightness of road wheel fasenings	•	•	•	•
Check tyres comply with manufacturer's specification	•	•	•	•
Check tyres for tread depth, visually for cuts in tyre fabric, exposure of ply or cord structure, lumps or bulges	•	•	•	•
Check output of charging system			•	•
Check function of original equipment, i.e., interior and exterior lamps. horns. warning indicators, wipers and washers	•	•	•	•
Check instrumentation	•	•	•	•
Check, if necessary renew, wiper blades		•	•	•
Check/adjust headlamp alignment	•	•	•	•
Check operation of all door locks and window controls	•			•
Check condition and security of seats, seat belts, and seat belt warning system	•	•	•	•
Test				
Road/roller test and check operation of all instrumentation; report additional work required	•		•	•

MINI

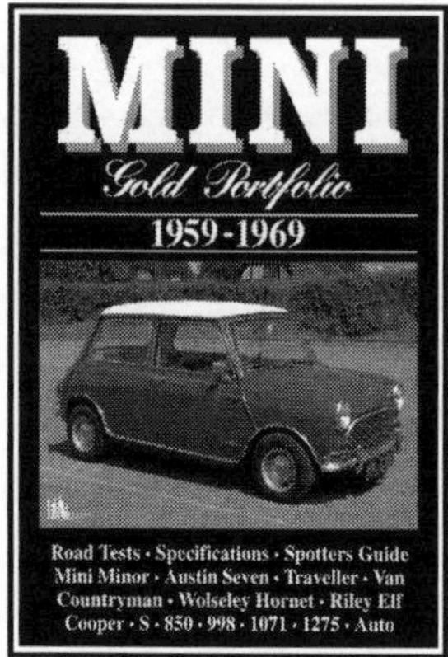

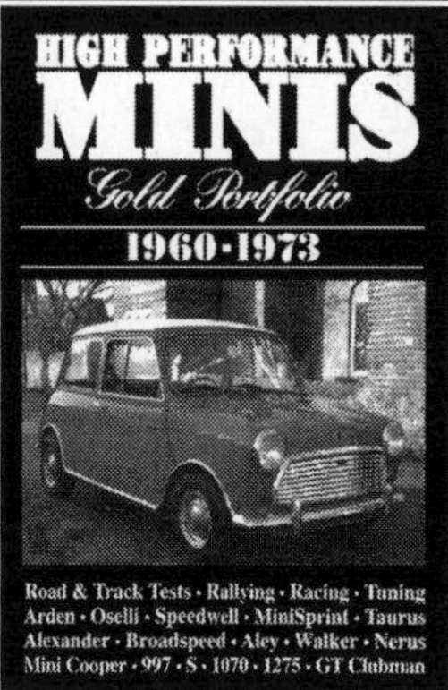

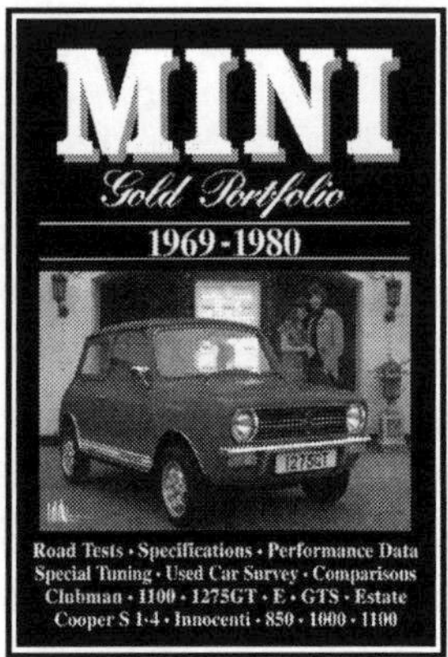

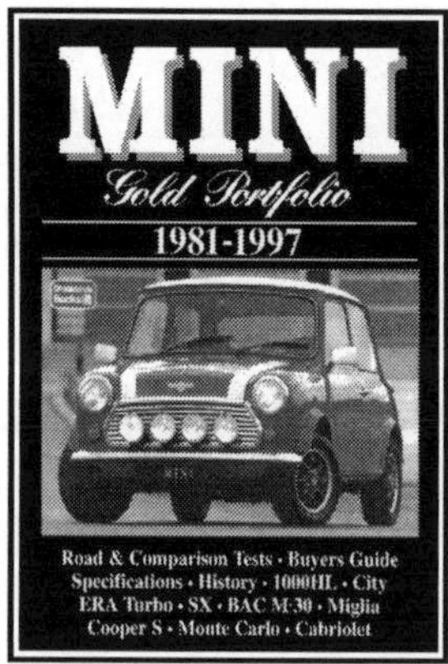

www.brooklandsbooks.com

Printed in Great Britain
by Amazon